Contemporary Business

Boone • Kurtz

Fourteenth Edition

The State College of Florida

To order books or for customer service, please call 1(800)-CALL-WILEY (225-5945).

Printed in the United States of America.

ISBN   978-1-118-41317-3

Printed and bound by IPAK.

10 9 8 7 6 5 4 3 2

Custom Brief Contents

SOLUTIONS AT THE SPEED

Business Weekly Updates

Save time every Monday morning with Business Weekly Updates. New and relevant business news stories and videos are posted to the website each Monday morning.
www.wileybusinessupdates.com

The Wiley Business Video Series

Brand new documentary-style video clips of successful companies like Zipcar, Seventh Generation, and Comet Skateboards accompany each chapter and reinforce key introduction to business concepts and expose students to innovative business practices.
(Available in WileyPLUS and on DVD)

OF BUSINESS

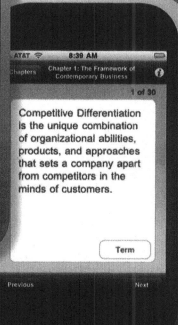

Study Faster. iPhone Apps.

Study on the go with Contemporary Business iPhone apps.

(available at the iTunes App Store)

WILEY

John Wiley & Sons, Inc.

David L. Kurtz

University of Arkansas

Boone & Kurtz's

Contemporary
BUSINESS

2012 UPDATE EDITION

. . . at the speed of business

"The 14th edition of Contemporary Business is dedicated to Joseph S. Heider, who brought me to John Wiley & Sons. Thank you, Joe."
—Dave

Vice President & Executive Publisher	George Hoffman
Senior Acquisitions Editor	Franny Kelly
Assistant Editor	Emily McGee
Production Manager	Dorothy Sinclair
Senior Production Editor	Valerie A. Vargas
Marketing Manager	Kelly Simmons
Creative Director	Harry Nolan
Senior Designer	Madelyn Lesure
Text Designer	4 Design Group
Cover Designer	Wendy Lai
Production Management Services	Integra–Chicago
Senior Illustration Editor	Anna Melhorn
Photo Editor	Hilary Newman
Photo Researcher	Teri Stratford
Editorial Assistant	Melissa Solarz
Executive Media Editor	Allison Morris
Media Editor	Elena Santa Maria
Back Cover	iStock

This book was set in Janson TextLTStd-Roman 10/13 by MPS Limited, a Macmillan Company, Chennai, India and printed and bound by Quad/Graphics. The cover was printed by Quad/Graphics.

This book is printed on acid free paper. ∞

Founded in 1807, John Wiley & Sons, Inc. has been a valued source of knowledge and understanding for more than 200 years, helping people around the world meet their needs and fulfill their aspirations. Our company is built on a foundation of principles that include responsibility to the communities we serve and where we live and work. In 2008, we launched a Corporate Citizenship Initiative, a global effort to address the environmental, social, economic, and ethical challenges we face in our business. Among the issues we are addressing are carbon impact, paper specifications and procurement, ethical conduct within our business and among our vendors, and community and charitable support. For more information, please visit our website: www.wiley.com/go/citizenship.

ISBN-13   978-1-118-01030-3

Printed in the United States of America

10 9 8 7 6 5 4 3 2

About the Author

During Dave Kurtz's high school days, no one in Salisbury, Maryland, would have mistaken him for a scholar. In fact, he was a mediocre student, so bad that his father steered him toward higher education by finding him a succession of backbreaking summer jobs. Thankfully, most of them have been erased from his memory, but a few linger, including picking peaches, loading watermelons on trucks headed for market, and working as a pipefitter's helper. Unfortunately, these jobs had zero impact on his academic standing. Worse yet for Dave's ego, he was no better than average as a high school athlete in football and track.

But four years at Davis & Elkins College in Elkins, West Virginia, turned him around. Excellent instructors helped get Dave on a sound academic footing. His grade point average soared—enough to get him accepted by the graduate business school at the University of Arkansas, where he met Gene Boone. Gene and Dave became longtime co-authors; together they produced more than 50 books. In addition to writing, Dave and Gene were involved in several entrepreneurial ventures.

This long-term partnership ended with Gene's death in 2005. But, this book will always be Boone & Kurtz's *Contemporary Business*.

Dave ended up back at the University of Arkansas, after tours of duty in Ypsilanti, Michigan; Seattle, Washington; and Melbourne, Australia. Dave and his wife, Diane, have six "perfect" grand children and four demanding canine companions. Dave can be reached at ProfKurtz@gmail.com.

WileyPLUS for Students

WileyPLUS builds students' confidence because it takes the guesswork out of studying by providing a clear roadmap to academic success. *WileyPLUS* provides an online environment that integrates relevant resources, including the entire digital textbook, in an easy-to-navigate framework that helps you study more effectively.

With *WileyPLUS*, you receive 24/7 access to resources that promote positive learning outcomes.

Throughout each study session, you can assess your progress and gain immediate feedback on your strengths and weaknesses so you can be confident you are spending your time wisely.

Powered by proven technology and built on a foundation of cognitive research, *WileyPLUS* has enriched the education of millions of students, in over 20 countries around the world.

WileyPLUS is filled with student resources including:

Business Weekly Updates

Stay up to date on the very latest in business news stories. Each week you will find links to 5 new articles, video clips, business news stories, and so much more.

Audio Chapter Review Summaries

Available in English and Spanish, these reviews provide a quick overview of the main chapter concepts, so you can review them in the car, on foot, at the gym – anywhere!

iPhone Apps

You can now review chapter concepts and key terms on the go with our iPhone flashcard and self-study quiz apps.

Student Study Guide

Review key business concepts and test your knowledge so you're ready for the next quiz or exam.

The Wiley Business Video Series

Brand new end-of-chapter video cases include companies like Zipcar, Seventh Generation, New Harvest Coffee Roasters, and Comet Skateboards.

What are Learning Styles?

Have you ever repeated something to yourself over and over to help remember it? Or does your best friend ask you to draw a map to someplace where the two of you are planning to meet, rather than just tell her the directions? If so, then you already have an intuitive sense that people learn in different ways, Researchers in learning theory have developed various categories of learning styles. Some people, for example, learn best by reading or writing. Others learn best by using various senses—seeing, hearing, feeling, tasting, or even smelling. When you understand how you learn best, you can make use of learning strategies that will optimize the time you spend studying. To find out what your particular learning style is, www.wiley.com/college/boone and take the learning styles quiz you find there. The quiz will help you determine your primary learning style:

Visual Learner	Auditory Learner	Haptic Learner	Olfactory Learner
Print Learner	Interactive Learner	Kinesthetic Learner	

Then, consult the information below and on the following pages for study tips for each learning style. This information will help you better understand your learning style and how to apply it to the study of business.

Study Tips for Visual Learners

If you are a Visual Learner, you prefer to work with images and diagrams. It is important that you see information.

Visual Learning
- Draw charts/diagrams during lecture.
- Examine textbook figures and graphs.
- Look at images and videos on *WileyPLUS* and other Web sites.
- Pay close attention to charts, drawings, and handouts your instructor uses.
- Underline; use different colors.
- Use symbols, flowcharts, graphs, different arrangements on the page, white spaces.

Visual Reinforcement
- Make flashcards by drawing tables/charts on one side and definition or description on the other side.
- Use art-based worksheets; cover labels on images in text and then rewrite the labels.
- Use colored pencils/markers and colored paper to organize information into types.
- Convert your lecture notes into "page pictures." To do this:
  - Use the visual learning strategies outlined above.

- Reconstruct images in different ways.
- Redraw pages from memory.
- Replace words with symbols and initials.
- Draw diagrams where appropriate.
- Practice turning your visuals back into words.

If visual learning is your weakness: If you are not a Visual Learner but want to improve your visual learning, try re-keying tables/charts from the textbook.

Study Tips for Print Learners

If you are a Print Learner, reading will be important but writing will be much more important.

Print Learning
- Write text lecture notes during lecture.
- Read relevant topics in textbook, especially textbook tables.
- Look at text descriptions in animations and Web sites.
- Use lists and headings.
- Use dictionaries, glossaries, and definitions.
- Read handouts, textbooks, and supplementary library readings.
- Use lecture notes.

Print Reinforcement
- Rewrite your notes from class, and copy classroom handouts in your own handwriting.
- Make your own flashcards.
- Write out essays summarizing lecture notes or textbook topics.
- Develop mnemonics.
- Identify word relationships.
- Create tables with information extracted from textbook or lecture notes.
- Use text based worksheets or crossword Puzzles.
- Write out words again and again.
- Reread notes silently.

- Rewrite ideas and principles into other words.
- Turn charts, diagrams, and other illustrations into statements.
- Practice writing exam answers.
- Practice with multiple choice questions.
- Write paragraphs, especially beginnings and endings.
- Write your lists in outline form.
- Arrange your words into hierarchies and points.

If print learning is your weakness: If you are not a Print Learner but want to improve your print learning, try covering labels of figures from the textbook and writing in the labels.

Study Tips for Auditory Learners

If you are an Auditory Learner, then you prefer listening as a way to learn information. Hearing will be very important, and sound helps you focus.

Auditory Learning
- Make audio recordings during lecture.
- Do not skip class; hearing the lecture is essential to understanding.

- Play audio files provided by instructor and textbook.
- Listen to narration of animations.
- Attend lecture and tutorials.

- Discuss topics with students and instructors.
- Explain new ideas to other people.
- Leave spaces in your lecture notes for later recall.

Study Tips for Auditory Learners (continued)

- Describe overheads, pictures, and visuals to somebody who was not in class.

Auditory Reinforcement

- Record yourself reading the notes and listen to the recording
- Write out transcripts of the audio files.
- Summarize information that you have read, speaking out loud.

- Use a recorder to create self-tests.
- Compose "songs" about information.
- Play music during studying to help focus.
- Expand your notes by talking with other and with information from your textbook.
- Read summarized notes out loud.
- Explain your notes to another auditory learner.
- Talk with the instructor.

- Spend time in quiet places recalling the ideas.
- Say your answers out loud.

If auditory teaming is your weakness: If you are not an Auditory Learner but want to improve your auditory learning, try writing out the scripts from pre-recorded lectures.

Study Tips for Interactive Learners

If you are an Interactive Learner, you will want to share your information. A study group will be important.

Interactive Learning

- Ask a lot of questions during lecture or TA review sessions.
- Contact other students, via e-mail or discussion forums, and ask them to explain what they learned.

Interactive Reinforcement

- "Teach" the content to a group of other students.
- Talking to an empty room may seem odd, but it will be effective for you.
- Discuss information with others, making sure that you both ask and answer questions.
- Work in small group discussions, making a verbal and written discussion of what others say.

If interactive learning is your weakness: If you are not an Interactive Learner but want to improve prove your interactive learning, try asking your study partner questions and then repeating them to the instructor.

Study Tips for Haptic Learners

If you are a Haptic Learner, you prefer to work with your hands. It is important to physically manipulate material.

Haptic Learning

- Take blank paper to lecture to draw charts/tables/diagrams.
- Using the textbook, run your fingers along the figures and graphs to get a "feel" for shapes and relationships.

Haptic Reinforcement

- Trace words and pictures on flashcards.
- Perform electronic exercises that involve drag-and-drop activities.
- Alternate between speaking and writing information.
- Observe someone performing a task that you would like to learn.

- Make sure you have freedom of movement while studying.

If haptic learning is your weakness: If you are not a Haptic Learner but want to improve your haptic learning, try spending more time in class working with graphs and tables while speaking or writing down information.

Study Tips for Kinesthetic Learners

If you are a Kinesthetic Learner, it will be important that you involve your body during studying.

Kinesthetic Learning

- Ask permission to get up and move during Lecture.
- Participate in role-playing activities in the classroom.
- Use all your senses.
- Go to labs; take field trips.
- Listen to real-life examples.
- Pay attention to applications.
- Use trial-and-error methods.
- Use hands-on approaches.

Kinesthetic Reinforcement

- Make flashcards; place them on the floor, and move your body around them.
- Move while you are teaching the material to others.
- Put examples in your summaries.
- Use case studies and applications to help with principles and abstract concepts.
- Talk about your notes with another Kinesthetic person.

- Use pictures and photographs that illustrate an idea.
- Write practice answers.
- Role-play the exam situation.

If kinesthetic learning is your weakness: If you are not a Kinesthetic Learner but want to improve your kinesthetic learning, try moving flash cards to reconstruct graphs and tables, etc.

Study Tips for Olfactory Learners

If you are an Olfactory Learner, you will prefer to use the senses of smell and taste to reinforce learning. This is a rare learning modality.

Olfactory Learning

- During lecture, use different scented markers to identify different types of information.

Olfactory Reinforcement

- Rewrite notes with scented markers.

- If possible, go back to the computer lab to do your studying.
- Burn aromatic candles while studying.
- Try to associate the material that you're studying with a pleasant taste or smell.

If olfactory learning is your weakness: If you are not an Olfactory Learner but want to improve your olfactory learning, try burning an aromatic candle or incense while you study, or eating cookies during study sessions.

LEARNING STYLES SURVEY CHART

Resources	Visual	Print	Auditory	Interactive	Haptic	Kinesthetic
Hit & Miss	✔	✔		✔		
Launching Your Career	✔	✔		✔		
Learning Goals	✔	✔		✔		
They Said It	✔	✔				
BusinessEtiquette	✔	✔		✔		
Solving an Ethical Controversy	✔	✔				
Assessment Checks	✔	✔		✔		
Review Questions	✔	✔		✔		
Cases	✔	✔		✔		
Project / Teamwork Applications	✔	✔		✔		
Flashcards	✔	✔		✔	✔	✔
Business Terms	✔	✔		✔		
Interactive Quizzes	✔	✔		✔		
Student PowerPoints	✔	✔		✔	✔	
Audio Summary (English / Spanish)	✔	✔	✔	✔	✔	
Animated Figures	✔	✔	✔	✔	✔	
Case Study Animations	✔	✔	✔	✔	✔	✔
E-lectures	✔	✔	✔	✔	✔	
Greensburg, KS Continuing Case	✔	✔	✔	✔	✔	✔
End-of-Chapter Videos	✔	✔	✔	✔	✔	✔
Final Exam Questions	✔	✔		✔		
Quiz Questions	✔	✔		✔		
Pre-lecture Questions	✔	✔		✔		
Post-lecture Questions	✔	✔		✔		
Video Questions	✔	✔	✔	✔		✔
Drop-box Questions	✔	✔		✔		

Acknowledgements

Contemporary Business has long benefited from the instructors who have offered their time as reviewers. Comprehensive reviews of the 14th edition and ancillary materials were provided by the following colleagues:

Danielle Blesi
Hudson Valley Community College

Margaret Dunfee
Northern Arizona University

Joanne Frazier
Montgomery College, Rockville

Connie Golden
Lakeland Community College

Frank Harber
Indian River State University

Joe Molina
MiraCosta College

Chris Osuanah
J. Sargeant Reynolds Community College

Angela Rabatin
Prince George's Community College

Tim Rogers
Ozark Technical Community College

John Streibich
Monroe Community College

Colette Wolfson
Ivy Tech Community College, South Bend

Lisa Zangaro
Oakton Community college

Thanks also to all of our colleagues who have assisted us in previous editions in our continuing efforts to make the best business text even better. The new edition continues to reflect so many of their recommendations. Among the hundreds of reviewers and focus group participants who contributed to the book during previous editions, we acknowledge the special contributions of the following people:

Nathaniel R. Calloway
University of Maryland University College

Gary Cohen
University of Maryland

Kellie Emrich
Cuyahoga Community College

Gil Feiertag
Columbus State Community College

Janice Feldbauer
Schoolcraft College

Chuck Foley
Columbus State Community College

Karen Halpern
South Puget Sound Community College

Tim Hatten
Mesa State College

Linda Hefferin
Elgin Community College

John Hilston
Brevard Community College

Martin Karamian
Pierce College

Cynthia Miree-Coppin
Oakland Unversity

David Oliver
Edison State College

Sally Proffitt
Tarrant County College

Jayre Reaves
Rutgers University

David Robinson
University of California, Berkeley

Patricia Setlik
Harper College

John Striebich
Monroe Community College

Rodney Thirion
Pikes Peak Community College

Sal Veas
Santa Monica College

Collette Wolfson
Ivy Tech Community College

Lisa Zingaro
Oakton Community College

Brenda Anthony
Tallahassee Community College

Lorraine P. Bassette
Prince George's Community College

Barbara Ching
Los Angeles City College

Rachna Condos
American River College

Susan J. Cremins
Westchester Community College

Tamara Davis
Davenport University

Colleen Dunn
Bucks County Community College

Joyce Ezrow
Anne Arundel Community College

Kathleen K. Ghahramani
Johnson County Community College

Connie Golden
Lakeland Community College

Susan Greer
Horry-Georgetown Technical College

James V. Isherwood
Community College of Rhode Island

Mary Beth Klinger
College of Southern Maryland

Claudia Levi
Edmonds Community College

Kathy Lorencz
Oakland Community College

Levi Richard
Citrus College

Jenny C. Rink
Community College of Philadelphia

Susan Roach
Georgia Southern University

Sandra Robertson
Thomas Nelson Community College

Barbara Rosenthal
Miami Dade College, Kendall Campus

JoDee Salisbury
Baker College

Rieann Spence-Gale
Northern Virginia Community College

Bob Urell
Irvine Valley College

Ed Becker
Housatonic Community College

Cathleen Behan
North Virginia Community College

Vicki Bjerke
Northeast Iowa Community College

Robert Brinkmeyer
University of Cincinnati

Ronald Cereola
James Madison University

Leo Chiantelli
Shasta College

John Cicero
Shasta College

Robert M. Clark
Horry-Georgetown Technical College

Douglas Crowe
Bradley University

Charles R. Fenner
State University of New York- Canton

Susan Greer
Horry-Georgetown Technical College

William Harvey
Henry Ford Community College

David Hollomon
Victor Valley College

Clark Lambert
Farmingdale State College

James R. Lashley
Bowie State University

Victor Lipe
Trident Technical College

Michael Mandel
Housatonic Community College

Gina McConoughey
Illinois Central College

Dennis R. Murphy
Horry-Georgetown Technical College

John Muzzo
Harold Washington University

Jack Partlow
Northern Virginia Community College

W.J. Patterson
Sullivan University

Michael Quinn
James Madison University

Rama Ramaswamy
Minneapolis Community and Technical College

JoAnn Rawley
Reading Area Community College

Donna Scarlett
Iowa Western Community College—Clarinda

Charles Smith
Horry-Georgetown Technical College

Michael Thomas
Henry Ford Community College

LaVena Wilkin
Sullivan University

Jamil Ahmad
Los Angeles Trade—Technical College

Sylvia Allen
Los Angeles Valley College

Kenneth F. Anderson
Borough of Manhattan Community College

Andrea Bailey
Moraine Valley Community College

Norman E. Burns
Bergen Community College

Diana Carmel
Golden West College

Barbara Ching
Los Angeles City College

Ron Colley
South Suburban College

Scott Colvin
Naugatuck Community College

Peter Dawson
Collin County Community College

Dr. Richard L. Drury
Northern Virginia Community College

John A. Fawcett
Norwalk Community College

Dr. Barry Freeman
Bergen Community College

Richard Ghidella
Fullerton College

Ross Gittell
University of New Hampshire

Clark Hallpike
Elgin Community College

Carnella Hardin
Glendale College—Arizona

Britt Hastey
Los Angeles City College

Dave Hickman
Frederick Community College

Nathan Himelstein
Essex County College

Scott Homan
Purdue—West Lafayette

Howard L. Irby, Jr.
Bronx Community College

Robert Ironside
North Lake College

Charlotte Jacobsen
Montgomery College

Bruce Johnson
College of the Desert

Judith Jones
Norwalk Community College

Marce Kelly
Santa Monica College

Gregory Kishel
Cypress College—Santa Ana College

Patricia Kishel
Cypress College

Andy Klein
DeVry University

Mary Beth Klinger
College of Southern Maryland

John S. Leahy
Palomar College

Delores Linton
Tarrant County College-Northwest Campus

Stacy Martin
Southwestern Illinois College

Theresa Mastrianni
Kingsborough Community College

Bob Matthews
Oakton Community College

Hugh McCabe
Westchester Community College

Tricia McConville
Northeastern University

Rebecca Miles
Delaware Tech

Linda Morable
Richland College

Linda Mosley
Tarrant County College

Carol Murphy
Quinsigamond Community College

Andrew Nelson
Montgomery College

Greg Nesty
Humboldt College

Linda Newell
Saddleback College

Emmanuel Nkwenti
Pennsylvania College of Technology

Paul Okello
Tarrant County College

Lynn D. Pape
Northern Virginia Community College—Alexandria Campus

Charles Pedersen
Quinsigamond Community College

John Pharr
Cedar Valley—Dallas County Community College District

Jeff Podoshen
DeVry University

Jude A. Rathburn
University of Wisconsin—Milwaukee

Levi Richard
Citrus College

Joe Ryan
Valley College

Althea Seaborn
Norwalk Community College

John Seilo
Orange Coast Community College

Richard Sherer
Los Angeles Trade—Technical College

Gerald Silver
Purdue University—Calumet

Leon Singleton
Santa Monica College

Malcolm Skeeter
Norwalk Community College

Robert Smolin
Citrus College

Darrell Thompson
Mountain View College

Sandra Toy
Orange Coast College

Phil Vardiman
Abilene Christian University

Gina Vega
Merrimack College

Michelle Vybiral
Joliet Junior College

Rick Weidmann
Prince George's Community College

S. Martin Welc
Saddleback College

Steve Wong
Rock Valley College

Greg Akins
Lansing Community College

Ken Anderson
Borough of Manhattan Community College

Nancy Bailey
Middlesex Community College

Mary Barnum
Grand Rapids Community College

Sherry Bell
Ferris State University

Ellen Benowitz
Mercer Community College

Mike Bento
Owens Community College

Pat Bernson
County College of Morris

Trudy Borst
Ferris State University

David Braun
Pierce College

David England
John A. Logan College

Barry Freeman
Bergen Community College

Eric Glohr
Lansing Community College

Karen Hawkins
Miami Dade Community College

Nate Himelstein
Essex Community College

Kim Hurns
Washtenaw Community College

Dmitriy Kalyagin
Chabot College

Elias Konwufine
Keiser College

Carl Kovelowski
Mercer Community College

Pierre Laguerre
Bergen Community College

Stacy Martin
Southwestern Illinois College

Duane Miller
Utah Valley State College

Ed Mitchell
Hillsborough Community College

Frank Novakowski
Davenport University

Tom Passero
Owens Community College

Tom Perkins
Lansing Community College

Robert Reck
Western Michigan University

Paul Ricker
Broward Community College

Jenny Rink
Community College of Philadelphia

Susan Roach
Georgia Southern University

Edith Strickland
Tallahassee Community College

Keith Taylor
Lansing Community College

Joyce Thompson
Lehigh-Carbon Community College

Bob Urell
Irvine Valley College

Richard Warner
Lehigh-Carbon Community College

David Woolgar
Santa Ana College

Chuck Zellerbach
Orange Coast College

Alison Adderly-Pitman
Brevard Community College

David Alexander
Angelo State University

Kenneth Anderson
Mott Community College

Charles Armstrong
Kansas City Kansas Community College

Donald B. Armstrong
Mesa College

Nathaniel Barber
Winthrop University

Alan Bardwick
Community College of Aurora

Keith Batman
Cayuga Community College

Robb Bay
Community College of Southern Nevada

Charles Beem
Bucks County Community College

Carol Bibly
Triton College

Daniel Biddlecom
Erie Community College—North Campus

Joseph Billingere
Oxnard College

Larry Blenke
Sacramento City College

Paula E. Bobrowski
SUNY Oswego

Charlane Bomrad Held
Onandaga Community College

Brenda Bradford
Missouri Baptist College

Steven E. Bradley
Austin Community College

Willie Caldwell
Houston Community College

Barney Carlson
Yuba College

Bonnie Chavez
Santa Barbara City College

Felipe Chia
Harrisburg Area Community College

Rowland Chidomere
Winston-Salem State University

Marie Comstock
Allan Hancock College

Ronald C. Cooley
South Suburban College

Suzanne Counte
Jefferson College

Robert Cox
Salt Lake Community College

Pam Crader
Jefferson College

Norman B. Cregger
Central Michigan University

Dana D'Angelo
Drexel University

Dean Danielson
San Joaquin College

Kathy Daruty
Los Angeles Pierce College

David DeCook
Arapahoe Community College

Richard L. Drury
Northern Virginia Area Community College—Annandale

Linda Durkin
Delaware County Community College

Lance J. Edwards
Otero Junior College

William Ewald
Concordia University

Carol Fasso
Jamestown Community College

Jodson Faurer
Metropolitan State College at Denver

Jan Feldbauer
Austin Community College

Sandie Ferriter
Harford Community College

Steven H. Floyd
Manatee Community College

Nancy M. Fortunato
Bryant and Stratton

John G. Foster Jr.
Montgomery College—Rockville

William D. Foster
Fontbonne College

Blane Franckowiak
Tarrant County Community College

Edward Friese
Okaloosa-Walton Community College

Atlen Gastineau
Valencia Community College—West Campus

Milton Glisson
North Carolina A&T State University

Bob Googins
Shasta Community College

Robert Gora
Catawba Valley Community College

Don Gordon
Illinois Central College

Gary Greene
Manatee Community College

Blaine Greenfield
Bucks County Community College

Stephen W. Griffin
Tarrant County Community College

Maria Carmen Guerrero-Caldero
Oxnard College

Annette L. Halpin
Beaver College

Michael Hamberger
Northern Virginia Area Community College—Annandale

Neal Hannon
Bryant College

Douglas Heeter
Ferris State University

Paul Hegele
Elgin Community College

Chuck Henry
Coastline Community College

Thomas Herbek
Monroe Community College

Tom Heslin
Indiana University, Bloomington

Joseph Ho
College of Alameda

Alice J. Holt
Benedict College

Vince Howe
University of North Carolina, Wilmington

Eva M. Hyatt
Appalachian State University

Kathy Irwin
Catawba Valley Community College

Gloria M. Jackson
San Antonio College

Ralph Jagodka
Mount San Antonio College

Chris Jelepis
Drexel University

Steven R. Jennings
Highland Community College

Geraldine Jolly
Barton College

Dave Jones
LaSalle University

Don Kelley
Francis Marion University

Bill Kindsfather
Tarrant County Community College

Charles C. Kitzmiller
Indian River Community College

B. J. Kohlin
Pasadena City College

Carl Kovelowski
Mercer Community College

Ken Lafave
Mount San Jacinto College

Rex Lambrecht
Northeastern Junior College

Fay D. Lamphear
San Antonio College

Bruce Leppine
Delta College

Thomas Lloyd
Westmoreland County Community College

Jim Locke
Northern Virginia Area Community College—Annandale

Paul Londrigan
Mott Community College

Kathleen J. Lorencz
Oakland County Community College

John Mack
Salem State College

Paul Martin
Aims College

Lori Martynowicz
Bryant and Stratton

Michael Matukonis
SUNY Oneonta

Virginia Mayes
Montgomery College—Germantown

Joseph E. McAloon
Fitchburg State College

James McKee
Champlain College

Michael McLane
University of Texas, San Antonio

Ina Midkiff
Austin Community College

Rebecca Mihelcic
Howard Community College

Richard Miller
Harford Community College

Joseph Mislivec
Central Michigan University

Kimberly K. Montney
Kellogg Community College

Gail Moran
Harper College

Linda S. Munilla
Georgia Southern University

Kenneth R. Nail
Pasco-Hernando Community College

Joe Newton
Buffalo State College

Janet Nichols
Northeastern University

Frank Nickels
Pasco-Hernando Community College

Sharon Nickels
St. Petersburg Junior College

Nnamdi I. Osakwe
Livingstone College

Tibor Osatreicher
Baltimore City Community College

George Otto
Truman College

Thomas Paczkowski
Cayuga Community College

Alton Parish
Tarrant County Community College

Jack Partlow
Northern Virginia Area Community College—Annandale

Jeff Penley
Catawba Valley Community College

Robert Pollero
Anne Arundel Community College

Alton J. Purdy
Solano Community College

Surat P. Puri
Barber Scottia College

Linda Reynolds
Sacramento City College

Brenda Rhodes
Northeastern Junior College

Merle Rhodes
Morgan Community College

Pollis Robertson
Kellogg Community College

Robert Ross
Drexel University

Benjamin Sackmary
Buffalo State College

Catherina A. Sanders
San Antonio College

Lewis Schlossinger
Community College of Aurora

Gene Schneider
Austin Community College

Raymond Shea
Monroe Community College

Nora Jo Sherman
Houston Community College

Leon J. Singleton
Santa Monica College

Jeff Slater
North Shore Community College

Candy Smith
Folsom Lakes College

Solomon A. Solomon
Community College of Rhode Island

R. Southall
Laney College

Martin St. John
Westmoreland County Community College

E. George Stook
Anne Arundel Community College

James B. Stull
San Jose State University

Bill Syverstein
Fresno City College

Thomas Szezurek
Delaware County Community College

Daryl Taylor
Pasadena City College

John H. Teter
St. Petersburg Junior College

Gary Thomas
Anne Arundel Community College

Michael Thomas
Henry Ford Community College

Frank Titlow
St. Petersburg Junior College

Roland Tollefson
Anne Arundel Community College

Sheb True
Loyola Marymount University

Robert Ulbrich
Parkland College

Ariah Ullman
SUNY Binghamton

Sal Veas
Santa Monica College

Steven Wade
Santa Clara University

Dennis Wahler
San Jacinto Evergreen Community College District

W. J. Walters
Central Piedmont Community College

Timothy Weaver
Moorpark College

Richard Wertz
Concordia University

Darcelle D. White
Eastern Michigan University

Jean G. Wicks
Bowie State University

Tom Wiener
Iowa Central Community College

Dave Wiley
Anne Arundel Community College

Richard J. Williams
Santa Clara University

Joyce Wood
Northern Virginia Community College

Gregory Worosz
Schoolcraft College

Martha Zennis
Jamestown Community College

In Conclusion

I would like to thank Ingrid Benson, Debbie Meyer and the staff at Integra-Chicago. Their unending efforts on behalf of *Contemporary Business* were truly extraordinary. I would also like to thank Tim Hatten at Mesa State College for his valuable feedback.

Let me conclude by noting that this new edition would never have become a reality without the outstanding efforts of the Wiley editorial, production, and marketing teams. Special thanks to George Hoffman, Lisé Johnson, Franny Kelly, Kelly Simmons, and Emily McGee.

Dave Kurtz

| Brief Contents |

Contents

PART 2 Starting and Growing Your Business

143

[**Chapter 6**]

Opening Vignette
Elon Musk Launches Space X into the Final Frontier

BusinessEtiquette
Communicating By Email, Text Message, or Social Networking Updates: You Don't Have to Be All Thumbs

Hit & Miss
Meyer Wells: New Life for Old Wood

Hit & Miss
Businesses Based at Home Are Booming

Solving an Ethical Controversy
Entrepreneurs and Ethics: It's Good Business

Going Green
Adam Lowry and Eric Ryan: There's a Method to Their Madness

PART 3 Management: Empowering People to Achieve Business   215

Chapter 7

Opening Vignette
Ursula Burns: Moving
Xerox Forward

**Solving an Ethical
Controversy**
Google Stands Alone: When
Ethics and Business Don't Mix

Going Green
Johnson & Johnson: Caring for
the World

Hit & Miss
Jeff Immelt Tries to Lead GE in
a New Direction

Hit & Miss
Southwest Airlines: "We Love
Your Bags"

BusinessEtiquette
Managing a Millennial
Workforce

[Chapter 8]

Opening Vignette
After the Flood: Gaylord Opryland Hotel Stays Afloat.

Hit & Miss
Stop Demotivating Employees—And They'll Be Motivated

Solving an Ethical Controversy
Should Paid Sick Leave Be Required by Law?

BusinessEtiquette
How to Ask for a Raise

Hit & Miss
AOL Employees Don't Exit Voluntarily

Going Green
Labor Unions and Green Construction

PART 4 Marketing Management   349

[**Chapter 12**]

Opening Vignette
Bag Balm: A Simple Product with Hundreds of Uses

Hit & Miss
Buick: Making an Old Brand New Again

Hit & Miss
PortionPac Makes More By Selling Less

Going Green
Testa Produce Sells—and Builds—Green

Solving an Ethical Controversy
Teens at the Mall: Good or Bad for Business?

BusinessEtiquette
Minding Your Social Media Manners

PART 5 Managing Technology and Information   465

PART 6 Managing Financial Resources   497

PART 1

Business in a Global Environment

Jacob Wackerhausen/iStockphoto

Chapter 1

Learning Objectives

[1] Distinguish between business and not-for-profit organizations.

[2] Identify and describe the factors of production.

[3] Describe the private enterprise system, including basic rights and entrepreneurship.

[4] Identify the six eras of business, and explain how the relationship era—including alliances, technology, and environmental concerns—influences contemporary business.

[5] Explain how today's business workforce and the nature of work itself is changing.

[6] Identify the skills and attributes managers need to lead businesses in the 21st century.

[7] Outline the characteristics that make a company admired by the business community.

The Changing Face of Business

Google and Android: Fast and Faster

Technology is constantly changing the way we communicate and conduct business, which means that firms involved in either of these arenas must innovate at an equally rapid pace. Soon, half of all the cell phones in the United States will be smart phones. In another couple of years, the market for smart phone apps will total more than $40 billion. In the space of a few recent months, the Google Android operating system surpassed the Apple iPhone in total number of U.S. subscribers—surprising even the keenest of industry watchers. Android didn't start out as a big hit. In fact, when the first Android arrived on the market, it was considered by many to be something of a dud. But Google kept improving on the software, and as it got better, major phone manufacturers like Motorola, HTC, and Samsung took notice and signed up for the ride. Android began to catch on, and within a few months more than 250,000 new phones were activated each day. Then the unthinkable happened: Google Android surged past Apple iPhone to become the largest smart phone platform in the U.S. and the third-largest in the world. How did Google Android manage this, when Apple iPhone had reigned supreme?

One research firm reports that Google Android, which was sitting in second place behind Apple iPhone, expanded its market shares so strategically that it was able to slide past Apple iPhone in market share without Apple losing any of its own share. Although many firms attempt to succeed by taking aim directly at their competitors' products, Google Android instead adopted the strategy of developing products that suited what Google does best: search. In addition, the firm found ways to enter new markets without wasting resources on trying to knock Apple aside. Google took a risk by entering the smart phone market that had been dominated by Apple, but the firm developed a system with features that dovetail neatly with its other capabilities as a search engine. For example, the Nexus S, one of the new generation Androids, integrates easily with Google Apps, Google Voice, Google Maps, and others. Users have discovered that the Nexus S works beautifully as a GPS when used with Google Maps. Along with its Android platform—which now powers more than 100 smart phone models—Google has been offering a continous barrage of user-friendly apps, many of which are free, to attract new users and retain those who are already onboard.

Android apps include such popular choices as Double Twist, Kindle Reader for Android, Ski Report, Movies by Flixster, Shazam, and Urbanspoon. Double Twist allows users to sync their iTunes playlists, songs, and videos wirelessly to their Android phones. Flixster posts information about movie hits, new films, and DVD releases. Users can tap on the "theaters" section for information on local show times or to buy tickets. Urbanspoon not only helps users find restaurants, it allows them to make reservations and then helps them get there with its internal GPS tracker.

The Android software program itself is tiny by comparison to those of its rivals, yet it has managed to shape the near future of the mobile industry. In addition, it has turned Google and its previous ally Apple into direct competitors. The rapid and unexpected rise to the top by Google Android sends a message to businesses everywhere: innovation reigns supreme.[1]

Chris Ratcliffe/Bloomberg/Getty Images, Inc.

Overview

Business is the nation's engine for growth. A growing economy—one that produces more goods and services with fewer resources over time—yields income for business owners, their employees, and stockholders. So a country depends on the wealth its businesses generate, from large enterprises like the Walt Disney Company to tiny online startups, and from venerable firms like 150-year-old jeans maker Levi Strauss & Company to powerhouses like Google. What all these companies and many others share is a creative approach to meeting society's needs and wants.

Businesses solve our transportation problems by marketing cars, tires, gasoline, and airline tickets. They bring food to our tables by growing, harvesting, processing, packaging, and shipping everything from spring water to cake mix and frozen shrimp. Restaurants buy, prepare, and serve food, and some even deliver. Construction companies build our schools, homes, and hospitals, while real estate firms bring property buyers and sellers together. Clothing manufacturers design, create, import, and deliver our jeans, sports shoes, work uniforms, and party wear. Entertainment for our leisure hours comes from hundreds of firms that create, produce, and distribute films, television shows, videogames, books, and music CDs and downloads.

To succeed, business firms must know what their customers want so that they can supply it quickly and efficiently. That means they often reflect changes in consumer tastes, such as the growing preference for sports drinks and vitamin-fortified water. But firms can also *lead* in advancing technology and other changes. They have the resources, the know-how, and the financial incentive to bring about new innovations as well as the competition that inevitably follows, as in the case of Apple's iPhone and Google's Android.

You'll see throughout this book that businesses require physical inputs like auto parts, chemicals, sugar, thread, and electricity, as well as the accumulated knowledge and experience of their managers and employees. Yet they also rely heavily on their own ability to change with the times and with the marketplace. Flexibility is a key to long-term success—and to growth.

In short, business is at the forefront of our economy—and *Contemporary Business* is right there with it. This book explores the strategies that allow companies to grow and compete in today's interactive marketplace, along with the skills that you will need to turn ideas into action for your own success in business. This chapter sets the stage for the entire text by defining business and revealing its role in society. The chapter's discussion illustrates how the private enterprise system encourages competition and innovation while preserving business ethics.

What Is Business?

What comes to mind when you hear the word *business?* Do you think of big corporations like ExxonMobil or Target? Or does the local bakery or shoe store pop into your mind? Maybe you recall your first summer job. The term *business* is a broad, all-inclusive term that can be applied to many kinds of enterprises. Businesses provide the bulk of employment opportunities, as well as the products that people enjoy.

Business consists of all profit-seeking activities and enterprises that provide goods and services necessary to an economic system. Some businesses produce tangible goods, such as automobiles, breakfast cereals, and digital music players; others provide services such as insurance, hair styling, and entertainment ranging from Six Flags theme parks and sports events to concerts.

A business, such as this cell phone store, survives through the exchange between buyer and seller. In this case, the customer and the salesperson.

Business drives the economic pulse of a nation. It provides the means through which its citizens' standard of living improves. At the heart of every business endeavor is an exchange between a buyer and a seller. A buyer recognizes a need for a good or service and trades money with a seller to obtain that product. The seller participates in the process in hopes of gaining profits—a main ingredient in accomplishing the goals necessary for continuous improvement in the standard of living.

Profits represent rewards for businesspeople who take the risks involved in blending people, technology, and information to create and market want-satisfying goods and services. In contrast, accountants think of profits as the difference between a firm's revenues and the expenses it incurs in generating these revenues. More generally, however, profits serve as incentives for people to start companies, expand them, and provide consistently high-quality competitive goods and services.

The quest for profits is a central focus of business because without profits, a company could not survive. But businesspeople also recognize their social and ethical responsibilities. To succeed in the long run, companies must deal responsibly with employees, customers, suppliers, competitors, government, and the general public.

Not-for-Profit Organizations

What do Ohio State's athletic department, the U.S. Postal Service, the American Red Cross, and your local library have in common? They are all classified as **not-for-profit organizations**, businesslike establishments that have primary objectives other than returning profits to their owners. These organizations play important roles in society by placing public service above profits, although it is important to understand that these organizations need to raise money so that they can operate and achieve their social goals. Not-for-profit organizations operate in both the private and public sectors. Private-sector not-for-profits include museums, libraries, trade associations, and charitable and religious organizations.

business all profit-seeking activities and enterprises that provide goods and services necessary to an economic system.

profits rewards for businesspeople who take the risks involved to offer goods and services to customers.

not-for-profit organizations organization that has primary objectives such as public service rather than returning a profit to its owners.

Government agencies, political parties, and labor unions, all of which are part of the public sector, are also classified as not-for-profit organizations.

Not-for-profit organizations are a substantial part of the U.S. economy. Currently, more than 1.5 million nonprofit organizations are registered with the Internal Revenue Service in the United States, in categories ranging from arts and culture to science and technology.[2] These organizations control more than $2.6 trillion in assets and employ more people than the federal government and all 50 state governments combined.[3] In addition, millions of volunteers work for them in unpaid positions. Not-for-profits secure funding from both private sources, including donations, and government sources. They are commonly exempt from federal, state, and local taxes.

Although they focus on goals other than generating profits, managers of not-for-profit organizations face many of the same challenges as executives of profit-seeking businesses. Without funding, they cannot do research, obtain raw materials, or provide services. St. Jude Children's Research Hospital's pediatric treatment and research facility in Memphis treats nearly 5,000 children a year for catastrophic diseases, mainly cancer, immune system problems, and infectious and genetic disorders. Patients come from all 50 states and all over the world and are accepted without regard to the family's ability to pay. To provide top-quality care and to support its research in gene therapy, chemotherapy, bone marrow transplantation, and the psychological effects of illness, among many other critical areas, St. Jude relies on contributions, with some assistance from federal grants and investments.[4]

Other not-for-profits mobilize their resources to respond to emergencies. When the massive earthquake and tsunami hit Japan, it left vast amounts of people throughout the country without shelter, food, and drinking water. The Red Cross took immediate action to provide medical care and relief assistance.[5]

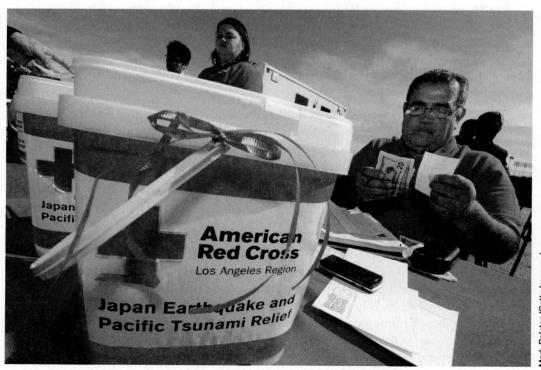

Mark Ralston/Getty Images, Inc.

■ The Red Cross mobilizes its efforts to respond to the earthquake disaster relief in Japan.

Some not-for-profits sell merchandise or set up profit-generating arms to provide goods and services for which people are willing and able to pay. College bookstores sell everything from sweatshirts to coffee mugs with school logos imprinted on them, while the Sierra Club and the Appalachian Mountain Club both have full-fledged publishing programs. The Lance Armstrong Foundation has sold more than 40 million yellow LiveStrong wristbands as well as sports gear and accessories for men, women, and children in the United States and abroad, with the money earmarked to fight cancer and support patients and families.[6] Handling merchandising programs like these, as well as launching other fund-raising campaigns, requires managers of not-for-profit organizations to develop effective business skills and experience. Consequently, many of the concepts discussed in this book apply to not-for-profit organizations as well as to profit-oriented firms.

Factors of Production

An economic system requires certain inputs for successful operation. Economists use the term **factors of production** to refer to the four basic inputs: natural resources, capital, human resources, and entrepreneurship. Table 1.1 identifies each of these inputs and the type of payment received by firms and individuals who supply them.

Natural resources include all production inputs that are useful in their natural states, including agricultural land, building sites, forests, and mineral deposits. The largest wind farm in the world, the Roscoe Wind Complex near Roscoe, Texas, generates enough power to support almost a quarter million homes. Natural resources are the basic inputs required in any economic system.

Capital, another key resource, includes technology, tools, information, and physical facilities. *Technology* is a broad term that refers to such machinery and equipment as computers and software, telecommunications, and inventions designed to improve production. Information, frequently improved by technological innovations, is another critical factor because both managers and operating employees require accurate, timely information for effective performance of their assigned tasks. Technology plays an important role in the success of many businesses. Sometimes technology results in a new product, such as hybrid autos that run on a combination of gasoline and electricity. Most of the major car companies have introduced hybrid versions of their best-sellers in recent years.

Technology often helps a company improve its own products. Recently Amazon announced an update to its free Kindle app for the iPad and iPhone that allows users to

<table>
<tr><td>Table
1.1</td><td colspan="2">**Factors of Production and Their
Factor Payments**</td></tr>
<tr><th>FACTOR OF PRODUCTION</th><th>CORRESPONDING FACTOR PAYMENT</th></tr>
<tr><td>Natural resources</td><td>Rent</td></tr>
<tr><td>Capital</td><td>Interest</td></tr>
<tr><td>Human resources</td><td>Wages</td></tr>
<tr><td>Entrepreneurship</td><td>Profit</td></tr>
</table>

Assessment Check ☑

1. What activity lies at the heart of every business endeavor?
2. What are the primary objectives of a not-for-profit organization?

factors of production four basic inputs for effective operation: natural resources, capital, human resources, and entrepreneurship.

natural resources all production inputs that are useful in their natural states, including agricultural land, building sites, forests, and mineral deposits.

capital production inputs consisting of technology, tools, information, and physical facilities.

access millions of free book titles from an array of Internet sources, including files from Project Gutenberg and Internet Archive. Already in its second generation, it's also small and comfortable enough to be held in your hands with improved battery life and storage capacity. Weighing in at considerably less than a pound, the Kindle reflects light for ease of reading and generates little heat.[7]

And sometimes firms rely on technology to help move and track their products more efficiently. Delivery firm UPS recently launched a marketing campaign to promote its logistics business, which uses technology to assist companies in such tasks as operating warehouses, shipping goods, and clearing customs. UPS has also partnered with the Red Cross to launch logistics emergency teams in several U.S. cities.[8]

To remain competitive, a firm needs to continually acquire, maintain, and upgrade its capital, and businesses need money for that purpose. A company's funds may come from owner-investments, profits plowed back into the business, or loans extended by others. Money then goes to work building factories; purchasing raw materials and component parts; and hiring, training, and compensating workers. People and firms that supply capital receive factor payments in the form of interest.

human resources
production inputs consisting of anyone who works, including both the physical labor and the intellectual inputs contributed by workers.

<u>**Human resources**</u> represent another critical input in every economic system. Human resources include anyone who works, from the chief executive officer (CEO) of a huge corporation to a self-employed editor. This category encompasses both the physical labor and the intellectual inputs contributed by workers. Companies rely on their employees as a valued source of ideas and innovation, as well as physical effort. Some companies solicit employee ideas through traditional means, such as an online "suggestion box" or in staff meetings. Others encourage creative thinking during company-sponsored hiking or rafting trips or during social gatherings. Effective, well-trained human resources provide a

Plesea Petre/iStockphoto

Competent, effective human resources can be a company's best asset. Providing perks to those employees to keep them is in a company's best interest, as software provider SAS has proven.

significant competitive edge because competitors cannot easily match another company's talented, motivated employees in the way they can buy the same computer system or purchase the same grade of natural resources.

Hiring and keeping the right people matters, as we'll see later in the case at the end of this chapter. SAS continues to be a great place to work in part due to the attention the firm pays to retain their employees.[9]

Entrepreneurship is the willingness to take risks to create and operate a business. An entrepreneur is someone who sees a potentially profitable opportunity and then devises a plan to achieve success in the marketplace and earn those profits. By age 20, Jessica Mah was CEO of inDinero, a Web site that helps small businesses keep track of their money. Mah had "noticed that anything that touches money is much harder for entrepreneurs than it should be," so she took a risk and started a firm designed to help them.[10]

U.S. businesses operate within an economic system called the *private enterprise system*. The next section looks at the private enterprise system, including competition, private property, and the entrepreneurship alternative.

entrepreneurship willingness to take risks to create and operate a business.

Assessment Check ☑

1. Identify the four basic inputs to an economic system.
2. List four types of capital.

The Private Enterprise System

No business operates in a vacuum. All operate within a larger economic system that determines how goods and services are produced, distributed, and consumed in a society. The type of economic system employed in a society also determines patterns of resource use. Some economic systems, such as communism, feature strict controls on business ownership, profits, and resources to accomplish government goals.

In the United States, businesses function within the **private enterprise system**, an economic system that rewards firms for their ability to identify and serve the needs and demands of customers. The private enterprise system minimizes government interference in economic activity. Businesses that are adept at satisfying customers gain access to necessary factors of production and earn profits.

Another name for the private enterprise system is **capitalism**. Adam Smith, often identified as the father of capitalism, first described the concept in his book *The Wealth of Nations*, published in 1776. Smith believed that an economy is best regulated by the "invisible hand" of **competition**, the battle among businesses for consumer acceptance. Smith thought that competition among firms would lead to consumers' receiving the best possible products and prices because less efficient producers would gradually be driven from the marketplace.

The "invisible hand" concept is a basic premise of the private enterprise system. In the United States, competition regulates much of economic life. To compete successfully, each firm must find a basis for **competitive differentiation**, the unique combination of organizational abilities, products, and approaches that sets a company apart from competitors in the minds of customers. Businesses operating in a private enterprise system face a critical task of keeping up with changing marketplace conditions. Firms that fail to adjust to shifts in consumer preferences or ignore the actions of competitors leave themselves open to failure. Apple and Microsoft have long been known for their rivalry, despite the fact that on occasion they have teamed up in alliances. For instance, Microsoft recently announced plans to unveil tablet software designed to compete directly with the iPad.[11]

private enterprise system economic system that rewards firms for their ability to identify and serve the needs and demands of customers.

capitalism economic system that rewards firms for their ability to perceive and serve the needs and demands of consumers; also called the private enterprise system.

competition battle among businesses for consumer acceptance.

competitive differentiation unique combination of organizational abilities, products, and approaches that sets a company apart from competitors in the minds of customers.

Microsoft and Google Square Off on the Web

Google took a big step into Microsoft-dominated territory with its introduction of home and office tools like Gmail and Google Docs, and especially with its own operating system, Chrome OS, to challenge Microsoft's long-running Windows series. Google even has a Web browser, also called Chrome, to compete with Microsoft's entrenched Internet Explorer, while Microsoft challenges Google's dominance in Internet searches with its new search engine, Bing.

Google has long supported Web-based applications, as opposed to the desk-top applications that have been Microsoft's specialty, but Microsoft is fighting back. It's creating browser-based versions of its desktop Office products including Word, Excel, and PowerPoint to compete with Google's cloud-computing tools. Microsoft's applications, often known for growing by adding more and more features in each new generation, will have to match Google's successful focus on speed and ease of use. Google has used these characteristics to promote a great user experience with its PC products, an advantage it hopes to import into the business applications market. "We want to spoil people like heck in their personal lives," says Google's vice president of product management. "Then when they go to work, they should be asking the question, 'Why are things so hard?'"

Google credits some of its success to its design teams' unwillingness to settle for the status quo. "I don't think our Docs team has ever been fundamentally happy with their product," said the president of the company's enterprise group. That restlessness means shortfalls in any Google product's performance may be short-lived. Google Docs,

for instance, can't yet match Microsoft Word's editing and page layout features, while Google Spreadsheets offers limited performance and scaling capabilities.

Google is so determined to solve such problems, however, that it's helping to shape the creation of the World Wide Web's new HTML5 language, the standard for structuring and presenting content on Web pages and Web-based documents. "We view the Web as a platform," says Google's enterprise product management director. "We don't view it as a companion to the desktop. . . . We want the vast majority of users of Microsoft Office to be able to easily switch to Google Docs."

Critical Thinking Questions

1. What feature or features do you think Google has identified as its basis for competitive differentiation?

2. Some companies are considering using Google's Android operating system for their tablet PCs and netbooks. How would you expect Microsoft to react if Google succeeds in entering the market for desktop applications in this way?

Sources: Carl Brooks, "Online Office App Wars: Microsoft vs. Google vs. IBM," *SearchCloudComputing.com*, accessed June 14, 2011, http://searchcloudcomputing.techtarget.com; M. Merrill, "Microsoft Bing, Google Compete with Health Maps," Healthcare IT News, www.healthcareitnews.com, June 2, 2010; Thomas Claburn, "Microsoft Web Apps Will Force Google's Hand," InformationWeek, www.informationweek.com, April 10, 2010; Nick Bilton, "A Big-Picture Look at Google, Microsoft, Apple and Yahoo," *The New York Times,* www.nytimes.com, January 22, 2010.

Another of Microsoft's competitors, Google, launched Chrome in an effort to compete in the web browser market; see the "Hit & Miss" feature.

Throughout this book, our discussion focuses on the tools and methods that 21st-century businesses apply to compete and differentiate their goods and services. We also discuss many of the ways in which market changes will affect business and the private enterprise system in the years ahead.

Basic Rights in the Private Enterprise System

For capitalism to operate effectively, the citizens of a private enterprise economy must have certain rights. As shown in Figure 1.1, these include the rights to private property, profits, freedom of choice, and competition.

The right to **private property** is the most basic freedom under the private enterprise system. Every participant has the right to own, use, buy, sell, and bequeath most forms of property, including land, buildings, machinery, equipment, patents on inventions, individual possessions, and intangible properties.

private property most basic freedom under the private enterprise system; the right to own, use, buy, sell, and bequeath land, buildings, machinery, equipment, patents, individual possessions, and various intangible kinds of property.

The private enterprise system also guarantees business owners the right to all profits—after taxes—they earn through their activities. Although a business is not assured of earning a profit, its owner is legally and ethically entitled to any income it generates in excess of costs.

Freedom of choice means that a private enterprise system relies on the potential for citizens to choose their own employment, purchases, and investments. They can change jobs, negotiate wages, join labor unions, and choose among many different brands of goods and services. People living in the capitalist nations of North America, Europe, and other parts of the world are so accustomed to this freedom of choice that they sometimes forget its importance. A private enterprise economy maximizes individual prosperity by providing alternatives. Other economic systems sometimes limit freedom of choice to accomplish government goals, such as increasing industrial production of certain items or military strength.

The private enterprise system also permits fair competition by allowing the public to set rules for competitive activity. For this reason, the U.S. government has passed laws to prohibit "cutthroat" competition—excessively aggressive competitive practices designed to eliminate competition. It also has established ground rules that outlaw price discrimination, fraud in financial markets, and deceptive advertising and packaging. The Federal Communications Commission (FCC) recently closed a loophole in its rules that will help increase competition in the cable industry by forcing major companies to give up their exclusive rights to broadcast certain sports channels. "Consumers who want to switch video providers shouldn't have to give up their favorite team in the process," the FCC chairperson said. "Today the Commission levels the competitive playing field."[12]

FIGURE
1.1 **Basic Rights within a Private Enterprise System**

The Entrepreneurship Alternative

The entrepreneurial spirit beats at the heart of private enterprise. An **entrepreneur** is a risk taker in the private enterprise system. You hear about entrepreneurs all the time—two college students starting a software business in their dorm room or a mom who invents a better baby carrier. Many times their success is modest, but once in a while, the risk pays off in huge profits. Individuals who recognize marketplace opportunities are free to use their capital, time, and talents to pursue those opportunities for profit. The willingness of individuals to start new ventures drives economic growth and keeps pressure on existing companies to continue to satisfy customers. If no one were willing to take economic risks, the private enterprise system wouldn't exist.

By almost any measure, the entrepreneurial spirit fuels growth in the U.S. economy. Of all the businesses operating in the United States, about one in seven firms started operations during the past year. These newly formed businesses are also the source of many of the nation's new jobs. Every year, they create more than one of every five new jobs in the economy. Most measures of entrepreneurship count the smallest or youngest businesses on the assumption that they are the enterprises in which entrepreneurship is most significant. These companies are a significant source of employment or self-employment. Of the nearly 27 million U.S. small businesses currently in operation, more than 20 million are self-employed people without any employees. More than 21 million U.S. employees currently work for a business with fewer than 20 employees.[13] Does starting a business require higher education? Not necessarily, although it can help. Figure 1.2 presents the results of a survey of small-business owners, which shows that about 24 percent of all respondents had graduated from college, and 19 percent had postgraduate degrees.

entrepreneur person who seeks a profitable opportunity and takes the necessary risks to set up and operate a business.

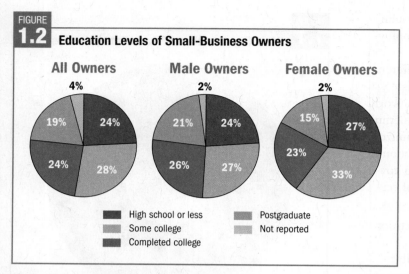

FIGURE 1.2 Education Levels of Small-Business Owners

All Owners

- 4%
- 19%
- 24%
- 24%
- 28%

Male Owners

- 2%
- 21%
- 24%
- 26%
- 27%

Female Owners

- 2%
- 15%
- 27%
- 23%
- 33%

- High school or less
- Some college
- Completed college
- Postgraduate
- Not reported

Note: Numbers may not total to 100 percent due to rounding.

Source: Data from "Survey of Business Owners (SBO): Owner's Education Levels at Start-Up, Purchase, or Acquisition of the Business," U.S. Census Bureau, http://www.census.gov, accessed June 14, 2011.

Besides creating jobs and selling products, entrepreneurship provides the benefits of innovation. In contrast to more established firms, start-up companies tend to innovate most in fields of technology that are new and uncrowded with competitors, making new products available to businesses and consumers. Because small companies are more flexible, they can make changes to products and processes more quickly than larger corporations. Entrepreneurs often find new ways to use natural resources, technology, and other factors of production. Often, they do this because they have to—they may not have enough money to build an expensive prototype or launch a nationwide ad campaign. Sometimes an entrepreneur may innovate by simply tweaking an existing idea. Eric Hansen, owner of Competitive Lawn Care, a small lawn-care service in Illinois, wanted to prepare his business for a potential downturn during the recent recession. He came up with the idea of running all the company's lawnmowers on propane, which would save money and reduce noise. A year-long journey to make his idea a reality took him from local government offices to obtain approval for opening the first private propane filling station in the country, to Kentucky to search for new equipment, and all the way to Europe to research technology from around the world. Says Hansen, "I am proud to say that after a year of hard work, Competitive Lawn Service Inc. will be the first company in the country to have a commercial lawn maintenance crew to operate 100 percent on propane as an alternative fuel, as well as a private propane fill station at our location. And our growing list of commercial and residential clients are listening and applauding. The future looks bright . . . and we are ready. Ready to branch out, expand, open new locations, and go where no company has gone before in the direction of alternative fuels, quality service, and a passion for making a difference in this world."[14]

Entrepreneurship is also important to existing companies in a private enterprise system. More and more, large firms are recognizing the value of entrepreneurial thinking among their employees, hoping to benefit from enhanced flexibility, improved innovation, and new market opportunities. eBay has used mobile technology to reinvent itself and its business customers—many of whom are entrepreneurs. Using augmented reality—which allows such activities as virtually "trying on" clothes via smart phone—eBay sellers have extended their reach to consumers' hands even when they aren't thinking about a purchase. "Mobile commerce is eBay's chance to become ubiquitous without brick-and-mortar outlets," observes one analyst.[15]

As the next section explains, entrepreneurs have played a vital role in the history

Competitive Lawn Care's mowers all run on propane—the efforts to make this happen came from the entrepreneurial spirit of the company's owner, Eric Hansen.

Dmitrijs Dmitrijevs/Shutterstock

of U.S. business. They have helped create new industries, developed successful new business methods, and improved U.S. standing in global competition.

Six Eras in the History of Business

In the roughly 400 years since the first European settlements appeared on the North American continent, amazing changes have occurred in the size, focus, and goals of U.S. businesses. As Figure 1.3 indicates, U.S. business history is divided into six distinct time periods: (1) the Colonial period, (2) the Industrial Revolution, (3) the age of industrial entrepreneurs, (4) the production era, (5) the marketing era, and (6) the relationship era. The next sections describe how events in each of these time periods have influenced U.S. business practices.

The Colonial Period

Colonial society emphasized rural and agricultural production. Colonial towns were small compared with European cities, and they functioned as marketplaces for farmers and craftspeople. The economic focus of the nation centered on rural areas, because prosperity depended on the output of farms and plantations. The success or failure of crops influenced every aspect of the economy.

Colonists depended on England for manufactured items as well as financial backing for their infant industries. Even after the Revolutionary War (1776–1783), the United States maintained close economic ties with England. British investors continued to provide much of the financing for developing the U.S. business system, and this financial influence continued well into the 19th century.

The Industrial Revolution

The Industrial Revolution began in England around 1750. It moved business operations from an emphasis on independent, skilled workers who specialized in building products one by one to a factory system that mass-produced items by bringing together large numbers of semiskilled workers. The factories profited from the savings created by large-scale production, bolstered by increasing support from machines over time. As businesses grew, they could often purchase raw materials more cheaply in larger lots than

Assessment Check ✓

1. What is an alternative term for *private enterprise system*?
2. What is the most basic freedom under the private enterprise system?
3. What is an entrepreneur?

FIGURE 1.3 **Six Eras in Business History**

Era	Main Characteristics	Time Period
Colonial	Primarily agricultural	Prior to 1776
Industrial Revolution	Mass production by semiskilled workers, aided by machines	1760–1850
Industrial entrepreneurs	Advances in technology and increased demand for manufactured goods, leading to enormous entrepreneurial opportunities	Late 1800s
Production	Emphasis on producing more goods faster, leading to production innovations such as assembly lines	Through the 1920s
Marketing	Consumer orientation, seeking to understand and satisfy needs and preferences of customer groups	Since 1950s
Relationship	Benefits derived from deep, ongoing links with individual customers, employees, suppliers, and other businesses	Began in 1990s

before. Specialization of labor, limiting each worker to a few specific tasks in the production process, also improved production efficiency.

Influenced by these events in England, business in the United States began a time of rapid industrialization. Agriculture became mechanized, and factories sprang up in cities. During the mid-1800s, the pace of the revolution was increased as newly built railroad systems provided fast, economical transportation. In California, for example, the combination of railroad construction and the gold rush fueled a tremendous demand for construction.

The Age of Industrial Entrepreneurs

Building on the opportunities created by the Industrial Revolution, entrepreneurship increased in the United States. In 1900, Arthur R. Wilson and several partners paid $10,000 in gold coins for a 27-acre parcel of granite-rich land in California. This natural resource was the basis for the Granite Rock Co., which provided the material for roads and buildings in California's booming economy. The company, now called Graniterock, evolved in response to technological, competitive, and marketplace demands and continues to survive in the 21st century. Today the firm, which has stores throughout California, offers consumer products such as granite countertops as well as many "green" products made from recycled materials.[16]

Inventors created a virtually endless array of commercially useful products and new production methods. Many of them are famous today:

- Eli Whitney introduced the concept of interchangeable parts, an idea that would later facilitate mass production on a previously impossible scale.

- Robert McCormick designed a horse-drawn reaper that reduced the labor involved in harvesting wheat. His son, Cyrus McCormick, saw the commercial potential of the reaper and launched a business to build and sell the machine. By 1902, the company was producing 35 percent of the nation's farm machinery.

- Cornelius Vanderbilt (railroads), J. P. Morgan (banking), and Andrew Carnegie (steel), among others, took advantage of the enormous opportunities waiting for anyone willing to take the risk of starting a new business.

The entrepreneurial spirit of this golden age in business did much to advance the U.S. business system and raise the overall standard of living of its citizens. That market transformation, in turn, created new demand for manufactured goods.

Slobo Mitic/iStockphoto

Granite Rock Co., started in the Age of Industrial Entrepreneurs, has evolved in response to 21st-century demands.

The Production Era

As demand for manufactured goods continued to increase through the 1920s, businesses focused even greater attention on the activities involved in producing those goods. Work became increasingly specialized, and huge, labor-intensive factories dominated U.S. business. Assembly lines, introduced by Henry Ford, became commonplace in major industries. Business owners turned over their responsibilities to a new class of managers trained in operating established companies. Their activities emphasized efforts to produce even more goods through quicker methods.

During the production era, business focused attention on internal processes rather than external influences. Marketing was almost an afterthought, designed solely to distribute items generated by production activities. Little attention was paid to consumer wants or needs. Instead, businesses tended to make decisions about what the market would get. If you wanted to buy a Ford Model T automobile, your color choice was black—the only color produced by the company.

The Marketing Era

The Great Depression of the early 1930s changed the shape of U.S. business yet again. As incomes nose-dived, businesses could no longer automatically count on selling everything they produced. Managers began to pay more attention to the markets for their goods and services, and sales and advertising took on new importance. During this period, selling was often synonymous with marketing.

Demand for all kinds of consumer goods exploded after World War II. After nearly five years of doing without new automobiles, appliances, and other items, consumers were buying again. At the same time, however, competition also heated up. Soon businesses began to think of marketing as more than just selling; they envisioned a process of determining what consumers wanted and needed and then designing products to satisfy those needs. In short, they developed a **consumer orientation**.

Businesses began to analyze consumer desires before beginning actual production. Consumer choices skyrocketed. Automobiles came in a wide variety of colors and styles, and car buyers could choose among them. Companies also discovered the need to distinguish their goods and services from those of competitors. **Branding**—the process of creating an identity in consumers' minds for a good, service, or company—is an important marketing tool. A **brand** can be a name, term, sign, symbol, design, or some combination that identifies the products of one firm and differentiates them from competitors' offerings.

Branding can go a long way toward creating value for a firm by providing recognition and a positive association between a company and its products. Some of the world's most famous—and enduring—brands include Coca-Cola, IBM, Microsoft, McDonald's, Disney, Toyota, Mercedes Benz, and Samsung.[17]

The marketing era has had a tremendous effect on the way business is conducted today. Even the smallest business owners recognize the importance of understanding what customers want and the reasons they buy.

The Relationship Era

As business continues in the 21st century, a significant change is taking place in the ways companies interact with customers. Since the Industrial Revolution, most businesses have concentrated on building and promoting products in the hope that enough customers will buy them to cover costs and earn acceptable profits, an approach called **transaction management**.

consumer orientation business philosophy that focuses first on determining unmet consumer wants and needs and then designing products to satisfy those needs.

branding process of creating an identity in consumers' minds for a good, service, or company; a major marketing tool in contemporary business.

brand name, term, sign, symbol, design, or some combination that identifies the products of one firm and differentiates them from competitors' offerings.

transaction management building and promoting products in the hope that enough customers will buy them to cover costs and earn profits.

relationship era the business era in which firms seek ways to actively nurture customer loyalty by carefully managing every interaction.

In contrast, in the **relationship era**, businesses are taking a different, longer-term approach to their interactions with customers. Firms now seek ways to actively nurture customer loyalty by carefully managing every interaction. They earn enormous paybacks for their efforts. A company that retains customers over the long haul reduces its advertising and sales costs. Because customer spending tends to accelerate over time, revenues also grow. Companies with long-term customers often can avoid costly reliance on price discounts to attract new business, and they find that many new buyers come from loyal customer referrals.

Business owners gain several advantages by developing ongoing relationships with customers. Because it is much less expensive to serve existing customers than to find new ones, businesses that develop long-term customer relationships can reduce their overall costs. Long-term relationships with customers enable businesses to improve their understanding of what customers want and prefer from the company. As a result, businesses enhance their chances of sustaining real advantages through competitive differentiation.

The relationship era is an age of connections—between businesses and customers, employers and employees, technology and manufacturing, and even separate companies. The world economy is increasingly interconnected, as businesses expand beyond their national boundaries. In this new environment, techniques for managing networks of people, businesses, information, and technology are critically important to contemporary business success. As you begin your own career, you will soon see how important relationships are, including your online presence; see the "Business Etiquette" feature for suggestions on presenting yourself in a positive way through social networking.

Managing Relationships through Technology

relationship management collection of activities that build and maintain ongoing, mutually beneficial ties with customers and other parties.

technology business application of knowledge based on scientific discoveries, inventions, and innovations.

Increasingly, businesses focus on **relationship management**, the collection of activities that build and maintain ongoing, mutually beneficial ties with customers and other parties. At its core, relationship management involves gathering knowledge of customer needs and preferences and applying that understanding to get as close to the customer as possible. Many of these activities are based on **technology**, or the business application of knowledge based on scientific discoveries, inventions, and innovations. In managing relationships with customers, technology most often takes the form of communication, via the Internet and cell phone. The "Hit & Miss" feature describes the importance of tablet technology in business today.

Blogs are growing more influential as a link between companies and their customers, and more companies are beginning to take advantage of their directness. Some that are connecting with customers in a positive way through their company blogs are Kodak, Walmart, Patagonia, and LinkedIn.[18] Google recently used its corporate blog both to announce its new Buzz social networking product and to calm angry users with announcements about needed changes in the service.

Strategic Alliances

strategic alliance partnership formed to create a competitive advantage for the businesses involved; in international business, a business strategy in which a company finds a partner in the country where it wants to do business.

Businesses are also finding that they must form partnerships with other organizations to take full advantage of available opportunities. One form of partnership between organizations is a **strategic alliance**, a partnership formed to create a competitive advantage for the businesses involved.

E-business has created a whole new type of strategic alliance. A firm whose entire business is conducted online, such as Amazon or Overstock.com, may team up with traditional retailers that contribute their expertise in buying the right amount of the right merchandise, as well as their knowledge of distribution. Overstock.com, based in Salt Lake City, Utah, is an online-only retailer designed for bargain hunters looking for brand-name consumer goods including clothing, appliances, electronics, and sporting goods at discount prices. The manufacturers and distributors that Overstock .com partners with gain a new avenue for reducing their inventory and allow the firm to carry over 2 million different products on its Web site. Overstock.com earned revenues of more than $800 million in one recent year and has received several workplace and customer service awards.[19]

The Green Advantage

Another way of building relationships is to incorporate issues that your customers care about into your business. As environmental concerns continue to influence consumers' choices of everything from yogurt to clothing to cars and light bulbs, many observers say the question about "going green" is no longer whether, but how. The need to develop environmentally friendly products and processes is becoming a major new force in business today. Companies in every industry are researching ways to save energy, cut emissions and pollution, reduce waste, and, not incidentally, save money and increase profits as well. The family-owned Bigelow Tea Company is working with Connecticut's Clean Energy Fund to install solar panels on four different building levels at its headquarters in Fairfield. The panels are expected to supply almost 7 percent of the building's electrical energy needs, equivalent to the power used by 22 average homes.[20]

Energy is among the biggest costs for most firms, and carbon-based fuels such as coal are responsible for most of the additional carbon dioxide in the atmosphere. Many companies have begun to address this issue, none perhaps with

Hit & Miss

How Tablets Will Change Business

When Apple's iPad first appeared on the market, only the diehard technology lovers were willing to spend the money for a device that lacked features such as a camera, multitasking capability, USB port, GPS, and the like—not to mention the fact that it was exclusive to the AT&T network. But businesspeople who are adept at seeing into the near feature quickly grasped the tablet's potential, once the bugs were worked out, features were added, and the price dropped. Apple was already planning the next generation of iPads when the first version hit the shelves. The firm faced two major challenges: convincing buyers to adopt the new technology and staying steps ahead of the competition.

Marketing the iPad correctly has been a major point. Some businesspeople view tablets as a potential replacement for the smart phone, while others do not. At its core, the iPad is a multimedia reader that could propel firms much farther toward paperless operation than any previous technology by providing access to a vast array of content. The tablet offers mobility and is user friendly to the extent that it will likely overshadow netbooks and notebooks. Some IT departments will be rethinking whether their employees need PCs or even smart phones—when an iPad or one of its competitors could do the job.

Although Apple dominates the tablet market, competitors are close behind. Some analysts predict that sales of Google's Android tablet will match those of the iPad sooner rather than later. Others disagree, arguing that Apple will reign at the top of the tablet market for some time, largely because of Apple's unparalleled skill at offering innovative new products coupled with apps and service. Either way, businesspeople who use these devices will benefit as the tablets are packed with more features and capabilities, and their prices begin to drop.

Questions for Critical Thinking

1. What strategic alliances might Apple make to give its iPad a continued competitive advantage over competitors?
2. Tablet devices such as the iPad can allow businesses to move toward the goal of becoming paperless. How might this create an advantage for these firms?

Sources: Tim Bajarin, "Why Competing Tablets Will Struggle Against the iPad," *PCMag.com*, January 11, 2011, http://www.pcmag.com; Don Reisinger, "Tablets in Business: 10 Ways They Are Changing the Corporate World," *Channel Insider*, January 10, 2011, http://www.channelinsider.com; Elizabeth Woyke, "Analyst: Android Tablet Shipments Will Match iPad in Second Half of 2011," *Forbes*, January 10, 2011, http://www.forbes.com; Molly Wood, "The iPad: It's Just Ahead of Its Time," *CNET*, January 28, 2010, http://www.news.cnet.com.

more flair that Greensulate, a small business that insulates rooftops with beautiful meadows of lavender, native grasses, and a hardy plant called sedum. The firm's efforts to date have eliminated more than 3,000 pounds of carbon from the atmosphere.[21] Clean solar energy is coming into its own and may soon be more viable and more widely available. SolarCity, a California installer of rooftop solar cells, is having trouble keeping up with growing demand. "It is hard to find installers," says the company's CEO. "We're at the stage where if we continue to grow at this pace, we won't be able to sustain the growth."[22]

Some "green" initiatives can themselves be costly for firms. General Electric, however, with its Ecomagination line of environmentally friendly products, is among those that have realized thinking "green" can satisfy not only consumers' environmental concerns but also those of shareholders by saving money and earning profits. As evidence of the company's success, GE has been ranked by the Toronto media company *Corporate Knights* as the world's top company for sustainability. This means that GE fulfills criteria for financial performance, energy productivity, waste management, and transparency in operations. *Corporate Knights* head Toby Heaps notes that the top companies "squeeze four times more wealth out of every resource they use."[23]

Each new era in U.S. business history has forced managers to reexamine the tools and techniques they formerly used to compete. Tomorrow's managers will need creativity and vision to stay on top of rapidly changing technology and to manage complex relationships in

Exelon Bets on Nuclear

"Time is not our friend with respect to global climate change. . . . the usual approach—doing too much, too late—will not work." So says John Rowe, CEO of the utility company Exelon, a recent winner of the National Safety Council's Green Cross for Safety. Exelon is betting on the world's growing demand for renewable energy sources to create a sound financial future for the company and its stakeholders while minimizing its environmental impact.

Created in 2000 from a merger between utility companies in Chicago and Philadelphia, Exelon sold most of its underperforming coal plants to focus on nuclear power generation. Its fleet of 17 reactors is the world's third-largest, topped only by utilities in France and Russia. Exelon earns $17 billion in sales and close to $3 billion in profits a year, returning more than twice as much to shareholders as other utilities. Its nuclear plants produce about 130 billion kilowatt-hours of electricity each year and have reduced greenhouse gas emissions more than 35 percent from earlier levels. That's equivalent to taking a million passenger cars off the road.

Legislation to cap or more heavily regulate carbon emissions will force Exelon's carbon-dependent competitors to raise prices. "I thought climate legislation would come sooner or later and that I'd rather have my money in the nuke fleet," says Rowe. The company plans to further shrink its carbon footprint by 2020 by eliminating more than 15 million metric tons of potential greenhouse gas emissions every year.

Questions for Critical Thinking

1. Exelon has tried and failed to acquire three smaller rival companies. What role, if any, do you think strategic partnerships might play in the company's future?

2. Exelon is the most valuable U.S. utility company in terms of market value and derives 92 percent of its power from nuclear plants. Do you think being environmentally aware and being profitable are compatible goals for a business? Why or why not?

Sources: Company Web site, www.exeloncorp.com, accessed January 14, 2011; Julie Schmit, "Exelon CEO: Deal with Emissions Now," *USA Today*, January 25, 2010, www.usatoday.com; Jonathan Fahey, "Exelon's Carbon Advantage," *Forbes*, January 18, 2010, http://www.forbes.com; "National Safety Council Names Exelon Nuclear as Recipient of 2010 Green Cross for Safety Medal," *PR Newswire*, January 5, 2010, prnewswire.com

RENEWABLE ENERGY. WATER DESALINATION.

FUEL CONSERVATION. IT'S NOT

A VISION OF THE FUTURE.

IT'S ECOMAGINATION

RIGHT

NOW.

ecomagination.com

GE
imagination at work

©General Electric Co.

Going green doesn't have to be expensive. General Electric's Ecomagination line has shown that green products can save money and earn profits as well as respond to consumers' environmental concerns.

Assessment Check ☑

1. What was the Industrial Revolution?

2. During which era was the idea of branding developed?

3. What is the difference between transaction management and relationship management?

the global business world of the fast-paced 21st century. As green operations become more cost-effective, and consumers and shareholders demand more responsive management, few firms will choose to be left behind. For a look at management issues in the energy industry, see the "Going Green" feature.

Today's Business Workforce

A skilled and knowledgeable workforce is an essential resource for keeping pace with the accelerating rate of change in today's business world. Employers need reliable workers who are dedicated to fostering strong ties with customers and partners. They must build workforces capable of efficient, high-quality production needed to compete in global markets. Savvy business leaders also realize that the brainpower of employees plays a vital role in a firm's ability to stay on top of new technologies and innovations. In short, a first-class workforce can be the foundation of a firm's competitive differentiation, providing important advantages over competing businesses.

Changes in the Workforce

Companies now face several trends that challenge their skills for managing and developing human resources. Those challenges include aging of the population and a shrinking labor pool, growing diversity of the workforce, the changing nature of work, the need for flexibility and mobility, and the use of collaboration to innovate.

Aging of the Population and Shrinking Labor Pool By 2030, the number of U.S. workers 65 or older will reach 72 million—double what it is today—and many of them will retire from the workforce, taking their experience and expertise with them. As Table 1.2 shows, the U.S. population as a whole is trending older. Yet today, many members of the Baby Boom generation, the huge number of people born between 1946 and 1964, are still hitting the peaks of their careers. At the same time, members of so-called Generation X (born from 1965 to 1981) and Generation Y (born from 1982 to 2005) are building their careers, so employers are finding more generations in the workforce simultaneously than ever before. This broad age diversity brings management challenges with it, such as accommodating a variety of work-life styles, changing expectations of work, and varying levels of technological expertise. Still, despite the widening age spectrum of the workforce, some economists predict the U.S. labor pool could soon fall short by as many as 10 million people as the Baby Boomers retire.

More sophisticated technology has intensified the hiring challenge by requiring workers to have ever more advanced skills. Although the number of college-educated workers has doubled in the past 20 years, the demand is still greater than the supply of these individuals. Because of these changes, companies are increasingly seeking—and finding—talent at the extreme ends of the working-age spectrum. Teenagers are entering the workforce sooner, and some seniors are staying longer—or seeking new careers after retiring from their primary careers. Many older workers work part-time or flexible hours. Dick Chevrette

⌐1.2⌐ Aging of the U.S. Population

AGE	2010	2020	2025
16–64	203 million	214 million	218 million
	66% of total	63% of total	61% of total
65 and older	40 million	55 million	64 million
	13% of total	16% of total	18% of total
Median	37 years	38 years	38.5 years

Source: U.S. Census Bureau, "Resident Population Projections by Sex and Age: 2010 to 2050," *Statistical Abstract of the United States,* http://www.census.gov, accessed May 2011.

worked for 38 years as a manager at Massachusetts General Hospital. When he hit 62, he wanted to still be mentally challenged and active so he scaled back his hours but didn't stop working. Meanwhile, for those older employees who do retire, employers must administer a variety of retirement planning and disability programs, retraining, and insurance benefits.

Increasingly Diverse Workforce The U.S. workforce is growing more diverse, in age and in every other way as well. The two fastest-growing ethnic populations in the U.S. are Hispanics and people of Asian origin. By the year 2050, the number of Hispanics in the U.S. will grow from a current 35 million to 102 million, or 24 percent of the total population. The Asian population will increase from 10 million to 33 million, or 8 percent of the total U.S. population.[24] Considering that minority groups will make up half the total U.S. population by the year 2050, managers must learn to work effectively with diverse ethnic groups, cultures, and lifestyles to develop and retain a superior workforce for their company.

Diversity, blending individuals of different genders, ethnic backgrounds, cultures, religions, ages, and physical and mental abilities, can enhance a firm's chances of success. Some of the firms that made the top ten in a recent list of "Top 50 Companies for Diversity" were also leaders and innovators in their industries, including Sodexo, Johnson & Johnson, AT&T, Marriott International, Coca-Cola, and Procter & Gamble.[25] Several studies have shown that diverse employee teams and workforces tend to perform tasks more effectively and develop better solutions to business problems than homogeneous employee groups. This result is due in part to the varied perspectives and experiences that foster innovation and creativity in multicultural teams.

Practical managers also know that attention to diversity issues can help them avoid damaging legal battles. Losing a discrimination lawsuit can be very costly, yet in a recent survey, 72 percent of respondents who were members of racial or ethnic minorities reported they had been the target of workplace discrimination.[26]

diversity blending individuals of different genders, ethnic backgrounds, cultures, religions, ages, and physical and mental abilities to enhance a firm's chances of success.

Outsourcing and the Changing Nature of Work Not only is the U.S. workforce changing, but so is the very nature of work. Manufacturing used to account for most of U.S. annual output, but the balance has now shifted to services such as financial management and communications. This means firms must rely heavily on well-trained service workers with knowledge, technical skills, the ability to communicate and deal with people, and a talent for creative thinking. The Internet has made possible another business tool for staffing flexibility—**outsourcing**, using outside vendors to produce goods or fulfill services and functions that were previously handled in-house. In the best situation, outsourcing allows a firm to reduce costs and concentrate its resources on the things it does best while gaining access to expertise it may not have. But outsourcing also creates its own challenges, such as differences in language or culture.

Offshoring is the relocation of business processes to lower-cost locations overseas. This can include both production and services. In recent years, China has emerged as a dominant location for production offshoring for many firms, while India has become the key player in offshoring services. Some U.S. companies are now structured so that entire divisions or functions are developed and staffed overseas—the jobs were never in the United States to start with. Another trend in some industries is **nearshoring**, outsourcing production or services to nations near a firm's home base.

Flexibility and Mobility Younger workers in particular are looking for something other than the work-comes-first lifestyle exemplified by the Baby Boom generation. But workers of all ages are exploring different work arrangements, such as telecommuting from remote locations and sharing jobs with two or more employees. Employers are also hiring growing numbers of temporary and part-time employees, some of whom are less interested in advancing up the career ladder and more interested in using and developing their skills. While the cubicle-filled office will likely never become entirely obsolete, technology makes productive networking and virtual team efforts possible by allowing people to work where they choose and easily share knowledge, a sense of purpose or mission, and a free flow of ideas across any geographical distance or time zone.

Managers of such far-flung workforces need to build and earn their trust, in order to retain valued employees and to ensure that all members are acting ethically and contributing their share without the day-to-day supervision of a more conventional work environment. These managers, and their employees, need to be flexible and responsive to change while work, technology, and the relationships between them continue to evolve.

Innovation through Collaboration Some observers also see a trend toward more collaborative work in the future, as opposed to individuals working alone. Businesses using teamwork hope to build a creative environment where all members contribute their knowledge and skills to solve problems or seize opportunities.

The old relationship between employers and employees was pretty simple: workers arrived at a certain hour, did their jobs, and went home every day at the same time. Companies rarely laid off workers, and employees rarely left for a job at another firm. But all that—and more—has changed. Employees are no longer likely to remain with a single company throughout their entire careers and do not necessarily expect lifetime loyalty from the companies they work for. They do not expect to give that loyalty either. Instead, they build their own careers however and wherever they can. These changes mean that many firms now recognize the value of a partnership with employees that encourages creative thinking and problem solving and that rewards risk taking and innovation.

outsourcing using outside vendors to produce goods or fulfill services and functions that were previously handled in-house or in-country.

offshoring relocation of business processes to lower-cost locations overseas.

nearshoring outsourcing production or services to locations near a firm's home base.

Assessment Check ✔

1. Define *outsourcing, offshoring,* and *nearshoring.*
2. Describe the importance of collaboration and employee partnership.

The 21st-Century Manager

Today's companies look for managers who are intelligent, highly motivated people with the ability to create and sustain a vision of how an organization can succeed. The 21st-century manager must also apply critical-thinking skills and creativity to business challenges and lead change.

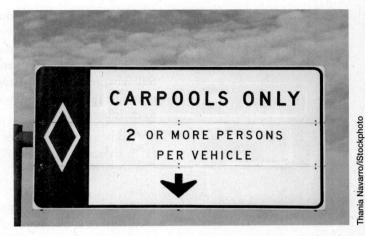

Nobis Engineering employees are rewarded for carpooling and reducing energy use in other ways as well.

Importance of Vision

To thrive in the 21st century, businesspeople need **vision**, the ability to perceive marketplace needs and what an organization must do to satisfy them. Nannu Nobis, co-founder and CEO of Nobis Engineering, is recognized for his firm's environmental work as well as its efforts to convert its own business operations to the highest standards of sustainability. Nobis Engineering—which employs only 100 people—recently won prestigious major contracts with the Army Corps of Engineers and EPA valued at $40 million. When the firm expanded to meet client needs, Nobis authorized $5 million to renovate a 20,000-square-foot historic mill building according to the U.S. Green Building Council LEED process. The building achieved LEED gold status, which serves as an inspiration to clients. Nobis Engineering employees are rewarded for carpooling and reducing energy use in other ways as well. So far, Nobis Engineering has reduced its carbon emissions by more than 13,000 pounds. "You have to walk the walk," Nannu Nobis says. "Our clients take this [sustainability] seriously and are proud to be with a firm that takes it seriously."[27]

> **vision** the ability to perceive marketplace needs and what an organization must do to satisfy them.

Importance of Critical Thinking and Creativity

Critical thinking and creativity are essential characteristics of the 21st-century workforce. Today's businesspeople need to look at a wide variety of situations, draw connections between disparate information, and develop future-oriented solutions. This need applies not only to top executives, but to midlevel managers and entry-level workers as well.

Critical thinking is the ability to analyze and assess information to pinpoint problems or opportunities. The critical-thinking process includes activities such as determining the authenticity, accuracy, and worth of information, knowledge, and arguments. It involves looking beneath the surface for deeper meaning and connections that can help identify critical issues and solutions. Without critical thinking, a firm may encounter serious problems.

> **critical thinking** ability to analyze and assess information to pinpoint problems or opportunities.

Creativity is the capacity to develop novel solutions to perceived organizational problems. Although most people think of it in relation to writers, artists, musicians, and inventors, that is a very limited definition. In business, creativity refers to the ability to see better and different ways of doing business. A computer engineer who solves a glitch in a software program is executing a creative act; so is a shipping clerk who finds a way to speed delivery of the company's overnight packages. Sometimes a crisis calls for creative leadership. Captain Chesley Sullenberger, who famously guided US Airways Flight 1549 to a safe landing in New York's Hudson River, had to make immediate and critical decisions when both his engines quit after hitting birds upon take-off. His passengers' and crew members'

> **creativity** capacity to develop novel solutions to perceived organizational problems.

lives—and lives on the ground—depended on his quick thinking and years of training. As the jet lost thrust in both engines and drifted at low speed and low altitude over one of the most densely populated areas in the world, Sullenberger faced the challenge of his life. But with quick thinking he managed a safe emergency landing in the Hudson. Later, when Sullenberger retired, he stated that, "My message going forward is that I want to remind everyone in the aviation industry that we owe it to our passengers to keep learning how to do it better."[28]

Some practice and mental exercise can cultivate your own ability to think creatively. Here are some exercises and guidelines:

- In a group, brainstorm by listing ideas as they come to mind. Build on other people's ideas, but don't criticize them. Wait until later to evaluate and organize the ideas.

- Think about how to make familiar concepts unfamiliar. A glue that doesn't stick very well? That's the basis for 3M's popular Post-it® notes.

- Plan ways to rearrange your thinking with simple questions such as, "What features can we leave out?" or by imagining what it feels like to be the customer.

- Cultivate curiosity, openness, risk, and energy as you meet people and encounter new situations. View these encounters as opportunities to learn.

- Treat failures as additional opportunities to learn.

- Get regular physical exercise. When you work out, your brain releases endorphins, and these chemicals stimulate creative thinking.

- Pay attention to your dreams and daydreams. You might find that you already know the answer to a problem.

Creativity and critical thinking must go beyond generating new ideas, however. They must lead to action. In addition to creating an environment in which employees can nurture ideas, managers must give them opportunities to take risks and try new solutions.

Ability to Lead Change

Today's business leaders must guide their employees and organizations through the changes brought about by technology, marketplace demands, and global competition. Managers must be skilled at recognizing employee strengths and motivating people to move toward common goals as members of a team. Throughout this book, real-world examples demonstrate how companies have initiated sweeping change initiatives. Most, if not all, have been led by managers comfortable with the tough decisions that today's fluctuating conditions require.

Factors that require organizational change can come from both external and internal sources; successful managers must be aware of both. External forces might include feedback from customers, developments in the international marketplace, economic trends, and new technologies. Internal factors might arise from new company goals, emerging employee needs, labor union demands, or production problems.

Assessment Check ✔

1. Why is vision an important managerial quality?
2. What is the difference between creativity and critical thinking?

What Makes a Company Admired?

Who is your hero? Is it someone who has achieved great feats in sports, government, entertainment, or business? Why do you admire the person—does he or she run a company, earn a lot of money, or give back to the community and society? Every year, business magazines and organizations publish lists of companies that they consider to be "most admired." Companies, like individuals, may be admired for many reasons. Most people would mention solid profits, stable growth, a safe and challenging work environment, high-quality goods and services, and business ethics and social responsibility. *Business ethics* refers to the standards of conduct and moral values involving decisions made in the work environment. *Social responsibility* is a management philosophy that includes contributing resources to the community, preserving the natural environment, and developing or participating in nonprofit programs designed to promote the well-being of the general public. You'll find business ethics and social responsibility examples throughout this book, as well as a deeper exploration of these topics in Chapter 2. For businesses to behave ethically and responsibly, their employees need to have strong moral compasses that guide them. The "Solving an Ethical Controversy" feature debates the responsibility that watchdogs have when they fail to perform their duties.

As you read this text, you'll be able to make up your mind about why companies should—or should not—be admired. *Fortune* publishes two lists of most-admired companies each year, one for U.S.-based firms and one for the world. The list is compiled from surveys and other research conducted by the Hay Group, a global human resources and organizational consulting firm. Criteria for making the list include innovation, people management, use of corporate assets, social responsibility, quality of management, and quality of products and services.[29] Table 1.3 lists the top ten "Most Admired Companies" for a recent year.

Assessment Check ✓

1. Define *business ethics* and *social responsibility*.
2. Identify three criteria used to judge whether a company might be considered admirable.

What's Ahead

As business speeds along in the 21st century, new technologies, population shifts, and shrinking global barriers are altering the world at a frantic pace. Businesspeople are catalysts for many of these changes, creating new opportunities for individuals who are prepared to take action. Studying contemporary business will help you prepare for the future.

Table
⌐1.3⌐ *Fortune's* Top Ten Most Admired Companies

1 Apple	**4** Johnson & Johnson	**7** Toyota Motor
2 Google	**5** Amazon.com	**8** Goldman Sachs
3 Berkshire Hathaway	**6** Procter & Gamble	**9** Walmart
		10 The Coca-Cola Company

Source: "World's Most Admired Companies 2010," *Fortune*, http://money.cnn.com, accessed January 14, 2011. Copyright 2010 by Time, Inc. Used by permission and protected by the Copyright laws of the United States. The printing, copying redistribution, or retransmission of the Material without express permission is prohibited.

Solving an Ethical Controversy

SEC Lax on Oversight?

The Securities and Exchange Commission (SEC) was created by Congress in 1934 to protect investors by monitoring the securities industry. According to the SEC's Web site, "The laws and rules that govern the securities industry in the United States derive from a simple and straightforward concept: all investors, whether large institutions or private individuals, should have access to certain basic facts about an investment prior to buying it, and so long as they hold it. To achieve this, the SEC requires public companies to disclose meaningful financial and other information to the public."

Recently, however, a whopping $65 billion securities fraud came to light when the investment company run by Bernard Madoff turned out to be the biggest Ponzi scheme of all time. Madoff used new

investors' funds to pay off the older ones. All the investment profits Madoff claimed were an illusion. Independent investigator Harry Markopolos told Congress he had been warning the SEC about Madoff's activities for years. "I gift-wrapped and delivered the largest Ponzi scheme in history to them and somehow they couldn't be bothered to conduct a thorough and proper investigation because they were too busy on matters of higher priority," Markopolos testified. Thousands of individual and institutional investors faced financial ruin as Madoff's scheme evaporated.

Does the SEC bear part of the blame for investor losses if it is not doing its job?

PRO

1. A $65 billion fraud could flourish only under a flawed regulatory system. "Our current fragmented regulatory system can allow bad actors to engage in misconduct outside the view and reach of some regulators," said an officer of the securities industry's watchdog organization. "It is undeniable that . . . the system failed to protect investors."

2. "The SEC is . . . captive to the industry it regulates, and it is afraid of bringing big cases against the largest, most powerful firms," said Markopolos. "Clearly the SEC was afraid of Mr. Madoff."

CON

1. The SEC's director of enforcement told a Senate committee, "We don't turn a blind eye to fraud. If we see it and we suspect it, we pursue it. We don't want fraudsters out there."

2. The director also said the SEC doesn't have enough resources to pursue all the tip-offs of potential fraud that come before it: "If we had more resources we could clearly do more." Other regulators blamed lack of coordination among government agencies for the lapses in oversight that allowed Madoff to operate.

Summary

Madoff pled guilty to charges of felony securities fraud and was sentenced to 150 years in prison. Meanwhile, the SEC itself has proposed new rules to improve the oversight of investment advisers under the Dodd–Frank Act, which extends certain aspects of the Investment Advisers Act.

Sources: "SEC: Comment Deadline Nears for Adviser Oversight," *Investment News*, January 14, 2011, http://www.investmentnews.com; Suzanne Barlyn, "SEC Is Urged to Bolster Oversight of Registered Investment Advisers," *The Wall Street Journal*, January 12, 2011, http://online.wsj.com; "SEC Proposes Rules to Improve Oversight of Investment Advisers," *U.S. Securities and Exchange Commission*, November 19, 2010, http://www.sec.gov; Jenny Anderson and Zachery Kouwe, "SEC Enforcers Focus on Avoiding Madoff Repeat," *The New York Times*, February 8, 2010, http://www.nytimes.com; Linda Sandler, "Madoff Said Only Brother Could Do Audit, Witness Tells Congress," *Bloomberg News*, February 5, 2009, http://www.bloomberg.com; "Witness on Madoff Tells of Fear for Safety," *The New York Times*, February 4, 2009, http://www.nytimes.com.

Throughout this book, you'll be exposed to the real-life stories of many businesspeople. You'll learn about the range of business careers available and the daily decisions, tasks, and challenges that they face. By the end of the course, you'll understand how marketing, production, accounting, finance, and management work together to provide competitive advantages for firms. This knowledge can help you become a more capable employee and enhance your career potential.

Now that this chapter has introduced some basic terms and issues in the business world of the 21st century, Chapter 2 takes a detailed look at the ethical and social responsibility issues facing contemporary business. Chapter 3 deals with economic challenges, and Chapter 4 focuses on the difficulties and opportunities faced by firms competing in world markets.

Summary of Learning Objectives

1 **Distinguish between business and not-for-profit organizations.**

Business consists of all profit-seeking activities that provide goods and services necessary to an economic system. Not-for-profit organizations are business-like establishments whose primary objectives involve social, political, governmental, educational, or similar functions—instead of profits.

Assessment Check Answers ☑

1.1 What activity lies at the heart of every business endeavor? At the heart of every business endeavor is an exchange between a buyer and a seller.

1.2 What are the primary objectives of a not-for-profit organization? Not-for-profit organizations place public service above profits, although they need to raise money in order to operate and achieve their social goals.

2 **Identify and describe the factors of production.**

The factors of production consist of four basic inputs: natural resources, capital, human resources, and entrepreneurship. Natural resources include all productive inputs that are useful in their natural states. Capital includes technology, tools, information, and physical facilities. Human resources include anyone who works for the firm. Entrepreneurship is the willingness to take risks to create and operate a business.

Assessment Check Answers ☑

2.1 Identify the four basic inputs to an economic system. The four basic inputs are natural resources, capital, human resources, and entrepreneurship.

2.2 List four types of capital. Four types of capital are technology, tools, information, and physical facilities.

3 **Describe the private enterprise system, including basic rights and entrepreneurship.**

The private enterprise system is an economic system that rewards firms for their ability to perceive and serve the needs and demands of consumers. Competition in the private enterprise system ensures success for firms that satisfy consumer demands. Citizens in a private enterprise economy enjoy the rights to private property, profits, freedom of choice, and competition. Entrepreneurship drives economic growth.

Assessment Check Answers ☑

3.1 What is an alternative term for private enterprise system? Capitalism is an alternative word for private enterprise system.

3.2 What is the most basic freedom under the private enterprise system? The most basic freedom is the right to private property.

3.3 What is an entrepreneur? An entrepreneur is a risk taker who is willing to start, own, and operate a business.

4 **Identify the six eras of business, and explain how the relationship era—including alliances, technology, and environmental concerns—influences contemporary business.**

The six historical eras are the Colonial period, the Industrial Revolution, the age of industrial entrepreneurs, the production era, the marketing era, and the relationship era. In the Colonial period, businesses were small and rural, emphasizing agricultural production. The Industrial Revolution brought factories and mass production to business. The age of industrial entrepreneurs built on the Industrial Revolution through an expansion in the number and size of firms. The production era focused on the growth of factory operations through assembly lines and other efficient internal processes. During and following the Great Depression, businesses concentrated on finding markets for their products through advertising and selling, giving rise to the marketing era. In the relationship era, businesspeople focus on developing and sustaining long-term relationships with customers and other businesses. Technology promotes innovation and communication, while alliances create a competitive advantage through partnerships. Concern for the environment also helps build strong relationships with customers.

Assessment Check Answers ☑

4.1 What was the Industrial Revolution? The Industrial Revolution began around 1750 in England and moved business operations from an emphasis on independent, skilled workers to a factory system that mass-produced items.

4.2 During which era was the idea of branding developed? The idea of branding began in the marketing era.

4.3 What is the difference between transaction management and relationship management? Transaction management is an approach that focuses on building, promoting, and selling enough products to cover costs and earn profits. Relationship management is the collection of activities that build and maintain ongoing ties with customers and other parties.

5 **Explain how today's business workforce and the nature of work itself is changing.**

The workforce is changing in several significant ways: (1) it is aging and the labor pool is shrinking, and (2) it is becoming increasingly diverse. The nature of work has shifted toward services and a focus on information. More firms now rely on outsourcing, offshoring, and nearshoring to produce goods or fulfill services and functions that were previously handled in-house or in-country. In addition, today's workplaces are becoming increasingly flexible, allowing employees to work from different locations and through different relationships. And companies are fostering innovation through teamwork and collaboration.

Assessment Check Answers ✓

5.1 Define *outsourcing*, *offshoring*, and *nearshoring*.
Outsourcing involves using outside vendors to produce goods or fulfill services and functions that were once handled in-house. Offshoring is the relocation of business processes to lower-cost locations overseas. Nearshoring is the outsourcing of production or services to nations near a firm's home base.

5.2 Describe the importance of collaboration and employee partnership. Businesses are increasingly focusing on collaboration, rather than on individuals working alone. No longer do employees just put in their time at a job they hold their entire career. The new employer–employee partnership encourages teamwork and creative thinking, problem solving, and innovation. Managers are trained to listen to and respect employees.

⌐6⌐ Identify the skills and attributes that managers need to lead businesses in the 21st century.

Today's managers need vision, the ability to perceive marketplace needs and the way their firm can satisfy them. Critical-thinking skills and creativity allow managers to pinpoint problems and opportunities and plan novel solutions. Finally, managers are dealing with rapid change, and they need skills to help lead their organizations through shifts in external and internal conditions.

Assessment Check Answers ✓

6.1 Why is vision an important managerial quality? Managerial vision allows a firm to innovate and adapt to meet changes in the marketplace.

6.2 What is the difference between creativity and critical thinking? Critical thinking is the ability to analyze and assess information to pinpoint problems or opportunities. Creativity is the capacity to develop novel solutions to perceived organizational problems.

⌐7⌐ Outline the characteristics that make a company admired by the business community.

A company is usually admired for its solid profits, stable growth, a safe and challenging work environment, high-quality goods and services, and business ethics and social responsibility.

Assessment Check Answers ✓

7.1 Define *business ethics* and *social responsibility*. Business ethics refers to the standards of conduct and moral values involving decisions made in the work environment. Social responsibility is a management philosophy that includes contributing resources to the community, preserving the natural environment, and developing or participating in nonprofit programs designed to promote the well-being of the general public.

7.2 Identify three criteria used to judge whether a company might be considered admirable. Criteria in judging whether companies are admirable include three of the following: solid profits, stable growth, a safe and challenging work environment, high-quality goods and services, and business ethics and social responsibility.

■ Business Terms You Need to Know

business 5	entrepreneurship 9	branding 15	strategic alliance 16
profits 5	private enterprise system 9	brand 15	diversity 21
not-for-profit	capitalism 9	transaction	outsourcing 22
organizations 5	competition 9	management 15	offshoring 22
factors of production 7	competitive differentiation 9	relationship era 16	nearshoring 22
natural resources 7	private property 10	relationship	vision 23
capital 7	entrepreneur 11	management 16	critical thinking 23
human resources 8	consumer orientation 15	technology 16	creativity 23

■ Review Questions

1. Why is business so important to a country's economy?

2. In what ways are not-for-profit organizations a substantial part of the U.S. economy? What challenges do not-for-profits face?

3. Identify and describe the four basic inputs that make up factors of production. Give an example of each factor of production that an auto manufacturer might use.

4. What is a private enterprise system? What four rights are critical to the operation of capitalism? Why would capitalism function poorly in a society that does not ensure these rights for its citizens?

5. In what ways is entrepreneurship vital to the private enterprise system?

6. Identify the six eras of business in the United States. How were businesses changed during each era?

7. Describe the focus of the most recent era of U.S. business. How is this different from previous eras?

8. Define *partnership* and *strategic alliance*. How might a motorcycle dealer and a local radio station benefit from an alliance?

9. Identify the major changes in the workforce that will affect the way managers build a world-class work-force in the 21st century. Why is brainpower so important?

10. Identify four qualities that the "new" managers of the 21st century must have. Why are these qualities important in a competitive business environment?

■ Projects and Teamwork Applications

1. The entrepreneurial spirit fuels growth in the U.S. economy. Choose a company that interests you—one you have worked for or dealt with as a customer—and read about the company in the library or visit its Web site. Learn what you can about the company's early history: Who founded it and why? Is the founder still with the organization? Do you think the founder's original vision is still embraced by the company? If not, how has the vision changed?

2. Brands distinguish one company's goods or services from its competitors. Each company you purchase from hopes that you will become loyal to its brand. Some well-known brands are Burger King, Coca-Cola, Hilton, and Old Navy. Choose a type of good or service you use regularly and identify the major brands associated with it. Are you loyal to a particular brand? Why or why not?

3. More and more businesses are forming strategic alliances to become more competitive. Sometimes, businesses pair up with not-for-profit organizations in a relationship that is beneficial to both. Choose a company whose goods or services interest you, such as Timberland, FedEx, General Mills, or Target. On your own or with a classmate, research the firm on the Internet to learn about its alliances with not-for-profit organizations. Then describe one of the alliances, including goals and benefits to both parties. Create a presentation for your class.

4. This chapter describes how the nature of the workforce is changing: the population is aging, the labor pool is shrinking, the workforce is becoming more diverse, the nature of work is changing, the workplace is becoming more flexible and mobile, and employers are fostering innovation and collaboration among their employees. Form teams of two to three students. Select a company and research how that company is responding to changes in the workforce. When you have completed your research, be prepared to present it to your class. Choose one of the following companies or select your own: State Farm Insurance, Archer Daniels Midland, 3M, Marriott, or Dell.

5. Many successful companies today use technology to help them improve their relationship management. Suppose a major supermarket chain's management team has asked you to assess its use of technology for this purpose. On your own or with a classmate, visit one or two local supermarkets and also explore their corporate Web sites. Note the ways in which firms in this industry already use technology to connect with their customers, and list at least three ideas for new ways or improvements to existing ones. Present your findings to the class as if they represented the management team.

■ Web Assignments

1. **Using search engines.** Gathering information is one of the most popular applications of the Web. Using two of the major search engines, such as Google and Bing, search the Web for information pertaining to brand and relationship management. Sort through your results—you're likely to gets thousands of "hits"—and identify the three most useful. What did you learn from this experience regarding the use of a search engine?

   http://www.google.com

   http://www.bing.com

2. **Companies and not-for-profits.** In addition to companies, virtually all not-for-profit organizations have Web sites. Four Web sites are listed below, two for companies (Alcoa and Sony) and two for not-for-profits (Cleveland Clinic and National Audubon Society). What is the purpose of each Web site? What type of information is available? How are the sites similar? How are they different?

   http://www.alcoa.com

   http://www.sony.com

   http://www.clevelandclinic.org

   http://www.audubon.org

3. **Characteristics of U.S. workforce.** Visit the Web site listed below. It is the home page for the *Statistical Abstract of the United States*. Published annually by the U.S. Census Bureau, the *Statistical Abstract* is a good source of basic demographic and economic data. Click on "Labor Force, Employment, and

Earnings." Use the relevant data tables to prepare a brief profile of the U.S. workforce (gender, age, educational level, and so forth). How is this profile expected to change over the next 10 to 20 years?

http://www.census.gov/compendia/statab/

Note: Internet Web addresses change frequently. If you don't find the exact sites listed, you may need to access the organization's home page and search from there or use a search engine such as Bing or Google.

CASE 1.1 SAS Is Still a Great Place to Work

The employee benefits and perks at SAS, a privately held business software company in Raleigh, North Carolina, are so many and varied it boggles the imagination. The company's 300-acre campus houses a gym, weight room, meditation garden, sauna, and Olympic-size swimming pool. It seems unlikely any of the complex's 4,200 employees would fall ill with such health-building options to choose from, but just in case, there's a health-care center with a staff of 56 including four doctors, ten nurses, physical therapists, and a psychologist. All care is free. "We charge you for one thing," says the health service director, "if you miss your appointment and don't give us notice. That's $10."

Free or subsidized programs include Pilates, Zumba, yoga, weight management, smoking cessation, Wii bowling, massage, and aerobics. Two subsidized daycare centers care for 600 children, and there's a summer camp. Job sharing, telecommuting, and domestic partner benefits for same-sex couples are offered. Employees can get their clothes dry cleaned, car detailed, and income tax return prepared while they work. They can eat in any of three subsidized cafeterias during the day (one has a piano player who takes requests) and grab take-out for the family at day's end. They can prepare their own snacks in one of the many kitchens. But with free snacks every day, including Krispy Kremes (Fridays) and M&Ms (a long-standing Wednesday tradition), why would they?

Jim Goodnight, the company's only CEO in its 34 years, believes treating employees well is simply good business. Rather than thinking it's unusual for SAS to be so generous, he wonders why other companies don't follow suit. And with revenues that have risen every year of the firm's existence, recently topping $2.3 billion despite the global recession, it appears he's right. SAS has been one of *Fortune's* best companies to work for in each of the last 13 years and recently earned the number-one spot on the list. "Some may think that because SAS is family-friendly and has great benefits we don't work hard," says a communications employee. "But people do work hard here, because they're motivated to take care of a company that takes care of them." That sentiment expresses the culture of trust Goodnight has worked to create. "What we don't do is treat our employees like they're all, you know, criminals," says his vice president of human resources.

Employee turnover among the 11,000 SAS employees worldwide is 2 percent, well below the industry average, and the company receives about 100 résumés for every open position. (About half its employees work in the United States.) The typical employee works 35 hours per week and many make their own schedules; no one counts sick days. Average tenure is ten years.

About 17,000 customers worldwide use SAS data mining software, including IBM, Microsoft, Oracle, national retailers, banks, insurance and pharmaceutical firms, universities, the Census Bureau, and even professional baseball teams. Goodnight spends much of his time on the road meeting and talking with these clients, though he sometimes admits he would rather be programming. But he's well aware of where the real value of the company lies, and that's the reason he's willing to spend so much on making SAS a great place to work. "My chief assets drive out the gate every day," he says. "My job is to make sure they come back."

Questions for Critical Thinking

1. Explain how flexible and family-friendly policies have played a role in SAS's success.

2. What kind of relationship does SAS seem to have with its employees? With its customers?

Sources: "100 Best Companies to Work For: #1 SAS," *CNNMoney .com*, http://money.cnn.com, accessed May 17, 2011; David A. Kaplan, "SAS: A New No. 1 Best Employer," *CNNMoney.com*, January 22, 2010, http://money.cnn.com; Stefan Stern, "A Good Day for Dr. Goodnight and SAS," *Financial Times*, January 22, 2010, http://blogs .ft.com; Rick Smith, "'We're Hiring' Sign Remains Out at SAS for 2010," *WRAL Tech Wire*, January 21, 2010, http://wraltechwire.com.

Kayak.com

Among the many business projects launched by entrepreneur Paul English is a Web site called gethuman .com, designed to help frustrated consumers short-cut their way through large companies' automated phone systems. English's main job, however, is running a popular travel search engine he co-founded with Steve Hafner called Kayak.com, and in keeping with his fanatical focus on good customer service (just what those automated phone systems often don't provide), he and Kayak's engineers take regular turns personally responding to customers' e-mails and telephone calls. To those who say he could get the customer service job done for much less than an engineer's salary, English says, "If you make the engineers answer e-mails and phone calls from the customers, the second or third time they get the same question, they'll actually stop what they're doing and fix the code. Then we don't have those questions any more."

When English, who is also the company's chief technology officer, takes the calls himself, he's likely to give out his personal cell phone number and tell the caller, "If you have any follow-up questions, my name is Paul English; I'm the co-founder of the company." Only a handful of people will call him back, he says, "but they're blown away when I do that."

Kayak's staff of about 100 employees all talk, Twitter, or e-mail customers every day. Their work supports a Web site that lets millions of users compare prices for air travel, hotels, vacation deals, and rental cars. There are offices in Connecticut, where Hafner lives, Massachusetts, where English lives, and California, where the two bought a competing firm in 2007, as well as local sites across Europe. Hafner and English phone or instant-message each other every day. "We can practically read each other's minds," says English. "If an issue comes up, I know how he's going to weigh in and vice versa. We trust each other." They also trust their engineers and encourage them to chime in with solutions to problems.

English, who has founded three other firms and sold one of them to Intuit several years ago, is an early riser who describes himself as having "more ideas than I can get done in a day." After checking e-mail, practicing yoga, and taking his son to school, he arrives at work for a day that might start with meetings, including with nonprofits like Partners in Health or Village Health Works in which he plays an advisory role. "There are certain fundamental rights that I believe all people should have," he says. "Kids shouldn't be dying of drinking dirty water." English likes to leave half his day free of scheduled appointments and spend the time walking around the office's open-plan environment to "see what's going on and work on product issues and design strategy."

Acknowledging the company's growing success, and mindful that it needed more sophisticated marketing to keep it in the forefront of travel customers' minds, Kayak recently launched a national advertising campaign, which the cofounders took an active part in shaping. With a new logo and the tagline, "Search one and done," Kayak.com hopes to make more people aware that, as their ad agency's founder says, "it doesn't make sense to start their travel search anywhere else."

Questions for Critical Thinking

1. How does Paul English typify an entrepreneur? In what ways do you think his experience, background, or attitudes are unusual for an entrepreneur?

2. How well do you think Kayak.com manages its relationships with its users? If it grows considerably larger over the next few years, how do you think this may change that relationship?

Sources: Company Web site, http://www.kayak.com, accessed May 17, 2011; "Kayak Launches National Advertising Campaign," *PR Newswire*, February 9, 2010; Paul English, "The Way I Work," *Inc.*, February 2, 2010, http://www.inc.com.

New Harvest Coffee Roasters Brews Up Fresh Business

If you're one of those people for whom the scent of freshly roasted coffee is irresistible, you have something in common with RikKleinfeldt. Kleinfeldt, the co-founder and president of New Harvest Coffee Roasters, is a self-proclaimed coffee fanatic. He dwells on the aroma and flavor of coffee. He measures the freshness of roasted coffee in hours and days, instead of weeks and months. Kleinfeldt started New Harvest Coffee Roasters ten years ago as a way to pay homage to fresh coffee and build a business around it.

Kleinfeldt observes Starbucks' tremendous success at creating gathering places for people to enjoy coffee and tea—as well as baked goods—in a relaxed social atmosphere. But he also notes with humor that, although cafes and coffee bars were thriving a decade ago, these popular hang-outs "weren't really about coffee. They were about smoothies and cookies. I thought, maybe it's time to get back to basics and roast some coffee." Kleinfeldt recalls that friends and colleagues—fellow coffee fans—felt the same way. He believed that he had a basis to start a business. "We're coffee people," he explains. "There is a like-minded group of people."

Kleinfeldt also points out that the movement toward locally grown or produced foods has been a big help in establishing and building support for his business. "The idea of local coffee starts with the local roaster," he explains. Although the coffee beans themselves are grown elsewhere—mostly on farms in Costa Rica—they are roasted at New Harvest's facility in Rhode Island, where the company is based. "Freshness is a huge factor" in a good cup of coffee, says Kleinfeldt. "Once it's roasted, it's good for about two to twelve days, which is a good incentive to buy local."

Buying local is exactly what retailers and coffee shops like Blue State Coffee do, creating a collaborative relationship with New Harvest. Alex Payson, COO of Blue State Coffee—a thriving shop in Rhode Island—observes that most of his customers live within a five or ten-minute walk from his business. Blue State customers are educated about the coffee they drink. "They want to *know*," says Payson smiling. "We connect with our coffee farmers. Our customers ask about the story *behind* our coffee," including farming practices and working conditions. Payson and his colleagues from New Harvest have traveled together to some of the coffee farms in Costa Rica that grow the beans they purchase. In fact, loyal customers can view the progress of trips like this on New Harvest's Facebook page.

Relationships with companies like Blue State Coffee as well as with consumers are the basis for New Harvest's growth as a business. "We need strategic alliances," says RikKleinfeldt. "Blue State is a great example of that. They buy into what we're doing and we support what they are doing. They collaborate with us—what's good for Blue State is also good for New Harvest." Blue State educates its customers and employees about the benefits of buying from a local firm like New Harvest, which in turn works with certified organic, free trade growers. When Blue State's workers are able to discuss their products knowledgeably with customers—including where and how they are grown, harvested and roasted—a relationship is developed.

Sharing activities, comments, news, and anecdotes with customers, retailers, and coffee shops through social media such as Facebook and Twitter allows New Harvest to broaden its base without spending more dollars on marketing and advertising. These connections also put a personal face on the company and allow New Harvest to gain important knowledge about the views and preferences of its customers. In addition, they provide valuable opportunities to showcase some of the company's work in the community as well as its support for organizations such as the Rainforest Alliance and New England GreenStart.

"Our mission is to be the leader in our region in developing the palate and expectations of coffee drinkers, in order to create a permanent market for the coffee produced by passionate and skilled growers," states the New Harvest Web site. For RikKleinfeldt's company and customers, coffee is much more than a hot cup of joe in the morning. Coffee—organically grown, freshly roasted, and served locally—represents a sustainable way to do business.

Questions for Critical Thinking

1. Give examples of each of the four factors of production that New Harvest must rely on to be a successful operation. How does each contribute to the firm's success?
2. Visit New Harvest's Facebook page. Note specific examples of the ways in which the firm is using social media to manage its relationships.
3. RikKleinfeldt notes the importance of strategic alliances with firms like Blue State Coffee. Describe how you think New Harvest benefits from alliances with not-for-profit organizations such as Rainforest Alliance, New England GreenStart, and Rhode Island PBS.
4. New Harvest builds much of its reputation on its efforts toward environmental sustainability. How does this reputation affect its relationship with consumers?

Sources: New Harvest Web site, http://www.newharvestcoffee.com, accessed May 17, 2011; Blue State Coffee Web site, http://www.bluestatecoffee.com, accessed May 17, 2011.

Chapter 2

Learning Objectives

[1] Explain the concepts of business ethics and social responsibility.

[2] Describe the factors that influence business ethics.

[3] List the stages in the development of ethical standards, and discuss how organizations shape ethical behavior.

[4] Describe how businesses' social responsibility is measured, and summarize the responsibilities of business to the general public, customers, and employees.

[5] Explain why investors and the financial community are concerned with business ethics and social responsibility.

Business Ethics and Social Responsibility

PharmaJet Jumps from Doing Good to Doing Well

Courtesy Kathleen Callender, founder, PharmaJet, Inc.

Kathy Callender is a business founder who wants to change the world one injection at a time. For the 15 to 20 billion people worldwide who receive vaccinations or injectable medications each year, the technology her firm has developed—needleless injections—could mean the difference between life and death. That's because needles are the main cause of the spread of HIV and hepatitis, and they're also more expensive to use than PharmaJet's needle-free injectors cartridges. With a PharmaJet injector, the medicine or vaccine travels at lightning speed through the skin from a small, disposable cartridge. The cartridge is thrown away, and there's no needle to stick a nurse accidentally or to be reused on another patient in haste or to save money. The implications for healthcare—both in the United States and abroad—are huge.

It's one thing to develop a truly innovative, beneficial product; but it's another to bring that product to market and make a profit. Callender, a former dental hygienist who worked periodically with her orthodontist husband to provide dental care to patients in developing countries, struggled for more than a decade to obtain enough financing and marketplace support to launch PharmaJet's injector. "I didn't talk about what I was doing," recalls Callender, "because people thought I was nuts." But Callender was determined to make a difference *and* a profit—if the company could thrive, she could continue to make a difference in people's health, particularly in those developing areas, such as Honduras, where she and her husband had worked. "For me, that was the defining moment," says Callender. "The developing world is my passion."

Callender suffered some major setbacks, including demonstrations during which the PharmaJet injector failed. But she was not deterred. Instead, Callender and her team went back to the lab and redesigned the device. Meanwhile, Callender persisted with potential investors who routinely dismissed her ideas as too simple or dreamy. The fact that she was focused on the developing world and was a former dental hygienist instead of an executive added strikes against her business credibility. Callender never backed down, managed to raise $14 million in backing, and PharmaJet is beginning to prove Callender's skeptics wrong.

Brazil is very interested in MMR delivery with the PharmaJet technology. PharmaJet is completing a clinical trial in infants and young children to deliver measles-mumps-rubella vaccinations to children in Brazil. At the other end of the spectrum, prison officials in the United States have begun to use it as a safer, cleaner alternative for vaccinating inmates. In addition to the attractiveness of needle-free technology, Callender recognizes that landing large-volume contracts—such as the vaccinations in Brazil—means that PharmaJet can sell its injectors at a much lower price than the price of a needle delivery system. This means that patients receive clean, safe injections at an affordable price—and PharmaJet can make enough profit to survive and grow.

PharmaJet has been receiving a lot of positive press recently, including features in the news and through medical media. Health departments in New Jersey and California have struck agreements with PharmaJet. Pharmacy and supermarket chains have agreed to try the PharmaJet system in their flu-shot clinics.[1]

Kathy Callender's efforts to improve worldwide healthcare through the use of one small device proves that a single small business can make a difference in society. Many companies—large and small—are concerned with improving both society and the environment. Sometimes that means growing more slowly than they might or reducing short-term profits for longer, sustained benefits. In other cases it means persisting in the face of skepticism, as Kathy Callender did.

Although most organizations strive to combine ethical behavior with profitable operation, some have struggled to overcome major ethical lapses in recent years. Ethical failures in a number of large or well-known firms led to lawsuits, indictments, and judgments against firms. The image of the CEO—and of business in general— suffered as the evening news carried reports of executives pocketing millions of dollars in compensation while their companies floundered.

But sometimes bad news is a prelude to good news. In the wake of such stories, both the government and companies have renewed their efforts to conduct themselves in an ethical manner and one that reflects a responsibility to society, to consumers, and to the environment. In 2004 the Federal Sentencing Commission strengthened its guidelines for ethics compliance programs, and more and more firms began to pay attention to formulating more explicit standards and procedures for ethical behavior. Companies also began to recognize the enormous impact of setting a good example rather than a bad one. Today you are likely to hear about the goodwill that companies such as Target Corporation, Ford Motor Company, and Starbucks generate when they give back to their communities through youth reading programs, undertake recycling or energy-conservation programs, or seek to pay fair prices to suppliers.

As we discussed in Chapter 1, the underlying aim of business is to serve customers at a profit. But most companies today try to do more than that, looking for ways to give back to customers, society, and the environment. Sometimes they face difficult questions in the process. When does a company's self-interest conflict with society's and customers' well-being? And must the goal of seeking profits conflict with upholding high principles of right and wrong? In response to the second question, a growing number of businesses of all sizes are answering no.

Concern for Ethical and Societal Issues

business ethics
standards of conduct and moral values regarding right and wrong actions in the work environment.

An organization that wants to prosper over the long term is well advised to consider **business ethics**, the standards of conduct and moral values governing actions and decisions in the work environment. Businesses also must take into account a wide range of social issues, including how a decision will affect the environment, employees, and customers.

These issues are at the heart of *social responsibility*, whose primary objective is the enhancement of society's welfare through philosophies, policies, procedures, and actions. In short, businesses must find the delicate balance between doing what is right and doing what is profitable. Home Depot has developed a sophisticated system through which certain goods—such as gas cans, generators, plywood, flashlights, and batteries—are stocked in specific distribution locations so they are readily available for shipment to areas that need them in the event of a hurricane. Using its supply chain effectively not only benefits society, it boosts Home Depot's bottom line.[2]

In business, as in life, deciding what is right or wrong in a given situation does not always involve a clear-cut choice. Firms have many responsibilities—to customers, to employees, to investors, and to society as a whole. Sometimes conflicts arise in trying to serve the different needs of these separate constituencies. The ethical values of executives and individual employees at all levels can influence the decisions and actions a business takes. Throughout your own career, you will encounter many situations in which you will need to weigh right and wrong before making a decision or taking action. So we begin our discussion of business ethics by focusing on individual ethics.

Business ethics are also shaped by the ethical climate within an organization. Codes of conduct and ethical standards play increasingly significant roles in businesses in which doing the right thing is both supported and applauded. This chapter demonstrates how a firm can create a framework to encourage—and even demand—high standards of ethical behavior and social responsibility from its employees. The chapter also considers the complex question of what business owes to society and how societal forces mold the actions of businesses. Finally, it examines the influence of business ethics and social responsibility on global business.

Assessment Check ☑

1. To whom do businesses have responsibilities?

2. If a firm is meeting all its responsibilities to others, why do ethical conflicts arise?

PhotoAlto/Frederic Cirou/Getty Images, Inc.

You will encounter many decisions in your career. How you choose to handle them will shape your ethical values.

The Contemporary Ethical Environment

Business ethics are now in the spotlight as never before. Companies realize that they have to work harder to earn the trust of the general public, and many have taken on the challenge as if their very survival depends on it. This movement toward *corporate social responsibility* should benefit all—consumers, the environment, and the companies themselves.

Most business owners and managers have built and maintained enduring companies without breaking the rules. One example of a firm with a longstanding commitment to ethical practice is Johnson & Johnson, the giant multinational manufacturer of healthcare products. The most admired pharmaceutical maker and the ninth-most-admired company in the world, according to *Fortune*, Johnson & Johnson has abided by the same basic code of ethics, its well-known Credo, for more than 50 years. The Credo, reproduced in Figure 2.1, remains the ethical standard against which the company's employees periodically evaluate how well their firm is performing. Management is pledged to address any lapses that are reported. This pledge was recently put to the test when the company recalled several popular drugs, including Tylenol, Benadryl, and Sudafed, when it learned that equipment at one of its manufacturing plants had not been cleaned properly.[3]

Many companies are conscious of how ethical standards can translate into concern for the environment. Recently, Walmart announced a plan to pursue three sustainability goals:

1. to use only renewable energy sources

2. to recycle all of its waste

3. to sell products that "sustain people and the environment," according to Matt Kistler, the company's senior vice president for sustainability.

The company conducted a survey of its suppliers on their sustainability practices as a first step in developing a "sustainability index" to help its customers assess the impact—on the environment and on society—of products in its stores.[4]

Although not all companies set and meet high ethical standards, the ethical climate seems to be improving despite the recent recession. The National Business Ethics Survey, conducted by the Ethics Resource Center, recently found that workplace misconduct has decreased over the last few years, with more employees willing to report such behavior when they witnessed it. Workers said that although ethical cultures were stronger,

FIGURE 2.1 Johnson & Johnson Credo

Our Credo

We believe our first responsibility is to the doctors, nurses and patients, to mothers and fathers and all others who use our products and services. In meeting their needs everything we do must be of high quality. We must constantly strive to reduce our costs in order to maintain reasonable prices. Customers' orders must be serviced promptly and accurately. Our suppliers and distributors must have an opportunity to make a fair profit.

We are responsible to our employees, the men and women who work with us throughout the world. Everyone must be considered as an individual. We must respect their dignity and recognize their merit. They must have a sense of security in their jobs. Compensation must be fair and adequate, and working conditions clean, orderly and safe. We must be mindful of ways to help our employees fulfill their family responsibilities. Employees must feel free to make suggestions and complaints. There must be equal opportunity for employment, development and advancement for those qualified. We must provide competent management, and their actions must be just and ethical.

We are responsible to the communities in which we live and work and to the world community as well. We must be good citizens—support good works and charities and bear our fair share of taxes. We must encourage civic improvements and better health and education. We must maintain in good order the property we are privileged to use, protecting the environment and natural resources.

Our final responsibility is to our stockholders. Business must make a sound profit. We must experiment with new ideas. Research must be carried on, innovative programs developed and mistakes paid for. New equipment must be purchased, new facilities provided and new products launched. Reserves must be created to provide for adverse times. When we operate according to these principles, the stockholders should realize a fair return.

Source: "Our Company Credo," Johnson & Johnson Web site, http://www.jnj.com, accessed January 19, 2011, © Johnson & Johnson.

some felt more pressure to cut corners to save money and get the job done, particularly in a difficult economy.[5]

The **<u>Sarbanes-Oxley Act of 2002</u>** established new rules and regulations for securities trading and accounting practices. Companies are now required to publish their code of ethics, if they have one, and inform the public of any changes made to it. The law may actually motivate even more firms to develop written codes and guidelines for ethical business behavior. The federal government also created the U.S. Sentencing Commission to institutionalize ethics compliance programs that would establish high ethical standards and end corporate misconduct. The requirements for such programs are shown in Table 2.1.

The current ethical environment of business also includes the appointment of new corporate officers specifically charged with deterring wrongdoing and ensuring that ethical standards are met. Ethics compliance officers, whose numbers are rapidly rising, are responsible for conducting employee training programs that help spot potential fraud and abuse within the firm, investigating sexual harassment and discrimination charges, and monitoring any potential conflicts of interest. But practicing corporate social responsibility is more than just monitoring behavior. Many companies now adopt a three-pronged approach to ethics and social responsibility:

1. engaging in traditional corporate philanthropy, which involves giving to worthy causes

2. anticipating and managing risks

3. identifying opportunities to create value by doing the right thing.[6]

Table 2.1 **Minimum Requirements for Ethics Compliance Programs**

- Compliance standards and procedures. Establish standards and procedures, such as codes of ethics and identification of areas of risk, capable of reducing misconduct or criminal activities.

- High-level personnel responsibility. Assign high-level personnel, such as boards of directors and top executives, the overall responsibility to actively lead and oversee ethics compliance programs.

- Due care in assignments. Avoid delegating authority to individuals with a propensity for misconduct or illegal activities.

- Communication of standards and procedures. Communicate ethical requirements to high-level officials and other employees through ethics training programs or publications that explain in practical terms what is required.

- Establishment of monitoring and auditing systems and reporting system. Monitor and review ethical compliance systems, and establish a reporting system employees can use to notify the organization of misconduct without fear of retribution.

- Enforcement of standards through appropriate mechanisms. Consistently enforce ethical codes, including employee discipline.

- Appropriate responses to the offense. Take reasonable steps to respond to the offense and to prevent and detect further violations.

- Self-reporting. Report misconduct to the appropriate government agency.

- Applicable industry practice or standards. Follow government regulations and industry standards.

Sources: "An Overview of the United States Sentencing Commission and the Federal Sentencing Guidelines," Ethics and Policy Integration Centre, http://www.epic-online.net; "The Relationship between Law and Ethics, and the Significance of the Federal Sentencing Guidelines for Organizations," Ethics and Policy Integration Centre, http://www.ethicaledge.com; U.S. Sentencing Commission, "Sentencing Commission Toughens Requirements for Corporate Compliance and Ethics Programs," USSC news release, http://www.ussc.gov.

Sarbanes-Oxley Act of 2002 federal legislation designed to deter and punish corporate and accounting fraud and corruption and to protect the interests of workers and shareholders through enhanced financial disclosures, criminal penalties on CEOs and CFOs who defraud investors, safeguards for whistleblowers, and establishment of a new regulatory body for public accounting firms.

Individuals Make a Difference

In today's business environment, individuals can make the difference in ethical expectations and behavior. As executives, managers, and employees demonstrate their personal ethical principles—or lack of ethical principles—the expectations and actions of those who work for and with them can change.

What is the current status of individual business ethics in the United States? Although ethical behavior can be difficult to track or define in all circumstances, evidence suggests that unfortunately some individuals act unethically or illegally on the job. The National Business Ethics Survey identifies such behaviors as putting one's own interests ahead of the organization, lying to employees, misreporting hours worked, Internet abuse, and safety violations, among others.[7]

Technology seems to have expanded the range and impact of unethical behavior. For example, anyone with computer access to data has the potential to steal or manipulate the data or to shut down the system, even from a remote location. Banks and other financial institutions are often targeted for such attacks. The identity Theft Resource Center recently reported as many as 2.6 million customer records were exposed in one bank data breach alone.[8] While some might shrug these occurrences away, in fact they have an impact on how investors, customers, and the general public view a firm. It is difficult to rebuild a tarnished image, and long-term customers may be lost.

Nearly every employee, at every level, wrestles with ethical questions at some point or another. Some rationalize questionable behavior by saying, "Everybody's doing it." Others act unethically because they feel pressured in their jobs or have to meet performance quotas. Yet some avoid unethical acts that don't mesh with their personal values and morals. To help you understand the differences in the ways individuals arrive at ethical choices, the next section focuses on how personal ethics and morals develop.

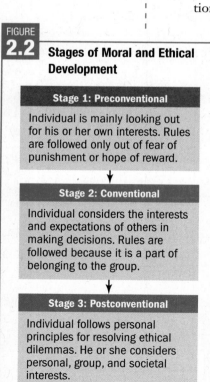

FIGURE 2.2

Stages of Moral and Ethical Development

Stage 1: Preconventional

Individual is mainly looking out for his or her own interests. Rules are followed only out of fear of punishment or hope of reward.

↓

Stage 2: Conventional

Individual considers the interests and expectations of others in making decisions. Rules are followed because it is a part of belonging to the group.

↓

Stage 3: Postconventional

Individual follows personal principles for resolving ethical dilemmas. He or she considers personal, group, and societal interests.

Development of Individual Ethics

Individuals typically develop ethical standards in the three stages shown in Figure 2.2: the preconventional, conventional, and postconventional stages. In stage 1, the preconventional stage, individuals primarily consider their own needs and desires in making decisions. They obey external rules only because they are afraid of punishment or hope to receive rewards if they comply.

In stage 2, the conventional stage, individuals are aware of and act in response to their duty to others, including their obligations to their family members, coworkers, and organizations. The expectations of these groups influence how they choose between what is acceptable and unacceptable in certain situations. Self-interest, however, continues to play a role in decisions.

Stage 3, the postconventional stage, represents the highest level of ethical and moral behavior. The individual is able to move beyond mere self-interest and duty and take the larger needs of society into account as well. He or she has developed personal ethical principles for determining what is right and can apply those principles in a wide variety of situations. One issue that you may face at work is an ethically compromised or "sticky" situation; the "Business Etiquette" feature lists some tips to consider in deciding how to handle such a dilemma.

An individual's stage in moral and ethical development is determined by a huge number of factors. Experiences help shape responses to different situations.

A person's family, educational, cultural, and religious backgrounds can also play a role, as can the environment within the firm. Individuals can also have different styles of deciding ethical dilemmas, no matter what their stage of moral development.

To help you understand and prepare for the ethical dilemmas you may confront in your career, let's take a closer look at some of the factors involved in solving ethical questions on the job.

On-the-Job Ethical Dilemmas

In the fast-paced world of business, you will sometimes be called on to weigh the ethics of decisions that can affect not just your own future but possibly the futures of your fellow workers, your company, and its customers. As already noted, it's not always easy to distinguish between what is right and wrong in many business situations, especially when the needs and concerns of various parties conflict. In the recent past, some CEOs (or their companies) who were accused of wrongdoing simply claimed that they had no idea crimes were being committed, but today's top executives are making a greater effort to be informed of all activities taking place in their firms.

Many clothing retailers donate unworn, unsold garments to charities such as clothing banks. In one recent year, a graduate student discovered that the H&M store on New York's 34th Street was destroying unsold clothing instead. When she contacted store officials and then the company's headquarters in Sweden, her requests for information and offers of help to put H&M in contact with aid organizations went unanswered. She then contacted *The New York Times*, which published a story detailing how H&M—among other retailers—routinely mutilated unsold garments before discarding them to render them unsalable by street vendors or other black-market sellers. The New York City Clothing Bank, founded by the city's mayor during the 1980s, accepts unsold garments and slightly defaces them—not to destroy them but to protect retailers by negating the garments' street value. When

BusinessEtiquette

How to Handle Ethical Dilemmas at Work

How Can Business Support an Ethical Environment?

"Doing well begins with doing right," according to Sharon Allen, Deloitte LLP's chairman of the board. Her advice to companies in the current economy is to concentrate on ethics and by encouraging employees to work to high ethical standards, the organization will end up with strong performers.

Unethical behavior in the workplace can lead to lost earnings and damaged personal lives. In a recent survey the Association of Certified Fraud Examiners discovered that U.S. companies lose approximately 7 percent of their annual revenues to fraud. On the reverse side, companies that were deemed highly ethical on *Ethisphere*'s list saw increased growth.

Employees are eager to work for those companies that demonstrate good corporate social responsibility and high standards for ethical business conduct and customers put more trust into those organizations as well. To ensure the good ethical conduct for both employees and customers, companies should have ethical leaders, a code of ethics or similar policies, and ethics training for employees.

What Can You Do about an Ethical Dilemma?

The business journalist Suzy Welch claims that ethical dilemmas are difficult to resolve because we tend to jump to conclusions based on insufficient information. Welch suggests the following steps if you suspect unethical behavior in the office:

1 Get all the facts. Ask tactful questions of people you know are trustworthy—not sources of rumors or gossip. In return, beware of revealing anything told to you in confidence. Talk to your company's human resources department. Be investigative, not aggressive.

2 When you have the facts, ask yourself, Is this really a moral dilemma? Or is it a case of office politics? What may look like an ethical problem could be a power play in disguise.

3 If the situation really is an ethical dilemma, explain the issue to a trusted friend outside the company—and outside your family. That person may be able to take an unbiased view and advise you about what to do next.

Sources: Suzy Welch, "What to Do When Facing Ethical Problems at Work," *CNN*, www.cnn.com, accessed June 21, 2011; Sharon Allen, "The New ROE: Return On Ethics," *Forbes.com*, www.forbes.com, July 21, 2009.

FIGURE
2.3

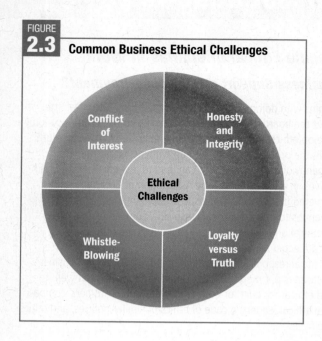

Common Business Ethical Challenges

Ethical Challenges

Conflict of Interest

Honesty and Integrity

Whistle-Blowing

Loyalty versus Truth

the story was published, H&M promised that it would stop destroying unsold clothing and instead donate the garments to charity. A company spokeswoman in New York declared, "It will not happen again. We are committed 100 percent to make sure this practice is not happening anywhere else, as it is not our standard practice."[9]

Businesses may sometimes refuse to purchase goods or services from a particular country because of civil rights abuses by the government of that country. The diamond industry has been plagued with such issues. For a number of years, there has been an international ban on the trade of diamonds from the Marange fields of Zimbabwe because of civil rights abuses against the workers in those mines. While the United Arab Emirates more recently joined the UN-backed ban, talks have begun to resume a level of restricted trade.[10]

Solving ethical dilemmas is not easy. In many cases, each possible decision can have both unpleasant consequences and positive benefits that must be evaluated. The ethical issues that confront manufacturers with unsold merchandise are just one example of many different types of ethical questions encountered in the workplace. Figure 2.3 identifies four of the most common ethical challenges that businesspeople face: conflict of interest, honesty and integrity, loyalty versus truth, and whistle-blowing.

conflict of interest
situation in which an employee must choose between a business's welfare and personal gain.

Conflict of Interest A <u>conflict of interest</u> occurs when a businessperson is faced with a situation in which an action benefiting one person or group has the potential to harm another. Conflicts of interest may pose ethical challenges when they involve the businessperson's own interests and those of someone to whom he or she has a duty or when they involve two parties to whom the businessperson has a duty. Lawyers, business consultants, or advertising agencies would face a conflict of interest if they represented two competing companies: a strategy that would most benefit one of the client companies might harm the other client. Similarly, a real estate agent would face an ethical conflict by representing both the buyer and seller in a transaction. Handling the situation responsibly would be possible, but it would also be difficult. A conflict may also exist between someone's personal interests and those of an organization or its customers. An offer of gifts or bribes for special treatment creates a situation in which the buyer, but not necessarily the company, may benefit personally.

A conflict of interest may also occur when one person holds two or more similar jobs in two different workplaces. Ethical ways to handle conflicts of interest include (1) avoiding them and (2) disclosing them. Some companies have policies against taking on clients who are competitors of existing clients. Most businesses and government agencies have written policies prohibiting employees from accepting gifts or specifying a maximum gift value. Or a member of a board of directors or committee might abstain from voting on a decision in which he or she has a personal interest. In other situations, people state their potential conflict of interest so that the people affected can decide whether to get information or help they need from another source instead.

integrity adhering to deeply felt ethical principles in business situations.

Honesty and Integrity Employers highly value honesty and integrity. An employee who is honest can be counted on to tell the truth. An employee with **integrity** goes beyond truthfulness. Having integrity means adhering to deeply felt ethical principles in business situations. It includes doing what you say you will do and accepting responsibility for mistakes. Behaving with honesty and integrity inspires trust, and as a result, it can help build long-term relationships with customers, employers, suppliers, and the public. Employees, in turn, want their managers and the company as a whole to treat them honestly and with integrity.

Unfortunately, violations of honesty and integrity are all too common. Some people misrepresent their academic credentials and previous work experience on their résumés or job applications. Although it may seem tempting to embellish a résumé in a competitive job market, the act shows a lack of honesty and integrity—and eventually it will catch up with you. A recent news report details a city worker in Ohio, who after years of listing a bachelor's degree on her résumé had to admit that she only attended the school for six months and never graduated. She stepped down from her position.[11]

Employers and employees value honesty and integrity, but what should happen when employees misuse Internet privileges for personal purposes?

Others steal from their employers by taking home supplies or products without permission or by carrying out personal business during the time they are being paid to work. For example, Internet misuse during the work day is increasing. Employees use the Internet for personal shopping, email, gaming, and social networking. This misuse costs U.S. companies an estimated $85 billion annually in lost productivity.[12] While the occurrence of such activity varies widely—and employers may feel more strongly about cracking down on some activities than others—most agree that Internet misuse is a problem. Some have resorted to electronic monitoring and surveillance. Compliance with laws regarding the privacy and security of client information is another major reason given for the continuing increase in such monitoring.

Loyalty versus Truth Businesspeople expect their employees to be loyal and to act in the best interests of the company. But when the truth about a company is not favorable, an ethical conflict can arise. Individuals may have to decide between loyalty to the company and truthfulness in business relationships. People resolve such dilemmas in various ways. Some place the highest value on loyalty, even at the expense of truth. Others avoid volunteering negative information but answer truthfully if someone asks them a specific question. People may emphasize truthfulness and actively disclose negative information, especially if the cost of silence is high, as in the case of operating a malfunctioning aircraft or selling tainted food items.

Whistle-Blowing When an individual encounters unethical or illegal actions at work, that person must decide what action to take. Sometimes it is possible to resolve the problem by working through channels within the organization. If that fails, the person should weigh the potential damages to the greater public good. If the damage is significant, a person may conclude that the only solution is to blow the whistle. <u>Whistle-blowing</u> is an employee's disclosure to company officials, government authorities, or the media of illegal, immoral, or unethical practices.

A whistle-blower must weigh a number of issues in deciding whether to come forward. Resolving an ethical problem within the organization can be more effective, assuming

whistle-blowing
employee's disclosure to company officials, government authorities, or the media of illegal, immoral, or unethical practices committed by an organization.

higher-level managers cooperate. A company that values ethics will try to correct a problem, and staying at a company that does not value ethics may not be worthwhile. In some cases, however, people resort to whistle-blowing because they believe the unethical behavior is causing significant damage that outweighs the risk that the company will retaliate against the whistle-blower. Those risks have been real in some cases. State and federal laws protect whistle-blowers in certain situations, such as reports of discrimination, and the Sarbanes-Oxley Act of 2002 now requires that firms in the private sector provide procedures for anonymous reporting of accusations of fraud. Under the act, anyone who retaliates against an employee for taking concerns of unlawful conduct to a public official can be prosecuted. In addition, whistle-blowers can seek protection under the False Claims Act, a law that was passed in the 1800s, under which they can file a lawsuit on behalf of the government if they believe that a company has somehow defrauded the government. Charges against healthcare companies for fraudulent billing for Medicare or Medicaid are examples of this type of lawsuit. The American Recovery and Reinvestment Act of 2009—also known as the "stimulus package"—grants protection to other whistle-blowers. If an employee of a nonfederal organization (including state or local government) believes that organization has misused funds it received under the stimulus package, he or she will be protected against retaliation after reporting this information.[13]

Despite these protections, whistle-blowing still has its risks. When employee Hector Aldana reported safety concerns to his supervisor and the human resources director at Virgin America Airlines, his worries fell on deaf ears. After making numerous attempts to alert management officials about his observation that the airline was not adhering to FAA regulations regarding maintenance records for its airbus fleet, Aldana warned that he would have to contact the FAA. Aldana was immediately fired. Within a short time, he was not only jobless but also bankrupt and homeless. When later asked if the current whistle-blowing laws protected him, Aldana replied with an emphatic "no."[14]

Obviously, whistle-blowing and other ethical issues arise relatively infrequently in firms with strong organizational climates of ethical behavior. The next section examines how a business can develop an environment that discourages unethical behavior among individuals.

How Organizations Shape Ethical Conduct

No individual makes decisions in a vacuum. Choices are strongly influenced by the standards of conduct established within the organizations where people work. Most ethical lapses in business reflect the values of the firms' corporate cultures.

As shown in Figure 2.4, development of a corporate culture to support business ethics happens on four levels:

1. ethical awareness

2. ethical reasoning

3. ethical action

4. ethical leadership.

Assessment Check ☑

1. What role can an ethics compliance officer play in a firm?
2. What factors influence the ethical environment of a business?

If any of these four factors is missing, the ethical climate in an organization will weaken.

Ethical Awareness

The foundation of an ethical climate is ethical awareness. As we have already seen, ethical dilemmas occur frequently in the workplace. So employees need help in identifying ethical problems when they occur. Workers also need guidance about how the firm expects them to respond.

One way for a firm to provide this support is to develop a **code of conduct**, a formal statement that defines how the organization expects employees to resolve ethical questions. Johnson & Johnson's Credo, presented earlier, is such a code. At the most basic level, a code of conduct may simply specify ground rules for acceptable behavior, such as identifying the laws and regulations that employees must obey. Other companies use their codes of conduct to identify key corporate values and provide frameworks that guide employees as they resolve moral and ethical dilemmas.

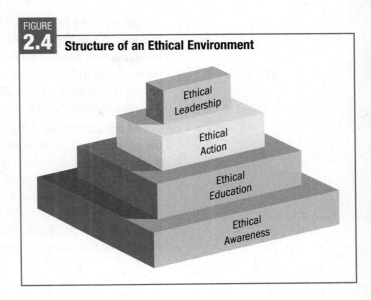

FIGURE 2.4 Structure of an Ethical Environment

The aerospace giant Lockheed Martin, headquartered in Bethesda, Maryland, and with branch offices around the world, has issued a code of conduct to define its values and help employees put them into practice. The code of conduct emphasizes "maintaining a culture of integrity" and defines three basic core values: "do what's right; respect others; perform with excellence." The code applies to "all Lockheed Martin employees, members of the Board of Directors, agents, consultants, contract labor or others, when they are representing or acting for the corporation." All employees at every level are expected to treat fellow employees, suppliers, and customers with dignity and respect and to comply with environmental, health, and safety regulations. The code reminds leaders that their language and behavior must not put or even seem to put pressure on subordinates that might induce them to perform in a way that is contrary to the standards set forth in the code. The code also outlines procedures for reporting violations to a local company ethics officer, promising confidentiality and nonretaliation for problems reported in good faith. Lockheed Martin issues a copy of this code of conduct to each employee and also posts it (in more than 20 languages) on its Web site.[15]

Other firms incorporate similar codes in their policy manuals or mission statements; some issue a code of conduct or statement of values in the form of a small card that employees and managers can carry with them. Harley-Davidson has developed a brief code of ethics that employees can apply both at work and in their personal lives. It reads: "Tell the truth, keep your promises, be fair, respect the individual and encourage intellectual curiosity."

code of conduct formal statement that defines how an organization expects its employees to resolve ethical issues.

Ethical Education

Although a code of conduct can provide an overall framework, it cannot detail a solution for every ethical situation. Some ethical questions have black-and-white answers, but others do not. Businesses must provide the tools employees need to evaluate the options and arrive at suitable decisions.

Many firms have either instituted their own ethics training programs or hired organizations such as Syrus Global, which provides outsourced ethics and compliance programs to businesses. Among other services, Syrus hosts employee reporting services with an anonymous hotline and an ethics case management system. It also helps companies develop appropriate ethics codes with ethics training customized to each company's needs, including specialized online, interactive training systems.[16]

Many authorities debate whether ethics can be taught, but training can give employees the chance to practice applying ethical values to hypothetical situations before they face real-world situations. Similar strategies are being used in many business school ethics programs, where case studies and practical scenarios work best. Convicted white-collar criminal Walter Pavlo, a former employee at telecommunications firm MCI, speaks at colleges and universities about his experiences in the firm and prison. Pavlo, who along with other MCI associates stashed $6 million in offshore accounts, speaks about his actions in an effort to warn students of the consequences of cheating.

Ethical Action

Codes of conduct and ethics training help employees recognize and reason through ethical problems. In addition, firms must provide structures and approaches that allow decisions to be turned into ethical actions. Texas Instruments gives its employees a reference card to help them make ethical decisions on the job. The size of a standard business card, it lists the following guidelines:

- Is the action legal?
- Does it comply with our values?
- If you do it, will you feel bad?
- How will it look in the newspaper?
- If you know it's wrong, don't do it!
- If you're not sure, ask.
- Keep asking until you get an answer.

Goals set for the business as a whole and for individual departments and employees can affect ethical behavior. A firm whose managers set unrealistic goals for employee performance may find an increase in cheating, lying, and other misdeeds, as employees attempt to protect themselves. In today's Internet economy, the high value placed on speed can create a climate in which ethical behavior is sometimes challenged. Ethical decisions often require careful and quiet thought, a challenging task in today's fast-paced business world.

Some companies encourage ethical action by providing support for employees faced with dilemmas. One common tool is an employee hotline, a telephone number that employees can call, often anonymously, for advice or to report unethical behavior they have witnessed. Ethics compliance officers at some firms, as mentioned previously, guide employees through ethical minefields.

Ethical Leadership

Executives must not only talk about ethical behavior but also demonstrate it in their actions. This requires employees to be personally committed to the company's core values and be willing to base their actions on them. The recent recession exposed executive-level misdeeds that damaged or even destroyed entire organizations and wiped out people's life savings. In the aftermath, two students at the Harvard Business School interviewed corporate leaders in their native India and Pakistan whom they regarded as highly moral. The students concluded that these "ethical mavericks" follow a moral code with three simple characteristics:

1. use clear, explicit language rather than euphemisms for corrupt behavior

2. encourage behavior that generates and fosters ethical values

3. practice moral absolutism, insisting on doing right, even if it proves financially costly.[17]

However, ethical leadership should also go one step further and charge each employee at every level with the responsibility to be an ethical leader. Everyone should be aware of problems and be willing to defend the organization's standards.

Unfortunately, not all organizations are able to build a solid framework of business ethics. Because the damage from ethical misconduct can powerfully affect a firm's **stakeholders**—customers, investors, employees, and the public—pressure is exerted on businesses to act in acceptable ways. But when businesses fail, the law must step in to enforce good business practices. Many of the laws that affect specific industries or individuals are described in other chapters in this book. For example, legislation affecting international business operations is discussed in Chapter 4. Laws designed to assist small businesses are examined in Chapter 5. Laws related to labor unions are described in Chapter 8. Legislation related to banking and the securities markets is discussed in Chapters 16 and 17. Finally, for an examination of the legal and governmental forces designed to safeguard society's interests when businesses fail at self-regulation, see Appendix A, "Business Law."

Acting Responsibly to Satisfy Society

A second major issue affecting business is the question of social responsibility. In a general sense, **social responsibility** is management's acceptance of the obligation to consider profit, consumer satisfaction, and societal well-being of equal value in evaluating the firm's performance. It is the recognition that business must be concerned with the qualitative dimensions of consumer, employee, and societal benefits, as well as the quantitative measures of sales and profits, by which business performance is traditionally measured. Businesses may exercise social responsibility because such behavior is required by law, because it enhances the company's image, or because management believes it is the ethical course of action. The "Going Green" feature discusses the efforts of Starbucks to implement environmentally sound practices.

stakeholders customers, investors, employees, and public affected by or with an interest in a company.

Assessment Check ✓

1. What is the preconventional stage in the development of ethical standards?

2. How can loyalty and truth come into conflict for an employee?

3. How does ethical leadership contribute to ethical standards throughout a company?

social responsibility business's consideration of society's well-being and consumer satisfaction, in addition to profits.

Going Green

Starbucks Re-Designs Its Stores. Now, What About the Cup?

In June 2009, the coffee-selling giant Starbucks announced that as it builds new stores and renovates existing ones worldwide, the company plans to design them with two goals in mind: reflecting the character of the neighborhood and striving for a reduced environmental impact.

The project is part of Starbucks' efforts to reposition itself. The company will employ local artisans and materials and use recycled and reclaimed materials to make each store unique. It has also commited itself to conserving water and energy, recycling where possible, and using "green" construction methods. Among its goals are:

- to use renewable resources for 50 percent of the energy used in its stores
- to make its stores 25 percent more energy efficient to reduce greenhouse gas emissions
- to meet U.S. Green Building Code LEED (Leadership in Energy and Environmental Design) certification standards for all its new stores
- to have recycling in stores where it controls waste collection by 2015.

The company has already put some of these goals into practice. The next challenge is those ubiquitous disposable cups. About 3 billion Starbucks paper cups are thrown in the trash each year. Starbucks is determined to change that. The firm launched an outside design contest, looking for innovative ways to solve the problem. And the company has partnered with Georgia Pacific paper mill to recycle some of the cups into Starbucks napkins. The goal is to have a 100-percent recyclable cup by 2015. Meanwhile, customers are helping out: some are already toting their own reusable travel mugs into Starbucks for a fill-up.

Questions for Critical Thinking

1. How do Starbucks' new plans for its stores reflect its sense of social responsibility?
2. How has Starbucks reached out to customers and the community in order to reach its sustainability goals? Why is this an important step for the business?

Sources: Company Web site, http://www.starbucks.com, accessed January 19, 2011; Anya Kamenetz, "What Are You Going to Do About This Damn Cup?" *Fast Company*, November 2010, pp. 116–120, 174–175; "Starbucks Recycling Cups at Chicago, Seattle Stores," *Environmental Leader*, June 29, 2010, http://www.environmentalleader.com.

Historically, a company's social performance has been measured by its contribution to the overall economy and the employment opportunities it provides. Variables such as total wages paid often indicate social performance. Although profits and employment remain important, today many factors contribute to an assessment of a firm's social performance, including providing equal employment opportunities; respecting the cultural diversity of employees; responding to environmental concerns; providing a safe, healthy workplace; and producing high-quality products that are safe to use.

A business is also judged by its interactions with the community. To demonstrate their social responsibility, many corporations highlight charitable contributions and community service in their annual reports and on their Web sites. The Mercadien Group, a business and accounting firm based in Princeton, New Jersey participates in the Toys for Tots program with the U.S. Marine Corps. The company's office is the official drop-off site for the program, and employees at all levels take part. During one recent collection year, the Marines collected and distributed nearly 20 million toys nationwide, of which Mercadien was proud to be a part.[18]

Firms such as Full Circle Coupons are based almost entirely on the premise of social responsibility. Full Circle is an Internet-based business that allows subscribers to log on to its Web site, choose a fundraiser or charity they want to support, and print out discount coupons for local businesses. Full Circle then donates half the annual subscriber fee of $25 to charity. Owners Martha and Brett Bogart believe they have found a business opportunity that not only generates a profit, but automatically gives back to the community.[19]

Some firms measure social performance by conducting **social audits**, formal procedures that identify and evaluate all company activities that relate to social issues such as conservation,

social audits formal procedure that identifies and evaluates all company activities that relate to social issues such as conservation, employment practices, environmental protection, and philanthropy.

employment practices, environmental protection, and philanthropy. The social audit informs management about how well the company is performing in these areas. Based on this information, management may revise current programs or develop new ones.

Outside groups may conduct their own evaluations of businesses. Various environmental, religious, and public-interest groups have created standards of corporate performance. Reports on many of these evaluations are available to the general public. The New York–based Council on Economic Priorities is one such group. Other groups publicize their evaluations and include critiques of the social responsibility performance of firms.

Photo courtesy of Mercadien

Mercadien's participation in the Toys for Tots program highlights its commitment to the community in which they work and allows the firm to fulfill its social responsibility.

As Figure 2.5 shows, the social responsibilities of business can be classified according to its relationships to the general public, customers, employees, and investors and other members of the financial community. Many of these relationships extend beyond national borders.

Responsibilities to the General Public

The responsibilities of business to the general public include dealing with public health issues, protecting the environment, and developing the quality of the workforce. Many would argue that businesses also have responsibilities to support charitable and social causes and organizations that work toward the greater public good. In other words, they should give back to the communities in which they earn profits. Such efforts are called *corporate philanthropy*.

Public-Health Issues One of the most complex issues facing business as it addresses its ethical and social responsibilities to the general public is public health. Central to the public-health debate is the question of what businesses should do about dangerous products such as tobacco and alcohol. Tobacco products represent a major health risk, contributing to heart disease, stroke, and cancer among smokers. Families and coworkers of smokers share this danger as well, as their exposure to secondhand smoke increases their risks for cancer, asthma, and respiratory infections. Many cities have not only banned smoking in public places, but also commercial businesses such as restaurants.

Heart disease, diabetes, and obesity have become major public health issues as the rates of these three conditions have been rising. A reported 5 million American children between the ages of 6 and 17 are

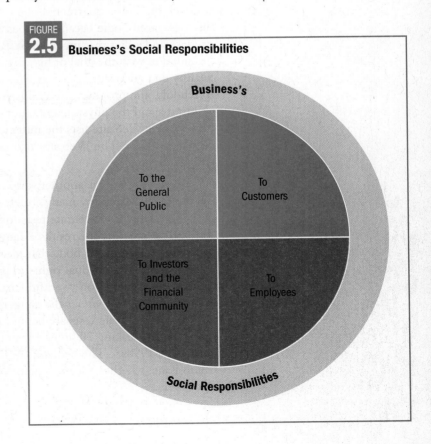

FIGURE

2.5 Business's Social Responsibilities

Business's

| To the General Public | To Customers |
| To Investors and the Financial Community | To Employees |

Social Responsibilities

| To do their part to aid the general public, SUBWAY and the Jared Foundation focus on encouraging children to eat healthfully in the hopes of avoiding obesity problems later in life.

overweight. Three-quarters of obese teenagers will become obese adults at risk for these diseases. Jared Fogle became famous for losing 245 pounds over a two-year period through exercise and a diet that included SUBWAY sandwiches. He has since set up the Jared Foundation with the goal of fighting childhood obesity by encouraging children to develop healthy diet and exercise habits. Spreading his message through speaking tours, grants to schools, and programs for children and their families, Fogle says, "My goal is to help children avoid the physical and emotional hardships I went through living with obesity." SUBWAY's Web site lists the nutritional values of its menu items and sources of diet and nutrition advice. The Web site also features a linked page supporting the Jared Foundation and its mission.[20]

Substance abuse is another serious public health problem worldwide. Revelations of the use of illegal steroids by many athletes, particularly in professional baseball, highlights the difficulty of devising accurate tests for performance-enhancing and muscle-building drugs and fairly evaluating the results. Many of the drugs in question are so similar to compounds naturally present in the body that identification is extremely difficult. With regard to drug testing, athletes' individual rights to privacy have been questioned, particularly due to their widespread influence on youthful fans. Steroid use is on the rise among high school athletes, despite the publicity about the dangers of such drugs. Tougher penalties for professional players who fail drug tests are being formulated. Baseball slugger Mark McGwire, who had hit a record-breaking 70 home runs in the 1998 season, admitted that he had used steroids during the 1990s.[21] The "Solving an Ethical Controversy" feature explores a related public health issue: whether advertisements for prescription drugs are informative or harmful to consumers.

Solving an Ethical Controversy

Are Prescription Drug Advertisements Helpful or Harmful to Consumers?

Since 1985 in the United States, drug manufacturers have used direct-to-consumer advertising (DTCA) to market name-brand prescription drugs. DTCA increased dramatically after 1997, when the Food and Drug Administration (FDA) no longer required detailed lists of possible side effects. A little more than a decade later, pharmaceutical companies spent $4.5 billion on advertising. New Zealand is the only other developed country where DTCA is legal.

Americans now spend more on prescription drugs than on any other area of health care. One reason is the sheer number of prescriptions. Another is that advertising costs have raised the prices of brand-name prescription drugs. Drug companies also market heavily to doctors. The medical community has voiced concern that DTCA may be harming both the public and the healthcare system.

Does direct-to-consumer advertising benefit the American public?

PRO

1. DTCA encourages people to ask their doctors about potentially harmful conditions that may be helped by nonsurgical treatment if caught early enough.

2. Drug companies use their profits to develop new drugs. This process involves considerable research and testing to win FDA approval of drugs that can improve or even save lives.

CON

1. Drug advertisements appeal to people's emotions while minimizing potential side effects. Advertisements may even persuade people to ask for unnecessary treatments.

2. Pharmaceutical companies usually advertise new drugs that have not been tested over time and are more expensive than slightly different, older drugs with well-known side effects. DTCA sometimes backfires.

Summary

Congress has repeatedly tried and failed to curb DTCA. Some proposals would end tax deductions for drug companies' advertising expenses or require a waiting period before advertising a new drug. Pharmaceutical companies have tried to introduce DTCA in Europe, but European Union countries voted overwhelmingly against even an "information to patients" section of a proposed regulation.

Sources: "Prescription Drug TV Ads," *Vaughn's Summaries,* http://www.vaughns-1-pagers.com, accessed January 19, 2011; "What Are Your Thoughts on Drug Ads on TV?" *Toluna,* January 17, 2011, http://us.toluna.com; "U.S. Ad Spending Down Nine Percent . . . Nielsen Says," The Nielsen Company, February 24, 2010, http://nielsen.com; "Should Prescription Drugs Be Advertised Directly to Consumers?" ProCon.org, http://prescriptiondrugs.procon.org, accessed February 12, 2010.

Protecting the Environment Businesses impact the environment in a variety of ways—through the energy they consume, the waste they produce, the natural resources they use, and more. Today, many businesses have built goals into their corporate philosophy for taking steps toward protecting the environment. Some have taken even greater steps, such as launching initiatives toward sustainability—operating in such a way that the firm not only minimizes its impact on the environment, but actually regenerates or replaces used resources. Two such firms are consumer-goods manufacturer Procter & Gamble and healthcare giant Kaiser Permanente. Recently the two companies issued mandatory assessments of sustainability to their suppliers—rating them on energy and water use, recycling, waste production, greenhouse gases produced, and other factors. "We're sending a message to our vendors loud and clear," stated Dean Edward, vice-president and chief procurement officer at Kaiser Permanente. Both companies expect their suppliers to meet green standards—or risk losing them as customers.[22]

Recycling can help companies do their part to protect the environment. Best Buy stores will take your old TVs, DVD players, computers, cell phones, and other electronic devices to avoid having them end up in landfills.

Nathan Gleave/iStockphoto

recycling reprocessing of used materials for reuse.

green marketing a marketing strategy that promotes environmentally safe products and production methods.

For many managers, finding ways to minimize pollution and other environmental damage caused by their products or operating processes has become an important economic and legal issue as well as a social one. When General Motors unveiled the Chevrolet Volt, the new car instantly vaulted past conventional hybrids that run on a combination of electricity and gasoline. The Volt is entirely electric. After its battery runs down, a gasoline engine powers an on-board generator that recharges the battery. General Motors settled on a 40-mile range for the battery because Department of Transportation studies have shown that over three-quarters of commuters drive about that distance to and from work every day, and half of all American households drive even less per day. GM's Vehicle Line Director Tony Posawatz notes, "The beauty of the Volt is the size of the battery."[23]

Despite the efforts of companies like Procter & Gamble, Kaiser Permanente, General Motors, and thousands of others, production and manufacturing methods still leave behind large quantities of waste materials that can further pollute the air, water, and soil. Some products themselves, such as electronics that contain lead and mercury, are difficult to recycle or reuse—although scientists and engineers are finding ways to do this. In other instances, the action (or lack of action) on the part of a firm results in an environmental disaster, as in the case of the explosion and large-scale spill from BP's offshore drilling rig in the Gulf of Mexico. The months-long spill not only affected the ocean and coastal environments, but also the lives of residents and local economies. Nearly a year of investigation revealed risky mistakes and cost-cutting measures made by BP and its associates resulting in tens of billions of dollars in fines to the firms and a push from critics for greater reform.[24] Despite the difficulty, however, companies are finding that they can be environmentally friendly and profitable, too. Another solution to the problems of pollutants is **recycling**—reprocessing used materials for reuse. Recycling can sometimes provide much of the raw material that manufacturers need, thereby conserving the world's natural resources and reducing the need for landfills. The "Hit & Miss" feature describes a company with a creative twist on recycling, turning used restaurant oil and grease into clean, biodegradable biodiesel fuel.

According to the Environmental Protection Agency, discarded electronic items now make up as much as 40 percent of the lead in landfills in the United States. The Institute of Scrap Recycling Industries estimates that about 2.8 billion pounds (1.4 million tons) of electronic equipment were recycled in a recent year.[25] Firms such as Best Buy are trying to make it easier for consumers to recycle their unwanted electronics. Free of charge, consumers can drop small items like CDs, DVDs, cell phones, and rechargeable batteries in kiosks at store entrances. Customers can leave larger items, such as CPUs, VCRs, DVD players, TVs, and computer monitors, at the customer service desk. Best Buy charges a $10 recycling fee for items with screens, but gives customers a $10 store gift card on the spot. Other retailers such as Target and Apple offer trade-in programs, while service providers such as AT&T and Verizon also have drop-off locations for phones. Not-for-profit organizations have joined the effort as well. Goodwill Industries recently partnered with Dell Computer to make it easier for consumers to donate their old computer equipment.[26]

Many consumers have favorable impressions of environmentally conscious businesses. To target these customers, companies often use **green marketing**, a marketing strategy that

Hit & Miss

Pacific Biodiesel Recycles Oil from French Fries to Fuel

In 1980, Robert King founded King Diesel on the island of Maui in Hawaii. The company used conventional diesel fuel to run the generators at the Central Maui Landfill, but in 1995, King became concerned at the large amounts of used cooking oil being dumped. He contacted Daryl Reece at the University of Idaho. Reece helped develop a process that successfully converted used restaurant oils into biodiesel fuel. Together they founded Pacific Biodiesel, using biodiesel to run the generators at the landfill in one of America's first commercially viable, community-based biodiesel plants. Today Pacific Biodiesel and its associated companies produce and sell biodiesel fuel and design, build, and support biodiesel plants around the country.

Biodegradable and nontoxic, biodiesel fuel can be used in any diesel engine. It is produced from renewable resources such as cooking oil and soybean oil, which would otherwise be dumped in landfills or down drains. Biodiesel significantly cuts down on many pollutants and reduces dependence on foreign oil. In addition, the company has pledged not to import any oil—such as soybean oil from South America or palm oil from Southeast Asia—for its product, nor does it export biodiesel outside the United States.

On Maui, restaurants pay haulers to take their used cooking oil to the landfill. The haulers pay the county of Oahu for the right to dump garbage at waste facilities. Pacific Biodiesel's facility at the landfill is rent free. The haulers' fees cover most of the county's payment to Pacific Biodiesel for processing the waste. Shipping this waste off island would be much more expensive; recycling it prolongs the useful life of the landfills and guarantees a local source of energy. On Maui alone, Pacific Biodiesel recycles about 200,000 gallons of oil and grease each year.

Recently Pacific Biodiesel announced the production of the first commercial biodiesel in Alaska at a plant that the firm constructed in Oregon and shipped for reassembly to Anchorage, Alaska, where it will be run by Alaska Green Waste Solutions.

Questions for Critical Thinking

1. How might Pacific Biodiesel spread the message that recycling is good business as well as good for the environment? How might it reach out to other industries?

2. How does Pacific Biodiesel fulfill its responsibilities to the general public?

Sources: Company Web site, http://www.biodiesel.com, accessed January 19, 2011; "Official Pacific Biodiesel, Inc. Position on Imported Oil," December 3, 2010, http://www.biodiesel.com; "First Commercial Biodiesel Produced in Alaska," *Biodiesel Magazine*, June 18, 2010, http://www.biodieselmagazine.com.

---

promotes environmentally safe products and production methods. A business cannot simply claim that its goods or services are environmentally friendly, however. The Federal Trade Commission (FTC) has issued guidelines for businesses to follow in making environmental claims. A firm must be able to prove that any environmental claim made about a product has been substantiated with reliable scientific evidence. In addition, as shown in Figure 2.6, the FTC has given specific directions about how various environmental terms may be used in advertising and marketing.

Other environmental issues—such as finding renewable sources of clean energy and developing **sustainable** agriculture—are the focus of many firms' efforts. Vinod Khosla, founder of Sun Microsystems, is now working with a group of high-powered entrepreneurs and investors in Silicon Valley to develop a new generation of energy.[27] Solar energy, geothermal energy, biodiesel, and wind power are just a few of the renewable sources of energy being developed by entrepreneurs, large energy firms, and small engineering companies. As we have seen in the "Hit & Miss" feature above, Pacific Biodiesel started with one plant and now has branches nationwide.

Mars Incorporated, the maker of Dove Chocolate and other candies, has committed to buying 100,000 tons of cocoa from Rainforest Alliance–certified farms. It is also working in conjunction with the market-oriented sustainability program UTZ Certified and intends to use sustainably grown cocoa in all of its chocolate products by 2020.[28]

sustainable the capacity to endure in ecology.

FIGURE
2.6

FTC Guidelines for Environmental Claims in Green Marketing

If a business says a product is...	The product or package must . . .
Biodegradable	break down and return to nature in a reasonably short period of time.
Recyclable	be entirely reusable as new materials in the manufacture or assembly of a new product or package.
Refillable	be included in a system for the collection and return of the package for refill. If consumers have to find a way to refill it themselves, it is not **refillable**.
Ozone Safe/Ozone Friendly	must not contain any ozone-depleting ingredient.

Developing the Quality of the Workforce

In the past, a nation's wealth has often been based on its money, production equipment, and natural resources. A country's true wealth, however, lies in its people. An educated, skilled workforce provides the intellectual know-how required to develop new technology, improve productivity, and compete in the global marketplace. It is becoming increasingly clear that to remain competitive, U.S. business must assume more responsibility for enhancing the quality of its workforce, including encouraging diversity of all kinds.

In developed economies like that of the United States, many new jobs require college-educated workers. With demand high for workers with advanced skills, the difference between the highest-paid and lowest-paid workers has been increasing. Education plays an important role in earnings, despite success stories of those who dropped out of college or high school to start businesses. Workers with professional degrees earn an average of $2,749 a week, whereas those with some high school but no diploma earn about $449.[29] Businesses must encourage students to stay in school, continue their education, and sharpen their skills. Cheerios supports Spoonfuls of Stories, a national program to encourage young children and their parents to read together by distributing more than 50 million books in specially marked cereal boxes. The company has also contributed more than $3.5 million to First Book, a not-for-profit that gives children from low-income families the chance to own their first new books.[30]

Organizations also face enormous responsibilities for helping women, members of various cultural groups, and those who are physically challenged to contribute fully to the economy. Failure to do so is not only a waste of more than half the nation's workforce but also devastating to a firm's public image. Some socially responsible firms also encourage diversity in their business suppliers. Retail giant JCPenney's Partnership Program is designed to foster relationships with minority- and women-owned businesses—an effort the company has worked at for more than 30 years.

Through a commitment to developing employee diversity, Walmart's president and CEO Mike Duke recently reiterated the company's emphasis on inclusion. "There isn't a single part of our business that can't benefit from people of all backgrounds contributing different skills, different ideas, and different points of view," said Duke. One area that Duke believes is crucial for Walmart to focus on is the advancement of women in the company worldwide.[31]

Corporate Philanthropy

As Chapter 1 pointed out, not-for-profit organizations play an important role in society by serving the public good. They provide the human resources that enhance the quality of life in communities around the world. To fulfill this mission, many not-for-profit organizations rely on financial contributions from the business community. Firms respond by donating billions of dollars each year to not-for-profit organizations. This **corporate philanthropy** includes cash contributions, donations of equipment and products, and supporting the volunteer efforts of company employees. Recipients

corporate philanthropy
effort of an organization to make a contribution to the communities in which it earns profits.

include cultural organizations, adopt-a-school programs, community development agencies, and housing and job training programs.

Corporate philanthropy can have many positive benefits beyond the purely "feel-good" rewards of giving, such as higher employee morale, enhanced company image, and improved customer relationships. General Mills, for instance, is a major contributor to the Susan G. Komen Breast Cancer Foundation, through its line of yogurt products marketed under the Yoplait brand name. Yoplait's target market is health-conscious women, the same group most likely to know of or become involved with the Komen Foundation's fund-raising efforts. The firm also sponsors its My Hometown Helper program, a nationwide initiative that provides grants to communities, not-for-profit groups, and public schools for community improvement projects.[32]

Corporate philanthropy can enhance a company's customer relationships. Through sales of its Yoplait yogurt line, General Mills contributes to the Susan G. Komen Breast Cancer Foundation, a charity that is important to the health-conscious consumers who buy Yoplait.

Companies often seek to align their marketing efforts with their charitable giving. Many contribute to the Olympics and create advertising that features the company's sponsorship. This is known as *cause-related marketing*. In a recent survey, nearly nine out of ten young people said they believed companies had a duty to support social causes, and nearly seven in eight said they would switch brands in order to reward a company that did so. Consumers are often willing to pay even more for a product, such as Newman's Own salad dressings and salsa, because they know the proceeds are going to a good cause.

Another form of corporate philanthropy is volunteerism. In their roles as corporate citizens, thousands of businesses encourage their employees to contribute their efforts to projects as diverse as Habitat for Humanity, the Red Cross, and the Humane Society. In addition to making tangible contributions to the well-being of fellow citizens, such programs generate considerable public support and goodwill for the companies and their employees. In some cases, the volunteer efforts occur mostly during off-hours for employees. In other instances, firms permits their workforces to volunteer during regular working hours. Sometimes volunteers with special skills are indispensable. After the devastating earthquake in Haiti, the pilots' union at the shipping giant UPS volunteered to transport supplies and personnel in the relief effort.[33]

Responsibilities to Customers

Businesspeople share a social and ethical responsibility to treat their customers fairly and act in a manner that is not harmful to them. **Consumerism**—the public demand that a business consider the wants and needs of its customers in making decisions—has gained widespread acceptance. Consumerism is based on the belief that consumers have certain rights. A frequently quoted statement of consumer rights was made by President John F. Kennedy in 1962. Figure 2.7 summarizes these consumer rights. Numerous state and federal laws have been implemented since then to protect these rights.

consumerism public demand that a business consider the wants and needs of its customers in making decisions.

The Right to Be Safe Contemporary businesspeople must recognize obligations, both moral and legal, to ensure the safe operation of their products. Consumers should feel assured that the products they purchase will not cause injuries in normal use. **Product liability** refers to the responsibility of manufacturers for injuries and damages caused by their products. Items that lead to injuries, either directly or indirectly, can have disastrous consequences for their makers.

Many companies put their products through rigorous testing to avoid safety problems. Still, testing alone cannot foresee every eventuality. Companies must try to consider all possibilities and provide adequate warning of potential dangers. When a product does

product liability the responsibility of manufacturers for injuries and damages caused by their products.

FIGURE
2.7

Consumer Rights as Proposed by President Kennedy

pose a threat to customer safety, a responsible manufacturer responds quickly to either correct the problem or recall the dangerous product. Although we take for granted that our food—and our pets' food—is safe, sometimes contamination leaks in, which can cause illness or even death. Recently a concern about salmonella, a microorganism that produces dangerous infections, caused several manufacturers of pet foods and supplements to recall their products. Natural Balance Pet Foods issued a voluntary recall of its Sweet Potato & Chicken dry food, while the United Pet Group recalled its Pro-Pet Adult Daily Vitamin products. No illnesses or deaths were reported, but the companies wanted to be certain its products were safe for pets to consume.[34]

The Right to Be Informed Consumers should have access to enough education and product information to make responsible buying decisions. In their efforts to promote and sell their goods and services, companies can easily neglect consumers' right to be fully informed. False or misleading advertising is a violation of the Wheeler-Lea Act, a federal law enacted in 1938. The FTC and other federal and state agencies have established rules and regulations that govern advertising truthfulness. These rules prohibit businesses from making unsubstantiated claims about the performance or superiority of their merchandise. They also require businesses to avoid misleading consumers. Businesses that fail to comply face scrutiny from the FTC and consumer protection organizations. For instance, Dannon Company settled a class-action lawsuit that charged the firm with false advertising for two of its yogurt products, DanActive and Activia. The advertising claimed that the yogurt products had been "clinically" and "scientifically" proven to regulate the digestive system and improve immunity. Dannon agreed to a settlement of $45 million and to change the wording of its advertisements.[35]

The Food and Drug Administration (FDA), which sets standards for advertising conducted by drug manufacturers, eased restrictions for prescription drug advertising on television. In print ads, drug makers are required to spell out potential side effects and the proper uses of prescription drugs. Because of the requirement to disclose this information, prescription drug television advertising was limited. Now, however, the FDA says drug ads on radio and television can directly promote a prescription drug's benefits if they provide a quick way for consumers to learn about side-effects, such as displaying a toll-free number or Internet address. As we have seen, the "Solving an Ethical Controversy" feature on page 51 discusses the pros and cons of such advertising.

The FDA also monitors "dietary supplements," including vitamins and herbs. This includes protecting consumers against fake and sometimes harmful versions of name-brand supplements. In 2010, the FDA issued a public alert to warn consumers about counterfeit versions of Alli, an over-the-counter weight-loss supplement. Instead of the correct active ingredient, the counterfeit Alli contained a controlled substance that should not be used without a doctor's supervision and that may actually harm certain patients. In addition, the packaging of the counterfeit was missing a "lot" code and differed in other, subtle ways from the genuine packaging. The fake capsules were different in size and shape from the real ones, too. Apparently all the fake Alli had been sold over the Internet rather than in stores, so customers could not inspect the packaging or the capsules before receiving the product.[36]

The responsibility of business to preserve consumers' right to be informed extends beyond avoiding misleading advertising. All communications with customers—from salespeople's comments to warranties and invoices—must be controlled to clearly and accurately inform customers. Most packaged-goods firms, personal-computer makers, and other makers of products bought for personal use by consumers include toll-free customer service numbers on their product labels so that consumers can get answers to questions about a product.

To protect their customers and avoid claims of insufficient disclosure, businesses often include warnings on products. As Figure 2.8 shows, sometimes these warnings go far beyond what a reasonable consumer would expect. Others are downright funny.

The Right to Choose Consumers should have the right to choose which goods and services they need and want to purchase. Socially responsible firms attempt to preserve this right, even if they reduce their own sales and profits in the process. Brand-name drug makers have recently gone on the defensive in a battle being waged by state governments, insurance companies, consumer groups, unions, and major employers such as General Motors and Verizon. These groups want to force down the rising price of prescription drugs by ensuring that consumers have the right and the opportunity to select cheaper generic brands.

The Right to Be Heard Consumers should be able to express legitimate complaints to appropriate parties. Many companies expend considerable effort to ensure full hearings for consumer complaints. The auction Web site eBay assists buyers and sellers who believe they were victimized in transactions conducted through the site. It deploys a 200-employee team to work with users and law enforcement agencies to combat fraud. The company has strict guidelines for buyers and sellers and rules for leaving feedback about a buyer or seller. For example, buyers must operate within a list of acceptable goods for sale and may not offer such items as alcohol, pornography, drugs, counterfeit currency, or artifacts from cave formations, graves, or Native American sites. The protection of copyrights is also an important part of eBay's policy.[37]

Responsibilities to Employees

Companies that can attract skilled and knowledgeable employees are better able to meet the challenges of competing globally. In return, businesses have wide-ranging responsibilities to their employees, both here and abroad. These include workplace safety, quality-of-life issues, ensuring equal opportunity on the job, avoiding age discrimination, and preventing sexual harassment and sexism.

FIGURE 2.8

Actual Wacky Warning Labels

Workplace safety is an important business responsibility. In potentially dangerous areas workers are required to wear hard hats.

Vedran Vidovic/Shutterstock

Workplace Safety A century ago, few businesses paid much attention to the safety of their workers. In fact, most business owners viewed employees as mere cogs in the production process. Workers—many of whom were young children—toiled in frequently dangerous conditions. In 1911, a fire at the Triangle Shirtwaist Factory in New York City killed 146 people, mostly young girls. Contributing to the massive loss of life were the sweatshop working conditions at the factory, including overcrowding, blocked exits, and a lack of fire escapes. This horrifying tragedy forced businesses to begin to recognize their responsibility for their workers' safety.

The safety and health of workers on the job is now an important business responsibility. The Occupational Safety and Health Administration (OSHA) is the main federal regulatory force in setting workplace safety and health standards. These mandates range from broad guidelines on storing hazardous materials to specific standards for worker safety in industries such as construction, manufacturing, and mining. OSHA tracks and investigates workplace accidents and has the authority to fine employers who are found liable for injuries and deaths that occur on the job.

One unsettling fact is that about 70 teens die every year in the United States as a result of work injuries. Most of these fatalities occur because of unsafe equipment, inadequate safety training, and dangerous work that is illegal or inappropriate for youth. OSHA is taking steps to educate employers and teen workers about safety, health, and a positive work environment. The OSHA Web site has a special section for teens with the answers to most frequently asked questions about such issues as wages, labor standards, harassment issues, and safety at work. In addition, the U.S. Department of Labor has rolled out a new initiative called YouthRules!, a project designed to further educate and empower young workers. The YouthRules! Web page offers information and activities for teens, parents, educators, and employers.[38]

Quality-of-Life Issues Balancing work and family is becoming harder for many employees. They find themselves squeezed between working long hours and handling child-care problems, caring for elderly parents, and solving other family crises. A *sandwich generation* of households, those caring for two generations—their children and their aging parents—has arisen. As the population ages, the share of American households providing some type of care to a relative or friend age 50 or older has grown dramatically in the early years of the 21st century. At the same time, as married women spend more time working outside the home, they have fewer hours per week to spend on family. The employees juggling work with life's other demands aren't just working mothers. Childless couples, single people, and men all express frustration with the pressures of balancing work with family and personal needs. To help with the work–life balance, some employers are offering flexible work schedules so that parents can meet the needs of their children (or aging parents) as well as their jobs. *Working Mother* magazine offers up their list of 100 best companies to work for offering work–life balance. Criteria for selection include the option to telecommute, flexible scheduling, job sharing, and access to childcare. Some of the magazine's top choices are Bank of America, Deloitte, Discovery Communications, General Mills, and IBM.[39] Increasingly, women are starting their own businesses so they can set their own hours and goals. The "Hit & Miss" feature portrays one woman who started her own business to provide her ailing son the care he needed.

Some companies have come up with truly innovative ways to deal with work schedules, including paid time off for vacation or illness. At some of its locations, IBM has done away

Balancing Life and Work with a Cup of Tea

In 2000, Zhena Muzyka was living in Ojai, California, a 25-year-old single mother whose infant son needed kidney surgery. Muzyka had no health insurance and only a few dollars in the bank. From watching her Rom (gypsy) grandmother tend a huge garden and blend teas, she had always been interested in herbal medicine, so she borrowed money from her parents and her brother and started Zhena's Gypsy Tea from a cart in a friend's antique store. At first, she was able to keep her son, Sage, with her in a baby carrier. When her teas proved popular—and Sage outgrew the carrier—she realized she had reached a turning point.

Muzyka searched for new sources and started blending her own loose-leaf teas, adding essential oils for their medicinal value. She discovered that none of the teas she was buying were organic or **fair trade**. She made the change to fair trade teas after learning that infant mortality rates among tea pickers on non–fair trade farms can reach 70 percent. Fair trade tea workers have guaranteed health care, clean water, education, and maternity leave and child care.

As Zhena's Gypsy Tea has grown and diversified, Muzhaka has searched for new ways to put her values into practice. Her Pink Tea for Women's Health is a partner of the Breast Cancer Research Foundation.

The company now uses corn silk for its teabags. It buys wind credits, even though that lowers profits. Muzyka says, "[Zhena's Gypsy Tea] is the most 'worth it' thing I've ever done. Knowing that we're sincerely making a difference for people and helping them out of poverty—while providing a delicious cup of tea for consumers here—is pretty satisfying."

And Sage? After three operations, he got a clean bill of health in 2007.

Questions for Critical Thinking

1. How did Zhena Muzyka translate her life experiences into her company's ethics culture?
2. Do you have an idea for starting your own business? If so, brainstorm some ideas for balancing your life and values with your work.

Sources: Company Web site, http://www.gypsytea.com, accessed June 21, 2011; Eve Gumpel, "Gypsy Tea Steeped in Health and Fun," *Women Entrepreneur.com*, January 24, 2010, http://www.womenentrepreneur.com; "Oh, That's So Yesterday: A California Tea Company Gets a Brand Makeover," *Inc.*, December 2009/January 2010.

---

with prescribed vacation time altogether—the focus is on results. Employees have an informal agreement with their supervisors about when they will be out of the office, based on their ability to complete their work on schedule. The number of days they take off is not tracked; instead vacation time is considered open ended. But the catch is, the work has to be done. Perhaps surprisingly, the firm found that employees put in just as many hours, if not more, under the new program. According to an IBM representative, ". . . there is no policing, and employees are empowered to take vacation when they want."[40]

Another solution has been to offer **family leave** to employees who need to deal with family matters. Under the Family and Medical Leave Act of 1993, businesses with 50 or more employees must provide unpaid leave annually for any employee who wants time off for the birth or adoption of a child; to become a foster parent; or to care for a seriously ill relative, spouse, or self if he or she has a serious health condition or injury. The law requires employers to grant up to 12 weeks of leave each year, and leave may be taken intermittently as medical conditions make necessary. This unpaid leave also applies to an employee who has a serious illness. Workers must meet certain eligibility requirements. Employers must continue to provide health benefits during the leave and guarantee that employees will return to equivalent jobs. The issue of who is entitled to health benefits can also create a dilemma as companies struggle to balance the needs of their employees against the staggering costs of health care.

Ensuring Equal Opportunity on the Job Businesspeople face many challenges managing an increasingly diverse workforce in the 21st century. Technological advances are expanding the ways people with physical disabilities can contribute in the workplace. Businesses also need to find ways to responsibly recruit and manage older workers and workers with varying lifestyles. In addition, beginning with Lotus Development in 1982, companies have begun to extend benefits equally to employees, regardless of sexual orientation. In particular, that means the company offers benefits such as health insurance to

fair trade a market-based approach to pay higher prices to producers on exports from developing countries to developed countries in order for the developing countries to obtain better trading conditions and promote sustainability.

family leave the Family and Medical Leave Act of 1993 states that businesses with 50 or more employees must provide unpaid leave up to 12 weeks annually for any employee who wants time off for the birth or adoption of a child, to become a foster parent, or to care for a seriously ill relative, spouse, or self if he or she has a serious health condition or injury.

unmarried domestic partners if it offers them to spouses of married couples. Companies that now offer these gender-neutral benefits include Avon Products, Costco Wholesale, Disney, General Mills, and Mattel.

To a great extent, efforts at managing diversity are regulated by law. The Civil Rights Act (1964) outlawed many kinds of discriminatory practices, and Title VII of the act specifically prohibits **discrimination**—biased treatment of a job candidate or employee—in the workplace. As shown in Table 2.2, other nondiscrimination laws include the Equal Pay

Table 2.2 Laws Designed to Ensure Equal Opportunity

LAW	KEY PROVISIONS
Title VII of the Civil Rights Act of 1964 (as amended by the Equal Employment Opportunity Act of 1972)	Prohibits discrimination in hiring, promotion, compensation, training, or dismissal on the basis of race, color, religion, sex, or national origin.
Age Discrimination in Employment Act of 1967 (as amended)	Prohibits discrimination in employment against anyone age 40 or older in hiring, promotion, compensation, training, or dismissal.
Equal Pay Act of 1963	Requires equal pay for men and women working for the same firm in jobs that require equal skill, effort, and responsibility.
Vocational Rehabilitation Act of 1973	Requires government contractors and subcontractors to take affirmative action to employ and promote qualified disabled workers. Coverage now extends to all federal employees. Coverage has been broadened by the passage of similar laws in more than 20 states and, through court rulings, to include people with communicable diseases, including AIDS.
Vietnam Era Veterans Readjustment Act of 1974	Requires government contractors and subcontractors to take affirmative action to employ and retain disabled veterans. Coverage now extends to all federal employees and has been broadened by the passage of similar laws in more than 20 states.
Pregnancy Discrimination Act of 1978	Requires employers to treat pregnant women and new mothers the same as other employees for all employment-related purposes, including receipt of benefits under company benefit programs.
Americans with Disabilities Act of 1990	Makes discrimination against the disabled illegal in public accommodations, transportation, and telecommunications; stiffens employer penalties for intentional discrimination on the basis of an employee's disability.
Civil Rights Act of 1991	Makes it easier for workers to sue their employers for alleged discrimination. Enables victims of sexual discrimination to collect punitive damages; includes employment decisions and on-the-job issues such as sexual harassment, unfair promotions, and unfair dismissal. The employer must prove that it did not engage in discrimination.
Family and Medical Leave Act of 1993	Requires all businesses with 50 or more employees to provide up to 12 weeks of unpaid leave annually to employees who have had a child or are adopting a child, are becoming foster parents, are caring for a seriously ill relative or spouse, or are themselves seriously ill. Workers must meet certain eligibility requirements.
Uniformed Services Employment and Reemployment Rights Act of 1994	Prohibits employers from denying employment benefits on the basis of employees' membership in or obligation to serve in the uniformed services and protects the rights of veterans, reservists, and National Guard members to reclaim their jobs after being absent due to military service or training.
Genetic Information Nondiscrimination Act of 2008	Prohibits employers from discriminating against employees or applicants on the basis of genetic information, including genetic tests of an individual or family member or an individual's personal or family medical history.

Act (1963), the Age Discrimination in Employment Act (1967), the Equal Employment Opportunity Act (1972), the Pregnancy Discrimination Act (1978), the Civil Rights Act of 1991, and numerous executive orders. The Americans with Disabilities Act (1990) protects the rights of physically challenged people. The Vietnam Era Veterans Readjustment Act (1974) protects the employment of veterans of the Vietnam War. The Genetic Information Nondiscrimination Act (2008) prohibits discrimination on the basis of genetic tests or the medical history of an individual or that individual's family.

The **Equal Employment Opportunity Commission (EEOC)** was created to increase job opportunities for women and minorities and to help end discrimination based on race, color, religion, disability, gender, or national origin in any personnel action. To enforce fair-employment laws, it investigates charges of discrimination and harassment and files suit against violators. The EEOC can also help employers set up programs to increase job opportunities for women, minorities, people with disabilities, and people in other protected categories.

Fair treatment of employees is more than a matter of complying with EEOC regulations, however. All employees want to be treated with respect. A minority employee who misses out on a plum assignment may miss out on the big raise that goes with it. As the employee's salary grows more slowly, managers may eventually begin to use the size of the salary as an indicator that the employee contributes less to the organization. While in the past the EEOC has focused on this type of individual situation, currently it is addressing what it terms "systemic discrimination," which it defines as "a pattern or practice, policy and/or class cases where the alleged discrimination has a broad impact on an industry, profession, company, or geographic location." A systemic discrimination charge usually becomes a class-action suit, which costs considerably more to defend than an individual lawsuit. So firms are examining their employment practices carefully to make sure they are not open to discrimination charges.[41] Chapter 9 takes a closer look at diversity and employment discrimination issues as part of a discussion of human resource management.

Age Discrimination With the average age of U.S. workers steadily rising, more than half the workforce is projected to be age 40 or older in a few years. Yet some employers find it less expensive to hire and retain younger workers, who generally have lower medical bills as well as lower salary and benefits packages. At the same time, many older workers have training and skills that younger workers have yet to acquire. The Age Discrimination in Employment Act of 1967 (ADEA) protects individuals who are age 40 or older, prohibiting discrimination on the basis of age and denial of benefits to older employees.

Ruling in a lawsuit brought under the ADEA, the Supreme Court determined that employers can be held liable for age discrimination against older workers even if they intended no harm. At the same time, the court allowed employers to use "reasonable" factors such as cost cutting to defend business practices that might have more severe impacts on older than on younger workers. However, in June 2009, a new Court ruling shifted the burden of proof onto employees seeking to prove that age discrimination was a factor in their demotion or dismissal.[42]

Legal issues aside, employers might do well to consider not only the experience that older workers bring to the workplace but also their enthusiasm. Many surveys report that older workers who remain on the job by choice—not because they are forced to do so for economic reasons—are often happy with their employment. But other studies show that aging baby boomers are increasingly dissatisfied with the workplace due to the falling value of their retirement investments and diminishing options such as relocation. Still, employees with decades of work experience can be a valuable asset to any firm.[43]

In all cases, employers need to plan ahead for the aging of the workforce, finding ways to retain accumulated business wisdom, prepare for the demand for health services, and be

Equal Employment Opportunity Commission (EEOC) this commission was created to increase job opportunities for women and minorities and to help end discrimination based on race, color, religion, disability, gender, or national origin in any personnel action.

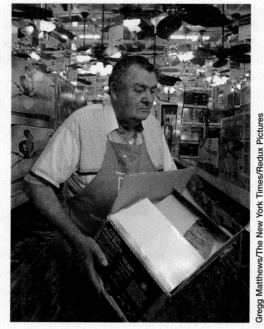

Employers are responsible for avoiding age discrimination in the workplace. As the average age of workers rises, employers will benefit from the older generation's knowledge.

ready for growth in the industries that serve seniors. The 55 to 64 age group will increase from just over 18 percent to almost 24 percent over the next few years, whereas the 35 to 44 age group will decrease by just over 4 percent. These numbers signify a coming shift in the workforce, as well as in the goods and services needed.[44]

Sexual Harassment and Sexism Every employer has a responsibility to ensure that all workers are treated fairly and are safe from sexual harassment. **Sexual harassment** refers to unwelcome and inappropriate actions of a sexual nature in the workplace. It is a form of sex discrimination that violates the Civil Rights Act of 1964, which gives both men and women the right to file lawsuits for intentional sexual harassment. Almost 14,000 sexual harassment complaints are filed with the EEOC each year, of which about 16 percent are filed by men.[45] Thousands of other cases are either handled internally by companies or never reported.

Two types of sexual harassment exist. The first type occurs when an employee is pressured to comply with unwelcome advances and requests for sexual favors in return for job security, promotions, and raises. The second type results from a hostile work environment in which an employee feels hassled or degraded because of unwelcome flirting, lewd comments, or obscene jokes. The courts have ruled that allowing sexually oriented materials in the workplace can create a hostile atmosphere that interferes with an employee's ability to do the job. Employers are also legally responsible to protect employees from sexual harassment by customers and clients. The EEOC's Web site informs employers and employees of criteria for identifying sexual harassment and how it should be handled in the workplace.

Preventing sexual harassment can be difficult because it involves regulating the conduct of individual employees. Sometimes victims, especially young employees, are intimidated or unaware of their rights, but the EEOC has set up a Youth@Work program (http://www.eeoc.gov/youth) to ensure that young workers can learn about the various types of discrimination and ways to avoid them.

sexual harassment
unwelcome and inappropriate actions of a sexual nature in the workplace.

The cost in settlements or fines can be enormous. So in addition to ethical and legal reasons, it makes good business sense for firms to prevent this kind of behavior from happening. To avoid sexual harassment problems, many firms have established policies and employee education programs aimed at preventing such violations. An effective harassment prevention program should include the following measures:

- Issue a specific policy statement prohibiting sexual harassment.

- Develop a complaint procedure for employees to follow.

- Create a work atmosphere that encourages sexually harassed staffers to come forward.

- Investigate and resolve complaints quickly and take disciplinary action against harassers.

Unless all these components are supported by top management, sexual harassment is difficult to eliminate.

Sexual harassment is often part of the broader problem of **sexism**—discrimination against members of either sex, but primarily affecting women. One important sexism issue is equal pay for equal work.

Lilly Ledbetter was near retirement when she found out that for a considerable length of time, men at her management level had been getting paid more than she had been. But the Supreme Court threw out her case because she did not sue within the statute of limitations—that is, within 180 days of the first instance of a lower paycheck. In January 2009, President Barack Obama signed a law that extended the statute of limitations in such cases.[46]

U.S. Census statistics show that overall, women still earn 77 cents for every 1 dollar earned by men. The number drops to 68 cents for African American women and 58 cents for Hispanic women. Education, occupation, work hours, and other factors don't seem to affect the gap, which remains unexplained other than the penalty of gender.[47] In some extreme cases, differences in pay and advancement can become the basis for sex discrimination suits, which, like sexual harassment suits, can be costly and time consuming to settle. As in all business practices, it is better to act legally and ethically in the first place.

Responsibilities to Investors and the Financial Community

Although a fundamental goal of any business is to make a profit for its shareholders, investors and the financial community demand that businesses behave ethically and legally. When firms fail in this responsibility, thousands of investors and consumers can suffer.

State and federal government agencies are responsible for protecting investors from financial misdeeds. At the federal level, the Securities and Exchange Commission (SEC) investigates suspicions of unethical or illegal behavior by publicly traded firms. It investigates accusations that a business is using faulty accounting practices to inaccurately portray its financial resources and profits to investors. Regulation FD ("Fair Disclosure") is an SEC rule that requires publicly traded companies to announce major information to the general public, rather than first disclosing the information to selected major investors. The agency also operates an Office of Internet Enforcement to target fraud in online trading and online sales of stock by unlicensed sellers. Recall that the Sarbanes-Oxley Act of 2002 also protects investors from unethical accounting practices. Chapter 17 discusses securities trading practices further.

sexism discrimination against members of either sex, but primarily affecting women.

Assessment Check ✓

1. What is meant by social responsibility, and why do firms exercise it?

2. What is green marketing?

3. What are the four main consumer rights?

Assessment Check ✓

1. Why do firms need to do more than just earn a profit?

2. What is the role of the Securities and Exchange Commission?

What's Ahead

The decisions and actions of businesspeople are often influenced by outside forces such as the legal environment and society's expectations about business responsibility. Firms also are affected by the economic environments in which they operate. The next chapter discusses the broad economic issues that influence businesses around the world. Our discussion will focus on how factors such as supply and demand, unemployment, inflation, and government monetary policies pose both challenges and opportunities for firms seeking to compete in the global marketplace.

Summary of Learning Goals

⌈1⌉ Explain the concepts of business ethics and social responsibility.

Business ethics refers to the standards of conduct and moral values that businesspeople rely on to guide their actions and decisions in the workplace. Businesspeople must take a wide range of social issues into account when making decisions. Social responsibility refers to management's acceptance of the obligation to put an equal value on profit, consumer satisfaction, and societal well-being in evaluating the firm's performance.

Assessment Check Answers ✓

1.1 To whom do businesses have responsibilities? Businesses are responsible to customers, employees, investors, and society.

1.2 If a firm is meeting all its responsibilities to others, why do ethical conflicts arise? Ethical conflicts arise because business must balance doing what is right and doing what is profitable.

⌈2⌉ Describe the factors that influence business ethics.

Among the many factors shaping individual ethics are personal experience, peer pressure, and organizational culture. Individual ethics are also influenced by family, cultural, and religious standards. Additionally, the culture of the organization where a person works can be a factor.

Assessment Check Answers ✓

2.1 What role can an ethics compliance officer play in a firm? Ethics compliance officers are charged with deterring wrongdoing and ensuring that ethical standards are met.

2.2 What factors influence the ethical environment of a business? Individual ethics and technology influence the ethical environment of a business.

⌈3⌉ List the stages in the development of ethical standards, and discuss how organizations shape ethical behavior.

In the preconventional stage, individuals primarily consider their own needs and desires in making decisions. They obey external rules only from fear of punishment or hope of reward. In the conventional stage, individuals are aware of and respond to their duty to others. Expectations of groups, as well as self-interest, influence behavior. In the postconventional stage, the individual can move beyond self-interest and duty to include consideration of the needs of society. A person in this stage can apply personal ethical principles in a variety of situations. Conflicts of interest occur when a businessperson is faced with a situation in which an action benefiting one person has the potential to harm another, as when the person's own interests conflict with those of a customer. Honesty and integrity are valued qualities that engender trust, but a person's immediate self-interest may seem to require violating these principles. Loyalty to an employer sometimes conflicts with truthfulness. Whistle-blowing is a possible response to misconduct in the workplace, but the personal costs of doing so may be high. Employees are strongly influenced by the standards of conduct established and supported within the organizations where they work. Businesses can help shape ethical behavior by developing codes of conduct that define their expectations. Organizations can also use this training to develop employees' ethics awareness and reasoning. They can foster ethical action through decision-making tools, goals consistent with ethical behavior, and advice hotlines. Executives must also demonstrate ethical behavior in their decisions and actions to provide ethical leadership.

Assessment Check Answers ✓

3.1 What is the preconventional stage in the development of ethical standards? In the preconventional stage, the individual looks out for his or her own interests and follows rules out of fear of punishment or hope of reward.

3.2 How can loyalty and truth come into conflict for an employee? Truth and loyalty can come into conflict when the truth about a company or situation is unfavorable.

3.3 How does ethical leadership contribute to ethical standards throughout a company? Employees more readily commit to the company's core values when they see that leaders and managers behave ethically.

┌4┐ Describe how businesses' social responsibility is measured, and summarize the responsibilities of business to the general public, customers, and employees.

Today's businesses are expected to weigh their qualitative impact on consumers and society, in addition to their quantitative economic contributions such as sales, employment levels, and profits. One measure is their compliance with labor and consumer protection laws and their charitable contributions. Another measure some businesses take is to conduct social audits. Public-interest groups also create standards and measure companies' performance relative to those standards. The responsibilities of business to the general public include protecting the public health and the environment and developing the quality of the workforce. Additionally, many would argue that businesses have a social responsibility to support charitable and social causes in the communities in which they earn profits. Business also must treat customers fairly and protect consumers, upholding their rights to be safe, to be informed, to choose, and to be heard. Businesses have wide-ranging responsibilities to their workers. They should make sure that the workplace is safe, address quality-of-life issues, ensure equal opportunity, and prevent sexual harassment and other forms of discrimination.

Assessment Check Answers ✔

4.1 What is meant by social responsibility, and why do firms exercise it? Social responsibility is management's acceptance of its obligation to consider profit, consumer satisfaction, and societal well-being to be of equal value

when evaluating the firm's performance. Businesses exercise it because it is required by law, because it enhances the company's image, or because management believes it is the right thing to do.

4.2 What is green marketing? Green marketing is a marketing strategy that promotes environmentally safe products and production methods.

4.3 What are the four main consumer rights? The four main consumer rights are the right to be safe, to be informed, to choose, and to be heard.

┌5┐ Explain why investors and the financial community are concerned with business ethics and social responsibility.

Investors and the financial community demand that businesses behave ethically as well as legally in handling their financial transactions. Businesses must be honest in reporting their profits and financial performance to avoid misleading investors. The Securities and Exchange Commission is the federal agency responsible for investigating suspicions that publicly traded firms have engaged in unethical or illegal financial behavior.

Assessment Check Answers ✔

5.1 Why do firms need to do more than just earn a profit? Firms need to do more than just earn a profit because the law requires them to behave in a legal and ethical manner and because investors and shareholders demand such behavior.

5.2 What is the role of the Securities and Exchange Commission? Among other functions, the Securities and Exchange Commission investigates suspicions of unethical or illegal behavior by publicly traded firms.

▉ Business Terms You Need to Know

business ethics 36	code of conduct 45	sustainable 53	discrimination 60
Sarbanes-Oxley Act of 2002 39	stakeholders 47	corporate philanthropy 54	Equal Employment Opportunity Commission (EEOC) 61
conflict of interest 42	social responsibility 47	consumerism 55	
integrity 42	social audits 48	product liability 55	
whistle-blowing 43	recycling 52	fair trade 59	sexual harassment 62
	green marketing 52	family leave 59	sexism 63

▉ Review Questions

1. What do the terms *business ethics* and *social responsibility* mean? Why are they important components of a firm's overall philosophy in conducting business?

2. In what ways do individuals make a difference in a firm's commitment to ethics? Describe the three stages in which an individual develops ethical standards.

3. What type of ethical dilemma does each of the following illustrate? (A situation might involve more than one dilemma.)

   a. Due to the breakup with a client, an advertising agency suddenly finds itself representing rival companies.

   b. A newly hired employee learns that the office manager plays computer games on company time.

   c. A drug manufacturer offers a doctor an expensive gift as an inducement to prescribe a new brand-name drug.

   d. An employee is asked to destroy documents that implicate his or her firm in widespread pollution.

   e. A company spokesperson agrees to give a press conference that puts a positive spin on his or her firm's use of sweatshop labor.

4. Describe how ethical leadership contributes to the development of each of the other levels of ethical standards in a corporation.

5. In what ways do firms demonstrate their social responsibility?

6. What are the four major areas in which businesses have responsibilities to the general public? In what ways can meeting these responsibilities give a firm a competitive edge?

7. Identify and describe the four basic rights that consumerism tries to protect. How has consumerism improved the contemporary business environment? What challenges has it created for businesses?

8. What are the five major areas in which companies have responsibilities to their employees? What types of changes in society are now affecting these responsibilities?

■ Projects and Teamwork Applications

1. Write your own personal code of ethics. Create standards for your behavior at school, in personal relationships, and on the job. Then assess how well you meet your own standards and revise them if necessary.

2. On your own or with a classmate, visit the Web site of one of the following firms, or choose another that interests you. On the basis of what you can learn about the company from the site, construct a chart or figure that illustrates examples of the firm's ethical awareness, ethical education, ethical actions, and ethical leadership. Present your findings to class.

   a. Sun Microsystems
   b. NFL, NHL, NBA, MLB, MLS (or any major professional sports league)
   c. Hewlett-Packard
   d. Foundation Health Systems
   e. Irving Oil

■ Web Assignments

1. **Ethical standards.** Go to the Web site listed below. It summarizes the ethical standards for all employees and suppliers of John Deere and Company. Review the material and then write a brief report relating Deere's ethical standards to the material on corporate ethics discussed in the chapter. In addition, consider how Deere's ethical standards are integrated with the firm's overall global citizenship efforts.

   http://www.deere.com/en_US/globalcitizenship/values/ethics.html

2. **Starting a career.** Each year *BusinessWeek* magazine rates the best companies to begin a career. Visit the *BusinessWeek* Web site and review the most recent list. What criteria did

9. Identify which Equal Opportunity law (or laws) protects workers in the following categories:

   a. an employee who must care for an elderly parent
   b. a National Guard member who is returning from deployment overseas
   c. a job applicant who is HIV positive
   d. a person who is over 40 years old
   e. a woman who has been sexually harassed on the job
   f. a woman with a family history of breast cancer

10. How does a company demonstrate its responsibility to investors and the financial community?

   f. Costco
   g. IKEA

3. Now take the company you studied for question 2 (or choose another one) and conduct a social audit on that firm. Do your findings match the firm's culture of ethics? If there are any differences, what are they and why might they occur?

4. On your own or with a classmate, go online, flip through a magazine, or surf television channels to identify a firm that is engaged in green marketing. If you see a commercial on television, go to the firm's Web site to learn more about the product or process advertised. Does the firm make claims that comply with the FTC guidelines? Present your findings in class.

5. As a consumer, you have come to expect a certain level of responsibility toward you on the part of companies with which you do business. Describe a situation in which you felt that a company did not recognize your rights as a consumer. How did you handle the situation? How did the company handle it? What was the final outcome?

BusinessWeek use when building this list? What role does ethics and social responsibility play?

http://www.businessweek.com

3. **Social responsibility.** Athletic footwear manufacturer New Balance is one of the few companies in its industry that still manufactures products in the United States. Go to the Web site listed below and learn more about the firm's commitment to U.S. manufacturing. Prepare a report that relates this commitment to the firm's other core values.

http://www.newbalance.com/company/

Note: Internet Web addresses change frequently. If you don't find the exact sites listed, you may need to access the organization's home page and search from there or use a search engine such as Bing or Google.

Cause-Related Marketing—Give a Day, Get a Disney Day

Pink ribbons for breast cancer research. Product Red merchandise for fighting HIV/AIDS and other diseases. Yellow LiveStrong bracelets for cancer research. These campaigns are examples of cause-related marketing. A typical cause-related marketing campaign teams one or more nonprofit organizations with for-profit ones. The for-profit organization announces publicly that it will donate some or all of the proceeds from a product or products to the nonprofit organization. For example, if you buy an iPod Nano Product [Red], a Starbucks [Red] card, or a Product [Red] T-shirt from the Gap, that corporation makes a contribution to the Global Fund to Fight AIDS, Tuberculosis, and Malaria. One hundred percent of the contribution goes to grants financed by the Global Fund for projects in Africa.

Cause-related marketing began in 1976 when the March of Dimes, which fights birth defects, wanted to raise funds in the West. It teamed with Marriott Corporation, which wanted to generate publicity for its new Great America theme park in California. The campaign was a huge success. Cause-related marketing has grown from almost nothing to roughly $1.57 billion. Social networking groups such as Facebook and Twitter have become official or unofficial resources for information and for spreading the word about causes such as education, fighting disease, clean water, and environmental issues.

After the recent recession, consumers spent less and turned to inexpensive, family-oriented activities. In this climate, a new type of cause-related partnership came into being.

Disney Parks announced its new "Give a Day, Get a Disney Day" program for 2010. In partnership with the HandsOn Network, a national volunteer network, Disney offered free one-day, one-park admission to the first million people who performed one day of certified volunteer work for a participating charity or other program. Habitat for Humanity and Ronald McDonald House Charities were just two of the nationwide programs, but volunteers could also clean up a local park; work at a homeless shelter, museum, or other institution; or walk or run for a cause such as diabetes or heart disease. Many of the activities were family oriented and were intended to help parents teach their children about volunteering. Families of up to

eight could volunteer together, and children as young as six could participate.

Jay Rasulo, the chairman of Walt Disney Parks and Resorts, said, ". . . we want to recognize . . . the contributions people make to their communities every day. We want to inspire 1 million volunteers—people who will invest time and energy to make their own communities and neighborhoods a better place."

Visitors can check the Disney Web site to find opportunities, arranged by location, for volunteering through the HandsOn network. So many people visited the sign-up page on that day that it crashed several times. Although Disney had no official social network pages, multiple unofficial ones were created. In addition, HandsOn publicized the program through its Facebook, Twitter, and YouTube accounts.

Tree Fresno's goal is to reforest areas near the San Joaquin Valley in California. More than 150 people, many in families, volunteered through the Disney program to spend a day planting seedlings. A thousand other people in family groups also signed up to volunteer. The program was closing in on its goal of 1 million volunteers. Although it is too soon to tell whether volunteer cause-related marketing will become more common, the success of "Give a Day, Get a Disney Day" has set a standard to which future projects can aspire.

Questions for Critical Thinking

1. **How does Disney fulfill its responsibility to the general public?**
2. **Which organization benefits more from the "Give a Day, Get a Disney Day" program—Disney or HandsOn? Explain your answer.**

Sources: Walt Disney Company and Affiliated Companies, "Give a Day of Volunteer Service in 2010, Get a Day of Disney Theme Park Fun—Free," September 29, 2009, http://disney.com/corporate, accessed February 2010; HandsOn Network, "Give a Day. Get a Disney Day," n.d., http://handsonnetwork.org; Carrie Urban Kapraun, "Disney and the HandsOn Network: Give a Day, Get a Disney Day," *IEG,* January 22, 2010, http://www.sponsorship.com; Nancy Osborne, "Give a Day, Get a Disney Day," *KFSN,* January 22, 2010; http://abclocal.go.com/kfsn; Rachael Chong, "Cause-Related Marketing: Just Plain Ol' Marketing?" *Huffington Post,* January 4, 2010; http://www.huffingtonpost.com; Product Red Web site, http://www.joinred.com; Joe Waters, "Why Social Media and Cause Marketing Belong Together," Selfish Giving, February 16, 2010, http://selfishgiving.com.

For many years, environmentalists have advocated slower driving and slower flying as ways to save fuel and cut down on emissions of greenhouse gases. This equation applies at sea as well as on land and in the air. When the price of oil reached $145 a barrel, the container shipping giant Maersk Line decided to take action.

Based in Copenhagen, Maersk is the largest shipping line in the world, with more than 500 vessels. Instead of the standard speed of 24 or 25 knots (just under 29 miles per hour), the *Ebba Maersk* sails at 12 knots (just under 14 miles per hour), a speed known in the industry as "super slow steaming." Super slow steaming reduces fuel consumption from 350 tons per day to 100 to 150 tons and saves $5,000 an hour. Maersk has shifted hundreds of its ships to super slow steaming. Other shipping lines resisted slowing their vessels down at first, but now many of them have adopted "slow steaming" speed (20 knots, or 23 miles per hour) or super slow steaming.

The recent recession created a further incentive for container shipping lines to reduce costs and save energy. Among other measures, Maersk's ships have lowered their interior lighting and substituted rolls of paper towels for paper napkins in their dining salons. "The previous focus has been on 'What will it cost?' and 'Get it to me as fast as possible,'" said Søren Stig Nielsen, the director of environmental sustainability at Maersk. "But now there is a third dimension. What's the CO_2 footprint?"

Then there are the containers themselves. Whether empty or full, they occupy the same amount of space. Made of steel, they are still heavy even when empty. The Dutch company Cargoshell has devised a container that, when empty, collapses in less than half a minute to one-quarter the size of a full one. Thus Cargoshells can be stacked more compactly than steel containers. Steel containers usually have outward-opening doors that take up an entire side panel. The Cargoshell's door simply rolls up or down. Cargoshells are made of fiber-reinforced composite materials, so they weigh 25 percent less than steel containers. They need no paint because they do not corrode. The composites are good insulators, important for temperature control. Manufacturing Cargoshells generates less carbon dioxide than manufacturing steel containers. All these factors add up to reduced costs, energy savings, and lower carbon emissions.

The ports where cargo ships arrive and depart are crowded with cranes, trucks, trains, tugboats, and ferries—all of which emit diesel exhaust into the atmosphere. The U.S. Environmental Protection Agency (EPA) has declared diesel exhaust to be a possible carcinogen. To reduce exposure to it, the EPA has initiated Clean Ports USA, a voluntary, incentive-based program to encourage ports and truck fleet owners to reduce emissions. Strategies include changing to cleaner-burning diesel fuels; retrofitting or repairing existing diesel engines (which can last 20 or 30 years); replacing aging engines or vehicles with newer, less-polluting ones; and reducing time that engines are left idling. In an unlikely alliance, the Teamsters union and environmentalists have joined forces to persuade the Port of Los Angeles to ban older trucks from transporting goods away from port and have the trucking companies buy newer, cleaner-running rigs.

Taken separately, all these measures are worthy efforts to fight global warming. Taken together, they could add up to a "green" integration of almost all aspects of the shipping industry.

Questions for Critical Thinking

1. How do Maersk and Cargoshell carry out their responsibilities to society?

2. Many of the goods you buy and use are imported from overseas and sold more cheaply than if they were made in the United States. But do they have hidden, nonmonetary costs? Use the information in this case as a guide.

Sources: Maersk Web site, http://www.maersk.com, accessed June 21, 2011; Steven Greenhouse, "Clearing the Air at American Ports," *The New York Times,* February 26, 2010, http://www.nytimes.com; "Maersk Cuts Fuel Use, Emissions 30% by Slowing Down," *Environmental Leader,* February 18, 2020, http://www.environmentalleader.com; Elisabeth Rosenthal, "Slow and Steady Across the Sea Aids Profit and the Environment," *The New York Times,* February 17, 2010, http://www.nytimes.com; John W. Miller, "Maersk: Container Ship Cuts Costs to Stay Afloat," Polaris Institute, February 2010, http://www.polarisinstitute.org; Cargoshell Web site, http://www.cargoshell.com, accessed February 12, 2010; Clean Ports USA, U.S. Environmental Protection Agency, http://epa.gov, accessed February 12, 2010; Jace Shoemaker-Galloway, "Cargoshell Collapsible Shipping Containers: A Greener and Flatter Way to Transport Goods," *Triple Pundit,* February 5, 2010, http://www.triplepundit.com.

Seventh Generation: Beyond Paper and Plastic

Seventh Generation was founded in Vermont twenty years ago on the premise that there's a better way to do business, one that protects both the planet and the people. The company's name is derived from the Great Law of the Iroquois, which mandates that "In every deliberation, we must consider the impact of our decision on the next seven generations." Co-founder and executive chairman Jeffrey Hollender takes this mandate literally.

Hollender refers to himself as "chief protagonist" of Seventh Generation. For two decades he has campaigned for environmentally responsible consumer products, manufacturing processes, and operations at Seventh Generation. In addition, he campaigns outside the company to raise awareness about the importance of consumerism in preservation of the environment.

Hollender admits to watershed moments in his own life that have led him to redirect his company. When his young son had a particularly severe asthma attack, the doctor told Hollender that the best way to controls his son's asthma was to control his environment—in particular, his household environment. Hollender recognized the enormity of this statement and took it on as a corporate challenge. EPA research had already revealed that the air in the average home is two to five times more polluted than outdoor air. "I realized then that Seventh Generation had a lot more to offer than protecting the outdoor environment, and it became the turning point for the company." If Seventh Generation could offer a broad spectrum of household products that did not contribute to indoor pollution—but performed cleaning and other tasks as effectively as products containing toxic chemicals—the company could achieve an entirely new level of corporate responsibility.

Senior chemist Cara Bondi describes the challenge she and her colleagues faced. "Prior to the last decade, companies would try to put out green products but they didn't really do the job," which resulted in these products failing in the marketplace. If they weren't effective at cleaning laundry or dishes, appealing to consumers' consciences wouldn't help. "If you expect someone to transition from a traditional cleaning product to green cleaning products, you need to have the performance that they expect," she explains. "It was a problem that needed to be addressed. We wanted to be able to give consumers a solution that was authentic and sustaining." In recent years, scientists have been able to isolate more naturally derived ingredients that are equal to chemically based ingredients. Now consumers must be re-educated about these products and convinced to give them another try. One such product has been developed by Seventh Generation in partnership with another firm, CleanWell. It is a disinfectant made from the garden herb thyme. The new product actually kills bacteria on surfaces without the use of toxic chemicals.

As chief executive, Hollender must consider his company as a whole organization—not just a chemistry lab. "When you think about sustainability and responsibility, you have to take a holistic approach," he notes. "You have to look at everything in your supply chain and the life cycle of the product." Hollender emphasizes that a socially responsible firm must consider every input and output, including raw materials, harvesting, manufacturing processes, warehousing, sales, and ultimate use—whether the consumer uses up the product, reuses or recycles it, or throws it away. Hollender describes how, in examining Seventh Generation's inputs and outputs, company researchers discovered that the single most energy-wasting feature of its soap products was the fact that they required hot water to perform effectively. So the firm's team reformulated them to function in cold water.

Seventh Generation continues to develop new and better products. The firm's Web site is filled with information on sustainability, including the blog "Ask the Science Man," where consumers can ask just about any question—such as how to find nontoxic nail polish. And though Hollender's involvement in day-to-day operations is reduced as he takes his message to a nationwide audience, he remains committed to his company's corporate responsibility. "Few businesses are willing to talk about their failures," he says. "But it's that level of transparency that will build deep loyalty with the consumer." Hollender is determined to build a loyalty that will last at least seven generations.

Questions for Critical Thinking

1. What might be some ethical issues faced by Seventh Generation managers, researchers, and employees?

2. What steps might Hollender take to ensure that ethical leadership continues as he spends more time away from Seventh Generation?

3. Give examples of ways in which Seventh Generation fulfills its social responsibilities in each of the four categories: to the general public; to customers; to investors; and to employees.

4. Visit the Seventh Generation Web site at http://www.seventhgeneration.com and read more about the firm's community involvement. Discuss the company's efforts. Do they match well with the Great Law of the Iroquois?

Sources: Seventh Generation Web site, http://www.seventhgeneration.com, accessed June 21, 2011; CleanWell Web site, http://www.cleanwelltoday.com, accessed June 21, 2011; "Seventh Generation and Walmart Announce Strategic Partnership," *Market Wire*, July 26, 2010, http://www.marketwire .com; Danielle Sacks, "Jeffrey Hollender: Seventh Generation, Triple Bottom Line Entrepreneur," *Fast Company.com*, February 2, 2010, http://www.fastcompany.com.

Learning Objectives

[1] Distinguish between microeconomics and macroeconomics. Explain the factors that drive demand and supply.

[2] Describe each of the four different types of market structures in a private enterprise system, and compare the three major types of economic systems.

[3] Identify and describe the four stages of the business cycle. Explain how productivity, price level changes, and employment levels affect the stability of a nation's economy.

[4] Discuss how monetary policy and fiscal policy are used to manage an economy's performance.

[5] Describe the major global economic challenges of the 21st century.

Economic Challenges Facing Contemporary Business

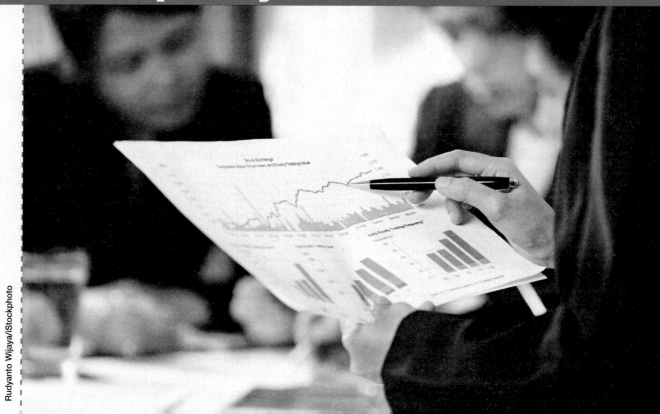

Rudyanto Wijaya/iStockphoto

NASCAR Tries to Restart Its Engine

NASCAR is widely known as the most popular spectator sport in the United States. Yet even its most diehard fans are tapping the brakes when it comes to buying tickets to their favorite speedway. Tracks in cities such as Phoenix and Talladega have reported double-digit percent declines in attendance. Just as worrisome is the fact that, instead of watching races at home, fans are changing the channel. Some critics of NASCAR blame a drop in dramatic action and a mandated car chassis design that leaves car models undifferentiated. Others say that the races are just too long and the broadcast commentary is boring. But NASCAR defenders argue that there's another huge obstacle: the economy. "We knew admissions would be down [this year]," admits Roger VanDerSnick, COO of International Speedway Corp, which operates a dozen tracks around the country. "The biggest impediment is the economy."

NASCAR is largely supported by middle-class fans who are now reluctant to open their wallets. They also want value for their entertainment dollar. If NASCAR doesn't live up to fans' expectations, they will find another form of entertainment. In response, NASCAR, Fox Sports, and TNT (NASCAR's broadcasters), are trying several measures to regain viewership and boost ticket sales. NASCAR officials have loosened the rules, encouraging drivers to be more aggressive in their driving style. Race officials have also introduced double-file restarts that crowd the leaders toward the front, eliminated lapped cars, and extended overtime finishes, among other changes. Fox Sports is asking NASCAR to shorten its races, some of which take up to four hours to complete, claiming that even the most loyal fans don't want to sit in front of the TV for that long. Tracks are slashing ticket prices and launching promotions in order to win back their fan base.

International Speedway Corp. announced last year that it would cut prices on more than 500,000 tickets for NASCAR's premier race series, the Sprint Cup. "A number of our ticketing strategies are working," says ISC's Roger VanDerSnick. "But our sport is comprised of middle America, and it's going to take time before the economy starts driving employment and consumer confidence."

Sunoco Inc., the official fuel of NASCAR, recently announced "Decal Race," a consumer promotion giving fans a chance to win a 2011 Ford Explorer or free fuel for an entire year. Contestants snap photos of cars with Sunoco/NASCAR decals on the bumpers and upload them to a Web site where they can win interim prizes, such as a $100 Sunoco gift card, and a chance at the big prize. And Texas Motor Speedway plans to open a new tailgating area called Pit Stop Park, where fans can set up tables and chairs, barbecue grills, and tailgate tents. The park will have restroom facilities, picnic tables, horseshoe pits, and even a catering option. "This concept caters to those fans that may not have RVs but still want an upscale and park-like alternative for tailgating with family and friends on race weekends," remarks TMS president Eddie Gossage. Finally, the tracks and TV executives are poised to scrap an old way of creating the sponsorships that are vital to NASCAR. Tracks used to sell race title sponsorships independently, then pass their partners to TV networks for the sale of supporting advertisements. While this created competition, it also resulted in fragmentation that doesn't work in this economy. So for the first time, the different parties are collaborating on joint sales of title sponsorships. "Economic realities dictate that we become more creative in our approach," notes Neil Mulcahy, executive vice president for Fox's sports sales. These steps could be the boost that NASCAR needs.[1]

Chapter

3   Overview

microeconomics study of small economic units, such as individual consumers, families, and businesses.

economics social science that analyzes the choices people and governments make in allocating scarce resources.

macroeconomics study of a nation's overall economic issues, such as how an economy maintains and allocates resources and how a government's policies affect the standards of living of its citizens.

When we examine the exchanges that companies and societies make as a whole, we are focusing on the *economic systems* operating in different nations. These systems reflect the combination of policies and choices a nation makes to allocate resources among its citizens. Countries vary in the ways they allocate scarce resources.

Economics, which analyzes the choices people and governments make in allocating scarce resources, affects each of us, because everyone is involved in producing, distributing, or simply consuming goods and services. In fact, your life is affected by economics every day. Whether you buy tickets to a NASCAR race or decide to stay home and watch TV instead, you are making an economic choice. Understanding how the activities of one industry affect those of other industries, and how they relate in the overall picture of a country, is an important part of understanding economics.

The choices you make actually may be international in scope. If you are in the market for a new car, you might visit several dealers in a row on the same street—Ford, Chrysler, Honda, Hyundai, and General Motors. You might decide on Hyundai—a Korean firm—but your car might very well be manufactured in the United States, using parts from all over the world. Although firms sometimes emphasize the American origin of their products in order to appeal to consumers' desire to support the U.S. economy, many items are made of components from a variety of nations.

Businesses and not-for-profit organizations also make economic decisions when they choose how to use human and natural resources; invest in equipment, machinery, and buildings; and form partnerships with other firms. Economists refer to the study of small economic units, such as individual consumers, families, and businesses, as **microeconomics.**

The study of a country's overall economic issues is called **macroeconomics** (*macro* means "large"). Macroeconomics addresses such issues as how an economy uses its resources and how government policies affect people's standards of living. The substitution of ethanol for gasoline or biodiesel for diesel fuel has macroeconomic consequences—affecting many parts of the U.S. economy and suppliers around the world. Macroeconomics examines not just the economic policies of individual nations, but the ways in which those individual policies affect the overall world economy. Because so much business is conducted around the world, a law enacted in one country can easily affect a transaction that takes place in another country. Although macroeconomic issues have a broad scope, they help shape the decisions that individuals, families, and businesses make every day.

This chapter introduces economic theory and the economic challenges facing individuals, businesses, and governments in the global marketplace. We begin with the microeconomic concepts of supply and demand and their effect on the prices people pay for goods and services. Next we explain the various types of economic systems, along with tools for comparing and evaluating their performance. Then we examine the ways in which governments seek to manage economies to create stable business environments in their countries. The final section in the chapter looks at some of the driving economic forces currently affecting people's lives.

Microeconomics: The Forces of Demand and Supply

Think about your own economic activities. You shop for groceries, subscribe to a cell phone service, pay college tuition, fill your car's tank with gas. Now think about your family's economic activities. When you were growing up, your parents might have owned a home or rented an apartment. You might have taken a family vacation. Your parents may have shopped at discount clubs or at local stores. Each of these choices relates to the study of microeconomics. They also help determine both the prices of goods and services and the amounts sold. Information about these activities is vital to companies because their survival and ability to grow depends on selling enough products priced high enough to cover costs and earn profits. The same information is important to consumers who must make purchase decisions based on prices and the availability of the goods and services they need.

At the heart of every business endeavor is an exchange between a buyer and a seller. The buyer recognizes that he or she needs or wants a particular good or service—whether it's a hamburger or a haircut—and is willing to pay a seller for it. The seller requires the exchange in order to earn a profit and stay in business. So the exchange process involves both demand and supply. **Demand** refers to the willingness and ability of buyers to purchase goods and services at different prices. The other side of the exchange process is **supply**, the amount of goods and services for sale at different prices. Understanding the factors that determine demand and supply, as well as how the two interact, can help you understand many actions and decisions of individuals, businesses, and government. This section takes a closer look at these concepts.

You shop for groceries, subscribe to a cell phone service, pay college tuition, fill your car's tank with gas. Each of these choices relates to the study of microeconomics. They also help determine the prices of goods and the amounts sold.

demand willingness and ability of buyers to purchase goods and services.

supply willingness and ability of sellers to provide goods and services.

Factors Driving Demand

For most of us, economics amounts to a balance between what we want and what we can afford. Because of this dilemma, each person must choose how much money to save and how much to spend. We must also decide among all the goods and services competing for our attention. Suppose you wanted to purchase a smart phone. You'd have to choose from a variety of brands and models. You'd also have to decide where you wanted to go to buy one. After shopping around, you might decide you didn't want a smart phone at all. Instead, you might purchase something else, or save your money.

Demand is driven by a number of factors that influence how people decide to spend their money, including price. It can be driven by consumer preferences. It may also be driven by outside circumstances or larger economic events. During the recent recession, the videogame industry—including portable players and consoles, software, and associated items—experienced an 8 percent decline in sales during one year. However, videogames such as *Kinect Adventures!* and *Wii Sports* have enjoyed sales of more than 200,000 units a year.[2]

Demand can also increase the availability of certain types of Web sites and services. Recognizing the enormous popularity of Google's YouTube, and believing the demand would grow, networks NBC and Fox teamed up to launch an online video site, which provides programming from different entertainment companies. The site, called Hulu.com, offers full-length movies and television shows. It also hosts programming from NBC, ABC, and Fox, along with shows from Sony and Metro Goldwyn-Mayer.[3]

Demand is driven by consumer tastes and preferences as well as by economic conditions. Consumers tend to fill up their gas tanks more frequently when the per-gallon price is low.

Eric Shelton/©AP/Wide World Photos

demand curve graph of the amount of a product that buyers will purchase at different prices.

In general, as the price of a good or service goes up, people buy smaller amounts. In other words, as price rises, the quantity demanded declines. At lower prices, consumers are generally willing to buy more of a good. A **demand curve** is a graph of the amount of a product that buyers will purchase at different prices. Demand curves typically slope downward, meaning that lower and lower prices attract larger and larger purchases.

Gasoline provides a classic example of how demand curves work. The left side of Figure 3.1 shows a possible demand curve for the total amount of gasoline that people will purchase at different prices. The prices shown may not reflect the actual price in your location at this particular time, but they still demonstrate the concept. When gasoline is priced at $3.56 a gallon, drivers may fill up their tanks once or twice a week. At $3.96 a gallon, many of them start economizing. They may combine errands or carpool to work. So the quantity of gasoline demanded at $3.96 a gallon is lower than the amount demanded at $3.56 a gallon. The opposite happens at $3.16 a gallon. More gasoline is sold at $3.16 a gallon than at $3.56 a gallon, as people opt to run more errands or take a weekend trip. However, as mentioned earlier, other factors may cause consumers to accept higher prices anyway. They may have made vacation plans in advance and do not want to cancel them. Or they may be required to drive to work every day.

Economists make a clear distinction between changes in the quantity demanded at various prices and changes in overall demand. A change in quantity demanded, such as the change that occurs at different gasoline prices, is simply movement along the demand curve. A change in overall demand, on the other hand, results in an entirely new demand curve. Businesses are constantly trying to make predictions about both kinds of demand, and a miscalculation can cause problems. In the case of gasoline, which is derived from crude oil, many factors come into play. One factor that is beginning to make a major impact is the investment in and development of alternative fuels such as biodiesel, wind, and solar power. If alternatives are developed and readily available, then demand for oil may level off. Another issue is the U.S. economy. When a downturn occurs, so does the demand for oil and other goods. But disruptions in energy sources have the opposite effect; political unrest in oil-rich nations such as Nigeria or extreme weather that takes refineries offline increase the demand for the oil that is available.[4]

We can illustrate how the increased demand for gasoline worldwide has created a new demand curve, as shown in Figure 3.1. The new demand curve shifts to the right of the old demand curve, indicating that overall demand has increased at every price. A demand curve can also shift to the left when the demand for a good or service drops. However, the demand curve still has the same shape.

Although price is the underlying cause of movement along a demand curve, many factors can combine to determine the overall demand for a product—that is, the shape and position of the demand curve. These influences include customer preferences and incomes, the prices of substitute and complementary items, the number of buyers in a market, and the strength of their optimism regarding the future. Changes in any of these factors produce a new demand curve.

Changes in household income also change demand. As consumers have more money to spend, firms can sell more products at every price. This means the demand curve has shifted

FIGURE 3.1 Demand Curves for Gasoline

A. Demand Curve for Gasoline and Change in Quantity Demanded

$3.96/gal.
$3.56/gal.
$3.16/gal.

Price per Gallon (P)
$4.30
3.90
3.50
3.10
2.70

Quantity (Q) (millions of gallons)
10   20   30

B. Shift in the Demand Curve for Gasoline—Change in Demand

New Demand Curve

Price per Gallon (P)
$4.30
3.90
3.50
3.10
2.70

Quantity (Q) (millions of gallons)
10   20   30

to the right. When income shrinks, nearly everyone suffers, and the demand curve shifts to the left. With the recent decline in new housing and home improvement, Home Depot and Lowe's experienced a drop in demand. Meanwhile, discount retailers like Walmart and Walgreens experienced an increase in sales, so their demand curve shifted to the right.[5] Table 3.1 describes how a demand curve is likely to respond to each of these changes.

For a business to succeed, management must carefully monitor the factors that may affect demand for the goods and services it hopes to sell. Costco has free sampling stations throughout its stores where customers can try small portions of various foods prepared on site. This practice encourages customers to buy something in the department where they are sampling.

Table 3.1 Expected Shifts in Demand Curves

FACTOR	DEMAND CURVE SHIFTS	
	TO THE RIGHT *IF*:	TO THE LEFT *IF*:
Customer preferences	Increase	Decrease
Number of buyers	Increase	Decrease
Buyers' incomes	Increase	Decrease
Prices of substitute goods	Increase	Decrease
Prices of complementary goods	Decrease	Increase
Future expectations become more	Optimistic	Pessimistic

Factors Driving Supply

Important economic factors also affect supply, the willingness and ability of firms to provide goods and services at different prices. Just as consumers must decide about how to spend their money, businesses must decide what products to sell, and how.

Sellers would prefer to charge higher prices for their products. A **supply curve** shows the relationship between different prices and the quantities that sellers will offer for sale, regardless of demand. Movement along the supply curve is the opposite of movement along the demand curve. So as price rises, the quantity that sellers are willing to supply also rises. At progressively lower prices, the quantity supplied decreases. In Figure 3.2, a possible supply curve for gasoline shows that increasing prices for gasoline should bring increasing supplies to market.

Businesses need certain inputs to operate effectively in producing their output. As discussed in Chapter 1, these *factors of production* include natural resources, capital, human resources, and entrepreneurship. Natural resources include land, building sites, forests, and mineral deposits. Capital refers to resources such as technology, tools, information, physical facilities, and financial capabilities. Human resources include the physical labor and intellectual inputs contributed by employees. Entrepreneurship is the willingness to take risks to create and operate a business. Factors of production play a central role in determining the overall supply of goods and services.

A change in the cost or availability of any of these inputs can shift the entire supply curve, either increasing or decreasing the amount available at every price. If the cost of land increases, a firm might not be able to purchase the site for a more efficient manufacturing plant, which would lower production levels, shifting the supply curve to the left. But if the company finds a way to speed up the production process, allowing it to turn out more products with less labor, the change reduces the overall cost of the finished products, which shifts the supply curve to the right.

Table 3.2 summarizes how changes in various factors can affect the supply curve. Sometimes forces of nature can affect the supply curve. During a record-breaking freeze

supply curve graph that shows the relationship between different prices and the quantities that sellers will offer for sale, regardless of demand.

FIGURE 3.2 Supply Curve for Gasoline

Table 3.2 Expected Shifts in Supply Curves

	SUPPLY CURVE SHIFTS	
FACTOR	**TO THE RIGHT *IF*:**	**TO THE LEFT *IF*:**
Costs of inputs	Decrease	Increase
Costs of technologies	Decrease	Increase
Taxes	Decrease	Increase
Number of suppliers	Increase	Decrease

one recent January, a significant percentage of Florida's citrus crop, including oranges and lemons, was severely damaged. Because the fruit could not be harvested and shipped, supply dropped. The U.S. Department of Agriculture estimated that the next harvest could be the second lowest since 2000. The freeze could also affect the following year's crop if trees are not able to flower in the spring. However, growers said that even the frozen fruit could still be used for juice.[6]

The worldwide fishing industry has often experienced such shifts in the supply curve. In the United States, tourists and locals who were accustomed to an abundance of seafood from the Gulf of Mexico were unable to enjoy their favorite catch during the months after the BP oil spill. Fishermen and restaurant owners experienced economic hardship first because they couldn't obtain the shrimp and fish, then because they could not overcome the stigma that the catch might be contaminated. Meanwhile, across the globe, Vietnam's shrimp industry was booming, hitting a record high of $2 billion for shrimp exports, including to the shrimp-starved United States.[7]

How Demand and Supply Interact

Separate shifts in demand and supply have obvious effects on prices and the availability of products. In the real world, changes do not alternatively affect demand and supply. Several factors often change at the same time—and they keep changing. Sometimes such changes in multiple factors cause contradictory pressures on prices and quantities. In other cases, the final direction of prices and quantities reflects the factor that has changed the most. Demand and supply can affect employment as well as products.

Figure 3.3 shows the interaction of both supply and demand curves for gasoline on a single graph. Notice that the two curves intersect at *P*. The law of supply and demand states that prices (*P*) are set by the intersection of the supply and demand curves. The point where the two curves meet identifies the **equilibrium price**, the prevailing market price at which you can buy an item.

If the actual market price differs from the equilibrium price, buyers and sellers tend to make economic choices that restore the equilibrium level. The price of gold hit a record high in December 2009, but when the Federal Reserve Bank raised interest rates and the dollar gained strength against the euro, gold prices fell. Investors always seem to return to gold as a safe standard, according to economists, and consumers who are intent on buying jewelry most likely will do so, but they may buy more or fewer pieces as the price of gold changes over time.[8]

In other situations, suppliers react to market forces by reducing prices. For a number of years, fast-food chains such as McDonald's and Wendy's attracted customers by offering everyday value menus and coupons. However, the recent economic downturn has meant that people are more likely to eat at home and go out less, so the chains experienced a drop in profits. Competition among the chains, already strong, could grow even fiercer, depending on the length of the economic recovery.[9] Included in that competition is the success of the Five Guys Burgers and Fries chain as the "Hit & Miss" feature discusses.

equilibrium price prevailing market price at which you can buy an item.

FIGURE 3.3 Law of Supply and Demand

Price per Gallon (P)

$4.30
3.90
3.50
3.10
2.70

Demand

Supply

P

Equilibrium Price

10   20   30

Quantity (Q) (millions of gallons)

Five Guys Burgers and Fries: A Simple Recipe for Success

When his two oldest sons declared they were not going to college, Jerry Murrell supported their decision. To keep the boys close to home and employed, he and his wife, Janie, used the money intended for their tuition to open a hamburger take-out shop in Arlington, Virginia. From this small beginning, Five Guys and a Burger (named for Murrell's five sons) grew to 570 franchises in the United States and Canada. All the Murrells' sons eventually joined the company, which the family still owns and runs.

Very early, Murrell realized that in order to compete with the fast-food chains, Five Guys would have to concentrate on food. All the restaurants feature the same simple, red-and-white-tile décor. The meat for the burgers—80 percent lean—is always fresh, never frozen. Burgers are made to order, with a selection of 15 free toppings including grilled mushrooms, barbecue and hot sauce, and jalapenos. The buns are toasted on a grill, and the fries are thick-cut from Idaho potatoes, cooked in peanut oil. Because Five Guys insists on top-quality ingredients, prices might change according to what the firm has to pay for its ingredients. But regular burgers still only run from $4.69 to $5.99, and little burgers are $3.49 to $5.49.

The family tried some experiments that failed, such as serving coffee and a chicken sandwich. Aside from a very few kinds of hot dogs, they have stayed with the original burger-and-fries formula that first brought them success.

The food-industry research firm Technomic named Five Guys the fastest growing chain for a recent year. That same year, the company took in an estimated $570 million—up 50 percent from the previous year. "We figure our best salesman is our customer," Murrell says. "Treat that person right, he'll walk out the door and sell for you."

Questions for Critical Thinking

1. Why do you think Five Guys and a Burger prospered during the recent recession?
2. How might supply and demand determine what the company pays its suppliers?

Sources: Company Web site, http://www.fiveguys.com, accessed January 26, 2011; Catherine Muccigrosso, "When You Need a Good Burger Fast, Try Five Guys," *Herald Online*, December 24, 2010, http://www.heraldonline.com. Jerry Murrell, "How I Did It," *Inc.com*, April 1, 2010, http://www.inc.com; "Business Opening: Five Guys Burgers and Fries," *greenbaypressgazette*, March 25, 2010, http://www.greenbaypressgazette.com; Ashley Miller, "Five Guys Named Fastest Growing Chain Restaurant," *examiner.com*, March 30, 2010, http://www.examiner.com.

Assessment Check ✔

1. Define microeconomics and macroeconomics.

2. Explain demand and supply curves.

3. How do factors of production influence the overall supply of goods and services?

As pointed out earlier, the forces of demand and supply can be affected by a variety of factors. One important variable is the larger economic environment. The next section explains how macroeconomics and economic systems influence market forces and, ultimately, demand, supply, and prices.

Macroeconomics: Issues for the Entire Economy

Every country faces decisions about how to best use the four basic factors of production. Each nation's policies and choices help determine its economic system. But the political, social, and legal environments differ in every country. So no two countries have exactly the same economic system. In general, however, these systems can be classified into three categories: private enterprise systems; planned economies; or combinations of the two, referred to as mixed economies. As business becomes an increasingly global undertaking, it is important to understand the primary features of the various economic systems operating around the world.

Capitalism: The Private Enterprise System and Competition

Most industrialized nations operate economies based on the *private enterprise system*, also known as *capitalism* or a *market economy*. A private enterprise system rewards businesses for meeting the needs and demands of consumers. Government tends to favor a hands-off attitude toward controlling business ownership, profits, and resource allocations. Instead, competition regulates economic life, creating opportunities and challenges that businesspeople must handle to succeed.

The relative competitiveness of a particular industry is an important consideration for every firm because it determines the ease and cost of doing business within that industry. Four basic types of competition take shape in a private enterprise system: pure competition, monopolistic competition, oligopoly, and monopoly. Table 3.3 highlights the main differences among these types of competition.

Pure competition is a market structure, like that of small-scale agriculture or fishing, in which large numbers of buyers and sellers exchange homogeneous products and no single participant has a significant influence on price. Instead, prices are set by the market as the forces of supply and demand interact. Firms can easily enter or leave a purely competitive market because no single company dominates. Also, in pure competition, buyers see little difference between the goods and services offered by competitors.

Fishing and agriculture are good examples of pure competition. The wheat grown and sold by one farmer in the Midwest is virtually identical to that sold by others. As rainfall and

pure competition
market structure in which large numbers of buyers and sellers exchange homogeneous products and no single participant has a significant influence on price.

Table

⌐3.3⌐ Types of Competition

	TYPES OF COMPETITION			
CHARACTERISTICS	**PURE COMPETITION**	**MONOPOLISTIC COMPETITION**	**OLIGOPOLY**	**MONOPOLY**
Number of competitors	Many	Few to many	Few	No direct competition
Ease of entry into industry by new firms	Easy	Somewhat difficult	Difficult	Regulated by government
Similarity of goods or services offered by competing firms	Similar	Different	Similar or different	No directly competing products
Control over price by individual firms	None	Some	Some	Considerable in a pure monopoly; little in a regulated monopoly
Examples	Small-scale farmer in Indiana	Local fitness center	Boeing Aircraft	Rawlings Sporting Goods, exclusive supplier of major-league baseballs

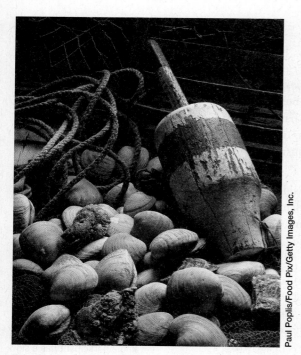

Fishing is a good example of pure competition. Because clams gathered by one individual are virtually identical to those gathered by others, the price rises and falls with changes in supply and demand. Whenever a poisonous "red tide" of algae infests the clam beds off the coast of New England, the supply of fresh clams plummets and the price skyrockets.

temperatures affect the crop growth, the price for this commodity rises or falls according to the law of supply and demand. The same concept applies to the fishing industry gathering clams and mussels off the coast of New England. The region's notorious "red tide" of algae sometimes contaminates part of the season's supply of shellfish just when summer tourists want them the most—and prices skyrocket.

Monopolistic competition is a market structure, like that for retailing, in which large numbers of buyers and sellers exchange differentiated (heterogeneous) products, so each participant has some control over price. Sellers can differentiate their products from competing offerings on the basis of price, quality, or other features. In an industry that features monopolistic competition, it is relatively easy for a firm to begin or stop selling a good or service. The success of one seller often attracts new competitors to such a market. Individual firms also have some control over how their goods and services are priced.

One example of monopolistic competition is the market for pet food. Consumers can choose from private-label (store brands such as Walmart's Ol'Roy) and brand-name products like Purina in bags, boxes, and cans. Producers of pet food and the stores that sell it have wide latitude in setting prices. Consumers can choose the store or brand with the lowest prices, or sellers can convince them that a more expensive offering, for example the Fromm brand, is worth more because it offers better nutrition, more convenience, or other benefits.

An **oligopoly** is a market situation in which relatively few sellers compete and high start-up costs form barriers to keep out new competitors. In some oligopolistic industries, such as paper and steel, competitors offer similar products. In others, such as aircraft and automobiles, they sell different models and features. The huge investment required to enter an oligopoly market tends to discourage new competitors. The limited number of sellers also enhances the control these firms exercise over price. Competing products in an oligopoly usually sell for very similar prices because substantial price competition would reduce profits for all firms in the industry. So a price cut by one firm in an oligopoly will typically be met by its competitors. However, prices can vary from one market to another, as from one country to another.

The final type of market structure is a **monopoly**, in which a single seller dominates trade in a good or service for which buyers can find no close substitutes. A pure monopoly occurs when a firm possesses unique characteristics so important to competition in its industry that they serve as barriers to prevent entry by would-be competitors. After presiding over what many called monopolies in their respective areas, Microsoft and Google are expanding into each other's territory. Microsoft launched Bing to compete with Google Search. Google countered with Google Chrome OS, aimed at MS Windows. These efforts cost millions not only to develop, but also to promote—Microsoft has spent an estimated $100 million on marketing for Bing. Although Google still dominates, Bing's market share has reportedly been growing at a steady pace.[10]

Many firms create short-term monopolies when research breakthroughs permit them to receive exclusive patents on new products. In the pharmaceuticals industry, drug giants such as Merck and Pfizer invest billions in research and development programs. When the research leads to successful new drugs, the companies can enjoy the benefits of their

monopolistic competition market structure in which large numbers of buyers and sellers exchange heterogeneous products so each participant has some control over price.

oligopoly market situation in which relatively few sellers compete and high start-up costs form barriers to keep out new competitors.

monopoly market situation in which a single seller dominates trade in a good or service for which buyers can find no close substitutes.

Microsoft and Google are expanding into each other's territory. Microsoft launched its own search engine, Bing, and Google countered with Google Chrome OS.

patents: the ability to set prices without fear of competitors undercutting them. Once the patent expires, generic substitutes enter the market, driving down prices.

Because a monopoly market lacks the benefits of competition, many governments regulate monopolies. Besides issuing patents and limiting their life, the government prohibits most pure monopolies through antitrust legislation such as the Sherman Act and the Clayton Act. The U.S. government has applied these laws against monopoly behavior by Microsoft and by disallowing proposed mergers of large companies in some industries. In other cases, the government permits certain monopolies in exchange for regulating their activities.

With **regulated monopolies**, a local, state, or federal government grants exclusive rights in a certain market to a single firm. Pricing decisions—particularly rate-increase requests—are subject to control by regulatory authorities such as state public service commissions. An example is the delivery of first-class mail, a monopoly held by the U.S. Postal Service. The USPS is a self-supporting corporation wholly owned by the federal government. Although it is no longer run by Congress, postal rates are set by a Postal Commission and approved by a Board of Governors.

During the 1980s and 1990s, the U.S. government trended away from regulated monopolies and toward deregulation. Regulated monopolies that have been deregulated include long-distance and local telephone service, cable television, cell phones, and electric utilities. The idea is to improve customer service and reduce prices for customers through increased competition. The Federal Communications Commission (FCC) recently adopted a ban on exclusive access agreements between cable providers and apartment building owners. However, owners and cable operators may enter into exclusive bulk billing agreements, under which apartment residents receive a single provider's service at a discount rate. Meanwhile, residents may opt to contract with another provider.[11]

regulated monopolies local, state, or federal government grants exclusive rights in a certain market to a single firm.

Planned Economies: Socialism and Communism

planned economy
government controls
determine business owner-
ship, profits, and resource
allocation to accomplish
government goals rather
than those set by individual
firms.

socialism economic
system characterized by
government ownership
and operation of major
industries such as
communications.

communism economic
system in which all
property would be shared
equally by the people of
a community under the
direction of a strong central
government.

In a **planned economy**, government controls determine business ownership, profits, and resource allocation to accomplish government goals rather than those set by individual firms. Two forms of planned economies are communism and socialism.

Socialism is characterized by government ownership and operation of major industries such as communications. Socialists assert that major industries are too important to a society to be left in private hands and that government-owned businesses can serve the public's interest better than private firms. However, socialism allows private ownership in industries considered less crucial to social welfare, such as retail shops, restaurants, and certain types of manufacturing facilities. Scandinavian countries such as Denmark, Sweden, and Finland have many socialist features in their societies, as do some African nations and India.

The writings of Karl Marx in the mid-1800s formed the basis of communist theory. Marx believed that private enterprise economies created unfair conditions and led to worker exploitation because business owners controlled most of society's resources and reaped most of the economy's rewards. Instead, he suggested an economic system called **communism**, in which all property would be shared equally by the people of a community under the direction of a strong central government. Marx believed that elimination of private ownership of property and businesses would ensure the emergence of a classless society that would benefit all. Each individual would contribute to the nation's overall economic success, and resources would be distributed according to each person's needs. Under communism, the central government owns the means of production, and the people work for state-owned enterprises. The government determines what people can buy because it dictates what is produced in the nation's factories and farms.

Several nations adopted communist-like economic systems during the early 20th century in an effort to correct abuses they believed existed in their previous systems. In practice, however, these new governments typically gave less freedom of choice in regard to jobs and purchases. These governments might be best described as totalitarian socialism. These nations often made mistakes in allocating resources to compete in the growing global marketplace. Government-owned monopolies often suffer from inefficiency.

Consider the former Soviet Union, where large government bureaucracies controlled nearly every aspect of daily life. Shortages became chronic because producers had little or no incentive to satisfy customers. The quality of goods and services also suffered for the same reason. When Mikhail Gorbachev became the last president of the dying Soviet Union, he tried to improve the quality of Soviet-made products. Effectively shut out of trading in the global marketplace and caught up in a treasury-depleting arms race with the United States, the Soviet Union faced severe financial problems. Eventually, these events led to the collapse of Soviet communism and the breakup of the Soviet Union itself.

Today, communist-like systems exist in just a few countries, such as North Korea. By contrast, the People's Republic of China has shifted toward a more market-oriented economy. The national government has given local government and individual plant managers more say in business decisions and has permitted some private businesses. Households now have more control over agriculture, in contrast to the collectivized farms introduced during an earlier era. In addition, Western products such as McDonald's restaurants and Coca-Cola soft drinks are now part of Chinese consumers' lives, and Chinese workers manufacture products for export to other countries.

Mixed Market Economies

Private enterprise systems and planned economies adopt basically opposite approaches to operating economies. In reality, though, many countries operate **mixed market economies**, economic systems that draw from both types of economies, to different degrees. In nations generally considered to have a private enterprise economy, government-owned firms frequently operate alongside private enterprises. In the United States, programs like Medicare are government run.

France has blended socialist and free enterprise policies for hundreds of years. The nation's energy production, public transportation, and defense industries are run as nationalized industries, controlled by the government. Meanwhile, a market economy operates in other industries. Over the past two decades, the French government has loosened its reins on state-owned companies, inviting both competition and private investment into industries previously operated as government monopolies.

The proportions of private and public enterprise can vary widely in mixed economies, and the mix frequently changes. Dozens of countries have converted government-owned and operated companies into privately held businesses in a trend known as **privatization**. Even the United States has seen proposals to privatize everything from the postal service to Social Security.

Governments may privatize state-owned enterprises in an effort to raise funds and improve their economies. The objective is to cut costs and run the operation more efficiently. For most of its existence, Air Canada was a state-owned airline. But in 1989 the airline became fully privatized, and in 2000 the firm acquired Canadian Airlines International, becoming the world's tenth-largest international air carrier. Air Canada now maintains an extensive global network, with destinations in the United States, Europe, the Middle East, Asia, Australia, the Caribbean, Mexico, and South America. It offers such amenities as à la carte pricing, personal entertainment systems in seat backs, and fold-flat beds for transatlantic flights.[12]

Table 3.4 compares the alternative economic systems on the basis of ownership and management of enterprises, rights to profits, employee rights, and worker incentives.

Evaluating Economic Performance

Ideally, an economic system should provide two important benefits for its citizens: a stable business environment and sustained growth. In a stable business environment, the overall supply of needed goods and services is aligned with the overall demand for these items. No wild fluctuations in price or availability to complicate economic decisions. Consumers and businesses not only have access to ample supplies of desired products at affordable prices but also have money to buy the items they demand.

Growth is another important economic goal. An ideal economy incorporates steady change directed toward continually expanding the amount of goods and services produced from the nation's resources. Growth leads to expanded job opportunities, improved wages, and a rising standard of living.

mixed market economy economic system that draws from both types of economies, to different degrees.

privatization conversion of government-owned and operated companies into privately held businesses.

Assessment Check ✔

1. What is the difference between pure competition and monopolistic competition?

2. On which economic system is the U.S. economy based?

3. What is privatization?

3.4 Comparison of Alternative Economic Systems

SYSTEM FEATURES	CAPITALISM (PRIVATE ENTERPRISE)	PLANNED ECONOMIES		
		COMMUNISM	SOCIALISM	MIXED ECONOMY
Ownership of enterprises	Businesses are owned privately, often by large numbers of people. Minimal government ownership leaves production in private hands.	Government owns the means of production with few exceptions, such as small plots of land.	Government owns basic industries, but private owners operate some small enterprises.	A strong private sector blends with public enterprises.
Management of enterprises	Enterprises are managed by owners or their representatives, with minimal government interference.	Centralized management controls all state enterprises in line with three- to five-year plans. Planning now is being decentralized.	Significant government planning pervades socialist nations. State enterprises are managed directly by government bureaucrats.	Management of the private sector resembles that under capitalism. Professionals may also manage state enterprises.
Rights to profits	Entrepreneurs and investors are entitled to all profits (minus taxes) that their firms earn.	Profits are not allowed under communism.	Only the private sector of a socialist economy generates profits.	Entrepreneurs and investors are entitled to private-sector profits, although they often must pay high taxes. State enterprises are also expected to produce returns.
Rights of employees	The rights to choose one's occupation and to join a labor union have long been recognized.	Employee rights are limited in exchange for promised protection against unemployment.	Workers may choose their occupations and join labor unions, but the government influences career decisions for many people.	Workers may choose jobs and labor union membership. Unions often become quite strong.
Worker incentives	Considerable incentives motivate people to perform at their highest levels.	Incentives are emerging in communist countries.	Incentives usually are limited in state enterprises but do motivate workers in the private sector.	Capitalist-style incentives operate in the private sector. More limited incentives influence public-sector activities.

Flattening the Business Cycle

A nation's economy tends to flow through various stages of a business cycle: prosperity, recession, depression, and recovery. No true economic depressions have occurred in the United States since the 1930s, and most economists believe that society is capable of preventing future depressions through effective economic policies. Consequently, they

Solving an Ethical Controversy

Should Alternative Energy Development Be Relied on to Create New Jobs?

Eventually, we will run out of fossil fuels such as oil and coal. The development of alternative energy sources—solar, wind, ethanol, biodiesel, geothermal, and nuclear—could create thousands of new jobs, help revive the economy, and slow down global warming.

A study sponsored by American renewable-energy corporations urges Congress to enact a federal standard of 25 percent reliance on alternative energy by 2025. Supporters claim that a national Renewable Electricity Standard (RES) of 25 percent would create hundreds of thousands of jobs in renewable energy fields. such as solar, geothermal, and hydro power.

Should we develop alternative energy sources to aid economic recovery and create jobs?

PRO

1. With national unemployment still hovering over 9 percent, many industries continue to shrink and shed jobs. Clean energy, on the other hand is growing, and could represent as many as 2.5 million new jobs over the next fifteen years.

2. Clean, renewable energy will help end America's unsustainable dependence on foreign oil. Fossil fuels cause environmental destruction and their prices fluctuate.

CON

1. Fossil fuels will last for many more years. Continual advances could keep them the more energy-efficient, economical choice.

2. Alternative energy sources are still in early development. Some, such as wind power, have not yet lived up to their expected potential. It will take more time—and costly research—before they become economical and viable on a national scale.

Summary

Several European countries along the North Sea have joined to create an environmentally clean "supergrid" that will get its energy from green sources in Scotland, Germany, and Norway, connected by a network of energy-efficient undersea cables. At home, the U.S. is expected to become the world leader in the development of biofuels and other biobased products, generating up to 800,000 new jobs by the year 2022.

Sources: Jennifer Runyon, "2011 Outlook for Clean Energy Jobs in the U.S.—Beating the Trend," *Renewable Energy World*, accessed June 21, 2011, http://www.renewableenergyworld.com; "Stronger National Renewable Electricity Standard Needed for Significant Clean Energy Job Stability and Growth, Study Finds," American Wind Energy Association, February 4, 2010, http://www.awea.org; "Can Alternative Energy Effectively Replace Fossil Fuels?" ProCon, http://alternativeenergy.procon.org, accessed February 4, 2010; Keith Bradsher, "China Leading Global Race to Make Clean Energy," *The New York Times*, January 30, 2010, http://www.nytimes.com.

---

expect recessions to give way to periods of economic recovery. The "Solving an Ethical Controversy" feature explores whether developing alternative sources of energy will create new jobs to stimulate the economy.

Both business decisions and consumer buying patterns differ at each stage of the business cycle. In periods of economic prosperity, unemployment remains low, consumer confidence about the future leads to more purchases, and businesses expand—by hiring more employees, investing in new technology, and making similar purchases—to take advantage of new opportunities.

As recent events show, during a **recession**—a cyclical economic contraction that lasts for six months or longer—consumers frequently postpone major purchases and shift buying patterns toward basic, functional products carrying low prices. Businesses mirror these changes in the marketplace by slowing production, postponing expansion plans, reducing inventories, and often cutting the size of their workforces. During recessions, people facing layoffs and

recession cyclical economic contraction that lasts for six months or longer.

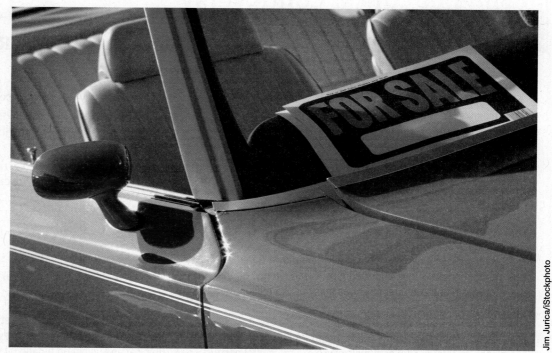

Jim Jurica/iStockphoto

During a recession, consumers may shift buying patterns toward basic, functional products carrying low prices. People facing layoffs and depletions of household savings become much more conservative in their spending and often sell cars, jewelry, and stocks to make ends meet.

depletions of household savings become much more conservative in their spending, postponing luxury purchases and vacations. They often turn to lower-priced retailers like Target, Kohl's, and JC Penney for the goods they need. And they have sold cars, jewelry, and stocks to make ends meet. They also sold everything from old books to artwork to kitchenware on eBay.

If an economic slowdown continues in a downward spiral over an extended period of time, the economy falls into depression. Many Americans have grown up hearing stories about their great-grandparents who lived through the Great Depression of the 1930s, when food and other basic necessities were scarce and jobs were rare.

In the recovery stage of the business cycle, the economy emerges from recession and consumer spending picks up steam. Even though businesses often continue to rely on part-time and other temporary workers during the early stages of a recovery, unemployment begins to decline as business activity accelerates and firms seek additional workers to meet growing production demands. Gradually, the concerns of recession begin to disappear, and consumers start eating out at restaurants, booking vacations, and purchasing new cars again.

Productivity and the Nation's Gross Domestic Product

An important concern for every economy is **productivity**, the relationship between the goods and services produced in a nation each year and the inputs needed to produce them. In general, as productivity rises, so does an economy's growth and the wealth of its citizens. In a recession, productivity stalls or even declines.

Productivity describes the relationship between the number of units produced and the number of human and other production inputs necessary to produce them. Productivity is a

productivity relationship between the number of units produced and the number of human and other production inputs necessary to produce them.

ratio of output to input. When a constant amount of inputs generates increased outputs, an increase in productivity occurs.

Total productivity considers all inputs necessary to produce a specific amount of outputs. Stated in equation form, it can be written as follows:

$$\text{Total Productivity} = \frac{\text{Output (goods or services produced)}}{\text{Input (human / natural resources, capital)}}$$

Many productivity ratios focus on only one of the inputs in the equation: labor productivity or output per labor-hour. An increase in labor productivity means that the same amount of work produces more goods and services than before. Many of the gains in U.S. productivity are attributed to technology, and in recent years the United States appears to be enjoying the fruits of technology and productivity.

Productivity is a widely recognized measure of a company's efficiency. In turn, the total productivity of a nation's businesses has become a measure of its economic strength and standard of living. Economists refer to this measure as a country's **gross domestic product (GDP)**—the sum of all goods and services produced within its boundaries. The GDP is based on the per-capita output of a country—in other words, total national output divided by the number of citizens. As Figure 3.4 shows, only the European Union—which contains twenty-seven member nations and has a GDP of $14.8 trillion—has a GDP higher than that of the United States.[13]

In the United States, GDP is tracked by the Bureau of Economic Analysis (BEA), a division of the U.S. Department of Commerce. Current updates and historical data on the GDP are available at the BEA's Web site (http://www.bea.gov).

gross domestic product (GDP) sum of all goods and services produced within a country's boundaries during a specific time period, such as a year.

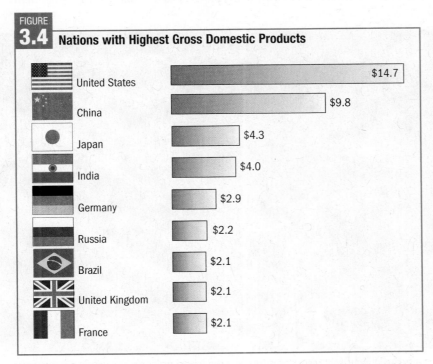

FIGURE 3.4 **Nations with Highest Gross Domestic Products**

Nation	GDP
United States	$14.7
China	$9.8
Japan	$4.3
India	$4.0
Germany	$2.9
Russia	$2.2
Brazil	$2.1
United Kingdom	$2.1
France	$2.1

Source: *World Factbook*, Central Intelligence Agency, https://www.cia.gov, accessed January 26, 2011.

Price-Level Changes

inflation rising prices caused by a combination of excess consumer demand and increases in the costs of raw materials, component parts, human resources, and other factors of production.

core inflation rate inflation rate of an economy after energy and food prices are removed.

hyperinflation economic situation characterized by soaring prices.

Another important indicator of an economy's stability is the general level of prices. For the last 100 years, economic decision makers concerned themselves with **inflation**, rising prices caused by a combination of excess consumer demand and increases in the costs of raw materials, component parts, human resources, and other factors of production. The **core inflation rate** is the inflation rate of an economy after energy and food prices are removed. This measure is often an accurate prediction of the inflation rate that consumers, businesses, and other organizations can expect to experience during the near future.

Excess consumer demand generates what is known as demand-pull inflation while increases in the costs of factors of production generates cost-push inflation. America's most severe inflationary period during the last half of the 20th century peaked in 1980, when general price levels jumped almost 14 percent in a single year. In extreme cases, an economy may experience **hyperinflation**—an economic situation characterized by soaring prices. This situation has occurred in South America, as well as in countries that once formed the Soviet Union.

Inflation devalues money as persistent price increases reduce the amount of goods and services people can purchase with a given amount of money. This is bad news for people whose earnings do not keep up with inflation, who live on fixed incomes, or who have most of their wealth in investments paying a fixed rate of interest. Inflation can be good news to people whose income is rising or those with debts at a fixed rate of interest. A homeowner with a fixed-rate mortgage during inflationary times is paying off that debt with money that is worth less and less each year. However, despite the changes in the stock and housing markets, the number of U.S. households with a net worth of at least $1 million grew 16 percent in one recent year to reach 7.8 million. The number of households worth $5 million or more increased 17 percent to 980,000.[14]

When increased productivity keeps prices steady, it can have a major positive impact on an economy. In a low-inflation environment, businesses can make long-range plans

When increased productivity keeps prices steady, it can have a major positive impact on an economy. Low interest rates encourage firms to invest in capital improvements—such as building a new company headquarters or expanding its existing space—which are likely to produce productivity gains.

without the constant worry of sudden inflationary shocks. Low interest rates encourage firms to invest in research and development and capital improvements, both of which are likely to produce productivity gains. Consumers can purchase growing stocks of goods and services with the same amount of money, and low interest rates encourage major acquisitions such as new homes and autos. But there are concerns. The fluctuating cost of oil—which is used to produce many goods—is a continuing issue. Businesses need to raise prices to cover their costs. Also, smaller firms have gone out of business or have been merged with larger companies, reducing the amount of competition and increasing the purchasing power of the larger corporations. Business owners continue to keep a watchful eye on signs of inflation.

The opposite situation—**deflation**—occurs when prices continue to fall. In Japan, where deflation has been a reality for several years, shoppers pay less for a variety of products ranging from groceries to homes. While this situation may sound ideal to consumers, it can weaken the economy. For instance, industries such as housing and auto manufacturing need to maintain strong prices in order to support all the related businesses that depend on them.

deflation opposite of inflation, occurs when prices continue to fall.

Measuring Price Level Changes In the United States, the government tracks changes in price levels with the **Consumer Price Index (CPI)**, which measures the monthly average change in prices of goods and services. The federal Bureau of Labor Statistics (BLS) calculates the CPI monthly based on prices of a "market basket," a compilation of the goods and services most commonly purchased by urban consumers. Figure 3.5 shows the categories included in the CPI market basket. Each month, BLS representatives

Consumer Price Index (CPI) measurement of the monthly average change in prices of goods and services.

FIGURE
3.5 **Contents of the CPI Market Basket**

Transportation
automobiles, airline fares, gasoline

Recreation
televisions, pets and pet products, sports equipment, movie tickets

Medical Care
prescription drugs, medical supplies, doctor's office visits, eyeglasses

Apparel
men's shirts, women's dresses, jewelry

Education and Communication
tuition, postage, telephone services, computers

Housing
rent, fuel oil, furniture

Food and Beverages
breakfast cereal, milk, coffee, wine, chicken, snacks

Other Goods and Services
tobacco, haircuts, legal expenses

Source: Information from Bureau of Labor Statistics, "Consumer Price Indexes: Frequently Asked Questions," accessed January 26, 2011, http://www.bls.gov/cpi.

Hit & Miss

Microloans Aid Women's Businesses

Almost half of American workers are women, including working mothers. Regardless of income, all saw their economic status deteriorate during the recession. In a recent survey, although most women thought conditions would improve eventually, more than half of working mothers are living below the poverty line.

In response to the demands of childcare and earning a living, many women have started their own businesses. After a career in the fashion industry, Tory Burch launched a successful design company. Learning from her own experience as a working mother, she later established the Tory Burch Foundation. Her research revealed some grim statistics: the majority of poor people in the United States are women. Having a child is one of the leading factors when a woman's income falls below the cost of living. Single mothers are most likely to be self-employed—but are also in the greatest danger of poverty.

Inspired by microloan organizations in the developing world, Burch formed a partnership with ACCION USA, a microlender in the United States. At $500 to $50,000, ACCION USA's loans are somewhat larger than those in developing nations, but many have the same purpose: "to economically empower women." Their clients have low to moderate incomes and are more likely to be rejected by traditional banks,

so these microloans are essential to their success. Forty percent are women, and more than 80 percent are members of minority groups. ACCION USA reports that more than 90 percent of these microloans have been repaid.

Burch remarks that financing women's companies is more than social responsibility, it's good business and good for the economy. "Women are the hardest hit by the economy," says Burch. "And they repay their loans more often than not."

Questions for Critical Thinking

1. Why might having a baby cause a single mother's income to fall?
2. Why do you think that the payback rate on microloans is so high?

Sources: Tory Burch Foundation, http://www.toryburchfoundation.org, accessed January 27, 2011; "Tory Burch Foundation, National Women's Business Week and a Free CD," *The Clothes Whisperer*, October 18, 2010, http://www.theclotheswhisperer.co.uk; Marshall Heyman, "Fashion Designer Shares the Wealth," *The Wall Street Journal*, August 26, 2010, http://online.wsj.com.

---

visit thousands of stores, service establishments, rental units, and doctors' offices all over the United States to price the multitude of items in the CPI market basket. They compile the data to create the CPI. Thus, the CPI provides a running measurement of changes in consumer prices.

Employment Levels People need money to buy the goods and services produced in an economy. Because most consumers earn that money by working, the number of people in a nation who currently have jobs is an important indicator of how well the economy is doing. In general, employment has been on the rise in the United States the past few years, although there have been some dips. Areas that have seen gains include professional and technical services, as well as education, healthcare, and social assistance.[15] The "Hit & Miss" feature discusses a foundation that helps working women and their families.

Economists refer to a nation's **unemployment rate** as an indicator of its economic health. The unemployment rate is usually expressed as a percentage of the total workforce actively seeking work but are currently unemployed. The total labor force includes all people who are willing and available to work at the going market wage, whether they currently have jobs or are seeking work. The U.S. Department of Labor, which tracks unemployment rates, also measures so-called discouraged workers. These individuals want to work but have given up looking for jobs, for various reasons. Unemployment can be grouped into the four categories shown in Figure 3.6: frictional, seasonal, cyclical, and structural.

Frictional unemployment applies to members of the workforce who are temporarily not working but are looking for jobs. This pool of potential workers includes new graduates, people who have left jobs for any reason and are looking for other employment, and former workers who have decided to return to the labor force. **Seasonal unemployment**

unemployment rate percentage of the total workforce actively seeking work but are currently unemployed.

frictional unemployment applies to members of the workforce who are temporarily not working but are looking for jobs.

seasonal unemployment joblessness of workers in a seasonal industry.

is the joblessness of people in a seasonal industry. Construction workers, farm laborers, fishing boat operators, and landscape employees may contend with bouts of seasonal unemployment when wintry conditions make work unavailable.

Cyclical unemployment includes people who are out of work because of a cyclical contraction in the economy. During periods of economic expansion, overall employment is likely to rise, but as growth slows and a recession begins, unemployment levels commonly rise. At such times, even workers with good job skills may face temporary unemployment. Workers in high-tech industries, air travel, and manufacturing have all faced unemployment during economic contraction.

Structural unemployment applies to people who remain unemployed for long periods of time, often with little hope of finding new jobs like their old ones. This situation may arise because these workers lack the necessary skills for available jobs or because the skills they have are no longer in demand. For instance, technological developments have increased the demand for people with computer-related skills but have created structural unemployment among many types of manual laborers or workers who may have been injured and unable to return to work.

FIGURE
3.6 **Four Types of Unemployment**

Frictional Unemployment
· Temporarily not working
· Looking for a job
Example: New graduates entering the workforce

Seasonal Unemployment
· Not working during some months
· Not looking for a job
Example: Farm workers needed only when a crop is in season

Structural Unemployment
· Not working due to no demand for skills
· May be retraining for a new job
Example: Assembly line employees whose jobs are now done by robots

Cyclical Unemployment
· Not working due to economic slowdown
· Looking for a job
Example: Executives laid off during corporate downsizing or recessionary periods

Managing the Economy's Performance

Government can use both monetary policy and fiscal policy in its efforts to fight unemployment, increase business and consumer spending, and reduce the length and severity of economic recessions. For instance, the Federal Reserve System can increase or reduce interest rates, and the federal government can enact tax cuts and rebates, or propose other reforms.

Monetary Policy

A common method of influencing economic activity is **monetary policy**, government actions to increase or decrease the money supply and change banking requirements and interest rates to influence spending by altering bankers' willingness to make loans.

cyclical unemployment people who are out of work because of a cyclical contraction in the economy.

structural unemployment people who remain unemployed for long periods of time, often with little hope of finding new jobs like their old ones.

Assessment Check ✔

1. Describe the four stages of the business cycle.
2. What are some measures that economists use to determine the health of an economy?

monetary policy government actions to increase or decrease the money supply and change banking requirements and interest rates to influence bankers' willingness to make loans.

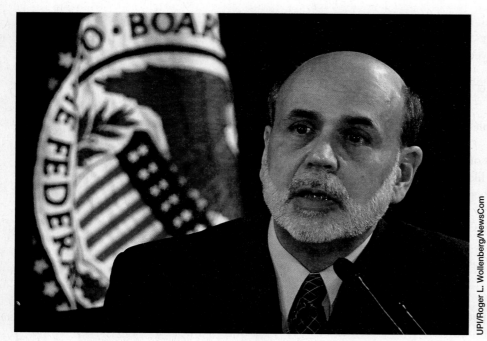

The Federal Reserve uses a number of tools to regulate the economy. The Fed lends money to member banks, which in turn make loans to business and individual borrowers.

UPI/Roger L. Wollenberg/NewsCom

An **expansionary monetary policy** increases the money supply in an effort to cut the cost of borrowing, which encourages business decision makers to make new investments, in turn stimulating employment and economic growth. By contrast, a **restrictive monetary policy** reduces the money supply to curb rising prices, overexpansion, and concerns about overly rapid economic growth.

In the United States, the Federal Reserve System ("the Fed") is responsible for formulating and implementing the nation's monetary policy. It is headed by a chairman and board of governors, all of whom are nominated by the president. The current chairman is Ben Bernanke, who also serves as chairman of the Federal Open Market Committee, the Fed's main agency for monetary policymaking. All national banks must be members of this system and keep some percentage of their checking and savings funds on deposit at the Fed.

The Fed's board of governors uses a number of tools to regulate the economy. By changing the required percentage of checking and savings accounts that banks must deposit with the Fed, the governors can expand or shrink funds available to lend. The Fed also lends money to member banks, which in turn make loans at higher interest rates to business and individual borrowers. By changing the interest rates charged to commercial banks, the Fed affects the interest rates charged to borrowers and, consequently, their willingness to borrow.

Fiscal Policy

Governments also influence economic activities by making decisions about taxes and spending. Through revenues and expenses, the government implements **fiscal policy**. This is the second technique that officials use to control inflation, reduce unemployment, improve the general standard of living, and encourage economic growth. Increased taxes may restrict economic activities, while lower taxes and increased government spending usually boost spending and profits, cut unemployment rates, and fuel economic expansion. On some occasions, the U.S. federal government has issued tax rebates to its citizens and businesses in an effort to stimulate investment and spending. The "Going Green" feature discusses federal tax credits for energy-efficient products.

International Fiscal Policy Nations in the industrial world, including the United States, are currently struggling to find ways to help developing nations modernize their economies. One proposal is to forgive the debts of some of these countries, particularly

expansionary monetary policy increases the money supply in an effort to cut the cost of borrowing, which encourages business decision makers to make new investments, in turn stimulating employment and economic growth.

restrictive monetary policy reducing the money supply to curb rising prices, overexpansion, and concerns about overly rapid economic growth.

fiscal policy government spending and taxation decisions designed to control inflation, reduce unemployment, improve the general welfare of citizens, and encourage economic growth.

Tax Credits for an Energy Star

To encourage Americans to save energy and reduce pollution, the Environmental Protection Administration (EPA) launched the "ENERGY STAR" program in 1992. Later, the Energy Department and the EPA began granting makers of appliances and building materials the familiar ENERGY STAR seal if their products met federal standards for energy efficiency. The American Recovery and Reinvestment Act of 2009 revised a program begun earlier that awards federal income-tax credits to consumers who buy these products. The stimulus package also contains funds for rebates to consumers who buy new, ENERGY STAR–qualified appliances. Each U.S. state and territory has developed its own rebate plan.

Hybrid gas-electric vehicles and those using alternative fuels are eligible for tax credits, as are plug-in electric vehicles. You can also get a tax credit equivalent to 10 percent of the cost if you convert a conventional vehicle to a plug-in, electric-drive motor.

In the state-administered rebate program, replacing certain appliances with qualified ones will not only get you a rebate but will also lower your utility bills. Depending on climate, geography, and other factors, your state may choose from among boilers, central or room air conditioners, washing machines, dishwashers, freezers, oil and gas furnaces, heat pumps (air source and geothermal), refrigerators, and water heaters.

Certain kinds of home improvements are eligible for tax credits. You might invest in a new, qualified central air-conditioning system, heat pump, or furnace. If you live in a cold climate, you might choose to insulate or seal your windows. You might install a biomass stove that burns agricultural and wood waste, plants and residues, or wood pellets. Not only will you get a tax credit, you will also see long-run savings on your fuel bill and help protect the environment.

Questions for Critical Thinking

1. How will paying out rebates and granting tax credits stimulate the economy?
2. Which would you prefer to receive—an income-tax credit or a rebate? Why?

Sources: U.S. Department of Energy, "Consumer Energy Tax Incentives: What the American Recovery and Reinvestment Act Means to You," http://www.energy.gov, accessed June 21, 2011; Alliance to Save Energy, "Energy-Efficient Home and Vehicle Tax Credits," http://ase.org, accessed February 4, 2010; "Federal Tax Credits for Consumer Energy Efficiency," http://www.energystar.gov, accessed February 4, 2010; Environmental Protection Administration, "Environmental Progress," http://www.epa.gov, accessed February 4, 2010; U.S. Department of Energy, "Rebates for ENERGY STAR Appliances," http://www.energysavers.gov, accessed February 4, 2010.

---

those in Africa, to stimulate their economies to grow. But not all fiscal experts agree with this idea. They suggest that any debt forgiveness should come with certain conditions so that these countries can build their own fiscal policies. Countries should encourage and allow citizens to own property, lower their tax rates, avoid devaluing their currencies, lay a path for new businesses to start, and reduce trade barriers. In addition, they must improve agriculture, education, and health care so their citizens can begin to set and reach financial goals. The World Bank is an organization that offers such programs as low-interest loans and interest-free credit and grants to developing countries. The World Bank has been involved in helping Haiti recover from the catastrophic earthquake of 2010.[16]

The Federal Budget Each year, the president proposes a **budget** for the federal government, a plan for how it will raise and spend money during the coming year, and presents it to Congress for approval. A typical federal budget proposal undergoes months of deliberation and many modifications before receiving approval. The federal budget includes a number of different spending categories, ranging from defense and Social Security to interest payments on the national debt. The decisions about what to include in the budget have a direct effect on various sectors of the economy. During a recession, the federal government may approve increased spending on interstate highway repairs to improve transportation and increase employment in the construction industry. During prosperity, the government may allocate more money for scientific research toward medical breakthroughs or alternative fuels.

budget organization's plan for how it will raise and spend money during a given period of time.

Assessment Check ✔

1. What is the difference between an expansionary monetary policy and a restrictive monetary policy?

2. What are the three primary sources of government funds?

3. Does a balanced budget erase the federal debt?

The primary sources of government funds to cover the costs of the annual budget are taxes, fees, and borrowing. Both the overall amount of these funds and their specific combination have major effects on the economic well-being of the nation. One way governments raise money is to impose taxes on sales, income, and other sources. But increasing taxes leaves people and businesses with less money to spend. This might reduce inflation, but overly high taxes can also slow economic growth. Governments then try to balance taxes to give people necessary services without slowing economic growth.

Taxes don't always generate enough funds to cover every spending project the government hopes to undertake. When the government spends more than the amount of money it raises through taxes, it creates a **budget deficit**. To cover the deficit, the U.S. government borrows money by selling Treasury bills, Treasury notes, and Treasury bonds to investors. All of this borrowing makes up the **national debt**. If the government takes in more money than it spends, it is said to have a **budget surplus**. A **balanced budget** means total revenues raised by taxes equal the total proposed spending for the year.

Achieving a balanced budget—or even a budget surplus—does not erase the national debt. U.S. legislators continually debate how fast the nation should use revenues to reduce its debt. Most families want to wipe out debt—from credit cards, automobile purchases, and college, to name a few sources. To put the national debt into personal perspective, with roughly 308 million U.S. citizens, each one owes about $40,260 as his or her share.

But for the federal government, the decision is more complex. When the government raises money by selling Treasury bills, it makes safe investments available to investors worldwide. If foreign investors cannot buy Treasury notes, they might turn to other countries, reducing the amount of money flowing into the United States. U.S. government debt has also been used as a basis for pricing riskier investments. If the government issues less debt, the interest rates it commands are higher, raising the overall cost of debt to private borrowers. In addition, the government uses the funds from borrowing, at least in part, to invest in such public services as education and scientific research.

Global Economic Challenges of the 21st Century

Businesses face a number of important economic challenges in the 21st century. As the economies of countries around the globe become increasingly interconnected, governments and businesses must compete throughout the world. Although no one can predict the future, both governments and businesses will likely need to meet several challenges to maintain their global competitiveness. Table 3.5 identifies five key challenges: (1) the economic impact of the continuing threat of international terrorism, (2) the shift to a global information economy, (3) the aging of the world's population, (4) the growth of China and India, and (5) efforts to enhance the competitiveness of every country's workforce.

No country is an economic island in today's global economy. Not only is an ever-increasing stream of goods and services crossing national borders, but a growing number of businesses have become true multinational firms, operating manufacturing plants and other facilities around the world. As global trade and investments grow, events in one nation can reverberate around the globe. The "Business Etiquette" feature offers some tips for international travel.

Despite the risks of world trade, global expansion can offer huge opportunities to U.S. firms. With U.S. residents accounting for just over 1 in every 22 of the world's nearly 7 billion people, growth-oriented American companies cannot afford to ignore the world market.[17] U.S. businesses also benefit from the lower labor costs in other parts of the world, and some are finding successful niches importing goods and services provided by foreign firms. Still, it is extremely important for U.S. firms to keep close track of the foreign firms that supply their products. A number of U.S. companies have tried having their goods manufactured in China because production costs are significantly lower than they would be in the United States. But there have been so many product recalls of Chinese-made goods during the past several years—ranging from toys and pet food to construction drywall and drinking glasses—that the U.S. Consumer Products Safety Commission (CPSC) has opened an office in Beijing. The goal is to provide the CPSC with closer observation and better communication between U.S. and Chinese firms about manufacturing standards.[18]

U.S. firms must also develop strategies for competing with each other and with foreign firms to meet the needs and wants of consumers overseas. In the huge and fragmented beverage industry, experts predict that the Japanese and Chinese markets for healthy soft drinks, including juice-based and tea-based drinks, will grow significantly over the next few years.[19]

BusinessEtiquette

Tips for International Travel

Good manners and good communication have always been important in business and are becoming even more crucial as global business increases. If your work takes you to a foreign country—or even to an international videoconference—it is essential for you to understand the manners and etiquette of the place you are visiting, either actually or virtually. Here are some useful tips for international business travel, based on suggestions by Dana Persia of DP Image Consulting.

Before Leaving

1 Do as much research as you can on the business etiquette and customs of the country you will visit. For example, the conventional handshake greeting is avoided in many countries. Books and Web sites on international business etiquette as well as the U.S. State Department Web site are helpful.

2 Try to learn a few key phrases of the language whose country you are visiting. Your hosts will appreciate the effort.

3 Compare American business and casual dress with what is appropriate in the country you are visiting. Standards of modesty for women are stricter in many countries. In general, try to fit in as best you can.

Getting There

1 If possible, arrive enough in advance to adapt to time-zone changes, especially before an important conference or meeting.

2 Be sure to get enough sleep before you travel to help mitigate the effects of jet lag.

3 Drinking water before, during, and after your flight will also help with jet lag. Avoid alcohol and caffeine, which are dehydrating.

When You Arrive

Your pretravel research should include gender roles, especially for women; when and where talking about business is permissible; and the etiquette surrounding business cards, alcohol, and gifts. What is appropriate in one country may be unacceptable somewhere else!

Sources: "Business Etiquette—Touchy About Handshakes," *Ravenwerks*, January 9, 2011, http://www.ravenwerks.com; DP Image Consulting Web site, http://www.dpimageconsulting.com, accessed February 4, 2010; International Business Etiquette and Manners, http://www.cyborlink.com, accessed February 4, 2010; U.S. Department of State Web site, http://www.state.gov, accessed February 4, 2010.

3.5 Global Economic Challenges

CHALLENGE	FACTS AND EXAMPLES
International terrorism	• Assistance in locating and detaining known terrorists by dozens of nations • Cooperation in modifying banking laws in most nations in an effort to cut off funds to terrorist organizations. • Concerns over the safety of mass-transit systems following bombings in Moscow and elsewhere.
Shift to a global information economy	• Half of all American workers hold jobs in information technology or in industries that intensively use information technology, goods, and services. • Software industry in India expects to employ more than 2.3 million people. • Internet users in Asia and western Europe have more than doubled in five years.
Aging of the world's population	• Median age of the U.S. population is 36 plus, and by 2025, more than 64 million Americans will be age 65 or older—nearly double today's number. This will increase demands for health care, retirement benefits, and other support services, putting budgetary pressure on governments. • As Baby Boomers, now reaching their early 60s, begin to retire, businesses around the globe will need to find ways to replace their workplace skills.
Growth of India and China straining commodity prices	• China and India now make up more than one-third of the world's population. China's economic growth has been in the industrial sector, and India's focused more in services. Both countries are now consumers of oil and other commodities, affecting prices.
Enhancing competitiveness of every country's workforce	• Leaner organizations (with fewer supervisors) require employees with the skills to control, combine, and supervise work operations.

Assessment Check ✓

1. Why is virtually no country an economic island these days?

2. Describe two ways in which global expansion can benefit a U.S. firm.

What's Ahead

Global competition is a key factor in today's economy. In Chapter 4, we focus on the global dimensions of business. We cover basic concepts of doing business internationally and examine how nations can position themselves to benefit from the global economy. Then we describe the specific methods used by individual businesses to expand beyond their national borders and compete successfully in the global marketplace.

Summary of Learning Objectives

⌈1⌉ Distinguish between microeconomics and macroeconomics. Explain the factors that drive demand and supply.

Microeconomics is the study of economic behavior among individual consumers, families, and businesses whose collective behavior in the marketplace determines the quantity of goods and services demanded and supplied at different prices. Macroeconomics is the study of the broader economic picture and how an economic system maintains and allocates its resources; it focuses on how a government's monetary and fiscal policies affect the overall operation of an economic system.

Demand is the willingness and ability of buyers to purchase goods and services at different prices. Factors that drive demand for a good or service include customer preferences, the number of buyers and their incomes, the prices of substitute goods, the prices of complementary goods, and consumer expectations about the future. Supply is the willingness and ability of businesses to offer products for sale at different prices. Supply is determined by the cost of inputs and technology resources, taxes, and the number of suppliers operating in the market.

Assessment Check Answers ✔️

1.1 Define *microeconomics* and *macroeconomics*.
Microeconomics is the study of economic behavior among individual consumers, families, and businesses whose collective behavior in the marketplace determines the quantity of goods and services demanded and supplied at different prices. *Macroeconomics* is the study of the broader economic picture and how an economic system maintains and allocates its resources.

1.2 Explain demand and supply curves. A demand curve is a graph of the amount of a product that buyers will purchase at different prices. A supply curve shows the relationship between different prices and the quantities that sellers will offer for sale, regardless of demand.

1.3 How do factors of production influence the overall supply of goods and services? A change in the cost or availability of any of the inputs considered to be factors of production can shift the entire supply curve, either increasing or decreasing the amount available at every price.

⌐2⌐ Describe each of the four different types of market structures in a private enterprise system, and compare the three major types of economic systems.

Four basic models characterize competition in a private enterprise system: pure competition, monopolistic competition, oligopoly, and monopoly. Pure competition is a market structure, like that in small-scale agriculture, in which large numbers of buyers and sellers exchange homogeneous products and no single participant has a significant influence on price. Monopolistic competition is a market structure, like that of retailing, in which large numbers of buyers and sellers exchange differentiated products, so each participant has some control over price. Oligopolies are market situations, like those in the steel and airline industries, in which relatively few sellers compete and high start-up costs form barriers to keep out new competitors. In a monopoly, one seller dominates trade in a good or service, for which buyers can find no close substitutes.

The major economic systems are private enterprise economy, planned economy (such as communism or socialism), and mixed market economy. In a private enterprise system, individuals and private businesses pursue their own interests—including investment decisions and profits—without undue governmental restriction. In a planned economy, the government exerts stronger control over business ownership, profits, and resources to accomplish governmental and societal—rather than individual—goals. Socialism, one type of planned

economic system, is characterized by government ownership and operation of all major industries. Communism is an economic system without private property; goods are owned in common, and factors of production and production decisions are controlled by the state. A mixed market economy blends government ownership and private enterprise, combining characteristics of both planned and private enterprise economies.

Assessment Check Answers ✔️

2.1 What is the difference between pure competition and monopolistic competition? Pure competition is a market structure in which large numbers of buyers and sellers exchange homogeneous products. Monopolistic competition is a market structure in which large numbers of buyers and sellers exchange differentiated products.

2.2 On which economic system is the U.S. economy based? The U.S. economy is based on the private enterprise system.

2.3 What is privatization? Privatization is the conversion of government-owned and operated agencies into privately held businesses.

⌐3⌐ Identify and describe the four stages of the business cycle. Explain how productivity, price level changes, and employment levels affect the stability of a nation's economy.

The four stages are prosperity, recession, depression, and recovery. Prosperity is characterized by low unemployment and strong consumer confidence. In a recession, consumers often postpone major purchases, layoffs occur, and household savings may be depleted. A depression occurs when an economic slowdown continues in a downward spiral over a long period of time. During recovery, consumer spending begins to increase and business activity accelerates, leading to an increased number of jobs.

As productivity rises, so do an economy's growth and the wealth of its citizens. In a recession, productivity stalls or possibly declines. Changes in general price levels—inflation or deflation—are important indicators of an economy's general stability. The U.S. government measures price-level changes by the Consumer Price Index. A nation's unemployment rate is an indicator of both overall stability and growth. The unemployment rate shows, as a percentage of the total labor force, the number of people actively seeking employment who are unable to find jobs.

Assessment Check Answers ✔️

3.1 Describe the four stages of the business cycle. The four stages are prosperity, recession, depression, and recovery. Prosperity is characterized by low unemployment and strong consumer confidence. Recession may include consumers postponing major purchases, layoffs, and decreased household savings. A depression occurs when an economic slowdown continues in a downward spiral over a long period of time. In recovery, consumer spending increases and business activity accelerates.

3.2 What are some measures that economists use to determine the health of an economy? Gross domestic product (GDP), general level of prices, core inflation rate, the Consumer Price Index, and the unemployment rate are all measures used to determine the health of an economy.

⌐4⌐ Discuss how monetary policy and fiscal policy are used to manage an economy's performance.

Monetary policy encompasses a government's efforts to control the size of the nation's money supply. Various methods of increasing or decreasing the overall money supply affect interest rates and therefore affect borrowing and investment decisions. By changing the size of the money supply, government can encourage growth or control inflation. Fiscal policy involves decisions regarding government revenues and expenditures. Changes in government spending affect economic growth and employment levels in the private sector. However, a government must also raise money, through taxes or borrowing, to finance its expenditures. Because tax payments represent funds that might otherwise have been spent by individuals and businesses, any taxation changes also affect the overall economy.

Assessment Check Answers ✔

4.1 What is the difference between an expansionary monetary policy and a restrictive monetary policy? An expansionary monetary policy increases the money supply in an effort to cut the cost of borrowing. A restrictive monetary policy reduces the money supply to curb rising prices, overexpansion, and concerns about overly rapid economic growth.

4.2 What are the three primary sources of government funds? The U.S. government acquires funds through taxes, fees, and borrowing.

4.3 Does a balanced budget erase the federal debt? No, a balanced budget does not erase the national debt; it just doesn't increase it.

⌐5⌐ Describe the major global economic challenges of the 21st century.

Businesses face five key challenges in the 21st century: (1) the threat of international terrorism; (2) the shift to a global information economy; (3) the aging of the world's population; (4) the growth of India and China, which compete for resources; and (5) efforts to enhance the competitiveness of every country's workforce.

Assessment Check Answers ✔

5.1 Why is virtually no country an economic island these days? No business or country is an economic island because many goods and services travel across national borders. Companies now are becoming multinational firms.

5.2 Describe two ways in which global expansion can benefit a U.S. firm. A firm can benefit from global expansion by attracting more customers and using less expensive labor and production to produce goods and services.

■ Business Terms You Need to Know

economics 72	monopoly 80	inflation 88	monetary policy 91
microeconomics 72	regulated monopolies 81	core inflation rate 88	expansionary monetary policy 92
macroeconomics 72	planned economy 82	hyperinflation 88	restrictive monetary policy 92
demand 73	socialism 82	deflation 89	fiscal policy 92
supply 73	communism 82	Consumer Price Index (CPI) 89	budget 93
demand curve 74	mixed market economy 83	unemployment rate 90	budget deficit 94
supply curve 76	privatization 83	frictional unemployment 90	national debt 94
equilibrium price 77	recession 85	seasonal unemployment 90	budget surplus 94
pure competition 79	productivity 86	cyclical unemployment 91	balanced budget 94
monopolistic competition 80	gross domestic product (GDP) 87	structural unemployment 91	
oligopoly 80			

■ Review Questions

1. How does microeconomics impact business? How does macroeconomics affect business? Why is it important for businesspeople to understand the fundamentals of each?

2. Draw supply and demand graphs that estimate what will happen to demand, supply, and the equilibrium price of coffee if these events occur:

a. Widely reported medical studies suggest that coffee drinkers are less likely to develop certain diseases.

b. The cost of manufacturing paper cups increases.

c. The state imposes a new tax on takeout beverages.

d. The biggest coffee chain leaves the area.

3. Describe the four different types of competition in the private enterprise system. In which type of competition would each of the following businesses be likely to engage?

a. large drug stores chain

b. small yoga studio

c. steel mill

d. large farm whose major crop is corn

e. Microsoft

4. Distinguish between the two types of planned economies. What factors do you think keep them from flourishing in today's environment?

5. What are the four stages of the business cycle? In which stage do you believe the U.S. economy is now? Why?

6. What is the gross domestic product? What is its relationship to productivity?

7. What are the effects of inflation on an economy? What are the effects of deflation? How does the Consumer Price Index work?

8. What does a nation's unemployment rate indicate? Describe what type of unemployment you think each of the following illustrates:

a. discharged armed forces veteran

b. bus driver who has been laid off due to cuts in his or her city's transit budget

c. worker who was injured on the job and must start a new career

d. lifeguard

e. dental hygienist who has quit one job and is looking for another

9. Explain the difference between monetary policy and fiscal policy. How does the government raise funds to cover the costs of its annual budget?

10. What is the difference between the budget deficit and the national debt? What are the benefits of paying down the national debt? What might be the negative effects?

■ Projects and Teamwork Applications

1. Describe a situation in which you have had to make an economic choice in an attempt to balance your wants with limited means. What factors influenced your decision?

2. Choose one of the following products and describe the different factors that you think might affect its supply and demand.

a. UGG boots

b. Kindle

c. Miles by Discover credit card

d. newly created name-brand drug

e. bicycling tour in Europe

3. Go online to research one of the following government agencies—its responsibilities, its budget, and the like. Then make the case for privatizing it:

a. Veterans Administration

b. Bureau of the Census

c. Smithsonian Institution

d. Transportation and Security Administration

e. Social Security

4. Some businesses automatically experience seasonal unemployment. Increasingly however, owners of these businesses are making efforts to increase demand—and employment—during the off-season. Choose a classmate to be your business partner, and together select one of the following businesses. Create a plan for developing business and keeping employees for a season during which your business does not customarily operate:

a. children's summer camp

b. ski lodge

c. inn located near a beach resort

d. house painting service

e. greenhouse

5. On your own or with a classmate, go online to research the economy of one of the following countries. Learn what you can about the type of economy the country has, its major industries, and its competitive issues. (Note which industries or services are privatized and which are government owned.) Take notes on unemployment rates, monetary policies, and fiscal policies. Present your findings to the class.

a. China

b. New Zealand

c. India

d. Sweden

e. Mexico

f. Canada

g. Brazil

Web Assignments

1. **Credit card regulations.** Several new federal regulations governing credit cards went into effect recently. Visit the Web site listed here and click on "New Credit Card Rules." After reviewing these rules, prepare a brief report highlighting the most significant changes.

   http://federalreserve.gov/creditcard/

2. **Unemployment.** In the United States, the Bureau of Labor Statistics (BLS) compiles and publishes data on unemployment. Go to the BLS Web site (http://www.bls.gov) and click on "Unemployment." Read through the most recent report and answer the following questions:

   a. What is the current unemployment rate in the United States? How does it compare to other developed countries?

   b. Which state has the highest unemployment rate? Which state has the lowest unemployment rate?

   c. What is the so-called underemployment rate?

3. **Gross domestic product.** Visit the Web site of the Bureau of Economic Analysis (http://www.bea.gov) and access the most recent statistics on the U.S. GDP. Prepare a brief report. What is the current GDP? What is the difference between real and nominal GDP? What are the individual components that make up GDP?

Note: Internet Web addresses change frequently. If you don't find the exact sites listed, you may need to access the organization's home page and search from there or use a search engine such as Bing or Google.

CASE 3.1 Nuclear Energy: Making a Comeback?

In the 2010 State of the Union address, the president called for more clean-energy jobs, with expansion of nuclear power as an alternative energy source. He declared, "To create more of these clean energy jobs, we need more production, more efficiency, more incentives. And that means building a new generation of safe, clean nuclear power plants in this country."

Other countries, such as Great Britain, are already planning to build new nuclear plants. Although none have been built in the United States for many years, the 104 currently operating plants generate almost 20 percent of America's electricity. Wind and solar energy together generate less than 5 percent.

An alloy of enriched uranium powers nuclear reactors. How large is the world's supply of uranium? How long will it last?

Uranium, a metal, is relatively common and can be found in rocks and even seawater as well as in ore deposits in the earth. With 24 percent, Australia has the largest supply overall, but Kazakhstan recently declared that it had surpassed Australia's output. Canada has less than 10 percent of the world's supply, but has the highest concentration of top-quality ore. Worldwide, about 67,00 tons of uranium are used each year. At current demand, that supply is expected to last about 70 years. The World Nuclear Association (WNA) predicts that nuclear reactor capacity will increase by about 27 percent in the next decade and that the demand for uranium will grow by 33 percent in response.

There is some debate about when the demand for uranium will be greater than the supply that can be mined economically. Antinuclear activists point out that mineral resources are nonrenewable. Just as the world will eventually run out of oil and coal, it will also run out of uranium. Some analysts believe that this will happen sooner rather than later.

Environmentalists object to destructive mining techniques. In Australia, activists are concerned with the land rights of indigenous Australians. Another potential roadblock is that uranium mining in general is impeded by a lack of infrastructure and a shortage of experienced workers, factors that drive up processing costs. And, a still-unsolved and crucial problem is how to manage safe, long-term storage of spent nuclear rods, which continue to emit radioactivity.

The World Nuclear Association disagrees with these assessments. First, not all uranium deposits have been discovered. Since 1975, the number of known deposits has tripled. Advances in geological research and more exploration will detect many more. As mining techniques improve, known deposits that are currently unreachable will become economically accessible. The WNA predicts that at *current* rates of usage, known supplies will last 200 years rather than 70 or 80.

Second, ore deposits are not the only sources of uranium. It is also found in nuclear weapons, available because of various disarmament treaties. The end of the Cold War in the late 1980s also meant the end of the nuclear arms race. Nuclear warheads contain high-quality enriched uranium. Utility companies and governments also have stockpiles of the metal.

Third, research is ongoing to make enrichment facilities and reactors more energy efficient.

Fourth, unlike oil or coal, uranium can be recycled from spent nuclear fuel rods and from tailings (uranium left over from the enrichment process). These techniques should also improve over time. Other sources, such as phosphates and seawater, could become economically viable in the future.

Questions for Critical Thinking

1. What factors do you think will affect the supply and demand curve for nuclear energy?

2. Describe what type of competition you predict will arise in the nuclear energy industry.

Sources: Barack Obama, State of the Union address, January 27, 2010, http://www.whitehouse.gov; "Is Nuclear Power the Future? Obama Calls for More Plants," *USA Today,* January 26, 2010, http://usatoday.com; "The Nuclear Reactor—How They Are Constructed," *Virtual Nuclear Tourist,* http://www.nucleartourist.com, accessed February 4, 2010; Toni Johnson, "Global Uranium Supply and Demand," Council on Foreign Relations, January 14, 2010, http://www.cfr.org; Chanyaporn Chanjaroen, "Uranium Supply to Fall Short of Demand after 2015, Baobab Says," *Bloomberg.com,* August 26, 2009, http://www.bloomberg.com; "Supply of Uranium," World Nuclear Association, September 2009, http://www.world-nuclear.org.

Smart Phones: Recession Proof and Growing

The ascent of the smart phone has been one of the most revolutionary developments in electronics. Among the many models available are the the Nokia N900, the Apple iPhone, Research in Motion's BlackBerry, the Palm Treo, and the Motorola Droid, with others in the works. Microsoft is planning to launch smart phone software to rival Apple's.

Despite the recent recession, smart phones have remained wildly popular in the United States and abroad. The numbers are staggering. In one recent quarter, 53 million smart phones were shipped worldwide. Nokia led the global market with almost 40 percent of market share. The BlackBerry was second, with just over 20 percent. The iPhone was third, with over 16 percent. Other smart phones had a combined market share of just over 24 percent.

Competition among the smart phones will almost certainly remain strong and is likely to become stronger. Two influential factors are coverage and applications.

The new Droid from Motorola is giving the iPhone a run for its money. The Droid runs on the Verizon network, whereas AT&T has exclusive rights to the iPhone. Verizon has wider network coverage than AT&T, but AT&T allows iPhone users to multitask on one handset. At present, prospective buyers must choose between quality of coverage and multitasking. The coverage issue may become moot, however, because some predict that Apple may soon unlock the iPhone, and AT&T will no longer be the sole carrier.

In applications, or "apps," the iPhone has far surpassed any other smart phone. It leads in number of app developers, number of apps, and number of people who have downloaded those apps. Applications number in the hundreds of thousands; Apple alone has 75,000. Most are free; others (about 18 percent) cost just a few dollars. Apps range from weather to games to music to news. A typical user downloads 20 apps, with games far in the lead. Apple recently celebrated its one-billionth iPhone download.

Here are some predictions for the smart phone industry:

- Some analysts forecast that sales of smart phones will increase four-fold by 2013, and fees for smart phone apps in the United States alone will increase ten-fold to $4.2 billion. As they grow ever more powerful and more versatile, smart phones could very well replace laptops in the future.

- Smart phones will account for an increasing share of the mobile-phone market. In a recent year, 1.2 billion mobile phones were shipped worldwide; of these, 190 million were smart phones. That percentage is expected to rise.

- As we have seen, application stores will experience a boom. The iPhone already has plenty of games, so analysts suggest app writers should develop other types of software, such as business apps. The BlackBerry has plenty of business applications, so writers should develop more games.

- Location-based services, which already include GPS, will increase. Droid users can download step-by-step spoken directions via Google. You'll be able to use your smart phone to trace a package or find your friends so you can meet for a movie. Advertisers may be able to have pop-up ads on the maps you download.

Manufacturers are expected to launch other devices in addition to smart phones. Some are already available. Amazon's e-reader Kindle is facing competition from the

Barnes & Noble Nook. Apple's iPad tablet is expected to function as a media viewer as well as an e-reader. As this decade unfolds, devices and applications will be limited only by the developers' imaginations.

Questions for Critical Thinking

1. How has the rapid development of technology affected competition in the mobile-phone industry?

2. How does this technology affect supply and demand in the mobile-phone industry?

Sources: Apple Web site, http://www.apple.com, accessed June 21, 2011; Amazon Web site, http://www.amazon.com, accessed June 21, 2011; Barnes & Noble Web site, http://barnesandnoble.com, accessed June 21, 2011; Marguerite Reardon, "Microsoft Readies Smartphone Assault on Apple," *cnet news,* February 9, 2010, http://news.cnet.com; "Smart phones Leading the Handset Industry Out of Recession," *Mobile Entertainment,* February 1, 2010, http://www.mobile-ent.biz; Matt Hamblen, "7 Smartphone Predictions for 2010," *Computerworld Mobile & Wireless,* December 4, 2009, http://www.computerworld.com; Matt Hamblen, "Big Money Seen for iPhone, Smartphone App Developers," *InfoWorld,* September 22, 2009, http://www.infoworld.com; Sarah Perez, "The State of the Smartphone: iPhone Is Way, Way Ahead," *ReadWriteWeb,* April 20, 2009, http://www.readwriteweb.com.

CASE 3.3

Secret Acres: Selling Comics Is Serious Business

Just about everyone remembers a favorite comic book from childhood—whether it was *Spiderman, Tin Tin,* or even *Garfield.* Leon Avelino and Barry Matthews readily acknowledge that they are kids in grown-up bodies with real day jobs (Avelino works for *Sports Illustrated* and Matthews is an accountant for an e-commerce firm) who happen to love comic books and their latest incarnation, graphic novels. Their love for comics in all forms—along with the desire to start their own business—led them to found Secret Acres, a comic book and graphic novel publisher based in New York City. In addition to publishing several works from up-and-coming authors (they have eight books on their list so far), the Secret Acres duo sells books from independent distributors. Often asked whether they think Secret Acres will succeed or fail in the next few years, Avelino quips, "People think we're too small to fail anyway." He laughs but then adds, "That pisses me off. I think we can totally fail."

But Avelino and Matthews have no intention of failing. Acknowledging that Secret Acres faces many economic challenges if it's going to hang on and eventually succeed, Matthews observes, "Every decision we make, we know what the outcome is going to be because it's all small and it's very close to us." Right now, Secret Acres can use its small size to build relationships with its customers. "We are able, because we're small, to produce a very specific kind of comic book, a specific kind of graphic novel, that appeals to a specific audience," explains Matthews. "I love that. We have a lot of control over what we do and we're not doing anything specifically to turn a buck." That said, the accountant in Matthews knows that in order to stay in business, Secret Acres must sell enough books to push unit costs down, keeping production expenses and prices as low as possible.

Matthews also refers to relationships with book stores, which are personal because he and Avelino do all the communicating themselves. "When you have a small group of stores you are selling from, you have to collect from them on a one-to-one basis," says Matthews. Sometimes the relationship becomes awkward when Matthews or Avelino has to remind a book store owner personally of an unpaid balance.

Another challenge facing the duo is the uncertain future of the print publishing market. The introduction of e-readers such as Amazon's Kindle and Barnes & Noble's Nook creates a new delivery system for printed work. While the e-reader hasn't created the sensation among consumers that its manufacturers had hoped (some competing models have already disappeared from the marketplace), online delivery of printed matter is alive and well—and it's likely that some form of e-reader will eventually catch on. "Publishers are nervous because no one knows how popular e-readers will be in the long run," says Matthews.

Another phenomenon that has taken hold over the last decade is the graphic novel, the fiction genre that combines comic book techniques with the longer, more complex structure of a novel. Graphic novels are particularly popular among teens and college students, but they have received serious attention from the literary world. College courses are now taught around the graphic novel, and the American Library Association publishes a list of recommended graphic novels for teens each year. A firm like Secret Acres could capitalize on a literary trend that continues to gain ground.

Matthews and Avelino haven't quit their day jobs yet. They know it will be awhile before they can call themselves full-time publishers. But they love the comic book business and they are willing to wait for the good times they believe are ahead. "We have faith in the fact that if these books find the right audience, they'll do fine," says Avelino. "I'm OK with being patient. We need to keep going long enough to build a back list that is self-supporting." And Secret Acres already has a following among comic fans—their secret is out.

Questions for Critical Thinking

1. What steps might Matthews and Avelino take to create demand for their books? How must a small business like Secret Acres balance supply with demand?

2. How might Secret Acres make the most of an economy that is recovering slowly? What advantages and disadvantages might the firm have over a large publishing company?

3. How would you categorize the competition that Secret Acres faces?

4. Do you think Secret Acres should pursue online distribution through e-readers and other delivery systems? Why or why not?

Sources: Secret Acres Web site, http://www.secretacres.com, accessed June 21, 2011; "Great Graphic Novels for Teens," *Young Adult Library Services Association,* http://www.ala.org/yalsa, accessed August 19, 2010; Harry McCracken, "E-Readers May Be Dead, But They're Not Going Away Yet," *PC World,* August 17, 2010, http://www.pcworld.com.

Chapter

4

Learning Objectives

[1] Explain the importance of international business and the primary reasons nations trade, and discuss the concepts of absolute and comparative advantage in international trade.

[2] Describe how nations measure international trade and the significance of exchange rates.

[3] Identify the major barriers that confront global businesses.

[4] Explain how international trade organizations and economic communities reduce barriers to international trade.

[5] Compare the different levels of involvement used by businesses when entering global markets.

[6] Distinguish between a global business strategy and a multidomestic business strategy.

Competing in World Markets

UPI/Stephen Shaver/NewsCom

Ford Figo: India's Cool New Car

The Ford Figo isn't sleek or fast. It's a compact car designed for the middle of the road. But don't yawn yet. The Figo is Ford's first vehicle designed specifically for the automobile market in India—which is a big deal for the company, given the fact that there are more than one billion Indian consumers. Perhaps that is why Ford India, which was established in 1995, has recently gone all out—pouring more than $500 million into India to double its production capacity to 200,000 cars per year. And it looks like the investment is beginning to pay off. The Figo sold 60,000 units within the first 10 months of its launch and received various accolades, including "Car of the Year" from the *Economic Times-Zig Wheels Car Awards* and the BBC Top Gear's "Small Car of the Year."

What's so great about the Figo—whose name means "cool" in colloquial Italian—and why is its success so important to Ford Motor Company? U.S. automakers have struggled for the last decade, plagued by lack of innovation, the consequences of soaring fuel costs, and drooping sales. Ford Motor Company was the only major U.S. automaker to refuse government assistance during the recession, but the company still faced huge challenges. Launching a winning vehicle to the world marketplace could boost Ford's sales and image as a competitor around the globe. Built on the same platform as the popular Fiesta, the Figo is a modest, compact hatchback that handles well along the narrow, crowded streets of India. Despite its simple design and relatively low cost, the Figo offers luxury features such as rapid deceleration warning, intelligent central locking, six-speed intermittent wipers, distance to empty tank, and a smart programmable remote key. In addition, the car comes in both gasoline and diesel models and offers a choice of seven exterior paint colors, ranging from Moon Dust Silver to Metallic Chili. The Figo is built for easy repairs and priced starting at $7,680—making it affordable and attractive to Indian consumers.

The Figo still has a few hills to climb in order to completely win over the Indian market. Although $7,680 is a low price tag by U.S. economic standards, it is about twice the cost of India's least expensive cars, the Tata Nano and Maruti-Suzuki 800. India's per capita income hovers around $1,000, so for many, any car purchase at all is a luxury. But Figo's first-year sales and popularity with the media will help the car gain momentum in the marketplace. Ford India plans to export the Figo to additional Asia-Pacific countries and to Africa as well. Currently Ford has no plans to bring the Figo to the United States, but if it performs up to expectations internationally, the Figo could easily be considered the foundation of Ford's small-car strategy worldwide.

Upon receiving the ET-Zig Wheels award, Ford India's president and managing director Michael Boneham said, "We would like to dedicate this award to all our customers and our employees for making the Figo a grand success." That was just the first year in the product life cycle of an unassuming hatchback that could prove to be Ford's next big thing.[1]

Consider for a moment how many products you used today that came from outside the United States. Maybe you drank Brazilian coffee with your breakfast, wore clothes manufactured in Honduras or Malaysia, drove to class in a German or Japanese car fueled by gasoline refined from Venezuelan crude oil, and watched a movie on a television set assembled in Mexico for a Japanese company such as Sony. A fellow student in Germany may be wearing Zara jeans, using a Samsung cell phone, and drinking Pepsi.

U.S. and foreign companies alike recognize the importance of international trade to their future success. Economic interdependence is increasing throughout the world as companies seek additional markets for their goods and services and the most cost-effective locations for production facilities. No longer can businesses rely only on domestic sales. Today, foreign sales are essential to U.S. manufacturing, agricultural, and service firms as sources of new markets and profit opportunities. Foreign companies also frequently look to the United States when they seek new markets.

Thousands of products cross national borders every day. The computers that U.S. manufacturers sell in Canada are **exports**, domestically produced goods and services sold in markets in other countries. **Imports** are foreign-made products purchased by

domestic consumers. Together, U.S. exports and imports make up about a quarter of the U.S. gross domestic product (GDP). The United States is fourth in the world among exporting nations, with exports near $1 trillion, and annual imports of about $1.5 trillion. That total amount is more than double the nation's imports and exports of just a decade ago.[2]

Transactions that cross national boundaries may expose a company to an additional set of factors such as new social and cultural practices, economic and political environments, and legal restrictions. Before venturing into world markets, firms like Ford Motor Company must adapt their business strategies as they plan to launch products like the Figo overseas.

This chapter travels through the world of international business to see how both large and small companies approach globalization. First, we consider the reasons nations trade, the importance and characteristics of the global marketplace, and the ways nations measure international trade. Then we examine barriers to international trade that arise from cultural and environmental differences. To reduce these barriers, countries turn to organizations that promote global business. Finally, we look at the strategies firms implement for entering foreign markets and the way they develop international business strategies.

exports domestically produced goods and services sold in other countries.

imports foreign goods and services purchased by domestic customers.

Why Nations Trade

As domestic markets mature and sales growth slows, companies in every industry recognize the increasing importance of efforts to develop business in other countries. Walmart operates stores in Mexico, Boeing sells jetliners in Asia, and soccer fans in Britain watch their teams being bought by U.S. billionaires. These are only a few of the thousands of U.S. companies taking advantage of large populations, substantial resources, and rising standards of living abroad that boost foreign interest in their goods and services. Likewise, the U.S. market, with the world's highest purchasing power, attracts thousands of foreign companies to its shores.

International trade is vital to a nation and its businesses because it boosts economic growth by providing a market for its products and access to needed resources. Companies can expand their markets, seek growth opportunities in other nations, and make their production and distribution systems more efficient. They also reduce their dependence on the economies of their home nations.

International Sources of Factors of Production

Business decisions to operate abroad depend on the availability, price, and quality of labor, natural resources, capital, and entrepreneurship—the basic factors of production—in the foreign country. Indian colleges and universities produce thousands of highly qualified computer scientists and engineers each year. To take advantage of this talent, many U.S. computer software and hardware firms have set up operations in India, and many others are outsourcing information technology and customer service jobs there.

Trading with other countries also allows a company to spread risk because different nations may be at different stages of the business cycle or in different phases of development. If demand falls off in one country, the company may still enjoy strong demand in other nations. Companies such as Kellogg's and IKEA have long used international sales to offset lower domestic demand.

Size of the International Marketplace

In addition to human and natural resources, entrepreneurship, and capital, companies are attracted to international business by the sheer size of the global marketplace. Only one in six of the world's nearly 6 billion people live in a relatively well-developed country. The share of the world's population in the less developed countries will increase over the coming years because more developed nations have lower birthrates. But the U.S. Census Bureau says the global birthrate is slowing overall, and the average woman in today's world bears half as many children as her counterpart did 35 years ago.[3]

As developing nations expand their involvement in global business, the potential for reaching new groups of customers dramatically increases. Firms looking for new revenue are inevitably attracted to giant markets such as China and India, with respective populations of about 1.3 billion and 1.2 billion. However, people alone are not enough to create a market. Consumer demand also requires purchasing power. As Table 4.1 shows, population size is no guarantee of economic prosperity. Of the ten most populous countries, only the United States appears on the list of those with the highest per-capita GDPs.

Although people in the developing nations have lower per-capita incomes than those in the highly developed economies of North America and western Europe, their huge

Table
4.1

The World's Top Ten Nations Based on Population and Wealth

COUNTRY	POPULATION (IN MILLIONS)	COUNTRY	PER-CAPITA GDP (IN U.S. DOLLARS)
China	1,323	Qatar	$87,717
India	1,156	Luxembourg	$78,723
United States	308	Norway	$53,269
Indonesia	240	Brunei	$50,103
Brazil	199	Singapore	$49,433
Pakistan	175	United States	$46,443
Bangladesh	156	Switzerland	$42,948
Nigeria	150	Hong Kong	$42,574
Russia	140	Ireland	$39,441
Japan	127	Netherlands	$39,278

Sources: International Monetary Fund, "World Economic Outlook Database—October 2009," www.imf.org, accessed February 24, 2011; U.S. Census Bureau, International Data Base, "Countries and Areas Ranked by Population" www.census.gov, accessed March 8, 2010.

populations do represent lucrative markets. Even when the higher-income segments are only a small percentage of the entire country's population, their sheer numbers may still represent significant and growing markets.

Also, many developing countries have typically posted high growth rates of annual GDP. Until the recent economic slowdown, U.S. GDP grew at an annual rate of about 4.4 percent. By contrast, GDP growth in less developed countries was much greater—China's GDP growth rate averaged 10.1 percent over a recent three-year period, and India's averaged 7.5 percent.[4] These markets represent opportunities for global businesses, even though their per-capita incomes lag behind those in more developed countries. Many firms are establishing operations in these and other developing countries to position themselves to benefit from local sales driven by expanding economies and rising standards of living. Walmart is one of those companies. As the largest retail firm in the world, Walmart employs more than 2 million workers worldwide. Walmart International is growing fast, with more than 4,000 stores and 700,000 employees in 15 countries as far-ranging as Brazil. More than 75 percent of Walmart's overseas stores operate under a local banner.[5]

The United States trades with many other nations. As Figure 4.1 shows, the top five are Canada, China, Mexico, Japan, and the Federal Republic of Germany. With the United Kingdom, South Korea, France, Taiwan, and Brazil, they represent nearly two-thirds of U.S. imports and exports every year.[6] Foreign trade is such an important part of the U.S. economy that it makes up a large portion of the business activity in many of the country's individual states as well. Texas exports more than $163 billion of goods annually, and California exports more than $120 billion. Other big exporting states include Florida, Illinois, New York, and Pennsylvania.[7]

Absolute and Comparative Advantage

Few countries can produce all the goods and services their people need. For centuries, trading has been the way that countries can meet the demand. If a country focuses on producing what it does best, it can export surplus domestic output and buy foreign products that it lacks or cannot efficiently produce. The potential for foreign sales of a particular item depends largely on whether the country has an absolute advantage or a comparative advantage.

A country has an *absolute advantage* in making a product for which it can maintain a monopoly or that it can produce at a lower cost than any competitor. For centuries, China enjoyed an absolute advantage in silk production. The fabric was woven from fibers recovered from silkworm cocoons, making it a prized raw material in high-quality clothing. Demand among Europeans for silk led to establishment of the famous Silk Road, a 5,000-mile link between Rome and the ancient Chinese capital city of Xian.

FIGURE 4.1 Top Ten Trading Partners with the United States

Country	Total U.S. Imports and Exports per Month
Canada	$40 billion
China	$35
Mexico	$29
Japan	$14
Germany	$11
United Kingdom	$8
South Korea	$6
France	$5
Taiwan	$4.6
Brazil	$4.3

Source: Data from U.S. Census Bureau, "Top Ten Countries with which the U.S. Trades," http://www.census.gov/ foreign-trade/top/dst/current/balance.html, accessed January 31, 2011.

Absolute advantages are rare these days. But some countries manage to approximate absolute advantages in some products. Climate differences can give some nations or regions an advantage in growing certain plants. Saffron, perhaps the world's most expensive spice at around $130 per ounce, is the stigma of a flowering plant in the crocus family. It is native to the Mediterranean, Asia Minor, and India. Today, however, saffron is cultivated primarily in Spain, where the plant thrives in its soil and climate. Attempts to grow saffron in other parts of the world have generally been unsuccessful.[8]

A nation can develop a *comparative advantage* if it can supply its products more efficiently and at a lower price than it can supply other goods, compared with the outputs of other countries. China is profiting from its comparative advantage in producing textiles. On the other hand, ensuring that its people are well educated is another way a nation can develop a comparative advantage in skilled human resources. India offers the services of its educated tech workers at a lower wage. But sometimes these strategies backfire. Recently U.S. firms have pulled back from manufacturing or locating customer service operations overseas because of consumer complaints about quality.

To boost its longstanding advantage in research and innovation as global competition increases, IBM recently took the unusual step of forming several global research laboratories with other companies, universities, and governments as widespread as Saudi Arabia, Switzerland, China, Taiwan, India, and Ireland. Australia was then added to the list, with the establishment of the first IBM lab that combines research and development in a single organization. The new lab focuses on smarter natural resource and disaster management.[9]

Assessment Check ✓

1. Why do nations trade?
2. Cite some measures of the size of the international marketplace.
3. How does a nation acquire a comparative advantage?

Saffron, possibly the world's most expensive spice, is extracted from crocus flowers. Because the plants grow well in very few places outside Spain, that country enjoys a near absolute advantage in saffron production.

Measuring Trade between Nations

Clearly, engaging in international trade provides tremendous competitive advantages to both the countries and individual companies involved. But how do we measure global business activity? To understand what the trade inflows and outflows mean for a country, we need to examine the concepts of balance of trade and balance of payments. Another important factor is currency exchange rates for each country.

A nation's **balance of trade** is the difference between its exports and imports. If a country exports more than it imports, it achieves a positive balance of trade, called a *trade surplus*. If it imports more than it exports, it produces a negative balance of trade, called a *trade deficit*. The United States has run a trade deficit every year since 1976. Despite being one of the world's top exporters, the United States has an even greater appetite for foreign-made goods, which creates a trade deficit.

A nation's balance of trade plays a central role in determining its **balance of payments**—the overall flow of money into or out of a country. Other factors also affect the balance of payments, including overseas loans and borrowing, international investments, profits from such investments, and foreign aid payments. To calculate a nation's balance of payments, subtract the monetary outflows from the monetary inflows. A positive balance of payments, or a *balance-of-payments surplus*, means more money has moved into a country than out of it. A negative balance of payments, or *balance-of-payments deficit*, means more money has gone out of the country than entered it.

balance of trade difference between a nation's exports and imports.

balance of payments overall money flows into and out of a country.

Major U.S. Exports and Imports

The United States, with combined exports and imports of about $2.5 trillion, leads the world in the international trade of goods and services. As listed in Table 4.2, the leading categories of goods exchanged by U.S. exporters and importers range from machinery and vehicles to crude oil and chemicals. Strong U.S. demand for imported goods is partly a reflection of the nation's prosperity and diversity.

Although the United States imports more goods than it exports, the opposite is true for services. U.S. exporters sell more than $507 billion in services annually. Much of that money comes from travel and tourism—money spent by foreign nationals visiting the United States.[10] The increase in that figure is especially significant because the dollar has declined and continues to fluctuate in terms of foreign currencies in recent years. U.S. service exports also include business and technical services such as engineering, financial services, computing, legal services, and entertainment, as well as royalties and licensing fees. Major service exporters include Citibank, Walt Disney, Allstate Insurance, and Federal Express, as well as retailers such as McDonald's and Starbucks.

Businesses in many foreign countries want the expertise of U.S. financial and business professionals. Accountants are in high demand in Russia, China, the Netherlands, and Australia—Sydney has become one of Asia's biggest financial centers. Entertainment is

Table

4.2 Top Ten U.S. Merchandise Exports and Imports

EXPORTS	AMOUNT (IN BILLIONS)	IMPORTS	AMOUNT (IN BILLIONS)
Agricultural commodities	$11.52	Crude oil	$353.5
Motor vehicles	98.9	Motor vehicles	190.8
Electrical machinery	82.0	Television, VCR	133.2
Alcoholic beverages	80.2	Electrical machinery	112.6
Mineral fuel	76.0	Automated data processing equipment	96.5
General industrial machinery	55.2	Petroleum preparations	87.1
Specialized industrial machinery	51.9	Agricultural commodities	80.7
Petroleum preparations	51.4	Clothing	78.9
Scientific instruments	42.5	General industrial machinery	66.9
Chemicals—plastics	34.3	Chemicals—medicinal	59.2

Source: U.S. Census Bureau, "U.S. Exports and General Imports by Selected SITC Commodity Groups," *Statistical Abstract of the United States: 2010,* http://www.census.gov, accessed January 31, 2011.

another major growth area for U.S. service exports. The Walt Disney Company already has theme parks in Europe and Asia. But the firm now has plans to build a multi-billion-dollar park in Shanghai, China, pending final approval from central authorities.[11]

With annual imports reaching nearly $2 trillion, the United States is by far the world's leading importer. American tastes for foreign-made goods for everything from clothing to consumer electronics show up as huge trade deficits with the consumer-goods-exporting nations of China and Japan.

Exchange Rates

A nation's **exchange rate** is the rate at which its currency can be exchanged for the currencies of other nations. It is important to learn how foreign exchange works because we live in a global community and the value of currency is an important economic thermometer for every country. Each currency's exchange rate is usually quoted in terms of another currency, such as the number of Mexican pesos needed to purchase one U.S. dollar. Roughly 12 pesos are needed to exchange for a dollar. A Canadian dollar can be exchanged for approximately $1 in the United States. The euro, the currency used in most of the European Union (EU) member countries, has made considerable moves in exchange value during its few years in circulation. European consumers and businesses now use the euro to pay bills by check, credit card, or bank transfer. Euro coins and notes are also used in many EU member-countries.

Foreign exchange rates are influenced by a number of factors, including domestic economic and political conditions, central bank intervention, balance-of-payments position, and speculation over future currency values. Currency values fluctuate, or "float," depending on the supply and demand for each currency in the international market. In this system of

exchange rate value of one nation's currency relative to the currencies of other countries.

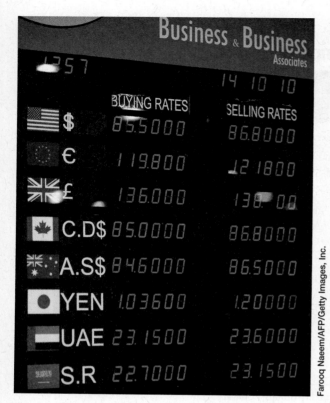

Because we live in a global community it is important to understand how currency exchange rates work. Those rates can be influenced by a variety of factors.

Farooq Naeem/AFP/Getty Images, Inc.

floating exchange rates, currency traders create a market for the world's currencies based on each country's relative trade and investment prospects. In theory, this market permits exchange rates to vary freely according to supply and demand. In practice, exchange rates do not float in total freedom. National governments often intervene in currency markets to adjust their exchange rates.

Nations influence exchange rates in other ways as well. They may form currency blocs by linking their exchange rates to each other. Many governments practice protectionist policies that seek to guard their economies against trade imbalances. For instance, nations sometimes take deliberate action to devalue their currencies as a way to increase exports and stimulate foreign investment. **Devaluation** describes a drop in a currency's value relative to other currencies or to a fixed standard. In Brazil, a currency devaluation made investing in that country relatively cheap, so the devaluation was followed by a flood of foreign investment. Pillsbury bought Brazil's Brisco, which makes a local staple, *pao de queijo*, a cheese bread formed into rolls and served with morning coffee. Other foreign companies invested in Brazil's construction, tourism, banking, communications, and other industries.

For an individual business, the impact of currency devaluation depends on where that business buys its materials and where it sells its products. Business transactions are usually conducted in the currency of the particular region in which they take place. When business is conducted in Japan, transactions are likely to be in yen. In the United Kingdom, transactions are in pounds. With the adoption of the euro in the EU, the number of currencies in that region has been reduced. At present, the EU member-countries using the euro include Austria, Belgium, Finland, France, Germany, Greece, Ireland, Italy, Luxembourg, the Netherlands, Portugal, Slovenia, and Spain. Other countries' currencies include the British pound, Australian dollar, the Indian rupee, the Brazilian real, the Mexican peso, the Taiwanese dollar, and the South African rand.

Exchange rate changes can quickly create—or wipe out—a competitive advantage, so they are important factors in decisions about whether to invest abroad. In Europe, a declining dollar means that a price of ten euros is worth more, so companies are pressured to lower prices. At the same time, if the dollar falls it makes European vacations less affordable for U.S. tourists because their dollars are worth less relative to the euro.

On the Internet you can find currency converters such as those located at http://beginnersinvest.about.com/od/currencycalc/Currency_Calculator.htm, which can help in your monetary conversions. It also helps you understand how much spending power a U.S. dollar has in other countries.

Currencies that owners can easily convert into other currencies are called *hard currencies*. Examples include the euro, the U.S. dollar, and the Japanese yen. The Russian ruble and many central European currencies are considered soft currencies because they cannot be readily converted. Exporters trading with these countries sometimes prefer to barter, accepting payment in oil, timber, or other commodities that they can resell for hard-currency payments.

The foreign currency market is the largest financial market in the world, with a daily volume in excess of 3 trillion U.S. dollars.[12] This is about ten times the size of all the world's stock markets combined, so the foreign exchange market is the most liquid and efficient financial market in the world.

devaluation reduction in a currency's value relative to other currencies or to a fixed standard.

Assessment Check ✓

1. Compare balance of trade and balance of payments.

2. Explain the function of an exchange rate.

3. What happens when a currency is devalued?

Barriers to International Trade

All businesses encounter barriers in their operations, whether they sell only to local customers or trade in international markets. Countries such as Australia and New Zealand regulate the hours and days retailers may be open. Besides complying with a variety of laws and exchanging currencies, international companies may also have to reformulate their products to accommodate different tastes in new locations. By focusing on cookie products that Chinese consumers like, Kraft Foods has quadrupled its revenues in China over the past four years. The next frontier: the Chinese breakfast market. "There's a hole in the breakfast market now, and we're moving to fill it," says Lorna Davis, president and chairman of Kraft China.[13]

In addition to social and cultural differences, companies engaged in international business face economic barriers as well as legal and political ones. Some of the hurdles shown in Figure 4.2 are easily breached, but others require major changes in a company's business strategy. To successfully compete in global markets, companies and their managers must understand not only how these barriers affect international trade but also how to overcome them.

Social and Cultural Differences

The social and cultural differences among nations range from language and customs to educational background and religious holidays. Understanding and respecting these differences are critical to pave the way for international business success. Businesspeople with knowledge of host countries' cultures, languages, social values, and religious attitudes and practices are well equipped for the marketplace and the negotiating table. Sensitivity to such elements as local attitudes, forms of address, and expectations regarding dress, body language, and timeliness also helps them win customers and achieve their business objectives. It is not only U.S. executives who are adapting to the global business environment. Considering the number of transactions that are sealed on the golf links, Chinese students at Xiamen University must learn golf, as well as business and law, and Peking University is building a practice green. The "Business Etiquette" feature offers suggestions for understanding the Japanese culture.

Language English is the second most widely spoken language in the world, followed by Hindustani, Spanish, Russian, and Arabic. Only Mandarin Chinese is more commonly used. It is not uncommon for students abroad for whom English is not their first language to spend eight years of elementary and high school in English language classes. Understanding a business colleague's primary language may prove to be the difference between closing an

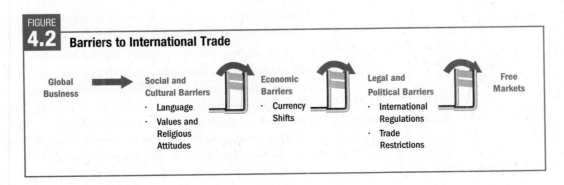

FIGURE 4.2 Barriers to International Trade

Global Business → Social and Cultural Barriers
· Language
· Values and Religious Attitudes

Economic Barriers
· Currency Shifts

Legal and Political Barriers
· International Regulations
· Trade Restrictions

Free Markets

BusinessEtiquette

Tips for Understanding Japanese Culture

Japan's 125 million people live in a fairly small area and tend to be reserved and introverted; their culture emphasizes conformity more than in the United States. Their literacy rate is nearly 100 percent; 95 percent of the population has completed high school. Buddhism and Shintoism are the dominant religions. Here are some tips for respecting Japanese culture that can help you in your global business dealings.

- Dress to impress. Casual wear is not appropriate in work situations.

- Because you will often remove your shoes indoors in Japan, choose slip-on styles that are easy to get on and off.

- Avoid large hand gestures and pointing; the Japanese do not talk with their hands and may find it distracting.

- Respect others' personal space. While handshakes are becoming more common, bowing is still the traditional greeting.

- Remember that in Japan a smile can legitimately mean many things, including anger, sorrow, or embarrassment.

- Keep in mind that the Japanese don't make frequent eye contact and are very comfortable with silence. Don't feel you need to fill conversational gaps.

- Business entertaining most often occurs in bars and restaurants after the end of the workday. Tipping is not required.

- If you are invited to a Japanese home, consider yourself honored.

- Remember to give and receive business cards with both hands. Show respect for a business card you are given by examining it carefully.

- Always wrap gifts. In Japan it's safest to have the store wrap your gifts to ensure the paper and other details are appropriate. White, for instance, symbolizes death.

- Keep in mind that the Japanese dislike criticism. They also prefer not saying no and may say yes when they mean otherwise.

Sources: "Japanese Etiquette," *Cultural Savvy.com*, www.culturalsavvy.com, accessed February 24, 2011; "Japan," *Cyborlink.com*, www.cyborlink.com, accessed February 24, 2011; Emily Maltby, "Expanding Abroad? Avoid Cultural Gaffes," *The Wall Street Journal*, January 19, 2010, p. B5.

international business transaction and losing the sale to someone else. Company representatives operating in foreign markets must not only choose correct and appropriate words but also translate words correctly to convey the intended meanings. Firms may also need to rename products or rewrite slogans for foreign markets.

Potential communication barriers include more than mistranslation. Companies may present messages through inappropriate media, overlook local customs and regulations, or ignore differences in taste. One U.S. executive recently lost a deal in China by giving the prospective client a set of four antique clocks wrapped in white paper. Unfortunately, the number four and the Chinese word for clock are similar to the word "death," while white is the traditional color for funerals.[14] Cultural sensitivity is especially critical in cyberspace. Web site developers must be aware that visitors to a site may come from anywhere in the world. Some icons that seem friendly to U.S. Internet users may shock people from other countries. A person making a high-five hand gesture would be insulting people in Greece; the same is true of making a circle with the thumb and index finger in Brazil, a thumbs-up sign in Egypt, and a two-fingered peace sign with the back of the hand facing out in Great Britain.

Gift-giving traditions employ the language of symbolism. For example, in Latin America, knives and scissors should not be given as gifts because they represent the severing of friendship. Flowers are generally acceptable, but Mexicans use yellow flowers in their Day of the Dead festivities, so they are associated with death.

Values and Religious Attitudes

Even though today's world is shrinking in many ways, people in different countries do not necessarily share the same values or religious attitudes. Marked differences remain in workers' attitudes from country to country, for instance.

U.S. society places a higher value on business efficiency and low unemployment than European society, where employee benefits are more valued. The U.S. government does not regulate vacation time, and employees typically receive no paid vacation during their first year of employment, then two weeks' vacation, and eventually up to three or four weeks if they stay with the same employer for many years. In contrast, the EU mandates a minimum paid vacation of four weeks per year, and most Europeans get five or six weeks. In these countries, a U.S. company that opens a manufacturing plant would not be able to hire any local employees without offering vacations in line with a nation's business practices.

U.S. culture values national unity, with tolerance of regional differences. The United States is viewed as a national market with a single economy. European countries that are part of the 27-member EU are trying to create a similar marketplace. However, many resist the idea of being European citizens first and British, Danish, or Dutch citizens second. British consumers differ from Italians in important ways, and U.S. companies that fail to recognize this variation will run into problems with brand acceptance.

Religion plays an important role in every society, so businesspeople must also cultivate sensitivity to the dominant religions in countries where they operate. Understanding religious cycles and the timing of major holidays can help prevent embarrassing moments when scheduling meetings, trade shows, conferences, or events such as the opening of a new manufacturing plant. People doing business in Saudi Arabia must take into account Islam's month-long observance of Ramadan, when work ends at noon. Friday is the Muslim Sabbath, so the Saudi workweek runs from Saturday through Thursday. Also, many Muslims abstain from alcohol and consider pork unclean, so gifts of pigskin or liquor would be offensive.

Economic Differences

Business opportunities are flourishing in densely populated countries such as China and India, as local consumers eagerly buy Western products. Although such prospects might tempt American firms, managers must first consider the economic factors involved in doing business in these markets. A country's size, per-capita income, and stage of economic development are among the economic factors to consider when evaluating it as a candidate for an international business venture. Tata, for instance, has an eye on Western auto buyers, even as it shapes its low-budget Nano car for the home market in India. See the "Hit & Miss" feature for details.

Infrastructure Along with other economic measures, businesses should consider a country's **infrastructure**. Infrastructure refers to basic systems of communication (telecommunications, television, radio, and print media), transportation (roads and highways, railroads, and airports), and energy facilities (power plants and gas and electric utilities). The Internet and technology use can also be considered part of infrastructure.

India's growing industrialization and its latest projections of 30 million air passengers a year mean the country will soon need at least 400 new airports, according to the country's civil aviation minister. With the Indian aviation industry growing at nearly 20 percent a year, 3,000 new planes will also be needed. Bidding for contractors to work on construction of a new airport in the capital city of Mumbai will take about a year to complete. Part of India's new air travel security is a CT scanner to inspect luggage at the country's biggest new airport, built in a record three years in New Delhi.[15]

Financial systems also provide a type of infrastructure for businesses. In the United States, buyers have widespread access to checks, credit cards, and debit cards, as well as electronic systems for processing these forms of payment. In many African countries, such as Ethiopia, local businesses do not accept credit cards, so travelers to the capital city, Addis Ababa, are warned to bring plenty of cash and traveler's checks.

infrastructure basic systems of communication, transportation, and energy facilities in a country.

The Tiny Nano—A Potential Hit for Tata Motors

When the Tata Nano, a tiny new car for sale in India for $2,500, arrived in the United States recently, it wasn't on the road; it was on display at the Cooper-Hewitt National Design Museum in New York. "As the world's most affordable car, it is a design achievement," said a museum director.

The Nano is also a safe and sturdy vehicle. More, it is a potential revolution in transportation for millions of Indian families that can't otherwise afford a car. In building its "people's car," Tata has relied on existing parts and a highly simplified design to limit costs.

"My particular fascination about the Nano is what I refer to as the 'Nano effect' on the rest of the world's vehicle industry," said one research director. He predicts people everywhere will ask, "If Indians can buy a four-door car for $2,500, why can't I?"

Perhaps they soon can. Tata, a $63 billion Indian conglomerate, backed the Nano through legal troubles over the land needed for a manufacturing plant that delayed production for two years. The recent recession also brought Tata its first financial losses in seven years, just when it faced heavy debts incurred when it bought the money-losing Jaguar and Land Rover brands from Ford Motor.

But Tata's strategic plan is still to achieve international stature by solving the transportation problems of low-income car markets in the developing world. It will sell the Nano in Nigeria next and has already hurdled Europe's crash-safety test. U.S. drivers can now own the Nano CX, and the first diesel Nano is expected to roll out of assembly in the fall of 2011.

Questions for Critical Thinking

1. Do you think Tata's goal of making transportation affordable in developing countries is realistic? Why or why not?

2. Can you think of any disadvantages for low-income markets of having a sudden influx of cars on the road?

Sources: "Tata Nano Diesel May Launch by September 2011," *Auto News India,* January 19, 2011, http://www.autonewsindia.info; Alan Gell, "The World's Cheapest Car: 2011 Tata Nano," *Examiner.com,* January 13, 2011, http://www.examiner.com; Phil Patton, "A Tata Nano Takes Manhattan," *The New York Times,* February 11, 2010, http://www.nytimes.com; April K. Gupta and Haiyan Wang, "Tata Nano: Not Just a Car But Also a Platform," *Business Week,* January 20, 2010, http://www.businessweek.com.

Currency Conversion and Shifts Despite growing similarities in infrastructure, businesses crossing national borders encounter basic economic differences: national currencies. Foreign currency fluctuations may present added problems for global businesses. As explained earlier in the chapter, the values of the world's major currencies fluctuate—sometimes drastically—in relation to each other. Rapid and unexpected currency shifts can make pricing in local currencies difficult. Shifts in exchange rates can also influence the attractiveness of various business decisions. A devalued currency may make a nation less desirable as an export destination because of reduced demand in that market. However, devaluation can make the nation desirable as an investment opportunity because investments there will be a bargain in terms of the investor's currency.

Political and Legal Differences

Like social, cultural, and economic differences, legal and political differences in host countries can pose barriers to international trade. To compete in today's world marketplace, managers involved in international business must be well versed in legislation that affects their industries. Some countries impose general trade restrictions. Others have established detailed rules that regulate how foreign companies can operate.

Political Climate An important factor in any international business investment is the stability of the political climate. The political structures of many nations promote stability similar to that in the United States. Other nations, such as Indonesia, Congo, and Bosnia, feature quite different—and frequently changing—structures. Host nations often pass laws designed to protect their own interests, sometimes at the expense of foreign businesses. See the "Ethical Controversy" feature for a look at how fair trade laws work.

Solving an Ethical Controversy

How Fair Is Fair Trade?

While demand for candy remains high, the price of cocoa is near a 30-year-high. One reason is that to win the coveted "fair trade" designation for their products, chocolate makers must pay small cocoa farmers an extra $150 per ton for the raw ingredient and accept a price of at least $1,600 a ton overall. Nestlé recently announced its popular Kit Kat chocolate bars, which represent about a quarter of the company's U.K. candy sales, will now include only fair trade chocolate from West Africa. Still, the company has come under criticism for allegedly lagging on other possible problems such as child labor.

Is "fair trade" fair enough?

PRO

1. As one of the world's largest buyers of cocoa beans for Kit Kat, Nestlé is taking a strong lead in social responsibility, even though high fair-trade cocoa prices are "going to put pressure on our business," according to the firm's U.K. head.

2. Nestlé's efforts will provide poor cocoa farmers with cash, trees, and training, and help them keep children in school.

CON

1. If a company allows the use of child labor on its behalf abroad, its fair trade claims are not credible. A firm can and should make sure that all of its actions are socially responsible, at home and abroad.

2. While big companies can more easily afford to engage in fair trade practices, smaller firms—with less negotiating power—often lose out.

Summary

Nestlé has promised to plant millions of disease-resistant cocoa trees in Africa over the next few years and to spend at least $445 million on sustainable farming projects in the same period. It has also agreed to a global initiative to improve cocoa farmers' access to health care and to combat child labor. Meanwhile, proponents of fair trade encourage consumers to buy as many certified fair trade products as possible, which will motivate retailers to continue carrying them.

Sources: "Banana Wars: Who Are the Real Winners?" *Guardian Word of Mouth Blog*, February 4, 2011, http://www.guardian.co.uk; "Resolve to Buy Fair, Be Fair in 2011," *Fair Trade USA*, January 1, 2011, http://www.transfairusa.org; Roberta Cruger, "Is Fair Trade Chocolate Fair Enough?" The *Independent/RelaxNews*, www.treehugger.com, February 14, 2010; Thomas Muller, "Nestle Sees Stagnant U.K. Chocolate Market as Cocoa Prices Soar," *Bloomberg.com*, www.bloomberg.com, December 12, 2009; "Organizations Question Nestlé's Commitment to Fair Trade Cocoa," Laborrights.org, www.laborrights.org, December 7, 2009; Deborah Ball, "Nestle Moves to Fair-Trade Chocolate for KitKat Candy in U.K.," *The Wall Street Journal*, www.online.wsj.com, December 7, 2009.

During violent protests in Egypt, under government orders Vodafone (with headquarters in England) cut off its Internet and mobile phone services to 28 million customers because, the company stated, "there were no legal or practical options open but to comply with the authorities." The move angered free-speech advocates, but Vodafone stood firm in its decision because officials from the crumbling Egyptian government could have ordered violence toward Vodafone employees or cell towers. Although service was restored a day later, Vodafone stated further that, "Any actions we take in Egypt will be judged in light of [our employees'] continued well-being."[16]

Legal Environment When conducting business internationally, managers must be familiar with three dimensions of the legal environment: U.S. law, international regulations, and the laws of the countries in which they plan to trade. Some laws protect the rights of foreign companies to compete in the United States. Others dictate actions allowed for U.S. companies doing business in foreign countries.

The *Foreign Corrupt Practices Act* forbids U.S. companies from bribing foreign officials, political candidates, or government representatives. Although the law has been in effect since 1977, in the past few years, the U.S. government has increased its enforcement, including major proceedings in the pharmaceutical, medical device, and financial industries. In addition, German automaker Daimler, A.G. agreed to pay $185 million in fines to resolve FCPA charges.[17] The United States, United Kingdom, France, Germany, and 36 other countries have signed the Organization for Economic Cooperation and Development Anti-Bribery Convention.

Still, corruption continues to be an international problem. Its pervasiveness, combined with U.S. prohibitions, creates a difficult obstacle for U.S. businesspeople whom want to do business in many foreign countries. Chinese pay *huilu*, and Russians rely on *vzyatka*. In the Middle East, palms are greased with *baksheesh*. Figure 4.3 compares 179 countries based on surveys of perceived corruption. This Corruption Perceptions Index is computed by Transparency International, a Berlin-based organization that rates the degree of corruption observed by businesspeople and the general public.

The growth of online business has introduced new elements to the legal climate of international business. Patents, brand names, trademarks, copyrights, and other intellectual property are difficult to police, given the availability of information on the Internet. However, some countries are adopting laws to protect information obtained by electronic contacts.

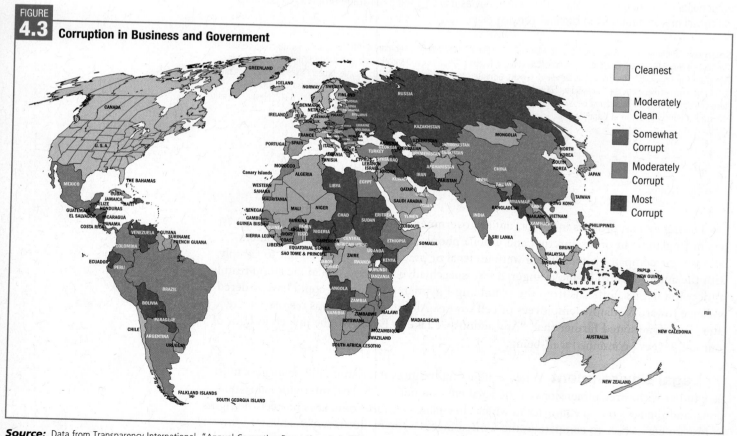

FIGURE 4.3 Corruption in Business and Government

Cleanest

Moderately Clean

Somewhat Corrupt

Moderately Corrupt

Most Corrupt

Source: Data from Transparency International, "Annual Corruption Perceptions Index," http://www.transparency.org, accessed January 31, 2011.

IBM Helps Keep Water Flowing

Did you know it takes 11 gallons of water to manufacture one slice of bread, and 35 gallons to make a single cup of coffee? Water, one of our most abundant resources, is under ever-greater stress. One in five people worldwide lack access to safe drinking water.

IBM is taking major steps to protect the Earth's finite supply of water. Though this essential resource exists worldwide, there is no global market for it and little international or even national exchange of information about how to conserve it. "Water is about quantity, quality, space, and time," says IBM's Global Innovation Outlook report on the world's water management problems. "Whether you have a big problem or not depends entirely on where you live."

IBM is addressing the future of water management in several ways. It is setting up networks of meters and sensors with special IBM software to monitor the capacity and quality of water systems that serve nations, communities, organizations, and individual homes. The company is working to ensure that treated drinking water is subject to less waste from thousands of miles of aging underground pipes and IBM's acoustic technology helps locate the worst leaks for priority repairs. IBM is also collecting data on pollution, marine life, and waves for commercial fishermen, and improving filters to inexpensively eliminate arsenic and salt from drinking water in developing countries.

"We're not going to create water where there is none," says the vice president of IBM's Big Green Innovations. "But where we know water is under stress, we need to monitor what's going on and better manage it."

Questions for Critical Thinking

1. For its water-management efforts, *Fast Company* magazine recently voted IBM 18th in the world in innovation. What do you think makes IBM particularly suited for this award?

2. IBM is an information services company. What do you think other socially responsible firms could learn from its water-management efforts?

Sources: Company Web site, http://www.ibm.com, accessed February 4, 2011; "Advanced Water Management," www.ibm.com, accessed March 23, 2010; "Smarter Water Management," www.ibm.com, accessed March 23, 2010; "Chuck Salter, #18. IBM," *Fast Company*, www.fastcompany.com, February 17, 2010.

Malaysia imposes stiff fines and long jail terms on those convicted of illegally accessing computers and using information that passes through them.

International Regulations To regulate international commerce, the United States and many other countries have ratified treaties and signed agreements that dictate the conduct of international business and protect some of its activities. The United States has entered into many *friendship, commerce, and navigation treaties* with other nations. Such treaties address many aspects of international business relations, including the right to conduct business in the treaty partner's domestic market. Other international business agreements involve product standards, patents, trademarks, reciprocal tax policies, export controls, international air travel, and international communications. One area in which there are no international regulations involves the use/protection of water supplies. IBM is stepping in to help provide the international community with water-management methods and tools as we see in the "Going Green" feature.

When Congress granted China full trade relations with the United States, China agreed to lower trade barriers, including subsidies that held down the prices of food exports, restrictions on where foreign law firms can open offices, and taxes charged on imported goods. In exchange for China's promise to halve these taxes, called *tariffs*, the United States granted Chinese businesses equal access to U.S. markets enjoyed by most other countries.

Many types of regulations affect the actions of managers doing business in international markets. Not only must worldwide producers and marketers maintain required minimum quality levels for all the countries in which they operate, but they must comply with numerous specific local regulations. Britain prevents advertisers from encouraging children to engage in such unhealthy behavior as overeating or replacing regular meals with candy and snack foods. Malaysia's Censorship Board prohibits nudity and profanity on TV. Germany and France allow publishers to set prices that retailers charge for their books.

Italian clothing manufacturers, who have long enjoyed high status for their fabrics and workmanship, say they are suffering from the consequences of a lax labeling system. Until recently, international clothing designers could buy cheaper fabric in China or Bulgaria and have the garments cut in countries with lower labor costs, then send them to Italy for final sewing, tack the prestigious "Made in Italy" label on them, and charge a high price for the goods. A new Italian law states that two of the four stages of clothing production must take place in Italy in order to earn the "Made in Italy" label. The law isn't stringent enough for some Italian manufacturers, who worry that Italy's fashion brand will continue to suffer.[18]

Types of Trade Restrictions

Trade restrictions such as taxes on imports and complicated administrative procedures create additional barriers to international business. They may limit consumer choices while increasing the costs of foreign-made products. Trade restrictions are also imposed to protect citizens' security, health, and jobs. A government may limit exports of strategic and defense-related goods to unfriendly countries to protect its security, ban imports of insecticide-contaminated farm products to protect health, and restrict imports to protect domestic jobs in the importing country.

Other restrictions are imposed to promote trade with certain countries. Still others protect countries from unfair competition. Regardless of the political reasons for trade restrictions, most take the form of tariffs. In addition to tariffs, governments impose a number of nontariff—or administrative—barriers. These include quotas, embargoes, and exchange controls.

tariffs tax imposed on imported goods.

Tariffs Taxes, surcharges, or duties on foreign products are referred to as **tariffs**. Governments assess two types of tariffs—revenue and protective tariffs—both of which make imports more expensive for domestic buyers. Revenue tariffs generate income for the government. Upon returning home, U.S. leisure travelers who are out of the country more than 48 hours and who bring back goods purchased abroad must pay import taxes on their value in excess of $200 to $1,600, depending on the country of origin. This duty goes directly to the U.S. Treasury. The sole purpose of a protective tariff is to raise the retail price of imported products to match or exceed the prices of similar products manufactured in the home country. In other words, protective tariffs seek to limit imports and level the playing field for local competitors.

Of course, tariffs create a disadvantage to companies that want to export to the countries imposing the tariffs. In addition, governments do not always agree on the reasons behind protective tariffs. So they do not always have the desired effect. The United States imposes a tariff on foreign competitors accused of selling products at lower prices in the United States than U.S. manufacturers charge. The government passed a bill giving the money from these tariffs directly to U.S. plaintiff companies, instead of to the Treasury as in the past. The European Union recently agreed to an order that it comply with the Information Technology Agreement (ITA) by eliminating all tariffs on imported electronics goods such as computers and computer parts, flat-panel screens, and fax machines.[19]

Nontariff Barriers Nontariff, or administrative, trade barriers restrict imports in more subtle ways than tariffs. These measures may take such forms as quotas on imports, restrictive standards for imports, and export subsidies. Because many countries have recently substantially reduced tariffs or eliminated them entirely, they increasingly use nontariff barriers to control flows of imported products.

Quotas limit the amounts of particular products that countries can import during specified time periods. Limits may be set as quantities, such as number of cars or bushels of wheat, or as values, such as dollars' worth of cigarettes. Governments regularly set quotas for agricultural products and sometimes for imported automobiles. The United States, for example, sets a quota on imports of sugar. Imports under the quota amount are subject to a lower tariff than shipments above the quota. Sugar and related products imported at the higher rate may enter the country in unlimited quantities, however.[20]

International trade restrictions include *quotas,* or limits, on the amount of a product that can be imported into a country. In the United States, sugar is subject to import quotas.

Richardo Azoury/iStockphoto

Quotas help prevent **dumping**. In one form of dumping, a company sells products abroad at prices below its cost of production. In another, a company exports a large quantity of a product at a lower price than the same product in the home market and drives down the price of the domestic product. Dumping benefits domestic consumers in the importing market, but it hurts domestic producers. It also allows companies to gain quick entry to foreign markets.

More severe than a quota, an **embargo** imposes a total ban on importing a specified product or even a total halt to trading with a particular country. The United States has a longstanding trade embargo with Cuba. Embargo durations can vary to accommodate changes in foreign policy.

Another form of administrative trade restriction is **exchange control**. Imposed through a central bank or government agency, exchange controls affect both exporters and importers. Firms that gain foreign currencies through exporting are required to sell them to the central bank or another agency. Importers must buy foreign currencies to pay for their purchases from the same agency. The exchange control authority can then allocate, expand, or restrict foreign exchange in accordance with national policy.

Reducing Barriers to International Trade

Although tariffs and administrative barriers still restrict trade, overall the world is moving toward free trade. Several types of organizations ease barriers to international trade, including groups that monitor trade policies and practices and institutions that offer monetary assistance. Another type of federation designed to ease trade barriers is the multinational economic community, such as the European Union. This section looks at the roles these organizations play.

quota limit set on the amounts of particular products that can be imported.

dumping selling products abroad at prices below production costs or below typical prices in the home market to capture market share from domestic competitors.

embargo total ban on importing specific products or a total halt to trading with a particular country.

exchange control restriction on importation of certain products or against certain companies to reduce trade and expenditures of foreign currency.

Assessment Check ✓

1. How might values and attitudes form a barrier to trade, and how can they be overcome?

2. What is a tariff? What is its purpose?

3. Why is dumping a problem for companies marketing goods internationally?

Organizations Promoting International Trade

For the 60-plus years of its existence, the **General Agreement on Tariffs and Trade (GATT)**, an international trade accord, sponsored a series of negotiations, called rounds, which substantially reduced worldwide tariffs and other barriers. Major industrialized nations founded the multinational organization in 1947 to work toward reducing tariffs and relaxing import quotas. The last set of completed negotiations—the Uruguay Round—cut average tariffs by one-third, in excess of $700 billion; reduced farm subsidies; and improved protection for copyright and patent holders. In addition, international trading rules now apply to various service industries. Finally, the new agreement established the **World Trade Organization (WTO)** to succeed GATT. This organization includes representatives from 153 countries.

World Trade Organization Since 1995, the WTO has monitored GATT agreements among the member-nations, mediated disputes, and continued the effort to reduce trade barriers throughout the world. Unlike provisions in GATT, the WTO's decisions are binding on parties involved in disputes.

The WTO has grown more controversial in recent years as it issues decisions that have implications for working conditions and the environment in member nations. Concerns have been expressed that the WTO's focus on lowering trade barriers encourages businesses to keep costs down through practices that may increase pollution and human rights abuses. Particularly worrisome is the fact that the organization's member-countries must agree on policies, and developing countries tend not to be eager to lose their low-cost advantage by enacting stricter labor and environmental laws. Other critics claim that if well-funded U.S. firms such as fast-food chains, entertainment companies, and Internet retailers can freely enter foreign markets, they will wipe out smaller foreign businesses serving the distinct tastes and practices of other countries' cultures.

Trade unions in developed nations complain that the WTO's support of free trade makes it easier to export manufacturing jobs to low-wage countries. U.S. glassmaking has been on a long decline as an industry, replaced by increased imports. But some artisans are determined to see a comeback. Glass blower Greg Lueck (also COO of a tech consulting firm) opened Firehouse Studio in Vancouver, Washington, to provide workspace and equipment to local glass blowers.[21]

But many small and midsize firms have benefited from the WTO's reduction of trade barriers and lowering of the cost of trade. They currently make up 97 percent of all firms that export goods and services, according to the Department of Commerce.

The most recent round of WTO talks was called the *Doha Round* after the city in Qatar where it began. After several years of heated disputes and collapsed negotiations, the eight leading industrial nations recommitted themselves to successful conclusion of the talks. Under discussion were ways to improve global agricultural trade and trade among developing countries. The leaders worked to reduce domestic price supports, eliminate export subsidies, and improve market access for goods. Such changes could help farmers in developing countries compete in the global marketplace.[22]

World Bank Shortly after the end of World War II, industrialized nations formed an organization to lend money to less developed and developing countries. The **World Bank** primarily funds projects that build or expand nations' infrastructure such as transportation, education, and medical systems and facilities. The World Bank and other development banks provide the largest source of advice and assistance to developing nations. Often, in exchange for granting loans, the World Bank imposes requirements intended to build the economies of borrower nations.

General Agreement on Tariffs and Trade (GATT) international trade accord that substantially reduced worldwide tariffs and other trade barriers.

World Trade Organization (WTO) 153-member international institution that monitors GATT agreements and mediates international trade disputes.

World Bank organization established by industrialized nations to lend money to less developed countries.

The World Bank has been criticized for making loans with conditions that ultimately hurt the borrower nations. When developing nations are required to balance government budgets, they are sometimes forced to cut vital social programs. Critics also say that the World Bank should consider the impact of its loans on the environment and working conditions.

International Monetary Fund Established a year after the World Bank, the **International Monetary Fund (IMF)** was created to promote trade through financial cooperation and, in the process, eliminate barriers. The IMF makes short-term loans to member nations that are unable to meet their expenses. It operates as a lender of last resort for troubled nations. In exchange for these emergency loans, IMF lenders frequently require significant commitments from the borrowing nations to address the problems that led to the crises. These steps may include curtailing imports or even devaluing currencies. Throughout its existence, the IMF has worked to prevent financial crises by warning the international business community when countries encounter problems meeting their financial obligations. Often, the IMF lends to countries to keep them from defaulting on prior debts and to prevent economic crises in particular countries from spreading to other nations.

However, some countries owe far more money than they can ever hope to repay, and the debt payments make it impossible for their governments to deliver desperately needed services to their citizens. Following a devastating earthquake in Haiti, the G7 countries (the world's most industrialized nations including the United States, Canada, France, and Brazil) promised to cancel any remaining debt owed them by Haiti. The World Bank not only pledged financial support as Haiti struggled to get back on its feet but also waived payment on Haiti's debt for five years while it sought a way to cancel the remaining debt.[23]

International Economic Communities

International economic communities reduce trade barriers and promote regional economic integration. In the simplest approach, countries may establish a *free-trade area* in which they trade freely among themselves without tariffs or trade restrictions. Each maintains its own tariffs for trade outside this area. A *customs union* sets up a free-trade area and specifies a uniform tariff structure for members' trade with nonmember nations. In a *common market*, or economic union, members go beyond a customs union and try to bring all of their trade rules into agreement.

One example of a free-trade area is the **North American Free Trade Agreement (NAFTA)** enacted by the United States, Canada, and Mexico. Other examples of regional trading blocs include the MERCOSUR customs union (joining Brazil, Argentina, Paraguay, Uruguay, Chile, and Bolivia) and the ten-country Association of South East Asian Nations (ASEAN).

NAFTA

NAFTA became effective in 1994, creating the world's largest free-trade zone with the United States, Canada, and Mexico. With a combined population of more than 450 million and a total GDP of more than $15 trillion, North America represents one of the world's most attractive markets. The United States—the single largest market—dominates North America's business environment. Although fewer than 1 person in 20 lives in the United States, the nation's more than $14 trillion GDP represents about one-fifth of total world output.[24]

International Monetary Fund (IMF) organization created to promote trade, eliminate barriers, and make short-term loans to member nations that are unable to meet their budgets.

North American Free Trade Agreement (NAFTA) agreement among the United States, Canada, and Mexico to break down tariffs and trade restrictions.

With NAFTA allowing free trade for the United States, Canada, and Mexico, the amount of goods and services traded is healthy for Canada's economy as well as the United States.

Canada is far less densely populated but has achieved a similar level of economic development. In fact, Canada's economy has been growing at a faster rate than the U.S. economy in recent years. More than two-thirds of Canada's GDP is generated in the services sector, and three of every four Canadian workers are engaged in service occupations. The country's per-capita GDP places Canada among the top nations in terms of its people's spending power. Canada's economy is fueled by trade with the United States, and its home markets are strong as well. The United States and Canada are each other's biggest trading partners. About 78 percent of Canada's exports and about 53 percent of its imports are to or from the United States.[25] U.S. business is also attracted by Canada's human resources. For instance, all major U.S. automakers have large production facilities in Canada.

Mexico is moving from developing nation to industrial nation status, thanks largely to NAFTA. Mexico's trade with the United States and Canada has tripled since the signing of NAFTA, although 18 percent of the country's 111 million people live below the poverty line and per-capita income is about a quarter that of the United States. But Mexico's border with the United States is busy with a nearly endless stream of traffic transporting goods from Mexican factories into the United States. The United States is Mexico's largest trading partner by far, accounting for about 80 percent of total exports and almost 50 percent of all Mexico's imports.[26]

By eliminating all trade barriers and investment restrictions among the United States, Canada, and Mexico over a 15-year period, NAFTA opened more doors for free trade. The agreement also eased regulations governing services, such as banking, and established uniform legal requirements for protection of intellectual property. The three nations can now trade with one another without tariffs or other trade barriers, simplifying shipments of goods across the partners' borders. Standardized customs and uniform labeling regulations create economic efficiencies and smooth import and export procedures. Trade among the partners has increased steadily, more than doubling since NAFTA took effect.

CAFTA-DR

Central America–Dominican Republic Free Trade Agreement (CAFTA-DR) agreement among the United States, Costa Rica, the Dominican Republic, El Salvador, Guatemala, Honduras, and Nicaragua to reduce tariffs and trade restrictions.

The **Central America–Dominican Republic Free Trade Agreement (CAFTA-DR)** created a free-trade area among the United States, Costa Rica, the Dominican Republic (the DR of the title), El Salvador, Guatemala, Honduras, and Nicaragua. The agreement ends most tariffs on nearly $33 billion in products traded between the United States and its Latin American neighbors. Agricultural producers such as corn, soybean, and dairy farmers stand to gain under the relaxed trade rules. U.S. sugar producers, which were supported by subsidies keeping their prices higher than the rest of the world, fought against CAFTA-DR's passage. And labor unions complained that the agreement would lower labor standards and export millions more jobs to lower-wage countries. But overall, CAFTA-DR's effects should be positive, increasing both exports and imports substantially, much as NAFTA did.

European Union

Perhaps the best-known example of a common market is the **European Union (EU)**. The EU combines 27 countries, nearly 500 million people, and a total GDP of roughly $12.28 trillion to form a huge common market. As Figure 4.4 shows, 12 countries—Cyprus, Malta, Estonia, Latvia, Lithuania, Hungary, Poland, the Czech Republic, Slovakia, Slovenia, Bulgaria, and Romania—are the latest EU members. Current candidate countries are Croatia, Turkey, Iceland, and the former Yugoslav Republic of Macedonia. The Treaty of Lisbon took effect in 2009, with a goal of increasing efficiency.[27]

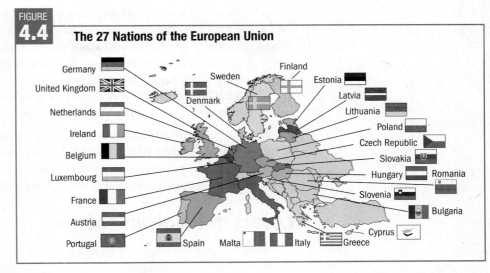

FIGURE 4.4

The 27 Nations of the European Union

Germany, United Kingdom, Netherlands, Ireland, Belgium, Luxembourg, France, Austria, Portugal, Sweden, Denmark, Spain, Malta, Italy, Greece, Finland, Estonia, Latvia, Lithuania, Poland, Czech Republic, Slovakia, Hungary, Romania, Slovenia, Bulgaria, Cyprus

The EU's goals include promoting economic and social progress, introducing European citizenship as a complement to national citizenship, and giving the EU a significant role in international affairs. To achieve its goal of a borderless Europe, the EU is removing barriers to free trade among its members. This highly complex process involves standardizing business regulations and requirements, standardizing import duties and taxes, and eliminating customs checks so that companies can transport goods from England to Italy or Poland as easily as from New York to Boston.

Unifying standards and laws can contribute to economic growth. But just as NAFTA sparked fears in the United States about free trade with Mexico, some people in western Europe worried that opening trade with such countries as Poland, Hungary, and the Czech Republic would cause jobs to flow eastward to lower-wage economies.

The EU also introduced the euro to replace currencies such as the French franc and Italian lira. For the 13 member-states that have adopted the euro, potential benefits include eliminating the economic costs of currency exchange and simplifying price comparisons. Businesses and their customers now make check and credit card transactions in euros and use euro notes and coins in making cash purchases.

Going Global

While expanding into overseas markets can increase profits and marketing opportunities, it also introduces new complexities to a firm's business operations. Before deciding to go global, a company faces a number of key decisions, beginning with the following:

- determining which foreign market(s) to enter
- analyzing the expenditures required to enter a new market
- deciding the best way to organize the overseas operations.

These issues vary in importance depending on the level of involvement a company chooses. Education and employee training in the host country would be much more important for an electronics manufacturer building an Asian factory than for a firm that is simply planning to export American-made products.

European Union (EU) 27-nation European economic alliance.

Assessment Check ✔

1. What international trade organization succeeded GATT, and what is its goal?

2. Compare and contrast the goals of the World Bank and the International Monetary Fund.

3. What are the goals of the European Union, and how do they promote international trade?

The choice of which markets to enter usually follows extensive research focusing on local demand for the firm's products, availability of needed resources, and ability of the local workforce to produce world-class quality. Other factors include existing and potential competition, tariff rates, currency stability, and investment barriers. A variety of government and other sources are available to facilitate this research process. A good starting place is the CIA's *World Factbook*, which contains country-by-country information on geography, population, government, economy, and infrastructure.

U.S. Department of Commerce counselors working at district offices offer a full range of international business advice, including computerized market data and names of business and government contacts in dozens of countries. As Table 4.3 shows, the Internet provides access to many resources for international trade information.

Levels of Involvement

After a firm has completed its research and decided to do business overseas, it can choose one or more strategies:

- exporting or importing
- entering into contractual agreements such as franchising, licensing, and subcontracting deals
- direct investment in the foreign market through acquisitions, joint ventures, or establishment of an overseas division.

Although the company's risk increases with the level of its involvement, so does its overall control of all aspects of producing and selling its goods or services.

Table 4.3
International Trade Research Resources on the Internet

WEB SITE AND ADDRESS	GENERAL DESCRIPTION
Europages http://www.europages.com	Directory of and links to Europe's top 500,000 companies in 33 European countries
World Trade Organization http://www.wto.org	Details on the trade policies of various governments
CIA *World Factbook* https://www.cia.gov/cia/library/publications/the-world-factbook	Basic facts about the world's nations, from geography to economic conditions
STAT-USA http://www.stat-usa.gov	Extensive trade and economic data, information about trends, daily intelligence reports, and background data (access requires paid subscription to the service)
U.S. Commercial Service http://trade.gov/cs	Information about Commerce Department counseling services, trade events, and U.S. export regulations
U.S. Business Advisor http://www.SBA.gov	One-stop access to a range of federal government information, services, and transactions
U.S. State Department http://www.travel.state.gov/travel/cis_pa_tw/tw/tw_1764.html	Listing of the State Department's latest travel warnings about conditions that may affect safety abroad, supplemented by the list of consulate addresses and country information

For Jeffery Adler, it was an offer too good to refuse. His California-based business, Dlush Beverage Joints, a small chain of shops that served fruit smoothies, tea, and baked goods was paid a visit one day by several members of the wealthy Alghanim family from Kuwait. The Alghanims liked the experience so much they proposed a sweet business deal to Adler and his firm: Alghanim Sons Group would become the Persian Gulf franchisees of Dlush. Alghanim now has a 20-year franchise agreement to develop an unlimited number of Dlush stores in six countries throughout the region. Adler receives a percentage of the stores' revenues and a steady income, and the Dlush brand has an immediate international presence.

Zazzle, on the other hand, has worked to develop an international presence via the Internet. The California company offers specialized T-shirts, mugs, hats, and other such items. Zazzle has tailored its business to each specific country by building individual Web sites (in different languages) for fifteen countries and offering shipping to another seventy. Michael Karns, head of Zazzle's international development, keeps a close watch on all aspects of the company's overseas e-commerce.[28]

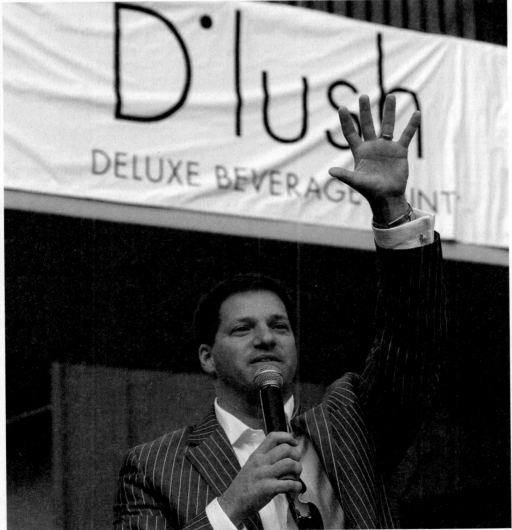

Marsaili McGraph/Getty Images, Inc.

Jeffery Adler, head of Dlush Beverage Joints, joined with Alghanim Sons Group, from Kuwait, to expand his business into the Persian Gulf.

Importers and Exporters When a firm brings in goods produced abroad to sell domestically, it is an importer. Conversely, companies are exporters when they produce—or purchase—goods at home and sell them in overseas markets. An importing or exporting strategy provides the most basic level of international involvement, with the least risk and control.

Fuel Systems Solutions Inc. is a U.S. firm headquartered in New York that provides propane and natural gas fuel systems and components for use in industry and transportation. It has sales facilities on five continents and distributors and dealers in more than 70 countries.[29]

Exports are frequently handled by special intermediaries called export trading companies. These firms search out competitively priced local merchandise and then resell it abroad at prices high enough to cover expenses and earn profits. When a retail chain such as Dallas-based Pier 1 Imports wants to purchase West African products for its store shelves, it may contact an export trading company operating in a country such as Ghana. The local firm is responsible for monitoring quality, packaging the order for transatlantic shipment, arranging transportation, and arranging for completion of customs paperwork and other steps required to move the product from Ghana to the United States.

Firms engage in exporting of two types: indirect and direct. A company engages in *indirect exporting* when it manufactures a product, such as an electronic component, that becomes part of another product sold in foreign markets. The second method, *direct exporting*, occurs when a company seeks to sell its products in markets outside its own country. Often the first step for companies entering foreign markets, direct exporting is the most common form of international business. Firms that succeed at this may then move to other strategies. Crops are imported and exported globally.

In addition to reaching foreign markets by dealing with export trading companies, exporters may choose two other alternatives: export management companies and offset agreements. Rather than simply relying on an export trading company to assist in foreign markets, an exporting firm may turn to an *export management company* for advice and expertise. These international specialists help the exporter complete paperwork, make contacts with local buyers, and comply with local laws governing labeling, product safety, and performance testing. At the same time, the exporting firm retains much more control than would be possible with an export trading company.

An *offset agreement* matches a small business with a major international firm. It basically makes the small firm a subcontractor to the larger one. Such an entry strategy helps a new exporter by allowing it to share in the larger company's international expertise. The small firm also benefits in such important areas as international transaction documents and financing, while the larger company benefits from the local expertise and capabilities of its smaller partner.

Countertrade A sizable share of international trade involves payments made in the form of local products, not currency. This system of international bartering agreements is called **countertrade**.

A common reason for resorting to international barter is inadequate access to needed foreign currency. To complete an international sales agreement, the seller may agree to accept part or all of the purchase cost in merchandise rather than currency. Because the seller may decide to locate a buyer for the bartered goods before completing the transaction, a number of international buyers and sellers frequently join together in a single agreement.

Countertrade may often be a firm's only opportunity to enter a particular market. Many developing countries simply cannot obtain enough credit or financial assistance to afford

countertrade barter agreement whereby trade between two or more nations involves payment made in the form of local products instead of currency.

the imports that their people want. Countries with heavy debt burdens also resort to countertrade. Russian buyers, whose currency is often less acceptable to foreign traders than the stronger currencies of countries such as the United States, Great Britain, Japan, and EU countries, may resort to trading local products ranging from crude oil to diamonds to vodka as payments for purchases from foreign companies unwilling to accept Russian rubles. Still, other countries such as China may restrict imports. Under such circumstances, countertrade may be the only practical way to win government approval to import needed products.

Contractual Agreements Once a company, large or small, gains some experience in international sales, it may decide to enter into contractual agreements with local parties. These arrangements can include franchising, foreign licensing, and subcontracting.

Franchising Common among U.S. companies, franchising can work well for companies seeking to expand into international markets, too. A **franchise**, as described in detail in Chapter 5, is a contractual agreement in which a wholesaler or retailer (the franchisee) gains the right to sell the franchisor's products under that company's brand name if it agrees to the related operating requirements. The franchisee can also receive marketing, management, and business services from the franchisor. While these arrangements are common among leading fast-food brands such as McDonald's and KFC, other kinds of service providers also often look to franchising as an international marketplace option.

Domino's Pizza has expanded to more than 9,000 stores in more than 60 international markets around the world. Its largest international market is in Mexico, but wherever it operates, the company fine-tunes its menus to meet local tastes with such specialties as barbecued chicken in the Bahamas, black bean sauce in Guatemala, squid in Japan, and chorizo in Mexico.[30]

Foreign Licensing In a **foreign licensing agreement**, one firm allows another to produce or sell its product, or use its trademark, patent, or manufacturing processes, in a specific geographical area. In return, the firm gets a royalty or other compensation.

Licensing can be advantageous for a small manufacturer eager to launch a well-known product overseas. Not only does it get a proven product from another market, but little or no investment is required to begin operating. The arrangement can also allow entry into a market otherwise closed to imports due to government restrictions. Sometimes a licensing agreement can ensure product freshness by allowing manufacturing to take place in the local market. Morinaga, a Japanese food manufacturer, holds licenses to produce Lipton teas, Kraft cheeses, and Sunkist fruit drinks and desserts in Japan.[31]

Subcontracting The third type of contractual agreement, **subcontracting**, involves hiring local companies to produce, distribute, or sell goods or services. This move allows a foreign firm to take advantage of the subcontractor's expertise in local culture, contacts, and regulations. Subcontracting works equally well for mail-order companies, which can farm out order fulfillment and customer service functions to local businesses. Manufacturers practice subcontracting to save money on import duties and labor costs, and businesses go this route to market products best sold by locals in a given country. Some firms, such as Maryland-based Pacific Bridge Medical, help medical manufacturers find reliable subcontractors and parts suppliers in Asia.

A key disadvantage of subcontracting is that companies cannot always control their subcontractors' business practices. Several major U.S. companies have been embarrassed by reports that their subcontractors used child labor to manufacture clothing.

franchise contractual agreement in which a franchisee gains the right to produce and/or sell the franchisor's products under that company's brand name if they agree to certain operating requirements.

foreign licensing agreement international agreement in which one firm allows another to produce or sell its product, or use its trademark, patent, or manufacturing processes, in a specific geographical area in return for royalties or other compensation.

subcontracting international agreement that involves hiring local companies to produce, distribute, or sell goods or services in a specific country or geographical region.

Offshoring While it is not generally considered a way of initiating business internationally, *offshoring*, or the relocation of business processes to a lower-cost location overseas, has become a widespread practice. China has emerged as the preferred destination for production offshoring and India for services offshoring. Many business leaders argue, in favor of offshoring, that global firms must keep their costs as low as possible to remain competitive. But the apparent link between jobs sent overseas and jobs lost at home has made the practice controversial. Legislatures of various states have tried to slow the tide of offshoring through new laws, but many observers believe the real goal should be to improve corporate research and development efforts in the United States.

Offshoring shows no signs of slowing down, but it is changing, particularly for manufacturers. Mexico, India, and Vietnam are now the countries with the lowest manufacturing costs. "There was huge momentum and almost herd behavior around going to China back in 2005 or 2006," says one consultant. "China was more competitive than other low-cost countries and had more infrastructure. Now, some of that has changed. Rising transportation costs and material costs, which hurt China in 2007 and 2008, applied to a much lesser degree in Mexico." If companies are manufacturing abroad to sell to foreign markets, offshoring may make more sense than making heavy or bulky products abroad and transporting them to North American markets for sale. Time in transport is also a factor. Not surprisingly, maintaining flexibility by offshoring to a few different low-cost locations may be U.S. firms' lowest-risk strategy for the future. "If the rupee strengthens," says the consultant, "you can shift some work to Vietnam. If transportation costs go crazy, you can move some more work to Mexico."[32]

International Direct Investment Investing directly in production and marketing operations in a foreign country is the ultimate level of global involvement. Over time, a firm may become successful at conducting business in other countries through exporting and contractual agreements. Its managers may then decide to establish manufacturing facilities in those countries, open branch offices, or buy ownership interests in local companies. Because of its focus on offering consumer deals for local businesses, Groupon must invest directly in its operations overseas. See the "Hit & Miss" feature for a description of Groupon's ups and downs in foreign markets.

In an *acquisition*, a company purchases another existing firm in the host country. An acquisition permits a largely domestic business operation to gain an international presence very quickly. Polaris Industries Inc., a U.S. firm, recently acquired Swissauto Powersports, a Swiss designer of high-performance engines for recreational and racing vehicles founded in 1987. The two companies had a long history of partnering together, but the acquisition will brighten Polaris's international profile. It "directly supports our stated objectives to be the best in powersports and a global market leader," said Polaris's CEO.[33]

Joint ventures allow companies to share risks, costs, profits, and management responsibilities with one or more host country nationals. By setting up an *overseas division*, a company can conduct a significant amount of its business overseas. This strategy differs from that of a multinational company in that a firm with overseas divisions remains primarily a domestic organization with international operations. Matsushita established Panasonic Automotive Systems Asia Pacific to develop and sell new technology products in India, Thailand, Indonesia, Malaysia, the Philippines, and Vietnam.

From Multinational Corporation to Global Business

A **multinational corporation (MNC)** is an organization with significant foreign operations. As Table 4.4 shows, firms headquartered in the United States make up half the list of

joint venture partnership between companies formed for a specific undertaking.

multinational corporation (MNC) firm with significant operations and marketing activities outside its home country.

Groupon's Goal: Spread Deals Around the World

Groupon, the Chicago-based online coupon company, has been called one of the hottest Internet start-ups in the world. Within its first two years, the firm has developed the Internet's largest ad network and has rebuffed a $6 billion buyout offer from Google. Its 30-year-old CEO, Andrew Mason, is already considered a business superstar because of his innovative—yet simple—way of connecting buyers and sellers. "What we're trying to do is fundamentally change the way that people buy from local businesses in the same way that e-commerce has changed the way that people buy products," explains Mason. Groupon—for group coupon—works by numbers: if enough buyers sign up online for its daily coupon deal, the deal is activated. Everyone wins: participating businesses, consumers, and Groupon. Different deals are available to its 50 million subscribers in 35 different countries.

But despite all the excited buzz about billions in earnings and plans for an initial public offering (IPO), Groupon has stumbled a few times in its efforts to establish itself globally. In Japan, Groupon offered a deal for the delivery of *osechi*, a traditional New Year's meal. The meal requires painstaking preparation and meticulous presentation. Because the local restaurant was overwhelmed by the volume of orders, many of the *osechi* meals arrived late and damaged, at a price that consumers did not feel was worthwhile. Mason immediately apologized for the mistake and promised to rebuild his company's reputation in Japan.

Chinese officials recently criticized Groupon for hiring employees away from Chinese competitors such as Ftuan.com and Shuangtuan.com. In addition, the Chinese Internet market, which serves approximately 457 million users, is already jammed with an estimated 1,000 group-buying sites, which will make successful entry into China a challenge for Groupon. "The China market is very different," explains Wan Wenshuo, the director of operations for Shuangtuan.com. "The culture and the Internet habits are all different. So it will take longer for [Groupon] to adapt itself to fit China."

Going forward, Groupon must take on rapidly growing competition around the world, from Europe to South America to Asia. In some cases, Groupon has already bought out the competition. Mason is not afraid of these challenges. Nor is he afraid to admit his company's mistakes—as he did in Japan—and learn from them. "We created Groupon to help enrich people's lives," he says.

Questions for Critical Thinking

1. Why is it an important strategy for Groupon to establish itself locally in each market that it serves?

2. In addition to apologizing, what steps might Mason and his firm take to rebuild its image in Japan? What lessons might be learned from this as the company seeks to gain ground in China?

Sources: Company Web site, http://www.groupon.com, accessed January 31, 2011; Michael Kan, "Chinese Group-Buying Sites Fight Groupon's Alleged Poaching," *PC World*, January 26, 2011, http://www.pcworld.com; "Google to Launch Groupon Competitor," *Mashable*, January 20, 2011, http://mashable.com; "Groupon Apologizes to Customers in Japan," *Associated Press*, January 17, 2011, http://www1.cw.56.com; Bari Weiss, "Groupon's $6 Billion Gambler," *The Wall Street Journal*, December 20, 2010, http://online.wsj.com; "Groupon Versus the World," *Inc.*, October 2010, pp.116–118.

---

the world's largest multinationals. China, the Netherlands, Spain, and the United Kingdom make up the other half. Note that the two top industries are banking and oil and gas.

Many U.S. multinationals, including Nike and Walmart, have expanded their overseas operations because they believe that domestic markets are peaking and foreign markets offer greater sales and profit potential. Other MNCs are making substantial investments in developing countries in part because these countries provide low-cost labor compared with the United States and western Europe. In addition, many MNCs are locating high-tech facilities in countries with large numbers of technical school graduates.

Developing a Strategy for International Business

In developing a framework in which to conduct international business, managers must first evaluate their corporate objectives, organizational strengths and weaknesses, and strategies for product development and marketing. They can choose to combine these elements in either a global strategy or a multidomestic strategy.

Assessment Check ✓

1. Name three possible strategies for beginning overseas operations.

2. What is countertrade?

3. Compare and contrast licensing and subcontracting.

4. Describe joint ventures.

Table 4.4 The World's Top Ten Leading Companies (Based on a Combined Ranking for Sales, Profits, Assets, and Market Value)

RANK	COMPANY	INDUSTRY	COUNTRY OF ORIGIN
1	JPMorgan Chase	Banking	United States
2	General Electric	Conglomerates	United States
3	Bank of America	Banking	United States
4	ExxonMobil	Oil & Gas	United States
5	ICBC	Banking	China
6	Banco Santander	Banking	Spain
7	Wells Fargo	Banking	United States
8	HSBC Holdings	Banking	United Kingdom
9	Royal Dutch Shell	Oil & Gas	Netherlands
10	BP	Oil & Gas	United Kingdom

Source: "The Global 2000," *Forbes*, April 21, 2010, http://www.forbes.com.

Global Business Strategies

In a **global business** (or *standardization*) **strategy**, a firm sells the same product in essentially the same manner throughout the world. Many companies simply modify their domestic business strategies by translating promotional brochures and product-use instructions into the languages of the host nations.

A global marketing perspective can be appropriate for some goods and services and certain market segments that are common to many nations. The approach works for products with nearly universal appeal, for luxury items such as jewelry and for commodities like chemicals and metals. Alcoa, for instance, is the world's biggest producers of aluminum for markets that include aerospace, automotive, building and construction, consumer electronics, packaging, and commercial transportation. Because in many applications aluminum's strength and light weight mean there are no good substitutes for it, the company forecasts a long-term increase in global demand, especially in China, India, Russia, the Middle East, and Latin America. It also views itself as committed to a global strategy that incorporates the highest ethical and sustainability practices. Recently Alcoa was awarded the top spot for its use of basic resources by the annual Covalence Ethical Rankings, a prestigious international survey that ranks the ethical performance of multinational companies.[34]

Multidomestic Business Strategies

Under a **multidomestic business** (or *adaptation*) **strategy**, the firm treats each national market in a different way. It develops products and marketing strategies that appeal to the customs, tastes, and buying habits of particular national markets. Companies that

Assessment Check ✓

1. What is a global business strategy? What are its advantages?

2. What is a multidomestic business strategy? What are its advantages?

neglect the global nature of the Internet can unwittingly cause problems for potential customers by failing to adapt their strategy. European consumers, for instance, were at first hesitant to adopt online ordering of products ranging from books to railroad tickets. But in recent years, Internet use in western Europe has grown dramatically. Companies as diverse as the European divisions of Amazon.com; Egg PLC of London, an online financial services company; and the French national railroad have seen the numbers of visitors to their Web sites climbing, along with Internet revenues.

What's Ahead

Examples in this chapter indicate that both large and small businesses are relying on world trade, not just major corporations. Chapter 5 examines the special advantages and challenges that small-business owners encounter. In addition, a critical decision facing any new business is the choice of the most appropriate form of business ownership. Chapter 5 also examines the major ownership structures—sole proprietorship, partnership, and corporation—and assesses the pros and cons of each. The chapter closes with a discussion of recent trends affecting business ownership, such as the growing impact of franchising and business consolidations through mergers and acquisitions.

Internet users in western Europe are no longer as concerned making purchases for such items as railroad tickets online. As this businessman enjoys the ability to work on the train, he may be purchasing his return ticket through his online connection.

Tomas Bercic/iStockphoto

Summary of Learning Objectives

1 Explain the importance of international business and the primary reasons nations trade, and discuss the concepts of absolute and comparative advantage in international trade.

The United States is both the world's largest importer and the largest exporter, although less than 5 percent of the world's population lives within its borders. With the increasing globalization of the world's economies, the international marketplace offers tremendous opportunities for U.S. and foreign businesses to expand into new markets for their goods and services. Doing business globally provides new sources of materials and labor. Trading with other countries also reduces a company's dependence on economic conditions in its home market. Countries that encourage international trade enjoy higher levels of economic activity, employment, and wages than those that restrict it.

Nations usually benefit if they specialize in producing certain goods or services. A country has an absolute advantage if it holds a monopoly or produces a good or service at a lower cost than other nations. It has a comparative advantage

if it can supply a particular product more efficiently or at a lower cost than it can produce other items.

Assessment Check Answers ✓

1.1 Why do nations trade? Nations trade because trading boosts economic growth by providing a market for products and access to needed resources. This makes production and distribution systems more efficient and reduces dependence on the economy of the domestic market.

1.2 Cite some measures of the size of the international marketplace. Although developing countries have lower per-capita incomes than developed nations in North America and western Europe, their populations are large and growing. China's population is about 1.3 billion and India's is roughly 1.1 billion.

1.3 How does a nation acquire a comparative advantage? Comparative advantage exists when a nation can supply a product more efficiently and at a lower price than it can supply other goods, compared with the outputs of other countries.

⌐2⌐ Describe how nations measure international trade and the significance of exchange rates.

Countries measure the level of international trade by comparing exports and imports and then calculating whether a trade surplus or a deficit exists. This is the balance of trade, which represents the difference between exports and imports. The term *balance of payments* refers to the overall flow of money into or out of a country, including overseas loans and borrowing, international investments, and profits from such investments. An exchange rate is the value of a nation's currency relative to the currency of another nation. Currency values typically fluctuate, or "float," relative to the supply and demand for specific currencies in the world market. When the value of the dollar falls compared with other currencies, the cost paid by foreign businesses and households for U.S. products declines, and demand for exports may rise. An increase in the value of the dollar raises the prices of U.S. products sold abroad, but it reduces the prices of foreign products sold in the United States.

Assessment Check Answers ☑

2.1 Compare balance of trade and balance of payments. Balance of trade is the difference between exports and imports; balance of payments is the overall flow of money into or out of a country.

2.2 Explain the function of an exchange rate. A nation's exchange rate is the rate at which its currency can be exchanged for the currencies of other nations to make it easier for them to trade with one another.

2.3 What happens when a currency is devalued? Devaluation describes a fall in a currency's value relative to other currencies or to a fixed standard.

⌐3⌐ Identify the major barriers that confront global businesses.

Businesses face several obstacles in the global marketplace. Companies must be sensitive to social and cultural differences, such as languages, values, and religions, when operating in other countries. Economic differences include standard-of-living variations and levels of infrastructure development. Legal and political barriers are among the most difficult to judge. Each country sets its own laws regulating business practices. Trade restrictions such as tariffs and administrative barriers also present obstacles to international business.

Assessment Check Answers ☑

3.1 How might values and attitudes form a barrier to trade, and how can they be overcome? Marked differences in values and attitudes, such as religious attitudes, can form barriers between traditionally capitalist countries and those adapting new capitalist systems. Many of these can be overcome by learning about and respecting such differences.

3.2 What is a tariff? What is its purpose? A tariff is a surcharge or duty charged on foreign products. Its purpose is to protect domestic producers of those items.

3.3 Why is dumping a problem for companies marketing goods internationally? Dumping is selling products abroad at prices below the cost of production or exporting products at a lower price than charged in the home market. It drives the cost of products sharply down in the market where they are dumped, thus hurting the domestic producers of those products.

⌐4⌐ Explain how international trade organizations and economic communities reduce barriers to international trade.

Many international organizations seek to promote international trade by reducing barriers among nations. Examples include the World Trade Organization, the World Bank, and the International Monetary Fund. Multinational economic communities create partnerships to remove barriers to the flow of goods, capital, and people across the borders of members. Three such economic agreements are the North American Free Trade Agreement, CAFTA-DR, and the European Union.

Assessment Check Answers ☑

4.1 What international trade organization succeeded GATT, and what is its goal? The World Trade Organization (WTO) succeeded GATT with the goal of monitoring GATT agreements, mediating disputes, and continuing the effort to reduce trade barriers throughout the world.

4.2 Compare and contrast the goals of the World Bank and the International Monetary Fund. The World Bank funds projects that build or expand nations' infrastructure such as transportation, education, and health systems and facilities. The International Monetary Fund makes short-term loans to member nations that are unable to meet their budgets. The fund operates as a lender of last resort.

4.3 What are the goals of the European Union, and how do they promote international trade? The European Union's goals include promoting economic and social progress, introducing European citizenship as a complement to national citizenship, and giving the EU a significant role in international affairs. Unifying standards and laws is expected to contribute to international trade and economic growth.

⌐5⌐ Compare the different levels of involvement used by businesses when entering global markets.

Exporting and importing, the first level of involvement in international business, involves the lowest degree of both risk and control. Companies may rely on export trading or management companies to help distribute their products. Contractual agreements such as franchising, foreign licensing, and subcontracting offer additional options. Franchising and licensing are especially appropriate for services. Companies may also choose local subcontractors to produce goods for local sales. International direct investment in production and marketing facilities provides the highest degree of control but also the greatest risk. Firms make direct investments by acquiring foreign companies or facilities, forming joint ventures with local firms and setting up their own overseas divisions.

Assessment Check Answers ☑

5.1 Name three possible strategies for beginning overseas business operations. Strategies are exporting or importing; contractual agreements such as franchising, licensing, or subcontracting; and making direct investments in foreign markets through acquisition, joint venture, or establishment of an overseas division.

5.2 What is countertrade? Countertrade consists of payments made in the form of local products, not currency.

5.3 Compare and contrast licensing and subcontracting. In a foreign licensing agreement, one firm allows another to produce or sell its product or use its trademark, patent, or manufacturing process in a specific geographical area in return for royalty payments or other compensations. In subcontracting a firm hires local companies abroad to produce, distribute, or sell its goods and services.

5.4 Describe joint ventures. Joint ventures allow companies to share risks, costs, profits, and management responsibilities with one or more host-country nationals.

⌐6⌐ **Distinguish between a global business strategy and a multidomestic business strategy.**

A company that adopts a global (or standardization) strategy develops a single, standardized product and marketing strategy for implementation throughout the world. The firm sells the same product in essentially the same manner in all countries in which it operates. Under a multidomestic (or adaptation) strategy, the firm develops a different treatment for each foreign market. It develops products and marketing strategies that appeal to the customs, tastes, and buying habits of particular nations.

Assessment Check Answers ☑

6.1 What is a global business strategy? What are its advantages? A global business strategy specifies a standardized competitive strategy in which the firm sells the same product in essentially the same manner throughout the world. It works well for goods and services that are common to many nations and allows the firm to market them without making significant changes.

6.2 What is a multidomestic business strategy? What are its advantages? A multidomestic business strategy allows the firm to treat each foreign market in a different way to appeal to the customs, tastes, and buying habits of particular national markets. It allows the firm to customize its marketing appeals for individual cultures or areas.

■ Business Terms You Need to Know

■ Review Questions

1. How does a business decide whether to trade with a foreign country? What are the key factors for participating in the information economy on a global basis?

2. Why are developing countries such as China and India becoming important international markets?

3. What is the difference between absolute advantage and comparative advantage? Give an example of each.

4. Can a nation have a favorable balance of trade and an unfavorable balance of payments? Why or why not?

5. Identify several potential barriers to communication when a company attempts to conduct business in another country. How might these be overcome?

6. Identify and describe briefly the three dimensions of the legal environment for global business.

7. What are the major nontariff restrictions affecting international business? Describe the difference between tariff and nontariff restrictions.

8. What is NAFTA? How does it work?

9. How has the EU helped trade among European businesses?

10. What are the key choices a company must make before reaching the final decision to go global?

▌ Projects and Teamwork Applications

1. When Britain transferred Hong Kong to China in 1997, China agreed to grant Hong Kong a high degree of autonomy as a capitalist economy for 50 years. Do you think this agreement is holding up? Why or why not? Consider China's economy, population, infrastructure, and other factors in your answer.

2. The tremendous growth of online business has introduced new elements to the legal climate of international business. Patents, brand names, copyrights, and trademarks are difficult to monitor because of the boundaryless nature of the Internet. What steps could businesses take to protect their trademarks and brands in this environment? Come up with at least five suggestions, and compare your list with your classmates'.

3. The WTO monitors GATT agreements, mediates disputes, and continues the effort to reduce trade barriers throughout the world. However, widespread concerns have been expressed that the WTO's focus on lowering trade barriers may encourage businesses to keep costs down through practices that may lead to pollution and human rights abuses. Others argue that human rights should not be linked to international business. Do you think environmental and human rights issues should be linked to trade? Why or why not?

4. Describe briefly the EU and its goals. What are the pros and cons of the EU? Do you predict that the European alliance will hold up over the next 20 years? Why or why not?

5. Use the most recent edition of "The *Fortune* Global 500," which is published in *Fortune* magazine normally in late July or early August, or go to *Fortune*'s online version at http://money.cnn.com/magazines/fortune/global500, to answer the following questions.

   a. On what is the Global 500 ranking based (e.g., profits, number of employees, revenues)?

   b. Among the world's ten largest corporations, list the countries in which they are based.

   c. Identify the top-ranked company, along with its Global 500 ranking and country, for the following industry classifications: Food and Drug Stores; Industrial and Farm Equipment; Petroleum Refining; Utilities: Gas and Electric; Telecommunications; Pharmaceuticals.

▌ Web Assignments

1. **WTO.** Visit the Web site of the World Trade Organization (http://www.wto.org). Research two current trade disputes. Which countries and products are involved? What, if anything, do the two disputes have in common? What procedures does the WTO follow in resolving trade disputes between member-countries?

2. **EU.** Europa.eu is the Web portal for the European Union. Go to the following Web site (http://europa.eu/index_en.htm) and answer the following questions:

   a. What are the steps a country must take to become a member of the EU?

   b. How many EU members have adopted the euro? Which countries will be adopting the euro over the next few years?

   c. What is the combined GDP of EU members? Which EU member has the largest GDP? Which has the smallest GDP?

3. **Nestlé.** Nestlé is one of the world's largest global corporations. Visit the firm's Web site (http://www.nestle.com). Where is the company headquartered? What are some of its best-known brands? Are these brands sold in specific countries or are they sold worldwide? Make a list of three of four issues Nestle faces as a global corporation.

Note: Internet Web addresses change frequently. If you do not find the exact sites listed, you may need to access the organization's or company's home page and search from there or use a search engine such as Bing or Google.

Google and Facebook Face Off in India's Social Networking Wars

India is the world's largest democracy and, with 1.2 billion people, the second-most populous country (after China). It is considered a major growth Internet market, with a tradition of free speech, a growing middle class that is still discovering the Internet (only about 5 percent of the Indian population is online so far), and huge market opportunities for providers of Web search and advertising.

Orkut, owned by Google, has long been India's most popular social networking site, growing 35 percent a year and averaging 15 to 16 million unique visitors a month. Facebook, its closest rival, was launched around the same time in 2004. Despite steady growth, Facebook has since been running a fairly distant second to Orkut, recently reaching 7.5 to 8.2 million visitors a month. But Facebook has been turning up the heat in the social networking wars, and in one recent month it gained 700,000 visitors. Orkut's numbers dropped by 800,00 for the same month, the largest dip in a year. Many observers of India's Internet scene believe these two statistics signal a leap forward for Facebook that may put it on track to soon surpass Google's Orkut as India's premier online social network.

In fact, Facebook grew its audience about 230 percent in one recent year. What accounts for its success? One factor is a special software tool the site is promoting to let new users easily import their friends from Orkut and other sites. The tool speeds the process of establishing a Facebook presence and was created especially for Orkut. Facebook is also available in a number of widely used Indian languages, including Hindi, Punjabi, Bengali, Telugu, Tamil, and Malayalam. And Facebook hired away a top Google advertising executive and has been buying ads on Google's India portal. Finally, a "lite" version of Facebook, designed for users in developing countries that have limited access to high-speed Internet connections, was also added recently.

Meanwhile, Google faces some potential problems in India that are common to many multinational and Internet companies. Fearing a backlash in the midst of emotional public mourning for an Indian official killed in a helicopter crash, it recently removed offensive comments posted about him on Orkut, along with the entire user group to which they were posted. Says one leading India civil liberties lawyer, "Communal tensions become largely an excuse for denial of civil liberties and denial of freedom of speech. It's a very thin line that's being tread."

"In those gray areas it is really hard," agrees Google's deputy general counsel. Company policy is to review posted material that Orkut users have flagged. Anything that violates its global bans on child pornography and hate speech, or the laws of the country in which it is operating, is removed.

Questions for Critical Thinking

1. Do you think Facebook can become India's leading social networking site? Why or why not? What else can Facebook do to ensure success?

2. How well do you think Google is handling the problem of censoring content on its international sites such as Orkut? How do you think its solutions of these problems affect its plans to keep ahead of Facebook?

Sources: Robin Wauters, "In India Facebook Uses Google AdWords to Leapfrog Orkut," *Tech Crunch*, http://techcrunch.com, January 22, 2010; Amol Sharma and Jessica E. Vascellaro, "Google and India Test the Limits of Liberty," *The Wall Street Journal*, www.online.wsj.com, January 2, 2010; Leena Rao, "Facebook's Plan to Trounce Orkut in India May Be Working," *Tech Crunch*, http://techcrunch.com, November 30, 2009; "Orkut Vs. Facebook: What the Indians Are Looking For," *Social Media News*, http://socialmedia.globalthoughtz.com, November 19, 2009.

TOMS Shoes Takes One Step at a Time

On a trip to Argentina, a young U.S. entrepreneur named Blake Mycoskie saw firsthand how a simple pair of shoes, beyond the means of many of the world's poor, could provide everything from the ability to attend school to protection from life-threatening infections. Moved by the experience, Mycoskie had a striking insight: that a revenue-based business was more likely than a charity to sustain itself over the long term. And so TOMS Shoes was born.

TOMS Shoes, which stands for "tomorrow's shoes," makes simple, lightweight, and inexpensive but stylish shoes with a unique business model called One for One. For every pair it sells, TOMS gives a pair of shoes away to a child in need somewhere in the world. In just a few years it has given away some 400,000 pairs of shoes to kids in Argentina, South Africa, Ethiopia, and the United States, 28 countries in all. Some were able to own shoes for the first time in their lives. "When you give some of these children a pair of shoes," says Mycoskie, " . . . it is like a prized possession. It's not an accessory. It's a necessity, really."

To those who have difficulty understanding his business model, Mycoskie tells this story: "I got to meet Bill Gates. And he said, 'You know, 50 percent of the infectious diseases in the world can be prevented by two things. Toilets and shoes. So, keep doing what you're doing.'"

With only 50 full-time employees and a crew of enthusiastic volunteers, TOMS recently turned its first profit, in a year in which it hoped to give away another 300,000 pairs. Several times a year, Mycoskie himself travels with several employees to different parts of the world to lead "shoe drops." He says it's the best part of his job. "When we're in these countries, we are in the field at least once a day hand-placing shoes on kids' feet. It's really important for us to go back and do that. It's a renewable energy source for me." On these trips, Mycoskie also meets with representatives from local public-health organizations.

TOMS' current focus is on preventing a debilitating soil-borne disease, common in Ethiopia, which attacks the lymphatic system, effectively isolating its victims who are mostly women and children. Simply wearing shoes prevents the transmission of the disease. Donated shoes are also helping to prevent hookworm in Guatemala. And children who wear shoes can more readily walk to school.

To give away more shoes, of course, TOMS must sell more. Its products have been featured in *Teen Vogue,*

Marie Claire, Star, and *LA Confidential* magazines and promoted through "shoe drops," a pop-up store (a temporary retail outlet backed by a marketing blitz), fashion shows, campus appearances, and other trendy events. The company has extended its original canvas espadrilles (modeled on Argentinean *alpargatas),* to include more styles and colors for men and women, and a kids' line called Youth TOMS.

Mycoskie, who recently gave away most of his possessions to live on a small sailboat docked on the California coast, keeps his entrepreneurial hand in everything the company does. "It turns out doing the things you enjoy and having fun with them often create the best message."

Questions for Critical Thinking

1. Do you think TOMS' One for One business model is sustainable in the long term? Why or why not?

2. Mycoskie says his customers provide "the best type of marketing you can have" because when asked about their footwear, "they never say 'TOMS.' They tell the whole story. They say, 'When I bought this pair of shoes, a child got a pair.'" What lesson do you think other socially responsible firms can learn from TOMS' business practices?

Sources: Company Web site, http://www.toms.com, accessed February 4, 2011; Tamara Schweitzer, "The Way I Work," *Inc.,* June 2010, pp. 113–115; Kellie Doligale, "Good for the Sole: Toms Founder Set to Visit UK," *The Kentucky Kernel* (University of Kentucky at Lexington), March 7, 2010, http://kykernel.com; Daniel Seberg, "Giving Kids Their First Pair of Shoes," *CBS News,* October 28, 2009, http://www.cbsnews.com; Karen Leo and Lindsay Goldwert, "TOMS Shoes Saving Lives, One Sole at a Time," *ABC News,* September 3, 2009, http://www.abcnews.com; Shannon Cook, "These Shoes Help Others Get a Step Up," *CNN.com,* March 25, 2009, http://www.cnn.com.

CASE 4.3 | ## Smart Design: Life Is In the Details

When you peel a potato or run your pizza cutter through to cut a slice, it's likely that you only notice the tool you are using if it doesn't work—if it sticks or snags, gouges the potato or tears the pizza crust. The team at Smart Design doesn't mind not being noticed. They operate quietly behind the scenes, developing a wide range of designs for products made and sold by companies around the world. They come up with designs that make everything from toothbrushes to automobiles function better in human hands. Smart Design engineers developed the

popular OXO Good Grips line of kitchen utensils as well as the SmartGauge instrument cluster for the Ford Fusion Hybrid.

"Smart Design is about designing products for people in their everyday life," explains Richard Whitehall, vice president of industrial design for Smart Design. "There are little things you might see in a product that you'd think, 'I wish I'd thought of that—it's a great idea.'" Sometimes it's the simplest or smallest detail in the engineering of a product that makes a difference in whether consumers will continue to use the product or purchase it again. Smart Design tries to make products that work well universally for a wide range of people in different situations. This is where the global challenge comes in—differences in cultural preferences, product use, language, and other factors can make universal product development difficult. But Smart Design has offices in both the U.S. and abroad, with testing locations in Europe and Asia, and employees representing more than 20 different countries.

Ted Booth, director of interactive design says, "Interactive design is anything with a 'chip' in it. I can't imagine approaching interactive design without a global perspective." Booth explains how Smart Design develops the design for a mobile phone. "The way people use it varies from country to country," he notes. "So what might look like a new feature in one country is really old hat in another." Booth observes that it is very common for consumers in Finland and South Korea to pay for most goods and services from their mobile phones, whereas this is not a common practice among U.S. consumers. Some of this practice is driven by industry standards, but much of it has to do with cultural expectations. "It's important to have a global perspective [in design] so you know the trends in other countries. You need to design and shape the experience to hit the market and bring something new to the market, but also adapt to individual markets," concludes Booth.

Booth describes his company's work on the "Q" control for HP—a single navigation controller that can be used across all HP products, ranging from TV remotes to printers to cameras. Smart Design tested the Q control in the U.S., Germany, Spain, and South Korea. Researchers discovered that, while a few local adaptations were necessary, there was one universal preference among all consumers: everyone needed a "back" button in order to go forward. Booth explains that there is a universal need for people to know that there is an escape, undo—or back—for every function in order for users to feel comfortable completing an interactive task.

Smart Design has an impressive list of worldwide clients, including Ford, Bell Canada, ESPN, World Kitchen, Microsoft, Samsung, and Kellogg's among many others. The firm has won many accolades, including nationally recognized design awards. But Smart Design remains focused on the details. The firm recently developed the Reach Wondergrip children's toothbrush for Johnson & Johnson when it became apparent that traditional children's toothbrushes were just scaled down from the adult models. Kids couldn't hold them easily and were less likely to brush their teeth. The new Wondergrip children's model changed the industry standard for children's toothbrushes—and brushing habits. Smart Design also developed a women's sports watch for Nike—based on needs and preferences of women runners. And there's that line of kitchen tools that make food preparation and cooking just a little bit easier and more fun.

Richard Whitehall, who actually began his career working for a firm that manufactured mountaineering gear, describes the importance of design in every product used by consumers. "We were trying to think of a situation people were in and trying to design a product in a way that people from different countries—whether they were stuck in the Alps or on a boat—could use in all these different situations." Whether you are climbing a mountain in Switzerland or cutting your pizza in Boston, you want your gear to work flawlessly—and that is the goal of Smart Design.

Questions for Critical Thinking

1. Ted Booth and Richard Whitehall mention some of the cultural barriers that Smart Design faces in developing products for worldwide use. Give examples of other barriers the firm might face in international trade.

2. Describe what you believe would be the best level of involvement for Smart Design to have when doing business in Europe. Remember to take into consideration the European Union.

3. Smart Design already has a presence in South Korea. How might the firm best approach developing products for the market in India? In China?

4. Do you believe it is possible to develop truly universal products? Why or why not?

Sources: Smart Design Web site, http://www.smartdesignworldwide.com, accessed June 21, 2011; "National Design Awards," *Cooper-Hewitt, National Design Museum,* http://www.nationaldesignawards.org, accessed August 19, 2010; Alissa Walker, "Biomimicry Challenge: For IBM, Smart Design Draws Water Inspiration from Ecosystems," *Fast Company.com,* May 17, 2010, http://www.fastcompany.com.

GREENSBURG, KS
New Ways to Be a Better Town

Greensburg, Kansas, had been struggling for years. Located along Highway 54, a major trucking route, the town was merely a pit stop for people on their way somewhere else. It did have a few tourist attractions: the Big Well, the world's largest hand-dug well, and a 1,000-pound meteorite that fell from the sky in 2006.

Lonnie McCollum, the town's mayor, had been looking into ways to breathe new life into the town. McCollum wanted to add a little vintage charm to its quaint Main Street, but could not raise the money. And he had launched a campaign to put the "green" back in Greensburg by promoting green building technology. But the idea, which many residents associated with hippies and tree-huggers, did not go over well.

Then everything changed. "My town is gone," announced Town Administrator Steve Hewitt on May 5, 2007, after surveying the damage caused by a devastating tornado. "I believe 95 percent of the homes are gone. Downtown buildings are gone, my home is gone." With a clean slate and 700 homes to replace, Hewitt vowed to rebuild Greensburg using sustainable materials. He believed the town had a unique opportunity to control its environmental impact and reduce operating costs through increased energy efficiency.

"What if we turned this tragedy into something beautiful?" asked resident Dan Wallach in a new business plan he wrote shortly after the disaster. Wallach and his wife had long been interested in sustainable Green living. Using their experience in developing nonprofits, the two launched Greensburg GreenTown, an organization designed to support Greensburg's green building efforts through education, fund-raising, and public relations management.

One of Wallach's favorite new projects was BTI Greensburg, the local John Deere dealership. Owners Kelly and Mike Estes had decided to replace their ruined building with an energy-efficient, technologically state-of-the-art showroom featuring radiant heat, solar energy, passive cooling, and wind power. With corporate support from John Deere, BTI Greensburg would become a flagship green dealership.

Long-term plans for Greensburg include a business incubator, to help displaced businesses get back on their feet and bring new businesses to town; a green industrial park, green museum, and green school system; green building codes and zoning restrictions; and a community of green homes and businesses.

Questions

After viewing the video, answer the following questions:

1. In what ways is the town of Greensburg like any other business?
2. In what ways is the town of Greensburg a socially responsible organization?
3. What might be the effects of the town's new green building guidelines on residents and businesses? On the regional economy?
4. What kind of business is Greensburg GreenTown? How does its structure differ from John Deere's?

LAUNCHING YOUR
[Global Business and Economics Career]

In Part 1, "Business in a Global Environment," you learned about the background and current issues driving contemporary business. The part includes four chapters covering such issues as the changing face of business, business ethics and social responsibility, economic challenges facing contemporary business, and competing in world markets. Business has always been an exciting career field, whether you choose to start your own company, work at a local business, or set your sights on a position with a multinational corporation. But today's environment is especially attractive because businesses are expanding their horizons to compete in a global economy—and they need dedicated and talented people to help them accomplish their goals. In fact, professional and business service jobs are found in some of the fastest-growing industries in the U.S. economy and are projected to grow by more than 23 percent over a decade.[1] So now is the time to explore several different career options that can lead you to your dream job. Each part in this text profiles the many opportunities available in business. Here are a few related to Chapters 1 through 4.

If you're good at number crunching and are interested in how societies and companies function, then maybe a career as an *economist* is in your future. Economists study how resources are allocated, conduct research by collecting and analyzing data, monitor economic trends, and develop forecasts.

They look into such vital areas as the cost of energy, foreign trade and exchange between countries, the effect of taxes, and employment levels—both from a big-picture national or global viewpoint and from the perspective of individual businesses. Economists work for corporations to help them run more efficiently, for consulting firms to offer special expertise, or for government agencies to oversee economic decision making. Typically, advanced degrees are needed to climb to top-level positions. Economists usually earn about $83,590 per year.[2]

Or perhaps you are interested in global business. Companies increasingly search the world for the best employees, supplies, and markets. So you could work in the United States for a foreign-based firm such as Nokia or Toyota; abroad in Australia, Asia, Europe, or Latin America for a U.S.-based firm such as Microsoft; or with overseas coworkers via computer networks to develop new products for a firm such as General Electric. With technology and telecommunications, distance is no longer a barrier to conducting business. Global business careers exist in all the areas you'll be reading about in this text—business ownership, management, marketing, technology, and finance.

Global business leaders are not born but made—so how can you start on that career path? Here are the three areas that businesses consider when selecting employees for overseas assignment:

- *competence*—including technical knowledge, language skills, leadership ability, experience, and past performance

- *adaptability*—including interest in overseas work, communication and other personal skills, empathy for other cultures, and appreciation for varied management styles and work environments

- *personal characteristics*—level of education, experience, and social compatibility with the host country.[3]

Solid experience in your field or company ranks at the top of the list of needed skills. Firms want to send employees who have expertise in their business and loyalty to the firm to represent them overseas. Those who obtain their master's of business administration (MBA) degree are reaping rewards financially: in a recent year, the average median base salary for MBA graduates reached $78,820.[4] Companies are reluctant to send new graduates abroad immediately. Instead, they invest in training to orient employees to the new assignment.

Knowledge of and interest in other languages and cultures is the second-highest priority. Businesspeople need to function smoothly in another society, so they are selected based on their familiarity with other languages and cultures. Because China is a business hotspot, some people have become fluent in Mandarin Chinese to boost their career prospects. Also, some school systems are offering Chinese language classes in addition to their standard offerings of Spanish, French, German, and Russian.

Finally, employees are evaluated on their personal characteristics to be certain that they will fit well in their new country. A person's talent is still foremost in making assignments, but executives with cross-cultural skills are in high demand.[5]

Career Assessment Exercises in Economics and Global Business

1. With the ups and downs in the U.S. economy, economists have been highlighted in the news. The head of the Federal Reserve, Benjamin Bernanke, has been managing the country's general financial condition. To get an idea of the role economists play in a federal government agency, research Bernanke's background and qualifications. Assess how he is performing at the Fed. Now make a list of your own skills. Where is

there a match of your skills to his? What do you need to change?

2. To see the effect of the global economy in your community, go to a major retailer. Look at the number of different countries represented in the products on the shelves. Compare your list with those of your classmates to see who found the most countries and what goods those countries provided. Go online to research the career opportunities at the retailer's Web site.

3. To learn more about other countries, do research online for a country in which you are interested. Here are some sources that may be useful:

- *The World Factbook*, published by the Central Intelligence Agency, https://www.cia.gov/library/publications/the-world-factbook/. This publication, updated yearly, contains a wealth of information about countries—geography and climate, population statistics, cultural and political information, transportation and communications methods, and economic data.

- *BusinessWeek* magazine, http://www.businessweek.com. The Web site has links to Asia and Europe, where you can explore breaking news or information on global companies.

- Online news sites Yahoo! News and Google News, http://news.yahoo.com and http://news.google.com. Both of these online news sites have links to global business news. The Yahoo! site has a link for "Business" and then "Global Economy." The Google site has a "Business" link and then lists sites for many countries and many languages.

Write a one-page summary of what you found. Make a list of abilities you would need to function well as a businessperson in that country. Concentrate on the areas of competence, adaptability, and personal characteristics. Now formulate a plan to gain those skills.

PART [2]

Starting and Growing Your Business

Chapter 5

Learning Objectives

1. Distinguish between small and large businesses.
2. Discuss the contributions of small businesses to the economy.
3. Discuss the survival rate of small businesses.
4. Describe the features of an effective business plan.
5. Describe funding opportunities for small businesses, including the role of the Small Business Administration (SBA).
6. Explain how franchising can provide opportunities for both franchisors and franchisees.
7. Outline the three main legal forms of business ownership, and summarize the features of businesses owned by employees and families, as well as not-for-profit organizations.
8. Describe public and collective (cooperative) business ownership.
9. Identify types of corporations and the levels of corporate management.
10. Describe mergers, acquisitions, and joint ventures.

Forms of Business Ownership and Organization

Masterfile

Dewey Weber Makes Surfing a Family Business

©Weber Family Photo

There are lots of small surfboard shops and manufacturers dotting the U.S. coast. The nature of the sport—and the industries that support it—keep it a small, close-knit community. After all, there are only a limited number of people with regular access to waves. Surfers like to think of themselves as free spirits riding the waves. And those who manufacture and sell surfing equipment are usually surfers. So, when a sea change occurs in the surfing business environment, its effect may be felt worldwide. The Weber family, manufacturers of Dewey Weber Surf Boards since the 1960s, knows this all too well. Several years ago, Clark Foam, the main supplier of the raw material for surfboards, shut its doors. Roughly 80 percent of U.S. surfboard manufacturers—including Dewey Weber—relied on Clark's polyurethane "blanks" for their boards. Companies were forced either to lay off workers or close their shops altogether. Manufacturers in Asia, who could make surfboards for less, began to ramp up production and send their less-expensive finished products to the United States "I think a lot of domestic producers have been hurting because of the economy," notes Shea Weber, president of Dewey Weber Surf Boards and son of company founder, the late Dewey Weber. "But what affected us more was the day Clark Foam closed."

The Weber family remained undaunted by the situation, determined instead to turn it into a wave of good fortune. "What I have seen over the last few years is more design development, more willingness to create exciting shapes and designs than I ever remember before," observes Weber. They decided to remain true to their brand's high quality and focused on their ability as a small business to create custom surfboards to meet the needs of dedicated surfers. In addition, Dewey Weber gives its shapers—the artisans who actually make the boards—the freedom to innovate with new designs, shapes, and materials. As a customer, "being able to work with your shaper will never lose its value," Shea Weber points out. "The ability to customize any aspect of your new board is something that I believe was taken for granted for too many years. Remember, not all surfboards are created equal, and neither are all surfers."

Building a relationship with their customers is just as important to the Weber family as building surfboards. The company's motto, "Stay Close to the Soul," refers to family, customers, and the total surfing experience. "We believe that the 'Weber Experience' is more than just a high quality surfboard," says Weber. A company representative takes the time to get to know each customer's needs and wants before taking an order for a board.

Running a family business—and keeping it successful as it transfers from one generation to the next—is a challenge. But Shea Weber says that the secret to his company's longevity is the fact that "at Dewey Weber, our employees and our customers are our extended family. We believe on some level we are all connected, and that if you treat people like family, you will be linked on a much higher level than just an employee or just a customer." So when the next big economic wave breaks, Dewey Weber Surf Boards plans to be riding its crest.[1]

Do you hope to work for a big company or a small one? Do you plan to start your own business? If you're thinking about striking out on your own, you're not alone. On any given day in the United States, more people are in the process of starting a new business than getting married or having a baby. But before you enter the business world—as an employee or an owner—you need to understand the industry in which a company operates, as well as the size and framework of the firm's organization. For example, Dewey Weber Surf Boards is a small, family-owned business that operates in an industry that was recently affected by the availability of raw materials. Its customers include hobbyists and professional athletes. It's important to remember that most larger businesses—like Ford and Apple—began as small businesses.

Several variables affect the way a business is organized, including how easily it can be set up, access to financing, tolerance of financial risk, and strengths and weaknesses that exist in competing firms, as well as the strengths and weaknesses of your firm.

This chapter begins by focusing on small-business ownership, including the advantages and disadvantages of small-business ventures, the contributions of small business to the economy, and the reasons small businesses fail. The chapter examines the services provided by the U.S. government's Small Business Administration, the role of women and minorities in small business, as well as alternatives for small businesses such as franchising.

The chapter then moves on to an overview of the forms of private business ownership—sole proprietorships, partnerships, and corporations. In addition, the features of businesses owned by employees and families, as well as not-for-profit organizations, are discussed. Public and collective ownership are examined. The chapter concludes with an explanation of structures and operations typical of larger companies and a review of the major types of business alliances.

Most Businesses Are Small Businesses

Although many people associate the term *business* with corporate giants such as Kraft, Target, Disney, and ExxonMobil, 98 percent of all U.S. companies are considered small businesses. These firms have generated 64 percent of new jobs during the past 15 years and employ more than half of all private-sector (nongovernment) workers.[2] Small business is also the launching pad for new ideas and products. They hire 40 percent of high-tech workers such as scientists, engineers, and computer programmers, who devote their time to developing new goods and services.[3]

What Is a Small Business?

How can you tell a small business from a large one? The Small Business Administration (SBA), the federal agency most directly involved with this sector of the economy, defines a **small business** as an "independent business having fewer than 500 employees." However, those bidding for government contracts or applying for government assistance may vary in size according to industry. For example, small manufacturers fall in the 500-worker range, whereas wholesalers must employ fewer than 100. Retailers may generate up to $6 million in annual sales and still be considered small businesses, while farms or other agricultural businesses are designated small if they generate less than $750,000 annually.[4]

Logan Green and John Zimmer started Zimride, a California-based service that would let carpoolers connect with each other online. At the beginning, Zimride's customers, who pay about $10,000 a year to use the platform, were mostly colleges and universities, but its 35 clients now include Cigna and Walmart. Zimride employs six people and reports that its annual revenues are around $400,000—and making a profit.[5] Already, Zimride has won awards for its green innovations. By SBA standards, Zimride is a small business.

Because government agencies offer benefits designed to help small businesses compete with larger firms, small-business owners want to determine whether their companies meet the standards for small-business designation. If it qualifies, a company may be eligible for government loans or for government purchasing programs that encourage proposals from smaller suppliers. With assistance like this, Zimride might eventually expand to other areas of the country and become a larger business.

small business independent business with fewer than 500 employees, not dominant in its market.

Typical Small-Business Ventures

Small businesses have always competed against each other as well as against some of the world's largest organizations. ModCloth, an online clothing retailer founded by husband-and-wife team Eric and Susan Koger, does both. Launched while the owners were still in college, the business offers trendy fashions by independent designers. The Kogers say they compete successfully against other clothing e-tailers because they develop a close relationship with designers and sell their inventory well before they have to pay for it. Their 104 employees are mostly young women who buy the types of clothes ModCloth sells. Because of these relationships, ModCloth can compete against other clothing e-tailers of any size.[6]

The past 15 years have seen a steady erosion of small businesses in some industries as larger firms have bought out small independent businesses and replaced them with larger operations. The number of independent home improvement stores has fallen dramatically as Lowe's and other national discounters have increased the size and number of their stores. But as Table 5.1 reveals, the businesses least likely to be gobbled up are those that sell personalized services, rely on certain locations, and keep their overhead costs low.

Nonfarming-related small firms create more than half the nation's gross domestic product (GDP). In the past, many of these businesses focused on retailing or

In California, Logan Green and John Zimmer started Zimride, a service that lets carpoolers connect with each other online. This small business creates a social network for sharing rides.

Courtesy John Zimmer, Zimride, Inc.

Table 5.1 Business Sectors Most Dominated and Least Dominated by Small Firms

MOST LIKELY TO BE A SMALL FIRM	FEWER THAN 20 WORKERS
Home builders	97%
Florists	97%
Hair salons	96%
Auto repair	96%
Funeral homes	94%

LEAST LIKELY TO BE A SMALL FIRM	FEWER THAN 20 WORKERS
Hospitals	14%
Nursing homes	23%
Paper mills	33%
Electric utilities	38%
Oil pipelines	38%

Source: U.S. Census Bureau, "Number of Firms, Number of Establishments, Employment, and Annual Payroll by Employment Size of the Enterprise for the United States, All Industries," accessed March 31, 2011, http://www.census.gov.

a service industry such as insurance. More recently, however, small firms have carved out an important niche for themselves: providing busy consumers with customized services that range from pet-sitting to personal shopping. These businesses cater to the needs of individual customers in a way that big firms can't.

As Figure 5.1 shows, small businesses provide most jobs in the construction, agricultural services, wholesale trade, services, and retail trade industries. Retailing to the consumer is another important industry for small firms. Retailing giants such as Amazon and Macy's may be the best-known firms, but smaller stores and Web sites outnumber them. And these small firms can be very successful, as the owners of ModCloth illustrate, often because they can keep their overhead expenses low.

Small business also plays a significant role in agriculture. Although most farm acreage is in the hands of large corporate farms, most U.S. farms are owned by individual farmers or families, not partners or shareholders.[7] The family farm is a classic example of a small-business operation. It is independently owned and operated, with a limited number of employees, including family members. Cider Hill Farm in Massachusetts is one such farm. Three generations of the Cook family operate the farm together—it produces fruit and vegetables, including a wide variety of cooking and eating apples from its orchards, and honey from its on-site beehives. In addition, Cider Hill makes its own fresh cider and cider doughnuts every day and operates a well-stocked country store on the property. During growing season, the farm hosts field trips for schools, offers hay rides, and creates a corn maze in its fields. All of these activities contribute to the income of the farm. The Cooks are also dedicated to environmentally friendly farming technologies. Cider Hill operates three wind turbines and uses solar cells to help power its buildings.[8]

Fifty-two percent of small businesses in the United States are **home-based businesses**—firms operated from the residence of the business owner. There are about 16 million such businesses in the United States.[9] People who operate home-based firms often do so because this type of work allows them more control over their business as well as their personal time. Whether you're a morning person or a night owl, in many cases you can structure your business hours accordingly. Access to the Internet and availability of communications devices such as the BlackBerry and other smart phone technology makes it convenient to run a home-based business. Freedom from overhead costs such as leasing office or warehouse space is another major attraction of home-based businesses. Drawbacks include isolation and less visibility to customers—except, of course, if your customers visit you online. In that case, they don't care where your office is located.

Many small-business start-ups are more competitive because of the Internet. The Internet doesn't guarantee success—there are so many Web sites that a small firm needs to find ways to make its online presence effective. But establishing a Web site is generally less expensive than opening a retail store and reaches a broader spectrum of potential customers. Connecticut-based eBeanstalk.com is an online toy store. How does this small business compete with the likes of online giants such as Amazon and Toys 'R' Us? The company specializes in learning toys that "help plant the seeds that help children grow." Two teams of experts (including 700 moms) hired by eBeanstalk evaluate more than 10,000 toys from manufacturers, to narrow the selection down to around 600 of what they consider to be the best learning toys. That group may shrink even further. Only the selected toys are included on the site. Consumers appreciate this screening process, knowing they can go straight to eBeanstalk for the toys they want.[10]

American business history is filled with inspirational stories of great inventors who launched companies in barns, garages, warehouses, and attics. For young visionaries such as Apple Computer founders Steve Jobs and Steve Wozniak, the logical option for transforming their technical idea into a commercial reality was to begin work in a family garage. The impact of today's entrepreneurs, including home-based businesses, is discussed in more depth in Chapter 6.

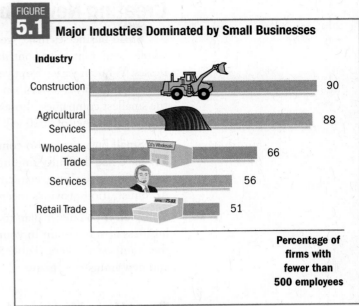

FIGURE 5.1 Major Industries Dominated by Small Businesses

Industry

Construction	90
Agricultural Services	88
Wholesale Trade	66
Services	56
Retail Trade	51

Percentage of firms with fewer than 500 employees

Source: Office of Advocacy, U.S. Small Business Administration, "Small Business Profile: United States," accessed March 31, 2011, http://www.sba.gov/advocacy.

home-based business firm operated from the residence of the business owner.

Assessment Check ✔

1. How does the Small Business Administration (SBA) define *small business?*

2. In what industries do small businesses play a significant role?

Contributions of Small Business to the Economy

Small businesses form the core of the U.S. economy. Businesses with fewer than 500 employees generate more than half the nation's gross domestic product (GDP). These companies account for more than 97 percent of known U.S. exporters, shipping more than 30 percent of all exported goods overseas each year.[11] Small firms are credited with U.S. competitiveness in a number of world markets.[12]

Creating New Jobs

Small businesses make tremendous contributions to the U.S. economy and to society as a whole. One impressive contribution is the number of new jobs created each year by small businesses. While it varies from year to year, on average three of every four new jobs are created by companies with fewer than 500 employees.[13] A significant share of these jobs are created by the smallest companies, those with four or fewer employees. It is hopeful that the Small Business Jobs Act of 2010 will give a further boost to these numbers.[14]

Small businesses also contribute to the economy by hiring workers who traditionally have had difficulty finding jobs at larger firms, such as women returning to the workforce, former welfare recipients, and workers with various challenges. The Small Business Administration provides incentives for companies to hire these types of workers.

Even if you never plan to start your own company, you will probably work for a small business at some point in your career, particularly at the beginning. Small firms often hire the youngest workers. Table 5.2 illustrates some of the newest jobs within both traditional and new industries, many of which can be found in small businesses.

Creating New Industries

Small firms give businesspeople the opportunity and outlet for developing new ideas. Sometimes these new ideas become entirely new industries. Many of today's largest and most successful firms, such as Whole Foods, Google, and Amazon, began as small businesses. Facebook co-founders Mark Zuckerberg, Dustin Moskovitz, Chris Hughes, and Eduardo Saverin launched their new business from their college dorm room. Within a few years, Facebook had logged more than 500 million active users and positioned itself as a leader in the new industry of social networking.[15]

New industries are sometimes created when small businesses adapt to provide needed services to a larger corporate community. Corporate downsizing has created a demand for other businesses to perform activities previously handled by in-house employees. These

Table
5.2 New Job Opportunities for Small Businesses

INDUSTRY	JOBS
Green energy and construction	Wind-farm engineers; solar installers and technicians; green-collar specialists and consultants; green construction specialists
Healthcare	Home health care specialists; informatics specialists (workers cross-trained in healthcare and technology)
Self-improvement	Yoga instructors and studio managers; spa managers; nutrition specialists
Education technology	Tech and trade school teachers and administrators; creators of online education materials; specialists in software and hardware for use in schools
Other growing industries	Temporary staffing agencies; repair services; fast-casual dining

Sources: Jason Del Ray and Tamara Schweitzer, "Best Industries for Starting a Business Right Now," *Inc.,* accessed January 4, 2011, http://www.inc.com; "11 Big Ideas to Watch in 2011," *Inc.,* accessed January 4, 2011, http://www.inc.com; "Small Business Jobs Act of 2010," *U.S. Small Business Administration,* http://www.sba.gov, accessed January 4, 2011.

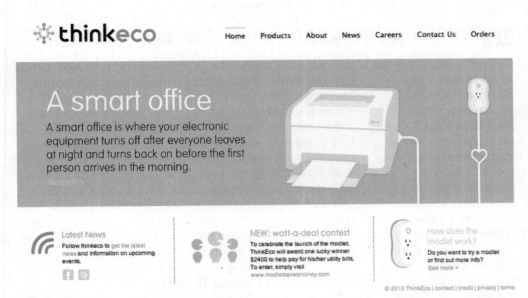

New industries can be created when small businesses adapt to shifts in consumer interests and preferences. ThinkEco wants to make it easier for consumers to save money and energy.

support businesses may become an industry themselves. The need for wireless communication devices and services to support businesses has resulted in a proliferation of small businesses to fill this niche.

New industries can be created when small businesses adapt to shifts in consumer interests and preferences. For example, the idea of offering accessories for men—dubbed "mancessories" by marketers—has taken root in the U.S. economy, with small businesses at the forefront selling goods ranging from shapewear for bellies to bacon-flavored toothpicks. Online sites and newsletters like UrbanDaddy and Thrillist that feature such products report accelerating growth.[16]

Finally, new industries may be created when both the business world and consumers recognize a need for change. The recent emphasis on environmental responsibility—ranging from recycling and reuse of goods to reducing the amount of energy consumed—has fostered a whole new industry of green goods and services, many produced by small companies. ThinkEco is a small firm that has created a device that regulates outlet power, allowing its business customers to save as much as 20 percent on their energy bills. ClearEdge Power offers a fuel-cell power energy system that is particularly effective for other small businesses, such as boutique hotels and restaurants.[17] The "Going Green" feature describes one small-business owner who is pouring her passion and talent into environmentally responsible services.

Innovation

Small businesses are adept at developing new and improved goods and services. Innovation is often the entire reason for the founding of a new business. In a typical year, small firms develop twice as many product innovations per employee as larger firms. They also produce 13 times more patents per employee than larger firms.[18]

Green Mama: Small Business with a Big Message

The Green Mama isn't a mythical figure. She's a consultant, writer, and environmentalist who believes the world can be made a more sustainable place one mom at a time. Manda Aufochs Gillespie had been living and promoting an environmentally conscious lifestyle for several years when she was featured in a *Chicago Tribune* article. Suddenly, Gillespie became a guru for like-minded parents who simply wanted to improve the health and lives of their families while reducing their impact on the planet. Since then she has launched a Web site, www.thegreenmama.com; hosts a weekly playgroup/seminar for parents called the Green Mama Café; writes a regular blog; consults for daycare businesses and educational institutions; gives workshops; appears on television; and provides everyday advice to consumers. She's also a mom.

The Web site is the center of Gillespie's green universe. "The site is for people who are trying to be green parents in any major city," she explains. "It's a tool for living." Visitors to the site can get shopping tips for the best cloth diapers, learn how to clean their floors with white vinegar (instead of commercial cleaners), become informed about buying local produce, and get the real scoop on everything from the effectiveness of hand sanitizers to the cost of organic produce. No question is too elementary for Gillespie. In addition, she offers suggestions for saving money—as well as reducing waste—such as re-gifting a gently used child's garment to another child instead of buying a new piece of clothing for a birthday gift.

How does all of this philosophy translate to business? It's not just the $5 that each mom pays to attend one of Gillespie's workshops in person at the Green Mama Café, or any consulting fees she may charge. It's the fact that, according to marketing experts, these moms represent a group of about 20 million consumers who are beginning to demand green goods and services. It's not just cloth diapers and natural floor cleaners. These consumers are now scrutinizing every item they put in their reusable shopping bags. If they have to pay a bit more for those products, they will—because in many cases they are saving money elsewhere. "It turns out that what saves money also saves resources and what is better for the environment can also make parenting easier, if you have the right mindset," says one mom who attends Gillespie's Green Mama seminars. It is estimated that these green moms wield nearly $210 billion in purchasing power—something that manufacturers, media, and service providers have begun to notice.

Questions for Critical Thinking

1. Manda Gillespie is part of a movement of small businesses that are creating a whole new industry: green goods and services for parents. What factors do you believe will contribute to the success of this movement? What pitfalls might they face?

2. As a consumer, have you embraced any green goods or services? Why or why not? Have they been offered by small or large companies?

Sources: Green Mama Web site, http://www.thegreenmama.com, accessed March 31, 2011; "Green Your School in 5 Easy Steps," Green Mama blog in *Chicago Now*, September 6, 2010, http://www.chicagonow.com/blogs; "Four-Leaf Clovers, Leprechauns and Mamas," *YoYo Mama*, March 17, 2010, http://www.yoyomama.ca.

Assessment Check ✓

1. What are the three key ways in which small businesses contribute to the economy?

2. How are new industries formed?

Key 20th-century innovations developed by small businesses include the airplane, the personal computer, soft contact lenses, and the zipper. Innovations that already drive small businesses in the 21st century include those that fall into social networking, security, and green energy industries. The "Business Etiquette" feature offers tips for using online social networking successfully.

Why Small Businesses Fail

Small businesses play a huge role in the U.S. economy. But one of the reasons they are so successful is also the reason they may fail—their founders are willing to take a risk. Some of the most common shortcomings that plague a small firm include management inexperience, inadequate financing, and the challenge of meeting government regulations.

As Figure 5.2 shows, 7 out of every 10 new businesses survive at least two years. About 50 percent make it to the five-year mark. But by the tenth year, 82 percent will have closed.[19] Let's look a little more closely at why this happens.

Management Shortcomings

One of the most common causes of small-business failure is the shortcomings of management. These may include lack of people skills, inadequate knowledge of finance, inability to track inventory or sales, poor assessment of the competition, or simply the lack of time to do everything required. Whereas large firms often have the resources to recruit specialists in areas such as marketing and finance, the owner of a small business often winds up wearing too many hats at once.

This could result in bad decision making that could end in the firm's failure. Krispy Kreme was once a small business that expanded too fast as a result of poor decisions made by management. The company's near failure had nothing to do with the quality of its doughnuts. Instead, as the company grew bigger, so did its debt. Allegations of management misconduct were made. Meanwhile, consumers turned their tastebuds toward more healthful snacks and breakfast foods produced by competitors. Now under new management, operating at a leaner size, and rolling out strategies such as new offerings and upgraded packaging for its grocery store products, the firm is recovering.[20]

Owners of small businesses can increase their chances of success if they become educated in the principles of business; know the industry in which they intend to operate; develop good interpersonal skills; understand their own limitations; hire motivated employees; and seek professional advice on issues like finance, regulations, and other legal matters.[21]

Inadequate Financing

Money is the foundation of any business. Every business—large or small—needs a certain amount of financing in order to operate, thrive, and grow. Another leading problem of small businesses is inadequate financing. First-time business owners often assume that their firms will generate enough funds from their initial sales to finance continuing operations. But building a business takes time. Products need to be developed, employees have to be hired, a Web site must be constructed, distribution has to be determined, office or retail space might have to be secured,

BusinessEtiquette

How to Use Social Networking in Your Job Search

Online social networking is likely part of your every day life. But you can put this technology to powerful use when you are looking for a job. During one recent year, networking sites such as LinkedIn registered about 1 million new users per month. Worried about getting lost in the social-networking shuffle? Use a few simple tips from the pros to help you stand out from the millions of other job-seekers who have discovered the benefits of social networking.

- *Research a network before jumping in.* Some networks, such as Facebook, exist mostly to connect friends with each other. Others, such as LinkedIn, have a stronger employment focus. Twitter, on the other hand, attracts both types of users. To adopt the right approach—and make the most of a site—learn something about it before you log on to search for an employer.

- *Complete your online profile.* Help prospective employers by filling out your online profile. Update your bio as frequently as possible. Provide a link to your own blog or Web page if you have one. Don't mix business and personal information in one account or profile. Post an accurate photo of yourself, not one of a pet or you as a child.

- *Share information.* Be willing to share information about companies or career opportunities with like-minded job-seekers. You can help an online recruiter find the right person—even if it's not you.

- *Search for people.* Look for companies that interest you, then try to make connections with friends, family members, classmates, alumni—anyone who might be able to help you establish contact within those companies. A specific job might not be available at the moment, but a personal connection could help you when that job does open up.

- *Respect privacy.* Just as you only want to present certain information about yourself online, respect the privacy of potential employers and colleagues. Familiarize yourself with the privacy settings of a social networking site and abide by them.

Sources: DeLynn Senna, "Recruiters Reveal Pet Peeves About Job Seekers," *Yahoo! Hot Jobs*, http://www.monster.com, accessed March 21, 2011; Daer Glista, "Etiquette Tips for Social Networking," *EzineMark.com*, December 1, 2010, http://business.ezinemark.com; Lydia Ramsay, "Social Networking Etiquette Tips," February 24, 2010, http://mts.typepad.com/blog.

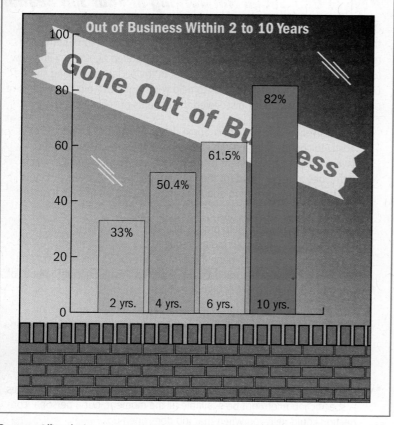

FIGURE 5.2 Rate of Business Failures

Out of Business Within 2 to 10 Years

Gone Out of Business

	2 yrs.	4 yrs.	6 yrs.	10 yrs.
	33%	50.4%	61.5%	82%

Source: Office of Advocacy, U.S. Small Business Administration, "Frequently Asked Questions: Advocacy Small Business Statistics and Research," accessed March 31, 2011, www.sba.gov.

and so forth. Most small businesses—even those with minimal start-up costs—sometimes don't turn a profit for months or even years.[22]

Although there are stories about business founders starting firms with just a few hundred dollars loaned by a friend or with a cash advance from a credit card, commercial banks and other financial institutions are the largest lenders to small businesses, accounting for 65 percent of total traditional credit to small firms. This type of financing includes credit lines and loans for nonresidential mortgages, vehicles, specialized equipment, and leases.[23]

Figure 5.3 shows that despite their relatively high interest rates, credit cards do remain an important source of financing for small businesses. The heaviest users of credit cards for business financing are firms with fewer than ten employees. Inadequate financing can compound management shortcomings by making it more difficult for small businesses to attract and keep talented people. Typically, a big company can offer a better benefits package and a higher salary.

With less money to spend on employees, marketing, inventory, and other business costs, successful small companies need to be creative. Cindy Francis is a former interior designer. When the real estate market took a downturn, she knew she had to come up with another way to make a living. So she followed her passion for baking and started Fantastic Fortunes—giant fortune cookies baked fresh from all natural ingredients, with customized fortunes for any occasion, ranging from new baby to retirement. A local New Hampshire restaurant owner gave Francis the use of his kitchen one day a week, in which she whipped up her cookies and packaged them. Local media picked up on Francis's unique product and within a year, Fantastic Fortunes had a following among consumers, upscale grocery markets, and corporate events. Francis and her husband, who helps out with the business, say their current goal is to reach 100 outlets for the Fantastic Fortunes cookies.[24]

Government Regulation

Small-business owners cite their struggle to comply with government regulations as one of the biggest challenges they face. Some firms fold because of this burden alone. Paperwork costs account for billions of small-business dollars each year. A large company can better cope with requirements for forms and reports. Larger firms often find that it makes economic sense to hire or contract with specialists in specific types of

©Fantastic Fortune Cookies

Cindy Francis from Fantastic Fortunes took a unique fortune cookie recipe from her home and turned it into a successful business.

regulation, such as employment law and workplace safety regulations. By contrast, small businesses often struggle to absorb the costs of government paperwork because of their more limited staff and budgets. The smallest firms—those with fewer than 20 employees—spend 45 percent more per employee than larger firms just to comply with federal regulations.[25]

Recognizing the burden of regulation on small businesses, Congress sometimes exempts the smallest companies from certain regulations. For example, small businesses with 49 or fewer employees are exempt from the Family and Medical Leave Act, which gives employees up to 12 weeks of unpaid leave each year to take care of a newborn child, adopt a child, or care for a family member who has serious health problems.[26] Most small-business owners comply with employment and other laws, believing that such compliance is ethically correct and fosters better employee relations than trying to determine which regulations don't apply to a small business.

Taxes are another burdensome expense for a small business. In addition to local, state, and federal income taxes, employers must pay taxes covering workers' compensation insurance, Social Security payments, and unemployment benefits. Although large companies have similar expenses, they generally have more resources to cover them. But there are also tax incentives designed to help small businesses. These incentives cover a broad range including tax credits for use of biodiesel and renewable fuels, increased research activities, pension plan start-up, and access for individuals with disabilities.[27]

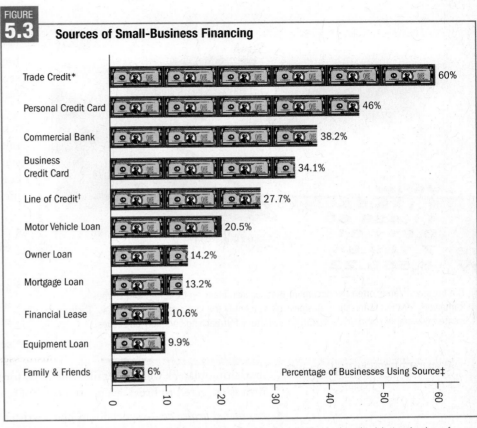

FIGURE 5.3

Sources of Small-Business Financing

Source	Percentage
Trade Credit*	60%
Personal Credit Card	46%
Commercial Bank	38.2%
Business Credit Card	34.1%
Line of Credit†	27.7%
Motor Vehicle Loan	20.5%
Owner Loan	14.2%
Mortgage Loan	13.2%
Financial Lease	10.6%
Equipment Loan	9.9%
Family & Friends	6%

Percentage of Businesses Using Source‡

*Trade credit is purchasing goods or equipment from a supplier who finances the purchase by delaying the date of payment for those goods.

†A line of credit is an agreement between a bank and a borrower, indicating the maximum amount of credit the bank will extend to the borrower.

Note: Total exceeds 100 percent because businesses typically use more than one source of financing.

Source: Small Business Administration, Office of Advocacy, "Financing Patterns of Small Firms," accessed January 3, 2011, http://www.sba.gov/advocacy; Susan Coleman, "Free and Costly Trade Credit: A Comparison of Small Firms," Academy of Entrepreneurial Finance, February 2008, www.google.com, accessed June 23, 2010.

The Business Plan: A Foundation for Success

Large or small, every business needs a plan in order to succeed. While there are tales of firms launched from an idea scribbled on a napkin at a restaurant or sketched out on graph paper in a dorm room, the idea must be backed by a solid plan in order to become reality. A **business plan** is a written document that provides an orderly statement of a company's

The business plan is often the document that secures financing for a firm and creates a framework for the organization. Business plans identify the firm's mission and goals. They create measurable standards and outline a strategy for reaching company objectives.

Dimitrije Paunovic/iStockphoto

goals, the methods by which it intends to achieve these goals, and the standards by which it will measure its achievements. The business plan is often the document that secures financing for a firm and creates a framework for the organization.

Business plans give the organization a sense of purpose. They identify the firm's mission and goals. They create measurable standards and outline a strategy for reaching company objectives. A typical business plan includes the following sections:

- an *executive summary* that briefly answers the who, what, where, when, why, and how questions for the business

- an *introduction* that includes a general statement of the concept, purpose, and objectives of the proposed business

- separate *financial* and *marketing sections* that describe the firm's target market and marketing plan as well as detailed financial forecasts of the need for funds and when the firm is expected to break even—the level of sales at which revenues equal costs

- *résumés of principals*—especially in plans written to obtain financing.

Within this structure, an effective business plan contains the written soul of a firm. A good plan addresses the following issues:

- *The company's mission and the vision of its founders.* Look at the home page of any firm's Web site and you will find its mission. At the Web site for TOMs Shoes, visitors learn that "TOMs shoes was founded on a simple premise: With every pair you purchase, TOMs will give a pair of new shoes to a child in need. One for one. Using the purchasing power of individuals to benefit the greater good is what we're all about."[28] This simple declaration states why the company was founded and what it intends to accomplish.

- *An outline of what makes the company unique.* Why start a business that's just like hundreds of others? An effective business plan describes what distinguishes the firm and its products from the rest of the pack. TOMs Shoes illustrates a unique business model with its "one-for-one" donation program.

- *The customers.* A business plan identifies who the firm's customers will be and how it will serve their needs.

- *The competition.* A business plan addresses its existing and potential competitors as legitimate entities, with a strategy for creating superior or unique offerings. Studying the competition can provide valuable information about what works and what doesn't in the marketplace.

- *Financial evaluation of the industry and market conditions.* This knowledge helps develop a credible financial forecast and budget.

- *Assessment of the risks.* Every business undertaking involves risks. A solid business plan acknowledges these and outlines a strategy for dealing with them.[29]

Assessment Check ☑

1. What are the five main sections of a business plan?

2. Why is an effective business plan important to the success of a firm?

Whether a firm's intention is to revolutionize an entire industry on a global scale or improve the lives of children by providing them with shoes, the business plan is a major factor in its success. For more detailed information on how to write a business plan, see Appendix D, "Developing a Business Plan," on page A-43.

Assistance for Small Businesses

An important part of organizing a small business is financing its activities. Once a business plan has been created, various sources can be tapped for loans and other types of financing. These include government agencies as well as private investors. In the scramble for dollars, sometimes government allocation of funds to certain firms is subject to criticism, as discussed in the "Solving an Ethical Controversy" feature.

Small Business Administration

Small businesses can benefit from using the resources provided by the **Small Business Administration (SBA)**. The SBA is the principal government agency concerned with helping small U.S. firms, and it is the advocate for small businesses within the federal government. More than 2,100 employees staff the SBA's Washington headquarters and its regional and field offices.[30] The SBA is "committed to helping small businesses, which are the backbone of the nation's economy, thrive. Working closely with a wide range of lending partners across the country, SBA has developed a number of financial programs that address the various needs of small businesses."[31]

Small Business Administration (SBA) principal government agency concerned with helping small U.S. firms.

Phil McCarton/Reuters/Landov LLC

Fisker Automotive received government loans to build a plug-in hybrid sports car called the Karma. That sounds like a win–win situation—investment in alternative energy vehicles, creation of new jobs, rejuvenation of the auto industry—but the new car will be built in Finland and priced around $89,000, out of reach for the average car buyer.

Solving an Ethical Controversy

Good Karma or Bad Karma?

During the recent economic downturn, many businesses—large and small—received funds from the federal government to survive and ultimately grow. One such business was Fisker Automotive, a California start-up automaker that received $528 million in government loans to build a plug–in hybrid sports car called the Karma. That sounds like a win-win situation for everyone—investment in vehicles powered by alternative energy, the creation of new jobs, rejuvenation of the auto industry. But the allocation has its critics, largely because the new car will be built in Finland—and will be priced at about $89,000, out of reach for the average car buyer.

Should federal funds be allocated to support firms that manufacture luxury goods overseas?

PRO

1. According to Fisker Automotive, no federal funds will be used for operations overseas. Instead, much of the loan money will be used for the purchase of components from U.S. suppliers, as well as engineering and design, which will be done in the U.S. The Department of Energy estimates that the loans will save or create about 5,000 jobs.

2. Although the Karma carries a hefty sticker price, the design of the car should attract buyers who might otherwise purchase traditional sports cars whose fuel consumption and emissions are high. Fisker claims that with projected tax credits, the Karma will ultimately cost around $39,000.

CON

1. Investing in a product that can only be purchased by the wealthiest car buyers is not an equitable distribution of government funds. "This is not for average Americans," argues a spokesperson for Citizens Against Government Waste. "It's a status symbol thing."

2. Other firms, including those that applied for much smaller loans to develop alternatively powered vehicles at a lower price point, were rejected by the government. More companies could have been supported, with more jobs created, and more hybrid cars could have been sold to average car buyers if the funds had been distributed more equitably.

Summary

Fisker has pledged to repay the government loans with interest and to offer a superior product to luxury car buyers. The firm claims that the launch of the Karma, the world's first production plug-in hybrid car, will "put the American auto industry ahead of foreign competition." But detractors say that federal funds should be reserved for firms that produce goods and services to benefit a wider range of consumers. Recently Fisker announced that it would partner with the Chinese Grand Automotive Group to distribute, market, and service the Karma in China.

Sources: Company Web site, http://karma.fiskerautomotive.com, accessed March 31, 2011; Tiffany Hsu, "Fisker Automotive to Sell Electric Vehicles in China and Start U.S. Deliveries in Spring," *Los Angeles Times,* December 15, 2010, http://latimesblogs.latimes.com; Sebastian Blanco, "After a Visit to Fisker HQ, Jim Motavalli Frustrated by Lack of Information," *Autoblog Green,* August 18, 2010, http://green.autoblog.com; "Gore-Backed Car Firm Gets Large U.S. Loan," *The Wall Street Journal,* September 25, 2009, http://onlinewsj.com.

Financial Assistance from the SBA Contrary to popular belief, the SBA seldom provides direct business loans. Nor does it provide outright grants to start or expand small businesses.[32] Instead, the SBA *guarantees* small-business loans made by private lenders, including banks and other institutions. To qualify for an SBA-backed loan, borrowers must be "unable to secure conventional commercial financing on reasonable terms and be a 'small business' as defined by SBA size standards."[33] Direct SBA loans are available in only a few special situations, such as natural disaster recovery and energy conservation or development programs. Under the 2009 Recovery Act, the SBA temporarily eliminated specific loan fees and raised the guarantee level on some of its loans.[34] The previously mentioned Small Business Jobs Act of 2010 was also intended to make more capital available to entrepreneurs and small business owners.

The SBA also guarantees **microloans** of up to $35,000 to start-ups and other very small firms. The average loan is $13,000 with a maximum term of six years.[35] Microloans may be used to buy equipment or operate a business but not to buy real estate or pay off other loans.

microloans small-business loans often used to buy equipment or operate a business.

These loans are available from nonprofit organizations located in most states. Other sources of microloans include the federal Economic Development Administration, some state governments, and certain private lenders, such as credit unions and community development groups. The most frequent suppliers of credit to small firms are banks.

Small-business loans are also available through SBA-licensed organizations called *Small Business Investment Companies (SBICs)*, which are run by experienced venture capitalists. SBICs use their own capital, supplemented with government loans, to invest in small businesses. Like banks, SBICs are profit-making enterprises, but they are likely to be more flexible than banks in their lending decisions. Large companies that used SBIC financing when they were small start-ups include Apple, Federal Express, and Staples.

Other Specialized Assistance Although government purchases represent a huge market, small companies have difficulty competing for this business with giant firms, which employ specialists to handle the volumes of paperwork involved in preparing proposals and completing bid applications. Today, many government procurement programs set aside portions of government spending for small companies; an additional SBA role is to help small firms secure these contracts. With set-aside programs for small businesses, up to 23 percent of certain government contracts are designated for small businesses.

Every federal agency with buying authority must maintain an Office of Small and Disadvantaged Business Utilization to ensure that small businesses receive a reasonable portion of government procurement contracts. To help connect small businesses with government agencies, the SBA's Web site offers Central Contractor Registration, which includes a search engine for finding business opportunities as well as a chance for small businesses to provide information about themselves. Set-aside programs are also common in the private sector, particularly among major corporations.

In addition to help with financing and government procurement, the SBA delivers a variety of other services to small businesses. It provides information and advice through toll-free telephone numbers and its Web site, http://www.sba.gov. Through its Small Business Training Network, the SBA offers free online courses; sponsors inexpensive training courses on topics such as taxes, networking, and start-ups in cities and small towns throughout the nation; and provides a free online library of more than 200 SBA publications and additional business resources. Business owners can find local resources by logging on to the SBA Web site and searching for SBA partners in their region. Local resource partners include small-business development centers, women's business centers, U.S. export assistance centers, and veterans business outreach centers.[36]

Local Assistance for Small Businesses

In conjunction with the federal government or on their own, state and local governments often have programs in place to help small businesses get established and grow. One such region is Washington state's Thurston County. The Thurston County Economic Development Council was founded more than 25 years ago with the mission of "creating a vital and sustainable economy throughout our County that supports the livelihood and values of our residents."[37] The Thurston County EDC provides information and assistance in business planning, licenses and registrations, taxes, and employment considerations. In addition, the council works to connect local businesses with each other and with industry experts, create marketing messages that attract new businesses and customers, and ensure that Thurston County plays an important role in the region's economy.[38] Organizations like the Thurston County EDC offer important resources and links for small businesses around the country.

Business Incubators Some community agencies interested in encouraging business development have implemented a concept called a **business incubator** to provide low-cost shared business facilities to small start-up ventures. See the "Hit and Miss" feature to read about Turning Technologies' incubator experience. A typical incubator might section off space in an abandoned plant and rent it to various small firms. Tenants often share clerical staff, computers, and other business services. The objective is that, after a few months or years, the fledgling business will be ready to move out and operate on its own.

More than 1,400 business incubator programs operate in the United States, with about 7,000 worldwide. Ninety-four percent are run by not-for-profit organizations focused on economic development. Nearly half of all incubators focus on new technology businesses, and more than half operate in urban areas.[39]

Private Investors

A small business may start with cash from a personal savings account or a loan from a family member. But small-business owners soon begin to look for greater sums of money in order to continue operating and eventually grow. They may want to continue with assistance from private investors. **Venture capital**—money invested in the small business by another business firm or group of individuals in exchange for an ownership share—can give the small business a boost. As the economy has improved recently, so has the confidence of venture capitalists. The National Venture Capital Association reports that more than half of venture capitalists express optimism about the near future and expect to focus on information technology in general, focusing on consumer Internet and digital media, cloud computing, and mobile/telecom. These investors are tough in their requirements for a solid business plan and expect small-business owners to run lean operations.[40]

Shama Kabani researched the power of social networking suggesting that businesses could use these tools to market their goods and services. When she couldn't convince larger corporations of this powerful tool, she started her own full-time online consulting firm.

Small-Business Opportunities for Women and Minorities

In the United States today, more than 10 million firms are owned by women, employing more than 13 million workers and generating nearly $2 trillion in sales. In fact, 40 percent of all privately held companies are owned by women. Further, nearly 2 million businesses are owned by women of color, employing 1.2 million people and generating $165 billion in annual revenues.[41]

Women, like men, have a variety of reasons for starting their own companies. Some have a unique business idea that they want to bring to life. Others decide to strike out on their own when they lose their jobs or become frustrated with the bureaucracies in large companies. When Shama Kabani wrote her master's thesis on the power of social networking, her research suggested that businesses could use these tools to market their goods and services. But when she pitched her idea to a large consulting firm, the company rejected it as a fad. So Kabani set out on her own. She founded her own full-time online consulting firm, which is now called The Marketing Zen Group. The company is positioned as a full-service digital marketing firm that is dedicated to offering other small firms strategies and implementations for operating on the Internet. Clients include such diverse organizations as K9 Cuisine, Arthur Murray Dance Schools, and Phoneraiser.[42]

Turning Technologies Creates High-Tech Jobs

Young companies that grow and add jobs to boost their local economies make a lot of people happy about their success. That's why so many people are smiling in Youngstown, Ohio, since a new technology company came to town.

Helped along by a business organization that provides start-up tech firms with free rent and utilities, Turning Technologies was founded in Youngstown. Its breathtaking growth brought dozens of new jobs to a city with 18 percent unemployment that is haunted by the decline of its old steel mills. Turning pays corporate income taxes on more than $30 million annual revenue, and it has already been called the fastest growing privately held software company in the United States—ranked at 18th overall. The firm boasts more than 6,500 clients, and more than a million people use its audience-response products.

Audience-response systems are the wireless keypads you've probably seen spectators using on TV game shows to register their opinions or answers to questions. Thanks to Turning's affordable hardware and the availability of both its free and licensed software programs, teachers from kindergarten through college are now enjoying the benefits of audience-response technology. Instructors can ask questions in class using other programs like PowerPoint, Blackboard, and WebCT; have students key in answers—anonymously or not—using their remotes; and instantly collate the responses to see how many students answered correctly.

Government agencies and not-for-profit organizations also use the systems for their training programs. "Audience involvement boosts focus and comprehension levels," says Turning's CEO Mike Broderick, and instructors agree. "It gives you the opportunity to reteach if you need to and then move on if you don't," says one middle school teacher. Adds a school principal about applications of the Turning program, "We have some teachers that are working hard to find the many avenues they can go beyond. You're really only limited by your creativity."

And it gets better. "Not only can we identify how each student is responding," says Turning's vice president for education sales, "but we can compile that data by classroom, by building, and by district and tag the data to specific standards." Among the impressive results already confirmed is "an increase of 15 points in test scores when our technology is used frequently and effectively."

Most of Turning's 120 employees are young Ohioans who enjoy some of the same benefits as their Silicon Valley counterparts, such as in-house foosball and air hockey for work breaks. The firm takes pride in being the kind of success story people have long thought "doesn't happen here." It has had double- or triple-digit growth since its launch. "I would not be surprised to see Turning Technologies at 2,000 workers in three to four years," says the CEO of the organization that helped the company get its start. The release of new products, including the program called TurningKey, will help spur this growth. TurningKey allows the creation of digital keys for new or existing tests or quizzes and the delivery of self-paced assessments to participants via another new product, ResponseCard NXT.

The bottom line? Good products that are affordable, easy to use, and well marketed can help small companies become engines of growth and job creators.

Questions for Critical Thinking

1. Why might a company such as Turning Technologies locate outside the high-tech hotspots where most firms are? List some possible advantages and disadvantages to that strategy.

2. What should a company like Turning Technologies do if, as it grows, it needs to hire people with technical experience or skills that are hard to find in a depressed area?

Sources: Company Web site, http://www.turningtechnologies.com, accessed March 31, 2011; Anthony Ponce and Shawna Prince, "Classrooms Evolve Beyond Chalkboards, No. 2 Pencils," *NBC Chicago*, December 1, 2010, http://www.nbcchicago.com/news; "Turning Technologies Releases New Polling Tools," *Successful Meetings*, October 26, 2010, http://www.successfulmeetings.com; "In Ohio, You Can Maintain Your Balance No Matter How Fast You Grow," *Ohio Means Business*, http://www.ohiomeansbusiness.com, accessed April 2, 2010.

In other cases, women leave large corporations when they feel blocked from opportunities for advancement. Sometimes this occurs because they hit the so-called glass ceiling. Because women are more likely than men to be the primary caregivers in their families, some may seek self-employment as a way to achieve flexible working hours so they can spend more time with their families.

Many nationwide business assistance programs are geared toward women-owned firms. Among the programs offered by the Small Business Administration are the Contract Assistance for Women Business Owners program, which teaches women how to market to the federal government, and the Women's Network for Entrepreneurial Training, which matches experienced businesswomen with women trying to get started. Organizations like the Center for Women's Business Research provide information, contacts, and other resources as well.

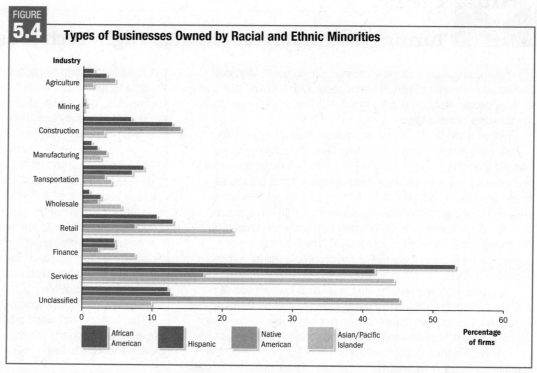

FIGURE 5.4 Types of Businesses Owned by Racial and Ethnic Minorities

Legend: African American · Hispanic · Native American · Asian/Pacific Islander

Industry (vertical axis): Agriculture, Mining, Construction, Manufacturing, Transportation, Wholesale, Retail, Finance, Services, Unclassified

Percentage of firms (horizontal axis): 0, 10, 20, 30, 40, 50, 60

Source: Data from Office of Advocacy, U.S. Small Business Administration, "Minorities in Business," accessed January 3, 2011, http://www.sba.gov/advocacy.

Assessment Check ✔

1. What are the various ways the SBA helps small businesses?

2. What are business incubators?

3. Why are small businesses good opportunities for women and minorities?

franchising contractual business arrangement between a manufacturer or other supplier, and a dealer such as a restaurant operator or retailer.

Business ownership is also an important opportunity for America's racial and ethnic minorities. In recent years, the growth in the number of businesses owned by African Americans, Hispanics, and Asian Americans has far outpaced the growth in the number of U.S. businesses overall. Figure 5.4 shows the percentages of minority ownership in major industries. The relatively strong presence of minorities in the services and retail industries is especially significant because these industries contain the greatest number of businesses.

The Small Business Administration has programs targeted to minority-owned small businesses. One is the Mentor-Protégé Program, which pairs an established, financially healthy business with a small minority-owned business. Through the program, the protégé firm gains technical and financial assistance as well as subcontract support.[43]

Franchising

Franchising combines large and small businesses into a single entity and is a major factor in the growth of small businesses. **Franchising** is a contractual business arrangement between a manufacturer or another supplier and a dealer such as a restaurant operator or a retailer. The contract specifies the methods by which the dealer markets the product of the supplier. Franchises can involve both goods and services, such as food and wait staff. The top ten franchises are shown in Table 5.3.

Starting a small, independent company can be a risky, time-consuming endeavor, but franchising can reduce the amount of time and effort needed to expand. The parent company has already developed and tested the concept, and the brand is often familiar to prospective customers.

Table 5.3	Top Ten Franchises		
1 Hampton Hotels (hotel)	**4** 7-Eleven (convenience store)	**7** Vanguard Cleaning Systems (commercial cleaning)	
2 Ampm (convenience store/ gas station)	**5** Supercuts (hair salon)	**8** Servpro (insurance/disaster cleaning & restoration)	
3 McDonald's (fast-food restaurant)	**6** Days Inn (hotel)	**9** SUBWAY (submarine sandwiches & salads)	
		10 Denny's (full-service family restaurant)	

Source: "2011 Franchise 500," *Entrepreneur*, http://entrepreneur.com/franchise500, accessed March 31, 2011. http://www.entrepreneur.com/franchises/franchise500/index.html with permission of Entrepreneur Media, Inc. © 2011 by Entrepreneur Media, Inc. All rights reserved.

The Franchising Sector

Franchised businesses are a huge part of the U.S. economy, accounting for nearly 50 percent of all retail sales. The International Franchise Association reported that franchising is responsible for about 900,000 businesses at a gross value of nearly $870 billion. The business sectors currently experiencing the most growth are quick-service restaurants, retail food, and personal and business services.[44]

Franchising overseas is also a growing trend for businesses whose goal is to expand into foreign markets. It seems that anywhere you go in the world, you can get a McDonald's burger. But other international franchises are becoming more common. Baskin-Robbins, now owned by Dunkin' Brands, has more than 5,800 stores worldwide, including such countries as Australia, Canada, China, Japan, Malaysia, and Russia. There are more than 850 Baskin-Robbins ice cream stores in Japan, and 2,700 in the United States.[45]

International franchises are becoming more common. Baskin-Robbins has more than 6,000 stores in more than 35 countries including Australia, Canada, China, Japan, Vietnam, and Russia.

Franchising Agreements

The two principals in a franchising agreement are the franchisee and the franchisor. The individual or business firm purchasing the franchise is called the **franchisee**. This business owner agrees to sell the goods or services of the franchisor under certain terms. The **franchisor** is the firm whose products are sold by the franchisee. For example, McDonald's Corp. is a franchisor. Your local McDonald's restaurant owner is a franchisee.

Franchise agreements can be complex. They involve an initial purchase fee plus agreed-upon start-up costs. Because the franchisee is representing the franchisor's brand, the franchisor usually stipulates the purchase of certain ingredients or equipment, pricing, and marketing efforts. McDonald's is one of the more expensive franchises—total start-up costs

franchisee individual or business firm purchasing a franchise.

franchisor firm whose products are sold to customers by the franchisee.

can run more than $1 million. In contrast, the total start-up cost for a SUBWAY franchise may reach $228,000.[46] For this reason, businesspeople interested in purchasing a more expensive franchise often group together.

Benefits and Problems of Franchising

As with any other type of business arrangement, franchising has its benefits and drawbacks. Benefits for the franchisor include opportunities for expansion that might not otherwise be available. A franchised business can move into new geographic locations, including those overseas, at less expense and with the advantages of employing local workers and businesspeople who have intimate knowledge of consumer preferences. A good franchisor can manage a much larger and more complex business—with fewer direct employees—than could be handled without the franchise option. In most cases, franchisees will be highly attentive to the management of their franchises because of their stake as business owners. If the business is run efficiently, the franchisor will probably experience a greater return on investment than if the firm were run entirely as a company-owned chain of retail shops, restaurants, or service establishments.

Finally, a successful franchisor can usually negotiate better deals on ingredients, supplies, even real estate, because of its financial strength. This clout also benefits the franchisees if the savings are passed along to them.[47]

Franchising can be the quickest way to become a business owner. Some people contend that it's also the least risky. Franchisees have the benefit of name recognition—McDonald's, SUBWAY, Pizza Hut, and Super 8—that usually includes a loyal following of customers. The management system of the franchisor has already been established and a performance record is readily available. In addition, franchisors provide a wide range of support to franchisees, including financing, assistance in obtaining a location, business training, supplies, and marketing tools.[48]

Franchisees themselves say they are drawn to the idea of franchising because it combines the freedom of business ownership with the support of a large company. Like other small-business owners, franchisees want to make their own business decisions and determine their own work hours. And they want to have more control over the amount of wealth they can possibly accumulate, as opposed to what they might earn in a salaried job. In an economic slowdown, franchisees might very well be executives who have been laid off during a downsizing or reorganization effort by previous employers. These are highly trained and motivated businesspeople looking for a way to restart their careers.[49] Sometimes the ideas or successes of individual franchisees can benefit the entire company, as was the case with SUBWAY, described in the "Hit & Miss" feature.

Franchising can have its downside—for both franchisors and franchisees. For the franchisor, if its franchisees fail in any way, that failure reflects on the brand as well as the bottom line. The same holds true for the franchisee: a firm that is mismanaged at the top level can spell doom for the smaller business owners who are actually running the individual units. Krispy Kreme, mentioned earlier, is an example of a franchised company that stumbled due to overexpansion. When a firm initially decides to offer franchise opportunities, the company overall may lose money for several years. Of course, in offering franchise opportunities, the franchisor—often the founder of what was once a small business—loses absolute control over every aspect of the business. This uncertainty can make the process of selecting the right franchisees to carry out the company's mission a difficult one.[50]

One Small Franchise Produces One Big Idea

SUBWAY has enjoyed top franchise rankings consistently for more than a decade. With 30,000 sandwich restaurants in nearly 80 countries, the firm is poised to become the single largest fast-food chain in the world. But SUBWAY is made up of many small businesses—franchises—and sometimes what seems to be an insignificant idea on the part of one franchisee can change the shape of the entire organization.

Stuart Frankel is one such franchisee, and his idea was simple: on weekends, charge a special price of $5 for a footlong SUBWAY sandwich. Since this was a price decrease of about $1 per sandwich, it took awhile for Frankel and two other local Florida SUBWAY franchisees to convince corporate leadership that the idea was a good one. The economy was sluggish, food costs had crept upward, and SUBWAY shops were virtually empty because consumers were eating at home instead of dining out. Frankel's employees stood idle at their stations as sandwich sales declined. But after pressing hard, Frankel got the OK from corporate headquarters. From there, a chain reaction began.

"I like round numbers," quipped Frankel about the $5 price. SUBWAY customers liked the number too. As soon as the special pricing was announced, they returned in droves. Sales increased by double digits. Employees made sandwiches as fast as their fingers could fly. Meanwhile, SUBWAY's corporate marketing team pushed the $5 promotion nationwide—franchises from New York to New Orleans began offering $5 footlongs. When the initial four-week time span for the promotion was up, marketing executives extended it to seven weeks. When that time lapsed, they decided to extend it indefinitely, with eight footlong sandwiches from which to choose, including the Meatball Marinara, Cold Cut Combo, Veggie Delite, and Black Forest Ham.

Something else happened. Demand for the $5 footlongs was so great that franchise owners began to experience shortages of certain ingredients. They couldn't get enough bread, turkey, ham, or tuna. One franchisee recalls being in a panic. "The whole thing took on a life of its own," notes Jeff Moody, CEO of SUBWAY's advertising arm.

With one motion, Stuart Frankel struck a chord with consumers who were looking for ways to enjoy themselves and stretch each dollar at the same time. "There are only a few times when a chain has been able to scramble up the whole industry, and this is one of them," notes restaurant consultant Jeffrey T. Davis. "It's huge." Sometimes a small idea is really big.

Questions for Critical Thinking

1. Why do you think Stuart Frankel's idea was so successful with consumers? Would it have been as successful during different economic circumstances? Why or why not?

2. A franchise company is only as good as its franchisees. And a franchisee's success is based in part on the decisions and support of corporate leadership. If the $5 footlong promotion had failed, how do you think the outcome would have affected Frankel's franchise business? How might it have affected SUBWAY?

Sources: Company Web site, http://www.subway.com, accessed March 31, 2011; "2011 Franchise 500," *Entrepreneur*, http://www.entrepreneur.com, accessed March 31, 2011; "SUBWAY Shows Off Outfits Made from Restaurant Chain's Recycled Packaging," September 10, 2010, http://www.subway.com; "$5 Footlong Subs Are an Every Day Value at SUBWAY Restaurants," April 1, 2010, http://www.subway.com.

The franchisee faces an outlay of cash in the form of an initial investment, franchise fees, supplies, maintenance, leases, and the like. The most expensive franchises generally are those that involve hotels and resorts, which can run in the millions.[51] Start-up costs for McDonald's restaurants can also top several million, depending on the location. For this reason, it is not unusual for groups of businesspeople to purchase a franchise (or several franchise locations).[52] Payments to the franchisor can add to the burden of keeping the business afloat until the owner begins to earn a profit. Choosing a low-cost start up such as Heaven's Best might be a good alternative. Heaven's Best, a cleaning company that specializes in carpet and upholstery for both businesses and residences. The firm offers top-quality methods, equipment, and products along with training, brand awareness, and marketing tools. Businesspeople can purchase a franchise for an investment of as little as $25,000.[53] But it is important for franchisees always to evaluate carefully how much profit they can make once their cost obligations are met.

Because franchises are so closely linked to their brand, franchisors and franchisees must work well together to maintain standards of quality in their goods and services. If customers are unhappy with their experience at one franchise location, they might avoid stopping at another one several miles away, even if the second one is owned and operated by someone else. This is especially true where food is involved. The discovery of tainted meat or produce at one franchise restaurant can cause panic to spread throughout the entire chain. A potential franchisee would be wise to thoroughly research the financial performance and reputation of the franchisor, using resources such as other franchisees and the Federal Trade Commission.

Some franchisees have found the franchising agreement to be too confining. As the saying goes, you can't add a tuna salad sandwich to the menu at McDonald's no matter how many stores you own. The agreements are usually fairly strict, and that generally helps to maintain the integrity of the brand. Toward this end, some franchise companies control promotional activities, select the site location, or even become involved in hiring decisions. But these activities may seem overly restrictive to some franchisees, especially those seeking independence and autonomy.

Restrictions can also cost franchisees more than they feel is fair. Recently, the National Franchise Association, a group that represents more than 80 percent of Burger King's U.S. franchisees, sued the hamburger company for forcing its members to offer consumers a $1 double cheeseburger on its menu, complying with the company's promotional efforts. While the $1 burger offering may seem like a great way to attract and serve hungry consumers, BK franchisees claim that the promotion has cost them a loss of at least 10 cents per burger. In other words, it costs most franchises $1.10 to make and serve a cheeseburger for which they must charge $1. However, a judge dismissed the lawsuit, siding with Burger King.[54]

Assessment Check ✓

1. What is the difference between a franchisor and a franchisee?
2. What are the benefits to both parties of franchising?
3. What are the potential drawbacks of franchising for both parties?

Forms of Private Business Ownership

Regardless of its size, every business is organized according to one of three categories of legal structure: sole proprietorship, partnership, or corporation. As Figure 5.5 shows, sole proprietorships are the most common form of business ownership, accounting for more than 70 percent of all firms in the United States. Although far fewer firms are organized as corporations, the revenues earned by these companies are 19 times greater than those earned by sole proprietorships.

Each legal structure offers unique advantages and disadvantages. But because there is no universal formula for every situation, some business owners prefer to organize their companies further as S corporations, limited-liability partnerships, and limited-liability companies. In some cases, corporations are owned by their employees.

In addition to the three main legal structures, several other options for ownership exist. These include employee-owned businesses, family-owned businesses, and not-for-profit organizations.

Sole Proprietorships

sole proprietorship business ownership in which there is no legal distinction between the sole proprietor's status as an individual and his or her status as a business owner.

The most common form of business ownership, the **sole proprietorship** is also the oldest and the simplest. In a sole proprietorship, no legal distinction separates the sole proprietor's status as an individual from his or her status as a business owner. Although sole proprietorships are common in a variety of industries, they are concentrated primarily among small businesses such as repair shops, small retail stores, and service providers such as plumbers, hair stylists, and photographers.

Sole proprietorships offer some unique advantages. Because such businesses involve a single owner, they are easy to form *and* dissolve. A sole proprietorship gives the owner maximum management flexibility, along with the right to all profits after payment of business-related bills and taxes. A highly motivated owner of a sole proprietorship directly reaps the benefits of his or her hard work.

Minimal legal requirements simplify entering and exiting a sole proprietorship. The owner registers the business or trade name—to guarantee that two firms do not use the same name—and takes out any necessary licenses. Local governments require certain licenses for businesses such as restaurants, motels or hotels, and retail stores. In addition, some occupational licenses require business owners to obtain specific insurance such as liability coverage.

Sole proprietorships are also easy to dissolve. This advantage is particularly important to temporary or seasonal businesses that set up for a limited period of time. It's also helpful if the owner needs or wants to close the business for any reason—say, to relocate or to accept a full-time position with a larger firm.

Management flexibility is another advantage of a sole proprietorship. The owner can make decisions without reporting to a manager, take quick action, and keep trade secrets. A sole proprietorship always bears the individual "stamp" or flair of its owner, whether it's a certain way of styling hair or the way a store window is decorated.

The greatest disadvantage of the sole proprietorship is the owner's personal financial liability for all debts of the business. Also, the business must operate with financial resources limited to the owner's personal funds and money that he or she can borrow. Such financing limitations can keep the business from expanding.

Another disadvantage is that the owner must wear many hats, handling a wide range of management and operational responsibilities. He or she may not have expertise in every area, which may inhibit the firm's growth or even cause the firm damage. In addition, sole proprietors may face a higher chance of being audited by the Internal Revenue Service than other types of business owners. Finally, a sole proprietorship usually lacks long-term continuity because a change in personal circumstances or finances can terminate the business on short notice.

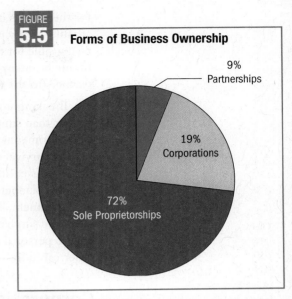

FIGURE 5.5

Forms of Business Ownership

- 9% Partnerships
- 19% Corporations
- 72% Sole Proprietorships

Source: Data from U.S. Census Bureau, "Statistical Abstract," accessed January 3, 2011, http://www.census.gov.

Partnerships

Another option for organizing a business is to form a partnership. The Uniform Partnership Act, which regulates this ownership form in most states, defines a **partnership** as an association of two or more persons who operate a business as co-owners by voluntary legal agreement. Many small businesses begin as partnerships between co-founders.

Partnerships are easy to form. All the partners need to do is register the business name and obtain any necessary licenses. Having a partner generally means greater financial capability and someone to share in the tasks and decision making of a business. It's even better if one partner has a particular skill such as design, while the other has a knack for financials.

Most partnerships have the disadvantage of being exposed to unlimited financial liability. Each partner bears full responsibility for the debts of the firm, and each is legally liable

partnership association of two or more persons who operate a business as co-owners by voluntary legal agreement.

for the actions of the other partners. If the firm fails and is left with debt—no matter who is at fault—every partner is responsible for those debts. If one partner defaults, the others are responsible for the firm's debts, even if it means dipping into personal funds. To avoid these problems, many firms establish a limited-liability partnership, which limits the liability of partners to the value of their interests in the company.

Breaking up a partnership is more complicated than dissolving a sole proprietorship. Rather than simply withdrawing funds from the bank, the partner who wants out may need to find someone to buy his or her interest in the firm. The death of a partner also threatens the survival of a partnership. A new partnership must be formed, and the estate of the deceased is entitled to a share of the firm's value. To ease the financial strains of such events, business planners recommend life insurance coverage for each partner, combined with a buy-sell agreement. The insurance proceeds can be used to repay the deceased partner's heirs and allow the surviving partner to retain control of the business. Because partnerships are vulnerable to personal conflicts that can quickly escalate, it's important for partners to choose each other carefully—not just because they are best friends—and try to plan for the future.

Corporations

corporation legal organization with assets and liabilities separate from those of its owner(s).

A **corporation** is a legal organization with assets and liabilities separate from those of its owner(s). A corporation can be a large or small business. It can be Ford Motor Corp. or a local auto repair shop.

Corporate ownership offers considerable advantages. Because a corporation is a separate legal entity, its stockholders have only limited financial risk. If the firm fails, they lose only the money they have invested. This applies to the firm's managers and executives as well. Because they are not the sole proprietors or partners in the business, their personal savings are not at risk if the company folds or goes bankrupt. This protection also extends to legal risk. Class-action suits involving automakers, drug manufacturers, and food producers are filed against the companies, not the owners of those companies. Though companies such as GE recently experienced class-action suits, their employees and stockholders were not required to pay the settlements from their own bank accounts.[55]

Corporations offer other advantages. They gain access to expanded financial capabilities based on the opportunity to offer direct outside investments such as stock sales. A large corporation can legally generate internal financing for many projects by transferring money from one part of the corporation to another.

One major disadvantage for a corporation is the double taxation of corporate earnings. After a corporation pays federal, state, and local income taxes on its profits, its owners (stockholders) also pay personal taxes on any distributions of those profits they receive from the corporation in the form of dividends.

S corporations corporations that do not pay corporate taxes on profits; instead, profits are distributed to shareholders, who pay individual income taxes.

S Corporations and Limited Liability Corporations
To avoid double taxation of business income while minimizing financial liability for their owners, many smaller firms (those with fewer than 100 stockholders) organize as **S corporations.** These companies can elect to pay federal income taxes as partnerships while retaining the liability limitations typical of corporations. S corporations are only taxed once. Unlike regular corporations, S corporations do not pay corporate taxes on their profits. Instead, the untaxed profits of S corporations are paid directly as dividends to shareholders, who then pay the individual tax rate. This tax advantage has resulted in a tremendous increase in the number of S corporations. Consequently, the IRS is closely auditing S corporations because some businesses don't meet the legal requirements to form S corporations.[56]

Business owners may also form **limited-liability companies (LLCs)** to secure the corporate advantage of limited liability while avoiding the double taxation characteristic of corporations. An LLC combines the pass-through taxation of a partnership or sole proprietorship with the limited liability of a corporation.

An LLC is governed by an operating agreement that resembles a partnership agreement, except that it reduces each partner's liability for the actions of the other owners. Corporations of professionals, such as lawyers, accountants, and physicians, use a similar approach, with the letters *PC* attached to the business name. LLCs appear to be the wave of the future. Immediately after the first LLC law was passed, most major CPA (certified public accountant) firms in the U.S. converted to LLC status. Today you'll see the LLC or PC designation attached to small businesses ranging from bowling alleys to veterinary hospitals. On a much larger scale, Amazon.com is also an LLC.

limited-liability corporation (LLC) corporation that secures the corporate advantage of limited liability while avoiding the double taxation characteristic of a traditional corporation.

Employee-Owned Corporations

Another alternative for creating a corporation is **employee ownership**, in which workers buy shares of stock in the company that employs them. The corporate organization stays the same, but most stockholders are also employees.

employee ownership business ownership in which workers buy shares of stock in the company that employs them.

The popularity of this form of corporation is growing. The number of employee ownership plans has increased dramatically. Today about 20 percent of all employees of for-profit companies report owning stock in their companies; approximately 25 million Americans own employer stock through *employee stock ownership plans (ESOPs)*, options, stock purchase plans, 401(k) plans, and other plans.

Several trends underlie the rise in employee ownership. One is that employees want to share in whatever profit their company earns. Another is that company executives want employees to care deeply about their firm's success and contribute their best effort. These firms remain committed to this kind of involvement and compensation for their workers. Because human resources are so essential to the success of a modern business, employers want to build their employees' commitment to the organization. However, managers also admit that often employees below the executive level are not as informed about the programs as they should be, and their companies could do a better job of educating employees at all levels.[57] Some of the country's most successful public corporations, including Procter & Gamble, Lowe's, and Southwest Airlines, have embraced employee ownership and watched their stock values hold up better than other companies.

Family-Owned Businesses

Family-owned firms are considered by many to be the backbone of American business. The Waltons and the Fords are viewed as pioneers because each of these firms—Walmart and Ford Motor Corp.—was once a small, family-owned company. Family-owned firms come in a variety of sizes and legal structures. But because of the complex nature of family relationships, family-owned firms experience some unique challenges.

Whether a family-owned business is structured as a partnership, limited liability corporation, or traditional corporation, its members must make decisions regarding succession, marriages and divorces, compensation, hierarchy and authority, shareholder control, and the like. Whereas some family members may prefer a loose structure—perhaps not even putting certain agreements in writing—experienced businesspeople caution that failing to choose the right legal structure for a family-owned firm can doom the business from the start.

Family-owned companies are considered by many to be the backbone of American business. Walmart's Walton family started with Walton's 5-10 store.

Jb Reed/Bloomberg/Getty Images, Inc.

"For family-owned businesses, especially those with multi-generational owners, lack of a formal structure is a frequent cause of turmoil and legal disputes which often result in very contentious litigation and, ultimately, the dissolution of the business," asserts one expert in family businesses.[58]

Succession is a major benefit—and drawback—to family-owned firms. On the one hand, a clearly documented plan for succession from one generation to the next is a huge source of security for the firm's continuity. But lack of legal planning, or situations in which succession is challenged, can cause chaos. In fact, only a small percentage of family-owned businesses survive into the second or even third generation.

A small family firm that has managed to thrive for five generations is Squamscott Beverages. Originally called Connermade, the company was founded in 1883 when William H. Conner began producing his own "tonic" beverage—a spruce beer that came in glass bottles with porcelain and wire stoppers. Conner ran the company until his son Alfred took over in 1911. Alfred remained in charge until 1948, when he handed the reins to his own son, Alfred Jr. Today, Tom Conner and his son Dan manage most aspects of running the firm, which is still headquartered on the family's rural property. Squamscott Beverages produces soda drinks in a variety of flavors, including birch beer, cola, cream, orange, grape, and ginger ale. Bottles are distributed to small grocery outlets, or customers can visit the bottling plant to select whatever flavors they want. Recently the company sent its first shipment of soda to California and is considering further expanding its distribution. "We have made it through the Great Depression," notes Dan Conner. "We made it through the early '80s housing crunch. We're always going to be here."[59] The Conners are not as famous or as wealthy as the Waltons or Fords, but the chance of their business surviving through future generations is strong.

Not-for-Profit Corporations

not-for-profit corporation organization whose goals do not include pursuing a profit.

The same business concepts that apply to commercial companies also apply to **not-for-profit corporations**—organizations whose goals do not include pursuing a profit. About 1.5 million not-for-profits operate in the United States, including charitable groups, social-welfare organizations, government agencies, and religious congregations. This sector also includes museums, libraries, hospitals, conservation groups, private schools, and the like.

Most states set out separate legal provisions for organizational structures and operations of not-for-profit corporations. These organizations do not issue stock certificates, because they pay no dividends to owners, and ownership rarely changes. They are also exempt from paying income taxes. However, they must meet very strict regulations in order to maintain their not-for-profit status.

City Year Inc. is a not-for-profit organization that supports community service efforts by young people in their late teens and early twenties. City Year has a number of programs in which volunteers can participate. Its signature program, the City Year Youth Corps, invites 1,750 volunteers between the ages of 17 and 24 to commit to a year of full-time community service in activities such as mentoring and tutoring inner-city school children, helping to restore and reclaim public spaces, and staffing youth summer camps. The organization also partners with for-profit corporations such as Timberland, Comcast, and Pepsi to fund and implement its efforts.[60]

Public and Collective Ownership of Business

Though most businesses in the U.S. are owned by the private sector, some firms are actually owned by local, state, or the federal government. Alaskan Railroad Corp., East Alabama Medical Center, and the Iowa Lottery are all government-owned businesses.[61]

In another type of ownership structure, groups of customers may collectively own a company. Recreational Equipment Inc. (REI) is a collectively owned retailer that sells outdoor gear and apparel. Finally, groups of smaller firms may collectively own a larger organization. Both of these collective ownership structures are also referred to as cooperatives.

Public (Government) Ownership

One alternative to private ownership is some form of *public ownership*, in which a unit or agency of government owns and operates an organization. In the United States, local governments often own parking structures and water systems. The Pennsylvania Turnpike Authority operates a vital highway link across the Keystone State. The federal government operates Hoover Dam in Nevada to provide electricity over a large region.

Sometimes public ownership results when private investors are unwilling to invest in a high-risk project—or find that operating an important service is simply unprofitable. The National Railroad Passenger Corporation—better known as Amtrak—is a for-profit corporation that operates inter-city passenger rail service in 46 states and the District of Columbia. Congress created Amtrak in the Rail Passenger Service Act of 1970, thereby removing from private railroads the obligation of transporting passengers, because passenger rail travel was generally unprofitable. In exchange, the private railroads granted Amtrak access to their existing tracks at a low cost. The Amtrak board of directors is made up of seven voting members appointed for five-year terms by the President of the United States.[62]

Collective (Cooperative) Ownership

Collective ownership establishes an organization referred to as a *cooperative* (or *co-op*), whose owners join forces to operate all or part of the activities in their firm or industry. Currently, there are about 100 million people worldwide employed by cooperatives.[63] Cooperatives allow small businesses to pool their resources on purchases, marketing, equipment, distribution, and the like. Discount savings can be split among members. Cooperatives can share equipment and expertise. During difficult economic times, members find a variety of ways to support each other.

Cooperatives are frequently found among agricultural businesses. Cabot Creamery is a cooperative of 1,500 small dairy farms spread throughout New England and upstate New York. Cabot is owned and operated by its members—farmers and their families. In addition, Cabot works with other cooperatives around the country to produce and distribute high-quality cheese, butter, and other dairy products.[64]

Assessment Check ✓

1. What are the key differences between sole proprietorships and partnerships?

2. What is a corporation?

3. What is the main distinction of a not-for-profit corporation?

Assessment Check ✓

1. What is public ownership?

2. What is collective ownership? Where are cooperatives typically found, and what benefits do they provide small businesses?

Organizing a Corporation

A corporation is a legal structure, but it also requires a certain organizational structure that is more complex than the structure of a sole proprietorship or a partnership. This is why people often think of a corporation as a large entity, even though it does not have to be a specific size.

Types of Corporations

Corporations fall into three categories: domestic, foreign, and alien. A firm is considered a *domestic corporation* in the state where it is incorporated. When a company does business in states other than the one where it has filed incorporation papers, it is registered as a *foreign corporation* in each of those states. A firm incorporated in one nation that operates in another is known as an *alien corporation* where it operates. Some firms—particularly large corporations with operations scattered around the world—may operate under all three of these designations.

Where and How Businesses Incorporate

Businesses owners who want to incorporate must decide where to locate their headquarters and follow the correct procedure for submitting the legal document that establishes the corporation.

Where to Incorporate Deciding where to incorporate—and establish headquarters—may be based on a number of factors. Most businesses want to be near their customers. Real estate prices as well as services such as public transportation and communications networks are other variables. Access to a good labor pool is another reason for choosing a location. Online businesses such as Amazon.com and eBay don't need to worry about positioning themselves near their customers, but they should consider the local labor pool.

Although most small- and medium-sized businesses are incorporated in the states in which they operate, a U.S. firm can actually incorporate in any state it chooses. The founders of large corporations, or of those that will do business nationwide, often compare the benefits—such as tax incentives—provided by each state. Some states are considered to be more "business friendly" than others. Delaware is one of the easiest states in which to incorporate.

The Corporate Charter Each state has a specific procedure for incorporating a business. Most states require at least three *incorporators*—the individuals who create the corporation. In addition, the new corporation must select a name that is different from names used by other businesses. Figure 5.6 lists the ten elements that most states require for chartering a corporation.

The information provided in the articles of incorporation forms the basis on which a state grants a *corporate charter*, which is the legal document that formally establishes a corporation. After

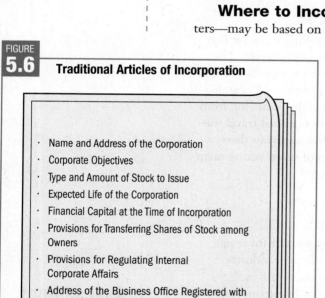

FIGURE 5.6

Traditional Articles of Incorporation

- Name and Address of the Corporation
- Corporate Objectives
- Type and Amount of Stock to Issue
- Expected Life of the Corporation
- Financial Capital at the Time of Incorporation
- Provisions for Transferring Shares of Stock among Owners
- Provisions for Regulating Internal Corporate Affairs
- Address of the Business Office Registered with the State of Incorporation
- Names and Addresses of the Initial Board of Directors
- Names and Addresses of the Incorporators

securing the charter, the owners prepare the company's bylaws, which describe the rules and procedures for its operation.

Corporate Management

Regardless of its size, every corporation has levels of management and ownership. Figure 5.7 illustrates those that are typical—although a smaller firm might not contain all five of these. These levels range from stockholders down to supervisory management.

Stock Ownership and Stockholder Rights

At the top of Figure 5.7 are **stockholders**. They buy shares of stock in the corporation, becoming part owners of it. Some companies, such as family businesses, are owned by relatively few stockholders, and the stock is generally unavailable to outsiders. In such a firm, known as a *closed* or *closely held corporation*, the stockholders also control and manage all of the company's activities. S.C. Johnson & Son is one such firm.

In contrast, an open corporation, also called a *publicly held corporation*, sells stock to the general public, establishing diversified ownership and often leading to a broader scope of operations than those of a closed corporation. Publicly held corporations usually hold annual stockholders' meetings. During these meetings, managers report on corporate activities, and stockholders vote on any decisions that require their approval, including elections of officers. Walmart holds the nation's largest stockholder meeting at the University of Arkansas Bud Walton Arena. Approximately 16,000 people attend. In addition to standard shareholder business, the Walmart meeting has featured celebrities and entertainers such as Tim McGraw, Mary J. Blige, and Jamie Foxx.

Stockholders' role in the corporation depends on the class of stock they own. Shares are usually classified as common or preferred stock. Although owners of **preferred stock** have limited voting rights, they are entitled to receive dividends before holders of common stock. If the corporation is dissolved, they have first claims on assets, once debtors are repaid. Owners of **common stock** have voting rights but only residual claims on the firm's assets, which means they are last to receive any income distributions. Because one share is typically worth only one vote, small stockholders generally have little influence on corporate management actions.

Board of Directors

Stockholders elect a **board of directors**—the governing body of a corporation. The board sets overall policy, authorizes major transactions involving the corporation, and hires the chief executive officer (CEO). Most boards include both inside directors (corporate executives) and outside directors—people who are not otherwise employed by the organization. Sometimes the corporation's top executive also chairs the board. Generally, outside directors are also stockholders, so they have a financial stake in the company's performance.

Corporate Officers and Managers

The CEO and other members of top management, such as the chief operating officer (COO), chief financial officer (CFO), and the chief information officer (CIO) make most major corporate decisions. Managers at the next level down the hierarchy, middle management, handle the ongoing operational

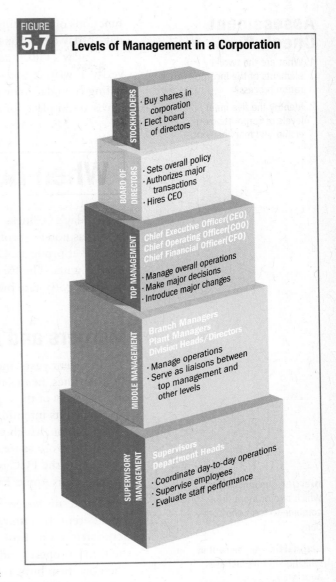

FIGURE 5.7 Levels of Management in a Corporation

STOCKHOLDERS
- Buy shares in corporation
- Elect board of directors

BOARD OF DIRECTORS
- Sets overall policy
- Authorizes major transactions
- Hires CEO

TOP MANAGEMENT
Chief Executive Officer (CEO)
Chief Operating Officer (COO)
Chief Financial Officer (CFO)
- Manage overall operations
- Make major decisions
- Introduce major changes

MIDDLE MANAGEMENT
Branch Managers
Plant Managers
Division Heads/Directors
- Manage operations
- Serve as liaisons between top management and other levels

SUPERVISORY MANAGEMENT
Supervisors
Department Heads
- Coordinate day-to-day operations
- Supervise employees
- Evaluate staff performance

stockholders owners of a corporation due to their purchase of stock in the corporation.

preferred stock shares that give owners limited voting rights, and the right to receive dividends or assets before owners of common stock.

common stock shares that give owners voting rights but only residual claims to the firm's assets and income distributions.

board of directors governing body of a corporation.

Assessment Check ✓

1. What are the two key elements of the incorporation process?
2. Identify the five main levels of corporate ownership and management.

functions of the company. At the first tier of management, supervisory personnel coordinate day-to-day operations, assign specific tasks to employees, and evaluate job performance.

Today's CEOs and CFOs are bound by stricter regulations than in the past. They must verify in writing the accuracy of their firm's financial statements, and the process for nominating candidates for the board has become more complex. In short, more checks and balances are in place for the governance of corporations.

When Businesses Join Forces

Today's business environment contains many complex relationships among businesses as well as not-for-profit organizations. Two firms may team up to develop a product or co-market products. One company may buy out another. Large corporations may split into smaller units. The list of alliances is a varied as the organizations themselves, but the major trends in corporate ownership include mergers and acquisitions and joint ventures.

Mergers and Acquisitions (M&A)

In recent years, mergers and acquisitions among U.S. corporations have hit an all-time high. Airlines, financial institutions, telecommunications companies, and media corporations are just a few of the types of businesses that have merged into giants. Recently, Comcast announced its intention to buy a majority stake in NBC Universal from General Electric for $13.75 billion, which would give the nation's largest cable company 51 percent control of the TV network as well as lucrative cable channels and a major movie studio. The deal was required by the FCC to meet certain conditions, such as sharing content with new Web platforms such as Apple TV and Netflix, firms that want to offer TV over the Internet.[65]

merger agreement in which two or more firms combine to form one company.

acquisition agreement in which one firm purchases another.

The terms *merger* and *acquisition* are often used interchangeably, but their meanings are different. In a **merger**, two or more firms combine to form one company. In an **acquisition**, one firm purchases the other. This means that not only does the buyer acquire the firm's property and assets, it also takes on any debt obligations. Acquisitions also occur when one firm buys a division or subsidiary from another firm. Drug manufacturer Pfizer recently bought Synbiotics, maker of veterinary immunodiagnostics, in order to expand its presence in the animal pharmaceutical market.[66]

vertical merger merger that combines firms operating at different levels in the production and marketing process.

Mergers can be classified as vertical, horizontal, or conglomerate. A **vertical merger** combines firms operating at different levels in the production and marketing process—the combination of a manufacturer and a large retailer, for instance. A vertical merger pursues one of two primary goals: (1) to ensure adequate flows of raw materials and supplies needed for a firm's products or (2) to increase distribution. Software giant Microsoft is well known for acquiring small firms that have developed products with strong market potential, such as Teleo, a provider of voice over Internet protocol (VoIP) software and services that can be used to make phone calls via the Internet.

horizontal merger merger that joins firms in the same industry for the purpose of diversification, increasing customer bases, cutting costs, or expanding product lines.

A **horizontal merger** joins firms in the same industry. This is done for the purpose of diversification, increasing customer bases, cutting costs, or expanding product lines. This type of merger is particularly popular in the auto and healthcare industries. Volkswagen now owns the Porsche brand, while CVS Caremark recently purchased another firm's Medicaid prescription business.

A **conglomerate merger** combines unrelated firms. The most common reasons for a conglomerate merger are to diversify, spur sales growth, or spend a cash surplus that might otherwise make the firm a tempting target for a takeover effort. Conglomerate mergers may join firms in totally unrelated industries. General Electric is, in fact, well known for its conglomerate mergers—including its ownership of healthcare services and household appliances. Experts debate whether conglomerate mergers are beneficial. The usual argument in favor of such mergers is that a company can use its management expertise to succeed in a variety of industries. But the obvious drawback is that a huge conglomerate can spread its resources too thin to be dominant in any one market.

Joint Ventures: Specialized Partnerships

A **joint venture** is a partnership between companies formed for a specific undertaking. Sometimes a company enters into a joint venture with a local firm, sharing the operation's costs, risks, management, and profits with its local partner. This is particularly common when a firm wants to enter into business in a foreign market. A joint venture also may enable companies to solve a mutual problem. Nokia and an educational publisher formed a joint venture in China to grow MobilEdu, a wireless education service first launched by Nokia several years earlier. MobilEdu feeds English-language learning materials from multiple content providers directly to customers via their mobile phones. China is now the world's largest mobile phone market, with the greatest number of consumers learning English.[67]

Joint ventures between for-profit firms and not-for-profit organizations are becoming more and more common. These partnerships provide great benefits for both parties. Not-for-profit organizations receive the funding, marketing exposure, and sometimes manpower they might not otherwise generate. City Year, mentioned earlier, enjoys these benefits from partnerships with Timberland, Pepsi, and Comcast along with other firms such as Starbucks and MSNBC. Recently, Starbucks partnered with MSNBC to publicize a program of community involvement called Brewing Together a Day of Service, in which Starbucks employees participated in shorter-term City Year projects.[68]

What's Ahead

The next chapter focuses on the driving forces behind the formation of new businesses: entrepreneurs. It examines the differences between a small-business owner and an entrepreneur and identifies certain personality traits typical of entrepreneurs. The chapter also details the process of launching a new venture, including identifying opportunities, locating needed financing, and turning good ideas into successful businesses. Finally, the chapter explores a method for infusing the entrepreneurial spirit into established businesses—intrapreneurship.

Cheryl Gerber/MSNBC/NBCUPB/©AP/Wide World Photos

Joint ventures between for-profit firms and not-for-profit organizations provide great benefits for both parties. Starbucks partnered with MSNBC to publicize a program of community involvement called Brewing Together Day of Service, in which Starbucks employees participated in shorter-term City Year (a not-for-profit organization) projects.

Summary of Learning Objectives

⌐1⌐ Distinguish between small and large businesses.

A small business is an independently owned business having fewer than 500 employees. Generally it is not dominant in its field and meets industry-specific size standards for income or number of employees. A business is classified as large when it exceeds these specifications.

Assessment Check Answers ✔

1.1 How does the Small Business Administration (SBA) define *small business*? A small business is defined as an independent business having fewer than 500 employees. However, those bidding for government small contracts or applying for government assistance may vary in size according to industry.

1.2 In what industries do small businesses play a significant role? Small businesses provide most jobs in construction, agriculture, wholesale trade, services, and retail trade. In addition, home-based businesses make up 52 percent of small businesses in the U.S.

⌐2⌐ Discuss the contributions of small businesses to the economy.

Small businesses create new jobs and new industries. They often hire workers who traditionally have had difficulty finding employment at larger firms. Small firms give people the opportunity and outlet for developing new ideas, which can turn into entirely new industries. Small businesses also develop new and improved goods and services.

Assessment Check Answers ✔

2.1 What are the three key ways in which small businesses contribute to the economy? Small businesses create new jobs, new industries, and provide innovation.

2.2 How are new industries formed? New industries are formed when small businesses adapt to shifts in consumer interests and preferences. Innovation and new technology can play a significant role. In addition, new industries may be created when both the business world and consumers recognize a need for change.

⌐3⌐ Discuss the survival rate of small businesses.

About seven of every ten new (small) businesses survive at least two years. But by the tenth year, 82 percent have closed. Failure is often attributed to management shortcomings, inadequate financing, and difficulty meeting government regulations.

Assessment Check Answers ✔

3.1 What percentage of small businesses remain in operation five years after starting? Ten years? About 50 percent are in business after five years; about 82 percent have folded by the ten year mark.

3.2 What are the three main causes of small-business failure? The three main causes of small-business failure are management shortcomings, inadequate financing, and difficulty complying with government regulations.

⌐4⌐ Describe the features of an effective business plan.

A complete business plan contains an executive summary, an introduction, financial and marketing sections, and resumes of the business principals. Within this structure, an effective business plan includes the company's mission, an outline of what makes the company unique, identification of customers and competitors, financial evaluation of the industry and market, and an assessment of the risks.

Assessment Check Answers ✔

4.1 What are the five main sections of a business plan? The five sections are the executive summary, introduction, financial section, marketing section, and resumes of principals.

4.2 Why is an effective business plan important to the success of a firm? The business plan puts in writing all the reasons the firm can be successful. It contains the written soul of the firm. It is the document that secures financing and creates a framework for the organization.

⌐5⌐ Describe funding opportunities for small businesses, including the role of the Small Business Administration (SBA).

The SBA guarantees loans made by private lenders, including microloans and those funded by Small Business Investment Companies. It offers training and information resources, so business owners can improve their odds of success. The SBA also advocates small-business interests within the federal government and provides specific support for businesses owned by women and minorities. State and local governments also have programs designed to help small businesses get established and grow. Venture capitalists are firms that invest in small businesses in return for an ownership stake.

Assessment Check Answers ✔

5.1 What are the various ways the SBA helps small businesses? The SBA guarantees business loans; helps small businesses compete for government set-aside programs; and provides business information, advice, and training to owners of small businesses.

5.2 What are business incubators? Business incubators are programs organized by community agencies that provide such services as rental space, clerical staff, and office equipment in an effort to help small businesses get started.

5.3 Why are small businesses good opportunities for women and minorities? Women feel they can achieve more as small-business owners and can balance family and work more easily if they own their own firms. Minority business owners can receive special assistance from programs like the Mentor-Protégé program provided by the SBA.

⌐6⌐ Explain how franchising can provide opportunities for both franchisors and franchisees.

A franchisor is a large firm that permits a small-business owner (franchisee) to market and sell its products under its brand name, in return for a fee. Benefits to the franchisor include opportunities for expansion and greater profits. Benefits to the franchisee include name recognition, quick start-up, support from the franchisor, and the freedom of small-business ownership.

Assessment Check Answers ✅

6.1 What is the difference between a franchisor and a franchisee? A franchisor permits a small-business owner (franchisee) to market and sell its products under its brand name, in return for a fee.

6.2 What are the benefits to both parties of franchising? Benefits to the franchisor include opportunities for expansion and greater profits. Benefits to the franchisee include name recognition, quick start-up, support from the franchisor, and the freedom of small-business ownership.

6.3 What are the potential drawbacks of franchising for both parties? The drawbacks for the franchisor include mismanagement and failure on the part of any of its franchisees, overexpansion, and loss of absolute control over the business. Drawbacks for the franchisee include an initial outlay of expenses, problems due to failure on the part of the franchisor or other franchisees; and restrictive franchise agreements.

⌐7⌐ Outline the three legal forms of business ownership, and summarize the features of businesses owned by employees and families, as well as not-for-profit organizations.

A sole proprietorship is owned and operated by one person. While sole proprietorships are easy to set up and offer great operating flexibility, the owner remains personally liable for all of the firm's debts and legal settlements. In a partnership, two or more individuals share responsibility for owning and running the business. Partnerships are relatively easy to set up, but they do not offer protection from liability. When a business is set up as a corporation, it becomes a separate legal entity. Investors receive shares of stock in the firm. Owners have no legal and financial liability beyond their individual investments. In an employee-owned business, most stockholders are also employees. Family-owned businesses may be structured legally in any of these three ways but face unique challenges, including succession and complex relationships. The legal structure of a not-for-profit corporation stipulates that its goals do not include earning a profit.

Assessment Check Answers ✅

7.1 What are the key differences among sole proprietorships and partnerships? Sole proprietorships and partnerships expose their owners to unlimited financial liability from their businesses. Sole proprietorships are more flexible and easier to dissolve than partnerships. Partnerships involve shared work load and decision making, whereas sole proprietorships are entirely the responsibility of one business owner.

7.2 What is a corporation? A corporation is a legal organization with assets and liabilities separate from those of its owners. A corporation can be a large or small business.

7.3 What is the main distinction of a not-for-profit corporation? A not-for-profit organization is set up legally so that its goals do not include pursuing a profit. Most states set out specific legal provisions for organizational structures and operations of not-for-profit corporations. They are exempt from paying income taxes.

⌐8⌐ Describe public and collective (cooperative) business ownership.

Public ownership occurs when a unit or agency of government owns and operates an organization. Collective ownership establishes an organization referred to as a cooperative, whose owners join forces to operate all or part of the functions in their firm or industry.

Assessment Check Answers ✅

8.1 What is public ownership? Public ownership occurs when a unit or agency of government owns and operates an organization.

8.2 What is collective ownership? Where are cooperatives typically found, and what benefits do they provide small businesses? Collective ownership establishes an organization referred to as a cooperative (co-op), whose owners join forces to operate all or part of the functions in their firm or industry. Cooperatives are frequently found among agricultural businesses. They can also occur in retail. Cooperatives allow small firms to pool their resources, share equipment and expertise, and help each other through difficult times.

⌐9⌐ Identify types of corporations and the levels of corporate management.

There are three types of corporations: domestic, foreign, and alien. Stockholders, or shareholders, own a corporation. In return for their financial investments, they receive shares of stock in the company. Stockholders elect a board of directors, who set overall policy. The board hires the chief executive officer (CEO), who then hires managers.

Assessment Check Answers ✅

9.1 What are the two key elements of the incorporation process? The two key elements are where to incorporate and the corporate charter.

9.2 Identify the five main levels of corporate ownership and management. The five levels are: stockholders, board of directors, top management, middle management, and supervisory management.

10. Describe mergers, acquisitions, and joint ventures.

In a merger, two or more firms combine to form one company. A vertical merger combines firms operating at different levels in the production and marketing process. A horizontal merger joins firms in the same industry. A conglomerate merger combines unrelated firms. An acquisition occurs when one firm purchases another. A joint venture is a partnership between companies formed for a specific undertaking.

Assessment Check Answers ✓

10.1 Distinguish between a merger and an acquisition. In a merger, two or more firms combine to form one company. In an acquisition, one firm purchases the property and assumes the obligations of another. Acquisitions also occur when one firm buys a division or subsidiary from another firm.

10.2 What are the different kinds of mergers? Mergers can be classified as vertical, horizontal, or conglomerate.

10.3 What is a joint venture? A joint venture is a partnership between organizations formed for a specific undertaking.

■ Key Terms

small business 147
home-based business 149
business plan 155
Small Business
    Administration (SBA) 157
microloans 158
business incubator 160
venture capital 160

franchising 162
franchisee 163
franchisor 163
sole proprietorship 166
partnership 167
corporation 168
S corporations 168

limited-liability corporation
    (LLC) 169
employee ownership 169
not-for-profit corporation 170
stockholders 173
preferred stock 173
common stock 173

board of directors 173
merger 174
acquisition 174
vertical merger 174
horizontal merger 174
conglomerate merger 175
joint venture 175

■ Review Questions

1. Describe how a small business might use innovation to create new jobs.

2. Why do so many small businesses fail before they reach their tenth year?

3. What are the benefits of developing and writing an effective business plan?

4. What is the Small Business Administration? How does it assist small companies, financially and in other specialized ways?

5. Describe how local governments and business incubators help small firms get established and grow.

6. Why are so many small-business owners attracted to franchising? Under what circumstances might it be better

to start an entirely new business instead of purchasing a franchise?

7. What are the benefits and drawbacks to traditional corporate structure? How do S corporations and limited liability corporations enhance the corporate legal structure?

8. Cooperatives appear frequently in agriculture. Describe another industry in which you think collective ownership would be beneficial, and explain why.

9. In a proprietorship and in partnerships the owners and the managers of the business are the same people. How are ownership and management separated in corporations?

10. How might a joint venture between a commercial firm and a not-for-profit organization help both achieve their goals?

■ Projects and Teamwork Applications

1. Research a large firm to find out more about its beginnings as a small business. Who founded the company? Does the firm still produce its original offerings, or has it moved entirely away from them?

2. Go to the Web site Entrepreneur.com and research information on franchises. Choose one that interests you and evaluate the information about its start-up requirements. Would you consider a partnership in your franchise with someone

you know? Why or why not? Present your findings in class.

3. Brainstorm a small business idea. Research the industry and major competition online. Draft a business plan. Include your decision on whether your firm will be a sole proprietorship or a partnership.

4. Identify an organization—such as Americorps or the United States Postal Service—that is owned by a unit or agency of

government. Imagine that you have been hired by that agency as a consultant to decide whether the organization should remain publicly owned. Research its successes and failures, and write a memo explaining your conclusion.

Web Assignments

1. **Small-business successes.** Visit the Web site at http://www.businessweek.com/smallbiz/successstories/. Scroll through the titles of success stories and choose one that interests you. Read the feature and prepare a brief report answering these questions:

   a. What does the firm do?

   b. Where did the idea originate?

   c. What expertise does the owner have?

   d. How did the business begin?

   e. Who are its competitors?

2. **Great small workplaces.** Winning Workplaces is a not-for-profit organization that is "committed to helping small and midsize organizations create high-performance workplaces." Visit the organization's Web site at

5. Identify a business and a not-for-profit organization that could form a joint venture beneficial to both. Either draft a written proposal or create an advertisement for the event that would result.

http://www.winningworkplaces.com and read at least two postings or articles there that interest you. Summarize the articles and explain how they help fulfill the Winning Workplaces' mission of helping small businesses succeed.

3. **Family-business tips for success.** Go to the Web site for *Family Business Magazine* at http://www.familybusinessmagazine.com and click on the feature article. Read the piece to learn about a particular family-owned business. Alternatively, choose a family-owned business such as S.C. Johnson (large) or Cider Hill Farm (small) and visit the firm's Web site to learn how the company has grown over the years and achieved success.

Note: Internet Web addresses change frequently. If you do not find the exact sites listed, you may need to access the organization's or company's home page and search from there.

Leslie Blodgett: The Bare Escentuals of Business   CASE 5.1

Leslie Blodgett was always passionate about color, cosmetics, and making people feel good. After college she went to work for Max Factor, a small firm that was acquired by Revlon and then Procter & Gamble. When Blodgett got a call from one of the investors who owned a little makeup company called Bare Escentuals, she had never heard of the firm. The company was the first to offer a mineral-based powder makeup that might actually succeed—and Blodgett was intrigued. "A powder foundation that was good for your skin made great sense," recalls Blodgett. "But the shades Bare Escentuals had created weren't working. They were gross. I knew complexions and how to match skin tones—and I saw a huge opportunity." Blodgett went to work for the small firm and became CEO within a few months.

"There were seven of us in the office just winging it," Blodgett admits. With her cosmetics knowledge, Blodgett immediately relaunched the line as bareMinerals, which included six eye shadows, six blushes, five powder foundations, and brushes—all designed to work together. But by the end of the first two years, Blodgett worried that the company wasn't going to make it. As she was channel-surfing late one night, she stopped at the TV shopping channel QVC. As she watched, Blodgett formulated

a plan—if she could get bareMinerals on the air, she knew she could sell the products. It turned out that QVC agreed with her, and Blodgett sold $45,000 of products in her first airing. The shopping channel immediately re-booked her on a regular basis.

Blodgett continuously looks to her customers for inspiration—both for product and marketing ideas. She began hosting events at the boutiques, inviting customers to share their ideas and tips—after which she began to name new products after specific customers. Blodgett then expanded Bare Escentuals' TV presence with infomercials that gave her more time to explain the products and application processes. Looking for a wider distribution network, she hounded Sephora until they offered her space in their stores. Shortly after that, Nordstrom came calling. Meanwhile, Blodgett decided that if small in-store events were good, bigger events were better—and she organized cruises for customers.

Over the next fifteen years, Blodgett brought Bare Escentuals, step-by-step, from small-business status with six stores in northern California to its recent sale to Japanese beauty giant Shiseido for $1.7 billion, with 130 boutiques across the nation and 2,200 employees.

Blodgett herself became a cosmetics and small-business celebrity. But the company was growing too quickly and she recognized that Bare Escentuals couldn't keep up with the demand for new products. So she hired a new chief financial officer who, with the sale of the firm to Shiseido has become CEO, while Blodgett has assumed the position of executive chairman. She continues to be well-known for her approachability, answering her own emails from customers, always striving for the personal touch that makes her business style unique.

Throughout the company's growth, Blodgett never lost sight of her own passion or her company's mission to offer the highest-quality cosmetics that not only look natural but benefit the skin. She believes that making people feel good about themselves is her most important task. "I don't want to be a business," Blodgett says. "I want to be a community."

Questions for Critical Thinking

1. What specific factors do you believe led Leslie Blodgett and her small firm to success?
2. Bare Escentuals is now part of a much larger company. What kinds of changes might take place at Bare Escentuals over the next few years?

Sources: "Meet Leslie," http://www.bareescentuals.com, accessed March 31, 2011; "Leslie Blodgett," *Women's Conference Organization*, http://www.womensconference.org, accessed March 31, 2011; "How I Did It: Leslie Blodgett of Bare Escentuals," from *Inc.*, July 1, 2010. Copyright © 2010 by MANSUETO VENTURES LLC. Reproduced with permission of MANSUETO VENTURES LLC via Copyright Clearance Center.

CASE 5.2

Small Meets Big: Patagonia and Walmart Join Forces for the Environment

When Yvon Chouinard started rock climbing as a teenager, he never dreamed his passion would lead to the ownership of two companies and a lifelong passion for preserving the planet. But 55 years later, the climber-businessman has joined forces with Walmart—a seemingly unlikely partner—to spread the word that sustainability is cool.

Chouinard founded Chouinard Equipment to make safer, more environmentally friendly equipment for rock climbers and mountaineers. He didn't like the way previous generations of climbers had destroyed mountain environments. Patagonia, founded in 1972, offered the "soft" side of the outdoors—specialized clothing, boots, packs, luggage, and other gear. From the very beginning, Chouinard and his design team worked hard to develop products whose materials and manufacturing processes were eco-friendly. "The reason I am in business is I want to protect what I love," Chouinard explains. "I used to spend 250 days a year sleeping on the ground. I've climbed on every continent. I'm old enough to have seen the destruction."

In fact, in the mid-1990s Chouinard discovered that the cotton Patagonia was using for many of its garments came from industrial farms that used toxic chemicals. His response was swift and definite. He gave his company just 18 months to change completely to organic cotton. Chouinard has also been successful at persuading other businesses to go green.

For the past few years, Chouinard's team has been working with Walmart to develop a sustainability index for its products, sharing valuable information that Patagonia has gained over the years. Walmart is 1,300 times as large as Patagonia, but Patagonia has knowledge and experience that Walmart can use to reinvent itself as an environmentally responsible firm. Chouinard doesn't mind sharing with a company that has such a monumental impact on the marketplace as well as the planet. And Walmart officials are eager to learn. The company plans to post scorecards in its stores, rating products on eco-friendliness and social impact. And it is developing a system to give preference to suppliers who comply with these steps. At one conference of Walmart buyers and executives, Chouinard pointed out that Walmart's use of little LED lights in its stores—which seem to use minimal energy—actually requires 19 plants in California to power them. At this statement, a Walmart buyer stood in the audience and shouted, "We're going to get rid of those!"

Questions for Critical Thinking

1. The alliance between Patagonia and Walmart is an excellent example of a small business and a large business working together to achieve an objective. Do you think the same results would be possible if Walmart acquired Patagonia? Why or why not?
2. Walmart is learning from Patagonia. But what might Patagonia learn from Walmart?

Sources: "What We Do," Patagonia Web site, http://www.patagonia.com, accessed March 31, 2011; "Patagonia," in "*Inc.* Top Workplaces 2010," http://www.inc.com, accessed March 31, 2011; Monte Burke, "Walmart, Patagonia, Team to Green Business," *Forbes,* May 6, 2010, http://www.forbes.com.

Seventh Generation isn't as old as its company name suggests. In fact, the firm has been in business for a bit more than two decades, merely allowing time for a second generation of employees to move the company's mission forward. But the firm is focused clearly on the future—seven generations in the future, to be precise. Seventh Generation's mission is based on the Great Law of the Iroquois, which states: "In every deliberation, we must consider the impact of our decision on the next seven generations." With that in mind, the company manufactures and sells household products carefully designed and produced to leave as little impact on the natural environment as possible.

Jeffrey Hollender, Seventh Generation's cofounder and executive chairman, is passionate about the planet. "This is a moment in time that we may not have again," he says of his company's efforts to educate consumers about the impact of the products they buy and use—and its alternative offerings. It's true that Seventh Generation is now a large enough company that Hollender can speak with a voice heard by media, legislators, and the general public. But it wasn't always this way. "We started in 1988 selling energy products like compact fluorescent lightbulbs (CFLs) that cost about $28 a piece," recalls Hollender. His company operated out of a single room in Vermont with half a dozen employees. At first, most consumers were reluctant to pay the high price for CFLs or the firm's organic bedding and cleaning products. But Hollender and his staff remained committed. "We basically sold products we needed to live a more responsible, natural lifestyle," explains Hollender.

Despite the company's small size, word about its fresh ideas in household cleaning and energy use spread quickly, despite the fact that many people thought Seventh Generation was a nonprofit organization. "We grew a lot the first three years," says Hollender. "We went from $100,000 to $1 million to $8 million in sales—then we crashed, we hit a wall." Seventh Generation experienced the growing pains that nearly every small business goes through. Hollender admits that the most difficult aspect of growth was realizing it had happened too fast. He cut his own salary, but the decision that caused Hollender the most pain was the layoffs necessary to keep the firm running. "Letting someone go because we had failed to be financially viable enough to employ them, that's my failing," he asserts. "Letting people go has to be the absolute last resort."

But the firm regained its balance and began to grow again with a new sense of purpose. Today, Seventh Generation is nearing $200 million in sales, with its laundry detergent and diapers as its top-selling products. This figure that allows the company to hire experts in research and development, build stronger relationships with suppliers and customers, engage in business practices that promote sustainability, and market products that fulfill its promise to reduce human impact on the natural environment. "Growth brings credibility," observes Dave Rappaport, Seventh Generation's director of corporate consciousness.

Hollender agrees. "Our size allows a platform to influence the way business is done in America," he comments. Hollender, who recently turned the job of CEO over to Chuck Maniscalco, now uses his clout to spend more time on not-for-profit environmental initiatives such as the Sustainability Institute.

In addition, Seventh Generation has entered into a strategic partnership with retail giant Walmart to offer environmentally friendly products at more than 1,500 of its stores nationwide as well as on Walmart.com. As part of the alliance, Walmart stores will now carry a range of Seventh Generation's cleaning products, including its best-selling laundry detergent, dish soap, and cleaning spray. An expanded array of products, including baby diapers and wipes, are offered on Walmart.com. CEO Maniscalco is enthusiastic about the partnership. "Seventh Generation and Walmart are committed to helping people learn about natural alternatives and ways to protect themselves and their families," he remarked recently.

Jeffrey Hollender notes that Seventh Generation's work is far from finished. "We need to become a business that is all good rather than less bad," he states. When his company reaches that point, he predicts, its growth could have no limits.

Questions for Critical Thinking

1. Describe specific contributions that you believe Seventh Generation makes to the economy.

2. Given the high failure rate of small businesses, why do you think Seventh Generation has survived?

3. Seventh Generation is a privately held company. Create a chart showing possible benefits and pitfalls for the company if its management decided to sell stock to the general public.

4. Seventh Generation has entered into a strategic partnership with Walmart. Do you think this partnership will be a successful match for both parties? Why or why not?

Sources: Company Web site, http://www.seventhgeneration.com, accessed March 31, 2011; Ronnie Ribitzky, "7 Facts About Seventh Generation," *Portfolio.com,* http://www.portfolio.com, accessed March 31, 2011; "Seventh Generation and Walmart Announce Strategic Partnership," *MarketWire,* July 26, 2010, http://www.marketwire.com; Danielle Sacks, "Jeffrey Hollender: Seventh Generation, Triple Bottom Line Entrepreneur," *Fast Company.com,* February 2, 2010, http://fastcompany.com.

Learning Objectives

[1] Define the term *entrepreneur,* and distinguish among entrepreneurs, small-business owners, and managers.

[2] Identify the different types of entrepreneurs.

[3] Explain why people choose to become entrepreneurs.

[4] Discuss factors that support and expand opportunities for entrepreneurs.

[5] Identify personality traits that typically characterize successful entrepreneurs.

[6] Summarize the process of starting a new venture.

[7] Explain how organizations promote intrapreneurship.

Starting Your Own Business: The Entrepreneurship Alternative

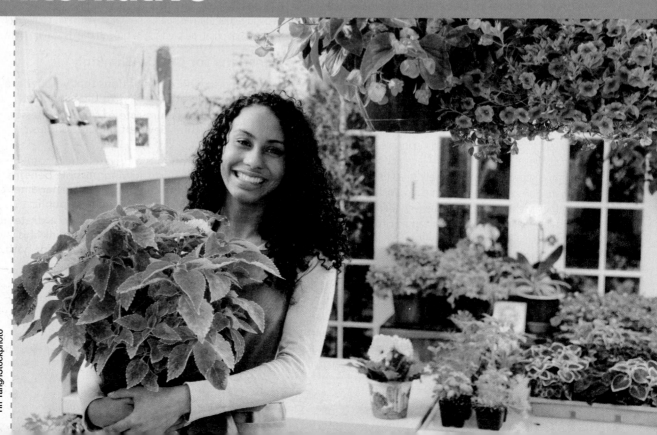

Elon Musk Launches SpaceX into the Final Frontier

Gary I. Rothstein/EPA/Landov LLC

Elon Musk founded PayPal when skeptics still thought Internet shopping was a fad. And he founded Tesla Motors because he believes that the automobile industry will be entirely electric within the next two decades. But Musk's latest venture is out of this world—literally. SpaceX, short for Space Exploration Technologies, recently launched the first commercially developed space capsule into orbit, then successfully recovered it at sea.

SpaceX, a small California-based start-up powered by the vision of an entrepreneur, accomplished something that none of the major aerospace firms and only five national space programs—including NASA—had managed to do. Designed and built by SpaceX's own engineers, the unmanned capsule—called Dragon—held up under the battering of a launch and then navigated itself back to Earth. The business ramifications of this achievement for Musk are huge: SpaceX will be the only company on the planet capable of carrying cargo to and from space—and the International Space Station—in the near future. Dragon's launch proved that "government and industry can leverage expertise and resources to foster a new and vibrant space economy," notes one NASA administrator. But for Elon Musk, a former physics student from South Africa, this is about more than the potential millions that will land in his bank account. It is the next frontier, the forgoing of a new industry that will ultimately include not just cargo transport but also astronaut travel and surveillance satellites.

Meanwhile, back on Earth, Musk continues to tend to California-based Tesla Motors because people still need to drive cars, and he has no doubt about the future of electric vehicles. Within two years of hitting the road, the Tesla Roadster hit sales of 1,500 cars in 30 countries. That number is tiny when compared to the hundreds of thousands of cars sold by each of the large automakers, but Musk is convinced that sales of his vehicles signal the coming trend—and as with all of his other ventures, Musk wants to be in the lead, even if it means mistakes and failures along the way. At a price tag of $100,000, the Tesla Roadster is unlikely to find itself parked in every driveway. But Tesla plans to introduce a midsize sports sedan—at a more competitive price—in the coming year. And with a huge infusion of cash, in the form of a $50 million investment from Toyota, Tesla will begin developing an electric SUV. Panasonic, which makes Tesla's battery cells, recently pumped $30 million into the firm. Backing from Toyota and Panasonic indicates that the big companies agree with Musk's foresight—and they want to be part of the next wave.

Musk isn't content to wait for the market to come to him; instead, he takes his products to the most likely market. Tesla already has six dealerships in Europe and is making a grand entrance in Japan. "We do believe Japan will be our Number 2 country in terms of sales over time," says Musk. "Japan is a key market for the kind of product we produce."

And what about outer space? Musk seems somehow to maintain his enthusiasm for two businesses, two industries, and two frontiers—all at the same time. He travels from one firm to the other by jet, and he is quick to list the attributes of his Tesla vehicles. But perhaps he's most proud of the coolest product of all: a rocket. "If there had been people sitting in the Dragon today," he said of its initial launch, "they would've had a nice ride."[1]

Overview

You think you want to start and run your own company. Like Elon Musk who has founded multiple firms, you've got a great idea for a new business and you dream of achieving fame and fortune. If you've been bitten by the entrepreneurial bug, you're not alone. More than ever, people like you, your classmates, and your friends are choosing the path of entrepreneurship.

How do you become an entrepreneur? Experts advise aspiring entrepreneurs to learn as much as possible about business by completing academic programs such as the one in which you are currently enrolled and by gaining practical experience by working part- or full-time for businesses. In addition, you can obtain valuable insights about the pleasures and pitfalls of entrepreneurship by reading newspaper and magazine articles and biographies of successful entrepreneurs. These sources will help you learn how entrepreneurs handle the challenges of starting their businesses. For advice on how to launch and grow a new venture, turn to magazines such as *Entrepreneur, Forbes, Fast Company, Success, Black Enterprise, Hispanic,* and *Inc.* Entrepreneurship associations such as the Association of African-American Women Business Owners and the Entrepreneurs'

Organization also provide valuable assistance. Finally, any aspiring entrepreneur should visit these Web sites:

- U.S. Chamber of Commerce (http://www.uschamber.com)
- Entrepreneur.com (http://www.entrepreneur.com)
- Kauffman Foundation (http://www.kauffman.org)
- The Small Business Administration (http://www.sba.gov)
- *The Wall Street Journal* Small Business (http://online.wsj.com/small-business)

In this chapter, we focus on pathways for entering the world of entrepreneurship, describing the activities of entrepreneurs, the different kinds of entrepreneurs, and the reason a growing number of people choose to be entrepreneurs. It discusses the business environment in which entrepreneurs work, the characteristics that help entrepreneurs succeed, and the ways they start new ventures. The chapter ends with a discussion of methods by which large companies try to incorporate the entrepreneurial spirit.

What Is an Entrepreneur?

entrepreneur person who seeks a profitable opportunity and takes the necessary risks to set up and operate a business.

An **entrepreneur** is a risk taker in the private enterprise system, a person who seeks a profitable opportunity and takes the necessary risks to set up and operate a business. Consider Sam Walton, Walmart's founder, who started by franchising a few small Ben Franklin variety stores, and then opened his own Walton Five and Dime stores. Forty-five years later, this small venture has grown into a multibillion-dollar global business that is the largest company on earth.

Entrepreneurs differ from many small-business owners. Although many small-business owners possess the same drive, creative energy, and desire to succeed, what makes entrepreneurs different is that one of their major goals is expansion and growth. (Many small-business owners prefer to keep their businesses small.) Sam Walton wasn't satisfied with just one successful Ben Franklin franchise, so he purchased others. And when that wasn't enough, he started and grew his own stores. Entrepreneurs combine their ideas and drive with money, employees, and other resources to create a business that fills a market need. That entrepreneurial role can make something significant out of a small beginning. Walmart, the company that Sam Walton started, reported net sales in excess of $405 billion for one recent year.[2]

Entrepreneurs also differ from managers. Managers are employees who direct the efforts of others to achieve an organization's goals. Owners of some small start-up firms serve as owner-managers to implement their plans for their businesses and to offset human resource limitations at their fledgling companies. Entrepreneurs may also perform a managerial role, but their overriding responsibility is to use the resources of their organizations—employees, money, equipment, and facilities—to accomplish their goals. When Hollywood socialite Bobbie Weiner found herself struggling for cash, she signed up for a special-effects makeup course, hoping that she could earn just a few dollars working for the movie industry. But the result has been a huge success. She realized that specialized makeup is needed by many categories of people—actors, the military, Halloween revelers, sports fans, and funeral directors. After doing a few makeup jobs on horror films, Weiner was recruited to work on the blockbuster *Titanic*. That led to a rush of other movies, a contract with the military for camouflage paint, worldwide requests from funeral homes, and her own product line. Although Weiner is now worth millions and employs 250 people at her company—called Bloody Mary—she is still very much in charge of the firm's mission, goals, and image.[3]

Studies have identified certain personality traits and behaviors common to entrepreneurs that differ from those required for managerial success. One of these traits is the willingness to assume the risks involved in starting a new venture. Some, like Bobbie Weiner, take that risk out of necessity—they've left or lost previous jobs or simply need a way to generate cash. Others want a challenge or a different quality of life. Entrepreneurial characteristics are examined in detail in a later section of this chapter.

Categories of Entrepreneurs

Entrepreneurs apply their talents in different situations. These differences can be classified into distinct categories: classic entrepreneurs, serial entrepreneurs, and social entrepreneurs.

Classic entrepreneurs identify business opportunities and allocate available resources to tap those markets. Dana Hood is a classic entrepreneur. She recognized that dog owners want special attention for their pets when they leave those animals in the care of others. She also knew that pet owners spent $3.4 billion for boarding and daycare centers during one recent year. So, when she founded her daycare center for dogs in Denver, she made certain that her services stood out from the average kennel. At For the Love of Dog, Hood and her staff offer customized services such as grooming and anesthesia-free teeth-cleaning, a treadmill, swimming pools, and water misters to cool off her customers' pets during hot weather. In addition, pet owners can purchase high-end organic foods and treats, beds and toys, as well as other retail goods. "It's a great way to take advantage of a captive audience," notes Hood.[4]

Assessment Check ☑

1. What tools do entrepreneurs use to create a new business?
2. How do entrepreneurs differ from managers?

classic entrepreneur person who identifies a business opportunity and allocates available resources to tap that market.

Courtesy Dana Hood

Dana Hood recognized that dog owners were willing to pay for special attention to be paid to their pets. When she founded her daycare center for dogs, she included custom services. Hood is a classic entrepreneur, who identified a business opportunity and then marshalled the resources to pursue it.

serial entrepreneur
person who starts one business, runs it, and then starts and runs additional businesses in succession.

social entrepreneur
person who recognizes societal problems and uses business principles to develop innovative solutions.

Assessment Check ✔

1. What do classic entrepreneurs and social entrepreneurs have in common?

2. Is a social entrepreneur simply a philanthropist?

While a classic entrepreneur starts a new company by identifying a business opportunity and allocating resources to tap a new market, <u>**serial entrepreneurs**</u> start one business, run it, and then start and run additional businesses in succession. Elon Musk is a serial entrepreneur, having founded PayPal, Tesla Motors, and SpaceX. Jessica Herrin is also a serial entrepreneur. When Herrin graduated from college with an economics degree, she joined a software startup firm where she got hooked on the idea of "unlimited potential." At age 24, Herrin founded WeddingChannel.com, which grew within a few years to 100 employees and $21 million in revenues. When her firm was purchased by The Knot, Herrin went on to found Stella & Dot, a high-quality fashion jewelry business sold by 7,500 independent representatives at parties and online. Already, Stella & Dot has hit $33 million in revenues, and the jewelry has been featured in business and fashion press—and perhaps more importantly, on celebrities. "I want to build a company that is the next great global brand that changes the lives of women around the world," asserts Herrin.[5]

Some entrepreneurs focus on solving society's challenges through their businesses. <u>**Social entrepreneurs**</u> recognize a societal problem and use business principles to develop innovative solutions. Social entrepreneurs are pioneers of innovations that benefit humanity. When a group of seven Indian women gathered one afternoon more than 50 years ago to roll out dough for traditional crackers, they recognized a potential opportunity to produce and market this popular food for a wider audience. They established a women's cooperative based on this idea called Lijjat Papad, with the intent to empower Indian women entrepreneurs. Since then, the cooperative has become one of India's most successful business ventures. The company now produces a wide variety of bakery products, spices, and flour, along with cleaning products such as detergent and liquid soap. Headquartered in Mumbai, Lijjat Papad has 73 branches around the country and has become one of the most popular and trusted brands in India.[6]

Reasons to Choose Entrepreneurship as a Career Path

If you want to run your own business someday, you'll have plenty of company. During one recent year, about 530,000 new businesses were created each month in the United States, with services and the construction industry experiencing the highest rates of activity.[7]

The past few decades have witnessed a heightened interest in entrepreneurial careers, spurred in part by publicity celebrating the successes of entrepreneurs such as Michael Dell, who launched what would become computer giant Dell following his freshman year at the University of Texas; Oprah Winfrey, who parlayed her career as a reporter into the media-production empire Harpo; and Bill Gates, who left Harvard to start Microsoft with friend Paul Allen.

People choose to become entrepreneurs for many different reasons. Some are motivated by dissatisfaction with the traditional work world—they want a more flexible schedule or freedom to make all the decisions. Others launch businesses to fill a gap in goods or services that they could use themselves. Still others start their own firms out of financial necessity, like Bobbie Weiner did with her makeup business. Carol Craig is another such entrepreneur. Craig was a flight officer and computer engineer, specializing in anti-submarine and subsurface warfare for the U.S. Navy. When unsuccessful knee surgery left her with a disabled veteran discharge, she didn't know what to do. She followed her husband, also a naval officer, around to military posts and discovered that the military needed her after all—as a civilian consultant. So she founded Craig Technologies headquartered in Florida, which provides avionic software development, project management, software systems engineering, Web design, and data warehousing services to the military. In one decade, the firm has grown from one employee—Carol Craig—to more than 170 employees and $20 million in income. Although Craig didn't plan this to be her career, she says "I was never afraid of trying new things. I'm an accidental entrepreneur."[8]

As pointed out in Figure 6.1, people become entrepreneurs for one or more of four major reasons: a desire to be their own boss, succeed financially, attain job security, and improve their quality of life. Each of these reasons is described in more detail in the following sections.

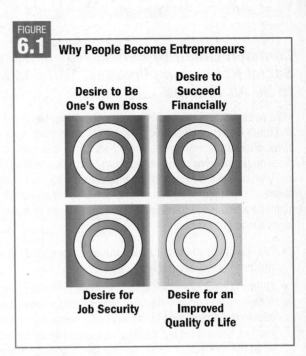

FIGURE 6.1 Why People Become Entrepreneurs

Desire to Be One's Own Boss

Desire to Succeed Financially

Desire for Job Security

Desire for an Improved Quality of Life

Being Your Own Boss

The freedom to make all the decisions—being your own boss—is one of the biggest lures of entrepreneurship. After 20 years of working in the fitness industry, Peter Taunton wanted out of the big-box health club scene. But he wasn't finished with fitness. He decided to create a different kind of gym, one for average people who prefer to work out without wearing Spandex shorts or being bombarded by loud music and big-screen TVs. Taunton founded Taunton's Snap Fitness—small, neighborhood-oriented fitness clubs based on affordability, convenience, and cleanliness. Snap Fitness clubs—there are now nearly 2,000 franchised locations—are smaller than the average gym but are open 24 hours a day. They feature up-to-date cardio and training equipment, but that's about all. There are no childcare facilities or smoothie bars, no pools or racquetball courts. This means that the cost of membership falls way below the national average. Taunton likes the fact that he had the authority to put his dreams into action. And his customers seem to agree with his decisions. "People see us, I think, as a breath of fresh air," Taunton observes.[9]

Being your own boss generally means getting to make all the important decisions. It also means engaging in much—if not all—of the communication related to your business, including

After 20 years in the fitness industry, Peter Taunton wanted a change, but he wasn't finished with fitness. He created small, neighborhood-oriented fitness clubs based on affordability, convenience, and cleanliness. For many entrepreneurs, controlling when, where, and how they work is a major motivator.

Frank Couch/Birmingham News/Landov LLC

Communicating by E-mail, Text Message, or Social Networking Updates: You Don't Have to Be All Thumbs

Most entrepreneurs rely heavily on e-mail, texting, social networking updates, and other modes of electronic communication to reach their customers, suppliers, distributors, employees, and others. Often that communication takes place on the run; when you're your own boss, you are busy taking care of many tasks at once. Although you may consider yourself adept with the cell phone or smart phone keyboard, and can whip off an e-mail in no time, it might be a good idea to review a few etiquette tips to make sure your messages sound professional.

- Don't write in all caps. It makes the message sound frenetic, or as if you meant to be yelling at the recipient.

- On the subject line, don't write "Important—Please Read." Your message is likely to end up in someone's "delete" box, unread. Likewise, try to avoid sending any kind of "forwarded" messages—for the same reason. Instead, use a short but descriptive subject line so the recipient knows what the message is about. An example might be "Review of Tuesday's Meeting."

- Avoid slang expressions and shorthand such as "LOL," "ru," and "L8." Also avoid smiley or sad-face icons.

- Be friendly but not overly familiar. Never include jokes in a business e-mail or text message.

- Be brief. A short message is much more helpful than a long one. If more discussion is necessary, conclude with a note that you will follow up with a phone call.

- Remember that your computer or your phone is like a tape recorder. Messages can be saved and stored. For that reason, you don't want to make an unprofessional comment that could come back to haunt you. Never include personal messages within professional ones, and refrain from insults or criticisms that could damage your company's image or the reputation of others.

Sources: Mark Grossman, "Email Etiquette Is Important," *Grossman Law Group,* http://www
.ecomputerlaw.com, accessed July 5, 2011; "Business Email Etiquette: What You Should Know
BEFORE You Hit Send," http://www.evancarmichael.com/Women-Entrepreneurs, accessed March
16, 2010; Karl Stolley and Allen Brizee, "Email Etiquette," *Purdue Owl,* http://owl.english.purdue
.edu, accessed March 16, 2010; Nina Kaufman, "Making it Legal," *Entrepreneur.com,* http://legal
.entrepreneur.com, accessed March 16, 2010.

customers, suppliers, distributors, retailers, and the like. The "Business Etiquette" feature offers tips for professional-style communication—even if you're on the run and using your thumbs.

Financial Success

Entrepreneurs are wealth creators. Many start their ventures with the specific goal of becoming rich—or at least financially successful. Often they believe they have an idea for a superior product and they want to be the first to bring it to market, reaping the financial rewards as a result. Entrepreneurs believe they won't achieve their greatest success by working for someone else, and they're generally right. Of course, the downside is that when they fail, they don't have the cushion of employment.

John Vechey recalls growing up without luxuries. "I bond with anyone who has ever eaten government cheese," he quips. While in college, Vechey and a friend developed an online game called ARC that the pair eventually sold to Sierra for $100,000. After coming up with popular games such as Bejeweled and Plants vs. Zombies—based on the idea that online games should be simple and fun for everyone—the three co-founders of PopCap (John Vechey, Jason Kapalka, and Brian Fiete) turned down a $60 million offer for the Seattle-based company. Vechey believes they still have much more to accomplish, as PopCap nears the $100 million mark in sales.[10]

Job Security

Although the demand for skilled employees remains high in many industries, working for a company, even a *Fortune* 500 firm, is no guarantee of job security. In fact, over the past ten years, large companies sought efficiency by downsizing and actually eliminated more jobs than they created. As a result, a growing number of American workers—both first-time job seekers and laid-off long-term employees—are deciding to create their own job security by starting their own businesses. While running your own business doesn't guarantee job security, the U.S. Small Business

Administration has found that most newly created jobs come from small businesses, with a significant share of those jobs coming from new companies.[11]

Overseas, as economies are changing, workers are discovering the benefits of entrepreneurship compared to employment by big firms. In China, where entire industries such as banking, steel, and telecommunications, are government-owned, young businesspeople are starting their own small firms. There are nearly 500 million people under the age of 30 in China, and their role models are Bill Gates and Michael Dell, reports an entrepreneurship professor at the Europe International Business School in Shanghai.[12]

Quality of Life

Entrepreneurship is an attractive career option for people seeking to improve their quality of life. Starting a business gives the founder independence and some freedom to decide when, where, and how to work. A **lifestyle entrepreneur** is a person who starts a business to gain flexibility in work hours and control over his or her life. But this does *not* mean working fewer hours or with less intensity. Generally it is the opposite—people who start their own businesses often work longer and harder than ever before, at least in the beginning. But they enjoy the satisfaction of success, both materially and in the way they live their lives.

Dan Abrams wanted it all—wealth and the freedom to do the things he loves. An avid backcountry skier, Abrams faced a serious problem: On just about every strenuous run, he was ripping the seams on his ski pants and jackets. "Fortunately, the manufacturers who made that stuff were good about honoring their warranties," acknowledges Abrams. But Abrams wondered, why not make clothes that could withstand the rigors of the backcountry? So Abrams and his friend Greg Steen borrowed $38,000 on their credit cards and launched FlyLow Gear, starting with durable new t-shirts. Then they added triple-stitched ski pants and sold out their entire first production run. FlyLow's revenues are on course to break $1 million soon. Abrams and Steen are still skiing. "I could build a $1 million company or ski 100 days a year," says Abrams. "I choose to do both and have it all."[13] Two other entrepreneurs who have chosen to build a company based on their lifestyle values are Seth Meyer and John Wells, as described in the "Hit & Miss" feature.

The Environment for Entrepreneurs

Are you ready to start your own company? Do some research about the environment in which you will be conducting business. There are several important overall factors to consider. There's the economy—whether it is lagging or booming, you may find opportunities. Consider where you want to locate your business. Currently, the states with the highest rate of entrepreneurial activity are Georgia, New Mexico, Montana, Arizona, Alaska, and California. And the metropolitan area with the highest rate of activity is Atlanta.[14]

Overall, the general attitude toward entrepreneurs in the United States is positive. In addition to favorable public attitudes toward entrepreneurs and the growing number of financing options, several other factors—identified in Figure 6.2—also support and expand

lifestyle entrepreneur person who starts a business to reduce work hours and create a more relaxed lifestyle.

Assessment Check ✔

1. What are the four main reasons people choose to become entrepeneurs?
2. What factors affect the entrepreneur's job security?

Meyer Wells: New Life for Old Wood

When a single tree falls in the forest—or in the backyard, some people really do care. In fact, they care so much that they want to preserve the tree. They don't want to see it cut up into firewood, or left to rot. Seth Meyer and John Wells feel that way about trees, and they have put that passion to work. Several years ago they started Meyer Wells, a Seattle-based business that salvages downed trees and transforms them into one-of-a-kind pieces of furniture. Make no mistake about it—these are not lumberjacks, nor are they landscapers. They are fine furniture makers whose raw materials are sometimes as dear to their owners as members of the family.

One family paid the pair to create several pieces of furniture from a tree that had split open in a windstorm. "This fellow's father and he planted this [tree] years ago," explains Meyer. So Meyer and Wells moved the tree to their shop where they and their employees milled and dried the wood. They designed the furniture in consultation with the family. "There's nothing like opening up a tree and seeing the beauty of the wood inside," notes Wells. "Every one of them is an artifact." That's how the partners' customers view trees as well.

Meyer Wells also harvests local trees that are marked to be cut down due to development, or those that have died of disease or storm damage. The shop sometimes houses these trees until they find a suitable home. Recently the firm acquired some elm trees that had been planted along a road in Iowa as a memorial to fallen WWI soldiers—

the trees had been cut down both because of disease and to clear the way for a bike path. Meyer and Wells want to continue to honor the memory of the soldiers by turning the trees into beautiful, functional furniture.

Meyer Wells doesn't just serve individual consumers. They have some business customers as well, including Starbucks.

Meyer Wells' products are goods that people are willing to pay for, even in a sluggish economy. The company was profitable right from the beginning, with steady growth since then. Within four years, revenues reached $850,000, with a realistic goal of $1 million the following year. The company now employs nearly 20 workers.

Meyer Wells exemplifies the new entrepreneurs: its business model is based on sustainability. They are proving that companies can actually profit from operating with green practices. They are also demonstrating that their passion for craftsmanship, modern design, and community involvement can be successfully incorporated into a business. "I really believe a designer can influence people and move us in a direction that's more sustainable," observes Seth Meyer. "That's what I've chosen to do, and I think it's what's made us a successful business."

Sources: Meyer Wells Web site, http://www.meyerwells.com, accessed February 7, 2011; "Local Biz Turns Downed Trees Into One-of-a-Kind Treasures," *KOMO News*, December 27, 2010, http://www.komonews.com; Lawrence W. Cheek, "Finding New Life (and Profit) in Doomed Trees," *The New York Times*, August 7, 2010, http://www.nytimes.com.

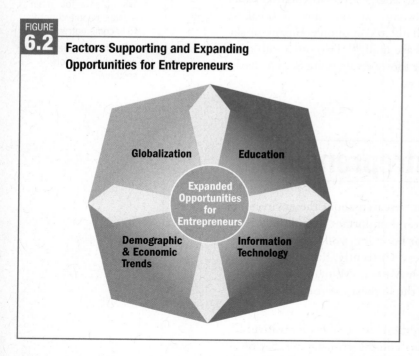

FIGURE 6.2

Factors Supporting and Expanding Opportunities for Entrepreneurs

opportunities for entrepreneurs: globalization, education, information technology, and demographic and economic trends. Each of these factors is discussed in the following sections.

Globalization

The rapid globalization of business has created many opportunities for entrepreneurs. Entrepreneurs market their products abroad and hire international talent. Among the fastest-growing small U.S. companies, almost two of every five have international sales. Despite her location in Wisconsin, Margaret Maggard sells her yoga-inspired, handmade jewelry—called Bhati Beads—all over the world, including to celebrities. The jewelry, which often features hand-carved beads strung on a soft leather cord, has been showcased on models in magazines ranging from *Lucky* and *Sports Illustrated* to the European fashion magazine *Grazia*.[15]

Growth in entrepreneurship is a worldwide phenomenon. The role of entrepreneurs is growing in most industrialized and newly industrialized nations, as well as in the emerging

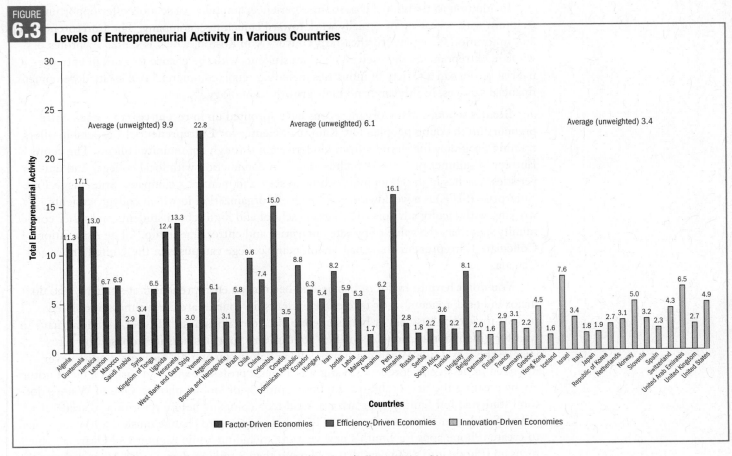

FIGURE 6.3

Levels of Entrepreneurial Activity in Various Countries

Average (unweighted) 9.9   Average (unweighted) 6.1   Average (unweighted) 3.4

Total Entrepreneurial Activity

Countries

■ Factor-Driven Economies   ■ Efficiency-Driven Economies   □ Innovation-Driven Economies

Source: Neils Bosma and Jonathan Levie, "2009 Executive Report," *Global Entrepreneurship Monitor*, 2010, p. 21

free-market countries in central and eastern Europe. However, as shown in Figure 6.3, the level of entrepreneurship varies considerably. Worldwide, more than 9 percent of adults are starting or managing a new business. Thailand leads in the number of adults engaged in entrepreneurial activity (27 percent), followed by Peru (26 percent), Colombia (23 percent), Venezuela (20 percent), Dominican Republic (17 percent), and China (16 percent). The United States, with more than 9 percent of adults qualifying as entrepreneurs, is currently in 13th place.[16]

Organizations worldwide recognize the importance of developing the next generation of entrepreneurs. Global Enterpreneurship Week (GEW) is one way of reaching out to students as well as recent graduates to encourage entrepreneurship. Founded by the Kauffman Organization and Enterprise UK, the recent week-long GEW held 40,000 events in 100 countries for 10 million participants. More than 18,000 companies and organizations planned youth-oriented business events in countries ranging from the United States to South Africa. But Brazil earned top honors with 4,324 events and more than 7 million participants.[17]

Education

The past two decades have brought tremendous growth in the number of educational opportunities for would-be entrepreneurs. Today, more than 100 U.S. universities offer full-fledged majors in entrepreneurship, dozens of others offer an emphasis in entrepreneurship, and hundreds more offer one or two courses in how to start a business.

In addition to traditional classroom experience, a number of schools offer opportunities to intern with a start-up or actually work toward launching a company. The Entrepreneurship and Innovation Group at Northeastern University in Boston, which is staffed by professors who are entrepreneurs themselves, provides students with the chance to work in entrepreneurial settings in a variety of industries including retail, commercial real estate development, financial services, health care, and high-growth technology.[18]

Besides schools, many organizations have sprouted up in recent years to teach entrepreneurship to young people. The Kauffman Center for Entrepreneurial Leadership offers training programs for learners from kindergarten through community college. The center's Entreprep summer program, which is taught in conjunction with local colleges and universities, teaches high school juniors how to start and manage a company. Students in Free Enterprise (SIFE) is a worldwide not-for-profit organization in which college students, working with faculty advisors, teach grade school and high school students and other community members the value of private enterprise and entrepreneurship.[19] The Association of Collegiate Entrepreneurs has chapters on many college campuses in the United States and Canada.

You don't have to major in business to become an entrepreneur, but students who do major in entrepreneurship or take entrepreneurship courses are three times more likely to start their own business or help someone else start a business.[20] In fact, you don't have to wait for graduation to launch your first startup, and your business idea doesn't have to change the world. Ge Wang did finish college before starting his business, but he never intended to be an entrepreneur. Wang was a music professor who had earned a bit of notoriety by creating the first orchestra composed entirely of mobile phones. One of Wang's doctoral students, Jeff Smith, had started a small tech company before returning to academics. When Smith met Wang he thought, "This dude is going to change music." So Wang began to create iPhone apps for Smith's new venture, including Sonic Lighter and Ocarina (which turns an iPhone into a flute and has sold more than 3 million downloads). More recent creations are Magic Piano and Glee karaoke. "We want to make apps that make people feel less inhibited—to play music by accident," explains Wang. "There's a little creativity in everyone. We just think we need to nudge them."[21]

Information Technology

The explosion in information technology (IT) has provided one of the biggest boosts for entrepreneurs. As computer and communications technologies have merged and dropped dramatically in cost, entrepreneurs have gained tools that help them compete with large companies. Information technology helps entrepreneurs work quickly and efficiently, provide immediate and attentive customer service, increase sales, and project professional images. In fact, technology has leveled the playing field to the point that, with the use of smartphones and other wireless devices, along with instant Web distribution, a dorm-room innovator can compete with a much larger firm. Technology has also assisted in the tremendous increase of homepreneurs—entrepreneurs who run home-based businesses. These successful ventures are described in the "Hit & Miss" feature.

Social networking has further transformed the business environment for entrepreneurs. According to a recent study, more than 90 percent of successful companies now use at least one social media tool. One entrepreneur who embraces the full impact of social media on his business is Adam Kidron, who runs an upscale, health-conscious burger joint in New York

Hit & Miss

Businesses Based at Home Are Booming

The idea itself makes perfect sense: you're laid off from your full-time job, or you've recently moved to a new area, or you just had a baby. Working from home seems like the ideal solution. But until a few years ago, home-based businesses were not really considered legitimate by the business community in general. Most people viewed home-based work as no more challenging—or lucrative—than stuffing envelopes. All that has changed. Today, more than 6.6 million home-based businesses contribute at least half of their owners' household income. It is estimated that homepreneurs employ about one in every ten private-sector workers—and their businesses are as competitive as any other. Technology has made all this possible.

Some homepreneurs run businesses entirely based on technology, such as Web development. Stephen Labuda, president of Agency3, is a former programmer for Deutsche Bank, a large international banking firm. He built Web sites on the side for several years before he quit his job and made Agency3 his full-time, home-based career in Boston. The firm's revenues are now in the millions and Labuda has about half a dozen employees. Labuda loves working from home. "I'm not intending to go rent office space," he notes.

Other homepreneurs rely on technology to reach customers, fulfill orders, ship goods, or provide other services. When Michael and Mary Ferrari retired, they realized they needed to supplement their savings—and they didn't necessarily want to stop working. So they formed UnusualThreads.com based in California, which sells fashions worn by celebrities. The couple still only works the site part time, but they earn enough money to augment their savings and can take time off to travel. Another such homepreneur is Marco Barberini, who launched OvernightPetTags.com in Michigan several years ago and now grosses more than $8,000 a month. Barberini discovered a way to manufacture and ship pet-identification tags cheaper than his competition. His goal is to tag every pet in the United States Barberini echoes the advice of every successful homepreneur. "Most people give up too quickly," he says. "Just make sure that [your product] is going to be something that's in demand, and do it."

Questions for Critical Thinking

1. Could any of these home-based businesses succeed without the heavy use of information technology? Why or why not?
2. Outline your own idea for a home-based business that would rely on technology.

Sources: Steven Berglas, "Wake-up Call for Newly Hatched Entrepreneurs," *Forbes.com*, February 6, 2010, http://www.forbes.com; Carol Tice, "Homepreneur Winners Keep Growing Despite Downturn," *Entrepreneur.com*, February 1, 2010, http://blog.entrpreneur.com; John Tozzi, "The Rise of the Homepreneur," *BusinessWeek*, accessed January 8, 2010, http://www.businessweek.com.

City, called 4food. Customers "design" their own burgers on one of the iPads in the restaurant or on their home computers or smart phones. Then they save the burger recipe to 4food's database. They can go further by posting their creation on Twitter or Facebook, or they can create their own YouTube commercial about it. "Really, social media is part of the fundamentals of the product," Kidron observes. "The idea that social media is some kind of fad is ridiculous. It's how we communicate. New companies will have social media in their DNA."[22]

Demographic and Economic Trends

Who might be starting a business alongside you? Immigrants to the United States are the most likely to start their own businesses, as well as those between the ages of 55 and 64.[23] As Baby Boomers continue to age and control a large share of wealth in this country, the trend can only be expected to continue. Older entrepreneurs will also have access to their retirement funds and home equity for financing. Many Boomers also plan to work after retirement from traditional jobs or careers, either because they want to or in order to boost income and savings.

As mentioned earlier, college students are jumping on the entrepreneurial wagon in greater numbers too. Alfonso Olvera started RailTronix while a student at the University of Houston. RailTronix is a Web-based software system that helps rail shippers in the oil industry track their shipments in real time. RailTronix produced $250,000 in revenues in its first year. Now Olvera is developing a similar system for the grain industry.[24] Chrissie Harsh launched Chrissie's Cookies while at the University of Texas at Austin, simply because word of her exceptional baking traveled around campus. Harsh's classmates could order Finger-Lickin Peanut Butter or Cranberry White Chocolate Chip cookies online or request special ingredients. Harsh uses Facebook to market her business and keep in touch with customers. Her Facebook page cites a bold mission statement: "Changing the world one cookie at a time." Every year, Harsh bakes cookies for a local benefit that raises funds to dig drinking wells in Africa.[25]

Demographic trends—including the aging of the U.S. population, the growth of ethnic groups, and the predominance of two-income families—create opportunities for entrepreneurs. Convenience products for busy parents, foods that cater to ethnic preferences, and services designed specifically for older consumers all enjoy an opportunity for success. And as the economy fluctuates, entrepreneurs who are flexible enough to adapt quickly stand the best chance for success. Bobby Flam, owner of Jumbo's Restaurant in Miami, has kept his restaurant in the same location for 44 years despite hurricanes, riots, economic downturns, and the flight of other business. "I stayed because I wanted to be an example that business could succeed here," says Flam. He admits that not much has changed. "I ought to be selling more," Flam observes. "But the person who used to spend $20 is spending $5." Flam never turns away someone who is hungry and feeds an average of 10 homeless people a day. Flam also helps new local entrepreneurs get started in the neighborhood—and enjoys regular visits by sports stars from the Miami Heat and Miami Dolphins.[24]

Assessment Check ✔

1. To what extent is entrepreneurship possible in different countries, and what opportunities does globalization create for today's entrepreneurs?

2. Identify the educational factors that help expand current opportunities for entrepreneurs.

3. Describe current demographic trends that suggest new goods and services for entrepreneurial businesses.

Characteristics of Entrepreneurs

People who strike out on their own are pioneers in their own right. They aren't satisfied with the status quo and want to achieve certain goals on their own terms. Successful entrepreneurs are often likely to have had parents who were entrepreneurs—or dreams of starting their own business. They also tend to possess specific personality traits. Researchers who study successful entrepreneurs report that they are more likely to be curious, passionate, self-motivated, honest, courageous, and flexible. The eight traits summarized in Figure 6.4 are especially important for people who want to succeed as entrepreneurs.

FIGURE 6.4

Characteristics of Entrepreneurs

Entrepreneurial Personality

Vision

High Energy Level

Need to Achieve

Self-Confidence and Optimism

Tolerance for Failure

Creativity

Tolerance for Ambiguity

Internal Locus of Control

Vision

Entrepreneurs generally begin with a *vision*—an overall idea for how to make their business idea a success. Then they pursue this vision with relentless passion. Bill Gates and Paul Allen launched Microsoft with the vision of a computer on every desk and in every home, all running Microsoft software. Their vision helped Microsoft become the world's largest marketer of computer software. It guided the company and provided clear direction for employees as Microsoft grew, adapted, and prospered in an industry characterized by tremendous technological change.

Arguably, every invention from the light bulb to the cell phone originated from a person with vision—someone who viewed the world in a slightly different way. Sometimes inventions have occurred out of necessity or even a mistake. True entrepreneurs know how to turn these situations into opportunities. It's well known that penicillin was created by accident; so was champagne. The heating potential for microwaves was discovered by their inventor while working on another project. Play-Doh was intended to be a cleaning product, and Velcro was created by a hunter who noticed that burrs stuck to his socks as he walked through the wilderness.[27]

High Energy Level

Entrepreneurs work long and hard to realize their visions. Many entrepreneurs work full-time at their regular day jobs and spend weeknights and weekends launching their start-ups. Many entrepreneurs work alone or with a very small staff, which means that they often wear most—if not all—of the hats required to get the business going, filling design, marketing, sales, and financial roles. Most entrepreneurs spend at least 70 hours a week on their new business, which can affect their other job (if they have one) and the quality of their personal life—at least in the beginning.[28] Thus, they need a high level of energy in order to succeed.

Need to Achieve

Entrepreneurs work hard because they want to excel. Their strong competitive drive helps them enjoy the challenge of reaching difficult goals and promotes dedication to personal success. A poll conducted by About.com showed Oprah Winfrey as the most admired entrepreneur among adults. The first African American woman billionaire, Winfrey has built an empire stretching from television to magazines to radio. Her own words best illustrate her strong drive: "I don't think of myself as a poor, deprived ghetto girl who made good. I think of myself as somebody who from an early age knew I was responsible for myself, and had to make good."[29] But when teens were polled for their favorite entrepreneurs, Apple co-founder Steven Jobs got the top spot, followed by *Harry Potter* author J.K. Rowling. Oprah Winfrey came in third. Facebook founder Mark Zuckerberg was fifth in line.[30]

Self-Confidence and Optimism

Entrepreneurs believe in their ability to succeed, and they instill their optimism in others. Often their optimism resembles fearlessness in the face of difficult odds. They see opportunities where others see danger lurking. Robbie Vitrano is one such entrepreneur. Owner of Trumpet, a marketing agency based in New Orleans, Vitrano refuses to give up on the small business that were wiped out in Hurricane Katrina. Several years after other types of aid have disappeared, Vitrano continues to support his business neighbors—believing that his investment will pay off in the revitalization of the city. Trumpet is now headquartered in the Icehouse, a 12,000-square-foot commercial real estate development

©Richard Drew/AP/Wide World Photos

Entrepreneurs often succeed simply because they won't give up. When sales of Bobbi Brown's cosmetics line stalled, she moved the company to a new location and revamped its advertising. In the process, she successfully differentiated her company from the competition.

in a building that once lay under water. The Icehouse is home to ten small business, start-ups, and not-for-profit organizations that otherwise would have been left without office space. Elsewhere in town, Vitrano has jump-started Naked Pizza, which is now so popular he has begun to sell franchises.[31]

Tolerance for Failure

Entrepreneurs often succeed by sheer will and the ability to try and try again when others would give up. They also view setbacks and failures as learning experiences and are not easily discouraged or disappointed when things don't go as planned. Bobbi Brown has built a big name in the cosmetics industry. Estée Lauder bought her company, and Brown stayed on in an active role. The brand faced some setbacks after its acquisition and sales went flat, but Brown never gave up. She met with the CEO, who said the problem was that the cosmetics were not setting themselves apart from the competition. Brown took the criticism in stride, learned from the setback, and decided to change the culture of the company. She moved out of the GM building to a loft in the SoHo section of Manhattan, made advertising photographs more editorial, and approached the cosmetics business as if it were a magazine. The company's numbers vastly improved and eventually hit half a billion dollars.[32]

When things go well, it's easy to take personal credit. But when poor business decisions result in failure, it's a bit more difficult. Truly successful entrepreneurs are willing to take responsibility for their mistakes. That is why an important part of launching any new business is establishing a code of ethics, as discussed in the "Solving an Ethical Controversy" feature.

Creativity

Entrepreneurs typically conceive new ideas for goods and services, and they devise innovative ways to overcome difficult problems and situations. If we look at the top entrepreneurs in the world, we can see that creativity is the common denominator. *Inc.* magazine presents an annual list of the 500 top small businesses, most of which were started by entrepreneurs. The word *solution* is one of the most common to appear in the names of these companies.

Some entrepreneurs find creative solutions to problems; others find creative ways to accomplish a task or provide a service. Still others create entirely new products. The Lubbers family started a sustainable farm—instead of buying groceries with unknown or potentially toxic ingredients—in order to address the health issues suffered by their young daughter. Today the thriving Vermont farm offers grass-fed beef and lamb, whey-free pork, artisan cheeses, and fresh baked goods. Lubbers Farm also hosts educational workshops and offers a cow-share leasing program.[33]

Solving an Ethical Controversy

Entrepreneurs and Ethics: It's Good Business

When you're starting a new business, it's easy to get caught up in the excitement of it: a fresh start, a new idea, visions of fame and fortune. It might seem harmless to present an overly optimistic sales picture or be a bit vague about where and how your product will be produced—after all, once your invention hits the stores, sales will skyrocket and all will be forgiven. But experts in every industry warn against such fuzzy communication and decision making. Not only might your venture fall flat as a result, but failure may come in the form of a damaged reputation or legal ramifications. And while you might be someone who can tolerate some failures, a wise entrepreneur knows how to prevent others—such as a failure of ethics.

Should every new business have a formal code of ethics?

PRO

1. A code of ethics "embodies the ethical commitments of your organization," writes business author Chris MacDonald. "It tells the world who you are, what you stand for, and what to expect when conducting business with you." It also demonstrates leadership.

2. A code of ethics is a necessity in today's business environment. Without it, if there is a difficult incident or event, a small firm may be exposed to "greater risk from regulatory and prosecutorial authorities," observes Michael Connor, publisher of *Business Ethics.*

CON

1. Not every entrepreneurial enterprise, particularly those run by one person, needs a formal code of ethics. A person's word or a handshake is just as effective. The important thing is to convey integrity about the way your firm will do business.

2. There are too many stories in the media about businesspeople who have failed to make ethical decisions—and not enough accounts of the many entrepreneurs who conduct business every day in an ethical manner. A code of ethics will not make a bad person good; nor will lack of a code turn a good person bad.

Summary

Some people argue that writing a formal code of ethics takes too much time; others recommend outsourcing it to a consultant or another third party. However, the overwhelming majority of business experts advise taking the time and effort to develop these formal guidelines. If a company has more than one employee, then all employees should be required to become familiar with the code. As an entrepreneur, you will face many challenges and probably a few failures; but none should be a failure of ethics.

Sources: "Business Ethics," Small Business Administration, http://www.sba.gov, accessed March 16, 2010; Carter McNamara, "Complete Guide to Ethics Management," *Management Help,* http://www.managementhelp.org, accessed March 16, 2010; Chris MacDonald, "Considerations for Writing a Code of Ethics," *Streetwise Small Business Book of Lists,* accessed March 16, 2010; Josh Spiro, "How To Write a Code of Ethics for Business," *Inc.com,* February 24, 2010, http://www.inc.com; Don Knauss, "The Role of Business Ethics in Relationships with Customers," *Forbes.com,* January 19, 2010, http://www.forbes.com.

Aaron Patzer started Mint.com in California because he and his friends and family were frustrated with Intuit's Quicken products. He insisted that he could develop more user-friendly personal-finance software, and he did. Two years later, Patzer sold his Web site to Intuit for $170 million.[34]

When his grandmother died, college student Curtis Funk got the idea to record the proceedings and memories of funerals onto CDs and sell them to families through funeral homes. Families of deceased loved ones appreciated the CDs so much that Funk's company, FuneralRecording.com located in Utah now has several employees and coordinates with more than 200 funeral homes around the United States to provide live streaming audio and video, transcripts, CDs, and other services. The firm also offers updates through Twitter, under the name "funeraltech."[35]

Tolerance for Ambiguity

Entrepreneurs take in stride the uncertainties associated with launching a venture. Dealing with unexpected events is the norm for most entrepreneurs. Tolerance for ambiguity is different from the love of risk taking that many people associate with entrepreneurship. Successful entrepreneurship is a far cry from gambling because entrepreneurs look for strategies that they believe have a good chance of success, and they quickly make adjustments when a strategy isn't working. An important way entrepreneurs manage ambiguity is by staying close to customers so that they can adjust their offerings in keeping with customer desires. One such entrepreneur is Kevin Mitnick. In the mid-1990s, Mitnick was arrested by the FBI for computer hacking, after which he served five years in prison. When he was released, Mitnick could have hidden his identity and started a new life—or gone on to further crimes. Instead, Mitnick went legitimate, opening his own computer security consulting company. He maintains a solid relationship with the businesses whose systems he once might have compromised. As head of his own firm, Mitnick Security Consulting, Mitnick is often asked to speak on security issues to government officials and business owners. "I was running from these people [before] and now they are wanting autographs," quips Mitnick.[36]

Internal Locus of Control

Entrepreneurs have an internal locus of control, which means they believe that they control their own destinies. You won't find entrepreneurs blaming others or outside events for their successes or failures—they own it all.

Ralph Braun was diagnosed with a degenerative illness when he was 6 years old. By the time he was 14, he was confined to a wheelchair. Braun attended college for one year but had to drop out because he just couldn't navigate the large campus in his traditional wheelchair. So he decided to design his own transportation. Within about four months, he had built his first scooter. Then he got a job at a local automotive supply factory, where he was able to get around quite easily on his scooter. People noticed, told him about friends or family members who needed such a scooter, and he built them to order. Braun began to focus on the cumbersome van he was driving—and redesigned the interior of that as well, including a lift that is now standard on buses and mass transit. Again, he received requests to convert the vans of other wheelchair-bound drivers. Eventually Braun quit his factory job so he could focus on his business full-time. BraunAbility, located in Indiana, is now a $200 million empire. As he began building scooters, Braun recalls "everyone told me it wasn't going to work. But when it comes to commonsense engineering, I'm very blessed. I think it is a [natural] ability." Braun is clearly in charge of his fate.[37]

After reading this summary of typical personality traits, maybe you're wondering if you have what it takes to become an entrepreneur. Take the test in Figure 6.5 to find out. Your results may help you determine whether you would succeed in starting your own company.

Assessment Check ☑

1. What is meant by an entrepreneur's vision?

2. Why is it important for an entrepreneur to have a high energy level and a strong need for achievement?

3. How do entrepreneurs generally feel about the possibility of failure?

FIGURE
6.5 **Quiz for Small Business Success**

Choose the answer you think is best for each question. There are no "wrong" answers.

1. What is the key to business success:
a. business knowledge
b. market awareness
c. hands on management
d. sufficient capital
e. hard work

2. If a relative ever asks me for advice about starting a business I will tell them to:
a. work for someone else in the field first
b. write a business plan
c. study marketing
d. give up the idea
e. learn about budgeting

3. Which is the largest potential trouble spot:
a. too much growth
b. too little growth
c. too fast growth
d. too slow growth
e. sporadic growth

4. I trust: (select as many as apply)
a. nobody
b. myself
c. my partner
d. a few key employees
e. my customers

5. I am unhappy when my employees are:
a. late
b. unhappy
c. abrupt with customers
d. resigning
e. less dedicated than me

6. My customers are: (select as many as apply)
a. always right
b. too fussy
c. demanding
d. worth listening to
e. dumb

7. Rank these in order of importance for small-business marketing success:
a. word-of-mouth
b. advertising
c. signs
d. location
e. community events

8. When it comes to money I am:
a. careful
b. too carefree
c. emotional
d. shrewd
e. hardnosed

9. Financially my firm:
a. has trouble with cash-flow
b. has a good line of credit
c. is financed totally by receipt—no credit
d. is making better profits this year than last
e. knows exactly where it is all the time

10. In hiring people:
a. I take far too long
b. I look for the cheapest person
c. personality is more Important than experience
d. I look for the best person, and am willing to pay
e. I only hire at the trainee level

11. With my employees:
a. I treat everybody the same
b. I try to talk privately to everybody once a week
c. To whatever extent possible I tailor assignments to personalities
d. I encourage them to talk to me about the business
e. I try to work alongside them whenever possible

12. The real key to business success is:
a. hard work and perseverance
b. fine products and service
c. advertising
d. knowing the fundamentals of business
e. employees

13. Competition is:
a. dumb
b. smart
c. cunning
d. everywhere
e. a constant threat

14. The best competitive advantage is:
a. experience
b. understanding what the market wants
c. confidence
d. conducting a business ethically
e. a detailed plan

15. I keep:
a. careful financial records
b. in touch with my customers
c. in touch with my employees
d. trying new techniques
e. wanting to retire

16. My dream is:
a. to grow the business until someone else can run it
b. to work until I drop
c. to give up these headaches and have more fun at work
d. to try another business
e. to take a vacation

17. I think business plans are:
a. for the birds
b. nice but not necessary
c. something I can do with my accountant
d. useful and informative
e. essential—wouldn't do business without them

18. What makes a terrific entrepreneur?
a. creativity
b. discipline
c. consumer orientation
d. technical proficiency
e. flexibility

19. What does a business need most?
a. money
b. market research
c. help
d. time
e. a solid business plan

20. What is essential to marketing?
a. "a sixth sense"
b. market research
c. customer awareness
d. experience
e. testing

Source: U.S. Small Business Administration, http://www.sba.gov/small/businessplanner/manage/makedecisions/serv_manage_q4.html, accessed February 12, 2011.

Starting a New Venture

The examples of entrepreneurs presented so far have introduced many ways to start a business. This section discusses the process of choosing an idea for a new venture and transforming the idea into a working business.

Selecting a Business Idea

In choosing an idea for your business, the two most important considerations are (1) finding something you love to do and are good at doing and (2) determining whether your idea can satisfy a need in the marketplace. People willingly work hard doing something they love, and the experience will bring personal fulfillment. The old adages "Do what makes you happy" and "Be true to yourself" are the best guidelines for deciding on a business idea.

Success also depends on customers, so would-be entrepreneurs must also be sure that the idea they choose has interest in the marketplace. The most successful entrepreneurs tend to operate in industries in which a great deal of change is taking place and in which customers have difficulty pinpointing their precise needs. These industries allow entrepreneurs to capitalize on their strengths, such as creativity, hard work, and tolerance of ambiguity, to build customer relationships. Nevertheless, examples of outstanding entrepreneurial success occur in every industry. Whether you want to build a business based on your grandmother's cookie recipes or know that you have a better idea for tax-preparation software, you are more likely to succeed if you ask yourself the right questions from the beginning.

Consider the following guidelines as you think about your business ideas:

- List your interests and abilities. Include your values and beliefs, your goals and dreams, things you like and dislike doing, and your job experiences.

- Make another list of the types of businesses that match your interests and abilities.

- Read newspapers and business and consumer magazines to learn about demographic and economic trends that identify future needs for products that no one yet offers.

- Carefully evaluate existing goods and services, looking for ways you can improve them.

- Decide on a business that matches what you want and offers profit potential.

- Conduct marketing research to determine whether your business idea will attract enough customers to earn a profit.

- Learn as much as you can about the industry in which your new venture will operate, your merchandise or service, and your competitors. Read surveys that project growth in various industries.

Eric Casaburi already knew that he loved the fitness industry—he had owned two licensed fitness centers and liked the energy of the business. But he thought he could do a better job. "I felt there was a niche for a low-cost provider that gave a high-end experience," Casaburi explains. And he wanted to do it with a twist. "Nostalgia for the 1980s has never disappeared," he observes. So Casaburi developed the idea for Retro Fitness—a chain of gyms along the East Coast with a 1980s theme. The gyms, which feature Retro Cardio Movie Theaters, RetroBlends, juice bars, bright red-and-yellow weight machines, and Rubik's Cubes at the front desk. Retro Fitness is a hit. While traditional gyms are struggling to hang onto customers, Retro Fitness is swelling with new members. Why? "If you keep people entertained," says Casaburi, "they don't mind the sweat." Casaburi doesn't mind the sweat either—with the help of franchising agreements, he plans to expand his business to several hundred locations over the next few years.[38]

Many entrepreneurs who start new businesses invent new products or processes. When that happens, the inventor–entrepreneur needs to protect the rights to his or her invention by securing a patent. The U.S. Patent and Trademark Office's Web site (http://www.uspto.gov) provides information about this process, along with forms to apply for a patent. Inventors can also apply for a patent online.

Adam Lowry and Eric Ryan started their firm, Method, because they believed they could make better household cleaning supplies than the larger firms. Today, they are credited with reinventing an industry, as described in the "Going Green" feature.

Adam Lowry and Eric Ryan: There's a Method to Their Madness

To most people, the household cleaning industry would seem to be as dull as dishwater—but not childhood buddies Adam Lowry and Eric Ryan. Where others saw dreariness, the two entrepreneurs saw green—in both senses of the word. They believed they could create more eco-friendly soaps, dishwashing liquids, and laundry detergents than the big companies; package them more attractively; and make huge profits. With their Califonia-based company Method, they have achieved these goals.

More than a decade ago, the budding entrepreneurs brainstormed about products they could reinvent that would challenge industry giants. What could evoke more drudgery than cleaning? Even the products were boring. They were made with harsh chemicals and packaged in dull plastic bottles. But they pulled in the profits for their manufacturers. So Lowry and Ryan's solution was simple: come up with nontoxic products and package them in cool-looking bottles and jars.

Method wasn't an overnight success. The partners' economic timing was off—their first cleaning product hit the market just as the economy stumbled, and they ran through the $100,000 in savings they had put up as seed capital. They found themselves mixing batches of the cleaning brew in a bathtub and delivering orders in a pick-up truck. Then they maxed out their credit cards and couldn't pay their vendors. "We had to appeal to the inner entrepreneur in each of our vendors," recalls Lowry. "We had to sell them on the fact that Eric and I could do something that had never been done before."

Slowly the cleaning tide began to turn, and a year later Method products were beginning to appear in about 800 stores—including Target. But this wasn't enough for Lowry and Ryan; they wanted to make a bold statement about nontoxic cleaners. To build visibility for their brand, they went to well-known product designer Karim Rashid, who liked the idea and came aboard Method as the company's chief creative officer. From there, the business took off. Because the company was so small, its innovations in product and design could reach the marketplace in weeks instead of months or years. Method now markets about 150 products ranging from hand soap to bathroom cleaners, which are sold at retailers or online through Method's Web site. The firm's marketing slogan, "People against dirty," has caught on with consumers around the country. Avid consumers can blog or post reviews of Method's products at the firm's site as well. As for a business idea, Ryan and Lowry have found their Method.

Questions for Critical Thinking

1. Adam Lowry and Eric Ryan set challenging goals when they selected their business idea. They could have failed. Why do you think they have succeeded?

2. You often hear the advice to "do what makes you happy." No one loves washing dishes or doing laundry. Why do you think Lowry and Ryan chose household cleaners as their business—what is there about the business that could make them happy?

Sources: Method Web site, http://methodhome.com, accessed February 12, 2011; "How Two Friends Built a $100 Million Company," *Inc.com,* http://www.inc.com, accessed March 16, 2010; Stuart Elliott, "A Clean Break With Staid Detergent Ads," *The New York Times,* February 3, 2010, http://www.nytimes.com; Julie Scelfo, "Begone, Carbon Footprint!," *The New York Times,* January 27, 2010, http://www.nytimes.com.

Buying an Existing Business Some entrepreneurs prefer to buy established businesses rather than assume the risks of starting new ones. Buying an existing business brings many advantages: employees are already in place to serve established customers and deal with familiar suppliers, the good or service is known in the marketplace, and the necessary permits and licenses have already been secured. Getting financing for an existing business also is easier than it is for most start-ups. Some sellers may even help the buyers by providing financing and offering to serve as consultants. Most people want to buy a healthy business so that they can build on its success, but an experienced entrepreneur might purchase a struggling business with the intent of turning it around. There are many resources for entrepreneurs who are considering the purchase of a business, ranging from information provided by government agencies such as the Small Business Administration to Web sites listing actual companies for sale.

Buying a Franchise Like buying an established business, buying a franchise offers a less risky way to begin a business than starting an entirely new firm. But franchising, which was discussed in detail in Chapter 5, still involves risks, and it is wise to do thorough research before taking the plunge. While there are a multitude of franchises from which to

Preparing a business plan is advisable and necessary, particularly if an entrepreneur is seeking funds from outside sources. When Shez Zamrudeen felt she was ready to open her Jersey City boutique in New Jersey, called Deen, she developed a plan for her new business.

Courtesy Shez Zamrudeen

choose, one area that is experiencing tremendous growth is firms whose goods and services are targeted for children and their parents. These businesses offer everything from photography to tutoring to security. "They are pretty much recession resistant," says Jeff Elgin, CEO of FranChoice, "since people are going to scrimp in a lot of areas before they start cutting stuff for their children."[39]

Creating a Business Plan

In the past, many entrepreneurs launched their ventures without creating formal business plans. Although planning is an integral part of managing in contemporary business, entrepreneurs typically seize opportunities as they arise and change course as necessary. Flexibility seems to be the key to business start-ups, especially in rapidly changing markets. But because of the risks inherent in starting a business, it has become apparent that at least some planning is not only advisable but necessary, particularly if an entrepreneur is seeking funds from outside sources.

When Shez Zamrudeen felt she was ready to put her passion for fashion to work in the form of her own boutique called Deen, she developed a plan for her new business. A major part of Zamrudeen's plan involved finding a way to distinguish her shop from many others in her New Jersey area. She decided to place her flagship store in New Jersey's Powerhouse Arts District in Jersey City—complete with original art work decorating the walls. "There is no other boutique in the area that has an art gallery and clothing store in one," claims Zamrudeen. When the recession hit, Zamrudeen was undaunted. "I had to adjust my current business plan and long-term goals," she admits. "I had to be smarter and more careful with my inventory." But Zamrudeen says she still plans to achieve all her business goals within the next five to ten years.[40]

Chapter 5 and Appendix D discuss business plans in more detail. The Internet also offers a variety of resources for creating business plans. Table 6.1 lists some of these online resources.

Table 6.1 **Online Resources for Preparing a Business Plan**

AllBusiness.com http://www.allbusiness.com	The "Business Advice" page provides links to examples, templates, and tips for writing a plan.
Inc. http://www.inc.com	Under "Departments," click "How-To-Guides" and then "Writing a Business Plan," which links to 150+ articles about how to write a business plan.
Kauffman eVenturing http://www.kauffman.org/eventuring	The "Explore Topics" section has links to information and resources for researching and writing a plan, as well as presenting it to lenders or investors.
MoreBusiness.com http://www.morebusiness.com	To see a sample plan, select "Business & Marketing Plans" from the list of templates.

Finding Financing

A key issue in any business plan is financing. Requirements for **seed capital**, funds used to launch a company, depend on the nature of the business. They can range as high as several million—say, for the purchase of a McDonald's franchise in a lucrative area—or as low as $1,000 for Web site design. Many entrepreneurs rely on personal savings or loans from business associates, family members, or even friends for start-up funds. Table 6.2 lists the common sources of start-up capital.

Debt Financing When entrepreneurs use **debt financing**, they borrow money that they must repay. Loans from banks, finance companies, credit-card companies, and family or friends are all sources of debt financing. Although some entrepreneurs charge business expenses to personal credit cards because they are relatively easy to obtain, high interest rates make this source of funding expensive, and the Small Business Administration (SBA) recommends finding alternative methods of funding.

Many banks turn down requests for loans to fund start-ups, fearful of the high risk such ventures entail. This has been particularly true over the last several years. Only a small percentage of start-ups raise seed capital through bank loans, although some new firms can get SBA-backed loans, as discussed in Chapter 5. Applying for a bank loan requires careful preparation. Bank loan officers want to see a business plan and will evaluate the entrepreneur's credit history. Because a start-up has not yet established a business credit history, banks often base lending decisions on evaluations of entrepreneurs' personal credit histories. Banks are more willing to make loans to entrepreneurs who have been in business for a while, show a profit on rising revenues, and need funds to finance expansion. Some entrepreneurs have found that local community banks are more interested in their loan applications than are the major national banks.

seed capital initial funding needed to launch a new venture.

debt financing borrowed funds that entrepreneurs must repay.

Table

⌐6.2⌐ Funding Used by Entrepreneurs for Start-ups

SOURCE	PERCENTAGE OF ENTREPRENEURS*
Self-financing	82%
Loans from family, friends, or business associates	22%
Bank loans	18%
Lines of credit	18%
Venture capital	8%
SBA or other government funds	4%

*Percentages do not total 100 because entrepreneurs often use multiple sources to finance start-ups.

Source: "Entrepreneurial America: A Comprehensive Look at Today's Fastest-Growing Private Companies," *Inc. The Handbook of the American Entrepreneur,* http://www.inc.com, accessed July 5, 2011.

Even entrepreneurs who have previously received funding from banks—and have maintained a good relationship with their lenders—have experienced a credit crunch in recent years. After several years in business, Kevin Semcken got a call from his loan officer informing him that the bank would no longer fund his $2.5 million line of credit. A line of credit is an approved loan that a business can borrow from when funds are needed. Without that money, Colorado-based Able Planet could not buy the raw materials or manufacture its products—headsets, headphones, and assistive listening devices for people with varied levels of hearing. Large retailers like Costco and Walmart had already placed orders. So Semcken reevaluated his business plan and found alternative funding.[41]

equity financing funds invested in new ventures in exchange for part ownership.

Equity Financing To secure <u>equity financing</u>, entrepreneurs exchange a share of ownership in their company for money supplied by one or more investors. Entrepreneurs invest their own money along with funds supplied by other people and firms that become co-owners of the start-ups. An entrepreneur does not have to repay equity funds. Rather, the investors share in the success of the business. Sources of equity financing include family and friends, business partners, venture capital firms, and private investors. Kevin Semcken, owner of Able Planet, was able to secure some equity funding.[42]

Teaming up with a partner who has funds to invest may benefit an entrepreneur with a good idea and skills but little or no money. Investors may also have business experience, which they will be eager to share because the company's prosperity will benefit them. Like borrowing, however, equity financing has its drawbacks. One is that investment partners may not agree on the future direction of the business, and in the case of partnerships, if they cannot resolve disputes, one partner may have to buy out the other to keep operating.

venture capitalists business firms or groups of individuals that invest in new and growing firms in exchange for an ownership share.

Some entrepreneurs find creative ways to obtain equity financing. Gavin McClurg did that when he came up with a timeshare business model for his start-up. His venture, called Offshore Odysseys, is actually a five-year sailing expedition aboard a $1.2 million catamaran named *Discovery* that will cover the world. Investors buy timeshare segments for between $20,000 and $30,000 on the journey, during which they might swim across the equator or paraglide above Tahiti. Shareholders may purchase more than one segment—a prominent Australian anesthesiologist has eight, and a former Wall Street executive owns six. Shareholders also pay annual fees to cover operating expenses as well as food and beverages on the trip. Shares and fees cover McClurg's salary and living expenses—so at the end of the journey, he will likely have pocketed about $500,000 after taxes. He hopes to turn the *Discovery* into a fleet of several boats.[43]

Jody MacDonald Photography

Some entrepreneurs find creative ways to obtain equity financing. Gavin McClurg's venture, Offshore Odysseys, is a sailing expedition aboard a catamaran named *Discovery*. Investors buy timeshare segments for between $20,000 and $30,000 on the journey, during which they might swim across the equator or paraglide above Tahiti.

<u>Venture capitalists</u> are business organizations or groups of private individuals that invest in early-stage, high-potential, growth companies. Venture capitalists typically back companies in high technology industries such as biotechnology. In exchange for taking a risk with their own funds, these investors expect high rates of return, along with a stake in the company. Typical terms for accepting venture capital include agreement on how much the company is worth, how much stock both the investors and the founders will retain, control of the company's board, payment of dividends, and the period of time during which the founders are prohibited from "shopping" for further investments.[44] Venture capitalists

require a combination of extremely rare qualities, like innovative technology, potential for rapid growth, a well-developed business model, and an impressive management team.

Angel investors, wealthy individuals who invest money directly in new ventures in exchange for equity, are a larger source of investment capital for start-up firms. In contrast to venture capitalists, angels focus primarily on new ventures. Many angel investors are successful entrepreneurs who want to help aspiring business owners through the familiar difficulties of launching their businesses. Angel investors back a wide variety of new ventures. Because most entrepreneurs have trouble finding wealthy private investors, angel networks form to match business angels with start-ups in need of capital.

The Small Business Administration's Active Capital provides online listings to connect would-be angels with small businesses seeking financing. Venture capitalists that focus on women include Isabella Capital (http://www.fundisabella.com) and Springboard Enterprises (http://springboardenterprises.org). Those interested in minority-owned business include the U.S. Hispanic Chamber of Commerce (http://www.ushcc.com).

Government Support for New Ventures

Federal, state, and local governments support new ventures in a number of ways, as discussed in Chapter 5. The Small Business Administration (SBA), state and local agencies, as well as business incubators all offer information, resources, and sometimes even access to financing for entrepreneurs.

Another way to encourage entrepreneurship is through *enterprise zones*, specific geographic areas designated for economic revitalization. Enterprise zones encourage investment, often in distressed areas, by offering tax advantages and incentives to businesses locating within the boundaries of the zone. The state of Florida has 56 enterprise zones and allows a business located within urban zones to take tax credits for 20 or 30 percent of wages paid to new employees who reside within the urban enterprise zone. Colorado has 16 zones, while Ohio has designated 19 zones.

Government legislation can also encourage investment in the U.S. economy. The Immigration Act of 1990 (IMMACT 90) recognizes the growing globalization of business. It contains a provision that sets aside visas for immigrants wishing to invest money in a new venture in a *targeted employment area*—a rural area or an area that has experienced an unemployment rate of at least 150 percent of the national average. In addition, IMMACT 90 enables more experts in the fields such as science, engineering, and computer programming to be hired by U.S. firms.[45]

Intrapreneurship

Established companies try to retain the entrepreneurial spirit by encouraging **intrapreneurship**, the process of promoting innovation within their organizational structures. Today's fast-changing business climate compels established firms to innovate continually to maintain their competitive advantages.

Many companies encourage intrapreneurship—30 percent of large firms now allocate funds toward intrapreneurship.[46] 3M is a firm that has long been known for its innovative products. Ranging from Post-It Notes and Scotch Tape to Nutri-Dog Chews and

Thinsulate insulation, there are more than 55,000 3M products either on store shelves or embedded in other firms' goods.[47]

Coming up with the ideas for these products, developing them, and testing them before bringing them to market takes time and resources. CEO George Buckley believes that the only way to do this is to allocate both in support of intrapraneurship. Despite the recent recession, Buckley maintained $1 billion for research and development. 3M allows its researchers to devote 15 percent of their time to pursue their own ideas. One recent successful product that resulted from this is the first electronic stethoscope with Bluetooth technology. The company also awards annual Genesis Grants, worth up to $100,000, to 3M scientists for research. "Our business model is literally new-product innovation," comments Larry Wendling, head of 3M's corporate research.[48]

Assessment Check ✓

1. Why would large companies support intrapreneurship?
2. What is a skunkworks?

What's Ahead

In upcoming chapters, we look at other trends that are reshaping the business world of the 21st century. For example, in the next part of *Contemporary Business* we explore the critical issues of how companies organize, lead, and manage their work processes; manage and motivate their employees; empower their employees through teamwork and enhanced communication; handle labor and workplace disputes; and create and produce world-class goods and services.

Summary of Learning Objectives

⌐1⌐ Define the term *entrepreneur,* and distinguish among entrepreneurs, small-business owners, and managers.

Unlike many small-business owners, entrepreneurs typically own and run their businesses with the goal of building significant firms that create wealth and add jobs. Entrepreneurs are visionaries. They identify opportunities and take the initiative to gather the resources they need to start their businesses quickly. Both managers and entrepreneurs use the resources of their companies to achieve the goals of those organizations.

Assessment Check Answers ✓

1.1 What tools do entrepreneurs use to create a new business? Entrepreneurs combine their ideas and drive with money, employees, and other resources to create a business that fills a market need.

1.2 How do entrepreneurs differ from managers? Managers direct the efforts of others to achieve an organization's goals. The drive and impatience that entrepreneurs have to make their companies successful may hurt their ability to manage.

⌐2⌐ Identify the different types of entrepreneurs.

A classic entrepreneur identifies a business opportunity and allocates available resources to tap that market. A serial entrepreneur starts one business, runs it, and then starts and runs additional businesses in succession. A social entrepreneur uses business principles to solve social problems.

Assessment Check Answers ✓

2.1 What do classic entrepreneurs and social entrepreneurs have in common? They both identify opportunities and allocate resources to pioneer new innovations.

2.2 Is a social entrepreneur simply a philanthropist? A philanthropist generally promotes human welfare through charitable donations, while a social entrepreneur pioneers new ways to advance social causes and thus enhance social welfare.

⌐3⌐ Explain why people choose to become entrepreneurs.

There are many reasons people choose to become entrepreneurs. Some reasons are: desire to be one's own boss; desire to achieve financial success, desire for job security; desire to improve one's quality of life.

Assessment Check Answers ✓

3.1 What are the four main reasons people choose to become entrepreneurs? People generally choose to become entrepreneurs because they want to be their own boss, they believe they will achieve greater financial success, they believe they have more control over job security, and they want to enhance their quality of life.

3.2 What factors affect the entrepreneur's job security? An entrepreneur's job security depends on the decisions of customers and investors and on the cooperation and commitment of the entrepreneur's own employees.

⌐4⌐ Discuss factors that support and expand opportunities for entrepreneurs.

A favorable public perception, availability of financing, the falling cost and widespread availability of information technology, globalization, entrepreneurship education, and changing demographic and economic trends all contribute to a fertile environment for people to start new ventures.

Assessment Check Answers ✓

4.1 To what extent is entrepreneurship possible in different countries, and what opportunities does globalization create for today's entrepreneurs? More than 9 percent of adults worldwide are starting or managing a new business. As for globalization opportunities, entrepreneurs market their products abroad and hire international talent. Among the fastest-growing small U.S. companies, almost two of every five have international sales.

4.2 Identify the educational factors that help expand current opportunities for entrepreneurs. More than 100 U.S. universities offer majors in entrepreneurship, dozens of others offer an entrepreneurship emphasis, and hundreds more offer courses in how to start a business. Also, organizations such as the Kauffman Center for Entrepreneurial Leadership, Entreprep, and Students in Free Enterprise encourage and teach entrepreneurship.

4.3 Describe current demographic trends that suggest new goods and services for entrepreneurial businesses. The aging of the U.S. population, the emergence of Hispanics as the nation's largest ethnic group, and the growth of two-income families are creating opportunities for entrepreneurs to market new goods and services.

⌐5⌐ Identify personality traits that typically characterize successful entrepreneurs.

Successful entrepreneurs share several typical traits, including vision, high energy levels, the need to achieve, self-confidence and optimism, tolerance for failure, creativity, tolerance for ambiguity, and an internal locus of control.

Assessment Check Answers ✓

5.1 What is meant by an entrepreneur's vision? Entrepreneurs begin with a vision, an overall idea for how to make their business idea a success, and then passionately pursue it.

5.2 Why is it important for an entrepreneur to have a high energy level and a strong need for achievement? Because start-up companies typically have a small staff and struggle to raise enough capital, the entrepreneur has to make up the difference by working long hours. A strong need for achievement helps entrepreneurs enjoy the challenge of reaching difficult goals and promotes dedication to personal success.

5.3 How do entrepreneurs generally feel about the possibility of failure? They view failure as a learning experience and are not easily discouraged or disappointed when things don't go as planned.

⌐6⌐ Summarize the process of starting a new venture.

Entrepreneurs must select an idea for their business, develop a business plan, obtain financing, and organize the resources they need to operate their start-ups.

Assessment Check Answers ✓

6.1 What are the two most important considerations in choosing an idea for a new business? Two important considerations are finding something you love to do and are good at doing and determining whether your idea can satisfy a need in the marketplace.

6.2 What is the difference between debt financing and equity financing? Debt financing is money borrowed that must be repaid. Equity financing is an exchange of ownership shares in their company for money supplied by one or more investors.

6.3 What is seed capital? Seed capital is the money that is used to start a company.

⌐7⌐ Explain how organizations promote intrapreneurship.

Organizations encourage intrapreneurial activity within the company in a variety of ways, including hiring practices, dedicated programs such as skunkworks, access to resources, and wide latitude to innovate within established firms.

Assessment Check Answers ✓

7.1 Why would large companies support intrapreneurship? Large firms support intrapreneurship to retain an entrepreneurial spirit and to promote innovation and change.

7.2 What is a skunkworks? A skunkworks project is initiated by an employee who conceives an idea and then recruits resources from within the company to turn that idea into a commercial product.

Business Terms You Need to Know

entrepreneur 184
classic entrepreneur 185
serial entrepreneur 186

social entrepreneur 186
lifestyle entrepreneur 189
seed capital 203

debt financing 203
equity financing 204
venture capitalists 204

angel investors 205
intrapreneurship 205

Review Questions

1. Identify the three categories of entrepreneurs. How are they different from each other? How might an entrepreneur fall into more than one category?

2. People often become entrepreneurs because they want to be their own boss, and be in control of most or all of the major decisions related to their business. How might this relate to potential financial success? If there are downsides, what might they be?

3. How have globalization and information technology created new opportunities for entrepreneurs? Describe current demographic trends that suggest new goods and services for entrepreneurial businesses.

4. Identify the eight characteristics that are attributed to successful entrepreneurs. Which trait or traits do you believe are the most important for success? Why? Are there any traits that you think might actually contribute to potential failure? If so, which ones—and why?

5. When selecting a business idea, why is the advice to "do what makes you happy" and "be true to yourself" so important?

6. Suppose an entrepreneur is considering buying an existing business or franchise. Which of the eight entrepreneurial traits do you think would most apply to this person, and why?

7. Imagine that you and a partner are planning to launch a business that sells backpacks, briefcases, and soft luggage made out of recycled materials. You'll need seed capital for your venture. Outline how you would use that seed capital.

8. Describe the two main types of financing that entrepreneurs may seek for their businesses. What are the risks and benefits involved with each?

9. What is an enterprise zone? Describe what types of businesses might benefit from opening in such a zone—and how their success might be interconnected.

10. What is intrapreneurship? How does it differ from entrepreneurship?

Projects and Teamwork Applications

1. Interview an entrepreneur—you can do this in person, by e-mail, or on the phone. The person can be a local shop or restaurant owner, a hair salon owner, a pet groomer, a consultant—any field is fine. Find out why that person decided to become an entrepreneur. Ask whether his or her viewpoint has changed since starting a business. Decide whether the person is a classic, serial, or social entrepreneur. Present your findings to the class.

2. Certain demographic trends can represent opportunities for entrepreneurs—the aging of the U.S. population, the increasing diversity of the U.S. population, the growth in population of some states, and the predominance of two-income families to name a few. On your own or with a classmate, choose a demographic trend and brainstorm for business ideas that could capitalize on the trend. Create a poster or PowerPoint presentation to present your idea—and its relationship to the trend—to your class.

3. Review the eight characteristics of successful entrepreneurs. Which characteristics do you possess? Do you think you would be a good entrepreneur? Why or why not? Create an outline of the traits you believe are your strengths—and those that might be your weaknesses.

4. Many entrepreneurs turn a hobby or area of interest into a business idea. Others get their ideas from situations or daily problems for which they believe they have a solution—or a better solution than those already offered. Think about an area of personal interest—or a problem you think you could solve with a new good or service—and create the first part of a potential business plan, the introduction to your new company and its offerings. Then outline briefly what kind of financing you think would work best for your business, and what steps you would take to secure the funds.

5. Enterprise zones are designed to revitalize economically distressed areas. Choose an area with which you are familiar—it may be as close as a local neighborhood, or as far away as a city in which you might like to live someday. Do some online research about the area. Then outline your own plan for an enterprise zone—including businesses that you think would do well in the area, jobs that might be created, housing creation, and other factors.

Web Assignments

1. **Tools for entrepreneurs.** American Express has established something it calls "Open Forum" to allow entrepreneurs and small business owners to communicate with one another and share ideas. Visit the Open Forum Web site and review the available material. Prepare a short report on how Open Forum could help an entrepreneur start and grow a business.

   http://www.openforum.com/

2. **Venture capitalists.** Venture capital firms are an important source of financing for entrepreneurs. Most actively solicit funding proposals. Go to the Web site shown here to learn more about venture capital. What are some of the famous businesses that were originally financed by venture capitalists?

   http://www.nvca.org/

3. **Getting started.** Visit the Web site of *Entrepreneur* magazine and click on "Starting a Business." How should you go about researching a business idea? What are the steps involved in getting a product to market?

   http://www.entrepreneur.com

Note: Internet Web addresses change frequently. If you don't find the exact sites listed, you may need to access the organization's home page and search from there or use a search engine such as Bing or Google.

Marco Giannini's Dogswell: A Healthy Company after All   CASE 6.1

There's no question that pet lovers around the United States are willing to spend whatever it takes to enhance their companions' lives—they'll purchase gourmet food and treats, a variety of toys, and even services such as "day camp" for dogs. Marco Giannini himself is a dog lover. He is also a serial entrepreneur whose previous business—Clear Day (a natural beverage company)—went bust about ten years ago. Giannini learned a lot from that experience, and when he started his new company in California, Dogswell, he implemented those lessons.

Dogswell is a manufacturer and marketer of natural dog treats with catchy names like Happy Hips and Mellow Mut. The treats contain supplemental ingredients intended to help fight conditions like arthritis and hip dysplasia, both of which are common among medium-sized to larger dogs. The treats have been a hit—within five years, Dogswell sales topped $17 million.

But Giannini wasn't satisfied with just a small bite of the pet-care market. An entrepreneur who is well known for his high energy and self-confidence, Giannini also likes the high-stakes gamble of thinking big. So he decided to introduce a line of dog food. "I wanted to become a household name, and I figured, food was the way to get us there," recalls Giannini. Dogswell's new kibble performed beautifully in taste tests—dogs chowed it down. Dogswell was already a national brand with a presence at chains like Whole Foods and Target, so it wasn't difficult to get the new kibble to the shelves. But Giannini decided to offer coupons for a free $10.99 bag of kibble with every purchase of a 15-ounce bag of treats, which sells for about $16 to $20. The coupon promotion ended up costing the company $100,000 a month and failed to attract repeat buyers quickly enough to cover the loss.

As his company began to crumble, Giannini frantically searched for private-equity investors who would continue to believe in him and his products. His optimism paid off in the form of TSG, an investment group willing to take the risk as along as Giannini went back to his core business—healthy dog treats—with food following more conservatively. "With all the success, I had gotten cocky," admits Giannini." He acknowledges his own mistakes and vows to learn from them, as he did with Clear Day.

Despite the ups and downs of owning a company, Giannini wouldn't be happy in any other kind of job. "Tolerance of small business and taking chances—doing what you want to do—is something that runs in my family," Giannini says proudly.

Questions for Critical Thinking

1. Describe the entrepreneurial traits that Giannini has. How have these benefited him? In what ways might these same traits be a burden?

2. Giannini secured financing from a private equity group. How will this affect his control over the business? What other types of financing might have been appropriate for Dogswell?

Sources: Company Web site, http://www.dogswell.com, accessed March 4, 2011; "Dogswell," *Pet Product News*, http://www.petproductnews.com, accessed March 4, 2011; Nitasha Tiku, "Case Study: Lining Up Investors for a Turnaround," *Inc.com*, December 1, 2009, http://www.inc.com; Deborah Coeh, "Putting a Financial Spin on a Dog's Domain," *Reuters*, April 14, 2009, http://in.reuters.com.

Small Businesses Are Big into Social Networking

One of the biggest challenges for an entrepreneur is getting the word out about a new business to potential investors, suppliers, the media, and customers. Perhaps that is why entrepreneurs have been so quick to embrace social media as a tool for communication to as many people as possible.

If used skillfully, many believe, social media can help level the playing field between small businesses and their giant competitors. David avRutick, co-owner of Folbot, a small kayak retailer, claims that without Twitter, he wouldn't have as many sales as he does. "You can't buy that kind of exposure," avRutick says. Folbot competes against such household names as L.L. Bean and Cabela's—there's no way the smaller company could challenge the larger ones without widespread interactive communication. Stephen Bailey, who tracks social-media marketing for the footwear retailer John Fluevog Boots & Shoes notes, "The people coming from social media have been buying." How could Bailey's company lure customers away from Zappos.com without social media?

However, critics point out that the use of such sites as Facebook, Twitter, LinkedIn, and the more recent Yelp have a wide range of value to small businesses. "The hype right now exceeds the reality," observes Larry Chiagouris, a professor of marketing at Pace University's Lubin School of Business. Despite the fact that the use of social media by firms with fewer than 100 employees doubled in one recent year, only 22 percent of those who responded to a separate survey reported a direct increase in profits as a result of social media use, while half said they broke even on the investment. Others caution that social media networking eats up valuable time, particularly for an entrepreneur whose day is usually chock full of tasks ranging from design to distribution, and manufacturing to marketing.

"If you spend two hours a day on Twitter and Facebook, that's 25 percent of your day!" points out Chaitanya Sagar, founder of a small business outsourcing company called p2w2. (http://www.p2w2.com).

Most experts, including experienced entrepreneurs, support the use of social media, but with moderation. Chris Lindland, owner of Cordarounds.com, an online clothing retailer, advises patience. "My business has been visited millions of times, but I haven't made millions of sales," he comments. But he believes that his patience will pay off. "People have told me they finally got around to buying from my business after reading about it on social media two years ago." Chaitanya Sagar agrees. "If you expect immediate sales from social media, you will be disappointed," he counsels. Sagar suggests that entrepreneurs focus instead on marketing their brands instead of expecting direct sales. "If you have this perspective, you will be able to use social media for the right reasons and save a lot of time."

Questions for Critical Thinking

1. How do you foresee social networking changing the business environment for entrepreneurs?
2. How might entrepreneurs use social networking media to secure financing for their businesses?

Sources: Kasey Wehrum, "Is Social Media Worth Your Time?," *Inc.com,* March 16, 2010, http://www.inc.com; Sarah E. Needleman, "Entrepreneurs Question Value of Social Media," *The Wall Street Journal,* March 16, 2010, http://online.wsj.com; Ross Kimarovsky, "10 Small Business Social Media Marketing Tips," *Mashable.com,* http://mashable.com, accessed March 4, 2011; Paul Frederic, "Smart Social Networking for Your Small Business," *Forbes.com,* June 5, 2009, http://www.forbes.com; Claire Cain Miller, "Yelp Will Let Businesses Respond to Web Reviews," *The New York Times,* April 10, 2009, http://www.nytimes.com.

Comet Skateboards: It's a Smooth Ride

Jason Salfi loves skateboarding. This is how many small businesses begin. The founder has a passion for something—whether it's cooking or surfing or creating video games—and wants to turn it into a business. In Salfi's case, it's skateboarding. The company, now in

business for more than a decade, is Comet Skateboards. When Salfi graduated from Cornell University, he did what a lot of recent graduates do: he headed west. He lived on a boat off the coast of California for awhile and partnered with a friend tinkering around with skateboards, which the pair sold to other skateboard fans among their circle of friends. Salfidesired something more. He wanted to find a better way to manufacture skateboards as well as the means to support his newly started family. "Back then, skateboards were made with 7 layers of maple and sprayed with a lacquer based coating," he recalls. "Skateboards were accounting for 35 to 40 percent of the natural maple being harvested each year." Salfi loved skateboarding, but he didn't like the way boards were made. He believed that a skateboard could be built with more environmentally sustainable processes and materials. "I wanted to start a company that would make an impression on people and build an awareness around the use of natural resources," Salfi says.

Not long after he established Comet Skateboards, Salfi moved his company and his family back east to Ithaca, New York where he partnered with e2e Materials, a small start-up out of Cornell. The firm specializes in regionally sourced bio-composite materials; they manufacture their own soy-based resin and bio-composites that Salfi describes as "incredibly strong *and* biodegradable." The formula was exactly what Salfi was looking for. He set up shop and hired several employees, including Bob Rossi, who is head of Web development for Comet as well as president of the Green Resource Hub, an organization that focuses on finding ways for businesses to practice sustainability.

Rossi is impressed with Salfi's total commitment to finding the best way to manufacture his products, even if it means moving cross country. "To move your business into the opportunity, to create a greener product, that is pretty impressive to me," observes Rossi. "There's a lot of green-washing out there," says Rossi. He knows the difference. Comet goes much farther than simply purchasing e2e's materials; the firm has adopted a closed-loop manufacturing process, which means that it reduces or eliminates waste by examining the life cycle of all the materials used in its manufacturing process.

It might seem like Salfi and Rossi aren't cut from the same cloth as the previous generation of skateboarders—they're busy doing good things for the environment and for their community instead of rolling along the fringes of society like the bad boys of original skateboarding. But Salfi remains true to his skateboarding heritage (Rossi admits to being new to the sport). Comet boards have names like The Voodoo Doll and Shred City, and are built for specialists who prefer downhill or freeriding. Riders are invited to contribute ideas for the shapes, graphics, and names of new boards. Comet, which has found a way to actually increase profit potential by using green materials, receives kudos from business bloggers as well as diehard boarding bloggers. It appears that Salfi has found a way to blend doing good with doing good business—in a sport that was once considered far out of the mainstream.

Salfi hopes that Comet Skateboards will ultimately serve as an example of a small business that can make a big difference—while making products that provide fun. "We look at everything we do through the lens of how we can create a model that people can replicate in the future," he says. Salfi observes proudly that although Comet has only been in Ithaca for a few years, so far the company has a 100-percent retention rate of employees. He wants Comet to be a company that is known for its positive working environment, a place where people can develop long-term careers.

"We know that in the grand scheme of things, we're a small company, but through the many means of getting the message out—the Internet, video, music, and photography—we can actually have a broad footprint and make the idea of sustainability and social justice appealing to a broader market," predicts Salfi. While the bottom line—turning a profit—is vital to Comet's survival and growth, Salfi believes that this new way of doing business is more important in the long run. "We like to think we're creating a blueprint for the kind of company that will be around for 100 or 200 years," he muses. Then the skateboarder emerges. With a grin Salfi adds, "At the end of the day we're making skateboards, and we don't want to bum anybody out."

Questions for Critical Thinking

1. In which category (or categories) would you place Jason Salfi as an entrepreneur? Why? Give examples.

2. Salfi notes that the use of information technology—part of the environment for entrepreneurs—can help Comet Skateboards reach a broader audience. Can you identify any demographic and economic trends that might provide opportunities for Comet Skateboard's growth as a business?

3. Which of the traditional characteristics of entrepreneurs do you believe best describe Jason Salfi? Why?

4. As Comet Skateboards reaches the next level of growth, where might the firm have the best chance of obtaining further financing? Why?

Sources: Comet Skateboards Web site, http://www.cometskateboards .com, accessed March 4, 2011; "GOOD Products," Halogen TV, http://www.halogentv.com, accessed March 4, 2011; Nadia Hosni, "Triple Bottom Line: Comet Skateboards," *Tonic,* April 27, 2010, http://www.tonic.com.

KANSAS

GREENSBURG, KS

Greensburg: A Great Place to Start

Ashley Petty started taking massage therapy classes while studying for her business degree. After graduating, she worked for several years as a massage therapist, until the spa where she worked closed. Ashley was job hunting when the tornado hit her hometown of Greensburg, Kansas. Watching volunteers, residents, and relief workers exhaust themselves cleaning up the devastated town, she saw an opportunity. She would return home to start her own spa in Greensburg.

It was definitely a risky venture—the last thing she would have expected to find in Greensburg before the storm. Armed with a business plan she had written in college, Ashley drove to Town Hall and applied for one of the temporary trailers that were brought in to house displaced businesses. She got her trailer—a 1970s singlewide, complete with imitation wood paneling, stinky carpet, and a leaky roof. Not exactly the luxe spa she had envisioned in her business plan, but a good enough start. With a fresh coat of paint, some scented candles, and new drapes, she opened Elements Therapeutic Massage and Day Spa.

Ashley had expected that her spa would be a hard sell. The storm had destroyed the town's communications, so traditional advertising was out. To build a client base, Ashley turned to word of mouth. She went to town meetings, talked to old friends, met with volunteers from all over the country. Still, months went by and she still had barely enough clients to pay her expenses.

Winter hit. It was cold, the ancient furnace ran constantly, drafts blew in the new curtains, and rain soaked the freshly steamed carpet. Elements was the last place anyone would want to go to escape the stress of rebuilding—even Ashley couldn't stand to be there. Under normal circumstances, she would have considered more extensive capital improvements, but the trailer was only temporary and she was out of money.

At one town meeting, green architecture firm BNIM presented a plan for the new Downtown Greensburg, including a business incubator to sustain old businesses and promote new ones. Traditionally, a business incubator is reserved for start-ups, but in Greensburg, once-successful businesses needed help getting back on their feet. The incubator would be housed in a totally energy-efficient retail/office building with space for approximately ten new businesses. The rent would be reasonable, and the utility costs next to nothing. Ashley jumped at the chance to apply for a place in the building.

Questions

After viewing the video, answer the following questions:

1. What major challenges does Ashley Petty face in starting her business?

2. How will Greensburg's business incubator stimulate economic development?

3. What are some of the challenges Greensburg faces in recruiting new businesses? What incentives would you offer to encourage new business development there?

4. Would you start a new business in Greensburg? Why or why not?

LAUNCHING YOUR
[Entrepreneurial Career]

2

In Part 2, "Starting and Growing Your Business," you learned about the many ways that business owners have achieved their dreams of owning their own company and being their own boss. The part's two chapters introduced you to the wide variety of entrepreneurial or small businesses; the forms they can take—sole proprietorship, partnership, or corporation—and the reasons that some new ventures succeed and others fail. You learned that entrepreneurs are visionaries who build firms that create wealth and that they share traits such as vision and creativity, high energy, optimism, a strong need to achieve, and a tolerance for failure. By now you might be wondering how you can make all this information work for you. Here are some career ideas and opportunities in the small-business and e-business areas.

First, whatever field attracts you as a future business owner, try to acquire experience by working for someone else in the industry initially. The information and skills you pick up will be invaluable when you start out on your own. Lack of experience is often cited as a leading reason for small-business failure.[1]

Next, look for a good fit between your own skills, abilities, and characteristics and a market need or niche. For instance, the U.S. Department of Labor reports that opportunities in many healthcare fields are rising with the nation's increased demand for health services.[2] As the population of older people rises, and as young families find themselves increas-ingly pressed for time, the need for child care and elder services will also increase—and so will the opportunities for new businesses in those areas. So keep your eyes on trends to find ideas that you can use or adapt.

Another way to look for market needs is to talk to current customers or business associates. When the owner of Michigan-based Moon Valley Rustic Furniture wanted to retire, he went to see Rick Detkowski, who was in the real estate business. The owner intended to offer the buildings to Detkowski and close the business down. But the real estate agent, who owned several pieces of Moon Valley furniture himself, instead decided to buy, not just the buildings, but the furniture business, too. Before the sale was completed—and to determine whether he could run Moon Valley profitably—Detkowski talked with existing customers and furniture dealers, who had been hoping for years that the company would expand its line of sturdy cedar and pine items from the traditional summer lawn furniture into more innovative designs. Further research showed that the general environmental trend among consumers was boosting demand for rustic furniture, in contrast with the overall housing slump. So Detkowski took the plunge and is now in the furniture manufacturing business. He has expanded the company's product lines and reorganized the factory floor for more efficiency—and cost savings.[3]

Are you intrigued by the idea of being your own boss but worried about risking your savings to get a completely new and untried business off the ground? Then owning a franchise, such as Quiznos or Dunkin' Donuts, might be for you. The Small Business Administration advises aspiring entrepreneurs that while franchising can be less risky than starting a new business from scratch, it still requires hard work and sacrifice. In addition, you need to completely understand both the resources to which you'll be entitled and the responsibilities you'll assume under the franchise agreement. Again, filling a market need is important for success. To find more information about franchising, access the Federal Trade Commission's consumer guide to buying a franchise at http://www.ftc.gov/bcp/edu/pubs/consumer/invest/inv05.shtm.

Are you skilled in a particular area of business, technology, or science? The consulting industry will be a rapidly growing area for several years, according to the Bureau of Labor Statistics.[4] Consulting firms offer their expertise to clients in private, government, not-for-profit, and even foreign business operations. Business consultants influence clients' decisions in marketing, finance, manufacturing, information systems, e-business, human resources, and many other areas including corporate strategy and organization. Technology consultants support businesses in all fields, with services ranging from setting up a secure Web site or training employees in the use of new software to managing an off-site help desk or planning for disaster recovery. Science consulting firms find plenty of work in the field of environmental consulting, helping businesses deal with pollution cleanup and control, habitat protection, and compliance with government's environmental regulations and standards.

But perhaps none of these areas appeal to you quite so much as tinkering with gears and machinery or with computer graphics and code. If you think you have the insight and creativity to invent something completely new, you need to make sure you're informed about patents, trademarks, and copyright laws to protect your ideas.[5] Each area offers different protections for your work, and none will guarantee success. Here again, hard work, persistence, and a little bit of luck will help you succeed.

Career Assessment Exercises in Entrepreneurship and Business Ownership

1. Find out whether you have what it takes to be an entrepreneur. Review the material on the SBA's Web site http://www.sba.gov/smallbusinessplanner/index.html. or take the Brigham Young University's Entrepreneurial Test at http://marriottschool.byu.edu/cfe/startingout/test.cfm. Answer the questions there. After you've finished, use the scoring guides to determine how ready you are to strike out on your own. What weak areas did your results disclose? What can you do to strengthen them?

2. Find an independent business or franchise in your area, and make an appointment to talk to the owner about his or her start-up experience. Prepare a list of questions for a 10- to 15-minute interview, and remember to ask about details such as the number of hours worked per week, approximate start-up costs, goals of the business, available resources, lessons learned since opening, and rewards of owning the business. How different are the owner's answers from what you expected?

3. Search online for information about how to file for a patent, trademark, or copyright. A good starting point is http://www.uspto.gov. Assume you have an invention you wish to protect. Find out what forms are required; what fees are necessary; how much time is typically needed to complete the legal steps; and what rights and protections you will gain.

PART [3]

Management: Empowering People to Achieve Business

[Chapter 7]

Management, Leadership, and the Internal Organization

[Chapter 8]

Human Resource Management: From Recruitment to Labor Relations

[Chapter 9]

Top Performance through Empowerment, Teamwork, and Communication

[Chapter 10]

Production and Operations Management

Chapter 7

Learning Objectives

1. Define *management* and the three types of skills necessary for managerial success.

2. Explain the role of vision and ethical standards in business success.

3. Summarize the major benefits of planning, and distinguish among strategic planning, tactical planning, and operational planning.

4. Describe the strategic planning process.

5. Contrast the two major types of business decisions, and list the steps in the decision-making process.

6. Define *leadership,* and compare different leadership styles.

7. Discuss the meaning and importance of corporate culture.

8. Identify the five major forms of departmentalization and the four main types of organization structures.

Management, Leadership, and the Internal Organization

Masterfile

Ursula Burns: Moving Xerox Forward

Ramin Talaie/Bloomberg/
Getty Images, Inc.

Ursula Burns is a corporate superstar. The CEO of Xerox, based in Norwalk, CT, took over the chairmanship of the company when Anne Mulcahy stepped down, becoming the first African American woman to run a Fortune 500 company. A few weeks after taking on the CEO job, Burns lauched the biggest deal in Xerox history—the acquisition of Affiliated Computer Services (ACS) for the hefty sum of $6.4 billion, a price that investors and analysts believed Xerox couldn't afford. But Burns was adamant about the decision as a major part of her company's future. She views the purchase as the way for Xerox to extend its ability to manage business processes for clients. Her ability to make bold decisions is one characteristic that landed Burns in the top seat at a major corporation.

Burns has been employed at Xerox her entire career—an unusual phenomenon in today's workplace. She joined the firm in 1980 as a mechanical engineering summer intern. From there Burns never looked back. She led business team, headed up the manufacturing and supply chain operations, led Xerox's global research, and more. Burns has always been known to be blunt and outspoken as a manager. But her firm has needed several bold moves, and Burns has managed to shepherd it through the recent recession by making these moves, including the acquisition of ACS. "What I learned is that [the recession] could be, and was for us, a good time to change. We changed the inside operations to ensure that we were liquid and profitable. We hunkered down, but we wanted to make sure we kept investing to differentiate ourselves."

Burns has not been deterred by the challenges of leading a firm of 134,000 employees. She is positive about the strong culture at Xerox. "We are nice," Burns observes. "And I mean that in a very good way. We are real people working with real people. It's phenomenal. We are also a team-based company. Diversity is important . . . differences in how you work, what your points of view are, are things that we love." Burns also points out that "this niceness sometimes leads to lack of motion, lack of decision." She emphasizes the importance of empowering managers to make their own decisions in order to get things done.

Despite the fact that Xerox already has 10,100 active patents, Burns is passionate about the importance of constant innovation. She pumped $781 million into research and development during one recent year. She believes that despite the digital age, the need for printed documents will not disappear. Instead, as she puts it, "the value of paper will change." Recent Xerox product launches include ColorQube, a solid-ink technology that produces 90 percent less solid waste with considerably less energy use that its liquid counterparts; and new smart-document technologies. "One of the biggest investments we have is in trying to make color more affordable." Burns offers advice to young managers who want to succeed. "Don't start out wanting to be a CEO," she says. "You're going to be really disappointed if you do that because you may end up doing things you don't love. Find something that you love to do, and find a place that you really like to do it." Burns really loves her job and her company. She's been there for thirty years.[1]

When asked about their professional objectives, many students say, "I want to be a manager." You may think that the role of a manager is basically being the boss. But in today's business world, companies are looking for much more than bosses. They want managers who understand technology, can adapt quickly to change, can skillfully motivate employees, and realize the importance of satisfying customers. Managers who can master those skills will continue to be in great demand because their commitment strongly affects their firms' performance. And they may end up running their firms, as has Ursula Burns of Xerox.

This chapter begins by examiningv how successful organizations use management to turn visions into reality. It describes the levels of management, the skills that managers need, and the functions that managers perform. The chapter explains how the first of these functions, planning, helps managers meet the challenges of a rapidly changing business environment and develop strategies that guide a company's future. Other sections of the chapter explore the types of decisions that managers make, the role of managers as leaders, and the importance of corporate culture. The chapter concludes by examining the second function of management—organizing.

What Is Management?

management process of achieving organizational objectives through people and other resources.

Management is the process of achieving organizational objectives through people and other resources. The manager's job is to combine human and technical resources in the best way possible to achieve the company's goals.

Management principles and concepts apply to not-for-profit organizations as well as profit-seeking firms. A city mayor, the president of the Appalachian Mountain Club, and a superintendent of schools all perform the managerial functions described later in this chapter. Management happens at many levels, from that of a family-owned restaurant manager to a national sales manager for a major manufacturer.

The Management Hierarchy

Your local supermarket works through a fairly simple organization that consists of a store manager, several assistant or department managers, and employees who may range from baggers to cashiers to stock clerks. However, if your supermarket is part of a regional or national chain, there will be corporate managers above the store manager. The Stop & Shop Supermarket Company has more than 350 supermarkets located from New Hampshire to New Jersey, as well as headquarters located in Massachusetts. Within each store there are managers for everything from the meat department to human resources. But at

Stop & Shop headquarters, you'll find top-level managers for such functions as finance, consumer affairs, real estate, information technology, sales and operations, and pharmacy among others.[2]

All of these people are managers because they combine human and other resources to achieve company objectives. Their jobs differ, however, because they work at different levels of the organization.

A firm's management usually has three levels: top, middle, and supervisory. These levels of management form a management hierarchy, as shown in Figure 7.1. The hierarchy is the traditional structure found in most organizations. Managers at each level perform different activities.

The highest level of management is *top management*. Top managers include such positions as chief executive officer (CEO), chief financial officer (CFO), and executive vice president. Top managers devote most of their time to developing long-range plans for their organizations. They make decisions such as whether to introduce new products, purchase other companies, or enter new geographical markets. Top managers set a direction for their organization and inspire the company's executives and employees to achieve their vision for the company's future.

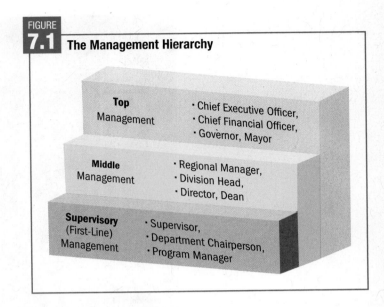

FIGURE 7.1 The Management Hierarchy

Top Management
- Chief Executive Officer,
- Chief Financial Officer,
- Governor, Mayor

Middle Management
- Regional Manager,
- Division Head,
- Director, Dean

Supervisory (First-Line) Management
- Supervisor,
- Department Chairperson,
- Program Manager

The job isn't easy. Many top managers must steer their firms through the storms of an economic downturn, a slump in sales, a quality crisis, and the like. Sometimes the storm involves selling big dream to investors, stockholders, and managers during a economic downturn. Laura Ipsen, senior vice president and general manager of the Smart Grid Business Unit of Cisco, has met with this challenge. Her idea for San Jose-based Cisco is to create a new energy ecosystem for the 21st century. If she's successful, Ipsen's firm could claim a significant share of what is predicted to be a $100-billion smart-grid market. It's not easy to convince all parties that the gamble is a wise one when the future isn't clear. "My job is like having to put together a 1,000-piece puzzle," says Ipsen, "but I don't have the box top with the picture of what it looks like, and some pieces are missing."[3]

Middle management, the second tier in the management hierarchy, includes positions such as general managers, plant managers, division managers, and branch managers. Middle managers' attention focuses on specific operations, products, or customer groups within an organization. They are responsible for developing detailed plans and procedures to implement the firm's strategic plans. If top management decided to broaden the distribution of a product, a sales manager would be responsible for determining the number of sales personnel required. Middle managers are responsible for targeting the products and customers who are the source of the sales and profit growth expected by their CEOs. To achieve these goals, middle managers might budget money for product development, identify new uses for existing products, and improve the ways they train and motivate salespeople. Because they are more familiar with day-to-day operations than CEOs, middle managers often come up with new ways to increase sales or solve company problems.

Supervisory management, or first-line management, includes positions such as supervisor, section chief, and team leader. These managers are directly responsible for assigning nonmanagerial employees to specific jobs and evaluating their performance. Managers at

L.L. Bean ranks in the top tier of *BusinessWeek*'s annual top customer-service providing companies. The first-line managers make sure that customer service is a priority for all employees.

this first level of the hierarchy work directly with the employees who produce and sell the firm's goods and services. They are responsible for implementing middle managers' plans by motivating workers to accomplish daily, weekly, and monthly goals. In *BusinessWeek's* most recent annual ranking of customer service champs, all of the top-ranked firms have first-line managers who implement the firms' strategies to provide superior customer service. L.L. Bean, Nordstrom, the Ritz-Carlton, and Ace Hardware all have in common first-line managers who see that customer service is a top priority among its employees.[4]

Skills Needed for Managerial Success

Managers at every level in the management hierarchy must exercise three basic types of skills: technical, human, and conceptual. All managers must acquire these skills in varying proportions, although the importance of each skill changes at different management levels.

Technical skills are the manager's ability to understand and use the techniques, knowledge, and tools and equipment of a specific discipline or department. Technical skills are especially important for first-line managers and become less important at higher levels of the management hierarchy. But most top executives started out as technical experts. The résumé of a vice president for information systems probably lists experience as a computer analyst and that of a vice president for marketing usually shows a background in sales. Many firms, including Home Depot and Dell have increased training programs for first-line managers to boost technical skills and worker productivity. Cold Stone Creamery, which operates franchises for its premium ice-cream stores nationwide, carefully trains managers and crew members in the art of preparing its specialty ice cream for hungry customers. "We don't interview potential crew members, we *audition* them," says the company.[5]

Human skills are interpersonal skills that enable managers to work effectively with and through people. Human skills include the ability to communicate with, motivate, and lead employees to complete assigned activities. Managers need human skills to interact with people both inside and outside the organization. It would be tough for a manager to succeed without such skills, even though they must be adapted to different forms—for instance, mastering and communicating effectively with staff through e-mail, cell phones, pagers, faxes, and text messaging, all of which are widely used in today's offices. As you can imagine, it is important for managers of Cold Stone Creamery ice cream stores to have excellent human skills not only with customers but also with employees.

Conceptual skills determine a manager's ability to see the organization as a unified whole and to understand how each part of the overall organization interacts with other parts. These skills involve an ability to see the big picture by acquiring, analyzing, and interpreting information. Conceptual skills are especially important for top-level managers, who must develop long-range plans for the future direction of their organization. After selling his own company, LinkExchange, to Microsoft for $265 million, Tony Hsieh joined Zappos as an advisor and eventually became its CEO. Hsieh's conceptual skills helped Zappos to grow sales to more than $1 billion annually while at the same time winning accolades for being an excellent place to work. Recently, Hsieh helped engineer the sale of Zappos to Amazon in a deal worth $1.2 billion.[6]

Managerial Functions

In the course of a typical day, managers spend time meeting and talking with people, reading, thinking, and sending text or e-mail messages. As they perform all these activities, managers are carrying out four basic functions: planning, organizing, directing, and controlling. Planning activities lay the groundwork, and the other functions are aimed at carrying out the plans.

Planning Planning is the process of anticipating future events and conditions and determining courses of actions for achieving organizational objectives. Effective planning helps a business focus its vision, avoid costly mistakes, and seize opportunities. Planning should be flexible and responsive to changes in the business environment, and should involve managers from all levels of the organization. As global competition intensifies, technology expands, and the speed at which firms bring new innovations to market increases, planning for the future becomes even more critical. For example, a CEO and other top-level managers need to plan for succession—those who will follow in their footsteps. Some CEOs resist this kind of planning, fearing that doing so might shorten their time at the helm of a company. But management experts encourage planning ahead for the next generation of management, in order to keep the company's position in the marketplace strong.[7]

Business mogul Warren Buffet is now in his 80s and showing little signs of slowing down. But it's clear that someone (or several people) must be in place to take the reins of his huge diversified company, Berkshire Hathaway, which has significant holdings in businesses ranging from Geico Insurance to Helzberg Diamonds to NetJets. Recently Buffet tapped Todd Combs, who is half Buffett's age, as an investment manager and potential successor to manager Berkshire's $100 billion investment portfolio, which includes holdings in American Express, The Coca-Cola Company, Procter & Gamble, and other major firms. But no one has yet been named to succeed Buffet as Berkshire's CEO.[8]

Organizing Once plans have been developed, the next step in the management process typically is organizing—the process of blending human and material resources through a formal structure of tasks and authority; arranging work, dividing tasks among employees, and coordinating them to ensure implementation of plans and accomplishment of objectives.

planning process of anticipating future events and conditions and determining courses of action for achieving organizational objectives.

organizing process of blending human and material resources through a formal structure of tasks and authority; arranging work, dividing tasks among employees, and coordinating them to ensure implementation of plans and accomplishment of objectives.

Organizing involves classifying and dividing work into manageable units with a logical structure. Managers staff the organization with the best possible employees for each job. Sometimes the organizing function requires studying a company's existing structure and determining whether to restructure it in order to operate more efficiently, cost effectively, or sustainably.

Directing   Once an organization has been established, managers focus on **directing**, or guiding and motivating employees to accomplish organizational objectives. Directing might include training (or retraining), setting up schedules, delegating certain tasks, and monitoring progress. To fulfill the objective of reducing the office electricity bill, an office manager might have incandescent light bulbs replaced by compact fluorescents, ask employees to turn off the lights when they leave a room and direct the IT staff to program all the office computer screens to turn off after 15 minutes of inactivity.[9]

Often when managers take time to listen to their employees, the manager gains insight and the employee gets a motivational boost. Christopher Mills, co-owner of Prime Debt Services in Dallas, meets with employees each week. "I found the more I listened, the better they pepped up," he says.[10]

Controlling   The **controlling** function evaluates an organization's performance against its objectives. Controlling assesses the success of the planning function and provides feedback for future rounds of planning.

The four basic steps in controlling are to establish performance standards, monitor actual performance, compare actual performance with established standards, and make corrections if necessary. Under the provisions of the Sarbanes-Oxley Act, for example, CEOs and CFOs must monitor the performance of the firm's accounting staff more closely than has been done in the past. They must personally attest to the truth of financial reports filed with the Securities and Exchange Commission.

Setting a Vision and Ethical Standards for the Firm

A business begins with a **vision**, its founder's perception of marketplace needs and the ways a firm can satisfy them. Vision serves as the target for a firm's actions, helping direct the company toward opportunities and differentiating it from its competitors. When 18-year-old Ben Lewis started his water retailing business, Give Water, headquartered in Pennsylvania, he wanted to make it easy for consumers to donate to their favorite causes: as easy as drinking a bottle of water. So he manufactured bottles in different colors that corresponded to certain types of charities—for example, green for environmental organizations and pink for breast cancer research. When customers bought a bottle of water, 10 cents of the purchase would go toward the chosen charity. "This makes activism really easy for people," said Lewis. "All they have to do is buy the water."[11]

Serveral years later, Give Water reports that it has donated more than $50,000 to various causes since it began, which means that it has earned about $650,000 in sales. Give Water now has a deal with Whole Foods to carry its water, and founder Ben Lewis is hoping to achieve nationwide sales in the coming year. Lewis now has a new vision: donating $1,000,000 a year to charity through sales of his products.[12]

A company's vision must be focused and yet flexible enough to adapt to changes in the business environment. Also critical to a firm's long-term relationship with its customers,

directing guiding and motivating employees to accomplish organizational objectives.

controlling function of evaluating an organization's performance against its objectives.

Assessment Check ✔

1. What is management?
2. How do the jobs of top managers, middle managers, and supervisory managers differ?
3. What is the relationship between the manager's planning and controlling functions?

vision perception of marketplace needs and the ways a firm can satisfy them.

Solving an Ethical Controversy

Google Stands Alone: When Ethics and Business Don't Mix

When Google first entered the Chinese market, the firm was battered by criticism for its agreement to a compromise on censorship with the Chinese government, which controls the distribution of information to its public. Google did so in the hope that the Chinese government would eventually relax its stand and allow its citizens the same access to Internet information as others have around the world. But that didn't happen—in fact, censorship seemed to grow tighter, along with evidence that someone was using Google to identify Chinese dissidents.

So, Google announced that it was shutting down operations in China and rerouting users to a safe site in Hong Kong. While Google received praise from the Internet community for its move, the firm got little support from the business world and criticism from Chinese students.

Should the ethical standards set by a U.S. business override repressive laws and regulations established by any of the countries in which it operates?

PRO

1. Many multinational firms now have global ethics policies that apply to each country in which they do business, regardless of national law. This helps managers make consistent decisions, even if it means losing some profits.

2. Ethical standards must always take precedence over practices that compromise human rights. "If any corporate executive finds that he or she is actually considering putting profit ahead of humanity," argues Mickey Edwards, vice president of the international nonprofit Aspen Institute, "it is time for that person to reflect seriously on how and when the moral compass, and one's own claim to humanity, got lost."

CON

1. Ethical standards are not always the same from one country to the next. Google's move may, in fact, have a negative impact on Chinese consumers who at least had access to some information while Google was there. "Leaving may look and feel great to those of us in the West, but exiting a market may not always have the desired impact," writes one expert.

2. Companies willing to compromise with such governments could actually use their influence with consumers to drive change. One way to do this is to create demand for their goods and services. Another is to become active in the community through service projects such as building schools.

Summary

Despite efforts by the U.S. government, confusion and conflict over Google's move continued. Chinese students now view Google as intertwined with the U.S. government and that any further decisions by either would be a backslide. "The Chinese government won and Google lost," said one student. "Not only did they lose money and the Chinese market, but they also lost their spirit." But analysts point out that the Chinese market of 1 billion potential consumers is difficult to harness under any circumstances. One analyst points out, "There is a barrage of new rules and regulations for foreign companies operating in China. Everybody is trying to figure out what it means."

Sources: James Fallows and Brian Glucroft, "Google, China, and Chinese College Student—Part III," *The Atlantic*, February 2011, http://www.theatlantic.com. Alexei Oreskovic and Paul Eckert, "Google Finds Few Allies in China Battle," *Reuters*, March 25, 2010, http://www.reuters.com; Steve Pearlstein and Raju Narisetti, "Doing Right at What Cost?" *The Washington Post*, March 25, 2010, http://views.washingtonpost.com; Aron Cramer and Dunstan Allison Hope, "Google and China: When Should Business Leave On Human Rights Grounds?" *Huffington Post*, March 22, 2010, http://www.huffingtonpost.com.

suppliers, and the general public are the ethical standards that top management sets. Sometimes ethical standards are set in compliance with industry or federal regulations, such as safety or quality standards. Sometimes new standards are set in response to unethical actions by managers, such as the financial accounting activities that resulted in the Sarbanes-Oxley Act. Currently, firms are taking a closer look at large compensation packages received by their CEOs and other top executives. Due to public outcry, compensation committees are reevaluating their criteria for salaries, bonuses, and other benefits.[13]

The ethical tone that a top management team establishes can reap monetary as well as nonmonetary rewards. Setting a high ethical standard does not merely restrain employees

Courtesy Troy Rhodes

A firm's vision serves as the target for its actions, helping direct the company toward opportunities and differentiating it from its competitors. Troy Rhodes Jr. of MyBookBorrow.com states his vision is "to build an online empire."

from doing wrong, but it encourages, motivates, and inspires them to achieve goals they never thought possible. Such satisfaction creates a more productive, stable workforce—one that can create a long-term competitive advantage for the organization. In practice, ethical decisions are not always clear-cut, and managers must make difficult decisions. Sometimes a firm operates in a country where standards differ from those in the United States. In other situations, a manager might have to make an ethical decision that undermines profits or even causes people to lose their jobs. And while it's tempting to think that a large firm—by virtue of its size—will have a harder time adopting ethical practices than a small firm, consider toymaker giant Mattel, which has repeatedly earned recognition for its ethical standards. Named one of the "World's Most Ethical Companies" by the Ethisphere Institute, California-based Mattel consistently demonstrates high standards in a number of areas. "Our commitment to 'play fair' is at the core of our organization's culture and is the cornerstone of our ethical compliance program," notes chairman and CEO Robert A. Eckert.

Alex Brigham, executive director of the New York–based Ethisphere Institute, observes the connection between ethics and good business. "Mattel's promotion of a sound ethical environment shines within its industry and shows a clear understanding that operating under the highest standards for business behavior goes beyond goodwill and is intimately linked to performance and profitability," he says.[14]

Sometimes taking an ethical stand can actually cost a firm in lost revenues and other support. When Google announced a reversal of its original stance on censorship in China—essentially shutting down operations there and rerouting traffic to an uncensored site in Hong Kong—not only did the company lose business, it found itself standing eerily alone on the issue. Google's decision and the consequences are discussed in the "Solving an Ethical Controversy" feature.

Assessment Check ✔

1. What is meant by a vision for the firm?

2. Why is it important for a top executive to set high ethical standards?

Importance of Planning

Although some firms manage to launch without a clear strategic plan, they won't last long if they don't' map out a future. Facebook founder Mark Zuckerberg says that he didn't have a major plan for the site at the beginning. But Facebook's nearly global reach and membership of more than 500 million and counting—means that Zuckerberg must plan the firm's next moves in order to outrun competitors and avoid major stumbles. Currently Zuckerberg is studying the Chinese market, a difficult one to enter successfully. "China is extremely complex," he notes, because of political, economic, and infrastructural issues. But Zuckerberg is undaunted. "How can you connect the whole world if you leave out 1.6 billion people?"[15]

Types of Planning

Planning can be categorized by scope and breadth. Some plans are very broad and long range, while others are short range and very narrow, affecting selected parts of the organization rather than the whole thing. Planning can be divided into the following categories: strategic, tactical, operational, and contingency, with each step including more specific information than the last. From the mission statement (described in the next section) to objectives to specific plans, each phase must fit into a comprehensive planning framework. The framework also must include narrow, functional plans aimed at individual employees and work areas relevant to individual tasks. These plans must fit within the firm's overall planning framework and help it reach objectives and achieve its mission.

Strategic Planning The most far-reaching level of planning is *strategic planning*—the process of determining the primary objectives of an organization and then acting and allocating resources to achieve those objectives. Generally, strategic planning is undertaken by top executives in a company. As part of its strategy of using company resources to raise environmental awareness—and develop or improve products—Staples sponsors its annual Staples Global EcoEasy Challenge, a competition in which college students develop new products or redesign existing ones in a way that represents an innovative approach to sustainability.[16]

Tactical Planning *Tactical planning* involves implementing the activities specified by strategic plans. Tactical plans guide the current and near-term activities required to implement overall strategies. The Staples Global EcoEasy Challenge is a tactic that reflects strategic planning around environmentally responsible products. Another tactic for the same strategy is Staples' development of its EcoEasy and Sustainable Earth product lines. "Staples' commitment to designing more environmentally responsible products as compared to conventional products is evident by our own EcoEasy and Sustainable Earth brands," notes Staples' vice president of environmental affairs Mark Buckley.[17]

Operational Planning

Operational planning creates the detailed standards that guide implementation of tactical plans. This activity involves choosing specific work targets and assigning employees and teams to carry out plans. Unlike strategic planning, which focuses on the organization as a whole, operational planning deals with developing and implementing tactics in specific functional areas. Operational planning related to the Staples EcoEasy Challenge might include identifying competition categories such as creating a product using eco-innovative materials; selecting judges; setting deadlines; reviewing contestant applications; and the like.

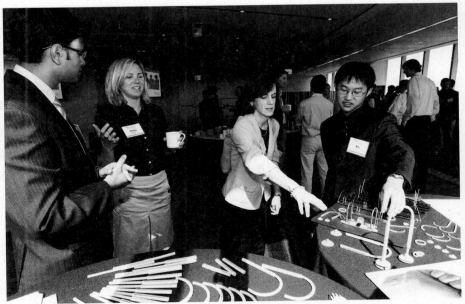

As an example of strategic planning, Staples is using its company resources to raise environmental awareness, and develop and improve products through its annual Staples Global EcoEasy Challenge competition for college students.

©Brian Ach Photography 2010

Contingency Planning Planning cannot foresee every possibility. Major accidents, natural disasters, and rapid economic downturns can throw even the best-laid plans into chaos. To handle the possibility of business disruption from events of this nature, many firms use *contingency planning*, which allows them to resume operations as quickly and as smoothly as possible after a crisis while openly communicating with the public about what happened. This planning activity involves two components: business continuation and public communication. Many firms have developed management strategies to speed recovery from accidents such as loss of data, breaches of security, product failures, and natural disasters such as floods or fire. If a major disaster or business disruption occurs, a company's contingency plan usually designates a chain of command for crisis management, assigning specific functions to particular managers and employees in an emergency. But crisis more often occurs on a less global scale. For example, a product delivery might go astray, a key person might be sick and unable to attend an important customer meeting, or the power might go out for a day. These instances require contingency planning as well.

When more than 1.3 million government nurses, teachers, and office workers in South Africa went on strike to demand higher wages, the government was forced to deploy office administrators to keep essential health services running. And when British Airways cabin crews went on strike, the movement spread to pilots and additional personnel at other airlines, canceling hundreds of flights across Europe. British Airways officials had anticipated the strike, however, and lessened some of its effects by installing retrained, on-ground staff as cabin crew. "The contingency plans are going well," noted a British Airways spokesperson.[18]

Assessment Check ✔

1. Outline the planning process.
2. Describe the purpose of tactical planning.
3. Compare the kinds of plans made by top managers and middle managers. How does their focus differ?

Planning at Different Organizational Levels

Although managers spend some time on planning virtually every day, the total time spent and the type of planning done differ according to the level of management. As Table 7.1 points out, top managers, including a firm's board of directors and CEO, spend a great deal of time on long-range planning, while middle-level managers and supervisors focus on short-term, tactical and operational planning. Employees at all levels can benefit themselves and their company by making plans to meet their own specific goals.

Table

7.1 Planning at Different Management Levels

PRIMARY TYPE OF PLANNING	MANAGERIAL LEVEL	EXAMPLES
Strategic	Top management	Organizational objectives, fundamental strategies, long-term plans
Tactical	Middle management	Quarterly and semiannual plans, departmental policies and procedures
Operational	Supervisory management	Daily and weekly plans, rules, and procedures for each department
Contingency	Primarily top management, but all levels contribute	Ongoing plans for actions and communications in an emergency

The Strategic Planning Process

Strategic planning often makes the difference between an organization's success and failure. Strategic planning has formed the basis of many fundamental management decisions. Successful strategic planners typically follow the six steps shown in Figure 7.2: defining a mission, assessing the organization's competitive position, setting organizational objectives, creating strategies for competitive differentiation, implementing the strategy, and evaluating the results and refining the plan.

Defining the Organization's Mission

The first step in strategic planning is to translate the firm's vision into a **mission statement**. A mission statement is a written explanation of an organization's business intentions and aims. It is an enduring statement of a firm's purpose, possibly highlighting the scope of operations, the market it seeks to serve, and the ways it will attempt to set itself apart from competitors. A mission statement guides the actions of employees, and publicizes the company's reasons for existence.

mission statement
written explanation of an organization's business intentions and aims.

Mission statements can be short or long:

- Starbucks: "To inspire and nurture the human spirit—one person, one cup and one neighborhood at a time."

- Disney: "We create happiness by providing the finest in entertainment for people of all ages, everywhere."

- Nike: "To bring inspiration and innovation to every athlete in the world."

- Sony: "To experience the joy of advancing and applying technology for the benefit of the public."

FIGURE
7.2 **Steps in the Strategic Planning Process**

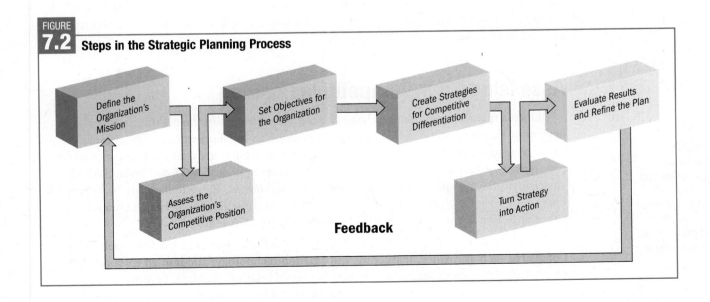

Define the Organization's Mission → Set Objectives for the Organization → Create Strategies for Competitive Differentiation → Evaluate Results and Refine the Plan

Assess the Organization's Competitive Position

Turn Strategy into Action

Feedback

Going Green

Johnson & Johnson: Caring for the World

In its company statement of values, Johnson & Johnson promises that "We must maintain in good order the property we are privileged to use, protecting the environment and natural resources." That's a simple statement, but a complex pledge to fulfill. Johnson & Johnson makes a wide range of consumer products such as Band-Aids, Listerine, and Johnson's Baby Lotion. It also produces medical devices and prescription drugs. Doing so can result in a giant carbon footprint made by manufacturing emissions, chemicals in products and processes, and a tremendous use of energy. Yet Johnson & Johnson is committed to reaching its environmental goals and has put the management in place to do so.

The firm sets new long-term goals every five years, under its "Healthy Planet" program. Some of these have included using direct purchase of low-impact hydro and wind power, on-site solar power and landfill gas, and purchasing renewable energy certificates from wind power and biomass facilities. Johnson & Johnson believes these practices not only benefit the environment, but also the company because it provides the firm with reliable, affordable sources of energy. In addition, Johnson & Johnson operates the largest fleet of hybrid vehicles owned by a corporation in the world.

Part of the "Healthy Planet" program also involves being truthful about green advertising—avoiding so-called greenwashing. Company management believes in transparency—informing employees, suppliers, consumers, and shareholders of what's green and what's not. This also means being specific about sustainability measures. "Provide your consumers with real numbers that inform and empower them," says the Web site. And while Johnson & Johnson refuses to overstate its accomplishments, the firm is beginning to publicize its efforts so that consumers can share in them. For example, the company is the second-largest producer of solar panels in the United States, and it has received the Leadership in Energy and Environmental Design (LEED) Gold certification for its Spring House research facility in Pennsylvania.

None of these goals could be achieved without support from Johnson & Johnson's leadership. Chairman and CEO William Weldon is committed to his company's sustainability initiatives as they relate to people and the planet. He writes, "More than ever, we know that caring for the health and well-being of people is not only an outstanding business but a mission that truly touches lives."

Questions for Critical Thinking

1. What role does the CEO's leadership play in accomplishing Johnson & Johnson's green goals?
2. How does the company's mission relate to sustainability?

Sources: Michael Christel, "J&J's New Lean, Green Lab to Be Key R&D Hub," *PharmaLive*, February 8, 2011, http://blog.rddirections.com; Company Web site, http://www.jnj.com, accessed April 12, 2010; "To Our Shareholders," *Annual Report*, http://www.investor.jnj.com, accessed April 12, 2010; "Partner Profile," *Green Power Partnership*, March 22, 2010, http://www.epa.gov.

A good mission statement states the firm's purpose for being in business and its overall goal. The most effective mission statements are memorable as well. The "Going Green" feature describes the mission of Johnson & Johnson, a global manufacturer of pharmaceuticals and healthcare products.

Assessing Your Competitive Position

Once a mission statement has been created, the next step in the planning process is to determine the firm's current—or potential—position in the marketplace. The company's founder or top managers evaluate the factors that may help it grow or could cause it to fail. A frequently used tool in this phase of strategic planning is the <u>**SWOT analysis**</u>. SWOT is an acronym for *strengths*, *weaknesses*, *opportunities*, and *threats*. By systematically evaluating all four of these factors, a firm can then develop the best strategies for gaining a competitive advantage. The framework for a SWOT analysis appears in Figure 7.3.

To evaluate a firm's strengths and weaknesses, its managers may examine each functional area such as finance, marketing, information technology, and human resources. Or they might evaluate strengths and weaknesses of each office, plant, or store. Entrepreneurs may focus on the individual skills and experience they bring to a new business.

SWOT analysis SWOT is an acronym for *strengths, weaknesses, opportunities,* and *threats.* By systematically evaluating all four of these factors, a firm can then develop the best strategies for gaining a competitive advantage.

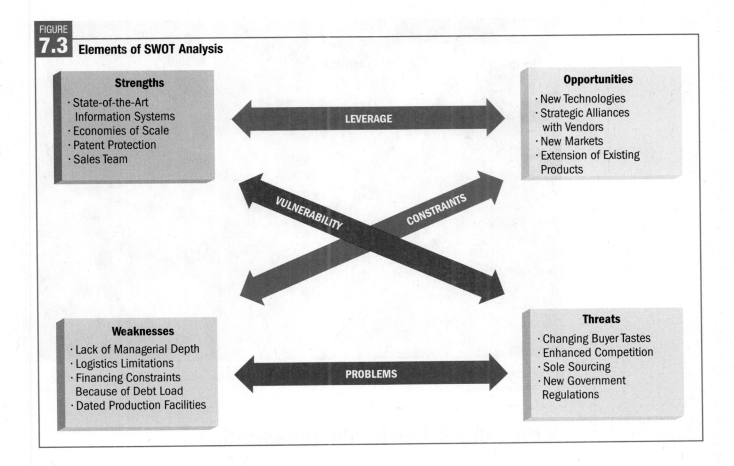

FIGURE 7.3 Elements of SWOT Analysis

Strengths
- State-of-the-Art Information Systems
- Economies of Scale
- Patent Protection
- Sales Team

LEVERAGE

VULNERABILITY

CONSTRAINTS

Opportunities
- New Technologies
- Strategic Alliances with Vendors
- New Markets
- Extension of Existing Products

Weaknesses
- Lack of Managerial Depth
- Logistics Limitations
- Financing Constraints Because of Debt Load
- Dated Production Facilities

PROBLEMS

Threats
- Changing Buyer Tastes
- Enhanced Competition
- Sole Sourcing
- New Government Regulations

For Starbucks, a key strength is consumers' positive image of the company's brand, which gets them to stand in line to pay premium prices for coffee. That positive image comes from Starbucks's being one of the best 100 companies to work for in the United States, according to *Fortune*, and from its socially responsible corporate policies. The company's strategic plans have included various ways to build on Starbucks's strong brand loyalty by attaching it to new products and expanding into new markets. The expansion efforts have included creating a Music WiFi Community on its Web site; offering bottled Frappuccino drinks in grocery stores; and opening thousands of Starbucks outlets in Europe, Asia, and the Middle East. Weaknesses include saturating some markets with too many stores and not paying attention to store design. Starbucks eventually addressed these weaknesses by closing some stores and redesigning others.[19]

SWOT analysis continues with an attempt to define the major opportunities and threats the firm is likely to face. Threats might include an economic recession—during which consumers are not willing to pay a premium for products—or a change in federal regulations. Starbucks addressed the threat of an economic downturn by beginning to offer less-expensive, instant coffee in stores like Costco and Target. Opportunities include such phenomena as the growth of social media. So Starbucks added links to Facebook and Twitter from its Web site.[20]

A SWOT analysis isn't carved in stone. Strengths and weaknesses, like opportunities and threats, may shift over time. A strength may eventually become a weakness and a threat may turn into an opportunity. But the analysis gives managers a place to start.

Extending Starbucks' strong brand loyalty to new products and markets is one example of the company's strategic turnaround plan.

Kevork Djansezian/©AP/WideWorld Photos

Setting Objectives for the Organization

objectives guideposts by which managers define the organization's desired performance in such areas as new-product development, sales, customer service, growth, environmental and social responsibility, and employee satisfaction.

The next step in planning is to develop objectives for the firm. **Objectives** set guideposts by which managers define the organization's desired performance in such areas as new-product development, sales, customer service, growth, environmental and social responsibility, and employee satisfaction. While the mission statement identifies a company's overall goals, objectives are more concrete.

Piperlime, a division of San Francisco-based Gap Inc., was created to sell apparel, accessories, and other fashion products outside of Gap's traditional line, which also includes Banana Republic and Old Navy. Offering trendy skirts, top, boots, jewelry, and bags, Piperlime's Web site also features blogs by shoppers and "picks" by celebrity stylist Rachel Zoe.[21] Gap's objectives for the site are twofold. "It's about growth," says Piperlime's general manager Jennifer Gosselin. And it's about being "relevant to the 20s and 30s customers."[22]

Creating Strategies for Competitive Differentiation

Developing a mission statement and setting objectives point a business in a specific direction. But the firm needs to identify the strategies it will use to reach its destination ahead of the competition. The underlying goal of strategy development is *competitive differentiation*—the unique combination of a company's abilities and resources that set it apart from its competitors. A firm might differentiate itself by being the first to introduce a product such as the iPad to a widespread market; or by offering exceptional customer service such as Nordstrom; or by offering bargains such as Costco. Brett Skoda founded Ohio-based CollegeFitness.com when he was a college student specifically to help fellow students lose the "freshman 15" and band together to live healthier lifestyles.[23]

Implementing the Strategy

Once the first four phases of the strategic planning process are complete, managers are ready to put those plans into action. Often, it's the middle managers or supervisors who actually implement a strategy. But studies show that top company officials are still reluctant to empower these managers with the authority to make decisions that could benefit the company. Companies that are willing to empower employees generally reap the benefits.[24]

In an effort to accomplish the strategy of cutting costs, avoiding layoffs, and maintaining a high level of customer service, insurance and financial services giant USAA started cross-training its call-center representatives. As a result, when customers place calls about certain issues, they don't automatically have to be transferred to someone else. A call rep who answers investment queries can also answer questions about insurance. While this may seem an obvious solution—without much tangible effect—in fact, the cross-training has reduced the cost of running the call center, saved jobs, and increased customer satisfaction. Call reps are now more empowered to help customers directly, which also boosts employee morale.[25]

Monitoring and Adapting Strategic Plans

The final step in the strategic planning process is to monitor and adapt plans when the actual performance fails to meet goals. Monitoring involves securing feedback about performance. Managers might compare actual sales against forecasts; compile information from surveys; listen to complaints from the customer hot line; interview employees who are involved; and review reports prepared by production, finance, marketing, or other company units. If an Internet advertisement doesn't result in enough response or sales, managers might evaluate whether to continue the advertisement, change it, or discontinue it. If a retailer observes customers buying more jeans when they are displayed near the front door, likely the display area will stay near the door—and perhaps be enlarged. Ongoing use of such tools as SWOT analysis and forecasting can help managers adapt their objectives and functional plans as changes occur.

Managers as Decision Makers

Managers make decisions every day, whether it involves shutting down a manufacturing plant or adding grilled cheese sandwiches to a lunch menu. **Decision making** is the process of recognizing a problem or opportunity, evaluating alternative solutions, selecting and implementing an alternative, and assessing the results. Managers make two basic kinds of decisions: programmed decisions and nonprogrammed decisions.

decision making process of recognizing a problem or opportunity, evaluating alternative solutions, selecting and implementing an alternative, and assessing the results.

Programmed and Nonprogrammed Decisions

A *programmed decision* involves simple, common, and frequently occurring problems for which solutions have already been determined. Examples of programmed decisions include reordering office supplies, renewing a lease, and referring to an established discount for bulk orders. Programmed decisions are made in advance—the firm sets rules, policies, and procedures for managers and employees to follow on a routine basis. Programmed decisions actually save managers time and companies money because new decisions don't have to be made each time the situation arises.

The release of the iPad was a nonprogrammed decision made by Apple involving a complex and unique opportunity with important consequences for the company.

A *nonprogrammed decision* involves a complex and unique problem or opportunity with important consequences for the organization. Examples of nonprogrammed decisions include entering a new market, deleting a product from the line, or developing a new product. Apple's decision to develop and launch its new product the iPad was a nonprogrammed decision that involved research and development, finances, technology, production, and marketing. Decisions were made about everything from what kinds of apps and accessories the iPad would offer to how much the new device would cost consumers.[26]

How Managers Make Decisions

In a narrow sense, decision making involves choosing among two or more alternatives, with the chosen alternative becoming the decision. In a broader sense, decision making involves a systematic, step-by-step process that helps managers make effective choices. This process begins when someone recognizes a problem or opportunity, develops possible courses of action, evaluates the alternatives, selects and implements one of them, and assesses the outcome. It's important to keep in mind that managers are *human* decision makers, and while they can follow the decision-making process as shown in Figure 7.4 step-by-step, the outcome of their decisions depends on many factors, including the accuracy of their information and the experience, creativity, and wisdom of the person.

Making good decisions is never easy. A decision might hurt or help the sales of a product; it might offend or disappoint a customer or coworker; it might affect the manager's own career or reputation. Managers' decisions can have complex legal and ethical dimensions. *CRO Magazine* publishes an annual list of "The 100 Best Corporate Citizens." These companies make decisions that are ethical, environmentally responsible, fair toward employees,

FIGURE 7.4 Steps in the Decision-Making Process

Recognize Problem or Opportunity → Develop Alternative Courses of Action → Evaluate Alternatives → Select and Implement Chosen Alternative → Follow Up to Determine Effectiveness of Decision

and accountable to local communities and that provide responsible goods and services to customers and a healthy return to investors. These organizations prove that good corporate citizenship is good behavior. The top ten corporate citizens named one recent year were: Hewlett-Packard, Intel, General Mills, IBM, Kimberly-Clark, Abbott Laboratories, Bristol-Myers Squibb, The Coca-Cola Company, Gap Inc., and Hess Corporation.[27]

Assessment Check ✓

1. Distinguish between programmed and non-programmed decisions.
2. What are the steps in the decision-making process?

leadership ability to direct or inspire people to attain certain goals.

Managers as Leaders

A manager must demonstrate **leadership**, directing or inspiring people to attain certain goals. Great leaders do not all share the same qualities, but three traits are often mentioned: empathy (the ability to imagine yourself in someone else's position), self-awareness, and objectivity. While it might seem as though empathy and objectivity are opposite traits, they do balance each other. Many leaders share other traits—courage, passion, commitment, innovation, and flexibility to name a few.

Leadership involves the use of influence or power. This influence may come from one or more sources. One source of power is the leader's position in the company. A national sales manager has the authority to direct the activities of the sales force. Another source of power is a leader's expertise and experience. A first-line supervisor with expert machinist skills will most likely be respected by employees in the machining department. Some leaders derive power from their personalities. Employees may admire a leader because they recognize an exceptionally kind and fair, humorous, energetic, or enthusiastic person. Admiration, inspiration, and motivation are especially important during difficult economic times or when a leader has to make tough decisions for the company. This has been true of Jeffrey Immelt, chairman and CEO of General Electric (GE), as described in the "Hit & Miss" feature.

When Doug Conant took over the CEO job at Campbell's Soup, headquartered in Camden, New Jersey, the company was decidedly ho-hum. Instead of boiling with innovation, the firm had left new ideas simmering on the back burner. Conant looked around his company, which produces one of the best-known brands in the world, with frustration. "The microwave was invented in 1947, but

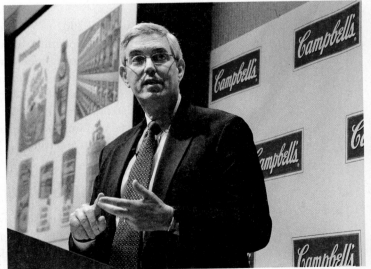

Doug Conant, Campbell's Soup former CEO, believes that action is the best demonstration of leadership.

Jeff Immelt Tries to Lead GE in a New Direction

GE, once considered one of the nation's most recognizable and respected firms, has fallen on hard times. The company, which manufactures everything from toasters to washing machines to jet engines, has been forced to pull the plug on various ventures in order to save itself. The man in charge of the power at GE is its CEO, Jeffrey Immelt.

Over the years, GE has grown into a conglomerate, straying far from its roots as a manufacturer of electrical appliances. Its GE Capital unit, which accounted for more than half of the company's overall profits, is now burdened with a huge number of bad loans. GE's stake in NBC Universal and the NBC network will likely be sold to cable operator Comcast. But shareholders and others are asking, "Why was GE involved in these businesses in the first place?"

Jeffrey Immelt has vowed to change the direction of the company. "GE must be an industrial company first," he notes. "We need a new strategy for this economy. We should clear away any arrogance, false assumptions, or a sense that things will be OK just because we are [in] America."

Financially, GE can't just walk away from its GE Capital commitments. But Immelt has promised to reduce its size and renew the firm's focus on its industrial roots, including a significant investment in clean energy projects. He takes his leadership role, as well as the leadership role of GE itself, very seriously. "We need to invest more in innovation. We need to target this innovation toward fulfilling big needs like clean energy," he says. "Nothing of consequence is accomplished without leadership."

Immelt observes that today's leaders must adopt a democratic style that encourages input from employees. "Twenty-first century leaders listen. They use external inputs as a catalyst. They put their ego in check. They ask more questions than they answer. They welcome dissent and debate, and are constantly seeking more intelligence."

Immelt has been spending his weekends listening to the 185 officers of GE—one at a time. The weekend sessions create personal connections with his team.

He also points out the importance of delegating in order to innovate more easily and regain a competitive standing in the marketplace. "GE is a big organization. The problem with size is that it can be too slow. At GE, we must push decision-making down in the organization and we must delegate more."

When Immelt was asked to lead the President's Council on Jobs and Competitiveness, he accepted without hesitation. "We've got to invest and we've got to drive exports," Immelt said. "Ninety-five percent of the world's population is outside the U.S. Ultimately to create manufacturing jobs, we've got to be innovating and we've got to be exporting."

Questions for Critical Thinking

1. How would you characterize Immelt's leadership style? Is it appropriate for a big organization like GE? Why or why not?
2. Do you think Immelt is an effective motivator? Would you want to work for him? Why or why not?

Sources: Allan Chernoff, "Obama's Chief Job Promoter: Jeffrey Immelt," *CNN Money.com*. January 24, 2011, http://money.cnn.com; Diane Brady, "Can GE Still Manage?" *Bloomberg BusinessWeek*, April 25, 2010, 26–32; GE Web site, http://www.ge.com, accessed April 9, 2010; "Renewing American Leadership: Immelt at West Point," *GE Reports*, http://www.gereports.com, accessed April 9, 2010; Stephen Manning, "GE's CEO Declines Bonus for 2nd Year," *BusinessWeek*, March 5, 2010, http://www.businessweek.com.

it took us until 2002 to put together a microwaveable soup pack," he pointed out. So Conant got to work on updating the world's largest soup company. He cut all products that were not number one or number two in their categories. He poured resources into developing products that shrieked value, nutrition, and convenience to consumers. And he engineered a new focus on two of the world's largest soup-eating nations: China and Russia. When Conant stepped down, he was praised by company chairman Paul Charron as someone who "conceived and implemented a strategic vision that transformed Campbell into the focused, highly competitive business it is today."[28]

Leadership Styles

The way a person uses power to lead others determines his or her leadership style. Leadership styles range along a continuum with autocratic leadership at one extreme end and free-rein leadership at the other. *Autocratic leadership* is centered on the boss. Autocratic leaders make decisions on their own without consulting employees. They reach decisions, communicate them to subordinates, and expect automatic implementation.

Democratic leadership includes subordinates in the decision-making process. This leadership style centers on employees' contributions. Democratic leaders delegate assignments, ask employees for suggestions, and encourage participation. An important outgrowth of democratic leadership in business is the concept of **empowerment**, in which employees share authority, responsibility, and decision making with their managers.

At the other end of the continuum from autocratic leadership is *free-rein leadership*. Free-rein leaders believe in minimal supervision. They allow subordinates to make most of their own decisions. Free-rein leaders communicate with employees frequently, as the situation warrants. For the first decade of its existence, Google was proud of its free-rein leadership style. Engineers were encouraged to pursue any and all ideas; teams formed or disbanded on their own; employees spent as much or as little time as they wanted to on any given project. But as the firm entered its second decade, it became apparent that not every innovation was worth pursuing—and some valuable ideas were getting lost in the chaos. Executive Chairman Eric Schmidt noted, "We were concerned that some of the biggest ideas were getting squashed." So the firm established a process for reviewing new project ideas in order to identify those most likely to succeed.[29]

When US Airways flight 1549 was forced to ditch into the Hudson River, the quick thinking and decision-making leadership style of Chesley Sullenberger (now retired) saved the lives of everyone on that flight.

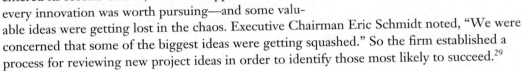

Which Leadership Style Is Best?

No single leadership style is best for every firm in every situation. Sometimes leadership styles require change in order for a company to grow, as has been the case for Google. In a crisis, an autocratic leadership style might save the company—and sometimes the lives of customers and employees. This was the case when US Airways flight 1549 was forced to ditch into the Hudson River after hitting a wayward flock of Canada geese. Quick, autocratic decisions made by pilot Chesley Sullenberger resulted in the survival of everyone on board the flight. But US Airways management on the ground activated a democratic style of leadership in which managers at many levels were empowered to take actions to help the passengers and their families. For example, one executive arrived on the scene with a bag of emergency cash for passengers and credit cards for employees so they could purchase medicines, food, or anything else they needed.[30] A company that recognizes which leadership style works best for its employees, customers, and business conditions is most likely to choose the best leaders for its particular needs.

Corporate Culture

An organization's **corporate culture** is its system of principles, beliefs, and values. The leadership style of its managers, the way it communicates, and the overall work environment influence a firm's corporate culture. A corporate culture is typically shaped by the leaders who founded and developed the company and by those who have succeeded them. Although

Charlotte Observer/MCT/Landov LLC

empowerment giving employees shared authority, responsibility, and decision making with their managers.

Assessment Check ☑

1. How is *leadership* defined?
2. Identify the styles of leadership as they appear along a continuum of greater or lesser employee participation.

corporate culture organization's system of principles, beliefs, and values.

Google has grown by leaps and bounds since its launch, the firm still tries to maintain the culture of innovation, creativity, and flexibility that its co-founders Larry Page and Sergey Brin promoted from the beginning. Google now has offices around the world, staffed by thousands of workers who speak a multitude of languages. "We are aggressively inclusive in our hiring, and we favor ability over experience," states the Web site. "The result is a team that reflects the global audience Google serves. When not at work, Googlers pursue interests from cross-country cycling to wine tasting, from flying to Frisbee."[31]

Managers use symbols, rituals, ceremonies, and stories to reinforce corporate culture. The corporate culture at the Walt Disney Company is almost as famous as the original Disney characters themselves. In fact, every Disney employee is known as a cast member. All new employees attend training seminars in which they learn the language, customs, traditions, stories, product lines—everything there is to know about the Disney culture and its original founder, Walt Disney.[32]

Corporate cultures can be very strong and enduring, but sometimes they are forced to change to meet new demands in the business environment. A firm that is steeped in tradition and bureaucracy might have to shift to a leaner, more flexible culture in order to respond to shifts in technology or customer preferences. A firm that grows quickly—like Google—generally has to make some adjustments in its culture to accommodate more customers and employees.

In an organization with a strong culture, everyone knows and supports the same principles, beliefs, and values, as is the case at Southwest Airlines, described in the "Hit & Miss" feature. To achieve its goals, a business must also provide structure, which results from the management function of organizing.

Assessment Check ✓

1. What is the relationship between leadership style and corporate culture?
2. What is a strong corporate culture?

organization structured group of people working together to achieve common goals.

Organizational Structures

An **organization** is a structured group of people working together to achieve common goals. An organization features three key elements: human interaction, goal-directed activities, and structure. The organizing process, much of which is led by managers, should result in an overall structure that permits interactions among individuals and departments needed to achieve company goals.

The steps involved in the organizing process are shown in Figure 7.5. Managers first determine the specific activities needed to implement plans and achieve goals. Next, they

FIGURE 7.5 Steps in the Organizing Process

1. Determine Specific Work Activities Necessary to Implement Plans and Achieve Objectives
2. Group Work Activities into a Logical Pattern or Structure
3. Assign Activities to Specific Positions and People and Allocate Necessary Resources
4. Coordinate Activities of Different Groups and Individuals
5. Evaluate Results of the Organizing Process

Southwest Airlines: "We Love Your Bags"

Southwest Airlines is well known for its reasonable fares, cheerful service, convenient schedules, and a genuine interest in its passengers. When other airlines started charging customers for checked baggage, Southwest flatly refused to get on board. Instead, the airline stood firm against this kind of additional charge, poking fun at it with an advertising campaign whose tagline was, "We Love Your Bags." Customers just love Southwest for decisions like this.

Southwest has a corporate culture filled with humor and energy that spills over to its customers, begun with its founder Herb Kelleher. "Southwest Airlines has built its culture and its reputation from the inside out," says the company Web site. The idea is that if the company's 32,000 employees are happy, they will be motivated to ensure their customers' happiness as well. This simple strategy has been very effective. "Southwest likes to think of itself as a customer service organization that happens to fly airplanes," explains president Colleen Barrett.

One of the characteristics that Southwest looks for in potential employees is a "servant's heart." When considering a pool of flight-attendant candidates, Southwest managers conduct group interviews to see how the candidates interact with one another—generally it is a good indicator of how they will react to customers. Believing that strong relationships within the company is important to the firm's long-term success, Southwest gives employees every opportunity to voice their opinions, receive education and training, and move up the career ladder.

Southwest empowers its middle managers, supervisors, and front-line employees with the authority to make decisions that strengthen relationships with customers. "In the airline industry, a company is only as good as its customers' last travel experience," notes Ginger Hardage, Southwest's senior vice president for corporate communication. "At Southwest, employees are encouraged to make decisions from the heart, and in turn, these proactive gestures provide positive benefits to the customers and the company."

Although a strong corporate culture is clearly part of an overall strategy, at Southwest it is more than that—frequently employees and passengers refer to Southwest as a company with "heart." That heart originated with Southwest's founder and long-time CEO Herb Kelleher, who is known for his love of fun. Even after Kelleher stepped down from the CEO position, the company runs on his spirit. Current CEO Gary Kelly observes that Southwest strives to keep its culture "supportive, active, and fun."

Questions for Critical Thinking

1. How would you describe the principles, beliefs, and values at Southwest?
2. Herb Kelleher is no longer CEO of Southwest, yet the company's original corporate culture seems to have survived. Why do you think this is?

Sources: Company Web site, http://www.southwest.com, accessed July 5, 2011; "Southwest's Secret to a Positive Corporate Culture: Its Employees," Business Civic Leadership Center, http://www.uschamber.org, accessed March 29, 2010; Dan Oswald, "Corporate Culture Done Right: Southwest Airlines," *Employment Law Post*, accessed January 8, 2010, http://employmentlawpost.com.

---

group these work activities into a logical structure. Then they assign work to specific employees and give the people the resources they need to complete it. Managers coordinate the work of different groups and employees within the firm. Finally, they evaluate the results of the organizing process to ensure effective and efficient progress toward planned goals. Evaluation sometimes results in changes to the way work is organized.

Many factors influence the results of organizing. The list includes a firm's goals and competitive strategy, the type of product it offers, the way it uses technology to accomplish work, and its size. Small firms typically create very simple structures. The owner of a dry-cleaning business generally is the top manager, who hires several employees to process orders, clean the clothing, and make deliveries. The owner handles the functions of purchasing supplies such as detergents and hangers, hiring and training employees and coordinating their work, preparing advertisements for the local newspaper, and keeping accounting records.

As a company grows, its structure increases in complexity. With increased size comes specialization and growing numbers of employees. A larger firm may employ many

FIGURE
7.6 Sample Organization Chart

salespeople, along with a sales manager to direct and coordinate their work, or organize an accounting department.

An effective structure is one that is clear and easy to understand: employees know what is expected of them and to whom they report. They also know how their jobs contribute to the company's mission and overall strategic plan. An *organization chart* can help clarify the structure of a firm. Figure 7.6 illustrates a sample organization chart.

Not-for-profit organizations also organize through formal structures so they can function efficiently and carry out their goals. These organizations, such as the Salvation Army and the American Society for Prevention of Cruelty to Animals (ASPCA), sometimes have a blend of paid staff and volunteers in their organizational structure.

Departmentalization

departmentalization
process of dividing work activities into units within the organization.

Departmentalization is the process of dividing work activities into units within the organization. In this arrangement, employees specialize in certain jobs—such as marketing, finance, or design. Depending on the size of the firm, usually an executive runs the department, followed by middle-level managers and supervisors. The five major forms of departmentalization subdivide work by product, geographical area, customer, function, and process.

- *Product departmentalization.* This approach organizes work units based on the goods and services a company offers. California's Activision Blizzard Inc. recently restructured its organization by product. The videogame publisher is now divided into four divisions: "Call of Duty," a military game; internally owned games such as

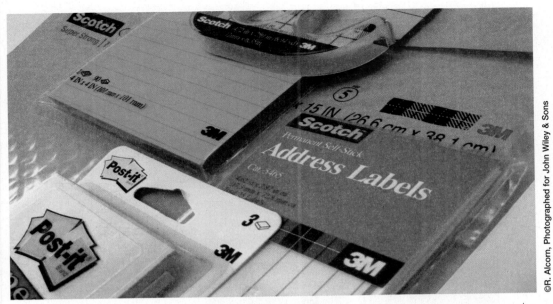

These familiar office products represent only one of 3M Corporation's many product lines. Because 3M serves such a broad spectrum of customers, it is organized on the basis of customer departmentalization.

"Guitar Hero" and "Tony Hawk"; licensed properties; and Blizzard Entertainment, maker of the online game "World of Warcraft."[33]

- *Geographical departmentalization.* This form organizes units by geographical regions within a country or, for a multinational firm, by region throughout the world. The Web site Petswelcome.com makes it easy for traveling pet owners to locate hotel chains, rentals, amusement parks, and other recreational locations around the country that welcome pets. Users can search by type of lodging, route planned, and destination.[34]

- *Customer departmentalization.* A firm that offers a variety of goods and services targeted at different types of customers might structure itself based on customer departmentalization. Management of Procter & Gamble's wide array of products is divided among three major business units: Beauty and Grooming (Fusion, CoverGirl, Braun, Ivory); Health and Well-Being (Crest, lams); and Household Care (Pampers, Tide, Mr. Clean).[35]

- *Functional departmentalization.* Some firms organize work units according to business functions such as finance, marketing, human resources, and production. An advertising agency may create departments for creative personnel (say, copywriters), media buyers, and account executives.

- *Process departmentalization.* Some goods and services require multiple work processes to complete their production. A manufacturer may set up separate departments for cutting material, heat-treating it, forming it into its final shape, and painting it.

As Figure 7.7 illustrates, a single company may implement several different departmentalization schemes. In deciding on a form of departmentalization, managers take into account the type of product they produce, the size of their company, their customer base, and the locations of their customers.

FIGURE 7.7 Different Forms of Departmentalization within One Company

Chief Executive Officer

Vice President Production — Vice President Marketing — Chief Financial Officer → **Functional Departmentalization**

Domestic Sales Manager — International Sales Manager → **Geographical Departmentalization**

Sales Manager for Business Markets — Sales Manager for Consumer Markets → **Customer Departmentalization**

Delegating Work Assignments

delegation managerial process of assigning work to employees.

Managers assign work to employees, a process called **delegation**. Employees might be responsible for answering customer calls, scooping ice cream, processing returns, making deliveries, opening or closing a store, cooking or serving food, contributing to new-product design, calculating a return on investment, or any of thousands of other tasks. Just as important, employees are given a certain amount of authority to make decisions.

Companies like Zappos, the online shoe retailer, that empower their workers to make decisions that could better serve their customers generally have happier employees and more satisfied customers.[36] As employees receive greater authority, they also must be accountable for their actions and decisions—they receive credit when things go well, and must accept responsibility when they don't. Managers also must figure out the best way to delegate responsibilities to employees who belong to different age groups, including Millennials, as discussed in the "Business Etiquette" feature.

Span of Management
The *span of management*, or span of control, is the number of employees a manager supervises. These employees are often referred to as direct reports. First-line managers have wider spans of management, monitoring the work of many employees. The span of management varies depending on many factors, including the type of work performed and employees' training. In recent years, a growing trend has brought wider spans of control, as companies have reduced their layers of management to flatten their organizational structures, in the process increasing the decision-making responsibility they give employees.

Centralization and Decentralization
How widely should managers disperse decision-making authority throughout an organization? A company that emphasizes *centralization* retains decision making at the top of the management hierarchy. A company

that emphasizes *decentralization* locates decision making at lower levels. A trend toward decentralization has pushed decision making down to operating employees in many cases. Firms that have decentralized believe that the change can improve their ability to serve customers. For example, the front desk clerk at a hotel is much better equipped to fulfill a guest's request for a crib or a wake-up call than the hotel's general manager.

Types of Organization Structures

The four basic types of organization structures are line, line-and-staff, committee, and matrix. While some companies do follow one type of structure, most use a combination.

Line Organizations
A *line organization*, the oldest and simplest organization structure, establishes a direct flow of authority from the chief executive to employees. The line organization defines a simple, clear *chain of command*—a hierarchy of managers and workers. With a clear chain of command, everyone knows who is in charge and decisions can be made quickly. This structure is particularly effective in a crisis situation. But a line organization has its drawbacks. Each manager has complete responsibility for a range of activities; in a medium-sized or large organization, however, this person can't possibly be expert in all of them. In a small organization such as a local hair salon, or dentist's office, a line organization is probably the most efficient way to run the business.

Line-and-Staff Organizations
A *line-and-staff organization* combines the direct flow of authority of a line organization with staff departments that support the line departments. Line departments participate directly in decisions that affect the core operations of the organization. Staff departments lend specialized technical support. Figure 7.8 illustrates a line-and-staff organization. Accounting, engineering, and human resources are staff departments that support the line authority extending from the plant manager to the production manager and supervisors.

FIGURE 7.8 Line-and-Staff Organization

Plant Manager

Accounting

Engineering

Human Resources

Production Manager

Supervisor

Supervisor

Supervisor

——— Line Relationships
▬▬▬ Staff Relationships

A line manager and a staff manager differ significantly in their authority relationships. A line manager forms part of the primary line of authority that flows throughout the organization. Line managers interact directly with the functions of production, financing, or marketing—the functions needed to produce and sell goods and services. A staff manager provides information, advice, or technical assistance to aid line managers. Staff managers do not have authority to give orders outside their own departments or to compel line managers to take action.

The line-and-staff organization is common in midsize and large organizations. It is an effective structure because it combines the line organization's capabilities for rapid decision making and direct communication with the expert knowledge of staff specialists.

Committee Organizations

A *committee organization* is a structure that places authority and responsibility jointly in the hands of a group of individuals rather than a single manager. This model typically appears as part of a regular line-and-staff structure.

Committees also work in areas such as new-product development. A new-product committee may include managers from such areas as accounting, engineering, finance, manufacturing, marketing, and technical research. By including representatives from all areas involved in creating and marketing products, such a committee generally improves planning and employee morale because decisions reflect diverse perspectives.

Committees tend to act slowly and conservatively, however, and may make decisions by compromising conflicting interests rather than by choosing the best alternative. The definition of a camel as "a racehorse designed by committee" provides an apt description of some limitations of committee decisions. At Nordstrom, the six-person office of the co-presidency was eventually abandoned for a more traditional structure.

Matrix Organizations

Some organizations use a matrix or product management design to customize their structures. The *matrix structure* links employees from different parts of the organization to work together on specific projects. Figure 7.9 diagrams a matrix structure. A project manager assembles a group of employees from different functional areas. The employees keep their ties to the line-and-staff structure, as shown in the vertical white lines. As the horizontal gold lines show, employees are also members of project teams. When the project is completed, employees return to their "regular" jobs.

In the matrix structure, each employee reports to two managers: one line manager and one project manager. Employees who are chosen to work on a special project receive instructions from the project manager (horizontal authority), but they continue as employees in their permanent functional departments (vertical authority). The term *matrix* comes from the intersecting grid of horizontal and vertical lines of authority.

FIGURE 7.9 Matrix Organization

The matrix structure is popular at high-technology and multinational corporations, as well as hospitals and consulting firms. Dow Chemical and Procter & Gamble have both used matrix structures. The major benefits of the matrix structure come from its flexibility in adapting quickly to rapid changes in the environment and its capability of focusing resources on major problems or products. It also provides an outlet for employees' creativity and initiative. However, it challenges project managers to integrate the skills of specialists from many departments into a coordinated team. It also means that team members' permanent functional managers must adjust their employees' regular workloads.

The matrix structure is most effective when company leaders empower project managers to use whatever resources are available to achieve the project's objectives. Good project managers know how to make the project goals clear and keep team members focused. A firm that truly embraces the matrix structure also nurtures a project culture by making sure staffing is adequate, the workload is reasonable, and other company resources are available to project managers.[37]

Assessment Check ✓

1. What is the purpose of an organization chart?
2. What are the five major forms of departmentalization?
3. What does *span of management* mean?

What's Ahead

In the next chapter, we sharpen our focus on the importance of people—the human resource—in shaping the growth and profitability of the organization. We examine how firms recruit, select, train, evaluate, and compensate employees in their attempts to attract, retain, and motivate a high-quality workforce. The concept of motivation is examined, and we will discuss how managers apply theories of motivation in the modern workplace. The next chapter also looks at the important topic of labor–management relations.

Summary of Learning Objectives

⌐1¬ Define *management* and the three types of skills necessary for managerial success.

Management is the process of achieving organizational objectives through people and other resources. The management hierarchy is generally as follows: top managers provide overall direction for company activities, middle managers implement the strategies of top managers and direct the activities of supervisors, and supervisors interact directly with workers. The three basic managerial skills are: technical, human or interpersonal, and conceptual.

Assessment Check Answers ☑

1.1 What is management? Management is the process of achieving organizational objectives through people and other resources. The manager's job is to combine human and technical resources in the best way possible to achieve the company's goals.

1.2 How do the jobs of top managers, middle managers, and supervisory managers differ? Top managers develop long-range plans, set a direction for their organization, and inspire all employees to achieve the company's vision. Middle managers focus on specific operations, products, or customers. They develop procedures to implement the firm's strategic plans. Supervisory managers interact directly with nonmanagerial employees who produce and sell the firm's goods and services. They are responsible for implementing the plans developed by middle managers and motivating workers to accomplish immediate goals.

1.3 What is the relationship between the manager's planning and controlling functions? Controlling is evaluating an organization's performance to determine whether it is accomplishing its objectives. The basic purpose of controlling is to assess the success of the planning function.

Controlling also provides feedback for future rounds of planning.

⌐2¬ Explain the role of vision and ethical standards in business success.

Vision is the founder's perception of the marketplace needs and the firm's methods for meeting them. Vision helps clarify a firm's purpose and the actions it can take to make the most of opportunities. High ethical standards can help build success for a firm through job satisfaction and customer loyalty.

Assessment Check Answers ☑

2.1 What is meant by a vision for the firm? A vision serves as the target for a firm's actions, helping direct the company toward opportunities and differentiating it from its competitors.

2.2 Why is it important for a top executive to set high ethical standards? High ethical standards often result in a stable workforce, job satisfaction, and customer loyalty.

⌐3¬ Summarize the major benefits of planning, and distinguish among strategic planning, tactical planning, and operational planning.

The planning process identifies organizational goals and develops the actions necessary to reach them. Planning helps a company turn vision into action, take advantage of opportunities, and avoid costly mistakes. Strategic planning is a far-reaching process. It views the world through a wide-angle lens to determine the long-range focus and activities of the organization. Tactical planning focuses on the current and short-range activities required to implement the organization's strategies. Operational planning sets standards and work targets for functional areas such as production, human resources, and marketing.

Assessment Check Answers ✓

3.1 Outline the planning process. Some plans are very broad and long range, focusing on key organizational objectives; others are more detailed and specify how particular objectives will be achieved. From the mission statement to objectives to specific plans, each phase must fit into a comprehensive planning framework.

3.2 Describe the purpose of tactical planning. The purpose of tactical planning is to determine which short-term activities should be implemented to accomplish the firm's overall strategy.

3.3 Compare the kinds of plans made by top managers and middle managers. How does their focus differ? Top managers focus on long-range, strategic plans. In contrast, middle-level managers and supervisors focus on short-term, tactical planning.

⌐4¬ Describe the strategic planning process.

The first step of strategic planning is to translate the firm's vision into a mission statement that explains its overall intentions and aims. Next, planners must assess the firm's current competitive position using tools such as SWOT analysis. Managers then set specific objectives. The next step is to develop strategies for reaching objectives that will differentiate the firm from its competitors. Managers then develop an action plan that outlines the specific methods for implementing the strategy. Finally, the results achieved by the plan are evaluated, and the plan is adjusted as needed.

Assessment Check Answers ✓

4.1 What is the purpose of a mission statement? A mission statement is a public declaration of a firm's purpose, the reason it exists, the customers it will serve, and the way it is different from competitors. A mission statement guides the actions of company managers and employees.

4.2 Which of the firm's characteristics does a SWOT analysis compare? A SWOT analysis determines a firm's strengths, weaknesses, opportunities, and threats relative to its competitors. A SWOT analysis helps determine a firm's competitive position in the marketplace.

4.3 How do managers use objectives? Objectives, which are derived from the firm's mission statement, are used to define desired performance levels in areas such as profitability, customer service, and employee satisfaction.

⌐5¬ Contrast the two major types of business decisions, and list the steps in the decision-making process.

A programmed decision applies a company rule or policy to solve a frequently occurring problem. A nonprogrammed

decision forms a response to a complex and unique problem with important consequences for the organization. The five-step approach to decision making includes recognizing a problem or opportunity, developing alternative courses of action, evaluating the alternatives, selecting and implementing an alternative, and following up the decision to determine its effectiveness.

Assessment Check Answers ✓

5.1 Distinguish between programmed and nonprogrammed decisions. Programmed decisions, such as reordering office supplies, are simple and happen frequently, so procedures for these can streamline the process. Nonprogrammed decisions, such as the purchase of real estate or equipment, require more individual evaluation.

5.2 What are the steps in the decision-making process? The decision-making steps are recognition of a problem or opportunity, development of alternatives, evaluation of alternatives, selection and implementation of the chosen alternative, and follow-up to determine effectiveness of the decision.

⌐6¬ Define *leadership,* and compare different leadership styles.

Leadership is the act of motivating others to achieve certain goals. The basic leadership styles are autocratic, democratic, and free-rein leadership. The best leadership style depends on three elements: the leader, the followers, and the situation.

Assessment Check Answers ✓

6.1 How is *leadership* defined? Leadership means directing or inspiring people to attain organizational goals. Effective leaders share several traits, such as empathy, self-awareness, and objectivity in dealing with others. Leaders also use the power of their jobs, expertise, and experience to influence others.

6.2 Identify the styles of leadership as they appear along a continuum of greater or lesser employee participation. At one end of the continuum, autocratic leaders make decisions without consulting employees. In the middle of the continuum, democratic leaders ask employees for suggestions and encourage participation. At the other end of the continuum, free-rein leaders leave most decisions to their employees.

⌐7¬ Discuss the meaning and importance of corporate culture.

Corporate culture refers to an organization's principles, beliefs, and values. It is typically shaped by a firm's founder and perpetuated through formal programs such as training, rituals, and ceremonies, as well as through informal discussions among employees. Corporate culture can influence a firm's success by giving it a competitive advantage.

Assessment Check Answers ✔

7.1 What is the relationship between leadership style and corporate culture? The best leadership style to adopt often depends on the organization's corporate culture and its system of principles, beliefs, and values. Managerial philosophies, communications networks, and workplace environments and practices all influence corporate culture.

7.2 What is a strong corporate culture? A corporate culture is an organization's system of principles, beliefs, and values. In an organization with a strong culture, everyone knows and supports the same principles, beliefs, and values.

┌─┐
│8│ **Identify the five major forms of departmentalization and**
└─┘ **the four main types of organization structures.**

The subdivision of work activities into units within the organization is called *departmentalization*. It may be based on products, geographical locations, customers, functions, or processes. Most firms implement one or more of four structures: line, line-and-staff, committee, and matrix structures.

Assessment Check Answers ✔

8.1 What is the purpose of an organization chart? An organization chart is a visual representation of a firm's structure that illustrates job positions and functions.

8.2 What are the five major forms of departmentalization? Product departmentalization organizes units by the different goods and services a company offers. Geographical departmentalization organizes units by geographical regions. Customer departmentalization organizes units by different types of customers. Functional departmentalization organizes units by business functions such as finance, marketing, human resources, and production. Process departmentalization organizes units by the steps or work processes it takes to complete production or provide a service.

8.3 What does *span of management* mean? The span of management, or span of control, is the number of employees a manager supervises.

▉ Business Terms You Need to Know

management 218	controlling 222
planning 221	vision 222
organizing 221	mission statement 227
directing 222	SWOT analysis 228

objectives 230	corporate culture 235
decision making 231	organization 236
leadership 233	departmentalization 238
empowerment 235	delegation 240

▉ Review Questions

1. What are the three levels of management hierarchy? For each level, which management skills might be considered most important, and why?

2. Identify the four basic managerial functions. Suppose you were hired to be the manager of a local restaurant. Which managerial functions would likely be the biggest part of your job? In what ways?

3. Describe the link between a company's vision and its ethical standards. Why is it important for top management to put forth a clear vision and ethical standards for a company?

4. Identify the four types of planning, then think about the following scenario. Suppose you planned a large cookout with your friends, but when you woke up on the morning of the party, it was pouring rain. What type of planning would you use prior to the storm? What type of planning would allow you to cope with the rain? Specifically, what could you do?

5. What is the link between a firm's vision and its mission statement? Think about your own career as a start-up venture. What is your vision? What might be your mission statement?

6. Define *objectives*. Outline objectives you might have for your own college education and career. How might this outline help you implement your own career strategy?

7. Identify each of the following as a programmed or nonprogrammed decision:
   a. reordering printer cartridges
   b. selecting a cell phone provider
   c. buying your favorite toothpaste or shampoo at the supermarket
   d. selecting a college to attend
   e. filling your car with gasoline

8. From what sources might a leader derive power? Which leadership style might work best for a manager whose firm is forced to make cost-cutting decisions? Why?

9. Why is a strong corporate culture important to a company's success? How might the corporate culture be linked to leadership style?

10. Which type of organization structure provides a firm with the most flexibility to respond to changes in the marketplace and engage in innovation? What might be the drawbacks of this structure?

▮ Projects and Teamwork Applications

1. Imagine that you've been hired as a supervisor by a bakery shop called Claire's Cakes that is beginning to grow. The founder, whose name is Claire, is looking for ways to increase production capacity, expand its deliveries, and eventually open several more shops in the area. Create a job description for yourself, including the managerial functions you think you'll need and skills you believe you'll need for success.

2. On your own or with a classmate, create a mission statement for Claire's Cakes. Think about the type of company it is, the products it offers customers (cakes for special occasions or milestones), and the type of growth it is planning.

3. Contingency planning requires a combination of foresight and adaptability. Josh James, founder of Omniture, the Web analytics firm he recently sold to Adobe, recalls the importance of being able to adapt when his company seemed on the brink of disaster. "There were times when I lay down on the floor at night, close to crying. Then my wife would come over and kick me and say, 'Get up and figure it out.' "[38] Research the news headlines for situations that could (or did) require contingency planning. Report to the class what the challenge was, and how the managers involved handled it. Remark on whether the planning was effective or successful.

4. Identify someone who you think is a good leader—it can be someone you know personally or a public figure. Describe the traits that you think are most important in making this person an effective leader. Would this person's leadership style work in situations other than his or her current position? Why or why not?

5. Research a firm whose goods or services you purchase or admire. Learn what you can about the organization's culture. Do you think you would be an effective manager in this culture? Why or why not? Share your findings with the class.

▮ Web Assignments

1. **Strategic planning.** Visit the Web site listed below. It summarizes Johnson & Johnson's strategic planning philosophy. Review several recent acquisitions by Johnson & Johnson and prepare a brief report discussing how the acquisitions resulted from the company's strategic planning process.

   http://www.investor.jnj.com/strategic.cfm

2. **Mission statements.** Go to the Web sites of two organizations, a for-profit firm and a not-for-profit organization. Print out both organization's mission statements. Take the material with you to class to participate in a discussion on mission statements.

3. **Management structure.** Visit the Web site listed below. Click on "corporate governance" and answer the following questions:

   a. How would you characterize Target's organizational structure?

   b. What is the composition of Target's board of directors?

   http://investors.target.com/phoenix.zhtml?c=65828&p=irol-IRHome

Note: Internet Web addresses change frequently. If you don't find the exact sites listed, you may need to access the organization's home page and search from there or use a search engine such as Bing or Google.

Ford Drives Out of the Financial Mud

Recently, when the other major U.S. automakers accepted federal funds in order to stay in business, Ford Motor Company—in the voice of CEO Alan R. Mulally—said no. The federal funds were to come in the form of short-term loans, which Ford determined that it didn't need at the time to survive. Several years earlier, the firm had faced financial decisions and restructured its debt in such a way that, when the economy slowed down, Ford didn't.

Mulally observes that this timing was a bit of luck and a bit of strategic planning. "I go back to the fundamental point of view that the Ford Motor Company has taken about the future going forward, and the actions that we have taken to create that future," he observes. "[Several years] ago we decided that fuel efficiency was going to be very, very important going forward, along with quality and safety and good value. We also decided that we wanted to provide customers with an absolutely clear vision of Ford and focus on the Ford brand." As part of this overall strategy, Ford sold off its luxury brands Aston Martin, Jaguar, and Land Rover. Meanwhile, it invested in the development of moderately priced, fuel-efficient cars and trucks. Ford took on some extra debt at the time as a hedge against a recession—and had the cash on hand when the other two automakers didn't.

Decisions like this are typical of the responsibilities that are faced by top managers like Mulally. They require strong leadership qualities that include a willingness to persist during tough times. But Mulally wasn't always CEO of Ford. His first management position was as an engineering supervisor at Boeing. He overmanaged his employees so closely that one engineer finally quit. Mulally says that this was an important experience early in his management career. He realized that his job as a manager was "to help connect people to a bigger goal, a bigger program and help them move forward to even bigger contributions. That experience stayed with me forever on what it really means to manage and lead."

Mulally believes that every employee has something to offer an organization and that each worker must be clear about the firm's mission. "I think the most important thing is coming to a shared view about what we're trying to accomplish," he says. "What are we? What is our real purpose? And then, how do you include everybody so you know where you are on that plan?"

As the company's leader, Mulally says that his job is to focus on four things: (1) the process of connecting his firm to the outside world, (2) keeping track of the firm's identity in the marketplace, (3) balancing short-term objectives with long-term goals, and (4) the values and standards of the organization. Mulally notes that keeping his eye on these four variables keeps Ford on the road. "I'm the one who needs to focus on those four things, because if I do that, the entire team will have a collective point of view and an understanding of all four of these areas." When asked what career advice he would give to young recruits to the business world, Mulally answers without hesitation: "Don't manage your career. Follow your dream and contribute."

Questions for Critical Thinking

1. How does Alan Mulally's "focus on four things" help him with strategic planning for Ford? Do you believe it made a difference in the firm's decision to decline the federal loan?
2. Mulally emphasizes the importance of having every employee understand the firm's mission. How might this understanding help employees contribute to the company's performance?

Sources: Paul Ingrassia, "Ford's Renaissance Man," *The Wall Street Journal,* http://www.online.wsj.com; accessed March 29, 2010; Keith Naughton and Ian King, "Mulally: Ford Marking Tremendous Progress," *BusinessWeek,* January 7, 2010, http://www.businessweek.com; Adam Bryant, "Planes, Cars, and Cathedrals," *The New York Times,* September 9, 2009, http://www.nytimes.com; John Hockenberry, "Interview with Ford CEO Alan Mulally," *PRI/WNYC,* April 3, 2009, http://www.pri.org; Excerpt from "Interview with Ford CEO Alan Mulally," from The Takeaway, a co-production of Public Radio International and WNYC. Reprinted with permission.

It might seem like an odd match at first: military officers as business managers. But a number of firms, including retail giant Walmart, are discovering the benefits of military leadership as part of their management team. Recently Walmart faced a management problem: not enough junior managers in training. So Bill Simon, President and CEO of Walmart U.S. presented an idea: begin hiring junior military officers as management candidates. Simon, himself a 25-year veteran of the Navy and Naval Reserves thought the strategy made perfect sense. Walmart's human resources department set out to implement the plan. "The thinking was that we could bring in world-class leadership talent that was already trained and ready to go," explains Jennifer Seidner, a senior recruiting manager. "and then we could teach them retail, because we know that pretty well."

Within a few months, Walmart realized it was mining a huge vein of golden talent. The retailer hired retired Army brigadier general Gary Profit to expand military recruiting throughout the business. Now, recruiting from the military is standard procedure. "It's been a fairly dramatic change," observes Jennifer Seidner. The benefit to veterans is also dramatic. For the first time since World War II, veterans returning from combat are welcomed by businesses who want to hire them.

One project manager for GE Oil & Gas is a former Army captain. He manages a team of 50 people as they build a structure—they are ahead of schedule and under budget. When asked what his role is on the project, the manager says without hesitation, "leader, absolutely. To get the pieces where they need to be at the right time takes someone out there motivating, directing, organizing. It takes a leader to do it."

Bill Simon's initial idea has caught and spread like wildfire throughout the business world. Firms such as Home Depot, Lowe's, State Farm Insurance, AT&T, Bank of America, and Merck all now routinely hire veterans as managers. In fact, companies actually compete with each other to locate and tap the best of the talent. Noel Tichy, director of the Global Business Partnership at the University of Michigan observes, "There's a big pool of these officers who have had the kind of under-fire judgment experience that makes them really valuable. Whoever has the best screening and development is going to get some great leaders." Larry Siegel, senior vice president for the headhunting firm RecruitMilitary, agrees. "It's sort of blood in the water," he quips. "Companies really want these folks."

Managers don't necessarily arrive fully formed from the military. Often these job candidates lack certain technical skills such as budgeting. So, business schools have begun to attract these students—and MBA programs are happy to enroll them. In all, it's a positive outcome for everyone. Many of tomorrow's business leaders are already training—sometimes halfway around the world, in a tank or a tent.

Questions for Critical Thinking

1. What kind of leadership style are military recruits most likely to adopt? Why? Do you think this could ever become a problem?

2. How might planning in the military translate itself to planning in the business world?

Sources: "What Business Can Learn at West Point," *The Washington Post*, http://views.washingtonpost.com, accessed March 29, 2010; Brian O'Keefe, "Battle-tested: From Soldier to Business Leader," *CNN Money.com*, March 8, 2010, http://money.cnn.com; Colonel Tom Kolditz, "Why the Military Produces Great Leaders," *Harvard Business Review*, February 6, 2009, http://blogs.hbr.org.

Dan Formosa: At the Forefront of Smart Design

Like many new businesses, Smart Design was founded by a collection of college classmates who wanted to change something. Dan Formosa, along with several college friends, had a background in design and ergonomics. The group believed that design should be about people, not things—and Smart Design was born. In the beginning, it was a hard sell—not the designs themselves, but the idea that the needs of individual *people* should be involved in the development of design. Formosa was interested in "how design can affect our quality of life, improve performance, and affect behavior." The original Smart Design team "pulled together techniques in biomechanics and cognitive psychology," recalls Formosa. "This was a type of an approach that no other design group was undertaking in the U.S. at the time, so it was an early test of our beliefs about what and where design should be." Smart Design was successful throughout the 1980s, but Formosa admits that it was an uphill battle to convince clients that design was, indeed, for everyone.

Then came OXO. Around 1990, Smart Design acquired the manufacturing firm OXO as a client, giving Formosa's team a chance to re-invent the design of common household products ranging from can openers to scissors, resulting in the OXO Good Grips line of kitchen utensils. Because of the mundane nature of these products—consumers weren't accustomed to shopping for a potato peeler that actually felt comfortable in the hand—once they caught on, the idea that everyday design matters began to take hold in the marketplace. Smart Design's client base grew significantly, as did the company. Firms such as Ford, ESPN, Samsung, Nike, and Microsoft began to request Smart Design's services, and the number of employees increased.

No matter how much talent lies in the firm, though, managing a company of designers can be like trying to herd cats. Everyone has an idea, and everyone is running headlong in a different direction. So leadership is critical to the firm's success. Paulette Bluhm-Sauriol, director of brand communication, observes that while most designers are detail oriented, "Someone has to make sure that the team is keeping the big picture in mind, not just the details." That's part of her job as well as Formosa's:

maintaining the overall vision. She also notes that, as a leader, Formosa has the natural gift of connecting and empathizing with people, whether it is employees or potential end-users of Smart Design's products. "Dan has the ability to make going into people's lives and becoming part of their lives comfortable," she observes.

This was particularly true during the development of a new type of pre-filled medical syringe that Smart Design undertook for UCB/OXO Cimzia. The medication Cimzia is a solution that alleviates chronic pain in patients with certain conditions. If patients could administer the solution themselves in a comfortable way, it would enhance their lives. When the pharmaceutical maker UCB and OXO partnered to develop the new product, they went to Smart Design for the design. Formosa asked his team to go straight to the patients themselves to ask them what they needed. Designers met and observed patients in their own environment, giving them a chance to express their wishes. "It can be uncomfortable, but it's amazing how you can get to the big ideas by approaching the project his way," says Paulette Bluhm-Sauriol.

The syringe has met with marketplace success, and has even won an International Design Excellence Award. Most important, patients are getting what they need, which is exactly what Formosa strives for in each product his firm designs. "If someone buys a product or signs up for a service, they expect it to work. If you actually encounter a product or service that exceeds expectations, that is the sign of a great design," he says. Formosa also contends that the same principles can be applied to the design of a delicate hospital instrument as are applied to a pizza cutter. "Since our focus is designing for people, then that is the common ground," he asserts.

At Smart Design, the corporate culture supports the notion that the ideas of every employee are important. Regardless of job title, each person is considered a designer, with something valuable to contribute to the process. Formosa doesn't mind the potential chaos of this kind of organization—it's how he operates. "When we have everybody thinking everything, it's a positive sign," he says. It's a formula that works.

Questions for Critical Thinking

1. Describe Dan Formosa's vision for Smart Design. Why do you think it took so long to gain popularity in the marketplace?

2. Identify Smart Design's strategy for competitive differentiation.

3. How would you describe Dan Formosa's leadership style? Do you think it is the best style for Smart Design? Why or why not?

4. Discuss Smart Design's corporate culture. Do you think it is effective for the kind of business the company engages in? Why or why not?

Sources: Smart Design Web site, http://www.smartdesignworldwide.com, accessed July 5, 2011; "Smart Design," National Design Awards, http://www.nationaldesignawards.org/2010, accessed August 19, 2010; Ralph Goldsworthy, "Dan Formosa of Smart Design, Designer Q&A," *Design Droplets.com,* April 28, 2010, http://designdroplets.com.

Chapter 8

Learning Objectives

[1] Explain the role and responsibilities of human resource management.

[2] Describe how recruitment and selection contribute to placing the right person in a job.

[3] Discuss how orientation, training programs, and performance appraisals help companies develop their employees.

[4] Describe how firms compensate employees through pay systems and benefit programs.

[5] Discuss employee separation and the impact of downsizing and outsourcing.

[6] Explain the different methods and theories of motivation.

[7] Discuss the role of labor unions, the collective bargaining process, and methods for settling labor–management disputes.

Human Resource Management: From Recruitment to Labor Relations

Troels Graugaard/iStockphoto

After the Flood: Gaylord Opryland Hotel Stays Afloat

Jeff Gentner/Getty Images, Inc.

When the Cumberland River spilled over its banks in a recent May, the levees built for a 100-year-old flood couldn't hold back the water. Before waves rushed into the Gaylord Opryland Hotel in Nashville, officials evacuated more than 1,500 guests to a nearby high school and other locations. Employees took quick action to save every item they could of historic value from the hotel and Nashville's Grand Old Opry. And when danger subsided, workers wielded cleaning equipment and giant humidifiers to reduce subsequent damage from problems such as mold and mildew from damp air. Still, much of the Gaylord Opryland was submerged under 10 feet of water, with repair estimates as high as $200 million.

Initially, Gaylord executives were hoping to retain all of the hotel's staff during the renovation period. For the first month, employees were provided with full pay and benefits. But as the true extent of the damage was assessed, including the time it would take to repair and reopen the hotel, CEO Colin V. Reed reluctantly announced layoffs of more than 1,700 workers. "We are deeply sorry to have to make this incredibly difficult decision, as our employees are and have always been the driving force behind the success of our business," said Reed. "We are grateful for everything our employees have done to make Gaylord Opryland a wonderful place to work and visit, and thank them for the courage and commitment they have shown over the last month."

Some employees accepted the decision while others felt betrayed. "They sideswiped us bad here," said one staffer who had worked more than 24 hours straight during the hours of the flood, transporting guests to other hotels, shelters, and the airport. But the same employee admitted without hesitation, "I would love to go back to work for them" when the hotel reopens. Those who were laid off were given two weeks of pay, plus payment for any unused vacation days, and the company pledged to make healthcare benefits available at the same cost through September. Nearby hotels hired some of the Opryland workers, with the understanding the those employees could return to the Opryland if they chose to once it reopened.

Meanwhile, hundreds of construction workers logged 16-hour days for nearly six months to repair and restore the hotel in time for the planned November 15 reopening—scheduled to welcome guests for the holidays. Opryland intended to dazzle the public with a grand reopening that included a show featuring Radio City's Rockettes, a playground created from ice, and fireworks. In addition, the company committed to spending $12 million to raise the height of its nearby levee to a 500-year level. When Opryland reopened its doors, the hotel was once again fully staffed with all the former employees who wanted to return. "This flood has brought our company together," said Pete Weien, Gaylord's general manager. "It has brought out stars together in a great sense of community."[1]

The importance of employees to the success of any organization is the very basis of management. In this chapter, we explore the important issues of human resource management and motivation. We begin with a discussion of the ways organizations attract, develop, and retain employees. Then we describe the concepts behind motivation and the way human resource managers apply them to increase employee satisfaction and organizational effectiveness.

We also discuss the reasons why labor unions exist, and focus on legislation that affects labor–management relations. The process of collective bargaining is then discussed, along with tools used by unions and management in seeking their objectives.

human resource management function of attracting, developing, and retaining employees who can perform the activities necessary to accomplish organizational objectives.

Human Resources: The People Behind the People

A company is only as good as its workers. If people come to work each day eager to see each other, to do their very best on the job, to serve their customers, and to help their firm compete, then it's very likely that company will be a success. The best companies value their employees just as much as their customers—without workers, there would be no goods or services to offer customers. Firms like Children's Creative Learning Centers (CCLC) understand this. Gaylord Opryland's management knew that despite a huge natural disaster, assisting its top-quality employees—and rehiring them as soon as possible—was vital to the company's survival. Achieving the highest level of job satisfaction and dedication among employees is the goal of **human resource management**, which attracts, develops, and retains the employees who can perform the activities necessary to accomplish organizational objectives.

Not every firm is large enough to have an entire human resources department. But whoever performs this function generally does the following: plan for staffing needs, recruit and hire workers, provide for training and evaluate performance, determine compensation and benefits, and oversee employee separation. In accomplishing these five tasks, shown in Figure 8.1, human resource managers achieve their objectives of

Blend/Getty Images, Inc.

The best companies value their employees just as much as their customers. Firms like Children's Creative Learning Centers (CCLC) understand this, and do their best to hire top-quality employees and support them while they provide top-quality child care to customers.

1. providing qualified, well-trained employees for the organization;

2. maximizing employee effectiveness in the organization; and

3. satisfying individual employee needs through monetary compensation, benefits, opportunities to advance, and job satisfaction.

Human resource plans must be based on an organization's overall competitive strategies. In conjunction with other managers, human resource managers predict how many employees a firm or department will need, and what skills those workers should bring to the job—along with what skills they might learn on the job. Human resource managers are often consulted when a firm is considering reducing costs by laying off workers, or increasing costs by hiring new ones. They may be involved in both long-term and short-term planning.

FIGURE 8.1 Human Resource Management Responsibilities

Recruitment and Selection

Human resource managers recruit and help select the right workers for a company. To ensure that job candidates bring the necessary skills to the job or have the desire and ability to learn them, most firms implement the recruitment and selection process shown in Figure 8.2.

Finding Qualified Candidates

When the economy dips and jobs are lost, many people compete for a limited number of positions. When a company develops a great reputation for benefits or working conditions, it might be inundated with applications. But even with a large number of job candidates competing for a small number of openings, companies sometimes have trouble finding the right person for each position. According to a recent survey by the National Association of Colleges and Employers, firms are currently looking for candidates with the following top five skills and strengths: verbal communication skills, strong work ethic, teamwork skills, analytical skills, and initiative.[2]

In addition to traditional methods of recruiting, such as college job fairs, personal referrals, and want ads, most companies now rely on their Web sites. A firm's Web site might contain a career section with general employment information and a listing of open positions. Applicants are often able to submit a résumé and apply for an open position online. Appendix E, Careers in Contemporary Business, points out that some firms also post job openings on sites such as Monster.com.

Internet recruiting is such a quick, efficient, and inexpensive way to reach a large pool of job seekers that the vast majority of companies currently use the Internet, including social networking sites, to fill job openings. This is also the best way for firms to reach new college graduates and workers in their 20s and even 30s. Using a social media site such as Facebook allows firms to communicate directly with candidates and get feedback. But it's also important

Assessment Check ✓

1. What are the five main tasks of a human resource manager?

2. What are the three overall objectives of a human resource manager?

FIGURE
8.2

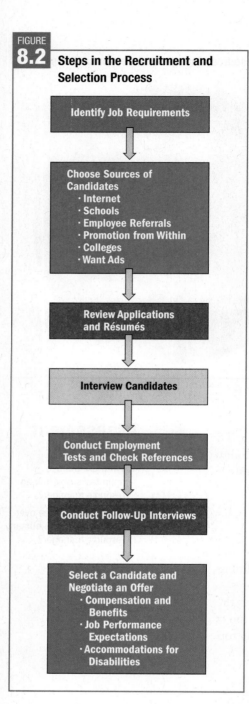

Steps in the Recruitment and Selection Process

Identify Job Requirements

Choose Sources of Candidates
- Internet
- Schools
- Employee Referrals
- Promotion from Within
- Colleges
- Want Ads

Review Applications and Résumés

Interview Candidates

Conduct Employment Tests and Check References

Conduct Follow-Up Interviews

Select a Candidate and Negotiate an Offer
- Compensation and Benefits
- Job Performance Expectations
- Accommodations for Disabilities

for jobseekers to be as specific as possible when using the Internet to look for a job. For example, if possible, they should apply through the firm's Web site instead of one of the large, third-party job sites. "Employers see that the vast majority of applicants coming through these [third-party] sites have not done sufficient research, and often are questionable fits for the advertised positions," notes one human resource expert.[3]

Recruiting techniques continue to evolve as technology advances. JobsinPods.com is an online library of podcast interviews with hiring managers and employees at a variety of U.S. companies, including AT&T, Intel, and IBM. New podcasts, also called jobcasts, are posted in a blog format, and older podcasts are archived. Some describe employers' hiring needs, while others talk about what it's like to work at a particular company. Job seekers can also download the podcasts to an iPod and listen to them at their leisure.[4]

Selecting and Hiring Employees

It's the human resource manager's job to select and hire employees, often in conjunction with department managers or supervisors. Every firm must follow state and federal employment laws. Title VII of the Civil Rights Act of 1964 prohibits employers from discriminating against applicants based on their race, religion, color, sex, or national origin. The Americans with Disabilities Act of 1990 prohibits employers from discriminating against disabled applicants. The Civil Rights Act created the *Equal Employment Opportunity Commission (EEOC)* to investigate discrimination complaints. The Uniform Employee Selection Guidelines were adopted by the EEOC in 1978 to further clarify ways in which employers must ensure that their employees will be hired and managed without discrimination.[5] The EEOC also helps employers set up *affirmative action programs* to increase job opportunities for women, minorities, people with disabilities, and other protected groups. The Civil Rights Act of 1991 expanded the alternatives available to victims of employment discrimination by including the right to a jury trial, punitive damages, and damages for emotional distress. At the same time, opponents to such laws have launched initiatives to restrict affirmative action standards and protect employers against unnecessary litigation.

These laws, which are designed to level the playing field for all job seekers, have been the basis for thousands of legal cases over the years. Recently, UPS Freight agreed to pay a $46,000 settlement to a former employee because of religious discrimination. The employee, who is a Rastafarian, was told to shave his beard and cut his hair to comply with company grooming policy. Because long hair and a beard are part of Rastafarian worship, the employee requested accommodation. UPS fired him, which was a violation of his civil rights.[6] Failure to comply with equal employment opportunity legislation can result in costly legal fees, expensive fines, bad publicity, and poor employee morale.

Because of the high cost of such lawsuits and settlements, human resource managers must understand the laws in order to prevent unintended violations. Even the process of interviewing a job candidate is covered by law. An interviewer may not ask any questions about marital status, children, race or nationality, religion, age, criminal records, mental illness, medical history, or alcohol and substance abuse problems. For more information about employment law, visit the Web sites of the Society for Human Resource Management (http://www.shrm.org) and the EEOC (http://www.eeoc.gov).

Navigating the maze of hiring restrictions is a challenge. Some firms try to screen out high-risk employees by requiring drug testing for job applicants, particularly in industries that deal with public safety—such as air travel or truck driving. But drug testing is controversial because of privacy issues. Also, positive test results may not be accurate. Another issue is whether employees can be required to speak a particular language—usually English—in the workplace. Although the EEOC views this as discrimination, a bill was recently introduced in the Tennessee legislature that would allow businesses to make this requirement as "an allowable employment practice."[7] Employers may legally establish requirements for specific jobs—a bona fide occupational qualification (BFOQ)—that may cut across EEOC protected classes. For example, a designer of women's clothes by necessity is permitted to hire only female models to show off new designs.

Internet recruiting is such a quick, efficient, and inexpensive way to reach a large pool of job seekers that the vast majority of companies currently use the Internet, including social-networking sites, to fill job openings. Aerospace giant Boeing recently began posting job ads on Facebook.

Daniel Acker/Bloomberg/Getty Images, Inc.

Recruitment and selection are expensive. There are costs for advertising, interviewing, administering employment tests and even medical exams. Once an applicant is hired, there are costs for training and perhaps equipment such as a computer. But a bad hiring decision is even more expensive, because the firm has to go through the whole process again to find the right person. One estimate states that the cost of mis-hiring top-level managers amounts to 24 times the candidate's annual pay. "Every minute spent making sure you have the right person in the right job will save you week of time later on," advises Allied Signal CEO Larry Bossidy.[8]

To avoid these mistakes—and to get the right person for the job—many employers require applicants to complete employment tests. These tests may verify certain skills, including mechanical, technical, language, and computer skills. One example is the Wonderlic Basic Skills Test, which measures basic math and verbal skills. The Wonderlic is a cognitive ability test, which measures a person's abilities in understanding words, numbers, and logic. Cognitive ability tests accurately predict job performance on many types of jobs.

Orientation, Training, and Evaluation

Once hired, employees need to know what is expected of them and how well they are performing. Companies provide this information through orientation, training, and evaluation. A new hire may complete an orientation program administered jointly by the human resource personnel and the department in which the employee will work. During orientation, employees learn about company policies regarding their rights and benefits. They might receive an employee manual that includes the company's code of ethics and code of conduct. And they'll usually receive some form of training.

Training Programs

Training is a good investment for both employers and employees. Training provides workers with an opportunity to build their skills and knowledge, preparing them for new job

Assessment Check ✓

1. Describe several recruiting techniques used by human resource managers.

2. What is the function of the Equal Employment Opportunity Commission (EEOC)?

opportunities within the company. It also provides employers with a better chance at retaining long-term, loyal, high-performing workers. Companies of all sizes take creative approaches to training. Nugget Market, a nine-store California supermarket chain that was recently ranked in the top ten of *Fortune's* "100 Best Companies to Work For," rolls out continuous information about products, the company, and updates from executives, on a large, flat screen monitor in each store. Employees who watch—and absorb—the information are eligible for bonus rewards that range from $20 to $1,000.[9]

On-the-Job Training One popular teaching method is *on-the-job training*, which prepares employees for job duties by allowing them to perform tasks under the guidance of experienced employees. A variation of on-the-job training is apprenticeship training, in which an employee learns a job by serving for a time as an assistant to a trained worker. While American apprenticeships usually focus on blue-collar trades—such as plumbing and heating services—in Europe, many new entrants to white-collar professions complete apprenticeships. McDonald's now has apprenticeship-training programs in its U.K. restaurants as part of an economic stimulus plan launched by the British government. McDonald's offered 6,000 apprenticeships in the first year of its program, increasing the number to 10,000 the following year. "We're letting people know that we're as serious about education as we are about burgers and fries," notes the company's Web site.[10]

Classroom and Computer-Based Training Many firms offer some form of classroom instruction such as lectures, conferences, and workshops or seminars. Ernst & Young, a large tax-service firm, offers a training program called Ernst & Young and You (EYU), focusing on classroom learning, experiential learning, and coaching.[11]

Many firms are replacing classroom training with computer-based training programs, which can significantly reduce the cost of training. Computer-based training offers consistent presentations, along with videos that can simulate the work environment. Employees can learn at their own pace without having to sign up for a class. Through online training programs, employees can engage in interactive learning—they might conference with a mentor or instructor who is located elsewhere; or they might participate in a simulation requiring them to make decisions related to their work. An extension of computer-based training is multimedia training, which may combine text with sound, 3-D animation, high-resolution graphics, games, simulations, and the like. Sony uses a multimedia program developed by QuickStart, "If you've got training that's entertaining and does the job, you've got a sure winner," says Will Grasse of California-based QuickStart. People learn more if they have fun while they train."[12]

Management Development A *management development program* provides training designed to improve the skills and broaden the knowledge of current or future managers and executives. Training may be aimed at increasing specific technical knowledge or more general knowledge in areas such as leadership and interpersonal skills. Glimmerglass Consulting Group, based in New Hampshire, provides management training in leadership, team development, and strategic implementation. After assessing a client's work environment as well as the strengths and weaknesses of its management team, Glimmerglass coaches design a program intended to strengthen management's leadership and team skills. The program may involve an outdoor learning experience such as rock climbing. Glimmerglass's client list includes such firms as Wyeth Pharmaceuticals, Shell International, Eastern Mountain Sports, and Big Brothers/Big Sisters.[13]

Despite the importance of training talented employees for managerial jobs, many companies are searching for new hires to fill gaps in their executive ranks because they failed to develop future managers. In a move that surprised the international banking world, David de

Rothschild appointed a successor from outside his family—the first in 200 years—to take over running the group of financial advisory and wealth management companies that make up the Rothschild banking empire. Nigel Higgins is no stranger to the firm; he has worked there for 27 years. But Rothschild chose Higgins because there was no family member ready to handle the job. "If you're not totally self-centered, which I hope I am not, one thinks about how to increase the stability of the firm internally and externally," explains Rothschild, who is only semi-retiring.[14]

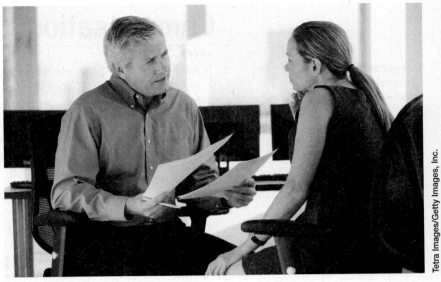

Employees value face-to-face feedback on their performance. Evaluations that are fair and consistent can improve an organization's productivity and profitability.

Performance Appraisals

Feedback about performance is the best way for a company—and its employees to improve. Most firms use annual **performance appraisals** to evaluate an employee's job performance and provide feedback about it. A performance appraisal can include assessments of everything from attendance to goals met. Based on this evaluation, a manager will make decisions about compensation, promotion, additional training needs, transfers, or even termination. While performance appraisals are common, not everyone agrees about their usefulness. Some management experts argue that a performance review is skewed in favor of a single manager's subjective opinion—whether it's positive or negative—and that most employees are afraid to speak honestly to their managers during a performance review.[15] If a performance review is to be at all effective, it should meet the following criteria:

- take place several times a year;
- be linked to organizational goals;
- be based on objective criteria;
- take place in the form of a two-way conversation.[16]

Some firms conduct peer reviews, in which employees assess the performance of their coworkers, while other firms ask employees to review their supervisors and managers. One such performance appraisal is the *360-degree performance review*, a process that gathers feedback from a review panel of 8 to 12 people, including coworkers, supervisors, team members, subordinates, and sometimes even customers. The idea is to get as much frank feedback from as many perspectives as possible. By its very nature, this kind of review involves a lot of work, but employees benefit from it because they are more involved with the process and ultimately better understand their own strengths, weaknesses, and roles in the company. Managers benefit because they get much more in-depth feedback from all parts of the organization. Companies such as Halogen Software offer computer programs to help firms gather and sift through this type of data. Organizations as diverse as Dole, Quiznos, Princess Cruises, and the San Diego Zoo use products from Canada-based Halogen. However, a potential weakness of this type of review is its anonymous nature.[17]

performance appraisal evaluation of and feedback on an employee's job performance.

Assessment Check ☑

1. What are the benefits of computer-based training?
2. What is a management development program?
3. What are the four criteria of an effective performance appraisal?

Tetra Images/Getty Images, Inc.

Compensation

Compensation—how much employees are paid in money and benefits—is one of the most highly charged issues faced by human resource managers. The amount employees are paid, along with whatever benefits they receive, has a tremendous influence on where they live, what they eat, and how they spend their leisure time. It also has an effect on job satisfaction. Balancing compensation for employees at all job levels can be a challenge for human resource managers. And while compensation certainly is a factor in job satisfaction, it isn't the only one, as discussed in the "Hit & Miss" feature.

Everyone likes to read about the companies—or the jobs—that pay their employees the most in cash and benefits. *Fortune* magazine lists an annual "100 Best Companies to Work For," which includes information on compensation. Among the current compensation leaders are Salesforce.com, where senior account executives earn an average total pay of $318,000 annually and enjoy unique perks such as trips to Hawaii and shopping sprees; and worldwide law firm Bingham McCutchen, where attorneys earn an average of $200,000 in salary and another 7.5 percent in matched pension funds.[18] Of course, top executives at large companies earn a lot more than this—which has been brought up as an issue among employees and shareholders.

The terms *wages* and *salary* are often used interchangeably, but actually are different. Wages are based on an hourly pay rate or the amount of work accomplished. Typical wage earners are factory workers, construction workers, auto mechanics, retail salespeople, and restaurant wait staff. Salaries are calculated periodically, such as weekly or monthly. Salaried employees receive a set amount of pay that does not fluctuate with the number of hours worked. Whereas wage earners receive overtime pay, salaried workers do not. Office personnel, executives, and professional employees usually receive salaries.

An effective compensation system should attract well-qualified workers, keep them satisfied in their jobs, and inspire them to succeed. It's also important to note that certain laws, including minimum wage, must be taken into account. The Lilly Ledbetter Fair Pay Act of 2009 is one such law, which now gives workers more time to file a complaint for pay discrimination.[19]

Most firms base their compensation policies on the following factors: (1) what competing companies are paying, (2) government regulation, (3) cost of living, (4) company profits, and (5) an employee's productivity. Many firms try to balance rewarding workers with maintaining profits by linking more of their pay to superior performance. Firms try to motivate employees to excel by offering some type of incentive compensation in addition to salaries or wages. These programs include the following:

- profit sharing, which awards bonuses based on company profits;
- gain sharing, when companies share the financial value of productivity gains, cost savings, or quality improvements with their workers;
- lump-sum bonuses and stock options, which reward one-time cash payments and the right to purchase stock in the company based on performance;
- pay for knowledge, which distributes wage or salary increases as employees learn new job tasks.

Figure 8.3 summarizes the four types of incentive compensation programs.

Hit & Miss

Stop Demotivating Employees—And They'll Be Motivated

A lot of discussion among managers and human resource professionals centers on employee motivation: What's the secret to coaxing the best performance from every employee at a firm? While there are some common sense rules—such as fair compensation and recognition for accomplishments—some experts believe that the secret lies not in motivating workers, but in *stopping their demotivation*. What does this mean? The fact is that most employees start their jobs with great enthusiasm; but their morale drops off significantly after only six months on the job and continues to decline sometimes for years. The challenge for managers is to staunch this flow of their companies' lifeblood.

First, managers must find out what keeps employees engaged and happy at work. It turns out that employees aren't necessarily concerned with an extra two weeks' vacation or an expensive, onsite gym—although those are nice. Instead, they care about things that don't cost companies a dime: a sense of pride in achievement, respect from coworkers and managers, and supportive relationships with fellow employees. Everyone who goes to work needs a sense of purpose—a connection to their company's mission and "reason for being." It's a manager's job to convey that purpose—the way in which each employee's job fits the organization's mission. A manager must also be sure to take the time to provide recognition for employees' accomplishments. Sometimes a simple "thank you" or "good job" is enough. Managers also need communicate clearly and frequently with employees and should promote teamwork whenever possible, which fosters camaraderie.

When employees become discouraged, they start thinking about looking for employment elsewhere. When a worker finds a new job—and the original company doesn't want to lose that employee—often he or she receives a counteroffer from the original firm, in the form of a pay raise, a promotion, or the like. But this is rarely successful because the employee feels that his or her manager should have recognized the problem and addressed it well beforehand. Instead of letting things reach this point, a savvy manager can be on the lookout for signs that morale is drooping and try to counteract this by meeting with one or more employees to learn how the workplace atmosphere in general might be improved. If one employee has low morale, then it's likely that others do as well.

In the end, one of the most important things a manager can do to stop the demotivation of their own employees is to listen to them, involve them in decisions about their own jobs, and provide reinforcement and recognition for top performance. Smart managers promote the idea that "the past is not good enough" and encourage creative thinking and innovation from their employees. Giving employees a little more rein often results in winning the race in a competitive marketplace.

Sources: Kishore Krishnan, "Stop Demotivating Employees," *Ezine Articles,* http://ezinearticles.com, accessed February 22, 2011; Dan Ariely, "(De)motivating Employees," February 5, 2011, http://danariely.com; David Sirota, Louis A. Mischkind, and Michael Irwin Seltzer, "Stop Demotivating Your Employees!" *Harvard Business Review,* Summer 2010, pp. 14–15.

Employee Benefits

In addition to wages and salaries, firms provide benefits to employees and their families as part of their compensation. **Employee benefits**—such as vacation, retirement plans, profit-sharing, health insurance, gym memberships, child and elder care, and tuition reimbursement—are paid entirely or in part by the company. Benefits represent a large component of an employee's total compensation. Although wages and salaries account for around 70 percent of the typical employee's earnings, the other 30 percent takes the form of employee benefits.[20] Table 8.1 shows the breakdown of an average worker's benefits as compared to wages or salary.

Some benefits are required by law. U.S. firms are required to make Social Security and Medicare contributions, as well as payments to state unemployment insurance and workers' compensation programs, which protect workers in case of job-related injuries or illnesses. The Family and Medical Leave Act of 1993 requires covered employers to offer up to 12 weeks of unpaid, job-protected leave to eligible employees. Firms voluntarily provide other employee benefits, such as child care and health insurance, to help them attract and retain employees. California is the first state to make paid family leave into law.[21] As the "Solving an Ethical Controversy" feature discusses, some advocates are pressing state and federal lawmakers to require businesses to provide paid sick leave.

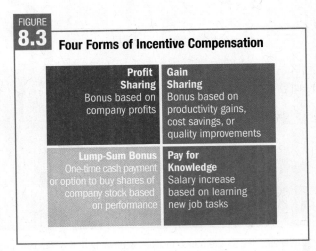

FIGURE 8.3 Four Forms of Incentive Compensation

Profit Sharing	Gain Sharing
Bonus based on company profits	Bonus based on productivity gains, cost savings, or quality improvements
Lump-Sum Bonus One-time cash payment or option to buy shares of company stock based on performance	**Pay for Knowledge** Salary increase based on learning new job tasks

employee benefits
additional compensation such as vacation, retirement plans, profit-sharing, health insurance, gym memberships, child and elder care, and tuition reimbursement, paid entirely or in part by the company.

⌐8.1⌐ Costs for Employee Compensation

TYPE OF COMPENSATION	PERCENTAGE OF TOTAL COMPENSATION
Wages and salaries	70. 8
Benefits	29.2
Paid leave	6.8
Supplemental pay	3.0
Insurance	7.8
Health benefits	7.3
Retirement and savings	3.4
Legally required benefits	8.2

Source: "Legally Required Benefits Costs in Private Industry," Bureau of Labor Statistics, July 5, 2011, http://www.bls.gov.

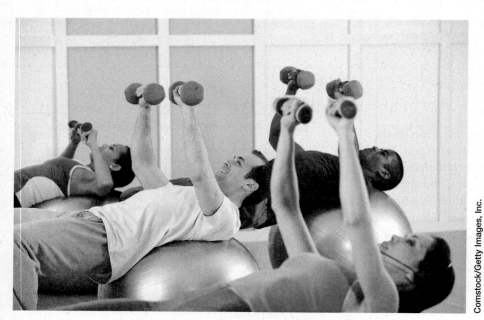

Benefits like on-site fitness facilities improve both the company's health and that of employees.

Comstock/Getty Images, Inc.

In the past, companies have picked up most of the tab for healthcare benefits, with employees paying little of the cost. However, with costs soaring nearly 15 percent each year, employers are passing along premium increases to employees. Many companies now offer incentives for workers to live healthier lives. Gym memberships, nutrition programs, wellness visits to the doctor, and smoking-cessation classes are all examples of these incentives. SAS has its own medical center, along with a free on-site gym. The firm provides an abundance of other employee benefits as well, including on-site daycare, unlimited sick days, and a summer camp for kids. In addition to all of that, SAS still pays 90 percent of its employees' monthly insurance premiums.[22]

Pensions and other retirement plans make up a chunk of employee benefits. Recently, some companies have shrunk the matching contributions they will make to workers' *401(k) plans*—retirement savings plans to which employees can make pretax contributions. Some firms have cut back on cash contributions to their employees' plans and now contribute company stock instead. However, others have managed to continue with a higher rate of funding. Raytheon Solipsys offers a 401(k) with a 200 percent match on employee contributions.[23]

Solving an Ethical Controversy

Should Paid Sick Leave Be Required by Law?

The United States is the only one of the world's major economic powers that does not require employers to provide paid sick days. Advocates say the country should follow the lead of other developed nations and make paid sick days a basic labor standard.

U.S. businesses voluntarily provide paid sick days for about 86 percent of full-time workers. The Family and medical Leave Act (FMLA) requires that all businesses with more than 50 employees provide their workers with up to 12 weeks of unpaid leave for illness, childbirth or adoption, or care of a family member who is sick. The proposed Healthy Families Act (HFA) is an attempt to close the gap between these two situations. The HFA would require employers to provide their workers with a specified number of paid sick days each year.

Should businesses be required to provide paid sick leave for their employees?

PRO

1. A healthy workforce is vital to the competitiveness of any firm. When an employee is unable to seek time off for medical treatment for an illness, it puts the company at risk. "Not only is this situation bad for sick workers and their families, but it puts other workers and the public at risk of contracting infectious illnesses," points out one public official.

2. No worker should be penalized for being ill. "The purpose of this bill [HFA] is that you cannot be fired because you're sick," notes Maine Senate President Elizabeth Mitchell.

CON

1. Requiring firms to pay for sick leave adds to the cost of doing business, and employers may be forced to cut other benefits, institute a hiring freeze, or lay people off because they can't afford the added expense.

2. Workers may be encouraged to misuse their sick leave, and when one takes unplanned time off, an employer may be forced to pay a temporary worker in addition to the permanent employee who is out sick.

Summary

Those in favor of paid sick leave argue that it is a matter of basic workers' rights, and would benefit mostly low-income employees who are already struggling to make ends meet. Opponents say that the burden is too great for most businesses and would result in lost productivity, a reduction in wages to offset the cost, and perhaps a loss in the number of jobs altogether.

Sources: James Sherk, "Understanding Mandatory Paid Sick Leave," *The Heritage Foundation*, February 22, 2011, http://www.heritage .org; "Editorial: Reject Mandate for Paid Sick Leave," *The New Haven Register*, April 1, 2010, http://www.nhregister.com; A. J. Higgins, "Paid Sick Leave Bill Significantly Weakened," *Maine Public Broadcasting Network*, March 29, 2010, http://www.mpbn.net; Laura Fishman, "Paid Sick Leave Strikes Debate," *The Houston Employment Law Blog*, February 12, 2010, http://houstonemploymentlawsblog.com; Christine Stuart, "Lamont Not Sold on Paid Sick Days for Small Businesses," *CTNewsjunkie.com*, February 9, 2010, http://www.ctnewsjunkie.com.

Flexible Benefits

In response to increasing diversity in the workplace, firms are developing creative ways to tailor their benefit plans to the needs of employees. One approach sets up *flexible benefit plans*, also called cafeteria plans. This system offers employees a choice of benefits, including different types of medical insurance, dental and vision plans, and life and disability insurance. This flexibility allows one working spouse to choose medical coverage for the entire family, while the other spouse uses benefit dollars to buy other types of coverage. Typically, each employee receives a set allowance (called flex dollars or credits) to pay for benefits depending on his or her needs. Contributions to cafeteria accounts can be made by both the employee and employer. Cafeteria plans also offer tax benefits to both employees and employers.

Another way of increasing the flexibility of employee benefits involves time off from work. Instead of establishing set numbers of holidays, vacation days, and sick days, some

A two-career couple heads for the daycare center and work. Many employees use flextime to mesh their work schedules with opening and closing times at schools and daycare programs.

employers give each employee a bank of *paid time off (PTO)*. Employees use days from their PTO accounts without having to explain why they need the time. The greatest advantage of PTO is the freedom it gives workers to make their own choices; the greatest disadvantage is that it is an expensive benefit for employers.[24]

Flexible Work

Some firms are moving toward the option of *flexible work plans*, which are benefits that allow employees to adjust their working hours or places of work according to their needs. Flexible work plan options include flextime, compressed workweeks, job sharing, and home-based work (tele-commuting). These benefit programs have reduced employee turnover and absenteeism, and boosted productivity and job satisfaction. Flexible work has become critical in attracting and keeping talented human resources.

Flextime allows employees to set their own work hours within certain constraints. Rather than scheduling everyone to work between 8:00 a.m. and 5:00 p.m., a manager might stipulate that all employees be at work between the core hours of 10:00 a.m. and 3:00 p.m. Outside the core hours, employees can choose to start and end early, or start and end late. Flextime works well in jobs that are independent, but not so well when teams or direct customer service are involved. Flextime has gained popularity in the accounting industry. Ernst & Young builds flexibility into its workplace, believing it fosters greater productivity in the long run.[25]

With the help of programs from BidShift, a San Diego company that specializes in Internet-based scheduling software, the logistic problems of flexible scheduling are solved for users such as the San Angelo Community Medical Center. BidShift's programs allow managers to post schedules online, where employees log in and request certain shifts or schedule changes.[26]

Some companies offer a *compressed workweek*, which allows employees to work longer hours on fewer days. Employees might work four 10-hour days and then have three days off each week. Such arrangements not only reduce the number of hours employees spend commuting each week, but can stretch out the company's overall workday, providing more availability to customers in other time zones. Hospitals, police and fire departments, and airlines often offer work schedules that allow several long days matched by several days off. About 40 percent of retailer Macy's 30,000 employees opt for a compressed workweek. Starwood Hotels offers this option to its employees at corporate headquarters, but cannot do so for most of its hotel workers because shift work is common.[27]

A *job sharing program* allows two or more employees to divide the tasks of one job. This plan appeals to a growing number of people who prefer to work part-time rather than full-time—such as older workers, students, working parents, and people of all ages who want to devote time to personal interests or leisure. Job sharing requires a lot cooperation and communication between the partners, but a company can benefit from the talents of both people. Some economists believe that a federal job-sharing program, which would give workers access to emergency unemployment insurance, would help prevent layoffs during times when unemployment is high. Seventeen states have already adopted such legislation. However, opponents disagree because of the cost.[28]

Home-based work programs allow employees to perform their jobs from home instead of at the workplace. These *telecommuters* are connected to their employers via the Internet, voice and video conferencing, and mobile devices. Working from home generally appeals to employees who want freedom, but also to persons with disabilities, older workers, and parents. Companies benefit from telework arrangements because they can expand their pool of talent and increase productivity without increasing costs.[29] Telecommuters need to be self-disciplined and reliable employees. They also need managers who are comfortable with setting goals and managing from afar. Forrester Research predicts that telecommuting will grow from 34 million workers to 63 million by the 2016, with the help of such promotions as Telework Week, which encourages businesses to "go green, give your car a rest, and telework."[30]

More than 70 percent of Generation Y professionals—those just entering the workforce—are concerned with balancing career with personal life. Most simply reject the idea of sitting in an office cubicle for 8 to 10 hours a day. They want the flexibility to do their jobs anywhere, any time.[31] This is placing increasing pressure on companies to offer options like job sharing, compressed workweeks, and telecommuting.

Employee Separation

<u>Employee separation</u> is a broad term covering the loss of an employee for any reason, voluntary or involuntary. Voluntary separation includes workers who resign to take a job at another firm or start a business. Involuntary separation includes downsizing and outsourcing.

Voluntary and Involuntary Turnover

Turnover occurs when an employee leaves his or her job. Voluntary turnover occurs when the employee decides to resign—perhaps to take another job, start a new business, or retire. The human resource manager might ask the employee for an exit interview to find out why he or she is leaving; this conversation can provide valuable information to a firm. An employee might decide to resign because of lack of career opportunities. Learning this, the human resource manager might offer ongoing training.[32] Another might resign because of low pay. In that case, the human resource manager might offer a raise. The "Business Etiquette" feature offers some advice on how to ask for a raise. Sometimes employees choose to resign and accept jobs at other firms because they fear upcoming layoffs. In this case, the human resource manager might be able to allay fears about job security.

Involuntary turnover occurs when employees are terminated because of poor job performance or unethical behavior in business practices or in the workplace. No matter how necessary a termination may be, it is never easy for either the human resource manager or the employee. The employee may react with anger or tears; coworkers may take sides. Human resource managers should remain calm and professional, and must be educated in employment laws. Protests against wrongful dismissal are often involved in complaints filed by the EEOC or by lawsuits brought by fired employees. Involuntary turnover also occurs when firms are forced to eliminate jobs as a cost-cutting measure, as in the case of downsizing or outsourcing.

Downsizing

As the economy tightens, companies are often faced with the hard choice of terminating employees in order to cut costs or streamline the organization. **Downsizing** is the process of reducing the number of employees within a firm by eliminating jobs. Downsizing can be

Assessment Check ☑

1. Explain the difference between *wage* and *salary*.
2. What are flexible benefit plans? How do they work?

employee separation broad term covering the loss of an employee for any reason, voluntary or involuntary.

downsizing process of reducing the number of employees within a firm by eliminating jobs.

How to Ask for a Raise

Just thinking about asking your boss for a raise might cause your hands to sweat. You fear rejection or worse, retaliation. But if you know that you are doing a superior job—including taking the initiative when it's not required—or it's been more than a year since your last increase, then perhaps it's time to make a case for yourself. You should be able to at least open the conversation with your boss. Here are a few tips for making your effort successful:

- *Be prepared.* Find out whether there is a policy for raises at your company, including a range or sliding scale for each position. Learn where your current pay lies along the scale.

- *Gather important data about yourself.* Consistently document your work accomplishments, including extra projects or tasks you've undertaken and done well. Keep a log of positive feedback from coworkers, other supervisors, and customers. If the praise is already in writing, that's even better.

- *Think through exactly what you want.* Is it a percentage increase? A dollar amount? Or perhaps expanded vacation time or time off for career education? Make sure your request is reasonable. When you meet with your supervisor, be as specific as possible.

- *Don't be pushy or hasty in your conversation.* At the same time, put forth your argument with confidence. Your goal is to get your supervisor to open up to thinking about the possibility of meeting your request.

- If your supervisor turns down your request, *ask for specifics about what you need to do in order to qualify for the raise*—and when. If possible, ask for a follow-up meeting within a certain period of time, such as two months.

- When you return to your desk or office, *send your supervisor an e-mail thanking him or her for meeting with you,* and politely recap the results of the conversation. If your request has been granted, make sure your performance lives up to it. If your supervisor has deferred a decision, don't give up. Get back to work, document everything, and earn that raise.

Sources: Smantha Maziarz Christmann, "Asking For More: Don't Be Afraid to Ask for a Raise," *Buffalo News,* March 15, 2010, http://www.buffalonews.com; "How to Negotiate for a Raise—Even in a Bad Economy," *EmploymentDigest.net,* March 4, 2010, http://www.employment digest.net; Mary Sevinsky, "Is a Raise in Your Future for 2010?," *CareerRealism.com,* January 15, 2010, http://www.careerealism.com.

accomplished through early retirement plans or voluntary severance programs. But these options don't always accomplish the goal, as was the case for AOL in a recent downsizing effort described in the "Hit & Miss" feature.

While some firms report improvements in profits, market share, employee productivity, quality, and customer service after downsizing, research is beginning to show that downsizing doesn't guarantee those improvements. "Much of the conventional wisdom about downsizing—like the fact that it automatically drives a company's stock price higher, or increases profitability—turns out to be wrong," notes Jeffrey Pfeffer of Stanford University.[33] Downsizing can have the following negative effects:

- Anxiety, health problems, and lost productivity among remaining workers.

- Expensive severance packages paid to laid-off workers.

- A domino effect on the local economy—unemployed workers have less money to spend, creating less demand for consumer goods and services, increasing the likelihood of more layoffs and other failing businesses.[34]

If downsizing is ultimately the only alternative for company survival, then there are steps that managers can take to make sure it is done the best way possible. If a firm is committed to its workforce as part of its mission, then it will do everything it can to support both the workers who must leave and those who will stay. "Employees tend to fear change," notes Jeremy Galbraith, CEO of Europe-based Burson-Marsteller. "But change can offer opportunities." His firm predicts that one in five European companies will downsize in the coming year. Sometimes firms downsize in the hope of attracting a buyer, as in the case of MySpace. The social network announced layoffs of about half of its 1,100 employees in an effort to achieve a sale.[35]

Hit & Miss

AOL Employees Don't Exit Voluntarily

People don't want to leave their jobs, especially when the economy is tighter than usual and unemployment numbers are already high. But that's what AOL asked its workers to do in a recent effort to downsize the company and control costs. AOL asked for 2,500 volunteer separations and only received 1,100. That left a gap of 1,400 workers. The goal was to reduce the firm's workforce by more than 30 percent, from 6,900 to about 4,400.

AOL, which had been struggling for several years under the merger with Time Warner, finally spun off as an independent company—but a damaged one. AOL management decided that the only way to turn the company around was to trim as much expense as possible. The turnaround initiative, dubbed Project Everest, was led by new CEO Tim Armstrong, a former sales executive for Google. After downsizing the workforce, Armstrong planned to refocus AOL's business in a few select areas, including content, online advertising, and communications.

If all of this sounds a bit cold-hearted and short-sighted to you, it does to others as well. One of the greatest blows to a company in the wake of layoffs is to the remaining workers' morale. Layoffs are devastating to those who are let go and just as traumatic to those who remain. Productivity often slides, as does the image of the company. "There's substantial research into the physical and health effects of downsizing on employees—research that reinforces the notion that layoffs are literally killing people," warns Jeffrey Pfeffer of Stanford University. In the case of AOL, the firm actually hired new salespeople to ensure continued advertising client coverage. In addition, AOL managers held meetings with advertisers to inform them of the actions being taken, and sent notes to certain clients containing private contact information for top executives. Despite these measures, some advertising clients have decided to take their business elsewhere. In an effort to rebuild its business, AOL may have lost one of its most valuable assets— its best people. And AOL is considering even more layoffs, as it plans to incorporate the acquisition of *The Huffington Post* into its organization.

Questions for Critical Thinking

1. Do you think it was a good decision for AOL to ask for volunteers to resign before making layoffs? Why or why not?

2. Could AOL managers have better prepared their clients for the downsizing?

Sources: J. P. Mangalindan, "Today in Tech: iPad Loses Features, AOL Layoffs Coming?" *CNN Money,* February 25, 2011, http://tech.fortune.cnn.com; Dustin Ensinger, "Why Layoffs Are Not Beneficial to Companies," *Economy in Crisis,* February 8, 2010, http://www.economyincrisis.org; Nicholas Carlson, "AOL Is Hiring Sales People to Make Sure Layoffs Don't Interrupt Coverage," *Business Insider,* January 13, 2010, http://www.businessinsider.com; "AOL Layoffs Begin: 1,400 Jobs to be Slashed," *Mashable.com,* January 11, 2010, http://www.mashable.com; Miguel Helft, "AOL Begins 1,200 Layoffs," *The New York Times,* January 11, 2010, http://bits.blogs.nytimes.com; Juan Carlos Perez, "AOL Voluntary Layoff Program Falls Short," *ComputerWorld,* January 5, 2010, http://www.computerworld.com.

Outsourcing

Another way that firms shrink themselves into leaner organizations is by **outsourcing**. Outsourcing involves transferring jobs from inside a firm to outside the firm. Jobs that are typically outsourced include office maintenance, deliveries, food service, and security. However, other job functions can be outsourced as well, including manufacturing, design, information technology (IT), and accounting. In general, in order to save expenses and remain flexible, companies will try to outsource functions that are not part of their core business.

Although outsourcing might work on paper, the reality might be different. Industry watchers believe that the Virgin brand suffered damage when its IT supplier allowed the airline's reservation system to collapse for 21 hours—stranding hundreds of passengers, including the business travelers that Virgin has been trying to attract. And although Australia has been getting a lot of attention lately as a potential solution for the outsourcing needs of U.S. firms, skeptics warn that labor costs will be high.[36]

outsourcing transferring jobs from inside a firm to outside the firm.

Assessment Check ✔

1. What is the difference between voluntary and involuntary turnover?

2. What is downsizing? How is it different from outsourcing?

Motivating Employees

Everyone wants to enjoy going to work. Smart employers know that and look for ways to motivate workers to commit to their company's goals and perform their best. Motivation starts with high employee morale—a positive attitude towards the job. Each year, *Fortune* announces their rankings for the "100 Best Companies to Work For." The most recent top

Table

8.2 *Fortune's* Top Ten Companies to Work For

1. SAS
2. Boston Consulting Group
3. Wegmans Food Markets
4. Google
5. NetApp
6. Zappos.com
7. Camden Property Trust
8. Nugget Market
9. REI (Recreational Equipment, Inc.)
10. Dreamworks

Source: "100 Best Companies to Work For," *Fortune*, http://money.cnn.com, accessed February 25, 2011.

ten are listed in Table 8.2. Employees at these companies have high morale because they feel valued and empowered.

High morale generally results from good management, including an understanding of human needs and an effort to satisfy those needs in ways that move the company forward. Low employee morale, on the other hand, usually signals a poor relationship between managers and employees and often results in absenteeism, voluntary turnover, and a lack of motivation.

Generally speaking, managers use rewards and punishments to motivate employees. Extrinsic rewards are external to the work itself, such as pay, fringe benefits, and praise. Intrinsic rewards are feelings related to performing the job, such as feeling proud about meeting a deadline or achieving a sales goal. Punishment involves a negative consequence for such behavior as being late, skipping staff meetings, or treating a customer poorly.

There are several theories of motivation, all of which relate back to the basic process of motivation itself, which involves the recognition of a need, the move toward meeting that need, and the satisfaction of that need. For instance, if you are hungry you might be motivated to make yourself a peanut butter sandwich. Once you have eaten the sandwich, the need is satisfied and you are no longer hungry. Figure 8.4 illustrates the process of motivation.

Maslow's Hierarchy of Needs Theory

The studies of psychologist Abraham H. Maslow suggest how managers can motivate employees. **Maslow's hierarchy of needs** has become a widely accepted list of human needs based on these important assumptions:

- People's needs depend on what they already possess.

- A satisfied need is not a motivator; only needs that remain unsatisfied can influence behavior.

- People's needs are arranged in a hierarchy of importance; once they satisfy one need, at least partially, another emerges and demands satisfaction.

Maslow's hierarchy of needs theory of motivation proposed by Abraham Maslow. According to the theory, people have five levels of needs that they seek to satisfy: physiological, safety, social, esteem, and self-actualization.

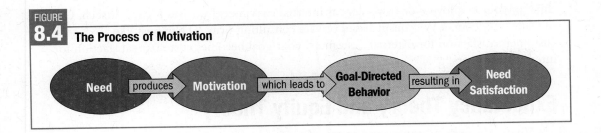

FIGURE 8.4 The Process of Motivation

Need —produces→ Motivation —which leads to→ Goal-Directed Behavior —resulting in→ Need Satisfaction

In his theory, Maslow proposed that all people have basic needs such as hunger and protection that they must satisfy before they can consider higher-order needs such as social relationships or self-worth. He identified five types of needs:

1. *Physiological needs.* These basic human needs include food, shelter, and clothing. On the job, employers satisfy these needs by paying salaries and wages and providing a heated or cooled workspace.

2. *Safety needs.* These needs refer to desires for physical and economic protection. Companies satisfy these needs with benefits like health insurance and meeting safety standards in the workplace.

3. *Social (belongingness) needs.* People want to be accepted by family, friends and coworkers. Managers might satisfy these needs through teamwork and group lunches.

4. *Esteem needs.* People like to feel valued and recognized by others. Managers can meet these needs through special awards or privileges.

5. *Self-actualization needs.* These needs drive people to seek fulfillment of their dreams and capabilities. Employers can satisfy these needs by offering challenging or creative projects, along with opportunities for education and advancement.[37]

According to Maslow, people must satisfy the lower-order needs in the hierarchy (physiological and safety needs) before they are motivated to satisfy higher-order needs (social, esteem, and self-actualization needs).

Herzberg's Two-Factor Model of Motivation

More than 50 years ago, Frederick Herzberg—a social psychologist and consultant—came up with a theory of motivation and work that is still popular today. Herzberg surveyed workers to find out when they felt good or bad about their jobs. He learned that certain factors were important to job satisfaction though they might not contribute directly to motivation. These *hygiene factors* (or maintenance factors) refer to aspects of work that are not directly related to a task itself but related to the job environment, including pay, job security, working conditions, status, interpersonal relations, technical supervision, and company policies.

Motivator factors, on the other hand, can produce high levels of motivation when they are present. These relate directly to the specific aspects of a job, including job responsibilities, achievement and recognition, and opportunities for growth. Hygiene factors are extrinsic, while motivators are intrinsic. Managers should remember that hygiene factors, though not motivational, can result in satisfaction. But if managers wish to motivate employees, they should emphasize recognition, achievement, and growth. Companies that make the various lists of "best places to work" always have managers who understand what it takes to motivate employees, regardless of how large or small the firms are. *Madison Magazine* ranks its top companies based on criteria such as trust, rewards, and work–life balance. "You need to think of your employees or coworkers as internal customers," advises Moses Altsech, CEO of CallMoses.com, a Wisconsin-based private consulting firm. "Then, just like your goal is customer satisfaction for external customers, your goal becomes customer satisfaction for internal customers, too."[38]

Expectancy Theory and Equity Theory

expectancy theory the process people use to evaluate the likelihood that their efforts will yield the results they want, along with the degree to which they want those results.

Victor Vroom's **expectancy theory** of motivation describes the process people use to evaluate the likelihood that their efforts will yield the results they want, along with the degree to which they want those results. Expectancy theory suggests that people use three factors to determine how much effort to put forth. First is a person's subjective prediction that a certain effort will lead to the desired result. This is the "can do" component of an employee's approach to work. Second is the value of the outcome (reward) to the person. Third is the person's assessment of how likely a successful performance will lead to a desirable reward. Vroom's expectancy theory is summarized in Figure 8.5. In short, an employee is motivated if he or she thinks he or she can complete a task. Next, the employee assesses the reward for accomplishing the task and is motivated if the reward is worth the effort.

equity theory an individual's perception of fair and equitable treatment.

Equity theory is concerned with an individual's perception of fair and equitable treatment. In their work, employees first consider their effort and then their rewards. Next, employees compare their results against those of their coworkers. As shown in Figure 8.6, if employees feel they are under-rewarded for their effort in comparison with others doing similar work, equity theory suggests they will decrease their effort to restore the balance. Conversely, if employees feel they are over-rewarded, they will feel guilty and put more effort into their job to restore equity and reduce guilt.

Many workers are willing to work hard as long as the burden is shared. Income inequality is higher in the United States than in any other developed society in the world. The top 10 percent of U.S. employees now earn 50 percent of all income. Many employees who, arguably, work just as hard as top managers, believe this is unfair. A bill called the Income Equity Act has been introduced several times in Congress, but has been defeated.[39]

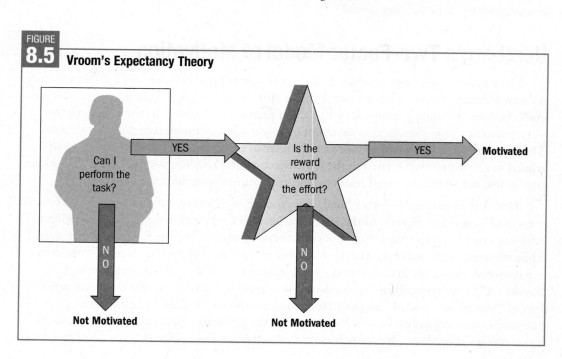

FIGURE 8.5 Vroom's Expectancy Theory

Can I perform the task? — YES → Is the reward worth the effort? — YES → **Motivated**

NO ↓ **Not Motivated**

NO ↓ **Not Motivated**

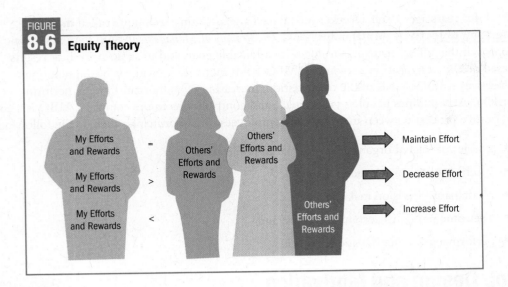

FIGURE 8.6 **Equity Theory**

My Efforts and Rewards	=	Others' Efforts and Rewards		→	Maintain Effort
My Efforts and Rewards	>			→	Decrease Effort
My Efforts and Rewards	<			→	Increase Effort

(Others' Efforts and Rewards)

Goal-Setting Theory and Management by Objectives

Needs motivate people to direct their behavior toward something that will satisfy their needs. That something is a goal. A goal is a target, objective, or result that someone tries to accomplish. **Goal-setting theory** says that people will be motivated to the extent to which they accept specific, challenging goals and receive feedback that indicates their progress toward goal achievement. As shown in Figure 8.7, the basic components of goal-setting theory are goal specificity, goal difficulty, goal acceptance, and performance feedback.

Goal specificity is the extent to which goals are clear and concrete. A goal such as "we want to reduce our carbon footprint" is vague and hard to pin down. But, "we want to reduce our carbon footprint by 2 percent" gives employees a clear target. Goal difficulty outlines how hard the goal is to reach. A more difficult goal, such as "we want to reduce our carbon footprint by 5 percent in three years" is actually more motivating than the easier goal.

Goal acceptance is the extent to which people understand and agree to the goal. If a goal is too challenging—such as reducing the firm's carbon footprint by 20 percent in two years—people are likely to reject it. Finally, performance feedback is information about performance and how well the goal has been met. Goal setting typically won't work unless performance feedback is provided.

Goals help focus workers' attention on the important parts of their jobs. Goals also energize and motivate people. They create a positive tension between the current state of affairs and the desired state. This tension is satisfied by meeting the goal or abandoning it.

goal-setting theory says that people will be motivated to the extent to which they accept specific, challenging goals and receive feedback that indicates their progress toward goal achievement.

FIGURE 8.7 **Components of Goal-Setting Theory**

Goal Specificity | Goal Difficulty

Performance Feedback | Goal Acceptance

management by objectives systematic approach that allows managers to focus on attainable goals and to achieve the best results based on the organization's resources.

Fifty years ago, Peter Drucker introduced a goal-setting technique called **management by objectives (MBO)** in his book, *The Practice of Management*. MBO is a systematic approach that allows managers to focus on attainable goals and to achieve the best results based on the organization's resources. MBO helps motivate individuals by aligning their objectives with the goals of the organization, increasing overall organizational performance. MBO clearly outlines people's tasks, goals, and contributions to the company. MBO is a collaborative process between managers and employees. MBO principles include the following:

- a series of related organizational goals and objectives;
- specific objectives for each person;
- participative decision making;
- a set time period to accomplish goals; and
- performance evaluation and feedback.

Job Design and Motivation

Today's human resource managers constantly search for ways to motivate employees through their jobs. Three ways that jobs can be restructured to be more motivating are through job enlargement, job enrichment, and job rotation.

Job enlargement is a job design that expands an employee's responsibilities by increasing the number and variety of tasks. Redesigning the production process is one way to accomplish this. Instead of having an assembly line on which each worker repeatedly completes the same task, modular work areas allow employees to complete a variety of tasks, which may result in the construction of an entire product.

Job enrichment involves an expansion of job duties that empowers an employee to make decisions and learn new skills leading toward career growth. The Pampered Chef is a direct seller of kitchen tools and housewares that gives its managers and sales consultants the power to make decisions about many aspects of their work. Kitchen consultants, who organize home sales parties, can decide how much or how little they want to work and receive various incentive rewards for performance. The company's mission is to provide "opportunities for individuals to develop their talents and skills to their fullest potential for the benefit of themselves, their families, our customers, and the company."[40]

Job rotation involves systematically moving employees from one job to another. Job rotation increases the range of activities by introducing workers to more jobs and therefore more tasks. The goal is to increase employees' interest in their jobs and allow them to learn more about the company. Nurses might rotate from oncology to the ICU in a hospital. Job rotation is often part of a training program, as is the case at EMC, a global provider of business solutions for data backup, information security, risk and compliance, and many other products. EMC offers motivated employees the chance to participate in rotational training programs in business, leadership, finance, and other areas.[41]

Managers' Attitudes and Motivation

A manager's attitude toward his or her employees greatly influences their motivation. Maslow's theory, described earlier, has helped managers understand that employees have a range of needs beyond their paychecks. Psychologist Douglas McGregor, a student of Maslow, studied motivation from the perspective of how managers view employees. After observing managers' interactions with employees, McGregor created two basic labels for the assumptions that different managers make about their workers' behavior, and how these assumptions affect management styles.

- *Theory X* assumes that employees dislike work and try to avoid it whenever possible, so management must coerce them to do their jobs. Theory X managers believe that the average worker prefers to receive instructions, avoid responsibility, take little initiative, and views money and job security as the only valid motivators—Maslow's lower order of needs.

- *Theory Y* assumes that the typical person actually likes work and will seek and accept greater responsibility. Theory Y managers assume that most people can think of creative ways to solve work-related problems, and should be given the opportunity to participate in decision making. Unlike the traditional management philosophy that relies on external control and constant supervision, Theory Y emphasizes self-control and self-direction—Maslow's higher order of needs.

Another perspective on management, proposed by management professor William Ouchi, has been labeled *Theory Z*. Organizations structured on Theory Z concepts attempt to blend the best of American and Japanese management practices. This approach views worker involvement as the key to increased productivity for the company and improved quality of work life for employees. Many U.S. firms have adopted the participative management style used in Japanese firms by asking workers for suggestions to improve their jobs and then giving them the authority to implement proposed changes.

Assessment Check ☑

1. What are the four steps in the process of motivation?

2. Explain how goal setting works.

3. Describe the three ways that managers structure jobs for increased motivation.

Labor–Management Relations

The U.S. workplace is far different from what it was a century ago, when child labor, unsafe working conditions, and a 72-hour workweek were common. The development of labor unions, labor legislation, and the collective bargaining process have contributed to the changed environment. Today's human resource managers must be educated in labor-management relations, the settling of disputes, and the competitive tactics of unions and management.

Development of Labor Unions

A <u>labor union</u> is a group of workers who have banded together to achieve common goals in the areas of wages, hours, and working conditions. The organized efforts of Philadelphia printers in 1786 resulted in the first U.S. minimum wage—$1 a day. One hundred years later, New York City streetcar conductors were able to negotiate a reduction in their workday from 17 to 12 hours.

Labor unions can be found at the local, national, and international levels. A *local union* represents union members in a specific area, such as a single community, while a *national union* is a labor organization consisting of numerous local chapters. An *international union* is a national union with membership outside the United States, usually in Canada. More

labor union group of workers who have banded together to achieve common goals in the areas of wages, hours, and working conditions.

than 15 million U.S. workers—about 12 percent of the nation's full-time workforce—belong to labor unions.[42] Although only about 8 percent of workers in the private sector are unionized, more than one-third of government workers belong to unions. The largest union in the United States is the 3.2 million-member National Education Association (NEA), representing public school teachers and other support personnel. Other large unions include the 2.2 million members of the Service Employees International Union (SEIU), the 1.4 million members of the International Brotherhood of Teamsters, the 1.3 million members of the United Food and Commercial Workers, and the 640,000 members of the United Auto Workers.

Labor Legislation

Over the past century, some major pieces of labor legislation have been enacted, including the following:

- *National Labor Relations Act of 1935 (Wagner Act).* Legalized collective bargaining and required employers to negotiate with elected representatives of their employees. Established the National Labor Relations Board (NLRB) to supervise union elections and prohibit unfair labor practices such as firing workers for joining unions, refusing to hire union sympathizers, threatening to close if workers unionize, interfering with or dominating the administration of a union, and refusing to bargain with a union.

- *Fair Labor Standards Act of 1938.* Set the first federal minimum wage (25 cents an hour), and maximum basic workweek for certain industries. Also outlawed child labor.

- *Taft-Hartley Act of 1947 (Labor–Management Relations Act).* Limited unions' power by banning such practices as coercing employees to join unions, coercing employers to discriminate against employees who are not union members, discrimination against non-union employees, picketing or conducting secondary boycotts or strikes for illegal purposes, and excessive initiation fees.

- *Landrum-Griffin Act of 1959 (Labor–Management Reporting and Disclosure Act).* Amended the Taft-Hartley Act to promote honesty and democracy in running unions' internal affairs. Required unions to set up a constitution and bylaws and to hold regularly scheduled elections of union officers by secret ballot. Set forth a bill of rights for members. Required unions to submit certain financial reports to the U.S. Secretary of Labor.

The Collective Bargaining Process

Labor unions work to increase job security for their members and to improve wages, hours, and working conditions. These goals are achieved primarily through **collective bargaining**, the process of negotiation between management and union representatives.

Union contracts, which typically cover a two- or three-year period, are often the result of weeks or months of discussion, disagreement, compromise, and eventual

collective bargaining
process of negotiation between management and union representatives.

agreement. Once agreement is reached, union members must vote to accept or reject the contract. If the contract is rejected, union representatives may resume the bargaining process with management representatives, or union members may strike to obtain their demands.

Settling Labor–Management Disputes

Strikes make the headlines, but most labor–management negotiations result in a signed contract. If a dispute arises, it is usually settled through a mechanism such as a grievance procedure, mediation, or arbitration. Any of these alternatives is quicker and less expensive than a strike.

The union contract serves as a guide to relations between the firm's management and its employees. The rights of each party are stated in the agreement. But no contract, regardless of how detailed, will eliminate the possibility of disagreement. Such differences can be the beginning of a *grievance*, a complaint—by a single employee or by the entire union—that management is violating some portion of the contract. Almost all union contracts require these complaints to be submitted through a formal grievance procedure similar to the one shown in Figure 8.8. A grievance might involve a dispute about pay, working hours, or the workplace itself. The grievance procedure usually begins with an employee's supervisor and then moves up the company's hierarchy. If the highest level of management can't settle the grievance, it is submitted to an outside party for mediation or arbitration.

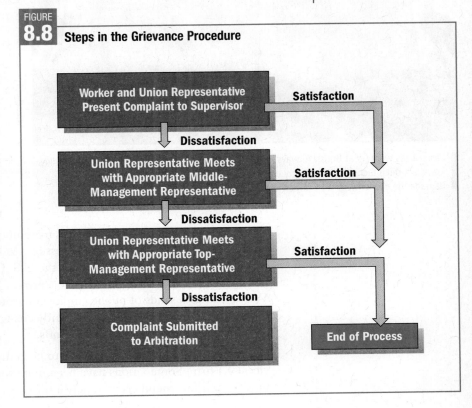

FIGURE 8.8 Steps in the Grievance Procedure

Mediation is the process of settling labor–management disputes through an impartial third party. Although the mediator does not make the final decision, he or she can hear the whole story and make objective recommendations. If the dispute remains unresolved, the two parties can turn to *arbitration*—bringing in an outside arbitrator, who renders a legally binding decision. The arbitrator must be acceptable both to the union and to management, and his or her decision is final. Most union negotiations go to arbitration if union and management representatives fail to reach a contract agreement.

Competitive Tactics of Unions and Management

Both unions and management use tactics to make their views known and to win support.

Picket lines went up at British Airways as members of the cabin crews went on strike. Strikes are a last-ditch tactic that can empty union coffers, injure an entire industry, and even damage the economy.

Union Tactics The chief tactics of unions are strikes, picketing, and boycotts. The *strike*, or walkout, is one of the most effective tools of the labor union. It involves a temporary work stoppage by workers until a dispute has been settled or a contract signed. A strike generally seeks to disrupt business as usual, calling attention to workers' needs and union demands. Strikes can last for days or weeks and can be costly to both sides. Although a strike is powerful, it can also be damaging to the very people it is trying to help. Surrounding businesses may suffer too. If striking workers aren't eating at their usual lunch haunts, those businesses will lose profits. Strikes seem to be on the decline, however. During the past decade, there have been only 17 major work stoppages on average per year, as compared to the decade spanning from 1971 to 1980, when there were nearly 270 major stoppages per year.[43]

Picketing, which involves workers marching in a public protest against their employer, is another effective form of union pressure. As long as picketing does not involve violence or intimidation, it is protected under the U.S. Constitution as freedom of speech. Picketing may accompany a strike, or it may be a protest against alleged unfair labor practices. In Wisconsin, thousands of public employees protested the governor's bill that limited their union bargaining power and significantly changed their healthcare costs and pension plans. The bill was passed despite the standoffs.[44]

A *boycott* is an organized attempt to keep the public from purchasing the goods or services of a firm. Some unions have been quite successful in organizing boycotts, and some unions even fine members who defy a boycott.

Management Tactics Management also has tactics for competing with organized labor when negotiations break down. In the past, it has used the lockout—a management "strike" to put pressure on union members by closing the firm. However, companies more commonly try to recruit strikebreakers in highly visible fields such as professional sports, or transfer supervisors and other nonunion employees to continue operations during strikes. In the British Airways strike, management leased aircraft from other airlines and used volunteer pilots and managers to take the place of the striking cabin crews.[45]

The Future of Labor Unions

Union membership and influence grew through most of the 20th century by giving industrial workers a voice in decisions about their wages, benefits, and working conditions. However, as the United States, western Europe, and Japan have shifted from manufacturing economies to information and service economies, union membership and influence has declined. Today, 52 percent of all union members are government employees; three times more union members now work for the U.S. Postal Service than work in the auto industry.[46]

Assessment Check ✓

1. What is a labor union? What is collective bargaining?

2. What are the three main tactics used by unions to win support for their demands?

Labor Unions and Green Construction

The construction industry has nearly unlimited opportunities to change the look of the world—or at least, make it greener. One labor union, the Operative Plasterers and Cement Masons International Association (OPCMIA) has already recognized this and is training its members in the use of new green technologies and processes that will ultimately improve the energy efficiency and reduce the carbon footprint of the nation's infrastructure. As the construction industry begins implementing these new technologies, particularly to achieve LEED status, workers need to know how to use them.

The OPCMIA training program is called Green Five. It is now being incorporated into existing training curricula in order to reach about 5,400 participants in 70 programs spread across local chapters, community colleges, vocational/technical schools, and OPCMIA Joint Apprenticeship and Training Centers. The Green Five program is training plasterers and cement masons in the sustainable use and application of the following materials: polished concrete, pervious concrete, exterior insulation finish systems, and American Clay. American Clay is a color mineral coating that is toxin free, VOC (volatile organic compound) free, and mold resistant. Training in the use of this product involves the preparation, mixing the material, hand application, primers, additives and sealers, and maintaining and repairing walls.

The Green Five program includes Green Awareness Training, which deals with energy-efficient building construction in general, addresses the process of energy assessment and retrofitting existing buildings, and provides an overview of environmentally sustainable products and manufacturing processes. Leadership training and "train-the-trainer" courses are offered as well.

But while many such positive steps are being taken, competition for green contracts is also heating up—with potentially damaging results. In California, conflict between the building trade unions and the California Unions for Reliable Energy has strained relationships and stalled projects.

Questions for Critical Thinking

1. In what ways does adopting a progressive stance toward "green" training help secure an important industry role for OPCMIA going forward?
2. In addition to construction, what other industries might benefit from unions taking a leadership role in sustainability training? How might these steps benefit workers, unions, and management?

Sources: Marc Lifsher, "Unions Cry Foul Over Green Contracts," *ENR California*, February 5, 2011, http://california.construction.com; David Bradley, "TR10: Green Concrete," *Technology Review*, May/June 2010, http://www.technologyreview.com; "About OPCMIA," OPCMIA Web site, http://www.opcmia.org, accessed April 29, 2010; Gerry Ryan, "The Green Five Program," *Green Labor Journal*, April 29, 2010, http://greenlaborjournal.com.

How can labor unions change to maintain their relevance? They can be more flexible and adapt to a global economy and diverse workforce. They can respond to the growing need for environmentally responsible business and manufacturing processes, as the Operative Plasterers and Cement Masons International Association (OPCMIA) is doing, described in the "Going Green" feature. Unions can establish collaborative relationships with human resource managers and other management officials. And they can recognize the potential for prosperity for all—management and union workers included.

What's Ahead

Treating employees well by enriching the work environment will continue to gain importance as a way to recruit and retain a highly motivated workforce. In addition, managers can tap the full potential of their employees by empowering them to make decisions, leading them to work effectively as teams, and fostering clear, positive communication. The next chapter covers these three means of improving performance. By involving employees more fully through empowerment, teamwork, and communication, companies can benefit from their knowledge while employees enjoy a more meaningful role in the company.

Summary of Learning Objectives

[1] Explain the role and responsibilities of human resource management.

Human resource managers are responsible for attracting, developing, and retaining the employees who can perform the activities necessary to accomplish organizational objectives. They plan for staffing needs, recruit and hire workers, provide for training, evaluate performance, determine compensation and benefits, and oversee employee separation.

Assessment Check Answers ✓

1.1 What are the five main tasks of a human resource manager? The five main tasks are planning for staffing needs, recruiting and hiring workers, providing for training, and evaluating performance, determining compensation and benefits, and overseeing employee separation.

1.2 What are the three overall objectives of a human resource manager? The three overall objectives are providing qualified, well-trained employees for the organization; maximizing employee effectiveness; and satisfying individual employee needs through monetary compensation.

[2] Describe how recruitment and selection contribute to placing the right person in a job.

Human resource managers use internal and external methods to recruit qualified employees. They may use college job fairs, personal referrals, want ads, and other resources. Internet recruiting is now the fastest, most efficient, and inexpensive way to reach a large pool of job seekers. Firms must abide by employment laws during selection in order to avoid lawsuits. Before hiring candidates, human resource managers may require employment tests that evaluate certain skills or aptitudes. When all of this is complete, there is a better chance that the right person will be hired for the job.

Assessment Check Answers ✓

2.1 Describe several recruiting techniques used by human resource managers. Techniques include college job fairs, personal referrals, want ads, company Web sites, online job sites, and online interviews such as jobcasts.

2.2 What is the function of the Equal Employment Opportunity Commission (EEOC)? The EEOC investigates discrimination complaints and helps employers set up affirmative action programs.

[3] Discuss how orientation, training programs, and performance appraisals help companies develop their employees.

New employees often participate in an orientation where they learn about company policies and practices. Training programs provide opportunities for employees to build their skills and knowledge and prepare them for new job opportunities within the company. They also give employers a better chance of retaining employees. Performance appraisals give employees feedback about their strengths and weaknesses and how they can improve.

Assessment Check Answers ✓

3.1 What are the benefits of computer-based training? Computer-based training offers consistent presentations, interactive learning, and employees can learn at their own pace. It is also less expensive than other types of training.

3.2 What is a management development program? A management development program provides training designed to improve the skills and broaden the knowledge of current and potential executives.

3.3 What are the four criteria of an effective performance appraisal? A performance appraisal should take place several times a year, be linked to organizational goals, be based on objective criteria, and be a two-way conversation.

[4] Describe how firms compensate employees through pay systems and benefit programs.

Firms compensate employees with wages, salaries, incentive pay systems, and benefits. Benefit programs vary among firms, but most companies offer healthcare programs, insurance, retirement plans, paid time off, and sick leave. A growing number of companies are offering flexible benefit plans and flexible work plans, such as flextime, compressed workweeks, job sharing, and home-based work.

Assessment Check Answers ✓

4.1 Explain the difference between *wage* and *salary*. Wages are based on an hourly pay rate or the amount of work accomplished. Salaries are paid periodically, such as weekly or monthly. Salaries do not fluctuate with hours worked.

4.2 What are flexible benefit plans? How do they work? Flexible benefit plans offer a choice of benefits, including different types of medical insurance, dental and vision, and life and disability insurance. Typically, each employee receives a set allowance to pay for these benefits depending on his or her needs.

[5] Discuss employee separation and the impact of downsizing and outsourcing.

Employee separation occurs when a worker leaves his or her job, voluntarily or involuntarily. Sometimes an employee is terminated because of poor job performance or unethical behavior. Downsizing is the process of reducing the number of employees within a firm in order to cut costs and achieve a leaner organization. However, some negative effects include anxiety and lost productivity among remaining workers; expensive severance packages; and a domino effect in the local economy. Outsourcing involves transferring jobs from inside a firm to outside the firm. While some expenses may be cut, a firm may experience a backlash in performance and public image.

Assessment Check Answers ✔

5.1 What is the difference between voluntary and involuntary turnover? Voluntary turnover occurs when employees leave firms to start their own businesses, take jobs with other firms, move to another community, or retire. Involuntary turnover occurs because of poor job performance or unethical behavior in business practices or the workplace. It can also occur when a company is forced to eliminate jobs.

5.2 What is downsizing? How is it different from outsourcing? Downsizing is the process of reducing the number of employees within a firm by eliminating jobs. Downsizing is done to cut overhead costs and streamline the organizational structure. With outsourcing, companies contract with other firms to perform noncore jobs or business functions, such as housekeeping, maintenance, or relocation services. This allows companies to focus on what they do best, and can result in a downsized workforce.

⌐6⌐ Explain the different methods and theories of motivation.

Employee motivation starts with high employee morale. According to Maslow's hierarchy of needs, people satisfy lower-order needs (such as food and safety) before moving to higher-order needs (such as esteem and fulfillment). Herzberg's two-factor model of motivation is based on the fulfillment of hygiene factors and motivation factors. Expectancy theory suggests that people use these factors to determine whether to put forth the effort to complete a task. Equity theory refers to a person's perception of fair and equitable treatment. Goal-setting theory says that people will be motivated to the extent to which they accept specific, challenging goals. Job design is also used by managers for motivation.

Assessment Check Answers ✔

6.1 What are the four steps in the process of motivation? The four steps are need, motivation, goal-directed behavior, and need satisfaction.

6.2 Explain how goal setting works. People will be motivated to the extent to which they accept specific, challenging goals and receive feedback that indicates their progress toward goal achievement.

6.3 Describe the three ways that managers structure jobs for increased motivation. Three ways that employers apply motivational theories to restructure jobs are job enlargement, job enrichment, and job rotation. Job enlargement is a job design that expands an employee's responsibilities by increasing the number and variety of tasks they entail. Job enrichment is a change in job duties to increase employees' authority in planning their work, deciding how it should be done, and learning new skills that help them grow. Job rotation involves systematically moving employees from one job to another.

⌐7⌐ Discuss the role of labor unions, the collective bargaining process, and methods for settling labor–management disputes.

Labor unions have resulted in the improvement of wages and working conditions for many workers over the past century, along with the passage of significant labor laws. Unions achieve these improvements through the collective bargaining process, resulting in an agreement. Most labor–management disputes are settled through the grievance process, in which sometimes mediation or arbitration is necessary.

Assessment Check Answers ✔

7.1 What is a labor union? What is collective bargaining? A labor union is a group of workers who have banded together to achieve common goals in the areas of wages, hours, and working conditions. Collective bargaining is the process of negotiation between management and union representatives.

7.2 What are the three main tactics used by unions to win support for their demands? Unions use strikes (walkouts), picketing, and boycotts.

■ Business Terms You Need to Know

Review Questions

1. Why has Internet recruiting become such an important tool for human resource managers?

2. Recruitment and selection are expensive. So, what precautions do human resource managers take to make sure they are hiring the right person for each job?

3. Give an example of a type of job that would be appropriate for on-the-job training. Then describe specifically how you think this type of training would work for your selected job, including types of tasks a new hire might learn this way.

4. On what five factors are compensation policies usually based? Name at least three employee benefits that are required by law and three more that are provided voluntarily by many firms.

5. Describe four types of flexible work plans. Identify an industry that would be well suited to each type of plan, and explain why.

6. Why do companies downsize? What are some of the drawbacks to downsizing? Why do companies outsource? What are some of the drawbacks to outsourcing?

7. Select three different theories of motivation, and explain how each can be used by managers to motivate employees.

8. Suppose a manager of a popular sandwich shop maintains a Theory X assumption about employees. At the beginning of each workweek, what types of things might the manager tell his or her employees? Now suppose the manager has a Theory Y assumption; then Theory Z. Describe what he or she might say to employees.

9. In what major ways has labor legislation changed the workplace over the past century? How might the workplace be different today without this legislation?

10. What are mediation and arbitration? Describe a situation that you think might result in arbitration.

Projects and Teamwork Applications

1. On your own or with a classmate, research consulting firms that provide management training programs—like Glimmerglass Consulting Group, described in the chapter. Prepare a presentation about one of these firms, describing the approach it takes as well as some of the specific elements of the program.

2. Choose one of the following companies, or one that you think you might like to work for sometime in the future. Using the firm's Web site and one of the job Web sites such as Monster.com (if applicable), research the company's benefits. Outline the firm's benefits and then determine if you still want to work for that company, and why. Suggested firms:

   a. Timberland

   b. SAS

   c. NextEra Energy Resources

   d. Kraft Foods

   e. FedEx

3. With a classmate, choose an on-campus job and outline how you would share that job. Create a schedule and division of tasks.

4. Choose what you think would be your dream job five years from now. Then create a chart according to Maslow's hierarchy of needs, and identify the ways in which you envision this job fulfilling each level of need.

5. Research one of the major labor laws outlined in the text to learn more about the circumstances that led to its proposal and passage. In what ways do you believe this law has (or has not) affected the working world that you expect to enter when you graduate?

Web Assignments

1. **Human resources (HR) as a profession.** Go to the Web site listed here and review the material. Answer the following questions:

   a. How many people are employed in HR?

   b. What are the educational requirements to become an HR manager?

   c. How rapidly is the occupation expected to grow over the next decade?

   http://www.bls.gov/oco/ocos021.htm

2. **Performance reviews.** Visit the Web sites listed here. Each lists some tips for conducting employee performance reviews. Print out the material and bring it to class to participate in a class discussion on performance reviews.

   http://www.squidoo.com/employeeperformancereview

   http://articles.techrepublic.com.com/5100-10878_11-1049853.html

   http://smallbusiness.dnb.com/human-resources/workforce-management/1385-1.html

3. **Teamsters.** The Teamsters is one of the nation's largest and oldest labor unions. Go to the union's Web site (http://www.teamster.org) and review the material. When was the union founded? Originally, the union represented workers in what industry? How many members do the Teamsters currently have? Other than the United States, in what other country does the union represent workers?

Note: Internet Web addresses change frequently. If you don't find the exact sites listed, you may need to access the organization's home page and search from there or use a search engine such as Bing or Google.

The Coca-Cola Company: Training for the Future Right Now

Coca-Cola is one of the most recognizable brands in the world—it has also stood the test of time, having survived more than 65 years. But the firm has come a long way from its first fizzy drink; it is now a global empire with products sold in more than 200 countries. The Coca-Cola Company maintains that the key to its success and longevity isn't its secret recipe for the famous cola in the red can; it's the people behind the fizz. The company has become especially expert in two areas of human resource management: wellness benefits and training. As a result, they employ healthy, skilled, and knowledgeable workers.

Several years ago, The Coca-Cola Company revamped its health and wellness programs so that they became an integral part of the firm's overall strategy. "We now have a strategy in which our health care benefits and our wellness programs are mixed together," explains Mary Williams, senior counsel of global compensation and benefits. Prior to the new initiative, "we had no communication with the employee that having a healthy worker within our workforce was important to the company."

The company now provides real incentives for employees to participate in its wellness programs. For example, one recent year they gave $120 to any worker who completed a wellness assessment. The following year, the company upped the ante, offering up to $180 to any employee who agreed to participate in health coaching. Fitness challenges, in which workers earn redeemable points for logging enough sleep at night or eating fruits and vegetables, are also included. Perhaps the most important part of the wellness effort is reaching employees with the right information, encouraging them to participate—there are now e-mail blasts and ads running on in-house television monitors, promoting wellness benefits. The new company mantra is "Live Positively," observes Mary Williams.

Just as important as keeping employees healthy is the effort to train and educate them, preparing them for future innovations and leadership roles. A few years ago, the company founded Coca-Cola University (CCU) as part of an overall strategy to develop the global workforce to reach its greatest potential. "No longer can we think of career development as a step up in job grade or organization level, or of training as the sole source of skill development," explains Katharine Nisbet, head of the management university. "Today, career development is about gathering critical experiences, necessary skills, and leadership capabilities that will be vital to the company's and individual's success today and in the future."

Coca-Cola University operates on a 70-20-10 model of employee development. This means that 70 percent of learning takes place on the job, 20 percent occurs through coaching and mentoring, and 10 percent is acquired through formal, structured training. Within this model, The Coca-Cola Company human resource managers strive to match the right training to each worker's needs. One employee might receive classroom teaching, online lessons, and on-the-job support while another might receive a different combination of training methods.

An important aspect of CCU's management training strategy is that it encompasses everyone. "Our leadership training applies to every Coca-Cola associate," says Katharine Nisbet. "It is helping them build core competencies such as innovation, collaboration, and teamwork." Some of the seminars in which all staff are invited to participate are: "Driving Innovative Business Improvements," "Collaborating to Win," and "Developing and Inspiring Others." At their performance appraisal meetings, employees are encouraged to sign up for these and other offerings through CCU. This means that The Coca-Cola Company always has a deep pool from which to draw management talent that is already knowledgeable about the company's strategies and objectives, now and for the future.

Questions for Critical Thinking

1. In addition to cash payments, what other incentives do you think might motivate The Coca-Cola Company employees to participate in its wellness programs?

2. The Coca-Cola Company has developed a comprehensive, worldwide training program. In addition to increasing its leadership pool, what other positive effects do you predict this may have on the company's future success?

Sources: "Associate Training," The Coca-Cola Company, http://www.thecoca-colacompany.com, accessed March 4, 2011; "Behind the Fizz," HRM, April 12, 2010, http://wwwhrmasia.com; Lydell C. Bridgeford, "Coca-Cola Retools Wellness Strategy," *SMB Human Resources*, March 15, 2010, http://smbhr.benefitnews.com.

CASE 8.2

Strikes: Who Wins, Who Loses?

As a consumer, there are many strikes you'll probably never notice. They won't affect your daily life, what you eat, how you get to work or to school, or your access to communication and information. But a strike that stops a major form of transportation generally has the effect that its union wants: people notice. That was the case in Britain recently when union railworkers threatened to strike over a major holiday weekend during which thousands of people were scheduled to travel by train.

The major issue leading to the strike vote was Network Rail's announcement that it would be eliminating 1,500 jobs in an effort to cut costs. Network Rail, which is state owned, maintains the track and signaling system over which private train operating companies run their train services. It also hires out track engineering and replacement contracts to private contractors. The workers involved in the dispute belong to the Rail Maritime Transport Workers Union (RMT). When RMT maintenance workers voted a 77 percent majority in favor of the strikes, Network Rail threatened to fire all 13,000 of them and reemploy a smaller number of them based on new terms and conditions. Because of budget cuts, a private subcontractor had already filed for bankruptcy—representing another 1,100 lost jobs.

Had the strike gone ahead as planned it would have been Britain's first in more than 16 years.

It would have disrupted travel throughout the nation, including passenger travel and the shipping of goods. But the strike was blocked by a British judge who cited irregularities in the union's strike ballot—a technicality. Union representatives were outraged by the decision. "This judgment is an attack on the whole trade union movement and twists the anti-union laws even further in favor of the bosses," argued Bob Crow, general secretary for RMT. Network Rail's head of operations, Robin Gisby, played to the general public. "This is good news for the millions of passengers who rely on us every day, and for our freight users and for the country as a whole," he said. "We have a responsibility to our people to continue talking to the unions to find a settlement."

Questions for Critical Thinking

1. If the RMT strike had gone ahead, what do you think might have been the result? How would the general public view RMT? How would Network Rail be viewed?

2. Do you think the union was a help or a hindrance to negotiations between workers and Network Rail? Why?

Sources: "UK Judge Blocks National Rail Strike," *The Star,* April 1, 2010, http://thestar.com.my; Adam Gabbatt, "Rail Strike Dates Announcement Likely Today," *Guardian,* March 25, 2010, http://www.guardian.co.uk.

CASE 8.3

Seventh Generation Promotes Company Ownership

Common sense dictates that companies who treat their employees well—from fair compensation to dignity in the workplace—will attract and retain the best workers. But from there, the picture becomes a bit murky. Traditional models of human resource management are being re-evaluated and sometimes tossed out by firms whose goals and values these models do not fit. Seventh Generation is one such company. "When we win an award for being one of the best places to work in America, that to me is the most important award we can win because it's the hardest thing we do," says co-founder Jeffrey Hollender.

Seventh Generation was founded on the premise of sustainability—that every product it manufactures, whether it is laundry detergent or paper towels, must be designed and produced in such a way that it leaves little or no impact on the environment. Sustainability includes its recruitment and development of human resources over the long term.

Most of the 100-plus employees at Seventh Generation have had at least some experience with another employer. Hollender points out that these employees arrive at Seventh Generation with all of the relationship patterns, values, and attitudes toward work they have learned elsewhere. "Most businesses teach us not to have a voice, not to speak up, not to challenge authority, not to unleash the maximum potential we have as individuals," he says. Because Seventh Generation incorporates a different set of values into its organizational culture, "the responsibility at Seventh Generation is to *unteach* people all of those habits and patterns, and unleash the potential that all of those other businesses have stifled," Hollender asserts.

Stephanie Lowe works in human resources at Seventh Generation. She notes that when she was hired, the company had only 30 employees—now there are more than 100. The increase in the number of employees has presented a challenge. Not only have people arrived from other firms with a variety of experience and expectations, the logistics of managing 100 employees are different from those of managing 30. "We can't do things as casually," says Lowe with some regret. "Things just wouldn't get done. It's a hard line to walk, and it's a challenge." In addition, the core value of sustainability is built into every decision the firm makes. "How do you do compensation in a socially responsible company?" asks Lowe. "How do you do that in a company that values different things, where people are asked to value themselves and bring more of themselves to work?"

Seventh Generation's answer to the compensation/social responsibility/sustainability question is ownership. Every person who works at Seventh Generation has a financial stake in the company. "The most significant way Seventh Generation's philosophy translates into HR is ownership," remarks Hollender. He points out that a firm can give employees health insurance, time off, grants for the purchase of hybrid vehicles, on-site fitness centers, and the like; but none of these benefits translates to ownership. "The most important thing is to let the people who are creating value by building the business participate in the value they create," Hollender asserts.

Stephanie Lowe echoes this philosophy. "We aren't trying to distinguish between the employees and the corporation," she explains. At Seventh Generation, the people are the company. Employees not only participate in company ownership, they are viewed as contributors in ways that reach outside their job descriptions. "We are shifting away from traditional performance management to personal development plans," says Lowe. "We do look at what employees need to work on to hit company goals, but also what each person needs to grow personally—and we

let them define that." Employees write personal initiatives that help the company recognize talents and potential that may not be readily evident during the performance of a particular job. "It's based on the concept that you measure what you value," explains Lowe. "We value volunteer time, making a difference in the world, raising more responsible global citizens." To that end, Seventh Generation encourages employees at every level to speak out with ideas for more sustainable products and processes.

When speaking about the Seventh Generation workforce, Hollender sounds more like a tribal elder than a business manager. Perhaps that's no coincidence, as Seventh Generation's mission is based on the Great Law of the Iroquois, which counsels each tribe member to consider the impact of all decisions on the next seven generations. "The thing I'm most proud of is the success of our employees at Seventh Generation," boastsHollender, "their growth, the things they have thought of that I would never have dreamed of, the tough questions that they ask me that I wouldn't ask myself. Unleashing that potential—that is the mostmagical thing about running a business."

Questions for Critical Thinking

1. Visit the Seventh Generation Web site at http://www.seventhgeneration.com and view the current job listings there. What kinds of qualities in job candidates does the firm look for that might be different from those at other companies?

2. What might be the potential benefits and pitfalls of Seventh Generation's view of performance and compensation?

3. Choose one of the motivational theories described in the chapter and discuss how the theory would pertain to Seventh Generation's approach to motivating employees.

4. Do you predict that employees at Seventh Generation will attempt to unionize? Why or why not? If they did, how do you think the firm would respond?

Sources: Seventh Generation Web site, http://www.seventhgeneration .com, accessed March 4, 2011; "Sustainability Study," *Accenture,* http:// microsite.accenture.com, accessed March 4, 2011; "Study Says Companies Should Train Managers in Sustainability," *7GenBlog,* July 2, 2010, http://www.seventhgeneration.com; Danielle Sacks, "Jeffrey Hollender: Seventh Generation, Triple Bottom Line Entrepreneur," *Fast Company.com,* February 2, 2010, http://www.fastcompany.com.

Chapter 9

Learning Objectives

[1] Describe why and how organizations empower employees.

[2] Distinguish among the five types of teams in the workplace.

[3] Identify the characteristics of an effective team, and summarize the stages of team development.

[4] Relate team cohesiveness and norms to effective team performance.

[5] Describe the factors that can cause conflict in teams and ways to manage conflict.

[6] Explain the importance and process of effective communication.

[7] Compare the different types of communication.

[8] Explain external communication and methods of managing a public crisis.

Top Performance through Empowerment, Teamwork, and Communication

Joshua Hodge Photography/iStockphoto

Innovation at Mayo Clinic through Teamwork

Innovation comes in many forms. Often when you think of innovation, you might imagine the latest high-tech gadgets or the newest generation of hybrid car. But you probably wouldn't think of Mayo Clinic. Mayo Clinic, which is located in Minnesota, is one of the premier healthcare facilities in the world, operating its own hospital, research laboratories, and medical school. One of the organization's primary objectives is to create innovations and solutions that will "transform the experience and delivery of healthcare." Mayo doctors, researchers, and administrators believe that the only way to achieve this is through collaboration and teamwork. "Many of history's greatest innovations resulted from the union of disciplines, from conversations that spanned schools of thought," notes Dr. David Rosenman, a Mayo Clinic physician. "The innovations in healthcare that help to foster population-level wellness will be no exception." Teamwork is an integral part of the Mayo organization. "Teamwork is the hallmark of Mayo Clinic Specialists," states the organization's Web site. "Specialists in many fields unite their areas of expertise to achieve a shared goal—providing the best care to every patient, every day. This sense of teamwork is a daily activity in the exam rooms, operating rooms, and hospitals of Mayo Clinic." Farther afield, Mayo-led teams work closely with their colleagues in such locations as China, South America, Haiti, and Russia to provide aid to victims of natural disasters, life-saving surgery to patients in remote areas, and education about healthcare and nutrition to populations that might otherwise not receive any care at all. "Volunteering is a great experience," says Dr. Kenton Zehr, who recently participated in a team effort in Russia that helped establish the capabilities for heart surgery there.

"You work together, you learn to be flexible, and you know you are helping to make a difference." Near home, Mayo Clinic employees use teamwork to promote health and wellness on the job as well as in the community. One member of Mayo's Systems and Procedures Team in Florida recently decided to walk the 17 miles to work in order to promote awareness for an upcoming Heart Walk sponsored by the American Heart Association and Mayo Clinic. In the process, he inspired several of his coworkers to participate in the Heart Walk, raising money as a team for the American Heart Association.

A recent study on innovation conducted by several universities and management firms acknowledged Mayo Clinic's collaborative approach as one of the key factors in its success, pointing out that teamwork has been part of its culture since it was established more than 100 years ago. Founded by William and Charles Mayo, the first Mayo hospital was built in the aftermath of a devastating tornado to serve survivors in the surrounding area. The Mayo brothers insisted on an open, collaborative atmosphere among the hospital's doctors that endures today, focusing on connectedness and cross-functional teams. In fact, they created the first known "group doctor" practice, which has since become the organizational standard in many hospitals and communities. It was also one of the first healthcare organizations to place doctors on salary in order to allow them to focus on the outcomes of their work (the wellness of patients) instead of the number of transactions (patients) they completed each day. Management experts note that the Mayo Clinic brand is now nearly as recognizable as that of The Coca-Cola Company. Around the world, people trust the Mayo name in healthcare. They might not think of it when they are healthy, but when they need help from the experts, they turn to the Mayo team.[1]

Photo courtesy of Mayo Clinic

Top managers at organizations like the Mayo Clinic recognize that teamwork and communication are essential for empowering employees to perform their best. This chapter focuses on how organizations involve employees by sharing information and empowering them to make critical decisions, allowing them to work in teams, and fostering communication. We begin by discussing the ways managers can empower their employees' decision-making authority and responsibility. Then we explain why and how a growing number of firms rely on teams of workers rather than individuals to make decisions and carry out assignments. Finally, we discuss how effective communication allows workers to share information that improves the quality of decision making.

Empowering Employees

empowerment giving employees authority and responsibility to make decisions about their work.

An important component of effective management is the **empowerment** of employees. Managers promote this goal by giving employees the authority and responsibility to make decisions about their work. Empowerment seeks to tap the brainpower of all workers to find improved ways of doing their jobs, better serving customers, and achieving organizational goals. Empowerment frees managers from hands-on control of workers. It also motivates workers by adding challenges to their jobs and giving them a feeling of ownership. Managers empower employees by sharing company information and decision-making authority and by rewarding them for their performance—as well as the company's. The topic of employee empowerment is discussed in the "Solving an Ethical Controversy" feature.

Sharing Information and Decision-Making Authority

One of the most effective methods of empowering employees is to keep them informed about the company's financial performance. Companies such as Virginia-based engineering firm Anderson & Associates (A&A) provide regular reports to their employees on key financial information, such as profit-and-loss statements. A&A designs roads, water and sewer lines, and water treatment plants for municipalities, along with private construction projects such as Warm Hearth Village, a retirement community, in which residents were consulted during the planning process. The firm practices open-book management, giving every employee access to the same financial information about their employer. Like other companies that practice this strategy, A&A also trains its employees to interpret financial statements so that they can understand how their work contributes to company profits. Using information technology to empower employees does carry some risks. One is that information may reach competitors. Although A&A considered this problem, management decided that sharing information was essential to the company's strategy.[2]

Solving an Ethical Controversy

Employee Empowerment: Yes or No?

Many firms today recognize the benefits of empowering employees—entrusting them with decision-making authority that may improve sales outcomes, relationships with customers, and the ultimate success of a firm. But not all managers are convinced that handing over the reins to their employees is the best way to run a company. They worry about the consequences of allowing employees to make decisions that could cost the company dearly if those choices turn out to be wrong.

Should firms empower employees to make decisions that could improve company relationships and overall performance?

PRO

1. Employees who are empowered to make decisions within their job descriptions and realm of expertise can help build relationships as well as sales. For example, an employee who has direct contact with customers can market products and solve customer problems more effectively if given the authority to do so. A salesperson who can authorize a return or a discount on the spot could cement a relationship with a customer and ensure repeat business.

2. Empowered employees are motivated to increase their own performance as well as that of the firm. Workers who are entrusted with making decisions about their own jobs are more invested in their company's overall performance. Employees who are motivated to display the commitment, initiative, and creativity that decision-making requires help propel their company to success.

CON

1. When things go wrong at a firm—such as a major product recall or the discovery of poor working conditions at an outsourced facility—customers, investors, and the public turn their attention immediately to the company's leadership. If the company's top management appears unaware of the decision making that led to these mistakes, then customers, investors, and the public quickly lose faith in the firm's credibility. Employee decision making can result in this type of communication breakdown within an organization.

2. When employees are empowered without proper training, customers or suppliers might receive insufficient or inaccurate information that could lead to failed solutions, damaged relationships, and lost sales.

Summary

While most firms are now practicing at least some degree of empowerment among employees, some managers are reluctant to delegate this kind of decision-making authority. However, even those managers who support empowerment agree that employees must be trained in decision-making skills and educated about the goods and services marketed by their firm. A firm can start along the right path toward empowerment by establishing decision-making criteria such as: Is this decision right for the customer *and* for the company? Is the decision ethical and in line with the firm's core values? A positive response to both these questions should lead to an empowered decision.

Sources: Kevin Rutkowski, "Employee Empowerment and Customer Service," *Catapult Systems,* January 13, 2011, http://blogs .catapultsystems.com; George N. Root, "Challenges of Employee Empowerment," *Small Business-Chron.com,* http://smallbusiness.chron .com, accessed August 16, 2010; Cameron Kauffman, "Employee Involvement: A New Blueprint for Success," *Journal of Accountancy,* May 2010, http://www.journalofaccountancy.com; Bob Reynolds, "Thoughts from the shower—Pros and Cons to Empowering Your Employees," *Snoitulos Ten,* April 30, 2010, http://www.snoitulosten.com; Stacy Blackman, "How to Empower Employees with the Illusion of Control," *Blogs Bnet.com,* April 16, 2010, http://blogs.bnet.com.

The second way in which companies empower employees is to give them broad authority to make workplace decisions that implement a firm's vision and its competitive strategy. Even among non-management staff, empowerment extends to decisions and activities traditionally handled by managers. Employees might be responsible for such tasks as purchasing supplies, making hiring decisions, scheduling production or work hours, overseeing the safety program, and granting pay increases.

This can be an especially powerful tool in many healthcare environments. At Lebanon Valley Brethren Homes, a long-term care facility in Pennsylvania, workers at all levels

A way in which companies empower employees is to give them broad authority to make workplace decisions that implement a firm's vision and its competitive strategy. At Lebanon Valley Brethren Homes, a long-term care facility in Pennsylvania, workers at all levels are empowered to do whatever it takes to improve the quality of their elderly residents' lives.

Yuri Arcurs/iStockphoto

are empowered to do whatever it takes to improve the quality of their elderly residents' lives. Each care worker attends to the same residents every day, so caregivers and residents form a strong personal bond. Caregivers are responsible for the overall management of their household including meals and housekeeping. They make decisions for individual residents ranging from sleep schedules to room lighting. As a result, each Green House—or household within the larger community—feels like a home.[3]

Empowerment can take other forms as well. GM recently announced an initiative in which GM workers could volunteer to take vehicles home and test drive them in real-life situations, as described in the "Hit & Miss" feature.

Linking Rewards to Company Performance

Perhaps the ultimate step in convincing employees of their stake in the prosperity of their firm is worker ownership. Two widely used ways that companies provide worker ownership are employee stock ownership plans and stock options. Table 9.1 compares these two methods of employee ownership.

Employee Stock Ownership Plans Almost 13 million workers participate in 10,500 *employee stock ownership plans (ESOPs)* worth more than $900 billion.[4] These plans benefit employees by giving them ownership stakes in their companies, leading to potential

Table
9.1 Employee Stock Ownership Plans and Stock Options

ESOP	STOCK OPTIONS
Company-sponsored trust fund holds shares of stock for employees	Company gives employees the option to buy shares of its stock
Usually covers all full-time employees	Can be granted to one, a few, or all employees
Employer pays for the shares of stock	Employees pay a set price to exercise the option
Employees receive stock shares (or value of stock) upon retiring or leaving the company	Employees receive shares of stock when (and if) they exercise the option, usually during a set period

Sources: "Employee Stock Options and Ownership (ESOP)," *Reference for Business,* http://www.referenceforbusiness.com, accessed March 9, 2011; "Employee Stock Options Fact Sheet," The National Center for Employee Ownership, http://www.nceo.org, accessed March 9, 2011.

Part 3 *Management: Empowering People to Achieve Business*

Hit & Miss

GM: Putting Workers in the Driver's Seat

There are lots of things that autoworkers at GM are used to doing as part of their jobs—operating machinery, running computer programs, managing schedules and logistics. But until recently, there's one thing GM workers hadn't been asked to do; at least, not to the extent they are now: drive the cars.

Workers at the GM assembly plant in Arlington, Texas, were recently given the chance to volunteer for a new program in which they could literally "check out" a vehicle from the plant lot, take it home for a night or a weekend, and drive it just as they would their own car or cross-over SUV. In return, the test drivers were asked for detailed feedback about the vehicles, for the first time giving them a powerful voice in the design and construction of the cars they spend hours and weeks building. "We had so much interest in [the program] we had to use a lottery to determine who would get to be a volunteer," reports Enrique Flores Jr., president of the United Auto Workers Local 276, the union representing 2,400 workers at the GM plant.

While the test-drive idea isn't new—executives and managers have participated in it for years—bringing the program to rank-and-file workers represents an updated attitude toward empowering employees. "We want to engage employees to do underground marketing," explains Wendy Stachowicz, coordinator of the GM Vehicle Advocate

Program. "You look at where the company has been and where it has to go. Everyone has to help."

In addition to a lottery, employees were selected based on their driving records. If they chose to purchase that vehicle or another one in the program, they qualified for discounts that reduced the price to near wholesale level. But participants didn't receive commissions or other rewards for test driving the cars—that wasn't the point. "This is a tool to empower people, to get them really engaged with our products," explains Stachowicz. Next, GM is considering expanding the program to include GM retirees and suppliers.

Questions for Critical Thinking

1. In what ways does the GM test-drive program empower workers?
2. How might GM benefit from this type of empowerment of its assembly plant workers?

Sources: "GM Employees Getting Up-Close Look at New Line-up," *FinChannel.com*, April 20, 2010, http://www.finchannel.com; "GM Launches Plant-City Tour to Showcase Line-up, Empower Employees to Promote New Vehicles," GM Web site, http://www.gm.com, accessed April 20, 2010; Terry Box, "Arlington GM Workers to Take Home New Cars to Try Out," *The Dallas Morning News*, February 27, 2010, http://www.dallasnews.com.

profits as the value of their firm increases. Under ESOPs, the employer buys shares of the company stock on behalf of the employee as a retirement benefit. The accounts continue to grow in value tax-free, and when employees leave the company, they can cash in their stock shares. Employees are motivated to work harder and smarter than they would without ESOPs because, as part owners, they share in their firm's financial success. About 60 percent of companies surveyed that offer ESOPs report an increase in employee productivity.[5]

As retirement plans, ESOPs must comply with government regulations designed to protect pension benefits. Because ESOPs can be expensive to set up, they are more common in larger firms than in smaller ones. Public companies with ESOPs average around 14,000 employees, while private companies average about 1,500 employees.[6] One danger with ESOPs is that if the majority of an employee's retirement funds are in company stock and the value falls dramatically, the employee may be financially harmed.[7]

Stock Options Another popular way for companies to share ownership with their employees is through the use of *stock options*, or rights to buy a specified amount of company stock at a given price within a given time period. In contrast to an ESOP, in which the company holds stock for the benefit of employees, stock options give employees a chance to own the stock themselves if they exercise their options by completing the stock purchase. If an employee receives an option on 100 shares at $10 per share and the stock price goes up to $20, the employee can exercise the option to buy those 100 at $10 each, sell them at the market price of $20, and keep the difference. If the stock price never goes above the option price, the employee isn't required to exercise the option.[8]

1. What is empowerment?

2. What kinds of information can companies provide employees to help them share decision-making responsibility?

3. How do employee stock ownership plans and stock options reward employees and encourage empowerment?

team group of people with certain skills who are committed to a common purpose, approach, and set of performance goals.

work teams relatively permanent group of employees with complementary skills who perform the day-to-day work of organizations.

Although options were once limited to senior executives and members of the board of directors, some companies now grant stock options to employees at all levels. Federal labor laws allow stock options to be granted to both hourly and salaried employees. It is estimated that 9 million employees in thousands of companies hold stock options.[9] About one-third of all stock options issued by U.S. corporations go to the top five executives at each firm. Much of the remainder goes to other executives and managers, who make up only about 2 percent of the U.S. workforce. Yet there is solid evidence that stock options motivate regular employees to perform better. Some argue that to be most effective as motivators, stock options need to be granted to a much broader base of employees.

Stock options have turned hundreds of employees at firms such as Home Depot, Microsoft, and Google into millionaires. But such success stories are no guarantee, especially when stock prices drop during economic downturns. As with ESOPs, employees face risks when they rely on a single company's stock to provide for them. In addition to stock options and ESOPs, many firms offer their executives other perks, or special privileges.

Teams

A **team** is a group of people with certain skills who are committed to a common purpose, approach, and set of performance goals. All team members hold themselves mutually responsible and accountable for accomplishing their objectives. Teams are widely used in business and in many not-for-profit organizations such as hospitals and government agencies.

Teams are one of the most frequently discussed topics in employee training programs, because teams require that people learn how to work effectively together. Many firms emphasize the importance of teams during their hiring processes, asking job applicants about their previous experiences as team members. Why? Because companies want to hire people who can work well with other people and pool their talents and ideas to achieve more together than they could achieve working alone. Figure 9.1 outlines five basic types of teams: work teams, problem-solving teams, self-managed teams, cross-functional teams, and virtual teams.

About two-thirds of U.S. firms currently use **work teams**, which are relatively permanent groups of employees. In this approach, people with complementary skills perform the day-to-day work of the organization. A work team might include all the workers involved in assembling and packaging a product—it could be anything from cupcakes to cars. Most of Walmart's major vendors maintain offices near its headquarters in Bentonville, Arkansas. Typically, the vendor offices operate as work teams, and the head of these vendor offices often has the title of "team leader."

FIGURE
9.1 **Five Types of Teams**

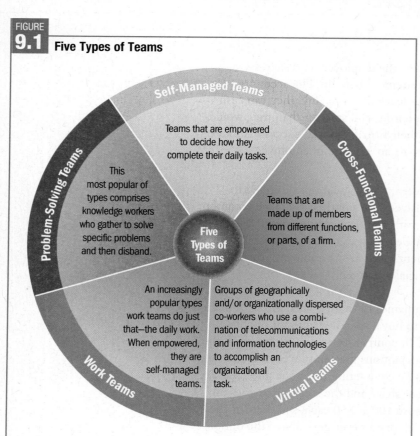

In contrast to work teams, a **problem-solving team** is a temporary combination of workers who gather to solve a specific problem and then disband. They differ from work teams in important ways, though. Work teams are permanent units designed to handle any business problem that arises, but problem-solving teams pursue specific missions. When Toyota was faced with serious quality problems—unintended acceleration, faulty brakes, and then questions about tires—and was forced to recall thousands of vehicles, the company formed Rapid Response Swift Market Analysis Response Teams (SMART) to deal with the technical problems. SMART were made up of field technology specialists, engineers from manufacturing and design, and product engineers from the United States with specialists from Japan on call. Together team members worked with dealers across the country to contact customers and arrange for on-site analyses of each problem vehicle to determine what went wrong and why. Teams were encouraged to "listen and react" to customers' descriptions of their experiences as part of their investigation.[10] Typically when a problem is solved, the team disbands—but in some cases, the team may develop a more permanent role within the firm.

A work team empowered with the authority to decide how its members complete their daily tasks is called a **self-managed team**. A self-managed team works most effectively when it combines employees with a range of skills and functions. Members are cross-trained to perform each other's jobs as needed. Distributing decision-making authority in this way can free members to concentrate on satisfying customers. Whole Foods Market has a structure based on self-managed work teams. Company managers decided that Whole Foods could be most innovative if employees made decisions themselves. Every employee is part of a team, and each store has about ten teams handling separate functions, such as groceries, bakery, and customer service. Each team handles responsibilities related to setting goals, hiring and training employees, scheduling team members, and purchasing goods to stock. Teams meet at least monthly to review goals and performance, solve problems, and explore new ideas. Whole Foods awards bonuses based on the teams' performance relative to their goals.[11]

A team made up of members from different functions, such as production, marketing, and finance, is called a **cross-functional team**. Most often, cross-functional teams work on specific problems or projects, but they can also serve as permanent work team arrangements. The value of cross-functional teams comes from their ability to bring different perspectives—as well as different types of expertise—to a work effort. Communication is key to the success of cross-functional teams. Chatter is a networking tool developed by Salesforce.com that allows internal information sharing across different business units and divisions of companies. Chatter "reduces email traffic, enhances access to internal experts, and encourages cross-functional teams to easily share findings and tools," observes one consultant.[12]

Virtual teams are groups of geographically or organizationally dispersed coworkers who use a combination of telecommunications and information technologies to accomplish an organizational task. Because of the availability of e-mail, videoconferencing, and group communication software, members of virtual teams rarely meet

problem-solving team temporary combination of workers who gather to solve a specific problem and then disband.

self-managed team work team that has the authority to decide how its members complete their daily tasks.

cross-functional team a team made up of members from different functions, such as production, marketing, and finance.

virtual teams group of geographically or organizationally dispersed coworkers who use a combination of telecommunications and information technologies to accomplish an organizational task.

Although members of a virtual team rarely meet in person, they stay in touch through new technologies, like videoconferencing. In today's global marketplace, the flexibility of virtual teams is a distinct advantage.

Image Source/Getty Images

Assessment Check ☑

1. What is a team?

2. What are the five types of teams, and how are they different?

face-to-face. The principal advantage of virtual teams is that they are very flexible. Employees can work with each other regardless of physical location, time zone, or organizational affiliation. Because of their very nature, virtual teams that are scattered across the globe can be difficult to manage. But firms that are committed to them believe that the benefits outweigh the drawbacks.

Team Characteristics

Effective teams share a number of characteristics. They must be an appropriate size to accomplish their work. In addition to size, teams also can be categorized according to the similarities and differences among team members, called *level* and *diversity*. We discuss these three characteristics next.

Team Size

Teams can range in size from as small as 2 people to as large as 150 people. In practice, however, most teams have fewer than 12 members. Although no ideal size limit applies to every team, research on team effectiveness indicates that they achieve their best results with about 6 or 7 members. A group of this size is big enough to benefit from a variety of diverse skills, yet small enough to allow members to communicate easily and feel part of a close-knit group.

Certainly, groups smaller or larger than this can be effective, but they also create added challenges for team leaders. Participants in small teams of two to four members often show a desire to get along with each other. They tend to favor informal interactions marked by discussions of personal topics, and they make only limited demands on team leaders. A large team with more than 12 members poses a different challenge for team leaders because decision making may work slowly and participants may feel less committed to team goals. Larger teams also tend to foster disagreements, absenteeism, and membership turnover. Subgroups may form, leading to possible conflicts among various functions. As a general rule, a team of more than 20 people should be divided into sub-teams, each with its own members and goals.

team level average level of ability, experience, personality, or any other factor on a team.

team diversity variances or differences in ability, experience, personality, or any other factor on a team.

Joe Gough/iStockphoto

Strong teams not only have talented members, but also members who are different in terms of ability, experience, or personality. Team diversity is an important consideration for teams that must complete a wide range of different tasks or particularly complex tasks. For instance, the British Broadcasting Corporation (BBC) routinely creates teams for a variety of events such as the FIFA World Cup or the Olympic Games.

Team Level and Team Diversity

Team level is the average level of ability, experience, personality, or any other factor on a team. Businesses consider team level when they need teams with a particular set of skills or capabilities to do their jobs well. For example, an environmental engineering firm might put together a team with a high level of experience to write a proposal for a large contract.

While team level represents the average level or capability on a team, **team diversity** represents the differences in ability, experience, personality, or any other factor on a

Team Diversity at Ernst & Young

Ernst & Young has seen it all—economic booms and busts, including the recent recession and fallout from the financial industry. But the company that provides tax, transaction, and advisory services is surviving, partly due to a new outlook about the business environment and the way it will operate going forward. One focus will be ways in which its 144,000 employees can contribute their talents more fully to the company's future.

Specifically, Ernst & Young is redefining the way it uses teams. A recent company survey entitled, "The New Global Mindset: Driving Innovation Through Diverse Perspective," revealed that companies operating in 25 or more countries base only 5 percent of their senior leadership in those countries. These companies are failing to make the most of the diverse cultures and ideas that could propel them forward. "The economic crisis has mandated that companies rethink the way they do business," observes James S. Turley, chairman and CEO of Ernst & Young. "Company leaders need to consider how a lack of diverse perspectives—at the top of their organization and at the individual team level—might affect plans for global growth, new products, or mergers and acquisitions."

So Ernst & Young has come up with a blueprint of thought behind its new team diversity. Managers who are planning or leading teams should consider the following:

- *The mindset.* Managers must think about what has to happen in order for a true cultural change to occur within the organization.
- *The talent.* Managers should search every corner of the organization for true talent—it might be in the cafeteria, at an assistant's desk, or in the human resources office.

- *Anticipation.* Creative managers need to use the diverse talents of team members to identify new products and services that could be the next "big thing."
- *Consensus.* Total agreement among team members isn't always necessary—or even the best thing. In fact, disagreement can boost a team's energy and force people to come up with new and better ideas and solutions.

"Innovation comes from constructive clashes of different ideas, and from that, the sparks create some brilliance," says CEO Jim Turley. "It's getting people in the room with different thoughts, who come from different experiences. It's getting all of our people to understand the direction of the world."

Questions for Critical Thinking

1. Why is team diversity so critical for a global firm like Ernst & Young?
2. Based on the nature of its business, at what level would you expect Ernst & Young's teams to operate? Why?

Sources: Luke Visconti, "CEO Chat: E&Y's Leader Tells How Global Diversity Drives Revenue," *Diversity Inc.*, November 1, 2010, http://www.diversityinc.com; Ernst & Young LLP Diversity Award," *BAP Forums,* http://www.bap.org, accessed April 19, 2010; "Diversity Drives Innovation," January 27, 2010, Ernst & Young Web site, http://www.ey.com; James S. Turley, "The New Global Mindset," *Bloomberg BusinessWeek,* January 26, 2010, http://www.businessweek.com; "Ernst & Young LLP Starts 2010 with a Three-Day Event for Minority Students and a Faculty Roundtable Focused on Campus Diversity," *PR Newswire*, January 6, 2010, http://www.printthis.clickability.com.

team. Strong teams not only have talented members—as demonstrated by their team level—but also members who are different in terms of ability, experience, or personality. Team diversity is an important consideration for teams that must complete a wide range of different tasks or particularly complex tasks. For instance, the British Broadcasting Corporation (BBC) routinely creates teams for a variety of events such as the FIFA World Cup or the Olympic Games. These teams involve production and broadcast groups larger than 100 people, many of whom are part-time employees. Team members typically come from more than 15 different countries, with skills ranging from electrician to statistician, or from scheduling to producing. And because an event at any of the sports venues only takes place once, the BBC teams have one chance to get it right.[13] Ernst & Young, a global firm that provides financial services, relies on team diversity, as described in the "Hit & Miss" feature.

Stages of Team Development

Teams typically progress through five stages of development: forming, storming, norming, performing, and adjourning. Although not every team passes through each of these stages, those teams that do are usually better performers. These stages are summarized in Figure 9.2.

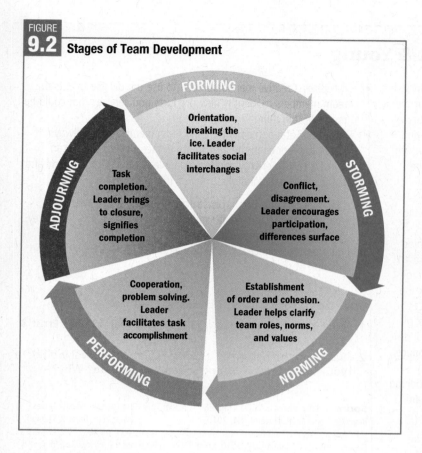

FIGURE
9.2 **Stages of Team Development**

FORMING

Orientation, breaking the ice. Leader facilitates social interchanges

STORMING

Conflict, disagreement. Leader encourages participation, differences surface

ADJOURNING

Task completion. Leader brings to closure, signifies completion

Cooperation, problem solving. Leader facilitates task accomplishment

PERFORMING

Establishment of order and cohesion. Leader helps clarify team roles, norms, and values

NORMING

Stage 1: Forming The forming is an orientation period during which team members get to know each other and find out what behaviors are acceptable to the group. Team members begin with curiosity about expectations of them and whether they will fit in with the group. An effective team leader provides time for members to become acquainted.

Stage 2: Storming The personalities of team members begin to emerge at the storming stage, as members clarify their roles and expectations. Conflicts may arise, as people disagree over the team's mission and jockey for position and control of the group. Subgroups may form based on common interests or concerns. At this stage, the team leader must encourage everyone to participate, allowing members to work through their uncertainties and conflicts. Teams must move beyond this stage to achieve real productivity.

Stage 3: Norming During the norming stage, members resolve differences, accept each other, and reach broad agreement about the roles of the team leader and other participants. This stage is usually brief, and the team leader should use it to emphasize the team's unity and the importance of its objectives.

Stage 4: Performing While performing, members focus on solving problems and accomplishing tasks. They interact frequently and handle conflicts in constructive ways. The team leader encourages contributions from all members. He or she should attempt to get any non-participating team members involved.

Stage 5: Adjourning The team adjourns after members have completed their assigned task or solved the problem. During this phase, the focus is on wrapping up and summarizing the team's experiences and accomplishments. The team leader may recognize the team's accomplishments with a celebration, perhaps handing out plaques or awards.

Team Cohesiveness and Norms

Teams tend to maximize productivity when they form into highly cohesive units. **Team cohesiveness** is the extent to which members feel attracted to the team and motivated to remain part of it. This cohesiveness typically increases when members interact frequently, share common attitudes and goals, and enjoy being together. Cohesive groups have a better chance of retaining their members than those that do not achieve cohesiveness. As a result, cohesive groups typically experience lower turnover. In addition, team cohesiveness promotes cooperative behavior, generosity, and a willingness on the part of team members to help each other. When team cohesiveness is high, team members are more motivated to contribute to the team, because they want the approval of other team members.

Assessment Check ☑

1. Explain team level and team diversity.

2. Explain how teams progress through the stages of team development.

team cohesiveness
extent to which team members feel attracted to the team and motivated to remain part of it.

Not surprisingly, studies have clearly established that cohesive teams quickly achieve high levels of performance and consistently perform better.

Team-building retreats are one way to encourage cohesiveness and improve satisfaction and retention. Firms that specialize in conducting these retreats offer a wide range of options. Sedona Spirit Yoga & Hiking offers yoga, hiking, and other activities geared toward team building surrounded by the red rocks of Arizona.[14] CEO Chef, based in California, offers the option of bringing its team-building program to its clients—which is typically less expensive than a traditional retreat. The culinary team from CEO Chef can travel to an off-site meeting location or to a company's own cafeteria for a team-building exercise in which participants work together to create a gourmet meal—then enjoy eating it.[15]

A **team norm** is a standard of conduct shared by team members that guides their behavior. Norms are not formal written guidelines; they are informal standards that identify key values and clarify team members' expectations. In highly productive teams, norms contribute to constructive work and the accomplishment of team goals. In Illinois, the Rockford Public Schools and Rock Valley College recently formed an alliance to create work teams of high school teachers and college faculty members to draft recommendations for the alignment of coursework so high school students would be better prepared to attend college.[16] In this case, team norms would include standards of conduct during meetings as well as a shared vision for the preparation of students.

Team Conflict

Conflict occurs when one person or group's needs do not match those of another, and attempts may be made to block the opposing side's intentions or goals. Conflict and disagreement are inevitable in most teams. But this shouldn't surprise anyone. People who work together are naturally going to disagree about what and how things are done. What causes conflict in teams? Although almost anything can lead to conflict—casual remarks that unintentionally offend a team member or fighting over scarce resources—the primary cause of team conflict is disagreement over goals and priorities. Other common causes of team conflict include disagreements over task-related issues, interpersonal incompatibilities, simple fatigue, and team diversity.

Earlier in this chapter we noted how teams can experience diversity among members. While diversity brings stimulation, challenge, and energy, it can also lead to conflict. The job of the manager is to create an environment in which differences are appreciated and in which a team of diverse individuals works productively together. Diversity awareness training programs can reduce conflict by bringing these differences out in the open and identifying the unique talents of diverse individuals.

Although most people think conflict should be avoided, management experts note that conflict can actually enhance team performance. The key to dealing with conflict is making sure that the team experiences the right kind of conflict. **Cognitive conflict** focuses on problem-related differences of opinion, and reconciling these differences strongly improves team performance. With cognitive conflict, team members disagree because their different experiences and expertise lead them to different views of the problem and its solutions. Cognitive conflict is also characterized by a willingness to examine, compare, and reconcile differences to produce the best possible solution. By contrast, **affective conflict** refers to the emotional reactions that can occur when disagreements become personal rather than professional, and these differences strongly decrease team performance. Because affective

team norm standard of conduct shared by team members that guides their behavior.

Assessment Check ☑

1. How does cohesiveness affect teams?
2. Explain how team norms positively and negatively affect teams.

conflict when one person or group's needs do not match those of another, and attempts may be made to block the opposing side's intentions or goals.

cognitive conflict disagreement that focuses on problem- and issue-related differences of opinion.

affective conflict disagreement that focuses on individuals or personal issues.

conflict often results in hostility, anger, resentment, distrust, cynicism, and apathy, it can make people uncomfortable, cause them to withdraw, decrease their commitment to a team, lower the satisfaction of team members, and decrease team cohesiveness. So, unlike cognitive conflict, affective conflict undermines team performance by preventing teams from engaging in activities that are critical to team effectiveness.

What can managers do to manage team conflict—and even make it work for them? Perhaps the team leader's most important contribution to conflict resolution can be facilitating good communication so that teammates respect each other and are free to disagree with each other. Ongoing, effective communication ensures that team members perceive each other accurately, understand what is expected of them, and obtain the information they need. Taking this a step further, organizations should evaluate situations or conditions in the workplace that might be causing conflict. Solving a single conflict isn't helpful if there are problems systemic to the team or to the company. Team-building exercises, listening exercises, and role-playing can help employees learn to become better team members.[17]

Assessment Check ✓

1. What is cognitive conflict, and how does it affect teams?

2. Explain affective conflict and its impact on teams.

The Importance of Effective Communication

Countries like China, India, and Mexico are home to businesses that provide goods and services to companies or consumers in the United States. But the more parties involved in the production process, the harder it is to coordinate communication. Toyota Motor Corp. became embroiled in miscommunication when it tried to establish a clear timeline for the reporting of the number of its vehicles that were affected by unintended acceleration worldwide. While the National Highway Traffic Safety Administration (NHTSA) investigated the issue, Toyota continued the recalls over a period of several years, reaching a total of more than 8 million total vehicles recalled.[18]

communication meaningful exchange of information through messages.

Communication can be defined as a meaningful exchange of information through messages. Few businesses can succeed without effective communication. In fact, as illustrated by the Toyota example, miscommunication can result in damage to the company. By the time the NHTSA closed its investigation, Toyota had been ordered to pay more than $16.4 million in fines for miscommunication alone and suffered additional losses related to the recalls and repairs on its vehicles.[19]

Managers spend about 80 percent of their time—6 hours and 24 minutes of every eight-hour day—in direct communication with others, whether on the telephone, in meetings, via e-mail, or in individual conversations. Company recruiters consistently rate effective communication, such as listening, conversing, and giving feedback, as the most important skill they look for when hiring new employees. In this last half of the chapter, you'll learn about the communication process, the basic forms of communication, and ways to improve communication within organizations.

The Process of Communication

Every communication follows a step-by-step process that involves interactions among six elements: sender, message, channel, audience, feedback, and context. This process is illustrated in Figure 9.3.

In the first step, the *sender* composes the message and sends it through a communication carrier, or channel. Encoding a message means that the sender translates its meaning into understandable terms and a form that allows transmission through a chosen channel. The sender can communicate a particular message through many different channels, including face-to-face conversations, phone calls, and e-mail or texting. A promotional message to the firm's customers may be communicated through such forms as radio and television ads, billboards, magazines and newspapers, sales presentations, and social media such as Facebook and Twitter. The audience consists of the people who receive the message. In decoding, the receiver of the message interprets its meaning. Feedback from the audience—in response to the sender's communication—helps the sender determine whether the audience has correctly interpreted the intended meaning of the message.

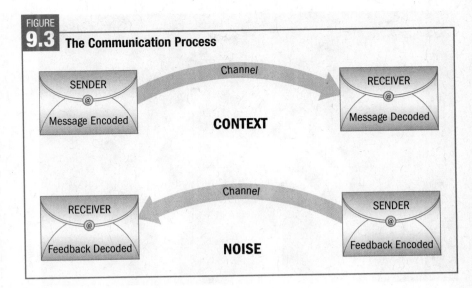

FIGURE 9.3 The Communication Process

Every communication takes place in some sort of situational or cultural context. The *context* can exert a powerful influence on how well the process works. A conversation between two people in a quiet office, for example, may be a very different experience from the same conversation held at a noisy party. An American who orders chips in an English tavern will receive French fries.

Anthropologists classify cultures as low context and high context. Communication in *low-context cultures* tends to rely on explicit written and verbal messages. Examples include Switzerland, Austria, Germany, and the United States. In contrast, communication in *high-context cultures*—such as those of Japan, Latin America, and India—depends not only on the message itself but also on the conditions that surround it, including nonverbal cues, past and present experiences, and personal relationships between the parties. Westerners must carefully temper their low-context style to the expectations of colleagues and clients from high-context countries. Although Americans tend to favor direct interactions and want to "get down to business" soon after shaking hands or sitting down to a business dinner, businesspeople in Mexico and Asian countries prefer to become acquainted before discussing details. When conducting business in these cultures, wise visitors allow time for relaxed meals during which business-related topics are avoided.

Senders must pay attention to audience feedback, even requesting it if none is forthcoming, because this response clarifies whether the communication has conveyed the intended message. Feedback can indicate whether the receiver heard the message and was able to decode it accurately. Even when the receiver tries to understand, the communication may fail if the message contained jargon or ambiguous words.

Noise during the communication process is some type of interference that influences the transmission of messages and feedback. Noise can result from simple physical factors such as poor reception of a cell phone message or static that drowns out a radio commercial. It can also be caused by more complex differences in people's attitudes and perceptions. Consequently, even when people are exposed to the same communications, they can end up with very different perceptions and understandings because of communication noise.

Noise during the communication process can result from simple physical factors such as poor reception of a cell phone message or static that drowns out a radio commercial. Consequently, even when people are exposed to the same communications, they may end up with very different perceptions and understandings because of communication noise.

YanLev/iStockphoto

Noise can be present at any point in the communication process. This is why managers must learn how to cut through noise when communicating with employees. Managers at i-level, a digital communications agency, found a creative way to cut through noise to communicate its plans to transition from a paper-based benefits process to an online system. First they distributed "i" character mugs to office staff. Then they sent messages to employees' mobile phones. Those with iPhones received animated messages. New hires and prospective employees without company phones received a USB stick with the messages. "The communications felt really innovative and it was good using digital media because at the end of the day, that's what we're about as a company," says James Miller, the company's human resource director. "People have found it really good fun and I'm really, really pleased with the concept we have come up with."[20]

Basic Forms of Communication

Managers and coworkers communicate in many different ways—by making a phone call, sending an e-mail, holding a staff meeting, or chatting in the hallway. They also communicate with facial expressions, gestures, and other body language. Subtle variations can significantly influence the reception of a message. As Table 9.2 points out, communication takes various forms: oral and written, formal and informal, and nonverbal.

Oral Communication

Managers spend a lot of time engaged in oral communication, both in person and on the phone. Some people prefer to communicate this way, believing that oral channels more accurately convey messages. Face-to-face oral communication allows people to combine words with such cues as facial expressions and tone of voice. Oral communication over the telephone lacks visual cues, but it does allow people to hear the tone of voice and provide immediate feedback by asking questions or restating the message. Because of its immediacy, oral communication has drawbacks. If one person is agitated or nervous during a conversation, noise enters the communication process. A hurried manager might brush off an employee who has an important message to deliver. A frustrated employee might feel compelled to fire a harsh retort at an unsupportive supervisor instead of thinking before responding.

In any medium, a vital component of oral communication is **listening**—receiving a message and interpreting its genuine meaning by accurately grasping the facts and feeling conveyed. Although listening may be the most important communication skill, most of us don't use it enough—or as well as we should.

listening receiving a message and interpreting its intended meaning by grasping the facts and feelings it conveys.

9.2 Forms of Communication

FORM	DESCRIPTION	EXAMPLES
Oral communication	Communication transmitted through speech	Personal conversations, speeches, meetings, voice mail, telephone conversations, videoconferences
Written communication	Communication transmitted through writing	Letters, memos, formal reports, news releases, e-mail, faxes, online discussion groups, Internet messaging
Formal communication	Communication transmitted through the chain of command within an organization to other members or to people outside the organization	Internal—memos, reports, meetings, written proposals, oral presentations, meeting minutes; external—letters, written proposals, oral presentations, speeches, news releases, press conferences
Informal communication	Communication transmitted outside formal channels without regard for the organization's hierarchy of authority	Rumors spread informally among employees via the grapevine
Nonverbal communication	Communication transmitted through actions and behaviors rather than through words	Gestures, facial expressions, posture, body language, dress, makeup

Listening may seem easy, because the listener appears to make no effort. But the average person talks at a rate of roughly 150 words per minute, while the brain can handle up to 400 words per minute. This gap can lead to boredom, inattention, and misinterpretation. In fact, immediately after listening to a message, the average person can recall only half of it. After several days, the proportion of a message that a listener can recall falls to 25 percent or less.

Certain types of listening behaviors are common in both business and personal interactions:

- *Cynical or defensive listening.* This type of listening occurs when the receiver of a message feels that the sender is trying to gain some advantage from the communication.

- *Offensive listening.* In this type of listening, the receiver tries to catch the speaker in a mistake or contradiction.

- *Polite listening.* In this mechanical type of listening, the receiver listens to be polite rather than to contribute to communication. Polite listeners are usually inattentive and spend their time rehearsing what they want to say when the speaker finishes.

- *Active listening.* This form of listening requires involvement with the information and empathy with the speaker's situation. In both business and personal life, active listening is the basis for effective communication.

Learning how to be an active listener is an especially important goal for business leaders because effective communication is essential to their role. Listening is hard work, but it pays off with increased learning, better interpersonal relationships, and greater influence.[21] Both managers and employees can develop skills to make them better listeners, as described in the "Business Etiquette" feature.

Written Communication

Listening may seem easy, because the listener appears to make no effort. But the average person talks at a rate of roughly 150 words per minute, while the brain can handle up to 400 words per minute. This gap can lead to boredom, inattention, and misinterpretation.

Channels for written communication include reports, letters, memos, online discussion boards and social media, e-mails, and text messages. Many of these channels permit only delayed feedback and create a record of the message. So it is important for the sender of a written communication to prepare the message carefully and review it to avoid misunderstandings—particularly before pressing that "send" button.

Effective written communication reflects its audience, the channel carrying the message, and the appropriate degree of formality. When writing a formal business document such as a complex marketing research report, a manager must plan in advance and carefully construct the document. The process of writing a formal document involves planning, research, organization, composition and design, and revision. Written communication via e-mail may call for a less-formal writing style, including short sentences, phrases, and lists.

E-mail is a very effective communication channel, especially for delivering straightforward messages and information. But e-mail's effectiveness also leads to its biggest problem: too much e-mail! Many workers find their valuable time being consumed with e-mail. To relieve this burden and leave more time for performing the most important aspects of the job, some companies are looking into ways to reduce the time employees spend sending and reading e-mail. To fulfill this need, there are now firms that provide e-mail management services. One such company is DakotaPro.biz, which provides customized e-mail solutions for firms that have been struggling to keep up with the volume of e-mail they receive and the time it takes to operate an in-house server.[22]

Other e-mail issues are security and retention. Because e-mail messages are often informal, senders occasionally forget that they are creating a written record. Even if the recipient deletes an e-mail message, other copies exist on company e-mail servers. E-mails on company servers can be used as evidence in a legal case or disciplinary action.

Formal Communication

A *formal communication channel* carries messages that flow within the chain of command structure defined by an organization. The most familiar channel, downward communication, carries messages from someone who holds a senior position in the organization to subordinates. Managers may communicate downward by sending employees e-mail messages, presiding at department meetings, giving employees policy manuals, posting notices on bulletin boards, and reporting news in company newsletters. The most important factor in formal communication is to be open and honest. "Spinning" bad news to make it look better almost always backfires. In a work environment characterized by open communication, employees feel free to express opinions, offer suggestions, and even voice complaints. Research has shown that open communication has the following seven characteristics:

1. *Employees are valued.* Employees are happier and more motivated when they feel they are valued and their opinions are heard.

2. *A high level of trust exists.* Telling the truth maintains a high level of trust; this forms the foundation for open communication and employee motivation and retention.

3. *Conflict is invited and resolved positively.* Without conflict, innovation and creativity are stifled.

4. *Creative dissent is welcomed.* By expressing unique ideas, employees feel they have contributed to the company and improved performance.

5. *Employee input is solicited.* The key to any company's success is input from employees, which establishes a sense of involvement and improves working relations.

6. *Employees are well informed.* Employees are kept informed about what is happening within the organization.

7. *Feedback is ongoing.* Both positive and negative feedback must be ongoing and provided in a manner that builds relationships rather than assigns blame.[23]

Many firms also define formal channels for upward communications. These channels encourage communication from employees to supervisors and upward to top management levels. Some examples of upward communication channels are employee surveys, suggestion boxes, and systems that allow employees to propose ideas for new products or voice complaints. Upward communication is also necessary for managers to evaluate the effectiveness of downward communication. Figure 9.4 illustrates the forms of organizational communication, both formal and informal.

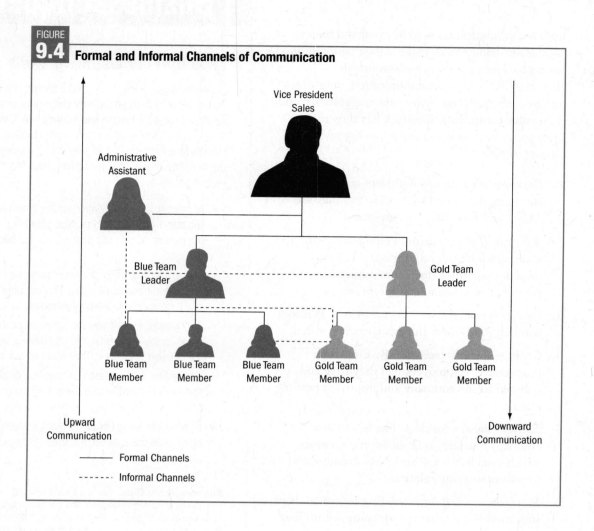

FIGURE 9.4 Formal and Informal Channels of Communication

Vice President Sales

Administrative Assistant

Blue Team Leader

Gold Team Leader

Blue Team Member

Blue Team Member

Blue Team Member

Gold Team Member

Gold Team Member

Gold Team Member

Upward Communication

Downward Communication

——— Formal Channels

------- Informal Channels

Informal Communication

grapevine internal information channel that transmits information from unofficial sources.

Informal communication channels carry messages outside formally authorized channels within an organization's hierarchy. A familiar example of an informal channel is the **grapevine**, an internal channel that passes information from unofficial sources. All organizations, large or small, have grapevines. Grapevines disseminate information with speed and economy and are surprisingly reliable. But company communications must be managed effectively so that the grapevine is not the main source of information. When properly nurtured, the grapevine can help managers get a feel for the morale of companies, understand the anxieties of the workforce, and evaluate the effectiveness of formal communications. Managers can improve the quality of information circulating through the company grapevine by sharing what they know, even if it is preliminary or partial information. By feeding information to selected people, smart leaders can harness the power of the grapevine.

Gossip—which usually travels along the grapevine—is the main drawback of this communication channel. Because gossip can spread misinformation quickly—particularly if it reaches the Internet—a manager should deal directly with the gossiper so the grapevine can become a legitimate source of information once again. Conversely, employees can nurture informal communication by taking the time to learn more about the communication needs of their managers.[24]

As organizations become more decentralized and more globally dispersed, informal communication—more than ever before—provides an important source of information, through e-mail, texting, and social media.

Nonverbal Communication

So far, this section has considered different forms of verbal communication, or communication that conveys meaning through words. Equally important is *nonverbal communication*, which transmits messages through actions and behaviors. Gestures, posture, eye contact, tone and volume of voice, and even clothing choices are all nonverbal actions that become communication cues. Nonverbal cues can have a far greater impact on communications than many people realize. In fact, it is estimated that 70 percent of interpersonal communication is conveyed through nonverbal cues. Top salespeople are particularly adept at reading and using these cues. For example, they practice "mirroring" a customer's gestures and body language in order to indicate agreement.[25]

Even personal space—the physical distance between people who are engaging in communication—can convey powerful messages. Figure 9.5 shows a continuum of personal space and social interaction with four zones: intimate, personal, social, and public. In the United States, most business conversations occur within the social zone, roughly between 4 and 12 feet apart. If one person tries to approach closer than that, the other will likely feel uncomfortable or even threatened.

Interpreting nonverbal cues can be especially challenging for people with different cultural backgrounds. Concepts of appropriate personal space differ dramatically throughout most of the world. Latin Americans conduct business discussions in positions that most Americans and northern Europeans would find uncomfortably close. Americans often back away to preserve their personal space, a gesture that Latin Americans perceive as a sign of

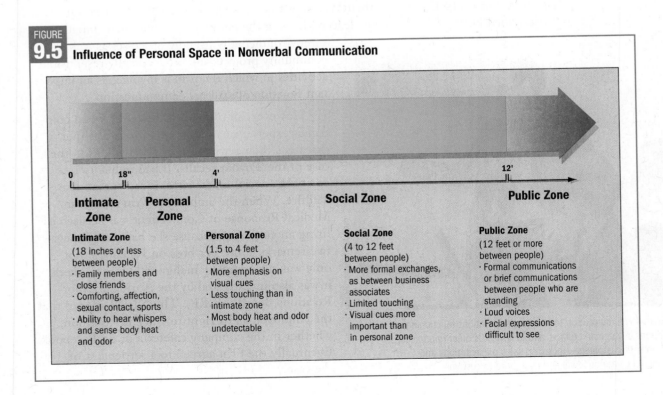

FIGURE 9.5 Influence of Personal Space in Nonverbal Communication

0	18"	4'		12'
Intimate Zone	**Personal Zone**	**Social Zone**		**Public Zone**

Intimate Zone
(18 inches or less between people)
· Family members and close friends
· Comforting, affection, sexual contact, sports
· Ability to hear whispers and sense body heat and odor

Personal Zone
(1.5 to 4 feet between people)
· More emphasis on visual cues
· Less touching than in intimate zone
· Most body heat and odor undetectable

Social Zone
(4 to 12 feet between people)
· More formal exchanges, as between business associates
· Limited touching
· Visual cues more important than in personal zone

Public Zone
(12 feet or more between people)
· Formal communications or brief communications between people who are standing
· Loud voices
· Facial expressions difficult to see

cold and unfriendly relations. To protect their personal space, some Americans separate themselves across desks or tables from their Latin American counterparts—at the risk of challenging their colleagues to maneuver around those obstacles to reduce the uncomfortable distance.

People send nonverbal messages even when they consciously try to avoid doing so. Sometimes nonverbal cues convey a person's true attitudes and thoughts, which may differ from spoken meanings. Generally, when verbal and nonverbal cues conflict, receivers of the communication tend to believe the nonverbal content. This is why firms seeking to hire people with good attitudes and a team orientation closely watch nonverbal behavior during job interviews in which job applicants participate in group sessions with other job candidates applying for the same job. If in those group interviews an applicant frowns or looks discouraged when a competing candidate gives a good answer, that nonverbal behavior suggests that this person may not be strongly team oriented.

Assessment Check ☑

1. Define the four common listening behaviors.
2. What are the differences between formal and informal communication?

external communication meaningful exchange of information through messages transmitted between an organization and its major audiences.

External Communication and Crisis Management

External communication is a meaningful exchange of information through messages transmitted between an organization and its major audiences, such as customers, suppliers, other firms, the general public, and government officials. Businesses use external communication to keep their operations functioning, to maintain their positions in the marketplace, and to build customer relationships by supplying information about topics such as product modifications and price changes. Every communication with customers—including sales presentations and advertisements—should create goodwill and contribute to customer satisfaction. Firms like Clorox use their Web sites to publish good news about the company, as described in the "Going Green" feature. Letting the public know about new initiatives for environmentally friendly processes as well as community projects and other socially responsible activities in which the firm is involved is an important function of external communication.

However, all of this is threatened when companies experience a public relations crisis that threatens their reputation or goodwill, as in the case of the Toyota recalls. If bad publicity hits any of the social media sites, it can spread like wildfire. When the ambulance firm American Medical Response of Connecticut was accused of firing an employee because she had posted negative remarks about her boss on Facebook, not only was the company maligned by the workers, it was also investigated by the National Labor Relations Board (NLRB). The NLRB alleged that the employee had a right to voice her opinion, whether in the company cafeteria or on Facebook. Eventually the firm agreed to a settlement of the case.[26]

Businesses use external communication to keep their operations functioning, to maintain their positions in the marketplace, and to build customer relationships. Every communication with customers—including sales presentations and advertisements—should create goodwill and contribute to customer satisfaction.

Yuri Arcurs/iStockphoto

Going Green

Clorox Comes Clean—Naturally

You've probably seen the Green Works brand of household and commercial cleaning solutions at your local supermarket—but you might not know that this line of natural, environmentally responsible cleaners is manufactured by the same people who make bleach. Clorox has committed itself wholeheartedly to ambitious initiatives aimed at reducing its impact on the environment through its manufacturing processes and the ingredients in its products. To accomplish this, the firm has established a department of Environmental Sustainability Strategy and an Eco Office. Its line of Green Works products meets strict environmental standards for ingredients, fragrances, packaging, and manufacturing processes. In addition, Clorox is working on similar efforts toward improving its traditional products.

One of the first bits of external communication about its new focus on product ingredients was literally a list of ingredients, so consumers would have more information about the products they were buying. The list has grown in detail—Clorox now provides more detailed information about its safety processes, guidelines used to screen ingredients, and data on fragrances (a major component of cleaning solutions). Clorox asks all of its fragrance suppliers to adhere to increasingly strict fragrance standards in the development of new products. In fact, Clorox is the first major consumer packaged goods company to go to such lengths to communicate to consumers exactly what its products contain and how they are made.

In order to spread the word farther, Clorox recently launched its own Corporate Social Responsibility (CSR) Web site that contains a wealth of information about its processes and products. The site is easy to navigate, offers access to a complete listing of product ingredients, and provides a comprehensive glossary of terms so consumers fully understand the function of each ingredient used in a product. Though the Web site is currently entirely in English, Clorox has plans for French and Spanish versions of the product ingredient section of the site.

Reaching even skeptical audiences, Clorox has gained the trust of the Sierra Club, with whom it has begun to partner on some of its programs. Together, Clorox and the Sierra Club trumpet the benefits of green cleaning. "Clorox is continuing to demonstrate the kind of progress we need companies to make," notes Sierra Club Chairman Carl Pope. "Since we began working with them on the Green Works brand, we've seen their commitment to important areas such as product innovation, ingredient communication, environmental stewardship and the transition to eliminate chlorine transportation from their U.S. supply chain. We applaud their approach to becoming even more open in communicating about their business practices and CSR commitments."

Questions for Critical Thinking

1. Clorox uses its CSR Web site to publish information and news about its green processes and products. How might the company use a social network such as Facebook to broaden its online external communication?

2. Do you think there is a downside to using the Internet for this type of communication? Why or why not?

Sources: Clorox Web site, "Corporation Responsibility," http://www.cloroxcsr.com, accessed March 3, 2011; "2010 Best Companies for America's Children," *Working Mother*, http://www.workingmother.com, accessed April 29, 1010; "Clorox's New CSR Web Site Features Upgraded 'Ingredients Inside' Product Information," *CSRwire*, February 1, 2010, http://www.csrwire.com.

How companies like Toyota or American Medical Response handle such events can determine whether its reputation can be restored. Putting together a plan of action and dealing with facts and rumors immediately could be the difference between regaining trust and disaster. The following communication steps can help calm a public relations crisis:

1. When a crisis occurs, a firm should respond quickly. Executives should prepare a written statement—and stick to it. The statement should mention the time, place, initial description of what occurred (not the cause), and the number and status of the people involved.

2. As soon as possible, top company management should appear in public—if possible, to the press. Because the public will hold top management accountable, it's best to have top managers responding to reporters' questions.

3. When answering questions at an initial press conference or in an interview, the management representative must stick to the facts. It's likely that details about the event, the cause, and people's roles will not yet be known; the spokesperson shouldn't speculate. As information becomes available, the firm can provide accurate updates.

4. If a question is currently unanswerable, the executive can offer to find out the answer, which should be delivered in a timely manner. It's not advisable to answer a question by saying, "No comment." It's much better to say, "I don't know."

5. The firm should acknowledge problems, explain solutions, and welcome feedback. If a question or factual statement puts the organization in a negative light, the manager should acknowledge the problem, and then explain how the firm is correcting it.

6. The press conference or interview will be most effective if the executive speaks briefly, clearly and provides positive visual images.[27]

Crises faced by firms such as Toyota and American Medical Response are generally exacerbated by widespread criticism on social media sites. By the time they have a chance to reply, the damage to their reputations is significant. Although the NHTSA has ended its probe of Toyota, the automaker continues to deal with negative publicity. American Medical Response has tried to bolster its image with news releases that create a positive image, such as information for consumers on how to prepare for cold winter temperatures and the warning signs of a heart attack. Management experts warn that companies should take the proliferation of social media seriously.[28]

What's Ahead

Today's consumers expect the products they buy to be of the highest value for the price. Firms ensure this value by developing efficient systems for producing goods and services, as well as maintaining high quality. The next chapter examines the ways in which businesses produce world-class goods and services, efficiently organize their production facilities, purchase what they need to produce their goods and services, and manage large inventories to maximize efficiency and reduce costs.

Assessment Check ✔

1. What is external communication?

2. What is the first thing a company should do when a public crisis occurs?

Summary of Learning Objectives

⌈1⌉ Describe why and how organizations empower employees.

Managers empower employees by giving them the authority and responsibility to make decisions about their work. Empowerment seeks to tap the brainpower of all workers to find improved ways of doing their jobs, better serving customers, and achieving organizational goals. Empowerment often includes linking rewards to company performance through employee stock ownership plans (ESOPs) and stock options.

Assessment Check Answers ✔

1.1 What is empowerment? Empowerment is giving employees authority and responsibility to make decisions about their work without traditional managerial approval and control.

1.2 What kinds of information can companies provide employees to help them share decision-making responsibility? Sharing information about company performance, particularly financial performance, is one of the best ways to share decision-making responsibility.

1.3 How do employee stock ownership plans and stock options reward employees and encourage empowerment? Employee stock ownership plans (ESOPs) benefit employees by giving them ownership stakes in their companies. Employees are motivated to work harder and smarter than they would without ESOPs because they share in their firm's financial success. In contrast to an ESOP, in which the company holds stock for the benefit of employees (when employees leave the company, they cash in their stock), stock options give employees a chance to own the stock themselves if they exercise their options by completing the stock purchase.

2 Distinguish among the five types of teams in the workplace.

The five basic types of teams are work teams, problem-solving teams, self-managed teams, cross-functional teams, and virtual teams. Work teams are permanent groups of coworkers who perform the day-to-day tasks necessary to operate the organization. Problem-solving teams are temporary groups of employees who gather to solve specific problems and then disband. Self-managed teams have the authority to make decisions about how their members complete their daily tasks. Cross-functional teams are made up of members from different units, such as production, marketing, and finance. Virtual teams are groups of geographically or organizationally dispersed coworkers who use a combination of telecommunications and information technologies to accomplish an organizational task.

Assessment Check Answers ✓

2.1 What is a team? A team is a group of employees who are committed to a common purpose, approach, and set of performance goals.

2.2 What are the five types of teams, and how are they different? Work teams are permanent, while problem-solving teams are temporary. Unlike work teams, self-managed teams have the authority to change how they get their work done. Cross-functional teams are composed of people from different backgrounds, while virtual teams are composed of people from different locations.

3 Identify the characteristics of an effective team, and summarize the stages of team development.

Three important characteristics of a team are its size, team level, and team diversity. The ideal team size is about six or seven members. Team level is the average level of ability, experience, personality, or any other factor on a team. Team diversity represents the variances or differences in ability, experience, personality, or any other factor on a team. Team diversity is an important consideration for teams that must complete a wide range of different tasks of particularly complex tasks. Teams pass through five stages of development: (1) Forming is an orientation period during which members get to know each other and find out what behaviors are acceptable to the group. (2) Storming is the stage during which individual personalities emerge as members clarify their roles and expectations. (3) Norming is the stage at which differences are resolved, members accept each other, and consensus emerges about the roles of the team leader and other participants. (4) Performing is characterized by problem solving and a focus on task accomplishment. (5) Adjourning is the final stage, with a focus on wrapping up and summarizing the team's experiences and accomplishments.

Assessment Check Answers ✓

3.1 Explain team level and team diversity. While team level represents the average level or capability on a team,

team diversity represents the variances or differences in ability, experience, personality, or any other factor on a team.

3.2 Explain how teams progress through the stages of team development. Teams pass through five stages of development: forming, storming, norming, performing, and adjourning.

4 Relate team cohesiveness and norms to effective team performance.

Team cohesiveness is the extent to which team members feel attracted to the team and motivated to remain on it. Team norms are standards of conduct shared by team members that guide their behavior. Highly cohesive teams whose members share certain standards of conduct tend to be more productive and effective.

Assessment Check Answers ✓

4.1 How does cohesiveness affect teams? Members of cohesive teams interact more often, share common attitudes and goals, have higher morale, and are more likely to help each other. Cohesive teams also perform better.

4.2 Explain how team norms positively and negatively affect teams. Norms are informal standards that identify key values and clarify team members' expectations. But those norms can be positive or negative. Positive norms contribute to constructive work and the accomplishment of team goals. Negative norms can, for example, contribute to reduced work effort, reduced quality, and poor job attendance.

5 Describe the factors that can cause conflict in teams and ways to manage conflict.

Conflict and disagreement are inevitable in most teams. Conflict can stem from many sources: disagreements about goals and priorities, task-related issues, interpersonal incompatibilities, scarce resources, and simple fatigue. The key to dealing with team conflict is not avoiding it, but making sure that the team experiences the right kind of conflict. Cognitive conflict focuses on problem-related differences of opinion and, when reconciled, strongly improves team performance. By contrast, affective conflict refers to the emotional reactions that can occur when disagreements become personal rather than professional, and these differences strongly decrease team performance. A team leader can manage team conflict by fostering good communication so team members perceive each other accurately, understand what is expected of them, and obtain the information they need.

Assessment Check Answers ✓

5.1 What is cognitive conflict, and how does it affect teams? With cognitive conflict, team members disagree because their different experiences and expertise lead them to different views of the problem and its solutions. Cognitive conflict is characterized by a willingness to examine, compare, and reconcile differences to produce the best possible solution.

5.2 Explain affective conflict and its impact on teams.
Because affective conflict often results in hostility, anger, resentment, distrust, cynicism, and apathy, it can make people uncomfortable, cause them to withdraw, decrease their commitment to a team, lower the satisfaction of team members, and decrease team cohesiveness.

⌐6⌐ Explain the importance and process of effective communication.

Managers spend about 80 percent of their time in direct communication with others. Company recruiters consistently rate effective communication—such as listening, conversing, and giving feedback—as the most important skill they look for when hiring new employees. The communication process follows a step-by-step process that involves interactions among six elements: sender, message, channel, audience, feedback, and context. The sender composes the message and sends it through the channel. The audience receives the message and interprets its meaning. The receiver gives feedback to the sender. The communication takes place in a situational or cultural context.

Assessment Check Answers ✓

6.1 What is the difference between communication in low-context and high-context cultures? Communication in low-context cultures tends to rely on explicit written and verbal messages. By contrast, communication in high-context cultures depends not only on the message itself but also on the conditions that surround it, including nonverbal cues, past and present experiences, and personal relationships between the parties.

6.2 In the context of the communication process, what is noise? Noise interferes with the transmission of messages and feedback. Noise can result from physical factors such as poor reception of a cell phone message or differences in people's attitudes and perceptions.

⌐7⌐ Compare the different types of communication.

People exchange messages in many ways: oral and written, formal and informal, verbal and nonverbal communication. Effective written communication reflects its audience, its channel, and the appropriate degree of formality. Formal communication channels carry messages within the chain of command. Informal communication channels, such as the grapevine, carry messages outside the formal chain of command. Nonverbal communication plays a larger role than most people realize. Generally, when verbal and nonverbal cues conflict, the receiver of a message tends to believe the meaning conveyed by nonverbal cues.

Assessment Check Answers ✓

7.1 Define the four common listening behaviors. Cynical listening occurs when the receiver of a message feels that the sender is trying to gain some advantage from the communication. Offensive listening occurs when the receiver tries to catch the speaker in a mistake or contradiction. Polite listening occurs when the receiver is rehearsing what he or she wants to say when the speaker finishes. Active listening requires involvement with the information and empathy with the speaker's situation.

7.2 What are the differences between formal and informal communication? Formal communication occurs within the formal chain of command defined by an organization. Informal communication occurs outside the organization's hierarchy.

⌐8⌐ Explain external communication and methods of managing a public crisis.

External communication is a meaningful exchange of information through messages transmitted between an organization and its major audiences, such as customers, suppliers, other firms, the general public, and government officials. Every communication with customers should create goodwill and contribute to customer satisfaction. However, all of this is threatened when companies experience a public crisis that threatens their reputations or goodwill. To manage a public crisis, businesses should respond quickly and honestly, with a member of top management present.

Assessment Check Answers ✓

8.1 What is external communication? External communication is a meaningful exchange of information through messages transmitted between an organization and its major audiences.

8.2 What is the first thing a company should do when a public crisis occurs? The firm should respond quickly by preparing a written statement that includes the time, place, description of the event, and the number and status of people involved.

■ Business Terms You Need to Know

empowerment 286	cross-functional	team cohesiveness 294	communication 296
team 290	team 291	team norm 295	listening 298
work teams 290	virtual teams 291	conflict 295	grapevine 302
problem-solving team 291	team level 292	cognitive conflict 295	external
self-managed team 291	team diversity 292	affective conflict 295	communication 304

Review Questions

1. How do companies benefit from empowering their employees? How do employees benefit from empowerment?

2. How might a firm that manufactures shoes use teams to determine ways to improve its environmental standards in terms of products and processes? What type (or types) of teams would be best for this initiative? Why?

3. How do team level and team diversity affect team performance?

4. What are the characteristics of an effective team? Why are these features so significant?

5. At what stages of development might a team not be able to move forward? How might a team leader or manager resolve the situation?

6. Describe the norms associated with your business class. How do these norms influence the way you behave?

7. What steps can managers take to manage team conflict?

8. In what ways is context a powerful influence on the effectiveness of communication? Describe an instance in which situational or cultural context influenced one of your communication processes.

9. What are the benefits and drawbacks of oral and written communication?

10. What is the role of external communication? Why is it so important to companies?

Projects and Teamwork Applications

1. Having the power and authority to make decisions about work is the essence of empowerment. For this project, the teacher steps back and gives the class free rein to plan and implement a day of classwork. The class might appoint a leader, divide into teams (to plan a lecture, come up with an assignment, plan a field trip, and the like). It's completely up to the students how to organize and conduct the one-day class. After the class, discuss the experience—including the upside and downside (if any) of empowerment.

2. Divide the class into teams of relatively equal size. Each team may select one of the following problems it intends to solve, or decide on one of its own: arranging for a certain speaker or expanding the vegetarian menu in the cafeteria. While it is not necessary to complete the entire problem-solving process, each team should go through the forming stage of team development and establish norms during which it outlines a plan for accomplishing the group's task. Is each team cohesive? Why or why not?

3. Try this listening exercise with a partner. First, spend a few minutes writing a paragraph or two about the most

important thing that happened to you this week. Second, read your paragraph out loud to your partner. Next, have your partner read his or her paragraph. Finally, each take turns summarizing the most important points in each other's stories. See how well you listened to each other.

4. On your own or with a classmate, visit the college library, mall, or anywhere else people gather. For about 10 or 15 minutes, observe the nonverbal cues that people give each other: Does the librarian smile at students? What is the body language of students gathered in groups? When you leave the venue, jot down as many of your observations as you can. Notice things like changes in nonverbal communication when someone joins a group or leaves it.

5. Choose a company with which you are familiar, or whose products you use. Research the company's offerings as well as some of its socially responsible and sustainability initiatives (e.g., if the firm has set a goal to reduce its energy consumption by 20 percent). Create an advertisement that focuses on one of these initiatives as an example of positive external communication from the company.

Web Assignments

1. **Team-building exercises.** The Web site Teampedia is "a collaborative encyclopedia of free team building activities, free icebreakers, teamwork resources, and tools for teams that anyone can edit!" You want to select a team-building exercise to help break down stereotypes. What are some of the suggested activities?

   http://www.teampedia.net/wiki/index.php?title=Main_Page

2. **Writing better business letters.** Assume you'd like to improve your business letter writing ability. Using a search engine, such as Google or Bing, search the Web for sites with tips and suggestions to improve letter writing skills.

(An example is shown here.) Select two of these sites and review the material. Prepare a brief summary.

http://www.askoxford.com/betterwriting/letterwriting/?view=uk

3. **Employee stock ownership plans.** Visit the Web site of the ESOP Association (http://www.esopassociation.org). Click on "use of ESOP." Print out the material and bring it to class to participate in a class discussion on employee stock ownership plans.

Note: Internet Web addresses change frequently. If you don't find the exact sites listed, you may need to access the organization's home page and search from there or use a search engine such as Bing or Google.

Over the years, thousands of Orlando's SeaWorld visitors have been enthralled by the skilled antics of resident whales and their trainers. Most people recognize that at least some risk to the whales' trainers is involved, partly because of the gigantic size and strength of these mammals. But no one expected the tragedy that unfolded when a veteran trainer was yanked into the water by her pony tail by one of her favorite partners, Tilikum the Orca whale. Within moments, the trainer lost her life.

SeaWorld faced a huge public crisis in which communication would prove to be crucial. The company was immediately bombarded with demands for answers. Were consumers in danger? Should all of SeaWorld be shut down? The fate of Tilikum ("Tilly") was called into question—should he be safely quarantined or put down? Were there other, equally dangerous animals performing at the theme park? All of these questions were overshadowed by the fact that SeaWorld, including its managers and employees, had lost a beloved colleague.

SeaWorld immediately halted all Orca whale shows at its Orlando location as well as its sister parks in San Antonio and San Diego while details of the tragedy were reviewed. Although Orlando SeaWorld President Dan Brown held a press conference shortly after the event, crisis experts pointed out that he faltered when he didn't correct the local sheriff's spokesman, who stated that the trainer had accidentally fallen into the water alongside the whale. Brown only said, "She drowned in an incident with one of our killer whales." When it was later revealed that Tilly had actually pulled the trainer into the water, Brown's credibility was tainted. Once the discrepancy was cleared up, SeaWorld made its head trainer available to answer further questions posed by the press and explain more thoroughly SeaWorld's training methods.

SeaWorld fielded accusations and attacks from all sides—from frightened families to animal rights advocates. As rumors began to swirl about Tilly's rambunctious history and his ultimate fate, it became apparent that there would be no easy solution. "If [SeaWorld] were to make even the slightest hint or suggestion that [Tilly] should be put down, I can only imagine the backlash that would come from animal rights groups from around the world on that one," observed Steve Huxter, the former head trainer at Sealand of the Pacific, where Tilly lived before being transferred to SeaWorld.

Meanwhile, another wave was gathering to sweep across SeaWorld's shore—this time in the form of Facebook and Twitter. SeaWorld was one of the early big companies to recognize the value of direct interaction with its customers by establishing a Facebook site and Twitter account. Both accounts were now deluged with comments from worried fans and barbs from critics. Eventually SeaWorld was forced to shut down its Facebook wall temporarily because of reportedly inappropriate photos relating to the tragedy. And @Shamu, the popular Twitter blog "ghostwritten" by Shamu the whale, was silenced.

But the Facebook site was reactivated shortly thereafter, and SeaWorld spokesman Fred Jacobs encouraged people to revisit it. He said that SeaWorld only censors postings that contain profanity or harassment, or would be insensitive to the trainer's family and friends. "If you were to get on Facebook right now and ask a question about the morality of keeping whales in captivity, we'll get back to you," Jacobs promised. "Now is not the time to circle the wagons. There's a value proposition between a company and the people who follow it on social media." While some people were skeptical about the wisdom of opening itself up to so much direct interaction with the public, SeaWorld officials were firm in their stance: this was their cue to listen.

Questions for Critical Thinking

1. How might SeaWorld's Dan Brown have better handled his initial press conference after the accident?

2. Going forward, how might SeaWorld use social media to heal and strengthen its relationship with the public?

Sources: "New Details About Whale Attack Responsible for SeaWorld Trainer's Death," *Radar,* March 1, 2010, http://www.radaronline.com; Laura Wides-Munoz, "SeaWorld Faces Major Public Relations Challenge," *The Examiner,* February 26, 2010, http://www.washingtonexaminer.com; Larry Rice, "Trainer: Orca Whale's Instinct Was to Play," *MyNorthwest.com,* February 26, 2010, http://www.mynorthwest.com; Beth Kassab, "Shamu Attack Exposes Social Media Risks," *OrlandoSentinel.com,* February 25, 2010, http://www.orlandosentinel.com.

Team building has become an industry unto itself—as more managers understand the importance of fostering strong, effective teams, companies that specialize in creative way to build teams. Chicago's Windy City Fieldhouse is one such firm. Even the name sounds like fun and games, and that's the intention.

Windy City Fieldhouse (WCF) develops and offers its corporate clients programs designed to bring people together in such a way that they don't even realize they are engaging in team-building and communication exercises. The WCF staff hosts outdoor corporate picnics, fun runs/walks, carnivals and block parties, even Grand Prix racing events. Of course, if a client wants a more traditional training program, WCF will do that too—but most companies go for the fun. "Striving to provide programs that enhance meaningful relationships and add tremendous value, WCF continues to develop a variety of corporate event packages in order to respond to its clients' needs," states the Web site.

WCF is perhaps best known for its "Scavenger Hunts in Chicago" (SHIC) division, which custom designs "Mission Impossible" scavenger hunts around the Chicago area for client teams. SHIC creates, organizes, and leads the corporate event in such a way that teams must collaborate to solve clues used to reach a destination chosen by the client company. The destination can be anything from a cocktail party to dinner at a Chicago Cubs game—it's up to the client. A Scavenger Hunt facilitator is provided for each team, and once they reach their final destination,

team members must complete certain missions such as taking funny photographs or finding special objects. With a facilitator acting as team leader, "Mission Impossible" team members learn how to set goals, establish norms, and make the most of diversity.

The response from participants is nearly always enthusiastic. "The feedback from my team was overwhelmingly positive," says one client. Another reports, "It has been a long time since this team has had a team gathering and when they did, we never had this much participation. Everyone really enjoyed the event." Windy City Fieldhouse is certainly on to something—the firm has been named "Best Teambuilding Company" in Chicago for three straight years.

Questions for Critical Thinking

1. Imagine that you had an opportunity to participate in one of SHIC's scavenger hunts. How do you think you would benefit from the experience as a team member?

2. Why is it important for SHIC to provide a facilitator for each team-building experience?

Sources: "Who Is Scavenger Hunts in Chicago?" and "Client Testimonials," Company Web site, http://www.scavengerhuntsinchicago .com, accessed March 8, 2011; "Scavenger Hunts in Chicago," *Here's Chicago*, http://www.hereschicago.com, accessed March 8, 2011; Toddi Gutner, "Applicants' Personalities Put to the Test," *Previsor*, http://www.previsor.com, accessed March 8, 2011.

The hotel and restaurant industry caters to its guests, but it has always had a reputation for being somewhat inhospitable to its employees. Traditionally, hotel and restaurant workers put in long hours for low pay and little or no recognition; they're the invisible hosts who fluff the pillows and sweep away crumbs. But Kimpton Hotels is setting a new example by treating its employees as something better than family: they are, in many ways, business partners.

Kimpton Hotels was founded in 1981 by Bill Kimpton, an investment banker with a vision for boutique hotels: small, luxurious hotels with impeccably intimate service and gourmet restaurants. Today, Kimpton operates 50 hotels and restaurants around the country, each beautifully designed and furnished. "But more than that," notes COONikiLeondakis, "the people really separate us" from other hotels. As COO, Leondakis knows first-hand the difference at Kimpton. Leondakis talks about her company's full-blown commitment to empowering employees to make decisions, to take part in running the business, to grow as professionals. "The employee of today wants more and expects more, and is not willing just to be a servant, loyal worker, or soldier," she says. Leondakis is proud of that fact and of the army of top-flight employees and managers who work at Kimpton's various locations.

One of those managers is Peggy Trott, the general manager of the Kimpton Hotel Palomar in Philadelphia. Trott explains how Kimpton empowers its employees. "Kimpton wants each general manager to be an entrepreneur," she says. "They want you to operate your hotel as if it is your own business. So there's a lot of leeway." While some managers might argue that this puts undue pressure on them to perform as business owners, Trott views the challenge as an opportunity. She notes that the attitude toward empowerment travels from the top down in the organization. She says that each of her employees is charged with being a hero every day, especially when it comes to guest service. If an employee is acting on behalf of a guest, then he or she is free to make the decision on the spot.

"I have high expectations, but I think that when you give people high expectations, they rise to the occasion," says Trott. For example, if a housekeeper sees that one of her guest rooms is housing a family of two parents and two children, the housekeeper is expected to stock the room with extra towels instead of waiting for the guests to call the front desk requesting more towels. No matter how large or small the task might seem, "We expect people to be self-leaders," notes NikiLeondakis. "We expect employees to use their heads."

Because each of the 50 Kimpton hotel and restaurant properties is unique to its location and local population, Kimpton actively recruits employees with diverse backgrounds and qualifications, then gives them the authority to serve their guests as they see best. Individuality is nurtured rather than squelched. NikiLeondakis observes that, because her employees come with a wide range of experience at different locations in the hospitality industry, sometimes it is difficult to get them to leave behind their previous assumptions about their role as hotel workers. "The biggest challenge with employee empowerment and communication is that we're all products of our past," Leondakis says. New employees often have to be retrained to think outside the box, make decisions, and "rock the boat," as Leondakis puts it.

The results of this retraining toward empowerment have not gone unnoticed. Kimpton Hotels consistently win awards for service, and the group has received many accolades for its approach to human resource management, including a recent award from the Human Rights Campaign for "Workplace Equality Innovation." In addition, Kimpton is regularly named to *Fortune's* list of "100 Best Companies to Work For."

Recent praise from the industry publication *Hospitality Design* included a statement from Kimpton CEO, Michael Depatie, crediting NikiLeondakis with much of the company's HR success. "Niki has an extraordinary ability to connect with people, from guests she meets on the road to each and every one of our employees," said Depatie. Leondakis, managers like Peggy Trott, and the entire staff, embody their company's assertion that "Our employees are our brand."

Questions for Critical Thinking

1. Give three specific reasons why empowerment is key to the success of a firm like Kimpton Hotels. How might this distinguish it from other hotel companies?

2. Select the concept of either a problem-solving team or a self-managed team. How might this team function at a Kimpton hotel? Who might be on the team, and what role might it play in the running of the hotel?

3. Give an example of a situation in which informal communication would function well among empowered employees at a Kimpton hotel.

4. Currently all Kimpton hotels are located in the U.S., which is a low-context culture. If the firm decided to open a hotel in a high-context culture such as Japan, how might communication between staff and guests differ?

Sources: Kimpton Hotels & Restaurants Web site, http://www.kimptonhotels.com, accessed July 5, 2011; "Why Work for Kimpton?," http://www.imkimpton.com, accessed August 22, 2010; Sam Guidino, Mike Desimone, Jeff Jenssen, Lynn Alley, "Kimpton Takes Philly," *Wine Spectator,* July 31, 2010; http://www.winespectator.com; "Kimpton Hotels Aim for 100 Percent Green Seal Certification," *GreenerBuildings,* March 31, 2010, http://www.greenbiz.com.

Chapter 10

Learning Objectives

[1] Explain the strategic importance of the production function.

[2] Identify and describe the four main categories of production processes.

[3] Explain the role of technology in the production process.

[4] Identify the factors involved in a plant location decision.

[5] Explain the major tasks of production and operations managers, and outline the three activities involved in implementing the production plan.

[6] Identify the steps in the production control process.

[7] Discuss the importance of quality control.

Production and Operations Management

Boeing's Next-Generation 737s Take to the Skies

When a Honda Accord or a Ford Explorer rolls out of the factory, it's usually put on a truck to be delivered to a dealership. But when a new Boeing 737 jet rolls onto the tarmac outside the manufacturing plant, someone has to fly it home to its new owner. Boeing, based in Chicago, is now producing more than 30 of its Next-Generation 737s a month—with plans to increase that number to 35 and 38 over the next few years—which means that its Seattle airfield has become a busy hub for airline crews that have been dispatched by airlines around the world to pick up their companies' shiny new jetliners.

The demand for single-aisle planes such as the 737 has risen recently—with signs of continued, steady increases worldwide. "We don't take [our production increase] lightly," notes Beverly Wyse, vice president and general manager of the Boeing 737 program. "We've worked very closely with the supply chain and our internal partners, and the team has used the innovation that they bring to work each and every day to ensure that we do it successfully." Boeing officials claim that its delivery slots are sold out for the coming year, with a backlog of more than 2,000 jet orders waiting to be filled. Industry analysts predict that airlines will need 21,000 single-aisle jets over the next two decades, and many of them are likely to be Boeing 737s.

"Our customers continue to show their preference for the Next-Generation 737 by exercising order options as well as by placing new orders," explains Boeing CEO Jim Albaugh. "We've managed our current backlog efficiently and increasing the rate is the product of our comprehensive planning and preparation."

Ramped up production also means an increase in jobs, particularly at the manufacturing plant near Seattle. Boeing plans to add about 1,200 new jobs at the 737 plant over the next few years in order to handle the record number of orders it has received for the jet from airlines around the world. The plant itself is undergoing a major expansion and adding new equipment. Local businesses and workers are happy about the growth. "The Boeing Company is a powerful engine in our economy and is responsible for creating thousands of jobs, attracting other companies and economic opportunities," says a spokesperson for a local Chamber of Commerce. At Boeing Field, crews from airlines representing nearly every continent—Australia, Europe, Asia, and North America—get their first look at the sparkling new jets they will be flying home to their employers. Monica Dustin, a Boeing customer relations manager, adds the finishing touch to each plane—a giant red bow attached to the handrail of the cranked-down staircase. She arranges for catered food and drinks to be served to the flight crews and makes sure that their brief visit is comfortable and pleasant. She's gotten to know several of them at least by sight, if not by name. Their airlines have taken delivery of so many planes in recent months that these crews are kept busy shuttling the new crafts home. "It gets quite busy around here," observes Dustin.

While Dustin looks after the creature comforts of her customers, flight dispatcher Erick Hall briefs the pilots on the route they should take from Seattle back to their home base, whether it is Norway or Japan. "We operate more like an airline operations center," quips Hall. "We're running flight plans, tracking flights."

As one Next-Generation 737 takes off into the sky, another one is readied for flight. Hall notes that many crews feel it is an honor to be entrusted with the pickup of a new jetliner for their company. "It's nice to feel that we can take part in that," says Hall.[1]

By producing and marketing the goods and services that people want, businesses satisfy their commitment to society as a whole. They create what economists call *utility*—the want-satisfying power of a good or service. Businesses can create or enhance four basic kinds of utility: time, place, ownership, and form. A firm's marketing operation generates time, place, and ownership utility by offering products to customers at a time and place that is convenient for purchase.

Production creates form utility by converting raw materials and other inputs into finished products, such as Boeing's 737 jet. **Production** uses resources, including workers and machinery, to convert materials into finished goods and services. This conversion process may make major changes in raw materials or simply combine already finished parts into new products. The task of **production and operations management** in a firm is to oversee the production process by managing people and machinery in converting materials and resources into finished goods and services, which is illustrated by Figure 10.1.

People sometimes use the terms *production* and *manufacturing* interchangeably, but the two are actually different. Production spans both manufacturing and nonmanufacturing industries. For instance, companies that engage in fishing or mining engage in production, as do firms that provide package deliveries or lodging. Figure 10.2 lists five examples of production systems for a variety of goods and services.

But whether the production process results in a tangible good such as a car or an intangible service such as cable television, it always converts inputs into outputs. A cabinetmaker combines wood, tools, and skill to create finished kitchen cabinets for a new home. A transit system combines buses, trains, and employees to create its output: passenger transportation. Both of these production processes create utility.

This chapter describes the process of producing goods and services. It looks at the importance of production and operations management and discusses the new technologies that are transforming the production function. It then discusses the tasks of the production and operations manager, the importance of quality, and the methods businesses use to ensure high quality.

production use of resources, such as workers and machinery, to convert materials into finished goods and services.

production and operations management oversee the production process by managing people and machinery in converting materials and resources into finished goods and services.

FIGURE 10.1 **The Production Process: Converting Inputs to Outputs**

INPUTS
· Resources
· Raw Materials

CONVERSION PROCESS
· Add Value

OUTPUTS
· Goods
· Services

FIGURE
10.2 Typical Production Systems

Example	Primary Inputs	Transformation	Outputs
Computer Factory	Hard drives, computer memory, computer chips, keyboards, cases, power supply, DVD drives, central circuit board, boards for network and Internet access and graphics, monitors, and software	Assembles components to meet customer orders, including specialized orders for hardware and software	Desktop or laptop computers
Trucking Firm	Trucks, personnel, buildings, fuel, goods to be shipped, packaging supplies, truck parts, utilities	Packages and transports goods from sources to destinations	Delivered goods
Retail Store	Buildings, displays, scanners, merchandise, personnel, supplies, utilities	Attracts customers, stores goods, sells products	Merchandise sold
Automobile Body Shop	Damaged autos, paints, supplies, machines, tools, buildings, personnel, utilities	Transforms damaged auto bodies into facsimiles of the originals	Repaired automobile bodies
County Sheriff's Department	Personnel, police equipment, automobiles, office furniture, buildings, utilities	Detects crimes and brings criminals to justice	Lower crime rates and peaceful communities

The Strategic Importance of Production

Along with marketing and finance, production is a vital business activity. Without products to sell, companies cannot generate money to pay their employees, lenders, and stockholders. And without the profits from products, firms quickly fail. The production process is just as crucial in nonprofit organizations, such as the St. Jude Children's Research Hospital and Goodwill Industries, because the goods or services they offer justify their existence. Effective production and operations management can lower a firm's costs of production, boost the quality of its goods and services, allow it to respond dependably to customer demands, and enable it to renew itself by providing new products. Let's look at the differences among mass, flexible, and customer-driven production.

Mass Production

From its beginnings as a colonial supplier of raw materials to Europe, the United States has evolved into an industrial giant. Much of this change has resulted from **mass production**, a system for manufacturing products in large quantities through effective combinations of employees with specialized skills, mechanization, and standardization. Mass production makes outputs (goods and services) available in large quantities at lower prices than individually crafted items would cost. It is mass production that brought cars, computers, televisions, books, and even homes to the majority of the population—that's right, even homes. William Levitt made homes affordable to the average American from the 1940s to the 1960s, by removing the most expensive items—the basements—and mass-producing them at the rate of one every 16 minutes. Levitt's first planned community, Levittown, brought his company a profit of about $5 million more than 60 years ago. Levitt, often called the Pioneer of Suburbs, followed a simple strategy. "Any fool can build homes," he quipped. "What counts is how many you can sell for how little."[2]

Mass production begins with the specialization of labor, dividing work into its simplest components so that each worker can concentrate on performing one task. By separating jobs into small tasks, managers create conditions for high productivity through mechanization, in which machines perform much of the work previously done by people. Standardization, the third element of mass production, involves producing uniform, interchangeable goods and parts. Standardized parts simplify the replacement of defective or worn-out components. For instance, if your car's windshield wiper blades wear out, you can easily buy replacements at a local auto parts store such as AutoZone.

A logical extension of these principles of specialization, mechanization, and standardization led to development of the *assembly line*. This manufacturing method moves the product along a conveyor belt past a number of workstations, where workers perform specialized tasks such as welding, painting, installing individual parts, and tightening bolts. Henry Ford's application of this concept revolutionized auto assembly. Before the assembly line, it took Ford's workers 12 hours to assemble a Model T car. But with an assembly line, it took just 1.5 hours to make the same car. Not surprisingly, dozens of other industries soon adopted the assembly-line process.

Although mass production has important advantages, it has limitations, too. While mass production is highly efficient for producing large numbers of similar products, it is highly inefficient when producing small batches of different items. This trade-off might tempt some companies to focus on efficient production methods rather than on making what customers really want. In addition, the labor specialization associated with mass production can lead to boring jobs, because workers keep repeating the same task. To improve their competitive capabilities, many firms adopt flexible production and customer-driven production systems. These methods won't replace mass production in every case, but in many instances might lead to improved product quality and greater job satisfaction. It might also enhance the use of mass production.

Flexible Production

While mass production is effective for creating large quantities of one item, *flexible production* is usually more cost-effective for producing smaller runs. Flexible production can take many forms, but it generally involves using information technology to share the details of customer orders, programmable equipment to fulfill the orders, and skilled people to carry out whatever tasks are needed to fill a particular order. This system is even more beneficial when combined with lean production methods that use automation and information technology to reduce requirements for workers and inventory. Flexible production requires a lot of communication among everyone in the organization.

Flexible production is now widely used in the auto industry; whereas Henry Ford revolutionized auto production in the early 20th century, automakers such as Toyota and Honda are innovating with new methods of production. Changing from mass production to flexible production has enabled these companies to produce different kinds of cars at the same plant. Honda's flexible manufacturing plant in Marysville, Ohio, now builds more than 90 percent of all Honda sedans sold in the United States. The facility accomplishes this through team-based operations, relying on the expertise and knowledge of individual workers to innovate and improve manufacturing processes. "No one is afraid to speak up and offer their opinions," says the Marysville plant Web site.[3]

This Honda auto plant uses flexible production techniques to turn out several different models. The auto industry, which developed mass production methods, now finds flexible production to be more efficient.

Customer-Driven Production

A *customer-driven production* system evaluates customer demands in order to make the connection between products manufactured and products bought. Many firms use this approach with great success. One method is to establish computer links between factories and retailers' scanners, using data about sales as the basis for creating short-term forecasts and designing production schedules to meet those forecasts. Another approach to customer-driven production systems is simply not to make the product until a customer orders it— whether it's a taco or a computer. Massachusetts-based Shibui Designs creates custom-made dresses in high-end fabrics for female executives and other women over 40. Each item of clothing is custom cut and fit to a single customer's measurements. Founder Elizabeth Nill, who is over 60, started the business because she couldn't find clothing that fit well. "I don't have the body of a model, and the bulges are real. Truly made classic clothing that is custom made-to-measure helps camouflage these inevitable imperfections and makes me feel more elegant." Nill's customers agree.[4]

Production Processes

Not surprisingly, the production processes and time required to make an Apple iPad and a gallon of gasoline are different. Production processes use either an analytic or synthetic system; time requirements call for either a continuous or an intermittent process.

An analytic production system reduces a raw material to its component parts in order to extract one or more marketable products. Petroleum refining breaks down crude oil into several marketable products, including gasoline, heating oil, and aviation fuel. When corn is processed, the resulting marketable food products include animal feed and corn sweetener.

A synthetic production system is the reverse of an analytic system. It combines a number of raw materials or parts or transforms raw materials to produce finished products. Canon's assembly line produces a camera by assembling various parts such as a shutter or a lens cap. Other synthetic production systems make drugs, chemicals, computer chips, and canned soup.

Assessment Check ✔

1. What is mass production?
2. What is the difference between flexible production and customer-driven production?

A continuous production process generates finished products over a lengthy period of time. The steel industry provides a classic example. Its blast furnaces never completely shut down except for malfunctions. Petroleum refineries, chemical plants, and nuclear power facilities also practice continuous production. A shutdown can damage sensitive equipment, with extremely costly results.

An intermittent production process generates products in short production runs, shutting down machines frequently or changing their configurations to produce different products. Most services result from intermittent production systems. For instance, accountants, plumbers, and dentists traditionally have not attempted to standardize their services because each service provider confronts different problems that require individual approaches. However, some companies such as Jiffy Lube (auto service), H&R Block (tax preparation service), and Lawn Dawg (lawn-care service), offer standardized services as part of a strategy to operate more efficiently and compete with lower prices. McDonald's, well-known for its nearly continuous production of food, has moved toward a more intermittent production model. The fast-food chain invested millions in new cooking equipment to set up kitchens for preparing sandwiches quickly to order, rather than producing large batches ahead of time and then keeping them warm under heat lamps.

Assessment Check ✔

1. What are the two main production systems?

2. What are the two time-related production processes?

Technology and the Production Process

Production continues to change rapidly as computer technologies develop. Many manufacturing plants are now "lights out" facilities that are completely automated—meaning no workers are required to build or make the products. While this signals a change in the types of jobs available in manufacturing, it also means that companies can design, produce, and adapt products more quickly to meet customers' changing needs.

Green Manufacturing Processes

More and more firms are pouring resources into the development of manufacturing processes that result in a reduction of waste, energy use, and pollution. Companies ranging in size from Walmart to the local café are finding ways to operate in a more sustainable manner—whether it is using biofuel to power a fleet of delivery trucks or eliminating unnecessary packaging, firms have begun to view the steps they take with pride. Chobani Greek Yogurt is manufactured in rural upstate New York with fresh ingredients obtained from local dairy farms, which reduces fuel consumption for refrigeration and transport. The yogurt contains no preservatives or artificial flavors, is made with milk free from synthetic growth hormones, and contains real fresh fruit.[5]

Firms that are involved in construction—or are thinking of building new offices or manufacturing plants—are turning their attention to **LEED (Leadership in Energy and Environmental Design)** certification for their facilities. LEED is a voluntary certification program administered by the U.S. Green Building Council, aimed at promoting the most sustainable construction processes available. The LEED certification process is rigorous and involves meeting standards in energy savings, water efficiency, CO^2 emissions reduction, improved indoor environmental quality (including air and natural light), and other

LEED (Leadership in Energy and Environmental Design) voluntary certification program administered by the U.S. Green Building Council, aimed at promoting the most sustainable construction processes available.

Drilling for Natural Gas—Clean Alternatives

Drilling for natural gas doesn't usually conjure up images of an undisturbed landscape. In fact, studies by the EPA as well as private environmental groups reveal that the major method for extracting natural gas from the earth—hydraulic fracturing—can result in contaminated water supplies. Hydraulic fracturing involves injecting millions of gallons of water, sand, and chemicals deep into the ground to crack open the beds of shale containing natural gas, allowing the gas to rise to the surface. Environmental scientists as well as residents of communities near where the drilling takes place are concerned about the amount of water being used as well as potential contamination of surrounding water supplies by the chemicals used in the process. The city of Buffalo, New York, recently banned hydraulic drilling, along with the storage, transfer, treatment, and disposal of the waste byproducts created by drilling.

A number of the energy companies—including those that drill for oil and natural gas—are paying attention to these concerns. Environmental Technologies Ltd. is making a nontoxic alternative to the toxic chemicals, stating that their product kills bacteria just as effectively. Ecosphere Technologies Inc., with headquarters in Florida, claims it can eliminate the need for anti-bacterial chemicals completely by killing the bacteria at the surface before water is injected into the gas wells. Ecosphere also helps energy producers reuse the water from hydraulic fracturing in order to reduce water use and waste. Traditionally, companies have paid to have millions of gallons of waste water shipped to treatment plants or disposal sites.

Although none of these firms plans to stop drilling, they are all researching and developing greener technologies. In fact, new companies—and divisions or subsidiaries of the larger energy firms—are forming rapidly to take advantage of this business opportunity. In response to this increase and concerns over environmental safety, the EPA recently announced the launch of a broad-based study on the effects of hydraulic fracturing. Despite local regulations such as the ban by Buffalo, "one thing I think EPA can do to add to the body of knowledge is to determine whether there are any holes in that regulatory structure," notes EPA spokesperson Lisa Jackson.

Questions for Critical Thinking

1. How would you classify the natural gas drilling production system? Explain why.
2. Do you predict that the firms that are investing in greener processes will ultimately be successful? Why or why not?

Sources: "City of Buffalo Bans Hydraulic Fracturing," *Reuters*, February 8, 2011, http://www.reuters.com; Jennifer A. Dlouhy, "EPA To Study Hydraulic Fracturing," *My San Antonio*, February 2, 2011, http://www.mysanantonio.com; "Hydraulic Fracturing," EPA Web site, http://www.epa.gov, accessed June 7, 2011; "Sustainable Technology," Baker Hughes Web site, http://www.bakerhughes.com, accessed June 7, 2011; Ben Casselman, "Firms See Green in Natural-Gas Production," *The Wall Street Journal*, March 30, 2010, http://www.wsj.com.

categories.[6] The "Going Green" feature describes how energy firms are developing new methods for drilling for natural gas that are much less damaging to the environment than traditional methods.

Robots

A growing number of manufacturers have freed workers from boring, sometimes dangerous jobs by replacing them with robots. A *robot* is a reprogrammable machine capable of performing a variety of tasks that require the repeated manipulation of materials and tools. Robots can repeat the same tasks many times without varying their movements. Many factories use robots today to stack their products on pallets and shrink-wrap them for shipping. Boston Scientific, a firm that makes medical devices, uses robots made by Kiva in two of its distribution centers. Saks Fifth Avenue recently purchased a Kiva robot system for its Maryland distribution center as the initial move in an effort to convert its fulfillment center from manual to automated operations.[7]

Historically, robots were most common in automotive and electronics manufacturing, but growing numbers of industries are adding robots to production lines as improvements in technology make them less expensive and more useful. Firms operate many different types of robots. The simplest kind, a pick-and-place robot, moves in only two or three directions as it picks up something from one spot and places it in another. So-called

Remote-controlled robots are especially well suited for work in dangerous environments. This field robot, developed for use by bomb squads, can photograph suspicious-looking devices, move them to a safer location, and blow them up.

Daniel Bringmann/iStockphoto

field robots assist people in nonmanufacturing, often hazardous, environments such as nuclear power plants, the international space station, and even battlefields. Police use robots to remotely dispose of suspected bombs. However, the same technology can be used in factories. Using vision systems, infrared sensors, and bumpers on mobile platforms, robots can automatically move parts or finished goods from one place to another, while either following or avoiding people, whichever is necessary to do the job. For instance, machine vision systems are being used more frequently for complex applications such as quality assurance in the manufacturing of medical devices. The advancements in machine vision components like cameras, illumination systems, and processors have greatly improved their capabilities. Companies like Minnesota-based PPT Vision help firms such as B. Braun Penang (Malaysia) boost productivity, manage risk, and improve quality across all of its product lines including syringe needles, pharmaceutical vials, and intravenous (IV) infusion bottles.[8]

Computer-Aided Design and Manufacturing

computer-aided design (CAD) process that allows engineers to design components as well as entire products on computer screens faster and with fewer mistakes than they could achieve working with traditional drafting systems.

A process called **computer-aided design (CAD)** allows engineers to design components as well as entire products on computer screens faster and with fewer mistakes than they could achieve working with traditional drafting systems. Using an electronic pen, an engineer can sketch three-dimensional (3-D) designs on an electronic drafting board or directly on the screen. The computer then provides tools to make major and minor design changes and to analyze the results for particular characteristics or problems. Engineers can put a new car design through a simulated road test to project its real-world performance. If they find a problem with weight distribution, for example, they can make the necessary changes virtually—without actually test-driving the car. With advanced CAD software, prototyping is as much "virtual" as it is "hands-on." Actual prototypes or parts aren't built until the engineers are satisfied that the required structural characteristics in their virtual designs have been met. Dentistry has benefited from CAD, which can design and create on-site such products as caps and crowns that fit a patient's mouth or jaw perfectly.[9]

computer-aided manufacturing (CAM) computer tools to analyze CAD output and enable a manufacturer to analyze the steps that a machine must take to produce a needed product or part.

The process of **computer-aided manufacturing (CAM)** picks up where the CAD system leaves off. Computer tools enable a manufacturer to analyze the steps that a machine must take to produce a needed product or part. Electronic signals transmitted to processing equipment provide instructions for performing the appropriate production steps in the correct order. Both CAD and CAM technologies are now used together at most modern production facilities. These so-called CAD/CAM systems are linked electronically to automatically transfer computerized designs into the production facilities, saving both time and effort. They also allow more precise manufacturing of parts.

Flexible Manufacturing Systems

flexible manufacturing system (FMS) production facility that workers can quickly modify to manufacture different products.

A **flexible manufacturing system (FMS)** is a production facility that workers can quickly modify to manufacture different products. The typical system consists of computer-controlled machining centers to produce metal parts, robots to handle the parts, and remote-controlled carts to deliver materials. All components are linked by electronic controls that dictate activities at each stage of the manufacturing sequence, even automatically replacing broken or worn-out drill bits and other implements.

Flexible manufacturing systems have been enhanced by powerful new software that allows machine tools to be reprogrammed while they are running. This capability allows the same machine to make hundreds of different parts without the operator having to shut the machine down each time to load new programs. The software also connects to the Internet to receive updates or to control machine tools at other sites. And because the software resides on a company's computer network, engineers can use it to diagnose production problems any time, from anywhere they can access the network. Pharmaceutical companies are constantly looking for new ways to use flexible manufacturing. Asia—especially India, China, and Singapore—has become an important location for this and other innovations in manufacturing.[10]

Computer-Integrated Manufacturing

Companies integrate robots, CAD/CAM, FMS, computers, and other technologies to implement **computer-integrated manufacturing (CIM)**, a production system in which computers help workers design products, control machines, handle materials, and control the production function in an integrated fashion. This type of manufacturing does not necessarily imply more automation and fewer people than other alternatives. It does, however, involve a new type of automation organized around the computer. The key to CIM is a centralized computer system running software that integrates and controls separate processes and functions. The advantages of CIM include increased productivity, decreased design costs, increased equipment utilization, and improved quality.

CIM is widely used in the printing industry to coordinate thousands of printing jobs, some very small. CIM saves money by combining many small jobs into one larger one and by automating the printing process from design to delivery. Global printing firm manroland AG uses CIM to provide printing solutions for its business customers. One of its products, PRINTVALUE, offers a complete line of solutions including customized 24/7 service and maintenance packages.[11]

The Location Decision

The decision of where to locate a production facility hinges on transportation, human, and physical factors, as shown in Table 10.1. Transportation factors include proximity to markets and raw materials, along with availability of alternative modes for transporting both inputs and outputs. Automobile assembly plants are located near major rail lines. Inputs—such as engines, plastics, and metal parts—arrive by rail, and the finished vehicles are shipped out by rail. Shopping malls are often located next to major streets and freeways in suburban areas, because most customers arrive by car.

Physical variables involve such issues as weather, water supplies, available energy, and options for disposing of hazardous waste. Theme parks, such as Walt Disney World, are often located in warm climates so they can be open, and attract visitors, year-round. A manufacturing business that wants to locate near a community must prepare an

computer-integrated manufacturing (CIM) production system in which computers help workers design products, control machines, handle materials, and control the production function in an integrated fashion.

Assessment Check ✓

1. List some of the reasons businesses invest in robots.
2. What is a flexible manufacturing system (FMS)?
3. What are the major benefits of computer-integrated manufacturing (CIM)?

Table
10.1

Factors in the Location Decision

LOCATION FACTOR	EXAMPLES OF AFFECTED BUSINESSES
Transportation	
Proximity to markets	Baking companies and manufacturers of other perishable products, dry cleaners, hotels, other services
Proximity to raw materials	Paper mills
Availability of transportation alternatives	Brick manufacturers, retail stores
Physical Factors	
Water supply	Computer chip fabrication plants
Energy	Aluminum, chemical, and fertilizer manufacturers
Hazardous wastes	All businesses
Human Factors	
Labor supply	Auto manufacturers, software developers
Local zoning regulations	Manufacturing and distribution companies
Community living conditions	All businesses
Taxes	All businesses

Ian Dagnall/Alamy

Deciding where to locate a production facility can often depend on the weather. Some theme parks, such as Walt Disney World, are located in warm climates so they can be open and attract visitors year-round.

environmental impact study that analyzes how a proposed plant would affect the quality of life in the surrounding area. Regulatory agencies typically require these studies to cover topics such as the impact on transportation facilities; energy requirements; water and sewage treatment needs; natural plant life and wildlife; and water, air, and noise pollution.

Human factors in the location decision include an area's labor supply, local regulations, taxes, and living conditions. Management considers local labor costs, as well as the availability of workers with needed qualifications. Software makers and other computer-related firms concentrate in areas with the technical talent they need, including California's Silicon Valley, Boston, and Austin, Texas. By contrast, some labor-intensive industries have located plants in rural areas with readily available labor pools and limited high-wage alternatives. And some firms with headquarters in the United States and other industrialized countries have moved production off-shore in search of low wages. But no matter what type of industry a firm is in, a production and operations manager's facility location decision must consider the following factors:

- proximity to suppliers, warehouses, and service operations

- insurance and taxes

- availability of such employee needs as housing, schools, mass transportation, day care, shopping, and recreational facilities

- size, skills, and costs of the labor force

- ample space for current and future needs of the firm

- distance to market for goods

- receptiveness of the community

- economical transportation for materials and supplies, as well as for finished goods

- climate and environment that matches the industry's needs and employees' lifestyle

- amount and cost of energy services

- government incentives.

A recent trend in location strategy is bringing production facilities closer to the final markets where the goods will be sold. One reason for this is reduced time and cost for shipping. Another reason is a closer cultural affinity between the parent company and supplier (in cases where production remains overseas). This has led some business developers to label Central America "the new Asia."[12] German automaker Volkswagen decided to build a $1 billion manufacturing plant in Chattanooga, Tennessee, for the construction of its new midsize sedan. The new Passat was engineered specifically for the U.S. market, featuring a clean diesel fuel option and a larger interior than competing models. Volkswagen plans to roll 150,000 vehicles out of the Chattanooga plant each year, with possibilities for a major expansion that would increase production capacity for even more.[13]

State and local governments may offer incentives to businesses that are willing to locate in their region. These incentives may take the form of tax breaks, agreements to improve infrastructure, and the like. The "Hit & Miss" feature describes how Twin Creeks Technologies teamed up with various agencies to bring a new solar panel plant to Senatobia, Mississippi.

Assessment Check ✓

1. How does an environmental impact study influence the location decision?

2. What human factors are relevant to the location decision?

The Sun Is Shining Brighter in Senatobia

Mississippi is becoming a new hub of high-tech manufacturing. Two major manufacturers recently agreed to build facilities in the state. One of these companies is Twin Creeks Technologies, which is locating its new solar panel production facility in Senatobia. Not only will the project generate new jobs for the local economy, its products—solar panels—represent the latest technology in generating solar power. In addition, its manufacturing processes are cleaner and greener than those used by other production plants. Carrying a price tag of more than $175 million, the facility will occupy 250,000 square feet when complete and create several hundred jobs for local workers, including administrative and factory jobs. "This facility will be the first renewable solar technology production plant in the state," declared Mississippi governor Haley Barbour, "and I commend this innovative start-up company for its commitment to doing business in the state and for creating over 500 jobs for the residents of Mississippi."

Twin Creeks isn't going it alone. The State of Mississippi is providing $50 million in loan assistance through the Mississippi Major Economic Impact Authority for the building project. In addition, the State and the City of Senatobia are providing $4 million toward improvement of infrastructure—roads, utilities, water, and so forth—at the building site. Twin Creeks considered 25 sites in six other states before deciding on the Senatobia location in Mississippi. The Mississippi governor's office helped complete the agreement quickly. "We are enthusiastic about hiring locally and making green energy products that are made in America," said Reza Nikfar of Twin Creeks at the groundbreaking ceremony.

Twin Creeks is also working with Northwest Mississippi Community College, the University of Mississippi's Center for Manufacturing Excellence, and UM's School of Engineering to recruit engineers and begin training other potential job candidates for the plant. This part of the location decision is particularly popular among residents of the area, where the unemployment rate topped 13 percent recently. "Twin Creeks was the first major economic development project to utilize Mississippi's new clean energy incentives program, which will open the door for new job opportunities in the clean energy sector for all Mississipians," notes Gray Swoope, executive director of the Mississippi Development Authority.

Questions for Critical Thinking

1. In addition to government incentives, what other factors did Twin Creeks likely consider in its decision to locate its plant in Senotobia?

2. In what ways does the community benefit from this decision? Might there be any drawbacks?

Sources: "Twin Creeks Technologies Breaks Ground on Solar Panel Manufacturing Facility in Senatobia, Miss.," *Press Release*, accessed June 7, 2011, http://www.mississippi .org; "Twin Creeks Technologies Locates Manufacturing Facility in Mississippi," *Solarbuzz*, April 5, 2010, http://www.solarbuzz.com; Robert Lee Long, "Solar Panel Plant to Net 512 Jobs," *Desoto Times Tribune*, April 5, 2010, http://desototimes.com; "Mississippi Lands $175 Solar Panel Plant," *Memphis Business Journal*, April 2, 2010, http://memphisbizjournals.com; "Mississippi Governor Says Senatobia to Get Solar Panel Manufacturing Facility, 500 Jobs," *The Commercial Appeal*, April 2, 2010, http://www.commercialappeal.com.

The Job of Production Managers

Production and operations managers oversee the work of people and machinery to convert inputs (materials and resources) into finished goods and services. As Figure 10.3 shows, these managers perform four major tasks.

1. Plan the overall production process.

2. Determine the best layout for the firm's facilities.

3. Implement the production plan.

4. Control the manufacturing process to maintain the highest possible quality.

Part of the control process involves continuous evaluation of results. If problems occur, managers return to the first step and make adjustments.

FIGURE 10.3 Tasks of Production Managers

PRODUCTION MANAGEMENT TASKS

Planning the Production Process → Selecting the Most Appropriate Layout → Implementing the Production Plan → Controlling the Production Process

Planning the Production Process

Production planning begins by choosing what goods or services to offer to customers. This decision is the essence of every company's reason for operating. Other decisions such as machinery purchases, pricing decisions, and selection of retail outlets all grow out of product planning. But with product planning, it's not enough to plan products that satisfy customers. Products must satisfy customers *and* be produced as efficiently and inexpensively as possible. So while marketing research studies determine consumer reactions to proposed products and estimate potential sales and profitability levels, production departments focus on planning the production process when they (1) convert original product ideas into final specifications and (2) design the most efficient facilities to produce those products.

It is important for production managers to understand how a project fits into the company's structure because this will affect the success of the project. In a traditional manufacturing organization, each production manager is given a specific area of authority and responsibility such as purchasing or inventory control. One drawback to this structure is that it may actually pit the purchasing manager against the inventory control manager. As more organizations have moved toward team-oriented structures, some organizations assign team members to specific projects reporting to the production manager. Each team is responsible for the quality of its products and has the authority to make changes to improve performance and quality. The major difference between the two approaches is that all workers on teams are responsible for their output, and teamwork avoids the competitiveness between managers often found in traditional structures.

Determining the Facility Layout

The next production management task is determining the best layout for the facility. An efficient facility layout can reduce material handling, decrease costs, and improve product flow through the facility. This decision requires managers to consider all phases of production and the necessary inputs at each step. Figure 10.4 shows three common layout designs: process, product, and fixed-position layouts. It also shows a customer-oriented layout typical of service providers' production systems.

A *process layout* groups machinery and equipment according to their functions. The work in process moves around the plant to reach different workstations. A process layout often

FIGURE 10.4 Basic Facility Layouts

(A) Process Layout

Laundry Receiving → Labeling and Sorting → Washing and Drying → Pressing

Delivery and Invoicing ← Loading ← Order Assembly

(B) Product Layout

(C) Fixed-Position Layout

Material Storage 1   Material Storage 2   Material Storage 3

Subcontractor A
Subcontractor B
Subcontractor C

Machine Group 1   Machine Group 2   Machine Group 3

Employee Group 1
Employee Group 2
Employee Group 3

(D) Customer-Oriented Layout

Enter ▼ ▲ Exit

Emergency Rooms, Acute Medicine, Patient Departure

Hospital Rooms
Hospital Rooms
Hospital Rooms
Hospital Rooms

Surgery, Radiology, Intensive Care, and Technical Services

Cafeteria

Doctors' Lounge/Offices   Nurses' Lounge/Offices   Business Office

Parking

Patient Receiving and Lobby

Parking

Exit ▼ ▲ Enter

facilitates production of a variety of nonstandard items in relatively small batches. Its purpose is to process goods and services that have a variety of functions. For instance, a typical machine shop generally has separate departments where machines are grouped by functions such as grinding, drilling, pressing, and lathing. Process layouts accommodate a variety of production functions and use general-purpose equipment that can be less costly to purchase and maintain than specialized equipment.

A *product layout*, also referred to as an assembly line, sets up production equipment along a product-flow line, and the work in process moves along this line past workstations. This type of layout efficiently produces large numbers of similar items, but it may prove inflexible and able to accommodate only a few product variations. Although product layouts date back at least to the Model T assembly line, companies are refining this approach with modern touches. Many auto manufacturers continue to use a product layout, but robots perform many of the activities that humans once performed. Automation overcomes one of the major drawbacks of this system—unlike humans, robots don't get bored doing a dull, repetitive job. European automaker Holland Car Plc uses an assembly-line approach called complete knockdown (CKD), in which all the parts of an auto are imported in pieces to be welded, painted, and assembled at its facility in Ethiopia.[14]

A *fixed-position layout* places the product in one spot, and workers, materials, and equipment come to it. This approach suits production of very large, bulky, heavy, or fragile products. For example, a bridge cannot be built on an assembly line. Fixed-position layouts dominate several industries including construction, shipbuilding, aircraft and aerospace, and oil drilling, to name a few. In all of these industries, the nature of the product generally dictates a fixed-position layout.

Service organizations also must decide on appropriate layouts for their production processes. A service firm should arrange its facilities to enhance the interactions between customers and its services—also called *customer-oriented layout*. If you think of patients as inputs, a hospital implements a form of the process layout. Banks, libraries, dental offices, and hair salons also use process layouts. Sometimes the circumstances surrounding a service require a fixed-position layout. For instance, doctors, nurses, and medical devices are brought to patients in a hospital emergency room.

Implementing the Production Plan

After planning the production process and determining the best layout, a firm's production managers begin to implement the production plan. This activity involves (1) deciding whether to make, buy, or lease components; (2) selecting the best suppliers for materials; and (3) controlling inventory to keep enough, but not too much, on hand.

Make, Buy, or Lease Decision One of the fundamental issues facing every producer is the **make, buy, or lease decision**—choosing whether to manufacture a product or component in house, purchase it from an outside supplier, or lease it. This decision is critical in many contemporary business situations.

Several factors affect the make, buy, or lease decision, including the costs of leasing or purchasing parts from vendors compared with the costs of producing them in house. The decision sometimes hinges on the availability of outside suppliers that can dependably meet a firm's standards for quality and quantity. The need for confidentiality sometimes affects the decision, as does the short- or long-term duration of the firm's need for supplies. A firm might not yet have the technology to produce certain components or materials, or the technology might be too costly. Goodyear Tire & Rubber Co. has teamed up with Genencor, an

make, buy, or lease decision choosing whether to manufacture a product or component in house, purchase it from an outside supplier, or lease it.

Goodyear Tire & Genencor: A Sweet Alliance

For many years, tire manufacturers like Goodyear have relied on synthetic rubber as a supplement to the natural rubber used to make truck and automobile tires. The basis of synthetic rubber, produced on a global scale, is a chemical called isoprene, which is a volatile, toxic hydrocarbon that is a byproduct from refining crude oil. Isoprene is bad for the environment and its production relies on the availability of crude oil for refining. Until recently, there wasn't a real alternative—Goodyear still needed to purchase its raw materials for the manufacture of its tires, including the isoprene-based synthetic rubber. But researchers at Genencor, an industrial biotechnology firm headquartered in Rochester, New York, have come up with the answer—a way to produce synthetic rubber from sugar instead of refined oil waste. Goodyear is so convinced of this solution that the firm has established a collaboration with Genencor.

"An intensive search has been underway for years for alternative sources of isoprene, in particular those from renewable resources such as biomass," explains Joseph McAuliffe, a scientist with Genencor. The method developed by Genencor involves the fermentation of sugar cane, corn, corn cobs, and switch grass to create a new product called BioIsoprene™, which will become the basis for synthetic rubber in the next few years. Goodyear, which makes 200 million tires annually, has been one of the world's largest users of iosoprene—so the conversion to Genencor's BioIsoprene™ will be significant.

"We want to make biochemicals from renewable materials," notes McAuliffe, "partially as a hedge against rising crude oil prices

and much more so because this approach moves us to a more sustainable future." Genencor has made the first delivery of BioIsoprene™ to Goodyear, which will begin to incorporate it into its manufacturing process, resulting in greener tires that will hit the road soon. Both firms see the collaboration as a win–win for all, including consumers. "We believe it's important to look at alternative renewable raw materials in our production processes," says Jesse Roeck of Goodyear. "We chose to work with Genencor based on our strategy of open innovation because they are one of the leaders in industrial biotechnology."

Questions for Critical Thinking

1. Describe the benefits of creating a research alliance for future raw materials or supplies.

2. Investing in a future with a supplier requires planning. How might this decision affect other aspects of the production process?

Sources: "Revolutionary Technology Promises Green Tires for a More Sustainable Future," *Clean Technology,* accessed June 7, 2011, http://www.azocleantech.com; "Genencor and Goodyear Partnering on Process to Develop BioIsoprene from Sugars," *Green Car Congress,* March 25, 2010, http://www.greencarcongress.com; "On the Road to Sweet Tires Made with a More Sustainable Process," *Physorg.com,* March 24, 2010, http://www.physorg.com; "BioIsoprene™ Product Begins Flowing from Genencor to Goodyear," *The Auto Channel,* March 9, 2010, http://www.theautochannel.com.

---

industrial biotechnology firm, to develop a cleaner alternative to the synthetic rubber now used as the raw material in many tires. The "Hit & Miss" feature describes how this alliance is contributing to the tires of the future.

Even when the firm decides to purchase from outside vendors, production managers should maintain access to multiple supply sources. An alternative supplier ensures that the firm can obtain needed materials despite strikes, quality-assurance problems, or other situations that may affect inputs. Outsourcing has its disadvantages. The main reason companies say they use outsourcing is to reduce costs and focus on their core business activities, but outsourcing also may trigger layoffs and compromise quality.[15]

In an industry where outsourcing is common, American Apparel chooses to keep all of its clothing production in the metropolitan Los Angeles area. Though the firm pays higher wages than rivals who outsource to other countries, American Apparel is able to offer quicker response times and maintain higher quality and better inventory control.[16]

Selection of Suppliers Once a company decides what inputs to purchase, it must choose the best vendors for its needs. To make this choice, production managers compare the quality, prices, dependability of delivery, and services offered by competing companies. Different suppliers may offer virtually identical quality levels and prices, so the final decision often rests on factors such as the firm's experience with each supplier, speed of delivery, warranties on purchases, and other services.

For a major purchase, negotiations between the purchaser and potential vendors may stretch over several weeks or even months, and the buying decision may rest with a number of colleagues who must say yes before the final decision is made. The choice of a supplier for an industrial drill press, for example, may require a joint decision by the production, engineering, purchasing, and quality-control departments. These departments often must reconcile their different views to settle on a purchasing decision.

The Internet has given buyers powerful tools for finding and comparing suppliers. Buyers can log on to business exchanges to compare specifications, prices, and availability. Ariba, with headquarters in California, offers organizations online software and other tools that allow them to source $120 billion worth of goods and services from suppliers around the world.[17]

Firms often purchase raw materials and component parts on long-term contracts. If a manufacturer requires a continuous supply of materials, a one-year or two-year contract with a vendor helps ensure availability. Today, many firms are building long-term relationships with suppliers and slashing the number of companies with which they do business. At the same time, they are asking their vendors to expand their roles in the production process.

Networking provides a way for production managers to learn about suppliers and get to know them personally. Trade shows, conferences, and seminars, and other meetings enable managers to meet suppliers, competitors, and colleagues. The "Business Etiquette" feature provides tips for making the most of these meetings.

Inventory Control Production and operations managers' responsibility for

BusinessEtiquette

Making the Most of Business Meetings

Some people love business meetings because they are a distraction from mundane tasks. Others find them tedious disruptions from more important matters. But business meetings—no matter what your outlook—are sometimes necessary. If you view a business meeting as part of your overall networking strategy—including staff meetings, sales meetings, appointments with customers, or conferences with colleagues—you can put it to work for you as a genuine career builder. Here are a few tips for making the most of your next business meeting:

- *Be on time.* Punctuality signifies that you value your own time as well as that of others. It also conveys the message that you intend to take the meeting seriously.
- *Turn off your cell phone and any other electronic devices.* Unless you are a doctor on call for emergencies, there is no need to have your cell phone turned on. Beeps and ringtones are a distraction to those who are trying to concentrate, and indicate to other participants that your attention is elsewhere.
- *Pay attention.* Listen actively to what others have to say. Take notes when appropriate.
- *Participate.* While dominating a conversation is not advisable, ask relevant questions and make brief, applicable points when appropriate. Stay on the subject.
- *Conduct yourself professionally.* Be polite to all other participants and be sure to thank them for their time at the end of the meeting.
- *Exchange business cards.* At the conclusion of the meeting, be sure to exchange business cards or obtain contact information from participants with whom you wish to continue communication.

Sources: Karyn Hill, "Business Meeting Etiquette—5 Essential Tips," *Business Coach Site,* http://www.bellaonline.com, accessed March 18, 2011; Donna Reynolds, "Practice Business Meeting Etiquette," *How To Do Things,* http://www.howtodothings.com, accessed March 18, 2011; Shaun Mangan, "7 Tips for More Effective Business Meetings," *Ezine Articles,* http://ezinearticles.com, accessed March 18, 2011.

inventory control
function requiring production and operations managers to balance the need to keep stock on hand to meet demand against the costs of carrying inventory.

inventory control requires them to balance the need to keep stock on hand to meet demand against the costs of carrying inventory. Among the expenses involved in storing inventory are warehousing costs, taxes, insurance, and maintenance. Firms waste money if they hold more inventory than they need. On the other hand, having too little inventory on hand may result in a shortage of raw materials, parts, or goods for sale that could lead to delays and unhappy customers.

Firms lose business when they consistently miss promised delivery dates or turn away orders. When Kansas farmer Jay Armstrong placed his order for a combine attachment—just as his family had done for 50 years—the dealer told Armstrong he wouldn't receive the equipment until August, when the farm's growing season was nearly over. So Armstrong was forced to make his purchase from a competitor, who promised delivery in May.[18]

Efficient inventory control can save a great deal of money. Many firms maintain *perpetual inventory* systems to continuously monitor the amounts and locations of their stock. Such inventory control systems typically rely on computers, and many automatically generate orders at the appropriate times. Many supermarkets link their scanning devices to perpetual inventory systems that reorder needed merchandise without human interaction. As the system records a shopper's purchase, it reduces the inventory count stored in the computer. Once inventory on hand drops to a predetermined level, the system automatically reorders the merchandise. Roundy's Supermarkets, headquartered in Wisconsin, uses a software system called SoftGrocer Inventory Management throughout its 154-store chain to manage its stock. The system is responsible for ordering and receiving inventory as well as counting and picking inventory in stockrooms. In addition, the software updates and verifies perpetual inventory balances. The company CIO says the software has helped Roundy's reduce its "out-of-stocks" while at the same time reducing "backroom and overall store inventory levels without impacting availability, which creates an immediate cost savings for our stores."[19]

Some companies go further and hand over their inventory control functions to suppliers. This concept is known as *vendor-managed inventory*. Trucking parts manufacturer and supplier Velvac, based in Wisconsin, uses a software program created by Ohio-based Datalliance to better serve its distributor customers. "VMI allows us to tailor inventory stocking plans for each individual distributor," explains Doug Mischock, Velvac's national sales manager.[20]

just-in-time (JIT) system broad management philosophy that reaches beyond the narrow activity of inventory control to influence the entire system of production and operations management.

Just-in-Time Systems

A **just-in-time (JIT) system** implements a broad management philosophy that reaches beyond the narrow activity of inventory control to influence the entire system of production and operations management. A JIT system seeks to eliminate anything that does not add value in operations activities by providing the right part at the right place at just the right time—right before it is needed in production.

JIT systems are being used in a wide range of industries, including medical supplies. Seattle Children's Hospital uses a JIT system to manage the distribution of its supplies, equipment, and clinical materials. The hospital partners with its key distributors to deploy the system. While the hospital does keep an inventory of certain emergency supplies on hand, the rest are distributed on a JIT basis, saving the hospital more than $2.5 million in its first year.[21]

Production using JIT shifts much of the responsibility for carrying inventory to vendors, which operate on

JIT systems are being used in a wide range of industries, including medical supplies.

Sean Locke/iStockphoto

forecasts and keep stock on hand to respond to manufacturers' needs. Suppliers that cannot keep enough high-quality parts on hand may be assessed steep penalties by purchasers. Another risk of using JIT systems is what happens if manufacturers underestimate demand for a product. Strong demand will begin to overtax JIT systems, as suppliers and their customers struggle to keep up with orders with no inventory cushion to tide them over.

Materials Requirement Planning Besides efficiency, effective inventory control requires careful planning to ensure the firm has all the inputs it needs to make its products. How do production and operations managers coordinate all of this information? They rely on **materials requirement planning (MRP)**, a computer-based production planning system that lets a firm ensure that it has all the parts and materials it needs to produce its output at the right time and place and in the right amounts.

Production managers use MRP programs to create schedules that identify the specific parts and materials required to produce an item. These schedules specify the exact quantities needed and the dates on which to order those quantities from suppliers so that they are delivered at the correct time in the production cycle. A small company might get by without an MRP system. If a firm makes a simple product with few components, a telephone call may ensure overnight delivery of crucial parts. For a complex product, however, such as a high-definition TV or aircraft, longer lead times are necessary.

Turtle Wax Ltd., an Illinois manufacturer of car care products including Turtle Wax, Color Magic, and Clear Vue, uses MRP software for a better picture of its operations. The software provides immediate production summaries, inventory levels, and sales and stock forecasts.[22]

Controlling the Production Process

The final task of production and operations managers is controlling the production process to maintain the highest possible quality. **Production control** creates a well-defined set of procedures for coordinating people, materials, and machinery to provide maximum production efficiency. Suppose that a watch factory must produce 80,000 watches during October. Production control managers break down this total into a daily production assignment of 4,000 watches for each of the month's 20 working days. Next, they determine the number of workers, raw materials, parts, and machines the plant needs to meet the production schedule. Similarly, a manager in a service business such as a restaurant must estimate how many dinners the outlet will serve each day and then determine how many people are needed to prepare and serve the food, as well as what food to purchase.

Figure 10.5 illustrates production control as a five-step process composed of planning, routing, scheduling, dispatching, and follow-up. These steps are part of the firm's overall emphasis on total quality management.

Production Planning

The phase of production control called *production planning* determines the amount of resources (including raw materials and other components) an organization needs to produce a certain output. The production planning process develops a bill of materials that lists all needed parts and materials. By comparing information about needed parts and materials

materials requirement planning (MRP) computer-based production planning system that lets a firm ensure that it has all the parts and materials it needs to produce its output at the right time and place and in the right amounts.

Assessment Check ✓

1. List the four major tasks of production and operations managers.
2. What is the difference between a traditional manufacturing structure and a team-based structure?
3. What factors affect the make, buy, or lease decision?

production control creates a well-defined set of procedures for coordinating people, materials, and machinery to provide maximum production efficiency.

FIGURE
10.5 Steps in Production Control

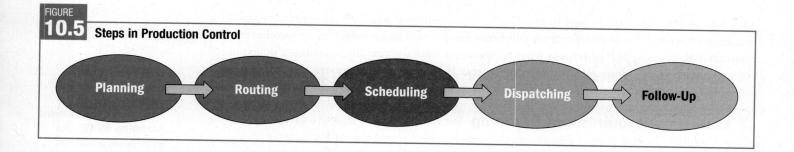

with the firm's perpetual inventory data, purchasing staff can identify necessary purchases. Employees or automated systems establish delivery schedules to provide needed parts and materials when required during the production process. Production planning also ensures the availability of needed machines and personnel. At the Wilson Sporting Goods Company factory in Ohio, there's a special excitement leading up to the Super Bowl each year: workers there have made every football that was ever used in a Super Bowl game. Each January, construction on the balls begins; the footballs are about 70 percent complete before the final playoff games are decided. But when the clock ticks down on those final games—and workers know which two team names will be printed on the balls—production goes into overdrive. The plant makes about 120 official game balls and around 6,000 replicas for sale to fans. "The market determines how many balls we will make," notes Gregory Miller, the plant controller.[23]

Although material inputs contribute to service-production systems, production planning for services tends to emphasize human resources more than materials.

Routing

Another phase of production control, called *routing*, determines the sequence of work throughout the facility and specifies who will perform each aspect of the work at what location. Routing choices depend on two factors: the nature of the good or service and the facility layouts discussed earlier in the chapter—product, process, fixed position, or customer oriented. JETCAM is a firm headquartered in Monaco that provides routing software to the aerospace composite industry, in which quality and accuracy is absolutely critical. One feature of the software is that it allows instructions for processes to be provided automatically instead of keyed in by workers—thus avoiding errors.[24]

Scheduling

In the *scheduling* phase of production control, managers develop timetables that specify how long each operation in the production process takes and when workers should perform it. Efficient scheduling ensures that production will meet delivery schedules and make efficient use of resources.

Scheduling is important whether the product is complex or simple to produce and whether it is a tangible good or a service. A pencil is simpler to produce than a computer, but each production process has scheduling requirements. A stylist may take 25 minutes to complete each haircut with just one or two tools, whereas every day a hospital has to schedule procedures and treatments ranging from X-rays to surgery to follow-up appointments. Sleepmaster is an Australian-based manufacturer of bedding products that recently moved some of its production offshore to China. Although the Chinese factory is completely owned and managed by Sleepmaster, the firm's MRP system did not have adequate scheduling capacity, and Chinese workers were not familiar with the technology. So Sleepmaster's operations manager implemented a new scheduling program called Resource Manager because it was more intuitive to use; it was easy to configure; it cost little to operate; and support was available via Skype.[25]

Production managers use a number of analytical methods for scheduling. One of the oldest methods, the *Gantt chart*, tracks projected and actual work progress over time. Gantt charts like the one in Figure 10.6 remain popular because they show at a glance the status of a particular project. However, they are most effective for scheduling relatively simple projects.

A complex project might require a *PERT (program evaluation and review technique)* chart, which seeks to minimize delays by coordinating all aspects of the production process. First developed for the military, PERT has been modified for industry. The simplified PERT diagram in Figure 10.7 summarizes the schedule for purchasing and installing a new robot in a factory. The heavy gold line indicates the *critical path*—the sequence of operations that requires the longest time for completion. In this case, the project cannot be completed in fewer than 17 weeks.

In practice, a PERT network may consist of thousands of events and cover months of time. Complex computer programs help production managers develop such a network and find the critical path among the maze of events and activities. The construction of a huge office building requires complex production planning of this nature.

Even small service businesses, like hair salons, use scheduling systems.

Dispatching

Dispatching is the phase of production control in which management instructs each department on what work to do and the time allowed for its completion. The dispatcher authorizes performance, provides instructions, and lists job priorities. Dispatching may be the responsibility of a manager or a self-managed work team.

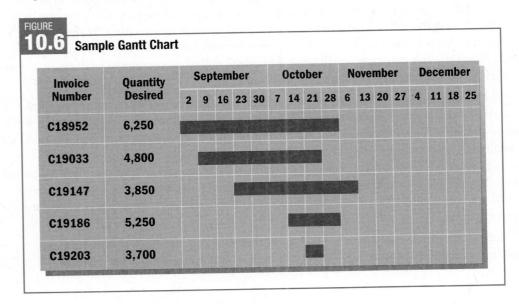

FIGURE 10.6 Sample Gantt Chart

Invoice Number	Quantity Desired	September					October				November				December			
		2	9	16	23	30	7	14	21	28	6	13	20	27	4	11	18	25
C18952	6,250	██	██	██	██	██	██	██										
C19033	4,800		██	██	██	██	██											
C19147	3,850			██	██	██	██	██	██	██								
C19186	5,250						██	██										
C19203	3,700							██										

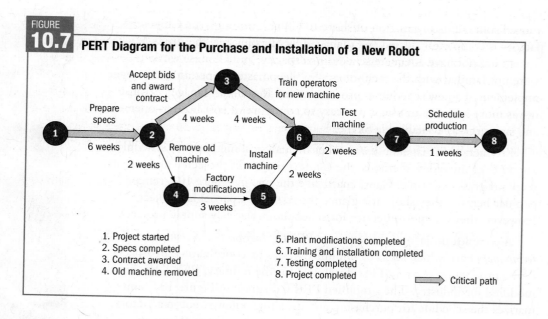

FIGURE 10.7 PERT Diagram for the Purchase and Installation of a New Robot

1. Project started
2. Specs completed
3. Contract awarded
4. Old machine removed
5. Plant modifications completed
6. Training and installation completed
7. Testing completed
8. Project completed

➡ Critical path

Follow-Up

Because even the best plans sometimes fail, production managers need to be aware of any problems. *Follow-up* is the phase of production control in which managers and employees or team members spot problems in the production process and come up with solutions. Problems take many forms: machinery malfunctions, delayed shipments, and employee absenteeism can all affect production. The production control system must detect and report these delays to managers or work teams so they can adjust schedules and correct the underlying problems.

Importance of Quality

Quality—as it relates to the production of goods and services—is defined as being free of deficiencies. Quality matters because fixing, replacing, or redesigning deficient products is costly. If Seagate makes a defective computer hard drive, it has to either fix the drive or replace it to keep a customer happy. If American Airlines books too many passengers for a flight, it has to offer vouchers worth several hundred dollars to encourage passengers to give up their seats and take a later flight.

For most companies, the costs of poor quality can amount to 20 percent of sales revenue, if not more. Some typical costs of poor quality include downtime, repair costs, rework, and employee turnover. Poor quality can also result in lost sales and a tarnished image. In an ironic twist, candymaker Candy Dynamics was forced to recall certain lots of its super sour candy bars called Toxic Waste Nuclear Sludge because it was discovered that they contained more than double the amount of lead considered allowable by law. It is possible that the candy, which is manufactured in Pakistan, was contaminated when ingredients were not correctly processed.[26]

One process that companies use to ensure that they produce high-quality products from the start is **benchmarking**—determining how well other companies perform

Assessment Check ☑

1. What five steps are involved in controlling the production process?
2. What is the difference between a PERT chart and a Gantt chart?

quality good or service that is free of deficiencies.

benchmarking process of determining how well other companies perform business functions or tasks.

business functions or tasks. In other words, benchmarking is the process of determining other firms' standards and best practices. Automobile companies routinely purchase each other's cars and then take them completely apart to examine and compare the design, components, and materials used to make even the smallest part. They then make improvements to match or exceed the quality found in their competitors' cars. Companies may use many different benchmarks, depending on their objectives. For instance, some organizations that want to make more money may compare their operating profits or expenses to those of other firms. Retailers concerned with productivity may want to benchmark sales per square foot.

It's important when benchmarking for a firm to establish what it wants to accomplish, what it wants to measure, and which company can provide the most useful benchmarking information. A firm might choose a direct competitor for benchmarking, or it might select a company in an entirely different industry—but one that has processes the firm wants to study and emulate.[27]

Quality Control

quality control measuring output against established quality standards.

Quality control involves measuring output against established quality standards. Firms need such checks to spot defective products and to avoid delivering inferior shipments to customers. Standards should be set high enough to meet customer expectations. A 90 or 95 percent success rate might seem to be a good number, but consider what your phone service or ATM network would be like if it worked only 90 percent of the time. You would feel frustrated and inconvenienced, and would probably switch your account to another bank or service provider.

Manufacturing firms can monitor quality levels through visual inspections, electronic sensors, robots, and X-rays. Surveys can provide quality-control information to services. Negative feedback from customers or a high rejection rate on a product or component sends a signal that production is not achieving quality standards. Firms that outsource operations may face a greater challenge in monitoring quality and assuring customers of the quality of their goods or services, especially if they are highly visible companies such as airlines. The "Solving an Ethical Controversy" feature discusses recent concerns over the quality of multivitamins manufactured for U.S. companies by facilities in China.

Because the typical factory can spend up to half its operating budget identifying and fixing mistakes, a company cannot rely solely on inspections to achieve its quality goals. Instead, quality-driven production managers identify all processes involved in producing goods and services and work to maximize their efficiency. The causes of problems in the processes must be found and eliminated. If a company concentrates its efforts on better designs of products and processes with clear quality targets, it can ensure virtually defect-free production.

General Electric, Heinz, 3M, Sears, and the U.S. military are just a few of the growing number of major organizations using the Six Sigma concept to achieve quality goals. *Six Sigma* means a company tries to make error-free products 99.9997 percent of the time—a tiny 3.4 errors per million opportunities. The goal of Six Sigma programs is for companies to eliminate virtually all defects in output, processes, and transactions. Motorola—also a Six Sigma firm—recently completed an initiative to redesign and simplify much of its software architecture in order to improve operational efficiencies and cut costs by reducing redundant IT applications.[28]

Solving an Ethical Controversy

Multivitamins Produced in China: Are Stricter Quality Controls Necessary?

Chinese manufacturing seems to be plagued by quality control issues, ranging from contamination of pet food and baby food to the paint on children's toys. Now it's multivitamins, which reportedly contain dangerous levels of lead and toxic bacteria—and are showing up in U.S. stores. In response, some legislators have called for stricter quality standards. Some vitamin firms have decided to seize the oppor-

tunity and source their ingredients elsewhere. One firm has begun offering Opurity, a new premium multivitamin whose ingredients come from other countries, labeling the bottle "China Free."

Should tighter quality controls be placed on Chinese manufacturing of U.S. goods?

PRO

1. According to the Chinese Ministry of Commerce, 85 percent of Chinese citizens rank quality concerns high for food and drugs made in their own country. Tighter controls would not only benefit U.S. and European consumers, they would benefit Chinese consumers as well.

2. Vitamins that are stamped "Made in Germany" or "Made in the USA" might still contain ingredients from China. Because it has already been demonstrated that these products contain high levels of toxic substances, tighter quality controls must be put into place.

CON

1. Many vitamins contain ingredients from multiple sources, so it is impossible to target China as the sole source of contamination.

2. Chinese production offers companies good value—labor and other services are far less expensive than in other countries, savings that can be passed along to the consumer.

Summary

Despite ongoing concerns, Swiss ingredients manufacturer Lonza recently announced that it would locate its new vitamin B3 manufacturing plant at its existing facility in China. Meanwhile, the Chinese government is considering new regulations on production of vitamin C—but with an emphasis on pricing power. For consumers who want assurance that the vitamins they purchase are free of ingredients from China, products like Opurity are available.

Sources: "China VC Industry to be Regulated in 2011," *Free Press Release*, January 26, 2011, http://www.free-press-release.com; "Lonza to Build Vitamin B3 Plant in China," *All About Feed*, May 4, 2010, http://www.allaboutfeed.net; "New Multivitamins Target Concern Over China's Quality Problems," *EIN*, April 27, 2010, http://www.einpresswire.com; "China Outsourcing: A Benefit to Companies Worldwide," *New Articles*, April 27, 2010, http://newarticles.co.tv.

International Organization for Standardization, (ISO) organization whose mission is to develop and promote International Standards for business, government and society to facilitate global trade and cooperation.

ISO Standards

For many goods and services, an important measure of quality is to meet the standards of the **International Organization for Standardization**, known as **ISO** for short—not an acronym but a shorter name derived from the Greek word *isos*, meaning "equal." Operating since 1947, ISO is a network of national standards bodies from 163 countries. Its mission is to develop and promote International Standards for business, government and society to facilitate global trade and cooperation. ISO has developed voluntary standards for everything from the format of banking and telephone cards to freight containers to paper sizes to metric screw threads. The U.S. member body of ISO is the American National Standards Institute.

The ISO 9000 family of standards give requirements and guidance for quality management to help organizations ensure that their products and services achieve customer satisfaction and also provide a framework for continual improvement. The ISO 14000 family of standards for environmental management helps organizations to ensure that their operations cause minimal harm to the environment and to achieve continual improvement of their environmental performance.

ISO 9001_2008 and ISO 14001:2004 respectively give the requirements for a quality management system and an environmental management system. Both can be used for certification, which means that the organization's management system (the way it manages its processes) is independently audited by a certification body (also known in North American as a registration body, or registrar) and confirmed as conforming to the requirements of the standard. The organization is then issued with an ISO 9001:2008 or an ISO 14001:2004 certificate.

Courtesy ISO

Many consumers prefer to buy from companies that are ISO 9000-certified.

It should be noted that certification is not a requirement of either standard, which can be implemented solely for the benefits it provides the organization and its customers. However, many organizations opt to seek certification because of the perception that an independent audit adds confidence in its abilities. Business partners, customers, suppliers and consumers may prefer to deal with or buy products and services from a certified organization. Certifications have to be periodically renewed through accompanying audits.

A second point is that ISO itself develops standards but does not itself carry out auditing and certification. This is done independently of ISO by hundreds of certification bodies around the world. The certificates they issue carry their own logo, but not ISO's because the latter does not approve or control their activities.

Whether or not an organization decides to seek certification of its management system, many have reported significant benefits from implementing ISO's management system standards, such as increased efficiency, better teamwork, improved customer satisfaction and reduced consumption of resources.[29]

Assessment Check ☑

1. What are some ways in which a company can monitor the quality level of its output?

2. List some of the benefits of acquiring ISO 9000 certification.

What's Ahead

Maintaining high quality is an important part of satisfying customers. Product quality and customer satisfaction are also objectives of the business function of marketing. The next part consists of three chapters that explore the many activities involved in customer-driven marketing. These activities include product development, distribution, promotion, and pricing.

Summary of Learning Objectives

[1] Explain the strategic importance of the production function.

Production and operations management is a vital business function. Without a quality good or service, a company cannot create profits, and it soon fails. The production process is also crucial in a not-for-profit organization, because the good or service it produces justifies the organization's existence. Production and operations management plays an important strategic role by lowering the costs of production, boosting output quality, and allowing the firm to respond flexibly and dependably to customers' demands.

Assessment Check Answers

1.1 What is mass production? Mass production is a system for manufacturing products in large quantities through effective combinations of employees with specialized skills, mechanization, and standardization.

1.2 What is the difference between flexible production and customer-driven production? Flexible production generally involves using technology to receive and fulfill orders and skilled people to carry out tasks needed to fill a particular order. Customer-driven production evaluates customer demands in order to make the connection between products manufactured and products bought.

[2] Identify and describe the four main categories of production processes.

The four main categories of production processes are the analytic production system, which reduces a raw material to its component parts in order to extract one or more marketable products; the synthetic production system, which combines a number of raw materials or parts to produce finished products; the continuous production process, which generates finished products over a lengthy period of time; and the intermittent production process, which generates products in short production runs.

Assessment Check Answers

2.1 What are the two main production systems? The two systems are analytic production and synthetic production.

2.2 What are the two time-related production processes? The two time-related production processes are the continuous production process and the intermittent production process.

[3] Explain the role of technology in the production process.

Computer-driven automation allows companies to design, create, and modify products rapidly and produce them in ways that effectively meet customers' changing needs. Important design and production technologies include robots, computer-aided design (CAD), computer-aided manufacturing (CAM), and computer-integrated manufacturing

(CIM). Many firms are pouring resources into the development of manufacturing processes that result in a reduction of waste, energy use, and pollution.

Assessment Check Answers

3.1 List some of the reasons businesses invest in robots. Businesses use robots to free people from sometimes dangerous assignments and to move heavy items from one place to another in a factory.

3.2 What is a flexible manufacturing system (FMS)? An FMS is a production facility that workers can quickly modify to manufacture different products.

3.3 What are the major benefits of computer-integrated manufacturing (CIM)? The main benefits are increased productivity, decreased design costs, increased equipment utilization, and improved quality.

[4] Identify the factors involved in a plant location decision.

Criteria for choosing the best site for a production facility fall into three categories: transportation, human, and physical factors. Transportation factors include proximity to markets and raw materials, along with availability of transportation alternatives. Physical variables involve such issues as water supply, available energy, and options for disposing of hazardous wastes. Human factors include the area's labor supply, local regulations, taxes, and living conditions.

Assessment Check Answers

4.1 How does an environmental impact study influence the location decision? An environmental impact study influences the location decision because it studies how transportation, energy use, water and sewer treatment needs, and other factors will affect plants, wildlife, water, air, and other features of the natural environment.

4.2 What human factors are relevant to the location decision? Human factors include an area's labor supply, labor costs, local regulations, taxes, and living conditions.

[5] Explain the major tasks of production and operations managers, and outline the three activities involved in implementing the production plan.

Production and operations managers use people and machinery to convert inputs (materials and resources) into finished goods and services. Four major tasks are involved. First, the managers must plan the overall production process. Next, they must pick the best layout for their facilities. Then they implement their production plans. Finally, they control the production process and evaluate results to maintain the highest possible quality.

Implementation involves deciding whether to make, buy, or lease components; selecting the best suppliers for materials; and controlling inventory to keep enough, but not too much, on hand.

Assessment Check Answers ✓

5.1 List the four major tasks of production and operations managers. The four tasks are planning overall production, laying out the firm's facilities, implementing the production plan, and controlling manufacturing to achieve high quality.

5.2 What is the difference between a traditional manufacturing structure and a team-based structure? In the traditional structure, each manager is given a specific area of authority. In a team-based structure, all workers are responsible for their output.

5.3 What factors affect the make, buy, or lease decision? The costs of leasing or purchasing parts from vendors, versus producing them in house, the availability of dependable outside suppliers, and the need for confidentiality affect this decision.

⌐6⌐ Identify the steps in the production control process.

The production control process consists of five steps: planning, routing, scheduling, dispatching, and follow-up. Quality control is an important consideration throughout this process. Coordination of each of these phases should result in high production efficiency and low production costs.

Assessment Check Answers ✓

6.1 What five steps are involved in controlling the production process? The five steps are planning, routing, scheduling, dispatching, and follow-up.

6.2 What is the difference between a PERT chart and a Gantt chart? PERT charts, which seek to minimize delays by coordinating all aspects of the production process, are used for more complex projects; Gantt charts, which track projected and actual work progress over time, are used for scheduling relatively simple projects.

⌐7⌐ Discuss the importance of quality control.

Quality control involves evaluating goods and services against established quality standards. Such checks are necessary to spot defective products and to see that they are not shipped to customers. Devices for monitoring quality levels of the firm's output include visual inspection, electronic sensors, robots, and X-rays. Companies are increasing the quality of their goods and services by using Six Sigma techniques and by becoming ISO 9000 and 14000 certified.

Assessment Check Answers ✓

7.1 What are some ways in which a company can monitor the quality level of its output? Benchmarking, quality control, Six Sigma, and ISO standards are ways of monitoring quality.

7.2 List some of the benefits of acquiring ISO 9000 certification. These standards define how a company should ensure that its products meet customers' requirements. Studies show that customers prefer to buy from companies that are ISO 9000 certified.

■ Business Terms You Need to Know

production 316	computer-aided	inventory	benchmarking 336
production and operations	manufacturing	control 332	quality control 337
management 316	(CAM) 322	just-in-time (JIT)	International
mass production 318	flexible manufacturing	system 332	Organization for
LEED (Leadership in Energy	system (FMS) 322	materials requirement	Standardization
and Environmental	computer-integrated	planning (MRP) 333	(ISO) 338
Design) 320	manufacturing (CIM) 323	production	
computer-aided design	make, buy, or lease	control 333	
(CAD) 322	decision 329	quality 336	

■ Review Questions

1. What is utility? How does production create utility?

2. Why is production such an important business activity? In what ways does it create value for the company and its customers?

3. Why are firms now moving more toward flexible production and customer-driven production instead of mass production? Describe a product that you think would be better suited to flexible production or customer-driven production than mass production. Explain your choice.

4. Identify which production system—analytic or synthetic—applies to each of the following products:

   a. logging

   b. medical care

   c. cotton farming

   d. fishing

   e. construction

5. Industries such as home construction and dentistry benefit from the use of CAD. In both of these, CAM could be used as well—in the manufacture of home components as well as dental implants, crowns, and the like. Choose another industry that seems like a candidate for the use of both CAD and CAM systems. Explain how the industry could use both.

Projects and Teamwork Applications

1. Imagine that you recently became the owner of a popular ice cream shop. You want to attract more customers and ultimately expand the business. Choose the type of production process—continuous or intermittent—you think would best fit your business. Then create a plan outlining specifically how you would use this process and why it would help you achieve your goal as a business owner.

2. On your own or with a classmate, imagine that you've been hired to help a business group design a shopping mall. Taking into account the factors listed in the chapter, come up with recommendations for where the mall should be located—and why. Present your plan to the class.

3. On your own or with a classmate, select one of the following businesses and sketch or describe the layout that you think would be best for attracting and serving customers:

Web Assignments

1. **Just-in-time inventory management systems.** Go to the Web sites listed here to learn more about just-in-time inventory management systems. Make some notes on what you learned and bring them to class to participate in a class discussion.

   http://www.wisegeek.com/what-is-a-just-in-time-inventory.htm

   http://smallbusiness.dnb.com/manage/finances/12375503-1.html

   http://www.smcdata.com/software-choices/just-in-time-inventory-control-systems-1.html

2. **Plant location decision.** Using an Internet news service, such as Google news (http://news.google.com) or Yahoo! news (http://news.yahoo.com), search for information on a recent plant location decision. An example is VW's recent

6. SeaWorld has facilities in Florida, Texas, and California. What specific factors might have contributed to these choices?

7. What would be the best facility layout for each of the following?

   a. movie rental shop

   b. nail salon

   c. car wash

   d. sandwich shop

8. What might be the factors involved in the selection of suppliers for a steakhouse restaurant?

9. What is inventory control? Why is the management of inventory crucial to a company's success?

10. What is benchmarking? How can it help a firm improve the quality of its goods and services?

   a. Mexican restaurant

   b. home furnishings store

   c. pet store

   d. motorcycle dealership

   e. dentist office

4. Suppose you and your best friend decided to operate a house-painting service. Draft a production plan for your business, including the following decisions: (a) make, buy, or lease; (b) suppliers; and (c) inventory control.

5. Choose two firms for comparison (one firm should provide a good benchmarking opportunity for its production processes). Keep in mind that the benchmarking firm doesn't necessarily have to be in the same industry as the other selected firm. Present your decisions to the class and explain why you made both choices.

decision to build a new production facility in Chattanooga, Tennessee. Research the decision and then prepare a brief report outlining the factors that went into the firm's decision to locate the plant where it did.

http://www.vw.com/vwbuzz/browse/en/us/detail/Volkswagen_Group_of_America_announces_it_will_produce_cars_in_Chattanooga/219.

3. **ISO certification.** Visit the Web site of the International Organization for Standardization (http://www.iso.org). Click on "standards development" and then "processes and procedures." What are some of the products for which ISO standards are currently being developed?

Note: Internet Web addresses change frequently. If you don't find the exact sites listed, you may need to access the organization's home page and search from there or use a search engine such as Bing or Google.

Macedonia: The New Hub of Apparel Manufacturing?

If you have to look twice on a map to find the Republic of Macedonia, you're probably not alone. But the small country with a population of about 2 million, nestled in the heart of eastern Europe (sharing borders with Bulgaria, Serbia, Kosovo, Albania, and Greece), is becoming a hotbed of apparel manufacturing. Although textiles and clothing already make up one of the largest industries in this country, Macedonian manufacturers are pushing for more, claiming that their factories are working at only half their capacity.

Currently, Macedonian factories are equipped to fulfill cut-make and cut-make-trim orders, but the goal is to offer full-package production, including design and domestic fabric procurement. "We need customers to move their design and product development here, so we become their partners in production, offering a fast, flexible approach and something cheaper than the client is used to," says Vladimir Icokaev, a manager at textile and clothing exporter Global Plus.

Macedonian factories already supply major European brands and retailers with everything from jackets and coats to skirts, pants, and shirts. The 500 textile and clothing firms in Macedonia are generally small by international standards—most employ from 30 to 500 workers. However, what they can't provide in volume they can offer in flexibility. Competitors from countries as nearby as Bulgaria and as far away as China and India are focusing on mass production, offering high volume at the lowest cost. Macedonian manufacturers, on the other hand, prefer to focus on short production runs and high quality. "If buyers want capacity they can get it anywhere in the world," says Ilijev Nikolco, general manager for manufacturer INT, which provides a range of services from design through finished garments. "The future for Macedonia is exclusively in higher quality, more complicated styles and lower lead times."

Unlike the competitive environment found in other countries, many of the small manufacturers in Macedonia work together to serve the same customers. "The appeal for buyers and retailers is that they can deal with one factory that has a network to put garments out to individual suppliers—a one-stop shop," notes Gabriela Pavloska, export manager at Okitex, a women's wear company that is headquartered in Germany. Okitex actually works with 20 factories in Macedonia to produce a complete collection of women's items—coats, blazers, blouses, and the like. "Our idea is to combine factories to provide a source because a client doesn't just want one type of garment," explains Pavloska.

Location is another factor that works in Macedonia's favor, particularly with its European customers. Delivery to the United Kingdom takes about three days, to Germany about two days. In addition, Macedonia is located near the high-end fabric producers in Turkey and Italy. So the average lead time from receipt of fabric to delivery of a product is around three weeks. The small, flexible Macedonian factories can easily produce minimum orders of just 100 pieces per style and color—and have them at a customer's doorstep anywhere in western Europe in less than a month.

Macedonia still has some obstacles to overcome. Workers do not always have the necessary technical skills, and Macedonia is not yet a member of the European Union. But some factories are sending workers to Germany and other countries for training, and the country recently held an international business event sponsored by USAID (the U.S. Agency for International Development) and the Macedonian Competitiveness Project. During the event, a group of 29 manufacturers showcased their capabilities to buyers that included such popular European brands as Topshop, Monsoon, Whistles, and BMB Clothing. Buyers were surprised—and impressed—by the facilities, the quality, the flexibility, and the easy location of Macedonian manufacturers. "It really is a brilliant way to meet a new manufacturing partner," said Leonie Barrie, an industry expert. So the next time you buy an item of clothing, check the label—it might read, "Made in Macedonia."

Questions for Critical Thinking

1. Do you think Macedonia's strategy of focusing on flexibility, quality, and proximity rather than trying to compete with the high-volume, low-price strategy of its rivals will be successful in the long run? Why or why not?

2. How might Macedonian apparel manufacturers attract U.S. buyers?

Sources: "Macedonian Apparel on Buyers' Radar," *Carana Corporation,* http://www.carana.com, accessed June 7, 2011; "Macedonia: Stip on Radar of UK Apparel Retailers," *Fibre2Fashion,* April 20, 2010, http://www.fibre2fashion.com; Leonie Barrie, "Analysis: Macedonian Makers Eye Fast Fashion Partnerships," *Just-Style,* March 23, 2010, http://www.just-style.com.

CASE 10.2 Zappos: How Not to Get Zapped by Customer Service

If you like shoes, you've heard of Zappos. Perhaps you've ordered a pair (or two or three) from the popular Web site, taking advantage of the free shipping and free returns. Tony Hsieh, CEO of Zappos, wants you to be happy. He wants to you be happy with your shoes, and if you're not, he wants to make returns easy for you. This is because he wants you to come back and order more shoes—which you probably will. Hsieh believes that the best way to attract and keep customers is to "wow" them with customer service. It's a formula that works—Zappos reports that nearly 75 percent of its business comes from repeat customers.

Although Zappos is now owned by Amazon, and has also grown to offer apparel, accessories, and other products, the company's commitment to customer service has not changed. Delivering top service, which includes fulfilling and shipping orders as quickly as possible, is a significant part of Zappos' production function. While Internet and other computer technology helps speed delivery and turnaround time, it also sets the bar higher than ever before. One survey recently revealed that consumers would be willing to pay nearly 11 percent more for superior customer service at online shopping sites. "Due to the seemingly distant and remote nature of online shopping, it makes sense that consumers would pay a higher premium to have the comfort and peace of mind that they will be taken care of in the case of a serious question, concern or problem," concluded the survey.

Customer service is also an investment in quality. Zappos currently has a Customer Loyalty department staffed by 380 employees whose job it is to communicate among the different departments of the company and with customers. The customer loyalty team interfaces with the resource desk, order verification (anti-fraud team),

quality assurance, kaizen (continuous training), and e-mail/live chat, along with other departments as necessary. Customer loyalty team members have the authority to send individual customers personal notes or request flowers for a wedding or anniversary celebration. They don't need to ask permission to issue refunds or coupons or to give out their contact information. At Zappos, the outlook is that everyone is a customer and should be treated with respect.

Constant improvement is also part of the company culture. "Let's take our learnings and improve, constantly," says marketing chief Aaron Magness. "If we rest, we'll be passed by the next more hungry business." Tony Hsieh agrees, adding that it is necessary to embrace change, recognizing opportunities in the industry and the marketplace. The formula must work—Zappos rakes in more than $1 billion each year selling shoes online to customers who haven't even tried them on to see if they can wiggle their toes.

Questions for Critical Thinking

1. Explain how customer service fulfills a significant portion of Zappos' production function.
2. What kind of firm might Zappos use for benchmarking? Why?

Sources: "Zappos' Customer Service Draws Raves in a New Report," *Internet Retailer,* accessed June 7, 2011, http://www.internetretailer.com; Sean Smith, "What Can Zappos CEO Tony Hsieh Teach You About Online Business Success?" *Power of More,* April 19, 2010, http://powerofmore.net; Brandon Gutman, "Zappos' Marketing Chief: Customer Service is the New Marketing!" *Fast Company,* March 15, 2010, http://www.fastcompany.com; Eric Friedman, "Zappos and the Continued Power of Customer Service," *Marketing,* March 12, 2010, http://www.marketing.fm; Graham Charlton, "Q&A: Zappos' Jane Judd on Customer Loyalty," *Ecoconsultancy,* November 4, 2009, http://ecoconsultancy.com.

CASE 10.3 Kimpton Hotels Puts Green Initiatives to Work

It's one thing for a company to talk about green initiatives; it's quite another for the firm to put those initiatives into practice. Kimpton Hotels & Restaurants began putting green initiatives to work in its hotels and restaurants nearly thirty years ago, long before these

practices became popular. Of course, it's the operations function of the business that implements this type of plan; it's the hotel manager, the dishwasher in the restaurant, the housekeeping staff, the front desk clerk. "*How* we do what we do defines us," observes NikiLeondakis, COO of

Kimpton Hotels & Restaurants, which runs 50 boutique-styleluxury hotels and restaurants across the U.S.

Although Kimpton began its green practices long ago, in 2005 the company launched a company-wide program called EarthCare in order to standardize these practices across all of its hotels and restaurants. Frank Kawecki, director of operations for KimptonRestaurants in the Northeast, recalls that Kimpton's green efforts started first in the restaurants with the chefs, then spread. When the EarthCare program began, the company asked for volunteers from each property who were devoted to the green effort because they were already committed to the idea and could communicate best between management and staff. Volunteers ranged from bartenders to general managers who were willing to meet once a month. One of the first initiatives—which came from restaurant servers—was to eliminate imported bottled water, shifting instead to locally bottled water and the use of recycled water bottles.

As EarthCare has expanded throughout the company, standard guidelines have been set for nearly every facet of the firm's operation. Home office materials and procedures include shifting to online publication of many documents; using post-consumer recycled paper and eco-friendly inks for those documents that are printed; making hotel keycards from recycled plastic; offering continuous education in green initiatives for staff, and more. At the hotels themselves, all hotel in-room materials and bills are printed on recycled paper; phone books are offered by request only; all plumbing is water-efficient; lighting is LED or CFL, and subject to motion sensors; rooms are stocked with green-certified linens and towels; guest room soaps are made of natural ingredients, and carpet cleaning is done with non-toxic products. If the list seems endless, it nearly is—and the complexity of the operations management required to implement standards such as these is daunting.

Waste management is a category unto itself, with hotel and restaurant-wide recycling and reuse of everything from cardboard and paper to batteries and computers. Restaurants in particular present a huge challenge. "There's an enormous amount of waste from a lot of restaurants," observes Frank Kawecki. "A lot of it can be composted, recycled, or reused. There can be a 40-percent savings in waste removal. Waste removal was traditionally a fixed expense that we have manipulated," through EarthCare. In addition to reducing waste and energy use, Kimpton restaurants purchase and serve as many certified organic products as possible, ranging from local produce and seafood to coffee, tea, and wine.

Saving the planet can be expensive. Running a business incurs costs as well. One of the challenges of implementing the EarthCare program is monitoring costs. "Green efforts can't compromise the experience for our guests and it can't cost our shareholders more money. If we go out of business, saving the planet as hoteliers goes away," notes NikiLeondakis. "So that premise was very good in helping us decide what we would tackle first—water savings, energy savings." Whatever is good for the planet has to be good for the bottom line. One way that Kimpton Hotels meets this goal is by looking at ways for certain costs to off-set each other. If purchasing recycled paper costs more, there might be a way to find savings in another area. "We put measurements on all of our efforts to see what impact they have on the bottom line," says Leondakis. "We've still been able to say that it saves us money."

Recently Kimpton Hotels announced its plan to seek third-party Green Seal certification on all 50 of its properties; ten properties have already been certified. Green Seal certification involves an application process and evaluation similar to LEED certification, which the company is also seeking for its new or renovated properties. "It will be an ongoing work in progress forever," predicts Leondakis. But Kimpton Hotels has a head start.

Questions for Critical Thinking

1. Location is certainly a production factor for Kimpton Hotels & Restaurants, which are located in cities such as New York, Los Angeles, Boston, Chicago, and Seattle. What location factors might Kimpton managers consider when thinking about whether to acquire or build a new Kimpton hotel and restaurant?

2. According to the EarthCare program, what factors might a Kimpton restaurant chef or manager consider when selecting suppliers?

3. A daily staff meeting at a Kimpton hotel can be considered part of production control, contributing to the smooth running of the hotel. Who might attend such a meeting? What kinds of topics might they discuss?

4. Quality is top priority at Kimpton Hotels & Restaurants. What steps can a Kimpton hotel manager take to balance quality and the initiatives of the EarthCare program?

Sources: Kimpton Hotels Web site, http://www.kimptonhotels. com, accessed June 7, 2011; Matt Courtland, "Environmental Mission Statements: A List of Hotel Sustainability Policies," *Environmental Leader,* March 18, 2010, http://www.environmentalleader.com; "Kimpton Hotels Aim for 100 Percent Green Seal Certification," *GreenerBuildings,* March 31, 2010, http://www.greenbiz.com.

GREENSBURG, KS

No Time to Micromanage

"This is a stepping stone for me," thought Greensburg's town administrator, Steve Hewitt. Hewitt, who had grown up in Greensburg, had moved back home and taken a position in the tiny rural town of 1,500. Standing in what was left of his kitchen on the night of Friday, May 4, 2007, he realized he had gotten more than he bargained for.

Across town, Mayor Lonnie McCollum and his wife had survived by clinging to a mattress as the storm ravaged their home. A write-in candidate in the past election, McCollum had accepted the job and set out to revive the dying town. Among his many ideas, the most innovative had been green building. McCollum was no tree-hugger; he was simply looking for a way to save money on fuel and utilities, to conserve the town's resources.

Like many people in town, Hewitt and McCollum had no idea of the extent of the damage. They would later learn that the two-mile-wide F5 tornado drove right through the two-mile-wide town. By the end of the weekend, though, they knew that Greensburg was gone. At a press conference, McCollum announced that the town would rebuild, and would do it using green technology.

By May 2008, the town was on its third mayor since the disaster, but Steve Hewitt was still the town administrator. He had expanded his staff from 20 to 35 people, establishing a full-time fire department, a planning department, and a community development department. Each week Hewitt spent hours giving interviews to reporters from all over the world. "He's very open as far as information," said Recovery Coordinator and Assistant Town Administrator Kim Alderfer. "He's very good about delegating authority. He gives you the authority to do your job. He doesn't have time to micromanage."

Meanwhile, residents Janice and John Haney had rebuilt their family farm on the outskirts of town. Although their new home, an earth berm structure, was full of energy-efficient features, Janice wasn't convinced that the plan to rebuild Greensburg using green technology was the right one. "I do worry that it will be a T-shirt slogan," said Haney. "I personally don't think the persons that are living in Greensburg right now are really committed to it. We didn't have a choice. You MUST go green. That's really not everybody's option." She added that many people feared higher taxes would force some families out of town.

Questions

After viewing the video, answer the following questions:

1. What kind of leader is Steve Hewitt?
2. How would you describe Greensburg's culture?
3. Do you believe that as town administrator, Hewitt had the right to impose green building codes on residents and businesses?
4. Perform a SWOT analysis of Greensburg's green initiative.

LAUNCHING YOUR
[Management Career]

Part 3, "Management: Empowering People to Achieve Business Objectives," covers Chapters 7 through 10, which discuss management, leadership, and the internal organization; human resource management, motivation, and labor–management relations; improving performance through empowerment, teamwork, and communication; and production and operations management. In those chapters, you read about top executives and company founders who not only direct their companies' strategy but lead others in their day-to-day tasks to keep them on track, middle managers who devise plans to turn the strategies into realities, and supervisors who work directly with employees to create strong teams that satisfy customers. An incredible variety of jobs is available to those choosing management careers. And the demand for managers will continue to grow. The U.S. Department of Labor estimates that managerial jobs will grow by nearly 15 percent over the next decade.[1]

So what kinds of jobs might you be able to choose from if you launch a management career? As you learned in Chapter 7, three types of management jobs exist: supervisory managers, middle managers, and top managers. Supervisory management, or first-line management, includes positions such as supervisor, office manager, department manager, section chief, and team leader. Managers at this level

work directly with the employees who produce and sell a firm's goods and services.

Middle management includes positions such as general managers, plant managers, division managers, and regional or branch managers. They are responsible for setting objectives consistent with top management's goals and planning and implementing strategies for achieving those objectives.

Top managers include such positions as chief executive officer (CEO), chief operating officer (COO), chief financial officer (CFO), chief information officer (CIO), and executive vice president. Top managers devote most of their time to developing long-range plans, setting a direction for their organization, and inspiring a company's executives and employees to achieve their vision for the company's future. Top managers travel frequently between local, national, and global offices as they meet and work with customers, suppliers, and company managers and employees.

Most managers start their careers in areas such as sales, production, or finance, so you likely will start in a similar entry-level job. If you do that job and other jobs well, you may be considered for a supervisory position. Then, if you are interested and have the technical, human, and conceptual skills to succeed, you'll begin your management career path. But what

kinds of supervisory management jobs are typically available? Let's review the exciting possibilities.

Administrative services managers manage basic services—such as clerical work, payroll, travel, printing and copying, data records, telecommunications, security, parking, and supplies—without which no organization could operate. On average, administrative service managers earn $75,000 a year.[2]

Construction managers plan, schedule, and coordinate the building of homes, commercial buildings such as offices and stores, and industrial facilities such as manufacturing plants and distribution centers. Unlike administrative service managers, who work in offices, construction managers typically work on building sites with architects, engineers, construction workers, and suppliers. On average, construction managers earn almost $78,000 a year.[3]

Food service managers run restaurants and services that prepare and offer meals to customers. They coordinate workers and suppliers in kitchens, dining areas, and banquet operations; are responsible for those who order and purchase food inventories; maintain kitchen equipment; and recruit, hire, and train new workers. Food service managers can work for chains such as Ruby Tuesday or Olive Garden, for local restaurants, and for corporate food service departments in organizations. On average, food service managers earn more than $49,500 a year.[4]

Human resource managers help organizations follow federal and local labor laws; effectively recruit, hire, train, and retain talented workers; administer corporate pay and benefits plans; develop and administer organizational human resource policies; and, when necessary, participate in contract negotiations or handle disputes. Human resource management jobs vary widely, depending on how specialized the requirements are. On average, human resource managers earn from $45,000 to $96,000 a year, depending on the area in which they specialize.[5]

Lodging managers work in hotels and motels but also help run camps, ranches, and recreational resorts. They may oversee guest services, front desk, kitchen, restaurant, banquet, house cleaning, and maintenance workers. Because they are expected to help satisfy customers around the clock, they often work long hours and may be on call when not at work. On average, lodging managers earn about $45,000 a year.[6]

Medical and health services managers work in hospitals, nursing homes, doctors' offices, and corporate and university settings. They run departments that offer clinical services; ensure that state and federal laws are followed; and handle decisions related to the management of patient care, nursing, surgery, therapy, medical records, and

financial payments. On average, medical and health service managers earn $75,000 a year.[7]

Purchasing managers lead and control organizational supply chains that ensure that companies have needed materials to produce the goods and services they sell, purchase materials at reasonable prices, and oversee deliveries when and where they are needed. Purchasing managers work with wholesale and retail buyers, buying goods that are then resold to others; purchasing agents, who buy supplies and raw materials for their organizations; and contract specialists, who negotiate and supervise purchasing contracts with key suppliers and vendors. On average, purchasing managers earn nearly $89,000 a year.[8]

Production managers direct and coordinate operations that manufacture goods. They work with employees who produce parts and assemble products, help determine which new machines should be purchased and when existing machines need maintenance, and are responsible for achieving production goals that specify the quality, cost, schedule, and quantity of units to be produced. On average, production managers earn almost $83,000 a year.[9]

Career Assessment Exercises in Management

1. The American Management Association is a global, not-for-profit

professional organization that provides a range of management development and educational services to individuals, companies, and government agencies. Access the AMA's Web site at http://www.amanet.org. Explore the "Free Resources" link there (you will have to register). Pick an article or research area that interests you. Provide a one-page summary of the management issues discussed in the feature.

2. Go online to a business news service, such as Yahoo! News or Google News, or look at the business section of your local newspaper. Find a story relating to a first-line supervisor, middle manager, or top executive. Summarize that person's duties. What decisions does that person make and how do those decisions affect his or her organization?

3. Pick a supervisory management position from the descriptions provided here that interests you. Research the career field. What skills do you possess that would make you a good candidate for a management position in that field? What work and other experience do you need to help you get started? Create a list of both your strengths and weaknesses and formulate a plan to add to your strengths.

PART 4

Marketing Management

R. Ian Lloyd/Masterfile

Learning Objectives

[1] Summarize the ways in which marketing creates utility.

[2] Discuss the marketing concept.

[3] Describe not-for-profit marketing, and identify the five major categories of nontraditional marketing.

[4] Outline the basic steps in developing a marketing strategy.

[5] Describe the marketing research function.

[6] Identify and explain each of the methods available for segmenting consumer and business markets.

[7] Outline the determinants of consumer behavior.

[8] Discuss the benefits of and tools for relationship marketing.

Customer-Driven Marketing

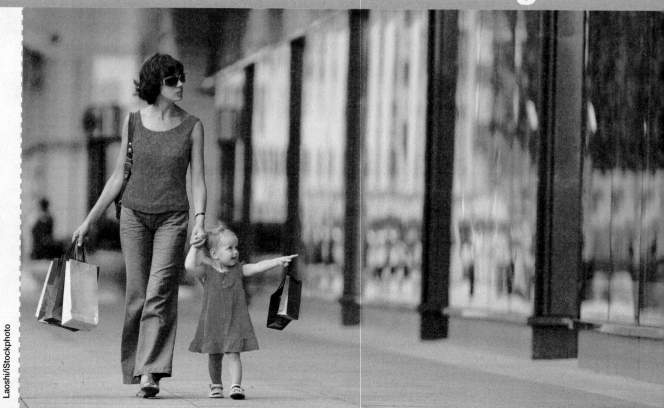

Laoshi/iStockphoto

Netflix: Streaming Versus DVDs

Do you like to stream movies to your laptop and watch them anywhere? Or do you prefer to plop onto the couch and watch a DVD on your roommate's flatscreen TV? Netfix, which made its name and its niche by offering mail-order subscriptions for DVDs, has now placed its bet on the streaming choice. With more than 17 million subscribers—66 percent of whom opted to stream 15 minutes or more of a TV show or movie last year—California-based Netflix is rolling out more of what it believes its customers want.

In addition to rising demand for content available through online streaming, the demand for devices that handle Netflix streaming for TV is increasing. Apple TV has sold 1 million of these devices, with the Roku and Boxee brands close behind. Most consumers say they are purchasing these devices in order to watch movies and shows streamed by Netflix. Perhaps even more significant is the deal Netflix recently made with Google's Android to offer instant streaming over its mobile phones. "I'm happy to announce we'll launch select Android devices that will instantly stream from Netflix," says Gret Peters of Netflix product development. "We will also continue to develop a standard, platform-wide solution that allows content providers to deliver their services to all Android-based devices." Android users who are also Netflix subscribers say they have been eagerly awaiting this option.

The big movie studios, which traditionally have been slow to adopt new choices for viewing, seem to be on board—at least partially. Recently Netfix agreed to pay nearly $1 billion over five years for the online streaming rights for movies from Paramount, Lionsgate, and MGM, which will stock the Netflix movie library with more titles—allowing the firm to continue its rapid growth in membership without keeping customers waiting for the titles they want to see. Netflix now has movie-streaming rights to approximately 46 percent of new releases in the United States. "We are giving people more and more reason to stream instead of waiting to get their DVDs through the mail," explains Ted Sarandos, chief content officer for Netflix.

What about DVD lovers—or customers who enjoy both methods of viewing? In its push to capture the streaming market (with the potential long-range goal of doing away entirely with DVDs), Netflix may have alienated some of these customers. When the firm announced that it was removing the option to "Add to DVD Queue" from customer's streaming devices, subscribers were quick to voice their discontent. Product development director Jamie Odell responded with a blog post explaining the benefits of the move—and was bombarded with 5,000 replies from customers, many of them negative. "You ought to leave this up to your subscribers to weigh in on," wrote one customer. In its enthusiasm for promoting the next big thing, Netflix seems to have forgotten to ask its customers first what they would prefer.

Despite this stumble, Netflix continues to dominate the home movie-watching market. A recent survey revealed that Netflix was one of the 50 most-searched terms on the Internet. Although the competitor that seems to be looming largest and closest is Facebook—because content providers can stream directly through their own Facebook pages—industry analysts have some doubt whether a Facebook presence can actually translate to rental sales and thus income, at least for the near future. Meanwhile, Netflix is positioning itself to be the number-one gateway for streaming movies and TV shows—and it is betting that you will be watching.[1]

Business success in the 21st century is directly tied to a company's ability to identify and serve its target markets. In fact, all organizations—profit-oriented and not-for-profit, manufacturing and retailing—*must* serve customer needs to succeed, just as Netflix does by offering multiple ways of viewing entertainment. Marketing is the link between the organization and the people who buy and use its goods and services. It is the way organizations determine buyer needs and inform potential customers that their firms can meet those needs by supplying a quality product at a reasonable price. And it is the path to developing loyal, long-term customers.

Although consumers who purchase goods for their own use and enjoyment, or business purchasers seeking products to use in their firm's operation, may seem to be a large number of undifferentiated masses, marketers see distinct wants and needs for each group. To understand buyers, from manufacturers to Web surfers to shoppers in the grocery aisles, companies gather mountains of data on every aspect of consumer lifestyles and buying behaviors. Marketers use the data to understand the needs and wants of both final customers and business buyers. Satisfying customers goes a long way toward building relationships with them. It's not always easy. To establish links with the buying public, Whole Foods CEO John Mackey invites e-mails from consumers who may—or may not—be customers. After several weeks of electronic debate with an animal welfare activist over Whole Foods's practice of selling duck meat from a particular source, Mackey asked the activist to help rewrite his firm's policies on farm animal treatment. This relationship, which developed through direct communication between the CEO and a consumer, has helped Whole Foods cement its relationship with customers who have certain food-source concerns.

This chapter begins with an examination of the marketing concept and the way businesspeople develop a marketing strategy. We then turn to marketing research techniques, leading to an explanation of how businesses apply data to market segmentation and understanding customer behavior. The chapter closes with a detailed look at the important role customer relationships play in today's highly competitive business world.

What Is Marketing?

Every organization—from profit-seeking firms such as McDonald's and Drugstore.com to such not-for-profits as the Make-a-Wish Foundation and the American Cancer Society—must serve customer needs to succeed. Perhaps retail pioneer J. C. Penney best expressed this priority when he told his store managers, "Either you or your replacement will greet the customer within the first 60 seconds."

According to the American Marketing Association Board of Directors, <u>marketing</u> is "the activity, set of institutions, and processes for creating, communicating, delivering, and exchanging offerings that have value for customers, clients, partners, and society at large."[2] In addition to selling goods and services, marketing techniques help people advocate ideas or viewpoints and educate others. The American Diabetes Association mails out questionnaires that ask, "Are you at risk for diabetes?" The documents help educate the general public about this widespread disease by listing its risk factors and common symptoms and describing the work of the association.

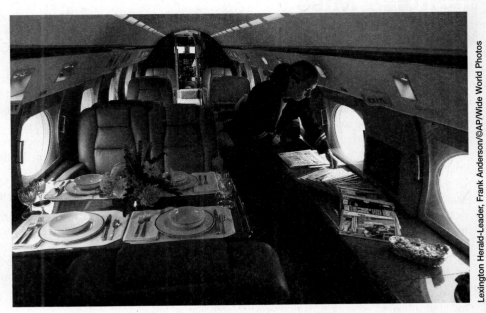

The best marketers give consumers what they want and anticipate their needs. NetJets offers fractional jet ownership to executives who want the luxury and flexibility of private ownership without the cost of owning their own plane.

Lexington Herald-Leader, Frank Anderson/©AP/Wide World Photos

Department store founder Marshall Field explained marketing quite clearly when he advised one employee to "give the lady what she wants." The phrase became the company motto, and it remains a business truism today. The best marketers not only give consumers what they want but even anticipate consumers' needs before those needs surface. Ideally, they can get a jump on the competition by creating a link in consumers' minds between the new need and the fulfillment of that need by the marketers' products. Principal Financial Group, with headquarters in Iowa, markets employee retirement plans to other firms that then custom tailor those plans to retain key employees. NetJets offers fractional jet ownership to executives who want the luxury and flexibility of private ownership without the cost of owning their own plane. Samsung offers its next generation of high-definition TV with its trademarked Internet@TV. Owners can connect their televisions to their home Internet connection, then add widgets to track the weather, check eBay, view Flickr albums, and check for Twitter updates—all in real time. In addition, they can get Video-on-Demand service through Blockbuster and Amazon. "Get the best of the Web right on your TV!" their promotion says.

As these examples illustrate, marketing is more than just selling. It is a process that begins with discovering unmet customer needs and continues with researching the potential market; producing a good or service capable of satisfying the targeted customers; and promoting, pricing, and distributing that good or service. Throughout the entire marketing process, a successful organization focuses on building customer relationships.

When two or more parties benefit from trading things of value, they have entered into an <u>exchange process</u>. When you purchase a cup of coffee, the other party may be a convenience store clerk, a vending machine, or a Dunkin' Donuts server. The exchange seems simple—some money changes hands, and you receive your cup of coffee. But the exchange process is more complex than that. It could not occur if you didn't feel the need for a cup of coffee or if the convenience store or vending machine were not available. You wouldn't choose Dunkin' Donuts unless you were aware of the brand. Because of marketing, your desire for a flavored blend, decaf, or plain black coffee is identified, and the coffee manufacturer's business is successful.

marketing organizational function and set of processes for creating, communicating, and delivering value to customers and for managing customer relationships in ways that benefit the organization and its stakeholders.

exchange process activity in which two or more parties give something of value to each other to satisfy perceived needs.

The Pepsi Refresh Project: Viral Marketing

PepsiCo recently launched the Pepsi Refresh Project, a year-long initiative in which consumers were invited to submit short videos of ideas that would benefit their communities. Pepsi accepted 1,000 videos each month and posted them online so that visitors to the Web site could vote on them. At the end of each month, Pepsi awarded grants of varying amounts to the winning projects, with the company giving away a total of $20 million over the year. Instead of costly advertising, Pepsi posted a video on the Web. The video quickly went viral, with visits to the Refresh Web site soaring 800 percent during one brief period, then staying consistent. Acknowledging that Facebook and Twitter have revolutionized marketing, Pepsi's CEO Indra Nooyi announced that the company is investing one-third of its marketing budget in social media.

Initial Web marketing for Refresh had advantages and disadvantages. Traffic to the Web site seemed to drop during the first three weeks of each month, then spike during the last week in the final round of voting, so announcing winners every month was an advantage. Also, people hoping to win grants set up their own local social media campaigns using Facebook and Twitter, thus generating more publicity for the project. However, as time went on, these contestants and some celebrity contestants became the sources of most of the publicity. SEO (search-engine optimization) firms watched the campaign closely to monitor its successes and to spot features that could be improved for future campaigns.

Despite the challenges, Pepsi announced that the Refresh Project would be renewed for a second year, pledging to fund twice as many projects as it had the first year. Consumers were invited to submit ideas in four categories—arts and music, communities, education, and the Pepsi Challenge. Voters could continue to cast their ballots for favorites via Facebook, Twitter, and mobile apps.

Questions for Critical Thinking

1. Choose an advertiser with a presence on Facebook and Twitter. Which social medium seems more successful at getting the advertiser's message across?

2. If you have a Facebook page, how would you use it to market either your own business or a cause that inspires you?

Sources: Bill Bruce, "Pepsi Refresh Project 2011 Programme Expands," *FoodBev.com*, February 1, 2011, http://www.foodbev.com; Pepsi Refresh Project Web site, http://www.refresheverything.com, accessed March 11, 2010; Michael Learmonth, "Pepsi's World Cup Campaign Infiltrates Viral Chart," *Advertising Age*, March 11, 2010, http://adage.com; "Pepsi Refresh Project: Social Media Marketing Splash or Flawed Strategy?" *Online PR News*, March 4, 2010, http://www.onlineprnews.com; Scott Moir, "Facebook vs. Twitter: A Social Media Internet Marketing Strategy and Benefit Comparison," *World Daily News*, February 23, 2010, http://www.jazzou.com "Pepsi Refresh Project—Huge Potential Viral Marketing Success," *Online PR News*, February 13, 2010, http://www.onlineprnews.com.

How Marketing Creates Utility

utility power of a good or service to satisfy a want or need.

Marketing affects many aspects of an organization and its dealings with customers. The ability of a good or service to satisfy the wants and needs of customers is called **utility**. A company's production function creates *form utility* by converting raw materials, component parts, and other inputs into finished goods and services. But the marketing function creates time, place, and ownership utility. *Time utility* is created by making a good or service available when customers want to purchase it. *Place utility* is created by making a product available in a location convenient for customers. *Ownership utility* refers to an orderly transfer of goods and services from the seller to the buyer. Firms may be able to create all three forms of utility. Target is the first nationwide retailer to offer bar-coded, scannable mobile coupons direct to cell phones. Guests can sign on to the program either on their personal computers or on their cell phones. Each month, they receive a text message with a link to a mobile Web site page where they will find offers for various products. They can use the mobile coupons at any Target store nationwide because Target is the first retailer to have point-of-sale scanning technology for the coupons in all of its stores. Steve Eastman, the president of Target.com, says, "At Target, we know that mobile phones are an integral part of our guests' lives, and mobile coupons are just another way we're providing convenient, on-the-go shopping solutions."[3] The soft-drink giant PepsiCo has also created several forms of utility for its customers through social networking media, as described in the "Hit & Miss" feature.

Assessment Check ✓

1. What is utility?
2. Identify ways in which marketing creates utility.

Evolution of the Marketing Concept

Marketing has always been a part of business, from the earliest village traders to large 21st-century organizations producing and selling complex goods and services. Over time, however, marketing activities evolved through the four eras shown in Figure 11.1: the production, sales, and marketing eras, and now the relationship era. Note that these eras parallel some of the time periods discussed in Chapter 1.

For centuries, organizations of the *production era* stressed efficiency in producing quality products. Their philosophy could be summed up by the remark, "A good product will sell itself." Although this production orientation continued into the 20th century, it gradually gave way to the *sales era*, in which businesses assumed that consumers would buy as a result of energetic sales efforts. Organizations didn't fully recognize the importance of their customers until the *marketing era* of the 1950s, when they began to adopt a consumer orientation. This focus has intensified in recent years, leading to the emergence of the *relationship era* in the 1990s, which continues to this day. In the relationship era, companies emphasize customer satisfaction and building long-term business relationships.

marketing concept companywide consumer orientation to promote long-run success.

Emergence of the Marketing Concept

The term **marketing concept** refers to a companywide customer orientation with the objective of achieving long-run success. The basic idea of the marketing concept is that marketplace success begins with the customer. A firm should analyze each customer's needs and then work backward to offer products that fulfill them. The emergence of the marketing

---

FIGURE 11.1   **Four Eras in the History of Marketing**

DEGREE OF EMPHASIS

High   Low

RELATIONSHIP
"Long-term relationships lead to success."

MARKETING
"The consumer is king! Find a need and fill it."

SALES
"Creative advertising and selling will overcome consumers' resistance and convince them to buy."

PRODUCTION
"A good product will sell itself."

1900   1950   2009

concept can be explained best by the shift from a *seller's market*, one with a shortage of goods and services, to a *buyer's market*, one with an abundance of goods and services. During the 1950s, the United States became a strong buyer's market, forcing companies to satisfy customers rather than just producing and selling goods and services.

Today, much competition among firms centers on the effort to satisfy customers. Amazon and Barnes & Noble have been battling for consumer preference for their e-readers, the Kindle and Nook. The two firms are continually adding features, making price adjustments, and offering new models of their products in order to satisfy consumers. Kindle's price has dropped from $349 to $139, and Amazon recently released Kindle software for Android users. Barnes & Noble followed its original Nook with Nook Color, touting its superiority at displaying magazines and children's books. Now both are facing competition from the Sony Reader and Apple's iPad.[4]

Assessment Check ✔

1. What is the marketing concept?
2. How is the marketing concept tied to the relationship era of marketing?

Not-for-Profit and Nontraditional Marketing

The marketing concept has traditionally been associated with products of profit-seeking organizations. Today, however, it is also being applied to not-for-profit sectors and other nontraditional areas ranging from religious organizations to political campaigns.

Not-for-Profit Marketing

Residents of every continent benefit in various ways from the approximately 20 million not-for-profit organizations currently operating around the globe. Nearly 1.6 million of them are located in the United States, where they employ nearly 13 million workers and benefit from volunteers representing the equivalent of 9 million full-time employees.[5] Women tend to volunteer at a higher rate than men, and people between the ages of 35 and 44 are also the most likely to volunteer.[6] The largest not-for-profit organization in the world is the Red Cross/Red Crescent. Other not-for-profits range from Habitat for Humanity to the Boys & Girls Clubs of America to the National Multiple Sclerosis Society. These organizations all benefit by applying many of the strategies and business concepts used by profit-seeking firms. They apply marketing tools to reach audiences, secure funding, and accomplish their overall missions. Marketing strategies are important for not-for-profit organizations because they are all competing for dollars—from individuals, foundations, and corporations—just as commercial businesses are.

Not-for-profit organizations operate in both public and private sectors. Public groups include federal, state, and local government units as well as agencies that receive tax funding. A state's department of natural resources, for instance, regulates land conservation and environmental programs; the local animal control officer enforces ordinances protecting people and animals; a city's public health board ensures safe drinking water for its citizens. The private not-for-profit sector comprises many different types of organizations, including the Houston Zoo, the United States Olympic Committee, and the American Academy of Pediatrics. Although some private not-for-profits generate surplus revenue, their primary

Sometimes, not-for-profit organizations form a partnership with a profit-seeking company to promote the firm's message or distribute its goods and services. This partnership usually benefits both organizations. The National Football League and the United Way formed the "Hometown Huddle."

goals are not earning profits. If they earn funds beyond their expenses, they invest the excess in their organizational missions.

In some cases, not-for-profit organizations form a partnership with a profit-seeking company to promote the firm's message or distribute its goods and services. This partnership usually benefits both organizations. The National Football League and the United Way joined to form one of the longest-running public-service partnerships in the United States. NFL athletes and other personalities appear in public-service advertisements and in person to promote community service and fundraising. Since 1999, the "Hometown Huddle" has been an NFL-wide day of service when team members, their families, coaches, and staff members participate in local community service activities.[7]

Celebrities are particularly visible campaigning for not-for-profit organizations—their own as well as others. The actress Reese Witherspoon is the Avon Global Ambassador and Honorary Chairperson of the Avon Foundation for Women. Witherspoon helped present a $500,000 grant to the Fund for Global Women's Leadership. The grant was intended to help the worldwide movement to end violence toward women.[8]

Nontraditional Marketing

Not-for-profit organizations often engage in one or more of five major categories of nontraditional marketing: person marketing, place marketing, event marketing, cause marketing, and organization marketing. Figure 11.2 provides examples of these types of marketing. As described in the "Going Green" feature, through each of these types of marketing,

The Tap Project

Recently, *Esquire* magazine challenged David Droga, the founder of the Droga5 advertising firm, to prove that his creative thinking deserved the magazine's "Best and Brightest" award. After seeing a documentary about New Orleans after Hurricane Katrina, Droga started thinking about how many people don't have access to clean, safe drinking water—which most Americans take for granted. When he was served the typical free glass of tap water at a New York City restaurant, he got the inspiration for his next advertising campaign. Droga remembers thinking, "We have to make people aware of the luxury we have and help others who don't have it." He presented his idea to UNICEF, and the Tap Project was born.

Approximately 900 million people around the world—about half of them children—lack safe, accessible drinking water. UNICEF and the Tap Project hope to cut that number in half by 2015. Every day, 4,100 children under age 5 die of water-borne diseases.

During the UN's World Water Week, top restaurants in New York City asked their patrons to donate one dollar or more for a glass of tap water. Since then, the Tap Project has raised almost $1.5 million in the United States. All donations go to UNICEF's water, sanitation, and hygiene programs. One dollar allows UNICEF to provide safe drinking water to one child for 40 days. Funds raised in 2010 went primarily to Haiti, the Central African Republic, Guatemala, Togo, and Vietnam. Caryl Stein, the president and CEO of the U.S. Fund for UNICEF, noted, "In Haiti alone, less than 60 percent of people had access to safe water even before the earthquake."

Leading advertising agencies in the United States have participated in the Tap Project. Casanova Pendrill Publicidad, which aims at the Hispanic market, won the top prize in *Advertising Age's* Non-Traditional/Guerrilla Marketing category. In its "Agua Sucia" ("dirty water") campaign, the firm bottled dirty water as if it were mineral water and sold the bottles for $1 from vending machines on New York City streets. "Customers" could choose from such "flavors" as cholera, typhoid, hepatitis, and dysentery. The agency's slogan was, "You'd never drink dirty water, the rest of the world shouldn't have to, either."

In succeeding years, the Tap Project spread to other U.S. cities and advertising agencies. In a recent year, 21 agencies produced advertisements that ran in 19 cities, in addition to efforts nationwide and on the Internet. For the most recent World Water Week, the Tap Project changed its focus. More than 1,000 restaurants participated, but volunteers also hosted 250 other fund-raising events around the country. The campaign established a presence on Facebook and Twitter as well as an online radio station. However, only five cities—Chicago, Los Angeles, New York, Seattle, and Washington, DC—and eight advertising agencies were involved. Ryu Mizuno, the director of marketing at the U.S. Fund for UNICEF, said the Tap Project was "maturing as a brand" and that the fund preferred "doing a few things in a great way instead of being all over the map."

Some observers claim that such changes are typical of nontraditional marketing campaigns, especially those where ad agencies have volunteered their services. Another difference from the first years is that the Tap Project's very success has spawned other water charities, all vying for donations and volunteers. The earthquake in Haiti also had an impact. However, UNICEF continues to grow the campaign and announced that funds for the coming year would be targeted for Togo, the Central African Republic, and Vietnam.

Questions for Critical Thinking

1. What types of nontraditional marketing does the Tap Project engage in?
2. As this feature mentions, fewer cities and advertisers participated in World Water Week. What steps would you suggest to improve participation in future years?

Sources: Tap Project Web site, http://www.tapproject.org, accessed March 21, 2011; Tap Project online radio station, http://www.tapprojectradio.org, accessed April 14, 2010; Droga5 Web site, http://www.droga5.com, accessed April 14, 2010; Karyn McCormack, "UNICEF: Tapping the Power of Water," *BusinessWeek*, http://www.businessweek.com, accessed April 14, 2010; Alessandra Bulow, "UNICEF Tap Project," *Food & Wine*, March 22, 2010, http://www.foodandwine.com; Helena Bottemiller, "Restaurants Join in Clean Water Project," *Food Safety News*, March 20, 2010, http://www.foodsafetynews.com; United States Fund for UNICEF, "2010 UNICEF Tap Project Launches to Help Provide Safe Water to Children Worldwide," March 11, 2010, http://www.unicefusa.org.

an organization seeks to connect with the audience that is most likely to offer time, money, or other resources. In some cases, the effort may reach the market the organization intends to serve.

person marketing use of efforts designed to attract the attention, interest, and preference of a target market toward a person.

Person Marketing Efforts designed to attract the attention, interest, and preference of a target market toward a person are called **person marketing**. Campaign managers for a political candidate conduct marketing research; identify groups of voters and financial supporters; and then design advertising campaigns, fund-raising events, and political rallies to reach them. Person marketing gained a lot of attention during a recent broadcast of the Academy Awards, during which commercials featured Ozzy Osbourne for Best Buy and Jennifer Lopez for the Venus razor brand.[9]

Many successful job seekers apply the tools of person marketing. They research the wants and needs of prospective employers, and they identify ways they can meet them. They seek employers through a variety of channels, sending messages that emphasize how they can benefit the employer.

Place Marketing

Place Marketing As the term suggests, **place marketing** attempts to attract people to a particular area, such as a city, state, or nation. It may involve appealing to consumers as a tourist destination or to businesses as a desirable business location. A strategy for place marketing often includes advertising.

Place marketing may be combined with event marketing, such as the Olympics. The official Web site for the London 2012 Olympics features photos of the various athletic venues around London, ticket sales, and videos about the mascots Wenlock and Mandeville more than a year before the games—all in an effort to get people to visit.[10]

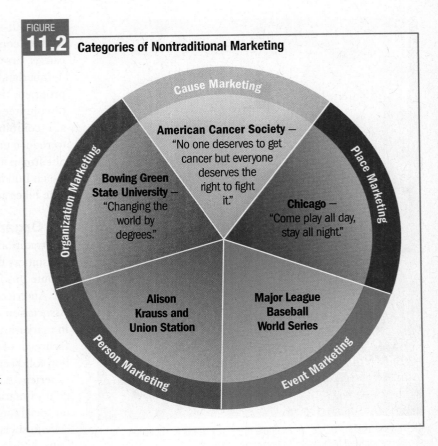

FIGURE 11.2 Categories of Nontraditional Marketing

Cause Marketing
Place Marketing
Event Marketing
Person Marketing
Organization Marketing

American Cancer Society — "No one deserves to get cancer but everyone deserves the right to fight it."

Bowing Green State University — "Changing the world by degrees."

Chicago — "Come play all day, stay all night."

Alison Krauss and Union Station

Major League Baseball World Series

Event Marketing

Event Marketing Marketing or sponsoring short-term events such as athletic competitions and cultural and charitable performances is known as **event marketing**. Target recently sponsored the first women's junior professional surfing competition. The American Diabetes Association sponsored the "Tour de Cure," a series of fund-raising cycling events held across the United States to raise funds to support its mission to prevent and cure diabetes.[11]

Event marketing often forges partnerships between not-for-profit and profit-seeking organizations. Many businesses sponsor events such as 10K runs to raise funds for health-related charities. These occasions require a marketing effort to plan the event and attract participants and sponsors. Events may be intended to raise money or awareness, or both.

Cause Marketing

Cause Marketing Marketing that promotes awareness of, or raises money for, a cause or social issue, such as drug abuse prevention or childhood hunger is **cause marketing**. Cause marketing seeks to educate the public and may or may not attempt to directly raise funds. An advertisement often contains a phone number or Web site address through which people can obtain more information about the organization or issue. Then they can either donate money or take other actions of support. The international accounting firm Deloitte sponsors the United Way's Alternative Spring Break program. Instead of heading for the beach, young adults and student volunteers participate in community service activities such as rebuilding communities devastated by hurricanes or tornadoes and helping low-income families with tax preparation.[12]

place marketing attempt to attract people to a particular area, such as a city, state, or nation.

event marketing marketing or sponsoring short-term events such as athletic competitions and cultural and charitable performances.

cause marketing marketing that promotes a cause or social issue, such as preventing child abuse, anti-littering efforts, and stop-smoking campaigns.

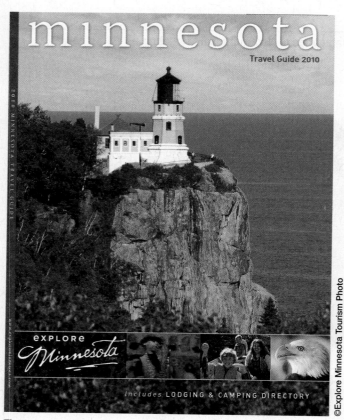

©Explore Minnesota Tourism Photo

The sightseeing guide, an example of *place marketing,* is published by the state of Minnesota to encourage tourism.

Profit-seeking companies look for ways to contribute to their communities by joining forces with charities and causes, providing financial, marketing, and human resources. Timberland is well known for participating in the City Year program, through which young adults contract to perform a year of volunteer service in their communities. For-profit firms can also combine their goods and services with a cause. In an effort to reduce energy use and pollution, entrepreneurs Jonathan Shriftman and Jake Medwell founded Solé Bicycles in California which builds hand-made, affordable bicycles from recycled parts. The bikes are popular among students and commuters.[13]

Organization Marketing The final category of nontraditional marketing, <u>organization marketing</u>, influences consumers to accept the goals of, receive the services of, or contribute in some way to an organization. The U.S. Postal Service, the American Cancer Society, and the National Basketball Association (NBA) are all examples of organizations that engage in marketing. Recently the NBA has turned to the social media for much of its marketing. The NBA claims more than 6.7 million followers on Facebook and Twitter. "Sports are communal experiences," says Melissa Rosenthal Brenner, NBA's vice president of marketing, explaining why the organization now focuses on social media marketing. NBA teams with the greatest presence in social media include the Los Angeles Lakers, the Phoenix Suns, and the Boston Celtics. "Twitter lets us grow our brand in a completely new way," remarks Jeramie McPeek, the Suns' vice president of digital marketing.[14]

organization marketing marketing strategy that influences consumers to accept the goals of, receive the services of, or contribute in some way to an organization.

Assessment Check ✅

1. Why do not-for-profit organizations engage in marketing?

2. What are the five types of nontraditional marketing used by not-for-profit organizations?

Developing a Marketing Strategy

Decision makers in any successful organization, for-profit or not-for-profit, follow a two-step process to develop a *marketing strategy*. First, they study and analyze potential target markets and choose among them. Second, they create a marketing mix to satisfy the chosen market. Figure 11.3 shows the relationships among the target market, the marketing mix variables, and the marketing environment. Later discussions refer back to this figure as they cover each topic. This section describes the development of a marketing strategy designed to attract and build relationships with customers. Sometimes, in an effort to do this, marketers use questionable methods, as described in the "Solving an Ethical Controversy" feature.

Earlier chapters of this book introduced many of the environmental factors that affect the success or failure of a firm's business strategy, including today's rapidly changing and highly competitive world of business, a vast array of social and cultural factors, economic challenges, political and legal factors, and technological innovations. Although these external forces frequently operate outside managers' control, marketers must still consider the impact of environmental factors on their decisions.

A marketing plan is a key component of a firm's overall business plan. The marketing plan outlines its marketing strategy and includes information about the target market, sales and revenue goals, the marketing budget, and the timing for implementing the elements of the marketing mix.

Solving an Ethical Controversy

When Free Credit Reports Aren't Free

When times are tough and credit is tight, consumers are more likely to search for and monitor their credit scores. The Fair Credit Reporting Act (FCRA) requires the three major consumer reporting companies—Equifax, Experian, and TransUnion—to provide consumers a free copy of their credit report once a year. Consumers must request the report through the official Annual Credit Report Request Service by phone or mail, or online at AnnualCreditReport.com. Credit report companies claim to offer free credit reports—but many offers contain hidden charges. Also, Experian has profited because consumers confuse its FreeCreditReport.com division with the federal government's AnnualCreditReport.com, the only truly free Web site.

Should firms be allowed to use the word "free" in advertising for credit reports if the service contains hidden charges?

PRO

1. If the credit score itself is free, but related services are not, then the advertising is truthful. Ty Taylor, the president of Experian's Consumer Direct Division, says, "You get a free credit report and free score for test-driving our services."

2. Some promotional offers contain free credit scores, with a tie-in to additional services for a fee. Other industries make similar offers for a free month of phone, cable, or Internet service.

CON

1. The word "free" is a powerful enticement in advertising. Some companies provide "free" reports, then bill consumers for services they have to cancel.

2. Consumer advocates say firms exploit people's fears. Edgar Dworsky, the founder of ConsumerWorld.org and formerly on Experian's consumer advisory panel, says, "Does the average person really need to see their credit reports more than once every four months? Do you need to look at it daily? That's paranoia."

Summary

The Federal Trade Commission's Free Credit Reports Rule requires credit report Web sites to carry the following across the top of each page: "THIS NOTICE IS REQUIRED BY LAW. Read more at FTC.GOV. You have the right to a free credit report from AnnualCreditReport.com or 877-322-8228, the ONLY authorized source under federal law." Very recently, rather than including this disclosure, Experian began charging $1 for a credit report and donating the fee to charity.

Sources: "FREE Annual Credit Reports," Federal Trade Commission, http://www.ftc.gov/freereports, accessed June 7, 2011; Ron Lieber, "Free Credit on Credit? No Longer," *The New York Times,* April 7, 2010, http://www.nytimes.com; Joe Taylor, "New Laws Crack Down on Free Credit Report Marketing," *CardRatings,* March 30, 2010, http://www.cardratings.com; Michelle Singletary, "Free Credit Reports Get Easier to Find," *The Washington Post,* March 4, 2010, http://www.boston.com.

Selecting a Target Market

The expression "find a need and fill it" is perhaps the simplest explanation of the two elements of a marketing strategy. A firm's marketers find a need through careful and continuing study of the individuals and business decision makers in its potential market. A market consists of people with purchasing power, willingness to buy, and authority to make purchase decisions.

Markets can be classified by type of product. **Consumer products**—often known as business-to-consumer **(B2C)** products—are goods and services, such as GPS systems, tomato sauce, and a haircut, that are purchased by end users. **Business products**—or business-to-business **(B2B)** products—are goods and services purchased to be used, either directly or indirectly, in the production of other goods for resale. Some products can fit either classification depending on who buys them and why. A computer or credit card can be used by a business or a consumer.

An organization's **target market** is the group of potential customers toward whom it directs its marketing efforts. Customer needs and wants vary considerably, and no single organization

consumer (B2C) product good or service that is purchased by end users.

business (B2B) product good or service purchased to be used, either directly or indirectly, in the production of other goods for resale.

target market group of people toward whom an organization markets its goods, services, or ideas with a strategy designed to satisfy their specific needs and preferences.

FIGURE
11.3

Target Market and Marketing Mix within the Marketing Environment

has the resources to satisfy everyone. *Popular Science* is geared toward readers who are interested in science and technology, whereas *Bon Appétit* is aimed at readers who are interested in fine food and cooking.

Decisions about marketing involve strategies for four areas of marketing activity: product, distribution, promotion, and pricing. A firm's **marketing mix** blends the four strategies to fit the needs and preferences of a specific target market. Marketing success depends not on the four individual strategies but on their unique combination.

Product strategy involves more than just designing a good or service with needed attributes. It also includes decisions about package design, brand names, trademarks, warranties, product image, new-product development, and customer service. Think about your favorite pair of jeans. Do you like them because they fit the best, or do other attributes—such as styling and overall image—also contribute to your brand preference? *Distribution strategy*, the second marketing mix variable, ensures that customers receive their purchases in the proper quantities at the right times and locations. *Promotional strategy*, another marketing mix element, effectively blends advertising, personal selling, sales promotion, and public relations to achieve its goals of informing, persuading, and influencing purchase decisions.

Pricing strategy, the final mix element, is also one of the most difficult areas of marketing decision making in setting profitable and justifiable prices for the firm's product offerings. Such actions are sometimes subject to government regulation and considerable public scrutiny. They also represent a powerful competitive weapon and frequently produce responses by the other firms in the industry, who match price changes to avoid losing customers. Think about your jeans again. Would you continue to purchase them if they were priced either much higher or much lower?

marketing mix blending of the four elements of marketing strategy—product, distribution, promotion, and pricing—to satisfy chosen customer segments.

Retail clinics are low-cost, walk-in medical facilities usually found in supermarkets, chain drugstores, and big-box stores. Patients typically see nurse practitioners or physician assistants, who can diagnose and treat minor medical conditions and prescribe some medications. The clinics are open late in the evenings and on weekends and also offer appropriate vaccinations and inexpensive sports and summer-camp physicals for children. They proved to be a popular alternative to primary care in areas where primary care physicians are scarce and because of their low cost, usually from $55 to $65 per visit. Retail clinics increased dramatically from just 200 to about 1,200 over the past few years. But after that, growth stalled, and both CVS and Walgreens closed some clinics. Some problems are the seasonality of such offerings as flu shots and the summer-camp physicals, oversaturation of the market in some areas, and difficulty in reaching potential patients who don't shop at the particular parent store. Retail clinics are evolving with the changing economic landscape, and how the operators of the clinics will solve these marketing problems remains to be seen.[15]

Developing a Marketing Mix for International Markets

Marketing a good or service in foreign markets means deciding whether to offer the same marketing mix in every market *(standardization)* or to develop a unique mix to fit each market *(adaptation)*. The advantages of standardizing the marketing mix include reliable marketing performance and low costs. This approach works best with B2B goods, such as steel, chemicals, and aircraft, which require little sensitivity to a nation's culture.

Adaptation, on the other hand, lets marketers vary their marketing mix to suit local competitive conditions, consumer preferences, and government regulations. Consumer tastes are often shaped by local cultures. Because consumer products generally tend to be more culture dependent than business products, they more often require adaptation. Subway, which already has 144 stores in China, plans to open 500 new stores in the next five years and hopes to match the Chinese presence of McDonald's in 10 years. As Subway opens stores in different regions, it plans to adapt its menu to local tastes with such offerings as Beijing roast duck sandwiches and "hot spicy Szechuan sauce." Why do these firms go out of their way to adapt to Chinese preferences? China is a market with 1.3 billion potential consumers.[16]

Marketers also try to build adaptability into the designs of standardized goods and services for international and domestic markets. *Mass customization* allows a firm to mass produce goods and services while adding unique features to individual or small groups of orders. For example, online firm Blank Label specializes in custom men's dress shirts and allows customers to choose their own fabric, style, individual features, and size. Spreadshirt, with U.S. headquarters in Boston, specializes in customized casual wear, accessories, and even personalized underwear.[17]

Assessment Check ✅

1. Distinguish between consumer products and business products.
2. What are the steps in developing a marketing strategy?

Karen Cowled/Alamy

Adaptation allows marketers to vary their marketing mix to suit local competitive conditions, consumer preferences, and government regulations. Because consumer products generally tend to be more culture dependent than business products, they more often require adaptation. Subway, which already has 144 stores in China, plans to open 500 new stores there.

Marketing Research

Marketing research involves more than just collecting data. Researchers must decide how to collect data, interpret the results, convert the data into decision-oriented information, and communicate those results to managers for use in decision making. **Marketing research** is the process of collecting and evaluating information to help marketers make effective decisions. It links business decision makers to the marketplace by providing data about potential target markets that help them design effective marketing mixes.

marketing research collecting and evaluating information to support marketing decision making.

Obtaining Marketing Research Data

Marketing researchers need both internal and external data. Firms generate *internal data* within their organizations. Financial records provide a tremendous amount of useful information, such as changes in unpaid bills; inventory levels; sales generated by different categories of customers or product lines; profitability of particular divisions; or comparisons of sales by territories, salespeople, customers, or product lines.

Researchers gather *external data* from outside sources, including previously published data. Trade associations publish reports on activities in particular industries. Advertising agencies collect information on the audiences reached by various media. National marketing research firms offer information through subscription services. Some of these professional research firms specialize in specific markets, such as teens or ethnic groups. This information helps companies make decisions about developing or modifying products. A recent report by the marketing research firm comScore on smart phone purchases indicates that Research in Motion's BlackBerry was still the best seller, with 43 percent of the market. Apple's iPhone was second, with 25 percent. In a surprising development, Palm's Pre, formerly in third place, was overtaken by Google's Android-based devices. Microsoft devices also showed a decline. Such data can give indirect but very clear indications of what consumers are looking for in a product.[18]

The largest consumer-goods manufacturer in the world, Procter & Gamble, has excelled in marketing research for a long time; it created its own marketing research department in 1923 and began conducting its research online in 2001. To help the company recover from the global recession, Bob McDonald, the company's chief executive officer, has set the goal of reaching 1 billion new customers by 2015. This expansion involves reaching customers in developing regions. As part of this strategy, he traveled undercover to 30 countries, posing as a marketing researcher.[19]

Secondary data, or previously published data, are low cost and easy to obtain. Federal, state, and local government publications are excellent data sources, and most are available online. The most frequently used government statistics include census data, which contain the population's age, gender, education level, household size and composition, occupation, employment status, and income. Even private research firms such as TRU (formerly Teenage Research Unlimited), which studies the purchasing habits of teens, provide some free information on their Web sites. This information helps firms evaluate consumers' buying behavior, anticipate possible changes in the marketplace, and identify new markets.

Even though secondary data are a quick and inexpensive resource, marketing researchers sometimes discover that this information isn't specific or current enough for their needs. If so, researchers may conclude that they must collect *primary data*—data collected firsthand through such methods as observation and surveys.

Observational studies view the actions of consumers either directly or through mechanical devices. As more retailers watch their customers via video cameras, they can solve problems such as widening a too-narrow aisle to allow shoppers easier access, but such close monitoring has also raised privacy concerns.[20] Procter & Gamble spends about $200 million on consumer observation each year, citing it as the firm's most important type of marketing research. CEO McDonald says, "If we can continue to innovate and continue to mind consumer needs and delight consumers, that ability outweighs any macroeconomic force."[21]

Simply observing customers cannot provide some types of information. A researcher might observe a customer buying a red sweater, but have no idea why the purchase was made—or for whom. When researchers need information about consumers' attitudes, opinions, and motives, they need to ask the consumers themselves. They may conduct surveys by telephone, in person, online, or in focus groups.

A *focus group* gathers 8 to 12 people in a room or over the Internet to discuss a particular topic. A focus group can generate new ideas, address consumers' needs, and even point out flaws in existing products. Pottery Barn Kids, a division of Pottery Barn, developed its Learning Toys Collection through observation, reading, and focus groups. Focus groups that included both parents and children were gathered and observed as they played with and talked about the new toys. Marketing researchers have also begun to take advantage of social media outlets such as Facebook, Twitter, and blogs as well as mobile marketing.[22]

Applying Marketing Research Data

As the accuracy of information collected by researchers increases, so does the effectiveness of resulting marketing strategies. One field of research is known as **business intelligence**, which uses various activities and technologies to gather, store, and analyze data to make better competitive decisions. Dell established its IdeaStorm Web site to gather information, criticism, compliments, and ideas for developing new computer products and improving existing ones. New users must register at the site and follow guidelines in order to post their ideas and reactions. Submitted ideas receive scores for their popularity, which helps Dell sort through material and decide which ideas to pursue. Recently, Dell added "Storm Sessions," where the company posts a topic and asks visitors to contribute their ideas. To make the discussions specific and relevant to the topic, each session is open only for a limited time. "Dream It. Share It. Make an Impact," says the IdeaStorm Web site.[23]

business intelligence activities and technologies for gathering, storing, and analyzing data to make better competitive decisions.

Data Mining

Once a company has built a database, marketers must be able to analyze the data and use the information it provides. **Data mining**, part of the broader field of business intelligence, is the task of using computer-based technology to evaluate data in a database and identify useful trends. These trends or patterns may suggest predictive models of real-world business activities. Accurate data mining can help researchers forecast recessions and pinpoint sales prospects.

Data mining uses **data warehouses**, which are sophisticated customer databases that allow managers to combine data from several different organizational functions. Companies such as San Franciso's Rapleaf Inc. collect publicly available personal information from social-networking sites such as Facebook, Twitter, and other forums. They then sell this

data mining computer searches of customer data to detect patterns and relationships.

data warehouse customer database that allows managers to combine data from several different organizational functions.

information to entities such as airlines and credit card companies that regard those individuals as potential customers. Such information can include everything from your blogging or posting habits to your credit rating. Among the issues arising from data mining are ownership of Web user data, the targeting capabilities of the Web, government supervision—and, of course, privacy.

A few days after Google launched its social network Google Buzz, it had to make some changes to protect users' privacy. More reprogramming may be needed, pending a petition to the Federal Trade Commission and a class-action lawsuit. However, Google Buzz does give users the choice of whether to state publicly who is following them and whom they are following. Some observers feel that privacy norms are changing, with confidentiality giving way to increasing openness.[24] Turiya Media's product Leafnode mines and analyzes the behavior of online game players by tracking the number of hours they spend on which games, then creating behavioral profiles. Game publishers pay a monthly fee for the resulting data, which enable them to "proactively identify and retain their best customers, and target them with personalized recommendations."[25]

Assessment Check ☑

1. What is the difference between primary data and secondary data?
2. What is data mining?

market segmentation process of dividing a total market into several relatively homogeneous groups.

Market Segmentation

Market segmentation is the process of dividing a market into several relatively homogeneous groups. Both profit-seeking and not-for-profit organizations use segmentation to help them reach desirable target markets. Market segmentation is often based on the results of research, which attempts to identify trends among certain groups of people. For instance, one recent survey revealed that social media use nearly doubled among older users in one year. Forty-seven percent of consumers between the ages of 50 and 64 now use social media, which is 88 percent higher than before. Younger adults are still the heaviest users at 86 percent, but the rise in use by older consumers is important information for businesses.[26] This kind of information can help marketers decide what types of products to develop and to whom they should be marketed.

Market segmentation attempts to isolate the traits that distinguish a certain group of customers from the overall market. However, segmentation doesn't automatically produce marketing success. Table 11.1 lists several criteria that marketers should consider. The effectiveness of a segmentation strategy depends on how well the market meets these criteria. Once marketers identify a market segment to target, they can create an appropriate marketing strategy.

Table

11.1 Criteria for Market Segmentation

CRITERION	EXAMPLE
A segment must be a measurable group.	Data can be collected on the dollar amount and number of purchases by college students.
A segment must be accessible for communication.	A growing number of seniors are going online, so they can be reached through Internet channels.
A segment must be large enough to offer profit potential.	In a small community, a store carrying only large-size shoes might not be profitable. Similarly, a specialty retail chain may not locate in a small market.

Companies that can identify trends in consumer preferences before their rivals do can benefit greatly; those that miss the boat generally suffer the consequences. Blockbuster lagged behind Netflix in capturing the segment of movie watchers who preferred traveling only as far as the mailbox to retrieve a DVD and wanted to keep it for an unspecified time period without paying a late fee. Netflix is now surging ahead with its online streaming option.[27]

How Market Segmentation Works

An immediate segmentation distinction involves whether the firm is offering goods and services to customers for their own use or to purchasers who will use them directly or indirectly in providing other products for resale (the so-called B2B market). Depending on whether their firms offer consumer or business products, marketers segment their target markets differently. Four common bases for segmenting consumer markets are geographical segmentation, demographic segmentation, psychographic segmentation, and product-related segmentation. By contrast, business markets can segment on three criteria: customer-based segmentation, end-use segmentation, and geographical segmentation. Figure 11.4 illustrates the segmentation methods for these two types of markets.

Segmenting Consumer Markets

Market segmentation has been practiced since people first began selling products. Tailors made some clothing items for men and others for women. Tea was imported from India for tea drinkers in England and other European countries. In addition to demographic and geographical segmentation, today's marketers also define customer groups based on psychographic—lifestyle and values—criteria as well as product-related distinctions.

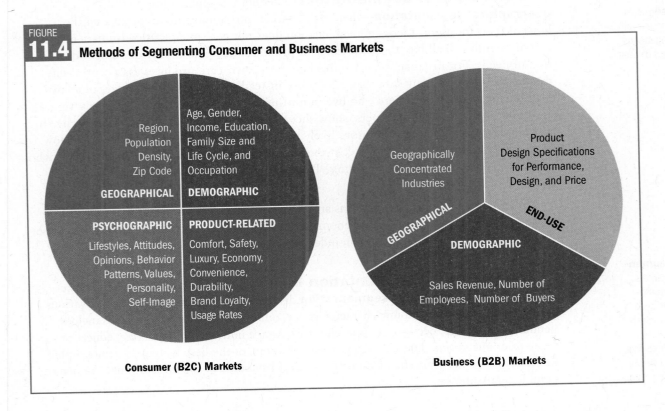

FIGURE 11.4 Methods of Segmenting Consumer and Business Markets

Consumer (B2C) Markets

GEOGRAPHICAL — Region, Population Density, Zip Code

DEMOGRAPHIC — Age, Gender, Income, Education, Family Size and Life Cycle, and Occupation

PSYCHOGRAPHIC — Lifestyles, Attitudes, Opinions, Behavior Patterns, Values, Personality, Self-Image

PRODUCT-RELATED — Comfort, Safety, Luxury, Economy, Convenience, Durability, Brand Loyalty, Usage Rates

Business (B2B) Markets

GEOGRAPHICAL — Geographically Concentrated Industries

END-USE — Product Design Specifications for Performance, Design, and Price

DEMOGRAPHIC — Sales Revenue, Number of Employees, Number of Buyers

A kids catalog, such as the one shown on the top of this pile, with this image on the cover would illustrate demographic segmentation by stage of the family life cycle.

geographical segmentation dividing an overall market into homogeneous groups on the basis of their locations.

Geographical Segmentation

The oldest segmentation method is **geographical segmentation**—dividing a market into homogeneous groups on the basis of their locations. Geographical location does not guarantee that consumers in a certain region will all buy the same kinds of products, but it does provide some indication of needs. For instance, suburbanites buy more lawn-care products than central-city dwellers. However, many suburbanites choose instead to purchase the services of a lawn maintenance firm. Consumers who live in northern states, where winter is more severe, are more likely to buy ice scrapers, snow shovels, and snowblowers than those who live in warmer climates. They are also more likely to contract with firms who remove the snow from driveways. Marketers also look at the size of the population of an area, as well as who lives there—are residents old or young? Do they reflect an ethnic background? What is the level of their income?

Job growth and migration patterns are important considerations as well. Some businesses combine areas or even entire countries that share similar population and product-use patterns instead of treating each as an independent segment.

demographic segmentation dividing markets on the basis of various demographic or socioeconomic characteristics such as gender, age, income, occupation, household size, stage in family life cycle, education, or ethnic group.

Demographic Segmentation

By far the most common method of market segmentation, **demographic segmentation** distinguishes markets on the basis of various demographic or socioeconomic characteristics. Common demographic measures include gender, income, age, occupation, household size, stage in the family life cycle, education, and racial or ethnic group. The U.S. Census Bureau is one of the best sources of demographic information for the domestic market. Figure 11.5 lists some of the measures used in demographic segmentation.

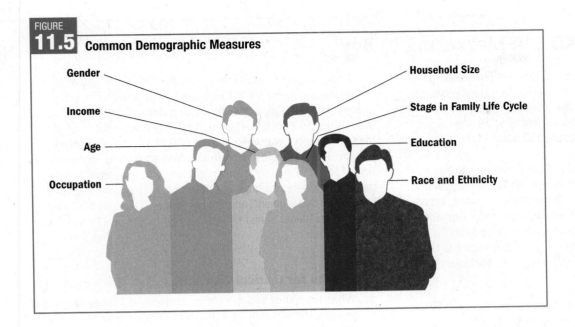

FIGURE 11.5 Common Demographic Measures

Gender

Income

Age

Occupation

Household Size

Stage in Family Life Cycle

Education

Race and Ethnicity

Police departments around the United States constitute a highly specialized occupational demographic group. Popular for its durability, the Ford Crown Victoria has long held 75 percent of the patrol-car market share. Ford plans to phase out the "Crown Vic," replacing it with the Police Interceptor, modeled on the Taurus sedan but modified for the extreme circumstances of police work. The Interceptor's fuel efficiency is 25 percent better than the Crown Vic's. Its 365-horsepower engine outguns the Crown Vic's by 115 horsepower. Ford's police advisory board helped develop the Interceptor, but it may face competition from General Motors, Chrysler, and Carbon Motors (based in Indiana), which produce or are planning police vehicles of their own.[28]

Gender used to be a simple way to define markets for certain products—jewelry and skin care products for women; tools and motorcycles for men. Much of that has changed—dramatically. Men now buy jewelry and skin care products, and women buy tools and motorcycles. But marketers have also found that even though these shifts have blurred the lines between products, there are still differences in the *way* that women and men shop. While men tend to identify an item and purchase it, women do more browsing. For example, a recent study revealed that 77 percent of women rely on peer recommendations when making a purchase; 68 percent search for online coupons; 61 percent refer to online product reviews; and 51 percent follow their favorite brands on Facebook and Twitter.[29]

Another shift involves purchasing power. Women now control an estimated 80 percent of consumer spending, or about $5 trillion per year.[30] With this knowledge in hand, Amazon recently purchased Zappos.com and launched a program called Amazon Mom.[31]

Age is perhaps the most volatile factor in demographic segmentation in the United States, with our rapidly aging population. Of the 308-plus million people who live in the United States, more than 97 million will be age 55 or older by the year 2020.[32] Based on these statistics, marketers for travel and leisure products, as well as retirement and business investments, are working hard to attract the attention of this age group, the aging Baby Boomers—those born between 1946 and 1964. Active-adult housing communities are one result of these efforts. Some developers built communities with a resort-style atmosphere

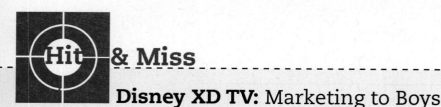

Disney XD TV: Marketing to Boys

Disney marketing aimed at young girls—the "Princesses" products, the Jonas Brothers, *High School Musical*—has been highly successful, although the Disney Channel audience is 40 percent male. In the United States alone, 30 million males are from 5 to 19 years old. Worldwide, boys (or their parents) spend $50 billion every year on clothes, toys, and videogames.

Recently, Disney bought Marvel Entertainment, hoping that Marvel's superheroes would bolster Disney's XD TV channel. Aimed at boys but not excluding girls, the channel offers animation, action-adventure, comedy, movies, sports-themed shows, and music videos. The Disney XD Web site has games, videos, and TV episodes.

How did Disney research a demographic that is known to be reluctant to talk about feelings? It hired a team of social scientists, who learned the following:

- Boys identify with protagonists who are trying to grow and want to see more characters like themselves in TV shows.
- Boys personalize their skateboards on the underside and carry them so the tag shows.
- Boys like to share small accomplishments.
- Boys shuttle quickly from one activity to another, moving among TV, videogames, sports, and so on.
- Boys want more variety and authenticity in TV shows aimed at them, not merely all action or all cartoons.

Disney implemented these results, by adding a trophy room to the games page at the XD Web site and by advising its actors to carry their skateboards so the tagging showed, for realism. Viewership at XD increased more than 25 percent—but most of the new audience was girls. Boys aged 6 to 14 increased only 10 percent. The economic downturn also hurt advertising, but when Disney added new programming for younger boys—ages 2 to 5—the results were much brighter. Viewing for Disney Junior jumped 55 percent for this segment, and the new show "Jake and the Never Land Pirates" leapt ahead to become the number-one TV series for the age group.

Questions for Critical Thinking

1. What type(s) of segmentation strategy is Disney applying? Do you think it will be effective? Why or why not?
2. What steps can Disney take to increase viewership of Disney XD among boys?

Sources: Company Web site, http://www.disney.go.com, accessed March 21, 2011; "Disney Portfolio of Brands Shines in Annual Presentation to Advertisers," *The Futon Critic*, March 16, 2011, http://www.thefutoncritic.com; Tom Lowry and Ronald Grover, "Disney's Marvel Deal and the Pursuit of Boys," *BusinessWeek*, March 9, 2010, http://www.businessweek.com; Seth Lubove and Andy Fixmer, "Disney Beefs Up Marketing to Boys," *The Ledger*, March 4, 2010, http://www.theledger.com.

---

in desirable locations such as Colorado ski country or the outskirts of a large city such as Chicago or San Francisco. However, because of the recession, many such communities have actually seen their populations decrease. According to Mark Mather, associate vice president of the Population Reference Bureau, "Baby boomers helped fuel housing and population growth in retirement areas earlier in the decade, and now they are playing an important role in the decline."[33]

Teens are another rapidly growing market. The entire scope of Generation Y—those born between 1976 and 1997—encompasses about 113 million young Americans, or a little more than one-third of the total population. Often called the Millennials, these consumers are tech-savvy shoppers who influence not only their own purchases but also those of their families and friends. They are educated consumers who comparison shop and usually avoid impulse purchases, partly because of the recession and partly because they are spending their own money. According to a Nielsen survey, compared with older generations, such as the Greatest Generation (those who lived through World War II) and the Baby Boomers, Generation Y consumers shop less often but buy more when they do, preferring megastores and big box-retailers.[34]

Statistics can be helpful, but they don't tell the whole story. Marketers must also learn where people live, how old they are, what language or languages they speak, and how much income they have in order to serve them well. Sometimes, marketers must do intensive research in order to reach a particular age or gender group, or both, as described in the "Hit & Miss" feature. Finally, they must learn cultural tastes and preferences.

Above all, companies must avoid stereotyping if they are going to market successfully to a diverse group of consumers. One way to do this is to break a large group into smaller segments. For instance, the Hispanic market is made up of many smaller segments, based on country of origin, language, lifestyle, and cultural values. In an attempt to target a younger Hispanic audience, three television networks have begun to offer bilingual, Spanish, and English-language programming with Hispanic themes. Because many Hispanic American teens and young adults are bilingual, the networks are trying to capture their attention while their parents and grandparents continue to watch Spanish-only programming. The mun2 (pronounced "moon-dos," for Telemundo 2) network targets young, bicultural Hispanics between 18 and 34. It recently launched a half-hour show, *The mun2 Look*, which explores the influence of American Hispanics on today's fashions. Gloria Medel, the executive producer of the network says that "mun2 understands that the young contemporary U.S. Latino experience is about standing out and embracing a personal style." "The mun2 Look" focuses on the culture's raw, edgy looks that are influencing today's runways.[35]

Teenagers are a rapidly growing market. Millennials are tech-savvy shoppers influencing their own purchases as well as those of their families and friends.

Matthew Ennis/iStockphoto

Entrepreneurs who are members of minority groups may start their own businesses out of frustration at not being able to find food, clothing, entertainment, or other goods and services that fit their tastes and needs. In fact, 12.5 percent of all businesses in the United States are owned by immigrants. Mexicans are the largest group, with 2.22 percent of immigrant-owned businesses. Motivated by the American dream that hard work will bring success and the good life, extended families often work in these businesses, which also support their ethnic communities. This localization makes them particularly vulnerable during hard times, but many immigrant entrepreneurs remain optimistic. In fact, during the recent economic downturn, immigrants started businesses at more than twice the rate of citizens born in America. Because these businesses are sometimes halted by immigration restrictions, a new bill has been introduced in Congress that could help entrepreneurs secure a green card more quickly.[36]

Psychographic Segmentation

Lifestyle is the sum of a person's needs, preferences, motives, attitudes, social habits, and cultural background. In recent years, marketing researchers have tried to formulate lifestyle portraits of consumers. This effort has led to another strategy for segmenting target markets, **psychographic segmentation**, which divides consumer markets into groups with similar psychological characteristics, values, and lifestyles.

Psychographic studies have evaluated motivations for purchases of hundreds of goods and services, ranging from soft drinks to healthcare services. Using the resulting data, firms tailor their marketing strategies to carefully chosen market segments. A frequently used

psychographic segmentation dividing consumer markets into groups with similar attitudes, values, and lifestyles.

method of developing psychographic profiles involves the use of *AIO statements*—people's verbal descriptions of various attitudes, interests, and opinions. Researchers survey a sample of consumers, asking them whether they agree or disagree with each statement. The answers are then tabulated and analyzed for use in identifying various lifestyle categories.

Another way to get current information from consumers about their lifestyles is to create *blogs* to which consumers may respond. Companies including Stonyfield Farm, Verizon, and Microsoft have hired bloggers to run online Web journals as a way to connect with and receive information from consumers. Other firms encourage employees at all levels to use blogs to communicate with consumers. General Motors has several blogs at its GMblogs.com site, each tailored to a specific brand or consumer interest. The FastLane blog discusses GM cars and trucks, inviting consumers to offer their thoughts and ideas. Chevrolet Voltage is aimed at fans of the Volt and other electric vehicles. The Lab is where GM's advanced design team talks about its work and invites feedback from community members.[37]

Although demographic classifications such as age, gender, and income are relatively easy to identify and measure, researchers also need to define psychographic categories. Often marketing research firms conduct extensive studies of consumers and then share their psychographic data with clients. In addition, businesses look to studies done by sociologists and psychologists to help them understand their customers. For instance, while children may fall into one age group and their parents in another, they also live certain lifestyles together. Recent marketing research reveals that today's parents are willing and able to spend more on goods and services for their children than parents were a generation or two ago. Spending on toys and videogames for children topped $41 billion for a recent year in the United States.[38] These are just a few trends identified by the researchers, but they provide valuable information to firms that may be considering developing games, designing the interiors of family vehicles, or implementing new wireless plans.

Product-Related Segmentation
Using <u>product-related segmentation</u>, sellers can divide a consumer market into groups based on buyers' relationships to the good or service. The three most popular approaches to product-related segmentation are based on benefits sought, usage rates, and brand loyalty levels.

Segmenting by *benefits sought* focuses on the attributes that people seek in a good or service and the benefits they expect to receive from it. As more firms shift toward consumer demand for products that are eco-friendly, marketers find ways to emphasize the benefits of these products. Swedish home-goods retailer IKEA follows strict guidelines for sourcing its solid wood furniture products. For example, the worldwide company does not accept any illegally felled wood. IKEA's own forest specialists trace batches of timber to their origins to ensure that the lumber is properly documented and certified by the Forest Stewardship Council (FSC). In addition, these specialists work with suppliers to promote more sustainably managed forests worldwide. IKEA uses its Web site and signage in its stores to educate consumers about its wood-source policies.[39]

Consumer markets can also be segmented according to the amounts of a product that people buy and use. Segmentation by *product usage rate* usually defines such categories as heavy users, medium users, and light users. The 80/20 principle states that roughly 80 percent of a product's revenues come from only 20 percent of its buyers. Companies can now pinpoint which of their customers are the heaviest users—and even the most profitable customers—and direct their heaviest marketing efforts to those customers.

The third technique for product-related segmentation divides customers by *brand loyalty*—the degree to which consumers recognize, prefer, and insist on a particular brand.

product-related segmentation dividing consumer markets into groups based on benefits sought by buyers, usage rates, and loyalty levels.

Marketers define groups of consumers with similar degrees of brand loyalty. They then attempt to tie loyal customers to a good or service by giving away premiums, which can be anything from a logo-emblazoned T-shirt to a pair of free tickets to a concert or sports event.

Segmenting Business Markets

In many ways, the segmentation process for business markets resembles that for consumer markets. However, some specific methods differ. Business markets can be divided through geographical segmentation; demographic, or customer-based, segmentation; and end-use segmentation.

Geographical segmentation methods for business markets resemble those for consumer markets. Many B2B marketers target geographically concentrated industries, such as aircraft manufacturing, automobiles, and oil field equipment. Especially on an international scale, customer needs, languages, and other variables may require differences in the marketing mix from one location to another.

Demographic, or *customer-based, segmentation* begins with a good or service design intended to suit a specific organizational market. Sodexho Marriott Services is the largest provider of food services in North America. Its customers include healthcare institutions, business and government offices, schools, and colleges and universities. Within these broad business segments, Sodexho identifies more specific segments, which might include colleges in the South or universities with culturally diverse populations—and differing food preferences or dining styles. Sodexho uses data obtained from surveys that cover students' lifestyles, attitudes, preferences for consumer products in general, services, and media categories. In addition, it uses targeted surveys that identify preferences for restaurant brands or certain foods, meal habits, amount of spending, and the like. Marketers evaluate the data, which sometime reveal surprising trends. At one university in the rural Northeast, students indicated that they liked foods with an international flavor. So Sodexho adapted its offerings accordingly.[40]

To simplify the process of focusing on a particular type of business customer, the federal government has developed a system for subdividing the business marketplace into detailed segments. The six-digit *North American Industry Classification System (NAICS)* provides a common classification system used by the member nations of NAFTA (the United States, Canada, and Mexico). It divides industries into broad categories such as agriculture, forestry, and fishing; manufacturing; transportation; and retail and wholesale trade. Each major category is further subdivided into smaller segments—such as gas stations with convenience food and warehouse clubs—for more detailed information and to facilitate comparison among the member-nations.

Another way to group firms by their demographics is to segment them by size based on their sales revenues or numbers of employees. Some firms collect data from visitors to its Web site and use the data to segment customers by size. Modern information processing also enables companies to segment business markets based on how much they buy, not just how big they are.

End-use segmentation focuses on the precise way a B2B purchaser will use a product. Resembling benefits-sought segmentation for consumer markets, this method helps small and mid-size companies target specific end-user markets rather than competing directly with large firms for wider customer groups. A company might also design a marketing mix based on certain criteria for making a purchase.

end-use segmentation marketing strategy that focuses on the precise way a B2B purchaser will use a product.

Assessment Check ☑

1. What is the most common form of segmentation for consumer markets?

2. What are the three approaches to product-related segmentation?

3. What is end-use segmentation in the B2B market?

Consumer Behavior

A fundamental marketing task is to find out why people buy one product and not another. The answer requires an understanding of consumer behavior, the actions of ultimate consumers directly involved in obtaining, consuming, and disposing of products and the decision processes that precede and follow these actions.

Determinants of Consumer Behavior

By studying people's purchasing behavior, businesses can identify consumers' attitudes toward and uses of their products. This information also helps marketers reach their targeted customers. Both personal and interpersonal factors influence the way buyers behave. Personal influences on **consumer behavior** include individual needs and motives, perceptions, attitudes, learned experiences, and self-concept. For instance, today people are constantly looking for ways to save time, so firms do everything they can to provide goods and services designed for convenience. However, when it comes to products such as dinner foods, consumers want convenience, but they also want to enjoy the flavor of a home-cooked meal and spend quality time with their families. So companies such as Stouffer's offer frozen lasagna or manicotti in family sizes, and supermarkets have entire sections devoted to freshly prepared take-out meals that range from roast turkey to filet mignon.

McDonald's is betting that consumers who drink premium coffee beverages also like to buy them at bargain prices. In many U.S. locations, McDonald's has placed McCafé coffee bars—serving cappuccinos, lattes, and mochas—near the cash register. The firm recently began offering fruit and oatmeal for breakfast, which, added to the McCafe beverages, resulted in an uptick in sales.[41]

The interpersonal determinants of consumer behavior include cultural, social, and family influences. In the area of convenience foods, cultural, social, and family influences come into play as much as an individual's need to save time. Understanding that many consumers value the time they spend with their families and want to care for them by providing good nutrition, marketers often emphasize these values in advertisements for convenience food products.

Sometimes external events influence consumer behavior. One study suggests that as a result of the recession, consumers may have permanently altered their buying and spending behavior. The survey found that 72 percent of consumers said that they had significantly or somewhat changed their shopping habits; only 7 percent said they had made no change. Manufacturers and retailers—and especially small businesses—will need to create new marketing strategies in response to these challenges.[42]

Determinants of Business Buying Behavior

Because a number of people can influence purchases of B2B products, business buyers face a variety of organizational influences in addition to their own preferences. A design engineer may help set the specifications that potential vendors must satisfy. A procurement manager may invite selected companies to bid on a purchase. A production supervisor may evaluate the operational aspects of the proposals that the firm receives, and the vice president of manufacturing may head a committee making the final decision.

consumer behavior actions of ultimate consumers directly involved in obtaining, consuming, and disposing of products and the decision processes that precede and follow these actions.

Steps in the Consumer Behavior Process

Consumer decision making follows the sequential process outlined in Figure 11.6, with interpersonal and personal influences affecting every step. The process begins when the consumer recognizes a problem or opportunity. If someone needs a new pair of shoes, that need becomes a problem to solve. If you receive a promotion at work and a 20 percent salary increase, that change may also become a purchase opportunity.

To solve the problem or take advantage of the opportunity, the consumer seeks information about his or her intended purchase and evaluates alternatives, such as available brands. The goal is to find the best response to the problem or opportunity.

Eventually, the consumer reaches a decision and completes the transaction. Later, he or she evaluates the experience by making a postpurchase evaluation. Feelings about the experience serve as feedback that will influence future purchase decisions. The various steps in the sequence are affected by both interpersonal and personal factors.

FIGURE 11.6 Steps in the Consumer Behavior Process

Evaluation of Alternatives — Purchase Decision — Purchase Act — Postpurchase Evaluation — Recognition of Problem or Opportunity — Search

Interpersonal Determinants

Cultural Influences
Family Influences
Social Influences

Personal Determinants

Needs and Motives
Perceptions
Attitudes
Learning
Self-Concept

FEEDBACK

Relationship Marketing

The past decade has brought rapid change to most industries, as customers have become better-informed and more-demanding purchasers through closely comparing competing goods and services. They expect, even demand, new benefits from the companies that supply them, making it harder for firms to gain a competitive advantage based on product features alone.

In today's hypercompetitive era, businesses need to find new ways of relating to customers if they hope to maintain long-term success. Businesses are developing strategies and tactics that draw them into tighter connections with their customers, suppliers, and even employees. As a result, many firms are turning their attention to the issues of relationship marketing. **Relationship marketing** goes beyond an effort toward making the sale. Instead, it develops and maintains long-term, cost-effective exchange relationships with partners. These partners include individual customers, suppliers, and employees. As its ultimate goal, relationship marketing seeks to achieve customer satisfaction.

Managing relationships instead of simply completing transactions often leads to creative partnerships. However, customers enter into relationships with firms only if they are assured that the relationship will somehow benefit them. As the intensity of commitment increases, so does the likelihood of a business continuing a long-term relationship with its customers.

Assessment Check ✓

1. Define *consumer behavior*.

2. What are some determinants of consumer behavior?

relationship marketing developing and maintaining long-term, cost-effective exchange relationships with partners.

Calming the Angry Customer

In any business, an angry customer is a challenge representing not only an immediate problem but also a potential loss of future business. The customer may be upset over poor service or a broken product, frustrated by lack of attention from the company, or just plain demanding. You, the businessperson, should view this customer not as a disruption but as an opportunity to see your company from the outside. With a little bit of common sense, good personal skills, and knowledge of your company and its products, you can very likely turn the customer's dissatisfaction into satisfaction.

- *Remain calm and professional.* The customer isn't angry with you personally. Let the customer speak first, and listen carefully as he or she states the problem. Make written notes. Acknowledge the customer's anger, then assure him or her that you will correct the situation.

- *Repeat the customer's stated problem.* Using your own words assures the customer that you have been listening. For example, you might say, "The shoes you received were the right color but the wrong size." Make sure you understand the problem before offering a solution.

- *Focus on the solution.* Having procedures in place beforehand can help you resolve a problem quickly. If you can't solve the problem yourself, immediately refer it to someone who can. Fast action will let the customer know that you are on his or her side.

- *Thank the customer for his or her patience.* By bringing the problem to your attention, the customer is actually giving you an opportunity to improve service to all your clients.

- *Follow up.* If appropriate, send an e-mail or make a phone call to make sure the correct pair of shoes arrived. Your professionalism will strengthen the customer's relationship with your firm—and positive word of mouth may even bring you new customers.

Sources: Lynne McClure, "Handling Angry Customers," Impact Publications, http://www.impactpublications.com, accessed June 7, 2011; Katy Tynan, "Conflict Management Part 2—Calming an Irate Customer," *Ezinearticles.com*, http://ezinearticles.com, accessed April 4, 2010; "How to Calm an Angry Customer," *BusinessKnowledgeSource.com*, http://www.businessknowledgesource.com, accessed April 4, 2010.

Businesses are building relationships by partnering with customers, suppliers, and other businesses. Timberland, maker of footwear and clothing, creates many partnerships that foster long-term relationships. The firm partners with not-for-profit organizations such as CARE, City Year, and Clean Air–Cool Planet to complete service projects for communities and the environment. Through its Serv-a-Palooza, hundreds of Timberland employees engage in volunteer tasks in their communities. Those opportunities even extend to customers who have expressed an interest in participating in programs in their own regions. If you want to volunteer for a food drive or to help restore a marsh, just log on to the Timberland Web site to see what's available. All of these activities help build relationships with customers, communities, and other organizations.[43]

Benefits of Relationship Marketing

Relationship marketing helps all parties involved. In addition to providing mutual protection against competitors, businesses that forge solid links with vendors and customers are often rewarded with lower costs and higher profits than they would generate on their own. Long-term agreements with a few high-quality suppliers frequently reduce a firm's production costs. Unlike one-time sales, these ongoing relationships encourage suppliers to offer customers preferential treatment, quickly adjusting shipments to accommodate changes in orders and correcting any quality problems that might arise.

Good relationships with customers can be vital strategic weapons for a firm. By identifying current purchasers and maintaining positive relationships with them, organizations can efficiently target their best customers. Studying current customers' buying habits and preferences can help marketers identify potential new customers and establish ongoing contact with them. Attracting a new customer can cost five times as much as keeping an existing one. Not only do marketing costs go down, but long-term customers usually buy more, require less service, refer other customers, and provide valuable feedback. Together, these elements contribute to a higher **lifetime value of a customer**—the revenues and intangible benefits (referrals and customer feedback) from the customer over the life of the relationship, minus the amount the company must spend to acquire and serve that customer. Keeping that customer may occasionally require some extra effort, especially if the customer has become upset or dissatisfied with a good or service. But good marketers can overcome this particular challenge, as described in the "Business Etiquette" feature.

Businesses also benefit from strong relationships with other companies. Purchasers who repeatedly buy from one business may find that they save time and gain service quality as the business learns their specific needs. Some relationship-oriented companies also customize items based on customer preferences. Because many businesses reward loyal customers with discounts or bonuses, some buyers may even find that they save money by developing long-term relationships. Alliances with other firms to serve the same customers also can be rewarding. The partners combine their capabilities and resources to accomplish goals that they could not reach on their own. In addition, alliances with other firms may help businesses develop the skills and experience they need to successfully enter new markets or improve service to current customers.

Tools for Nurturing Customer Relationships

Although relationship marketing has important benefits for both customers and businesses, most relationship-oriented businesses quickly discover that some customers generate more profitable business than others. If 20 percent of a firm's customers account for 80 percent of its sales and profits—the 80/20 principle mentioned earlier in the chapter—a customer in that category undoubtedly has a higher lifetime value than a customer who buys only once or twice or who makes small purchases.

While businesses shouldn't ignore any customer, they need to allocate their marketing resources wisely. A firm may choose to customize goods or services for high-value customers while working to increase repeat sales of stock products to less-valuable customers. Differentiating between these two groups also helps marketers focus on each in an effort to increase their commitment.

Frequency Marketing and Affinity Marketing Programs

Popular techniques through which firms try to build and protect customer relationships include frequent-buyer or -user programs. These so-called **frequency marketing** programs reward purchasers with cash, rebates, merchandise, or other premiums. Frequency programs have grown more sophisticated over the years. They offer more personalization and customization than in the past. Airlines, hotel groups, restaurants, and many retailers including supermarkets offer frequency programs. Vacationers who book three nights at the Atlantis resort in the Bahamas may earn a fourth night free along with a free breakfast and complimentary tickets for a dolphin-swim experience.[44]

Affinity programs are another tool for building emotional links with customers. An affinity program is a marketing effort sponsored by an organization that solicits involvement by individuals who share common interests and activities. Affinity programs are common in the credit card industry. For instance, a person can sign up for a credit card emblazoned with

lifetime value of a customer revenues and intangible benefits (referrals and customer feedback) from a customer over the life of the relationship, minus the amount the company must spend to acquire and serve that customer.

frequency marketing marketing initiative that rewards frequent purchases with cash, rebates, merchandise, or other premiums.

affinity program marketing effort sponsored by an organization that solicits involvement by individuals who share common interests and activities.

Courtesy Bank of America Corporation

Affinity programs are another tool for building emotional links with customers and common in the credit card industry. For instance, Bank of America offers credit cards featuring Major League Baseball® logos, like the one pictured here, as well as the logos of all the 30 MLB clubs.

the logo of a favorite charity, a sports or entertainment celebrity, or a photograph of his or her college. Bank of America offers credit cards featuring the logos of all the 30 Major League Baseball clubs.

Many businesses also use comarketing and cobranding. In a **comarketing** deal, two businesses jointly market each other's products. When two or more businesses link their names to a single product, **cobranding** occurs. When two seemingly unlikely businesses team up, the marketing sparks fly—and two very different groups of consumers may come together to buy the same product. Nike and iPod have marketed the Nike + iPod Sport kit, which allows a runner to insert a special sensor into a built-in pocket in a Nike+ shoe, which synchronizes the runner's activity with workout data and music that plays through the iPod. Enthusiasts can also purchase specially designed Nike workout apparel that has pockets designed to hold an iPod nano itself.[45]

comarketing cooperative arrangement in which two businesses jointly market each other's products.

cobranding cooperative arrangement in which two or more businesses team up to closely link their names on a single product.

One-on-One Marketing The ability to customize products and rapidly deliver goods and services has become increasingly dependent on technology such as computer-aided design and manufacturing (CAD/CAM). The Internet offers a way for businesses to connect with customers in a direct and intimate manner. Companies can take orders for customized products, gather data about buyers, and predict what items a customer might want in the future. Computer databases provide strong support for effective relationship marketing. Marketers can maintain databases on customer tastes, price-range preferences, and lifestyles, and they can quickly obtain names and other information about promising prospects. Amazon.com greets each online customer with a list of suggested books he or she might like to purchase. Many online retailers send their customers e-mails about upcoming sales, new products, and special events.

Small and large companies often rely on *customer relationship management (CRM)* software technology that helps them gather, sort, and interpret data about customers. Software firms develop this software in order to help businesses build and manage their relationships with customers. QueueBuster is one such product. The software offers callers the choice of receiving an automated return call instead of waiting on hold for the next available representative. After implementing the software, travel agency STA reported that its customer satisfaction ratings had improved to 98 percent. This simple solution to customers' frustration probably not only helped build customer loyalty but also helped save STA from lost business as well.[46]

Assessment Check ✔

1. What is the lifetime value of a customer?
2. Discuss the increasing importance of one-on-one marketing efforts.

What's Ahead

The next two chapters examine each of the four elements of the marketing mix that marketers use to satisfy their selected target markets. Chapter 12 focuses on products and their distribution through various channels to different outlets. Chapter 13 covers promotion and the various methods marketers use to communicate with their target customers, along with strategies for setting prices for different products.

Summary of Learning Goals

⌐1¬ **Summarize the ways in which marketing creates utility.**

Utility is the ability of a good or service to satisfy the wants and needs of customers. The production function creates form utility by converting inputs to finished goods and services. Marketing creates time, place, and ownership utility by making the product available when and where consumers want to buy and by arranging for orderly transfers of ownership.

Assessment Check Answers ☑

1.1 What is utility? Utility is the ability of a good or service to satisfy the wants and needs of customers.

1.2 Identify ways in which marketing creates utility. Marketing creates time utility by making a good or service available when customers want to purchase it, place utility by making the product available in a convenient location, and ownership utility by transferring the product from the buyer to the seller.

⌐2¬ **Discuss the marketing concept.**

The marketing concept refers to a companywide customer orientation with the objective of achieving long-run success. This concept is essential in today's marketplace, which is primarily a buyer's market, meaning buyers can choose from an abundance of goods and services. Marketing now centers on the satisfaction of customers and building long-term relationships with those customers.

Assessment Check Answers ☑

2.1 What is the marketing concept? The marketing concept is a companywide customer orientation with the objective of achieving long-run success. According to the marketing concept, success begins with the customer.

2.2 How is the marketing concept tied to the relationship era of marketing? Most marketing now centers on the satisfaction of customers and building long-term relationships with them, rather than simply producing and selling goods and services.

⌐3¬ **Describe not-for-profit marketing, and identify the five major categories of nontraditional marketing.**

Not-for-profit organizations must engage in marketing just as for-profit firms do. Not-for-profit organizations operate in both the public and private sectors, and use marketing to obtain volunteers and donations, make people aware of their existence, achieve certain goals for society, and so on. Not-for-profit organizations may engage in several types of nontraditional marketing—person, place, event, cause, or organization marketing. They may rely on one type or a combination.

Assessment Check Answers ☑

3.1 Why do not-for-profit organizations engage in marketing? Not-for-profit organizations use marketing to attract volunteers and donors, communicate their message, and achieve their societal goals.

3.2 What are the five types of nontraditional marketing used by not-for-profit organizations? The five types of nontraditional marketing are person, place, event, cause, and organization marketing.

⌐4¬ **Outline the basic steps in developing a marketing strategy.**

All organizations develop marketing strategies to reach customers. This process involves analyzing the overall market, selecting a target market, and developing a marketing mix that blends elements related to product, distribution, promotion, and pricing decisions.

Assessment Check Answers ☑

4.1 Distinguish between consumer products and business products. Business products are goods and services purchased to be used, either directly or indirectly, in the production of other goods for resale. Consumer products are purchased by end users.

4.2 What are the steps in developing a marketing strategy? The steps in developing a marketing strategy are to analyze the overall market, select a target market, and develop a marketing mix.

⌐5¬ **Describe the marketing research function.**

Marketing research is the information-gathering function that links marketers to the marketplace. It provides valuable information about potential target markets. Firms may generate internal data or gather external data. They may use secondary data or conduct research to obtain primary data. Data mining, which involves computer searches through customer data to detect patterns or relationships, is one helpful tool in forecasting various trends such as sales revenues and consumer behavior.

Assessment Check Answers ☑

5.1 What is the difference between primary data and secondary data? Secondary data are previously published facts that are inexpensive to retrieve and easy to obtain. Primary data are collected firsthand through observation or surveys.

5.2 What is data mining? Data mining involves computer searches through customer data in order to evaluate the data and identify useful trends.

6 Identify and explain each of the methods available for segmenting consumer and business markets.

Consumer markets can be divided according to four criteria: geographical factors; demographic characteristics, such as age and family size; psychographic variables, which involve behavioral and lifestyle profiles; and product-related variables, such as the benefits consumers seek when buying a product or the degree of brand loyalty they feel toward it. Business markets are segmented according to three criteria: geographical characteristics, customer-based specifications for products, and end-user applications.

Assessment Check Answers ☑

6.1 What is the most common form of segmentation for consumer markets? Demographics is the most commonly used consumer market segmentation method.

6.2 What are the three approaches to product-related segmentation? The three approaches to product-related segmentation are by benefits sought, product usage rate, and brand loyalty.

6.3 What is end-use segmentation in the B2B market? End-use segmentation focuses on the precise way a B2B purchaser will use a product.

7 Outline the determinants of consumer behavior.

Consumer behavior refers to the actions of ultimate consumers with direct effects on obtaining, consuming, and disposing of products, as well as the decision processes that precede and follow these actions. Personal influences on consumer behavior include an individual's needs and motives, perceptions, attitudes, learned experiences, and self-concept. The interpersonal determinants include cultural influences, social influences, and family influences. A number of people within a firm may participate in business purchase decisions, so business buyers must consider a variety of organizational influences in addition to their own preferences.

Assessment Check Answers ☑

7.1 Define *consumer behavior*. Consumer behavior refers to the actions of ultimate consumers directly involved in obtaining, consuming, and disposing of products, along with the decision processes surrounding these actions.

7.2 What are some determinants of consumer behavior? Determinants of consumer behavior include both personal influences and interpersonal influences. Personal influences include an individual's needs and motives; perceptions, attitudes, and experiences; and self-concept. Interpersonal influences include cultural, social and family influences.

8 Discuss the benefits of and tools for relationship marketing.

Relationship marketing is an organization's attempt to develop long-term, cost-effective links with individual customers for mutual benefit. Good relationships with customers can be a vital strategic weapon for a firm. By identifying current purchasers and maintaining a positive relationship with them, an organization can efficiently target its best customers, fulfill their needs, and create loyalty. Information technologies, frequency and affinity programs, and one-on-one efforts all help build relationships with customers.

Assessment Check Answers ☑

8.1 What is the lifetime value of a customer? The lifetime value of a customer incorporates the revenues and intangible benefits from the customer over the life of the relationship with a firm, minus the amount the company must spend to acquire and serve the customer.

8.2 Discuss the increasing importance of one-on-one marketing efforts. One-on-one marketing is increasing in importance as consumers demand more customization in goods and services. It is also increasingly dependent on technology such as computer-aided design and manufacturing (CAD/CAM). The Internet also offers a way for businesses to connect with customers in a direct and personal manner.

■ Key Terms

marketing 353	consumer (B2C) product 361	market segmentation 366	consumer behavior 374
exchange process 353		geographical segmentation 368	
utility 354	business (B2B) product 361		relationship marketing 375
marketing concept 355		demographic segmentation 368	
person marketing 358	target market 361		lifetime value of a customer 377
place marketing 359	marketing mix 362	psychographic segmentation 371	
event marketing 359	marketing research 364		frequency marketing 377
cause marketing 359	business intelligence 365	product-related segmentation 372	affinity program 377
organization marketing 360	data mining 365		comarketing 378
	data warehouse 365	end-use segmentation 373	cobranding 378

Review Questions

1. Define the four different types of utility and explain how marketing contributes to the creation of utility. Then choose one of the following companies and describe how it creates each type of utility with its goods or services:

   a. Burger King

   b. Polo Ralph Lauren

   c. Borders bookstore

   d. Supercuts hair salons

   e. Adobe Systems

2. Describe the shift from a seller's market to a buyer's market. Why was this move important to marketers?

3. Describe how an organization might combine person marketing and event marketing. Give an example.

4. Describe how an organization might combine cause marketing and organization marketing. Give an example.

5. Identify each of the following as a consumer product or a business product, or classify it as both:

   a. cup of coffee

   b. iPad

   c. gasoline

   d. boat trailer

   e. hand sanitizer

   f. hair gel

6. Identify and describe the four strategies that blend to create a marketing mix.

7. What is a target market? Why is target market selection usually the first step in the development of a marketing strategy?

8. Identify the two strategies that a firm could use to develop a marketing mix for international markets. What are the advantages and disadvantages of each?

9. Describe the types of data that someone who is thinking of starting an accounting service might choose to gather. How might this businessperson use the data in making the startup decision?

10. Explain each of the methods used to segment consumer and business markets. Which methods do you think would be most effective for each of the following and why? (Note that a combination of methods might be applicable.)

   a. supermarket featuring organic foods

   b. hair-care products

   c. tour bus company

   d. line of baby food

   e. dental insurance

   f. dry cleaner

11. What are the three major determinants of consumer behavior? Give an example of how each one might influence a person's purchasing decision.

12. What are the benefits of relationship marketing? Describe how frequency and affinity programs work toward building relationships.

Projects and Teamwork Applications

1. On your own or with a classmate, choose one of the following products and create an advertisement that illustrates how your firm creates time, place, and form utility in its delivery of the product to the customer.

   a. auto repair service

   b. hiking tours

   c. craft supply store

   d. pet-sitting service

2. Choose one of the following nonprofit organizations or find one on your own. Research the organization online to learn more about it. Outline your proposed contents for a fundraising event based on the chapter discussion of nontraditional marketing, such as cause marketing or organization marketing.

   a. ASPCA

   b. Prostate Cancer Foundation

   c. Red Cross

   d. Salvation Army

3. As a marketer, if you can find ways to classify your firm's goods and services as both business and consumer products, most likely your company's sales will increase as you build relationships with a new category of customers. On your own or with a classmate, choose one of the following products, and outline a marketing strategy for attracting the classification of customer that is *opposite* from the one listed in parentheses.

   a. hybrid car (consumer)

   b. LCD TV (consumer)

   c. limousine service (business)

   d. office furniture (business)

4. Think of two situations in which you have been a customer: one in which you were satisfied with the merchandise you received and one in which you were not. Make a list of the reasons you were satisfied in the first case and another list of the reasons you were not satisfied in the second case. Would you say that the failure was the result of the seller not understanding your needs?

5. Comarketing and cobranding are techniques that organizations often use to market their own and each other's products, such as Nike running shoes and the Apple iPod. On your own or with a classmate, choose two firms with goods and/or services you think would work well together for comarketing separate products or cobranding a single product. Then create an advertisement for your comarketing or cobranding effort.

▉ Web Assignments

1. **Demographic trends.** The *Statistical Abstract of the United States* is an excellent source of demographic and economic data about the United States. Visit the Web site listed here and click on "population." In terms of age and race, what does the U.S. population currently look like? What will the U.S. population look like in the decades to come?

   http://www.census.gov/compendia/statab/

2. **Market segmentation.** Go to the Web site of Canon USA and review the company's array of product offerings. Prepare a brief report on how Canon segments its markets.

   http://www.usa.canon.com/home

3. **Customer loyalty programs.** Airlines and hotel chains have extensive customer loyalty programs. Pick an airline and hotel chain and print out information on the firm's customer loyalty program. (Two examples are listed here.) Bring the material to class to participate in a discussion on this topic.

   http://www.southwest.com/rapid_rewards/

   http://www.marriott.com/rewards/rewards-program.mi

Note: Internet Web addresses change frequently. If you don't find the exact sites listed, you may need to access the organization's home page and search from there or use a search engine such as Bing or Google.

CASE 11.1 Advertising on Facebook: Unlimited Potential?

With 400 million members, Facebook is a global social network of unprecedented size—and untold potential revenue. Users are familiar with the advertisements in the right-hand margin of certain pages. Some big names, such as Walmart and PepsiCo, post ads, but so do many smaller companies. What users may not realize is that advertisers can use members' personal information—age, location, interests, level of education, and connections within Facebook—to refine the targeting of ads. For example, women who change their relationship status to "engaged" will suddenly start seeing ads from local caterers, planners, wedding-gown stores, photographers, and so on. In contrast, Google uses keywords and search histories to target ads.

Facebook recently surpassed Google as the most visited site in the United States. Eager to reach Facebook's much larger membership, advertisers are switching from Google to Facebook, which some predict will earn $2 billion from global advertising. One study found that 78 percent of Facebook users return to Facebook to see more news stories; only 67 percent of Google News users do so. Facebook traffic is up 185 percent; Google is up only 9 percent.

Facebook's "self-service" ads usually appear on a user's profile page and consist of a small photo and some text. An advertiser establishes a daily budget—there is no minimum—using Facebook's ad-creation tool. When the advertiser has spent the day's entire budget, Facebook stops running the ad. If money is left over, the advertiser can roll it over to the next day's budget. Advertisers pay either "by impression," every time a user views the ad, or "per click," every time a user actually clicks on the link in the ad to open the company's Web site.

Facebook members can become "fans" of an advertiser's Facebook page or can reply to an invitation to a company-sponsored event through Facebook. But as in other media, consumers have a deep mistrust of Web advertising as a credible source of information. With ads on Facebook becoming omnipresent, click-through rates (CTRs) have fallen to about 0.3 percent from close to 3 percent. Of course, the point is to get people to look at the ads, which most users ignore. When promoting a contest, one advertiser found that humor—and pictures of cute puppies and kittens—increased his CTR even more than did offers of prizes.

Some Facebook users find the ads off-putting—or worse—because advertisers can target them so precisely. But Dan Rose, the vice president for business development at Facebook, predicted that the quality of the ads would improve as more companies use the system.

Facebook requires the text and photo in an ad to be relevant to what is being advertised. However, Facebook does not review ads before they are posted. The only review system is user feedback. If a user reports an ad as misleading, offensive, uninteresting, irrelevant, repetitive, or "other," Facebook deletes the ad from that user's page. The more people ask for an ad to be removed, the less likely Facebook is to allow it be posted on other people's pages.

Some observers predict that Facebook will transform Web advertising and even the advertising industry itself. Facebook's "Connect" technology allows members to take their social networks with them as they browse the Internet. And just as in the real world, in the virtual world people are much more likely to value the opinions of their friends more than those of people—or advertisers—they don't know.

Questions for Critical Thinking

1. Why do advertisers continue to post ads on Facebook, even though the click-through response rate is so low?

2. How does Web advertising affect consumer behavior? Does it help build customer relationships or not?

Sources: Claire Cain Miller, "Twitter Unveils Plan to Draw Money from Ads," *The New York Times,* accessed June 7, 2011, http://www.nytimes.com; Courtney Rubin, "Should You Advertise on Facebook?" *Inc.com,* March 23, 2010, http://www.inc.com; Carmen Nobel, "Facebook Ad Model Is Friend to Small Business," *The Street,* March 22, 2010, http://www.thestreet.com; Steve Rubal, "Facebook Will Rule the Web During the Next Decade," *Advertising Age,* March 15, 2010, http://www.adage.com; Jonathan L. Yarmis, "How Facebook Will Upend Advertising," *BusinessWeek,* March 9, 2010, http://www.businessweek.com; Brad Stone, "Ads Posted on Facebook Strike Some as Off-Key," *The New York Times,* March 3, 2010, http://www.nytimes.com; Kunur Patel, "Will E-Commerce Help Facebook's Ad Sales?" *Advertising Age,* March 1, 2010, http://www.adage.com; Taylor Pratt, "Fun Ways to Improve Facebook Ad CTRs," *Search Engine Journal,* n.d. [March 2010], http://www.searchenginejournal.com.

Marketing Gone Wrong: Johnson & Johnson and Risperdal

CASE 11.2

Several years ago, the Food and Drug Administration (FDA) approved Johnson & Johnson's drug Risperdal to treat psychotic disorders, such as schizophrenia, in adults. However, the National Institute of Mental Health found that schizophrenia affects only about 1.1 percent of adults in the United States. According to a lawsuit by the state of Louisiana, Johnson & Johnson therefore decided to seek a wider market for the drug by indirectly promoting it for other purposes.

Under U.S. law, if the FDA has approved a drug for treating at least one disorder, doctors are permitted to prescribe it "off label," for any other disorder they think the drug will help—even if the FDA has not approved it for that disorder. (The condition the drug is intended to treat must be stated on the labeling.) However, drug manufacturers are forbidden to promote a drug for any other use than the FDA-approved one.

Recently, the U.S. Department of Justice charged Johnson & Johnson with paying hundreds of millions of dollars in kickbacks to Omnicare Inc. to buy and promote Risperdal, among other drugs, for off-label uses. Omnicare, the largest pharmacy for U.S. nursing-home patients, allegedly advocated prescribing Risperdal for elderly patients with Alzheimer's disease—even though the FDA never approved Risperdal for treating Alzheimer's. Johnson & Johnson stated, "We believe airing the facts will confirm that our conduct, including rebating programs like those the government now challenges, was lawful and appropriate. We look forward to the opportunity to present our evidence in court."

As far back as 1994—just one year after it approved Risperdal for psychotic disorders—the FDA ordered Johnson & Johnson to stop its claims that Risperdal was more effective than competing drugs. In 1999, the FDA warned the company that its marketing literature exaggerated Risperdal's benefits for elderly patients with Alzheimer's disease and understated the risks. Nonetheless, a Johnson & Johnson business plan revealed the company's intention to increase Risperdal's sales to these vulnerable patients well into the 21st century (as Baby Boomers age). Sales of Risperdal peaked at $4.5 billion in 2007, before the patent expired and other companies could legally manufacture cheaper, generic versions of the drug.

In 2005, the FDA issued a public health advisory, warning that Risperdal and similar drugs actually increased the chances of death among elderly Alzheimer's patients, usually from heart failure or pneumonia. The FDA has also required Risperdal to carry a "black box" warning, the most stringent in the FDA's arsenal.

Ten states have filed lawsuits against Johnson & Johnson for promoting Risperdal off label. Louisiana sued to force the company to pay millions of dollars in fines and to regain public money spent on Risperdal. Johnson & Johnson's lawyers argued that Louisiana did not cite any evidence of misrepresentation or off-label promotion. The company also claimed that there was no connection between its marketing and Louisiana doctors' decision to prescribe Risperdal. The judge rejected this argument, and the trial date was set. A spokesman for Johnson & Johnson said that the case "should be decided on the body of evidence, including testimony, not on the basis of excerpts from documents." The company has not put any money aside toward a settlement.

Omnicare paid $98 million to settle charges of running kickback plans with nursing homes and other drug manufacturers. Neither Omnicare nor Johnson & Johnson acknowledged doing anything wrong.

Questions for Critical Thinking

1. Do you think that recommending nonapproved uses of a drug is an appropriate marketing strategy? Why or why not?
2. Which market segmentation strategy do you think Johnson & Johnson was using when it decided to promote Risperdal for Alzheimer's patients? What did the company fail to take into account when developing this strategy?

Sources: Margaret Cronin Fisk, Jef Feeley, and David Voreacos, "Did J&J Plan to Break Rules?" *BusinessWeek,* June 7, 2011, http://www.businessweek.com; Margaret Cronin Fisk, Jeff Feeley, and David Voreacos, "J&J Pushed Risperdal for Elderly after U.S. Warning, Files Show," *Bloomberg.com,* March 10, 2010, http://www.bloomberg.com; Natasha Singer, "Johnson & Johnson Accused of Drug Kickbacks," *The New York Times,* January 16, 2010, http://www.nytimes.com; Michael Winter, "Johnson and Johnson Accused of Drug Kickbacks," *USA Today,* January 15, 2010, http://content.usatoday.com; Jim Edwards, "J&J Nursing Home Kickback Scheme Tripled Sales, DOJ Alleges," *BNET,* January 15, 2010, http://industry.bnet.com.

CASE 11.3 — Zipcar and UNH: Customer-Driven Marketing

When you're a college student, getting around campus (or off-campus) can sometimes be a challenge. You can walk. You can ride your bike or your skateboard. But when rain is pummeling your backpack or when you have to carry that heavy box of marketing flyers across campus, you wish you had a car—not to mention if you want to head off-campus for a weekend road trip. So you decide to bring a car to campus, but discover that you're forking over several hundred dollars for a parking permit and you can't find a place to park anyway. Then there's the expense of gas and insurance, and the nattering of friends who want a ride or who want to borrow your car—just for an hour or an evening. Depending on where you go to school, Zipcar has got you covered. If you happen to attend the University of New Hampshire, you're in luck.

Zipcar is a car-sharing network based in Cambridge, Massachusetts that operates in metropolitan areas and on university campuses around the U.S., Canada, and the United Kingdom. Car-sharing was already popular in Europe ten years ago when Zipcar founders decided to see if the idea would fly in the U.S. Shortly after its introduction to urban dwellers and U.S. students, Zipcar's message had wheels.

At the University of New Hampshire (UNH), students and faculty already had several transportation options, including an Amtrak station nearby and several bus services. But Brett Pasinella, who works for the University Office of Sustainability, wanted to find a way to link the different transportation options and expand them in a sustainable fashion. His research told him that Zipcar fit UNH's existing options. "We went through a bidding process to get the right company," Pasinella says. The firm had to meet UNH's requirement that membership include insurance and fuel. "Zipcar really stood out because of their technology and understanding of the services and what we were looking for," explainsPasinella. But UNH still had to sell the idea to budget-conscious students in order to make it work.

The Zipcar system is simple: for a $35 annual fee, UNH students or faculty get round-the-clock access to

Zipcars that are parked in designated parking spots around campus. When they join, members receive their own Zipcard (like a key card) that unlocks any Zipcar. Members reserve a car online, then use their Zipcard to access it. Gas and insurance are included with membership, as well as an average of 180 miles per day.

To sell the concept to UNH students, Brett Pasinella engaged a senior class of marketing students to develop a marketing plan for all the transportation systems available on campus. The class split into teams, one of which chose the Zipcar project. The marketing students created presentations designed to answer questions and help classmates overcome the hurdle of a $35 fee. Once they realized that an annual parking permit at UNH is $400—and that gas and insurance are included with Zipcar membership—they began to recognize the benefits. In addition, they saw Zipcars parked around the campus so they became familiar with the brand.

Brett Pasinella notes that UNH is also a sustainable campus, and that most of his job is focused on finding ways to reduce waste and energy use—including throughout the university's transportation system. Zipcar's entire fleet is EPA Smart Way certified and includes hybrids as well as other zero-emission vehicles. But Pasinella and UNH marketing student Erin Badger point out the realities of college life. "A lot of students will focus on the fact that Zipcar is easier for them and saves them money," concedes Erin Badger. "We have to promote Zipcar toward what students are looking for, and those are the two biggest factors."

After the first year in operation at UNH, Zipcar membership is growing. Pasinella plans to market the service proactively in coming years—sending Zipcar information to incoming students and faculty before they arrive on campus with their own vehicles. UNH conducted a survey of members and discovered that users like the convenience and visibility of the cars as well as the low cost. Erin Badger might be the Zipcar's best spokesperson at UNH. "I wish I'd figured it out a lot sooner," she admits. She accrued a lot of parking tickets around campus before she joined Zipcar. "I'd have saved myself a lot of money if I'd joined sooner," she says.

Questions for Critical Thinking

1. Who is Zipcar's target market? How might Zipcar's market be further segmented?

2. Describe how Zipcar might create a marketing mix for colleges and universities.

3. Just as Zipcar must market to UNH, UNH in turn must market the Zipcar concept to its customers—students and faculty. Describe how studying consumer behavior could help select a strategy for UNH's marketing effort.

4. What steps can Zipcar take to manage its relationship with UNH?

Sources: Zipcar Web site, http://www.zipcar.com, accessed June 7, 2011; University of New Hampshire Transportation Services, http://www.unh.edu/transportation, accessed June 7, 2011; "Zipcar, Inc.," *Bloomberg Businessweek*, http://investingbusinessweek.com, accessed June 7, 2011.

Chapter 12

Learning Objectives

[1] Explain marketing's definition of a product; differentiate among convenience, shopping, and specialty products; and distinguish between a product mix and a product line.

[2] Briefly describe each of the four stages of the product life cycle with their marketing implications.

[3] Explain how firms identify their products.

[4] Outline and briefly describe each of the major components of an effective distribution strategy.

[5] Distinguish between the different types of wholesaling intermediaries.

[6] Describe the various types of retailers, and identify retail strategies.

[7] Identify the various categories of distribution channels, and discuss the factors that influence channel selection.

Product and Distribution Strategies

Patrick Heagney/iStockphoto

Bag Balm: A Simple Product with Hundreds of Uses

Sometimes the simplest products have the most uses—and survive in the marketplace for the longest time. Bag Balm is one such product. Manufactured in Vermont, the gooey, sticky, green-yellow substance was formulated in the late 1800s as an ointment for softening cow udders; but more than a century later, Bag Balm has made its way into the medicine cabinets and kitchen drawers of households everywhere, with all kinds of uses. The company that manufacturers it couldn't be happier. Entrepreneur John Norris purchased the Bag Balm formula from its Vermont inventor in 1899 and traveled to Boston to design the original can—a green cube with red lettering that is still in use today. Once the product was packaged, Norris visited farms around the United States, peddling the miracle ointment to farmers, who quickly recognized the value of the product for their livestock. At some point, one of those farmers smeared a dab of Bag Balm on the chafed paws of a dog—with positive results. When it became apparent that minor cuts and abrasions healed more quickly with a bit of Bag Balm, veterinarians began to order the ointment in cases. Not surprisingly, pet owners tried the salve on themselves and their children, and Bag Balm worked its way from the barn to the house.

Today, consumers rub Bag Balm into scrapes and rashes on their pets and on themselves; they massage cracked skin on heels and hands with it; they apply it to chapped lips and baby skin with diaper rash. They use it to treat pimples, sunburns, bed sores, saddle sores, and eczema. They even turn to it when they need to lubricate door hinges and seal pruned trees. Farmers, construction workers, gardeners, painters, fishermen, mechanics, and professional athletes all use Bag Balm for skin irritations. Consumers don't care that Bag Balm hasn't been approved by the FDA for use by humans—only by animals. Loyal customers are convinced it works and continue to purchase it by the can and caseload. Winter is the most popular season for Bag Balm use, as the ointment soothes dry, wind-burned skin.

Bag Balm is still manufactured in Vermont by the family-owned Dairy Association Co. Inc., using the same formulation of petrolatum, lanolin, and antiseptic that was acquired by John Norris in 1899. The company occupies a few converted railroad buildings, and the plant itself fits entirely into one room. Six employees and two officers make the salve and run the firm. Cases of Bag Balm tins are shipped to retailers around the country such as Rite Aid, Fred Meyer, CVS Pharmacies, Walco, Costco, and Albertsons, where consumers can purchase the product. Those who don't liver near a retail location that carries Bag Balm can order it directly from distributor J J Smith & Company by emailing the firm or calling the toll-free number.

As today's marketplace is bombarded by increasingly complex goods and services, it is important to remember that a simple product that provides a variety of solutions for people's everyday lives may turn out to be the most successful and long-lasting of all. Despite the hundreds of daily problems Bag Balm may solve, however, there's one problem it can actually create. "Never put Bag Balm in your hair," advises one Bag Balm employee, "because you will not get it out."[1]

Toby Talbot/AP World Wide photos

In this chapter we examine ways in which organizations design and implement marketing strategies that address customers' needs and wants. Two of the most powerful such tools are strategies that relate to products, which include both goods and services, and those that relate to the distribution of those products.

As the story of Bag Balm illustrates, successful companies are keenly aware of their customers' needs. Bag Balm continues to publish new uses for its formula, connecting customers with each other to trade ideas. Bag Balm has chosen not to expand its product offerings, but instead to widen its distribution network over the years so that **consumers, veterinarians, and farmers** can find the product in retail locations across the country as well as order directly from the company. By publicizing the number of potential uses for the ointment and making it available in more outlets, Bag Balm has extended the life of its product well past the century mark.

This chapter focuses on the first two elements of the marketing mix: product and distribution. Our discussion of product strategy begins by describing

the classifications of goods and services, customer service, product lines and the product mix, and the product life cycle. Companies often shape their marketing strategies differently when they are introducing a new product, when the product has established itself in the marketplace, and when it is declining in popularity. We also discuss product identification through brand name and distinctive packaging, and the ways in which companies foster loyalty to their brands to keep customers coming back for more.

Distribution, the second mix variable discussed, focuses on moving goods and services from producer to wholesaler to retailer to buyers. Managing the distribution process includes making decisions such as what kind of wholesaler to use and where to offer products for sale. Retailers can range from specialty stores to factory outlets and everything in between, and they must choose appropriate customer service, pricing, and location strategies in order to succeed. The chapter concludes with a look at logistics, the process of coordinating the flow of information, goods, and services among suppliers and on to final consumers.

Product Strategy

product bundle of physical, service, and symbolic characteristics designed to satisfy consumer wants.

Most people respond to the question "What is a product?" by listing its physical features. By contrast, marketers take a broader view. To them, a **product** is a bundle of physical, service, and symbolic characteristics designed to satisfy consumer wants. The chief executive officer of a major tool manufacturer once startled his stockholders with this statement: "Last year our customers bought over 1 million quarter-inch drill bits, and none of them wanted to buy the product. They all wanted quarter-inch holes." Product strategy involves considerably more than just producing a good or service; instead, it focuses on benefits. The marketing conception of a product includes decisions about package design, brand name, trademarks, warranties, product image, new-product development, and customer service. Think, for instance, about your favorite soft drink. Do you like it for its taste alone? Or do other attributes, such as clever ads, attractive packaging, ease of purchase from vending machines and other convenient locations, and overall image, also attract you? These other attributes may influence your choice more than you realize.

Classifying Goods and Services

Marketers have found it useful to classify goods and services as either B2C or B2B, depending on whether the purchasers of the particular item are consumers or businesses. These classifications can be subdivided further, and each type requires a different competitive strategy.

Classifying Consumer Goods and Services

The classification typically used for ultimate consumers who purchase products for their own use and enjoyment and not for resale is based on consumer buying habits. *Convenience products* are items the consumer seeks to purchase frequently, immediately, and with little effort. Items stocked in gas-station markets, vending machines, and local newsstands are usually convenience products—for example, newspapers, snacks, candy, coffee, and bread.

Shopping products are those typically purchased only after the buyer has compared competing products in competing stores. A person intent on buying a new sofa or dining room table may visit many stores, examine perhaps dozens of pieces of furniture, and spend days making the final decision. *Specialty products*, the third category of consumer products, are those that a purchaser is willing to make a special effort to obtain. The purchaser is already familiar with the item and considers it to have no reasonable substitute. The nearest MINI dealer may be 75 miles away, but if you have decided you want one, you will make the trip.

Note that a shopping product for one person may be a convenience item for someone else. Each item's product classification is based on buying patterns of the majority of people who purchase it.

The interrelationship of the marketing mix factors is shown in Figure 12.1. By knowing the appropriate classification for a specific product, the marketing decision maker knows quite a bit about how the other mix variables will adapt to create a profitable, customer-driven marketing strategy.

IT'S TIME TO DRIVE LIKE THERE IS A TOMORROW.

To hug trees and corners at the same time. And for adrenaline to be regarded as a renewable resource. It's time for a little more turn and a little less burn. For the letters RPM to play nice with the letters MPG. And for the road and earth to finally find some middle ground. It's time to maximize our fun. To minimize our impact. And to start getting the most out of every single mile we drive. It's time to think about our Carfun Footprint.

MINIUSA.COM/MINIMALISM

Buying a *specialty product* takes extra effort. The MINI is sold in a limited number of places.

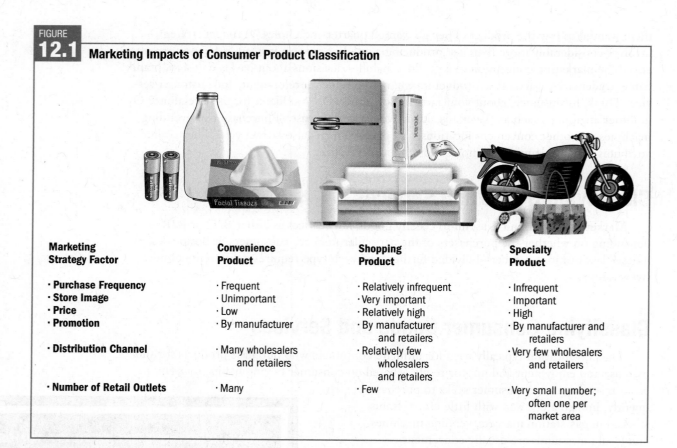

FIGURE 12.1 Marketing Impacts of Consumer Product Classification

Marketing Strategy Factor	Convenience Product	Shopping Product	Specialty Product
· Purchase Frequency	· Frequent	· Relatively infrequent	· Infrequent
· Store Image	· Unimportant	· Very important	· Important
· Price	· Low	· Relatively high	· High
· Promotion	· By manufacturer	· By manufacturer and retailers	· By manufacturer and retailers
· Distribution Channel	· Many wholesalers and retailers	· Relatively few wholesalers and retailers	· Very few wholesalers and retailers
· Number of Retail Outlets	· Many	· Few	· Very small number; often one per market area

Classifying Business Goods *Business products* are goods and services such as paycheck services and huge multifunction copying machines used in operating an organization; they also include machinery, tools, raw materials, components, and buildings used to produce other items for resale. While consumer products are classified by buying habits, business products are classified based on how they are used and by their basic characteristics. Products that are long-lived and relatively expensive are called *capital items.* Less costly products that are consumed within a year are referred to as *expense items.*

Five basic categories of B2B products exist: installations, accessory equipment, component parts and materials, raw materials, and supplies. *Installations* are major capital items, such as new factories, heavy equipment and machinery, and custom-made equipment. Installations are expensive and often involve buyer and seller negotiations that may last for more than a year before a purchase actually is made. Purchase approval frequently involves a number of different people—production specialists, representatives from the purchasing department, and members of top management—who must agree on the final choice.

Although *accessory equipment* also includes capital items, they are usually less expensive and shorter lived than installations and involve fewer decision makers. Examples include hand tools and fax machines. *Component parts and materials* are finished business goods that become part of a final product, such as disk drives that are sold to computer manufacturers or batteries purchased by automakers. *Raw materials* are farm and natural products used in producing other final products. Examples include milk, wood, leather, and soybeans. *Supplies* are expense items used in a firm's daily operation that do not become part of the final product. Often referred to as MRO (maintenance, repair, and operating supplies), they include paper clips, light bulbs, and copy paper.

Classifying Services Services can be classified as either B2C or B2B. Child and elder care centers and auto detail shops provide services for consumers, while the Pinkerton security patrol at a local factory and Kelly Services' temporary office workers are examples of business services. In some cases, a service can accommodate both consumer and business markets. For example, when ServiceMaster cleans the upholstery in a home, it is a B2C service, but when it spruces up the painting system and robots in a manufacturing plant, it is a B2B service.

Like tangible goods, services can also be convenience, shopping, or specialty products depending on the buying patterns of customers. However, they are distinguished from goods in several ways. First, services, unlike goods, are intangible. In addition, they are perishable because firms cannot stockpile them in inventory. They are also difficult to standardize, because they must meet individual customers' needs. Finally, from a buyer's perspective, the service provider is the service; the two are inseparable in the buyer's mind.

Marketing Strategy Implications

The consumer product classification system is a useful tool in marketing strategy. As described in Figure 12.1, because a new refrigerator is classified as a shopping good, its marketers have a better idea of its promotion, pricing, and distribution needs.

Each group of business products, however, requires a different marketing strategy. Because most installations and many component parts are frequently marketed directly from manufacturer to business buyer, the promotional emphasis is on personal selling rather than on advertising. By contrast, marketers of supplies and accessory equipment rely more on advertising, because their products are often sold through an intermediary, such as a wholesaler. Producers of installations and component parts may involve their customers in new-product development, especially when the business product is custom made. Finally, firms selling supplies and accessory equipment place greater emphasis on competitive pricing strategies than do other B2B marketers, who tend to concentrate more on product quality and customer service.

Product Lines and Product Mix

Few firms operate with a single product. If their initial entry is successful, they tend to increase their profit and growth chances by adding new offerings. The iPhone and iPad, with their touchscreen technology and App Stores, may be harbingers of things to come. Although most "mainstream knowledge workers" will probably continue to use conventional computers for some time, one IT research company predicts that by 2015, more than half of personal computers bought for users aged 15 and under will have touchscreens. The firm also predicts that touchscreen devices have a huge potential in education—which would mean that an entire generation will grow up with touchscreen technology.[2]

A company's **product line** is a group of related products marked by physical similarities or intended for a similar market. A **product mix** is the assortment of product lines and individual goods and services that a firm offers to consumers and business users. The Coca-Cola Company and PepsiCo both have product lines that include old standards—Coke Classic and Diet Coke, Pepsi and Diet Pepsi. But recently, PepsiCo announced it would start distributing Tampico Plus in selected states. Unlike other products from Tampico Beverages, Tampico Plus drinks contain vitamins A, C, and E. They also have half as much sugar as regular Tampico drinks. Thus, they meet the guidelines for beverages that can be sold in U.S. high schools, which want to limit the amount of sugar in drinks available to students.[3]

product line group of related products marked by physical similarities or intended for a similar market.

product mix the assortment of product lines and individual goods and services that a firm offers to consumers and business users.

A *product line* includes several related products designed to have the same appearance, like these PepsiCo products.

Marketers must assess their product mix continually to ensure company growth, to satisfy changing consumer needs and wants, and to adjust to competitors' offerings. To remain competitive, marketers look for gaps in their product lines and fill them with new offerings or modified versions of existing ones. A helpful tool that is frequently used in making product decisions is the product life cycle.

Product Life Cycle

Once a product is on the market, it usually goes through four stages known as the **product life cycle**: introduction, growth, maturity, and decline. As Figure 12.2 shows, industry sales and profits vary depending on the life-cycle stage of an item.

Product life cycles are not set in stone; not all products follow this pattern precisely, and different products may spend different periods of time in each stage. The concept, however, helps the marketing planner anticipate developments throughout the various stages of a product's life. Profits assume a predictable pattern through the stages, and promotional emphasis shifts from dispensing product information in the early stages to heavy brand promotion in the later ones.

Assessment Check ✔

1. How do consumer products differ from business products?

2. Differentiate among convenience, shopping, and specialty products.

product life cycle
four basic stages—introduction, growth, maturity, and decline—through which a successful product progresses.

Stages of the Product Life Cycle

In the *introduction stage*, the firm tries to promote demand for its new offering; inform the market about it; give free samples to entice consumers to make a trial purchase; and explain its features, uses, and benefits. Sometimes companies partner at this stage to promote new products. Others launch product offerings that enhance the use of products made by other companies, thus granting the start-up nearly immediate name recognition. Loopt

FIGURE 12.2 Stages in the Product Life Cycle

Sales and Profits

Introduction
Flex-Fuel vehicles, Internet TV broadcasts

(Early)
Satellite radio, Podcasting

Growth (Late)
iPhone, Internet video-conferencing

Maturity
Cell phones, DVD players

Decline
Hand-held PDAs, dial-up Internet connections

INDUSTRY SALES

INDUSTRY PROFITS

Time

is one such firm. Created by college sophomores Sam Altman and Nick Sivo, California-based Loopt transforms users' cell phones into GPS sharing system that alert them when friends are nearby. In addition, Loopt uses integrated content from Citysearch, Bing, and other Web services to provide more geographic search data to users. Recently, the firm also launched iPad and BlackBerry apps. "Explosive growth. Tons of users. Huge partnerships," says the Loopt Web site.[4]

New-product development costs and extensive introductory promotional campaigns to acquaint prospective buyers with the merits of the innovation, though essential to later success, are expensive and commonly lead to losses in the introductory stage. Some firms are seeking to lower these costs through ultra-low-cost product development, which involves meeting customer needs with the lowest-cost innovations possible, designing from scratch with a stripped-down budget, and the simplest engineering possible.[5] But all these expenditures are necessary if the firm is to profit later.

During the *growth stage*, sales climb quickly as new customers join early users who now are repurchasing the item. Word-of-mouth referrals and continued advertising and other special promotions by the firm induce others to make trial purchases. At this point, the company begins to earn profits on the new product. This success encourages competitors to enter the field with similar offerings, and price competition develops. After its initial success with the Kindle, Amazon faced competition from Barnes & Noble's Nook. Amazon rushed to launch its Kindle iPad Reader to the App Store, then Barnes & Noble countered with its popular NOOK color. Amazon announced that the Color Kindle 4 would be arriving soon.[6]

In the *maturity stage*, industry sales at first increase, but they eventually reach a saturation level at which further expansion is difficult. Competition also intensifies, increasing the availability of the product. Firms concentrate on capturing competitors' customers, often dropping prices to further the appeal. Cell phones are in the maturity stage: competitors compete not only on price but also on features such as calendars, e-mail and attachments, messaging capability, full-color screens, keyboards, and fax and word-processing functions. Flat-screen TVs are also in the maturity stage, so companies are trying to entice consumers to buy new ones by offering even bigger TVs than they have before, topping the 50-inch mark. As worldwide production of high-definition TVs increases dramatically, some observers predict that makers of LED backlight displays will lower their prices dramatically to stay competitive with other, less expensive display options.[7]

Sales volume fades late in the maturity stage, and some of the weaker competitors leave the market. During this stage, firms promote mature products aggressively to protect their market share and to distinguish their products from those of competitors. As discussed earlier in the chapter, Bag Balm has managed to do this with great success. More people use the product now than a century ago.[8]

Sales continue to fall in the *decline stage*, the fourth phase of the product life cycle. Profits decline and may become losses as further price-cutting occurs in the reduced overall market for the item. Competitors gradually exit, making some profits possible for the remaining firms in the shrinking market. The decline stage usually is caused by a product innovation or a shift in consumer preferences. Sometimes technology change can hasten the decline stage for a product. Eighty percent of U.S. residences contain at least one DVD player. High-definition DVDs, once touted as the ultimate in DVD technology, have been superseded by Blu-ray. Online sites where consumers can simply download movies or television shows are becoming another major competitor for entertainment as the link between computer and television is becoming faster and more reliable.[9]

Buick: Making an Old Brand New Again

When General Motors emerged from its financial troubles, many observers thought it might discontinue its Buick line. After all, the company had retired the hundred-year-old Oldsmobile several years ago. Once known as the "doctor's car" or the "banker's car," Buick gradually lost its prestige and became known for its older car buyers. But GM decided to regenerate the 106-year-old brand—with some success.

GM's strategy has been to aim at younger, upscale customers by offering only a few Buick models at first, but equipping them with the latest techology, from its OnStar system to DVD players, navigation systems, and the latest safety features. The Enclave, a large crossover vehicle, is popular with buyers about 55 years old; half of the buyers are women. The 2011 Buick Regal sedan is intended to compete with the Acura TSX and the Infiniti G37. Leather upholstery is standard, as are other luxury features. Designers of the revised LaCrosse sedan made sure the backseat has generous headroom and legroom. Buicks have always been popular in China, and GM hopes that the new LaCrosse will appeal to Chinese executives, who travel in chauffeur-driven cars. Many higher-income American buyers are trading in imports for the LaCrosse. By 2012, Buick plans to introduce two more models.

How successful has Buick's strategy been? It may be too soon to tell for sure. The average age of Buick buyers overall has fallen from 70 to 65. Buick sold more than 102,000 vehicles most recently, but that was fewer than the previous year and only about one-fourth as many as earlier in the decade. But Craig Bierly, Buick's product marketing director, says, "You have to change the product before you can change opinion. It's still too soon to really come to a verdict. . . . But nobody can say those are old person's cars anymore. Because they aren't."

Questions for Critical Thinking

1. What stage of its life cycle do you think the Buick brand has reached? How did General Motors extend Buick's life cycle?
2. How are Buick's new features part of General Motors' strategy for these cars?

Sources: Company Web site, http://www.buick.com, accessed March 29, 2011; Barry Silverstein, "Aging Buick Brand Is Young Again," *brandchannel*, April 12, 2010, http://www.brandchannel.com; Steven Cole Smith, "Test Drive: Regal Fuels Buick Revival," *Orlando Sentinel*, March 11, 2010, http://articles.orlandosentinel.com; Carguide editors, "2010 LaCrosse Breaks New Ground for Revived Buick Brand," *Carguide Canada*, February 17, 2010, http://www.carguidecanada.ca; James M. Amend, "Buick Revival Effort Showing Early Results, GM Marketers Say," *WardsAuto*, January 20, 2010, http://wardsauto.com.

Marketing Strategy Implications of the Product Life Cycle

Like the product classification system, the product life cycle is a useful concept for designing a marketing strategy that will be flexible enough to accommodate changing marketplace characteristics. These competitive moves may involve developing new products, lowering prices, increasing distribution coverage, creating new promotional campaigns, or any combination of these approaches. General Motors has decided to develop new versions of its Buick brand models, as the "Hit & Miss" feature explains. In general, the marketer's objective is to extend the product life cycle as long as the item is profitable. Some products can be highly profitable during the later stages of their life cycle, because all the initial development costs have already been recovered.

A commonly used strategy for extending the life cycle is to increase customers' frequency of use. Walmart and Meijer offer grocery sections in their stores in order to increase the frequency of shopper visits. Another strategy is to add new users. Despite the recent lending crunch, credit-card issuers are actively advertising for new—and viable—customers. Chase has been pushing its new line of credit cards designed for small businesses, called Ink. Each Ink card program has its own benefits and rewards, such as no interest (Ink Bold) and cash back (Ink Cash).[10]

A third product life cycle extension strategy is to find new uses for products, as Bag Balm has done. Post-it has also made successful use of this strategy. One recent blog posting lists 20 innovative ways students can use Post-it Notes, including wrapping the sticky edge around a cable to identify it and using the sticky edge to clean between the keys of a computer keyboard.[11] Finally, a firm may decide to change package sizes, labels, and product designs. Mattel has done this several times with its iconic Barbie doll.

Stages in New-Product Development

New-product development is expensive, time consuming, and risky, because only about one-third of new products become success stories. Products can fail for many reasons. Some are not properly developed and tested, some are poorly packaged, and others lack adequate promotional support or distribution or do not satisfy a consumer need or want. Even successful products eventually reach the end of the decline stage and must be replaced with new-product offerings.

Most of today's newly developed items are aimed at satisfying specific consumer demands. New-product development is becoming increasingly efficient and cost-effective because marketers use a systematic approach in developing new products. As Figure 12.3 shows, the new-product development process has six stages. Each stage requires a "go/no-go" decision by management before moving on to subsequent stages. Because items that go through each development stage only to be rejected at one of the final stages involve significant investments in both time and money, the sooner decision makers can identify a marginal product and drop it from further consideration, the less time and money will be wasted.

The starting point in the new-product development process is generating ideas for new offerings. Ideas come from many sources, including customer suggestions, suppliers, employees, research scientists, marketing research, inventors outside the firm, and competitive products. The most successful ideas are directly related to satisfying customer needs. Procter & Gamble recently expanded its Febreze home collection with the Flameless Luminary In-Home Scent Delivery System. Instead of a potentially dangerous candle, a battery-operated, flameless light diffuses fragrance from a decorative, scented shade. The light automatically turns off after four hours. The design was a finalist in the Consumer Packaged Goods—Household Segment category of the Edison Best New Product Awards.[12]

In the second stage, screening eliminates ideas that do not mesh with overall company objectives or that cannot be developed given the company's resources. Some firms hold open discussions of new-product ideas with specialists who work in different functional areas in the organization.

During the concept development and business analysis phase, further screening occurs. The analysis involves

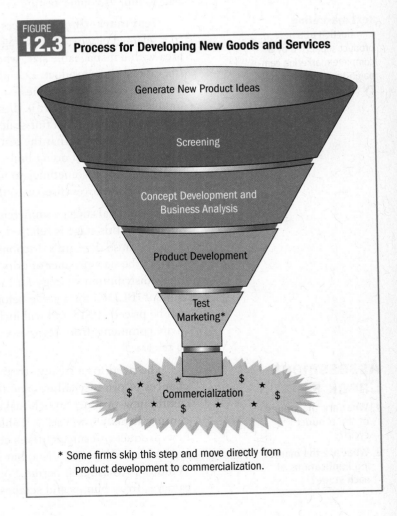

FIGURE 12.3 Process for Developing New Goods and Services

Generate New Product Ideas

Screening

Concept Development and Business Analysis

Product Development

Test Marketing*

Commercialization

* Some firms skip this step and move directly from product development to commercialization.

assessing the new product's potential sales, profits, growth rate, and competitive strengths and determining whether it fits with the company's product, distribution, and promotional resources. *Concept testing*—marketing research designed to solicit initial consumer reaction to new-product ideas—may be used at this stage. For example, potential consumers might be asked about proposed brand names and other methods of product identification. *Focus groups* are formal sessions in which consumers meet with marketers to discuss what they like or dislike about current products and perhaps test or sample a new offering to provide some immediate feedback.

Next, an actual product is developed, subjected to a series of tests, and revised. Functioning prototypes or detailed descriptions of the product may be created. These designs are the joint responsibility of the firm's development staff and its marketers, who provide feedback on consumer reactions to the proposed product design, color, and other physical features. Sometimes prototypes do not meet the stated requirements. When the U.S. military began looking for an improved helmet, it asked four companies to submit prototypes for helmets that would be 35 percent more effective against fragmentation as well as handgun and small-arms bullets. But all four prototypes failed. But a couple of years later, one firm submitted a prototype that was so strong that military engineers didn't have equipment powerful enough to penetrate the shell. "We don't know exactly [how strong] it is, but it's better than we've ever seen before," said one U.S. Army spokesman. The military then had to build stronger testing equipment.[13]

<u>**Test marketing**</u> introduces a new product supported by a complete marketing campaign to a selected city or TV coverage area. Marketers look for a location or television coverage area with a manageable size, where residents match their target market's demographic profile, to test their product. During the test marketing stage, the item is sold in a limited area while the company examines both consumer responses to the new offering and the marketing effort used to support it. Test market results can help managers determine the product's likely performance in a full-scale introduction. Some firms skip test marketing, however, because of concerns that the test could reveal their product strategies to the competition. Also, the expense of doing limited production runs of complex products such as a new auto or refrigerator is sometimes so high that the test marketing stage is skipped and the development process moves directly to the next stage.

In the final stage, commercialization, the product is made available in the marketplace. Sometimes this stage is referred to as a product launch. Considerable planning goes into this stage, because the firm's distribution, promotion, and pricing strategies must all be geared to support the new product offering. The videogame maker Electronic Arts (EA) announced a new distribution strategy for future games. EA will release premium downloadable content (PLDC) for a game before releasing the complete, packaged version. The PLDC will be priced at $15 and will include three to four hours of playing time. The company will invite comments from reviewers and players and make changes to the final version prior to release.[14]

The need for a steady stream of new products to offer the firm's customers, the chances of product failure, and the tens of millions of dollars needed to complete a successful new-product launch make new-product development a vital process for 21st-century firms. However, as Table 12.1 illustrates, success is not guaranteed until the new-product offering achieves customer acceptance. Microsoft introduced a new operating system, Windows Vista, but it just never caught on. The next version of Windows, Windows 7, has fared better. Sony's sock case for cameras is cute—but doesn't protect cameras from bumps and scrapes. And who needs a heated mouse pad? Yet a firm recently

test marketing
introduction of a new product supported by a complete marketing campaign to a selected city or TV coverage area.

Assessment Check ✓

1. What are the stages of the product life cycle?

2. What are the marketing implications of each stage?

12.1 The Worst-Made Cars on the Road

RANK	AUTO	TYPICAL OWNER COMMENT
1	Yugo	"I once test drove a Yugo, during which the radio fell out, the gear shift knob came off in my hand, and I saw daylight through the strip around the windshield."
2	Chevy Vega	"As near as I could tell, the car was built from compressed rust."
3	Ford Pinto	"The barbecue that seats four."
4	AMC Gremlin	"It was entirely possible to read a Russian novel during the pause between stepping on the gas and feeling any semblance of forward motion."
5	Chevy Chevette	"The ad didn't show the car going anywhere fast . . . because it couldn't."

Source: Reported in "Car Talk," http://www.cartalk.com, accessed June 7, 2011; Claire Martin, "The Worst Cars Ever," *MSN Autos*, April 22, 2010, http://editorial.autos.msn.com.

introduced one. Sometimes a name is enough to doom a product from the start—consider Chicken Poop lip gloss.[15]

Product Identification

A major aspect of developing a successful new product involves methods used for identifying a product and distinguishing it from competing offerings. Both tangible goods and intangible services are identified by brands, brand names, and trademarks. A **brand** is a name, term, sign, symbol, design, or some combination that identifies the products of one firm and differentiates them from competitors' offerings. Tropicana, Pepsi, and Gatorade are all made by PepsiCo, but a unique combination of name, symbol, and package design distinguishes each brand from the others.

A **brand name** is that part of the brand consisting of words or letters included in a name used to identify and distinguish the firm's offerings from those of competitors. The brand name is the part of the brand that can be vocalized. Many brand names, such as Coca-Cola, McDonald's, American Express, Google, and Nike, are famous around the world. Likewise, the "golden arches" brand mark of McDonald's also is widely recognized.

A **trademark** is a brand that has been given legal protection. The protection is granted solely to the brand's owner. Trademark protection includes not only the brand name but also design logos, slogans, packaging elements, and product features such as color and shape. A well-designed trademark, such as the Nike "swoosh," can make a difference in how positively consumers perceive a brand.

Selecting an Effective Brand Name

Good brands are easy to pronounce, recognize, and remember: Crest, Visa, and Dell are examples. Global firms face a real problem in selecting brand names, because an excellent brand name in one country may prove disastrous in another. Most languages have a short *a*, so Coca-Cola is pronounceable almost anywhere. But an advertising campaign for E-Z

brand name, term, sign, symbol, design, or some combination that identifies the products of one firm and differentiates them from competitors' offerings.

brand name part of the brand consisting of words or letters included in a name used to identify and distinguish the firm's offerings from those of competitors.

trademark brand that has been given legal protection.

To be effective, such *brand names* must be easy for consumers to pronounce, recognize, and remember.

Daniel Acker/Bloomberg/Getty Images, Inc.

washing machines failed in the United Kingdom because the British pronounce *z* as "zed."

Brand names should also convey the right image to the buyer. One effective technique is to create a name that links the product with its positioning strategy. The name Dial reinforces the concept of 24-hour protection; Dove soap and beauty products give an impression of mildness, and Taster's Choice instant coffee supports the promotional claim "Tastes and smells like ground roast coffee."

Brand names also must be legally protectable. Trademark law specifies that brand names cannot contain words in general use, such as *television* or *automobile*. Generic words—words that describe a type of product—cannot be used exclusively by any organization. On the other hand, if a brand name becomes so popular that it passes into common language and turns into a generic word, the company can no longer use it as a brand name. Once upon a time, aspirin, linoleum, and zipper were exclusive brand names, but today they have become generic terms and are no longer legally protectable.

Brand Categories

A brand offered and promoted by a manufacturer is known as a *manufacturer's* (or *national*) *brand*. Examples are Tide, Cheerios, Windex, Fossil, and Nike. But not all brand names belong to manufacturers; some are the property of retailers or distributors. A *private* (or *store*) *brand* identifies a product that is not linked to the manufacturer but instead carries a wholesaler's or retailer's label. Sears's Craftsman tools and Walmart's Ol' Roy dog food are examples.

Another branding decision marketers must make is whether to use a family branding strategy or an individual branding strategy. A *family brand* is a single brand name used for several related products. KitchenAid, Johnson & Johnson, Hewlett-Packard, and Arm & Hammer use a family name for their entire line of products. When a firm using family branding introduces a new product, both customers and retailers recognize the familiar brand name. The promotion of individual products within a line benefits all the products because the family brand is well known.

Other firms use an *individual branding* strategy by giving each product within a line a different name. For example, Procter & Gamble has individual brand names for its different laundry detergents, including Tide, Cheer, and Dash. Each brand targets a unique market segment. Consumers who want a cold-water detergent can choose Cheer over Tide or Dash, instead of purchasing a competitor's brand. Individual branding also builds competition within a firm and enables the company to increase overall sales.

Brand Loyalty and Brand Equity

Brands achieve varying consumer familiarity and acceptance. While a homeowner may insist on Anderson windows when renovating, the consumer buying a loaf of bread may not prefer any brand. Consumer loyalty increases a brand's value, so marketers try to strengthen brand loyalty. When a brand image suffers, marketers try to recreate a positive image.

Brand Loyalty Marketers measure brand loyalty in three stages: brand recognition, brand preference, and brand insistence. *Brand recognition* is brand acceptance strong enough that the consumer is aware of the brand, but not strong enough to cause a preference over other brands. A consumer might have heard of L'Oréal hair care products, for instance, without necessarily preferring them to Redken. Advertising, free samples, and discount coupons are among the most common ways to increase brand recognition.

Brand preference occurs when a consumer chooses one firm's brand over a competitor's. At this stage, the consumer usually relies on previous experience in selecting the product. Furniture and other home furnishings fall into this category. A shopper who purchased an IKEA dining room table and chairs and was satisfied with them is likely to return to purchase a bedroom set. While there, this shopper might pick up a set of mixing bowls for the kitchen or a lamp for the family room—because he or she knows and likes the IKEA brand.

Brand insistence is the ultimate degree of brand loyalty, in which the consumer will look for it at another outlet, special-order it from a dealer, order by mail, or search the Internet. Shoppers who insist on IKEA products for their homes may drive an hour or two—making a day excursion of the venture—to visit an IKEA store. The combination of value for the money and the concept of IKEA as a shopping destination have given the brand a unique allure for shoppers.[16]

Brand-building strategies were once limited to the consumer realm, but now they are becoming more important for B2B brands as well. Intel, Xerox, IBM, and service providers such as Krystal Klean and Cisco are among the suppliers who have built brand names among business customers.

Brand Equity Brand loyalty is at the heart of **brand equity**, the added value that a respected and successful name gives to a product. This value results from a combination of factors, including awareness, loyalty, and perceived quality, as well as any feelings or images the customer associates with the brand. High brand equity offers financial advantages to a firm, because the product commands a relatively large market share and sometimes reduces price sensitivity, generating higher profits. Figure 12.4 shows the world's ten most valuable brands and their estimated worth.

Brand awareness means the product is the first one that comes to mind when a product category is mentioned. If someone says "coffee," do you think of Starbucks, Dunkin' Donuts, or Folgers? Brand association is the link between a brand and other favorable images. A recent survey of small- and midsize-business owners and executives by American City Business Journals revealed that Southwest Airlines, Apple, UPS, Intuit, and the iPhone were the most recognizable brands in a field of 25.[17]

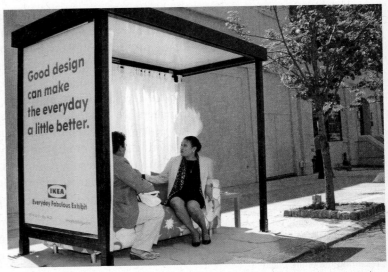

IKEA installed this clever showpiece, meant to look like a bus stop, in New York City during Design Week. The retailer of affordable, well-designed contemporary furniture enjoys *brand insistence*—the ultimate expression of brand loyalty. For devoted IKEA fans, no other brand will do.

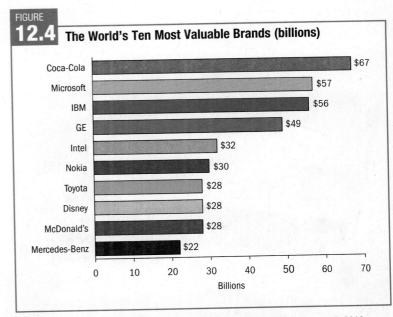

FIGURE **12.4** **The World's Ten Most Valuable Brands (billions)**

Brand	Value
Coca-Cola	$67
Microsoft	$57
IBM	$56
GE	$49
Intel	$32
Nokia	$30
Toyota	$28
Disney	$28
McDonald's	$28
Mercedes-Benz	$22

Source: Data from "100 Best Global Brands," *Bloomberg BusinessWeek,* February 25, 2010, http://bwnt.businessweek.com, accessed July 18, 2011.

brand equity added value that a respected and successful name gives to a product.

Large companies have typically assigned the task of managing a brand's marketing strategies to a *brand manager*, who may also be called a *product manager* at some firms. This marketing professional plans and implements the balance of promotional, pricing, distribution, and product arrangements that leads to strong brand equity. A *category manager*, a newer type of professional, oversees an entire group of products. Unlike traditional brand or product managers, category managers have profit responsibility for their product group. These managers are assisted by associates, usually called *analysts*. Part of the shift to category management was initiated by large retailers, when they realized there could be a benefit from the marketing muscle of large grocery and household goods producers such as Kraft and Procter & Gamble. As a result, producers began to focus their attention on in-store merchandising instead of mass-market advertising. A few years ago, Kraft reorganized its sales force so that each representative was responsible for a retailer's needs instead of pushing a single brand.

A **category advisor** functions in the B2B context. This vendor is the major supplier designated by a business customer to assume responsibility for dealing with all the other vendors for a project and presenting the entire package to the business buyer.

Packages and Labels

Packaging and labels are important in product identification. They also play an important role in a firm's overall product strategy. Packaging affects the durability, image, and convenience of an item and is responsible for one of the biggest costs in many consumer products. Due to a growing demand to produce smaller, more environmentally friendly packages, box manufacturers and chemical companies are now working harder to create more compact packaging that is made from renewable sources and is recyclable. One-third of America's waste consists of containers and packaging, much of it from fast-food chains. Quiznos recently launched its "Eat Toasty, Be Green" campaign, which introduced new, environmentally friendly packaging. Among the changes to reduce the chain's environmental impact are 100 percent compostable, wax-coated paper cups; salad containers made of renewable sugarcane; napkins made from 100 percent recycled materials; and plastic lids made from 30 percent recycled PET bottles. Even the employees' uniforms are being changed, with hats and aprons made from 100 percent recycled soda bottles.[18] PortionPac, maker of commercial cleaning solutions, has taken similar steps, as described in the **"Hit & Miss" feature**.

Choosing the right package is especially crucial in international marketing because marketers must be aware of such factors as language variations and cultural preferences. Consumers in African nations often prefer bold colors, but use of the country's flag colors may be problematic. Some countries frown on other uses of their flag. Also, in Africa red is often associated with death or witchcraft. Package size can vary according to the purchasing patterns and market conditions of a country. In countries with small

Due to a growing demand to produce more environmentally friendly packages, box manufacturers and chemical companies are now working harder to create more compact packaging that is made from renewable sources and is recyclable.

Courtesy PortionPac

PortionPac Makes More By Selling Less

It's hard to imagine a company that encourages its customers to buy fewer of its products. But that's exactly what PortionPac does—and the Chicago-based company has been successful since its establishment in 1964. In fact, the firm is so committed to its business model of selling *less*, it actually pays its salespeople bonuses for not selling more to customers than they need. Here's another surprise: PortionPac is a chemical company whose products and processes are actually good for the environment and the health of customers who use them.

PortionPac manufactures cleaning products for commercial use—the firm says its best customers are janitors. PortionPac cleaning systems are premeasured "doses" of concentrated, environmentally friendly cleaning solutions that ensure accurate and controlled use of the products. Instead of shipping a cleaning solution in a larger bottle that already contains a certain amount of water, PortionPac delivers a concentrated solution in a smaller bottle with instructions for dilution. Customers then reuse the original bottle, refilling it with subsequent packets of cleaning solution. "We teach our customers to use less product to achieve greater sanitation and greater labor efficiency," explains Burt Klein, president of PortionPac Chemical Corporation.

The system is based on the idea that, if recycling is good practice, then using less of a product to begin with is an even better practice. The PortionPac system is designed to reduce the resources required throughout a product's lifecycle to manufacture it, store it, distribute it, and dispose of it. PortionPac has won several green business awards for this seemingly simple solution. Thirteen of its twenty-two products have earned a green certification from the not-for-profit organization Green Seal, which rates products for their sustainability.

Customers such as school districts, office managers, health-care facilities, and state agencies are attracted to this philosophy because it reduces their costs and minimizes health hazards typically associated with cleaning products. "We're talking about saving the corporations money," notes Burt Klein. "We're talking about making their workers more productive. We're talking about standardizing production. All of these things made money for our customers, but also directly impacted the health of the environment." In addition, PortionPac addresses the issue of worker health, along with the health effects of others who are exposed to cleaning products—such as office workers, students, and hospital patients. "The people who work and are in those buildings [are the beneficiaries] because it becomes a safer, healthier environment for them also," observes Klein.

Although PortionPac currently sells only to organizations, the firm's long-term strategy includes a plan for retail sales so individual consumers can have access to the benefits of the company's cleaning system. "We believe in sustainability because we know caring about people and protecting the planet leads to prosperous communities and strong economies," says the company Web site. "We believe good things come in small Pacs. We believe less is more."

Sources: Company Web site, http://www.portionpaccorp.com, accessed March 24, 2011; Hosea Sanders, "Less Is More For Green Business," *ABC News*, January 21, 2011, http://abclocal.go.com; Leigh Buchanan, "The Un-Factory," *Inc.,* June 2010, pp. 63–67.

refrigerators, people may want to buy their beverages one at a time rather than in six-packs. Package weight is another important issue, because shipping costs are often based on weight.

Labeling is an integral part of the packaging process as well. In the United States, labeling must meet federal laws requiring companies to provide enough information to allow consumers to make value comparisons among competitive products and, in the case of food packaging, provide nutrition information on the label. Marketers who ship products to other countries have to comply with labeling requirements in those nations. This means knowing the answers to such questions as the following:

- Should the labels be in more than one language?

- Should ingredients be specified?

- Do the labels give enough information about the product to meet government standards?

Recently, the Food and Drug Administration (FDA) issued a statement by its commissioner, Dr. Margaret Hamburg, that encouraged food companies to ensure that their labeling complied with FDA regulations, and that the labeling was accurate and did not mislead the public. In the following year, the FDA informed 17 food companies that the labeling of almost two dozen of their products violated the Food, Drug, and Cosmetic Act. Among the violations were unauthorized health claims, unauthorized nutrient content claims, and unauthorized use of such terms as "healthy" and others that have strict regulatory definitions. In an open letter to the food industry, Dr. Hamburg stated, "Today, ready access to reliable information about the calorie and nutrient content of food is even more important, given the prevalence of obesity and diet-related diseases in the United States."[19]

Another important aspect of packaging and labeling is the *universal product code (UPC)*, the bar code read by optical scanners that print the name of the item and the price on a receipt. For many stores, these identifiers are useful not just for packaging and labeling but also for simplifying and speeding retail transactions and for evaluating customer purchases and controlling inventory. Radio-frequency identification (RFID) technology—embedded chips that can broadcast their product information to receivers—may replace UPC bar codes, however, as we'll discuss later in this chapter.

Distribution Strategy

The next element of the marketing mix, **distribution strategy**, deals with the marketing activities and institutions involved in getting the right good or service to the firm's customers. Distribution decisions involve modes of transportation, warehousing, inventory control, order processing, and selection of marketing channels. Marketing channels typically are made up of intermediaries such as retailers and wholesalers that move a product from producer to final purchaser.

The two major components of an organization's distribution strategy are distribution channels and physical distribution. **Distribution channels** are the paths that products—and legal ownership of them—follow from producer to consumer or business user. They are the means by which all organizations distribute their goods and services. **Physical distribution** is the actual movement of products from producer to consumers or business users. Physical distribution covers a broad range of activities, including customer service, transportation, inventory control, materials handling, order processing, and warehousing. As explained in the "Going Green" feature, Testa Produce, a food distributor, is building a new "green" facility to house its headquarters and its produce-distribution facility.

Distribution Channels

In their first decision for distribution channel selection, marketers choose which type of channel will best meet both their firm's marketing objectives and the needs of their customers. As shown in Figure 12.5, marketers can choose either a *direct distribution channel*, which carries goods directly from producer to consumer or business user, or distribution channels that involve several different marketing intermediaries. A *marketing intermediary* (also called a *middleman*) is a business firm that moves goods between producers and consumers or business users. Marketing intermediaries perform various functions that help the distribution channel operate smoothly, such as buying, selling, storing, and transporting products; sorting and grading bulky items; and providing information to other channel members. The two main categories of marketing intermediaries are wholesalers and retailers.

No one channel suits every product. The best choice depends on the circumstances of the market and on customer needs. The most appropriate channel choice may also change over time as new opportunities arise and marketers strive to maintain their competitiveness.

Testa Produce Sells—and Builds—Green

Since 1912, when Dominick Testa began selling fruits and vegetables door to door, Testa Produce Inc. has grown to become the Chicago area's premier independent produce distributor. The current generation is making changes that Dominick could not have imagined. As ground was broken for a new headquarters and warehouse, Testa Produce anticipated having the first food-distribution facility with the Leadership for Energy and Environmental Development (LEED) Platinum certification—the highest granted to a "green" building by the U.S. Green Building Council.

At $20 million, the new space cost 20 percent more and will have a longer return on investment than a conventional design. But Peter Testa, the company president, said, "[W]e . . . committed from the start to raising the bar on sustainability in our industry, which has a fairly large carbon footprint."

Testa Produce's new headquarters is equipped with the most advanced sustainable technological features, with room for future expansion and further advances in green technology.

A 245-foot-tall wind turbine and solar panels generate half of the building's power. Solar collectors heat water for all sinks, showers, and sanitary facilities. Skylights provide natural, ambient lighting, and a solar tracking system adjusts the ambient light over the course of the day.

The roof is about 50 percent vegetated to prevent rain runoff and slopes down to form a dramatic green wall at the building's entrance. An internal filtered cistern and a retention pond outside capture rainwater

and recycle it for nondrinking purposes. Permeable paving materials on walkways and in parking areas allow rainwater to drain into live wetlands. The landscaping features native plants that don't need constant irrigation. Watering should be necessary only during severe droughts.

When Testa moved to the new facilities, customers immediately began requesting tours—to which company president Peter Testa replied yes, "this is one heck of a cool building!"

Questions for Critical Thinking

1. As a distributor, Testa Produce doesn't have direct contact with the public. How might the company go about alerting consumers to its "green" initiatives?
2. What are some ways that Testa Produce might encourage its employees to follow "green" practices?

Sources: Peter Testa, "OK It's Finally Here: Testa Produce is Moving," Company Web site, http://www.testaproduce.com, March 14, 2011; "Testa Produce Turns a Brighter Shade of Green with Its New HQ," *Refrigerated Transport,* April 12, 2010, http://refrigeratedtrans.com; Sam Carlson, "Construction Under Way on Testa's Green Distribution Center," *Packer,* April 9, 2010, http://thepacker.com; Testa Produce, Inc., "Testa Produce Turns a Brighter Shade of Green," press release, April 7, 2010, https://ssl117.alentus.com; Betsy Kraat, "Epstein Designs 'Green' Headquarters/Produce Distribution Facility for Testa Produce, Inc.," *metroGREEN+BUSINESS,* March 4, 2010, http://www.metrogreenbusiness.com.

Currently, most smart phones sold in the United States are tied to a single wireless carrier that controls all distribution of its particular phone. Consumers can choose a smart phone but can't choose a carrier. Recently, Google announced the release of its Nexus One smart phone, for sale at a new, Google-hosted Web store. The Nexus One offers some new features, but Google's long-range goal is to change the distribution channels for smart phones. Buyers have the option of buying a conventional version of the Nexus One that is locked to T-Mobile's service plan and therefore controlled by T-Mobile, or an unlocked version—that is, one that can be used with any wireless service plan. By offering an unlocked smart phone, Google is gambling that consumers will choose a distribution channel that isn't tied to a wireless carrier and that Google itself will be able to create software that can compete with that available for the iPhone. In this type of business model, buyers would be able to select a phone first and then sign up with a carrier, much as they can now buy any brand of computer regardless of their Internet service provider.[20]

Direct Distribution The shortest and simplest means of connecting producers and customers is direct contact between the two parties. This approach is most common in the B2B market. Consumers who buy fresh fruits and vegetables at rural roadside stands or farmers markets use direct distribution, as do services ranging from banking and ten-minute oil changes to ear piercing and Mary Kay Cosmetics.

Direct distribution is commonly found in the marketing of relatively expensive, complex products that may require demonstrations. Most major B2B products such as installations,

FIGURE 12.5 Alternative Distribution Channels

Consumer Goods

Producer → Consumer

Producer → Retailer → Consumer

Producer → Wholesaler → Retailer → Consumer

Producer → Agent/Broker → Wholesaler → Retailer → Consumer

Business Goods

Producer → Business User

Producer → Agent/Broker → Business User

Producer → Wholesaler → Business User

Producer → Agent/Broker → Wholesaler → Business User

Services

Service Provider → Consumer or Business User

Service Provider → Agent/Broker → Consumer or Business User

accessory equipment, component parts, business services, and even raw materials are typically marketed through direct contacts between producers and business buyers. The Internet has also made direct distribution an attractive option for many retail companies and service providers. FedEx customers have long used online tools to track conventional shipments. Fedex's new International Priority Direct Distribution service allows users to ship more than one package from a single country of origin to a different recipients in single destination country. The packages are cleared through customs as a single shipment. In addition, multiple shipments to multiple recipients in multiple European Union countries can be cleared through customs as a single shipment through Charles de Gaulle Airport near Paris.[21]

Distribution Channels Using Marketing Intermediaries Although direct channels allow simple and straightforward connections between producers and their customers, the list of channel alternatives in Figure 12.5 suggests that direct distribution is not the best choice in every instance. Some products sell in small quantities for relatively low prices to thousands of widely scattered consumers. Makers of such products cannot cost effectively contact each of their customers, so they distribute products through specialized intermediaries called *wholesalers* and *retailers*.

Although you might think that adding intermediaries to the distribution process would increase the final cost of products, more often than not this choice actually lowers consumer prices. Intermediaries such as wholesalers and retailers often add significant value to a product as it moves through the distribution channel. They do so by creating utility, providing additional services, and reducing costs.

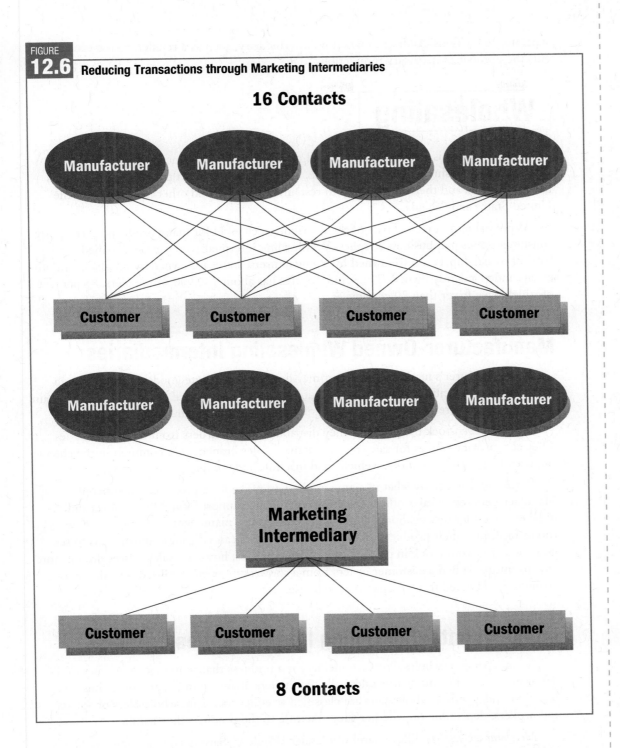

FIGURE 12.6 Reducing Transactions through Marketing Intermediaries

16 Contacts

Manufacturer Manufacturer Manufacturer Manufacturer

Customer Customer Customer Customer

Manufacturer Manufacturer Manufacturer Manufacturer

Marketing Intermediary

Customer Customer Customer Customer

8 Contacts

Marketing utility is created when intermediaries help ensure that products are available for sale when and where customers want to purchase them. If you want something warm to eat on a cold winter night, you don't call up Campbell's Soup and ask them to ship a can of chicken noodle soup. Instead, you go to the nearest grocery store, where you find utility in the form of product availability. In addition, intermediaries perform such important services as transporting merchandise to convenient locations. Finally, by representing numerous producers, a marketing intermediary can cut the costs of buying and selling. As Figure 12.6 shows, if four manufacturers each sold directly to four consumers, this would require 16

Assessment Check ☑

1. Define *distribution channels.*
2. What is a marketing intermediary?

separate transactions. Adding a marketing intermediary, such as a retailer, to the exchange cuts the number of necessary transactions to 8.

Wholesaling

wholesaler distribution channel member that sells primarily to retailers, other wholesalers, or business users.

A **wholesaler** is a distribution channel member that sells primarily to retailers, other wholesalers, or business users. For instance, Sysco is a wholesaler that buys food products from producers and then resells them to restaurants, hotels, and other institutions in the United States and Canada.

Wholesaling is a crucial part of the distribution channel for many products, particularly consumer goods and business supplies. Wholesaling intermediaries can be classified on the basis of ownership; some are owned by manufacturers, some are owned by retailers, and others are independently owned. The United States has about 430,000 wholesalers, 85 percent of which have fewer than 20 employees.[22]

Manufacturer-Owned Wholesaling Intermediaries

A manufacturer's marketing manager may decide to distribute goods directly through company-owned facilities to control distribution or customer service. Firms operate two main types of manufacturer-owned wholesaling intermediaries: sales branches and sales offices.

Sales branches stock the products they distribute and fill orders from their inventories. They also provide offices for sales representatives. Sales branches are common in the chemical, petroleum products, motor vehicle, and machine and equipment industries.

A *sales office* is exactly what its name implies: an office for a producer's salespeople. Manufacturers set up sales offices in various regions to support local selling efforts and improve customer service. Some kitchen and bath fixture manufacturers maintain showrooms to display their products. Builders and decorators can visit these showrooms to see how the items would look in place. Unlike sales branches, however, sales offices do not store any inventory. When a customer orders from a showroom or other sales office, the merchandise is delivered from a separate warehouse.

Independent Wholesaling Intermediaries

An independent wholesaling intermediary is a business that represents a number of different manufacturers and makes sales calls on retailers, manufacturers, and other business accounts. Independent wholesalers are classified as either merchant wholesalers or agents and brokers, depending on whether they take title to the products they handle.

Merchant wholesalers, like apparel wholesaler WholesaleSarong.com, are independently owned wholesaling intermediaries that take title to the goods they handle. Within this category, a *full-function merchant wholesaler* provides a complete assortment of services for retailers or industrial buyers, such as warehousing, shipping, and even financing. A subtype of full-function merchant is a *rack jobber*, such as Ohio-based Arrow Distributing, which handles distribution of CDs and DVDs to retail stores. This type of firm stocks, displays, and services particular retail products, such as paperback books or greeting cards in a drugstore or supermarket. Usually, the retailer receives a commission based on actual sales as payment for providing merchandise space to a rack jobber.

A *limited-function merchant wholesaler* also takes legal title to the products it handles, but it provides fewer services to the retailers to which it sells. Some limited-function merchant wholesalers only warehouse products but do not offer delivery service. Others warehouse and deliver products but provide no financing. One type of limited-function merchant wholesaler is a *drop shipper* such as Kate Aspen, an Atlanta-based wholesaler of wedding favors. Drop shippers also operate in such industries as coal and lumber, characterized by bulky products for which no single producer can provide a complete assortment. They give access to many related goods by contacting numerous producers and negotiating the best possible prices. Cost considerations call for producers to ship such products directly to the drop shipper's customers.

Another category of independent wholesaling intermediaries consists of *agents* and *brokers*. They may or may not take possession of the goods they handle, but they never take title, working mainly to bring buyers and sellers together. Stockbrokers such as Charles Schwab and real estate agents such as RE/MAX perform functions similar to those of agents and brokers, but at the retail level. They do not take title to the sellers' property; instead, they create time and ownership utility for both buyer and seller by helping carry out transactions.

Manufacturers' reps act as independent sales forces by representing the manufacturers of related but noncompeting products. These agent intermediaries, sometimes referred to as *manufacturers' agents*, receive commissions based on a percentage of the sales they make.

Retailer-Owned Cooperatives and Buying Offices

Retailers sometimes band together to form their own wholesaling organizations. Such organizations can take the form of either a buying group or a cooperative. The participating retailers set up the new operation to reduce costs or to provide some special service that is not readily available in the marketplace. To achieve cost savings through quantity purchases, independent retailers may form a buying group that negotiates bulk sales with manufacturers. Ace Hardware is a retailer-owned cooperative. The independent owners of it 4,400 stores have access to bulk merchandise purchases that save them—and their customers— money.[23] In a cooperative, an independent group of retailers may decide to band together to share functions such as shipping or warehousing.

Retailing

Retailers, in contrast to wholesalers, are distribution channel members that sell goods and services to individuals for their own use rather than for resale. Consumers usually buy their food, clothing, shampoo, furniture, and appliances from some type of retailer. The supermarket where you buy your groceries may have bought some of its items from a wholesaler such as Unified Grocers and then resold them to you.

Retailers are the final link—the so-called last three feet—of the distribution channel. Because they are often the only channel members that deal directly with consumers, it is essential that retailers remain alert to changing shopper needs. For instance, soaring gas prices affect consumers' budgets, so they may make fewer trips to the mall or cut back on nonessential purchases. As a result, retailers may need to offer special sales or events to lure customers to their shops. It is also important for retailers to keep pace with developments in the fast-changing business environment, such as the disruption in delivery of supplies from widespread wildfires or storms.

Assessment Check ✔

1. Define *wholesaling*.
2. Differentiate between a merchant wholesaler and an agent or broker in terms of title to the goods.

retailer distribution channel members that sell goods and services to individuals for their own use rather than for resale.

FIGURE
12.7 Types of Nonstore Retailing

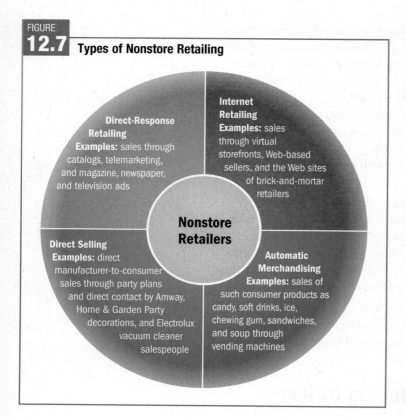

Direct-Response Retailing
Examples: sales through catalogs, telemarketing, and magazine, newspaper, and television ads

Internet Retailing
Examples: sales through virtual storefronts, Web-based sellers, and the Web sites of brick-and-mortar retailers

Nonstore Retailers

Direct Selling
Examples: direct manufacturer-to-consumer sales through party plans and direct contact by Amway, Home & Garden Party decorations, and Electrolux vacuum cleaner salespeople

Automatic Merchandising
Examples: sales of such consumer products as candy, soft drinks, ice, chewing gum, sandwiches, and soup through vending machines

This Zoom Shop kiosk dispenses Apple iPods and Sony PSPs automatically, just as an ATM dispenses cash. Automatic merchandising is a form of nonstore retailing.

©Jae C. Hong/AP/Wide World Photos

Nonstore Retailers

Two categories of retailers exist: store and nonstore. As Figure 12.7 shows, nonstore retailing includes four forms: direct-response retailing, Internet retailing, automatic merchandising, and direct selling. *Direct-response retailing* reaches prospective customers through catalogs; telemarketing; and even magazine, newspaper, and television ads. Shoppers order merchandise by mail, telephone, computer, and fax machine and then receive home delivery or pick the merchandise up at a local store. Lands' End has long stood out as a highly successful direct-response retailer; its well-known clothing catalog and stellar customer service have set the standard for this type of distribution channel. With the retailer's purchase by Sears, however, customers can now see, feel, and try on its clothing at Lands' End Shops in Sears locations around the country.

Internet retailing, the second form of nonstore retailing, has grown rapidly. Tens of thousands of retailers have set up shop online, with sales growing at a rate of about 5 percent a year (as compared with declines in total retail sales). Today, online sales account for about 3.8 percent of total retail sales.[24] A severe shakeout saw hundreds of Internet enterprises shut down during the first few years of the 21st century, but firms that survived have stronger business models than those that failed. Two examples of successful pure dot-coms are Amazon and eBay. A major shift in retailing has seen traditional brick-and-mortar retailers competing with pure dot-com start-ups by setting up their own Web sites as an option for shoppers. Nordstrom, JCPenney, and Walmart report strong online sales. Shopping sites are among the most popular Internet destinations, and sales of clothing and DVDs in particular have risen.

The last two forms of nonstore retailing are automatic merchandising and direct selling. *Automatic merchandising* provides convenience through the use of vending machines. ATMs may soon join the ranks of vending machines as banks find new ways to compete for customers. Some ATMs offer extra services such as check cashing and stamps, as well as concert tickets and road maps. Future ATMs will be able to connect wirelessly to cell phones to allow customers to download and pay for games and music. *Direct selling* includes direct-to-consumer sales by Pampered Chef kitchen representatives and salespeople for Silpada sterling silver jewelry through party-plan selling methods. Both are forms of direct selling.

Companies that previously relied heavily on telemarketing in generating new customers have encountered consumer resistance to intrusive phone calls. Among the growing barriers are caller ID, call-blocking devices such as the TeleZapper, and the National Do Not Call list, which made it illegal for most companies to call people who are registered. As a result, dozens of companies, including telecommunications and regional utilities, have sent direct-mail pieces to promote such services as phones, cable television, and natural gas distributors.

Store Retailers

In-store sales still outpace nonstore retailing methods like direct-response retailing and Internet selling. Store retailers range in size from tiny newsstands to multistory department stores and multiacre warehouselike retailers such as Sam's Club. Table 12.2 lists the different types of store retailers, with examples of each type. Clearly, there are many approaches to retailing and a variety of services, prices, and product lines offered by each retail outlet.

The Wheel of Retailing Retailers are subject to constant change as new stores replace older establishments. In a process called the *wheel of retailing*, new retailers enter the market by offering lower prices made possible through reductions in service. Supermarkets and discount houses, for example, gained their initial market footholds through low-price,

Table
12.2 Types of Retail Stores

STORE TYPE	DESCRIPTION	EXAMPLE
Specialty store	Offers complete selection in a narrow line of merchandise	Bass Pro Shops, Dick's Sporting Goods, Williams-Sonoma
Convenience store	Offers staple convenience goods, easily accessible locations, extended store hours, and rapid checkouts	7-Eleven, Mobil Mart, QuikTrip
Discount store	Offers wide selection of merchandise at low prices; off-price discounters offer designer or brand-name merchandise	Target, Walmart, Nordstrom Rack, Marshalls
Warehouse club	Large, warehouse-style store selling food and general merchandise at discount prices to membership card-holders	Costco, Sam's Club, BJ's
Factory outlet	Manufacturer-owned store selling seconds, production overruns, or discontinued lines	Adidas, Coach, Pottery Barn, Ralph Lauren
Supermarket	Large, self-service retailer offering a wide selection of food and nonfood merchandise	Safeway, Whole Foods Market, Kroger
Supercenter	Giant store offering food and general merchandise at discount prices	Walmart Supercenter, Super Target
Department store	Offers a wide variety of merchandise selections (furniture, cosmetics, housewares, clothing) and many customer services	Nordstrom, Macy's, Neiman Marcus

FIGURE
12.8 The Wheel of Retailing

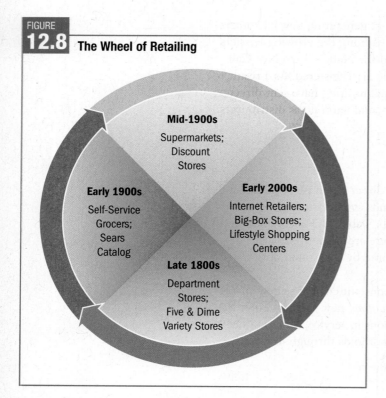

limited-service appeals. These new entries gradually add services as they grow and ultimately become targets for new retailers.

As Figure 12.8 shows, most major developments in retailing appear to fit the wheel pattern. The low-price, limited-service strategy characterized supermarkets, catalog retailers, discount stores, and, most recently, Internet retailers and giant "big-box" stores, such as PetSmart, Borders, and Office Depot. Corner grocery stores gave way to supermarkets and then to warehouse clubs such as Costco or BJ's. Department stores lost market share to discount clothing retailers such as Target and Marshalls. Independent bookstores have lost business to giant chains like Barnes & Noble, Borders, and such online-only sellers as Amazon.com and Buy.com.

Even though the wheel of retailing does not fit every pattern of retail evolution—for example, automatic merchandising has always been a relatively high-priced method of retailing—it does give retail managers a general idea of what is likely to occur during the evolution of retailing. It also shows that business success involves the "survival of the fittest." Retailers that fail to change fail to survive.

How Retailers Compete

Retailers compete with each other in many ways. Nonstore retailers focus on making the shopping experience as convenient as possible. Shoppers at stores such as Saks Fifth Avenue enjoy a luxurious atmosphere and personal service. In fact, those who visit the new shoe department at the flagship store in New York have the run of the entire eighth floor, which is entirely devoted to shoes—with its own Zip code. Saks recently began a new campaign called "Special Delivery to 10022-SHOE" to introduce shoes by new designers. Some of the shoes are exclusive to Saks. According to Cody Kondo, Saks senior vice president and general merchandising manager, "With Special Delivery, the team [of buyers] selected those styles that were unlike anything else being shown . . . those shoes that the merchants fell in love with."[25]

Like manufacturers, retailers must develop marketing strategies based on goals and strategic plans. Successful retailers convey images that alert consumers to the stores' identities and the shopping experiences they provide. To create that image, all components of a retailer's strategy must complement each other. After identifying their target markets, retailers must choose merchandising, customer service, pricing, and location strategies that will attract customers in those market segments.

Identifying a Target Market The first step in developing a competitive retailing strategy is to select a target market. This choice requires careful evaluation of the size and profit potential of the chosen market segment and the current level of competition for the segment's business. Bargain stores such as Family Dollar target consumers who are extremely price conscious, for example, while convenience stores like 7-Eleven target consumers who want an easy way to purchase items they buy frequently. Seventh Generation, which makes "green" home- and personal-care items, began as a mail-order company, then started selling at natural-food stores, then grew into a major business whose products are featured at supermarkets nationwide as well as at Target and at Amazon.com. Seventh Generation, which is committed to increasing consumer awareness of environmentally safe cleaning and household products, invites consumers to "Join the Seventh Generation Nation" at its Web site, where they can share information about sustainable practices, receive a free newsletter, and save on company products with coupons. The company's goal is to get 45 percent of American households to try at least one Seventh Generation product.[26]

Seventh Generation determined its *target market* was made up of the people committed to an environmentally safe cleaning and household products.

Selecting a Product Strategy Next, the retailer must develop a product strategy to determine the best mix of merchandise to carry to satisfy that market. Retail strategists must decide on the general product categories, product lines, and variety to offer. Sometimes that involves expanding the product mix and sometime it involves contracting it. Polaroid's parent company signed a five-year licensing agreement with Starlight, a leading consumer electronics manufacturer and distributer. Under the agreement, Starlight will develop a range of Polaroid-brand consumer electronics equipment, including Blu-ray players, stand-alone and portable DVD players, e-readers, iPod docking stations, and home theater systems.[27]

Shaping a Customer Service Strategy A retailer's customer service strategy focuses on attracting and retaining target customers to maximize sales and profits. Some stores offer a wide variety of services, such as gift wrapping, alterations, returns, interior design services, and delivery. Other stores offer bare-bones customer service, stressing low price instead. Some grocery shoppers, for instance, can find convenience online through a service like Peapod, which handles product selection, packing, and delivery. They can visit a supermarket and make their own selections. Or they can go to a discount supermarket like Minnesota-based Cub Foods, a division of SuperValu, where they not only assemble their orders but also bag their purchases.

Selecting a Pricing Strategy Retailers base their pricing decisions on the costs of purchasing products from other channel members and offering services to customers. Pricing can play a major role in consumers' perceptions of a retailer, and not just because they appreciate low prices. The grocery retailer Trader Joe's offers organic and gourmet foods under its own private labels at rock-bottom prices. Customers enjoy shopping for Trader Jose's Mexican specialties and Trader Darwin's nutritional supplements at prices lower than other gourmet or organic markets.[28] Pricing strategy is covered in more detail in Chapter 13.

Choosing a Location A good location often marks the difference between success and failure in retailing. The location decision depends on the retailer's size, financial resources, product offerings, competition, and, of course, its target market. Traffic patterns, the visibility of the store's signage, parking, and the location of complementary stores also influence the choice of a retail location. Consider the rivalry between PetSmart

Solving an Ethical Controversy

Teens at the Mall: Good or Bad for Business?

Some shopping malls have banned unsupervised minors on weekend evenings. Others are considering a total ban on teens who are not accompanied by adults. However, teenagers go to malls not only to hang out with their friends, but also to spend money—particularly if they have recently acquired a credit card. Mall merchants who used to complain about groups of unsupervised teenagers have now pinned their hopes on these young spenders to increase sales. Although they are more cautious shoppers than before the recession, teenagers are once again snacking at the food court and shopping at stores such as American Eagle and Abercrombie & Fitch.

Should malls that have essentially imposed curfews on teenagers consider lifting those bans to help boost business?

PRO

1. According to Thompson Reuters, spending by teenagers has increased, contrary to expectations after almost a year and a half of declining figures. Malls should encourage teens to shop.

2. Most teenagers are well behaved and should not be banned as a group because of the bad behavior of a few.

CON

1. Some merchants are still wary. One said, "Parents drop their kids off, and they don't know what their kids do while they are away."

2. The attractiveness of teenage free spending has to be considered in the light of crowd behavior. At one mall, more than a dozen teenagers were arrested after a fight broke out.

Summary

Just as adults spent much less during the recent recession, so did their children. Teenagers have now returned in some measure to previous spending habits, particularly if they are carrying credit cards—posing potential new problems as they learn about credit. Mall owners and civic leaders will need to find a balance between maintaining order and encouraging these consumers of tomorrow.

Sources: Pattie Kate, "What Are the Characteristics of Teenage Spending?" *wiseGEEK*, February 7, 2011, http://www.wisegeek.com; Andrea Chang, "Free-Spending Teens Return to Malls," *Los Angeles Times*, March 28, 2010, http://articles.latimes.com; Erica Shaffer, "City Leaders Recommend Total Ban of Unsupervised Teens at Mall," WTOL, February 18, 2010, http://www.wtol.com; Fran Daniel, "Mall May Limit Teens: Policy Expected to Require Parental Supervision on Friday, Saturday Evenings," *Winston-Salem Journal*, February 9, 2010, http://www2.journalnow.com.

---

and Petco. Petco tends to have smaller stores in greater numbers, located in strip malls, than PetSmart, whose strategy is to build bigger "power centers" right beside other large discount chains. PetSmart has added pet services—adoption, grooming, day care, and boarding—in some of its stores. Petco uses its stores to promote a broader selection of goods for offbeat pets, such as tarantulas and unusual reptiles. Both companies have implemented "green" initiatives.[29]

A *planned shopping center* is a group of retail stores planned, coordinated, and marketed as a unit to shoppers in a geographical trade area. By providing single convenient locations with free parking, shopping centers have largely replaced downtown shopping in many urban areas. But time-pressed consumers are increasingly looking for more efficient ways to shop, including catalogs, Internet retailers, and one-stop shopping at large free-standing stores such as Walmart Supercenters. To lure more customers, shopping centers are recasting themselves as entertainment destinations, with movie theaters, art displays, carousel rides, and musical entertainment. The giant Mall of America in Bloomington, Minnesota, features a seven-acre amusement park and an aquarium.

Shopping malls are well-known magnets for teens, who often meet there to socialize with friends. Businesses want to welcome their teen customers, but sometimes the cluster of teens hanging around the mall causes difficulties for other customers and some retailers, as described in the "Solving an Ethical Controversy" feature.

To varying degrees in recent years, large regional malls have also witnessed a growing shift in shopping center traffic to smaller strip centers, name-brand outlet centers, and *lifestyle centers*, open-air complexes containing retailers that often focus on specific shopper segments and product interests. Victoria Gardens, a lifestyle center in California, attributes some of its success to its partnerships with local businesses.[30]

Building a Promotional Strategy A retailer designs advertisements and develops other promotions to stimulate demand and to provide information such as the store's location, merchandise offerings, prices, and hours. When a recent year proved to be difficult, Starbucks turned to social media for a new promotional strategy. The chain launched MyStarbucksIdea.com, a forum where customers could ask questions, offer suggestions, and even voice their dislikes. The site's 180,000 registered users have offered 80,000 ideas, of which 50 have been implemented. The Starbucks Facebook page has some 5.7 million fans; the chain also has 775,000 Twitter followers. Charles Bruzzo, the chain's vice president for brand, content, and online, says the company is seeing the beginning of an "interesection between digital and physical."[31]

Nonstore retailers provide their phone numbers and Web site addresses. More recently, online retailers have scaled back their big advertising campaigns and worked to build traffic through word of mouth and clever promotions. Promotional strategy is also discussed in depth in Chapter 13.

Creating a Store Atmosphere A successful retailer closely aligns its merchandising, pricing, and promotion strategies with *store atmospherics*, the physical characteristics of a store and its amenities, to influence consumers' perceptions of the shopping experience. Atmospherics begin with the store's exterior, which may use eye-catching architectural elements and signage to attract customer attention and interest. Interior atmospheric elements include store layout, merchandise presentation, lighting, color, sound, and cleanliness. A high-end store such as Nordstrom, for instance, features high-ceilings in selling areas that spotlight tasteful and meticulously cared-for displays of carefully chosen items of obvious quality. Dick's Sporting Goods, on the other hand, carries an ever-changing array of moderately priced clothing and gear in its warehouselike settings furnished with industrial-style display hardware.

Assessment Check ☑

1. Define *retailer*.
2. What are the elements of a retailer's marketing strategy?

Distribution Channel Decisions and Logistics

Every firm faces two major decisions when choosing how to distribute its goods or services: selecting a specific distribution channel and deciding on the level of distribution intensity. In deciding which distribution channel is most efficient, business managers need to consider four factors: the market, the product, the producer, and the competition. These factors are often interrelated and may change over time. In today's global business environment, strong relationships with customers and suppliers are important for survival. One way to help cement such relationships online is to practice proper social media manners, as the "Business Etiquette" feature explains.

Minding Your Social Media Manners

More and more entrepreneurs are using social networking media to promote their small or medium-size businesses. Facebook, Twitter, LinkedIn, and myriad blogs and forums offer endless marketing opportunities. A recent survey found that 70 percent of small businesses planned to increase their use of social media. Seventy-nine percent did not plan to run TV commercials, and 70 percent didn't use radio.

Just as in the real business world, good manners, common courtesy, and common sense will take you far in the virtual business world. Here are a few tips on good manners for social media:

1 *Even though you join social networks to promote your business, don't make it too obvious.* Instead of promoting yourself or your business nonstop, use selected posts to indicate that you have something of value to offer to interested people. Otherwise, you run the risk of being considered a spammer.

2 *Be aware that you are in social networks for the long haul.* Group or forum members are real people with real interests and ideas. Get to know the members of your forums, find out what those interests are, and learn how the community as a whole works. Virtual networks of "friends" have unwritten rules, just as real networks do.

3 *It's not the numbers that count.* Getting your brand known or achieving other marketing goals doesn't necessarily depend on how many Twitter followers you have but on how you engage with them.

4 *Be careful of what you say.* Avoid vulgar language, off-color jokes, or any hint of racial or gender bias. Don't bring up religion, politics, or other delicate subjects. Leave any strong opinions out of your marketing profile.

5 *Remember that your customers will be discussing you on their own networks.* Your reputation may travel farther than you know!

Sources: Mickie Kennedy, "Do You Have Good Social Media Manners?" *eReleases,* accessed June 7, 2011, http://www.ereleases.com; Michelle Bowles, "5 Social Media Tips for ecommerce Marketing," *Online Marketing Blog,* March 12, 2010, http://www.toprankblog.com; Kim States, "Five Social Media Tips to Connect Small Businesses," *AzBiz.com,* January 2, 2010, http://www.azbiz.com; Sean Rasmussen.

Selecting Distribution Channels

Market factors may be the most important consideration in choosing a distribution channel. To reach a target market with a small number of buyers or buyers concentrated in a geographical area, the most feasible alternative may be a direct channel. In contrast, if the firm must reach customers who are dispersed or who make frequent small purchases, then the channel may need to incorporate marketing intermediaries to make goods available when and where customers want them.

In general, standardized products or items with low unit values usually pass through relatively long distribution channels. On the other hand, products that are complex, expensive, custom made, or perishable move through shorter distribution channels involving few—or no—intermediaries. The increasing prevalence of e-commerce is resulting in changes in traditional distribution practices. The European Commission recently issued a set of rules, effective until 2022, that permit makers of goods with less than a 30 percent market share—usually high-end manufacturers—to block Internet-only retailers from carrying their products. The commission declared that "suppliers should normally be free to decide on the number and type of distributors they want to have in their distribution systems. . . . More generally, suppliers may only want to sell to distributors that have one or more physical points of present [actual "bricks-and-mortar" stores] where the suppliers' goods can be touched, smelled, tried, etc." The European Alliance—which represents luxury goods manufacturers such as LVMH Louis Vuitton Moët Hennessey, Gucci, and Burberry—lobbied for and welcomed the new rules as a way to protect the quality image of their products. Online-only retailers, such as Amazon, eBay, and their European counterparts, called for repeal of the "bricks-and-mortar" requirement and warned that some manufacturers would use the new rules to "restrict the availability" of their products online and thus keep prices high.[32]

The Greek entrepreneur Stelios Haji-Ioannou, however, finds the Internet the perfect channel for easyGroup, the private investment group for his "easy" brand. The company represents a variety of businesses with the "easy" tag—including easyJet.com, easyCar.com, easyJobs.com, easyP-izza.com, and even an easyBus route between Gatwick Airport and London. Each business offers a no-frills, low-cost approach to services that consumers can order online. EasyJet is one of Europe's biggest Internet retailers, selling 95 percent of its seats online.[33]

Producers that offer a broad product line, with the financial and marketing resources to distribute and promote it, are more likely to choose a shorter channel. Instead of depending on marketing intermediaries, financially strong manufacturers with broad product lines typically use their own sales representatives, warehouses, and credit departments to serve both retailers and consumers.

In many cases, start-up manufacturers turn to direct channels because they can't persuade intermediaries to carry their products or because they want to extend their sales reach. Some companies employ direct channels to carry intangible goods as well. Based in New York City, Art Meets Commerce uses the Internet and social networking to promote small Broadway and off-Broadway shows with tight marketing budgets. The company posts short videos of its client shows on YouTube and takes advantage of Facebook and Twitter to amplify traditional word-of-mouth publicity. When celebrities see the shows and post favorable tweets, their followers may feel encouraged to see the shows too.[34]

Competitive performance is the fourth key consideration when choosing a distribution channel. A producer loses customers when an intermediary fails to achieve promotion or product delivery. Channels used by established competitors as well as new market entries also can influence decisions. Sometimes a joint venture between competitors can work well. Best Buy and Apple have teamed up to sell their products under the same roof. Under the agreement, Apple controls its own retail space within Best Buy stores. Although Apple has a well-established retail business, it can't match the size of electronics giant Best Buy. Best Buy benefits by generating more traffic from customers who want to see and buy Apple's innovative products in convenient locations. The strategy has worked well, as the sales of Macs in particular have increased. Consumers can log on to the Best Buy Website for product information, store locator, or to purchase the latest Apple items, ranging from the iPad2 to AppleTV.[35]

Selecting Distribution Intensity

A second key distribution decision involves *distribution intensity*—the number of intermediaries or outlets through which a manufacturer distributes its goods. Only one BMW dealership may be operating in your immediate area, but you can find Coca-Cola everywhere—in supermarkets, convenience stores, gas stations, vending machines, and restaurants. BMW has chosen a different level of distribution intensity than that used for Coca-Cola. In general, market coverage varies along a continuum with three different intensity levels:

1. *Intensive distribution* involves placing a firm's products in nearly every available outlet. Generally, intensive distribution suits low-priced convenience goods such as milk, newspapers, and soft drinks. This kind of market saturation requires cooperation by many intermediaries, including wholesalers and retailers, to achieve maximum coverage.

2. *Selective distribution* is a market-coverage strategy in which a manufacturer selects only a limited number of retailers to distribute its product lines. Selective distribution can reduce total marketing costs and establish strong working relationships within the channel.

Daniel Acker/Bloomberg/Getty Images, Inc.

Exclusive distribution limits market coverage in a specific geographical region. The approach suits expensive specialty products such as Rolex watches. Retailers are carefully selected to enhance the product's image to the market.

3. *Exclusive distribution,* at the other end of the continuum from intensive distribution, limits market coverage in a specific geographical region. The approach suits relatively expensive specialty products such as Rolex watches. Retailers are carefully selected to enhance the product's image to the market and to ensure that well-trained personnel will contribute to customer satisfaction. Although producers may sacrifice some market coverage by granting an exclusive territory to a single intermediary, the decision usually pays off in developing and maintaining an image of quality and prestige.

When companies are offloading excess inventory, even high-priced retailers may look to discounters to help them clear the merchandise from their warehouses. To satisfy consumers' taste for luxury goods, designer outlet malls offer shoppers a chance to buy status items at lower prices. Chicago Premium Outlets features 120 stores carrying such upscale brands as Michael Kors, Juicy Couture, and Diesel. Similar centers include Desert Hills Premium Outlets in California, Las Vegas Premium Outlets, and Seattle Premium Outlets.[36]

Logistics and Physical Distribution

supply chain complete sequence of suppliers that contribute to creating a good or service and delivering it to business users and final consumers.

A firm's choice of distribution channels creates the final link in the <u>**supply chain**</u>, the complete sequence of suppliers that contribute to creating a good or service and delivering it to business users and final consumers. The supply chain begins when the raw materials used in production are delivered to the producer and continues with the actual production activities that create finished goods. Finally, the finished goods move through the producer's distribution channels to end customers.

logistics process of coordinating the flow of goods, services, and information among members of the supply chain.

The process of coordinating the flow of goods, services, and information among members of the supply chain is called <u>**logistics**</u>. The term originally referred to strategic movements of military troops and supplies. Today, however, it describes all of the business activities involved in the supply chain with the ultimate goal of getting finished goods to customers.

Physical Distribution A major focus of logistics management—identified earlier in the chapter as one of the two basic dimensions of distribution strategy—is *physical distribution,* the activities aimed at efficiently moving finished goods from the production line to the consumer or business buyer. As Figure 12.9 shows, physical distribution is a broad concept that includes transportation and numerous other elements that help link buyers and sellers. An effectively managed physical distribution system can increase customer satisfaction by ensuring reliable movements of products through the supply chain. For instance, Walmart studies the speed with which goods can be shelved once they arrive at the store because

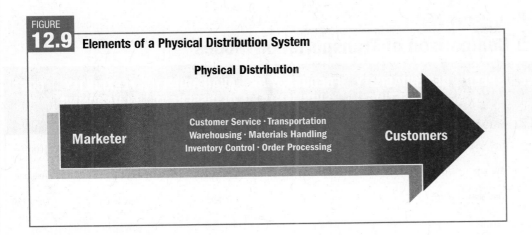

FIGURE
12.9 **Elements of a Physical Distribution System**

Physical Distribution

Marketer

Customer Service · Transportation
Warehousing · Materials Handling
Inventory Control · Order Processing

Customers

strategies that look efficient at the warehouse, such as completely filling pallets with goods, can actually be time-consuming or costly in the aisles.

Radio-frequency identification (RFID) technology relies on a computer chip implanted somewhere on a product or its packaging that emits a low-frequency radio signal identifying the item. The radio signal doesn't require a line of sight to register on the store's computers the way a bar code does, so a hand-held RFID reader can scan crates and cartons before they are unloaded. Because the chip can store information about the product's progress through the distribution channel, retailers can efficiently manage inventories, maintain stock levels, reduce loss, track stolen goods, and cut costs. The technology is similar to that already used to identify lost pets and speed vehicles through toll booths. Walmart, Target, the U.S. Department of Defense, and the German retailer Metro Group already require their suppliers to use RFID technology. The U.S. Army is now using solar power to activate battery-powered RFIDs, which are particularly useful in remote areas. Automakers are also using RFID technology to improve their production processes by tracking parts and other supplies. A new version of the RFID chip can be printed on paper or plastic. RFID technology brings with it privacy and counterfeiting concerns. Recently one company developed a process that uses unique silicon "fingerprints" to generate unclonable RFID chips.[37]

Warehousing is the physical distribution activity that involves the storage of products. *Materials handling* is moving items within factories, warehouses, transportation terminals, and stores. Inventory control involves managing inventory costs, such as storage facilities, insurance, taxes, and handling. The physical distribution activity of *order processing* includes preparing orders for shipment and receiving orders when shipments arrive.

The wide use of electronic data interchange (EDI) and the constant pressure on suppliers to improve their response time have led to **vendor-managed inventory**, in which the producer and the retailer agree that the producer (or the wholesaler) will determine how much of a product a buyer needs and automatically ship new supplies when needed.

The form of transportation used to ship products depends primarily on the kind of product, the distance involved, and the cost. The logistics manager can choose from a number of companies and modes of transportation. As Table 12.3 shows, the five major transport modes are—in order of total expenditures—trucks (with about 75 percent of total expenditures), railroads (approximately 12 percent), water carriers (6 percent), air freight

vendor-managed inventory process in which the producer and the retailer agree that the producer (or the wholesaler) will determine how much of a product a buyer needs and automatically ship new supplies when needed.

⌐12.3¬ Comparison of Transportation Modes

MODE	SPEED	DEPENDABILITY IN MEETING SCHEDULES	FREQUENCY OF SHIPMENTS	AVAILABILITY IN DIFFERENT LOCATIONS	FLEXIBILITY IN HANDLING	COST
Truck	Fast	High	High	Very extensive	Average	High
Rail	Average	Average	Low	Low	High	Average
Water	Very slow	Average	Very low	Limited	Very high	Very low
Air	Very fast	High	Average	Average	Low	Very high
Pipeline	Slow	High	High	Very limited	Very Low	Low

(4 percent), and pipelines (3 percent). The faster methods typically cost more than the slower ones. Speed, reliable delivery, shipment frequency, location availability, handling flexibility, and cost are all important considerations when choosing the most appropriate mode of transportation.

About 15.5 million trucks operate in the United States, carrying most finished goods all or part of the way to the consumer. Nearly 2 million of these are tractor trailers.[38] But railroads, which compete with many truck routes despite their recent loss of market share, are a major mode of transportation. The 565 freight railroads in the United States, Canada, and Mexico operate across more than 202,000 miles of track and earn almost $75 billion in revenues. Seventy percent of all autos manufactured in the United States travel to their destinations by train, as does 70 percent of the country's coal. A freight train needs only 1 gallon of diesel fuel to transport 1 ton of cargo almost 425 miles.[39]

Customer Service Customer service is a vital component of both product and distribution strategies. *Customer service standards* measure the quality of service a firm provides for its customers. Managers frequently set quantitative guidelines—for example, that all orders be processed within 24 hours after they are received or that salespeople approach shoppers within two minutes after they enter the store. Sometimes customers set their own service standards and choose suppliers that meet or exceed them.

The customer service components of product strategy include warranty and repair service programs. *Warranties* are firms' promises to repair a defective product, refund money paid, or replace a product if it proves unsatisfactory. Repair services are also important. Consumers want to know that help is available if something goes wrong. Those who shop for home computers, for example, often choose retailers that not only feature low prices but also offer repair services and tech support centers. Products with inadequate service backing quickly disappear from the market as a result of word-of-mouth criticism.

Consumers' complaints of the impersonal service they received at Web sites led dot-coms to take a number of steps to "humanize" their customer interactions and deal with complaints. Many Web sites contain button help icons that link the visitor to a representative.

Assessment Check ☑

1. What is distribution intensity?

2. Define *supply chain.*

3. What do customer service standards measure?

What's Ahead

This chapter covered two of the elements of the marketing mix: product and distribution. It introduced the key marketing tasks of developing, marketing, and packaging want-satisfying goods and services. It also focused on the three major components of an organization's distribution strategy: the design of efficient distribution channels; wholesalers and retailers who make up many distribution channels; and logistics and physical distribution. We now turn to the remaining two—promotion and pricing—in Chapter 13.

Summary of Learning Goals

⌐1⌐ **Explain marketing's definition of a product; differentiate among convenience, shopping, and specialty products; and distinguish between a product mix and a product line.**

A product is a bundle of physical, service, and symbolic attributes designed to satisfy consumer wants. The marketing conception of a product includes the brand, product image, warranty, service attributes, packaging, and labeling, in addition to the physical or functional characteristics of the good or service.

Goods and services can be classified as consumer (B2C) or business (B2B) products. Consumer products are those purchased by ultimate consumers for their own use. They can be convenience products, shopping products, or specialty products, depending on consumer habits in buying them. Business products are those purchased for use either directly or indirectly in the production of other goods and services for resale. They can be classified as installations, accessory equipment, component parts and materials, raw materials, and supplies. This classification is based on how the items are used and product characteristics. Services can be classified as either consumer or business services.

A product mix is the assortment of goods and services a firm offers to individual consumers and B2B users. A product line is a series of related products.

Assessment Check Answers ✅

1.1 How do consumer products differ from business products? Business products, such as drill presses, are sold to firms or organizations. Consumer products, such as personal-care items, are sold to final users.

1.2 Differentiate among convenience, shopping, and specialty products. Convenience products are items the consumer seeks to purchase frequently, immediately, and with little effort. Shopping products are typically purchased after the buyer has compared competing products in

competing stores. Specialty products are those a purchaser is willing to make a special effort to obtain.

⌐2⌐ **Briefly describe each of the four stages of the product life cycle with their marketing implications.**

Every successful new product passes through four stages in its product life cycle: introduction, growth, maturity, and decline. In the introduction stage, the firm attempts to elicit demand for the new product. In the product's growth stage, sales climb, and the company earns its initial profits. In the maturity stage, sales reach a saturation level. In the decline stage, both sales and profits decline. Marketers sometimes employ strategies to extend the product life cycle, including increasing the frequency of use, adding new users, finding new uses for the product, and changing package size, labeling, or product quality.

The new-product development process for most products has six stages: idea generation, screening, concept development and business analysis, product development, test marketing, and commercialization. At each stage, marketers must decide whether to continue to the next stage, modify the new product, or discontinue the development process. Some new products skip the test marketing stage due to the desire to quickly introduce a new product with excellent potential, a desire not to reveal new-product strategies to competitors, and the high costs involved in limited production runs.

Assessment Check Answers ✅

2.1 What are the stages of the product life cycle? In the introduction stage, the firm attempts to elicit demand for the new product. In the product's growth stage, sales climb, and the company earns its initial profits. In the maturity stage, sales reach a saturation level. In the decline stage, both sales and profits decline.

2.2 What are the marketing implications of each stage?
Marketers sometimes employ strategies to extend the product life cycle, including increasing frequency of use, adding new users, finding new uses for the product, and changing package size, labeling, or product quality.

3 Explain how firms identify their products.

Products are identified by brands, brand names, and trademarks, which are important elements of product images. Effective brand names are easy to pronounce, recognize, and remember, and they project the right images to buyers. Brand names cannot contain generic words. Under certain circumstances, companies lose exclusive rights to their brand names if common use makes them generic terms for product categories. Some brand names belong to retailers or distributors rather than to manufacturers. Brand loyalty is measured in three degrees: brand recognition, brand preference, and brand insistence. Some marketers use family brands to identify several related items in a product line. Others employ individual branding strategies by giving each product within a line a different brand name.

Assessment Check Answers ✅

3.1 Differentiate among a brand, a brand name, and a trademark. A brand is a name, term, sign, symbol, design, or some combination thereof used to identify the products of one firm and differentiate them from competitive offerings. A brand name is that part of the brand consisting of words or letters used to identify and distinguish the firm's offerings from those of competitors. A trademark is a brand that has been given legal protection.

3.2 Define *brand equity*. Brand equity is the added value that a respected and successful brand name gives to a product.

4 Outline and briefly describe each of the major components of an effective distribution strategy.

A firm must consider whether to move products through direct or indirect distribution. Once the decision is made, the company needs to identify the types of marketing intermediaries, if any, through which it will distribute its goods and services. The Internet has made direct distribution an attractive option for many retail companies. Another component is distribution intensity. The business must decide on the amount of market coverage—intensive, selective, or exclusive—needed to achieve its marketing strategies. Finally, attention must be paid to managing the distribution channel. It is vital to minimize conflict between channel members.

Assessment Check Answers ✅

4.1 Define *distribution channels*. Distribution channels are the paths that products, and title to them, follow from producer to consumer or business user.

4.2 What is a marketing intermediary? A marketing intermediary (also called a middleman) is a business firm that moves goods between producers and consumers or business users.

5 Distinguish between different types of wholesaling intermediaries.

Wholesaling is a crucial part of the distribution channel for many products, particularly consumer goods and business supplies. Wholesaling intermediaries can be classified on the basis of ownership; some are owned by manufacturers, some are owned by retailers, and others are independently owned. Firms operate two main types of manufacturer-owned wholesaling intermediaries: sales branches and sales offices.

An independent wholesaling intermediary is a business that represents a number of different manufacturers and makes sales calls on retailers, manufacturers, and other business accounts. Independent wholesalers are classified as either merchant wholesalers or agents and brokers, depending on whether they take title to the products they handle.

Retailers sometimes band together to form their own wholesaling organizations. Such organizations can take the form of either a buying group or a cooperative.

Assessment Check Answers ✅

5.1 Define *wholesaling*. Wholesaling is a crucial part of the distribution channel for many products, particularly consumer goods and business supplies.

5.2 Differentiate between a merchant wholesaler and an agent or broker in terms of title to the goods. Merchant wholesalers are independently owned wholesaling intermediaries that take title to the goods they handle. Agents and brokers may or may not take possession of the goods they handle, but they never take title, working mainly to bring buyers and sellers together.

6 Describe the various types of retailers, and identify retail strategies.

Retailers, in contrast to wholesalers, are distribution channel members that sell goods and services to individuals for their own use rather than for resale. Nonstore retailing includes four forms: direct-response retailing, Internet retailing, automatic merchandising, and direct selling. Store retailers range in size from tiny newsstands to multistory department stores and warehouselike retailers such as Sam's Club.

The first step in developing a competitive retailing strategy is to select a target market. Next, the retailer must develop a product strategy to determine the best mix of merchandise to carry to satisfy that market. A retailer's customer service strategy focuses on attracting and retaining target customers to maximize sales and profits. Retailers base their pricing decisions on the costs of purchasing products from other channel members and offering services to customers. A good location often marks the difference between success and failure in retailing. A retailer designs advertisements and develops other promotions to stimulate demand and to provide information such as the store's location, merchandise offerings, prices, and hours. A successful retailer closely aligns its merchandising, pricing, and promotion strategies with store atmospherics, the physical characteristics of a store and its amenities, to influence consumers' perceptions of the shopping experience.

Assessment Check Answers ✓

6.1 Define *retailer*. Retailers are distribution channel members that sell goods and services to individuals for their own use rather than for resale.

6.2 What are the elements of a retailer's marketing strategy? After identifying their target markets, retailers must choose merchandising, customer service, pricing, and location strategies that will attract customers in those market segments.

⌐7⌐ Identify the various categories of distribution channels, and discuss the factors that influence channel selection.

Marketers can choose either a direct distribution channel, which moves goods directly from the producer to the consumer, or indirect distribution channels, which involve marketing intermediaries in the paths through which products—and legal ownership of them—flow from producer to the final customer. Ideally, the choice of a distribution channel should support a firm's overall marketing strategy. Before selecting distribution channels, firms must consider their target markets, the types of goods being distributed, their own internal systems and concerns, and competitive factors.

Assessment Check Answers ✓

7.1 What is distribution intensity? Distribution intensity is the number of intermediaries or outlets through which a manufacturer distributes its goods.

7.2 Define *supply chain*. A supply chain is the sequence of suppliers that contribute to creating a good or service and delivering it to business users and final consumers.

7.3 What do customer service standards measure? Customer service standards measure the quality of service a firm provides for its customers.

◼ Business Terms You Need to Know

product 388	brand 397	distribution strategy 402	retailer 407
product line 391	brand name 397	distribution channels 402	supply chain 416
product mix 391	trademark 397	physical distribution 402	logistics 416
product life cycle 392	brand equity 399	wholesaler 406	vendor-managed inventory 417
test marketing 396	category advisor 400		

◼ Review Questions

1. Classify each of the following business-to-consumer (B2C) and business-to-business (B2B) goods and services. Then choose one and describe how it could be classified as both.

   a. *Runner's World* or *Esquire* magazine

   b. six-pack of apple juice

   c. limousine service

   d. tech support for a communications system

   e. golf course

   f. Thai restaurant

2. What is the relationship between a product line and a product mix? Give an example of each.

3. Identify and briefly describe the six stages of new-product development.

4. What is the difference between a manufacturer's brand and a private brand? What is the difference between a family brand and an individual brand?

5. What are the three stages of brand loyalty? Why is the progression to the last stage so important to marketers?

6. What are the advantages of direct distribution? When is a producer most likely to use direct distribution?

.7. What is the wheel of retailing? How has the Internet affected the wheel of retailing?

8. Identify and briefly describe the four different types of non-store retailers. Give an example of at least one type of good or service that would be suited to each type of nonstore retailer.

9. What are the three intensity levels of distribution? Give an example of two products for each level.

10. Define *logistics*. How does it relate to physical distribution?

■ Projects and Teamwork Applications

1. On your own or with a classmate, choose one of the following goods or services. Decide whether you want to market it as a consumer product or a business product. Now create a brand name and marketing strategy for your product.
   a. lawnmower repair service
   b. hardware store
   c. soft drink
   d. English-language class
   e. accounting firm

2. Choose one of the following products that is either in the maturity or decline stage of its life cycle (or select one of your own), and develop a marketing strategy for extending its life cycle.
   a. popcorn
   b. fast-food restaurant chain
   c. newspaper

   d. music CDs
   e. paper stationery or notecards

3. Where do you do most of your shopping—in stores or online? Choose your favorite retailer and analyze why you like it. Outline your reasons for shopping there, then add two or three suggestions for improvement.

4. Choose one of the following products and select a distribution intensity for the product. Describe specifically where and how your product would be sold. Then describe the reasons for your strategy.
   a. line of furniture manufactured from recycled or reclaimed materials
   b. custom-designed jewelry
   c. house-painting service
   d. handicraft supplies
   e. talk radio show

■ Web Assignments

1. **Product classification.** Visit the Web site of Johnson & Johnson (http://www.jnj.com) and click on "Our Products." Review the material in the chapter on product classification and then classify Johnson & Johnson's vast array of products.

2. **Shopping centers.** The Mall of America in Minnesota is the nation's largest shopping center. Go to the Mall's Web site (http://www.mallofamerica.com) to learn more about it. Make a list of five interesting facts you learned about the Mall of America.

3. **Railroad statistics.** Visit the Web site of the American Association of Railroads (http://www.aar.org). Click on

"Statistics and Publication" and then "Railroad Statistics." Review the material and answer the following questions:
   a. What is a so-called Class I railroad? How many are there?
   b. How many workers do these railroads employ?
   c. How much freight did Class I railroads carry during the most recent year for which data are available?

Note: Internet Web addresses change frequently. If you don't find the exact sites listed, you may need to access the organization's home page and search from there or use a search engine such as Bing or Google.

Luxury Brands Market to Millennials

Chanel. Armani. BMW. Cartier. These long-established, high-end brands are very interested in Generation Y, also known as the Millennials—those born during the 1980s and who are now between 18 and 28 years old. The newest challenge these once-exclusive brands face is marketing to this age group.

According to a recent marketing survey, Millennials are the "largest consumer group in U.S. history," even bigger than the baby-boom generation, the previous record holders. At 70 to 85 million, Millennials make up 25 percent of the American population. They are the most ethnically diverse group ever, as well as the least bound by gender stereotypes. They spend over $200 billion a year on purchases. As they enter the workforce and set up their own households, they will overtake the soon-to-retire baby boomers in spending power.

Even more important is how Millennials get information and communicate. Unlike any previous generation, they have grown up with digital technology and take cell phones, video games, and other high-speed electronic devices and media for granted. They are used to instantly available information and communication. A recent survey by the Pew Research Center notes that 75 percent of Generation Y uses social networking, in contrast to 50 percent of Generation X (30 to 45 years old) and 30 percent of baby boomers (46 to 64 years old).

Millennials are very aware of the value of what they buy. The marketing survey found that 65 percent of female Millennials and 61 percent of males describe themselves as brand conscious. But heritage and exclusivity, formerly effective marketing tools for prestige brands, mean little to Millennials, who instead value quality, authenticity, and image. They shun anything that resembles self-promotion in either brands or people, including prominently displayed corporate logos.

Burberry, a maker of high-end clothing and accessories established in 1836, recently began an ambitious multimedia effort to reach Millennials in the digital universe. One of the company's first moves was to hire the actress Emma Watson, world famous for playing Hermione Granger in the Harry Potter movies. A Millennial born in 1990, she was the new face of Burberry's spring–summer campaign. In addition to traditional print advertising and, of course, its home Web site, Burberry has employed live streaming and 3D filming of its fashion shows. With the photo blogger Scott Schuman, known as the Sartorialist, the company also launched a special Web site, Art of the Trench, to promote its classic trench coat. Burberry's Facebook page calls Art of the Trench "a living celebration of the trench coat and the people who wear it." The Web site, essentially a social networking blog, invites owners to submit photos of themselves wearing their trench coats—or to submit videos to its YouTube channel. Links allow visitors to "view details," "like," "share," and "leave comments" on the photos. They can also sort the photos by popularity, gender, styling, trench color, and weather. The site features music by the Maccabees, White Lies, and other groups, with links to their Web sites. Burberry's CEO, Angela Ahrendts, said, "Attracting the Millennial customer to luxury started two years ago—I said that we can either get crushed or ride the greatest wave of our life."

Scott Galloway of New York University's School of Business says, "Gen Y goodwill is arguably the closest thing to a crystal ball for predicting a brand's long-term prospects. Just as Boomers drove the luxury sector for the last 20 years, brands that resonate with Gen Y, whose purchasing power will surpass that of Boomers by 2017, will be the new icons of prestige."

Questions for Critical Thinking

1. Millennials are brand conscious but generally dislike conspicuous, flashy brand logos. How might this affect a company's brand equity?

2. Burberry is basing its product strategy on how Millennials use the Internet and social media, as opposed to how their elders do. Do you think this difference in use will continue as the Millennials mature? If so, how might Burberry change its product strategy?

Sources: Company Web site, http://us.burberry.com, accessed June 7, 2011; Art of the Trench, http://artofthetrench.com, accessed August 3, 2010; Sharalyn Hartwell, "Millennials Love Brands, Not Branding," Generation Y Examiner, May 6, 2010, http://www.examiner.com; Scott Galloway, "Gen Y Prestige Brand Ranking," May 3, 2010, http://l2thinktank.com/Gen_Y_Report.pdf; Pew Research Center, "The Millennials: Confident. Connected. Open to Change," February 24, 2010, http://pewresearch.org/pubs/1501/millennials-new-survey-generational-personality-upbeat-open-new-ideas-technology-bound; Jessica Bumpus, "Millennial Burberry," Vogue.com, March 3, 2010, http://www.vogue.co.uk; Suzy Menkes, "Marketing to the Millennials," New York Times, March 2, 2010, http://www.nytimes.com.

The Convergence of TV and the Internet

Nearly all observers are sure that someday soon, consumers will watch televisions anywhere, on any device—television, computer, or smartphone. Today, once major shows are aired, broadcast TV networks upload them onto their Web sites or to sites such as Hulu and YouTube. One survey reported that in one month alone, more than 178 million Americans watched 33 billion TV shows online.

Across the Atlantic, Britons use BBC's iPlayer to catch up with missed TV episodes online. The BBC and other British networks plan to unite broadcast television with online media in a new, hybrid configuration.

In the United States, viewers have enjoyed watching TV shows on their computers for free. Those days may be over soon—or then again, it may take a little longer.

Advertising fees bring a total of $70 billion to broadcast and cable television networks. Cable and satellite providers pay broadcast networks billions more in retransmission fees and make billions in fees from subscribers.

But when broadcast television networks upload their shows to the Internet, viewers don't have to pay cable and satellite providers, and the networks lose the revenue from cable and satellite licensing fees. Advertisers pay the networks for the right to embed their ads within the video content. But many advertisers shy away from online television because there is still no clear way to measure how effective their commercials will be. One observer says, "Advertisers aren't going to pay for the right to sponsor content [TV shows] unless they know how many people are watching it. The technology is available, but it is still in the process of being implemented."

Online television still has one major drawback: most of it is not live. CBS had live, online coverage of the recent NCAA basketball tournament, but that was an exception. Live broadcasts of shows such as *American Idol* and the Super Bowl charge the highest advertising fees. But online licensing problems and technical issues have made TV networks wary of live online broadcasting.

As viewers exercise their increasing options to watch what they want when they want it, some analysts predict that the only programs that large numbers of people will view at the same time will be sports events and news programs. Some viewers have even stopped their cable

subscriptions and watch TV exclusively online via downloads from Netflix, iTunes, and Amazon.

Another difficulty is that no one has yet developed a way to make the potentially infinite array of Internet programming available on television in a user-friendly manner. But as in Europe, Internet-ready televisions will be available in the United States. Best Buy has announced that soon all the Internet-ready televisions it sells will give buyers the option of subscribing to a Best Buy trove of downloadable broadcast materials. Other TV manufacturers will likely make similar offers.

Subscription television services may be the way of the future, although some generic shows, such as news, cooking shows, and how-to programs will remain free just because they are not unique. Recently, Microsoft unveiled its Mediaroom 2.0, which combines client software with cloud-based services to allow consumers to watch shows either on a flat-screen TV, a personal computer, or, in the future, on compatible smart phones. Enrique Rodriguez, Microsoft's corporate vice president for TV, Video and Music Business, says, "We want to make it easier for consumers to find and discover great content, to watch, listen and engage in new ways, and to do so anywhere and on any screen."

Questions for Critical Thinking

1. At what stage would you say broadcast television is in the product life cycle? What steps have the broadcast networks taken to prolong the life cycle of their product?

2. At this time, broadcast and cable television, Internet programming, and advertisers all have different distribution strategies. How might they bring these strategies closer together?

Sources: David Goldman, "Get Ready to Pay for Online TV," *CNN Money,* accessed June 7, 2011, http://money.cnn.com; Steve Plunkett, "Why 2010 Will Be the Year TV and the Web Really Converge," *Guardian,* February 16, 2010, http://guardian.co.uk; "Microsoft Mediaroom 2.0 Delivers the Future of TV," press release, January 6, 2010, http://www.microsoft.com; Holman W. Jenkins, Jr., "The Future on TV," *The Wall Street Journal,* January 5, 2010, http://online.wsj.com.

No matter how powerful they are, comic book heroes can't get themselves into bookstores—and readers' hands—without a little help. Leon Avelino and Barry Matthews, co-founders of Secret Acres, know that one of the greatest challenges of publishing is getting books onto the shelves and into readers' shopping carts. The task is even more difficult for small publishers—in this case, small publishers of comic books and graphic novels—because they don't have the wide distribution network of major publishers. But Avelino and Matthews, whose authors consider them the superheroes of comicbook publishing, are undaunted. They know what they are trying to achieve and work doggedly to make it happen.

"Distribution is a difficult thing right now," admits Matthews. "The publishing industry is changing and comic books themselves have a different distribution methodology and wholesale methodology than traditional books do." Unlike conventional book shops, comic book shops do not operate on a return basis. Conventional bookstores receive a small discount when they purchase books from a publisher, but then have the option to return any unsold books to the publisher. Comic book shops take a deeper discount but make no returns. Matthews also notes that currently there is only one major distributor of comic books—Diamond Distributors—which has the leverage to dictate much of what happens in the business of comic book distribution. In addition, Matthews observes that Secret Acres' graphic novels could easily be sold to the general book market, but many general book distributors prefer not to deal with smaller publishers because they simply don't produce enough books to be profitable.

All of that said, Matthews explains that they are learning alternative ways to distribute their books. "Amazon is great," he says. "They make it very easy for smaller publishers. They treat your books as if they are Amazon books, giving them the sheen of being part of a larger retail channel." Amazon does take a significant cut of sales, but Matthews says it's worth it to broaden the distribution of Secret Acres products. Of course, Secret Acres also sells its entire line directly through its Web site at http://www.secretacres.com, along with some books from other independent authors and publishers. This sales method is the most profitable for Secret Acres. More importantly, it allows Matthews and Avelino to keep closer tabs on their readers. Matthews explains that because orders are filled on an individual basis, he can slip promotional materials, notices of upcoming events or new books, and tie-ins right into the package of a customer whose preferences he knows. This one-on-one interaction helps in the management of customer relationships.

Matthews and Avelino also enjoy one other form of distribution—attending comic book conventions around the country, such as the Stumptown Comics Fest in Portland, Oregon. There, they have the opportunity to interact with readers, other publishers, comic book authors and artists, and even some smaller distributors who have begun to attend these events. They note that readers in particular love to meet the authors and artists. "It feeds the interest in what we're doing," says Matthews. While at an event, Matthews and Avelino try to carve out some time to meet with other small publishers. "A lot of small publishers are in the same position" with regard to distribution, Matthews explains. "So we have been talking with them to see if we can band together to share resources."

For the future, Matthews admits that he and Avelino have no idea how some of the new technologies, including e-readers, will ultimately affect distribution, but they plan to research the possibility of digitizing some of Secret Acres' titles for online distribution.

Despite its small size, Secret Acres' authors consider the firm a mighty one. Theo Ellsworth, author of such titles as *Capacity* and *Sleeper Car,* praises Secret Acres for its personal attention and efforts to market and distribute his books. "It feels good to have the distribution part in someone else's hands," says Ellsworth. He explains that having someone else take care of that aspect of publishing frees him up to concentrate on his art, producing more posters and books—which is, after all, the author's job.

Questions for Critical Thinking

1. Visit Secret Acres' web site at http://www.secretacres.com to learn more about the firm's product line. Write a marketing blurb describing the line to a potential distributor.
2. What steps can Secret Acres take to develop brand loyalty and ultimately brand equity for its products?
3. How might Secret Acres expand its Internet retailing presence?
4. Secret Acres is a tiny firm with limited distribution. How can the company use customer service to create a competitive advantage, increase distribution, and help it grow?

Sources: Secret Acres Web site, http://www.secretacres.com, accessed June 7, 2011; Stumptown Comics Fest, http://www.stumptowncomics.com, accessed June 7, 2011; "Great Graphic Novels for Teens," *Young Adult Library Services Association,* http://www.ala.org/yalsa, accessed June 7, 2011; Harry McCracken, "E-Readers May Be Dead, But They're Not Going Away Yet," *PC World,* August 17, 2010, http://www.pcworld.com.

Chapter 13

Learning Objectives

[1] Discuss how integrated marketing communications relates to a firm's overall promotional strategy, and explain the concept of a promotional mix along with outlining the objectives of promotion.

[2] Summarize the different types of advertising and advertising media.

[3] Outline the roles of sales promotion, personal selling, and public relations in a promotional strategy.

[4] Describe pushing and pulling promotional strategies.

[5] Outline the different types of pricing objectives.

[6] Discuss how firms set prices in the marketplace, and describe the four alternative pricing strategies.

[7] Discuss consumer perceptions of price.

Promotion and Pricing Strategies

Jitalia17/iStockphoto

San Francisco Giants Win With Pricing Strategy

Christian Petersen/Getty Images, Inc.

Gone are the days when a ticket for the windy bleachers out at remote Candlestick Park—former home of Major League Baseball's San Francisco Giants—could be bought for fifty cents. The stadium is gone, too. The Giants now swing their bats and run their bases at the sleek new AT&T Park, which is much more conveniently located near downtown San Francisco, not plagued by gusty winds. And the ticket prices are far, far beyond fifty cents. Yet Giants marketers believe they have hit a home run with their innovative pricing strategy. Called dynamic pricing, under the plan, ticket prices fluctuate with demand throughout the baseball season. Fans can lock in their ticket prices by purchasing early in the season—or wait to see how well the team does. For example, bleacher seats at AT&T Park range from $18 to $46 when purchased before opening day in April; but if the Giants do well and the stadium begins to fill up with advance ticket sales, those prices will increase. If the Giants aren't as successful that season, ticket prices could drop. The same principle holds true for the more expensive field club seats, which run between $89 and $195 per game. The other variable in the game date itself—if the Giants are playing an archrival on a weekend, the seats will be more expensive than if they are swinging bats against a lackluster team on a weekday.

In addition to individual ticket sales, the Giants offer a variety of packages, including season tickets, Giants gift cards, Giants road trips, ballpark tours, and special events like the Annual Slumber Party. For $200 per person (including a game ticket), after the game fans have the opportunity to set up camp on the baseball field, play catch under the lights, and enjoy games, movies, pizza, snacks, and other festivities—then eat breakfast together the following morning. A family of four pays a discounted rate of $750, and children under age five are admitted free with game ticket purchase. While this is certainly a splurge for many families, the cost is less than for some theme parks, and the baseball thrills are unmatched.

As the baseball season progresses, so do ticket sales. But when the team suddenly hits the playoffs—and makes it to the World Series as the Giants did in 2010, demand goes through the roof. During the playoffs against the San Diego Padres, the Giants exceeded expectations by sweeping three games in a row in front of stadium crowds that averaged nearly 38,000. Then they went on to defeat the Philadelphia Phillies for the National League championships. When the team found itself matched against the Texas Rangers, ticket brokers predicted intense demand because San Francisco had not won the World Series since 1954, and Texas had never been to the Series at all, "Anytime you have a first-time team in the World Series, it's unique, number one," explained Roger Jones, owner of Alliance Tickets. "Number two, you have a great geographical market in San Francisco. Number three is some tremendous pitching matchups." Before game one was even played, ticket seller StubHub posted its cheapest seats (standing room only) for $372, or more than 700 percent of the face value of $50.

San Francisco won the Series—thus increasing ticket demand for the following season. Fans didn't seem to mind.[1]

promotion function of informing, persuading, and influencing a purchase decision.

This chapter focuses on the different types of promotional activities and the way prices are established for goods and services. **Promotion** is the function of informing, persuading, and influencing a purchase decision. This activity is as important to not-for-profit organizations as it is to profit-seeking companies.

Some promotional strategies try to develop *primary demand*, or consumer desire for a general product category. The objective of such a campaign is to stimulate sales for an entire industry so that individual firms benefit from this market growth. A popular example is the dairy industry's "Got Milk?" campaign. Print and television messages about the nutritional benefits of milk show various celebrities. Other promotional campaigns aimed at increasing per-capita consumption have been commissioned by the California Strawberry Commission and the National Cattlemen's Beef Association.

Most promotional strategies, in contrast, seek to stimulate *selective demand*—desire for a specific brand. The San Francisco Giants try to stimulate loyalty with promotions like ballpark tours and their Annual Slumber Party. Country-Western star Toby Keith promotes Ford F-150 trucks, which encourages his fans to choose that brand over competitors.

Marketers choose from among many promotional options to communicate with potential customers. Each marketing

Most promotional strategies seek to stimulate *selective demand*—desire for a specific brand. Country-Western star Toby Keith wants to encourage his fans to choose Ford F-150 trucks over competitors.

Mike Cassese/Reuters/Landov LLC

message a buyer receives—through a television or radio commercial, newspaper or magazine ad, Web site, direct-mail flyer, or sales call—reflects the product, place, person, cause, or organization promoted in the content. Through **integrated marketing communications (IMC)**, marketers coordinate all promotional activities—media advertising, direct mail, personal selling, sales promotion, and public relations—to produce a unified, customer-focused promotional strategy. This coordination is designed to avoid confusing the consumer and to focus positive attention on the promotional message.

This chapter begins by explaining the role of IMC and then discusses the objectives of promotion and the importance of promotional planning. Next, it examines the components of the promotional mix: advertising, sales promotion, personal selling, and public relations. Finally, the chapter addresses pricing strategies for goods and services, as described in the chapter opener about the San Francisco Giants.

Integrated Marketing Communications

An integrated marketing communications strategy focuses on customer needs to create a unified promotional message in the firm's ads, in-store displays, product samples, and presentations by company sales representatives. To gain a competitive advantage, marketers that implement IMC need a broad view of promotion. Media options continue to multiply, and marketers cannot simply rely on traditional broadcast and print media and direct mail. Plans must include all forms of customer contact. Packaging, store displays, sales promotions, sales presentations, and online and interactive media also communicate information about a brand or organization. With IMC, marketers create a unified personality and message for the good, brand, or service they promote. Coordinated activities also enhance the effectiveness of reaching and serving target markets.

Marketing managers set the goals and objectives for the firm's promotional strategy with overall organizational objectives and marketing goals in mind. Based on these objectives, marketers weave the various elements of the strategy—personal selling, advertising, sales promotion, publicity, and public relations—into an integrated communications plan. This document becomes a central part of the firm's total marketing strategy to reach its selected target market. Feedback, including marketing research and sales reports, completes the system by identifying any deviations from the plan and suggesting improvements.

One of the most successful IMC campaigns recently was the Old Spice Guy. The campaign primarily focused on actor Isaiah Mustafa's six-pack abs, and the rest is advertising history. Marketing communications included: commercials for traditional broadcast TV; ads cued up on Old Spice's You Tube channel, which then spread to other social media channels; communication with the Old Spice Guy via Twitter; media buys on Google and Facebook; interactive digital treasure hunts; and more.[2]

The Promotional Mix

Just as every organization creates a marketing mix combining product, distribution, promotion, and pricing strategies, each also requires a similar mix to blend the many facets of promotion into a cohesive plan. The <u>promotional mix</u> consists of two components—personal and nonpersonal selling—that marketers combine to meet the needs of their firm's target customers and effectively and efficiently communicate its message to them. <u>Personal selling</u> is the most basic form of promotion: a direct person-to-person promotional presentation to a potential buyer. The buyer–seller communication can occur during a face-to-face meeting or via telephone, videoconference, or interactive computer link.

<u>Nonpersonal selling</u> consists of advertising, sales promotion, direct marketing, and public relations. Advertising is the best-known form of nonpersonal selling, but sales promotion accounts for about half of these marketing expenditures. Spending for sponsorships, which involves marketing messages delivered in association with another activity such as a golf tournament or a benefit concert, is on the rise as well. Marketers need to be careful about the types of promotion they choose or risk alienating the very people they are trying to reach.

Each component in the promotional mix offers its own advantages and disadvantages, as Table 13.1 demonstrates. By selecting the most effective combination of promotional mix elements, a firm may reach its promotional objectives. Spending within the promotional mix varies by industry. Manufacturers of many business-to-business (B2B) products typically spend more on personal selling than on advertising because those products—such as a new telecommunications system—may require a significant investment. Consumer-goods marketers may focus more on advertising and sponsorships. Later sections of this chapter discuss how the parts of the mix contribute to effective promotion.

Table

13.1 Comparing the Components of the Promotional Mix

COMPONENT	ADVANTAGES	DISADVANTAGES
Advertising	Reaches large consumer audience at low cost per contact Allows strong control of the message Message can be modified to match different audiences	Difficult to measure effectiveness Limited value for closing sales
Personal selling	Message can be tailored for each customer Produces immediate buyer response Effectiveness is easily measured	High cost per contact High expense and difficulty of attracting and retaining effective salespeople
Sales promotion	Attracts attention and creates awareness Effectiveness is easily measured Produces short-term sales increases	Difficult to differentiate from similar programs of competitors Nonpersonal appeal
Public relations	Enhances product or firm credibility Creates a positive attitude about the product or company	Difficult to measure effectiveness Often devoted to nonmarketing activities
Sponsorships	Viewed positively by consumers Enhances brand awareness	Difficult to control message

Objectives of Promotional Strategy

Promotional strategy objectives vary among organizations. Some use promotion to expand their markets, and others use it to defend their current positions. As Figure 13.1 illustrates, common objectives include providing information, differentiating a product, increasing sales, stabilizing sales, and accentuating a product's value.

Marketers often pursue multiple promotional objectives at the same time. To promote its Microsoft Office software, Microsoft has to convince business owners, who buy the software, and their employees, who use the software, that the product is a worthwhile investment.

Marketers need to keep their firm's promotional objectives in mind at all times. Sometimes the objectives are obscured by a fast-paced, creative ad campaign. In this case, the message—or worse, the brand name or image—is lost. The series of comic Geico ads that featured grumpy Neanderthals and the tag line "So easy a caveman could do it" were an instant hit. They were widely viewed on YouTube and even inspired a short-lived TV sitcom. But despite their quirky originality, the ads allowed humor to overtake the message; few viewers remembered the product—car insurance.

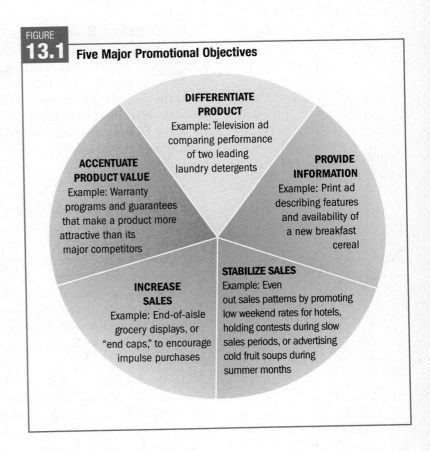

FIGURE 13.1 Five Major Promotional Objectives

DIFFERENTIATE PRODUCT
Example: Television ad comparing performance of two leading laundry detergents

PROVIDE INFORMATION
Example: Print ad describing features and availability of a new breakfast cereal

ACCENTUATE PRODUCT VALUE
Example: Warranty programs and guarantees that make a product more attractive than its major competitors

STABILIZE SALES
Example: Even out sales patterns by promoting low weekend rates for hotels, holding contests during slow sales periods, or advertising cold fruit soups during summer months

INCREASE SALES
Example: End-of-aisle grocery displays, or "end caps," to encourage impulse purchases

Providing Information A major portion of U.S. advertising is information oriented. Credit card ads provide information about benefits and rates. Ads for hair-care products include information about benefits such as shine and volume. Ads for breakfast cereals often contain nutritional information. Television ads for prescription drugs, a nearly $2 billion industry, are sometimes criticized for relying on emotional appeals rather than providing information about the causes, risk factors, and especially the prevention of disease.[3] But print advertisements for drugs often contain an entire page of warnings, side-effects, and usage guidelines.

Differentiating a Product Promotion can also be used to differentiate a firm's offerings from the competition. Applying a concept called **positioning**, marketers attempt to establish their products in the minds of customers. The idea is to communicate to buyers meaningful distinctions about the attributes, price, quality, or use of a good or service.

Marketers of luxury goods position their products as upscale, expensive, high quality, and exclusive. But how do they position goods that are intended for the vast number of "ordinary" consumers? Zappos recently met this challenge by using staff members in its marketing videos—wearing shoes, clothing, and handbags from the Zappos site. The message that real people can wear Zappos products was received positively by the firm's customers. "The consumer is likely to trust that communication more," explained one marketing expert.[4]

positioning concept in which marketers attempt to establish their products in the minds of customers by communicating to buyers meaningful distinctions about the attributes, price, quality, or use of a good or service.

Increasing Sales Increasing sales volume is the most common objective of a promotional strategy. Naturalizer became the third-largest seller of women's dress shoes by appealing to Baby Boomers. But as these women have grown older, they have bought fewer pairs of shoes each year. Naturalizer wants to keep these customers but also attract the younger generation. So the firm developed a new line of trendy shoes. The promotional strategy included ads in magazines read by younger women—such as *Elle* and *Marie Claire*—featuring young women in beach attire and Naturalizer shoes. The response to this strategy was a substantial increase in Naturalizer's sales through department stores.

Stabilizing Sales Sales stabilization is another goal of promotional strategy. Firms often use sales contests during slack periods, motivating salespeople by offering prizes such as vacations, TVs, smart phones, and cash to those who meet certain goals. Companies distribute sales promotion materials—such as calendars, pens, and notepads—to customers to stimulate sales during the off-season. Jiffy Lube puts that little sticker on your windshield to remind you when to have your car's next oil change—the regular visits help stabilize sales. A stable sales pattern brings several advantages. It evens out the production cycle, reduces some management and production costs, and simplifies financial, purchasing, and marketing planning. An effective promotional strategy can contribute to these goals.

McDonald's came up with a marketing campaign in San Diego for its mocha and caramel-flavor iced coffee drinks. Seventy taxis got new "extension tops" for greater product visibility. They show a two-dimensional image of the iced coffee drink—with the foamy topping actually emerging from the taxi top. On the back of each taxi receipt is a printed coupon for taxi customers. Almost 400 taxi drivers will have the coupons to hand out to their customers.[5]

Accentuating the Product's Value Some promotional strategies enhance product values by explaining hidden benefits of ownership. Carmakers offer long-term warranty programs; life insurance companies promote certain policies as investments. The creation of brand awareness and brand loyalty also enhances a product's image and increases its desirability. Advertising with luxurious images supports the reputation of premium brands like Jaguar, Tiffany, and Rolex.

Promotional Planning

Today's marketers can promote their products in many ways, and the lines between the different elements of the promotional mix are blurring. Consider the practice of **product placement**. A growing number of marketers pay placement fees to have their products showcased in various media, ranging from newspapers and magazines to television and movies. Coca-Cola gets prominent placement on *American Idol*, which features as many as 102 product placements in a single month. However, Chevrolet recently beat out Coca-Cola for its number of television placements in a month at 57; Coca-Cola grabbed second with 53, and Microsoft was third with 38 placements.[6] The top three shows for product placement were *American Idol* (Fox), *The Biggest Loser* (NBC), and *Gossip Girl* (CW).[7]

product placement
form of promotion in which marketers pay placement fees to have their products showcased in various media, ranging from newspapers and magazines to television and movies.

Coca-Cola gets prominent placement on *American Idol.* Product and brand placements have skyrocketed with the increasing number of reality TV shows and with improving technology that allows viewers to fast forward through conventional, stand-alone commercials.

Another type of promotional planning must be considered by firms with small budgets. Guerrilla marketing is innovative, low-cost marketing efforts designed to get consumers' attention in unusual ways. Guerrilla marketing is an increasingly popular tactic for marketers, especially those with limited promotional budgets. The Coca-Cola Company recently maximized a humorous guerrilla marketing effort by combining it with social media marketing. How many times have you tried to get a snack or a drink from a vending machine, only to have the machine keep your change, or worse, not give you your requested item? A vending machine at St. John's University in Queens, New York, was apparently broken. It gave the student customer a Coke—and then another, and another, and another. The pleased student handed out the unexpected bonus drinks, getting huge smiles from other students. The whole incident was filmed, guerrilla style, and posted on YouTube. It quickly went viral as viewers tweeted and blogged about it and sent the link to their friends.[8]

Marketers for larger companies have caught on and are using guerrilla approaches as well, with mixed success. The computer-game maker Electronic Arts (EA) faced an unusual challenge in marketing its videogame "Dante's Inferno," based on the first part of Dante Alighieri's medieval epic poem *The Divine Comedy.* In a survey EA conducted before starting its campaign, it found that fewer than 20 percent of those questioned knew anything about the "Inferno" besides the name. Not only did EA have to generate excitement about the game, it also had to educate prospective buyers about the poem. Dante assigned sinners to one of nine regions, or circles, of hell according to their sins. The circles descended from lust, gluttony, greed, and so on, down to treachery, the worst sin, in the lowest circle. The company's campaign, Nine Months of Hell, took as its theme Dante's imagined structure as adapted to EA's gaming needs. The campaign got off to a rocky start in the form of

guerrilla marketing
innovative, low-cost marketing efforts designed to get consumers' attention in unusual ways.

Assessment Check ☑️

1. What is the objective of an integrated marketing communications program?

2. Why do firms pursue multiple promotional objectives at the same time?

3. What are product placement and guerrilla marketing?

staged, phony protests against the game by phony religious groups. Although the protests were quickly unmasked as a hoax, they set up negative expectations about the rest of the campaign. Things went from bad to worse with the next circle, lust. The blatantly sexist contest at ComicCon, the biggest comic-book and gaming convention in the country, outraged female gamers—a large portion of the market—who already felt alienated and ignored by the gaming industry. The marketers apologized, learned from their mistakes, and tried for a somewhat more intellectual—though still edgy—approach. Phil Marineau, the senior product manager for the game, said, "[the contest] was a great eye-opener for us, and we're glad it happened early on, so we could learn from it." In the end, the campaign was both praised and criticized within the marketing industry.[9]

From this overview of the promotional mix, we now turn to discussions of each of its elements. The following sections detail the major components of advertising, sales promotion, personal selling, and public relations.

Advertising

Consumers receive from 4,000 to 5,000 marketing messages each day, many of them in the form of advertising.[10] Advertising is the most visible form of nonpersonal promotion—and the most effective for many firms. **Advertising** refers to paid nonpersonal communication usually targeted at large numbers of potential buyers. Although U.S. citizens often think of advertising as a typically American function, it is a global activity. Procter & Gamble leads the list of global advertisers, with measured media spending of $9.73 billion. The firm devotes two-thirds of its total advertising budget to international markets. Unilever, P&G's European competitor and the world's second largest global advertiser, recently allocated 86 percent of its advertising budget to non-U.S. markets. These two firms, along with other top global advertisers such as L'Oreal, Colgate-Palmolive, The Coca-Cola Company, and PepsiCo, aimed more than 10 percent of their spending at China, which accounts for 20 percent of the world's population.[11]

Advertising expenditures vary among industries, companies, and media. The top five categories for global advertisers are personal care, automotive, food, pharmaceuticals, and entertainment. But in the United States, pharmaceuticals take top honors, followed by entertainment, automotive, food, and personal care. Because advertising expenditures are so great, and because consumers around the world are bombarded with messages, advertisers need to be increasingly creative and efficient at attracting consumer's attention.[12]

Types of Advertising

The two basic types of ads are product and institutional advertisements. **Product advertising** consists of messages designed to sell a particular good or service. Advertisements for Nantucket Nectars juices, iPods, and Capital One credit cards are examples of product advertising. **Institutional advertising** involves messages that promote concepts, ideas, philosophies, or goodwill for industries, companies, organizations, or government entities. Each year, the Juvenile Diabetes Research Foundation promotes its "Walk for the Cure" fund-raising event, and your college may place advertisements in local papers or news shows to promote its activities. As the "Hit & Miss" feature describes, Heritage Oaks Bank's "Expect Success" campaign is an example of institutional advertising.

A form of institutional advertising that is growing in importance, **cause advertising**, promotes a specific viewpoint on a public issue as a way to influence public opinion and the

advertising paid nonpersonal communication usually targeted at large numbers of potential buyers.

product advertising consists of messages designed to sell a particular good or service.

institutional advertising involves messages that promote concepts, ideas, philosophies, or goodwill for industries, companies, organizations, or government entities.

cause advertising form of institutional advertising that promotes a specific viewpoint on a public issue as a way to influence public opinion and the legislative process.

Heritage Oaks: "Expect Success"

Heritage Oaks Bank is a community bank serving San Luís Obispo County on California's Central Coast. The bank recently launched a new and different advertising campaign. Called "Expect Success," the campaign highlights clients of the bank who have established personal and professional presences in the community.

The campaign takes the form of testimonials, giving the clients the opportunity to speak in their own words about their role models, the goals they have set for themselves, their favorite community moments, a saying they live by, and why Heritage Oaks Bank is their bank of choice. The bank advertises "Expect Success" in print and on television, with one-on-one interview testimonials available on its Web site. The campaign highlights a law firm partner, a furniture store owner, two winery owners, and a high-school sports coach, among others.

One example is the Meathead Movers. Aaron and Evan Steed started the business while they were teenagers. They began moving furniture for friends and neighbors after school, when they didn't have sports practice. They charged their customers whatever the customers wanted to pay for the work. Eventually the business grew with the help of Heritage Oaks Bank. "We work with Heritage Oaks Bank because in the recent difficult lending conditions they were able to finance a major project when no one else would," explain the entrepreneurs. "They believed in us, and now our storage facility has shattered industry fill-rate records and expectations." Mitch Massey, the bank's senior vice president for marketing, says, "I have always felt that the best way to tell our company's story is to have those who have grown their businesses, with our bank's involvement, share their success story."

Questions for Critical Thinking

1. What message does Heritage Oaks Bank's "Expect Success" campaign promote?
2. Imagine you are the marketing director for an institution such as a bank or a hospital. What message do you want to get across? How and where would you communicate it?

Sources: Company Web site, http://www.heritageoaksbank.com, accessed April 14, 2011; "Heritage Oaks Bank Kicks Off 'Expect Success' Ad Campaign," *slo-business. com,* January 19, 2010, http://www.slo-business.com; "Heritage Oaks Bank," *Bloomberg Businessweek,* n.d., http://investing.businessweek.com.

---

legislative process about issues such as literacy, hunger and poverty, and alternative energy sources. Both not-for-profit organizations and businesses use cause advertising, sometimes called *advocacy advertising.* As part of Avon's corporate responsibility, the Avon Foundation promotes its Speak Out Against Domestic Violence program with celebrity endorsements from Reese Witherspoon in its advertising.[13]

The Bill and Melinda Gates Foundation is a not-for-profit organization dedicated to raising public awareness and generating legislation and other efforts in the fight against poverty, lack of education, and disease. Funded through grants from the Gates fund and investment guru Warren Buffett, the foundation operates in all 50 states, the District of Columbia, and more than 100 countries. Through well-publicized grants of $1.37 billion to the United Negro College fund for its Millennium Scholars Program and tours abroad to personally oversee vaccination programs, the Gates fund generates interest in their causes. For their efforts they received a recent *Time* Person of the Year award.[14]

Advertising and the Product Life Cycle

Both product and institutional advertising fall into one of three categories based on whether the ads are intended to inform, persuade, or remind. A firm uses *informative advertising* to build initial demand for a product in the introductory phase of the product life cycle. Highly publicized new-product entries attract the interest of potential buyers who seek information about the advantages of the new products over existing ones, warranties provided, prices, and places that offer the new products. Ads for new cell phones boast of new features, colors, designs, and pricing options to attract new customers.

Product advertising consists of messages designed to sell a particular good or service.

Persuasive advertising attempts to improve the competitive status of a product, institution, or concept, usually in the growth and maturity stages of the product life cycle. One of the most popular types of persuasive product advertising, *comparative advertising*, compares products directly with their competitors—either by name or by inference. Tylenol advertisements mention the possible stomach problems that the generic drug aspirin could cause, stating that its pain reliever does not irritate the stomach. But advertisers need to be careful when they name competing brands in comparison ads because they might leave themselves open to controversy or even legal action by competitors. Notice that Tylenol does not mention a specific aspirin brand in its promotions.

Reminder-oriented advertising often appears in the late maturity or decline stages of the product life cycle to maintain awareness of the importance and usefulness of a product, concept, or institution. Triscuits have been around for a long time, but Nabisco attempts to mobilize sales with up-to-date advertising that appeals to health and fitness–conscious consumers. The advertising mentions its new no-trans-fat formulations.

Advertising Media

Marketers must choose how to allocate their advertising budgets among various media. All media offer advantages and disadvantages. Cost is an important consideration in media selection, but marketers must also choose the media best suited for communicating their message. As Figure 13.2 indicates, the three leading media outlets for advertising are television, newspapers, and magazines. However, Internet advertising is growing fast. Consumers now receive ads when they download news and other information to their hand-held wireless devices.

Advertising executives agree that firms need to rethink traditional ad campaigns to incorporate new media as well as updated uses of traditional media. Google is looking for ways to combine the targeting capabilities of Internet advertising and the richness of the television medium. Working with television manufacturer Sony, Google launched Google TV, which allows viewers to turn their sets into smart TVs—for downloading apps, browsing the entire Web, searching every cable and satellite channel, and more. Users can create a homepage for their TVs. Working with Logitech, Google now offers the capability for viewers to use their phone as a remote control.[15] The project has advanced to the point where Google is now offering the capability to search and record programs from the Dish Network Corp. Google is far from alone in the effort to bring the television and the Web together, however. It faces stiff competition from Microsoft and Apple, among others.[16]

Television Television is still one of America's leading national advertising media. Television advertising can be classified as network, national, local, and cable ads. The four major national networks—ABC, CBS, NBC, and Fox—along with the CW, broadcast almost one-fifth of all television ads. Despite a decline in audience share and growing competition from cable, network television remains the easiest way for advertisers to reach large numbers of viewers—10 million to 20 million with a single commercial. Automakers, fast-food restaurants, and food manufacturers are heavy users of network TV advertising.

About 58 percent of U.S. households with TVs now subscribe to cable, drawn to the more than 800 channels available through cable

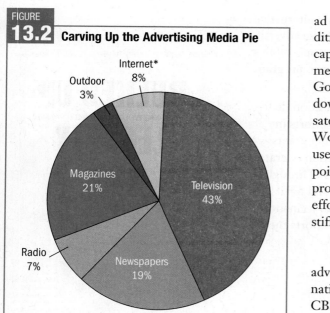

FIGURE 13.2 Carving Up the Advertising Media Pie

Internet* 8%
Outdoor 3%
Magazines 21%
Television 43%
Radio 7%
Newspapers 19%

Note: Percentages do not total to 100% due to rounding. Direct mail was not measured in these data.

*11 percent of all online ad spending is directed to social networking sites.

Sources: "Statistics: Social Networks Will Receive 11% of Online Ad Spending in 2011," *Wealthvest,* March 19, 2011, http://www.wealthvest .com; data from "100 Leading National Advertisers Index," *Advertising Age,* accessed April 7, 2011, http://adage.com.

or satellite services. But the cable and satellite networks are facing new competition. One survey indicates that 60 percent of American homes have one or more videogame consoles. People are using the consoles to download apps and video-on-demand offerings. And a small but growing number of viewers are discontinuing their cable service and opting for online services such as Netflix, Hulu, Apple's iTunes, and the networks' own Web sites. One recent survey found that 24 percent of the total U.S. population now watches at least some TV programming online. People still prefer free, advertising-supported downloads, although online network advertising made up only 2.5 percent of the yearly $62 billion in advertising revenues. However, the number of homes with digital video recorders (DVRs) and high-definition (HD) televisions is increasing steadily. Recent research suggests that even people who can use their DVRs to skip TV ads don't always do so. According to the Nielsen Company, many DVR users still watch shows at their scheduled times, when they must watch the ads, and even those who record shows for later viewing watch almost half the ads they could skip. With more people watching playbacks of their favorite shows, the networks' ratings—and commercial watching—increase too.[17]

Although—or perhaps because—television reaches the greatest number of consumers at once, it is the most expensive advertising medium. The Super Bowl is widely known for its hefty advertising price tag. Firms such as PepsiCo, GM, Volkswagen, Hyundai, and Teleflora paid as much as $3 million for a 30-second spot during one recent game. But the most expensive TV commercial of all time—so far—was the $6.5 million that Honda paid for an ad about its Accord.[18] Marketers want to be certain that their commercials reach the greatest number of viewers. Because of the high cost, advertisers may demand guarantees of audience size and receive compensation if a show fails to deliver the promised number of viewers.

Newspapers Daily and weekly newspapers continue to dominate local advertising. Marketers can easily tailor newspaper advertising for local tastes and preferences. Advertisers can also coordinate advertisements with other promotional efforts such as discount coupons from supermarkets and one-day sales at department stores. A disadvantage comes from the relatively short life span; people usually discard their newspapers soon after reading. Retailers and automobile dealers rank first among newspaper advertisers. Most newspapers now maintain Web sites, some of which offer separate material and features, to complement their print editions.

Radio Despite the proliferation of other media, the average U.S. household owns five radios—including those in cars—a market penetration that makes radio an important advertising medium. Advertisers like the captive audience of listeners as they commute to and from work. As a result, morning and evening drive-time shows command top ad rates. In major markets, many stations serve different demographic groups with targeted programming. Internet radio programming also offers opportunities for yet more focused targeting.

Satellite stations offer great potential for advertisers. Sirius and XM both offer commercial-free music, with advertising on news and talk shows. A recent study predicts that Internet radio will have 185 million listeners by 2020, although 250 million will still listen to AM/FM (sometimes referred to as terrestrial) radio. Internet advertising revenues reached $260 million in a year, with an additional $28 million from podcasting.[19] Google recently updated its AdWords application to include ads that can be broadcast by traditional radio stations. An advertiser fills out a questionnaire indicating the target audience and where and how often the ad should be run. The advertiser pays a fee each time the ad is aired and can have the ad tracked to find the best possible time to reach the desired audience.[20]

Magazines Magazines include consumer publications and business trade journals. *Time, Reader's Digest,* and *Sports Illustrated* are consumer magazines, whereas *Advertising Age* and *Oil & Gas Journal* fall into the trade category.

Magazines may customize their publications and target advertising messages to different regions of the country. One method places local advertising in regional editions of the magazines. Other magazines attach wraparounds—half-size covers on top of full-size covers—to highlight articles inside that relate to particular areas; different wraparounds appear in different parts of the country.

Magazines are a natural choice for targeted advertising. Media buyers study demographics of subscribers and select magazines that attract the desired readers. American Express advertises in *Fortune* and *Forbes* to reach businesspeople, while PacSun clothes and Clearasil skin medications are advertised in *teenVogue*.

Direct Mail The average U.S. household receives about 550 pieces of direct mail each year, including 100 catalogs. The huge growth in the variety of direct-mail offerings combined with the convenience they offer today's busy, time-pressed shoppers has made direct-mail advertising a multibillion-dollar business. Even consumers who like to shop online often page through a catalog before placing an online order. Although direct mail is expensive per person, a small business can afford a limited direct-mail campaign but not a television or radio ad. For businesses with a small advertising budget, a carefully targeted direct-mail effort can be highly effective. E-mail is a low-cost form of direct marketing. Marketers can target the most interested Internet users by offering Web site visitors an option to register to receive e-mail. Companies like Amazon.com, Spring Hill Nurseries, and Abercrombie & Fitch routinely send e-mails to regular customers.

Address lists are at the heart of direct-mail advertising. Using data-mining techniques to segment markets, direct-mail marketers create profiles that show the traits of consumers who are likely to buy their products or donate to their organizations. Catalog retailers sometimes experiment by sending direct-mail pieces randomly to people who subscribe to particular magazines. Next, they analyze the orders received from the mailings and develop profiles of purchasers. Finally, they rent lists of additional subscriber names that match the profiles they have developed.

Studies have shown that most U.S. consumers are annoyed by the amount of so-called "junk mail" they receive every day, including catalogs, advertising postcards, and flyers. Among Internet users, a major pet peeve is *spam*, or junk e-mail. Many states have outlawed such practices as sending e-mail promotions without legitimate return addresses, although it is difficult to track down and catch offenders.

The Direct Marketing Association (DMA; www.the-dma.org) helps marketers combat negative attitudes by offering its members guidelines on ethical business practices. The DMA also provides consumer information at its Web site, as well as services that enable consumers to opt out of receiving unsolicited offers. In addition, Federal Trade Commission regulations have taken effect for direct mail in certain industries. With the passage of the CARD Act of 2009, credit card issuers must follow stricter regulations in their direct mail practices. Unsolicited, preapproved applications that are sent to consumers must be accompanied by a prominent notice explaining how to get off the issuer's mailing list. Some issuers initially cut back on the number of mailings they sent, but recent figures show an increase in offers from 575 million to 1.4 billion, indicating an upswing in confidence.[21]

Outdoor Advertising In one year, outdoor advertising accounted for $6.1 billion in advertising revenues.[22] The majority of spending on outdoor advertising is for billboards, but spending for other types of outdoor advertising, such as signs in transit stations, stores, airports, and sports stadiums, is growing fast. Advertisers are exploring new forms of outdoor media, many of which involve technology: computerized paintings, video billboards, "trivision" that displays three revolving images on a single billboard, and moving billboards mounted on trucks. Other innovations include ads displayed on the Goodyear blimp, using an electronic system that offers animation and video.

Chicago's North Park University launched an outdoor advertising campaign featuring current students. The advertising invited viewers to a Web site where those students discussed how their education at North Park affected their lives. Digital advertising will soon be available on taxi tops. With almost 13,000 yellow medallion taxis in New York City alone, the potential visibility is enormous. Clear Channel Outdoor Advertising offers its Digital Outdoor Networks, a complete line of electronic advertising.[23] CBS Outdoor recently unveiled the first-ever high-definition, 3D projection display in New York City's Grand Central Station. And The Coca-Cola Company inaugurated its Digital Network, 28 electronic billboards that it owns in 27 locations. (The company leases the space from outdoor advertising firms such as Clear Channel Outdoor and Boardworks but owns the boards themselves.) Its first advertising on the billboards was a promotion of its special-edition Daytona 500 Coke cans. The Outdoor Advertising Association of America predicts that several hundred digital billboards will be introduced each year, with a total of 1,800 so far.[24] Outdoor advertising suffers from several disadvantages, however. The medium requires brief messages, and billboards are often attacked by preservation and conservation groups.

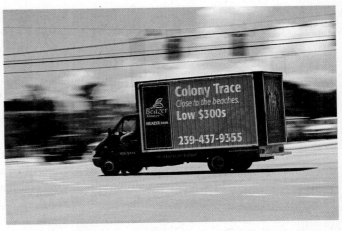

Naples Daily News

Advertisers are exploring new forms of outdoor media, many of which involve technology: computerized paintings, video billboards, "trivision" that displays three revolving images on a single billboard, and moving billboards mounted on trucks.

Internet Advertising Although online and interactive advertising revenues have already hit $21.7 billion annually—surpassing print media—they are expected to reach $42.5 billion by 2015. The number of smartphones and tablets is affecting this increase, as is the rapid multiplication of social media. "What we're seeing in terms of media share shifts and transformation is really unprecedented," observes Neal Polachek, president of BIA/Kelsey.[25]

Online and interactive media have already changed the nature of advertising. Starting with simple banner ads, Internet advertising has become much more complex and sophisticated. Miniature television screen images, called *widgets* or *gadgets*, can carry marketing messages only a few inches high on a Web site, blog, or desktop display. And they contain embedded links to their home sites. Online advertising can take other forms as well. Ford Motor Company's Fiesta subcompact was available in Europe but not in the United States. To educate the American public about the Fiesta, soon to become available, the company launched its Fiesta Movement by giving 100 consumers European Fiestas for six months and having them use the cars to complete various missions each month. (Ford paid for the gas.) Some people used the cars for charitable work, such as delivering Meals On Wheels. Others used them for real adventures or even for actually eloping. As part of the project, the consumers documented their missions and posted the results on YouTube, Flickr, Facebook, and Twitter. In the next phase of the Fiesta Movement, consumers will compete for cash prizes and the chance to win a Fiesta of their own. Google, which owns YouTube, predicts that the Web site will soon be in the black for the first time. Advertising on YouTube was nearly sold out. Eric Schmidt, Google's CEO, predicted that more advertisers would use YouTube in their ad campaigns. He said that YouTube "has gone from being a nice to have to an essential part of the media mix of any display campaign."[26]

Another example is *viral advertising*, which creates a message that is novel or entertaining enough for consumers to forward it to others, spreading it like a virus. The great advantage is that spreading the world online, which often relies on social networking sites like Facebook, YouTube, and Twitter, costs the advertiser nothing. While viral marketing can be risky, the best campaigns are edgy or funny. Among the most popular viral videos of late are Puma's "Hardchorus," Old Spice's "Smell Like a Man," and Levis' "The Guy Who Walks Across America." Salesforce.com recently decided to use YouTube as its video delivery platform because marketing surveys revealed that the site was "one of the most trusted" by users.[27]

Some viral campaigns rely on personal word-of-mouth promotions, and when ordinary consumers are recruited as "brand ambassadors" or "buzz agents" for pay, questions can arise about ethics. One company, BzzAgent, gives its members products instead of money. But these ambassadors are not required to tell others that they're being paid or receiving free gifts to discuss products, which some view as problematic.[28]

Sponsorship One of the hottest trends in promotion offers marketers the ability to integrate several elements of the promotional mix. <u>**Sponsorship**</u> involves providing funds for a sporting or cultural event in exchange for a direct association with the event. Sports sponsorships attract two-thirds of total sponsorship dollars in the United States alone. Entertainment, festivals, causes, and the arts divide up the remaining third of sponsorship dollars.

NASCAR, the biggest spectator sport in the United States, thrives on sponsorships. Sponsorships can run in the tens of millions. Hendricks Motorsports, based in North Carolina, is the wealthiest and most successful NASCAR team to date, with more than $115 million in sponsorships from firms such as PepsiCo, DuPont, Lowes, and GoDaddy.[29] Firms may also sponsor charitable or other not-for-profit awards or events. In conjunction with sports network ESPN, Gatorade sponsors its High School Athlete of the Year award, presented to the top male and female high school athletes who "strive for their best on and off the field."

Sponsors benefit in two major ways: exposure to the event's audience and association with the image of the activity. If a celebrity is involved, sponsors usually earn the right to use his or her name along with the name of the event in advertisements. They can set up signs at the event, offer sales promotions, and the like. Sponsorships play an important role in relationship marketing, bringing together the event, its participants, and the sponsoring firms.

Other Media Options As consumers filter out familiar advertising messages, marketers look for novel ways to catch their attention. In addition to the major media, firms promote through many other vehicles such as infomercials and specialized media. <u>**Infomercials**</u> are a form of broadcast direct marketing, also called *direct-response television (DRTV)*. These 30-minute programs resemble regular television programs but are devoted to selling goods or services such as exercise equipment, skin-care products, or kitchenware. The long format allows an advertiser to thoroughly present product benefits, increase awareness, and make an impact on consumers. Advertisers also receive immediate responses in the form of sales or inquiries because most infomercials feature toll-free phone numbers. Infomercial stars may become celebrities in their own right, attracting more customers wherever they go. The most effective infomercials tend to be for auto-care products, beauty and personal-care items, investing and business opportunities, collectibles, fitness and self-improvement products, and housewares and electronics.[30]

Advertisers use just about any medium they can find. They place messages on New York City MetroCard transit cards and toll receipts on the Massachusetts Turnpike. A more recent development is the use of ATMs for advertising. Some ATMs can play 15-second commercials on their screens, and many can print advertising messages on receipts. An ATM screen has a captive audience because the user must watch the screen to complete a transaction. Directory advertising includes the familiar Yellow Pages listings in telephone books and thousands of other types of directories, most presenting business-related promotions. Besides local and regional directories, publishers also have produced special printed and online versions of the Yellow Pages that target ethnic groups.

Sales Promotion

Traditionally viewed as a supplement to a firm's sales or advertising efforts, sales promotion has emerged as an integral part of the promotional mix. Promotion now accounts for more than half as many marketing dollars as are spent on advertising, and promotion spending is rising faster than ad spending. **Sales promotion** consists of forms of promotion such as coupons, product samples, and rebates that support advertising and personal selling.

Both retailers and manufacturers use sales promotions to offer consumers extra incentives to buy. Beyond the short-term advantage of increased sales, sales promotions can also help marketers build brand equity and enhance customer relationships. Examples include samples, coupons, contests, displays, trade shows, and dealer incentives.

Consumer-Oriented Promotions

The goal of a consumer-oriented sales promotion is to get new and existing customers to try or buy products. In addition, marketers want to encourage repeat purchases by rewarding current users, increase sales of complimentary products, and boost impulse purchases. Figure 13.3 shows how marketers allocate their consumer-oriented spending among the categories of promotions.

Promotions can also popularize an idea, such as the growing awareness of how much pollution plastic shopping bags contribute to the environment. The "Going Green" feature discusses the growing trend of banning plastic shopping bags.

Premiums, Coupons, Rebates, and Samples
Nearly six of every ten sales promotion dollars are spent on *premiums*—items given free or at a reduced price with the purchase of another product. Cosmetics companies such as Clinique offer sample kits with purchases of their products. Fast-food restaurants are also big users of premiums. McDonald's and Burger King include a toy with every children's meal—the toys often tie in with new movies or popular cartoon shows. In general, marketers choose premiums that are likely to get consumers thinking about and caring about the brand and the product. People who purchase health foods at a grocery store may find an offer for a free personal training session at a local health club printed on the back of their sales receipt.

Customers redeem *coupons* for small price discounts when they purchase the promoted products. Such offers may persuade a customer to try a new or different product. Some large supermarket

Assessment Check ✔

1. What are the two basic types of advertising? Into what three categories do they fall?
2. What is the leading advertising medium in the United States?
3. In what two major ways do firms benefit from sponsorship?

sales promotion consists of forms of promotion such as coupons, product samples, and rebates that support advertising and personal selling.

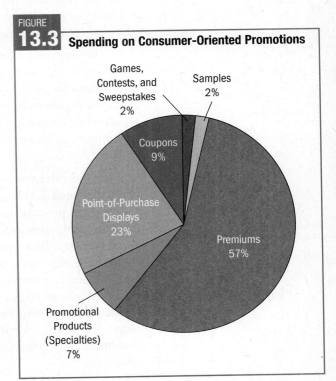

FIGURE 13.3 Spending on Consumer-Oriented Promotions

- Games, Contests, and Sweepstakes 2%
- Samples 2%
- Coupons 9%
- Point-of-Purchase Displays 23%
- Premiums 57%
- Promotional Products (Specialties) 7%

Source: Data from Kathleen M. Joyce, "Higher Gear," Promo Magazine, http://promomagazine.com, accessed April 26, 2010.

How Much Would You Pay for a Plastic Shopping Bag?

The U.S. Environmental Protection Agency estimates that almost 4 billion tons of plastics waste—in the form of bags, sacks, and wrapping—were generated in one year. Made from foreign oil, the plastic can take 1,000 years to degrade. Only about 1 percent is ever recycled.

A growing number of people want to reduce these statistics. For instance, San Francisco enacted an outright ban on plastic bags. New York City started requiring certain retailers to accept plastic bags for recycling. Los Angeles also banned plastic bags. In a first, Washington, D.C., imposed a tax of 5 cents on every plastic bag for supermarket customers. The city plans to use the revenue to restore a polluted local river.

But such laws have not always met with approval. In eco-friendly Seattle, voters overturned a law charging 20 cents per plastic bag, perhaps because they were already recycling and reusing the bags. The mayor of Washington, D.C., hopes that the tax on plastic bags will encourage shoppers to change their habits so they won't have to pay the tax at all.

The retailing giant Walmart already sells reusable bags for 50 cents. In three of its California stores, it is introducing the option of a 15 cent reusable bag that is expected to survive 75 shopping trips. The bag can then be recycled in existing bins in the stores.

Questions for Critical Thinking

1. Can stores that provide eco-friendly shopping bags or other ways to reduce the polluting effects of plastic reap promotional benefits from their efforts? How can cities that ban or tax plastic bags promote their actions?

2. What other ways can you think of to promote the idea of recycling plastic bags or reducing their use?

Sources: "NYCWasteLe$$," Plastic Bag Recycling, http://www.nyc.gov, accessed June 1, 2011; Dave Gram, "Vt. Plastic Bag Tax Proposal Seen Coming Too Late," *Rutland Herald,* April 16, 2010, http:// http://www.rutlandherald.com; Melissa Eddy, "Plastic Bag Ban: Would You Pay 5 Cents for a Bag?" *Huffington Post,* February 22, 2010, http://www.huffing-tonpost.com; Steve Painter, "3 Wal-Marts Testing Purge of Plastic Bags," *Arkansas Democrat-Gazette,* January 24, 2010, http://ww6.lexisnexis.com; Stephen Messenger, "Washington D.C.'s Plastic Bag Tax Takes Effect This Week," *TreeHugger.com,* January 3, 2010, http://www.treehugger.com.

chains double the face value of manufacturers' coupons. Coupons have the disadvantage of focusing customers on price rather than brand loyalty. While some consumers complain that clipping or printing out coupons is too time consuming, others relish the savings, particularly when money is tight and prices seem to be high.

American consumers' use of coupons increased 27 percent in a year, using 3.3 billion coupons to redeem $3.5 billion. Internet coupon use skyrocketed a whopping 360 percent. Marketers issued 367 billion coupons with a face value averaging $1.44, but shortened the expiration periods by some 10 percent. Some analysts predict that the growing use of paperless mobile coupons, which consumers can access on their Web-enabled cellphones while shopping and pioneered by such retailers as Target, could soon make clippable or even printed-out coupons obsolete.[31]

Rebates offer cash back to consumers who mail in required proofs of purchase. Rebates help packaged-goods manufacturers increase purchase rates, promote multiple purchases, and reward product users. Other types of companies also offer rebates, especially for electronics, computers and their accessories, and automobiles. Processing rebates gives marketers a way to collect data about their customers, but many shoppers find it inconvenient to collect the required receipts, forms, and UPC codes and then wait several weeks for their refund. Services such as RebateRemedy can cut the waiting time to days instead of weeks but take a 20 to 30 percent cut of the rebate, plus a processing fee. Some stores and manufacturers are phasing out mail-in rebates. After a brief period of testing mail-in rebates on some cell phones, Verizon found that customers preferred and expected instant online discounts, so the company has ended its mail-in rebate program on the Palm Pre and the Pixi Plus.[32]

A *sample* is a gift of a product distributed by mail, door to door, in a demonstration, or inside packages of another product. On any given day you might receive a sample moisturizer, a bar of soap, or a packet of laundry detergent. Three of every four consumers who receive samples will try them.

Games, Contests, and Sweepstakes Contests, sweepstakes, and games offer cash, merchandise, or travel as prizes to participating winners. Firms often sponsor these activities to introduce new goods and services and to attract additional customers. Games and contests require entrants to solve problems or write essays and sometimes provide proof of purchase. Sweepstakes choose winners by chance and require no product purchase. Consumers typically prefer them because games and contests require more effort. Companies like sweepstakes, too, because they are inexpensive to run and determine the number of winners from the beginning. With games and contests, the company cannot predict the number of people who will correctly complete a puzzle or gather the right number of symbols from scratch-off cards. Sweepstakes, games, and contests can reinforce a company's image and advertising message, but consumer attention may focus on the promotion rather than the product.

In recent years, court rulings and legal restrictions have limited the use of games and contests. Companies must proceed carefully in advertising their contests and games and the prizes they award. Marketers must indicate the chances of winning and avoid false promises such as implying that a person has already won.

Specialty Advertising Do you have any pens, T-shirts, or refrigerator magnets imprinted with a business name that you received for free? These offers are examples of <u>**specialty advertising**</u> or *advertising specialties*. This type of sales promotion involves the gift of useful merchandise carrying the name, logo, or slogan of a profit-seeking business or a not-for-profit organization. Because those products are useful and sometimes personalized with recipients' names, people tend to keep and use them, giving advertisers repeated exposure. Originally designed to identify and create goodwill for advertisers, advertising specialties now generate sales leads and develop traffic for stores and trade show exhibitors. Like premiums, these promotions should reinforce the brand's image and its relationship with the recipient.

specialty advertising promotional items that prominently display a firm's name, logo, or business slogan.

Trade-Oriented Promotions

Sales promotion techniques can also contribute to campaigns directed to retailers and wholesalers. <u>**Trade promotion**</u> is sales promotion geared to marketing intermediaries rather than to consumers. Marketers use trade promotion to encourage retailers to stock new products, continue carrying existing ones, and promote both new and existing products effectively to consumers. Successful trade promotions offer financial incentives. They require careful timing, attention to costs, and easy implementation for intermediaries. These promotions should bring quick results and improve retail sales. Major trade promotions include point-of-purchase advertising and trade shows.

trade promotion sales promotion geared to marketing intermediaries rather than to final consumers.

<u>**Point-of-purchase (POP) advertising**</u> consists of displays or demonstrations that promote products when and where consumers buy them, such as in retail stores. When the Swiffer floor cleaner was being introduced, Procter & Gamble used in-store demonstrations to show consumers how it worked. Marketing research has shown that consumers are more likely to purchase certain products when such displays are present. Sunscreen, painting supplies, and snacks are typically displayed this way. A high-tech version of POP advertising is digital advertising consoles mounted on grocery carts. With impulse purchases making up 53 percent of total buying, POP has already begun to evolve into what is being called "mobile advertising." Although privacy is still an issue, more and more Web sites and other

point-of-purchase (POP) advertising displays or demonstrations that promote products when and where consumers buy them, such as in retail stores.

BusinessEtiquette

How to Negotiate in a Difficult Economy

Despite the arrival of electronic media, many businesses still rely on personal selling. Even when the economy is weak, you can still find ways to negotiate effectively. Here are five tips for successful negotiation in good and difficult economic times:

1 *Be a good listener.* This is always a good idea. Like good detectives, good negotiators ask questions—and then listen as the other negotiator or prospect speaks. You'll establish trust—and learn whether your proposal will meet your prospect's needs.

2 *Be prepared.* Before you negotiate, do as much research as possible on your prospect, the prospect's business, what effect the economy has on his or her industry, and so on. Preparation is the only part of negotiation that is completely within your control.

3 *Be patient.* Americans seem always to be in a hurry, whereas in Asia, South America, or the Middle East, people realize that if you rush, you may make mistakes. Taking your time may also give you a psychological advantage over the other negotiator.

4 *Decide what is important to you.* What can you absolutely not do without? What would you be willing to give up, if you must compromise?

5 *Keep your options open.* If you feel you can't make a satisfactory agreement even with the best of intentions, leave yourself the option of walking away.

Sources: Ed Brodow, "Ten Tips for Negotiating in 2010," Ed Brodow Seminars, http://www.brodow.com, accessed June 7, 2011; Ken Dooley, "6 Tips for Negotiating in a Tough Economy," *BusinessBrief*, March 9, 2010, http://www.businessbrief.com; Ken Dooley, "The Keys to Successful Negotiation," *BusinessBrief*, February 16, 2010, http://www.businessbrief.com.

services are now able to locate Internet users, and location-based mobile spending is expected to increase from a current $34 million to $4 billion in 2015. About 25 percent of the 500 million Facebook members open the site via mobile electronic devices. Location-based advertising will not be directed primarily to stationary computers but to smart phones, iPads, Kindles, game consoles, and automobiles.[33]

Manufacturers and other sellers often exhibit at *trade shows* to promote goods or services to members of their distribution channels. These shows are often organized by industry trade associations. Each year, thousands of trade shows attract millions of exhibitors and hundreds of millions of attendees. Such shows are particularly important in fast-changing industries like those for computers, toys, furniture, and fashions. The annual Consumer Electronics Show, which is held in Las Vegas and attracts more than 100,000 visitors, is the nation's largest. But shows in the medical and healthcare, RV and camping, and even woodworking machinery fields remain strong. These shows are especially effective for introducing new products and generating sales leads.

Personal Selling

Many companies consider personal selling—a person-to-person promotional presentation to a potential buyer—the key to marketing effectiveness. Unless a seller matches a firm's goods or services to the needs of a particular client or customer, none of the firm's other activities produces any benefits. Today, sales and sales-related jobs employ about 16 million U.S. workers.[34] Businesses often spend five to ten times as much on personal selling as on advertising. Given the significant cost of hiring, training, benefits, and salaries, businesses are very concerned with the effectiveness of their sales personnel. One of their continuing concerns is with the way representatives communicate with others. The "Business Etiquette" feature discusses how to negotiate during difficult economic times.

How do marketers decide whether to make personal selling the primary component of their firm's marketing mix? In general, firms are likely to emphasize personal selling rather than advertising or sales promotion under four conditions:

1. Customers are relatively few in number and geographically concentrated.

2. The product is technically complex, involves trade-ins, or requires special handling.

3. The product carries a relatively high price.

4. It moves through direct-distribution channels.

Selling luxury items such as the Porsche 918 Spyder hybrid ($630,000) or a John Lennon-themed Steinway piano ($90,000) would require a personal touch. Then there's the $20,000 home theater device offered by California-based Prima Cinema, which automatically sends Hollywood films to customers' home systems the same day they premiere. Installation, including instructions on how to use the system, would require personal selling.[35]

The sales functions of most companies are experiencing rapid change. Today's salespeople are more concerned with establishing long-term buyer–seller relationships and acting as consultants to their customers than in the past. In the aftermath of the recession, salespeople face a new challenge—consumers who haggle over prices, even on retail items. One survey found that 88 percent of those questioned had haggled over at least one price in the preceding six months. Unlike in the Great Depression of the 1930s, the last time Americans engaged in serious amounts of haggling, today's consumers have advantages that would astound their predecessors. Anyone with a Web-enabled cell phone can Google competing prices of merchandise while standing in front of it in a retail store. Many have learned to bargain via Web sites such as eBay or have used Priceline to negotiate deals on travel. The survey found that hagglers had better than a 75 percent success rate in making deals on clothing, appliances, and jewelry. Consumers who negotiated medical bills were successful 58 percent of the time.[36]

Personal selling can occur in several environments, each of which can involve business-to-business or business-to-consumer selling. Sales representatives who make sales calls on prospective customers at their businesses are involved in *field selling*. Companies that sell major industrial equipment typically rely heavily on field selling. *Over-the-counter selling* describes sales activities in retailing and some wholesale locations, where customers visit the seller's facility to purchase items. *Telemarketing* sales representatives make their presentations over the phone. A later section reviews telemarketing in more detail.

Sales Tasks   All sales activities involve assisting customers in some manner. Although a salesperson's work can vary significantly from one company or situation to another, it usually includes a mix of three basic tasks: order processing, creative selling, and missionary selling.

Order Processing   Although both field selling and telemarketing involve this activity, order processing is most often related to retail and wholesale firms. The salesperson identifies customer needs, points out merchandise to meet them, and processes the order. Route sales personnel process orders for such consumer goods as bread, milk, soft drinks, and snack foods. They check each store's stock, report inventory needs to the store manager, and complete the sale. Most of these jobs include at least minor order-processing functions.

Creative Selling   Sales representatives for most business products and some consumer items perform creative selling, a persuasive type of promotional presentation. Creative selling promotes a good or service whose benefits are not readily apparent or whose purchase decision requires a close analysis of alternatives. Sales of intangible products such as insurance rely heavily on creative selling, but sales of tangible goods benefit as well.

order processing form of selling, mostly at the wholesale and retail levels, that involves identifying customer needs, pointing them out to customers, and completing orders.

creative selling persuasive type of promotional presentation.

Many retail salespeople just process orders, but many consumers are looking for more in the form of customer service, which is where creative selling comes in. Personal shoppers at Topshop—located in London and New York City—help customers create entire looks from three floors of clothing. They also offer customers refreshments and the option to ring up purchases at a special cash register without waiting in line.

Missionary Selling Sales work also includes an indirect form of selling in which the representative promotes goodwill for a company or provides technical or operational assistance to the customer; this practice is called **missionary selling**. Many businesses that sell technical equipment, such as Oracle and Fujitsu, provide systems specialists who act as consultants to customers. These salespeople work to solve problems and sometimes help their clients with questions not directly related to their employers' products. Other industries also use missionary selling techniques. Pharmaceutical company representatives—called *detailers*—visit physicians to describe the firm's latest offerings, although some firms are finding success with more subtle methods, including Web-based sales calls outside office hours. The pharmaceutical giant Pfizer recently cut back its sales force and has increasingly turned to electronic marketing. The company has found electronic detailing especially advantageous. With it, doctors can get the latest information on drugs when and where they choose. It also can be strictly controlled, and the company runs much less risk of its salespeople's being accused of marketing drugs for off-label uses—that is, for treating conditions other than those they were originally intended to help.[37] The actual sales, in any case, are handled through pharmacies, which fill the prescriptions.

Telemarketing **Telemarketing**, personal selling conducted by telephone, provides a firm's marketers with a high return on their expenditures, an immediate response, and an opportunity for personalized two-way conversation. Many firms use telemarketing because expense or other obstacles prevent salespeople from meeting many potential customers in person. Telemarketers can use databases to target prospects based on demographic data. Telemarketing takes two forms. A sales representative who calls you is practicing *outbound telemarketing*. On the other hand, *inbound telemarketing* occurs when you call a toll-free phone number to get product information or place an order.

Outbound telemarketers must abide by the Federal Trade Commission's 1996 Telemarketing Sales Rule. Telemarketers must disclose that they are selling something and on whose behalf they are calling before they make their presentations. The rule also limits calls to between 8 a.m. and 9 p.m., requires sellers to disclose details on exchange policies, and requires them to keep lists of people who do not want to receive calls. In some states, it is also against the law for telemarketers to leave messages on consumers' answering machines. Congress enacted another law in 2003 creating the National Do Not Call registry intended to help consumers block unwanted telemarketing calls. Consumers who want to be on the list must call a special number or visit a Web site to register. Telemarketers must stop calling registered numbers within 31 days or face stiff fines of up to $11,000 for each violation.[38] Charities, surveys, and political campaign calls are exempt from these restrictions. Businesses with which consumers already have a relationship, such as the bank where they have accounts or the dealership where they buy their cars, may conduct telemarketing calls under the guidelines of the Telemarketing Sales Rule.

The Sales Process The sales process typically follows the seven-step sequence shown in Figure 13.4: prospecting and qualifying, the approach, presentation, the demonstration, handling objections, closing, and the follow-up. Remember the importance of flexibility, though; a good salesperson is not afraid to vary the sales process based on a customer's responses and needs. The process of selling to a potential customer who is unfamiliar with a company's products differs from the process of serving a long-time customer.

Prospecting, Qualifying, and Approaching

At the prospecting stage, salespeople identify potential customers. They may seek leads for prospective sales from such sources as existing customers, friends and family, and business associates. The qualifying process identifies potential customers who have the financial ability and authority to buy.

Companies use different tactics to identify and qualify prospects. Some companies rely on business development teams, passing responses from direct mail along to their sales reps. Others believe in personal visits. Many firms are now using electronic social media, which cost little or nothing, to boost sales. Online newsletters, virtual trade shows, podcasts, Webinars, and blogs are good examples. Experts advice developing a clear strategy in order to be successful with social media.[39]

Successful salespeople make careful preparations, analyzing available data about a prospective customer's product lines and other pertinent information before making the initial contact. They realize the importance of a first impression in influencing a customer's future attitudes toward the selling company and its products.

Presentation and Demonstration

At the presentation stage, salespeople communicate promotional messages. They may describe the major features of their products, highlight the advantages, and cite examples of satisfied consumers. A demonstration helps reinforce the message that the salesperson has been communicating—a critical step in the sales process. Department-store shoppers can get a free makeover at the cosmetics counter. Anyone looking to buy a car will take it for a test drive before deciding whether to purchase it.

Some products are too large to transport to prospective buyers or require special installation to demonstrate. Using laptop computers, multimedia presentations, graphic programs like SmartDraw, Web conferences, and even podcasts, sales representatives can demonstrate these products for customers.[40] Others, such as services, are intangible. So a presentation including testimonials from satisfied customers or graphs illustrating results may be helpful.

Handling Objections

Some salespeople fear potential customers' objections because they view the questions as criticism. But a good salesperson can use objections as an opportunity to answer questions and explain how the product will benefit the customer. As a general rule, the key is to sell benefits, not features: How will this product help the customer?

Closing

The critical point in the sales process—the time at which the salesperson actually asks the prospect to buy—is the closing. If the presentation effectively matches

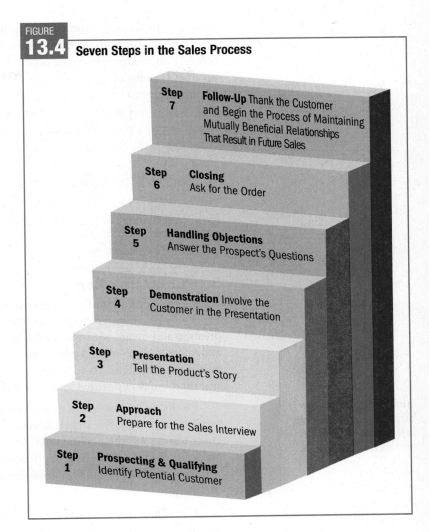

FIGURE 13.4 Seven Steps in the Sales Process

Step 7 Follow-Up Thank the Customer and Begin the Process of Maintaining Mutually Beneficial Relationships That Result in Future Sales

Step 6 Closing Ask for the Order

Step 5 Handling Objections Answer the Prospect's Questions

Step 4 Demonstration Involve the Customer in the Presentation

Step 3 Presentation Tell the Product's Story

Step 2 Approach Prepare for the Sales Interview

Step 1 Prospecting & Qualifying Identify Potential Customer product benefits to customer needs, the closing should be a natural conclusion. If there are more bumps in the process, the salesperson can try some different techniques, such as offering alternative products, offering a special incentive for purchase, or restating the product benefits. Closing the sale—and beginning a relationship in which the customer builds loyalty to the brand or product—is the ideal outcome of this interaction. But even if the sale is not made at this time, the salesperson should regard the interaction as the beginning of a potential relationship anyway. The prospect might very well become a customer in the future.

Follow-Up A salesperson's actions after the sale may determine whether the customer will make another purchase. Follow-up is an important part of building a long-lasting relationship. After closing, the salesperson should process the order efficiently. By calling soon after a purchase, the salesperson provides reassurance about the customer's decision to buy and creates an opportunity to correct any problems.

Public Relations A final element of the promotional mix, public relations (PR)—including publicity—supports advertising, personal selling, and sales promotion, usually by pursuing broader objectives. Through PR, companies attempt to improve their prestige and image with the public by distributing specific messages or ideas to target audiences. Cause-related promotional activities are often supported by public relations and publicity campaigns. In addition, PR helps a firm establish awareness of goods and services and then builds a positive image of them.

<u>Public relations</u> refers to an organization's communications and relationships with its various public audiences, such as customers, vendors, news media, employees, stockholders, the government, and the general public. Many of these communication efforts serve marketing purposes. Public relations is an efficient, indirect communications channel for promoting products. It can publicize products and help create and maintain a positive image of the company.

The public relations department links a firm with the media. It provides the media with news releases and video and audio clips, as well as holding news conferences to announce new products, the formation of strategic alliances, management changes, financial results, and similar developments. Publications issued by the department include newsletters, brochures, and reports.

Publicity The type of public relations that is tied most closely to promoting a company's products is **publicity**—nonpersonal stimulation of demand for a good, service, place, idea, event, person, or organization by unpaid placement of information in print or broadcast media. Press releases generate publicity, as does news coverage. Even criticism generates publicity, as in the case of the BP oil leak and the recent recalls of Johnson & Johnson's Tylenol products. Publicity can help save a struggling business. Fred Daley, owner of Fresh Fish Daley, faced the fact that he might have to close his New Hampshire business when state regulations governing the transportation of fish changed; he could not afford the upgrades to his van. When local news reported Daley's plight, his loyal customers came forward with donations; one man found an affordable van on eBay and helped Daley complete the purchase. "It's a story of goodwill," said Daley with gratitude.[41]

Not-for-profit organizations benefit from publicity when they receive coverage of events such as the Susan G. Komen Race for the Cure, which raises money for breast cancer research.[42] When a for-profit firm teams up with a not-for-profit firm in a fund-raising effort, the move usually generates good publicity for both organizations.

public relations organization's communications and relationships with its various public audiences.

publicity nonpersonal stimulation of demand for a good, service, place, idea, event, person, or organization by unpaid placement of information in print or broadcast media.

Assessment Check ☑

1. Why do retailers and manufacturers use sales promotions?

2. When does a firm use personal selling instead of nonpersonal selling?

3. How does public relations serve a marketing purpose?

Pushing and Pulling Strategies

pushing strategy personal selling to market an item to wholesalers and retailers in a company's distribution channels.

Marketers can choose between two general promotional strategies: a pushing strategy or a pulling strategy. A **pushing strategy** relies on personal selling to market an item to wholesalers and retailers in a company's distribution channels. So companies promote the product to members of the marketing channel, not to end users. Sales personnel explain to marketing intermediaries why they should carry particular merchandise, usually supported by offers of special discounts and promotional materials. Marketers also provide **cooperative advertising** allowances, in which they share the cost of local advertising of their firm's product or line with channel partners. All of these strategies are designed to motivate wholesalers and retailers to push the good or service to their own customers.

cooperative advertising allowances provided by marketers in which they share the cost of local advertising of their firm's product or product line with channel partners.

A **pulling strategy** attempts to promote a product by generating consumer demand for it, primarily through advertising and sales promotion appeals. Potential buyers will then request that their suppliers—retailers or local distributors—carry the product, thereby pulling it through the distribution channel. Dove used this strategy when it launched its new Men + Care line of men's personal-care products during a recent Super Bowl. The 30-second commercial, with its tagline "Be comfortable in your own skin," generated significant online response, with consumers searching such terms as "Super Bowl," "ad," and "men" to find retailers that stocked the products.[43]

pulling strategy promote a product by generating consumer demand for it, primarily through advertising and sales promotion appeals.

Most marketing situations require combinations of pushing and pulling strategies, although the primary emphasis can vary. Consumer products usually depend more heavily on pulling strategies than do B2B products, which favor pushing strategies.

Pricing Objectives in the Marketing Mix

price exchange value of a good or service.

Products offer utility, or want-satisfying power. However, we as consumers determine how much value we associate with each one. In the aftermath of a major storm, we may value electricity and food and water above everything else. If we commute a long distance or are planning a vacation, fuel may be of greater concern. But all consumers have limited amounts of money and a variety of possible uses for it. So the **price**—the exchange value of a good or service—becomes a major factor in consumer buying decisions.

Businesspeople attempt to accomplish certain objectives through their pricing decisions. Pricing objectives vary from firm to firm, and many companies pursue multiple pricing objectives. Some try to improve profits by setting high prices; others set low prices to attract new business. As Figure 13.5 shows, the four basic categories of pricing objectives are (1) profitability, (2) volume, (3) meeting competition, and (4) prestige.

At the makeup counter, salespeople provide a free makeup demonstration to reinforce the message of how their cosmetic products can enhance your look.

Robert Nystrom/iStockphoto

Profitability Objectives

Profitability objectives are the most common objectives included in the strategic plans of most firms. Marketers know that profits are the revenue the company brings in, minus its expenses. Usually a big difference exists between revenue and profit. Automakers try to produce at least one luxury vehicle for which they can charge $50,000 or more instead of relying entirely on the sale of $15,000 to $25,000 models.

Some firms maximize profits by reducing costs rather than through higher prices. Companies can maintain prices and increase profitability by operating more efficiently or by modifying the product to make it less costly to produce. One strategy is to maintain a steady price while reducing the size or amount of the product in the package—something that manufacturers of candy, coffee, and cereal have done over the years.

Volume Objectives

profitability objectives common objectives included in the strategic plans of most firms.

volume objectives bases pricing decisions on market share, the percentage of a market controlled by a certain company or product.

A second approach to pricing strategy—**volume objectives**—bases pricing decisions on market share, the percentage of a market controlled by a certain company or product. One firm may seek to achieve a 25 percent market share in a certain product category, and another may want to maintain or expand its market share for particular products. Family Dollar Stores relies on volume sales to make a profit. The nationwide chain of stores, which sells everything from ice cube trays to holiday decorations—for a dollar each—must find ways to attract as much traffic and sell as many products as possible on given day. Recently the North Carolina-based firm announced a strategy to increase the number of consumables, such as grocery items, health, and beauty products offered in its stores. Family Dollar plans to add more than 350 new items that consumers need to re-purchase on a regular basis, "leveraging slightly higher shelf heights and reducing space in some underperforming categories," according to Howard R. Levine, the company's chairman and CEO.[44]

Pricing to Meet Competition

A third set of pricing objectives seeks simply to meet competitors' prices so that price essentially becomes a nonissue. In many lines of business, firms set their own prices to match those of established industry leaders. However, companies may not legally work together to agree on prices.

Because price is such a highly visible component of a firm's marketing mix, businesses may be tempted to use it to obtain an advantage over competitors. But sometimes the race to match competitors' prices results in a *price war*, which has happened periodically in the airline and fast-food industries. The ability of competitors to match a price cut leads many marketers to try to avoid price wars by favoring other strategies, such as adding value, improving quality, educating consumers, and establishing relationships.

Although price is a major component of the marketing mix, it is not the only one. Electronic readers such as the Kindle and the iPad are in a fierce pricing competition for digital books, as the "Solving an Ethical Controversy" feature explains.

Solving an Ethical Controversy

Free E-Books: Good or Bad for Business?

When Amazon's Kindle electronic reader first became available, Amazon charged consumers $9.99 for each e-book they purchased. Publishers insisted that that price was too low to keep their business profitable. But Amazon actually gave some e-books away for free, including those of living authors who earn an income from their writing.

Amazon explained that the free e-books were a way to get consumers to check out unfamiliar writers. The hope was that they would then buy other works by those writers. But some publishers delay publication of electronic editions for several months after the hardcover books were issued, much as they delay paperback editions.

Should e-books be given away for free?

PRO

1. Some publishers regard free e-books as promotion to generate buzz about new or unknown authors.

2. Some publishers that give away e-books on a regular basis have noticed an increase in sales that's "all found money," as one executive says.

CON

1. "It is illogical to give books away for free," said David Young of Hachette Book Group, which publishes Stephanie Meyer's "Twilight" series.

2. The relatively low price of e-books may discourage consumers from buying actual books with suggested retail prices of $25 or more.

Summary

Both Amazon's Kindle and Barnes & Noble's Nook continue to offer free e-books. In addition, both offer the capability for customers to lend e-books to friends and family for 14 days by simply inputting a name and e-mail address. Although some publishers might cringe at these practices, it is likely that the trend will continue.

Sources: Alec Liu, "Kindle, Nook, Whatever: Here's How to Get Free E-Books," *FoxNews.com*, January 27, 2011, http://www.foxnews.com; Stan Schroeder, "The E-Book Price War Isn't Over Yet," *Mashable*, February 18, 2010, http://mashable.com; Motoko Rich, "Apple's Prices for E-Books May Be Lower Than Expected," *The New York Times*, February 18, 2010, http://www.nytimes.com; Motoko Rich, "With Kindle, the Best Sellers Don't Need to Sell," *The New York Times*, January 23, 2010, http://www.nytimes.com; "The Kindle Pricing Strategy & the Kindle Pricing History," *askDeb.com*, January 20, 2010, http://www.askdeb.com.

Prestige Objectives

The final category of objectives encompasses the effect of prices on prestige. **Prestige pricing** establishes a relatively high price to develop and maintain an image of quality and exclusiveness. Marketers set such objectives because they recognize the role of price in communicating an overall image for the firm and its products. People expect to pay more for a Lexus, a Louis Vuitton purse, or a vacation on St. Kitts or Nevis in the Caribbean. Despite a recession, the British retailer Selfridges has had a 60 percent increase in sales of "must-have" handbags by the luxury brand Mulberry. Mulberry even has waiting lists for some of its styles.[45]

Scarcity can create prestige. Products that are limited in distribution or so popular that they become scarce generate their own prestige—allowing businesses to charge more for them. Unfortunately, scarcity can also invite crime. Recently, federal prosecutors charged four men with hacking into the computer systems of Ticketmaster, Major League Baseball, Telecharge, and Live Nation Entertainment to highjack 1.5 million tickets to concerts by Bruce Springsteen and Miley Cyrus, baseball playoff games at Yankee Stadium, and other events. The men or their agents posed as individual online buyers, electronically bypassed the vendors' security systems, and bought blocks of tickets that they resold at hugely inflated

> **prestige pricing** establishes a relatively high price to develop and maintain an image of quality and exclusiveness.

> **Assessment Check** ✓
> 1. Define *price*.
> 2. What is a second approach to pricing strategy?

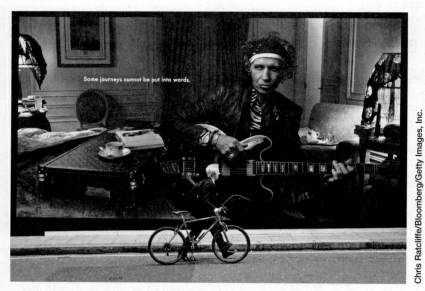

Prestige pricing establishes a relatively high price to develop and maintain an image of quality and exclusiveness. People expect to pay more for a Louis Vuitton bag, just like the rock star in the ad.

prices. The scam had been in operation since 2002 and had generated almost $29 million in illegal profits.[46]

Pricing Strategies

People from different areas of a company contribute their expertise to set the most strategic price for a product. Accountants, financial managers, and marketers provide relevant sales and cost data, along with customer feedback. Designers, engineers, and systems analysts all contribute important data as well.

Prices are determined in two basic ways: by applying the concepts of supply and demand discussed in Chapter 3 and by completing cost-oriented analyses. Economic theory assumes that a market price will be set at the point at which the amount of a product desired at a given price equals the amount that suppliers will offer for sale at that price. In other words, this price occurs at the point at which the amount demanded and the amount supplied are equal. Online auctions, such as those conducted on eBay, are a popular application of the demand-and-supply approach.

Price Determination in Practice

cost-based pricing formulas that calculate total costs per unit and then add markups to cover overhead costs and generate profits.

Economic theory might lead to the best pricing decisions, but most businesses do not have all the information they need to make those decisions, so they adopt **cost-based pricing** formulas. These formulas calculate total costs per unit and then add markups to cover overhead costs and generate profits.

Cost-based pricing totals all costs associated with offering a product in the market, including research and development, production, transportation, and marketing expenses. An added amount, the markup, then covers any unexpected or overlooked expenses and provides a profit. The total becomes the price. Although the actual markup used varies by such factors as brand image and type of store, the typical markup for clothing is determined by doubling the wholesale price (the cost to the merchant) to arrive at the retail price for the item.

Breakeven Analysis

breakeven analysis pricing-related technique used to determine the minimum sales volume a product must generate at a certain price level to cover all costs.

Businesses often conduct a **breakeven analysis** to determine the minimum sales volume a product must generate at a certain price level to cover all costs. This method involves a consideration of various costs and total revenues. *Total cost* is the sum of total variable costs and total fixed costs. *Variable costs* change with the level of production, as labor and raw materials do, while *fixed costs* such as insurance premiums and utility rates charged by water, natural gas, and electric power suppliers remain stable regardless of the production level. *Total revenue* is determined by multiplying price by the number of units sold.

Finding the Breakeven Point The level of sales that will generate enough revenue to cover all of the company's fixed and variable costs is called the *breakeven point*.

It is the point at which total revenue just equals total costs. Sales beyond the breakeven point will generate profits; sales volume below the breakeven point will result in losses. The following formulas give the breakeven point in units and dollars:

$$\text{Breakeven Point (in units)} = \frac{\text{Total fixed costs}}{\text{Contribution to fixed costs per unit}}$$

$$\text{Breakeven Point (in dollars)} = \frac{\text{Total fixed costs}}{1 - \text{Variable cost per unit/Price}}$$

A product selling for $20 with a variable cost of $14 per unit produces a $6 per-unit contribution to fixed costs. If the firm has total fixed costs of $42,000, then it must sell 7,000 units to break even on the product. The calculation of the breakeven point in units and dollars is as follows:

$$\text{Breakeven Point (in units)} = \frac{\$42,000}{\$20 - \$14} = \frac{\$42,000}{\$6} = 7,000 \text{ units}$$

$$\text{Breakeven Point (in dollars)} = \frac{\$42,000}{1 - \$14/\$20} = \frac{\$42,000}{1 - 0.7} = \frac{\$42,000}{0.3} = \$140,000$$

Marketers use breakeven analysis to determine the profits or losses that would result from several different proposed prices. Because different prices produce different breakeven points, marketers could compare their calculations of required sales to break even with sales estimates from marketing research studies. This comparison can identify the best price—one that would attract enough customers to exceed the breakeven point and earn profits for the firm.

Most firms add consumer demand—determining whether enough customers will buy the number of units the firm must sell at a particular price to break even—by developing estimates through surveys of likely customers, interviews with retailers that would be handling the product, and assessments of prices charged by competitors. Then the breakeven points for several possible prices are calculated and compared with sales estimates for each price. This practice is referred to as *modified breakeven analysis*.

FIGURE **13.6** **Breakeven Analysis**

Alternative Pricing Strategies

The strategy a company uses to set its prices should grow out of the firm's overall marketing strategy. In general, firms can choose from four alternative pricing strategies: skimming, penetration, discount or everyday low pricing, and competitive pricing.

Skimming Pricing
A <u>skimming pricing</u> strategy sets an intentionally high price relative to the prices of competing products. The term comes from the expression "skimming the cream." This pricing strategy often works for the introduction of a distinctive good or service with little or no competition, although it can be used at other stages of the product life cycle as well. A skimming strategy can help marketers set a price that distinguishes a firm's high-end product from those of competitors. It can also help a firm recover its product development costs before competitors enter the field. This is often the case with prescription drugs.

Penetration Pricing
By contrast, a <u>penetration pricing</u> strategy sets a low price as a major marketing weapon. Businesses may price new products noticeably lower than competing offerings when they enter new industries characterized by dozens of competing brands. Once the new product achieves some market recognition through consumer trial purchases stimulated by its low price, marketers may increase the price to the level of competing products. However, stiff competition might prevent the price increase.

Everyday Low Pricing and Discount Pricing
<u>Everyday low pricing (EDLP)</u> is a strategy devoted to maintaining continuous low prices rather than relying on short-term price-cutting tactics such as cents-off coupons, rebates, and special sales. This strategy has been used successfully by retailers such as Walmart and GNC to consistently offer low prices to consumers; manufacturers also use EDLP to set stable prices for retailers.

With *discount pricing*, businesses hope to attract customers by dropping prices for a set period of time. Automakers usually offer consumers special discounts on most or all of their

skimming pricing strategy that sets an intentionally high price relative to the prices of competing products.

penetration pricing strategy sets a low price as a major marketing weapon.

everyday low pricing (EDLP) is a strategy devoted to maintaining continuous low prices rather than relying on short-term price-cutting tactics such as cents-off coupons, rebates, and special sales.

Stores such as Walmart use an everyday low pricing strategy, devoted to maintaining continuous low prices rather than relying on short-term price-cutting tactics such as cents-off coupons, rebates, and special sales.

Will Lower Prices Help Nokia Regain Its Edge?

For years the Finnish electronics giant Nokia owned an enormous share of the world's cell phone market, easily beating out early competitors such as Motorola and Sony Ericsson. Recently, however, it has found itself facing competition from Apple's iPhone, which has begun to lower its prices, and from Research in Motion's BlackBerry devices.

The company seems to be trying various strategies, but some observers think Nokia has lost its strategic focus. Nokia's chief executive, Olli-Pekka Kallasvuo, announced that the company would focus on software, citing a deal with Microsoft to create business-oriented mobile applications. Another executive declared that Nokia would become the "world's biggest entertainment media network." Indeed, it recently launched its "Comes with Music" downloading service, which was the first of its kind in the Middle East. But it has done poorly elsewhere due to stiff competition from Apple's iTunes. Yet another executive announced the debut of the Booklet 3G, a laptop computer that would make the "personal computer more social, more helpful, and more personal."

At a meeting in New Delhi, India, Tuula Rytilä-Uotila, Nokia's vice president of products, announced that the company planned to lower the prices of Nokia's smart phones. "We want to take smart phones to a wider audience by bringing down the prices of such phones. The strategy is to be present in all price ranges." The company hopes to stimulate demand for its low-end mobile phones and perhaps put some indirect pressure on Apple and Research in Motion, whose handsets are more sophisticated.

Questions for Critical Thinking

1. Do you think Nokia will regain lost ground with its new pricing strategy? Why or why not?
2. Will Nokia's low-end cell phones make good loss leaders (a product sold at a low price to stimulate other sales)? Why or why not?

Sources: Company Web site, www.nokia.com, accessed April 21, 2011; Arik Hesseldahl, "Nokia's Kallasvuo: We Must 'Move Even Faster,'" *BusinessWeek*, April 22, 2010, http://www.businessweek.com; Mark Ritson, "Nokia Brand Needs Firm Direction," *Branding Strategy Insider*, April 5, 2010, http://www.brandingstrategyinsider.com; Abbas Jaffar Ali, "Nokia Announces the X6 and 'Comes with Music' Service for the Middle East," *T-Break Tech*, February 11, 2010, http://tech.tbreak.com; John Paczkowski, "Nokia Agitating for a Handset Price War?" *All Things Digital*, February 1, 2010, http://digitaldaily.allthingsd.com.

---

vehicles during the holiday shopping season. After the holidays, prices usual rebound. But experts warn that discounting must be done carefully, or profits can disappear. Businesses should offer discounts only for a specified period of time and with a clear understanding of what they are trying to accomplish with the strategy. They should advertise the discount, so customers know it is a special deal. When the time period has elapsed, so should the discount.

Seeing its market share erode, Nokia is trying various ways to lure consumers back, including lowering prices on some of its cell phones; this strategy is discussed in the "Hit & Miss" feature.

Competitive Pricing Although many organizations rely heavily on price as a competitive weapon, even more implement <u>competitive pricing</u> strategies. They try to reduce the emphasis on price competition by matching other firms' prices and concentrating their own marketing efforts on the product, distribution, and promotional elements of the marketing mix. In fact, in industries with relatively homogeneous products, competitors must match one another's price reductions to maintain market share and remain competitive. By pricing their products at the levels of competing offerings, marketers largely negate the price variable in their marketing strategies.

Consumer Perceptions of Prices

How do you perceive prices for certain products? Marketers must consider this. If large numbers of potential buyers consider a price too high or too low, businesses must correct the situation. Price–quality relationships and the use of odd pricing are important considerations in setting prices.

competitive pricing strategy that tries to reduce the emphasis on price competition by matching other firms' prices and concentrating their own marketing efforts on the product, distribution, and promotional elements of the marketing mix.

Assessment Check ✓

1. What is a cost-based pricing formula?
2. Why do companies implement competitive pricing strategies?

Price–Quality Relationships

Research shows that a consumer's perception of product quality is closely related to an item's price. Most marketers believe that this perceived price–quality relationship remains steady over a relatively wide range of prices, although extremely high or low prices have less credibility. The price–quality relationship can critically affect a firm's pricing strategy.

Many consumers associate prestige, quality, and high price together—believing that paying a high price for an item such as an Infiniti car or a Chanel bag not only conveys prestige but also ensures quality. Others believe that eating at an expensive restaurant automatically means the food will be better than food served at a modestly priced eating establishment. Conversely, consumers may view an extremely low price as an indication that corners have been cut and quality will suffer. But what about the perception associated with a sale? If a line of designer boots goes on sale for 50 percent off the original price, a bargain hunter will snap them up with a sense of victory—high quality at a rock bottom price. Still another shopper might buy two pairs, perceiving an even greater value at two for the price of one.

Marketing researchers also know that the verbal sound of a price influences consumers' perceptions of price, quality, and resulting value. The vowel sound "oo" (as in "two") makes people think of larger sizes ad prices, while the vowel sound "ee" (as in "three") evokes a smaller size and price. These perceptions can influence consumers' perception of the quality of the products they are considering buying.[47]

Odd Pricing

odd pricing pricing method using uneven amounts, which appear less than they really are to consumers.

Have you ever wondered why retailers set prices like $1.99 instead of $2 or $9.95 instead of $10? Before the age of cash registers and sales taxes, retailers reportedly followed this practice of **odd pricing**—pricing method using uneven amounts, which appear less than they really are to consumers—to force clerks to make correct change as part of their cash control efforts. But now **odd pricing** is commonly used because many retailers believe that consumers favor uneven amounts or amounts that sound less than they really are. However, some retailers also use this method to identify items that have been marked down. The odd price lets people know the item is on sale.

Assessment Check ✓

1. How does the price–quality relationship affect a firm's pricing strategy?
2. Why is odd pricing used?

What's Ahead

The chapters in Part 4 have explained the main principles underlying marketing management and described how each fits a firm's overall business strategy. The next few chapters will help you understand how companies manage the technology and information that are available to businesses to create value for their customers and enhance their competitiveness in the marketplace. You'll also learn how firms manage their financial resources.

⌐1⌐ Discuss how integrated marketing communications (IMC) relates to a firm's overall promotional strategy, and explain the concept of a promotional mix along with outlining the objectives of promotion.

In practicing IMC, a firm coordinates promotional activities to produce a unified, customer-focused message. IMC identifies consumer needs and shows how a company's products meet them. Marketers select the promotional media that best target and reach customers. Teamwork and careful promotional planning to coordinate IMC strategy components are important elements of these programs.

A company's promotional mix integrates two components: personal selling and nonpersonal selling, which includes advertising, sales promotion, and public relations. By selecting the appropriate combination of promotional mix elements, marketers attempt to achieve the firm's five major promotional objectives: provide information, differentiate a product, increase demand, stabilize sales, and accentuate the product's value.

Assessment Check Answers ✓

1.1 What is the objective of an integrated marketing communications program? An IMC strategy focuses on customer needs to create a unified promotional message about a firm's goods or services.

1.2 Why do firms pursue multiple promotional objectives at the same time? Firms pursue multiple promotional objectives because they may need to convey different messages to different audiences.

1.3 What are product placement and guerrilla marketing? Product placement involves paying a fee to have a product showcased in certain media. Guerrilla marketing is innovative, low-cost marketing efforts designed to get consumers' attention in unusual ways.

⌐2⌐ Summarize the different types of advertising and advertising media.

Advertising, the most visible form of nonpersonal promotion, is designed to inform, persuade, or remind. Product advertising promotes a good or service, while institutional advertising promotes a concept, idea, organization, or philosophy. Television, newspapers, and magazines are the largest advertising media categories. Others include direct mail, radio, and outdoor advertising. Interactive advertising directly involves the consumer, who controls the flow of information.

Assessment Check Answers ✓

2.1 What are the two basic types of advertising? Into what three categories do they fall? The two basic types are product and institutional. They fall into the categories of informative, persuasive, and reminder-oriented advertising.

2.2 What is the leading advertising medium in the U.S. According to the most recent statistics listed in Figure 13.2, television is the leading advertising medium in the U.S.

2.3 In what two major ways do firms benefit from sponsorship? Firms benefit from sponsorship in two ways: gain exposure to the event's audience, and association with the activity's image.

⌐3⌐ Outline the roles of sales promotion, personal selling, and public relations in promotional strategy.

Sales promotion accounts for greater expenditures than advertising. Consumer-oriented sales promotions such as coupons, games, rebates, samples, premiums, contests, sweepstakes, and promotional products offer an extra incentive to buy a product. Point-of-purchase advertising displays and trade shows are sales promotions directed to the trade markets. Personal selling involves face-to-face interactions between seller and buyer. The primary sales tasks are order processing, creative selling, and missionary selling. Public relations is nonpaid promotion that seeks to enhance a company's public image.

Assessment Check Answers ✓

3.1 Why do retailers and manufacturers use sales promotions? Retailers and manufacturers use sales promotions to offer consumers extra incentives to buy their products.

3.2 When does a firm use personal selling instead of nonpersonal selling? Personal selling is generally used when customers are few and geographically concentrated, the product is technically complex or requires special handling, the price is high, or the product moves through direct-distribution channels.

3.3 How does public relations serve a marketing purpose? Public relations can be an efficient, indirect communications channel for promoting products. It can publicize products and help create and maintain a positive image of the company.

⌐4⌐ Describe pushing and pulling promotional strategies.

A pushing strategy relies on personal selling to market a product to wholesalers and retailers in a company's distribution channels. A pulling strategy promotes the product by generating consumer demand for it, through advertising and sales promotion.

Assessment Check Answers ✓

4.1 Give an example of a pushing strategy. An example of a pushing strategy is that used by drug manufacturers, who used to market solely to physicians and hospitals. Today, they also use a pulling strategy by marketing directly to patients through advertising, which encourages patients to ask their doctors about medications.

4.2 Give an example of a pulling strategy. Pulling strategies are used by retailers and by manufacturers of consumer goods like cosmetics, automobiles, and clothing.

⌐5⌐ Outline the different types of pricing objectives.

Pricing objectives can be classified as profitability, volume, meeting competition, and prestige. Profitability objectives are the most common. Volume objectives base pricing decisions on market share. Meeting competitors' prices makes price a nonissue in competition. Prestige pricing establishes a high price to develop and maintain an image of quality or exclusiveness.

Assessment Check Answers ✅

5.1 Define *price.* Price is the exchange value of a good or service.

5.2 What is a second approach to pricing strategy? A second approach to pricing strategy is **volume objectives**, which bases pricing decisions on market share.

⌐6⌐ Discuss how firms set prices in the marketplace, and describe the four alternative pricing strategies.

Although economic theory determines prices by the law of demand and supply, most firms use cost-based pricing, which adds a markup after costs. They usually conduct a breakeven analysis to determine the minimum sales volume a product must generate at a certain price to cover costs. The four alternative pricing strategies are skimming, penetration, everyday low pricing and discounting, and competitive pricing. A skimming strategy sets a high price initially to recover costs and then lowers it; a penetration strategy sets a lower price and then raises it later. Everyday low pricing and discounting offers a lower price for a period of time. Competitive pricing matches other firms' prices and emphasizes nonprice benefits of a product.

Assessment Check Answers ✅

6.1 What is a cost-based pricing formula? A cost-based pricing formula calculates the total costs per unit and then adds markups to cover overhead costs and generate profits.

6.2 Why do companies implement competitive pricing strategies? Companies use competitive pricing strategies to reduce the emphasis on price competition by matching other firms' prices and concentrating their own marketing efforts on the product, distribution, and promotional elements of the marketing mix.

⌐7⌐ Discuss consumer perceptions of price.

Marketers must consider how consumers perceive the price–quality relationship of their products. Consumers may be willing to pay a higher price if they perceive a product to be of superior quality. Marketers often use odd pricing to convey a message to consumers.

Assessment Check Answers ✅

7.1 How does the price–quality relationship affect a firm's pricing strategy? Consumers must believe that the price of an item reflects its quality, except in extreme cases. So a firm must try to set its prices accordingly.

7.2 Why is odd pricing used? Retailers believe that consumers favor uneven amounts or amounts that sound like less than they really are. Odd pricing may also be used to indicate a sale item.

▌ Business Terms You Need to Know

promotion 428	institutional advertising 434	missionary selling 446	cost-based
integrated marketing	cause advertising 434	telemarketing 446	pricing 452
communications (IMC) 429	sponsorship 440	public relations 448	breakeven analysis 452
promotional mix 430	infomercial 440	publicity 448	skimming
personal selling 430	sales promotion 441	pushing strategy 449	pricing 454
nonpersonal selling 430	specialty advertising 443	cooperative advertising 449	penetration pricing 454
positioning 431	trade promotion 443	pulling strategy 449	everyday low
product placement 432	point-of-purchase (POP)	price 449	pricing (EDLP) 454
guerrilla marketing 433	advertising 443	profitability objectives 450	competitive
advertising 434	order processing 445	volume objectives 450	pricing 455
product advertising 434	creative selling 445	prestige pricing 451	odd pricing 456

▌ Review Questions

1. What is the purpose of integrated marketing communications?
2. What are the five major objectives of a promotional strategy?
3. Identify and define each of the three categories of advertising based on their purpose. Which type of advertising might marketers use for the following products?
   a. deodorant b. electronic reader
   c. organic produce d. healthcare insurance
4. What are the benefits of online and interactive advertising? What might be some drawbacks?
5. For each of the following, describe potential benefits and drawbacks of a sponsorship relationship:
   a. LG and the Snowboard FIS World Cup
   b. ING Bank and the New York City Marathon

   c. Wrangler and the Wrangler Football Golf Classic (a golf tournament that raises money for high school football programs)
6. If you were a marketer for Rolex, what kind of sales promotion might you use for high-end watches?
7. Under what circumstances are firms likely to emphasize personal selling?
8. Describe the seven-step sales process.
9. Define the four basic categories of pricing objectives.
10. What are the four alternative pricing strategies used by marketers? Give an example of the circumstances under which each might be selected.

Projects and Teamwork Applications

1. Choose a product that you purchased recently. Identify the various media that were used to promote the product and analyze the promotional mix. Do you agree with the company's marketing strategy, or would you recommend changes to the mix? Why? Create your own print ad for the product you chose, using any business strategies or knowledge you have learned in this course so far.

2. Evaluate the price of the product you selected in the preceding exercise. What appears to be the pricing strategy used by its manufacturer? Do you think the price is fair? Why or why not? Choose a different strategy and develop a new price for the product based on the strategy. Poll your classmates to learn whether they would purchase the product at the new price—and why.

3. Some schools have received financial benefits by allowing companies to promote their goods and services to students.

Others have decided against the practice, and some states have laws banning this type of promotion. Find some examples of corporate sponsors in public elementary and high schools and on college campuses. With your class, discuss the pros and cons of promotion in public schools and on college campuses. In your view, is there a distinction between a public school and a college campus? Why or why not?

4. On your own or with a classmate, research a recent situation that has caused a business, a not-for-profit organization, or a government agency to suffer from bad publicity. Evaluate the situation and create a program outlining steps the organization might take to build better public relations.

5. You are the marketing manager that is introducing a new line of video games. What approach would you take for establishing prices?

Web Assignments

1. **Top advertisers.** *Advertising Age* compiles data annually on the top national advertisers. Visit the Web site listed here and access the most recent year. Answer the following questions:

   a. Who were the top ten advertisers in that year?

   b. How much did they spend on advertising?

   c. What was the most advertised brand that year?

   http://adage.com/datacenter/article?article_id=106348

2. **Online coupon fraud.** Go to the Web sites listed to learn about online coupon fraud. Prepare a brief report. Make sure to answer the following: How big a problem is online coupon fraud? What are some changes marketers have made in an attempt to reduce online coupon fraud?

   http://www.newser.com/story/35962/hackers-spread-coupon-scam.html

   http://online.wsj.com/article/SB124641121217977575.html

   http://multichannelmerchant.com/retail/news/0308-curtailing-online-coupon-fraud/

3. **Yield management.** Assume you're interested in flying between Seattle and Houston. Visit some travel sites. Search for fares, varying such factors as advance purchase, day, time of departure, and so forth. What did this exercise teach you about yield management?

   http://www.expedia.com

   http://www.kayak.com

   http://www.travelocity.com

   Note: Internet Web addresses change frequently. If you don't find the exact sites listed, you may need to access the organization's home page and search from there or use a search engine such as Bing or Google.

Brand Names versus Store Brands

CASE 13.1

Shoppers who buy brand-name products usually cite quality as a reason. Shoppers who buy store-brand products usually cite price. Is it possible to have the best of both worlds?

Retailers such as Target, CVS, and Walgreens have found they had too many of the same products under different brand names. They saw that shoppers were buying less and looking for bigger bargains than usual. Items that weren't selling well were replaced by more popular brands or by in-house generics. This was particularly true of such basic items as household and personal products and food staples. As one observer said, "People don't

want to have to choose between among 15 or 20 different brands of toilet paper or paper towels or even basic food stuff." The retailers were confident that shoppers would be eager to snap up these bargains.

Target guessed that consumers would buy their in-house brands and it looks like they were correct. The high quality store lines that Target stocks have yielded a 2 percent increase in same-store sales for one recent month. The in-store brands of up & up, Archer Farms, and Market Pantry account for more than 20 percent of all food products sold at Target. A retailing analyst wrote in a recent report, "the company has unique top-line drivers that aren't dependent on macro recovery."

To some extent, this overall strategy has worked. The market share of store brands has grown between 2 and 6 percent. And 77 percent of consumers who bought less expensive store-brand items were satisfied with their choice.

Questions for Critical Thinking

1. Why do you think chain stores carry brand-name items alongside their own in-house brands?

2. What are some of the ways that stores such as Target are able to keep their prices low?

Sources: "Target's Comeback Plan on Track," *Store Brands Decisions,* August 10, 2010, http://www.storebrandsdecisions.com; Parija Kavilanz, "Dumped! Brand Names Fight to Stay in Stores," CNN Money.com, February 16, 2010, http://money.cnn.com; Kevin Cokeley, "Retailers Replacing Big Names with House Brands," NBC Dallas–Fort Worth, February 19, 2010, http://www.nbcdfw.com; Sara Zucker, "Wal-Mart Reintroduces Brands after Customer Complaints," Brandchannel.com, March 12, 2010, http://www.brandchannel.com.

CASE 13.2   Marketing to the Teenage Crowd

Today's teenagers were born shortly before the turn of the 21st century. They represent billions of dollars in buying power, but the big question for marketers is how to reach them.

Unlike their parents, today's teens have grown up in this electronic age and take it for granted. Like those of earlier generations, today's teens like to communicate with each other. Unlike their predecessors, they now can do so almost constantly. One study estimates that teenagers spend more than seven hours a day using media of various kinds, mostly electronic. How do they log this astonishing amount of time? By sacrificing sleep and multitasking. Some older teens can perform seven activities at once. Parents often find their teens listening to music, watching TV program, doing homework, playing a videogame, and text messaging.

What media do teenagers neglect or ignore? They hardly ever read newspapers. Jeffrey Cole, the director of the Center for the Digital Future at the University of Southern California, predicts that printed newspapers will eventually become extinct as social media steadily increase in power. Teens want news, he explains, but only about the narrowly focused community of their peers.

Teenagers don't contact their peers through e-mail. One survey indicates that although 73 percent of teens visit social-networking sites, only about 8 percent use Twitter. They do like smart phones, especially those with apps for constant status updates, but don't make many phone calls. Instead, they text message sometimes sending up to ten messages an hour.

Marketers will need to learn how to reach teenagers by recognizing that teens like to be invited to get involved, rather than being told. This means asking for their input, listening to them with genuine respect, adopting their suggestions, and continuing to ask for feedback. Morgan Stewart of ExactTarget conducted a survey asking teens which brand they thought did the best job of communicating with them. To his surprise, Amazon got more write-in votes than any other brand, including Facebook. He says of Amazon, "Teens can read reviews, they can

submit their own, and they can get recommendations based on what they like." Stewart believes that "managing your Amazon presence is more important than building out a Facebook strategy."

Of course, even Amazon is only one component of an integrated marketing plan. Teenagers are highly suspicious of anything that seems even remotely like advertising. When shopping, they depend heavily on the opinions of their peers. They also enjoy fun sites such as Sporcle.com, FunnyOrDie.com, and FailBlog.org. YouTube is another important tool for viral marketing, as well as being free.

Jeffrey Cole thinks that as today's teens move into adulthood, the allure of knowing everything about their friends will fade. What will endure will be something that every generation wants: they will still want to have "total control over their media" as a way of having "real control over their lives."

Questions for Critical Thinking

1. Do you think marketers can reach teens with specially tailored promotional campaigns for such goods and services as video games, smartphone apps, concert tickets, and so on? Why or why not?

2. How can marketers best target teens so as to appeal to them but without making them feel talked down to? Suggest a marketing or promotional theme for one product that you think would appeal to a teen.

Sources: Steve Bauer, "Reaching the Elusive Teenager," *Word of Mouth,* April 13, 2010, http://wom.fleishmanhilliard.com; Carol Phillips, "Where Teens Hang Out Digitally," *Millennial Marketing,* March 12, 2010, http://millennialmarketing.com; Tim Loc, "Teens Love Social Media, Detest Newspapers," *iMedia Connection,* March 3, 2010, http://www.imediaconnection.com; Steve McClellan, "Teens Into Social Media, Not Newspapers," *Mediaweek,* March 2, 2010, http://www.mediaweek.com; Tamar Lewin, "If Your Kids Are Awake, They're Probably Online," *The New York Times,* January 20, 2010, http://www.nytimes.com; "Teen Marketing: A Look Ahead," (Pangea Media,) January 1, 2010, http://www.pangeamedia.com.

Pet owners want the best for their dogs and cats, as evidenced by the $50 billion pet industry in the U.S., including everything from grooming services to squeaky toys. One area that has received little attention is travel. Although owners can find lodging that allows pets, and they can purchase travel carriers and gear, until recently there was little choice when it came to transport. If the animal had to travel long distance, it was relegated to the cargo hold of a plane. A couple of years ago, that changed when Dan Wiesel and Alysa Binder wanted to be able to transport their Jack Russell terrier safely and comfortably. So they started a pet transport business called Pet Airways.

"There are 80 million pets traveling around the U.S.," says Alysa Binder. "There's definitely a market for this. We're part of the pet community—we understand." Wiesel and Binder contracted with a firm that flies Beechcraft 1900 aircraft, selecting this plane for its versatility and safety record. They had the planes retrofitted to accommodate pet carriers in the main cabin. They launched their reservation system online and spread the word via social media. When traditional media heard of the new company, Wiesel and Binder appeared on such television shows as *Good Morning America* and *The Today Show,* as well as in magazines and newspapers. Because of this publicity, Pet Airways has spent nothing on advertising. Its greatest marketing challenge has been educating the public about their service. "Because we're the first to market, we have to tell people what we're all about," explains Binder.

Pet owners who want to book their animals on a Pet Airways flight make a reservation on the airline's Web site, http://www.petairways.com. One hour before departure, owners check in at the Pet Lounge. Pet passengers are boarded in their carriers, attended to by professional pet Attendants who accompany the animals on the flight, checking on them every 15 minutes to make sure they are secure and comfortable. Once the plane has landed, owners (or designated recipients) collect their pets in the Pet Lounge.

Pet Airways currently operates flights to nine cities around the U.S. Alysa Binder says the firm's goal is to reach 20 cities in the next 18 months. She notes that customers are willing and eager to pay for the service, considering it reasonable compared to traditional airlines.

Pet Airways fares start at $149. By comparison, American Airlines charges $100 for a pet to travel beneath a seat and $150 as baggage; Delta charges $150 and $275 respectively; and Northwest charges $150 and $225 respectively. Binder remarks that her customers don't usually consider price anyway because "we aren't the same as general carriers. It's a completely different service. People know that."

Pet Airways customers can register to receive the company's newsletter, which includes insider news on special flight deals and other promotions. They can join the MyPAWS Club, which offers a 40 percent discount on pet supplies at the Pet Airways online store, a 10 percent discount at pet-friendly hotels, 10 percent off at 1-800-PetMeds, 5 percent off on pet health insurance from Pets Best Insurance, and discounts and free samples from other Pet Airways partners.

Wiesel and Binder saw an opportunity in the marketplace and jumped at the chance to offer a safe, reliable solution for pet owners to transport their pets. "On Pet Airways, your pets aren't packages, they're passengers."

Questions for Critical Thinking

1. At this stage of Pet Airway's life cycle, what should be the company's primary promotional objectives? Why?

2. Pet Airways has not yet engaged in major advertising efforts. Which media would probably be most effective at reaching the firm's intended market? Why?

3. Pet Airways already offers some consumer-oriented promotions. Describe or outline an idea for a new promotion and explain your choice.

4. Outline Pet Airways' pricing objectives. How might these change over the next five years? Ten years? What do you think the best pricing strategy for Pet Airways should be? Why?

Sources: Pet Airways Web site, http://www.petairways.com, accessed June 7, 2011; "Pet Airways Combines with a Public Company Through Share Exchange with American Antiquities," *PR Newswire,* August 16, 2010, http://wwwprnewswire.com; "Doctors Call for Airline Pet Ban," *The Independent,* February 21, 2010, http://license.icopyright.net;" "Bone Voyage as Pets Get Airline," *BBC News,* April 17, 2009, http://news.bbc.co.uk.

GREENSBURG, KS
Think Green, Go Green, Save Green

Not long ago, the phrase "hybrid SUV" would have seemed an oxymoron. But in just a few short years, fuel-efficient hybrids of all shapes and sizes have appeared in showrooms. This new generation of vehicles combines fuel-efficient gas engines, natural gas engines, and hydrogen fuel cells. As gas prices soar and concern over the environment grows, consumers will become more and more interested in them.

Enter Lee Lindquist, Alternative Fuels Specialist at Scholfield Honda in Wichita, Kansas. A passionate environmentalist, Lee was researching alternative-fuel vehicles when he learned that Honda had been selling a natural gas Civic GX in New York and California since 1998. Originally marketed to municipalities and corporations as a way of addressing air quality issues, the Civic GX seemed the perfect way for cost-conscious Kansans to combat rising fuel prices. It was also a way to promote local resources, since Kansas is a major producer of natural gas.

Lee took the idea of the Civic GX to his boss, owner Roger Scholfield, who was skeptical of it at first. Scholfield had long promoted the Honda as a fuel-efficient vehicle and didn't want to muddy the waters with this new vehicle. But eventually he warmed to the idea and began offering the car to his corporate customers.

When the tornado hit Greensburg, the idea of going green took on a whole new life at Scholfield Honda. One of the problems with offering the Civic GX had been the lack of natural gas fueling stations, as well as the high cost of constructing one. Well aware of the media attention surrounding Greensburg, Scholfield decided to donate a natural gas Civic to the town, along with a fueling station.

Scholfield was up-front about the decision to donate the car. The investment was a costly one, and there were many less expensive ways of reaching his customers in Wichita. Scholfield admits he questioned his decision even as he drove into Greensburg for the presentation. But the bottom line was that it was the right thing to do. Today, when customers come into Scholfield's dealership, they are more interested in alternative-fuel and high-efficiency vehicles.

If you want to buy a Civic GX from Scholfield Honda today, get in line, because the staff can't keep them in stock. While you wait, enjoy a nice cup of coffee served in a compostable, corn-based disposable cup. Toss those old soda cans rattling around in your back seat into Scholfield's recycling bins. And on your way out, don't forget to take your complimentary Scholfield Honda reusable green shopping bag and water bottle.

Questions

After viewing the video, answer the following questions:

1. Do you think Scholfield's green marketing campaign will change consumers' opinions of hybrid and alternative-fuel cars?

2. Do you think Scholfield's donation of a natural gas Civic to the town of Greensburg will drive business to his dealership in Wichita? Why or why not?

LAUNCHING YOUR
[Marketing Career]

In Part 4, "Marketing Management," you learned about the goals and functions of marketing. The three chapters in this part emphasized the central role of customer satisfaction in defining value and developing a marketing strategy in traditional and nontraditional marketing settings. You learned about the part played by marketing research and the need for relationship marketing in today's competitive environment. You discovered how new products are developed and how they evolve through the four stages of the product life cycle, from introduction through growth and maturity to decline. You also learned about the role of different channels in creating effective distribution strategies. Finally, you saw the impact of integrated marketing communications on the firm's promotional strategy, the role of advertising, and the way pricing influences consumer behavior. Perhaps you came across some marketing tasks and functions that sounded especially appealing to you. Here are a few ideas about careers in marketing that you may want to pursue.

The first thing to remember is that, as the chapters in this part made clear, marketing is about a great deal more than personal selling and advertising. For instance, are you curious about why people behave the way they do? Are you good at spotting trends? *Marketing research analysts* seek answers to a wide range of questions about business competition, customer preferences, market trends, and past and future sales. They often design and conduct their own consumer surveys, using the telephone, mail, the Internet, or personal interviews and focus groups. After they analyze the data they've collected, their recommendations form input for managerial decisions about whether to introduce new products, revamp current ones, enter new markets, or abandon products or markets where profitability is low. As members of a new-product development team, marketing researchers often work directly with members of other business departments such as scientists, production and manufacturing personnel, and finance employees. Also, marketing researchers are increasingly asked to help clients implement their recommendations. With today's highly competitive economy, jobs in this area are expected to grow. Annual earnings for marketing research analysts average about $61,000.[1]

Another career path in marketing is sales. Do you work well with others and read their feelings accurately? Are you a self-starter? Being a *sales representative* might be for you. Selling jobs exist in every industry, and because many use a combination of salary and performance-based commissions, they can pay handsomely. Sales jobs are often a first step on the ladder to upper-management positions as well. Sales representatives work for wholesalers and manufacturing companies (and even for publishers such as the one that produces this book). They sell automobiles, computer systems and technology, pharmaceuticals, advertising, insurance, real estate, commodities and financial services, and all kinds of consumer goods and services.

If you're interested in mass communications, note that print and online magazines, newspapers, and broadcast companies such as ESPN and MTV generate most of their revenue from advertising, so sales representatives who sell space and time slots in the media contribute a great deal to the success of these firms.[2] And if you like to travel, consider that many sales jobs involve travel.

Advertising, marketing management, and *public relations* are other categories of marketing. In large companies, marketing managers, product managers, promotion managers, and public relations managers often work long hours under pressure; they may travel frequently or transfer between jobs at headquarters and positions in regional offices. Their responsibilities include directing promotional programs, overseeing advertising campaigns and budgets, and conducting communications such as press releases with the firm's publics. Thousands of new positions are expected to open up in the next several years; the field is expected to grow 14 percent over the next decade. Growth of the Internet and new media has especially increased demand for advertising and public relations specialists.[3]

Advertising and public relations firms employed about 458,000 people in a recent year.[4] About one in five U.S. advertising firms are located in New York or California, and more than a quarter of advertising industry workers live in those two states. Most advertising firms develop specialties; many of the largest are international in scope and earn a major proportion of their revenue abroad. Online advertising is just one area in which new jobs will be opening in the future, as more and more client firms expand their online sales operations.

Career Assessment Exercises in Marketing

1. Select a field that interests you. Use the Internet to research types of sales positions available in that field. Locate a few entry-level job openings and see what career steps that position can lead to. (You might wish to start with a popular job-posting site such as Monster. com.) Note the job requirements, the starting salary, and the form of compensation—straight salary? salary plus commission?—and write a one-page summary of your findings.

2. Use the Internet to identify and investigate two or three of the leading advertising agencies in the United States, such as Young & Rubicam or J. Walter Thompson. What are some of their recent ad campaigns, or who are their best-known clients? Where do the agencies have offices? What job openings do they currently list, and what qualifications should applicants for these positions have? Write a brief report comparing the agencies you selected, decide which one you would prefer to work for, and give your reasons.

3. Test your research skills. Choose an ordinary product, such as toothpaste or soft drinks, and conduct a survey to find out why people chose the brand they most recently purchased. For instance, suppose you wanted to find out how people choose their shampoo. List as many decision criteria as you can think of, such as availability, scent, price, packaging, benefits from use (conditioning, dandruff-reducing, and so on), brand name, and ad campaign. Ask eight to ten friends to rank these decision factors, and note some simple demographics about your research subjects such as their age, gender, and occupation. Tabulate your results. What did you find out about how your subjects made their purchase decision? Did any of your findings surprise you? Can you think of any ways in which you might have improved your survey?

PART

5

Managing Technology and Information

[Chapter 14]

Using Technology to
Manage Information

Chapter 14

Learning Objectives

[1] Distinguish between data and information, and explain the role of information systems in business.

[2] List the components and different types of information systems.

[3] Outline how computer hardware and software are used to manage information.

[4] Describe networking and telecommunications technology and the types of computer networks.

[5] Discuss the security and ethical issues involving computer information systems.

[6] Explain the steps that companies go through in anticipating, planning for, and recovering from information systems disasters.

[7] Review current trends in information systems.

Using Technology to Manage Information

Alexander Kirch/iStockphoto

The Shopkick App Kicks Shopping up a Notch

Just when you thought it couldn't possibly get any easier to shop—or harder to curb your shopping habit—along comes Shopkick. The Shopkick app is your own portable, personal shopper—as long you own a smart phone. Available first for iPhones, Shopkick will be accessible soon to Google Android phones as well.

The Shopkick app is a free mobile phone app that now links bricks-and-mortar retailers to the digital age. Users add the app to their phone, register, and when they walk into a participating retailer they automatically receive customized special discounts, loyalty points, and promotions via their phone. In addition, just by entering a store, Shopkick members receive "kickbucks" that are redeemable for rewards, such as gift cards or song downloads, or can be donated to charity. If they go a step further and scan a product with their phone or try on a clothing item, more kickbucks points are dropped in the bucket.

Electronics retailer Best Buy and department store behemoth Macy's were two of Shopkick's original launch partners, but Target, American Eagle, The Sports Authority, Crate & Barrel, and Simon Property Group, malls were quick to jump on board. "The retail environment is changing," acknowledges Margita Labhard, director of Best Buy's new customers solutions group. Best Buy recognized the opportunities offered by Shopkick and signed up early to "find new ways to bring people into our stores through the use of mobile technology, but more importantly, to know when they come into our store," says Labhard. Simon Property Group, which operates more than 100 malls nationwide, is Shopkick's biggest catch so far because it represents a presence in such a wide variety of stores. "It shows how excited our partners are about

Courtesy of Shopkick, Inc.

Shopkick's success, but it also shows how forward-thinking Simon Property Group is," claims Shopkick CEO Cyriac Roeding.

Shopkick does have its detractors, and some kinks will likely have to be worked out. The biggest objection comes from consumer advocacy groups, who are concerned about privacy. Shopkick technology "knows where you are, what you buy, your spending habits, passions, excesses," points out Jeffrey Chester, executive director of the Center for Digital Democracy. Unlike similar shopping apps such as Foursquare, Shopkick alerts retailers when users are inside a store, not just nearby. "That's unusual," notes Sucharita Mulpuru, a marketing analyst. "Will it lift sales? That remains to be seen, but everyone is eager to experiment."

Well, not everyone. Privacy advocates such as Chester are worried that the experiment could lead to data leaks that result in an invasion of consumers' privacy. "What appears to be a relatively harmless trade-off of your information for rewards or discounts is really misleading," Chester warns. But Shopkick's Roeding argues that shoppers should be rewarded for every bit of attention they devote to a retailer, even if it is just walking into a store and walking out again. "Foot traffic is so important," Roeding asserts. "Why does no one ever reward anyone for visiting a store?"

Within the first seven months of operation, Shopkick passed the one million users mark, indicating that consumers enjoy the convenience and customization the app offers, even if privacy concerns lurk in the shadows. It also indicates that, just like previous innovations—ranging from giving a credit-card number over the phone to shopping online to swiping a debit card at the grocery store—consumers will quickly adapt without worry. In fact, one million shoppers already have.[1]

This chapter explores how businesses manage information as a resource, particularly how they use technology to do so. Today, virtually all business functions—from human resources to production to supply chain management—rely on information systems. The chapter begins by differentiating between information and data and then defines an information system. The components of information systems are presented, and two major types of information systems are described. Because of their importance to organizations, the chapter discusses databases, the heart of all information systems. Then the chapter looks at the computer hardware and software that drive information systems. Today, specialized networks make information access and transmission function smoothly, so the chapter examines different types of telecommunications and computer networks to see how businesses like Shopkick are applying them for competitive advantage. The chapter then turns to a discussion of the ethical and security issues affecting information systems, followed by a description of how organizations plan for, and recover from, information system disasters. A review of the current trends in information systems concludes the chapter.

Data, Information, and Information Systems

Every day, businesspeople ask themselves questions such as the following:

- How well is our product selling in Atlanta compared with Tampa? Have sales among consumers aged 25 to 45 increased or decreased within the past year?

- How will rising energy prices affect production and distribution costs?

- If employees can access the benefits system through our network, will this increase or decrease benefit costs?

- Can we communicate more efficiently and effectively with our increasingly dispersed workforce?

data raw facts and figures that may or may not be relevant to a business decision.

information knowledge gained from processing data.

An effective information system can help answer these and many other questions. **Data** consist of raw facts and figures that may or may not be relevant to a business decision. **Information** is knowledge gained from processing those facts and figures. So although businesspeople need to gather data about the demographics of a target market or the specifications of a certain product, the data are useless unless they are transformed into relevant information that can be used to make a competitive decision. For instance, data might be the sizes of various demographic groups. Information drawn from those data could be how many of those individuals are potential customers for a firm's products. Technology has advanced so quickly that all businesses, regardless of size or location, now have access to data and information that can make them competitive in a global arena.

An **information system** is an organized method for collecting, storing, and communicating past, present, and projected information on internal operations and external intelligence. Most information systems today use computer and telecommunications technology. A large organization typically assigns responsibility for directing its information systems and related operations to an executive called the **chief information officer (CIO)**. Often, the CIO reports directly to the firm's chief executive officer (CEO). An effective CIO can understand and harness technology so that the company can communicate internally and externally in one seamless operation. But small companies rely just as much on information systems as do large ones, even if they do not employ a manager assigned to this area on a full-time basis.

The role of the CIO is both expanding and changing as the technology to manage information continues to develop. Over the past ten years, the role of a CIO has changed from being a technical one to that of a business partner who often exerts strong influence over his or her company's strategy. CIOs will need to adapt their roles even further in the future. Moreover, CIOs and former CIOs are beginning to appear on company boards more often.[2]

Information systems can be tailored to assist many business functions and departments—from marketing and manufacturing to finance and accounting. They can manage the overwhelming flood of information by organizing data in a logical and accessible manner. Through the system, a company can monitor all components of its operations and business strategy, identifying problems and opportunities. Information systems gather data from inside and outside the organization; they then process the data to produce information that is relevant to all aspects of the organization. Processing steps could involve storing data for later use, classifying and analyzing it, and retrieving it easily when needed.

Many companies—and nations—combine high-tech and low-tech solutions to manage the flow of information. E-mail, wireless communications, and videoconferencing haven't totally replaced paper memos, phone conversations, and face-to-face meetings, but they are increasingly common. Information can make the difference between staying in business and going bankrupt. Keeping on top of changing consumer demands, competitors' actions, and the latest government regulations will help a firm fine-tune existing products, develop new winners, and maintain effective marketing.

Components and Types of Information Systems

The definition of *information system* in the previous section does not specifically mention the use of computers or technology. In fact, information systems have been around since the beginning of civilization and were, by today's standards, very low tech. Think about your college or university's library. At one time the library probably had card catalog files to help you find information. Those files were information systems because they stored data about books and periodicals in an organized manner on 3-by-5-inch index cards. Users could flip through the cards and locate library materials by author, title, or subject, although the process could be tedious and time consuming.

Today, however, when businesspeople think about information systems, they are most likely thinking about **computer-based information systems**. These systems rely on computer and related technologies to store information electronically in an organized, accessible manner. So, instead of card catalogs, your college library probably uses a computerized information system that allows users to search through library holdings much faster and easier.

information system
organized method for collecting, storing, and communicating past, present, and projected information on internal operations and external intelligence.

chief information officer (CIO) executive responsible for managing a firm's information system and related computer technologies.

Assessment Check ☑

1. Distinguish between data and information.
2. What is an information system?

computer-based information systems information systems that rely on computer and related technologies to store information electronically in an organized, accessible manner.

Computer-based information systems consist of four components and technologies:

- computer hardware
- computer software
- telecommunications and computer networks
- data resource management.

Computer hardware consists of machines that range from supercomputers to smart phones. It also includes the input, output, and storage devices needed to support computing machines. Software includes operating systems, such as Microsoft's Windows 7 or Linux, and applications programs, such as Adobe Acrobat or Oracle's PeopleSoft Enterprise applications. Telecommunications and computer networks encompass the hardware and software needed to provide wired or wireless voice and data communications. This includes support for external networks such as the Internet and private internal networks. Data resource management involves developing and maintaining an organization's databases so that decision makers are able to access the information they need in a timely manner.

In the case of your college or university library, the computer-based information system is generally made up of computer hardware, such as monitors and keyboards, which are linked to the library's network and a database containing information on the library's holdings. Specialized software allows users to access the database. In addition, the library's network is likely also connected to a larger private network and the Internet. This connection gives users remote access to the library's database, as well as access to other computerized databases such as LexisNexis.

Databases

database centralized integrated collection of data resources.

The heart of any information system is its **database**, a centralized integrated collection of data resources. A company designs its databases to meet particular information processing and retrieval needs of its workforce. Businesses obtain databases in many ways. They can hire a staff person to build them on site, hire an outside source to do so, or buy packaged database programs from specialized vendors, such as Oracle. A database serves as an electronic filing cabinet, capable of storing massive amounts of data and retrieving it within seconds. A database should be continually updated; otherwise, a firm may find itself with data that are outdated and possibly useless. One problem with databases is that they can contribute to information overload—too much data for people to absorb or data that are not relevant to decision making. Because computer processing speed and storage capacity are both increasing rapidly, and because data have become more abundant, businesspeople need to be careful that their databases contain only the facts they need. If they don't, they can waste time wading through unnecessary data. Another challenge with databases is keeping them safe, as the "Hit & Miss" feature describes.

Masterfile

In the case of the *computer-based information system* in the library, it is generally made up of computer hardware linked to the library's network and a database containing information on the books in the library. Specialized software allows users to access the database.

Wyndham Hotels and Resorts Database Breached

In the third such incident in a year, Wyndham Hotels and Resorts—which owns Days Inn, Ramada, Super 8, and other hotel chains and restaurants—discovered that one of its secure databases had been compromised. From a single breach, a hacker gained access to customer information from several of the company's restaurants and other properties, then downloaded it to an off-site URL. The information included names and credit card numbers of guests, the cards' expiration dates, and other data from the magnetic strip on each card. Wyndham does not record customers' birth dates, Social Security numbers, addresses, or other identifying information, and those data were not included. The breach was discovered when a credit card processor and an issuer informed Wyndham that they had become concerned about "unusual fraud patterns" on the cards.

Wyndham took immediate steps to stop the break-in. In an open letter on its Web site, the company stated, "We deeply regret that this incident occurred," and detailed its investigation. The chain notified the U.S. Secret Service, which investigates counterfeiting, as well as the attorneys general of several states. It hired an outside investigator to appraise the damage and advise on improving security. It also hired a firm that specializes in credit card industry standards to look into each compromised property in order to improve compliance. In addition,

Wyndham notified American Express, Visa, MasterCard, and Discover of card numbers that may have been involved.

Wyndham assured guests that identity theft was unlikely, but warned them to monitor their credit card statements and reports vigilantly and to report any suspicious activity to the cards' issuers. It offered affected guests free credit monitoring and set up a special toll-free line that all guests could call for more information.

Questions for Critical Thinking

1. What can Wyndham do to assure its guests that it will protect them from credit card fraud?
2. The hotel industry in general is vulnerable to security breaches because of the huge volume of data that hotels collect and store during reservations and check-in. What steps might the industry take to prevent these breaches?

Sources: Sarah Braley, "Data Security a Top Priority for the Hotel Industry," *Meetings and Conventions*, April 6, 2011, http://www.meetings-conventions.com; Company Web site, http://www.wyndhamworldwide.com/customer_care, accessed May 24, 2010; Angela Moscaritolo, "Wyndham Hotels Suffers Another Data Breach," *SC Magazine*, March 9, 2010, http://www.scmagazineus.com; Larry Barrett, "Wyndham Hotels' Networks Hacked—Again," *eSecurity Planet*, March 9, 2010, http://www.esecurityplanet.com; Robert McMillan, "Wyndham Hotels Hacked Again," *IDG News Service*, February 26, 2010, http://www.cio.com.

Decision makers can also look up online data. Online systems give access to enormous amounts of government data, such as economic data from the Bureau of Labor Statistics and the Department of Commerce. One of the largest online databases is that of the U.S. Census Bureau. The census of population, conducted every ten years, attempts to collect data on more than 120 million households across the United States. After attempting to count everyone in the country, the Census Bureau has selected participants fill out forms containing questions about marital status, place of birth, ethnic background, citizenship, workplaces, commuting time, income, occupation, type of housing, number of telephones and vehicles, even grandparents as caregivers. Households receiving the most recent questionnaire can respond in English as well as a variety of other languages including Spanish, Chinese, Vietnamese, and Korean. Not surprisingly, sifting through all the collected data takes time. Although certain restrictions limit how businesspeople can access and use specific census data, the general public may access the data via the American FactFinder on the Census Bureau's Web site (http://factfinder.census.gov), as well as at state data centers and public libraries.

Another source of free information is company Web sites. Interested parties can visit firms' home pages to look for information about customers, suppliers, and competitors. Trade associations and academic institutions also maintain Web sites with information on topics of interest.

Types of Information Systems

Many different types of information systems exist. In general, however, information systems fall into two broad categories: operational support systems or management support systems.

Operational Support Systems

Operational support systems are designed to produce a variety of information on an organization's activities for both internal and external users. Examples of operational support systems include transaction processing systems and process control systems. **Transaction processing systems** record and process data from business transactions. For example, major retailers use point-of-sale systems, which link electronic cash registers to the retailer's computer centers. Sales data are transmitted from cash registers to the computer center either immediately or at regular intervals. **Process control systems** monitor and control physical processes. A steel mill, for instance, may have electronic sensors linked to a computer system monitoring the entire production process. The system makes necessary changes and alerts operators to potential problems.

Walmart quickly adopted an information system based on RFID (radio-frequency identification) technology to track supply chain activities. Today, many retailers use RFID. Truecount Corporation, based in Vermont, is one company that provides RFID software solutions to retailers so they can monitor shipping and receiving of goods, with the goal of achieving up-to-the-minute knowledge of inventory status. This "can be a huge competitive advantage for retailers," says Zander Livingston, CEO of Truecount.[3]

At American Airlines, the one thing we're not maintaining is the status quo.

AmericanAirlines

The complex process of airline maintenance is critical to passenger safety. To track parts, schedule inspections, and manage inventory levels, many airlines use an *operational support system*. In this ad, American Airlines reports that improved business processes have turned costly maintenance operations into a source of profit.

Management Support Systems

Information systems that are designed to provide support for effective decision making are classified as **management support systems**. Several different types of management support systems are available. A **management information system (MIS)** is designed to produce reports to managers and other professionals.

A **decision support system (DSS)** gives direct support to businesspeople during the decision-making process. For instance, a marketing manager might use a decision support system to analyze the impact on sales and profits of a product price change.

An **executive support system (ESS)** lets senior executives access the firm's primary databases, often by touching the computer screen, pointing and clicking a mouse, or using voice recognition. The typical ESS allows users to choose from many kinds of data, such as the firm's financial statements and sales figures, as well as stock market trends for the company and for the industry as a whole. If they wish, managers can start by looking at summaries and then access more detailed information when needed.

Finally, an **expert system** is a computer program that imitates human thinking through complicated sets of "if-then" rules. The system applies human knowledge in a specific subject area to solve a problem. Expert systems are used for a variety of business purposes: determining credit limits for credit card applicants, monitoring machinery in a plant to predict potential problems or breakdowns, making mortgage loans, and determining optimal plant layouts. They are typically developed by capturing the knowledge of recognized experts in a field whether within a business itself or outside it.

expert system computer program that imitates human thinking through complicated sets of "if-then" rules.

Computer Hardware and Software

It may be hard to believe, but only a few decades ago computers were considered exotic curiosities, used only for very specialized applications and understood by only a few people. The first commercial computer, UNIVAC I, was sold to the U.S. Census Bureau in the early 1950s. It cost $1 million, took up most of a room, and could perform about 2,000 calculations per second.[4] The invention of transistors and then integrated circuits (microchips) quickly led to smaller and more powerful devices. By the 1980s, computers could routinely perform several million calculations per second. Now, computers perform billions of calculations per second, and some fit in the palm of your hand.

When the first personal computers were introduced in the late 1970s and early 1980s, the idea of a computer on every desk, or in every home, seemed far-fetched. Today they have become indispensable to both businesses and households. Not only have computers become much more powerful and faster over the past 25 years, but they are less expensive as well. IBM's first personal computer (PC), introduced in 1981, cost well over $5,000 fully configured. Today, the typical PC sells for under $800.

Types of Computer Hardware

Hardware consists of all tangible elements of a computer system—the input devices, the components that store and process data and perform required calculations, and the output devices that present the results to information users. Input devices allow users to enter data and commands for processing, storage, and output. The most common input devices are the keyboard and mouse. Storage and processing components consist of the hard drive as well as various other storage components, including DVD drives and flash memory devices. Flash memory devices are becoming increasingly popular because they are small and can hold large amounts of data. Some, called thumb drives, can even fit on a keychain. To gain access to the data they hold, users just plug them into an unused USB (universal serial bus) port, standard on today's computers. Output devices, such as monitors and printers, are the hardware elements that transmit or display documents and other results of a computer system's work.

Different types of computers incorporate widely varying memory capacities and processing speeds. These differences define four broad classifications: mainframe computers, midrange systems, personal computers, and hand-held devices. A mainframe computer is the largest type of computer system with the most extensive storage capacity and the fastest processing speeds. Especially powerful mainframes called *supercomputers* can handle extremely rapid, complex calculations involving thousands of variables, such as weather modeling and forecasting. Today's supercomputers can perform a trillion or more calculations per second.

Midrange systems consist of high-end network servers and other types of computers that can handle large-scale processing needs. They are less powerful than mainframe computers

Assessment Check ✔

1. List the four components of a computer-based information system.
2. What is a database?
3. What are the two general types of information systems? Give examples of each.

hardware all tangible elements of a computer system.

server the heart of a midrange computer network.

but more powerful than most personal computers. A **server** is the heart of a midrange computer network, supporting applications and allowing the sharing of output devices, software, and databases among networked users. Many Internet-related functions at organizations are handled by midrange systems. Midrange systems are also commonly employed in process control systems, computer-aided manufacturing (CAM), and computer-aided design (CAD).

Personal computers are everywhere today—in homes, businesses, schools, nonprofit organizations, and government agencies. Recent estimates of PC ownership say that more than two-thirds of American households have at least one personal computer. They have earned increasing popularity because of their ever-expanding capability to handle many of the functions that large mainframes performed only a few decades ago. Most desktop computers are linked to networks, such as the Internet.

Desktop computers used to be the standard PC seen in offices and homes. While millions of desktop computers remain on the job, laptops—including notebooks and netbooks—now account for more than half of all PCs sold. The increasing popularity of these computers can be explained by their improved displays, faster processing speeds, ability to handle more intense graphics, larger storage capacities, and more durable designs. Last but not least is the most obvious advantage—they are portable. They are thinner and lighter than ever before. Business owners, managers, salespeople, and students all benefit from the constant innovation of the laptop.

While prices for full-size laptops, notebooks, and netbooks vary greatly—you can purchase a netbook for $300 or a MacBook Pro for $2,200—they still generally run less than a comparable desktop. A netbook doesn't have the computing capacity of a larger, more expensive notebook, but for a few hundred dollars it can perform basic tasks such as e-mail, word processing, and spreadsheet calculations.

Hand-held devices such as personal digital assistants (PDAs) and smart phones are even smaller. Although PDAs have limited software applications, they are good for keeping schedules and contact information. Smart phones, such as the iPhone, BlackBerry, Android, and BlackJack, essentially combine a phone with the Internet. Because of their ever-increasing capacity to surf the Internet, open and edit documents, send and receive messages, make calls, and more, sales of smart phones are rapidly outpacing PDAs as well as traditional cell phones.

Two other devices—tablets and e-readers—are also making inroads in business. In addition to the Apple iPad, there are now more than 75 tablet models on the market. Samsung, Motorola, and RIM (manufacturer of the BlackBerry) have all entered the tablet market with serious intentions and constant innovations designed to make them standard business tools. E-readers such as Amazon's Kindle and Barnes & Noble's Nook continue to expand their capacities as well—and will likely find their way into the business market before long.[5]

While smart phones can be terrific tools that boost productivity, some people overuse or even misuse them. The "Business Etiquette" feature describes some do's and don'ts of smart phone use in a business environment.

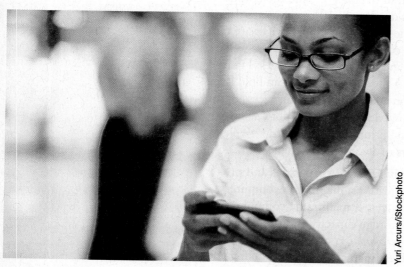

Yuri Arcurs/iStockphoto

While smart phones can boost productivity, some people overuse or even misuse them. Check out the "Business Etiquette" box for some helpful tips for courteous communication while using your hand-held device in a business environment.

In addition to PDAs and smart phones, specialized hand-held devices are used in a variety of businesses for different applications. Some restaurants, for example, have small wireless devices that allow servers to swipe a credit card and print out a receipt right at the customer's table. Drivers for UPS and FedEx use special hand-held devices to track package deliveries and accept delivery signatures. The driver scans each package as it is delivered, and the information is transmitted to the delivery firm's network. Within a few seconds, the sender, using an Internet connection, can obtain the delivery information and even see a facsimile of the recipient's signature.

Computer Software

Software includes all of the programs, routines, and computer languages that control a computer and tell it how to operate. The software that controls the basic workings of a computer system is its *operating system*. More than 90 percent of personal computers use a version of Microsoft's popular Windows operating system. Personal computers made by Apple use the Mac operating system. Most hand-held devices use either the Palm or Symbian operating system or a special version of Windows called Windows Mobile. But the Droid, iPhone, and BlackBerry models have their own operating systems. Other operating systems include Unix, which runs on many midrange computer systems, and Linux, which runs on both PCs and midrange systems.

A program that performs the specific tasks that the user wants to carry out—such as writing a letter or looking up data—is called *application software*. Examples of application software include Adobe Acrobat, Microsoft PowerPoint, and Quicken. Table 14.1 lists the major categories of application software. Most application programs are currently stored on individual computers. As the chapter's opening vignette discussed, the future of applications software is constantly changing. Some believe much of it will eventually become Web based, with the programs themselves stored in the "cloud," on Internet-connected servers. Others disagree, arguing that most computer users will not want to rely on an Internet connection to perform tasks such as preparing a spreadsheet using Microsoft Excel. The "Going Green" feature explains how some observers believe that cloud computing might help reduce greenhouse gases.

BusinessEtiquette

Courteous Communications via Wireless Devices

According to data from the U.S. Census Bureau and other sources, cell phone use in America has skyrocketed from about 3.5 million subscribers to about 285 million in a decade. With so many of us communicating instantly—and almost constantly—it is more important than ever to be courteous, whether speaking or e-mailing on a hand-held device.

1 *Be aware of your surroundings—and your neighbors.* If you're in a meeting or other place where a separate conversation would be disruptive, turn your ringtone off. If the call or e-mail simply can't wait, excuse yourself and leave the room before responding to it.

2 *Lower your voice when you're talking in public.* If the room you are in is quieter than your speaking voice, it's better to go somewhere else.

3 *When sending e-mail or texting, don't overabbreviate.* A business message can be concise without being cute or, worse, unintelligible. It is just as easy to say "See you at 3" as "cu@3."

4 *Before you send a text message or e-mail, read it over carefully.* Typos and grammatical errors don't look good, especially in a business message.

5 *Be careful about your Facebook profile photo.* Now that smart phones let users link all their contact information, your photo will appear on the other person's phone when you call. And people beyond those on your "friends" list will see it. Be sure your photo is appropriate for both friends and business callers.

Sources: Christopher Elliott, "E-Mail Etiquette for Wireless Devices: 7 Tips," Microsoft Small Business Center, http://www.microsoft.com, accessed June 21, 2011; Taya Flores, "Cell Phone Etiquette Is Important," *JC Online.com*, April 19, 2010, http://www.jconline.com; Mike Elgan, "Here Comes the New Cell Phone Etiquette," *IT World*, January 22, 2010, http://www.itworld.com.

---

software all the programs, routines, and computer languages that control a computer and tell it how to operate.

14.1 Common Types of Applications Software

TYPE	DESCRIPTION	EXAMPLES
Word processing	Programs that input, store, retrieve, edit, and print various types of documents.	Microsoft Word, Pages (Apple)
Spreadsheets	Programs that prepare and analyze financial statements, sales forecasts, budgets, and similar numerical and statistical data.	Microsoft Excel, Numbers (Apple)
Presentation software	Programs that create presentations. Users can create bulleted lists, charts, graphs, pictures, audio, and even short video clips.	Microsoft PowerPoint, Keynote (Apple)
Desktop publishing	Software that combines high-quality type, graphics, and layout tools to create output that can look as attractive as documents produced by professional publishers and printers.	Adobe Acrobat, Microsoft Publisher
Financial software	Programs that compile accounting and financial data to create financial statements, reports, and budgets; they perform basic financial management tasks such as balancing a checkbook.	Quicken, QuickBooks
Database programs	Software that searches and retrieves data from a database; it can sort data based on various criteria.	Microsoft Access, Approach
Personal information managers	Specialized database programs that allow people to track communications with personal and business contacts; some combine e-mail capability.	Microsoft Outlook, Lotus Organizer
Enterprise resource planning	Integrated cross-functional software that controls many business activities, including distribution, finance, and human resources.	SAP Enterprise Resource Planning

Assessment Check ✔

1. List two input and output devices.
2. What accounts for the increasing popularity of notebook computers?
3. What is software? List the two categories of software.

Computer Networks

As mentioned earlier, virtually all computers today are linked to networks. In fact, if your PC has Internet access, you're linked to a network. Local area networks and wide area networks allow businesses to communicate, transmit and print documents, and share data. These networks, however, require businesses to install special equipment and connections between office sites. But Internet technology has also been applied to internal company communications and business tasks, tapping a ready-made network. Among these new Internet-based applications are intranets, virtual private networks (VPNs), and voice over Internet protocol (VoIP). Each has contributed to the effectiveness and speed of business processes, so we discuss them next.

Local Area Networks and Wide Area Networks

local area networks (LANs), computer networks that connect machines within limited areas, such as a building or several nearby buildings.

Most organizations connect their offices and buildings by creating **local area networks (LANs),** computer networks that connect machines within limited areas, such as a building or several nearby buildings. LANs are useful because they link computers and allow them to share printers, documents, and information, as well as provide access to the Internet. Figure 14.1 shows what a small business computer network might look like.

wide area networks (WANs) tie larger geographical regions together by using telephone lines and microwave and satellite transmission.

Wide area networks (WANs) tie larger geographical regions together by using telephone lines and microwave and satellite transmission. One familiar WAN is long-distance

Can Cloud Computing Also Be "Green" Computing?

The rise in cloud computing has some observers hoping it will decrease the emission of greenhouse gases. However, others are concerned that it will cause emissions to increase because it will require larger and larger data storage centers that use more energy.

The environmental organization Greenpeace recently issued the "Cool IT Challenge" to the IT sector urging these firms to reduce emissions by using renewable electricity to power their data centers and to pressure utility companies to improve access to renewable energy. In a recent report, Greenpeace declared that IT energy solutions can even encourage the growth of local, decentralized energy centers as opposed to large grids. These smaller, local networks could result in better energy choices for consumers as well as improved efficiency and more use of renewable energy.

Greenpeace has also published a chart that rates major data centers' use of power sources. Google's data center in Oregon was the leading user of renewable energy, with almost 51 percent of its energy coming from renewable sources as opposed to coal and nuclear power.

GE has been investing in companies that develop software to make the data centers required for cloud computing more efficient, along with power companies such as Lineage Power Holdings, which works with alternative energy sources such as fuel cells, wind, and solar power.

Even Greenpeace has come under fire for relying on coal and nuclear energy at some of its data centers, due to long-term agreements with local utilities. Gary Cook, one of the Cool IT Campaign's policy advisors, declared, "We're definitely trying to run the greenest operation we can. . . . We're in the process of reworking some of our IT infrastructure, and we'll clean that up."

Questions for Critical Thinking

1. Why do you think devices such as smart phones or the iPad, which rely on cloud computing, might contribute to increased greenhouse gas emissions?

2. Do you think that data centers' voluntary actions will be enough to lower greenhouse gas emissions? Why or why not?

Sources: Martin LaMonica, "GE Buys Into Efficient Power for Cloud Computing," *CNET News*, January 14, 2011, http://news.cnet.com; Greenpeace Web site, http://www.greenpeace.org, accessed May 22, 2010; The Green Grid Web site, http://www.thegreengrid.org, accessed May 22, 2010; Rich Miller, "Greenpeace: Cloud Contributes to Climate Change," Data Center Knowledge, March 30, 2010, http://www.datacenterknowledge.com; Matthew Wheeland, "Cloud Computing Is Efficient, But It's Not Green—Yet," *GreenBiz*, March 30, 2010, http://www.greenbiz.com; Rich Miller, "Greenpeace's Hosting: Not 'Truly Green,' " Data Center Knowledge, March 3, 2010.

---

telephone service. Companies such as AT&T and Verizon provide WAN services to businesses and consumers. Firms also use WANs to conduct their own operations. Typically, companies link their own network systems to outside communications equipment and services for transmission across long distances.

WiFi wireless network that connects various devices and allows them to communicate with one another through radio waves.

Wireless Local Networks

A wireless network allows computers, printers, and other devices to be connected without the hassle of stringing cables in traditional office settings. The current standard for wireless networks is called WiFi. **WiFi**—short for *wireless fidelity*—is a wireless network that connects various devices and allows them to communicate with one another through radio waves. Any PC with a WiFi receptor can connect with the Internet at so-called hot spots—locations with a wireless router and a high-speed Internet modem. There are almost hundreds of thousands of hot spots worldwide today. They are found in a variety of places, including airports, libraries, and coffee shops. Examples include Panera Bread's 1,300 bakery-cafes in the United States and Kansai International Airport in Osaka, Japan. Some locations provide free access, while others charge a fee.

WiFi connections are often called *hot spots*—locations with a wireless router and a high-speed Internet modem. There are almost hundreds of thousands of hot spots worldwide today found in a variety of places, including airports, libraries, and coffee shops.

FIGURE
14.1

A Local Area Network

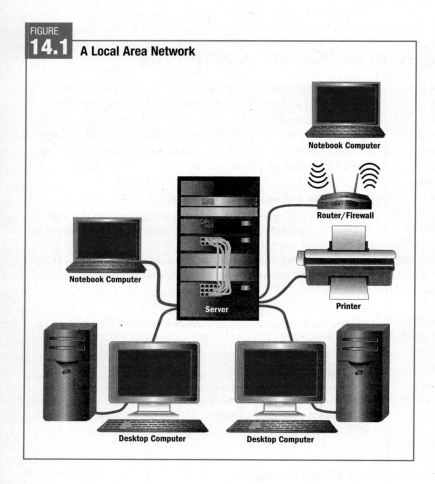

Many believe that the successor to WiFi will be *Wi-Max*. Unlike WiFi's relatively limited geographic coverage area—generally around 300 feet—a single Wi-Max access point can provide coverage over many miles. In addition, cell phone service providers, such as Sprint Nextel and AT&T, offer broadband network cards for notebook PCs. These devices allow users to access the provider's mobile broadband network from virtually any location where cell phone reception is available.

Intranets

A broad approach to sharing information in an organization is to establish a company network patterned after the Internet. Such a network is called an **intranet**. Intranets are similar to the Internet, but they limit access to employees or other authorized users. An intranet blocks outsiders without valid passwords from entering its network by incorporating both software and hardware known as a **firewall**. Firewalls limit data transfers to certain locations and log system use so that managers can identify attempts to log on with invalid passwords and other threats to a system's security. Highly sophisticated packages immediately alert system administrators about suspicious activities and permit authorized personnel to use smart cards to connect from remote terminals.

intranet computer network that is similar to the Internet but limits access to authorized users.

firewall limit data transfers to certain locations and log system use so that managers can identify attempts to log on with invalid passwords and other threats to a system's security.

Intranets solve the problem of linking different types of computers. Like the Internet, intranets can integrate computers running all kinds of operating systems. In addition, intranets are relatively easy and inexpensive to set up because most businesses already have some of the required hardware and software. For instance, a small business can simply purchase a DSL router and a few cables and create an intranet using phone jacks and internal phone lines. All the business's computers will be linked with each other and with the Internet.

Intranets can support teamwork among employees who are traveling or telecommuting. They can nurture innovation when designated for the development of creative ideas. They can be used to share marketing and brand information worldwide. Mobile intranets—with access from smart phones—are becoming increasingly popular for companies with employees who are often on the go. Mota-Engil, a leading construction firm in Portugal, recently won an award for its intranet called InnovCenter, which operates solely for the purpose of generating and capturing ideas for improving the firm's performance and services. InnovCenter receives employees' ideas via their mobile phones much like an old-fashioned suggestion box—even when workers are on the job at a faraway site.[6]

virtual private networks (VPNs) secure connections between two points on the Internet.

Virtual Private Networks

To gain increased security for Internet communications, companies often turn to **virtual private networks (VPNs)**, secure connections between two points on the Internet.

These VPNs use firewalls and programs that encapsulate data to make them more secure during transit. Loosely defined, a VPN can include a range of networking technologies, from secure Internet connections to private networks from service providers like IBM. A VPN is cheaper for a company to use than leasing several of its own lines. It can also take months to install a leased line in some parts of the world, but a new user can be added to a VPN in a day. Because a VPN uses the Internet, it can be wired, wireless, or a combination of the two.

Colorado-based Advanced Systems Group (ASG) provides data storage and management services to other companies. As the company expanded and opened branch offices, its own security became a concern. ASG turned to Check Point, which created a secure VPN connecting ASG's home office and five branch offices. The VPN allows ASG to add new sites and new remote users automatically.[7]

VoIP

VoIP—which stands for *voice over Internet Protocol*—is an alternative to traditional telecommunication services provided by companies such as Verizon and Qwest. The VoIP telephone is not connected to a traditional phone jack but rather is connected to a personal computer with any type of broadband connection. Special software transmits phone conversations over the Internet, rather than through telephone lines. A VoIP user dials the phone as usual. The person can make and receive calls to and from those with traditional telephone connections (landline or wireless).

A growing number of consumers and businesses have embraced VoIP, mainly due to its cost savings and extra features. As technology continues to advance, demand for the service has increased. AT&T and Verizon Wireless recently announced that they would permit VoIP on some smartphones. Google has been in the process of tying in VoIP to its Google Voice. The various VoIP providers are working together with the goal of creating a single VoIP standard that would permit seamless roaming worldwide.[8]

In spite of VoIP's apparent advantages, there are several potential drawbacks to replacing traditional telephony with Internet telephony. For one thing, your Internet phone service will be only as reliable as your broadband connection. If your broadband connection goes out, so will your phone service. Also, without extensive safeguards, VoIP can expose a phone system to the havoc that can affect the rest of the Internet, such as worms and viruses.

VoIP alternative to traditional telecommunication services provided by companies such as Verizon and Qwest.

Assessment Check ☑

1. What is a LAN?
2. What are the differences between an intranet and a VPN?
3. Briefly explain how VoIP works.

Security and Ethical Issues Affecting Information Systems

Numerous security and ethical issues affect information systems. As information systems become increasingly important business assets, they also become progressively harder and more expensive to replace. Damage to information systems or theft of data can have disastrous consequences. When computers are connected to a network, a problem at any individual computer can affect the entire network. Two of the major security threats are e-crime and so-called malware.

E-Crime

Computers provide efficient ways for employees to share information. But they may also allow people with more malicious intentions to access information. Or they may allow pranksters—who have no motive other than to see whether they can hack into a system—to gain access to private information. Common e-crimes involve stealing or altering data in several ways:

- Employees or outsiders may change or invent data to produce inaccurate or misleading information.

- Employees or outsiders may modify computer programs to create false information or illegal transactions or to insert viruses.

- Unauthorized people can access computer systems for their own benefit or knowledge or just to see if they can get in.

Individuals, businesses, and government agencies are all vulnerable to computer crime. Computer hackers—unauthorized users—sometimes work alone and sometimes work in groups. Hackers can break into computer systems just to show that they can do it; other times they have more sinister motives. A recent survey reported that although computer crime decreased slightly recently, the majority of such attacks may go undetected, because many firms have concentrated on foiling hackers and blocking pornography while leaving themselves open to cybercriminals who are developing increasingly sophisticated weapons. Even Apple computers, normally immune to cybercrime, are becoming vulnerable as more and more Mac users store data in the "cloud"—that is, on the Internet itself—rather than on hard drives. Until now there has been no single uniform system for reporting cyber crime, but the Internet Engineering Task Force (IETF) is working toward a common format that will have reliable time stamps, will be available in different languages, and will allow users to attach samples of malicious code. These automated tools will be able to analyze massive amounts of data much faster than human analysts can.[9]

Information system administrators implement two basic protections against computer crime: they try to prevent access to their systems by unauthorized users and the viewing of data by unauthorized system users. The simplest method of preventing access requires authorized users to enter passwords. The company may also install firewalls, described earlier. To prevent system users from reading sensitive information, the company may use encryption software, which encodes, or scrambles, messages. To read encrypted messages, users must use an electronic key to convert them to regular text. But as fast as software developers invent new and more elaborate protective measures, hackers seem to break through their defenses. Thus, security is an ongoing battle.

Recently consumers began receiving notification from credit-card issuers and retailers warning that Epsilon, the marketing services firm that sends more than 40 billion emails a year on behalf of its 2,500 business customers, had been compromised by hackers. In a statement, Epsilon said that the information obtained by hackers was limited to names and email addresses of consumers but that "no other personal identifiable information associated with the names was at risk." However, Epsilon's business clients—which included banks such as Chase, and retailers such as L.L. Bean and Walgreens—worried that consumers' privacy had been breached.[10]

As the size of computer hardware diminishes, it becomes increasingly vulnerable to theft. Hand-held devices, for instance, can easily vanish with a pickpocket or purse snatcher. Many notebook computers and hand-held devices contain special security software or passwords that makes it difficult for a thief or any unauthorized person to access the data stored in the computer's memory. If you have a notebook computer that contains sensitive personal information, you should consider having such safeguards.

Computer Viruses, Worms, Trojan Horses, and Spyware

Viruses, worms, Trojan horses, and spyware, collectively referred to as **malware**, are malicious software programs designed to infect computer systems. These programs can destroy data, steal sensitive information, and even render information systems inoperable. Recently, malware has been discovered in advertisements on major sites such as Yahoo, Fox, and Google as well as *The New York Times* and WhitePages.com. Malware attacks cost consumers and businesses billions of dollars annually. Although law enforcement has made progress against cybercrime, cybercriminals are now targeting social networking sites. A second search box recently began appearing on Facebook interfaces. This raised concern about a possible malware infection because Facebook reported that it had not inserted the second box.[11]

Computer **viruses** are programs that secretly attach themselves to other programs (called *hosts*) and change them or destroy data. According to the computer security company Symantec, there are currently almost 3 million active computer viruses worldwide.[12] Viruses can be programmed to become active immediately or to remain dormant for a period of time, after which the infections suddenly activate themselves and cause problems. A virus can reproduce by copying itself onto other programs stored in the same drive. It spreads as users install infected software on their systems or exchange files with others, usually by exchanging e-mail, accessing electronic bulletin boards, trading disks, or downloading programs or data from unknown sources on the Internet.

A **worm** is a small piece of software that exploits a security hole in a network to replicate itself. A copy of the worm scans the network for another machine that has a specific security hole. It copies itself to the new machine using the security hole and then starts replicating from there as well. Unlike viruses, worms don't need host programs to damage computer systems.

A **botnet** is a network of PCs that have been infected with one or more data-stealing viruses. Computer criminals tie the infected computers into a network, often without the owners being aware of it, and sell the botnet on the black market. They or others use the botnet to commit identity theft, send spam, buy blocks of concert tickets for scalping, and attack the Internet itself. About 4,000 to 6,000 botnets are active today. Spanish authorities recently brought down the Mariposa botnet, the world's largest to date, a network of 12.7 million infected computers. Some of the computers were inside *Fortune* 1,000 companies and major banks. Although the authorities made some arrests, the creator of the Mariposa botnet has not been caught.[13]

A **Trojan horse** is a program that claims to do one thing but in reality does something else, usually something malicious. For example, a Trojan horse might claim,

malware any malicious software program designed to infect computer systems.

viruses programs that secretly attach themselves to other programs (called *hosts*) and change them or destroy data.

worm small piece of software that exploits a security hole in a network to replicate itself.

botnet a network of PCs that have been infected with one or more data-stealing viruses.

Trojan horse program that claims to do one thing but in reality does something else, usually something malicious.

and even appear, to be a game. When an unsuspecting user clicks on the Trojan horse to launch it, the program might erase the hard drive or steal any personal data stored on the computer.

Spyware is software that secretly gathers user information through the user's Internet connection without his or her knowledge, usually for advertising purposes. Spyware applications are typically bundled with other programs downloaded from the Internet. Once installed, the spyware monitors user activity on the Internet and transmits that information in the background to someone else.

Attacks by malware are not limited to computers and computer networks; hand-held devices, including cell phones, have been affected as well. Smart phone users have reported a sharp increase in viruses, worms, and other forms of malware.[14] Firms such as IBM are directing more IT time toward issues of mobile phone security because skilled attackers can alter code to gain unauthorized access to a company's system, including sensitive information.[15]

As viruses, worms, botnets, and Trojan horses become more complex, the technology to fight them must increase in sophistication as well. The simplest way to protect against computer viruses is to install one of the many available antivirus software programs, such as Norton AntiVirus and McAfee VirusScan. These programs, which also protect against worms and some Trojan horses, continuously monitor systems for viruses and automatically eliminate any they spot. Users should regularly update them by downloading the latest virus definitions. In addition, computer users should also install and regularly update antispyware programs because many Trojan horses are forms of spyware.

But management must begin to emphasize security at a deeper level: during software design, in corporate servers, at Web gateways, and through Internet service providers. Because more than 90 percent of the world's PCs run on Microsoft operating systems, a single virus, worm, or Trojan horse can spread among them quickly. Individual computer users should carefully choose the files they load onto their systems, scan their systems regularly, make sure their antivirus software is up to date, and install software only from known sources. They should also be very careful when opening attachments to e-mails because many viruses, worms, and Trojan horses are spread that way.

Information Systems and Ethics

The scope and power of today's information systems not surprisingly raise a number of ethical issues and concerns. These affect both employees and organizations. For instance, it is not uncommon for organizations to have specific ethical standards and policies regarding the use of information systems by employees and vendors. These standards include obligations to protect system security and the privacy and confidentiality of data. Policies also may cover the personal use of computers and related technologies, both hardware and software, by employees.

Ethical issues also involve organizational use of information systems. Organizations have an obligation to protect the privacy and confidentiality of data about employees and customers. Employment records contain sensitive personal information, such as bank account numbers, which, if not protected, could lead to identity theft. Another ethical issue is the use of computer technology to monitor employees while they are working. The "Solving an Ethical Controversy" feature debates the issue of employee monitoring further.

spyware software that secretly gathers user information through the user's Internet connection without his or her knowledge, usually for advertising purposes.

Assessment Check ☑

1. Explain computer hacking.
2. What is malware?
3. How does a computer virus work?

Solving an Ethical Controversy

Should Employers Monitor Employees' Internet Use?

According to an American Management Association/ePolicy Institute survey, two-thirds of employers monitor employees' use of the Internet. Technology now allows them to check Web sites their employees visit on company time, keystrokes on individual computers, and the amount of time spent online. Employers can even track employees with GPS-enabled phones.

On-the-job access to the Internet and e-mail is indispensable. A certain amount of Internet surfing for research purposes is necessary in some fields. A company's Facebook page can be either a powerful marketing tool or a liability if employees use their own social media sites to complain about the company.

Should employers monitor their employees' time online?

PRO

1. Surveys have estimated that employees spend between one and two hours every day online for personal use. Some employees perform innocent tasks such as banking, but others visit inappropriate Web sites. Either way, those hours mean lost productivity for the company.

2. Inappropriate use of office computers could leave a company vulnerable to hacking, viruses, or other security compromises.

CON

1. Some employers are concerned that monitoring employees could endanger an atmosphere of trust, commitment, and motivation.

2. Employees do have a legitimate concern about privacy, especially if they have not been informed beforehand that their online activities are being monitored.

Summary

Although federal law clearly gives employers the right to monitor computer activity, a case pending before the U.S. Supreme Court concerns the permissible range of monitoring a worker's use of a company-provided electronic device. Most analysts suggest that companies should establish clear policies on computer, Internet, and e-mail use; train employees and have them sign a document saying they understand those policies; and then trust their employees.

Sources: "How Do Employers Monitor Internet Usage at Work," *wiseGEEK*, http://www.wisegeek.com, accessed June 21, 2011; Susan M. Heathfield, "Electronic Surveillance of Employees," *About.com* Human Resources, http://humanresources.about.com, accessed June 21, 2011; Karen Codere, "Managing Social Media in the Workplace," *The Business Ledger*, April 28, 2010, http://www.thebusiness ledger.com; Laura Petrecca, "More Employers Use Tech to Track Workers," *USA Today*, March 17, 2010, http://www.usatoday.com.

Disaster Recovery and Backup

Natural disasters, power failures, equipment malfunctions, software glitches, human error, and terrorist attacks can disrupt even the most sophisticated computer information systems. These disruptions can cost businesses and other organizations billions of dollars. Even more serious consequences can occur. For example, one recent study found that more than 93 percent of firms that lost their data centers for ten days or more went bankrupt within six months.[16]

FalconStor is a global firm that provides businesses with a variety of data back-up applications and sophisticated disaster recovery solutions. The firm's services go way beyond simply replicating data because after a major loss a company needs more than that, notes FalconStor product marketing manager Bobby Crouch. He explains that replicated

Cisco Systems Tackles Cloud Security

More and more businesses find themselves managing increasing amounts of e-mail and storing increasing amounts of data. Many save money and physical space by turning to cloud computing and storage, including software as a service (SaaS). Rather than installing software on site, with SaaS a business gains access to software over the Internet either by subscription or by a "pay as you go" plan. These businesses also need to protect their databanks from computer crime. In a traditional local area network, it is relatively easy to implement security applications at the network's borders. But in the borderless environment of cloud computing and with threats to security increasing, meeting this challenge is more difficult.

Cisco Systems has responded by developing security applications for cloud-based computing. One application directs a business's Web traffic to security towers located in 100 countries around the world. These locations use layers of antivirus and antimalware utilities to scan Web sites and quickly block access to them if they are compromised.

Another application offers both cloud-based and on-site e-mail security. The cloud-based application deletes spam and viruses. The on-site application provides data-loss prevention, e-mail encryption, and other services. Another e-mail encryption service provides cloud-based encryption for locally stored messages.

Other apps support security for off-site workers using desktops, laptops, tablets, and smart phones. One feature addresses the problem that occurs when an employee leaves a business. With one click of the mouse, an administrator can disable that person's access to every SaaS application he or she ever used. Also with one click, the administrator can enable access for a new employee.

As the vice president and general manager of Cisco's security technology unit states, "Securing the cloud is highly challenging. But it is one of the top challenges that the industry must rise to meet."

Questions for Critical Thinking

1. What are some advantages of storing data "in the cloud"? What are some disadvantages?
2. Why is it important to block a former employee's access to company data, e-mail, or applications?

Sources: "New Security Architecture Enables Context-Aware Capabilities in the Cisco ASA Firewall," press release, Cisco Systems Web site, February 16, 2011, http://newsroom .cisco.com; James Urquhart, "Cloud Computing and the Economy," *CNET News,* April 13, 2010, http://news.cnet.com; Margaret Steen, "Cloud Services and SaaS: A Smarter Way to Do Business," *Cisco News,* March 29, 2010, http://newsroom.cisco.com; Stuart Young, Andy Taylor, and James Macaulay, "Small Businesses Ride the Cloud: SMB Cloud Watch—U.S. Survey Results," Cisco Internet Business Solutions Group, February 2010, http://www .cisco.com; Mike Kirkwood, "Rulers of the Cloud: Will Cloud Computing Be the Second Coming of Cisco?" *ReadWriteWeb,* February 19, 2010, http://www.readwriteweb.com.

The "Hit & Miss" feature describes how Cisco Systems provides security for cloud-based applications.

Small and medium-size companies occasionally find themselves with jobs that require more computing power than their current systems offer. A cost-effective solution for these firms may be something called **grid computing**, which consists of a network of smaller computers running special software. The software breaks down a large, complex job into smaller tasks and then distributes them to the networked computers. The software then reassembles the individual task results into the finished job. By combining multiple small computers, grid computing creates a virtual mainframe or even a supercomputer.

grid computing consists of a network of smaller computers running special software.

Assessment Check ✔

1. What is an application service provider?
2. Explain on-demand computing.

What's Ahead

This is the first of two chapters devoted to managing technology and information. The next chapter, "Understanding Accounting and Financial Statements," focuses on accounting, financial information, and financing reporting. Accounting is the process of measuring, interpreting, and communicating financial information to enable people inside and outside the firm to make informed decisions. The chapter describes the functions of accounting and role of accountants; the steps in the accounting cycle; the types, functions, and components of financial statements; and the role of budgets in an organization.

Summary of Learning Goals

1. Distinguish between data and information, and explain the role of information systems in business.

It is important for businesspeople to know the difference between data and information. Data are raw facts and figures that may or may not be relevant to a business decision. Information is knowledge gained from processing those facts and figures. An information system is an organized method for collecting, storing, and communicating past, present, and projected information on internal operations and external intelligence. Most information systems today use computer and telecommunications technology.

Assessment Check Answers

1.1 Distinguish between data and information. Data consist of raw facts and figures that may or may not be relevant to a decision. Information is the knowledge gained from processing data.

1.2 What is an information system? An information system is an organized method for collecting, storing, and communicating past, present, and projected information on internal operations and external intelligence.

2. List the components and different types of information systems.

When people think about information systems today, they're generally thinking about computer-based systems, those that rely on computers and related technologies. Computer-based information systems rely on four components: computer hardware, software, telecommunications and computer networks, and data resource management. The heart of an information system is its database, a centralized integrated collection of data resources. Information systems fall into two broad categories: operational support systems and management support systems. Operational support systems are designed to produce a variety of information for users. Examples include transaction processing systems and process control systems. Management support systems are those designed to support effective decision making. They include management information systems, decision support systems, executive support systems, and expert systems.

Assessment Check Answers

2.1 List the four components of a computer-based information system. The four components of a computer-based information system are computer hardware, software, telecommunications and computer networks, and data resource management.

2.2 What is a database? A database is a centralized, integrated collection of data resources.

2.3 What are the two general types of information systems? Give examples of each. The two categories of information systems are operational support systems (such as transactions processing and process control systems) and management support systems (such as management information, decision support, executive support, and expert systems).

3. Outline how computer hardware and software are used to manage information.

Hardware consists of all tangible elements of a computer system, including input and output devices. Major categories of computers include mainframes, supercomputers, midrange systems, personal computers (PCs), and hand-held devices. Computer software provides the instructions that tell the hardware what to do. The software that controls the basic workings of the computer is its operating system. Other programs, called application software, perform specific tasks that users want to complete.

Assessment Check Answers

3.1 List two input and output devices. Input devices include the keyboard and mouse. Output devices include the monitor and printer.

3.2 What accounts for the increasing popularity of notebook computers? Notebook computers account for more than half of all new personal computers sold. Their increased popularity is due to better displays, lower prices, more rugged designs, increasing computing power, and slimmer designs.

3.3 What is software? List the two categories of software. Computer software provides the instructions that tell the hardware what to do. The software that controls the basic workings of the computer is its operating system. Other programs, called application software, perform specific tasks that users want to complete.

4. Describe networking and telecommunications technology and the types of computer networks.

Local area networks connect computers within a limited area. Wide area networks tie together larger geographical regions by using telephone lines, microwave, or satellite transmission. A wireless network allows computers to communicate through radio waves. Intranets allow employees to share information on a ready-made company network. Access to an intranet is restricted to authorized users and is protected by a firewall. Virtual private networks (VPNs) provide a secure Internet connection between two or more points. VoIP—voice over Internet protocol—uses a personal computer running special software and a broadband Internet connection to make and receive telephone calls over the Internet rather than over traditional telephone networks.

Assessment Check Answers

4.1 What is a LAN? A local area network (LAN) is a computer network that connects machines within a limited area, such as a building or several nearby buildings.

4.2 What are the differences between an intranet and a VPN? An intranet is a computer network patterned after the Internet. Unlike the Internet, access to an intranet is limited to employees and other authorized users. A virtual private network (VPN) is a way of gaining increased security for Internet connections.

4.3 Briefly explain how VoIP works. The VoIP phone is connected to a personal computer with any type of broadband connection. Special software transmits phone conversations over the Internet. A VoIP user can make and receive calls to and from those with traditional telephone connections (either landline or wireless).

⌐5⌐ Discuss the security and ethical issues involving computer information systems.

Numerous security and ethical issues affect information systems. Two of the main security threats are e-crime and malware. E-crimes range from hacking—unauthorized penetration of an information system—to the theft of hardware. Malware is any malicious software program designed to infect computer systems. Examples include viruses, worms, botnets, Trojan horses, and spyware. Ethical issues affecting information systems include the proper use of the systems by authorized users. Organizations also have an obligation to employees, vendors, and customers to protect the security and confidentiality of the data stored in information systems.

Assessment Check Answers ✔

5.1 Explain computer hacking. Computer hacking is a breach of a computer system by unauthorized people. Sometimes the hackers' motive is just to see if they can get in. Other times, hackers have more sinister motives, including stealing or altering data.

5.2 What is malware? Malware is any malicious software program designed to infect computer systems.

5.3 How does a computer virus work? A virus is a program that secretly attaches itself to another program (called a host). The virus then changes the host, destroys data, or even makes the computer system inoperable.

⌐6⌐ Explain the steps that companies go through in anticipating, planning for, and recovering from information systems disasters.

Information system disasters, whether human caused or due to natural causes, can cost businesses billions of dollars. The consequences of a disaster can be minimized by routinely backing up software and data, both at an organizational level and at an individual level. Organizations should back up critical data at an off-site location. Some may also want to invest in extra hardware and software sites, which can be accessed during emergencies.

Assessment Check Answers ✔

6.1 What are the types of disasters to which information systems are vulnerable? Natural disasters, power failures, equipment malfunctions, software glitches, human error, and even terrorist attacks can disrupt even the most powerful, sophisticated computer information systems.

6.2 List the tasks regarding off-site data storage. The five tasks are planning and deciding which data to back up, establishing and following a backup schedule, protecting data when they are transmitted off site, choosing the right vendor, and continually testing and refining the backup system.

⌐7⌐ Review the current trends in information systems.

Information systems are continually and rapidly evolving. Some of the most significant trends are the increasing demands of the distributed workforce, the increased use of application service providers, on-demand computing, and grid computing. Many people now work in virtual offices, including at home. Information technology makes this possible. Application service providers allow organizations to outsource most of their IT functions. Rather than buying and maintaining expensive software, on-demand computing offers users the option of renting software time from outside vendors and paying only for their usage. Grid computing consists of a network of smaller computers running special software creating a virtual mainframe or even supercomputer.

Assessment Check Answers ✔

7.1 What is an application service provider? An application service provider (ASP) is an outside vendor that provides both the computers and application support for managing an information system. By using an ASP, the organization effectively outsources some, or all, of its IT function.

7.2 Explain on-demand computing. Instead of purchasing and maintaining expensive software, some organizations use on-demand computing. In this arrangement, software is rented from a vendor and the organization only pays for its actual usage.

■ **Business Terms you need to Know**

data 468

information 468

information
   system 469

chief information
   officer (CIO) 469

computer-based
   information systems 469

database 470

operational
   support
   systems 472

transaction processing
   systems 472

process control
   systems 472

management support
systems 472
management information
system (MIS) 472
decision support
system (DSS) 472
executive support
system (ESS) 472
expert system 473

hardware 473
server 474
software 475
local area networks
(LAN) 476
wide area networks
(WAN) 476
WiFi 477
intranet 478

firewall 478
virtual private networks
(VPNs) 478
VoIP 479
malware 481
viruses 481
worm 481
botnet 481
Trojan horse 481

spyware 482
application service
provider (ASP) 485
on-demand
computing 485
cloud
computing 485
grid computing 486

■ Review Questions

1. Distinguish between data and information. Why is the distinction important to businesspeople in their management of information?

2. What are the four components of an information system?

3. Describe the two different types of information systems, and give an example of how each might help a particular business.

4. Explain decision support systems, executive support systems, and expert systems.

5. What are the major categories of computers? What is a smart phone?

6. What is an intranet? Give specific examples of benefits for firms that set up their own intranets.

7. What steps can organizations and individuals take to prevent computer crime?

8. How does a computer virus work? What can individuals and organizational computer users do to reduce the likelihood of acquiring a computer virus?

9. Why is disaster recovery important for businesses? Relate your answer to a natural disaster such as a hurricane or fire.

10. Describe four information system trends.

■ Projects and Teamwork Applications

1. Suppose you've been hired to design an information system for a midsize retailer. Describe what that information system might look like, including the necessary components. Would the system be an operational support system, a management support system, or both?

2. Select a local company and contact the person in charge of its information system for a brief interview. Ask that individual to outline his or her company's information system. Also, ask the person what he or she likes most about the job. Did this interview make you more or less interested in a career in information systems?

3. Working with a partner, research the current status of Wi-Max. Prepare a short report on its growth, its current uses, and its future for business computing.

4. Your supervisor has asked your advice. She isn't sure the company's information system needs any elaborate safeguards because the company has little Web presence beyond a simple home page. However, employees use e-mail extensively to contact suppliers and customers. Make a list of the threats to which the company's information system is vulnerable. What types of safeguards would you suggest?

5. Has your computer ever been hacked or attacked by a virus? What steps did you take to recover lost files and data? How would you prevent something similar from happening again?

■ Web Assignments

1. **Enterprise resource planning (ERP).** SAP is one of the world's largest enterprise resource planning software companies. Go to the firm's Web site (http://www.sap.com) and click on "Customer Testimonials." Choose one of the customers listed and read its testimonial. Prepare a brief summary and explain how this exercise improved your understanding of the business applications of ERP software.

2. **Computer security.** Visit the Web site listed below. Review the material and answer the following questions:

   a. What are two current malware threats? How serious are they?

   b. What is a potentially unwanted program (PUP)? What are two recent PUPs?

   http://www.mcafee.com/us/threat center/default.asp

3. **Cloud computing.** IBM is one of the largest providers of so-called cloud computing. Visit the IBM Web site (http://www.ibm.com) and click on "solutions" and then "cloud computing." Print out the material and bring it to class to participate in a class discussion on the subject.

Note: Internet Web addresses change frequently. If you don't find the exact sites listed, you may need to access the organization's home page and search from there or use a search engine such as Bing or Google.

Major installations, such as resorts or sports stadiums, have requirements well beyond those of, say, a small office. They must be able to provide a safe and secure environment for events involving thousands, or even tens of thousands, of guests or fans. They need to keep track of reservations or ticket sales and ensure well-stocked dining facilities or concession stands. Certain companies have made a specialty of meeting the information-technology needs of such immense venues.

MICROS Systems, with headquarters in Maryland, is a leading developer of information technology systems for the hospitality industry, with 90 distributors in 50 countries. The company provides hardware and software solutions for 310,000 restaurant clients, from Burger King to Hilton Hotels in the United States. Its MICROS-Fidelio subsidiary has more than 25,000 installations around the world for the hotel chains Travelodge and InterContinental Hotels Group, among others. The company's new MICROS-Retail group has enabled it to branch out into the retail industry, with clients such as Aéropostale, Starbucks, and IKEA.

One MICROS client is the M Resort Spa Casino in Las Vegas. This four-star resort has almost 400 hotel rooms and suites, a 92,000-square-foot casino, nine restaurants and five separate bars, meeting and conference space, a full spa, and a large plaza for special events. The hardware and software that MICROS installed coordinates into a single-system, 120 point-of-sale workstations, including the restaurants, bars, wine cellar, room service, and many other services. The system's hosted environment means lower emissions and use of electricity. MICROS's disaster recovery helps the resort come back online from outages in less time and using fewer resources. The resort will be able to expand the scale of this technology without additional infrastructure expenses as it plans for a large retail center and a 14-screen digital movie complex.

The Atlantis, Paradise Island resort in the Bahamas has used a MICROS hospitality management system package to institute a cashless environment. Previously, guests paid with cash or credit cards. The new system still allows credit card use but also offers another option. At check-in each guest is issued a magnetic-striped key card that operates the room door, keeps track of casino activity, and permits purchases. Each card has the guest's name imprinted on it. At transactions, employees ask the guest to confirm the room number. Guests no longer have to worry about keeping their cash secure. Revenues have increased, which also benefits the employees, who receive a percentage of each sale as a gratuity required by Bahamas law.

The New Meadowlands Stadium in New Jersey is twice as large as the stadium it replaced. With seating for 82,500, it is a showcase for the New York Giants and New Jersey Jets football teams, as well as for big-name concerts, college football, and international soccer. Due to a partnership with the U.S. Environmental Protection Agency, it is also one of the greenest American sports venues. MICROS Systems has installed hardware and software that will meet the large-scale requirements of the stadium. The hardware includes workstations, terminals, and hand-held devices. MICROS software applications manages the stadium's inventory and purchasing, the luxury suites and their catering needs, and the dining facilities. Customer relations software tracks sales, recognizes season-ticket holders and other core clientele, and cultivates new customers. Peter Brickman, the chief technology officer of the stadium, said, "The combination of innovative integrated solutions, advanced technology, security, reliable hardware, robust reporting, and open source friendly architecture made MICROS the only choice for our concession needs."

Questions for Critical Thinking

1. Visit the MICROS Systems Web site to learn more about its products for the global market. In what ways do you think the company can increase sales in Africa, Asia, and Latin America? How might the company have to adapt to conditions in these countries?

2. Imagine you are the manager of a sports arena. What sorts of hardware and software would help you manage such a large facility?

Sources: Company Web site, http://www.micros.com, accessed June 21, 2011; Diane Snyder, "At Atlantis, Cashless = Control," http://www.micros.com, accessed June 4, 2010; "The Revolutionary New Meadowlands Stadium to Open with MICROS," press release, May 4, 2010, http://www.micros.com; "MICROS Systems, Inc. Announces Deployment of MICROS 9700 HMS at M Resort Spa Casino in Las Vegas," press release, March 1, 2010, http://www.prnewswire.com.

Businesses both large and small, as well as most people with home computers or smart phones, have had unfortunate experiences with computer viruses. Once a virus has infiltrated a network or a device—a computer, tablet, PDA, or cell phone—it replicates and begins causing irritating slowdowns or worse, destroying data or stealing a user's identity.

Of the many software programs designed to catch and/or stop viruses and worms, those produced by Kaspersky Lab are among the most popular and the most effective. The company was founded by Russian-born Eugene Kaspersky. Kaspersky, an engineer, became interested in computer viruses when his own computer was attacked by the notorious Cascade virus in 1989. He developed a disinfection utility for it, then went on to compile a catalog of viruses and disinfection utilities. This database now includes 4 million entries. In 1997, he and several colleagues founded Kaspersky Lab.

With headquarters in Moscow and branches worldwide, the company has won many awards for its antivirus software packages. Only four years after establishing a presence in the Americas, Kaspersky Lab won an award for best e-mail security system. Today, Kaspersky Lab is the world's largest privately held antimalware company, with products for both corporate networks and home PC users in almost every country in the world. More than 300 million users rely on Kaspersky products for their security, and 150,000 new users join them every week.

One of Kaspersky Lab's success stories involves the Austrian National Tourist Office, the country's official tourist organization. It has 250 employees in 30 offices in Austria and in cities around the world, including New York, Sydney, Beijing, and Singapore. The tourist office's international Web site has pages in many languages and showcases Austria's many attractions for visitors. The office's travel services are Web based, and its employees rely constantly on the Internet for online research and e-mail from their colleagues in different branches. Well aware of the growing worldwide risk of viruses and other malware, the tourist office decided it needed a better security system.

The tourist office consulted the Austrian IT subsidiary Austrian Info Systems GmbH, which decided that the best solution would be to adopt the entire range of products in the Kaspersky Anti-Virus Business Optimal package. From the tourist bureau's home office in Vienna, the Kaspersky Administration Kit runs centralized monitoring and administration of all the office's servers and all of its antivirus protection. Other Kaspersky antivirus utilities protect all of the 250 workstations worldwide, the 25 file servers, and the 550 mailboxes making up the exchange infrastructure. A free administration kit helps Austrian Info Systems make regular searches of the tourist office's network for viruses.

For the home computer user, Kaspersky Lab offers programs that help prevent various forms of identity theft; offer protection against viruses, Trojan horses, spyware, and so on; and scan Web sites for malware. As more Mac users store data in the "cloud," on Internet servers, their computers can also become infected with viruses and other malware, so Kaspersky Lab also offers a Mac version of its antivirus software. And as smart phone users increasingly use their hand-held devices as PCs, they have a mobile security program as well.

As the company celebrated its 12th anniversary recently, its Web site declared that its "most valuable asset is the wealth of experience and knowledge it has gained in . . . combating viruses and other IT threats, enabling us to pre-empt trends in malware development. This helps us to remain one step ahead of the competition and provide our users with the most reliable protection from new types of attack."

Questions for Critical Thinking

1. Why is it so important for Kaspersky Lab—as a business—to stay ahead of new computer threats?

2. How do you protect your own computer or hand-held device from viruses and other malware? What steps would you take to improve your protection?

Sources: Company Web site, http://usa.kaspersky.com, accessed June 21, 2011; Austrian National Tourist Office Web site, http://www.austria.info, accessed June 21, 2011; Maxine Cheung, "Kaspersky CMO Outlines New Partner Initiatives and Resources," IT Business Canada, February 18, 2010, http://www.itbusiness.ca.

When you need a car, you want one. When you don't need a car, you don't want to be bothered with the hassle or the expense. That's what makes Zipcar so great. Zipcar is a car-sharing network based in Cambridge, Massachusetts that operates in urban and metropolitan areas and on university campuses around the U.S., Canada, and the United Kingdom. Currently, Zipcar serves more than 200 colleges and universities, and the number is growing steadily. "The service provides a new level of freedom for students, faculty, and staff," says Matthew Malloy, vice-president of international university operations for Zipcar. "Members can use Zipcars to run errands, attend meetings, or get away for the weekend on a pay-as-you-go basis. You no longer need to own to be free."

Once members sign up for the program, they receive a Zipcard that gives them access to any Zipcar parked around campus (or around town). The annual fee for the service is $35, and it includes fuel, insurance, and 180 travel miles per day. A member who wants to use a Zipcar simply goes online to reserve it, then picks up the designated car at the reserved time. "It's easy," says Erin Badger, a senior marketing student at the University of New Hampshire, where the Zipcar program is now in full swing. "You swipe your Zipcard [over a sensor] on the windshield and it unlocks the car. You get in, turn the key, and go." Each Zipcar comes equipped with an individually numbered Zipcard gas card that the driver uses to fill the tank with fuel. So members—especially budget-conscious students—don't need cash or their own credit cards when the gas gauge runs low. Members are asked to return each car with at least one-quarter of a tank of gas in it, so no one picks up a car with an empty tank.

Technology plays a huge role in the success of the Zipcar system. "When you think about the member experience, what makes it a seamless and enjoyable experience for the consumer is the technology infrastructure," observes Rob Weisberg, chief marketing officer at Zipcar. When marketing and setting up the system at colleges and universities,

Zipcar looks at how students use cars on campus, asking such questions as: Are there places on campus where use is more frequent, or do students want hybrids? "Any time you understand your consumers better, you are able to cater to them more effectively," says Weisberg. He notes that Zipcar puts a lot of effort into understanding demographic and psychographic (life style) trends on and around a campus.

Erin Badger likes the fact that she can use her iPhone app to reserve a Zipcar or extend the reservation if she is driving a car and isn't ready to return it. "The iPhone app relates to the student age group," she says. "They care about us." The Zipcar app was named to *Time* magazine's annual list of "Best Travel Gadgets" in one recent issue. "Beyond helping you manage reservations, find nearby pickup locations and browse car models available, the app offers clever capabilities like remote locking and unlocking and honking your car's horn from your phone when you inevitably forget what it looks like in a crowded lot," praises the *Time* review.

Zipcar is always looking toward the future and ways to better serve its customers. RobWeisberg predicts that eventually Zipcar technology will allow for customized seat settings and even pre-set radio station settings that automatically click into place when a member reserves a car. Still, Weisberg emphasizes the importance of the personal touch. He recalls that when a student member posted a note on Twitter joking that he loved everything about Zipcar except the fact that there wasn't a package of Skittles waiting for him when he unlocked the car, a Zipcar employee left a package of Skittles on the dashboard the next time the student reserved a car.

"Technology will never replace human interaction," warns Weisberg. "You'd never take the recommendation of a computer over the recommendation of a friend or family member or colleague. So our laser focus on the customer experience and ensuring that it is second to none is really where we need to play. Technology enables that, but it's never going to replace the human touch."

Questions for Critical Thinking

1. Through member surveys and social media postings, Zipcar collects information about members and their lifestyles in order to design the best system for a community. Write ten questions that you think might elicit useful information for Zipcar about students at your own college or university.

2. What kind of data would Zipcar's operational support systems likely collect? What kind of information might they provide?

3. The ZipcariPhone app already takes care of several tasks. If you were a Zipcar member, what new task would you add to the app?

4. Do you think your campus would be a good candidate for the Zipcar system? Why or why not? If your college or university already has Zipcar, are you a member? Why or why not?

Sources: Zipcar Web site, http://www.zipcar.com, accessed June 21, 2011; "Zipcar and SCVNGR, East Cambridge Neighbors, Partner on New Rewards Program," *Boston.com,* August 26, 2010, http://www.boston.com; "Zipcar, Inc.," *Bloomberg Business Week,* http://investing.businessweek.com, accessed August 24, 2010; University of New Hampshire Transportation Services, http://www.unh.edu/transportation, accessed August 24, 2010; PeterHa, "The Best Travel Gadgets of 2009," *Time,* November 2, 2009, http://www.time.com.

KANSAS

GREENSBURG, KS
The Dog Ate My Laptop

The night of the tornado, Superintendent of Schools Darin Headrick heard the storm sirens go off on his way home from work. He stopped at the home of High School Principal Randy Fulton and the two men headed for the basement, just in case. The next thing they knew, the entire school system was gone. Textbooks were scattered everywhere, computers destroyed.

For the first three months after the storm, no one could live in town. People stayed in shelters or with friends and family outside of town. No one had a home phone anymore, but people were eager to connect with each other and find out what was happening. Although the Federal Emergency Management Agency (FEMA) was distributing information at checkpoints on the edges of town, people had to go to town to get it.

Like 95 percent of the town's 1,500 residents, Headrick himself was homeless. With just four months to rebuild an entire school system, all he had were his laptop and cell phone, so he got into his truck and began searching for a wireless signal. Taking a lesson from his students, he used text messaging to distribute information. Although very few people still had computers, almost everyone had a cell phone. Residents who subscribed to the text service could receive updates and instant messages over the phone, wherever they were.

Rebuilding the schools was a bigger task. Headrick secured temporary trailers for grades K–12 and received generous donations of desks and school supplies. By August 15, he had the basics needed to start the school year, but he still lacked textbooks. Technology would have to fill in the gaps, so the students didn't fall behind.

One of the school system's existing programs was ITV, for Interactive Distance Learning Network. ITV allowed Greensburg's rural schools to log in to classrooms around the state via Web cam. This type of real-time distance learning is referred to as *synchronous learning*, as opposed to the asynchronous online courses given on college campuses. After the tornado, all that was needed to get the program up and running again were a computer, an Internet connection, and a Web cam.

Early in the winter each of Greensburg High's students got an unexpected gift: a laptop computer containing e-books, handwriting recognition software, and a tablet screen for note taking. The new laptops replaced their tattered textbooks. Students would hand in their assignments via e-mail and receive feedback from their teachers via instant messaging.

Questions

After viewing the video, answer the following questions:

1. Was Greensburg Public Schools' investment in technology a smart move?
2. Would you consider enrolling in an asynchronous online course? What might be the benefits and drawbacks?
3. Do you think hand-held devices and text messaging improve productivity and communication or distract their users?

LAUNCHING YOUR
[Information Technology and Accounting Career]

Part 5, "Managing Technology and Information," includes Chapters 14 and 15, which discuss using computers and related technology to manage information and accounting and financial statements. In Chapter 14, we discussed well-known technology companies such as Google and Oracle, as well as a host of smaller organizations that use computer technology to manage information. In Chapter 15, you read about accounting firms such as Ernst & Young and a variety of public and private organizations, large and small, that generate and use accounting data. These examples illustrate that all organizations need to manage technology and information. And with the complexity and scope of technology and information likely to increase in the years ahead, the demand for accounting and information systems professionals is expected to grow.

According to the U.S. Department of Labor, employment in occupations such as accounting, auditing, computer software engineering and support specialists, and network systems administrators is expected to grow faster than the average for all occupations in the next decade. In fact, two of the top five occupations in which employment is expected to grow the fastest over the next few years are related to information systems.[1] In addition, recent graduates with bachelor's degrees in accounting and information systems have among the highest average starting salaries of all business graduates. The median annual salary for accountants and auditors is almost $60,000, with the top 10 percent earning about $102,000.[2] Salaries in information systems vary widely based on education and experience. But starting salaries for computer science graduates average $61,000.[3] Those who are information systems managers earn about $112,000 per year.[4]

What types of jobs are available in information systems and accounting? What are the working conditions like? What are the career paths? Information systems and accounting are both fairly broad occupations and encompass a wide variety of jobs. In some cases you'll work in the accounting or information systems department of a business such as Procter & Gamble or Shell. In other cases, you'll work for a specialized accounting or information systems firm, such as PricewaterhouseCoopers or IBM, that provides these services to governments, not-for-profit organizations, and businesses.

Accounting and information systems are popular business majors, and many entry-level positions are available each year. For instance, many accounting graduates start their careers working for a public accounting firm. Initially, their job duties involve auditing or tax services, usually working with more senior accountants. As their careers progress, accounting graduates take on more and more supervisory responsibilities. Some may move from public accounting firms to take accounting positions at other organizations. Many accounting and information systems graduates spend their entire careers in these fields, while others move into other areas. People who began their careers in accounting or information systems are well represented in the ranks of senior management today. Let's look briefly at some of the specific jobs you might find after earning a degree in accounting or information systems.

Public accountants perform a broad range of accounting, auditing, tax, and consulting services for their clients, which include businesses, governments, not-for-profit organizations, and individuals. Auditing is one of the most important services offered by public accountants, and many accounting graduates begin their careers in this field. Auditors examine a client's financial statements and accounting procedures to make sure they conform with all applicable laws and regulations. Public accountants either own their own businesses or work for public accounting firms. Many public accountants are certified public accountants (CPAs). To become a CPA, you have to meet educational and experience requirements and pass a comprehensive examination.

Management accountants work for an organization other than a public accounting firm. They record and analyze financial information and financial statements for their organizations. Management accountants are also involved in budgeting, tax preparation, cost management, and asset management. Internal auditors verify the accuracy of their organization's internal controls and check for irregularities, waste, and fraud.

Technical support specialists are troubleshooters who monitor the performance of computer systems; provide technical support and solve problems for computer users; install, modify, clean, and repair computer hardware and software; and write training manuals and train computer users.

Network administrators design, install, and support an organization's computer networks, including its local area network, wide area network, Internet, and intranet systems. They provide administrative support for software and hardware users and ensure that the design of an organization's computer networks and all of the components fit together efficiently and effectively.

Computer security specialists plan, coordinate, and implement an organization's information security. They educate users about how to protect computer systems, install antivirus and similar software, and monitor the networks for security breaches. In recent years, the role and importance of computer security specialists have increased in response to the growing number of attacks on networks and data.

Career Assessment Exercises in Information Systems and Accounting

1. The American Institute of Certified Public Accountants is a professional organization dedicated to the enhancement of the public accounting profession. Visit the organization's Web site (http://www.aicpa.org). Review the information on CPA standards and examinations. Write a brief summary on what you learned about how to become a CPA.

2. Assume you're interested in a career as a systems administrator. Go to the following Web site: http://www.sage.org. Prepare a brief report outlining the responsibilities of a systems administrator, who hires for these positions, and what kind of educational background you need to become one.

3. Identify a person working in your local area in the accounting field and arrange an interview with that person (your college career center may be able to help you). Ask that person about his or her job responsibilities, educational background, and the best and worst aspects of his or her job as an accountant.

PART

Managing Financial Resources

6

Chapter 15

Learning Objectives

1 Explain the functions of accounting, and identify the three basic activities involving accounting.

2 Describe the roles played by public, management, government, and not-for-profit accountants.

3 Identify the foundations of the accounting system, including GAAP and the role of the Financial Accounting Standards Board (FASB).

4 Outline the steps in the accounting cycle, and define *double-entry bookkeeping* and the *accounting equation*.

5 Explain the functions and major components of the four principal financial statements: the balance sheet, the income statement, the statement of owners' equity, and the statement of cash flows.

6 Discuss how financial ratios are used to analyze a company's financial strengths and weaknesses.

7 Describe the role of budgets in a business.

8 Outline accounting issues facing global business and the move toward one set of worldwide accounting rules.

Understanding Accounting and Financial Statements

Deloitte Consulting Meets Challenges with Optimism

As consumers continue to try to figure out how to stretch a dollar, businesses are showing signs of recovering from the recent recession. Deloitte Consulting—a subsidiary of the major accounting firm Deloitte LLP—has managed to hold on and actually grow during difficult economic times. Deloitte offers a wide range of consulting services to businesses in just about every industry, from retail to finance, helping firms make management decisions that affect the tracking and reporting of their activities. For example, Deloitte's Consumer Pulse Survey helps retailers understand consumers' buying decisions and anticipate future trends. The most recent survey zeroed in on consumers' concern about high energy, food, and healthcare costs, concluding that average consumers are reluctant to buy big-ticket items until these prices level off. In addition, Deloitte tracks shopping patterns based on weather. "Weather can really impact consumer behavior," explains Alison Paul of Deloitte. Snowstorms, heavy rain, and even a prolonged heat wave will affect shoppers' behavior. Businesses use this information to help plan inventory needs, forecast sales, and track the results of these decisions.

In recent months, Deloitte Consulting has been focusing on the new, broader role of the chief financial officer (CFO) in its client organizations. Traditionally, financial organizations were established to focus on transactions and the administration of those transactions. Today's finance departments—in no matter what type of firm— must be able to gather and interpret data in ways that result in clearer business strategies and more effective decision making. Deloitte has developed a model called the Four Faces of the CFO: steward, operator, strategist, and catalyst. Using this model,

Deloitte creates customized solutions designed to maximize the capabilities of its clients' CFOs. "From strategy to operations, performance management to reporting, we help finance organizations become the valuable partners the business needs to win," notes the company's Web site. Deloitte's Financial Advisory Services division advises business clients on how to manage disputes, execute deals such as mergers and acquisitions, and meet regulatory requirements such as valuation and financial reporting. Deloitte's attitude toward the currently complex business environment is that beneath every stone is a potential opportunity—so no stone should be left unturned. "That's why it's so important to examine opportunities and challenges from every angle—accounting, assurance and advisory, risk, tax, strategy, financial, technology, and human capital," says its Web site. "And that's just what we help clients do."

With its variety of resources, Deloitte's consulting and advisory business managed to hold on through the recession. Punit Renjen, Deloitte's chairman and CEO, is optimistic about the firm's growth along with the global economy. "We are also committed to embedding quality in all aspects of our business, which not only is creating value for clients but also contributes to the profitability of engagements," says Renjen. "We will continue to anticipate market trends and invest in industries, services, and geographies where we see high-growth potential." In particular, Renjen predicts a focus on technological innovation, changing regulations, and global geopolitical shifts, as these factors affect markets. Helping customers navigate the financial complexities of today's ever-changing marketplace is what keeps Deloitte in business—and growing every day.[1]

Canadian Press/Steve White/ @AP/World Wide Photos

accounting process of measuring, interpreting, and communicating financial information to support internal and external business decision making.

Accounting professionals prepare the financial information that organizations present in their annual reports. Whether you begin your career by working for a company or by starting your own firm, you need to understand what accountants do and why their work is so important in contemporary business.

Accounting is the process of measuring, interpreting, and communicating financial information to enable people inside and outside the firm to make informed decisions. In many ways, accounting is the language of business. Accountants gather, record, report, and interpret financial information in a way that describes the status and operation of an organization and aids in decision making.

Millions of men and women throughout the world describe their occupation as accountant. In the United States alone more than 1.3 million people work as accountants. According to the Bureau of Labor Statistics, the number of accounting-related jobs is expected to increase by around 22 percent between now and 2018, a much faster rate of growth than the average for all occupations.[2] The availability of jobs and relatively high starting salaries for talented graduates have made accounting one of the most in-demand majors on college campuses. After the recent financial downturn, hiring levels fell, but the most recent report estimates that firms will hire 5.3 percent more accounting graduates this year over last year.[3]

This chapter begins by describing who uses accounting information. It discusses business activities involving accounting statements: financing, investing, and operations. It explains the accounting process, defines double-entry bookkeeping, and presents the accounting equation. We then discuss the development of financial statements from information about financial transactions. The methods of interpreting these statements and the roles of budgeting in planning and controlling a business are described next. The chapter concludes with a discussion of the development and implementation schedule of a uniform set of accounting rules for global business.

Users of Accounting Information

People both inside and outside an organization rely on accounting information to help them make business decisions. Figure 15.1 lists the users of accounting information and the applications they find for that information. Firms like Deloitte Consulting provide such information and help their customers make the best use of it.

Managers with a business, government agency, or not-for-profit organization are the major users of accounting information, because it helps them plan and control daily and long-range operations. Business owners and boards of directors of not-for-profit groups also rely on accounting data to determine how well managers are operating the organizations. Union officials use accounting data in contract negotiations, and employees refer to it as they monitor their firms' productivity and profitability performance.

To help employees understand how their work affects the bottom line, many companies share sensitive financial information with their employees and teach them how to understand and use financial statements. Proponents of what is often referred to as *open book management* believe that allowing employees to view financial information helps them better understand how their work contributes to the company's success, which, in turn, benefits them.

Outside a firm, potential investors evaluate accounting information to help them decide whether to buy a firm's stock. As we'll discuss in more detail later in the chapter, any company whose stock is traded publicly is required to report its financial results on a regular basis. So anyone, for example, can find out what Home Depot's sales were last year or how much money Research in Motion made during the last quarter. Bankers and other lenders use accounting information to evaluate a potential borrower's financial soundness. The Internal Revenue Service (IRS) and state tax officials use it to determine a company's tax liability. Citizens' groups and government agencies use such information in assessing the efficiency of operations such as Massachusetts General Hospital; the Topeka, Kansas, school system; Community College of Denver; and the Art Institute of Chicago.

Accountants play fundamental roles not only in business but also in other aspects of society. Their work influences each of the business environments discussed earlier in this book. They clearly contribute important information to help managers deal with the competitive and economic environments.

Less obvious contributions help others understand, predict, and react to the technological, regulatory, and social and cultural environments. For instance, thousands of people volunteer each year to help people with their taxes. One of the largest organized programs is Tax-Aide, sponsored by AARP (formally known as the American Association of Retired Persons). Its program has in excess of 34,000 IRS-trained volunteers in 6,600 locations nationwide helping middle- and low-income taxpayers over the age of 60 file their returns. More than 2.6 million clients use the free service each years.[4]

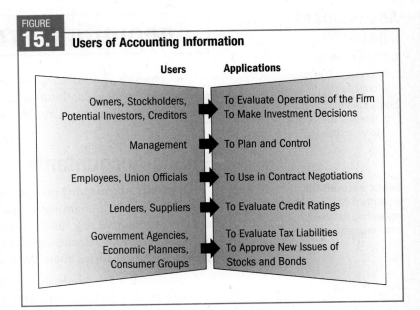

FIGURE 15.1 Users of Accounting Information

Users	Applications
Owners, Stockholders, Potential Investors, Creditors	To Evaluate Operations of the Firm / To Make Investment Decisions
Management	To Plan and Control
Employees, Union Officials	To Use in Contract Negotiations
Lenders, Suppliers	To Evaluate Credit Ratings
Government Agencies, Economic Planners, Consumer Groups	To Evaluate Tax Liabilities / To Approve New Issues of Stocks and Bonds

Accountants play a fundamental role in business and other areas of society by providing services to businesses, individuals, government agencies, and not-for-profit organizations.

Kathleen Finlay/Masterfile

Business Activities Involving Accounting

The natural progression of a business begins with financing. Subsequent steps, including investing, lead to operating the business. All organizations, profit oriented and not-for-profit, perform these three basic activities, and accounting plays a key role in each one:

1. **Financing activities** provide necessary funds to start a business and expand it after it begins operating.

2. **Investing activities** provide valuable assets required to run a business.

3. **Operating activities** focus on selling goods and services, but they also consider expenses as important elements of sound financial management.

Assessment Check ✓

1. Define *accounting.*

2. Who uses accounting information?

3. What are the three business activities that involve accounting?

public accountant
accountant who provides accounting services to other organizations.

Accounting Professionals

Accounting professionals work in a variety of areas in and for business firms, government agencies, and not-for-profit organizations. They can be classified as public, management, government, and not-for-profit accountants.

Public Accountants

A **public accountant** provides accounting services to individuals or business firms for a fee. Most public accounting firms provide three basic services to clients: (1) auditing, or examining, financial records; (2) tax preparation, planning, and related services; and (3) management consulting. Because public accountants are not employees of a client firm, they can provide unbiased advice about the firm's financial condition.

While there are hundreds of public accounting firms in the United States, a handful of firms dominate the industry. The four largest public accounting firms—Deloitte & Touche, Ernst & Young, KPMG, and PricewaterhouseCoopers (PwC)—collect almost $32 billion annually from U.S. clients alone. In contrast, the Minneapolis-based RSM McGladrey, the nation's fifth-largest accounting firm, has annual revenues of approximately $1.5 billion.[5]

One challenge faced by these firms is attracting and hiring the best talent. Ernst & Young recently adopted a new approach to reaching accounting students as wells as new grads: inviting them to meet on Facebook. E&Y's Facebook page now contains a six-question quiz that candidates can receive on their mobile phones. Participants may take the quiz—questions change regularly—as often as they want in an effort to win prizes such as an iPad. The quiz helps E&Y's human resources department identify potential trainees with whom the firm then makes contact. "We want to find the best and brightest, for internships and for full-time jobs," says Dan Black, director of the firm's campus recruiting effort. The quiz "adds to our accessibility and draws attention to our site." E&Y also reaches out to students via LinkedIn and Twitter. "This is just another way for people to meet us and learn about us and what we do," explains Black.[6]

Some years ago, public accounting firms came under sharp criticism for providing management consulting services to many of the same firms they audited. Critics argued that when a public accounting firm does both—auditing and management consulting—an inherent conflict of interest is created. In addition, this conflict of interest may undermine confidence in the quality of the financial statements accounting firms audit. The bankruptcies of some high-profile firms increased pressure on public accounting firms to end the practice. Legislation also established strict limits on the types of consulting services auditors can provide. For example, an accounting firm that audits a company's books cannot provide any other services to that company, including tax services. As a result, three of the four largest public accounting firms either sold large portions of their consulting practices or spun them off into separate companies, and they now concentrate on providing auditing and tax services. PwC, for instance, sold much of its consulting business to IBM.

As the "Hit & Miss" feature outlines, a growing number of public accountants are also certified as *forensic accountants,* and some smaller public accounting firms actually specialize in forensic accounting. These professionals, and the firms that employ them, focus on uncovering potential fraud in a variety of organizations.

Forensic Accountants: Fraud Busters

When most people think of accountants, they usually don't think of crime fighters. But that's exactly what forensic accountants are. People who work in this growing field investigate such white-collar crimes as business fraud, improper financial reporting, and illegal investment schemes.

Forensic accounting is accounting performed in preparation for legal review. Forensic accountants take the skeptical view, investigating below the surface of an organization's accounting system to find out what actually happened. They may also testify as expert witnesses if a case goes to trial. The job requires a bachelor's degree in accounting and CPA certification, with further training in investigative techniques for certification as a certified fraud examiner (CFE) or a certified forensic accountant (CrFA).

When the energy giant Enron Corporation collapsed, forensic accounting investigations revealed that for several years, company executives had issued false financial statements that exaggerated the company's earnings and thereby increased the firm's stock prices. The statements painted a rosy picture of steady profits that met earnings expectations. In reality, Enron's own investments were doing badly, and its profits were nonexistent. The company was actually losing money. Even after the truth began to leak out and the company's stock prices fell, the executives continued to issue false financial statements in the hope of slowing the fall. In a federal trial, two former executives were convicted of conspiracy, wire fraud, and securities fraud.

Forensic accounting is a rapidly growing profession. Each year, conferences are help around the nation focusing on issues faced by forensic accountants. RGL Forensics recently posted 10 percent growth during one year and has been named the fastest-growing forensic accounting firm in the United States. "Growth in accounting is dependent on changing with the market," notes RGL Forensics CFO Angie McPhee.

Questions for Critical Thinking

1. Describe how a shift in the economy has created a new career path for accounting students.

2. How might forensic accounting change the world of business?

Sources: "Marking a 10-Percent Growth, Forensic Accounting Firm Named Fastest Growing in U.S.," *Daily Business News*, April 14, 2011, http://accounting.dbusinessnews.com; Caleb Newquist, "What Are Your Questions for a Forensic Accounting Partner?" *Going Concern*, March 15, 2011, http://goingconcern.com; "Forensic Accounting," PricewaterhouseCoopers New Zealand, http://www.pwc.com/nz, accessed June 1, 2010; Tracy L. Coenen, "Enron: The Good, the Bad, and the Ugly," Sequence Inc., http://www.sequence-inc.com, accessed June 1, 2010; James A. DiGabriele, "Applying Forensic Skepticism to Lost Profits Valuations," *Journal of Accountancy*, April 2010, http://www.journalofaccountancy.com; Bob Trompeter, "Why Do You Need a Forensic Accountant Hired Gun?" Hutson Resource Group, February 23, 2010, http://hutsonresourcegroup.com; Rick Romell, "Accountants Who Focus on Fraud," *Milwaukee Journal Sentinel*, January 24, 2010, http://www.jsonline.com.

Certified public accountants (CPAs) demonstrate their accounting knowledge by meeting state requirements for education and experience and successfully completing a number of rigorous tests in accounting theory and practice, auditing, law, and taxes. Other accountants who meet specified educational and experience requirements and pass certification exams carry the title *certified management accountant, certified fraud examiner,* or *certified internal auditor.*

Management Accountants

An accountant employed by a business other than a public accounting firm is called a *management accountant.* Such a person collects and records financial transactions and prepares financial statements used by the firm's managers in decision making. Management accountants provide timely, relevant, accurate, and concise information that executives can use to operate their firms more effectively and more profitably than they could without this input. In addition to preparing financial statements, a management accountant plays a major role in interpreting them. A management accountant should provide answers to many important questions:

- Where is the company going?

- What opportunities await it?

- Do certain situations expose the company to excessive risk?

- Does the firm's information system provide detailed and timely information to all levels of management?

Management accountants frequently specialize in different aspects of accounting. A cost accountant, for example, determines the cost of goods and services and helps set their prices.

An internal auditor examines the firm's financial practices to ensure that its records include accurate data and that its operations comply with federal, state, and local laws and regulations. A tax accountant works to minimize a firm's tax bill and assumes responsibility for its federal, state, county, and city tax returns. Some management accountants achieve a *certified management accountant (CMA)* designation through experience and passing a comprehensive examination.

Management accountants are usually involved in the development and enforcement of organizational policies on such items as employee travel. As part of their job, many employees travel and accumulate airline frequent flyer miles and hotel reward points. While some organizations have strict policies over the personal use of travel perks, many do not.

Changing federal regulations affecting accounting and public reporting have increased the demand for management accountants in recent years. As a result, salaries for these professionals are rising.

Government and Not-for-Profit Accountants

Federal, state, and local governments also require accounting services. Government accountants and those who work for not-for-profit organizations perform professional services similar to those of management accountants. Accountants in these sectors concern themselves primarily with determining how efficiently the organizations accomplish their objectives. Among the many government agencies that employ accountants are the National Aeronautics and Space Administration, the Federal Bureau of Investigation, the Internal Revenue Service, the Commonwealth of Pennsylvania, and the City of Fresno, California. The federal government alone employs thousands of accountants.

Not-for-profit organizations, such as churches, labor unions, charities, schools, hospitals, and universities, also hire accountants. In fact, the not-for-profit sector is one of the fastest growing segments of accounting practice. An increasing number of not-for-profits publish financial information because contributors want more accountability from these organizations and are interested in knowing how the groups spend the money that they raise.

The Foundation of the Accounting System

To provide reliable, consistent, and unbiased information to decision makers, accountants follow guidelines, or standards, known as **generally accepted accounting principles (GAAP)**. These principles encompass the conventions, rules, and procedures for determining acceptable accounting and financial reporting practices at a particular time.

All GAAP standards are based on four basic principles: consistency, relevance, reliability, and comparability. Consistency means that all data should be collected and presented in the same manner across all periods. Any change in the way in which specific data are collected or presented must be noted and explained. Relevance states that all information being reported should be appropriate and assist users in evaluating that information. Reliability implies that the accounting data presented in financial statements are reliable and can be verified by an independent party such as an outside auditor. Finally, comparability ensures that one firm's financial statements can be compared with those of similar businesses. In the United States, the **Financial Accounting Standards Board (FASB)** is primarily responsible for evaluating, setting, or modifying GAAP. The U.S. Securities and Exchange Commission (SEC), the chief federal regulator of the financial markets and accounting industry, actually has the statutory authority to establish financial accounting and reporting standards for publicly held companies. (A publicly held company is one whose stock is publicly traded in a market such as the New York Stock Exchange.) However, the SEC's policy has been to rely on the accounting industry for this function, as long as the SEC believes the private sector is operating in the public interest. Consequently, the Financial Accounting Foundation—an organization made up of members of many different professional groups—actually appoints the members (currently five) of FASB, although the SEC does have some input. Board members are all experienced accounting professionals and serve five-year terms. They may be reappointed for a second five-year term. Board members must sever all connections with the firms they served prior to joining the board. The board is supported by a professional staff of more than 60 individuals.[7]

The FASB carefully monitors changing business conditions, enacting new rules and modifying existing rules when necessary. It also considers input and requests from all segments of its diverse constituency, including corporations and the SEC. One major change in accounting rules recently dealt with executive and employee stock options. Stock options give the holder the right to buy stock at a fixed price. The FASB now requires firms that give employees stock options to calculate the cost of the options and treat the cost as an expense, similar to salaries.

In response to well-known cases of accounting fraud, and questions about the independence of auditors, the Sarbanes-Oxley Act—commonly known as SOX—created the Public Accounting Oversight Board. The five-member board has the power to set audit standards and to investigate and sanction accounting firms that certify the books of publicly traded firms. Members of the Public Accounting Oversight Board are appointed by the SEC. No more than two of the five members of the board can be certified public accountants.

In addition to creating the Public Accounting Oversight Board, SOX also added to the reporting requirements for publicly traded companies. Senior executives including the CEO and chief financial officer (CFO), for example, must personally certify that the financial information reported by

Tips for Foreign Corrupt Practices Act Compliance

The Foreign Corrupt Practices Act is intended to prevent the bribery of foreign officials for the purpose of gaining or keeping business in another country. As more companies do business overseas, they are naturally concerned about becoming vulnerable to violations of this law. Federal enforcement of this act is at an all-time high and is expected to remain so. Penalties are severe and can include fines and imprisonment for anyone convicted. The Securities and Exchange Commission and the Department of Justice also expect strict compliance. The following are some ways that global firms can improve their compliance and mitigate risk:

1 Assess your firm's Foreign Corrupt Practices Act risk country by country. Does your firm do business with any state-owned foreign firms or foreign government officials? What risk is there of corruption and bribery?

2 Establish a Foreign Corrupt Practices Act compliance policy for your firm's employees in the United States and abroad. The policy should cover gifts and payments to foreign officials, charitable donations, accurate and complete records, and other areas vulnerable to risk.

3 Train your employees in the Foreign Corrupt Practices Act policy, and integrate it into your company's overall compliance. Have your HR department make it part of new-employee orientation.

4 Have a Foreign Corrupt Practices Act compliance team in place to monitor compliance and signal potential risks. The team should include company lawyers, accountants, and auditors and should be able to make both in-house and external investigations.

5 Plan any international investigations carefully. Many foreign countries do not recognize the attorney–client privilege as applying to company lawyers and employees.

Sources: "Foreign Corrupt Practices Act," Ernst & Young, http://www.ey.com, accessed June 21, 2011; U.S. Department of Justice, "Foreign Corrupt Practices Act: An Overview," http://www.justice.gov, accessed June 21, 2011; Gary Sturisky, "2010 Compliance Challenges: Three More Areas That Matter," *Corporate Compliance Insights*, March 4, 2010, http://www.corporatecomplianceinsights.com; Brian Loughman, Aaron Marcu, and Kerry Schalders, "Top Ten Tips for FCPA Compliance," Association of Corporate Counsel, March 1, 2010, http://www.acc.com; Nina Gross, "Foreign Corrupt Practices Act: Leading Practices to Consider," Deloitte, January 29, 2010, http://www.deloitte.com.

the company is correct. As we noted earlier, these requirements have increased the demand for accounting professionals, especially managerial accountants. One result of this increased demand has been higher salaries.

It is expensive for firms to adhere to GAAP standards and SOX requirements. Audits, for instance, can cost millions of dollars each year. These expenses can be especially burdensome for small businesses. Consequently, some have proposed modifications to GAAP and SOX for smaller firms, arguing that some accounting rules were really designed for larger companies. Others disagree.

The **Foreign Corrupt Practices Act** is a federal law that prohibits U.S. citizens and companies from bribing foreign officials in order to win or continue business. The law was later extended to make foreign officials subject to penalties if they in any way cause similar corrupt practices to occur within the United States or its territories. The "Business Etiquette" feature provides some tips on Foreign Corrupt Practices Act compliance.

The Accounting Cycle

Accounting deals with financial transactions between a firm and its employees, customers, suppliers, and owners; bankers; and various government agencies. For example, payroll checks result in a cash outflow to compensate employees. A payment to a vendor results in receipt of needed materials for the production process. Cash, check, and credit purchases by customers generate funds to cover the costs of operations and to earn a profit. Prompt payment of bills preserves the firm's credit rating and its future ability to earn a profit. The procedure by which accountants convert data about individual transactions to financial statements is called the **accounting cycle**.

Figure 15.2 illustrates the activities involved in the accounting cycle: recording, classifying, and summarizing transactions. Initially, any transaction that has a financial impact on the business, such as wages or payments to suppliers, should be documented. All of these

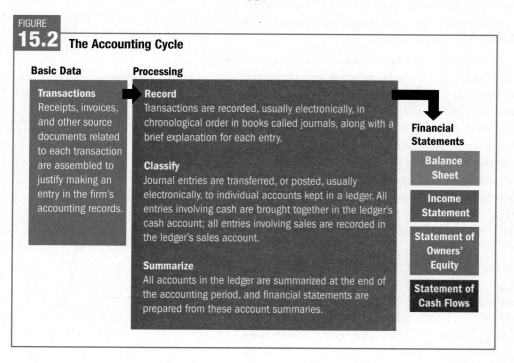

FIGURE 15.2 The Accounting Cycle

Basic Data

Transactions
Receipts, invoices, and other source documents related to each transaction are assembled to justify making an entry in the firm's accounting records.

Processing

Record
Transactions are recorded, usually electronically, in chronological order in books called journals, along with a brief explanation for each entry.

Classify
Journal entries are transferred, or posted, usually electronically, to individual accounts kept in a ledger. All entries involving cash are brought together in the ledger's cash account; all entries involving sales are recorded in the ledger's sales account.

Summarize
All accounts in the ledger are summarized at the end of the accounting period, and financial statements are prepared from these account summaries.

Financial Statements

Balance Sheet

Income Statement

Statement of Owners' Equity

Statement of Cash Flows

transactions are recorded in journals, which list transactions in chronological order. Journal listings are then posted to ledgers. A ledger shows increases or decreases in specific accounts such as cash or wages. Ledgers are used to prepare the financial statements, which summarize financial transactions. Management and other interested parties use the resulting financial statements for a variety of purposes.

The Accounting Equation

Three fundamental terms appear in the accounting equation: assets, liabilities, and owners' equity. An **asset** is anything of value owned or leased by a business. Assets include land, buildings, supplies, cash, accounts receivable (amounts owed to the business as payment for credit sales), and marketable securities.

Although most assets are tangible assets, such as equipment, buildings, and inventories, intangible possessions such as patents and trademarks are often some of a firm's most important assets. This kind of asset is especially essential for many companies, including computer software firms, biotechnology companies, and pharmaceutical companies. For instance, Johnson & Johnson—which has both biotechnology and pharmaceutical operations—reported more than $31 billion in intangible assets (including goodwill) in one recent year, out of a total of almost $95 billion in assets.[8]

Two groups have claims against the assets of a firm: creditors and owners. A **liability** of a business is anything owed to creditors—that is, the claims of a firm's creditors. When a firm borrows money to purchase inventory, land, or machinery, the claims of creditors are shown as accounts payable, notes payable, or long-term debt. Wages and salaries owed to employees also are liabilities (known as *wages payable* or *accrued wages*).

Owners' equity is the owner's initial investment in the business plus profits that were not paid out to owners over time in the form of cash dividends. A strong owners' equity position often is used as evidence of a firm's financial strength and stability.

asset anything of value owned by a firm.

liability claims against assets by creditors.

owners' equity funds contributed by owners plus profits not distributed to owners in the form of cash dividends.

Nikada/iStockphoto

Although tangible assets like buildings, equipment, and inventories may look impressive, they are sometimes less important to a company than intangible assets, such as patents and trademarks.

accounting equation
relationship that states that
assets must always equal
the sum of liabilities and
owners' equity.

The **accounting equation** (also referred to as the *accounting identity*) states that assets must equal liabilities plus owners' equity. This equation reflects the financial position of a firm at any point in time:

$$\text{Assets} = \text{Liabilities} + \text{Owners' equity}$$

Because financing comes from either creditors or owners, the right side of the accounting equation also represents the business's financial structure.

double-entry book-
keeping process by which
accounting transactions are
entered; each individual
transaction always has an
offsetting transaction.

The accounting equation also illustrates **double-entry bookkeeping**—the process by which accounting transactions are recorded. Because assets must always equal liabilities plus equity, each transaction must have an offsetting transaction. For example, if a company increases an asset, either another asset must decrease, a liability must increase, or owners' equity must increase. So if a company uses cash to purchase inventory, one asset (inventory) is increased while another (cash) is decreased by the same amount. Similarly, a decrease in an asset must be offset by either an increase in another asset, a decrease in a liability, or a decrease in owners' equity. If a company uses cash to repay a bank loan, both an asset (cash) and a liability (bank loans) decrease, and by the same amount.

Two simple numerical examples will help illustrate the accounting equation and double-entry bookkeeping. First, assume the owner of a photo studio purchases a new camera system for $5,000 using her personal funds. The accounting transaction would look as follows:

Increase plant, property, and equipment (an asset) by $5,000

Increase owners' equity by $5,000

So, the left side of the accounting equation would increase by $5,000 and be offset by a $5,000 increase on the right side.

Second, assume a firm has a $100,000 loan from a bank and decides to pay it off using some of its cash. The transaction would be recorded as:

Decrease bank loan (liability) by $100,000

Decrease cash (asset) by $100,000

In this second example, the left side and right side of the accounting equation would both decrease by $100,000.

The relationship expressed by the accounting equation underlies development of the firm's financial statements. Three financial statements form the foundation: the balance sheet, the income statement, and the statement of owners' equity. The information found in these statements is calculated using the double-entry bookkeeping system and reflects the basic accounting equation. A fourth statement, the statement of cash flows, is also prepared to focus specifically on the sources and uses of cash for a firm from its operating, investing, and financing activities.

The Impact of Computers and the Internet on the Accounting Process

For hundreds of years, bookkeepers recorded, or posted, accounting transactions as manual entries in journals. They then transferred the information, or posted it, to individual accounts listed in ledgers. Computers have streamlined the process, making it both faster and easier. For instance, point-of-sale terminals in retail stores perform a number of

Deloitte Educates Itself—and Others—on Sustainability

For many years, Deloitte has been one of the Big Four accounting and auditing firms. Recently the company decided not only to make its own internal operations greener but also to offer its clients training in green practices. It does seem logical for a firm that specializes in financial reporting to enter the realm of nonfinancial reporting as the business world changes course on green practices. Whereas firms once considered "going green" good public relations but financially unrewarding, many now see the importance of sustainability in an increasingly energy-limited environment.

Kathryn Pavlovsky, a co-leader of Deloitte's Enterprise Sustainability Group, says, "Nonfinancial reporting is evolving from voluntary communications to mandatory compliance, and the environmental regulatory and financial reporting worlds are converging." Activism by shareholders and changing consumer attitudes and behavior have also been heavily influential, as has the recent recession. Technological advances are making green practices increasingly feasible and affordable.

Deloitte's corporate responsibility policy declares that their U.S. firms will "advocate the sustainable use of natural resources and the environment." The company began its internal greening campaign by conducting a survey of its employees. Called "How green is your footprint?" the survey measured "greenness" on an individual basis, then made suggestions on how each employee could improve his or her performance. A second survey, "How green is your *other* footprint?" helps employees measure sustainability in their homes.

Deloitte also established a Green Leadership Council to maintain contact between the various company regions and management. The GLC educates employees about important green issues and promotes a unified message to all the company's offices. Deloitte employees now conduct virtual meetings and conferences whenever possible; when not, company travel offers green car-rental and hotel options. Deloitte has also adopted Leadership in Energy and Environmental Design (LEED) standards in building new offices and retrofitting existing ones. The company has focused on purchasing supplies that have a minimal impact on the environment, and worked with its suppliers for greater sustainability.

Deloitte's Center for Sustainability Performance (CSP) in Waltham, Massachusetts, is geared toward advising businesses on how to reduce their environmental impact and remain profitable. Among the areas covered are planning and strategy, revenue generation, tax incentives, and competitive branding. The CSP also explores sustainability opportunities for employees, offices, IT infrastructure, and communities. Among the center's activities are on-site training for client firms; research and development in sustainability measurement and reporting, publication of reports on these topics for corporate sustainability managers, and consulting and sales support.

One of the center's recent workshops for clients was "Sustainability Measurement and Reporting: Tools, Methods, and Metrics." The course was designed to help clients become acquainted with the current methods for measuring and reporting their own sustainability, as well as giving them a preview of new developments in these areas. According to Mark W. McElroy, the CSP's director, the course covered "tools, methods and metrics across all dimensions of corporate social responsibility and sustainability performance, including carbon, water, solid waste, social impacts, triple bottom line and nonfinancial measurement and reporting in general, both from an enterprise and product life cycle perspective."

In further developing its internal greening efforts, Deloitte recently introduced its Green Sync tool, which is intended to promote employee and stakeholder involvement. One reason for this is that energy may consume as much as 20 percent of a company's expenses. So including employees, customers, suppliers, and shareholders in sustainability efforts can affect a firm's bottom line. "Every company is an energy company," says Deloitte's Nick Main. "And if it isn't, it will be soon."

Questions for Critical Thinking

1. Why do you think Deloitte would find it relatively easy to expand from financial to nonfinancial reporting?
2. How would you go about answering the question, "How big is *your* carbon footprint?" What did you find that you could do to make your home and/or your workplace greener?

Sources: Nick Main and Joe Stanislaw, "Every Company Is an Energy Company," *Environmental Leader*, April 4, 2011; Deloitte Web site, http://www.deloitte.com, accessed June 21, 2011; Deborah Fleischer, "Deloitte: Best Practices for Going Green," *Triple Pundit*, February 1, 2010, http://www.triplepundit.com; Deborah Fleischer, "Deloitte: Green Training on Sustainability Measurement and Reporting," *Green Impact*, January 4, 2010, http://greenimpact.com.

---

functions each time they record sales. These terminals not only recall prices from computer system memory and maintain constant inventory counts of individual items in stock but also automatically perform accounting data entry functions.

Accounting software programs are used widely in both large and small businesses today. They allow a do-it-once approach, in which a single input leads to automatic conversion of a sale into a journal entry, which then is stored until needed. Decision makers can then request up-to-date financial statements and financial ratios instantly. Improvements in accounting software continue to make the process even faster and easier. In addition, accounting firms have begun to use mobile computing to better serve their clients. Smart phones provide connections between employees and their company's network, which means they can access current, vital information from anywhere. Accounting firms may also provide mobile computing to clients with branded applications allowing clients to access their financial information and services via their phones. As they increase their Internet capabilities, tablet computers are also emerging as important business tools for accounting firms.[9]

Because the accounting needs of entrepreneurs and small businesses differ from those of larger firms, accounting software makers have designed programs that meet specific user needs. Some examples of accounting software programs designed for entrepreneurs and small businesses, and designed to run on personal computers, include QuickBooks, Peachtree, and BusinessWorks. Software programs designed for larger firms, often requiring more sophisticated computer systems, include products from Oracle and SAP.

For firms that conduct business worldwide, software producers have introduced new accounting programs that handle all of a company's accounting information for every country in which it operates. The software handles different languages and currencies, as well as the financial, legal, and tax requirements of each nation in which the firm conducts business.

The Internet also influences the accounting process. Several software producers offer Web-based accounting products designed for small and medium-sized businesses. Among other benefits, these products allow users to access their complete accounting systems from anywhere using a standard Web browser. The "Going Green" feature explains how Deloitte is integrating sustainability into its infrastructure and its business services.

Assessment Check ✅

1. List the steps in the accounting cycle.
2. What is the accounting equation?
3. Briefly explain double-entry bookkeeping.

Financial Statements

Financial statements provide managers with essential information they need to evaluate the liquidity position of an organization—its ability to meet current obligations and needs by converting assets into cash; the firm's profitability; and its overall financial health. The balance sheet, income statement, statement of owners' equity, and statement of cash flows provide a foundation on which managers can base their decisions. By interpreting the data provided in these statements, managers can communicate the appropriate information to internal decision makers and to interested parties outside the organization.

Of the four financial statements, only the balance sheet is considered to be a permanent statement; its amounts are carried over from year to year. The income statement, statement of owners' equity, and statement of cash flows are considered temporary because they are closed out at the end of each year.

Public companies are required to report their financial statements at the end of each three-month period, as well as at the end of each fiscal year. Annual statements must be examined and verified by the firm's outside auditors. These financial statements

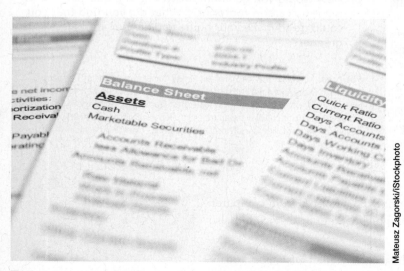

Mateusz Zagorski/iStockphoto

The balance sheet, the only permanent statement of the four financial statements, shows the firm's financial position on a particular date and its amounts are carried over from year to year.

Solving an Ethical Controversy

Should Whistle-Blowers Be Rewarded?

The Sarbanes-Oxley Act of 2002 (SOX) was intended to reduce fraud, partly by requiring CEOs and CFOs to sign off on the accuracy of their companies' financial statements. However, the largest percentage of reported fraud is revealed by anonymous whistle-blowers or by journalists, auditors, or others.

The U.S. False Claims Act allows citizens to file lawsuits alleging fraud against the federal government. The biggest settlements have involved hospital chains and drug manufacturers; the largest fine was $1 billion. Some whistle-blowers have collected almost $47 million in rewards. Provisions of the Foreign Corrupt Practices Act (FCPA) can also potentially result in huge rewards. But whistle-blowers are not always successful; some have been fired, forced to quit, or demoted.

Should whistle-blowers be rewarded for reporting financial fraud?

PRO

1. A recent survey found that "a strong monetary incentive to blow the whistle does motivate people with information to come forward."

2. Despite strict penalties for fraud, such as those under SOX and the FCPA, one survey reported that 83 percent of fraud examiners believe that internal corporate controls over fraud will actually decline.

CON

1. Some observers feel that certain "whistle-blower-friendly" provisions of the FCPA may discourage accused firms from simply settling with the federal government and paying a fine to avoid costly legal procedures.

2. Not all whistle-blowers are innocent. A former UBS banker exposed tax evasion at the firm but was sentenced to prison because he did not reveal at first that he had participated in the fraud himself.

Summary

Legislation before Congress would require the Securities and Exchange Commission (SEC) to award whistle-blowers up to 30 percent of fines the government collects on the basis of "original information." And nearly a decade after co-writing the Act, former congressman Michael Oxley registered as a lobbyist for the Financial Industry Regulatory Authority (FINRA), which promotes self-regulation of investment advisors. Currently, more than 1,000 whistle-blower cases are pending.

Sources: "Oxley of Sarbanes-Oxley to Lobby for Financial Self-Regulator," *Bloomberg.com,* March 18, 2011, http://www.bloomberg .com; "Sarbanes-Oxley Can Help Curb Company Fraud," McGladrey, http://rsmmcgladrey.com, accessed June 1, 2010; Michael Connor, "Finance Reform Bill Could Increase Big Payouts to Whistleblowers," *Business Ethics,* May 2, 2010, http://business-ethics.com; "Whistle blowers Making Money Thanks to Law," *NewsChannel 8,* May 1, 2010, http://cfc.news.8.net; Deloitte Webcast Poll, "Poll: More Financial Statement Fraud Expected to Be Uncovered in 2010, 2011," *Corporate Compliance Insights,* April 28, 2010, http://www.corporate complianceinsights.com; James Hyatt, "Who Detects Corporate Fraud? (Tip: It's Not Usually the SEC . . .)," *Business Ethics,* February 16, 2010, http://business-ethics.com; Michael Rubinkam, "UBS Tax Evasion Whistle-Blower Reports to Federal Prison," *USA Today,* January 8, 2010, http://www.usatoday.com.

---

are public information available to anyone. The "Solving an Ethical Controversy" feature discusses the problem of financial fraud.

A fiscal year does not have to coincide with the calendar year, and companies set different fiscal years. For instance, Starbucks's fiscal year runs from October 1 to September 30 of the following year. Nike's fiscal year consists of the 12 months between June 1 and May 31. By contrast, GE's fiscal year is the same as the calendar year, running from January 1 to December 31.

The Balance Sheet

A firm's **balance sheet** shows its financial position on a particular date. It is similar to a photograph of the firm's assets together with its liabilities and owners' equity at a specific moment in time. Balance sheets must be prepared at regular intervals, because a firm's

balance sheet statement of a firm's financial position—what it owns and claims against its assets—at a particular point in time.

managers and other internal parties often request this information every day, every week, or at least every month. On the other hand, external users, such as stockholders or industry analysts, may use this information less frequently, perhaps every quarter or once a year.

The balance sheet follows the accounting equation. On the left side of the balance sheet are the firm's assets—what it owns. These assets, shown in descending order of liquidity (in other words, convertibility to cash), represent the uses that management has made of available funds. Cash is always listed first on the asset side of the balance sheet.

On the right side of the equation are the claims against the firm's assets. Liabilities and owners' equity indicate the sources of the firm's assets and are listed in the order in which they are due. Liabilities reflect the claims of creditors—financial institutions or bondholders that have loaned the firm money; suppliers that have provided goods and services on credit; and others to be paid, such as federal, state, and local tax authorities. Owners' equity represents the owners' claims (those of stockholders, in the case of a corporation) against the firm's assets. It also amounts to the excess of all assets over liabilities.

Figure 15.3 shows the balance sheet for Diane's Java, a small California-based coffee wholesaler. The accounting equation is illustrated by the three classifications of assets, liabilities, and owners' equity on the company's balance sheet. Remember, total assets must always equal the sum of liabilities and owners' equity. In other words, the balance sheet must always balance.

The Income Statement

income statement
financial record of a company's revenues and expenses, and profits over a period of time.

Whereas the balance sheet reflects a firm's financial situation at a specific point in time, the **income statement** represents the flow of resources that reveals the performance of the organization over a specific time period. Resembling a video rather than a photograph, the income statement is a financial record summarizing a firm's financial performance in terms of revenues, expenses, and profits over a given time period, say, a quarter or a year.

In addition to reporting the firm's profit or loss results, the income statement helps decision makers focus on overall revenues and the costs involved in generating these revenues. Managers of a not-for-profit organization use this statement to determine whether its revenues from contributions and other sources will cover its operating costs. Finally, the income statement provides much of the basic data needed to calculate the financial ratios managers use in planning and controlling activities. Figure 15.4 shows the income statement for Diane's Java.

An income statement (some times called *a profit-and-loss*, or *P&L, statement*) begins with total sales or revenues generated during a year, quarter, or month. Subsequent lines then deduct all of the costs related to producing the revenues. Typical categories of costs include those involved in producing the firm's goods or services, operating expenses, interest, and taxes. After all of them have been subtracted, the remaining net income may be distributed to the firm's owners (stockholders, proprietors, or partners) or reinvested in the company as retained earnings. The final figure on the income statement—net income after taxes—is the so-called *bottom line*.

Keeping costs under control is an important part of running a business. Too often, however, companies concentrate more on increasing revenue than on controlling costs. Regardless of how much money a company collects in revenues, it won't stay in business for long unless it eventually earns a profit.

FIGURE
15.3 Diane's Java Balance Sheet (Fiscal Year, Ending December 31)

1 Current Assets:
Cash and other liquid assets that can or will be converted to cash within one year.

2 Plant, Property, and Equipment (net):
Physical assets expected to last for more than one year; shown net of accumulated depreciation—the cumulative value that plant, property, and equipment have been expensed (depreciated).

3 Value of assets such as patents and trademarks.

4 Current Liabilities:
Claims of creditors that are to be repaid within one year; accruals are expenses, such as wages, that have been incurred but not yet paid.

5 Long-Term Debt:
Debts that come due one year or longer after the date on the balance sheet.

6 Owners' (or shareholders') Equity:
Claims of the owners against the assets of the firm; the difference between total assets and total liabilities.

Diane's Java

Balance Sheet

($ thousands)	2013	2012
Assets		
1 Current Assets		
Cash	$ 800	$ 600
Short-term investments	1,250	940
Accounts receivable	990	775
Inventory	2,200	1,850
Total current assets	5,240	4,165
2 Plant, property, and equipment (net)	3,300	2,890
3 Goodwill and other intangible assets	250	250
Total Assets	8,790	7,305
Liabilities and Shareholders' Equity		
4 Current Liabilities		
Accruals	$ 350	$ 450
Accounts payable	980	900
Notes payable	700	500
Total current liabilities	2,030	1,850
5 Long-term debt	1,100	1,000
Total liabilities	3,130	2,850
6 Shareholders' equity	5,660	4,455
Total Liabilities and Equity	8,790	7,305

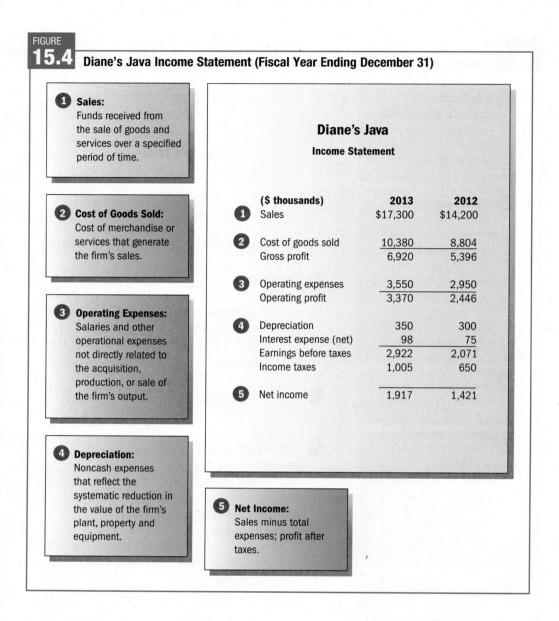

FIGURE 15.4 Diane's Java Income Statement (Fiscal Year Ending December 31)

① Sales:
Funds received from the sale of goods and services over a specified period of time.

② Cost of Goods Sold:
Cost of merchandise or services that generate the firm's sales.

③ Operating Expenses:
Salaries and other operational expenses not directly related to the acquisition, production, or sale of the firm's output.

④ Depreciation:
Noncash expenses that reflect the systematic reduction in the value of the firm's plant, property and equipment.

⑤ Net Income:
Sales minus total expenses; profit after taxes.

Diane's Java

Income Statement

($ thousands)	2013	2012
① Sales	$17,300	$14,200
② Cost of goods sold	10,380	8,804
Gross profit	6,920	5,396
③ Operating expenses	3,550	2,950
Operating profit	3,370	2,446
④ Depreciation	350	300
Interest expense (net)	98	75
Earnings before taxes	2,922	2,071
Income taxes	1,005	650
⑤ Net income	1,917	1,421

Statement of Owners' Equity

statement of owners' equity record of the change in owners' equity from the end of one fiscal period to the end of the next.

The **statement of owners'**, or shareholders', **equity** is designed to show the components of the change in equity from the end of one fiscal year to the end of the next. It uses information from both the balance sheet and income statement. A somewhat simplified example is shown in Figure 15.5 for Diane's Java.

Note that the statement begins with the amount of equity shown on the balance sheet at the end of the prior year. Net income is added, and cash dividends paid to owners are subtracted (both are found on the income statement for the current year). If owners contributed any additional capital, say, through the sale of new shares, this amount is added to equity. On the other hand, if owners withdrew capital, for example, through the repurchase of existing shares, equity declines. All of the additions and subtractions, taken together, equal the change in owners' equity from the end of the last fiscal year to the end of the current one. The new amount of owners' equity is then reported on the balance sheet for the current year.

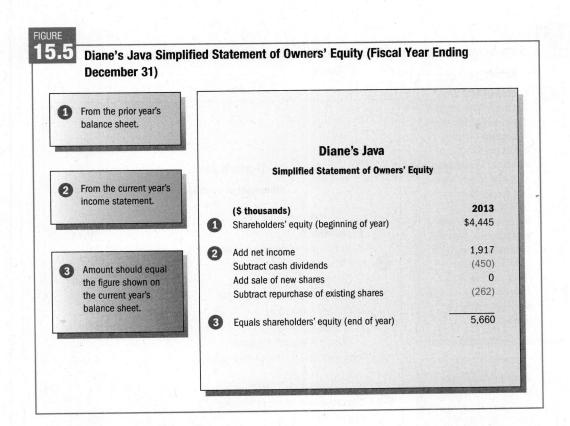

FIGURE 15.5 Diane's Java Simplified Statement of Owners' Equity (Fiscal Year Ending December 31)

1 From the prior year's balance sheet.

2 From the current year's income statement.

3 Amount should equal the figure shown on the current year's balance sheet.

Diane's Java

Simplified Statement of Owners' Equity

($ thousands)	2013
1 Shareholders' equity (beginning of year)	$4,445
2 Add net income	1,917
Subtract cash dividends	(450)
Add sale of new shares	0
Subtract repurchase of existing shares	(262)
3 Equals shareholders' equity (end of year)	5,660

The Statement of Cash Flows

In addition to the statement of owners' equity, the income statement, and the balance sheet, most firms prepare a fourth accounting statement—the **statement of cash flows**. Public companies are required to prepare and publish a statement of cash flows. In addition, commercial lenders often require a borrower to submit a statement of cash flows. The statement of cash flows provides investors and creditors with relevant information about a firm's cash receipts and cash payments for its operations, investments, and financing during an accounting period. Figure 15.6 shows the statement of cash flows for Diane's Java.

Companies prepare a statement of cash flows due to the widespread use of accrual accounting. **Accrual accounting** recognizes revenues and costs when they occur, not when actual cash changes hands. As a result, there can be differences between what is reported as sales, expenses, and profits, and the amount of cash that actually flows into and out of the business during a period of time. An example is depreciation. Companies depreciate fixed assets—such as machinery and buildings—over a specified period of time, meaning that they systematically reduce the value of the asset. Depreciation is reported as an expense on the firm's income statement—see Figure 15.4—but does not involve any actual cash. The fact that depreciation is a noncash expense means that what a firm reports as net income (profits after tax) for a particular period actually understates the amount of cash the firm took in, less expenses, during that period of time. Consequently, depreciation is added back to net income when calculating cash flow.

The fact that *cash flow* is the lifeblood of every organization is evidenced by the business failure rate. Many former owners of failed firms blame inadequate cash flow for their company's demise. Those who value the statement of cash flow maintain that its preparation and scrutiny

statement of cash flows statement showing the sources and uses of cash during a period of time.

accrual accounting accounting method that records revenues and expenses when they occur, not necessarily when cash actually changes hands.

FIGURE
15.6

Diane's Java Statement of Cash Flows (Fiscal Year Ending December 31)

① Operating Activities:
The nuts and bolts of day-to-day activities of a company carrying out its regular business; Increases in accounts receivable and inventory are uses of cash, while increases in accruals and accounts payables are sources of cash; in financially healthy firms, net cash flow from operating activities should be positive.

② Investing Activities:
Transactions to accumulate or use cash in ways that affect operating activities in the future; often a use of cash.

③ Financing Activities:
Ways to transfer cash to or from creditors and to or from owners; can be either positive or negative.

④ Net Cash Flow:
The sum of cash flow from operating, investing, and financing activities, a reconcilement of cash from the beginning to the end of the accounting period (one year in this example).

Diane's Java
Statement of Cash Flows

($ thousands)	2013
Cash Flow from Operating Activities	
① Net income	$1,917
Depreciation	350
Change in accounts receivable	(215)
Change in inventory	(350)
Change in accruals	(100)
Change in accounts payable	80
Total cash flow from operating activities	1,682
② **Cash Flow from Investing Activities**	
Capital expenditures	(760)
Change in short-term investments	(310)
Total cash flow from investing activities	(1,070)
③ **Cash Flow from Financing Activities**	
Cash dividends	(450)
Sale/repurchase of shares	(262)
Change in notes payable	200
Change in long-term debt	100
Total cash flow from financing activities	(412)
④ **Net Cash Flow**	200
Cash (beginning of year)	600
Cash (end of year)	800

by various parties can prevent financial distress for otherwise profitable firms, too many of which are forced into bankruptcy due to a lack of cash needed to continue day-to-day operations.

Even for firms for which bankruptcy is not an issue, the statement of cash flows can provide investors and other interested parties with vital information. For instance, assume that a firm's income statement reports rising earnings. At the same time, however, the statement of cash flows shows that the firm's inventory is rising faster than sales—often a signal that demand for the firm's products is softening, which may in turn be a sign of impending financial trouble.

Financial Ratio Analysis

Accounting professionals fulfill important responsibilities beyond preparing financial statements. In a more critical role, they help managers interpret the statements by comparing data about the firm's current activities to those for previous periods and to results posted by other companies in the industry. *Ratio analysis* is one of the most commonly used tools for measuring a firm's liquidity, profitability, and reliance on debt financing, as well as the effectiveness of management's resource utilization. This analysis also allows comparisons with other firms and with the firm's own past performance.

Ratios assist managers by interpreting actual performance and making comparisons to what should have happened. Comparisons with ratios of similar companies help managers understand their firm's performance relative to competitors' results. These industry standards are important yardsticks and help pinpoint problem areas, as well as areas of excellence. Ratios for the current accounting period also may be compared with similar calculations for previous periods to spot developing trends. Ratios can be classified according to their specific purposes. The four major categories of financial ratios are summarized in Table 15.1. The ratios for Diane's Java for the 2011 and 2012 fiscal years are shown in Table 15.2.

Table
⌞15.1⌟ Major Categories of Financial Ratios

CATEGORY	RATIO	DESCRIPTION
Liquidity ratios	Current ratio	Current assets divided by current liabilities
	Quick (acid-test) ratio	Current assets (minus inventory) divided by current liabilities
Efficiency ratios	Inventory turnover	Cost of goods sold divided by average inventory
	Receivables turnover	Credit sales divided by average accounts receivable
	Total asset turnover	Revenue or sales divided by average total assets
Leverage ratios	Debt ratio	Total liabilities divided by total assets
	Long term debt to equity	Long-term debt divided by owners' equity
Profitability ratios	Gross profit margin	Gross profit divided by revenue or sales
	Net profit margin	Net profit divided by revenue or sales
	Return on equity	Net profit divided by average owners' equity

Assessment Check ✅

1. List the four financial statements.
2. How is the balance sheet organized?
3. Define *accrual accounting*.

15.2 Financial Ratios for Diane's Java

FINANCIAL RATIO	2013 FISCAL YEAR	2012 FISCAL YEAR
Current ratio	2.58	2.25
Quick ratio	1.50	1.25
Inventory turnover	5.13	5.03
Receivables turnover	19.60	19.32
Total asset turnover	2.15	2.15
Debt ratio	35.6%	39.0%
Long-term debt to equity	19.4%	22.4%
Gross profit margin	40.0%	38.0%
Net profit margin	11.1%	10.0%
Return on equity	37.9%	36.6%

Liquidity Ratios

A firm's ability to meet its short-term obligations when they must be paid is measured by *liquidity ratios.* Increasing liquidity reduces the likelihood that a firm will face emergencies caused by the need to raise funds to repay loans. On the other hand, firms with low liquidity may be forced to choose between default or borrowing from high-cost lending sources to meet their maturing obligations.

Two commonly used liquidity ratios are the current ratio and the acid-test, or quick, ratio. The current ratio compares current assets to current liabilities, giving executives information about the firm's ability to pay its current debts as they mature. The current ratio of Diane's Java can be computed as follows (unless indicated, all amounts from the balance sheet or income statement are in thousands of dollars):

$$\text{Liquidity ratio} = \frac{\text{Current assets}}{\text{Current liabilities}} = \frac{5,240}{2,030} = 2.58$$

In other words, Diane's Java has $2.58 of current assets for every $1.00 of current liabilities. In general, a current ratio of 2:1 is considered satisfactory liquidity. This rule of thumb must be considered along with other factors, such as the nature of the business, the season, and the quality of the company's management team. Diane's Java's management and other interested parties are likely to evaluate this ratio of 2.58:1 by comparing it with ratios for previous operating periods and with industry averages.

The acid-test (or quick) ratio measures the ability of a firm to meet its debt payments on short notice. This ratio compares quick assets—the most liquid current assets—against current liabilities. Quick assets generally consist of cash and equivalents, short-term investments, and accounts receivable. So, generally quick assets equal total current assets minus inventory.

Diane's Java's current balance sheet lists total current assets of $5.24 million and inventory of $2.2 million. Therefore, its quick ratio is as follows:

$$\text{Acid-test ratio} = \frac{\text{Current assets} - \text{Inventory}}{\text{Current liabilities}} = \frac{(5,240 - 2,200)}{2,030} = 1.50$$

Because the traditional rule of thumb for an adequate acid-test ratio is around 1:1, Diane's Java appears to have a strong level of liquidity. However, the same cautions apply here as for the current ratio. The ratio should be compared with industry averages and data from previous operating periods to determine whether it is adequate for the firm.

Activity Ratios

Activity ratios measure the effectiveness of management's use of the firm's resources. One of the most frequently used activity ratios, the inventory turnover ratio, indicates the number of times merchandise moves through a business:

$$\text{Inventory turnover} = \frac{\text{Cost of goods sold}}{\text{Average inventory}} = \frac{10,380}{[(2,200 + 1,850)/2]} = 5.13$$

Average inventory for Diane's Java is determined by adding the inventory as of December 31, 2012 ($2.2 million) with the inventory as of December 31, 2011 ($1.85 million) and dividing it by 2. Comparing the 5.13 inventory turnover ratio with industry standards gives a measure of efficiency. It is important to note, however, that inventory turnover can vary substantially depending on the products a company sells and the industry in which it operates.

If a company makes a substantial portion of its sales on credit, measuring receivables turnover can provide useful information. Receivables turnover can be calculated as follows:

$$\text{Receivables turnover} = \frac{\text{Credit sales}}{\text{Average accounts receivable}}$$

Because Diane's Java is a wholesaler, let's assume that all of its sales are credit sales. Average receivables equals the simple average of 2012's receivables and 2011's receivables. The ratio for the company is:

$$\text{Receivables turnover} = \frac{17,300}{[(990 + 775)/2]} = 19.60$$

Dividing 365 by the figure for receivables turnover, 19.6, equals the average age of receivables, 18.62 days. Assume Diane's Java expects its retail customers to pay outstanding bills within 30 days of the date of purchase. Given that the average age of its receivables is less than 30 days, Diane's Java appears to be doing a good job collecting its credit sales.

Another measure of efficiency is total asset turnover. It measures how much in sales each dollar invested in assets generates:

$$\text{Total asset turnover} = \frac{\text{Sales}}{\text{Average total assets}}$$

$$= \frac{17,300}{[(8,790 + 7,305)/2]} = 2.15$$

Average total assets for Diane's Java equals total assets as of December 31, 2012 ($8.79 million) plus total assets as of December 31, 2011 ($7.305 million) divided by 2.

Diane's Java generates about $2.15 in sales for each dollar invested in assets. Although a higher ratio generally indicates that a firm is operating more efficiently, care must be taken when comparing firms that operate in different industries. Some industries simply require higher investment in assets than do other industries.

Profitability Ratios

Some ratios measure the organization's overall financial performance by evaluating its ability to generate revenues in excess of operating costs and other expenses. These measures are called *profitability ratios*. To compute these ratios, accountants compare the firm's earnings with total sales or investments. Over a period of time, profitability ratios may reveal the effectiveness of management in operating the business. Three important profitability ratios are gross profit margin, net profit margin, and return on equity:

$$\text{Gross profit margin} = \frac{\text{Gross profit}}{\text{Sales}} = \frac{6{,}920}{17{,}300} = 40.0\%$$

$$\text{Net profit margin} = \frac{\text{Net income}}{\text{Sales}} = \frac{1{,}917}{17{,}300} = 11.1\%$$

$$\text{Return on equity} = \frac{\text{Net income}}{\text{Average equity}} = \frac{1{,}1917}{\left[(5{,}660 + 4{,}455)/2\right]} = 37.9\%$$

All of these ratios indicate positive evaluations of the current operations of Diane's Java. For example, the net profit margin indicates that the firm realizes a profit of slightly more than 11 cents on each dollar of merchandise it sells. Although this ratio varies widely among business firms, Diane's Java compares favorably with wholesalers in general, which have an average net profit margin of around 5 percent. However, this ratio, like the other profitability ratios, should be evaluated in relation to profit forecasts, past performance, or more specific industry averages to enhance the interpretation of results. Similarly, while the firm's return on equity of almost 38 percent appears outstanding, the degree of risk in the industry also must be considered.

Leverage Ratios

Leverage ratios measure the extent to which a firm relies on debt financing. They provide particularly interesting information to potential investors and lenders. If management has assumed too much debt in financing the firm's operations, problems may arise in meeting future interest payments and repaying outstanding loans. As we discuss in Chapter 17, borrowing money does have advantages. However, relying too heavily on debt financing may lead to bankruptcy. More generally, both investors and lenders may prefer to deal with firms whose owners have invested enough of their own money to avoid overreliance

©Aflac

This AFLAC advertisement, aimed at investors rather than insurance buyers, notes the firm's ten-year total return to shareholders of 18.3 percent. *Return on equity* is one measure of a company's profitability.

on borrowing. The debt ratio and long-term debt to equity ratio help interested parties evaluate a firm's leverage:

$$\text{Debt ratio} = \frac{\text{Total liabilities}}{\text{Total assets}} = \frac{3,130}{8,790} = 35.6\%$$

$$\text{Long-term debt to equity} = \frac{\text{Long-term debt}}{\text{Owners' equity}} = \frac{1,100}{5,660} = 19.64\%$$

A total liabilities to total assets ratio greater than 50 percent indicates that a firm is relying more on borrowed money than owners' equity. Because Diane's Java's total liabilities to total assets ratio is 35.6 percent, the firm's owners have invested considerably more than the total amount of liabilities shown on the firm's balance sheet. Moreover, the firm's long-term debt to equity ratio is only 19.64 percent, indicating that Diane's Java has only about 19.6 cents in long-term debt to every dollar in equity. The long-term debt to equity ratio also indicates that Diane's Java hasn't relied very heavily on borrowed money.

The four categories of financial ratios relate balance sheet and income statement data to one another, help management pinpoint a firm's strengths and weaknesses, and indicate areas in need of further investigation. Large, multiproduct firms that operate in diverse markets use their information systems to update their financial ratios every day or even every hour. Each company's management must decide on an appropriate review schedule to avoid the costly and time-consuming mistake of overmonitoring.

In addition to calculating financial ratios, managers, investors, and lenders should pay close attention to how accountants applied a number of accounting rules when preparing financial statements. GAAP gives accountants leeway in reporting certain revenues and expenses. Public companies are required to disclose, in footnotes to the financial statements, how the various accounting rules were applied.

Budgeting

Although the financial statements discussed in this chapter focus on past business activities, they also provide the basis for planning in the future. A **budget** is a planning and controlling tool that reflects the firm's expected sales revenues, operating expenses, and cash receipts and outlays. It quantifies the firm's plans for a specified future period. Because it reflects management estimates of expected sales, cash inflows and outflows, and costs, the budget is a financial blueprint and can be thought of as a short-term financial plan. It becomes the standard for comparison against actual performance.

Budget preparation is frequently a time-consuming task that involves many people from various departments within the organization. The complexity of the budgeting process varies with the size and complexity of the organization. Large corporations such as United Technologies, Paramount Pictures, and Verizon maintain complex and sophisticated budgeting systems. Their budgets help managers integrate their numerous divisions in addition to serving as planning and controlling tools. But budgeting in both large and small firms is similar to household budgeting in its purpose: to match income and expenses in a way that accomplishes objectives and correctly times cash inflows and outflows.

Because the accounting department is an organization's financial nerve center, it provides much of the data for budget development. The overall master, or operating, budget is

Assessment
Check ☑

1. List the four categories of financial ratios.

2. Define the following ratios: *current ratio, inventory turnover, net profit margin,* and *debt ratio.*

budget organization's plans for how it will raise and spend money during a given period.

actually a composite of many individual budgets for separate units of the firm. These individual budgets typically include the production budget, cash budget, capital expenditures budget, advertising budget, and sales budget.

Technology has improved the efficiency of the budgeting process. The accounting software products discussed earlier—such as QuickBooks—all include budgeting features. Moreover, modules designed for specific businesses are often available from third parties. Many banks now offer their customers personal financial management tools (PFMs) developed by software companies. One such tool is FinanceWorks, an online finance program from Intuit's Digital Insight division. BBVA, a multinational Spanish banking group, offers Tu Cuentas ("you count"), based on a PFM program from Strands, a California software developer.[10]

One of the most important budgets prepared by firms is the *cash budget*. The cash budget, usually prepared monthly, tracks the firm's cash inflows and outflows. Figure 15.7 illustrates a sample cash budget for Birchwood Paper, a small Maine-based paper products company. The company has set a $150,000 target cash balance. The cash budget indicates months in which the firm will need temporary loans—May, June, and July—and how much it will need (close to $3 million). The document also indicates that Birchwood will generate

Assessment Check ☑

1. What is a budget?
2. How is a cash budget organized?

FIGURE 15.7 | **Four-Month Cash Budget for Birchwood Paper Company**

Birchwood Paper Company
Four-Month Cash Budget

($ thousands)	May	June	July	August
Gross sales	$1,200.0	$3,200.0	$5,500.0	$4,500.0
Cash sales	300.0	800.0	1,375.0	1,125.0
One month prior	600.0	600.0	1,600.0	2,750.0
Two months prior	300.0	300.0	300.0	800.0
Total cash inflows	1,200.0	1,700.0	3,275.0	4,675.0
Purchases				
Cash purchases	1,040.0	1,787.5	1,462.5	390.0
One month prior	390.0	1,040.0	1,787.5	1,462.5
Wages and salaries	250.0	250.0	250.0	250.0
Office rent	75.0	75.0	75.0	75.0
Marketing and other expenses	150.0	150.0	150.0	150.0
Taxes		300.0		
Total cash outflows	1,905.0	3,602.5	3,725.0	2,327.5
Net cash flow				
(Inflows – Outflows)	(705.0)	(1,902.5)	(450.0)	2,347.5
Beginnning cash balance	250.0	150.0	150.0	150.0
Net cash flow	(705.0)	(1,902.5)	(450.0)	2,347.5
Ending cash balance	(455.0)	(1,752.5)	(300.0)	2,497.5
Target cash balance	150.0	150.0	150.0	150.0
Surplus (deficit)	(605.0)	(1,902.5)	(450.0)	2,347.5
Cumulative surplus (deficit)	(605.0)	(2,507.5)	(2,957.5)	610.0

Hit & Miss

Accounting: Hong Kong Meets China

Hong Kong was a British colony for almost 200 years until 1997, when Britain ceded it to the People's Republic of China. China's rise to global power has brought difficulties to the intersection between its financial environment and Hong Kong's. Even after the turnover, Hong Kong and mainland China had two separate accounting systems with different standards and qualifying examinations. Hong Kong accounting is based on international standards and conducted in English; Chinese accounting is not.

At the beginning of 2010, Hong Kong accepted Chinese accounting standards. This step reflects China's growing attractiveness to international investors. It also advances China's ambition to be part of the international financial system, but until recently the Chinese accounting system has been notorious for its "book-cooking" scandals. And as Hong Kong's transition to Chinese standards progresses, Hong Kong accountants risk losing substantial business to Chinese firms.

Tim Lui, a tax partner at the Hong Kong branch of the worldwide accounting firm PricewaterhouseCoopers, believes that in the short run, at least, Hong Kong accountants have a competitive edge due to their training and international perspective. Foreign investors will be glad to see that Chinese companies will be audited by large, international accounting firms. But he warns against complacency: "The mainland's development is robust and fast and the market is immense." Another concern is that small and medium-sized Hong Kong accounting firms simply aren't big enough to succeed in China, especially in Shanghai, China's business and accounting center.

Tsingtao, a Chinese mainland brewery with operations in both Shanghai and Hong Kong, wants to become the first Hong Kong listed company to switch entirely to Chinese accounting standards. Tsingtao will probably be the first in a long line of such firms.

Questions for Critical Thinking

1. How might the convergence of Chinese and internationally accepted accounting methods affect Chinese firms' operations and ethical standards?

2. What can Hong Kong accounting firms do to increase their business in mainland China?

Sources: Malcolm Moore, "What Is So Great About Hong Kong Accounting Standards?" *China Economic Review,* January 12, 2011, http://www.chinaeconomicreview.com; Robert C. Sawhney, "The Competitiveness of Hong Kong & Asian Accounting Firms," white paper, March 2010, http://www.srchk.com; "The Demand for Accountants Is Always There," *China Daily,* January 8, 2010, http://www.chinadaily.com.

---

a cash surplus in August and can begin repaying the short-term loan. Finally, the cash budget produces a tangible standard against which to compare actual cash inflows and outflows.

International Accounting

Today, accounting procedures and practices must be adapted to accommodate an international business environment. The Coca-Cola Company and McDonald's both generate more than half their annual revenues from sales outside the United States. Nestlé, the giant chocolate and food products firm, operates throughout the world. It derives 98 percent of its revenues from outside Switzerland, its home country. International accounting practices for global firms must reliably translate the financial statements of the firm's international affiliates, branches, and subsidiaries and convert data about foreign currency transactions to dollars. Also, foreign currencies and exchange rates influence the accounting and financial reporting processes of firms operating internationally.

As market economies in countries such as Poland and China have developed, the demand for accountants has increased. The "Hit & Miss" feature describes recent developments in the accounting profession in China and Hong Kong.

In Pakistan, a truck driver delivers Nestlé food products. Because the Swiss corporation operates around the world, its profits and its financial statements are affected by foreign exchange rates.

Ilyas Dean/NewsCom

Exchange Rates

As defined in Chapter 4, an exchange rate is the ratio at which a country's currency can be exchanged for other currencies. Currencies can be treated as goods to be bought and sold. Like the price of any product, currency prices change daily according to supply and demand. So exchange rate fluctuations complicate accounting entries and accounting practices.

Accountants who deal with international transactions must appropriately record their firms' foreign sales and purchases. Today's sophisticated accounting software helps firms handle all of their international transactions within a single program. An international firm's consolidated financial statements must reflect any gains or losses due to changes in exchange rates during specific periods of time. Financial statements that cover operations in two or more countries also need to treat fluctuations consistently to allow for comparison.

In the United States, GAAP requires firms to make adjustments to their earnings that reflect changes in exchange rates. In general, a weakening dollar increases the earnings of a U.S. firm that has international operations because the same units of a foreign currency will translate into more U.S. dollars. By the same token, a strengthening dollar will have the opposite effect on earnings—the same number of units of a foreign currency will translate into fewer dollars. Recently the Mexican *peso* increased in value as the United States started to climb out of its recession. The U.S. recovery actually helped boost Mexican exports to nearly $300 billion in a year. "The *peso* tends to perform well as the U.S. improves," noted one strategist."[11]

International Accounting Standards

International Accounting Standards Board (IASB) established in 1973 to promote world-wide consistency in financial reporting practices.

International Financial Reporting Standards (IFRS) standards and interpretations adopted by the IASB.

The International Accounting Standards Committee (IASC) was established in 1973 to promote worldwide consistency in financial reporting practices. The IASC soon developed its first set of accounting standards and interpretations and, in 2001, became the **International Accounting Standards Board (IASB)**. **International Financial Reporting Standards (IFRS)** are the standards and interpretations adopted by the IASB. The IASB operates in much the same manner as the FASB does in the United States, interpreting and modifying IFRS.

Because of the boom in worldwide trade, there is a real need for comparability of and uniformity in international accounting rules. Trade agreements such as NAFTA and the expansion of the European Union have only heightened interest in creating a uniform set of global accounting rules. In addition, an increasing number of investors are buying shares in foreign multinational corporations, and they need a practical way to evaluate firms in other countries. To assist global investors, more and more firms are beginning to report their financial information according to international accounting standards. This practice helps investors make informed decisions.

Nearly 100 other countries currently require, permit the use of, or have a policy of convergence with IFRS. These nations include members of the European Union, India, Australia, Canada, and Hong Kong. At first, the United States was skeptical of IFRS, even though major American accounting organizations have been involved with the IASB since its inception. In fact, the SEC used to require all firms whose shares were publicly traded in the United States to report financial results using GAAP. This rule applied regardless of where firms were located.

This requirement started to change some years back, when the FASB and the IASB met and committed to the eventual convergence of IFRS with GAAP. This agreement was further clarified in 2005. Around the same time, the SEC began to loosen its rules on the use of IFRS by foreign firms whose shares trade in the United States. Today, many foreign companies can report results using IFRS as long as they reconcile these results to GAAP in a footnote. Some large U.S. companies were allowed to use international accounting standards beginning in 2009. By 2016, all U.S. firms will be required to do so. Almost half the companies polled in a recent survey said they wanted an option for early adoption of the standards.[12]

How does IFRS differ from GAAP? Although many similarities between IFRS and GAAP exist, there are some important differences. For example, under GAAP, plant, property, and equipment is reported on the balance sheet at the historical cost minus depreciation. Under IFRS, on the other hand, plant, property, and equipment is shown on the balance sheet at current market value. This gives a better picture of the real value of a firm's assets. Many accounting experts believe that IFRS is overall less complicated than GAAP and more transparent.[13]

Assessment Check ☑

1. How are financial statements adjusted for exchange rates?
2. What is the purpose of the IASB?

What's Ahead

This chapter describes the role of accounting in an organization. Accounting is the process of measuring, interpreting, and communicating financial information to interested parties both inside and outside the firm. The next two chapters discuss the finance function of an organization. Finance deals with planning, obtaining, and managing the organization's funds to accomplish its objectives in the most efficient and effective manner possible. Chapter 16 outlines the financial system, the system by which funds are transferred from savers to borrowers. Organizations rely on the financial system to raise funds for expansion or operations. The chapter includes a description of financial institutions, such as banks; financial markets, such as the New York Stock Exchange; financial instruments, such as stocks and bonds; and the role of the Federal Reserve System. Chapter 17 discusses the role of finance and the financial manager in an organization.

Summary of Learning Objectives

[1] Explain the functions of accounting, and identify the three basic activities involving accounting.

Accountants measure, interpret, and communicate financial information to parties inside and outside the firm to support improved decision making. Accountants gather, record, and interpret financial information for management. They also provide financial information on the status and operations of the firm for evaluation by outside parties, such as government agencies, stockholders, potential investors, and lenders. Accounting plays key roles in financing activities, which help start and expand an organization; investing activities, which provide the assets it needs to continue operating; and operating activities, which focus on selling goods and services and paying expenses incurred in regular operations.

Assessment Check Answers ☑

1.1 Define *accounting.* Accounting is the process of measuring, interpreting, and communicating financial information in a way that describes the status and operation of an organization and aids in decision making.

1.2 Who uses accounting information? Managers of all types of organizations use accounting information to help them plan, assess performance, and control daily and long-term operations. Outside users of accounting information include government officials, investors, creditors, and donors.

1.3 What are the three business activities that involve accounting? The three activities involving accounting are financing, investing, and operating activities.

[2] Describe the roles played by public, management, government, and not-for-profit accountants.

Public accountants provide accounting services to other firms or individuals for a fee. They are involved in such activities as auditing, tax return preparation, management consulting, and accounting system design. Management accountants collect and record financial transactions, prepare financial statements, and interpret them for managers in their own firms. Government and not-for-profit accountants perform many of the same functions as management accountants, but they analyze how effectively the organization or agency is operating, rather than its profits and losses.

Assessment Check Answers ✔

2.1 List the three services offered by public accounting firms. The three services offered by public accounting firms are auditing, management consulting, and tax services.

2.2 What tasks do management accountants perform? Management accountants work for the organization and are responsible for collecting and recording financial transactions, and preparing and interpreting financial statements.

⌐3⌐ Identify the foundations of the accounting system, including GAAP and the role of the Financial Accounting Standards Board (FASB).

The foundation of the accounting system in the United States is GAAP (generally accepted accounting principles), a set of guidelines or standards that accountants follow. There are four basic requirements to which all accounting rules should adhere: consistency, relevance, reliability, and comparability. The Financial Accounting Standards Board (FASB), an independent body made up of accounting professionals, is primarily responsible for evaluating, setting, and modifying GAAP. The U.S. Securities and Exchange Commission (SEC) also plays a role in establishing and modifying accounting standards for public companies, firms whose shares are traded in the financial markets.

Assessment Check Answers ✔

3.1 Define *GAAP*. GAAP stands for generally accepted accounting principles and is a set of standards or guidelines that accountants follow in recording and reporting financial transactions.

3.2 What are the four basic requirements to which all accounting rules must adhere? The four basic requirements to which all accounting rules must adhere are consistency, relevance, reliability, and comparability.

3.3 What is the role played by the FASB? The Financial Accounting Standards Board (FASB) is an independent body made up of accounting professionals and is primarily responsible for evaluating, setting, and modifying GAAP.

⌐4⌐ Outline the steps in the accounting cycle, and define *double-entry bookkeeping* and the *accounting equation*.

The accounting process involves recording, classifying, and summarizing data about transactions and then using this information to produce financial statements for the firm's managers and other interested parties. Transactions are recorded chronologically in journals, posted in ledgers, and then summarized in accounting statements. Today, much of this activity takes place electronically. The basic accounting equation states that assets (what a firm owns) must always equal liabilities (what a firm owes creditors) plus

owners' equity. This equation also illustrates double-entry bookkeeping, the process by which accounting transactions are recorded. Under double-entry bookkeeping, each individual transaction must have an offsetting transaction.

Assessment Check Answers ✔

4.1 List the steps in the accounting cycle. The accounting cycle involves the following steps: recording transactions, classifying these transactions, summarizing transactions, and using the summaries to produce financial statements.

4.2 What is the accounting equation? The accounting equation states that assets (what a firm owns) must always equal liabilities (what a firm owes) plus owners' equity. Therefore, if assets increase or decrease, there must be an offsetting increase or decrease in liabilities, owners' equity, or both.

4.3 Briefly explain double-entry bookkeeping. Double-entry bookkeeping means that every transaction must have an offsetting transaction.

⌐5⌐ Explain the functions and major components of the four principal financial statements: the balance sheet, the income statement, the statement of owners' equity, and the statement of cash flows.

The balance sheet shows the financial position of a company on a particular date. The three major classifications of balance sheet data are the components of the accounting equation: assets, liabilities, and owners' equity. The income statement shows the results of a firm's operations over a specific period. It focuses on the firm's activities—its revenues and expenditures—and the resulting profit or loss during the period. The major components of the income statement are revenues, cost of goods sold, expenses, and profit or loss. The statement of owners' equity shows the components of the change in owners' equity from the end of the prior year to the end of the current year. Finally, the statement of cash flows indicates a firm's cash receipts and cash payments during an accounting period. It outlines the sources and uses of cash in the basic business activities of operating, investing, and financing.

Assessment Check Answers ✔

5.1 List the four financial statements. The four financial statements are the balance sheet, the income statement, the statement of owners' equity, and the cash flow statement.

5.2 How is the balance sheet organized? Assets (what a firm owns) are shown on one side of the balance sheet and are listed in order of convertibility into cash. On the other side of the balance sheet are claims to assets, liabilities (what a firm owes), and owners' equity. Claims are listed in the order in which they are due, so liabilities are listed before owners' equity. Assets always equal liabilities plus owners' equity.

5.3 Define *accrual accounting*. Accrual accounting recognizes revenues and expenses when they occur, not when cash actually changes hands. Most companies use accrual accounting to prepare their financial statements.

⌐6⌐ **Discuss how financial ratios are used to analyze a company's financial strengths and weaknesses.**

Liquidity ratios measure a firm's ability to meet short-term obligations. Examples are the current ratio and the quick, or acid-test, ratio. Activity ratios, such as the inventory turnover ratio, accounts receivable turnover ratio, and the total asset turnover ratio, measure how effectively a firm uses its resources. Profitability ratios assess the overall financial performance of the business. The gross profit margin, net profit margin, and return on owners' equity are examples. Leverage ratios, such as the total liabilities to total assets ratio and the long-term debt to equity ratio, measure the extent to which the firm relies on debt to finance its operations. Financial ratios help managers and outside evaluators compare a firm's current financial information with that of previous years and with results for other firms in the same industry.

Assessment Check Answers ✔️

6.1 List the four categories of financial ratios. The four categories of ratios are liquidity, activity, profitability, and leverage.

6.2 Define the following ratios: *current ratio, inventory turnover, net profit margin,* **and** *debt ratio.* The current ratio equals current assets divided by current liabilities; inventory turnover equals cost of goods sold divided by average inventory; net profit margin equals net income divided by sales; the debt ratio equals total liabilities divided by total assets.

⌐7⌐ **Describe the role of budgets in a business.**

Budgets are financial guidelines for future periods reflecting expected sales revenues, operating expenses, and cash receipts and outlays. They reflect management expectations for future occurrences and are based on plans that have been made. Budgets serve as important planning and controlling tools by providing standards against which actual performance can be measured. One important type of budget is the cash budget, which estimates cash inflows and outflows over a period of time.

Assessment Check Answers ✔️

7.1 What is a budget? A budget is a planning and control tool that reflects the firm's expected sales revenues, operating expenses, cash receipts, and cash outlays.

7.2 How is a cash budget organized? Cash budgets are generally prepared monthly. Cash receipts are listed first. They include cash sales as well as the collection of past credit sales. Cash outlays are listed next. These include cash purchases, payment of past credit purchases, and operating expenses. The difference between cash receipts and cash outlays is net cash flow.

⌐8⌐ **Outline accounting issues facing global business and the move toward one set of worldwide accounting rules.**

One accounting issue that affects global business is exchange rates. An exchange rate is the ratio at which a country's currency can be exchanged for other currencies. Daily changes in exchange rates affect the accounting entries for sales and purchases of firms involved in international markets. These fluctuations create either losses or gains for particular companies. The International Accounting Standards Board (IASB) was established to provide worldwide consistency in financial reporting practices and comparability of and uniformity in international accounting standards. It has developed International Financial Reporting Standards (IFRS). Many countries have already adopted IFRS, and the United States is in the process of making the transition to it.

Assessment Check Answers ✔️

8.1 How are financial statements adjusted for exchange rates? An exchange rate is the ratio at which a country's currency can be exchanged for other currencies. Fluctuations of exchange rates create either gains or losses for particular companies because data about international financial transactions must be translated into the currency of the country in which the parent company resides.

8.2 What is the purpose of the IASB? The International Accounting Standards Board (IASB) was established to provide worldwide consistency in financial reporting practices and comparability and uniformity of international accounting rules. The IASB has developed the International Financial Reporting Standards (IFRS).

■ Business Terms You Need to Know

accounting 500
public accountant 502
generally accepted
   accounting principles
   (GAAP) 504
Financial Accounting
   Standards Board
   (FASB) 504

Foreign Corrupt Practices
   Act 506
accounting cycle 506
asset 507
liability 507
owners' equity 507
accounting
   equation 508

double-entry
   bookkeeping 508
balance sheet 511
income statement 512
statement of owners'
   equity 514
statement of cash
   flows 515

accrual accounting 515
budget 521
International Accounting
   Standards Board
   (IASB) 524
International Financial
   Reporting Standards
   (IFRS) 524

Review Questions

1. Define *accounting*. Who are the major users of accounting information?

2. What are the three major business activities in which accountants play a major role? Give an example of each.

3. What does the term *GAAP* mean? Briefly explain the roles of the Financial Accounting Standards Board and the Securities and Exchange Commission.

4. What is double-entry bookkeeping? Give a brief example.

5. List the four major financial statements. Which financial statements are permanent and which are temporary?

6. What is the difference between a current asset and a long-term asset? Why is cash typically listed first on a balance sheet?

7. List and explain the major items found on an income statement.

8. What is accrual accounting? Give an example of how accrual accounting affects a firm's financial statement.

9. List the four categories of financial ratios and give an example of each. What is the purpose of ratio analysis?

10. What is a cash budget? Briefly outline what a simple cash budget might look like.

Projects and Teamwork Applications

1. Contact a local public accounting firm and set up an interview with one of the accountants. Ask the individual what his or her educational background is, what attracted the individual to the accounting profession, and what he or she does during a typical day. Prepare a brief report on your interview. Do you now want to learn more about the accounting profession? Are you more interested in possibly pursuing a career in accounting?

2. Suppose you work for a U.S. firm that has extensive European operations. You need to restate data from the various European currencies in U.S. dollars in order to prepare your firm's financial statements. Which financial statements and which components of these statements will be affected?

3. Identify two public companies operating in different industries. Collect at least three years' worth of financial statements for the firms. Calculate the financial ratios listed in Table 15.1. Prepare an oral report summarizing your findings.

4. You've been appointed treasurer of a local not-for-profit organization. You would like to improve the quality of the organization's financial reporting to existing and potential donors. Describe the kinds of financial statements you would like to see the organization's accountant prepare. Why do you think better quality financial statements might help reassure donors?

5. Adapting the format of Figure 15.7, prepare on a sheet of paper your personal cash budget for next month. Keep in mind the following suggestions as you prepare your budget:

    a. *Cash inflows.* Your sources of cash would include your payroll earnings, if any; gifts; scholarship monies; tax refunds; dividends and interest; and income from self-employment.

    b. *Cash outflows.* When estimating next month's cash outflows, include any of the following that may apply to your situation:

        i. Household expenses (rent or mortgage, utilities, maintenance, home furnishings, telephone/cell phone, cable TV, household supplies, groceries)

        ii. Education (tuition, fees, textbooks, supplies)

        iii. Work (transportation, clothing)

        iv. Clothing (purchases, cleaning, laundry)

        v. Automobile (auto payments, fuel, repairs) or other transportation (bus, train)

        vi. Insurance premiums
        • Renters (or homeowners)
        • Auto
        • Health
        • Life

        vii. Taxes (income, real estate, Social Security, Medicare)

        viii. Savings and investments

        ix. Entertainment/recreation (health club, vacation/travel, dining, movies)

        x. Debt (credit cards, installment loans)

        xi. Miscellaneous (charitable contributions, child care, gifts, medical expenses)

    c. *Beginning cash balance.* This amount could be based on a minimum cash balance you keep in your checking account and should include only the cash available for your use; therefore, money such as that invested in retirement plans should not be included.

Web Assignments

1. **International Accounting Standards Board (IASB).** The IASB is responsible for setting and modifying international accounting rules. Go to the IASB's Web site (http://www.iasb.org) and click on "about us." Print out the material and bring it to class to participate in a class discussion on the IASB.

2. **Certified management accountant (CMA).** As noted in the chapter, managerial accountants often seek CMA certifications. Visit the Web site of the Institute of Management Accountants (http://www.imanet.org). Click on "certification" and then "getting started." What are the educational and experiential requirements to obtain a CMA? How

many exams does a CMA candidate have to pass? What do these exams cover?

3. **Financial reporting requirements.** The chapter discussed the financial reporting requirements of public companies in the U.S. Public companies are those whose shares are traded on a stock exchange. Visit the Web site listed here. Type in the name of a public company and then click on "financials" to view the firm's current financial statements. Prepare a brief report comparing those statements to the ones shown in the chapter.

http://www.google.com/finance

Note: Internet Web addresses change frequently. If you don't find the exact sites listed, you may need to access the organization's home page and search from there or use a search engine such as Bing or Google.

Intacct Provides Accounting Software as a Service

As more businesses turn to cloud computing, they are making use of SaaS, or software as a service, instead of buying, installing, and maintaining software packages. With SaaS, a company subscribes to a Web site that leases software. The software remains on that provider's servers. Any approved company employee can access it from anywhere—an in-office computer; an off-site notebook; or even a BlackBerry, iPhone, or other hand-held device with Internet capability. All data are saved and stored on the Web site's servers. Smaller companies find SaaS offers many benefits. They don't have to buy expensive software packages, administer the software and on-site servers, or hire IT personnel.

Intacct, based in San José, California, was one of the first online SaaS providers of accounting software. More than 30,000 people across 3,000 companies use its products. Intacct provides two basic packages: Intacct Accounting Edition allows accounting firms and their clients to work on the same financial data simultaneously. It is used mostly by accounting firms whose clients have from five to 100 employees. The second package, called simply Intacct, is used by businesses that have grown too large to use QuickBooks or similar applications from Microsoft or Sage. These businesses generally have 25 to 1,000 employees. In this case, the business has the software and controls access to it; the accounting firm logs in as a user.

Daniel Druker, a senior vice president at Intacct, says, "Our research with the AICPA [American Institute of Certified Public Accountants] shows a 50 percent productivity improvement for accounting firms that switch to SaaS—plus roughly doubling in proactive consultation hours. And firms can serve around 10 percent more clients with the same staff, by reducing time for travel and error fixing."

One of Intacct's clients is ASP Global Services (ASPGS), a warehouse management solutions provider.

Intacct's software has enabled ASPGS to modernize and streamline its financial processes. The General Ledger program has improved ASPGS's ability to plan, budget, report, and analyze its business. The software also enables ASPGS to enter data faster and more efficiently without having to export those data into a program such as Microsoft Excel. Intacct allows ASPGS to see a real-time income statement at any given moment. As a result, ASPGS has more accurate financial reporting and has saved a great deal of time and resources.

Mike Mullane, the CEO of ASPGS, says, "Intacct is a huge time saver for us. With Intacct, there are a lot of processes you can set up once and then let them run automatically going forward. This allows us to be more effective in managing the company and enables us to spend more time looking forward instead of constantly looking at what has already happened."

Recently Intacct unveiled the latest edition of its financial management and accounting package. The program, called Winter 2010, enables GAAP and analysis without the need for additional software. It also includes modules for such options as accounting, purchasing, business intelligence, multicurrency support, and sales-tax management, among many others. Druker says about the new edition, "Our mindset is: If you're a small business, why run a system like this yourself. You don't have to install or configure a thing. We turn it on for you, and you use it as you would use Google or Amazon."

Questions for Critical Thinking

1. Do you see any potential disadvantages in using software to automate administrative processes such as accounting and financial reporting? If so, what are they?

2. Why is it important for users of financial accounting and other software packages to restrict access to certain kinds of information in the system?

Sources: Intacct Web site, http://us.intacct.com, accessed June 21, 2011; ASPGS Web site, http://unicode.com, accessed June 1, 2010; "Using Cloud Financial Applications from intacct Cuts Monthly Close Process by More Than Two Weeks and Delivers $100,000 in Annual Salary Savings," *MarketWire,* March 29, 2010, http://www.marketwire.com; Daniel Dern, "Are You Being Served?" *Insight Magazine,* February–March 2010, http://www.icpas.org; "Intacct Launches Upgraded Online Accounting Program," *SmallBusinessComputing.com,* February 3, 2010, http://www.smallbusinesscomputing.com; "Intacct Winter 2010 Named One of the Top 10 Small Business Financial Applications by SmallBusinessComputing.com," press release, February 2, 2010, http://us.intacct.com.

CASE 15.2

BDO Seidman: Growing with the 20th Century and Beyond

In 1910, Maximillian Leonard Seidman (1888–1963), the son of Russian immigrants, founded the accounting firm of Seidman & Seidman in New York City. The profession of accounting was also brand new, but that situation soon changed.

When the income tax on individuals was established in 1913 by the Sixteenth Amendment to the U.S. Constitution, Seidman recognized the potential for growth as accountants took on a new role in tax planning for individuals. And when Congress enacted legislation in 1917 creating corporate income taxes, Seidman—now joined by two brothers—expanded the business to include corporations. The firm opened a second office in Michigan, just when the federal government converted furniture and woodworking factories to airplane manufacturing for WW I. Seidman & Seidman quickly became known for serving this industry when it developed a successful system for keeping track of furniture-plant costs.

Maximillian Seidman ran the firm for 45 years. He wrote many articles and served in many industry organizations. He advocated "Total Involvement" of his firm's employees in the business of their clients. In 1944 he declared, "It is the manner in which we serve our clients today that will determine whether we shall have them to serve as clients in the future."

Seidman & Seidman continued to expand, becoming a truly national firm by the 1960s. In 1963, it joined other accounting companies from Canada, Britain, the Netherlands and (then West) Germany in an international organization. In 1973, these firms formed a new group called BDO (Binder Dijker Otte & Co.). This group, now called BDO International, is the fifth largest accounting firm in the world, with 1,138 branches in 115 countries. The U.S. member, BDO Seidman LLP, has 17 branches and more than 400 independent locations.

Albert Lopez is the Southeast Regional Business Line Leader for Assurance Services at the Miami branch of BDO Seidman LLP. Its team-oriented approach and experience has enabled it to create and maintain long-term relationships as its many clients endure the recent ups and downs of the economy. Lopez says, "Success is about service. In this economy, it is especially important to be responsive and to bring a variety of offerings, including tax, assurance and consulting to the table . . . we want our clients to know that senior team members are always available."

As BDO celebrates its 100th anniversary, it has received a number of industry honors. BDO recently announced that 39 of its U.S. offices (including Miami) had won the Alfred P. Sloan Award for Business Excellence in Workplace Flexibility. This award acknowledges the personal and workplace advantages of flexibility programs when a firm uses them to improve its effectiveness and to benefit its employees. *Accounting Today* magazine and Best Companies Group named BDO one of the "best accounting firms." The Best Accounting Firms program identifies the best employers in the accounting industry and their benefits to the U.S. economy, workforce, and businesses. And, the American Society of Women Accountants (ASWA) and the American Woman's Society of CPAs (AWSCPA) both named BDO one of the "best 2010 CPA firms for women."

Questions

1. What historic and economic factors do you think might have contributed to the growth and expansion of the accounting industry, and Seidman's firm, from the early 20th century to today?

2. What advantages does BDO Seidman LLP enjoy in belonging to a large, international group?

Sources: Company Web site, http://www.bdo.com, accessed June 21, 2011; "Business Profile: BDO Seidman, LLP," *Business Leader,* http://www.businessleader.com, accessed June 1, 2010; "BDO Named a Best CPA Firm for Women by American Society of Women Accountants and American Woman's Society of CPAs," press release, April 29, 2010, http://eon.businesswire.com; "BDO Wins Alfred P. Sloan Award for Business Excellence," press release, *Career-Journal,* February 1, 2010, http://www.career-journal.com.

It's great to love the business you're in, as do Alysa Binder and Dan Wiesel, co-founders of Pet Airways. They not only love their business, they also care for their customers, who happen to be furry and four-legged. But Pet Airways, the only service devoted entirely to transporting cats and dogs around the country by air, is also a business—which means that Binder and Wiesel must pay attention to the financial aspects of their company. "We're doing something that's a feel-good, do-good service and it's absolutely rewarding," says Dan Wiesel. But Wiesel knows that, without a thorough accounting of finances, any small business is likely to crash shortly after takeoff.

Binder and Wiesel started Pet Airways based on personal experience—they wanted a better, safer travel option for their Jack Russell terrier than being stashed in the cargo hold. With fluctuating temperatures and dark, cramped quarters, a trip aboard a commercial airline can be unsafe and traumatic for many animals. Binder and Wiesel, both of whom had backgrounds in business, decided they could do a better job than the passenger airlines by offering pet owners a choice.

As soon as they agreed on their business idea, Wiesel jumped into the financial questions. "I had to ask, 'Is this a viable financial enterprise? What would people pay for a service like this?'" recalls Wiesel. He researched such issues as how much it would cost to retrofit the climate-controlled cabin of a plane to carry animals; how much it would cost to fly a plane from one location to another; and how much it would cost to staff the company. He also researched how much demand there would really be for a pet airline, and how many pets would have to be booked on each flight in order for the trip to be profitable. He put all of these variables—and more—onto a spreadsheet so he could see what he and Binder would need to do for Pet Airways to take off.

Wiesel says that financial modeling, financial spreadsheets, and good research on costs and pricing can make or break the launch of any small business. "Accounting itself is an absolute full-time, big job," he admits. He wants to "know how much money is coming in, how much is going out, and what's the bottom line." In addition there are taxes, payroll, benefits, and other financial documentation. Wiesel advises that in many cases it's a good idea for small businesses to contract out their accounting to professionals. He prefers this because outsourcing actually contains the cost of accounting.

Running a business is a balancing act, observes Wiesel. "You have to be able to reconcile how much cash you have with how you are going to spend it." For example, as Pet Airways looks to expand to more cities, the firm has to consider the cost of adding more flights and more staff as compared to how many more customers it might attract. Binder points out that, while it's exciting to think about growing, they have to factor in the expenditures of everything from additional hiring to developing a more sophisticated Web site and online reservation system.

All of this comes back to a sound financial plan, says Wiesel. "The financial plan is really the core of it because you can play the 'what if' game. You can look at the implications of certain decisions." For example, if Binder and Wiesel want to fly to a certain city, they can research which passenger airlines already serve that city. If it's United Airlines, they know that pet owners will be charged $175 for an animal to fly beneath a passenger's seat, or $250 to fly in the cargo hold. They can look at how many flights a day these airlines fly to the city, and probably learn how many pets are booked. And they can find out which terminal Pet Airways would use in addition to any airport taxes and fees. They can plug all this data into the financial plan and see if it works before making the final decision.

Binder and Wiesel usually agree on their company's goals and objectives. Wiesel says it all boils down to one question: "What's it going to cost you to achieve your plan?" Recently, Pet Airways announced its merger with the firm American Antiquities in a share-exchange agreement, a major step toward expansion. "We are delighted to complete this transaction . . . and believe this event represents a significant step in implementing our business plan and continued expansion," stated Wiesel.

Questions for Critical Thinking

1. In Pet Airways' accounting equation, what might be some of the firm's liabilities? What might be considered its assets?

2. Identify the types of costs that Pet Airways might list on its income statement.

3. Why is it important for a small company like Pet Airways to prepare a regular budget?

4. If Pet Airways decides to expand its operations overseas, what kinds of accounting issues would the firm have to take into consideration?

Sources: Pet Airways Web site, http://www.petairways.com, accessed June 21, 2011; "Pet Airways Combines with a Public Company Through Share Exchange with American Antiquities," *PR Newswire*, August 16, 2010, http://www.prnewswire.com; "Doctors Call for Airline Pet Ban," *The Independent*, February 21, 2010, http://license.icopyright.net.

Chapter 16

Learning Objectives

[1] Outline the structure and importance of the financial system.

[2] List the various types of securities.

[3] Define *financial market,* and distinguish between primary and secondary financial markets.

[4] Describe the characteristics of the major stock exchanges.

[5] Discuss the organization and functioning of financial institutions.

[6] Explain the functions of the Federal Reserve System and the tools it uses to control the supply of money and credit.

[7] Evaluate the major features of regulations and laws affecting the financial system.

[8] Describe the global financial system.

The Financial System

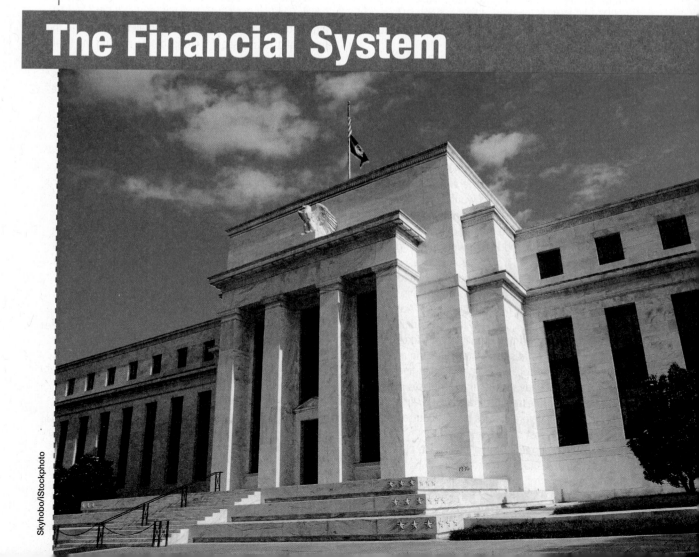

Sam's Club Lends to Small Businesses

Sam's Club, the members-only wholesaler that is part of Walmart, is selling more than bulk boxes of macaroni, patio furniture, and cashmere sweaters. Recognizing an opportunity during the recent credit crunch, Sam's Club has launched a lending program for small businesses. Many small firms have been unable to obtain the business credit they need to survive, let alone grow. On a survey, Sam's learned that 15 percent of its business customers were denied a loan in a recent year. So Sam's decided to offer discounted loans to qualified small business customers. "Access to capital is a major pain point for our members," explained Catherine Corley, vice president of membership at Sam's Club.

In collaboration with Superior Financial Group, one of only thirteen federally approved nonbank lenders of Small Business Administration loans, Sam's is making available loans from $5,000 to $25,000 to its small business members, for a period of 10 years. Firms who take out the loans are not required to spend this money at Sam's Club locations—they can use it for whatever they need. The program focuses on women-owned and minority-owned businesses, but any small business may apply.

Financial experts have praised the Sam's Club loan program because it is small-business friendly. Business owners can apply online for only $50 and receive approval and funding in as little as several days—which sometimes can mean the difference between life and death of a small firm. In addition, the program puts the Small Business Administration's Express Loan Program in the spotlight. The SBA has offered these loans for awhile, but many small business owners are not aware of them. Finally, the Sam's Club loan program supports a growing positive trend: the collaboration of large and small businesses, in particular, the support of smaller firms by larger ones.

What does Sam's Club—and its parent Walmart—get from lending small amounts of money to small businesses? While the program won't boost profits that much (at $50 per loan and an interest discount), it will strengthen relationships with its business customers, and the public relations surrounding the program are positive. Business customers will probably use some of the loan money to buy goods from Sam's Club, but the customer relationships and good PR are the real benefit to Walmart, particularly since the giant has been criticized in the past for taking over the territory of small, local retailers.

Walmart has tried a few times in the past to get into the financial services industry—in fact, the retailer tried to open a bank before Congress passed laws that prevent nonfinancial firms from operating banks—but this is the first such program to gain federal approval and traction in the marketplace. And while Sam's Club and Superior Financial are not licensed to offer small business customers a full range of banking services, such as checking accounts and electronic funds transfer, the loans might be exactly what some firms need in order to survive—at least until the banks loosen their lending belts.[1]

Slobo/iStockphoto

Businesses, governments, and individuals often need to raise capital. Assume the owner of a small business either forecasts a sharp increase or drop in sales; one might require more inventory and the other reduced production in order to survive. The owner might turn to a bank or a nonbank lender like Sam's Club for a loan that would provide the needed cash for either situation. On the other hand, some individuals and businesses have incomes that are greater than their current expenditures and wish to earn a rate of return on the excess funds. For instance, say your income this month is $3,000 but your expenditures are only $2,500. You can take the extra $500 and deposit it in your bank savings account, which pays you a rate of interest.

The two transactions just described are small parts of what is known as the **financial system**, the process by which money flows from savers to users. Virtually all businesses,

governments, and individuals participate in the financial system, and a well-functioning one is vital to a nation's economic well-being. The financial system is the topic of this chapter.

We begin by describing the financial system and its components in more detail. Then, the major types of financial instruments, such as stocks and bonds, are outlined. Next we discuss financial markets, where financial instruments are bought and sold. We then describe the world's major stock markets, such as the New York Stock Exchange.

Next, banks and other financial institutions are described in depth. The structure and responsibilities of the U.S. Federal Reserve System, along with the tools the Fed uses to control the supply of money and credit, are detailed. The chapter concludes with an overview of the major laws and regulations affecting the financial system and a discussion of today's global financial system.

financial system process by which money flows from savers to users.

Understanding the Financial System

Households, businesses, government, financial institutions, and financial markets together form what is known as the financial system. A simple diagram of the financial system is shown in Figure 16.1.

On the left are savers—those with excess funds. For a variety of reasons, savers choose not to spend all of their current income, so they have a surplus of funds. Users are the opposite of savers; their spending needs exceed their current income, so they have a deficit. They need to obtain additional funds to make up the difference. Savings are provided by some households, businesses, and the government, but other households, businesses, and the government are also borrowers. Households may need money to buy automobiles or homes. Businesses may need money to purchase inventory or build new production facilities. Governments may need money to build highways and courthouses.

Generally, in the United States, households are net savers—meaning that as a whole they save more funds than they use—whereas businesses and governments are net

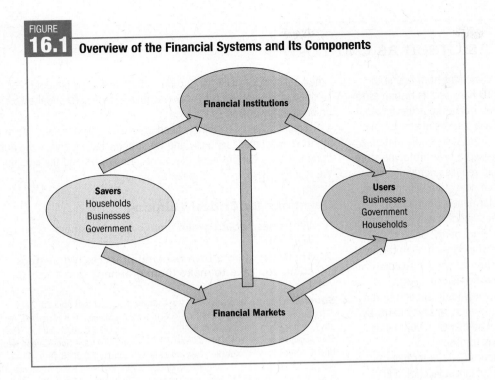

FIGURE 16.1 Overview of the Financial Systems and Its Components

users—meaning that they use more funds than they save. The fact that most of the net savings in the U.S. financial system are provided by households may be a bit of a surprise initially, because Americans do not have a reputation for being thrifty. Yet even though the savings rate of American households is low compared with those of other countries, American households still save hundreds of billions of dollars each year.

How much an individual saves is a function of many variables. One of the most important is the person's age. People often transition from net borrowers to net savers as they get older. When you graduate from college and begin a career, you likely have little in the way of savings. In fact, you may be deeply in debt. In the early years of your career, you may spend more than you make as you acquire major assets, such as a home. So in these early years your *net worth*—the difference between what you own and what you owe—is very low and may even be negative. However, as your career progresses and your income rises, you will begin to build a financial nest egg to fund retirement and other needs. Your net worth will also increase. It will continue to increase until you retire and begin drawing on your retirement savings.

Funds can be transferred between savers and users in two ways: directly and indirectly. A direct transfer means that the user raises the needed funds directly from savers. While direct transfers occur, the vast majority of funds flow through either financial markets or financial institutions. For example, assume a local school district needs to build a new high school. The district doesn't have enough cash on hand to pay for the school construction costs, so it sells bonds to investors (savers) in the financial market. The district uses the proceeds from the sale to pay for the new school and in return pays bond investors interest each year for the use of their money.

The other way in which funds can be transferred indirectly is through financial institutions—for example, a commercial bank such as Cincinnati-based Fifth Third Bank or Alabama-based Regions Bank. The bank pools customer deposits and uses the funds to make

Going Green

TD Bank: "As Green as Our Logo"

TD Bank's square, green logo is a familiar sight from Maine to Florida. With 1,000 branches or "stores," TD has used its resources to pursue an aggressive "green" policy. TD has worked to achieve carbon neutrality by reducing waste, using alternative sources of energy, and building environmentally friendly structures from sustainable materials.

To demonstrate its goal, TD bank unveiled a new prototype store. The 3,800-square-foot design is designed to reduce energy use by 50 percent, compared with earlier models. Each new store will make up to 20 percent of its own electricity with solar panels on the roof. To keep interior temperatures comfortable, the windows will have specially coated glass that reflects or absorbs heat energy. Sensors will control lighting over the course of the day. The drive-through facility will also have a translucent solar canopy. Outside, the landscaping will feature drought-resistant plants and water-efficient plumbing.

TD Bank has bought a block of wind energy large enough to run its 2,300 ATMs. It plans to encourage its customers to save energy by emphasizing online banking and paperless statements. TD Bank has also located many of its branches near public transportation.

In Maine, TD's 60,000-square-foot Auburn Call Center has achieved LEED-CI Platinum certification—the highest level of LEED certification—becoming the first building in the state to do so. TD is

"the largest U.S. based bank to be carbon neutral by building LEED-certified stores and offices," says Jacquelyn Henke, TD's real estate green strategy officer.

Fred Graziano, TD Bank's head of retail banking, says, "We're taking the environment seriously and we strongly believe this is the right thing to do for our business, customers, employees and the community. We want TD Bank to be as green as our logo."

Questions for Critical Thinking

1. Why does "going green" make good business sense for TD Bank?
2. Think about your own banking practices. What steps could you take to make them greener?

Sources: Company Web site, http://www.tdbank.com, accessed April 20, 2011; "TD Bank to Celebrate Opening of First 'Green' Stores in Maine," *Centre Daily Times,* April 19, 2011, http://www.centredaily.com; Patrick Lo, "TD Bank Goes Carbon Neutral," *Green Street Journal,* March 16, 2010, http://www.gsjournal.com; "TD Bank Goes Carbon Neutral, Unveils 'Green Store' Prototype," *Environmental Leader,* February 22, 2010, http://www.environmentalleader.com; "TD Bank, America's Most Convenient Bank, Announces It's Now Carbon Neutral and Unveils New 'Green Store' Prototype Design," press release, February 18, 2010, http://multivu.prnewswire.com.

Assessment Check ✓

1. What is the financial system?
2. In the financial system, who are the borrowers and who are the savers?
3. List the two most common ways in which funds are transferred between borrowers and savers.

securities financial instruments that represent obligations on the part of the issuers to provide the purchasers with expected stated returns on the funds invested or loaned.

loans to businesses and households. These borrowers pay the bank interest, and it, in turn, pays depositors interest for the use of their money.

The accompanying "Going Green" feature describes how TD Bank has begun transforming all its branches so that they will be "carbon neutral."

Types of Securities

For the funds they borrow from savers, businesses and governments provide different types of guarantees for repayment. **Securities**, also called financial instruments, represent obligations on the part of the issuers—businesses and governments—to provide the purchasers with expected or stated returns on the funds invested or loaned. Securities can be grouped into three categories: money market instruments, bonds, and stock. Money market instruments and bonds are both debt securities. Stocks are units of ownership in corporations like General Electric, Best Buy, 3M, and PepsiCo.

Money Market Instruments

Money market instruments are short-term debt securities issued by governments, financial institutions, and corporations. All money market instruments mature within one year from the date of issue. The issuer pays interest to the investors for the use of their funds. Money market instruments are generally low-risk securities and are purchased by investors when they have surplus cash. Examples of money market instruments include U.S. Treasury bills, commercial paper, and bank certificates of deposit.

Treasury bills are short-term securities issued by the U.S. Treasury and backed by the full faith and credit of the U.S. government. Treasury bills are sold with a maturity of 30, 90, 180, or 360 days and have a minimum denomination of $1,000. They are considered virtually risk free and easy to resell. Commercial paper is securities sold by corporations, such as Raytheon, that mature in from 1 to 270 days from the date of issue. Although slightly riskier than Treasury bills, commercial paper is still generally considered a very low-risk security.

A certificate of deposit (CD) is a time deposit at a financial institution, such as a commercial bank, savings bank, or credit union. The sizes and maturity dates of CDs vary considerably and can often be tailored to meet the needs of purchasers. CDs in denominations of $250,000 or less per depositor are federally insured. CDs in larger denominations are not federally insured but can be sold more easily before they mature.

Bonds

Bondholders are creditors of a corporation or government body. By selling bonds, a firm obtains long-term debt capital. Federal, state, and local governments also acquire funds through bonds. Bonds are issued in various denominations, or face values, usually between $1,000 and $25,000. Each issue indicates a rate of interest to be paid to the bondholder—stated as a percentage of the bond's face value—as well as a maturity date on which the bondholder is paid the bond's full face value. Because bondholders are creditors, they have a claim on the firm's assets that must be satisfied before any claims of stockholders in the event of the firm's bankruptcy, reorganization, or liquidation.

Types of Bonds A prospective bond investor can choose among a variety of bonds. The major types of bonds are summarized in Table 16.1. *Government bonds* are bonds sold by the U.S. Department of the Treasury. Because government bonds are backed by the full faith and credit of the U.S. government, they are considered the least risky of all bonds. The Treasury sells bonds that mature in 2, 5, 10, and 30 years from the date of issue.

Municipal bonds are bonds issued by state or local governments. Two types of municipal bonds are available. A *revenue bond* is a bond issue whose proceeds will be used to pay for a project that will produce revenue, such as a toll road or bridge. The Oklahoma Turnpike Authority has issued such bonds. A *general obligation bond* is a bond whose proceeds are to be used to pay for a project that will not produce any revenue, such as a new Indiana State Police Post. General obligation bonds can be sold only by states or local governmental units—such as Grand Rapids, Michigan, or Bergen County, New Jersey—that have the power to levy taxes. An important feature of municipal bonds is that their interest payments are exempt from federal income tax. Because of this attractive feature, municipal bonds generally carry lower interest rates than either corporate or government bonds.

Corporate bonds are a diverse group and often vary based on the collateral—the property pledged by the borrower—that backs the bond. For example, a *secured bond* is backed by a specific pledge of company assets. These assets are collateral, just like a home is collateral for a mortgage. However, many firms also issue unsecured bonds, called *debentures*. These bonds are backed only by the financial reputation of the issuing corporation.

Another popular type of bond is the *mortgage pass-through security*. These securities are backed by a pool of mortgage loans purchased from lenders, such as savings banks.

16.1 Types of Bonds

ISSUER	TYPES OF SECURITIES	RISK	SPECIAL FEATURES
U.S. Treasury (government bonds)	Notes: Mature in 10 years or fewer from date of issue.	Treasury bonds and notes carry virtually no risk.	Interest is exempt from state income taxes.
	Bonds: Mature in 30 years from date of issue.		
State and local governments (municipal bonds)	General obligation: Issued by state or local governmental units with taxing authority; backed by the full faith and credit of the state where issued.	Risk varies, depending on the financial health of the issuer.	Interest is exempt from federal income taxes and may be exempt from state income taxes.
	Revenue: Issued to pay for projects that generate revenue, such as water systems or toll roads; revenue from project used to pay principal and interest.	Most large municipal bond issues are rated in terms of credit risk (AAA or Aaa is the highest rating).	
Corporations	Secured bonds: Bonds are backed by specific assets.	Risk varies depending on the financial health of the issuer.	A few corporate bonds are convertible into shares of common stock of the issuing company.
	Unsecured bonds (debentures): Backed by the financial health and reputation of the issuer.	Most corporate bond issues are rated in terms of credit risk (AAA or Aaa is the highest rating).	
Financial institutions	Mortgage pass-through securities.	Generally very low risk.	They pay monthly income consisting of both interest and principal.

As borrowers make their monthly mortgage payments, these payments are "passed through" to the holders of the securities. Most mortgage pass-through securities are relatively safe because all mortgages in the pool are insured. However, in recent years, mortgage pass-through securities consisting of pools of so-called *subprime mortgages*, loans made to borrowers with poor credit ratings, were issued. Many of these securities turned out to be quite risky and, in part, triggered what became known as the *credit crisis*. The extent of the crisis forced the federal government to undertake a massive bailout of the financial system. The Office of Financial Stability—part of the U.S. Treasury department—was created to purchase poor-quality mortgage-backed and other securities from financial institutions.

Quality Ratings for Bonds Two factors determine the price of a bond: its risk and its interest rate. Bonds vary considerably in terms of risk. One tool bond investors use to assess the risk of a bond is its *bond rating*. Several investment firms rate corporate and municipal bonds, the best known of which are Standard & Poor's (S&P), Moody's, and Fitch. Table 16.2 lists the S&P bond ratings. Moody's and Fitch use similar rating systems. Bonds with the lowest level of risk are rated AAA. As ratings descend, risk increases. Bonds with ratings of BBB and above are classified as *investment-grade bonds*. By contrast, bonds with ratings of BB and below are classified as *speculative* or *junk bonds*. Junk bonds attract investors by

16.2 Standard & Poor's Bond Ratings

Highest	AAA	Investment grade
	AA	
	A	
	BBB	
	BB	Speculative grade
	B	
	CCC	
	CC	
Lowest	C	

Note: Standard & Poor's occasionally assigns a plus or minus following the letter rating. For instance, AA+ means that the bond is higher quality than most AA bonds but hasn't quite met AAA standards. Ratings below C indicate that the bond is currently not paying interest.

offering high interest rates in exchange for greater risk. Today, junk bonds pay about 50 percent more in interest than do investment-grade corporate bonds. The credit crisis of recent years generated a great deal of criticism of the ratings companies.

The second factor affecting the price of a bond is its interest rate. Other things being equal, the higher the interest rate, the higher the price of a bond. However, everything else often is not equal; the bonds may not be equally risky, or one may have a longer maturity. Investors must evaluate the trade-offs involved.

Another important influence on bond prices is the *market interest rate*. Because bonds pay fixed rates of interest, as market interest rates rise, bond prices fall, and vice versa. For instance, the price of a ten-year bond, paying 5 percent per year, would fall by about 8 percent if market interest rates rose from 5 percent to 6 percent.

Most corporate and municipal bonds, and some government bonds, are callable. A *call provision* allows the issuer to redeem the bond before its maturity at a specified price. Not surprisingly, issuers tend to call bonds when market interest rates are declining. For example, if York County, Pennsylvania, had $50 million in bonds outstanding with a 5 percent annual interest rate, it would pay $2.5 million annually in interest. If interest rates decline to 3 percent, the county may decide to call the 5 percent bonds, repaying the principal from the proceeds of newly issued 3 percent bonds. Calling the 5 percent bonds and issuing 3 percent bonds will save the county $1 million a year in interest payments. The savings in annual interest expense should more than offset the cost of retiring the old bonds and issuing new ones.

Stock

The basic form of corporate ownership is embodied in **common stock**. Purchasers of common stock are the true owners of a corporation. Holders of common stock vote on major company decisions, such as purchasing another company or electing a board of directors. In return for the money they invest, they expect to receive some sort of return.

common stock basic form of corporate ownership.

This return can come in the form of cash dividend payments, expected price appreciation, or both. Dividends vary widely from firm to firm. As a general rule, faster-growing companies pay less in dividends because they need more funds to finance their growth. Consequently, investors expect stocks paying little or no cash dividends to show greater price appreciation compared with stocks paying more generous cash dividends.

Sometimes unforeseen events can have a profound effect on dividends. On April 20, 2010, the oil-drilling rig *Deepwater Horizon*, leased by the British oil firm BP, exploded and caught fire, killing 11 oil workers and injuring others. The oil well, off the southeast coast of Louisiana, began leaking millions of gallons of crude oil and methane, endangering countless fish, birds, and other marine animals in the Gulf of Mexico. This is the first oil rig disaster of this magnitude to occur in the United States. Fishermen and others who made their living on the gulf saw their livelihoods threatened. The oil reached land, polluting the wetlands and beaches of Louisiana, Mississippi, Alabama, and Florida, harming wildlife there as well as damaging the tourist industry. Local residents, the media, and government figures were severe in condemning BP for not preventing the explosion and spill in the first place, for not capping the leaking well quickly and efficiently, for underestimating the quantities of leaking oil and methane, and for assembling insufficient forces and equipment for the cleanup.

Amid intense public and political pressure, BP launched an advertising campaign in print and on television, featuring its CEO, Tony Hayward, promising to "make this right." In early June, more than 40 members of Congress called on BP to suspend its dividends, stop the ad campaign, and instead use that money to clean up the oil spill. BP's stock began to fall, and Standard & Poor's downgraded BP's debt rating from AA-minus to A, hinting that it might downgrade that rating further. BP's chairman, Carl-Henric Svanberg, announced that BP would cancel dividend payments to shareholders for the first quarter of the fiscal year and suspend dividend payments to shareholders for the second and third quarters.

Before the disaster, BP had been Britain's largest company, but in the following months its value fell by half. Although the dividend suspension is not likely to have a severe affect on American shareholders, many investors and retirees in Britain rely on those dividends for income. In fact, BP's stock is the source of roughly 12 percent of all dividends paid on the London Stock Exchange. A year after the disaster, 43 percent of shareholders voted not to support Sir William Castell, the firm's safety committee chairman.

BP also agreed to create a fund to pay damages to fishermen, small-business owners, and others with financial losses caused by the oil spill. The fund, which will eventually total $20 billion and represents approximately one year's profit, will be administered by a neutral third party. Anyone whose claim is turned down will have the right of appeal. Scientists estimated the well was leaking more than 2.5 million gallons a day, making it the largest oil-related disaster in U.S. history.[2]

Common stockholders benefit from company success, and they risk the loss of their investments if the company fails. If a firm dissolves, claims of creditors must be satisfied before stockholders receive anything. Because creditors have the first (or senior) claim to assets, holders of common stock are said to have a residual claim on company assets.

The market value of a stock is the price at which the stock is currently selling. For example, Johnson & Johnson's stock price fluctuated between $59 and $69 per share during a recent year. What determines this market value is complicated; many variables cause stock prices to move up or down. However, in the long run stock prices tend to follow a company's profits.

Preferred Stock In addition to common stock, a few companies also issue preferred stock—stock whose holders receive preference in the payment of dividends. General

Motors and Ford are examples of firms with preferred stock outstanding. Also, if a company is dissolved, holders of preferred stock have claims on the firm's assets that are ahead of the claims of common stockholders. On the other hand, preferred stockholders rarely have any voting rights, and the dividend they are paid is fixed, regardless of how profitable the firm becomes. Therefore, although preferred stock is legally classified as equity, many investors consider it to be more like a bond than common stock.

Convertible Securities Companies may issue bonds or preferred stock that contains a conversion feature. Such bonds or stock are called *convertible securities*. This feature gives the bondholder or preferred stockholder the right to exchange the bond or preferred stock for a fixed number of shares of common stock. Convertible bonds pay lower interest rates than those lacking conversion features, helping to reduce the interest expense of the issuing firms. Investors are willing to accept these lower interest rates because they value the potential for additional gains if the price of the firm's stock increases. For instance, at a price of $61 per share, Peabody Energy's convertible bond would have a common stock value of at least $1,043 ($61 × 17.1). Should the price of Peabody's common stock increase by $10 per share, the value of the convertible will increase by at least $171.

Financial Markets

Securities are issued and traded in **financial markets**. While there are many different types of financial markets, one of the most important distinctions is between primary and secondary markets. In the **primary markets**, firms and governments issue securities and sell them initially to the general public. When a company needs capital to purchase inventory, expand a plant, make major investments, acquire another firm, or pursue other

Assessment Check ✓

1. What are the major types of securities?
2. What is a government bond? A municipal bond?
3. Why do investors purchase common stock?

financial markets
market in which securities are issued and traded.

primary markets
financial market in which firms and governments issue securities and sell them initially to the general public.

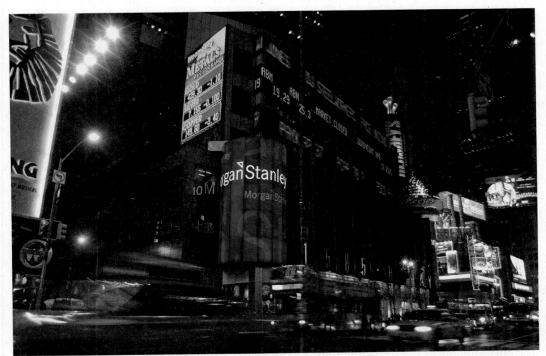

Richard Levine/Alamy

■ On the side of this building in Times Square, New York City, current stock prices and news updates are displayed.

Citigroup Spins Off Primerica Inc.

Not long ago, the banking giant Citigroup included not only banking but also insurance, among other interests. Following the recent financial crisis, Citigroup's CEO, Vikram Pandit, began to dispose of some of these holdings. He wanted to slim the company down to its original core banking business, focusing on large institutions and wealthy individuals.

Primerica Inc. was one of those holdings. Based in Duluth, Georgia, Primerica sells life insurance, mutual funds, and other financial products door-to-door. Its middle-class clients earn from $30,000 to $100,000 a year. The company never fit well with the rest of Citigroup, and its 100,000 fiercely independent salespeople liked it that way. As the financial crisis worsened, some of them called for cutting ties with the parent company.

Citigroup tried to sell Primerica but could not find a buyer willing to pay the asking price. So Citigroup announced that it would spin off Primerica instead. Primerica would issue an initial public offering (IPO), selling shares of stock for the first time. Primerica planned to sell 18 million shares at $12 to $14 a share. Under the terms of the IPO, Citigroup would take all the profits and keep Primerica's existing accounts. Primerica would emerge smaller but would keep any new policies. John Addison and Rick Williams, the co-CEOs of Primerica, said, "We're going to be a smaller, faster-growing company going forward."

The IPO exceeded expectations. Primerica sold more than 21 million shares at almost $20 each. Addison and Williams feel that the company's focus has contributed to its success. "No one else has our business model," Williams declared. "No one else focuses on the middle-income, middle market like we do." Analysts took the IPO's success as a sign that both the life insurance industry and the market were recovering from the recession.

Questions for Critical Thinking

1. Visit Citibank's and Primerica's Web sites. Why do you think these two companies did not mesh well together?
2. Although Citibank failed to find a buyer for Primerica, the IPO was very successful. Why do you think this was the case?

Sources: Primerica Web site, http://www.primerica.com, accessed June 21, 2011; Citigroup Web site, http://www.citigroup.com, accessed June 21, 2011; Kerri Shannon, "Citigroup Spin-Off Primerica Boasts Strong Stock Debut in Hot IPO Market," *Money Morning,* April 4, 2010, http://moneymorning.com; "Primerica IPO a Success as Shares Jump," *CNBC,* April 1, 2010, http://www.cnbc.com; Maria Aspan and Clare Baldwin, "Citi Spinoff Primerica Soars on Hopes for Economy," *Reuters,* April 1, 2010, http://www.reuters.com.

---

business goals, it may sell a bond or stock issue to the investing public. For example, the European Financial Stability Facility recently issued a bond whose proceeds will be allocated to a package designed to support the financial stability of Ireland. Similarly, with a massive budget deficit, California offered as much as $3.4 billion in Build America Bonds, which were part of the recent federal stimulus package.[3]

A stock offering gives investors the opportunity to purchase ownership shares in a firm and to participate in its future growth, in exchange for providing current capital. When a company offers stock for sale to the general public for the first time, it is called an *initial public offering (IPO)*. Analysts predicted three important IPOs from American companies during one recent year: AMC Entertainment, GNC Nutrition Centers, and Facebook.[4] The "Hit & Miss" feature describes an American company's IPO.

Both profit-seeking corporations and government agencies also rely on primary markets to raise funds by issuing bonds. For example, the federal government sells Treasury bonds to finance part of federal outlays such as interest on outstanding federal debt. State and local governments sell bonds to finance capital projects such as the construction of sewer systems, streets, and fire stations.

Announcements of new stock and bond offerings appear daily in business publications such as *The Wall Street Journal.* These announcements are often in the form of a simple black-and-white ad called a *tombstone.*

Securities are sold to the investing public in two ways: in open auctions and through investment bankers. Virtually all securities sold through open auctions consist of U.S. Treasury securities. A week before an upcoming auction, the Department of the Treasury announces the type and number of securities it will be auctioning. Treasury bills are auctioned weekly, but longer-term Treasury securities are auctioned once a month or once a quarter. Sales of most corporate and municipal securities are made via financial institutions such as Morgan Stanley. These institutions purchase the issue from the firm or government and then resell the issue to investors. This process is known as *underwriting*.

Financial institutions underwrite stock and bond issues at a discount, meaning that they pay the issuing firm or government less than the price the financial institutions charge investors. This discount is compensation for services rendered, including the risk financial institutions incur whenever they underwrite a new security issue. Although the size of the discount is often negotiable, it usually averages around 5 percent for all types of securities. The size of the underwriting discount, however, is generally higher for stock issues than it is for bond issues. For instance, underwriting discounts for IPOs are generally between 7 and 10 percent.

Corporations and governments are willing to pay for the services provided by financial institutions because they are financial market experts. In addition to locating buyers for the issue, the underwriter typically advises the issuer on such details as the general characteristics of the issue, its pricing, and the timing of the offering. Several financial institutions commonly participate in the underwriting process. The issuer selects a lead, or primary, financial institution, which in turn forms a syndicate consisting of other financial institutions. Each member of the syndicate purchases a portion of the security issue, which it resells to investors.

Media reports of stock and bond trading are most likely to refer to trading in the **secondary market**, a collection of financial markets in which previously issued securities are traded among investors. The corporations or governments that originally issued the securities being traded are not directly involved in the secondary market. They make no payments when securities are sold nor receive any of the proceeds when securities are purchased. The New York Stock Exchange (NYSE), for example, is a secondary market. In terms of the dollar value of securities bought and sold, the secondary market is four to five times as large as the primary market. Each day, roughly 1.6 billion shares worth about $45 billion are traded on the NYSE.[5] The characteristics of the world's major stock exchanges are discussed in the next section.

Understanding Stock Markets

Stock markets, or **exchanges**, are probably the best-known of the world's financial markets. In these markets, shares of stock are bought and sold by investors. The two largest stock markets in the world, the New York Stock Exchange and the Nasdaq stock market, are located in the United States.

The New York Stock Exchange

The New York Stock Exchange—sometimes referred to as the Big Board—is the most famous and one of the oldest stock markets in the world, having been founded in 1792. Today, more than 3,000 common- and preferred-stock issues are listed on the NYSE. These stocks represent most of the largest, best-known companies in the United States and have a total market value exceeding $13 trillion. In terms of the total value of stock traded, the NYSE is the world's largest stock market.

secondary market collection of financial markets in which previously issued securities are traded among investors.

Assessment Check ☑

1. What is a financial market?

2. Distinguish between a primary and a secondary financial market.

3. Briefly explain the role of financial institutions in the sale of securities.

stock markets (exchanges) market in which shares of stock are bought and sold by investors.

For a company's stock to be traded on the NYSE, the firm must apply to the exchange for listing and meet certain listing requirements. In addition, the firm must continue to meet requirements each year to remain listed on the NYSE. Corporate bonds are also traded on the NYSE, but bond trading makes up less than 1 percent of the total value of securities traded there during a typical year.

Trading on the NYSE takes place face-to-face on a trading floor. Buy and sell orders are transmitted to a specific post on the floor of the exchange. Buyers and sellers then bid against one another in an open auction. Only investment firms that are designated members of the NYSE and that own at least one trading license are allowed to trade on the floor of the exchange. The NYSE issues up to 1,366 trading licenses a year at a cost of about $40,000 each.[6]

Each NYSE stock is assigned to a specialist firm. Specialists are unique investment firms that maintain an orderly and liquid market in the stocks assigned to them. Specialists must be willing to buy when there are no other buyers and sell when there are no other sellers. Specialists also act as auctioneers and catalysts, bringing buyers and sellers together.

Some observers portray the NYSE and its trading practices as somewhat old fashioned, especially in this technological age. Most markets, they note, have abandoned their trading floors in favor of electronic trading. However, even though the NYSE still retains a trading floor, the exchange has become highly automated in recent years. Its computer systems automatically match and route most orders, which are typically filled within a few seconds.

The Nasdaq Stock Market

The world's second-largest stock market is the Nasdaq Stock Market. It is very different from the NYSE. Nasdaq—which stands for National Association of Securities Dealers Automated Quotation System—is actually a computerized communications network that links member investment firms. It is the world's largest intranet. All trading on Nasdaq takes place through its intranet, rather than on a trading floor. Buy and sell orders are entered into the network and executed electronically. All Nasdaq-listed stocks have two or more market makers—investment firms that perform essentially the same functions as NYSE specialists.

Around 5,000 companies have their stocks listed on Nasdaq. Compared with firms listed on the NYSE, Nasdaq-listed corporations tend to be smaller, less well-known firms. Some are relatively new businesses and cannot meet NYSE listing requirements. It is not uncommon for firms eventually to transfer the trading of their stocks from Nasdaq to the NYSE—16 did so in a recent year. However, dozens of major companies currently trade on Nasdaq—such as Amgen, Cisco Systems, Dell, Intel, and Microsoft—that would easily meet NYSE listing requirements. For a variety of reasons, these firms have decided to remain listed on Nasdaq.

Unlike the New York Stock Exchange, the Nasdaq does not have a trading floor; all transactions are done electronically. Firms listed on the Nasdaq tend to be smaller and younger than the large, established firms listed on the New York Stock Exchange.

Other U.S. Stock Markets

In addition to the NYSE and Nasdaq, several other stock markets operate in the United States. The American Stock Exchange, or AMEX, focuses on the stocks of smaller firms, as well as other financial instruments such as options. In comparison with the NYSE and Nasdaq, the AMEX is tiny. Daily trading volume is generally less than 100 million shares compared with the +1 billion shares on each of the larger two exchanges.

Several regional stock exchanges also operate throughout the United States. They include the Chicago, Pacific (San Francisco), Boston, Cincinnati, and Philadelphia stock exchanges. Originally established to trade the shares of small, regional companies, the regional exchanges now list securities of many large corporations as well. In fact, more than half of the companies listed on the NYSE are also listed on one or more regional exchanges.

Foreign Stock Markets

Stock markets exist throughout the world. Virtually all developed countries and many developing countries have stock exchanges. Examples include Mumbai, Helsinki, Hong Kong, Mexico City, Paris, and Toronto. One of the largest stock exchanges outside the United States is the London Stock Exchange. Founded in the early 17th century, the London Stock Exchange lists approximately 3,000 stock and bond issues by companies from more than 70 countries around the world. Trading on the London Stock Exchange takes place using a Nasdaq-type computerized communications network.

The London Stock Exchange is the most international of all stock markets. Approximately two-thirds of all cross-border trading in the world—for example, the trading of stocks of American companies outside the United States—takes place in London. It is not uncommon for institutional investors in the United States to trade NYSE- or Nasdaq-listed stocks in London.

Because stock markets around the world are so closely interconnected, changes in one country's economy can affect other countries too, as the "Hit & Miss" feature explains.

ECNs and the Future of Stock Markets

For years a so-called *fourth market* has existed. The fourth market is the direct trading of exchange-listed stocks off the floor of the exchange, in the case of NYSE-listed stocks, or outside the network, in the case of Nasdaq-listed stocks. Until recently, trading in the fourth market was limited to institutional investors buying or selling large blocks of stock.

Now the fourth market has begun to open up to smaller, individual investors through markets called *electronic communications networks* (ECNs). In ECNs, buyers and sellers meet in a virtual stock market and trade directly with one another. No specialist or market maker is involved. ECNs have become a significant force in the stock market in recent years. Around half of all trades involving Nasdaq-listed stocks take place on INET or Archipelago—the two largest ECNs—rather than directly through the Nasdaq system. Some have suggested that ECNs represent the future for stock markets, given that INET and Archipelago were acquired within the last few years by Nasdaq and the NYSE, respectively.

Hit & Miss

How News Lifts—or Sinks—World Stocks

The growth of computerized trading has closely connected all the developed nations and many of the developing nations. A snapshot of the world markets at the end of a recent month illustrates how events in one country influence stock markets everywhere.

In the spring of 2010, Americans grew hopeful that the country was starting to climb out of the worst financial crisis since the Great Depression. The Federal Reserve announced that although American households were not spending as much as before the recession, the U.S. economy was slowly improving. Some companies were making a profit from rising consumer demand. Earlier in the recovery, companies had made money by cutting costs. Prices of stock in U.S. companies such as Apple saw some increases. The computer giant Hewlett-Packard announced that it was buying the smart phone maker Palm.

The credit crisis that America seemed to be emerging from struck Greece, which warned that it might not be able to pay off its debts. As a member of the European Union, Greece has adopted the euro as its currency. Other euro countries, like Spain and Portugal, faced financial troubles as well. Standard & Poor's reduced the bond rating of all three countries. Recently, Standard & Poor reduced the United States' credit rating to AA+.

In an effort to recover, the Greek government enforced an austerity policy that reduced government spending on social programs despite public outrage. Nearly a year later, despite a bailout from the European Union and International Monetary Fund, economists predicted that the only way Greece could get back on its feet would be to restructure its debt, including a program of bond buybacks.

Questions for Critical Thinking

1. Why would a financial crisis on the other side of the world affect the U.S. economy?
2. Nearly a year after the crisis began, Greece was still struggling with its debt crisis. In what ways did its investors—including the European Union and International Monetary Fund—have to share the cost?

Sources: Tony Czuczka, "Greece Debt Buybacks Raised by Merkel's Economic Adviser Field," *Bloomberg Businessweek*, April 20, 2011, http://www.businessweek.com; Mark Rohner, "Greece Ahead of Targets, Will Not Default, Papandreou Says," *Bloomberg Businessweek*, June 22, 2010, http://www.businessweek.com; European Union Web site, http://europa.eu, accessed June 21, 2010; Will Swarts, "Stocks Surge as Earnings Stay Robust," *SmartMoney*, April 29, 2010, http://www.smartmoney.com; Christine Hauser, "Stocks Higher as Earnings Lift Sentiment," *The New York Times*, April 28, 2010, http://www.nytimes.com; Reuters, "Earnings Lift World Stocks, Greece Stays in Focus," *Economic Times*, April 21, 2010, http://economictimes.indiatimes.com.

Investor Participation in the Stock Markets

Because most investors aren't members of the NYSE, or any other stock market, they need to use the services of a brokerage firm to buy or sell stocks. Examples of brokerage firms include Edward Jones and TD Ameritrade. Investors establish an account with the brokerage firm and then enter orders to trade stocks. The brokerage firm executes the trade on behalf of the investor, charging the investor a fee for the service. While some investors phone in orders or visit the brokerage firm in person, many today use their PCs and trade stocks online. The requirements for setting up an account vary from broker to broker. Selecting the right brokerage firm is one of the most important decisions investors make.

The most common type of order is called a *market order*. It instructs the broker to obtain the best possible price—the highest price when selling and the lowest price when buying. If the stock market is open, market orders are filled within seconds. Another popular type of order is called a *limit order*. It sets a price ceiling when buying or a price floor when selling. If the order cannot be executed when it is placed, the order is left with the exchange's market maker. It may be filed later if the price limits are met.

Financial Institutions

One of the most important components of the financial system is **financial institutions**. They are an intermediary between savers and borrowers, collecting funds from savers and then lending the funds to individuals, businesses, and governments. Financial institutions greatly increase the efficiency and effectiveness of the transfer of funds from savers to users.

Assessment Check ✓

1. What are the world's two largest stock markets?
2. Why is the London Stock Exchange unique?
3. Explain the difference between a market order and a limit order.

financial institutions intermediary between savers and borrowers, collecting funds from savers and then lending the funds to individuals, businesses, and governments.

Because of financial institutions, savers earn more, and users pay less, than they would without them. In fact, it is difficult to imagine how any modern economy could function without well-developed financial institutions. Think about how difficult it would be for a businessperson to obtain inventory financing or an individual to purchase a new home without financial institutions. Prospective borrowers would have to identify and negotiate terms with each saver individually.

Traditionally, financial institutions have been classified into depository institutions—institutions that accept deposits that customers can withdraw on demand—and nondepository institutions. Examples of depository institutions include commercial banks, such as US Bancorp and Sun Trust; savings banks, such as Golden West Financial Corporation and Ohio Savings Bank; and credit unions, such as the State Employees Credit Union of North Carolina. Nondepository institutions include life insurance companies, such as Northwestern Mutual; pension funds, such as the Florida state employee pension fund; and mutual funds. In total, financial institutions have trillions of dollars in assets. Figure 16.2 illustrates the size of the most prominent financial institutions.

Commercial Banks

Commercial banks are the largest and probably most important financial institution in the United States, and in most other countries as well. In the United States, the approximately 6,800 commercial banks have total assets of more than $12 trillion. Commercial banks offer the most services of any financial institution. These services include a wide range of checking and savings deposit accounts, consumer loans, credit cards, home mortgage loans, business loans, and trust services. Commercial banks also sell other financial products, including securities and insurance.

Although 6,800 may sound like a lot of banks, the number of banks has actually declined dramatically in recent years; more than 25 years ago there were 14,000 commercial banks. At the same time, banks have grown larger: today, the typical commercial bank is about five times as large as it was ten years ago. Both changes can be explained by the fact that bank mergers are commonplace.

Although the overall trend in the banking industry has been toward fewer, larger banks, a countertrend has also emerged: the growth of small community banks. It is not uncommon for several dozen of these banks to begin operation in any one year. Community banks typically serve a single city or county and have millions, rather than billions, of dollars in assets and deposits. Many consumers and small-business owners prefer smaller banks because they believe they offer a higher level of personal service and often charge lower fees.

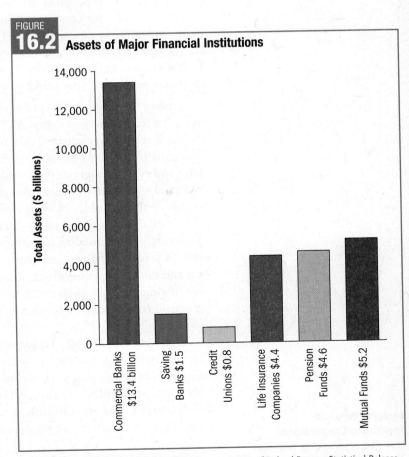

FIGURE 16.2 Assets of Major Financial Institutions

Total Assets ($ billions)

Commercial Banks $13.4 billion
Saving Banks $1.5
Credit Unions $0.8
Life Insurance Companies $4.4
Pension Funds $4.6
Mutual Funds $5.2

Source: Board of Governors of the Federal Reserve System, "Federal Reserve Statistical Release, Z.1, Flow of Funds Accounts of the United States," http://www.federalreserve.gov, accessed August 8, 2011.

FIGURE 16.3 **Distribution of Outstanding Commercial Bank Loans**

Other 7%

Consumer (not real estate) 15%

Single-Family Real Estate 34%

Commercial 18%

Other Real Estate 26%

Source: Federal Deposit Insurance Corporation (FDIC), Statistics on Depository Institutions Report, http://www2.fdic.gov, accessed April 19, 2011.

Federal Deposit Insurance Corporation (FDIC) federal agency that insures deposits at commercial and savings banks.

How Banks Operate Banks raise funds by offering a variety of checking and savings deposits to customers. The banks then pool these deposits and lend most of them out in the form of consumer and business loans. At the end of a recent year, banks held over $8.3 trillion in deposits and had almost $6.3 trillion in outstanding loans.[7] The distribution of outstanding loans is shown in Figure 16.3. As the figure shows, banks lend a great deal of money to both households and businesses for a variety of purposes. Commercial banks are an especially important source of funds for small businesses. When evaluating loan applications, banks consider the borrower's ability and willingness to repay the loan. Occasionally, banks reject applications.

Banks make money primarily because the interest rate they charge borrowers is higher than the rate of interest they pay depositors. Banks also make money from other sources, such as fees they charge customers for checking accounts and using automated teller machines.

In the aftermath of the recent credit crisis, many small business owners have suffered because banks have begun pulling their lines of credit. The "Business Etiquette" feature offers some suggestions if this happens to you.

Electronic Banking More and more funds each year move through electronic funds transfer systems (EFTSs), computerized systems for conducting financial transactions over electronic links. Millions of businesses and consumers now pay bills and receive payments electronically. Most employers, for example, directly deposit employee paychecks in their bank accounts, rather than issuing employees paper checks. Today nearly all Social Security checks and other federal payments made each year arrive as electronic data rather than paper documents.

One of the original forms of electronic banking, the automated teller machine (ATM) continues to grow in popularity. ATMs allow customers to make banking transactions at any time by inserting an electronic card into the machine and entering a personal identification number (PIN). Networked systems enable ATM users to access their bank accounts in distant states and even throughout the world. Most banks now offer customers debit cards—also called *check cards*—that allow customers to pay for purchases directly from their checking or savings account. A debit card looks like a credit card but acts like a check and replaces the customer's ATM card. Many large retailers—including Home Depot, Supervalu, Target, Walmart, and Walgreen's—have installed special terminals that allow customers to use their ATM or debit cards to make purchases. Customers are required to enter their personal identification numbers and can often get cash back. Consumers enjoy the convenience of this feature; at the same time, it eliminates the problem of bad checks for retailers. The number of annual ATM and debit card transactions is expected to exceed 46 billion within the next couple of years.[8]

Online Banking Today, many consumers do some or all of their banking on the Internet. According to a survey by the American Bankers Association, 36 percent of U.S. consumers of all age groups prefer Internet banking.[9] Two types of online banks exist: Internet-only banks, such as ING Direct, and traditional brick-and-mortar banks with Web sites, such as JPMorgan Chase and Citibank. A major reason people are attracted to online banking is convenience. Customers can transfer money, check account balances, and pay bills at any time.

Federal Deposit Insurance Most commercial bank deposits are insured by the **Federal Deposit Insurance Corporation (FDIC)**, a federal agency. Deposit insurance means that, in the event the bank fails, insured depositors are paid in full by the FDIC, up to $250,000. Federal deposit insurance was enacted by the Banking Act of 1933 as one of the measures designed to restore public confidence in the banking system. Before deposit insurance, so-called *runs* were common as people rushed to withdraw their money from a bank, often just on a rumor that the bank was in precarious financial condition. With more and more withdrawals in a short period, the bank was eventually unable to meet customer demands and closed its doors. Remaining depositors often lost most of the money they had in the bank. Deposit insurance shifts the risk of bank failures from individual depositors to the FDIC. Although banks still fail today, no insured depositor has ever lost any money.

Savings Banks and Credit Unions

Commercial banks are by far the largest depository financial institution in the United States, but savings banks and credit unions also serve a significant segment of the financial community. Today savings banks and credit unions offer many of the same services as commercial banks.

Savings banks used to be called *savings and loan associations* or *thrift institutions*. They were originally established in the early 1800s to make home mortgage loans. Savings and loans originally raised funds by accepting only savings deposits and then lent these funds to consumers to buy homes. Today, there are around 1,170 savings banks with total assets of about $1.26 trillion.[10] Although savings banks offer many of the same services as commercial banks, including checking accounts, they are not major lenders to businesses. About 82.6 percent of their outstanding loans are real estate loans.[11] Deposits in savings banks are now FDIC insured.

Credit unions are cooperative financial institutions that are owned by their depositors, all of whom are members. Around 90 million Americans belong to one of the nation's approximately 8,000 credit unions. Combined, credit unions have more than $825 billion in assets.[12] By law, credit union members must share similar occupations, employers, or membership in certain organizations. This

What to Do When Your Credit Gets Pulled

For years, banks have issued business credit cards to small business owners. The cards come with a line of credit—usually several thousand dollars or more—that gives these businesses a safety net in case a client was late in paying or some other emergency. After the credit crisis hit, millions of small business owners found themselves working without a net as banks began either to call those loans in or to cap credit lines at the amount outstanding. The National Small Business Association reported that thousands of small business owners reported that their credit lines had been decreased or that extensions of their loans had been rejected. Marilyn Landis of the NSBA said, "A few years ago, losing a line of credit was a crisis—today it's the new normal." Here are some steps to consider if this happens to you.

1 Be careful not to max out whatever credit you have left; this could have a negative impact on your credit score.

2 Make your current monthly payment as quickly as possible, either online or by phone.

3 Apply for a new credit card as quickly as possible. It usually takes several weeks for any changes in your credit limit to appear in your credit report. If you act fast, you may get a new card before your credit score is lowered.

4 If possible, pay down your existing credit card debt. However, if you know you'll need money in the short run, weigh that need against your credit score before you write the check.

5 Keep careful track of your credit score. AnnualCreditReport.com is the only government-authorized source for the free annual credit report that you are legally entitled to.

Sources: Federal Trade Commission, "Credit and Your Consumer Rights," http://www.ftc.gov, accessed June 21, 2011; Sam Thacker, "Steps to Take When Your Credit Line Is Pulled," *All-Business,* http://www.allbusiness.com, accessed June 21, 2010; Jeffrey Weber, "What to Do When Your Credit Limit Is Decreased," *SmartBalanceTransfers.com,* March 4, 2010, http://www.smartbalancetransfers.com; Julie Bennett, "What to Do When the Bank Pulls Your Line of Credit," *Entrepreneur,* February 2010, http://www.entrepreneur.com.

With credit unions growing in popularity, the National Credit Union Administration is a good place to start when looking for a credit union in your area.

National Credit Union Administration

law effectively caps the size of credit unions. In fact, the nation's largest bank—Bank of America—holds more deposits than all the country's credit unions combined.

Credit unions are designed to serve consumers, not businesses. Credit unions raise funds by offering members a number of demand and saving deposits—checking accounts at credit unions are referred to as share draft accounts—and then, in turn, lend these funds to members. Because credit unions are not-for-profit institutions, they often pay savers higher rates of interest, charge lower rates of interest on loans, and have fewer fees than other financial institutions. Credit unions can have either state or federal charters, and deposits are insured by a federal agency, the National Credit Union Administration (NCUA), which functions essentially the same way that the FDIC does.

Nondepository Financial Institutions

Nondepository financial institutions accept funds from businesses and households, much of which they then invest. Generally, these institutions do not offer checking accounts (demand deposits). Three examples of nondepository financial institutions are insurance companies, pension funds, and finance companies.

Insurance Companies Households and businesses buy insurance to transfer risk from themselves to the insurance company. The insurance company accepts the risk in return for a series of payments, called *premiums*. Underwriting is the process insurance companies use to determine whom to insure and what to charge. During a typical year, insurance companies collect more in premiums than they pay in claims. After they pay operating expenses, they invest this difference. Insurance companies are a major source of short- and long-term financing for businesses. Life insurance companies alone have total assets of more than $4.5 trillion invested in everything from bonds and stocks to real estate.[13] Examples of life insurers include Prudential and New York Life.

Pension Funds Pension funds provide retirement benefits to workers and their families. They are set up by employers and are funded by regular contributions made by employers and employees. Because pension funds have predictable long-term cash inflows and very predictable cash outflows, they invest heavily in assets, such as common stocks and real estate. At one time, pension funds owned more than 25 percent of all common stocks. One study that compared U.S. pension funds and those in other countries found that even after the financial crisis, U.S. pension funds had more than 61 percent of their assets invested in stocks but only about 23 percent in less risky bonds; Germany, which was second, had only 34.5 percent in stocks and more than 61 percent in bonds. Recently, U.S. companies have begun quietly moving their pension assets out of stocks and have begun buying more long-term bonds. In contrast, some states and other government agencies, wanting to make up for funds lost in the crisis, have begun investing in higher-risk categories. In total, pension funds have more than $4.6 trillion in assets.[14]

Finance Companies Consumer and commercial finance companies, such as Ford Credit, John Deere Capital Corporation, and the Pennsylvania-based Dollar Financial, offer short-term loans to borrowers. A commercial finance company supplies short-term funds to businesses that pledge tangible assets such as inventory, accounts receivable, machinery, or property as collateral for the loan. A consumer finance company plays a similar role for consumers. Finance companies raise funds by selling securities or borrowing funds from commercial banks. Many finance companies, such as GMAC, are actually subsidiaries of a manufacturer. GMAC finances dealer inventories of new cars and trucks, as well as providing loans to consumers and other buyers of General Motors products.

Mutual Funds

One of the most significant types of financial institutions today is the mutual fund. *Mutual funds* are financial intermediaries that raise money from investors by selling shares. They then use the money to invest in securities that are consistent with the mutual fund's objectives. For example, a stock mutual fund invests mainly in shares of common stocks. Mutual funds have become extremely popular over the last few decades. The United States' more than 7,600 mutual funds have more than $11 trillion in assets and more than 270 million shareholder accounts; 20 years ago, there were just over 3,000 funds with a total of just over $1 trillion in assets. One reason for this growth is the increased popularity of 401(k) and similar types of retirement plans. It is estimated that about 47 percent of all 401(k) assets are invested in mutual fund shares.[15]

Mutual fund investors are indirect owners of a portfolio of securities. As the value of the securities owned by the mutual fund changes, so too will the value of the mutual fund's shares. Moreover, investment income, such as bond interest and stock dividends, is passed through to fund shareholders.

Slightly less than half of mutual fund assets, around $5.2 trillion, are invested in stock funds. Money market mutual funds—those that invest in money market instruments such as commercial paper—are also popular. These funds have total assets of just over 2.6 trillion.[16]

The Role of the Federal Reserve System

Created in 1913, the **Federal Reserve System**, or **Fed**, or is the central bank of the United States and is an important part of the nation's financial system. The Fed has four basic responsibilities: regulating commercial banks, performing banking-related activities for the U.S. Department of the Treasury, providing services for banks, and setting monetary policy. Not all banks belong to the Fed. Banks with federal charters are required to belong to the Fed, but membership is optional for state-chartered banks. Because the largest banks in the country are all federally chartered, the bulk of banking assets is controlled by Fed members. The Fed acts as the bankers' bank for members. It provides wire transfer facilities, clears checks, replaces worn-out currency, and lends banks money.

Organization of the Federal Reserve System

The nation is divided into 12 federal reserve districts, each with its own federal reserve bank. Each district bank supplies banks within its district with currency and facilitates the clearing of checks. District banks are run by a nine-member board of directors, headed by a president.

Assessment Check ☑

1. What are the two main types of financial institutions?

2. What are the primary differences between commercial banks and savings banks?

3. What is a mutual fund?

Federal Reserve System (Fed) central bank of the United States.

The governing body of the Fed is the board of governors. The board consists of seven members, including a chair and vice chair, appointed by the president and confirmed by the Senate. A full term for a Fed governor is 14 years. If a governor serves a full term, he or she cannot be reappointed. A governor can be reappointed if he or she was initially appointed to an unexpired term. The chair and vice chair serve in those capacities for four years and can be reappointed. The chair of the board of governors is a very important position. Some have commented, only half jokingly, that the Fed chair is the second most powerful person in the nation.

The Fed is designed to be politically independent. Terms for Fed governors are staggered in such a way that a president cannot appoint a majority of members, assuming that all members serve their entire terms. The Fed also has its own sources of revenue and does not depend on congressional appropriations.

An important part of the Fed is the *Federal Open Markets Committee (FOMC)*. The FOMC sets most policies concerning monetary policy and interest rates. It consists of 12 members—the 7 Fed board governors plus 5 representatives of the district banks, who serve on a rotating basis. The Fed chair is also chair of the FOMC.

Check Clearing and the Fed

As mentioned earlier, one of the Fed's responsibilities is to help facilitate the clearing of checks. Even in this age of electronic and online banking, Americans still write billions of paper checks each year. The clearing of a check is the process by which funds are transferred from the check writer to the recipient.

Assume the owner of Gulf View Townhouses of Tampa buys a $600 carpet cleaner from the local Home Depot and writes a check. If Home Depot has an account at the same bank as Gulf View, the bank will clear the check in house. It will decrease the balance in the owner's account by $600 and increase the balance in Home Depot's account by $600. If Home Depot has an account at another bank in Tampa, the two banks may still clear the check directly with one another. This process is cumbersome, however, so it is more likely that the banks will use the services of a local check clearinghouse.

But if Home Depot has its account with a bank in another state—perhaps in Atlanta, where Home Depot is based—the check will likely be cleared through the Federal Reserve System. Home Depot will deposit the check in its Atlanta bank account. That bank, in turn, will deposit the check in the Federal Reserve Bank of Atlanta. The Atlanta Federal Reserve bank will present the check to Gulf View's bank for payment, which pays the check by deducting $600 from Gulf View's account. Regardless of the method used, the Check Clearing for the 21st Century Act allows banks and the Fed to use electronic images of checks—rather than the paper documents themselves—during the clearing process. Because these images are transferred electronically, the time it takes to clear a check has been reduced substantially, often to less than 48 hours.

Monetary Policy

The Fed's most important function is controlling the supply of money and credit, or monetary policy. The Fed's job is to make sure that the money supply grows at an appropriate rate, allowing the economy to expand and inflation to remain in check. If the money supply grows too slowly, economic growth will slow, unemployment will increase, and the risk of a recession will increase. If the money supply grows too rapidly, inflationary pressures will build. The Fed uses its policy tools to push interest rates up or down. If the Fed pushes interest rates up, the growth rate in the money supply will slow, economic growth will slow, and inflationary pressures will ease. If the Fed pushes interest rates down, the growth rate in the money supply will increase, economic growth will pick up, and unemployment will fall.

The two common measures of the money supply are called M1 and M2. M1 consists of currency in circulation and balances in bank checking accounts. M2 equals M1 plus balances in some savings accounts and money market mutual funds. Figure 16.4 shows the approximate breakdowns of M1 and M2. The Fed has four major policy tools for controlling the growth in the supply of money and credit: reserve requirements, the discount rate, open market operations, and Term Auction Facility loans.

The Fed requires banks to maintain reserves—defined as cash in their vaults plus deposits at district Federal Reserve banks or other banks—equal to a certain percentage of what the banks hold in deposits. For example, if the Fed sets the reserve requirement at 5 percent, a bank that receives a $500 deposit must reserve $25, so it has only $475 to invest or lend to individuals or businesses. By changing the reserve requirement, the Fed can affect the amount of money available for making loans. The higher the reserve requirement, the less banks can lend out to consumers and businesses. The lower the reserve requirement, the more banks can lend out. Because any change in the reserve requirement can have a sudden and dramatic impact on the money supply, the Fed rarely uses this tool. Reserve requirements range from 0 to 10 percent, depending on the type of account.

Another policy tool is the so-called *discount rate*, the interest rate at which Federal Reserve banks make short-term loans to member banks. A bank might need a short-term loan if transactions leave it short of reserves. If the Fed wants to slow the growth rate in the money supply, it increases the discount rate. This increase makes it more expensive for banks to borrow funds. Banks, in turn, raise the interest rates they charge on loans to consumers and businesses. The end result is a slowdown in economic activity. Lowering the discount rate has the opposite effect.

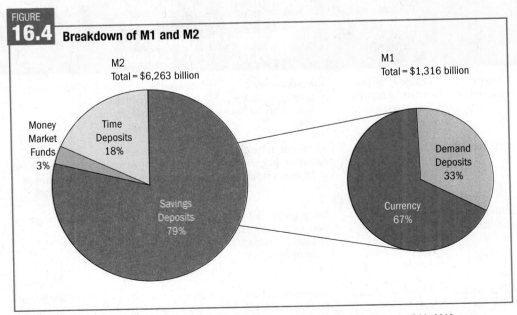

FIGURE 16.4 Breakdown of M1 and M2

M2
Total = $6,263 billion

M1
Total = $1,316 billion

Money Market Funds 3%

Time Deposits 18%

Savings Deposits 79%

Demand Deposits 33%

Currency 67%

Source: Board of Governors of the Federal Reserve System, Federal Reserve Statistical Release, April 29, 2010, http://www.federalreserve.gov, accessed August 8, 2011.

The third policy tool, and the one used most often, is *open market operations*, the technique of controlling the money supply growth rate by buying or selling U.S. Treasury securities. If the Fed buys Treasury securities, the money it pays enters circulation, increasing the money supply and lowering interest rates. When the Fed sells Treasury securities, money is taken out of circulation and interest rates rise. When the Fed uses open market operations it employs the so-called *federal funds rate*—the rate at which banks lend money to each other overnight—as its benchmark.

A relatively new monetary policy tool is the *term auction facility*. In these auctions, the Fed makes extra funds available to banks at low interest rates. During one three-year period, loans provided by the term auction facility and one other program totaled $13 trillion, roughly equal to the size of the nation's gross domestic product (GDP).[17] The more funds the Fed offers, and the lower the rate, the greater the impact on market interest rates, the supply of credit, and economic activity. Table 16.3 illustrates how the tools used by the Federal Reserve can stimulate or slow the economy.

The Federal Reserve has the authority to exercise selective credit controls when it thinks the economy is growing too rapidly or too slowly. These credit controls include the power to set margin requirements—the percentage of the purchase price of a security that an investor must pay in cash on credit purchases of stocks or bonds.

The Fed can also inject capital into the financial system in response to a financial crisis. During the recent credit crisis, the Fed pumped hundreds of billions of dollars into the financial system. The Fed even came to the rescue of AIG, a major insurance company, by purchasing some of the firm's stock.

Table 16.3

Tools Used by the Federal Reserve to Regulate the Growth in the Money Supply

TOOL	BRIEF DESCRIPTION	IMPACT ON THE GROWTH RATE OF THE MONEY SUPPLY	IMPACT ON INTEREST RATES AND THE ECONOMY	FREQUENCY OF USE
1. Reserve requirements	Change in the percentage of deposits held as reserves.	Increases in reserve requirements slow the growth rate in the money supply.	Increases in reserve requirements push interest rates up and slow economic growth.	Rarely used.
2. Discount rate	Change in the rate the Fed charges banks for loans.	An increase in the discount rate slows the growth rate in the money supply.	An increase in the discount rate pushes interest rates up and slows economic growth.	Used only in conjunction with open market operations.
3. Open market operations	Buying and selling government securities to increase or decrease bank reserves.	Selling government securities reduces bank reserves and slows the growth rate in the money supply.	Selling government securities pushes interest rates up and slows economic growth.	Used frequently.
4. Term auction facility loans	Fed auctions 28-day loans to banks.	Auctions boost bank reserves, leading to increased availability of credit.	Increased availability of credit pushes interest rates lower and spurs economic activity.	Relatively new; used frequently when first introduced.

Transactions in the foreign exchange markets also affect the U.S. money supply and interest rates. The Fed can lower the exchange value of the dollar by selling dollars and buying foreign currencies, and it can raise the dollar's exchange value by doing the opposite—buying dollars and selling foreign currencies. When the Fed buys foreign currencies, the effect is the same as buying securities because it increases the U.S. banking system's reserves. Selling foreign currencies, on the other hand, is like selling securities, in that it reduces bank reserves.

Regulation of the Financial System

Given the importance of the financial system, it is probably not surprising that many components are subject to government regulation and oversight. In addition, industry self-regulation is commonplace.

Bank Regulation

Banks are among the nation's most heavily regulated businesses. The main purpose of bank regulation is to ensure public confidence in the safety and security of the banking system. Banks are critical to the overall functioning of the economy, and a collapse of the banking system can have disastrous results. Many believe that one of the major causes of the Great Depression was the collapse of the banking system that started in the late 1920s.

All banks, whether commercial or savings, and credit unions have either state or federal charters. Most commercial banks are state chartered; however, federally chartered banks control more than half of all banking assets. State-chartered banks are regulated by the appropriate state banking authorities; federally chartered commercial banks are regulated by the Federal Reserve, the Federal Deposit Insurance Corporation, and the Comptroller of the Currency. Furthermore, state-chartered commercial banks that are federally insured—and virtually all are—are also subject to FDIC regulation.

At the federal level, savings banks are regulated by the Office of Thrift Supervision and the FDIC. Federal credit unions are subject to NCUA regulation. State-chartered savings banks and credit unions are also regulated by state authorities.

Banks and credit unions are subject to periodic examination by state or federal regulators. Examinations ensure that the institution is following sound banking practices and is complying with all applicable regulations. These examinations include the review of detailed reports on the bank's operating and financial condition, as well as on-site inspections. Regulators can impose various penalties on institutions deemed not in compliance with sound banking practices, including forcing the delinquent financial institution into a merger with a healthier one.

Government Regulation of the Financial Markets

Regulation of U.S. financial markets is primarily a function of the federal government, although states also regulate them. Federal regulation grew out of various trading abuses during the 1920s. To restore confidence and stability in the financial markets after the 1929 stock market crash, Congress passed a series of landmark legislative acts that have formed the basis of federal securities regulation ever since.

Assessment Check ✓

1. What is the Federal Reserve System?

2. How is the Fed organized?

3. List the four tools the Fed uses to control the supply of money and credit.

The Securities and Exchange Commission is a governmental agency charged with regulating financial markets. Its Web site featured here is a good source of information for would-be investors.

As noted in Chapter 15, the U.S. Securities and Exchange Commission, created in 1934, is the principal federal regulatory overseer of the securities markets. The SEC's mission is to administer securities laws and protect investors in public securities transactions. The SEC has broad enforcement power. It can pursue civil actions against individuals and corporations, but actions requiring criminal proceedings are referred to the U.S. Justice Department.

The SEC requires virtually all new public issues of corporate securities to be registered. As part of the registration process for a new security issue, the issuer must prepare a prospectus. The typical prospectus gives a detailed description of the company issuing the securities, including financial data, products, research and development projects, and pending litigation. It also describes the stock or bond issue and underwriting agreement in detail. The registration process seeks to guarantee full and fair disclosure. The SEC does not rule on the investment merits of a registered security. It is concerned only that an issuer gives investors enough information to make their own informed decisions.

Besides primary market registration requirements, SEC regulation extends to the secondary markets as well, keeping tabs on trading activity to make sure it is fair to all participants. Every securities exchange must by law follow a set of trading rules that have been approved by the SEC. In addition, the Market Reform Act of 1990 gave the SEC emergency authority to halt trading and restrict practices such as program trading—whereby computer systems are programmed to buy or sell securities if certain conditions arise—during periods of extreme volatility.

insider trading use of material nonpublic information about a company to make investment profits.

One area to which the SEC pays particular attention is insider trading. **Insider trading** is defined as the use of material nonpublic information about a company to make investment profits. Examples of material nonpublic information include a pending merger or a major oil discovery, which could affect the firm's stock price. The SEC's definition of insider trading goes beyond corporate insiders—people such as the company's officers and directors. It includes lawyers, accountants, investment bankers, and even reporters—anyone who uses nonpublic information to profit in the stock market at the expense of ordinary investors. Although some actions or communications are clearly insider trading, others are more ambiguous. Consequently, all employees of public companies have to be mindful of what is and isn't permitted.

Securities laws also require every public corporation to file several reports each year with the SEC; the contents of these reports become public information. The best known, of course, is the annual report. Public corporations prepare annual reports for their shareholders, and they file another report containing essentially the same information, Form 10-K, with the SEC. The SEC requires additional reports each time certain company officers and directors buy or sell a company's stock for their own accounts (Form 4) or anytime an investor accumulates more than 5 percent of a company's outstanding stock (Form 13-d). All of these reports are available for viewing and download at the Edgar Online Web site (http://www.freeedgar.com).

Industry Self-Regulation

The securities markets are also heavily self-regulated by professional associations and the major financial markets. The securities industry recognizes that rules and regulations designed to ensure fair and orderly markets promote investor confidence and benefit all participants. Two examples of self-regulation are the rules of conduct established by the various professional organizations and the market surveillance techniques used by the major securities markets.

Professional Rules of Conduct Prodded initially by federal legislation, the National Association of Securities Dealers (NASD) established and periodically updates rules of conduct for members—both individuals and firms. These rules are intended to ensure that brokers perform their basic functions honestly and fairly, under constant supervision. Failure to adhere to rules of conduct can result in disciplinary action. The NASD also established a formal arbitration procedure through which investors can attempt to resolve disputes with brokers without litigation.

Market Surveillance All securities markets use a variety of methods to spot possible violations of trading rules or securities laws. For example, the NYSE continuously monitors trading activity throughout the trading day. A key technical tool used by the NYSE is called Stock Watch, an electronic monitoring system that flags unusual price and volume activity. The NYSE then seeks explanations for unusual activity from the member firms and companies involved. In addition, all market participants must keep detailed records of every aspect of every trade (called an *audit trail*). The NYSE's enforcement division may impose a variety of penalties on members for rule violations. In addition, the exchange turns over evidence to the SEC for further action if it believes that violations of federal securities laws may have occurred.

Although self-regulation by the financial industry has been an important component of securities market regulation, some contend that the industry can never truly regulate itself effectively in today's market environment. The "Solving an Ethical Controversy" feature debates the pros and cons of industry self-regulation.

The Financial System: A Global Perspective

Not surprisingly, the global financial system is becoming more and more integrated each year. As we've noted, financial markets exist throughout the world. Shares of U.S. firms trade in other countries, and shares of international companies trade in the United States. In fact, investors in China and Japan own more U.S. Treasury securities than do domestic investors.

Financial institutions have also become a global industry. Major U.S. banks—such as JPMorgan Chase and Bank of America—have extensive international operations. They have offices, lend money, and accept deposits from customers throughout the world.

Assessment Check ☑

1. Who regulates banks?
2. Define *insider trading*.
3. List two ways in which the securities markets are self-regulated.

In Frankfurt, Germany, a sculpture of the euro—the symbol for the European Union's currency—stands outside the headquarters of Europe's central bank. The 12 gold stars represent all the peoples of Europe.

Alex Grimm/Reuters/Landov

Solving an Ethical Controversy

Can Wall Street Regulate Itself?

"Those of us who have looked to the self-interest of lending institutions to protect shareholders' equity, myself included, are in a state of shocked disbelief."

So said Alan Greenspan, the former chairman of the Federal Reserve Board, in testimony before Congress after the credit crisis. He had long supported the idea that the market could always be trusted to regulate itself and should be left free to do so. But with these words, he rejected that policy. The crisis brought an end to a Wall Street bubble that had flourished partly due to unlimited, unregulated speculation. Stricter government regulation of the financial industry seems inevitable.

Can Wall Street be trusted to regulate itself?

PRO

1. Regulation of Wall Street would give the government too much power over a private industry.

2. The mere idea of regulation has made some institutions change their behavior voluntarily. For example, Bank of America recently announced it would eliminate overdraft fees for consumer accounts.

CON

1. Some analysts feel that existing government regulation was too lax. They believe that the Securities and Exchange Commission, which is supposed to regulate the financial industry, was too lenient with some large financial institutions.

2. Some observers feel that commercial banking was concentrated in too few big banks. The four biggest banks had almost 40 percent of all deposits and two-thirds of all credit card accounts. These observers would also like to see banking and investment management separated.

Summary

Public disapproval of Wall Street is bound to continue as long as the effects of the financial crisis are felt. In July 2010, the Dodd-Frank Act became law, including the creation of a new Financial Services Oversight Council as well as tighter regulation of the financial industry as a whole.

Sources: Alan Zibel and Jessica Holzer, "House Republicans Go After Five Dodd-Frank Provisions," *The Wall Street Journal,* March 14, 2011, http://online.wsj.com; "President Obama Signs Dodd-Frank Act Into Law," *National Law Review,* July 21, 2010, http://www.natlaw review.com; Bill Singer, "Analyzing a Troubling Wall Street Double Standard," *Corporate Compliance Insights,* May 4, 2010, http://www.corporatecomplianceinsights.com; Felix Salmon, "How the SEC Cracks Down on Unethical Behavior," *Reuters,* April 20, 2010, http://blogs.reuters.com; Peter Hamby, "DNC Ad: Wall Street Lobbyists Trying to Block Reform," *CNN,* April 20, 2010, http://politicalticker.blogs.cnn.com; Roger Lowenstein, "*The End of Wall Street* by Roger Lowenstein: Book Excerpt," *Bloomberg Businessweek,* April 8, 2010, http://www.businessweek.com; Andrew Ross Sorkin, "Extreme Makeover, Wall Street Edition," *The New York Times,* April 1, 2010, http://dealbook.blogs.nytimes.com.

Assessment Check ✓

1. Where do U.S. banks rank compared with international banks?

2. Do other countries have organizations that play roles similar to those played by the Federal Reserve?

Although most Americans recognize large U.S. banks such as Citibank among the global financial giants, only two of the twenty largest banks in the world (measured by total assets) are U.S. institutions—JPMorgan Chase (ranked ninth) and Bank of America (ranked twelfth). The other eighteen are based in continental Europe, Great Britain, and Asia. The world's largest bank is BNP Paribas SA, based in Paris with $3 trillion in assets. These international banks operate worldwide, including locations in the United States.[18]

Virtually all nations have some sort of a central bank, similar to the U.S. Federal Reserve. Examples include the Banks of Canada, England, and Japan and the European Central Bank. These central banks play roles much like that of the Fed, such as controlling the money supply and regulating banks. Policymakers at other nations' central banks often respond to changes in the U.S. financial system by making similar changes in their own systems. For example, if the Fed pushes U.S. interest rates lower, central banks in Japan and Europe may also push their interest rates lower. These changes can influence events in countries around the world. Lower U.S. and European interest rates not only decrease the cost of borrowing for U.S. and European firms but also increase the amount of money available for loans to borrowers in other countries such as Chile and India.

What's Ahead

This chapter explored the financial system, a key component of the U.S. economy and something that affects many aspects of contemporary business. The financial system is the process by which funds are transferred between savers and borrowers and includes securities, financial markets, and financial institutions. The chapter also described the role of the Federal Reserve and discussed the global financial system. In the next chapter, we discuss the finance function of a business including the role of the financial managers, financial planning, asset management, and sources of short- and long-term funds.

Summary of Learning Goals

1 Outline the structure and importance of the financial system.

The financial system is the process by which funds are transferred between those having excess funds (savers) and those needing additional funds (users). Savers and users are individuals, businesses, and governments. Savers expect to earn a rate of return in exchange for the use of their funds. Financial markets, financial institutions, and financial instruments (securities) make up the financial system. Although direct transfers are possible, most funds flow from savers to users through the financial markets or financial institutions, such as commercial banks. A well-functioning financial system is critical to the overall health of a nation's economy.

Assessment Check Answers

1.1 What is the financial system? The financial system is the process by which funds are transferred between those having excess funds (savers) and those needing additional funds (users).

1.2 In the financial system, who are the borrowers and who are the savers? Savers and borrowers are individuals, businesses, and governments. Generally, individuals are net savers, meaning they spend less than they make, whereas businesses and governments are net borrowers.

1.3 List the two most common ways in which funds are transferred between borrowers and savers. The two most common ways funds are transferred are through the financial markets and through financial institutions.

2 List the various types of securities.

Securities, also called *financial instruments*, represent obligations on the part of issuers—businesses and governments—to provide purchasers with expected or stated returns on the funds invested or loaned. Securities can be classified into three categories: money market instruments, bonds, and stock. Money market instruments and bonds are debt instruments. Money market instruments are short-term debt securities and tend to be low-risk securities. Bonds are longer-term debt securities and pay a fixed amount of interest each year. Bonds are sold by the U.S. Department of the Treasury (government bonds), state and local governments (municipal bonds), and corporations. Mortgage pass-through securities are bonds backed by a pool of mortgage loans. Most municipal and corporate bonds have risk ratings. Common stock represents ownership in corporations. Common stockholders have voting rights and a residual claim on the firm's assets.

Assessment Check Answers

2.1 What are the major types of securities? The major types of securities are money market instruments, bonds, and stock.

2.2 What is a government bond? A municipal bond? A government bond is one issued by the U.S. Treasury. Municipal bonds are issued by state and local governments.

2.3 Why do investors purchase common stock? There are two primary motives for purchasing common stock. One is to receive dividends, cash payments to shareholders by the firm. The other is potential price appreciation of the shares.

⌐3⌐ **Define** *financial market,* **and distinguish between primary and secondary financial markets.**

A financial market is a market where securities are bought and sold. The primary market for securities serves businesses and governments that want to sell new security issues to raise funds. Securities are sold in the primary market either through an open auction or via a process called *underwriting.* The secondary market handles transactions of previously issued securities between investors. The New York Stock Exchange is a secondary market. The business or government that issued the security is not directly involved in secondary market transactions. In terms of the dollar value of trading volume, the secondary market is about four to five times larger than the primary market.

Assessment Check Answers ✔

3.1 What is a financial market? A financial market is a market in which securities are bought and sold.

3.2 Distinguish between a primary and a secondary financial market. The primary market for securities serves businesses and governments that want to sell new security issues to raise funds. The secondary market handles transactions of previously issued securities between investors.

3.3 Briefly explain the role of financial institutions in the sale of securities. Financial institutions purchase new securities issues from corporations or state and local governments and then resell the securities to investors. The institutions charge a fee for their services.

⌐4⌐ **Describe the characteristics of the major stock exchanges.**

The best-known financial markets are the stock exchanges. They exist throughout the world. The two largest—the New York Stock Exchange and Nasdaq—are located in the United States. The NYSE is bigger, measured in terms of the total value of stock traded. Larger and better-known companies dominate the NYSE. Buy and sell orders are transmitted to the trading floor for execution. The Nasdaq stock market is an electronic market in which buy and sell orders are entered into a computerized communication system for execution. Most of the world's major stock markets today use similar electronic trading systems. They may represent the future stock markets.

Assessment Check Answers ✔

4.1 What are the world's two largest stock markets? The world's two largest stock markets are the New York Stock Exchange and the Nasdaq Stock Market.

4.2 Why is the London Stock Exchange unique? The London Stock Exchange is probably the most international of the world's stock markets because a large percentage of the shares traded are not those of British firms.

4.3 Explain the difference between a market order and a limit order. A market order instructs the investor's

broker to obtain the best possible price when buying or selling securities. A limit order sets a maximum price (if the investor wants to buy) or a minimum price (if the investor wants to sell).

⌐5⌐ **Discuss the organization and functioning of financial institutions.**

Financial institutions act as intermediaries between savers and users of funds. Depository institutions—commercial banks, savings banks, and credit unions—accept deposits from customers that can be redeemed on demand. Commercial banks are the largest and most important of the depository institutions and offer the widest range of services. Savings banks are a major source of home mortgage loans. Credit unions are not-for-profit institutions offering financial services to consumers. Government agencies, most notably the Federal Deposit Insurance Corporation, insure deposits at these institutions. Nondepository institutions include pension funds and insurance companies. Nondepository institutions invest a large portion of their funds in stocks, bonds, and real estate. Mutual funds are another important financial institution. These companies sell shares to investors and, in turn, invest the proceeds in securities. Many individuals today invest a large portion of their retirement savings in mutual fund shares.

Assessment Check Answers ✔

5.1 What are the two main types of financial institutions? The two major types of financial institutions are depository institutions (those that accept checking and similar accounts) and nondepository institutions.

5.2 What are the primary differences between commercial banks and savings banks? Today commercial and savings banks offer many of the same services. However, commercial banks lend money to businesses as well as to individuals. Savings banks lend money primarily to individuals, principally in the form of home mortgage loans.

5.3 What is a mutual fund? A mutual fund is an intermediary that raises money by selling shares to investors. It then pools investor funds and purchases securities that are consistent with the fund's objectives.

⌐6⌐ **Explain the functions of the Federal Reserve System and the tools it uses to control the supply of money and credit.**

The Federal Reserve System is the central bank of the United States. The Federal Reserve regulates banks, performs banking functions for the U.S. Department of the Treasury, and acts as the bankers' bank (clearing checks, lending money to banks, and replacing worn-out currency). It controls the supply of credit and money in the economy to promote growth and control inflation. The Federal Reserve's tools include reserve requirements, the discount rate, open market operations, and term auction facility loans. Selective credit controls and purchases and sales of foreign currencies also help the Federal Reserve manage the economy.

Assessment Check Answers ☑

6.1 What is the Federal Reserve System? The Federal Reserve System is the U.S. central bank. It is responsible for regulating banks, providing banking-related services for the federal government, acting as the banker's bank, and setting monetary policy.

6.2 How is the Fed organized? The country is divided into 12 districts, each of which has a Federal Reserve Bank. The Fed is run by a seven-member board of governors headed by a chair and vice chair. An important part of the Fed is the Federal Open Markets Committee, which sets monetary and interest rate policy. The Fed is designed to be politically independent.

6.3 List the four tools the Fed uses to control the supply of money and credit. The four tools are reserve requirements, the discount rate, open market operations, and term auction facility loans.

⌐7⌐ Evaluate the major features of regulations and laws affecting the financial system.

Commercial banks, savings banks, and credit unions in the United States are heavily regulated by federal or state banking authorities. Banking regulators require institutions to follow sound banking practices and have the power to close noncompliant ones. In the United States, financial markets are regulated at both the federal and state levels. Markets are also heavily self-regulated by the financial markets and professional organizations. The chief regulatory body is the Securities and Exchange Commission. It sets the requirements for both primary and secondary market activity, prohibiting a number of practices, including insider trading. The SEC also requires public companies to disclose financial information regularly. Professional organizations and the securities markets also have rules and procedures that all members must follow.

Assessment Check Answers ☑

7.1 Who regulates banks? All banks have either state or federal charters. Federally chartered banks are regulated by the Federal Reserve, the FDIC, and the Comptroller of the Currency. State-chartered banks are regulated by state banking authorities and the FDIC.

7.2 Define _insider trading_. Insider trading is defined as the use of material nonpublic information to make an investment profit.

7.3 List two ways in which the securities markets are self-regulated. Professional organizations such as the National Association of Securities Dealers have codes of conduct that members are expected to follow. Major financial markets have trading rules and procedures to identify suspicious trading activity.

⌐8⌐ Describe the global financial system.

Financial markets exist throughout the world and are increasingly interconnected. Investors in other countries purchase U.S. securities, and U.S. investors purchase foreign securities. Large U.S. banks and other financial institutions have a global presence. They accept deposits, make loans, and have branches throughout the world. Foreign banks also operate worldwide. The average European or Japanese bank is much larger than the average American bank. Virtually all nations have central banks that perform the same roles as the U.S. Federal Reserve System. Central bankers often act together, raising and lowering interest rates as economic conditions warrant.

Assessment Check Answers ☑

8.1 Where do U.S. banks rank compared with international banks? Banks in Asia and Europe are generally much larger than U.S. banks. In fact, only 3 out of the world's 30 largest banks are based in the United States.

8.2 Do other countries have organizations that play roles similar to those played by the Federal Reserve? Yes, virtually all nations have central banks that perform many of the same functions that the U.S. Federal Reserve System does.

■ Business Terms You Need to Know

financial system 534	primary markets 541
securities 536	secondary market 543
common stock 539	stock markets
financial markets 541	(exchanges) 543

financial institutions 546	Federal Reserve
Federal Deposit	System (Fed) 551
Insurance Corporation	insider trading 556
(FDIC) 548	

■ Review Questions

1. What is the financial system? Why is the direct transfer of funds from savers to users rare?

2. What is a security? Give several examples.

3. List the major types of bonds. Explain a mortgage pass-through.

4. What are the differences between common stock and preferred stock?

5. Explain the difference between a primary financial market and a secondary financial market.

6. Why are commercial banks, savings banks, and credit unions classified as depository financial institutions? How do the three differ?

7. Why are life insurance companies, pension funds, and mutual funds considered financial institutions?

8. Briefly explain the role of the Federal Reserve and list the tools it uses to control the supply of money and credit.

9. What methods are used to regulate banks? Why are state-chartered banks also regulated by the FDIC?

10. Explain how the Federal Reserve, acting in conjunction with other central banks, could affect exchange rates.

■ Projects and Teamwork Applications

1. Collect current interest rates on the following types of bonds: U.S. Treasury bonds, AAA-rated municipal bonds, AAA-rated corporate bonds, and BBB-rated corporate bonds. Arrange the interest rates from lowest to highest. Explain the reasons for the ranking.

2. You've probably heard of U.S. savings bonds—you may even have received some bonds as a gift. What you may not know is that two different types of savings bonds exist. Do some research and compare and contrast the two types of savings bonds. What are their features? Their pros and cons? Assuming you were interested in buying savings bonds, which of the two do you find more attractive?

3. Working with a partner, assume you are considering buying shares of Lowe's or Home Depot. Describe how you would go about analyzing the two companies' stocks and deciding which, if either, you would buy.

4. Working in a small team, identify a large bank. Visit that bank's Web site and obtain its most recent financial statements.

Compare the bank's financial statements to those of a nonfinancial company, such as a manufacturer or retailer. Report on your findings.

5. Assume you're investing money for retirement. Specify several investment criteria you believe are most important. Go to the MSN Money Web Site (http://moneycentral .msn.com). Click "Fund Research" (under "Investing"), then choose either "Find top performers by category" or "Find using Easy Screener." Identify at least three mutual funds that most closely meet your criteria. Choose one of the funds and research it. Answer the following questions:

   a. What was the fund's average annual return for the past five years?

   b. How well did the fund perform relative to its peer group and relative to an index such as the Standard & Poor's 500?

   c. What are the fund's ten largest holdings?

■ Web Assignments

1. **Online stock trading.** Visit the Web site of a brokerage firm that offers online trading, such as E*Trade (www.etrade .com) or Charles Schwab (www.schwab.com), to learn more about online trading. Most electronic brokerage firms also offer a trading demonstration. Use the demonstration to see how you obtain price information, company news, place buy or sell orders, and check account balances. Make some notes about your experience and bring them to class to participate in a class discussion.

2. **Banking statistics.** Visit the Web site listed here. Access the most recent year you can find and answer the following questions:

   a. How many commercial banks were in operation at the end of the year? How many savings banks (institutions) were in operation?

   b. What were the total assets of commercial banks and savings banks at the end of the year?

   c. How many commercial banks had assets in excess of $5 billion at the end of the year? How many commercial banks had assets of less than $500 million at the end of the year?

   http://www2.fdic.gov/sdi/sob/

3. **Federal reserve system.** Go to the Web site of the Board of Governors of the Federal Reserve System (www.federalreserve.gov). Prepare a short report on the seven-member board. Who are the current members? What are their backgrounds? When were they appointed? When do their terms expire?

Note: Internet Web addresses change frequently. If you don't find the exact sites listed, you may need to access the organization's home page and search from there or use a search engine such as Bing or Google.

With the emergence of electronic trading, even a world-spanning transaction needs only the click of a mouse to take place. But this interconnected market also has its dark side, because almost all the nations of the world were affected by the financial crisis. Many of the developed nations struggled to recover, but some developing nations were more fortunate. Many of them did not participate in what turned out to be the housing market bubble and were relatively unaffected when it burst. Now the economies of nations in Asia and Latin America, as well as the oil-rich Russia and the former Soviet-bloc countries of eastern Europe, could very well move ahead of their counterparts.

Emerging markets—financial markets in developing nations—are not new. They have been around since the 19th century. Traditionally, developing nations provided raw materials, such as petroleum and other resources, to the industrialized West but imported relatively few goods in return. Until a few years ago, these nations' markets were best known for the extremes of their boom-and-bust cycles. As recently as 1997, many East Asian countries fell like dominoes under a series of bankruptcies, recessions, and other financial woes. In 1998, Russia defaulted on its debt, causing its market to tumble more than 80 percent. But since then, many developing countries have managed to balance their budgets and have improved in other ways that made their economies grow. This growth has brought prosperity. Low interest rates on loans have enabled local companies to prosper. These countries also have less national, corporate, and household debt than most developed nations do. People can afford to spend money on imported goods—and are ready and willing to invest in their own countries.

The Morgan Stanley Capital International (MSCI) Emerging Markets Index measures the performance of financial markets in 25 developing countries. They range from Egypt and the Czech Republic to Peru and Thailand, as well as Brazil, Russia, India, and China—also known as the BRIC countries. Recently, the MSCI Emerging Markets Index had grown 70 percent, in a single year.

Antoine Van Agtmael, the chairman of AshmoreEMM, coined the term *emerging markets.* He believes that after the crash of 2008 and the revival of 2009, "We have just had the best gains in the history of emerging markets, we need a bit of a breather. It's not going to be the panic of 2008 and it's not going to be the fabulous year we had last year."

Some investors warn that emerging markets also have a dark side. Perhaps best known to Americans for its palm-tree-shaped artificial islands, the small Middle Eastern country of Dubai spent lavishly on these and other fanciful construction projects and then fell heavily into debt. When it failed to attract buyers or even renters for these sites, Dubai's bubble economy burst and the country fell into a recession. Some investors also worry that housing bubbles like the one in the United States may be growing in China and Hong Kong.

But other investors, such as David Cohen of Action Economics in Singapore, are more hopeful. Cohen said, "The economic picture is brightening despite all the caution flagged by the central banks and finance ministry officials around the world. The data still continues [*sic*] to show a global recovery led by Asia."

So far, emerging markets account for less than 3 percent of assets managed by American investment firms. But if these markets continue to do well, that number could double over the next five years.

Questions for Critical Thinking

1. Suppose one or more developing nations falls into a recession. What effect might this have on world markets?
2. Why do you think Americans have invested so little in emerging markets? If you wanted to convince a friend to invest in an emerging market with you, what arguments would you use?

Sources: Ed Johnson and Ron Harui, "Emerging-Market Stocks Gain, Erasing 2010 Loss; Yen Weakens," *Bloomberg Businessweek,* accessed June 21, 2011, http://www.businessweek.com; "MSCI Emerging Markets Index," *Investopedia,* http://www.investopedia.com, accessed June 21, 2010; Jeremy Gaunt, "Global Investors Cut Stocks, Emerging Markets: Poll," *Reuters,* March 31, 2010, http://www.reuters.com; "Emerging Market Stocks May Need a 'Breather,' " *Economic Times,* March 17, 2010, http://economictimes.indiatimes.com; Tina Russo, "Big Upside for Small Stocks in Emerging Markets," *Forbes.com,* February 8, 2010, http://www.forbes.com; Heather Timmons, "Emerging Markets Soar Past Their Doubters," *The New York Times,* December 30, 2009, http://www.nytimes.com; "Dubai Property Prices Could Drop 20% More," *Property Frontiers,* July 2, 2009, http://news.propertyfrontiers.com.

Like the rest of the United States, mostly rural Meigs County, Tennessee, had suffered during the recent financial crisis and the recession that followed. As the three largest employers in the county heard many times, it was a bad year to try to start a credit union. But the Middle Tennessee Federal Credit Union, now worth $3 million, recently celebrated its first birthday.

The founders of the credit union, originally named the Mid East Tennessee Community Credit Union, had begun seeking a charter before the economic trouble. Their employees were resorting to predatory, high-interest payday loans to meet their financial needs, and the founders wanted to help them get small, short-term loans on more reasonable terms. The credit union opened for business in the midst of the recession. Jim Pitt, the chairman of the credit union's board and the CEO of Polyform Plastics, says, "Mostly I am proudest of our loans for the first year."

Whereas a bank is a for-profit institution beholden to its board members and shareholders, a credit union is a nonprofit cooperative owned by its members. Credit unions emphasize the basic finances of everyday life: savings and checking accounts, credit cards, and relatively small loans for homes or cars. Credit unions generally pay more interest on savings accounts and charge less interest on loans. Mark Wolff of the Credit Union National Association (CUNA) says, "The credit union channels any excess funds back to its members." Just as the FDIC does for banks, the federal government's National Credit Union Administration insures deposits of up to $250,000.

Credit unions are chartered to serve particular groups. Originally, most were affiliated with employers. For example, BECU (formerly the Boeing Employees' Credit Union) in Seattle once accepted only employees and their families. About ten years ago, credit unions began to ease their membership requirements. To join the Middle Tennessee Federal Credit Union, a person must simply either work, worship, live, or go to school in the local area.

With the big banks pulling or tightening consumer credit, consumers have had trouble getting even the most routine loans, for example, for a used car. Small-business owners have also suffered as banks have cut back. Credit unions have filled the gap. Around the country, credit unions now have 92 million members and have grown rapidly. In Michigan alone, they gained 59,000 new members in one year. Claudia York, the interim president and CEO of Chief Financial Federal Credit Union in Pontiac, Michigan, says, "We've been getting many more inquiries about [business loans]. We have not tightened up at all—we have money to loan. We're trying to be as generous as possible while still adhering to our [lending] guidelines."

Credit unions don't perform all the services of traditional banks, however. Only 59 percent of credit unions issue ATM cards. Those cards are usually part of a network of ATM machines at, for example, 7-Eleven, Walgreens, Costco, or even banks. Only 22 percent of credit unions have safe-deposit boxes. And most credit unions have only one branch, or even none.

Both the CUNA and NCUA Web sites have online tools to help you find a credit union near you. Allan McMorris, the president and CEO of Michigan's Oakland County Credit Union, said, "I'm very proud of the fact that in this tough economy, we are going to set a record in the number of loans disbursed. And of course, that's all local money on deposit and local loans. In our local economy, we think we're helping with the recovery."

Questions for Critical Thinking

1. Why is an organization such as the Credit Union National Association important to the credit union industry?

2. Use either the CUNA or the NCUA credit union locator tool to find a credit union near you. If you are eligible to join, compare the credit union with your current bank. What are the advantages to joining the credit union? What are the advantages to staying with your bank?

Sources: "Credit Union vs. Bank," Star Community Credit Union, http://www.starcreditunion.com, accessed June 21, 2011; Middle Tennessee Federal Credit Union Web site, http://www.midtenfcu.com, accessed June 21, 2010; National Credit Union Administration Web site, http://www.ncua.gov, accessed June 21, 2010; Credit Union National Association Web site, http://www.cuna.org, accessed June 21, 2010; David Morrison, "Year-Old Tenn. Credit Union Finds Success Despite Great Recession," *Credit Union Times,* April 28, 2010, http://www.cutimes.com; Bob Trebilcock, "Bye, Banks: Time to Join a Credit Union," *MoneyWatch/CBS News,* January 12, 2010, http://www.cbsnews.com; James Briggs, "Credit Unions Thrive as Big Banks Cut Back on Lending," *Oakland Press,* January 4, 2010, http://www.theoaklandpress.com.

"Fair Trade has always been part of my legacy in coffee," says RikKleinfeldt, president and co-founder of Rhode Island-based New Harvest Coffee Roasters. "That's where I started with New Harvest." But in less than a decade, New Harvest's business model has evolved beyond Fair Trade to something different.

New Harvest is a small-batch coffee roaster specializing in certified organic coffee that is grown and harvested by farms with sustainable practices. RikKleinfeldt notes that he built his company on two pillars: 1) the highest quality coffee, and 2) sustainable sourcing practices. "But these two weren't really gelling at first," he admits. At the beginning, Kleinfeldt tried to source from Fair Trade cooperatives, but this wasn't really fulfilling his objective. "Fair Trade is based on the commodity system," Kleinfeldt explains, "which creates a floor price at which coffee can't drop below. But it doesn't really address the issue of quality." The groups that work with Fair Trade are large cooperatives, sometimes encompassing several thousand small farms. All the coffee is blended together as a commodity, so it is impossible for a roaster like New Harvest to deal directly with each farm, selecting the specific harvest that it wants to buy.

Kleinfeldt is quick to point out that when Fair Trade began around a decade ago, it was a lifeline to small farmers because coffee prices were at an all-time low—these growers were selling their crops for less than it cost to produce them. Without Fair Trade, many of these farms would have gone out of business. With the coffee market somewhat stabilized though, commodity pricing brings its own set of problems. "The commodity pricing usually has nothing to do with the coffee itself," says Kleinfeldt. Prices are set at the New York Stock Exchange, not in the growing fields of Costa Rica or Colombia. He notes that roasters, retailers, and consumers may end up paying way too much or way too little for a particular year's crop.

So Kleinfeldt has become part of what he calls the Artisan Coffee movement—growers, roasters, and retailers who prefer to deal directly with each other as individual businesses. "We connect directly with our growers and determine price based on quality," he explains. Kleinfeldt and his staff, along with some of his retailers such as the owner of Blue State Coffee and the owner of Pejamajo Café, travel to the farms in Costa Rica and Colombia where they actually taste the coffee before purchasing a crop. Kleinfeldt believes this is the only way to get the best coffee on the market. These visits help develop strong relationships, find solutions to problems, and develop strategies for surviving and thriving as businesses. Through visiting, he says, "we can understand their challenges." One farm in particular is located in Colombia. The farmer

decided he didn't want to participate in a large Fair Trade cooperative—instead, he wanted to develop a market for his own coffee. So he approached New Harvest with the idea, and the match was ideal. He is now one of New Harvest's premier growers.

Sourcing the coffee beans directly from individual farms also helps New Harvest keep close track of organic and sustainability practices. GerraHarrigan, director of business development for New Harvest Coffee Roasters, notes that this is an important part of the firm's business. The owners of local coffee shops—and their customers—like the reassurance that New Harvest stands behind all of its claims. Harrigan takes the hands-on approach. "When we deal direct-trade coffee, the coffee has to be cared for a little more," she explains. Harrigan grades the coffee on several factors before pricing it for New Harvest.

Kleinfeldt wants consumers to know they are getting a great deal when they ask for New Harvest at their local shop. He points out that the price differentiation isn't as much as people might think. A visit to the supermarket reveals that Starbucks and Green Mountain sell for about $9 to $11 per pound, whereas most New Harvest coffee sells for about $11 to $13 a pound. Because of the richness of New Harvest, most customers actually get more cups of coffee from a pound of New Harvest than they do from the other premium brands.

Kleinfeldt hopes that the Artisan Coffee movement, as he refers to his company's practices, will flourish and grow. He believes that if you're going to drink a cup of coffee, it should be really fresh and of the highest quality—with beans preferably roasted by New Harvest.

Questions for Critical Thinking

1. What are the benefits and drawbacks of treating coffee as a commodity in the marketplace? What do you predict will be the future of Fair Trade?

2. Should the entire coffee market be regulated in any way? Why or why not? If so, how?

3. How would New Harvest change as a business if it made an initial public offering (IPO)?

4. What is your opinion of the so-called Artisan Coffee movement as a business model? Do you think it will be successful in the long run? Why or why not?

Sources: New Harvest Coffee Roasters Web site, http://www .newharvestcoffee.com, accessed June 21, 2011; "New Harvest Coffee Roasters," *GreenPeople,* http://www.greenpeople.org, accessed August 29, 2010; Richard Garcia, "Pejamajo Café & New Harvest Coffee Roasters," *Chefs Daily Food Bank,* May 4, 2010, http://www.chefsdailyfoodbank.com.

Chapter 17

Learning Objectives

[1] Define *finance,* and explain the role of financial managers.

[2] Describe the components of a financial plan and the financial planning process.

[3] Outline how organizations manage their assets.

[4] Compare the two major sources of funds for a business, and explain the concept of leverage.

[5] Identify sources of short-term financing for business operations.

[6] Discuss long-term financing options.

[7] Describe mergers, acquisitions, buyouts, and divestitures.

Financial Management

HP Buys Palm: Win or Lose?

REUTERS/Beck Diefenbach/
Landov LLC

When HP, the world's largest technology company (by revenue) announced its plans to purchase the struggling Palm for $1.2 billion, smartphones around the nation lit up with rumors, speculation, and perhaps even a little gossip. Why did HP plunk down a whopping 23 percent premium over Palm's previous closing stock price—in cash? What was HP so sure about?

More than a year later, the dust of acquisition hasn't exactly settled, but it has cleared enough to see what HP executives may have had in mind. Palm, which had once been a pioneer in the development of handheld devices and was well respected for its webOS platform, had failed to generate interest in its touch screen Pre and Pixi smartphones in a marketplace that was already jammed with products from Apple and Google. HP, which is known for its superior hardware, was tugging at its ties to Microsoft—the firm wanted its own operating system, one that didn't depend on the whims of Microsoft. HP had what Palm needed (cash), and Palm had what HP wanted in order to grow (a patented operating system). "Palm's innovative operating system provides an ideal platform to expand HP's mobility strategy and create a unique HP experience spanning multiple mobile connected devices," said Todd Bradley, HP's executive vice president.

For months, tech industry analysts speculated on HP's next move. Skeptics warned that the strategy would fail because consumers would have no need or desire to purchase HP/Palm devices instead of those from Apple or Android (Google). "Without unique apps, there's no reason to have a unique platform," said one writer. But others could see HP's longer-range goals and perhaps its vision as well. HP is a major supplier to businesses that use enterprise software, and developers have reported that they like Palm's webOS platform because of its similarities to the popular Linux. Thus, HP could capitalize on that market.

But there's more. Recently HP unveiled its new Palm Touchpad for the tablet market. It doesn't rely on Android, Windows, or iOS. Instead, it runs on its own Palm technology. This fact alone signals that HP insists on being recognized as a software company. The Palm Touchpad will not outsell the iPad any time soon. But Palm's webOS is well-regarded software, and HP now owns it—and has the financial and marketing resources to push it across the world. "All together [there are] 100 million devices with webOS deployed annually," observes HP's Todd Bradley. "That's the start of something pretty big."

And "big" is where HP is headed. The purchase of Palm is viewed by some as a major step toward building the next big thing in the tech industry, identified by Steven MacArthur, HP's head of Consumer Applications, as "the largest install base of connected users in the world."[1]

Previous chapters discuss two essential functions that a business must perform. First, the company must produce a good or service or contract with suppliers to produce it. Second, the firm must market its good or service to prospective customers. This chapter introduces a third, equally important, function: a company's managers must ensure that it has enough money to perform its other tasks successfully, in both the present and the future, and that these funds are invested properly. Adequate funds must be available to buy materials, equipment, and other assets; pay bills; and compensate employees. This third business function is **finance**—planning, obtaining, and managing the company's funds in order to accomplish its objectives as effectively and efficiently as possible.

An organization's financial objectives include not only meeting expenses and investing in assets but also maximizing its overall worth, often determined by the value of the firm's common stock. Financial managers are responsible for meeting expenses, investing in assets, and increasing profits to shareholders. Solid financial management is critical to the success of a business. The successful acquisition of Palm by HP could only take place with carefully planned financial management.

This chapter focuses on the finance function of organizations. It begins by describing the role of financial managers, their place in the organizational hierarchy, and the increasing importance of finance. Next, the financial planning process and the components of a financial plan are outlined. Then the discussion focuses on how organizations manage assets as efficiently and effectively as possible. The two major sources of funds—debt and equity—are then compared, and the concept of leverage is introduced. The major sources of short-term and long-term funding are described in the following sections. A description of mergers, acquisitions, buyouts, and divestitures concludes the chapter.

finance planning, obtaining, and managing the company's funds to accomplish its objectives as effectively and efficiently as possible.

The Role of the Financial Manager

Because of the intense pressures they face today, organizations are increasingly measuring and reducing the costs of business operations, as well as maximizing revenues and profits. As a result, **financial managers**—executives who develop and implement their firm's financial plan and determine the most appropriate sources and uses of funds—are among the most vital people on the corporate payroll.

Figure 17.1 shows what the finance function of a typical company might look like. At the top is the chief financial officer (CFO). The CFO usually reports directly to the company's chief executive officer (CEO) or chief operating officer (COO). In some companies, the CFO is also a member of the board of directors. In the case of the software maker Oracle,

financial managers executive who develops and implements the firm's financial plan and determines the most appropriate sources and uses of funds.

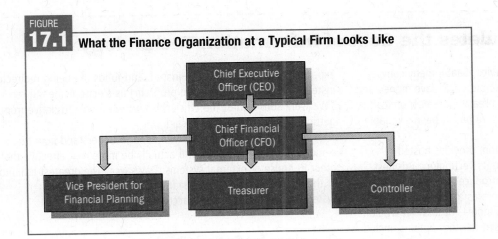

FIGURE 17.1 **What the Finance Organization at a Typical Firm Looks Like**

Chief Executive Officer (CEO)

Chief Financial Officer (CFO)

Vice President for Financial Planning

Treasurer

Controller

both the current CFO and the former CFO serve on that company's board, the latter as its chairman. Moreover, it's not uncommon for CFOs to serve as independent directors on other firms' boards, such as HP, Microsoft, and Target. As noted in Chapter 15, the CFO, along with the firm's CEO, must certify the accuracy of the firm's financial statements.

Reporting directly to the CFO are often three senior managers. Although titles can vary, these three executives are commonly called the *vice president for financial management* (or *planning*), the *treasurer*, and the *controller*. The vice president for financial management or planning is responsible for preparing financial forecasts and analyzing major investment decisions, such as new products, new production facilities, and acquisitions. The treasurer is responsible for all of the company's financing activities, including cash management, tax planning and preparation, and shareholder relations. The treasurer also works on the sale of new security issues to investors. The controller is the chief accounting manager. The controller's functions include keeping the company's books, preparing financial statements, and conducting internal audits. The "Hit & Miss" feature explains the increasing importance of financially sound IT management.

The growing importance of financial professionals is reflected in the growing number of CEOs who have been promoted from financial positions. Indra Nooyi, CEO of PepsiCo, and Jim Marsh, CEO of the British telecommunications company Cable and Wireless, both served as their firm's CFO prior to assuming the top job. The importance of finance professionals is also reflected in how much CFOs earn today. According to a survey by the executive compensation consulting firm Equilar, annual salaries for CFOs range from $840,000 to around $4 million.[2] These figures don't include bonuses, which in recent years have increased for CFOS even as their salaries dipped. Bonuses range from $145,000 to over half a million dollars.[3]

In performing their jobs, financial professionals continually seek to balance risks with expected financial returns. Risk is the uncertainty of gain or loss; return is the gain or loss that results from an investment over a specified period of time. Financial managers strive to maximize the wealth of their firm's shareholders by striking the optimal balance between risk and return. This balance is called the **risk-return trade-off**. For example, relying heavily on borrowed funds may increase the return

risk-return trade-off process of maximizing the wealth of the firm's shareholders by striking the optimal balance between risk and return.

Jin Lee/Bloomberg/Getty Images, Inc.

The growing importance of financial professionals is reflected in the growing number of CEOs who have been promoted from financial positions. Indra Nooyi, CEO of PepsiCo, served as CFO prior to assuming the top job.

Hit & Miss

Apptio Calculates the Cost of Information Technology

With the growth of software as a service (SaaS), many companies are making the transition to cloud computing to save money and increase efficiency. But is cloud computing really more economical and efficient in all cases? Until recently, there hasn't been a reliable way to find out.

Apptio, located in Bellevue, Washington, provides hosted Internet technology solutions, among them its Technology Business Management package. Recently, Apptio introduced its new Cost Transparency Template. This template generates the formulas necessary for a company to calculate how much more—or less—it would cost to invest in cloud computing as opposed to other options, including traditional in-house hardware and storage. Among Apptio's clients are BNP Paribas, Starbucks, Hallmark, and Expedia. Jeff Day, Apptio's director of marketing, says, "We see that cloud computing is going to change the way IT leaders think about how they manage IT."

St. Luke's Health System of Kansas City has 1,200 doctors among 9,000 total employees in 11 hospitals. The chief information officer, Debe Gash, wanted to eliminate nonessential IT-related costs. A spending-analytics tool from Apptio allowed Gash and her team to save millions of dollars by highlighting unnecessary or redundant spending. For example, St. Luke's had too many desktop software licenses, two full-time employees dealt only with spam management, and they were spending a lot of money on electronic storage. Those

expenses were reduced or eliminated, and funds are being redirected instead to finance such needed programs as electronic health records. "We were surprised at the efficiencies we were able to derive from getting those insights," Gash said.

In the future, IT managers will need to understand how the cloud works and whether it will actually be more cost effective than other in-house or external systems. Day says, "The greatest inhibitor of the cloud is a lack of understanding. IT leaders need better systems and tools to perform accurate analysis."

Questions for Critical Thinking

1. Why have companies recently become so concerned with cost management?
2. Why might it be difficult for very large companies to keep accurate account of spending on such items as computer hardware and software licenses?

Sources: Company Web site, http://www.apptio.com, accessed June 21, 2011; Denise Dubie, "IT Cost Management and the Cloud," *Network World,* April 13, 2010, http://www.networkworld.com; Bob Evans, "Global CIO: St. Luke's CIO Saves Millions with Apptio's Help," *InformationWeek,* April 6, 2010, http://www.informationweek.com; Brian Carlson, "Top 5 Financial Management Predictions for 2010," *CIO,* February 2, 2010, http://www.cio.com.

(in the form of cash) to shareholders, but the more money a firm borrows, the greater the risks to shareholders. An increase in a firm's cash on hand reduces the risk of being unable to meet unexpected cash needs. However, because cash in and of itself does not earn much, if any, return, failure to invest surplus funds in an income-earning asset—such as in securities—reduces a firm's potential return or profitability. Many illustrations of the risk-return trade-off are provided throughout this chapter.

Every financial manager must perform this risk-return balancing act. For example, in the late 1990s, Airbus wrestled with a major decision: whether to begin development and production of the giant A380 jetliner. The development costs for the aircraft—the world's largest jetliner—were initially estimated at more than $10 billion. Before committing to such a huge investment, financial managers had to weigh the potential profits of the A380 with the risk that the profits would not materialize. With its future on the line, Airbus decided to go ahead with the development of the A380, spending more than $15 billion on research and development. The A380 entered commercial service a few years ago. Airbus currently has 234 confirmed orders for its A380 jetliner, from 18 customers including Emirates (90 jets), Qantas Airways (20 jets), Singapore Airlines (19 jets), and Air France (12 jets).[4]

Financial managers must also learn to adapt to changes in the financial system. The recent credit crisis has made it more difficult for some companies to borrow money from traditional lenders such as banks. This, in turn, has forced firms to scale back expansion plans or seek funding from other sources such as commercial financing companies. In addition, financial managers must adapt to internal changes as well.

Assessment Check ✔

1. What is the structure of the finance function at the typical firm?
2. Explain the risk-return trade-off.

Financial Planning

Financial managers develop their organization's **financial plan**, a document that specifies the funds needed by a firm for a given period of time, the timing of inflows and outflows, and the most appropriate sources and uses of funds. Some financial plans, often called *operating plans*, are short-term in nature, focusing on projections no more than a year or two in the future. Other financial plans, sometimes referred to as *strategic plans*, have a much longer time horizon, perhaps up to five or ten years.

Regardless of the time period, a financial plan is based on forecasts of production costs, purchasing needs, plant and equipment expenditures, and expected sales activities for the period covered. Financial managers use forecasts to determine the specific amounts and timing of expenditures and receipts. They build a financial plan based on the answers to three questions:

1. What funds will the firm require during the planning period?

2. When will it need additional funds?

3. Where will it obtain the necessary funds?

Some funds flow into the firm when it sells its goods or services, but funding needs vary. The financial plan must reflect both the amounts and timing of inflows and outflows of funds. Even a profitable firm may face a financial squeeze as a result of its need for funds when sales lag, when the volume of its credit sales increases, or when customers are slow in making payments.

In general, preparing a financial plan consists of three steps. The first is a forecast of sales or revenue over some future time period. This projection is, in fact, the key variable in any financial plan because without an accurate sales forecast, the firm will have difficulty accurately estimating other variables, such as production costs and purchasing needs. The best method of forecasting sales depends on the nature of the business. For instance, a retailer's CFO might begin with the current sales-per-store figure. Then he or she would look toward the near future, factoring in expected same-store sales growth, along with any planned store openings or closings, to come up with a forecast of sales for the next period. If the company sells merchandise through other channels, such as online, the forecast is adjusted to reflect those additional channels.

Next, the CFO uses the sales forecast to determine the expected level of profits for future periods. This longer-term projection involves estimating expenses such as purchases, employee compensation, and taxes. Many expenses are themselves functions of sales. For instance, the more a firm sells, generally the greater its purchases. Along with estimating future profits, the CFO should also determine what portion of these profits will likely be paid to shareholders in the form of cash dividends.

After coming up with the sales and profit forecast, the CFO then needs to estimate how many additional assets the firm will need to support projected sales. Increased sales, for example, might mean the company needs additional inventory, stepped-up collections for accounts receivable, or even new plant and equipment. Depending on the nature of the industry, some businesses need more assets than do other companies to support the same amount of sales. The technical term for this requirement is *asset intensity*. For instance, the chemical manufacturer DuPont has approximately $0.68 in assets for every dollar in sales.

financial plan document that specifies the funds needed by a firm for a period of time, the timing of inflows and outflows, and the most appropriate sources and uses of funds.

Costco has a lower *asset intensity* than a typical manufacturing business might have.

So, for every $100 increase in sales, the firm would need about $68 of additional assets. The warehouse retailer Costco, by contrast, has only roughly $0.34 in assets for every dollar in sales. It would require an additional $34 of assets for every $100 of additional sales. This difference is not surprising; manufacturing is a more asset-intensive business than retailing.

A simplified financial plan illustrates these steps. Assume a growing company is forecasting that sales next year will increase by $40 million to $140 million. After estimating expenses, the CFO believes that after-tax profits next year will be $12 million and the firm will pay nothing in dividends. The projected increase in sales next year will require the firm to invest another $20 million in assets, and because increases in assets are uses of funds, the company will need an additional $20 million in funds. The company's after-tax earnings will contribute $12 million, meaning that the other $8 million must come from outside sources. So the financial plan tells the CFO how much money will be needed and when it will be needed. Armed with this knowledge, and given that the firm has decided to borrow the needed funds, the CFO can then begin negotiations with banks and other lenders.

The cash inflows and outflows of a business are similar to those of a household. The members of a household depend on weekly or monthly paychecks for funds, but their expenditures vary greatly from one pay period to the next. The financial plan should indicate when the flows of funds entering and leaving the organization will occur and in what amounts. One of the most significant business expenses is employee compensation.

A good financial plan also includes financial control, a process of comparing actual revenues, costs, and expenses with forecasts. This comparison may reveal significant differences between projected and actual figures, so it is important to discover them early to take quick action.

Bill Morrison is the CFO of Pittsburgh-based Genco Marketplace, which liquidates, or sells off, other companies' excess inventory. Genco buys inventory that is not selling well then resells it to wholesalers. In turn, the wholesalers sell the inventory to discount retailers. Always vigilant about the cost of freight, including fuel, Genco pays the transportation costs of taking the goods from their current location to where they will be liquidated. Some excess inventory is seasonal. When a retailer has winter coats left over in June, Genco will buy those coats, hold them in inventory, and sell them to a wholesaler in the fall, when demand rises again. But the longer a product remains unsold, the harder it will be to liquidate, even at a deep discount. In all cases, Morrison or members of his team have to prepare a financial plan that takes into account not only the benefits of buying the merchandise but the risks as well.[5]

Assessment Check ✓

1. What three questions does a financial plan address?

2. Explain the steps involved in preparing a financial plan.

Managing Assets

As we noted in Chapter 15, assets consist of what a firm owns. But assets also represent uses of funds. To grow and prosper, companies need to obtain additional assets. Sound financial management requires assets to be acquired and managed as effectively and efficiently as possible. The "Business Etiquette" feature offers tips for managing assets.

Short-Term Assets

Short-term, or current, assets consist of cash and assets that can be, or are expected to be, converted into cash within a year. The major current assets are cash, marketable securities, accounts receivable, and inventory.

Cash and Marketable Securities

The major purpose of cash is to pay day-to-day expenses, much as when individuals maintain balances in checking accounts to pay bills or buy food and clothing. In addition, most organizations strive to maintain a minimum cash balance in order to have funds available in the event of unexpected expenses. As noted earlier, because cash earns little, if any, return, most firms invest excess cash in so-called *marketable securities*—low-risk securities that either have short maturities or can be easily sold in secondary markets. Money market instruments—described in Chapter 16—are popular choices for firms with excess cash. The cash budget, which we discussed in Chapter 15, is one tool for managing cash and marketable securities because it shows expected cash inflows and outflows for a period of time. The cash budget indicates months when the firm will have surplus cash and can invest in marketable securities and months when it will need additional cash.

Critics of some companies' budgeting practices contend that occasionally firms hoard cash. Recently, Cisco Systems had more than $35 billion in cash and marketable securities. Yet firms may have good reasons for holding large amounts of cash and marketable securities. They may plan on using these funds shortly to make a large investment, pay dividends to shareholders, or repurchase outstanding bonds.

Accounts Receivable
Accounts receivable are uncollected credit sales and can be a significant asset. The financial manager's job is to collect the funds owed the firm as quickly as possible while still offering sufficient credit to customers to generate increased sales. In general, a more liberal credit policy means higher sales but also increased collection expenses, higher levels of bad debt, and a higher investment in accounts receivable.

Management of accounts receivable is composed of two functions: determining an overall

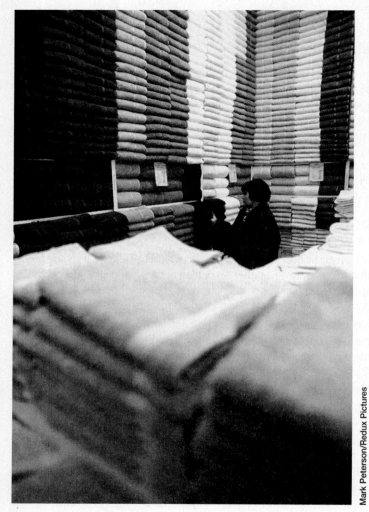

At Bed Bath & Beyond, inventory is the most valuable asset. Managing inventory can be a costly and highly complicated undertaking, especially for retailers.

Mark Peterson/Redux Pictures

credit policy and deciding which customers will be offered credit. Formulating a credit policy involves deciding whether the firm will offer credit and, if so, on what terms. Will a discount be offered to customers who pay in cash? Often, the overall credit policy is dictated by competitive pressures or general industry practices. If all your competitors offer customers credit, your firm will likely have to as well. The other aspect of a credit policy is deciding which customers will be offered credit. Managers must consider the importance of the customer as well as its financial health and repayment history.

One simple tool for assessing how well receivables are being managed is calculating accounts receivable turnover over successive time periods. We showed how this ratio is calculated in Chapter 15. If receivables turnover shows signs of slowing, it means that the average credit customer is paying later. This trend warrants further investigation.

Inventory Management For many firms, such as retailers, inventory represents the largest single asset. At the home furnishings retailer Bed Bath & Beyond, inventory makes up about 49 percent of total assets. Even for nonretailers, inventory is an important asset. At the heavy-equipment manufacturer Caterpillar, inventory is almost 12 percent of total assets. On the other hand, some types of firms, such as electric utilities and transportation companies, have no inventory. For the majority of firms, which do carry inventory, proper management of it is vital.

Managing inventory can be complicated. The cost of inventory includes more than just the acquisition cost. It also includes the cost of ordering, storing, insuring, and financing inventory, as well as the cost of stockouts, lost sales due to insufficient inventory. Financial managers try to minimize the cost of inventory. But production, marketing, and logistics also play important roles in determining proper inventory levels. The production considerations of inventory management were discussed in Chapter 10. In Chapter 12, we outlined the marketing and logistics issues surrounding inventory.

Trends in the inventory turnover ratio—described in Chapter 15—can be early warning signs of impending trouble. For instance, if inventory turnover has been slowing for several consecutive quarters, it indicates that inventory is rising faster than sales. In turn, this may suggest that customer demand is softening and the firm needs to take action, such as reducing production or increasing promotional efforts.

Capital Investment Analysis

In addition to current assets, firms also invest in long-lived assets. Unlike current assets, long-lived assets are expected to produce economic benefits for more than one year. These investments often involve substantial amounts of money. For example, as noted earlier in the chapter, Airbus invested more than $15 billion in development of the A380. In another example, a few years ago, auto manufacturer BMW spent $750 million to expand its production facility in Spartanburg, South Carolina, bringing its total investment in the state to $4.6 billion. Then the firm unveiled its first Super Bowl ad in many years—with scenes shot around South Carolina.[6]

The process by which decisions are made regarding investments in long-lived assets is called *capital investment analysis*. Firms make two basic types of capital investment decisions: expansion and replacement. The A380 and the BMW South Carolina plant investments are examples of expansion decisions. Replacement decisions involve upgrading assets by substituting new ones. A retailer, such as Walmart, might decide to replace an old store with a new Supercenter, as it did in Oxford, Ohio.

Financial managers must estimate all of the costs and benefits of a proposed investment, which can be quite difficult, especially for very long-lived investments. Only those investments that offer an acceptable return—measured by the difference between benefits and costs—should be undertaken. BMW's financial managers believed that the benefits of expanding the South Carolina production facility outweighed the high cost. The expansion will allow BMW to produce three new models designed mainly for the North American market, so the expected profit from the sale of these models would be considered in the decision. Some other benefits cited by BMW include lower production costs, improved logistics, and expanded use of renewable energy. The Spartanburg facility recently produced its 1 millionth BMW X5 and continues to emphasize its commitment to the U.S. market.[7]

Managing International Assets

Today, firms often have assets worldwide. Both McDonald's and The Coca-Cola Company generate more than half of their annual sales outside the United States. The vast majority of sales for Unilever and Nestlé occur outside their home countries (the Netherlands and Switzerland, respectively). Managing international assets creates several challenges for the financial manager, one of the most important of which is the problem of exchange rates.

As we discussed in several other chapters, an exchange rate is the rate at which one currency can be exchanged for another. Exchange rates can vary substantially from year to year, creating a problem for any company with international assets. As an example, assume a U.S. firm has a major subsidiary in the United Kingdom. Assume that the U.K. subsidiary earns an annual profit of £750 million (stated in British pounds). Over the past five years, the exchange rate between the U.S. dollar and the British pound has varied between 1.82 (dollars per pound) and 1.56.[8] This means the dollar value of the U.K. profits ranged from $1.37 billion to $1.17 billion.

Consequently, many global firms engage in activities that reduce the risks associated with exchange rate fluctuations. Some are quite complicated. However, one of the simplest and most widely used is called a *balance sheet hedge*. Essentially, a balance sheet hedge creates an offsetting liability to the non-dollar-denominated asset, one that is denominated in the same currency as the asset. In our example, the U.K. subsidiary is a pound-denominated asset. To create an offsetting liability, the firm could take out a loan, denominated in British pounds, creating a pound-denominated liability. If done correctly, this hedge will reduce or even eliminate the risk associated with changes in the value of the dollar relative to the pound. This will improve the financial performance of the firm, which can have a positive impact on its stock price.

Assessment Check ✓

1. Why do firms often choose to invest excess cash in marketable securities?

2. What are the two aspects of accounts receivable management?

3. Explain the difference between an expansion decision and a replacement decision.

Sources of Funds and Capital Structure

The use of debt for financing can increase the potential for return as well as increase loss potential. Recall the accounting equation introduced in Chapter 15:

$$\text{Assets} = \text{Liabilities} + \text{Owners' equity}$$

If you view this equation from a financial management perspective, it reveals that there are only two types of funding: debt and equity. *Debt capital* consists of funds obtained through borrowing. *Equity capital* consists of funds provided by the firm's owners when they reinvest earnings, make additional contributions, liquidate assets, issue stock to the general public, or raise capital from outside investors. The mix of a firm's debt and equity capital is known as its **capital structure**.

Companies often take very different approaches to choosing a capital structure. As more debt is used, the risk to the company increases since the firm is now obligated to make the interest payments on the money borrowed, regardless of the cash flows coming into the company. Choosing more debt increases the fixed costs a company must pay, which in turn makes a company more sensitive to changing sales revenues. Debt is frequently the least costly method of raising additional financing dollars, one of the reasons it is so frequently used.

Differing industries choose varying amounts of debt and equity to use when financing. Using the information provided by DataMonitor, the automotive industry has debt ratios (the ratio of liabilities to assets) of over 60 percent for both Toyota and Honda and over 90 percent for Ford. These companies are primarily using debt to finance their asset expenditures. Companies like the profit foodservice companies of McDonald's and Starbucks use only 49 percent debt and 27 percent debt, respectively. The mixture of debt and equity a company uses is a major management decision.

capital structure mix of a firm's debt and equity capital.

leverage increasing the rate of return on funds invested by borrowing funds.

Leverage and Capital Structure Decisions

Raising needed cash by borrowing allows a firm to benefit from the principle of **leverage**, increasing the rate of return on funds invested by borrowing funds. The key to managing leverage is to ensure that a company's earnings remain larger than its interest payments, which increases the leverage on the rate of return on shareholders' investment. Of course, if the company earns less than its interest payments, shareholders lose money on their original investments.

Figure 17.2 shows the relationship between earnings and shareholder returns for two identical hypothetical firms that choose to raise funds in different ways. Leverage Company obtains 50 percent of its funds from lenders who purchase

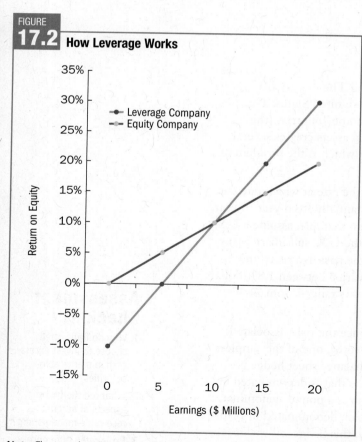

FIGURE 17.2 How Leverage Works

Note: The example assumes that both companies have $100 million in capital. Leverage company consists of $50 million in equity and $50 million in bonds (with an interest rate of 10 percent). Equity company consists of $100 million in equity and no bonds. This example also assumes no corporate taxes.

Solving an Ethical Controversy

Executive Pay: Should Shareholders Decide the Salaries of CEOs?

While the country was suffering through the financial crisis and its aftermath, the news media were filled with reports of astronomical salaries of CEOs and other top executives at large corporations.

Recently, General Electric (GE) implemented rules that would make it harder for CEO Jeffrey Immelt to cash in on the stock options he received as part of the previous year's pay package. Many believe that the board of directors made this move in order to avoid a "no" vote on the package from shareholders at the firm's annual meeting. This action illustrates the trend toward "say for pay" voting by shareholders.

Should company shareholders help determine how much top executives are paid?

PRO

1. Publicly held corporations are owned by their shareholders, who should have the opportunity to vote on compensation for top executives. Robert E. Denham and Rajiv L. Gupta, co-chairs of The Conference Board Task Force on Executive Compensation, said, "Shareholders . . . and the public deserve to see executive compensation programs that serve shareholders' interests and are explained to shareholders. . . ."

2. Some analysts believe that lopsided pay structures had a part in the financial crisis. Federal Reserve Chairman Ben Bernanke said, "Compensation practices at some banking organizations have led to misaligned incentives and excessive risk-taking. . . ."

CON

1. Shareholders may not necessarily know what appropriate pay is. Many don't have the time or resources to do their own analysis and judge whether a pay program is suitable—or whether it promotes a risk-taking, get-rich-quick mentality in executives.

2. Shareholders recently turned down the chance to vote on executive pay at companies such as Johnson & Johnson and Dow Chemical. Many prefer to discuss pay structures with management and board members before voting.

Summary

In its efforts to reform the financial industry as well as related business activities, the Dodd-Frank Act (signed into law in July 2010) requires that all public companies now hold "up-or-down" votes on CEO compensation. While these "say for pay" votes are actually nonbinding, they do carry a lot of weight with boards of directors. More firms are curtailing the perks received by chief executives, and making a greater effort to link top executive pay to company performance.

Sources: Jennifer Liberto, "CEO Pay: Shareholders Get a (Little) Say," *CNN Money*, April 21, 2011, http://money.cnn.com; Alix Stuart, "Reform Bill Mandates Say on Pay," *CFO.com*, June 29, 2010, http://www.cfo.com; Jim Kuhnhenn and Alan Fram, "Congress Agrees on Financial Oversight," *Philadelphia Inquirer*, June 26, 2010, http://www.philly.com; Ann Yerger, "Red Flags for Say-on-Pay Voting," Harvard Law School Forum on Corporate Governance and Financial Regulation, May 18, 2010, http://blogs.law.harvard.edu; A. G. Laffey, "Executive Pay: Time for CEOs to Take a Stand," *Harvard Business Review*, May 2010, http://hbr.org; Bryant Ruiz Switzky, "CEO Compensation Down in 2009," *Washington Business Journal*, May 7, 2010, http://washingtonbizjournals.com; Helen Coster, "The State of the CEO in 2010," *Forbes.com*, January 21, 2010, http://www.forbes.com.

company bonds. Leverage Company pays 10 percent interest on its bonds. Equity Company raises all of its funds through sales of company stock.

Notice that if earnings double, from, say, $10 million to $20 million, returns to shareholders of Equity Company also double—from 10 percent to 20 percent. But returns to shareholders of Leverage Company more than double—from 10 percent to 30 percent. However, leverage works in the opposite direction as well. If earnings fall from $10 million to $5 million, a decline of 50 percent, returns to shareholders of Equity Company also fall by 50 percent—from 10 percent to 5 percent. By contrast, returns to shareholders of

Leverage Company fall from 10 percent to zero. Thus, leverage increases potential returns to shareholders but also increases risk.

Another problem with borrowing money is that an overreliance on borrowed funds may reduce management's flexibility in future financing decisions. If a company raises equity capital this year and needs to raise funds next year, it will probably be able to raise either debt or equity capital. But if it raises debt capital this year, it may be forced to raise equity capital next year.

Equity capital has drawbacks as well. Because shareholders are owners of the company, they usually have the right to vote on major company issues and elect the board of directors. Whenever new equity is sold, the control of existing shareholders is diluted, and the outcome of these votes could potentially change. One contentious subject today between companies and shareholders is whether shareholders should be able to vote on executive pay packages. The "Solving an Ethical Controversy" feature debates this issue.

Another disadvantage of equity capital is that it is more expensive than debt capital. First, creditors have a senior claim to the assets of a firm relative to shareholders. Because of this advantage, creditors are willing to accept a lower rate of return than shareholders are. Second, the firm can deduct interest payments on debt, reducing its taxable income and tax bill. Dividends paid to shareholders, on the other hand, are not tax deductible. A key component of the financial manager's job is to weigh the advantages and disadvantages of debt capital and equity capital, creating the most appropriate capital structure for his or her firm.

Mixing Short-Term and Long-Term Funds

Another decision financial managers face is determining the appropriate mix of short- and long-term funds. Short-term funds consist of current liabilities, and long-term funds consist of long-term debt and equity. Short-term funds are generally less expensive than long-term funds, but they also expose the firm to more risk. This is because short-term funds have to be renewed, or rolled over, frequently. Short-term interest rates can be volatile. During a recent 12-month period, for example, rates on commercial paper, a popular short-term financing option, ranged from a high of 6 percent to a low of less than 2 percent.[9]

Because short-term rates move up and down frequently, interest expense on short-term funds can change substantially from year to year. For instance, if a firm borrows $50 million for ten years at 5 percent interest, its annual interest expense is fixed at $2.5 million for the entire ten years. On the other hand, if it borrows $50 million for one year at a rate of 4 percent, its annual interest expense of $2 million is only fixed for that year. If interest rates increase the following year to 6 percent, $1 million will be added to the interest expense bill. Another potential risk of relying on short-term funds is availability. Even financially healthy firms can occasionally find it difficult to borrow money.

Because of the added risk of short-term funding, most firms choose to finance all of their long-term assets, and even a portion of their short-term assets, with long-term funds. Johnson & Johnson is typical of this choice. Figure 17.3 shows a recent balance sheet broken down between short- and long-term assets, and short- and long-term funds.

Dividend Policy

Along with decisions regarding capital structure and the mix of short- and long-term funds, financial managers also make decisions regarding a firm's dividend

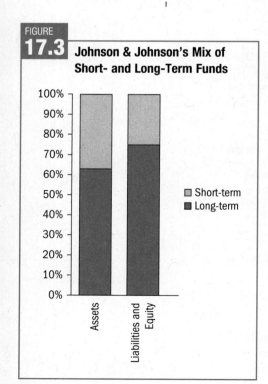

FIGURE 17.3 Johnson & Johnson's Mix of Short- and Long-Term Funds

■ Short-term
■ Long-term

Source: Johnson & Johnson balance sheet, Yahoo! Finance, http://finance.yahoo.com, accessed June 21, 2011.

policy. *Dividends* are periodic cash payments to shareholders. The most common type of dividend is paid quarterly and is often labeled as a *regular dividend*. Occasionally, firms make one-time special or extra dividend payments, as Microsoft did some years ago. Earnings that are paid in dividends are not reinvested in the firm and don't contribute additional equity capital.

Firms are under no legal obligation to pay dividends to shareholders. Although some companies pay generous dividends, others pay nothing. Until 2010, Starbucks never paid a dividend to its shareholders. In contrast, 3M has paid dividends for 30-plus consecutive years, during which time the amount has more than quadrupled. Companies that pay dividends try to increase them or at the very least hold them steady from year to year. However, in rare cases firms must cut or eliminate dividends. After heavily spending to launch and market its Nook e-reader, Barnes & Noble experienced a drop in profits despite the Nook's success. So the firm decided to temporarily suspend dividends to its shareholders, allowing it to continue pumping money into the business rather than increase its debt.[10]

Many factors determine a company's dividend policy, one of which is its investment opportunities. If a firm has numerous investment opportunities and wishes to finance some or all of them with equity funding, it will likely pay little, if any, of its earnings in dividends. Shareholders may actually want the company to retain earnings, because if they are reinvested, the firm's future profits, and the value of its shares, will increase faster. By contrast, a firm with more limited investment opportunities generally pays more of its earnings in dividends.

In addition to dividends, some firms buy back a portion of their outstanding stock. Home Depot, for instance, has repurchased more than $1 billion of stock over the past few years. Generally, shares are purchased on the secondary markets. The main purpose of share buy-backs is to raise the market value of the remaining shares, thus benefiting shareholders.

Jean Gill/iStockphoto

As a result of heavy spending for its Nook e-reader, Barnes & Noble temporarily suspended paying cash dividends.

Short-Term Funding Options

Many times throughout a year, an organization may discover that its cash needs exceed its available funds. Retailers generate surplus cash for most of the year, but they need to build up inventory during the late summer and fall to get ready for the holiday shopping season. Consequently, they often need funds to pay for merchandise until holiday sales generate revenue. Then they use the incoming funds to repay the amount they borrowed. In these instances, financial managers evaluate short-term sources of funds. By definition, short-term sources of funds are repaid within one year. Three major sources of short-term funds exist: trade credit, short-term loans, and commercial paper. Large firms often rely on a combination of all three sources of short-term financing.

Trade Credit

Trade credit is extended by suppliers when a firm receives goods or services, agreeing to pay for them at a later date. Trade credit is common in many industries such as retailing and manufacturing. Suppliers routinely ship billions of dollars of merchandise to retailers

Assessment Check ✓

1. Explain the concept of leverage.

2. Why do firms generally rely more on long-term funds than short-term funds?

3. What is an important determinant of a firm's dividend policy?

each day and are paid at a later date. Without trade credit, the retailing sector would probably look much different—with fewer selections. Under this system, the supplier records the transactions as an account receivable, and the retailer records it as an account payable. Target alone currently has more than $6.5 billion of accounts payable on its books. The main advantage of trade credit is its easy availability because credit sales are common in many industries. The main drawback to trade credit is that the amount a company can borrow is limited to the amount it purchases.

What is the cost of trade credit? If suppliers do not offer a cash discount, trade credit is effectively free. For example, assume a supplier offers trade credit under the terms net 30—meaning that the buyer has 30 days to pay. This is similar to borrowing $100 and repaying $100 in 30 days. The effective rate of interest is zero. However, some suppliers offer a discount if they are paid in cash. If a discount is offered, trade credit can get quite expensive. Now assume that a 2 percent discount is offered to cash buyers. If they do not take the discount, they have 30 days to pay. Essentially, then, if the buyer doesn't pay cash, it is borrowing $98 today and repaying $100 30 days from today. The annual interest rate on such a loan exceeds 24 percent.

Short-Term Loans

Loans from commercial banks are a significant source of short-term financing for businesses. Often businesses use these loans to finance inventory and accounts receivable. For example, late fall and early winter is the period of highest sales for a small manufacturer of ski equipment. To meet this demand, it has to begin building inventory during the summer. The manufacturer also has to finance accounts receivable (credit sales to customers) during the fall and winter. So it takes out a bank loan during the summer. As the inventory is sold and accounts receivable collected, the firm repays the loan.

There are two types of short-term bank loans: lines of credit and revolving credit agreements. A line of credit specifies the maximum amount the firm can borrow over a period of time, usually a year. The bank is under no obligation to actually lend the money, however. It does so only if funds are available. Most lines of credit require the borrower to repay the original amount, plus interest, within one year. By contrast, a revolving credit agreement is essentially a guaranteed line of credit—the bank guarantees that the funds will be available when needed. Banks typically charge a fee, on top of interest, for revolving credit agreements.

The cash budget is an important tool for determining the size of a line of credit because it shows the months when additional financing will be needed or when borrowed funds can be repaid. For instance, assume the ski manufacturer's cash budget indicates that it will need $2.5 million for the June through November period. The financial manager might set up a line of credit with the bank for $2.8 million. The extra $300,000 is for any unexpected cash outflows.

In addition to commercial banks, commercial finance companies also make short-term loans to businesses. While most bank loans are unsecured, meaning that no specific assets are pledged as collateral, loans from commercial finance companies are often secured with accounts receivable or inventory.

Another form of short-term financing using accounts receivable is called *factoring*. The business sells its accounts receivable to either a bank or finance company—called a *factor*—at a discount. The size of the discount determines the cost of the transaction. Factoring allows the firm to convert its receivables into cash quickly without worrying about collections.

The cost of short-term loans depends not only on the interest rate but also on the fees charged by the lender. In addition to fees, some lenders require the borrower to keep so-called *compensating balances*—5 to 20 percent of the outstanding loan amount—in a checking account. Compensating balances increase the effective cost of a loan since the borrower doesn't have full use of the amount borrowed.

Say, for example, that a firm borrows $100,000 for one year at 5 percent interest. The borrower will pay $5,000 in interest (5 percent × $100,000). If the lender requires that 10 percent of the loan amount be kept as compensating balance, the firm has use of only $90,000. However, because it still will pay $5,000 in interest, the effective rate on the loan is actually 5.56 percent ($5,000 divided by $90,000).

Commercial Paper

Commercial paper is a short-term IOU sold by a company; this concept was briefly described in Chapter 16. Commercial paper is typically sold in multiples of $100,000 to $1 million and has a maturity that ranges from 1 to 270 days. Most commercial paper is unsecured. It is an attractive source of financing because large amounts of money can be raised at rates that are typically 1 to 2 percent less that those charged by banks. At the end of a recent year, almost $1.15 trillion in commercial paper was outstanding.[11] Although commercial paper is an attractive short-term financing alternative, only a small percentage of businesses can issue it. That is because access to the commercial paper market has traditionally been restricted to large, financially strong corporations.

Assessment Check ✓

1. What are the three sources of short-term funding?
2. Explain trade credit.
3. Why is commercial paper an attractive short-term financing option?

Sources of Long-Term Financing

Funds from short-term sources can help a firm meet current needs for cash or inventory. A larger project or plan, however, such as acquiring another company or making a major investment in real estate or equipment, usually requires funds for a much longer period of time. Unlike short-term sources, long-term sources are repaid over many years.

Organizations acquire long-term funds from three sources. One is long-term loans obtained from financial institutions such as commercial banks, life insurance companies, and pension funds. A second source is bonds—certificates of indebtedness—sold to investors. A third source is equity financing acquired by selling stock in the firm or reinvesting company profits.

Public Sale of Stocks and Bonds

Public sales of securities such as stocks and bonds are a major source of funds for corporations. Such sales provide cash inflows for the issuing firm and either a share in its ownership (for a stock purchaser) or a specified rate of interest and repayment at a stated time (for a bond purchaser). Because stock and bond issues of many corporations are traded in the secondary markets, stockholders and bondholders can easily sell these securities. Recently, when a European debt crisis seemed likely, it caused a massive slowdown in bond sales. But as fears of a crisis eased later in the year, bond sales reached their highest level since the same time the previous year. As of midyear, companies had sold about $307 billion of U.S. corporate bonds.[12] Public sales of securities, however, can vary substantially from year to year depending on conditions in the financial markets. Bond sales, for instance, tend to be higher when interest rates are lower.

In Chapter 16, we discussed the process by which most companies sell securities publicly—through investment bankers via a process called *underwriting*. Investment bankers purchase the securities from the issuer and then resell them to investors. The issuer pays a fee to the investment banker, called an *underwriting discount*.

Private Placements

Some new stock or bond issues are not sold publicly but instead to a small group of major investors such as pension funds and insurance companies. These sales are referred to as *private placements*. Most private placements involve corporate debt issues. More than $120 billion in corporate bonds were sold privately in a recent year in the United States.[13]

It is often cheaper for a company to sell a security privately than publicly, and there is less government regulation with which to contend because SEC registration is not required. Institutional investors such as insurance companies and pension funds buy private placements because they typically carry slightly higher interest rates than publicly issued bonds. In addition, the terms of the issue can be tailored to meet the specific needs of both the issuer and the institutional investors. Of course, the institutional investor gives up liquidity because privately placed securities do not trade in secondary markets.

Venture Capitalists

venture capitalists raise money from wealthy individuals and institutional investors and invest the funds in promising firms.

Venture capitalists are an important source of long-term financing, especially to new companies. **Venture capitalists** raise money from wealthy individuals and institutional investors and invest these funds in promising firms. Venture capitalists also provide management consulting advice as well as funds. In exchange for their investment, venture capitalists become part owners of the business. If the business succeeds, venture capitalists can earn substantial profits. The "Going Green" feature describes how Intel has joined with two dozen venture capitalist firms to create the "Invest in America" alliance to fund research into clean technology among other innovations.

One of the largest venture capital firms is Draper Fisher Jurvetson, based in Menlo Park, California. During the past 20 years, DFJ has invested in hundreds of small start-ups including Hotmail (acquired by Microsoft) and Skype (acquired by eBay). Other firms in its $5.5 billion portfolio are Bright Source Energy, SpaceX, and Tumbleweed.[14]

Intel CEO, Paul Otellini, gives a speech in Washington, DC, announcing the creation of the Invest in America Alliance.

Justin Sullivan/Getty Images, Inc.

Private Equity Funds

Similar to venture capitalists, *private equity funds* are investment companies that raise funds from wealthy individuals and institutional investors and use those funds to make large investments

Going Green

Intel Invests in U.S. Technology

Paul Otellini, the CEO of Intel Corporation, the world's largest chip manufacturer, noted that other countries, among them China, India, and Taiwan, have overtaken the United States as centers of innovation in the technology industry. Concerned that the United States faces fierce competition from other countries worldwide, Otellini recently announced a new initiative. The "Invest in America Alliance" teams Intel with 17 technology companies—including Google, Microsoft, Dell, and General Electric—and 24 leading venture capital firms. The alliance plans to invest $3.5 billion in start-up technology companies in the United States over two years. Intel Capital, Intel's own investment sector, plans to invest $200 million. The money will go to businesses in innovative fields such as information technology, clean technology, and biotechnology. But the fund will also invest in newer industries such as molecular diagnostics, electric vehicle ecosystems, and wireless infrastructure.

Among the venture capital firms that have signed on are Advanced Technology Ventures, Kleiner Perkins Caufield & Byars, and Draper Fisher Jurvetson. Arvind Sodhani, the president of Intel Capital and Intel's executive vice president, said, "Venture capital investments have played an important role in creating jobs at home and keeping America at the leading edge of technology globally."

The alliance is also seeking commitments from the technology industry to increase their hiring of recent college graduates. Among those who have made the pledge are Google, Microsoft, Yahoo!, Adobe, and Dell. The alliance's goal is to create a total of about 10,500 jobs, mostly in computer science and engineering. But jobs will also be available in financial planning, marketing, and sales. Intel has promised to hire more recent graduates as well. "It would be a long-term mistake to let our future scientists and engineers sit idle after graduation," Otellini said.

Questions for Critical Thinking

1. Why does "going green" make good business sense for venture capitalists?
2. How are jobs in financial planning, marketing, and sales important to the technology industry?

Sources: Company Web site, http://www.intel.com, accessed June 21, 2011; Claire Cain Miller, "A $3.5 Billion Effort Aims to Help Tech Start-Ups," *The New York Times,* February 24, 2010, http://www.nytimes.com; Blake Ellis, "Intel Plans $3.5 Billion Investment Fund," *CNNMoney.com,* February 23, 2010, http://money.cnn.com; Lance Whitney, "Intel Alliance to Invest $3.5 Billion in U.S. Tech," *CNET News,* February 23, 2010, http://news.cnet.com; Chloe Albanesius, "Intel, Tech Giants Pledge $3.5B in U.S. Investment," *PCMag.com,* February 23, 2010, http://www.pcmag.com.

---

in both public and privately held companies. Unlike venture capital funds, which tend to focus on small, start-up companies, private equity funds invest in all types of businesses, including mature ones. For example, Cerberus Capital Management, a private equity fund, recently bought the military contractor DynCorp International for about $1.5 billion.[15] Often, private equity funds invest in transactions that take public companies private, or leveraged buyouts (LBOs). In these transactions, discussed in more detail in the next section, a public company reverts to private status. The "Hit & Miss" feature profiles another large private equity fund, Harvest Partners.

A variation of the private equity fund is the so-called *sovereign wealth fund.* These companies are owned by governments and invest in a variety of financial and real assets, such as real estate. Although sovereign wealth funds generally make investments based on the best risk-return trade-off, political, social, and strategic considerations also play roles in their investment decisions.

Recently, several sovereign wealth funds made large investments in major U.S. financial firms, including Morgan Stanley and Citigroup. For instance, the Abu Dhabi Investment Authority (ADIA) invested in Citigroup, buying $7.5 billion in "equity shares" and becoming the giant bank's largest single shareholder in the process. Subsequently, ADIA filed suit against Citigroup, claiming that the bank had misled ADIA about its financial health, which Citigroup denied. A year later, Citigroup announced the reinstatement of dividend payments and a reverse stock split, whereupon billionare Prince Alwaleed of neighboring Saudi Arabia declared his support.[16] The assets of the ten largest sovereign wealth funds are shown in Figure 17.4. Together, these ten funds have more than $2.3 trillion in assets.

Hit & Miss

Harvest Partners Grows Its Investments

Is it possible to have too much money to spend in too little time? Harvest Partners and other private equity firms have just a few years to invest about $500 billion.

Harvest Partners, based in New York City, is a private equity firm that specializes in leveraged buyouts and growth financing. It focuses on companies in the United States, the rest of North America, and western Europe that have well-established sales or operations in the United States. The firm manages funds emphasizing private equity and debt investments. Harvest Partners makes equity investments of anywhere from $30 million to $100 million in companies whose revenues run between $100 million and $750 million. It prefers to be a control investor and become a partner in the companies it finances. Those companies tend to be middle-market firms that need investment to adapt to changing times and markets.

Private equity firms usually have three to six years to reinvest funds they have raised from client investors. If they cannot or do not, they must return that money. During the boom years, Harvest Partners raised $815 million from client investors. So far it has reinvested about $293 million. Now the firm is facing a 2012 deadline to reinvest the remaining $522 million.

Not all private equity investments are successful. Harvest Partners had owned the equity of the Natural Products Group, a manufacturer of organic shampoos and soaps. But when NPG went bankrupt, Harvest Partners lost its entire investment.

Recently Harvest Partners joined MTP Energy Management to invest $80 million in Regency Energy Partners, a middle-market natural gas company. Michael DeFlorio, a senior managing director of Harvest Partners, said that Regency "embodies our investment strategy focused on exceptionally managed . . . midstream service providers participating in the most promising resource plays in the industry."

Questions for Critical Thinking

1. Describe some of the risks encountered by a firm such as Harvest Partners.
2. Why do you think Harvest Partners and other equity firms are required to invest their clients' funds within a limited time frame?

Sources: Company Web site, http://www.harvpart.com, accessed April 27, 2011; "Harvest Partners," profile from *Bloomberg Businessweek*, http://investing.businessweek.com, accessed June 24, 2010; Julie Cresswell, "On Wall Street, So Much Cash, So Little Time," *The New York Times*, June 23, 2010, http://www.nytimes.com; Emily Thornton, "LBO Firms Can't Spend $503 Billion as Deadlines Loom (Update 1)," *Bloomberg.com*, March 10, 2010, http://www.bloomberg.com; Brian Baxter, "The Bankruptcy Files: Curtain Drops on Movie Gallery, Air America Loses Frequency," *AM Law Daily*, February 4, 2010, http://amlawdaily.typepad.com "Harvest Partners, MTP Energy Invest in Regency Energy Partners," *iStockAnalyst*, September 7, 2009, http://www.istockanalyst.com.

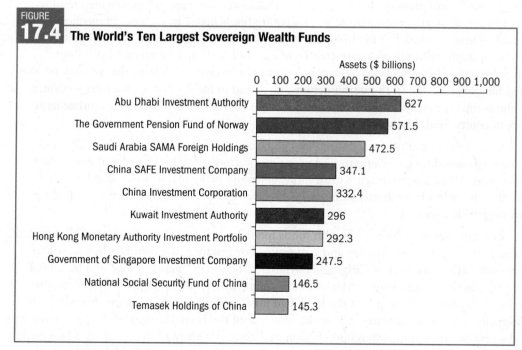

FIGURE 17.4 The World's Ten Largest Sovereign Wealth Funds

Assets ($ billions)

Fund	Assets
Abu Dhabi Investment Authority	627
The Government Pension Fund of Norway	571.5
Saudi Arabia SAMA Foreign Holdings	472.5
China SAFE Investment Company	347.1
China Investment Corporation	332.4
Kuwait Investment Authority	296
Hong Kong Monetary Authority Investment Portfolio	292.3
Government of Singapore Investment Company	247.5
National Social Security Fund of China	146.5
Temasek Holdings of China	145.3

Source: Sovereign Wealth Fund Institute, "Sovereign Wealth Fund Rankings," http://www.swfinstitute.org, accessed June 21, 2011.

Hedge Funds

Hedge funds are private investment companies open only to qualified large investors. In recent years, hedge funds have become a significant presence in U.S. financial markets. Before the recent recession, some analysts estimated that hedge funds accounted for about 60 percent of all secondary bond market trading and around one-third of all activity on stock exchanges. More recently, hedge fund providers have begun selling these funds, in the form of mutual funds, to smaller investors for as little as $1,000.[17] They are also significant investors in noninvestment grade, or junk, bonds. Hedge funds are estimated to have total assets that exceed $1.82 trillion.[18] Unlike mutual funds, hedge funds are not regulated by the SEC.

Traditionally, hedge funds, unlike venture capitalists and private equity funds, did not make direct investments in companies, preferring instead to purchase existing stock and bond issues.

Assessment Check ☑

1. What is the most common type of security sold privately?
2. Explain venture capital.
3. What is a sovereign wealth fund?

Mergers, Acquisitions, Buyouts, and Divestitures

Chapter 5 briefly described mergers and acquisitions. A merger is a transaction in which two or more firms combine into one company. In an acquisition, one firm buys the assets and assumes the obligations of another firm. Chapter 5 also listed the classifications of mergers and acquisitions—vertical, horizontal, and conglomerate—and noted that many of these transactions involve large sums of money. A recent example is Hewlett-Packard's acquisition of the smart phone maker Palm. In this section, we focus on the financial implications of not only mergers and acquisitions but also buyouts and divestitures.

Note that even in a merger, there is a buyer and seller. The seller is often referred to as the *target*. Financial managers evaluate a proposed merger or acquisition in much the same way they would evaluate any large investment—by comparing the costs and benefits. To acquire a company, a firm typically offers a higher price than the current market price for the target's shares. The action usually triggers a fluctuation in the stock prices of both firms. When Intel purchased Internet security firm McAfee, Intel's share price dropped 3.5 percent to $18.90, while McAfee's price rose 57 percent to $47.[19]

When the buyer makes what is known as a **tender offer** for the target's shares, it specifies a price and the form of payment. The buyer can offer cash, securities, or a combination of the two. The Intel offer to buy McAfee was a combination of cash and short-term investments totaling $7.68 billion. The tender offer can be friendly, meaning it is endorsed by the target's board of directors, or unfriendly. Shareholders of both the buyer and target must vote to approve a merger.

Justifying such a premium requires the financial manager also to estimate the benefits of a proposed merger. These benefits could take the form of cost savings from economies of scale or reduced workforces or the buyer getting a bargain price for the target's assets. Sometimes, a buyer finds that the most cost-effective method of entering a new market is simply to buy an existing company that serves the market. Johnson & Johnson has a long history of making such acquisitions. When it decided to enter the contact lens market several years ago, Johnson & Johnson bought Vistakon, the firm that invented disposable contact lenses under the brand name Acuvue. Whatever the reasons, the term used to describe the benefits produced by a merger or acquisition is *synergy*—the notion that the combined firm is worth more than the buyer and target are individually.

tender offer offer made by a firm to the target firm's shareholders specifying a price and the form of payment.

Leveraged buyouts, or **LBOs**, were briefly introduced in the preceding section. In an LBO, public shareholders are bought out, and the firm reverts to private status. The term *leverage* comes from the fact that many of these transactions are financed with high degrees of debt—often in excess of 75 percent. Private equity companies and hedge funds provide equity and debt financing for many LBOs. The firm's incumbent senior management is often part of the buyout group. LBO activity decreased sharply with the recent economic downturn. As the economy began to recover, LBO activity increased again. According to Standard & Poor's, LBO financing recently grew to $13.6 billion, about 15 times the amount from the same time a year before. With more than $500 billion in funds, private equity companies and others were looking for acquisitions.[20]

Why do so many LBOs occur? One reason is that private companies enjoy benefits that public companies do not. Private companies are not required to publish financial results, are subject to less SEC oversight, and are not pressured to produce the short-term profits often demanded by Wall Street. Some argue that LBOs, because of the high degree of debt, enforce more discipline on management to control costs. Although LBOs do have advantages, history has shown that many companies that go private reemerge as public companies several years later.

In a sense, a **divestiture** is the reverse of a merger. That is, a company sells assets such as subsidiaries, product lines, or production facilities. Two types of divestitures exist: sell-offs and spin-offs. In a *sell-off*, assets are sold by one firm to another. Verizon Wireless, an affiliate of Verizon Communications Inc., sold some of its wireless assets to AT&T. AT&T then announced plans to roll out its 3G wireless service to about 1.6 million former Verizon subscribers in rural areas across 18 states.

The other type of divestiture is a *spin-off*. In this transaction, the assets sold form a new firm. Shareholders of the divesting firm become shareholders of the new firm as well. For example, Motorola announced that it would split into two publicly traded firms. The parent company will handle its core business of mobile converged devices, digital home-entertainment devices, and video voice and data solutions. The spin-off firm will handle heavy-duty two-way radios, mobile computers, public security systems, wireless network infrastructure, and other business-oriented goods and services. Both entities will continue to use the Motorola brand name, with the parent company now named Motorola Mobile Devices and Home. Motorola shareholders will receive shares of the new company, Motorola Enterprise Mobility and Networks.

Firms divest assets for several reasons. Sometimes divestitures result from prior acquisitions that didn't work out as well as expected. In early 2001, America Online and Time Warner merged to create AOL Time Warner, Inc. Nine years later, Time Warner announced it would spin off AOL. The merger—now considered one of the worst mistakes in corporate history—failed to generate the much-heralded synergies between the two companies. Shortly after the merger, AOL had 27 million subscribers; more recently, that number had shrunk to about 6.3 million.

In other cases, a firm makes a strategic decision to concentrate on its core businesses and decides to divest anything that falls outside this core. That was the explanation that Motorola gave in response to criticism that the company had become too large and had seen its mobile-device business overtaken first by Nokia, then Samsung, and then Apple. Still another explanation relates to antitrust issues. Verizon originally wanted to buy Alltel. The U.S. Department of Justice required Verizon to divest itself of assets in markets where Alltel was already operating—mainly rural areas in many central states—before it would approve the purchase.

What's Ahead

Contemporary Business concludes with five appendixes. Appendix A, "Business Law," outlines the main legal issues concerning business. It reviews the types of laws, the regulatory environment of business, and the core of business law, including discussions of contract law and property law. Appendix B examines risk management and insurance. It describes the concept of risk, alternative ways of dealing with risk, and the various kinds of insurance available to business and individuals. Appendix C discusses some of the important components of personal financial planning, such as budgeting, credit, and retirement planning. Appendix D describes how to write an effective business plan, and Appendix E discusses career searches and options to help you prepare for your future in business.

Summary of Learning Goals

⌈1⌉ Define *finance,* and explain the role of financial managers.

Finance deals with planning, obtaining, and managing a company's funds to accomplish its objectives efficiently and effectively. The major responsibilities of financial managers are to develop and implement financial plans and determine the most appropriate sources and uses of funds. The chief financial officer (CFO) heads a firm's finance organization. Three senior executives reporting to the CFO are the vice president for financial management, the treasurer, and the controller. When making decisions, financial professionals continually seek to balance risks with expected financial returns.

Assessment Check Answers ✓

1.1 What is the structure of the finance function at the typical firm? The head of the finance function of a firm has the title of chief financial officer (CFO) and generally reports directly to the firm's chief executive officer. Reporting to the CFO are the treasurer, the controller, and the vice president for financial management.

1.2 Explain the risk–return trade-off. Financial managers strive to maximize the wealth of their firm's shareholders by striking the optimal balance between risk and return. Often, decisions involving the highest potential returns expose the firm to the greatest risks.

⌈2⌉ Describe the components of a financial plan and the financial planning process.

A financial plan is a document that specifies the funds needed by a firm for a given period of time, the timing of inflows and outflows, and the most appropriate sources and uses of funds. The financial plan addresses three questions: What funds will be required during the planning period? When will funds be needed? Where will funds be obtained? Three steps are involved in the financial planning process: forecasting sales over a future period of time, estimating the expected level of profits over the planning period, and determining the additional assets needed to support additional sales.

Assessment Check Answers ✓

2.1 What three questions does a financial plan address? The financial plan addresses three questions: What funds will be required during the planning period? When will funds be needed? Where will funds be obtained?

2.2 Explain the steps involved in preparing a financial plan. The first step is to forecast sales over a future period of time. Second, the financial manager must estimate the expected level of profits over the planning period. The final step is to determine the additional assets needed to support additional sales.

⌈3⌉ Outline how organizations manage their assets.

Assets consist of what a firm owns and also represent the uses of its funds. Sound financial management requires assets to be acquired and managed as effectively and efficiently as possible. The major current assets are cash, marketable securities, accounts receivable, and inventory. The goal of cash management is to have sufficient funds on hand to meet day-to-day transactions and pay any unexpected expenses. Excess cash should be invested in marketable securities, which are low-risk securities with short maturities. Managing accounts receivable, which are uncollected credit sales, involves collecting funds owed the firm as quickly as possible while also offering sufficient credit to customers to generate increased sales. The main goal of inventory management is to minimize the overall cost of inventory. Production, marketing, and logistics also play roles in determining proper inventory levels. Capital investment analysis is the process by which financial managers make decisions on long-lived assets. This involves comparing the benefits and costs of a proposed investment. Managing international assets poses additional challenges for the financial manager, including the problem of fluctuating exchange rates.

Assessment Check Answers ✔

3.1 Why do firms often choose to invest excess cash in marketable securities? Cash earns no rate of return, which is why excess cash should be invested in marketable securities. These are low-risk securities that have short maturities and can be easily sold in the secondary markets. As a result, they are easily converted back into cash, when needed.

3.2 What are the two aspects of accounts receivable management? The two aspects of accounts receivable management are deciding on an overall credit policy (whether to offer credit and, if so, on what terms) and determining which customers will be offered credit.

3.3 Explain the difference between an expansion decision and a replacement decision. An expansion decision involves decisions about offering new products or building or acquiring new production facilities. A replacement decision is one that considers whether to replace an existing asset with a new one.

⌜4⌟ Compare the two major sources of funds for a business, and explain the concept of leverage.

Businesses have two sources of funds: debt capital and equity capital. Debt capital represents funds obtained through borrowing, and equity capital consists of funds provided by the firm's owners. The mix of debt and equity capital is known as the firm's capital structure, and the financial manager's job is to find the proper mix. Leverage is a technique of increasing the rate of return on funds invested by borrowing. However, leverage increases risk. Also, overreliance on borrowed funds may reduce management's flexibility in future financing decisions. Equity capital also has drawbacks. When additional equity capital is sold, the control of existing shareholders is diluted. In addition, equity capital is more expensive than debt capital. Financial managers are also faced with decisions concerning the appropriate mix of short- and long-term funds. Short-term funds are generally less expensive than long-term funds but expose firms to more risk. Another decision involving financial managers is determining the firm's dividend policy.

Assessment Check Answers ✔

4.1 Explain the concept of leverage. Leverage is a technique of increasing the rate of return by borrowing funds. But leverage also increases risk.

4.2 Why do firms generally rely more on long-term funds rather than short-term funds? Although short-term funds are generally less expensive than long-term funds, short-term funds expose the firm to additional risks. The cost of short-term funds can vary substantially from year to year. In addition, at times short-term funds can be difficult to obtain.

4.3 What is an important determinant of a firm's dividend policy? The main determinant of a firm's dividend policy is its investment opportunities. Firms with more profitable investment opportunities often pay less in dividends than do firms with fewer such opportunities.

⌜5⌟ Identify sources of short-term financing for business operations.

The three major short-term funding options are trade credit, short-term loans from banks and other financial institutions, and commercial paper. Trade credit is extended by suppliers when a firm receives goods or services, agreeing to pay for them at a later date. Trade credit is relatively easy to obtain and costs nothing unless a supplier offers a cash discount. Loans from commercial banks are a significant source of short-term financing and are often used to finance accounts receivable and inventory. Loans can be either unsecured or secured, with accounts receivable or inventory pledged as collateral. Commercial paper is a short-term IOU sold by a company. Although large amounts of money can be raised through the sale of commercial paper, usually at rates below those charged by banks, access to the commercial paper market is limited to large, financially strong corporations.

Assessment Check Answers ✔

5.1 What are the three sources of short-term funding? The three sources of short-term funding are trade credit, short-term loans from banks and other financial institutions, and commercial paper.

5.2 Explain trade credit. Trade credit is extended by suppliers when a buyer agrees to pay for goods and services at a later date. Trade credit is relatively easy to obtain and costs nothing unless a cash discount is offered.

5.3 Why is commercial paper an attractive short-term financing option? Commercial paper is an attractive financing option because large amounts can be raised by selling commercial paper at rates that are generally lower than those charged by banks.

⌜6⌟ Discuss long-term financing options.

Long-term funds are repaid over many years. There are three sources: long-term loans obtained from financial institutions, bonds sold to investors, and equity financing. Public sales of securities represent a major source of funds for corporations. These securities can generally be traded in secondary markets. Public sales can vary substantially from year to year depending on the conditions in the financial markets. Private placements are securities sold to a small number of institutional investors. Most private placements involve debt securities. Venture capitalists are an important source of financing for new companies. If the business succeeds, venture capitalists stand to earn large profits. Private equity funds are investment companies that raise funds from wealthy individuals and institutional investors and use the funds to make investments in both public and private companies. Unlike venture capitalists, private equity funds invest in all types of businesses. Sovereign wealth funds are investment companies owned by governments.

Assessment Check Answers ✓

6.1 What is the most common type of security sold privately? Corporate debt securities are the most common type of security sold privately.

6.2 Explain venture capital. Venture capitalists are important sources of funding, especially for new companies. Venture capitalists invest in these companies by taking an ownership position. If the business succeeds, venture capitalists can earn substantial profits.

6.3 What is a sovereign wealth fund? A sovereign wealth fund is a government-owned investment company. These companies make investments in a variety of financial and real assets, such as real estate. Although most investments are based on the best risk-return trade-off, political, social, and strategic considerations play roles as well.

⌐7¬ **Describe mergers, acquisitions, buyouts, and divestitures.**
⌊ ⌋

A merger is a combination of two or more firms into one company. An acquisition is a transaction in which one company buys another. Even in a merger, there is a buyer and a seller (called the *target*). The buyer offers cash, securities, or a combination of the two in return for the target's shares. Mergers and acquisitions should be evaluated as any large investment is, by comparing the costs with the benefits. Synergy is the term used to describe the benefits a merger or acquisition is expected to produce. A leveraged buyout (LBO) is a transaction in which shares are purchased from public shareholders, and the company reverts to private status. Usually LBOs are financed with substantial amounts of borrowed funds. Private equity companies are often major financers of LBOs. Divestitures are the opposite of mergers, in which companies sell assets such as subsidiaries, product lines, or production facilities. A sell-off is a divestiture in which assets are sold to another firm. In a spin-off, a new firm is created from the assets divested. Shareholders of the divesting firm become shareholders of the new firm as well.

Assessment Check Answers ✓

7.1 Define *synergy*. Synergy is the term used to describe the benefits produced by a merger or acquisition. It is the notion that the combined firm is worth more than the buyer and the target are individually.

7.2 What is an LBO? An LBO—a leveraged buyout—is a transaction whereby public shareholders are bought out, and the firm reverts to private status. LBOs are usually financed with large amounts of borrowed money.

7.3 What are the two types of divestitures? A sell-off is a divestiture in which assets are sold to another firm. In a spin-off, a new firm is created from the assets divested. Shareholders of the divesting firm become shareholders of the new firm as well.

■ Business Terms You Need to Know

finance 568
financial managers 568
risk-return trade-off 569

financial plan 571
capital structure 576
leverage 576

venture
  capitalists 582
tender offer 585

leveraged
  buyouts (LBOs) 586
divestiture 586

■ Review Questions

1. Explain the risk-return trade-off and give two examples.
2. Describe the financial planning process. How does asset intensity affect a financial plan?
3. What are the principal considerations when determining an overall credit policy? How do the actions of competitors affect a firm's credit policy?
4. Why do exchange rates pose a challenge for financial managers of companies with international operations?
5. Discuss the concept of leverage. Use a numerical example to illustrate the effect of leverage.

6. What are the advantages and disadvantages of both debt and equity financing?
7. Compare and contrast the three sources of short-term financing.
8. Define *venture capitalist, private equity fund, sovereign wealth fund,* and *hedge fund*. Which of the four invests the most money in start-up companies?
9. Briefly describe the mechanics of a merger or acquisition.
10. Why do firms divest assets?

Projects and Teamwork Applications

1. Assume you would like to start a business. Put together a rough financial plan that addresses the three financial planning questions listed in the text.

2. Working with a partner, assume that a firm needs $10 million in additional long-term capital. It currently has no debt and $40 million in equity. The options are issuing a ten-year bond (with an interest rate of 7 percent) or selling $10 million in new equity. You expect next year's earnings before interest and taxes to be $5 million. (The firm's tax rate is 35 percent.) Prepare a memo outlining the advantages and disadvantages of debt and equity financing. Using the numbers provided, prepare a numerical illustration of leverage similar to the one shown in Figure 17.2.

3. Your new small business has really grown, but now it needs a substantial infusion of capital. A venture capital firm has agreed to invest the money you need. In return, the venture capital firm will own 75 percent of the business, and you will be replaced as CEO by someone chosen by the venture capitalist. You will retain the titles of founder and chairman of the board. Would you be willing to take the money but lose control over your business? Why or why not?

4. Working in a small team, select three publicly traded companies. Visit each firm's Web site. Most have a section devoted to information for investors. Review each firm's dividend policy. Does the company pay dividends? If so, when did it begin paying dividends? Have dividends increased each year, or have they fluctuated from year to year? Is the company currently repurchasing shares? Has it done so in the past? Prepare a report summarizing your findings.

5. As noted in the chapter, one of the most unfortunate mergers in corporate history involved Time Warner and America Online. Research this merger. Why did analysts expect it to be successful? Why did it fail? What has happened to AOL since then?

Web Assignments

1. **Jobs in financial management.** Visit the Web site listed here to explore careers in finance. How many people currently work as financial managers? What is the projected increase in employment over the next 10 to 20 years? What is the average level of compensation?

   http://www.bls.gov/oco/ocos010.htm

2. **Capital structure.** Go to the Web site listed here to access recent financial statements for the retailer Costco. Click on "balance sheet." What is the firm's current capital structure (the breakdown between debt and equity)? Has it changed significantly over the past five years? Why would a firm such as Costco choose to become more or less levered?

   http://moneycentral.msn.com/investor/invsub/results/statemnt.aspx?symbol=cost

3. **Mergers and acquisitions.** Using a news source, such as Google News (http://news.google.com) or Yahoo! News (http://news.yahoo.com), search for a recent merger or acquisition announcement. An example would be Hewlett-Packard's acquisition of Palm. (A link is shown here.) Print out the articles and bring them to class.

   http://www.hp.com/hpinfo/newsroom/press/2010/100428xa.html

Note: Internet Web addresses change frequently. If you don't find the exact sites listed, you may need to access the organization's home page and search from there or use a search engine such as Bing or Google.

CASE 17.1   ConocoPhillips Divests to Return to Its Core

ConocoPhillips, with headquarters in Houston, Texas, is the third largest American oil company. It has nearly 30,000 employees in offices in 30 countries around the world. But for two years running, Conoco did poorly in the New York Stock Exchange, with its shares losing 40 percent of their value. Conoco more than doubled its debt when it bought Burlington Resources Inc., a natural-gas producer, for $36 billion. At the end of a recent year, Conoco's debt was three times that of the largest U.S. oil company, ExxonMobil, even though ExxonMobil was almost twice Conoco's size in terms of revenue. How could Conoco turn itself around?

At its annual analyst meeting, the company announced plans to enhance its value to its shareholders by increasing dividends by 10 percent and buying back some shares of its stock. Another goal is to raise $10 billion by 2012.

ConocoPhillips will raise these funds through divestiture, selling off some of its noncore assets. The company said that these assets did not fit well strategically with its core operations, they had high operation costs, and they were marketable. The company acknowledged that it would lose from 80,000 to 120,000 barrels of oil production per day and 400 to 600 million barrels of oil equivalent in reserve. But it hoped to emerge leaner and stronger, with a renewed focus on core projects that would bring in a higher return on investment.

Jim Mulva, the chairman and CEO, said, "We are focused on creating and delivering value to our shareholders. We are taking decisive action to sell assets, reduce debt, build on our record of shareholder distributions, and improve returns while growing production and reserves per share,"

Some analysts believed that Conoco's first priority was to sell its 9 percent stake in Syncrude, which one analyst referred to as one of Conoco's "crown jewels." Syncrude Canada Ltd. is located in the province of Alberta, just north of Montana, and is the world's largest producer of synthetic crude oil from oil sand deposits. Conoco recently announced that it sold its share in Syncrude to China's Sinopec for $4.65 billion, pending approval by the Chinese and Canadian governments. Mulva declared, "[W]e are pleased that [Sinopec] has recognized the value of this quality asset."

Another of Conoco's noncore assets was its 20 percent share in Lukoil, Russia's biggest oil producer. Conoco had invested heavily in Lukoil in hopes of large profits on some joint projects with Lukoil, but those profits had never materialized. This was in part because of strict Russian regulations concerning foreign companies in important industries. Lukoil's CEO, Vagit Alekperov, commented, "Initially, we were aiming for a large package of joint

projects, but it turned out to be rather narrow, which probably also disappointed [Conoco]." At first, Conoco hoped Lukoil would buy back half of its stake, but Lukoil turned that offer down. Conoco then offered those shares for sale on the open market, keeping a 10 percent share in Lukoil. Conoco hopes to earn about $5 billion from that sale and use those funds to repurchase some of its stock from shareholders.

Conoco's 25 percent share in the Rockies Express Pipeline is another of the company's "crown jewels." This high-speed, natural-gas pipeline runs almost 1,700 miles from northwestern Colorado to eastern Ohio. Conoco has offered its stake in the Rockies Express Pipeline for sale. Will ConocoPhillips achieve its goal of raising $10 billion by 2012? Time will tell.

Questions for Critical Thinking

1. Why is it important for ConocoPhillips to increase the value of its shares for its investors?
2. Research ConocoPhillips. How close has it come to raising the desired $10 billion?

Sources: Company Web site, ConocoPhillips, http://www.conocophillips.com, accessed June 21, 2011; Company Web site, Syncrude Canada Ltd., http://www.syncrude.ca, accessed June 21, 2011; Company Web site, China Petroleum and Chemical Corporation (Sinopec), http://english.sinopec.com, accessed June 21, 2011; Company Web site, Lukoil Oil Company, http://www.lukoil.com, accessed June 21, 2011; Company Web site, Rockies Express Pipeline, http://www.kindermorgan.com, accessed June 21, 2011; "ConocoPhillips Sells Syncrude Stake to Sinopec," press release, *Trading Markets.com,* June 30, 2010, http://www.tradingmarkets.com; Nastassia Astrasheuskaya, "LUKOIL CEO Sees Conoco Keeping 10 Pct Stake-Paper," *Reuters,* June 24, 2010, http://af.reuters.com; Steve Gelsi, "ConocoPhillips Sells Syncrude Stake for $4.65 Billion," *MarketWatch,* April 12, 2010, http://www.marketwatch.com; Eric Fox, "ConocoPhillips Aims to Boost Returns," *Investopedia,* March 26, 2010, http://stocks.investopedia.com; "Conoco Phillips Ups Ante for Shareholders," *Rigzone,* March 24, 2010, http://www.rigzone.com; Bloomberg News, "Lukoil Doesn't Plan to Buy Shares from ConocoPhillips," *Houston Chronicle,* March 23, 2010, http://www.chron.com; Edward Klump, "Conoco's Divestiture Plan Seen Hinging on Syncrude (Update 2)," *Bloomberg Businessweek,* February 25, 2010, http://www.businessweek.com.

Top Hedge Fund Managers Earn Record Paychecks

CASE 17.2

Along with the rest of the banking and investment industry, hedge fund managers experienced steep drops in income during the recent recession. But as the economy

began to revive, the 25 top-earning hedge fund managers earned $25.3 billion. That figure shattered even the old record, set in the boom days before the crisis.

One of those managers was David Tepper of Appaloosa Management. Other investors feared that the banking sector would collapse again, but Tepper bet that the federal government would step in to prevent the biggest banks from failing. In late 2008 and early 2009, he invested heavily in preferred shares and bonds of the big banks, among other seemingly losing prospects. Tepper, formerly of Goldman Sachs, won big, earning $4 billion. "We bet on the country's revival," he said. "Those who keep their heads while others are panicking do well." The U.S. Treasury Department apparently agreed with him, because it also bought preferred stock in troubled banks to help shore them up. The Treasury has since sold many of those stocks at a handsome profit.

Hedge funds are elite, private investment companies that are open only to highly qualified, large investors. Unlike mutual funds, hedge funds are not regulated by the Securities and Exchange Commission. During the heady days before the financial crisis, hedge funds earned huge profits. Their managers did well, too, because they usually take a significant percentage of a hedge fund's annual earnings. When the crisis struck, even these funds experienced losses in the double digits, and their managers saw their income drop by as much as 50 percent. But when the market rallied, hedge funds resurged as well. Of the 25 top hedge fund managers, the lowest earner made $350 million.

As the United States and the rest of the world economies recovered, the news media reported the immense salaries of CEOs and other top corporate executives at banks and large brokerage houses. The stories stirred the critics, especially because ordinary people were losing their jobs, homes, and health insurance. But some analysts believe that hedge fund managers such as David Tepper earned their huge salaries because they dared to take big risks in the hope of big rewards.

Of course, not all hedge funds did well when the stock market revived. The gap between the highest-earning hedge funds and the losing ones grew wider. Nadia Papagiannis, a hedge fund analyst at Morningstar Inc., said, "The hedge funds that survived 2008 were able to capture the gains on the way up in 2009. This year is not going to be as lucrative as last year. There's not enough of room [*sic*] for another rally as big as we saw in '09."

Questions for Critical Thinking

1. Compare hedge funds with mutual funds.
2. Do you agree that the top hedge fund managers deserve their high salaries? Why or why not?

Sources: Jim Pavia, "Hedge Fund Manager Made $4B Last Year. And He Deserved It," *InvestmentNews,* April 8, 2010, http://www.investmentnews.com; Ben Rooney, "Hedge Fund Manager Paycheck: $4 Billion," *CNNMoney.com,* April 1, 2010, http://money.cnn.com; Jim Kim, "Hedge Fund Managers Earn Record Pay in 2009," *FierceFinance,* April 1, 2010, http://www.fiercefinance.com; Edward Helmore, "Hedge Fund Pay Soars—But 2010 Could be Tougher," *First Post,* April 1, 2010, http://www.thefirstpost.co.uk; Nelson D. Schwartz and Louise Story, "Pay of Hedge Fund Managers Roared Back Last Year," *The New York Times,* March 31, 2010, http://www.nytimes.com.

CASE 17.3 Comet Skateboards Rides the Triple Bottom Line

Jason Salfi, co-founder and president of Comet Skateboards, is the first to admit he can let the wheels get away from him. Since the inception of Comet Skateboards, he estimates that he has personally "tanked the company four times. I started the company with a friend and we would sacrifice everything for quality," Salfi admits. It's easy to see how this could happen. Salfi loves skateboarding and he's a fanatic about building the best skateboards on the market with the most sustainable materials available.

During the first years of production—when Comet moved from California to Ithaca, New York in order to source bio-composite materials—Salfi and his partner paid top dollar for all the materials they used in building the boards. "We weren't really watching how much money we were making," Salfi says sheepishly. They were so wrapped up in the excitement of developing and manufacturing an entirely new class of skateboard, they forgot to watch the bank account balance. Salfi recalls that they did all the stereotypical things that small start-ups do to obtain financing—maxed out their credit cards, got friends and family to co-sign for loans, found angel investors. But Comet Skateboards just seemed to roll through the money without enough return to ensure its survival.

Then the firm hired a manager to specialize in financial details. With a professional in place, Salfi began to understand the real and potential impacts certain buying decisions would have on the bottom line, and the way cash flow would affect getting products to the marketplace. Now, Comet can forecast better how a product release will affect cash flow, and how that in turn will affect the way they as a business can reach customers. "Ultimately we're trying to create a sustainable business platform to get our sustainable business vision out there in the marketplace," explains Salfi. But they couldn't do this without managing the company's financial resources.

Comet Skateboards is considered a triple bottom line company, carrying the B Corporation logo. This means that Comet strives to create benefit for the company owners (profit), the community (people), and the environment (planet). Currently there are more than two hundred B Corporations in thirty industries around the nation. Each company has submitted to rigorous evaluation and has put written standards in place addressing social and environmental responsibility. Everything that Comet does, from its closed-loop manufacturing process to its community involvement, refers to its triple bottom line commitment.

Jason Salfi insists that managing the finances for a triple bottom line company is pretty much the same as managing the finances for a traditional company. But there are some differences, particularly in the procurement of raw materials, energy use, and waste disposal. Also, triple bottom line companies are held accountable for the way they treat employees and how they are involved in the community. "The 'magic' is making sure we can afford all that," observes Salfi. "It's just a matter of prioritization. We're not going on $50,000 golf retreats. We're reinvesting the capital we have in the materials we use and the way we interact with people."

Despite the fact that he says he didn't pay attention to finances in the company's early days, Salfi has a good grasp on Comet's role in the larger economic picture. He likes the idea of projecting the impact Comet has on consumers' buying decisions, particularly young people. Teenagers who choose Comet skateboards are choosing products that are made by a triple bottom line firm. "If you look at the way a 14-year-old decides to buy things

for the rest of his or her life, and you look at the number of decisions that young person is going to make over the span of 50 or 60 years, you could extrapolate that we have impacted 1,000 people in a certain way that could eventually transfer billions of dollars toward socially responsible businesses," explains Salfi. "We're influencing the buying decisions of youth."

Salfi believes that, decades ago, "commerce used to be about improving the quality of life, but somewhere along the line, profits skewed motivations." He likes the idea of the triple bottom line rebalancing the priorities of business. "We like to think that as a B Corporation, we are part of a group that wants to bring back the original motivation for business, which was all about creating an improved quality of life for everyone, not just a select few." It might actually be possible for a few well-engineered skateboards to change the world.

Questions for Critical Thinking

1. Hiring a financial manager was a major step for Comet Skateboards. Identify some of the factors the manager would have to consider when creating a plan for risk-return trade-off.

2. What might be some short-term funding options for Comet? Some long-term options? Which would be best for this company, and why?

3. Suppose a larger firm approached Comet with an offer of acquisition. Create a chart outlining the major pros and cons of such an offer.

4. How might Comet's designation as a B Corporation affect the way it answers the three essential questions for building a financial plan?

Sources: Comet Skateboards Web site, http://cometskateboards.com, accessed June 21, 2011; "GOOD Products," Halogen TV, http://www.halogentv.com, accessed August 20, 2010; Nadia Hosni, "Triple Bottom Line: Comet Skateboards," *Tonic,* April 27, 2010, http://www.tonic.com.

GREENSBURG, KS
So Much to Do, So Little Cash

When Dan Wallach started Greensburg GreenTown, he knew it wouldn't be easy. A self-proclaimed idea guy, he admits that the details of high finance elude him. What he is good at is rallying people around a cause and getting them to write a few big checks. This time, though, Wallach decided to involve the largest number of people possible. Greensburg GreenTown's One Million $5.00 Donations campaign was the result.

The money that is raised will be used to cover GreenTown's operating expenses, as well as to fund gaps in municipal projects, build model green homes, and educate residents about green building practices. Another aspect of GreenTown's work is to provide information and access to media organizations. Shortly after the tornado, the Planet Green cable channel began production on a television series that would chronicle the town's rebuilding. Wallach thought the exposure created by that show and others like it would be valuable in his fund-raising efforts.

As a not-for-profit organization, Greensburg GreenTown is heavily regulated by the IRS, because the donations it receives are fully tax deductible. It falls into the same category as religious organizations and educational institutions, which are exempt from federal income taxes but must pay other federal taxes, such as employment taxes. Because working through the red tape required to obtain this IRS status can take time, many organizations, GreenTown included, work through an approved intermediary while their applications are processed.

Although Greensburg GreenTown supports and educates Greensburg's residents, the town itself must rely on other sources of funding. All towns have budgets for repairs and improvements, but no one expected to have to rebuild the entire town. After the tornado, Greensburg had no roads, no hospital, no school system, no utilities, or any of the other services one might expect to find in a town. Money was tight even before the tornado, so rebuilding seemed an impossible task.

Luckily, various government and corporate organizations chipped in. The Federal Emergency Management Agency (FEMA) and the U.S. Department of Agriculture (USDA) provided aid in the form of grants. Corporations like Frito-Lay donated significant amounts of money to support the town's innovative business incubator. With millions of dollars at stake and hundreds of projects under way at once, Assistant Town Administrator and Recovery Coordinator Kim Alderfer says the hardest part is keeping track of it all.

Questions

After viewing the video, answer the following questions:

1. What are the key legal and financial distinctions of Greensburg GreenTown?
2. If you were in Kim Alderfer's shoes, what kind of financial contingency plan would you put in place for Greensburg's future?
3. Should not-for-profit organizations be required to open their books to donors? Why or why not?

LAUNCHING YOUR
[Finance Career]

Part 6, "Managing Financial Resources," describes the finance function in organizations. Finance deals with planning, obtaining, and managing an organization's funds to accomplish its objectives in the most effective way possible. In Chapter 16, we discussed the financial system, including the various types of securities, financial markets and institutions, the Federal Reserve System, financial regulators, and global financial markets. In Chapter 17, we examined the role financial managers play in an organization; financial planning; short- and long-term financing options; and mergers, acquisitions, buyouts, and divestitures. Throughout both chapters, we described the finance functions of a variety of businesses, governments, and not-for-profit organizations. As Part 6 illustrates, finance is a very diverse profession and encompasses many different occupations. According to the U.S. Department of Labor, over the next decade most finance-related occupations are expected to experience employment growth that is a little better than average for all occupations. However, employment in several finance occupations is expected to grow faster than average. Employment in the financial investment industry should be strong because of the number of Baby Boomers in their peak earning years with funds to invest and the globalization of securities markets.[1]

In most business schools, finance is one of the most popular majors among undergraduates. Combining finance with accounting is a common double major. Those with degrees in finance also enjoy relatively high starting salaries. A recent survey found that the average starting salary for a person with an undergraduate degree in finance was nearly $50,500 per year.[2]

All organizations need to obtain and manage funds, so they employ finance professionals. Financial institutions and other financial services firms employ a large percentage of finance graduates. These businesses provide important finance-related services to businesses, governments, and not-for-profit organizations. Some graduates with finance degrees take jobs with financial services firms such as Bank of America and JP Morgan Chase, while others begin their careers working in the finance departments of businesses in other industries such as 3M and Boeing, governments, or not-for-profit organizations. You may begin your career evaluating commercial loan applications for a bank, analyzing capital investments for a business, or helping a not-for-profit organization decide how to invest its endowment. Often finance professionals work as members of a team, advising top management. Some individuals spend their entire careers working in finance-related occupations; others use their finance experience to move into other areas of the firm. Today, the chief financial officer—the senior finance executive—holds one of the most critical jobs in any organization. In addition, the number of CEOs who began their careers in finance is growing.

Finance is a diverse, exciting profession. Here are a few of the specific occupations you might find after earning a degree in finance.

Financial managers prepare financial reports, direct investment activities, raise funds, and implement cash management strategies. Computer technology has significantly reduced the time needed to produce financial reports. Many financial managers spend less time preparing reports and more time analyzing financial data. All organizations employ financial managers, although roughly 30 percent of all financial managers work for financial services firms such as commercial banks and insurance companies.[3] Specific responsibilities vary with titles. For instance, credit managers oversee the firm's issuance of credit, establish standards, and monitor the collection of accounts. Cash managers control the flow of cash receipts and disbursements to meet the needs of the organization.

Most *loan officers* work for commercial banks and other financial institutions. They find potential clients and help them apply for loans. Loan officers typically specialize in commercial, consumer, or mortgage loans. In many cases, loan officers act in a sales capacity, contacting individuals and organizations about their need for funds and trying to persuade them to borrow the funds from the loan officer's institution. Thus, loan officers often need marketing as well as finance skills.

Security analysts generally work for financial services firms such as Fidelity or Raymond James & Associates. Security analysts review economic data, financial statements, and other information to determine the outlook for securities such as common stocks and bonds. They make investment recommendations to individual and institutional investors. Many senior security analysts hold a chartered financial analyst (CFA) designation. Obtaining a CFA requires a specific educational background, several years of related experience, and a passing grade on a comprehensive, three-stage examination.

Portfolio managers manage money for an individual or institutional client. Many portfolio managers work for pension funds or mutual funds for which they make investment decisions to benefit the funds' beneficiaries. Portfolio managers generally have extensive experience as financial managers or security analysts, and many are CFAs.

Personal financial planners help individuals make decisions in areas such as insurance, investments, and retirement planning. Personal financial planners meet with their clients, assess their needs and goals, and make recommendations. Approximately 30 percent of personal financial planners are self-employed, and many hold certified financial planner (CFP) designations. Like the CFA, obtaining a CFP requires a specific educational background, related experience, and passing a comprehensive examination.

Career Assessment Exercises in Finance

1. Assume you're interested in pursuing a career as a security analyst. You've heard that the CFA is an important designation and can help enhance your career. Visit the CFA's Web site (http://www.cfainstitute.org) to learn more about the CFA. Specifically, what are the requirements to obtain a CFA, and what are the professional benefits of having a CFA?

2. Arrange for an interview with a commercial loan officer at a local bank. Ask the loan officer about his or her educational background, what a typical day is like, and what the loan officer likes and doesn't like about his or her job.

3. Ameriprise Financial offers financial planning services to individuals and organizations. Visit the firm's careers Web site (http:///www.ameriprise.com/careers). Review the material and write a brief summary of what you learned about being a personal financial planner. Does such a career interest you? Why or why not?

GREENSBURG, KS

The Bumpy Road to Recovery

The road to recovery from any disaster is paved with bumps and potholes. Sometimes, as in the case of Greensburg, Kansas, there are no roads at all. After being slammed by an F5 tornado, the town—which was already ailing economically—was forced to recreate its entire infrastructure. But city administrator Steve Hewitt observes that total devastation was, in fact, a silver lining to the black tornado cloud. "After the storm, we had a blank canvas," he says. Hewitt observes that the destruction forced each resident and business owner to ask, "What do we need to change to become this thriving new community?" The city council passed a resolution that every facility would build at the greenest, most sustainable level possible.

Several years into the recovery, Hewitt says that while he knew the town faced great challenges, he wasn't prepared for the emotional roller coaster of the entire community. As city administrator, he admits that this has been difficult to manage. Karen Alderfer, former recovery coordinator for the city, agrees. Her job—until the funding ran dry—was to keep the town's financial matters organized, recording and allocating government grants, loans, and any other funds that arrived for the recovery effort. Both Hewitt and Alderfer note that they had hoped to be farther along than at 60 percent of infrastructure completion by now—but they are also proud of Greensburg and its accomplishments thus far. While many small firms and organizations around the country have held benefits to raise funds for Greensburg, a large corporation—preferably one involved with green technology—hasn't yet agreed to locate in Greensburg, which would give the town a significant boost in terms of jobs and other resources. Hewitt and Alderfer believe this has been due to a sluggish economy.

Still, there are concrete results. Recently the new $50-million Kiowa County Schools building opened to students. The building has such green features as windows placed strategically for natural light, cisterns that catch rainwater for landscaping, and a wind turbine for power. Other municipal buildings, including town hall and the hospital, have been or will be built to sustainable standards. And the Silo House, a project undertaken by Greensburg Green Town—the not-for-profit organization that is helping to raise money, build, and educate the public about sustainable practices—is a model for future projects. Built with a $50,000 grant from AT&T, the Silo House has a visitor and education center along with a suite for eco-tourists.

A visitor walking through the town of Greensburg would notice signs of both devastation and recovery. Piles of rubble and debris, empty lots, and treeless streets recall disaster. Yet Main Street is filled with residents and visitors who are determined to raise Greensburg from its ashes. Their optimism, along with the positive attitude of Steve Hewitt, is catching. "This is the best job in America to have," he claims, "to build from the ground up."

Questions for Critical Thinking

1. Building from the ground up has many challenges. Create a chart outlining what you believe to be the benefits and drawbacks to Greensburg's approach.

2. Discuss how a small business might get started on the new Main Street of Greensburg.

3. Greensburg relies on its relationship with the media to provide good publicity about its projects. Why is communication so important to Greensburg's rebuilding efforts?

4. Hewitt and Alderfer express the town's wish for a large, green-technology corporation to become part of the Greensburg community. In what ways would this benefit the town? What are the potential drawbacks?

Sources: Greensburg Web site, http://www.greensburgks.org, accessed June 21, 2011; Jenny Deam, "After the Tornado: Stronger, Better, Greener," *Los Angeles Times*, August 31, 2010, http://www.latimes.com; Al Letson, "Town Rebuilds Green After Devastating Tornado," *National Public Radio*, May 14, 2010, http://www.npr.org.

GREENSBURG, KS
What Lies Ahead?

Greensburg was an agricultural community before it was leveled by an F5 tornado, and its leaders believe that its cultural roots will never die. "Agriculture will always play a huge part in the economy," predicts Councilman Jeanette Siemens, economic development director for Kiowa County, "but maybe in new ways." As the population of rural towns like Greensburg declines, new economic opportunities must replace some of the old traditions.

"There's a great opportunity for some synergy between new green tech companies to work closely with the agricultural sector," says Matt Christenson, recovery project coordinator and member of the Greensburg city council. One example would be a manufacturing firm whose processes use the straw left over from a wheat harvest to fortify building panels.

As Greensburg tries to incorporate agriculture into its greener future, the community is witnessing another change—in demographics. "It's a younger community," observes city administrator Steve Hewitt. Growth recovery is coming from young business people who want to take a chance. One such entrepreneur is Kari Kyle, owner of the Green Bean Coffee Company in Greensburg. Kyle and her husband were both born and raised in the Greensburg area, but moved away for fourteen years. When they decided to return, Kyle applied for a business loan from the local bank, received it, and opened her shop in the business incubator space downtown. When a larger space became available across the street, she grabbed it and expanded her menu offerings to include ice cream malts and shakes, soda fountain drinks and smoothies, as well as food. She says that business has tripled and is optimistic about the future. "Heck yeah, I know I'm going to make it," she insists.

Joah Bussert and Stephanie Paterson are also part of Greensburg's future. With degrees in architecture, as project managers they are helping to manage the construction of new buildings with green technologies. One building project is the Chain of Eco-Homes—a group of twelve homes with names like Meadowlark House and Homestead House, all constructed using the latest technologies. Bussert describes these houses as "testing grounds" to see how the technologies will perform specifically in the Midwest. Features include natural gas fuelmakers, double-skin walls, rooftop gardens, household composters, driveways made with permeable pavers, and of course tornado shelters. Peterson loves her job. "It's like no other place in the world," she says.

Each person involved with the reconstruction of Greensburg is looking far beyond its pre-tornado status, to a more prosperous, sustainable future. Councilman Jeanette Siemens sees a community that supports the entrepreneurial spirit and will ultimately become an educational tourist destination. Steve Hewitt acknowledges that every step of recovery must "have the things that attract families and businesses. The community will grow from young, innovative people." He continues to be upbeat about Greensburg's prospects. "I love what we do," he concludes.

Questions for Critical Thinking

1. Give an example of how the factors of demand and supply are currently at work in Greensburg.
2. Why do Greensburg community leaders consider entrepreneurship such a key element in the recovery and growth of the city?
3. What steps can the city administrator, project managers, and others take to change pre-tornado views about Greensburg?
4. Create an advertisement for Greensburg, targeting either tourists or businesses.

Sources: Greensburg Web site, http://www.greensburgks.org, accessed June 21, 2011; Jenny Deam, "After the Tornado: Stronger, Better, Greener," *Los Angeles Times,* August 31, 2010; http://www.latimes.com; Al Letson, "Town Rebuilds Green After Devastating Tornado," *National Public Radio,* May 14, 2010, http://www.npr.org.

Developing a Business Plan

What's Next? A New Business Model for Restaurants

You're accustomed to buying airline and concert tickets in advance—but what about meal tickets? We're not referring to fast-food chains; we're talking about fine dining restaurants. Traditionally, restaurant customers walk in the door and hope to find a vacant table; if they're planning ahead, they'll call for a reservation. But the idea of purchasing advance tickets for dining is new to most of us.

Grant Achatz, a well-known chef and restaurant owner in Chicago, has a new restaurant—based on a new kind of business plan. The restaurant is called Next, and instead of taking reservations, the restaurant is selling tickets. The plan makes sense for an eatery that is bound to be as popular as Achatz's other Chicago restaurant, Alina, which is sold out many weeks in advance. "We now pay three or four reservationists all day long to basically tell people they can't come to the restaurant," explains Achatz. When customers purchase tickets in advance, they are as assured of a ready table as they would be with a reservation. Achatz and his partner, Nick Kokonas, will be able to reduce the hidden cost of a full-time reservation staff. They plan to pass along savings like this to their diners. Selling tickets "allows us to give an experience that is actually a great value," notes Achatz.

Diners who want to enjoy a meal at Next simply visit the restaurant's Web site. They can look at the menu, which will change four times a year, and lock into the fixed price for the entire six-course meal. In addition, they can choose to dine at peak or off-peak hours, which will be reflected in the ticket price. That's the idea, anyway. But as soon as Next opened its virtual doors, tickets appeared on the secondary market—selling for as much as $500 to $3,000 on sites such as Craigslist and eBay. Those lucky enough to score original tickets from the restaurant's site itself would pay about $85 per person. Achatz and Kokonas decide how to distribute the gratuities among staff.

Achatz is known to offer unique dining experiences for which sophisticated customers are willing to pay. Next offers patrons total immersion in the cuisine of a specific place and time. It isn't just a theme; it's the recreation of an era, painstakingly researched by Achatz and his team. The first menu offering was based on spring in Paris around 1906, with food cooked from Escoffier's vague yet complicated cookbook of 1903. Dishes included cooked cucumber stuffed with chicken mousse and wrapped in bacon, clear turtle soup with Madeira, and apple cinnamon caramel soufflé. Three months later, the menu would shift its focus—perhaps to Palermo, Italy in 1949; or to a futuristic Hong Kong, in the year 2036.

Customers who become loyal fans the way sports fans buy season tickets may purchase a year's

Chicago Tribune/MCT/Landov LLC

Grant Achatz, a Chicago restauranteur, hopes his new idea for dining will take off. Get your tickets early!

subscription to Next, locking in the price and the reserved table for each of the seasonal menu changes. Achatz believes that once people get used to the idea of a prepaid meal, they will enjoy the experience. The dinner is paid for, and there's no fumbling in the wallet or waiting to sign the check. "There's no transaction in the restaurant at all," Achatz points out. "So you can literally come in, sit down, start your experience, and when you're done, you just get up and leave."[1]

Many entrepreneurs and small-business owners have written business plans to help them organize their businesses, get them up and running, and raise money for expansion. In this appendix, we cover the basics of business planning: what business plans are, why they're important, and who needs them. We also explain the steps involved in writing a good plan and the major elements it should contain. Finally, we cover additional resources to get you started with your own business plan—to help you bring your unique ideas to reality with a business of your own.

What Is a Business Plan?

You may wonder how the millions of different businesses operating in the United States and throughout the world today got their start. Often it is with a formal business plan. A *business plan* is a written document that defines what a company's objectives are, how these objectives will be achieved, how the business will be financed, and how much money the company expects to bring in. In short, it describes where a company is, where it wants to go, and how it intends to get there.

Why a Business Plan Is So Important

A well-written business plan serves two key functions:

1. It organizes the business and validates its central idea.
2. It summarizes the business and its strategy to obtain funding from lenders and investors.

First, a business plan gives a business formal direction, whether it is just starting, going through a phase of growth, or struggling. The business plan forces the principals—the owners—through rigorous planning, to think through the realities of running and financing a business. In their planning, they consider many details. How will inventory be stored, shipped, and stocked? Where should the business be located? How will the business use the Internet? And most important, how will the business make enough money to make it all worthwhile?

A business plan also gives the owners a well-reasoned blueprint to refer to when daily challenges arise, and it acts as a benchmark by which successes and disappointments can be measured. Additionally, a solid business plan will sell the potential owner on the validity of the idea. In some cases, the by-product of developing the plan is demonstrating to a starry-eyed person that he or she is trying to start a bad business. In other words, the process of writing a plan benefits a would-be businessperson as much as the final plan benefits potential investors.

Finally, a business plan articulates the business's strategy to financiers who may fund the business, and it is usually required to obtain a bank loan. Lenders and venture capitalists need to see that the business owner has thought through the critical issues and presented a promising idea before they will consider investing in it. They are, after all, interested in whether it will bring them significant returns.

Who Needs a Business Plan?

Every business owner who expects to be successful needs a business plan. Some people mistakenly believe that they need a business plan only if it will land on the desk of a venture capitalist or the loan committee of a bank. Others think that writing a plan is unnecessary if their bank or lending institution doesn't require it. Such assumptions miss the point of planning, because a business plan acts as a map to guide the way through the often tangled roads of running a business. Every small-business owner should develop a business plan because it empowers that person to take control.

How Do I Write a Business Plan?

Developing a business plan should mean something different to everyone. Think of a business plan as a clear statement of a business's identity. A construction company has a different identity from a newly launched magazine, which has yet a different identity from a restaurant hoping to expand its share of the market. Each business has unique objectives and processes, and each faces different obstacles.

At the same time, good business plans contain some similar elements no matter who the business owner is, what he or she sells, or how far the owner is into the venture. A savvy business owner molds the elements of a business plan into a professional and personal representation of the firm's needs and goals. The plan should also realistically assess the risks and obstacles specific to the business and present solutions for overcoming them.

Because the document is important, it takes time to collect needed information and organize it. Don't be misled into believing that you will simply sit down and begin writing. Before any writing begins, the business owner must become an expert in his or her field. Readying important information about the company and the market will make the writing easier and faster. Some critical pieces of information to have on hand are the following items:

- The company's name, legal form of organization, location, financial highlights, and owners or shareholders (if any).
- Organization charts, list of top managers, consultants or directors, and employee agreements.

- Marketing research, customer surveys, and information about the company's major competitors.

- Product information, including goods and services offered; brochures; patents, licenses, and trademarks; and research and development plans.

- Marketing plans and materials.

- Financial statements (both current and forecasted).

The business owner also must do a lot of soul searching and brainstorming to answer important questions necessary to build the backbone of a healthy business. Figure D.1 lists some critical questions to ask yourself.

Once equipped with these answers, you can begin writing the document, which can be anywhere between 10 and 50 pages long. The length of the plan depends on the complexity of the company, whether the company is a start-up (established companies have longer histories to detail), and what the plan will be used for. Regardless of size, the document should be well organized and easy to use, especially if the business plan is intended for external uses, such as to secure financing. Number all pages, include a table of contents, and make sure the format is attractive and professional. Include two or three illustrative charts or graphs and highlight the sections and important points with headings and bulleted lists. Figure D.2 outlines the major sections of a business plan.

FIGURE D.1 Self-Evaluation Questions

Take a few minutes to read and answer these questions. Don't worry about answering in too much detail at this point. The questions are preliminary and intended to help you think through your venture.

1. In general terms, how would you explain your idea to a friend?

2. What is the purpose or objective of your venture?

3. What service are you going to provide, or what goods are you going to manufacture?

4. Is there any significant difference between what you are planning and what already exists?

5. How will the quality of your product compare with competitive offerings?

6. What is the overview of the industry or service sector you are going to enter? Write it out.

7. What is the history, current status, and future of the industry?

8. Who is your customer or client base?

9. Where and by whom will your good or service be marketed?

10. How much will you charge for the product you are planning?

11. Where is the financing going to come from to initiate your venture?

12. What training and experience do you have that qualifies you for this venture?

13. Does such training or experience give you a significant edge?

14. If you lack specific experience, how do you plan to gain it?

The following paragraphs discuss the most common elements of an effective business plan. When you need additional instruction or information as you write, refer to the "Resources" section at the end of the appendix.

Executive Summary

The primary purpose of an executive summary is to entice readers sufficiently to read more about the business. An *executive summary* is a one- to two-page snapshot of what the overall business plan explains in detail. Consider it a business plan within a business plan. Through its enthusiasm and quick momentum, the summary should capture the reader's imagination. Describe your strategy for succeeding in a positive, intriguing, and realistic way and briefly yet thoroughly answer the first questions anyone would have about your business: who, what, why, when, where, and how. Financiers always turn to the executive summary first. If it isn't well presented or lacks the proper information, they will quickly move on to the next business plan in the stack. The executive summary is just as important to people funding the business with personal resources, however, because it channels their motivations into an articulate mission statement. It is a good idea to write the summary last, because it will inevitably be revised once the business plan takes final shape.

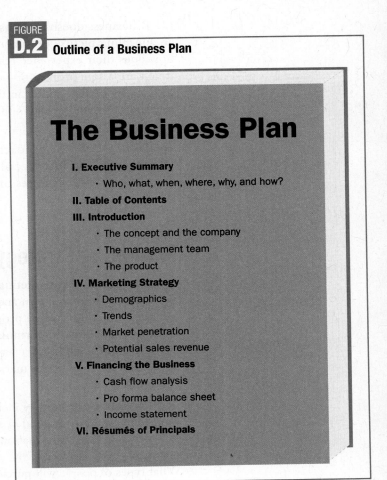

FIGURE D.2 Outline of a Business Plan

The Business Plan

I. Executive Summary
 · Who, what, when, where, why, and how?

II. Table of Contents

III. Introduction
 · The concept and the company
 · The management team
 · The product

IV. Marketing Strategy
 · Demographics
 · Trends
 · Market penetration
 · Potential sales revenue

V. Financing the Business
 · Cash flow analysis
 · Pro forma balance sheet
 · Income statement

VI. Résumés of Principals

To write an effective executive summary, focus on the issues that are most important to your business's success and save the supporting matters for the body. The executive summary should describe the firm's strategy and goals, the good or service it is selling, and the advantages it has over the competition. It should also give a snapshot of how much money will be required to launch the business, how it will be used, and how the lenders or investors will recoup their funds.

Introduction

The introduction follows the executive summary. After the executive summary has offered an attractive synopsis, the introduction should begin to discuss the fine details of the business. It should be crafted to include any material the upcoming marketing and financing sections do not cover. The introduction should describe the company, the management team, and the product in detail. If one of these topics is particularly noteworthy for your business, you may want to present that topic as its own section. Listen to what you write and respond as the plan takes shape.

Include basic information about the company—its past, present, and future. What are the company's roots, what is its current status, and what actions need to be taken to achieve its goals? If you are starting a company, include a description of the evolution of the concept. Be sure to tie all of the business's goals and plans to the industry in which it will operate, and describe the industry itself.

A business doesn't run itself, of course. People are the heart of a business, so write an appealing picture of the business's management team. Who are the key players and how does their experience resonate with the company's goals? Describe their—or your, if you are a sole proprietor—education, training, and experience, and highlight and refer to résumés included later in the plan. Be honest, however—not all businesses are started by experts. If you lack demonstrated experience in a certain area, explain how you plan to get it.

Also describe the product, the driving force behind the venture. What are you offering, and why is it special? What are the costs of the service or price tag on the good? Analyze the features of the offering and the effect these features have on the overall cost.

Marketing Strategy

Next comes the marketing strategy section. The *marketing strategy* describes the market's need for the item and the way the business will fulfill it. Marketing strategies are not based on informal projections or observations. They are the result of a careful market analysis. So formulating a marketing strategy allows the business owner to become familiar with every aspect of the particular market. If done properly, it will allow you to define your target market and position your business within that sector to get its share of sales.

The marketing strategy includes a discussion of the size of the customer base that will want to purchase your good or service and the projected rate of growth for the product or category. Highlight information on the demographics of your customers. *Demographics* are statistical characteristics of the segment of the market, such as income, gender, and age. What types of people will purchase your product? How old are they, and where do they live? What is their lifestyle like? For example, someone starting an interior design business will want to report how many homeowners live within a certain radius of the firm, as well as their median income. Of course, this section of the marketing analysis will be quite different for a company that conducts all of its business online. You will want to know the types of people who will shop at your Web site, but your discussion won't be limited to one geographic area. It is also a good idea to describe the trends in your product category. Trends are consumer and business tendencies or patterns that business owners can exploit to gain market share in an industry.

The marketing strategy should also detail your distribution, pricing, and promotional goals. Discuss the average price of your offering and the reasons behind the price you have chosen. How do you intend to let your potential customers know that you have a product to sell? How will you sell it—through a catalog, in a retail location, online, or perhaps a combination of all three? The effectiveness of your distribution, pricing, and promotional goals determines the extent to which you will be able to garner market share.

Competitors are another important part of your marketing strategy. What companies are already selling products similar to yours? Include a list of your competitors to show that you know exactly who they are and what you are up against. Describe what you think are their major strengths and weaknesses and how successful they have been within your market.

Also include the *market penetration*, which is the percentage of total customers who have purchased a company's product. If there are 10,000 people in your market, and 5,000 have purchased your product, your market penetration is 50 percent. The *potential sales revenue*, also an important figure to include, is the total revenue of a company if it captured 100 percent market penetration. In other words, this figure represents the total dollar value of sales you would bring in if everyone who is a potential customer purchased your product.

Financing the Business

The goal of a business is to make money. Everything in the business plan lays the foundation for the *financing section*. Business owners should not skip this section even if they are not seeking outside money. While it is crucial to have an accurate financial analysis to get financing, it also is a necessary exercise for business owners funding the venture themselves. The financing section demonstrates the cost of the product, operating expenses, expected sales revenue and profit, and the amount of the business owner's personal funds that will be invested to get the business up and running. The financial projections should be compelling but accurate and based on realistic assumptions. The owner should be able to defend them.

Any assumptions made in the body of the business plan should be tied into the financial section. For instance, if you think you will need a staff of five, your cash flow analysis should explain how you are going to pay them. A cash flow analysis, a mandatory component of a financial analysis, shows how much money will flow through your business throughout the year. It helps you plan for staggered purchasing, high-volume months, and slow periods. Your business may be cyclical or seasonal, so the cash flow projection lets you know if you need to arrange a line of credit to cover periodic shortfalls. In addition, an income statement is a critical component. The income statement is a statement of income and expenses your company has accrued over a period of time.

Remember that leaving out important details can undercut your credibility, so be thorough. The plan must include your assumptions about the conditions under which your business will operate. It should cover details such as market strength; date of start-up; sales buildup; gross profit margin; equipment, furniture, and fixtures required; and payroll and other key expenses that will affect the financial plan. In addition, a banker will want a pro forma balance sheet, which provides an estimate of what the business owns (assets), what it owes (liabilities), and what it is worth (owner's equity). Refer to Chapters 15, 16, and 17 of *Contemporary Business* for additional details on accounting, financial statements, and financial management.

Résumés of Principals

The final element of the business plan is the inclusion of the résumés of the principals behind the business: the management team. Each résumé should include detailed employment information and accomplishments. If applicable to your business, consider expanding on the traditional résumé by including business affiliations, professional memberships, hobbies, and leisure activities.

However you choose to develop a business plan, make sure that *you* develop the plan. It should sound as though it was written by the entrepreneur, not by some outside "expert."

Resources

A tremendous amount of material is available to help business owners—whether existing or prospective—write effective business plans. The biggest task is narrowing it down to which resources are right for you. The Internet delivers an abundance of sound business-planning tools and advice, much of which are free. It allows you to seek diverse examples and opinions, which is important because no one source will match your situation exactly. Your library and career center also have a wealth of resources. Following are some helpful resources for business planning.

Books

Dozens of books exist on how to write a business plan. Examples include the following:

- Edward Blackwell, *How to Prepare a Business Plan*, 7th ed. (London: Kogan Page Ltd., 2011).
- Steven D. Peterson, Peter E. Jaret, and Barbara Findlay Schenck, *Business Plans Kit for Dummies*, 3rd ed. (Wiley Publishing, 2010).
- Mike McKeever, *How to Write a Business Plan*, 10th ed. (Berkeley, CA: Nolo Press, 2010).
- John W. Mullins, *The New Business Road Test: What Entrepreneurs and Executives Should Do Before Writing a Business Plan*, 3rd ed. (*Prentice Hall Financial Times*, 2010).
- Michael Gerber, *The E-Myth Enterprise: How to Turn a Great Idea into a Thriving Business* (New York: Harper Collins, 2009); paperback edition 2010.

Web Sites

- *Entrepreneur, Inc.*, and *BusinessWeek* magazines offer knowledgeable guides to writing a business plan. *Entrepreneur*'s Web site also contains sample business plans.

  http://www.entrepreneur.com

  http://www.inc.com

  http://www.businessweek.com

- If you are hoping to obtain funding with your business plan, you should familiarize yourself with what investors are looking for. Two professional associations for the venture capital industry are the following:

  http://www.nvca.org (National Venture Capital Association)

  http://www.nasbic.org (National Association of Small Business Investment Companies)

- New Enterprise Associates and PricewaterhouseCoopers have useful Web sites:

  http://www.nea.com

  http://www.pwc.com ("The Second Key: Writing the Business Plan" link)

Software

Business-planning software can give an initial shape to your business plan. However, a word of caution is in order if you write a business plan using the software's template. Bankers and potential investors, such as venture capitalists, read so many business plans that those based on templates may sink to the bottom of the pile. Also, if you aren't looking for funding, using software can undercut a chief purpose of writing a plan—learning about your unique idea. So think twice before you deprive yourself of that experience. Remember, software is a tool. It can help you get started, stay organized, and build a professional-looking business plan, but it can't actually write the plan for you.

Associations and Organizations

Many government and professional organizations provide assistance to would-be business owners. Here is a partial list:

- The U.S. Small Business Administration offers planning materials, along with other resources.

  http://www.sba.gov/smallbusinessplanner

- The SBA also has a center specifically designed for female entrepreneurs.

  http://www.sba.gov/aboutsba/sbaprograms/onlinewbc

- One of the missions of the Ewing Marion Kauffman Foundation is to encourage entrepreneurship across the United States. The foundation's Web sites offer online resources for new and growing businesses.

  http://www.kauffman.org

©U.S. Small Business Administration

The Small Business Administration's Web site, www.sba.gov, offers a wealth of information on starting, managing, and expanding a small business.

Projects and Teamwork Applications

1. Visit the Web site for Next Restaurant at http://www .nextrestaurant.com to learn more about the restaurant's innovative method of selling tickets in advance. Now think of another business that doesn't usually sell tickets in advance—yet. Write a brief plan for converting that business to the pre-selling business model. Why do you think this would be successful? What might be the drawbacks?

2. Do you dream of starting your own business? Take your idea and answer as many of the self-evaluation questions in Figure D.1 as you can. Share your answers with the class. Then file your answers away to read at a future date—either when you have graduated from college or when you think you are ready to pursue your own business.

3. Write the executive summary portion of the business plan for your potential business. You may use the answers to the questions in Figure D.1 as a springboard.

WRITING AN EFFECTIVE BUSINESS PLAN

Nathaniel R. Calloway

Printed in the United States of America.

ISBN 978-1-118-28615-9

WRITING AN EFFECTIVE BUSINESS PLAN

OBJECTIVES

❖ Understand the primary advantages of developing an effective business plan

❖ Describe how the economic recession in the United States has led to increased entrepreneurial interest in individual proprietorships and the growth of small business

❖ Describe the basic components of a business plan, and the significance of each to an effective start-up business venture

❖ Explain the risk factors that the small business entrepreneur must clearly understand and carefully implement, in order to achieve financial and management success

❖ Discuss available resources that can provide assistance to the small business owner in creating and using a business plan

INTRODUCTION

"Above all, you want to create something you are proud of. That's always been my philosophy of business. I can honestly say that I have never gone into any business purely to make money. If that is the sole motive, then I believe you are better off doing nothing."

Richard Branson, Virgin Atlantic

First of all, let's define what is a *business plan*:

"A *business plan* is a written document that defines what a company's objectives are, how these objectives will be achieved, how the business will be financed, and how much money the company expects to bring in." [1]

Effective business planning has become increasingly more important to the success of starting a small business in the United States. But what are we talking about when we say "business planning"? There are different types of business (proprietorship, partnership, corporation), and different methods of operating a business (in a home office, in a physical store or office location, via telephone or postal mail order, or using the Internet). Already, we need to decide on a business type, and a method of operating the business – even though we may have an idea of what we would like to do in this business (sell products or provide services). Well, making these business decisions is called "business management", and operating your chosen business is the execution of your idea or plan. There's an old adage that states you should "Plan your work and work your plan". Effective business planning depends greatly upon how well you take your idea, and add to it the above business decisions we have discussed, and then the accumulated information being set forth clearly in the form of a written document, the business plan.

You might say – "I know now all of the details about my new business, and have them in my mind. Why can't I just tell people my idea, and explain verbally all of the things that I want to do and accomplish in my business?"

The principal focus of this writing is **small business**, although the concepts and procedures can be equally applicable to "large" firms (which you very likely want your business to become someday). For our purposes, *small business* will utilize the definition that is generally accepted by the United States Small Business Administration: a business operation that employs 500 or fewer people. [2]

Our assumption is that you are an aspiring entrepreneur who desires to start a business - that although will have its beginnings at home – will also need at some future time to obtain capital funding. The investment of money by either a financial organization (bank, credit union, venture capital firm) will permit growth by establishing the business location, hiring employees and arranging for advisory services, and acquiring the equipment and inventory that are sufficient to serve an identified consumer market with goods and/or services. Remember, Apple Computer, Incorporated today, a multi-billion dollar, multinational corporation, began as the combined ideas and work in a single home residential garage of Steve Jobs and Steve Wozniack. [3]

So - What is it so important for a company to *write an effective business plan*?

Let's look at why experts in the business/government world frown upon the lack of an effective business plan in the start-up of new business ventures.

According to the Home Business magazine, the growth rate of home-based businesses has been rising at a significantly high annual rate. [4]

In addition, the Small Business Administration (SBA) states that many new businesses fail within 4 years from start-up , providing for us a range that should be exceeded to achieve a successful launch.

The number of home-based businesses in the United States is a very fast-growing sector, although the foregoing data regarding this trend also varies by those small business research organizations, both private and public.

The number of U.S. households that currently are operating either a full or part-time business (home-based) exceeds 12 percent of all U.S. households (Office of Advocacy, Small Business Administration). The small business sector is a significant part of the U.S. economy, because of its ability, with proper capital infusions, to hire employees and generate sales revenue. [5]

Additionally, the International Data Corporation, a well-known research firm, between 34.3 million and 36.6 million U.S. households have active home offices, and these numbers are growing substantially.

Conversely, home-based businesses fall somewhere between 18.3 (U.S. Census Bureau)(CB) and 38 million (Bureau of Labor Statistics)(BLS) businesses. [6]

You have probably noticed, at this point, that the process of starting and successfully completing a project requires a number of steps could be completed more easily with a written plan. Architects use a written blueprint to plan a building structure before beginning construction. Vehicles that provide us transportation are first designed on paper according to a desired body style and specifically detailed electronic/mechanical specifications. After all, would anyone want to drive a car that placed controls for the radio by the vehicle's designer in the trunk? Without accurate plans or designs, the process of creation would be not only be needlessly time-consuming, but would also present many opportunities for mistakes that would not have been encountered otherwise.

In any event, the advent of computer technology and the World Wide Web has made the ability to create an effective business plan a much more efficient process. Given the failure rate mentioned earlier, it is clear that writing a business plan can provide the advantage of a document that can be a guide that will hopefully lead to the avoidance of such problems.

A significant advantage can be seen in personal business plans as well as in business planning. Although shopping (in everyday life) for one or two items in a store might not require a written list, it is very likely that shopping for five, ten, or more items without a written list may result in mistakes such as forgetting a desired item, or making an incorrect purchase. Similarly, a business plan contains numerous items relating to products, services, operations, financing, marketing, licensing, staffing, payroll, and budgeting that will be aided by the creation of an effective and efficiently written business plan.

Another very important function of a business plan is its ability to serve as a reference document throughout very significant stages in the life of the business. A completed business plan is expected by loan department approval officers at banks or financing institutions. Venture capitalists also require the entrepreneur to set forth in detail the projected financial needs of the entrepreneurial enterprise, in the initial start-up phase. Also, in future years, the revised business plan can be utilized to explain the planned implementation of expanded business operations in order to obtain additional capital. During the early years of operation, the business plan serves as a guide to assure that critical milestones are met, and that the commencement of operations will generate the desired level of sales while effectively maintaining control of expenses. During the succeeding years of managing the firm, the business plan can guide such important decisions as:

1) Are any changes needed to solve unexpected problems?
2) Is this a good time to expand/adjust the nature or level of operations (more new products/change the mix of products and services)?
3) If additional capital funding is needed, what amount should be requested, and how will the use of these funds advance the profitability of the business?

Finally, in the latter phase of business success, the business plan can be the basis for making important decisions on significant business format changes – such as going from a sole proprietorship to a partnership or corporation. There may be a need to expand from an Internet-based enterprise into "brick-and-mortar" (the opening of a store in a shopping center or commercial store location) – or vice-versa. There may be a time for decisions on whether to open more than one business location. The effective business plan – like the root of a mighty oak tree, should be the base from which all components of the business grow, and be a resource for the business for additional financing and management decision making throughout the life of the company.

Economists will be the first to note that the economic climate of a nation can have a profound impact upon the operations of both small and large business enterprises. Governmental policies pertaining to such U.S. business regulations as minimum wage employee payments, tax payments, licensing fees, payroll tax withholding requirements, and Social Security rules can be significant in the startup, continued operation, or the termination of a small business. The following section will investigate some factors within the U.S. economy that can influence the conduct of a small business plan.

THE U. S. ECONOMY AND SMALL BUSINESS

The difference between a successful person and others is not a lack of strength, not a lack of knowledge, but rather in a lack of will."

Vincent T. Lombardi, NFL Head Coach

When dramatic changes are occurring in a national economic recession, an entrepreneur might have certain questions:

How can I start my own small business when the U. S. consumer market and many business statistical indicators are at such a weak level now?

Will I be able to get a business startup loan?

Where will I find customers for my small business, when unemployment is at an all-time high, and business sales are not?

What is the value of creating a business plan when economic conditions can be apparently so unfavorable?

These are challenging questions, so let's look at what the statistics tell us about small business in the United States. The U.S. Small Business Administration (SBA), on its home page (www.sba.gov), makes the following statement:

"Many people dream of having their own business. To see if starting a business is right for you, ask yourself these important 20 questions. Your answers will help you determine if you are ready to become a small business owner or where you need to spend more time in planning." [6]

An entrepreneur must - without any doubt – be willing to spend a large amount of time *planning every component of the new business*. The *business plan* is an invaluable tool in this process, because it permits the owner to see each step of the process in writing.

The lack of proper planning is one of the most often-cited reasons for the failure of a business, either at startup, or during the early years of its operation.

Table 1: The Value of Small Business in the United States

Small Business (Percentage)	As a Percentage of all Employer Firms in the United States
50%	Small Businesses with Employees
64%	Net new jobs created since 1995

Source: Small Business Administration, Office of Advocacy

Indeed, small businesses with employees have increased at a far greater rate during recent years, due to a higher level of layoffs and unemployment brought about by the economic recession . In addition, approximately two-thirds of the net new jobs in the U.S. private enterprise system have come from small business operations, rather than major corporations and other large commercial and governmental organizations.[7]

The Small Business Administration (SBA) website is an excellent first step in the planning process, because of the numerous resources and advisory services freely made available by this U.S. Federal government agency.

There is a wealth of other resource information available to use as a guide in writing the business plan.

In addition to the SBA mentioned earlier, the Department of Commerce and the Census Bureau supply data on the status of business growth in the United States. The aforementioned agencies also offer special programs, that provide free advice to entrepreneurs from experienced and retired business executives. One of the best-known programs of this kind is the SCORE program, sponsored by the U.S. Small Business Administration (SBA). SCORE is a nonprofit association, educating entrepreneurs and helping small businesses start, grow, and succeed in the United States. SCORE has a partnership with SBA, mentoring small business owners for more than forty years. SCORE is a valuable network of over 13,000 volunteers. [8]

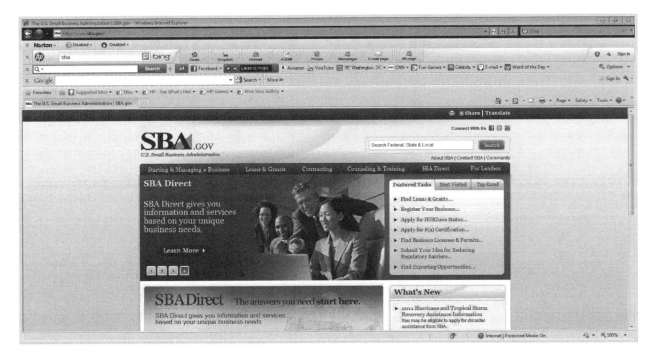

The SBA makes two important points for those entrepreneurs that desire to start their own business: 1) you must face the fact that you will have competition (many have this dream), and 2) you must very honestly answer questions to determine whether your dream can become a reality. The SBA website is an excellent starting point for any aspiring entrepreneur, and we will address some questions, and even more helpful information in later sections.

We have mentioned earlier that, even in a relatively normal business environment (minimal negative impact of inflation or recession), the business plan provides a view of how the new firm will meet customer needs. However, it must be remembered that *customers have wants and needs whether the state of the economy is good – or bad.*

How can I start my own small business when the U. S. consumer market and many business statistical indicators are at such a weak level now?

Consequently, the answer to our first question is "Yes". You can start your own business - **if you can first identify a customer need that will be provided to an unfulfilled, or less than fulfilled consumer market by your proposed enterprise.** Social networks, such as Facebook and Twitter – have attracted millions of both government, business, and individual users – because they found a communication need that previously was not provided by the Internet or other forms of electronic communication. Apple Computers, Inc., for example, began as a small business entrepreneurial effort to design and sell a personal computer, in a garage, by Steve Jobs and Steve Wozniak.[8]

The mortgage loan crisis in the U.S. (in the years 2008-2010) has forced lenders to make a much more strict assessment of the credit worthiness of both large and small business enterprises. You may have noticed that a shopping center that began construction a year or more ago suddenly stopped building operations for a period of time. This temporary delay could possibly have been due to the weakened state of the economy, which caused financial institutions to suspend financing until the pace of business and consumer spending began to show increased buying and selling activity. Venture capitalists, banks, and other business financing firms base their lending of such funds – the amount of small business loans that will be approved – upon a number of additional factors:

- How strong is the level of business (Sales, Assets, Income) in the industry?
- What are the industry financial statement analysis averages, based upon Pro Forma Financial Statements, and other financial data provided by the owner?
- For the business applicant under consideration, what is the credit rating for the firm, and what is the credit record for the years the business has been in operation?

Will I be able to get a business startup loan?

The answer to the second question posed earlier is also - Yes - the new small business can obtain a business loan – by successfully demonstrating a strong individual credit record rating among the manager (or managers) of the new company. The effective business plan of the new small business enterprise entrepreneur, in addition, *will be dependent upon the owner's ability to demonstrate outstanding personal credit worthiness, in order to obtain the initial loan request.*

Why? Because the lender has no previous business financial data to rely upon for a decision, the final decision on whether to approve capital funding must be based in large part upon whether the *prospective new business owner can utilize proven personal financial and credit management skills in the operation of a yet-unproven new business venture.*

The effective business plan is as much a "sales" plan as it is a "business" plan. The well-written business plan must set forth a process for how the business will generate an acceptable level of sales – in both strong and weak economic environments. To accomplish this task, the entrepreneur must do a lot of careful study – to thoroughly understand the market that the business will serve, comprehend the level of sales and costs that are estimated for future operations. The business plan must be able to convincingly explain what can be done to maintain an acceptable level of business in a period of a business downturn. Further, the effective business plan must be prepared to demonstrate in writing – with relevant charts, tables, and graphic depictions – the methods that the previously non-existent company will capture and maintain its share of the consumer market in the face of recognized competition. [9]

The high unemployment rate has been a discouraging situation for aspiring small business entrepreneurs, but not for those business sectors that provide needed services in markets that exist even in recessionary times within the United States. We will suggest in later sections the methods that can lead to a successful business startup.

Where will I find customers for my small business, when unemployment is at an all-time high, and business sales are not?

Finding customers for a small business is not impossible. However, that effort is an endeavor that demands a considerable amount of market research. A consumer market for each product or service is different in each geographical area of the nation – each state, each city, each town, and each neighborhood. If a market for a given product or service does not exist in the target area for the small business startup – the small business is doomed to failure.

An accurate search and selection of a consumer market might be compared to the job professions of a weather forecaster, budget analyst, or financial analyst. In each situation, for a new entrepreneur, the forecast or prediction should be based upon the best available information or trend indications for the prospective business startup given the time period in question. For a business plan to be effective, all possible formal and informal sources of information should be placed under consideration. However, it must be kept in mind that – like weather conditions can change monthly, weekly, and daily – so can the opinions of potential customers for your small business. The effective business plan *should always incorporate a "Plan B".* The alternative to "Plan A" (your first choice") will state a "what if" plan in case there are unexpected changes to the primary plan. Forecasters use the popular technique of the percentage of probability that the event will occur, for example, that there is a "60 percent chance of rain" (Plan A), meaning a 40 percent chance that there will be no rain.

The answer then to question three is - maybe – depending entirely upon how well the forecasted customer demand matches the ability of the business to "meet that demand". In reality, that "maybe " can become a ""Yes" only if you , the new owner, put on the hat of – you, the market analyst – to successfully define your target market.

What is the value of creating a business plan when economic conditions can be apparently so unfavorable

The answer to final question on the value of a business plan will be clearly "Yes" at this point, considering the factors we have seen thus far. Although many questions must be answered when contemplating the creation of a small business, it is possible to start a new business in both strong and weak economic conditions. Because customer needs always exist – so do business opportunities for the entrepreneur.

However, the following sections will examine even further the basic components of an effective business plan, to demonstrate more specifically what items you may want to incorporate into your small business plan.

THE BASIC COMPONENTS: BUSINESS PLAN

"Many of life's failures are people who did not realize how close they were to success when they gave up."

Thomas A. Edison, Inventor

A business plan is, in the beginning , *a written summary of the structure for a business* that the aspiring entrepreneur hopes *will exist in physical form at a future time. Once the business does exist*, and is in operation, *the business plan is*, or should be, *the primary reference document for any later changes that the owner might make to the enterprise, or desire to request for the benefit of the enterprise.* [10]

Before building a house, for example, someone (the architect) needs to make many decisions, and normally places the result of those decisions in writing. What decisions? First, where will the house be located? Other decisions can include: (1) how many floors? (2) how many rooms? (3) what materials are needed? (4) what workers will be needed to build it? In addition, other questions to be answered will be: (1) who will build it (building contractors – plumbers, electricians, etc.)? (2) when will it be built (schedule – start to finish)? Of course, a very important decision that must be made is: who will pay for the work (financing), and who will be paid how much for their work?

Now, imagine for a moment, that NONE of this building plan was written down!

What are the chances that this house could be constructed efficiently in a timely manner?

Clearly, even if it could be done – the likelihood is that it would take much longer, and be continually plagued with a significant amount of unnecessary mistakes and miscommunication.

Now, for your own small business, guess who is the "architect"?

That's right – you are!

Hopefully, you can see from this simplistic home construction example that as the "architect" of your future small business:

1. The decisions that you make, like those of a building architect, are very important to the successful creation of your enterprise.
2. The use of a written business plan can make the "construction" of your small business much more effective.

Another important point to be kept in mind is that there is no one business plan format that is used to create all business plans.

If you stand on one of the famous New York City bridges, looking at the high-rise skyscraper buildings in downtown Manhattan, you can see that each building has its own height and shape, because each building creator (i.e., architect) had a different concept about what that building would look like in its final form. The same is true for entrepreneurs: each small business has unique features, as do buildings – so there are many different ways to write a business plan.

THE BASIC COMPONENTS: THE EXECUTIVE SUMMARY - INTRODUCTION

"You must be very patient, very persistent. The world isn't going to shower gold coins on you just because you have a good idea. You're going to have to work like crazy to bring that idea to the attention of people. They're not going to buy it unless they know about it."

Herb Kelleher, Southwest Airlines

Simply put, the entrepreneur should choose to create, promote, and maintain that business which makes him happy, to have the best opportunity to achieve success.

There are several primary sections in a well-written business plan. The introductory section is known as the Executive Summary. The task of the six basic parts of the Executive Summary is to provide an overview of the content to be discussed in the business plan. The parts are, for the proposed small business enterprise: Who, What, Where, When, Why, and How. [11]

Here, we will describe each of the six parts in this section, and their role in an effective business plan.

However, one very important point should be made about the role this section should play in the success of the entire business plan document. Each paragraph, sentence, and word should be very carefully written – because it provides the "first impression", if you will, about every other part of the document that will follow in the business plan. The goal, at this point, is to stimulate the interest of the reader, so that there will be a strong desire to *know more about this prospective business*. Your description should capture and hold the attention of the reader from the very beginning. Clearly, the failure of the Executive Summary to generate this kind of interest can harm the effectiveness of everything that follows this section.

One especially helpful suggestion in writing this section (and all parts of the document) is to make an outline of the points that you wish to include in the section, before you begin to write the text.

Let's look now at what items might be included in your outline, for each part of the Executive Summary section for your business plan.

In order to introduce a generic version, this series of basic component sections will briefly describe the content that would likely be found within the parts of a small business plan. [12]

BASIC COMPONENTS: BUSINESS PLAN — THE "WHO" FACTOR

"Business needs more of the professional spirit. The professional spirit seeks professional integrity, from pride, not from compulsion."

Henry Ford

As mentioned earlier, there are several different formats that are termed a "business plan". For various sizes and types of business, each version can adequately serve its purpose.

The first part of the business plan under discussion is the Who Factor for the company.

The name of the prospective company should be chosen carefully, because it indicates a unique identity for the firm. It should be intended to cause anyone that views it to know, or be able to easily discover *your specific small business.*

It is important to keep in mind the old adage: "A picture is worth a thousand words." For your small business, using unique words is good, but the use of unique wording and a logo is even better!

In the mind of your customers, even the use one word — and one logo — can create a powerful identity.

For example, Facebook uses the one word - Facebook — and the small-case letter "f" (white in a blue square field) is its logo on the Internet. This trend has been followed by Twitter and MySpace with their own logos. This supports the earlier adage that it is not necessary to have several words in your chosen company name when one-or-two suffice well. [13]

Facebook Login

Facebook helps you connect and share with the people in your life.

It is certainly advisable to choose a name that is not commonly used by many other businesses.

"ABC Company" (using "ABC" with a variety of additional words) will bury your small business in any listing of small businesses.

Again, as with the study of your small business target market, the choice of a name for your business should involve some research of existing names. Sources for such names currently include the World Wide Web, in addition to computer databases compiled by business organizations such as the Chamber of Commerce, and government agencies.

The choice of a small business name (and possibly an optional business logo) should be designed to answer the question of: "Who am I?" The unique business name can be a significant advantage in establishing an effective identity of the small business.

THE BASIC COMPONENTS: BUSINESS PLAN – THE "WHAT" FACTOR

"Successful and unsuccessful people do not vary greatly in their abilities. They vary in their desires to reach their potential."

John Maxwell

Secondly, part of the business plan under discussion is the What Factor for the company.

There is a close link between the Who and What Factors. The ability of a business name (Who) should be supported strongly by the purpose (What) that the business will provide to its customer base. The failure of the owner to make clear what the line of business will be - selling products, services, or possibly both - can be a major cause of the company's demise.

The purpose of a small business has a number of parts. A business name identifies the total enterprise. However, the purpose should define and explain each of its components.

The owner of a business should be able to explain not only what the firm does, but how that is important to the customers served by the company.

This is why with many businesses, for many years, the tagline (also formerly known as a slogan or motto) has been extremely popular (instead of, or in addition to, the logo). For example, International Business Machines (IBM) developed and used in its advertising the following motto: "The System is the Solution". This tagline tells anyone that sees it that this company is in the systems business, and that they do find solutions for their customers – a very comforting thought. However, it should be noted that Ray Kroc, who started the very successful McDonald's Corporation, an internationally-famous hamburger chain, used systematic business planning techniques to build a multi-billion dollar empire. [14]

Looking at Table 1, other examples of business taglines and slogans are displayed that within a business plan, and in the minds of future customers, will confirm the identity of a business as a unique company. Notably, the taglines and slogans are not in each case describing the type of company. Their purpose is to bring to mind *the* name of the company based upon a phrase that remains associated with that customer or other business associate when the name is printed, spoken, or seen in an audio-visual format (advertising, television, radio, VCR video tape, Internet video, etc.).

For example, while the American Airlines slogan (*Something special in the air*) might clearly bring to mind an image of flying in a jet airliner, the Burger King tagline (*Have it your way*) might require the sight of a juicy hamburger, fries, and a soft drink. Although you may pay an advertising thousands of dollars to develop a tagline or logo for your small business plan, the beauty of these items is that you can freely develop them yourself, using nothing more than your own imagination. [15]

Table 1: Popular Business Taglines

Company	Business Taglines
American Airlines	*Something special in the air*
Apple Computers	*Think different*
BMW	*The ultimate driving machine*
Burger King	*Have it your way*
Coca Cola	*It's the real thing*
Kentucky Fried Chicken	*Finger-lickin' good!*
McDonalds	*We love to see you smile*
Sprite	*Obey your thirst*
United Airlines	*Fly the friendly skies*

Source: Famous Business Taglines and Company Slogans

THE BASIC COMPONENTS: BUSINESS PLAN – THE "WHEN" FACTOR

"Always bear in mind that your own resolution to success is more important than any other one thing."

Abraham Lincoln, U.S. President

The When Factor– depends on the type of business – no set rules

The time that a business should optimally begin operations is a matter of debate. As a new company, a startup during a time when business is not extremely busy could be an advisable plan.

How do I determine the best time to open the business? One way to find that answer is to observe similar businesses if possible.

Another method is to talk with advisors familiar with this type of business, or owners currently operating a business.

At what time(s) of the year is the business - which is similar to the firm that you intend to start – getting a higher level of sales? Weekends, Holidays, Spring, Summer, Fall, or Winter?

Your business plan should be able to answer with a reasonable level of confidence not only "when" you should start the business, but "when" the business is likely to be most profitable during the fiscal year. This forecast will be reflected in the section of your business plan known as the pro forma financial statements (to be discussed later in the Business Financing section).

THE BASIC COMPONENTS: BUSINESS PLAN – THE "WHERE" FACTOR

"Information technology and business are becoming inextricably interwoven. I don't think anybody can talk meaningfully about one without the talking about the other."

Bill Gates – Microsoft Corporation

One of the most important decisions to be made by the new entrepreneur is the answer to this question: Where will my new business serve its customers?

In the years prior to the advent of computer technology and the Internet, the decision was primarily one of a physical office or retail store location. The other alternatives might have involved a mail-order delivery, or a telephone-based customer sales operation. Each of these potential business locations will require a decision, and will then clearly affect the other factors discussed earlier within the owner's business plan.

Although the aforementioned location alternatives still are available for consideration - and decision – by the entrepreneur, the Internet has opened an online preference which has powerful potential. The dynamic electronic features of the World Wide Web have the ability to let the small business owner combine the Web with telecommunications, audio-visual, and postal mailing technologies to produce what we know as Internet business. Many businesses decide to operate both in the physical realm (face-to-face direct sales with customers, using telephone/fax communications), and also online business by launching/maintaining an Internet homepage that features the ability of customers to order products and services via the Web.

The business plan serves a critical function by defining which locations the entrepreneur intends to operate the firm. It is very important that the marketing strategy be illustrated that justifies the choices of business location, and the technology systems which will permit efficient communications – both off-line and online.

THE BASIC COMPONENTS: BUSINESS PLAN – THE "WHY" FACTOR

"Always bear in mind that your own resolution to success is more important than any other one thing."

Abraham Lincoln, U.S. President

The Why Factor involves the ability to show in your business plan why there is a compelling business need for the creation of this new small business. This area of the business plan is a marketing effort. As we have seen, and will further explore, this section goes directly to the heart of answering the question:

Why is this business so different from any other similar company, and why will it meet the wants and needs of the targeted consumer market?

Here is a primary reason why a business plan can assist the entrepreneur in providing such a well-written, clear and convincing explanation. Remember, a central purpose of the business plan is to, at least in part, provide the evidence which will bring an approval for the investment of capital funding into the enterprise. As such, it should be loaded with facts and figures which support the business owner's claim. Graphically, it should present forecasts, trends, and a plausible economic operating environmental "big picture". The verbal presentation of the entrepreneur should be strongly supported by the contents of the effective business plan. A well-prepared analysis within the business plan should anticipate and clearly answer any questions that might be asked by those reviewing the business plan. In other words, the business plan should be built upon the idea: If I am asked "why" about this topic – this will be my answer.

Anyone that has raised very young children knows that curiosity is an almost constant – and sometimes annoying – trait. Anyone who has prepared a business plan should expect similar treatment, being asked: "Why?" "Why?" "Why?" With parenthood and grandparenthood, the answers can sometimes lead to more questions. However, keep in mind that you are asking the banker, venture capitalist, and numerous other interested parties to invest money, time, resources, and most of all belief in the plan that you place before them. Truly, faith, persistence, hard work, determination, and patience are very necessary ingredients to this process.

THE BASIC COMPONENTS: BUSINESS PLAN – THE "HOW" FACTOR

"No one's a leader if there are no followers."

Malcolm Forbes - Forbes Magazine

Finally, the How Factor is where "the rubber meets the road", to quote an old adage.

Unless the prospective owner has thoroughly examined, understood, and committed in writing the business plan, there could be problems in the future operation. There is unfortunately, a reduced chance that the plan can result in the approval of capital funding, and the successful startup of the business enterprise.

The employment of a method known as: Planning Evaluation Review Technique, or PERT. This system forces the planner to place a project within a carefully written step-by-step order. For the new business owner, it can cause the assessment of the business operation that enables the learning of analytical skills necessary to determine the quality and value of data pertinent to effective business planning. It is worth stating that PERT-COST (the financial costing off-shoot of PERT) can do the same in the financial thinking about the enterprise. [16]

The How Factor involves many elements of the business operating plan. Accounting, Managing, Operating, Staffing, Licensing, and Consulting are some of the key parts of the business plan.

Using systematic charting methodologies in your business plan, each task and milestone can be successfully documented and accomplished, in the most efficient and cost-effective manner.

TABLE OF CONTENTS

The Table of Contents sets forth the order in which the detailed information pertaining to the primary elements of your small business operation.

It should be noted again that this business plan is one possible version. As illustrated earlier, the Internet and many other business resources provide different although equally acceptable business plan formats.

For our Table of Contents in the business plan, the sections to be included (with brief definition) are:

- Marketing Strategy – How your product or service can be a successful business enterprise.

- Marketing Demographics – Why your selected business location can geographically reach the target market
- Marketing Trends – Based upon known future business innovation, how your firm will be prepared to meet forecasted business market changes
- Marketing Penetration - What methodologies will be employed to make the business known to those customers to be served by its operation
- Business Financing - What amount of initial (or additional) capital will be required to enable the firm to successfully meet all operating requirements
- Business Management – What human resources will be employed for day-to-day leadership, consultation, and supply chain managerial supervision

MARKETING STRATEGY

A traditional saying states: "Build a better mousetrap, and the world will beat a path to your door." Your "mousetrap" – be it a product or a service – must be shown to be an improvement over any similar products already on the market.

The new business owner should use creativity and the ability to generate new ideas. Every product or service on the consumer market must endeavor to create in their business plan, as well as in the mind of the customer, that what is being offered is different, and hopefully better than others in that line of business.

The market strategy in the business plan should establish what is called *differentiation*. *Differentiation* can be based upon product features (what the product or service can do or provide), or by price (what a customer can pay), or by geographic location(cultural characteristics of the country/state/city, and town where the product is to be available).

In each of the aforementioned cases, the entrepreneur must be able to obtain the relevant information and understand the market within which the company will operate, in order to show what benefits can be achieved via the chosen market strategy.

For example, if a new company desires to offer pineapple-based food products: one might expect that the market strategy would first be to operate in the Hawaiian islands, or possibly the Caribbean /Pacific island chains. However, a strategy that could state in the business plan an Internet-based company with an advertising/promotional campaign. Although a physical business location would be a likely target for optimal sales revenue, a Web-based company permits such a firm to market the products world-wide.

The impact of Internet technologies upon traditional business startup decisions has been significant during the age of the World Wide Web. Marketing capabilities brought forth by the ability of a customer to order and receive products and services online have been a key to many successful small business ventures.

MARKETING DEMOGRAPHY

What is a business plan, really?

Demography is defined as the study of human population characteristics. Previously, the subject has been discussed regarding why it is important to include within the business plan a wise geographic business decision choice. While a physical (i.e. "brick-and-mortar") or online (Internet) selection should be presented, that is only part of the effective business plan decision. [17]

The business owner can easily risk a loss of sales revenue and successful operations by not considering the cultural and economic factors inherent in the chosen business location. Questions that should be asked and answered with the business plan might include:

1. What are the laws regarding the sale of my business products in this demographic area?
2. Will there be tax laws and licensing requirements which affect the kind of business I wish to offer?
3. What is the state of the economy in this geographic location, and would a new business of the kind I wish to offer be received well?
4. Given the geographic location and economy, what price can I charge for my products or services?
5. Is there a Chamber of Commerce in this location, and if so who will my competitors be in this locale?

Large companies such as Wal-Mart have found that opening a superstore in a small town has been met by strong resistance from area businesses, due to the loss of sales that might result to existing small businesses. Small businesses in certain areas may need to successfully complete application and other licensing requirements which may take months or years before the business startup.

An effective business plan should take all of the foregoing questions into account, and set forth a reasonable time schedule, with target milestone dates, for the completion of all such known issues.

The *release date* for approved funding may rely upon the successful *completion date of certain objectives.*

That is, the approved amount of capital financing for such business startup circumstances may very likely be dependent upon *when such requirements have been completed by the company.*

Furthermore, documentation which verifies such completion may need to be submitted to the bank financing or venture capital investment firm prior to the release of approved funding. Remember, a large percentage of small businesses never reach their successful launch dates, because the funding is inadequate for the beginning of their operations. Therefore, the better an effective business plan not only addresses – but also completes the time schedule requirements – the lower the risk of this capital funding barrier for the entrepreneur.

MARKETING TRENDS AND RESOURCES

Let's take a look at some business trends that have been predicted in recent years, and see how they compare with some of today's marketing trend barriers: [18]

Marketing and Advertising Statistics

Companies are expected to spend $26 billion on internet classifieds by 2011.
U.S. spending on online local advertising will grow 26% to $3.2 billion in 2005 and is expected to reach $5.3 billion by 2010.
Companies are expected to spend $26 billion on internet classifieds by 2011.
U.S. spending on online local advertising will grow 26% to $3.2 billion in 2005 and is expected to reach $5.3 billion by 2010.

By 2010, online video ad spending is expected to garner 8% of the $29.4 billion spent on online advertising.

Graph 1

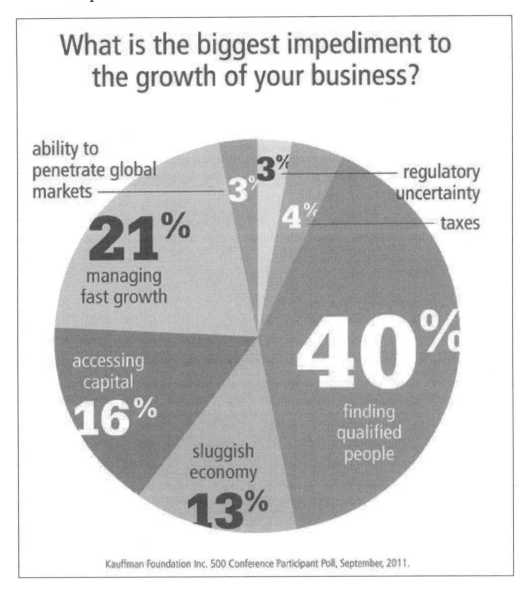

What is the biggest impediment to the growth of your business?

ability to penetrate global markets — 3%

21% managing fast growth

3% regulatory uncertainty

4% taxes

40% finding qualified people

accessing capital 16%

sluggish economy 13%

Kauffman Foundation Inc. 500 Conference Participant Poll, September, 2011.

Despite the positive growth trend forecasts in the U.S., there are potential barriers that business owners face in the future, based upon a Kauffman Survey. [18]

Survey results found that:

- Ninety-six percent of business owners plan to add employees in 2012.

- The location and hiring of qualified people is the biggest challenge standing that may block continued growth for 40 percent of companies. Managing growth (21 percent), accessing capital (16 percent), and the sluggish economy (13 percent) are also obstacles. Regulatory uncertainty and taxes were only 3 percent and 4 percent, respectively.

- Looking to the future, the respondents predict that mobile applications, cyber security and healthcare will be among the hottest industries.

The foregoing trend information illustrates the significant impact the Internet, email marketing, video marketing, and other online methods have had upon business advertising.

In addition, it is important for business entrepreneurs and owners to remain informed as new marketing trends are implemented both now and in the future. For example, the consumer market in recent years has seen the launch of several devices, including cellular Smartphones, netbook computers, and other wireless mobile device applications. The customer is able, using wireless programs (applications or "apps") to contact businesses online and make purchases/payments while "on the go".

Business plans should, as appropriate, reflect a marketing plan that is designed to provide the ability for customers to use these online tools to enhance the sales revenue potential. [18]

MARKETING PENETRATION

So, in the face of so many ways to "get the word out", and market business products and services – how do you choose those methods and techniques that will prove to be successful in your business plan?

Simply put, market penetration will probably be most successful for those companies that do not cling to a strict set of ideas – but change them as times change, and customer wants and needs change in the consumer market.

A perfect example of this adaptability to achieve market penetration is the way in which businesses now have established their individual Facebook and Twitter accounts. As these social networks exploded in popularity, those businesses began to recognize that using social networks was a new and powerful way to know what customers were thinking – both good and bad.

Businesses can become aware much more quickly about customer opinions regarding their public image, products, and services. Further, those "socially-networked" businesses can post their response to both positive – and especially negative – criticism.

The effective business plan will, for any given firm, provide an opportunity for convenient feedback from current and prospective customers. Customers are more likely to type a response in Facebook or Twitter than they are to provide answers to a printed, paper survey and send it back to the company in writing.

Market penetration is a hallmark of the successful business that is willing to keep a finger on the pulse of customer attitudes, and communicate on a frequent and regular basis with former, current, and new customers.

In any event, clearly both computer and Web-based technologies have had a significant impact on the conduct of business in the United States, and in the world. Those businesses that desire to more accurately understand and meet consumer market needs will utilize email and social network communication techniques in their business plan.

To distinguish their business plan image, the entrepreneur can improve the visibility of the company via appropriate email, telephone, and social networking methods.

THE BASIC COMPONENTS: BUSINESS FINANCING

Now that we have seen the importance of careful financial planning, one question comes to mind:

How do I convince an investor to loan me (as an entrepreneur) money for a new business that does not yet exist?

The answer: By including within your business plan a section that presents a series of **pro forma financial statements**.

Pro forma financial statements? What are those?

The American Heritage Dictionary defines "pro forma" as: "Done as a matter of or according to form."

When applied to financial statements (in accounting, generally the balance sheet and income statements), these statements are - simply put – predictions, forecasts, or best estimates of what the owner would expect future financial results to be using the capital funding (when and if) approved by investors. Pro forma financial statements do not represent operating results that have actually happened, as normally is the case with non-pro forma financial statements prepared by the accounting employees. [19]

However, when writing a business plan, properly prepared pro forma financial statements are required in an effectively prepared business. If the statements are not present in your business plan, approved funds will probably not be approved for your company. Table X explains what the advantages of pro forma financial statements are to the business plan:

Table 2: Business Plan Pro Forma Statements

Pro Forma Statement	Business Plan Advantage
Balance Sheet - Original	Forecasted Assets, Liabilities, Capital [1]
Income Statement - Original	Forecasted Income, Expenses, Net Income [1]
Balance Sheet – Worst Case	Forecasted Assets, Liabilities, Capital [2]
Income Statement – Worst Case	Forecasted Income, Expenses, Net Income [2]
Original Statements [1]	*Expected First Pro Forma Financial Statements [1]*
Worst Case Statements [1]	*Expected Worst Case Pro Forma Financial Statements [2]*

Source: Preparing Pro Forma Financial Statements [20]

The more effective business plans explain in very rigorous detail what each number of the pro forma statements means in terms of the company operation. The investors want to be absolutely certain that the entrepreneur has a total financial comprehension of the manner in which their investment will be utilized in the operation of the firm. If a prospective owner is not familiar with accounting fundamentals, it is recommended that a Certified Public Accountant (CPA) be consulted in the preparation of the statements. The use of best-estimate (worst-case scenario) statements provides a more realistic view of the consequences of less-than-ideal financial operations. A better insight can be gained by the investors of entrepreneurial decision making abilities if a commitment of funds receives their approval. [21]

PRINCIPAL STAFF BIOGRAPHICAL INFORMATION

Last, but certainly not least, is the selection of a team that will work with you to make this far-flung business dream a reality, and the presentation of that team in your business plan.

The first, and possibly most important step in the selection process, is the recognition that you – the entrepreneur – *do not* have the ability to do every necessary task in your company. You may be an expert in marketing – but know little or nothing about accounting, taxes, or payroll. Do you think it would be helpful to have an accountant available on staff? Good idea! What if you want to market your products or services online – but do not have a clue about how to *create and maintain* – the "care and feeding" of your business Internet homepage. This seems to require the ongoing availability of a Web design person or firm to handle those matters.

As the owner, you should first assess and determine what you can do in your company, and those necessary jobs that you will need to obtain either operating or advisory assistance. Investors do not expect the owner to be able to do everything for the business; however, the venture capitalists do expect that the honest entrepreneur acquire the human resources and the advice that will be enable a solution to be found for both known and unexpected problems that may arise during day-to-day operations.

Your efficiently-prepared business plan should contain the names, titles, years of experience, and biographical description of the benefits that will accrue to the business based upon the expertise of each staff member. If the staff member is being contracted as the member of a professional firm (i.e. CPA firm), then additional information regarding the firm should be provided, including the range of services that could be obtained if dictated by an appropriate situation.

Remember, your business plan should illustrate clearly that your business is prepared to resolve problems, both typical and unusual, in the areas of governmental regulations and licensing, accounting, taxation, staffing and payroll, marketing, sales, and customer service. The owner must realize that as a manager, the success of the enterprise depends upon the work done by a staff, acting as a team to meet the challenges of business operation.

BUSINESS PLAN RESOURCE INFORMATION

Business plans, as mentioned earlier, can be created in various formats for various types of business.

This section is intended as a brief quick-reference sample of the enormous number of Internet websites that are available for the aspiring business entrepreneur. Hopefully, the items shown here will lead to further research, for the preparation of an effective future business plan, and more importantly – a very successful future business.

RESOURCES

1. http://www.entrepreneur.com
2. http://www.inc.com
3. http://www.businessweek.com
4. http://www.blackenterprise.com
5. http://www.hispanicbusinessmagazine.com/
6. http://www.asianbusinesscentral.com/
7. http://www.www.kauffman.org/
8. http://www.sba.gov/
9. http://www.bls.gov/
10. http://www.commerce.gov/news/fact-sheets/

Bibliography

1. David L. Kurtz, Louis E. Boone, *Contemporary Business*, 14th Edition, 2011
2. David L. Kurtz, Louis E. Boone, *Contemporary Business*, 14th Edition, 2011
3. http://www.ehow.com/about_5372240_history-steve-wozniak.html
4. Home Business magazine , *Key Statistics on the Growing Home-Based Business Market,*
5. (http://homebusinessmag.com/newsstand/news/key-statistics-growing-home-based-business-market) http://www.entrepreneur.com/sbe/growth/index.html
6. http://www.sba.gov
7. http://www.sba.gov , Office of Advocacy
8. http://www.sba.gov
9. http://www.score.org
10. http://www.score.org/young_entrepreneurs
11. http://web.sba.gov/busplantemplate/BizPlanStart.cfm
12. David L. Kurtz, Louis E. Boone, Contemporary Business, 14th Edition, 2011, Appendix D
13. David L. Kurtz, Louis E. Boone, Contemporary Business, 14th Edition, 2011, Appendix D
14. http://www.facebook.com/
15. http://www.membershipsitebuilding.com/members/msb/blog/VIEW/00000010/00000060/The-System-is-the-Solution.html
16. http://businessaccent.com/2010/01/17/famous-business-taglines-and-company-slogans/
17. http://searchsoftwarequality.techtarget.com/definition/PERT-chart
18. American Heritage Dictionary, Second College Edition, 1983
19. http://www.entrepreneur.com/encyclopedia/businessstatistics/article82004.html /
20. http://www.kauffman.com
21. American Heritage Dictionary, Second College Edition, 1983
22. Read more: How to Prepare Pro Forma Financial Statements for a Business Plan | eHow.com http://www.ehow.com/how_2093871_prepare-pro-forma-financial-statements.html#ixzz1ZTh929OV
23. http://www.ehow.com/how_2093871_prepare-pro-forma-financial-statements.html

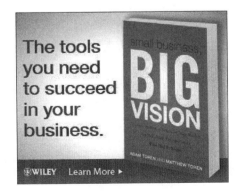

Bonus Content from
Resumes For Dummies

Resume Basics
Meant to Impress

In this part . . .

How do you show off your strengths and shine the best light on your not-so-strong abilities? This part of the book shows you how to handle less-than-ideal work histories or situations, from not enough experience to handling gaps in your employment record. It also explains how to give your content the zing it needs and how to make sure your resume's a looker. When you're ready to put together your resume, flip to the end of this part, which includes more than a dozen sample resumes.

If you want even more help with resume writing and design, pick up the most recent edition of *Resumes For Dummies* (Wiley), written by yours truly, Joyce Lain Kennedy. The chapter that follows is a selection of the best advice I have for creating a top-notch resume.

Putting Together a Top-Notch Resume

*H*ow much are you worth to employers? Are you a top pick, a maybe pick, or . . . gulp, a no-hire pick? Your resume inspires their first best guess, so make sure it's a compelling portrait of how your strengths and skills benefit the enterprise that you're hoping will write your next paycheck.

No matter the platform, you need to show your value via a well-written and well-constructed resume. After all, a prospective employer makes a leap of faith investing money in you as a new and untried employee. Are you really a good match for the position and company? The facts you include on your resume and how you present them are the first step toward answering that question.

In this chapter, I give you a quick rundown of three resume formats that play to different situations, provide advice on word choices that catch a reader or search engine's attention, offer design tips for a pleasing presentation, and leave you with some do's and don'ts of resume writing for recent grads and others in special circumstances. I've also included, at the end of this chapter, more than a dozen sample resumes that show you how to feature your knowledge and skills.

Resume Formats Make a Difference

Resume format refers not to the design or look of your resume but to how you organize and emphasize your information. Different format styles flatter different histories. At root, formats come in three family trees:

- ✔ The *reverse chronological* lists all employment and education, beginning with the most recent and working backward.

- ✔ The *skills-based functional* shouts what you can do instead of relaying what you've done and where you did it.

- ✔ The *hybrid* is a marriage of both formats.

Table 1 outlines how the preceding formats can enhance your personal curb appeal.

Table 1	Your Best Resume Formats at a Glance
Your Situation	*Suggested Formats*
Perfect career pattern	Reverse Chronological
Rookie or ex-military	Functional, Hybrid
Business	Reverse Chronological, Hybrid
Technical	Reverse Chronological, Hybrid
Professional	Reverse Chronological, Hybrid
Government	Reverse Chronological, Hybrid
Special issues	Functional, Hybrid

The following sections explore each type of resume format so you can choose the best style for you and your skills. If you're a recent graduate, a new civilian, a woman returning to the workplace, or someone with gaps in your work history, see the sections later in this chapter that relate to each of these situations for more tips.

As you peruse the following descriptions of resume formats, the big question to ask yourself is:

Does this format maximize my qualifications for the job I want?

If the format you're considering doesn't promote your top qualifications, take another look at the choices to select a format that helps you present your top-pick value.

Reverse Chronological Format

The *reverse chronological* (RC) format, shown in Figure 1, is straightforward: It cites your employments from the most recent back, showing dates as well as employers and educational institutions (college, vocational-technical schools, and career-oriented programs and courses). You accent a steady work history with a clear pattern of upward or lateral mobility.

Consider the strengths of the reverse chronological resume:

- ✔ This upfront format is by far the most popular with employers and recruiters because it is so, well, upfront.
- ✔ The RC format links employment dates, underscoring continuity. The weight of your experience confirms that you're a specialist in a specific career field.
- ✔ The RC format positions you for the next upward career step.
- ✔ As the most traditional of formats, RC is a good fit for traditional industries (such as banking, education, and accounting).

Use the reverse chronological format if you fall into any of these categories:

- ✔ You have a steady school and work record reflecting constant growth or lateral movement.
- ✔ Your most recent employer is a respected name in the industry, and the name may ease your entry into a new position.
- ✔ Your most recent job titles are impressive stepping stones.

Reverse Chronological Format

YOUR NAME
City, State
Home and Cell Phones
E-mail

Objective:
A position that uses your skills.

SUMMARY
- Years of work experience, paid and unpaid, relevant to target position's requirements
- Achievement that proves you can handle the target
- Another achievement that proves you can handle the target
- Skills, competencies, characteristics — facts that further your ability to handle target job
- Education and training relating to the target (if unrelated, bury in resume body)

PROFESSIONAL EXPERIENCE AND ACCOMPLISHMENTS

[dates]   **Job Title**   Employer, Employer's Location
A brief synopsis of your purpose in the company, detailing essential functions, products and customer base you managed.
- An achievement in this position relevant to objective (do not repeat summary)
- A second achievement in this position relevant to current objective
- More accomplishments, i.e., awards, recognition, promotion, raise, praise, training

[dates]   **Job Title**   Employer, Employer's Location
Detailed as above.

[dates]   **Job Title**   Employer, Employer's Location
A briefer synopsis of your purpose in the company, overviewing functions, products, customer base.
- An achievement made during this position relevant to current objective
- More accomplishments, i.e., awards, recognition, promotion, raise, praise, training

[dates]   **Job Title**   Employer, Employer's Location
An even briefer synopsis of your purpose in the company, overviewing functions, products, customer base.
- An achievement made during this position that's relevant to current objective

EDUCATION AND PROFESSIONAL TRAINING

Degree(s), classes, seminars, educational awards and honors
Credentials, clearances, licenses

Figure 1:
The tried-and-true, basic reverse chronological format.

To create a top-notch RC resume, focus on areas of specific relevance to your target position. List all pertinent places you've worked. Include for each the name of the employer and the city in which you worked, the years you were there, your title, your key responsibilities, and your measurable accomplishments.

Functional Format

The functional format (see Figure 2) is a resume of ability-focused topics — portable skills or functional areas. It ignores chronological order. Contemporary functional resumes briefly list employers, job titles, and sometimes even dates at the bottom of the resume to downplay their importance.

Functional Format

YOUR NAME
City, State
Home and Cell Phones
E-mail

Job Title You Desire

More than (# years paid and unpaid) work experience, in target area, contributing to an (achievement/result/high ranking in industry/top 5% of performance reviews). Add accomplishments, strengths, proficiencies, characteristics, education, brief testimonial — anything that supports your target job title.

PROFESSIONAL EXPERIENCE AND ACCOMPLISHMENTS

A TOP SKILL (Pertinent to objective and job requirements)
* An achievement illustrating this skill, and the location/employer of this skill*
* A second achievement illustrating this skill, and the location/employer of this skill*

A SECOND TOP SKILL (Pertinent to objective and job requirements)
* An achievement illustrating this skill, and the location/employer of this skill*
* A second achievement illustrating this skill, and the location/employer of this skill*

A THIRD TOP SKILL (Pertinent to objective and job requirements)
* An achievement illustrating this skill, and the location/employer of this skill*
* A second achievement illustrating this skill, and the location/employer of this skill*

A FOURTH SKILL (Optional — must relate to objective and job requirements)
* Detailed as above

A UNIQUE AREA OF PROFICIENCY (Pertinent to objective and job requirements)
* An achievement testifying to this proficiency, including the location/employer*
* A list of equipment, processes, software, or terms you know that reflect your familiarity with this area of proficiency
* A list of training experiences that document your qualifications and proficiency

EMPLOYMENT HISTORY

[dates]	**Job Title**	Employer, Location
[dates]	**Job Title**	Employer, Location
[dates]	**Job Title**	Employer, Location
[dates]	**Job Title**	Employer, Location

PROFESSIONAL TRAINING AND EDUCATION
Degrees, credentials, clearances, licenses, classes, seminars, training

* Omit locations/employers if your work history is obviously lacking in lockstep upward mobility

Figure 2:
No experience? Use the functional resume format.

The functional format is oriented toward what the job seeker can do for the employer, instead of narrating history. It is heaven-sent for new graduates, ex-military personnel, seasoned aces, and individuals with special-issue problems.

The following are the strengths of the functional format:

✔ A functional resume directs a reader's eyes to what you want him or her to notice. It helps the reader visualize what you can do instead of when and where you learned to do it. Functional resumes salute the future rather than embalm the past.

✔ The functional format — written after researching the target company — serves up the precise functions or skills that the employer wants. It's like saying, "You want budget control and turnaround skills — I offer budget control and turnaround skills." The skills sell is a magnet to reader eyes!

✔ It uses unpaid and nonwork experience to your best advantage.

✔ The functional format allows you to eliminate or subordinate work history that doesn't support your current objective.

The weaknesses of the functional format include the following:

✔ Recruiters and employers are more accustomed to RC formats than other types. Departing from the norm may raise suspicion that you're not the cream of the crop of applicants. Readers may assume that you're trying to hide inadequate experience, educational deficits, or who knows what.

✔ Functional styles may leave unclear which skills grew from which jobs or experiences.

✔ This format doesn't make a clear career path obvious.

When creating a functional resume, choose areas of expertise acquired during the course of your career, including education and unpaid activities. These areas become skill, competency, and functional headings, which vary by the target position or career field. Note accomplishments below each heading. A few examples of headings are: *Management, Sales, Budget Control, Cost Cutting, Project Implementation,* and *Turnaround Successes.*

List the headings in the order of importance and follow each heading with a series of short statements of your skills. Turn your statements into power hitters with measurable achievements.

Hybrid Format

The hybrid, a combination of reverse chronological and functional formats, satisfies demands for timelines as well as showcases your marketable skills and impressive accomplishments. Many people find the hybrid to be the most attractive of all formats.

Essentially, in a hybrid, a functional summary tops a reverse chronological presentation of dates, employers, and capsules of each position's duties. The hybrid style is similar to the contemporary functional format — so much so that making a case for distinction is sometimes difficult. Figure 3 gives you a template for this format.

Hybrid resumes appear to be rapidly gaining in popularity. A hybrid format combines the strengths of both the reverse chronological and functional formats, so check out those earlier sections. Its weakness is that, like a functional resume, it departs from the straightforward reverse chronological format that a very conservative employer may prefer.

The hybrid is a wise choice for rookies, ex-military personnel, seasoned aces, those with job history gaps or a multitrack job history, and individuals with special-issue problems. Additionally, job seekers who want to highlight their flexible qualifications for a variety of positions benefit from this format. Job seekers requiring a security clearance or the handling of large sums of money should stick to the straightforward reverse chronological format.

To create a hybrid resume, build a functional format of ability-focused topics and add employment documentation — employers, locations, dates, and role duties.

Hybrid Format

YOUR NAME
City, State
Home and Cell Phones
E-mail

Objective: Position as_____using your____ (#) years of experience in skills key to target.

SUMMARY OF QUALIFICATIONS
Number of years in area of target position
Related education, training and accreditation
An achievement pertinent to objective
Qualifications that reinforce your candidacy for this position
Other accomplishments, characteristics, proficiencies

SUMMARY OF SKILLS
• Technical skills   • Processes   • Computer software

ACCOMPLISHMENTS AND EXPERIENCE

Job Title, Top Qualifications Used   Employer, Location   [dates]

A Top Skill (Pertinent to objective/requirements)
• Accomplishments made while in this position
• Several apt achievements from position, pertinent to this skill and the objective
Another Skill (Pertinent to objective)
• Several achievements pertinent to this skill and the objective

Job Title, Top Qualifications Used   Employer, Location   [dates]

A Top Skill (Pertinent to objective/requirements)
• Accomplishments made while in this position, even more detailed
• Several apt achievements from this position, similar to above
Another Skill (Pertinent to objective)
• Several achievements pertinent to this skill and the objective

Job Title, Top Qualifications Used   Employer, Location   [dates]

A Top Skill (Pertinent to objective/requirements)
• Accomplishments made while in this position
• Several apt achievements from position, pertinent to this skill and the objective
Another Skill (Pertinent to objective)
• Several achievements pertinent to this skill and the objective

PROFESSIONAL TRAINING AND EDUCATION
Degrees, accreditations, licenses, clearances, courses

Figure 3:
The hybrid
format —
the best of
both worlds.

Wooing Employers with the Right Words

The words you use to describe your accomplishments on your resume speak volumes to the person looking at it. Vague, weak words don't convey your skills and achievements; they put the reader to sleep. Words that are specific and action-oriented showcase your qualifications and make the reader want to know more. Begin your hunt for the right words to build a top-notch resume, from action verbs and keyword nouns, to grammar and spelling tips.

Wow words are action verbs describing your strengths: *improved, upgraded, scheduled.* Keywords are usually nouns demonstrating essential skills: *technology transfers, PhD organic chemistry, multinational marketing.* A smattering of both can make your resume stand up and sing. An absence of either can make your resume sit down and shut up.

One way to sell your value and your benefits to an employer is to get specific. Communicate the importance of what you've done by using details — numbers, names, achievements, outcomes, volume of sales or savings, and size of contracts, for example.

Selling yourself with Wow words

Use lively, energetic verbs to communicate your abilities and accomplishments. The idea is to choose words of substance and power that zero in on what you're selling.

Try not to use the same word twice on your resume — an online thesaurus, such as Thesaurus. com, can give you a range of possibilities.

Take a look at the Wow words that follow and circle the words that are authentic for you.

Wow words for administration and management

advised	explained	mediated	referred
approved	governed	mentored	reorganized
authorized	guided	moderated	represented
chaired	headed	monitored	responded
consolidated	influenced	motivated	reviewed
counseled	initiated	negotiated	revitalized
delegated	inspired	originated	routed
determined	installed	oversaw	sponsored
developed	instituted	pioneered	streamlined
diagnosed	instructed	presided	strengthened
directed	integrated	prioritized	supervised
disseminated	launched	processed	taught
enforced	lectured	promoted	trained
ensured	listened	recommended	trimmed
examined	managed	redirected	validated

Wow words for sales and persuasion

arbitrated	inspired	negotiated	repositioned
catalogued	installed	obtained	researched
centralized	integrated	ordered	resolved
consulted	interpreted	performed	restored
dissuaded	investigated	planned	reviewed
documented	judged	processed	routed
educated	launched	produced	saved
established	lectured	promoted	served
expedited	led	proposed	set goals
familiarized	liaised	publicized	sold
identified	maintained	purchased	solved
implemented	manipulated	realized	stimulated
improved	marketed	recruited	summarized
increased	mediated	reduced	surveyed
influenced	moderated	reported	translated

Wow words for technical ability

analyzed	edited	instituted	programmed
broadened	educated	integrated	published
charted	eliminated	interfaced	reconstructed
classified	excelled	launched	networked
communicated	expanded	lectured	reduced
compiled	expedited	maintained	researched
computed	fabricated	marketed	restored
conceived	facilitated	mastered	revamped
conducted	forecast	modified	streamlined
coordinated	formed	molded	supplemented
designed	generated	operated	surveyed
detected	improved	packaged	systematized
developed	increased	pioneered	trained
devised	inspected	prepared	upgraded
drafted	installed	processed	wrote

Wow words for office support

adhered	coordinated	formulated	planned
administered	cut	hired	prepared
allocated	defined	identified	prescribed
applied	determined	implemented	processed
appropriated	dispensed	improved	provided
assisted	distributed	installed	recorded
assured	documented	instituted	repaired
attained	drafted	justified	reshaped
awarded	enacted	liaised	resolved
balanced	enlarged	maintained	scheduled
budgeted	evaluated	managed	screened
built	examined	operated	searched
charted	executed	ordered	secured
completed	followed up	organized	solved
contributed	formalized	packaged	started

Wow words for financial management

adjusted	developed	invested	returned
administered	disbursed	maintained	saved
allocated	dispensed	managed	shopped
analyzed	distributed	marketed	secured
appraised	doubled	merchandised	sold
audited	economized	planned	solicited
balanced	eliminated	projected	sourced
bought	exceeded	purchased	specified
budgeted	financed	reconciled	supplemented
calculated	forecast	reduced	tested
computed	funded	reported	tripled
conciliated	gained	researched	underwrote
cut	generated	reshaped	upgraded
decreased	increased	retailed	upsized

Wow words for many skills

accomplished	contributed	initiated	proposed
achieved	coordinated	integrated	remodeled
adapted	demonstrated	interpreted	repaired
adhered	dispensed	invented	reshaped
allocated	evaluated	launched	retrieved
appraised	executed	led	solved
arranged	facilitated	navigated	stimulated
articulated	forecast	organized	streamlined
assured	founded	originated	strengthened
collected	guided	overhauled	trained
communicated	illustrated	performed	upgraded
composed	improved	prioritized	won
conserved	increased	promoted	wrote

Using keywords to draw recruiters' attention

In the long-ago 1990s, recruiters and employers used keywords — nouns and short phrases — to search computer databases for qualified candidates. Today they type keywords into search engines to scour the entire Internet for the best people to select for a candidate pool.

That's why, when you're looking for a job, you can't afford to ignore the search engines, which seem to grow and grow. Take pains to feed those wooly-mammoth software creatures with effective keywords that shoot your resume to the top of recruiting search results. (In techie talk, the concept is called *search engine optimization,* or SEO.)

In computerized job searches, keywords describe not only your knowledge base and skills but also your experience and education. When writing keywords, focus on these categories:

- ✔ Skills
- ✔ Technical and professional areas of expertise
- ✔ Accomplishments and achievements
- ✔ Professional licenses, certifications, and affiliations
- ✔ Other distinguishing features of your work history
- ✔ Prestigious schools or former employers

Keywords are arbitrary and specific to the employer and each employer search. So the keywords (qualifications) — starting with the job title — in each job ad are the place to start as you customize your resume for the position.

In many human resource (HR) departments, resumes are screened by junior workers who lack the experience to read between the lines but work on a verbatim basis. That's why nearly matching word for word — rather than liberally paraphrasing — at least a portion of a job's requirements is the way to go.

If the job requirements state:

Ability to lead the development of staffing strategies and implementation plans and programs that identify talent internally and externally through the effective use of external sources.

You write:

Developed and implemented staffing strategies that identified talent internally and externally though the effective use of external sources.

By incorporating some of the employer's language, you strongly increase your odds of surviving the first cut. Your resume lives to fight another round for you when senior screeners look you over. The following lists provide examples of keywords for selected career fields and industries.

Keywords for administration and management

administrative processes
bachelor's degree
back office operations
benchmarking
budget administration
change management
crisis communications
data analysis
document management

facilities management
front office operations
office manager
operations manager
policy and procedure
production schedule
project planning
records management
regulatory reporting

Keywords for banking

branch manager
branch operations
commercial banking
construction loans
credit guidelines
debt financing
FILO (First In, Last Out)
financial management
investment management
investor relations

loan management
loan recovery
portfolio management
retail lending
ROE (Return On Equity)
ROI (Return On Investment)
trust services
turnaround management
Uniform Commercial Code Filing
workout

Keywords for customer service

account representative
call center
customer communications
customer focus groups
customer loyalty
customer needs assessment
customer retention
customer retention innovations
customer service manager
customer surveys
field service operation

Help desk
key account manager
order fulfillment
order processing
product response clerk
records management
sales administration
sales support administrator
service quality
telemarketing operations
telemarketing representative

Keywords for information technology

automated voice response (AVR)
chief information officer
client/server architecture
cross-functional team
data center manager
director of end-user computing
disaster recovery
end-user support

global systems support
Help desk
multimedia technology
network development analyst
project life cycle
systems configuration
technology rightsizing
vendor partnerships

Keywords for human resources

Bachelor of Science, Business Administration (BSBA)
college recruitment
compensation surveys
cross-cultural communications
diversity training
grievance proceedings
job task analysis
labor contract negotiations
leadership development

organizational development (OD)

recruiter
regulatory affairs
sourcing
staffing
succession planning
team leadership
training specialist
wage and salary administration

How can you find keywords for your occupation or career field? Use a highlighter to pluck keywords from these resources:

- ✔ **Online and printed help-wanted posts and ads:** Highlight the job skills, competencies, experience, education, and other nouns that employers request.

- ✔ **Job descriptions:** Ask employers for them, check at libraries for books or software with job descriptions, or search online. To find them online, just enter such terms as "job descriptions" or "job descriptions trainer" or "job descriptions electrical engineer" in a search engine.

Tailoring your writing

Resume language differs from normal speech in several ways. In general, keep the language tight and the tone professional, avoiding the following:

- ✔ **First-person pronouns (I, we):** Your name is at the top of each resume page, so the recruiter knows it's about *you*. Eliminate first-person pronouns. Simply start with a verb.

- ✔ **Articles (the, a, an):** Articles crowd sentences and don't clarify meaning. Substitute *retrained staff* for *retrained the staff*.

- ✔ **"Being" verbs (am, is, are, was, were):** Being verbs suggest a state of existence rather than a state of motion. Try *monitored requisitions* instead of *requisitions were monitored*. The active voice gives a stronger, more confident delivery.

- ✔ **Shifts in tense:** Use the present tense for a job you're still in and the past tense for jobs you've left. But, among the jobs you've left, don't switch back and forth between tenses. Another big mistake: dating a job as though you're still employed (2008–Present) and then describing it in the past tense.

- **Complex sentences:** Unless you keep your sentences lean and clean, readers won't take time to decipher them. Eliminate complex sentences by dividing ideas into sentences of their own and getting rid of extraneous details.

- **Overwriting:** Use your own voice; don't say *expeditious* when you want to say *swift*.

- **Abbreviations:** Abbreviations are informal and not universal — even when they're career-specific. Use *Internet* instead of *Net*.

  The exception is industry jargon — use it, especially in digital resumes. Knowledge and use of industry jargon adds to your credibility to be able to correctly and casually use terms common to the industry in which you're seeking employment.

After you've written your resume, check it for errors. Of all the reasons recruiters and hiring managers shoot down resumes, carelessness with spelling, grammar, and choice of words rank close to the top. Employers especially recoil from impaired spelling when the job seeker botches the interviewer's or the organization's name. (You can Google your way to the company's website to spell the organization's name; you can call to confirm the spelling of the interviewer's name.)

Know thy computer spell-checker. Know thy online dictionary. And know a human being who can carefully proofread your resumes to pick up grammar mistakes or misused words.

Crafting Resumes That Resonate

Pay plenty of attention to your resume's appearance in presenting your targeted content. A well-designed resume is like a guided tour — an employer's eyes are directed to the factual tip-offs that answer these three essential questions:

- Why are you contacting me?
- What can you do for me?
- How do I know you can do this

Here are some design suggestions for tree-and-ink resumes that will help you make the first cut in the employment screening process.

Paper selection

In a digital era, how good should your paper be? For professional, technical, and managerial jobs, the stock for a paper resume should be quality paper that contains rag content of perhaps 25 percent, as well as a watermark (a faint image ingrained in the paper). For lower-level positions, any decent-looking paper will do.

What color should you choose? Stick to white or off-white, eggshell, or the palest of gray. Print on only one side of the sheet.

Consistency, consistency, consistency

Make reading easy on employers by deciding on a style and sticking to it. Don't

- Mix differently spaced tabs and indentations.
- Mix bullet styles without thought. You can mix bullets and checkmarks if the result is tasteful and doesn't look cluttered.

> ✔ Use different spacing between lines. Keep your line spaces the same between headings and the body text for each data point. You're going for a finished look, which means no careless placement of content.

Come on, break it up!

How often have you tried to read a solid block of text and given up because it makes you want to run for the eyedrops? Employers and recruiters also space out on dense text, especially in small type. The solution is to break it up, to segment your data points in related groups. For example, break up a list of eight bullet points by dividing the related points into categories under corresponding headings.

Open spaces

White space is the master graphic attention-getter; it makes recruiters want to read a resume. Too often, job seekers hearing that they must not exceed one page (untrue!) try to cram too much information in too little space.

In addition to white space, consider the vital issue of line spacing — the space between lines in a paragraph and the space between paragraphs. Thoughtful line spacing is important because it impacts a document's overall look.

An overcrowded page almost guarantees your resume won't be read by younger recruiters and hiring managers who grew up in an age of television and quick-reading stories in newspapers, magazines, and web content. And older eyes won't take the wear and tear of too many words jammed into a small space.

If you're concerned that your resume is overstuffed, it's probably too hard to read. A ratio of one-quarter white space to text is about right.

Typefaces

No more than two typefaces (families of characters) should appear on one resume, but if you don't have an eye for good design, stick to one typeface. Times New Roman, Arial, Verdana, or Helvetica used alone is a fine choice for your resume.

If you want to mix two typefaces, I like Helvetica for headings and Times New Roman for text and lesser headings. Printing your name in small capital letters can be pleasing. Use italics sparingly; italicized words lose readability in blocks of text.

A few more tips on appearance

When wrapping up the fair face of your resume, bear these factors in mind:

> ✔ Your name and contact information can be flush left, centered, or flush right.

> ✔ Important information jumps out when set off by bullets, asterisks, and dashes.

> ✔ Don't staple together a two- or three-page resume or put it in a folder or plastic insert. The resume may be photocopied and distributed, or it may be scanned into a database.
>
> To minimize the risk of a page becoming an orphan, put a simple heading or footer on each page after the first with your name and page number. In a multiple-page resume, you may want to indicate the total number of pages (for example, Page 1 of 2).

Boosting Your Chance for an Interview as a Recent Graduate

When you've just walked the cap-and-gown line, you can sidestep "no experience" potholes by impressing employers with your vim and vigor, accomplishments, and up-to-date knowledge. Here's a primer on newbie strengths and weaknesses.

Quick take: Rookie strengths

As a recent graduate, you have three main selling points and various minor ones:

- ✔ You're energetic and fired up to tackle assigned tasks. With no kids, you're more likely to smile when asked to work long hours than are older employees who have family obligations.
- ✔ You're more current in technical skills than older competitors.
- ✔ You're available for the right price. You cost much less than an older, experienced person. Maybe half as much.

Throw in assertions that you're a fast learner, are untarnished by earlier workplace habits that may be anathema to new employers, and that, as a rookie, you're prime material to be molded according to a prospective employer's needs. Provide real-life examples of each claim or you risk coming off as a windbag who merely memorized slick-talking points.

Quick take: Rookie soft spots

Weaknesses you have to wrestle include the stereotyping of recent grads as inept greenhorns who can't find their butts with both hands. In fact, multiple surveys raise the decibel level on what many employers have long suspected or complained about: Most college students lack marketable skills. What can you do to offset this image of incompetence?

 If you have a grade point average (GPA) above 3.5 or have worked as a tutor, emphasize that fact on your resume and at the beginning of job interviews. You're trying to create the *halo effect;* that is, if you lead with an attention-grabbing accomplishment, potential employers swayed by that first great impression apply it to the rest of your qualifications.

If your GPA is poor or marginal, omit it from your resume but bring it up midway through a job interview. Comment that you had to work to pay for your school and living expenses. And, for jobs working with people, explain that you devoted much time to "real-life" experiences, such as leadership in campus organizations. Ideally, you also can show that your grades in your major are excellent, and that your GPA rose as you learned better study habits.

Tips for recent graduates

When writing a resume to land your first post-college job, you need to tailor it to specific job ads. Yes, I know this takes time, but I promise you that it's worth it. You can also customize your resume for posting in resume databases maintained by different industries, like banking and healthcare. Take care to match an employer's job requirements with your qualifications. Keep the following resume boosters in mind, as well.

Amp up your sales pitch

Thicken your work experience by including all unpaid positions — internships, special projects, and volunteer jobs. List them in reverse chronological order in your "Work Experience" section. Statements like these are powerful agents on your resume:

Sales: Sold $1,200 worth of tickets to college arts festival

Counseling: Advised 16 freshman students as peer counselor

Public Policy Coordination: Coordinator for student petition drive to save California Cougar from sports hunting, gaining 2,000 signatures in 35 days

Highlight the work experience most relevant to your intended future. If you have at least one year of full-time professional experience, place education after experience — unless your education is changing your career path.

Data-mine your college experience

Need a job? Get experience! Need experience? Get a job! This predicament has frustrated new graduates since the Industrial Revolution.

You have a difficult resume challenge when you have nothing but education to work with. Only dedicated job research and customizing each resume gives you a chance of producing a persuasive product. Perhaps you overlooked something; even child-sitting or pet-sitting demonstrates reliability and offers experience in accepting responsibility.

Consider the following factors to identify the experience and skills you garnered in college and match your information with the job you hope to land:

- ✔ **Work:** Internships, summer jobs, part-time jobs, campus jobs, entrepreneurial jobs, temporary work, and volunteer work
- ✔ **Sports:** Proven ability to achieve goals in a team environment
- ✔ **Awards and honors**
- ✔ **Research papers and projects**
- ✔ **Campus leadership**
- ✔ **Grade Point Average (GPA):** If it's 3.0 or above; otherwise, omit it (some advisers set the GPA floor at 3.5)
- ✔ **Technical skills and software facility**

Include an activity only if it reveals skills, competencies, accomplishments, results, or other qualifications to support your intended job. Omit high school data unless it adds a unique fact to the total impression that you're creating.

Gaffes common to new graduates

New graduates are more likely than experienced job seekers to make the following mistakes:

- ✔ **Falling short of image standards:** If you present an online resume blemished with the shorthand used for tweets and texting, a paper resume flawed with typos, a persona degraded with whoopee pictures, or a goofy profile on a social media site, you flunk.

- ✔ **Making employers guess:** Employers hate being asked to decipher your intent. Merely presenting your declared major and transcript excerpts is not enough to kick off a productive job search. Add either an objective to your resume and/or a skills summary directed at a specific career field.

- ✔ **Omitting heavy-hitter points:** You distinguish yourself by creating a summary that calls to mind an image of your brand. For example:

  > *As team captain, used strong influencing skills and tremendous personal energy. Got marketplace experience through multiple internships and 6 student jobs, including tutoring. GPA 3.8 despite heavy course load.*

- ✔ **Overcompensating with gimmicky language:** Don't tart up your resume to compensate for a lack of qualifications. Avoid using exotically original language, such as "eyelinered genius," a term used by a business graduate applying for an entry-level marketing position in the cosmetics industry. The term may be colorful, but charm communicates better in an interview.

- ✔ **Leveling the experience field:** Your resume is no place to give every job equal billing. Many rookie resumes are little more than rote listings of previous jobs — TV satellite dish sales representative, waiter, and computer coach, for example.

  Separate your jobs into an A list and a B list. The A list contains the jobs that relate to what you want to do next, even if you have to stretch their importance to make a connection. Briefly mention jobs on the B list in a section called "Other Experience" or "Other Jobs."

- ✔ **Stopping with bare bones:** Some rookies look at a sheet of paper and then at their embarrassing, bedraggled collection of jobs in their paid-experience stew. Desperate to get *anything* written, they settle for employer, job title, and dates of employment.

  The solution is to pull together *all* experience, including volunteer and part-time gigs. Think about your background and add all your relevant competencies and skills that point in the direction of your goals. One strategy is to sign up for a postgraduate internship. Speak with your college's career counselors or internship counselors about this possibility.

- ✔ **Hiding hot information:** Data entombed is data forgotten. Employers remember best the information you give first in a resume, not the data folded into the middle.

- ✔ **Highlighting the immaterial:** Many first-time resume writers feature the wrong skills and knowledge acquired on each job. Highlight the skills that help employers imagine you playing a role for their benefit in their company.

- ✔ **Ignoring employers' needs:** At this moment in time, no one cares what you want — the only thing that matters is the value you bring to the employer.

Winning Interviews as a New Civilian

If you're trading military life for your first civilian gig, be sure to sign up for the federal government's invaluable Transition Assistance Program (TAP). TAP offers a three-day class to help active-duty personnel write resumes and prepare for interviews.

Transition coaches say that a lot of young military retirees overlook TAP — perhaps the very ones who need it the most. As one TAP coach wryly observed: "Some of those we don't see here think they're gun fighters who will go out into the world and do great things and just aren't interested in resumes." That attitude is dead-wrong and self-defeating. The following sections, written by Don Orlando, a retired Air Force colonel, tell you how to present your military background in terms that folks with little military knowledge can understand.

Quick take: Transitioning military strengths

With a chest full of selling points, you've got six super marks of merit:

- ✔ You have exceptionally good training. And military bosses required you to master dozens of new, complex skills quickly and well. You're trainable.

- ✔ As you relate your substantial problem-solving experience, always go beyond *what* you did to show *how* you did it. Some brief stories show how you improved lives; others draw a straight line between what you did and why it made a difference to the mission.

- ✔ You know how to be a team player, and you show up on time. You perform well under pressure. You know how to accomplish assignments in a structured organization.

- ✔ You may have experience with a direct fit to the civilian job market: operations management, supply chain procurement, human resource management, systems administration, or financial planning.

- ✔ You have a strong work ethic to get it right the first time.

- ✔ You're flexible and able to quickly adapt to changing situations.

Quick take: Transitioning military soft spots

Communication is the biggest reason recruiters or hiring managers overlook well-qualified military candidates. They don't get what your resume says when you speak military-ese (also called *milspeak* and addressed later in this chapter) instead of civilian-ese.

When you're finished writing your resume, put it through the civilian translation wringer by asking friends and neighbors who know not a whit about things military to read it and see whether they understand what you're talking about.

Admittedly, some employers do hold a stigmatized stereotype of military service members as being rough, tough, rigid, and hard-headed types whose idea of leadership is command and control. Don't expect a resume to alter that perception, but a well-built resume helps get you inside an interview room where your pleasing personality can reverse false notions.

Tips for new civilians

Many employers appreciate vets as employees and give you preference over a comparable non-vet competitor. The federal government awards 5 to 10 extra points (beyond a passing score of 70 points) to a veteran's application — good news if you're applying for a federal position.

Government contractors hire big numbers of former military members. That's why it's especially important when preparing your resume to factor in federal requirements in online recruiting processes designed to promote equal employment procedures. Federal contractors must play by the rules set by the Office of Federal Contract Compliance Programs (OFCCP).

Here are other resume pointers to keep you moving ahead.

✔ **Advertise what you're selling:** Avoid building your resume around your military rank or title. Employers and recruiters may not understand what you did while in the military and fail to comprehend why they should hire you. Instead, emphasize the qualifications you bring to the employer.

✔ **Consider your best format:** A hybrid resume is a good choice, say many career coaches who work with transitioning military, because it features competencies and skills in professional categories rather than chronological history by rank or job title. But this doesn't mean a reverse chronological resume format can't be used to your advantage.

If you're working with a third-party recruiter, use the format that the recruiter — who is carrying your immediate future in his or her hands — advises.

✔ **Quantify, quantify, quantify:** Measure your results in numbers, percentages, and dollars whenever you can. In the civilian job market, the candidate who wins the numbers game often wins the job.

✔ **Place your accomplishment in context:** Context is a powerful platform on which to display your outstanding performance and accomplishments. For example, in citing an impressive performance, was the task remarkable because you did it with no experience in that area? Did you accomplish the task in three days instead of five days? How many members in your unit scored as well as you in producing the accomplishment? Include these details to help the employer see how your past experience may transfer to his opening.

✔ **Promote your promotions:** Were you sought out by a senior officer for a specific job? If so, do you know how many others may have been considered for that position? *Remember:* Not all promotions are formal. Maybe you received a de facto promotion by being given an assignment tagged as one to be filled by a higher rank. Similarly, perhaps you were promoted "below the zone" (before you normally would have been considered for advancement), which doesn't happen often and recognizes talent you can use to impress employers.

Get the message about milspeak

Bill Gaul, a former military officer and placement specialist, popular media commentator, and acknowledged expert on the military transitioning job market, answers questions about demilitarizing your resume.

Q: Can you give an example of what you call *milspeak?*

A: An Army officer's resume read: "As commanding officer of a 500-person organization, I was responsible for the health, morale, and welfare of all personnel." Health, morale, and welfare? Just think of the incredible range of skills and experience completely overlooked in that milspeak phrase. Far-reaching accomplishments and important responsibilities are whitewashed into boilerplate terms that mean nothing to a civilian hiring manager.

For example, digging into "health, morale, and welfare," we found "policy development, human resource management, budget planning and administration, process improvement, operations management, and staff development."

Q: What's the deal with job titles?

A: Some military job titles are ambiguous, some misleading. Translate your job title without misleading the employer:

✔ Mess cook (food service specialist)

✔ Fire control technician (electronic weapons systems technician)

- Motor pool specialist (automotive maintenance technician)
- Provost marshal (law enforcement officer)
- Quartermaster (supply clerk)
- Base commander (mayor of a small city)

Q: What can you do in situations where your specific work experience doesn't closely relate to the job you're applying for?

A: You can communicate your organizational position instead of your job title. An E-5 Marine Corps embassy guard applying for a management position in the security industry listed his job title as "facility supervisor." He added the details of his experience within the body of his resume. This drew readers because it represented more of a fit than someone who kept people in proper lines applying for visas.

Q: Aren't most military members in combat-related jobs?

A: Yes, and that can be a problem, trying to relate the job you've had to the job you want, unless you're applying for law enforcement positions. But the straight combat MOS (military occupational specialty) — infantry, tank gunner, reconnaissance Marine, and the like — has several options.

List your relative position in an organization — "unit supervisor" instead of "platoon sergeant" as your title. Your work in collateral duties may be the key. A platoon sergeant seeking a position in staff development and training, based on duty as a training NCO (noncommissioned officer), can list "training supervisor" as her title.

The dates listed must accurately reflect the time you spent in the specific collateral duties. As you know, you often have more than one collateral duty while performing a key role for an organization.

Q: How should you list your level of authority?

A: Omit references to rank or grade like "NCO, "petty officer," and "sergeant." Unless an employer has military experience, these terms won't communicate your relative position within an organization. Instead, list civilianized equivalents appropriate to your level of authority:

- Safety Warrant Officer OSHA (coordinator)
- Training NCO (training supervisor)
- Barracks sergeant (property manager)

Q: What about education and training?

A: Many courses and schools leave recruiters wondering exactly what you trained for because the course titles can be esoteric and arcane. The rule is this: List your training in a way that will provide immediately apparent support for your job objective.

If the name of a school or course doesn't communicate exactly what you were able to do after the course that you couldn't do before, show that value because you are trying to inform, not mystify. You are trying to demilitarize the language to help resume reviewers understand the nature of your military training. Some examples:

- SNAP II Maintenance School (Honeywell Computer Server Maintenance School)
- NALCOMIS Training (Automated Maintenance and Material Control System Training)
- Mess Management School (Food Service Management School)
- NCO Leadership Training (Leadership and Management Training)

Q: Is that all there is to civilizing a military background?

A: Not quite. To help resume reviewers understand the depth of your training, list the number of classroom hours you studied. To determine the number of hours, multiply the number of course days by 8, or the number of weeks by 40. If you completed the course within the past 10 years, list the completion date. If the course is older, leave off the date. Here are two examples:

Leadership and Management Training, 3/10 (160 hours)

Leadership and Management Training (160 hours)

Too Long Gone: For Women Only

The "on-ramping" woman still has an uphill climb. After taking a career break to care for her family, trying to re-enter the workforce — whether by choice or economic necessity — may make her feel as though she's been living on another planet.

As a mother, you possess in-demand skills — intelligence, willingness to work hard, creativity, attention to detail, efficiency, grace under pressure, initiative, leadership, persistence, resourcefulness, responsibility, teamwork, and a sense of humor — but the burden is on you to interpret these virtues as marketable skills:

- Grace under pressure, for example, translates to *crisis manager,* a valuable person when the electricity fails in a computer-driven office.

- Resourcefulness translates to *office manager,* someone who is able to ward off crank calls from credit collection agencies.

- A sense of humor translates to *data communications manager,* the person who joshes a sleepy technical whiz into reporting for work at 2 a.m. for emergency repair of a busted satellite hovering over Europe.

You can't, of course, claim those job titles on your resume, but you can make equivalency statements:

Like a crisis manager, I've had front-lines experience handling such problems as electrical failures, including computer crashes.

If you're a returning woman, use the following tips to develop a great resume that connects what you can do with what an employer wants done.

- **Sift through your past:** Identify transferable skills that you gained in volunteer, civic, hobby, and domestic work. Scout for adult and continuing education experiences, both on campus and in nontraditional settings.

- **Use professional terms:** In recounting civic and volunteer work, avoid the weak verbs: *worked with* or *did this or that.* Instead say *collaborated with* or *implemented.* The use of professional words can help de-emphasize informal training or work experience. See the earlier section "Selling yourself with Wow words" for ideas.

  Professionalizing your domestic experience is a tightrope walk: Ignoring it leaves you looking like a missing person, yet you can't be pretentious or naive. I suggest using the term *family caretaker* because it sounds modern and describes your role well. Refer to *home management* to minimize gaps in time spent as a homemaker.

Fill the home-management period with skills relevant to the targeted position. Examples include time management (developing the ability to do more with less time), budgeting experience (developing a sophisticated understanding of priority allocation of financial resources) and leadership positions in the PTA (developing a sense of authority and the ability to guide others).

Gaps in Your Record

Periods of unemployment leave hiccups in your work history. The best strategy is to tell the truth about what you were doing but sugarcoat it in a dignified, positive way. A few examples: *independent study, foreign travel, career renewal through study and assessment.*

An info-blizzard of tips has been published on how to repair resume interruptions. The principles are simple:

- ✔ Present the time gap as a positive event.

- ✔ Detail why it made you a better worker — not a better *person,* but a better worker — with more favorable characteristics, polished skills, and mature understanding, all of which you're dying to contribute to your new employer.

How can these principles be applied? Take the case of a student who dropped out of college to play in a band and do odd jobs for four years before coming back to finish his biology degree and look for a job. The student knows that employers may perceive him as uncommitted. In the resume, he should treat the band years like any other job: Describe the skills that were polished as a band leader. Identify instances of problem-solving, teamwork, leadership, and budgeting.

Do the real problem-solving in the cover letter that accompanies such a resume. You might say something like this:

> *After completing two years of undergraduate study, it was necessary for me to work to continue my education. Using my talents as a musician, I organized a band and after four years was able to continue my education. I matured and learned much about the real world and confirmed that an education is extremely important in fulfilling my career goals.*

The chief mistake people make is assuming that a positive explanation won't sell. Instead, they fudge dates from legitimate jobs to cover the gaps. You may get away with it in the beginning. But ultimately, you'll be asked to sign a formal application — a legal document. When a company wants to chop staff without paying severance benefits, the first thing that happens is an intense investigation of the company's database of application forms. People who lied on their applications can be sent out into the mean streets with nothing but their current paychecks on their backs. Lying isn't worth the risk — it's a mistake.

Another method of papering-over glaring gaps is to include all your work under "Work History" and cite unpaid and volunteer work as well as paid jobs. Use a functional or hybrid format to make the break less obvious. In the final analysis, if you can't find a positive explanation for a gap, say nothing.

If you have gaps in your work history caused by disability, you can no longer hide them. New computer databases make it easy for suspicious employers to research your medical history. And with health insurance costs so high, they may do exactly that.

If your illness-related job history has so many gaps that it looks like a hockey player's teeth, write "Illness and Recovery" next to the dates. It's honest, and the "recovery" part says, "I'm back and ready to work!"

A Sampling of Resumes

I can think of no better way to start your resume than by looking at some examples. By studying how other job-seekers have listed their qualifications, explained their achievements, and wrapped it all up in a neat package, you come up with ideas for your own resume; plus you gain a can-do attitude and the experience of putting together a resume is no longer so overwhelming.

I've included two categories of resumes in this section. First, I give you resumes that reflect the job market by the type of expertise and the work skills being recruited or offered. Then I offer resumes that downplay negative perceptions about your experience or your age.

A text box atop each sample resume contains a mission statement — that is, what the job seeker aims to accomplish, which usually is a better job. The mission statement also includes the requirements for a specific position — or a summary of the typically requested requirements for an occupation or career field.

Within the mission statement, each of the job's requirements has a number next to it. The same number also appears in the body of the resume next to the job seeker's matching qualification for that requirement.

The cross-matched numbers between a job's requirements and the candidate's qualifications shown here are for just for illustration, *not for your actual resume*.

These samples are intended to laser your attention to requirement-and-qualification matching, the single most important factor in causing your candidacy to get noticed in an online swarm of resumes.

Office Work. <u>Administrative Assistant</u>. Hybrid. College graduate seeks Executive Assistant position in chemical industry. Requirements: Bachelor's Degree,[1] 3-5 years in responsible administrative role for chemical manufacturer,[2] strong computer skills,[3] excellent written and verbal communication skills.[4]

ERIN KINGSTON

Phone: 443.555.8989   Baltimore, MD   emkingston@aol.com

ADMINISTRATIVE/OPERATIONS ASSISTANT

Highly-motivated, personable Administrative Professional with over 3 years' experience in chemical industry.[2] Recognized for enhancing productivity through exemplary operational, client service, and sales support. Efficient with exceptional time management, problem-solving, and analytical skills. Very strong oral communication[4] and interpersonal skills. Flexible and adaptable to changing priorities.

CORE STRENGTHS
- ➤ **Administrative Operations:** Special event, meeting, and travel logistics; correspondence, file, records, and database management; project administration and executive-level support.
- ➤ **Sales Support:** Client service, accounts management, problem trouble-shooting and resolution; contract administration, order review, and shipping management; sales tracking and reporting.
- ➤ **Communications:** Polished telephone skills. Experienced business writer, proofreader, and editor.[4]
- ➤ **Financial/Budget Administration:** Budget oversight, invoice verification, and expense tracking; purchasing, supply, and inventory management.
- ➤ **Computer Expertise:** Skilled in creating reports, spreadsheets, presentations, and graphs. Proficient in MS Windows, Word, Excel, PowerPoint, and Outlook.[3]

PROFESSIONAL EXPERIENCE

ADMINISTRATIVE ASSISTANT, BioProducts, Inc. - Columbia, Maryland   [dates]

Provide high level of administrative, sales operations, and client service support for leading manufacturer and supplier of biopesticides and chemical pesticides. Directly support VP of Sales and Marketing and 19 regional sales managers and field development researchers. After 2 months, promoted to permanent position.
- ➤ **Administrative Support:** Effectively orchestrate a full range of strategic administrative functions, including correspondence and publications management; database and file management; travel, special events, and meeting planning; and general purchasing/budget oversight. Create scientific/technical PowerPoint presentations, spreadsheets, graphs, and reports for managers.
- ➤ **Sales, Operations & Customer Service:** Direct liaison between customers and sales. Field 20+ calls per day for product and order information. Input domestic sales orders into database, updating contracts, pricing information, and customer account data. Schedule and track shipments; troubleshoot problems. Conduct operations and management process analyses.

Accomplishments:
- ➤ Independently developed new sales report/pivot table, now company's primary tracking tool.
- ➤ Developed and implemented a linked paper-and-computer-based filing system, incorporating an Excel spreadsheet, to provide fast and easy access to new product and regulatory information.

ADDITIONAL WORK EXPERIENCE

Target, Ellicott City, Maryland - Backroom Stocker/Flow/Replenishment.   [dates]
Kohl's, Ellicott City, Maryland - Overnight Sales Floor Stocker.   [dates]

EDUCATION & TRAINING

B.A.,[1] History, University of Maryland Baltimore County, Baltimore, Maryland.   [date]

Sales. Sales Representative. Reverse chronological. College grad seeks Manufacturer's Representative position in home theater/electronics equipment industry. Requirements: Bachelor's Degree,[1] 3-5 years in consultative sales,[2] relationship development skills,[3] product knowledge,[4] and experience in sales management.[5]

CHARLES A. TRENTON

Cell: (555) 999-9999 • Email: catrenton@gmail.com • Detroit, MI

OBJECTIVE: SALES CONSULTANT – HOME THEATER/ELECTRONICS

SYSTEM EXPERTISE

Audio Formats[4]– Dolby Digital, Dolby Pro Logic II, and DTS; encoding surround sound.

Media Formats[4]– Introduce home theater systems with integrated video and audio sources such as HD (720p, 1080i, 1080p) and Standard (480p) video, DVD-Jukebox (Fireball) systems, Hard-Drive based (Kaleidoscope) systems and AV distribution including Cable, Satellite, WiFi, Bluetooth and Cat5e (Control-4, Elan).

Speaker Recommendations[4]– Satellite, center channel and subwoofers to achieve optimum sound. Advise on room placement to achieve maximum sound experience.

Sound Engineering License – Omega Studio, Detroit, Mich. [date]

SALES EXPERIENCE

Supreme Home Theater and Audio, Detroit, Mich.

SENIOR AUDIO VIDEO CONSULTANT – SYSTEM DESIGNER [dates][2]

- Identify and analyze customer's home theater project interests and budget, understanding and anticipating needs and wants and recommending appropriate products and systems.[3] Discover unrealized music, home theater, and projection interests to grow sale.
- Build customer relationships based on trust;[3] personally manage sale and installation coordination.
- Develop innovative approaches to sales, such as demonstration CDs, to feature audio and visual equipment, resulting in increased enthusiasm and commitment to total quality system.
- Prepare and present sales proposals to decision makers and negotiate purchase agreement.

SYSTEM DESIGNER [dates]

- Member, architect/interior design team, planning total installation of new and renovated homes.
- Conducted site inspections, including planning wiring, special construction and cabinetry.
- Designed whole-house audio and video networking solutions and home automation, including lighting, security, CCTV and HVAC control.
- Developed relationships with architects, general contractors, builders and interior designers.

SALES MANAGER, AUDIO VIDEO CONSULTANT – SYSTEM DESIGNER [dates]

- Drove strategic business initiatives and managed daily operations.[5] Set standards and trained staff on customer assessments, product knowledge and introduction, sales techniques, relationship development and demo presentations.
- Motivated and mentored sales team on current technology and advanced applications.

Sales Accomplishments: Beat quota by 5-25% annually, increasing gross sales totals by $100,000+ per year for year-on-year growth. Top seller for [year] and [year]; Number 2 for [year].

Piano Town, Chicago, Ill. [dates]

SALES CONSULTANT – RETAIL SALES. Achieved 105-135% of sales quota in keyboard department.

EDUCATION: B.A.,[1] Psychology, Wayne State University, Detroit, Mich., [date]

Healthcare. Medical Technologist. Reverse chronological. Medical Technologist I seeks level II position. Requirements: Bachelor's degree in Medical Technology, Biology, or Clinical Laboratory Sciences,[1] 2-4 years' experience in clinical laboratory setting,[2] and excellent computer, verbal and written communication skills.[3]

CELESTE PEREZ

9084 Robinson Road • San Francisco, CA 94107
Cellular: 777-222-5757 • Email: celesteperez@yahoo.com

PROFILE: Dedicated **Medical Technologist** with over 3 years' experience.[2] Skilled in clinical laboratory methodology and activities, including performing complex analyses using sophisticated instruments and good judgement. Strong computer proficiencies, with excellent communication skills.[3] Customer service focused, with polished interpersonal skills. Organized and detail-oriented; reliable and able to take the initiative. Energetic and hardworking; able to work well under pressure.

~ **B.S.,**[1] Medical Technology, San Francisco State University, San Francisco, Calif. [date] ~

Completed six-week rotation, performing all aspects of analytical testing within clinical laboratory sections, including Blood Bank, Hematology, Microbiology, and Chemistry.

PROFESSIONAL EXPERIENCE

Medical Technologist I
LabCenter, San Francisco, Calif.   [dates]

- Specimen Testing: Perform complex qualitative and quantitative immunochemistry analyses and testing; prepare detailed reports summarizing findings. Anticipate and plan work to complete assigned tasks in allotted time. Ensure compliance with company policies, as well as federal, state, and local regulations. (Also possess 2 years' experience conducting virology assays.)

- Quality Control/Troubleshooting: Perform and document all instrument checks and quality control tests. Conduct daily preventative maintenance and troubleshooting; recognize, analyze, and take corrective action to resolve instrument and clinical testing problems. Contact manufacturers' technical service departments to troubleshoot and correct equipment problems, as needed. Assist co-workers in resolving similar problems.

- Administration: Perform clerical functions associated with designated laboratory area. Review reports for clerical accuracy and clinical indications, help maintain files, and accurately input results into computer database. Track inventory and reagent use; request supplies from supervisor on weekly basis.

- Training: Attend and participate in regular department staff meetings and volunteer for cross-training. Train other laboratory personnel and students within designated area.

Accomplishments:

- Consistently receive highest rating on quarterly and annual reviews. Contributed to achievement of annual laboratory goals and objectives; awarded bonus.

- Volunteered to attend week-long new equipment training; upon return, trained select group of employees on new procedures and machinery.

- Routinely volunteer to work hard-to-cover shifts.

Retailing. Retail sales worker. Reverse chronological. Retail worker seeks assistant manager position. Requirements: 1-2 years of retail experience,[1] positive sales attitude and proven sales leadership,[2] strong verbal and written communication skills,[3] strong customer service skills,[4] and basic computer skills.[5]

CYNTHIA MARIE ROMANI

Alexandria, VA   Cell: 555-444-0909   Email: cmromani@gmail.com

OBJECTIVE: Assistant Manager, Retail Beauty Company

PROFILE: Motivated **retail sales professional** with three years[1] of outstanding customer service experience.[4] Demonstrated sales leader,[2] with ability to consistently surpass goals and build client base. Positive attitude,[2] able to go above and beyond for customer satisfaction. Skilled in problem resolution, time and asset management and team leadership. Strong administrative and visual merchandising skills, with keen attention to detail. Excellent verbal and written communication skills.[3] Prior management experience in food service.

RETAIL EXPERIENCE

Key Holder, Sales Representative
Perfect Skin Co., Arlington, Va.   [dates][1]

> Customer Service:[4] Build customer base through friendly, attentive service. Educate customers in skin care and make-up products and techniques. Perform facials and color makeovers. Drive revenue by communicating and demonstrating benefits of products and special offers to new and returning customers. Maintain customer files and follow up on sales to create brand loyalty and increase customer retention. Answer questions and resolve customer complaints and problems.

> Merchandising/Loss Prevention: Plan and organize displays to correspond with current promotions and best-selling products. Maintain store appearance and stock shelves; identify and respond to security risks and thefts.

> Sales Administration: As Key Holder, open/close store; prepare daily deposits and sales reports. Process customer payments, balance cash drawers and maintain sales records. Interact with other stores as needed. Motivate staff to meet goals.[2]

Key Accomplishments:
> Promoted three times in 18 months, from part time to full time, then to Key Holder.
> Exceeded personal daily, weekly and monthly sales goals. Ranked top seller for [year].

OTHER EXPERIENCE

Administrative Assistant, National Fleet Leasing, Co., Fairfax, Va.   [dates]

Teacher, KinderCare Learning Center, Kingstowne, Va.   [dates]
> *Key Accomplishment:* Employee of the Quarter [date]

EDUCATION: Howard University, Washington, D.C., General Education   [dates]

COMPUTER SKILLS: MS Word, Excel, Outlook, PowerPoint; Internet; proprietary databases; hardware, software and peripheral troubleshooting.[5]

Nursing. Nurse R.N. Reverse chronological. Healthcare professional seeks advancement. Requirements: current appropriate R.N. licensure,[1] graduate of accredited School of Nursing,[2] minimum of one-year medical-surgical nursing and hemodialysis experience,[3] ability to assist in lifting patients and equipment,[4] and ability to provide coverage at area facilities during times of short staffing.[5]

SOPHIE McCALL, R.N. [1]
St. Paul, MN • Cell: 333-444-1010 • Email: nursesophie@hotmail.com

PROFILE: Dedicated **Nurse R.N.** [1] with over 11 years' medical experience providing superior clinical care to broad-based patient populations. Skilled leader and team-member, able to maintain positive attitude and productive work environment.[5] Strong interpersonal, administrative and patient/family education skills. Demonstrated ability to establish trust, emote genuine patient caring, and manage crisis situations. Highly organized and able to efficiently prioritize multiple tasks. Able to lift 60 lbs.[4]

PROFESSIONAL EXPERIENCE

Charge Nurse/Clinical Nurse
Med-Surg/Renal Unit,[3] Medical Care North America, St. Paul, Minn.   [dates]
- Provide specialized care for renal patients on 32-bed unit on human dialysis floor. Rotate as charge nurse, overseeing staff members (LPNs, NAs, Nurse Extenders, and Unit Secretaries) and participating in team/unit meetings.
- Conduct patient assessments, and develop, implement, and evaluate individualized care plans. Provide appropriate care and achieve patient outcomes by combining patient involvement and education into total care plan. Adjust treatment plan as needed.
- Perform technical aspects of hemodialysis,[3] assessing and documenting response to therapy. Administer medications, monitor patient progress, develop discharge plans, provide health and nutrition education, and maintain charts and documentation.
- Key team member of unit study project to assess quality of patient care. Analyzed 12 months of patient records to review care, treatment plan, and outcome. Drafted revised policies to improve care and ensure best practices.

Staff Nurse/Charge Nurse
Medical Specialty Unit, Oakdale Rehabilitation Center, Oakdale, Minn.   [dates]
- On 28-bed subacute care unit, rotated as charge nurse. Scheduled and supervised staff.
- Provided primary nursing care and educated patients and family. Assessed patients; developed and implemented treatment plans. Performed variety of procedures and treatments including paritometrial dialysis, ventilator care, central lines and IV therapy.
- Administered medications and monitored patient response. Maintained charts and worked with other healthcare professionals to provide total quality care.

Charge Nurse
Valley Creek Convalescent Center, Woodbury, Minn.   [dates]
- Oversaw all phases of night shift clinical care on 46-bed specialized care unit. Scheduled and supervised LPNs and Nursing Assistants.

EDUCATION
B.S.,[2] Nursing, College of St. Catherine, School of Nursing, St. Paul, Minn.   [dates]

Information Technology. Information Technology Help Desk Analyst. Hybrid. Recent MBA graduate with sales and IT experience seeks Technical Sales Analyst position. Requirements: Bachelor's Degree,[1] 1-2 years IT experience and/or training,[2] excellent customer service skills, knowledge of Microsoft Access, Word, mail merge, Excel, Internet and graphic design,[3] and excellent oral and written communication skills.[4]

WILLIAM J. FRANKLIN, JR.

billjfranklin@comcast.net

Catonsville, MD   Cell: (888) 777-3434

OBJECTIVE: Technical Sales Analyst, Solimar Systems, Inc.

QUALIFICATIONS SUMMARY

Accomplished technical marketing and sales value for employer with over two years' progressively responsible experience in sales, customer support, and end-user training for telecommunications technologies and services.[2] Strong technical background with proven success building and managing customer relationships with major corporate and government clients. Keen problem solving, analytical, and negotiation skills. Excellent presentation and oral/written communications skills.[4] BS Marketing degree.[1]

Business, marketing, sales, & technology expertise:

➢ Business Development, Client Relationship Management, & Needs Assessment
➢ Competitive Product Positioning, Technical Support & Troubleshooting, Technology Training
➢ Strategic Alliances, Government & Corporate Partnerships
➢ Strategic Sales & Marketing Planning/Research, Presentations, & New Product Launch
➢ Managing Vendor/Supplier Relationships
➢ Statistical Analyses, Graphical Presentation of Data, & Competitive Benchmarking
➢ Wireless Voice and Data Communications, including Pagers, PDAs, and BlackBerry Products
➢ PC hardware, Software & Peripheral devices, including all Microsoft applications

PROFESSIONAL EXPERIENCE

Help Desk IT Analyst
NET SOLUTIONS, INC. International Unit, Washington, D.C.   [dates]

Provide first tier end-user technical support via telephone to over 8,000 staff. Assist and resolve complex technical issues and questions on Lotus Notes; MS Office XP; remote access; BlackBerry devices; and other internal software applications. Conduct remote diagnostics to troubleshoot and resolve desktop application issues.

Accomplishment:
➢ Currently facilitating seamless migration of windows 2000 Enterprise Desktop (ED3) to XP (ED4) and Lotus Notes R5 to Notes ND6 with virtually no interruption to workflow.

SPRINT COMMUNICATIONS, Vienna, Va.   [dates]

Fast-track promotion through positions of increasing challenge and responsibility, based on consistently strong performance in sales support, account management and technical support of multi-million dollar wireless technology contracts with Fortune 1000 companies and federal government agencies, including the Department of Defense, the CIA, and the Federal Energy Regulatory Commission.

William J. Franklin, Jr. ~ Cell: (888) 777-3434

National Account Sales Consultant [dates]

Established and fostered relationships with government and corporate clients to promote integrated wireless data and messaging services, including pagers, PDAs, and BlackBerry products. Directly supported four Account Executives.

➢ Expanded and strengthened sales and marketing efforts through new product and training presentations. Contributed to new product development of key accounts.
➢ Challenged to identify, evaluate, and capture opportunities for upgrade or expansion of contracts.
➢ Provided technical support and problem resolution and led end-user training.
  Accomplishments:
  ➢ Consistently achieved or surpassed team quota at 100% each month for 3 years.
  ➢ Coordinated and managed up to 30 strategic accounts simultaneously and provided direct customer support to 40-50 individual customers.
  ➢ Monitored, researched, and summarized market trends and competitor data and developed integrated product analyses for accounts executives that drove sales growth.

Team Customer Account Executive [dates]

Integral member of four-person account service team that developed and orchestrated multi-media presentations and on-site technical training sessions for clients nationwide. Fostered open communications with customers to gather vital feedback on products, pinpoint problems, and end-user issues. Resolved diverse range of technical, service, and billing problems.

  Accomplishments:
  ➢ Contributed sales support to government channel to reach over 137% of plan for [years].
  ➢ Improved customer satisfaction and retention by responding promptly to user and billing issues, staying alert to potential problem areas, and developing creative solutions.

Regional Implementation Specialist [dates]

Integral member of a seven-person team that supported pre-sales and closing presentations for federal and corporate accounts.

  Accomplishments:
  ➢ Successfully implemented over 60 accounts, improved customer satisfaction by 50%.
  ➢ Closed 20 new government and corporate accounts.

ADDITIONAL WORK EXPERIENCE

Credit Manager, MBNA, Baltimore, Md. [dates]
Managed up to 500 customer loan and real estate accounts. Generated new business leads, cross-sold financial services, and refinanced loans through cold-calling, telemarketing, and field sales.

EDUCATION

Bachelor's Degree, Marketing,[1] Temple University, Philadelphia, Pa. [date]

COMPUTER SKILLS [3]

Proficient in popular applications, including Microsoft Windows, Excel, Word, Access, PowerPoint, Outlook, and Works; Lotus Notes; WordPerfect; Adobe Acrobat, Illustrator; Internet applications. Expertise with specialized data management, mail merge and analytical software.

New Graduate. <u>Veterinary Technician</u>. Reverse chronological. Worked in field while student; now seeks better job in larger vet hospital. Requirements: Medically assist veterinarians,[1] bachelor's degree,[2] instrumentation,[3] office software.[4]

DONNA LUNA

4214 Kensington Rd. • Dallas, TX 99999
Cell: 111-869-4716 • E-mail: DLuna@hotmail.com

PROFILE: Recent BS Biology plus 8 years' experience in veterinary and medical fields. Skilled in latest technology. Work cheerfully on team or independently. PC proficient. Dependable, conscientious veterinary paraprofessional ready for senior level veterinary hospital staff position.

LABORATORY SKILLS

✓ Dexterous use of laboratory equipment and instrumentation, including isolating environmental samples, performing assays, and identifying samples. Prepare, analyze, and test laboratory specimens. Stain slides to microscopic test for specific disease pathogens and unknowns.

✓ Assist with veterinary surgical and autopsy procedures. Perform micro animal surgeries and anesthetizations.

✓ Collect blood, and other samples from animals. Perform red/white blood cell counts.

✓ Keep comprehensive lab notes and researched, prepared, and presented detailed reports and papers. Lead and organized group project work.

WORK EXPERIENCE

Veterinary Technician   [dates]
Westview Animal Hospital, Dallas, Tx.

<u>Veterinary Support</u>:[1] Assist veterinarians to diagnose and treat variety of animal diseases and conditions including surgeries. Take and test blood, urine, and fecal samples, testing for disease, viruses, and parasites. Skilled with instrumentation, including radiograph and ultrasound.[3] Use Avimark, MS Word, & QuickBooks software.[4]

<u>Reception</u>: Receive and direct calls and visitors, answering customer inquiries and resolving problems. Assure customer satisfaction, exercising empathy and tact. Take and relay detailed messages regarding animal patients. Collect and process payments. Set appointments and send reminder notices. Update and maintain electronic and paper filing systems. Direct and provide guidance to Animal Care Assistants.

Receptionist   [dates]
Dr. Roger Lax, Plano, Tx.
<u>Administration</u>: Receptionist for busy private practice. Answered phones and received patients. Created and updated medical files. Gained competence with medical terminology.

EDUCATION

Bachelor of Science,[2] Biology; Towson University, Towson, Md.   [dates]

Relevant Coursework: Biostatistics, Biology: Ecology, Evolution, & Behavior, Botany, Chemistry, Comparative Animal Physiology, Dangerous Diseases, Fish Biology, Genetics, Medical Microbiology, Organic Chemistry, Physics, Zoology.

New Graduate. <u>Business Administration degree</u>. Hybrid. Candidate seeks Junior Financial Analyst position. Requirements: BS Business or Finance,[1] 1-3 years' relevant experience,[2] strong Excel skills,[3] independent work style,[4] highly motivated,[5] strong problem-solving skills,[6] excellent communication skills[7] and team player.[8]

JOSHUA GANSL

Charleston, SC 29401   Tel: 555.111.1712   joshgansl@yahoo.com

OBJECTIVE: Junior Financial Analyst

SKILLS & QUALIFICATIONS

- Strong financial, quantitative/qualitative analytical, and problem-solving skills.[6]
- International and domestic summer work experience. Gained essential knowledge evaluating properties, structuring financing, conducting pro-forma cash flow analysis, and executing leases for residential and commercial real estate sales and acquisitions.
- Poised, self-confident. Proven public speaking, interpersonal and multicultural communications skills.[7]
- Highly motivated with strong work ethic.[5] Well-developed team player abilities.[8] Able to prioritize tasks, work independently,[4] and meet deadlines.
- Competitive and ambitious. Welcome new challenges.
- Computer Skills: Advanced proficiencies in Microsoft Windows, Word, Excel,[3] and PowerPoint.

EDUCATION

B.S.,[1] Business Administration, Clemson University, Clemson, S.C., GPA 4.0   [date]

- **Relevant Courses:** Corporate Finance, Accounting, Financial Statement Analysis, Micro/Macro Economics, Business Statistics, and Management Information Systems
- **Team Project:** In-depth business case analysis of sporting goods industry. Conducted top-down financial statement analysis to determine predictors of future stock prices.

WORK EXPERIENCE

Tillman Securities, PLC, London, England [2]   [dates]

Worked directly with CFO on commercial real estate acquisitions and financing. Reviewed properties and conducted future cash flow analysis. Prepared and presented regulatory and financial documentation to financial institutions.

- Involved in executing purchase of over $100 million in commercial real estate properties.
- Part of team that refinanced several multimillion dollar real estate properties.

JOSHUA GANSL

Seaside Realty Partners, Inc., Los Angeles, Calif. [dates]

Summer [year]: Participated in successful acquisition of 18 commercial properties leased to U.S. Drugstore Corporation in upstate New York. Created Excel spreadsheets, performed due diligence, analyzed and prepared leasing agreements, conducted pro-forma cash flow analysis, and conducted on-site inspections with acquisition team.

- Presented summary financial data to outside investors and the company's executives to be used for acquisition decision-making.

Summer [year]: Shadowed Vice Chairman. Gained valuable experience evaluating real estate properties, and predicting future cash flow and property income. Developed passion and talent for identifying, structuring, and executing sound commercial real estate investments.

Gansl and Greenberg, LLP, Los Angeles, Calif. [dates]

- Delivered administrative and operational support for high-volume law firm. Ensured all documents were accurately filed. Provided customer service and supported legal staff.

Camp International, Jerusalem, Israel [dates]

Camp counselor at an international summer camp for 200 campers from all over the Americas and Europe; including England, France, and Belgium.
- Led broad range of team activities and supervised tours throughout Israel.
- Promoted open communications and camaraderie among all campers. Reinforced importance of respecting cultural differences.
- Developed talent for fostering communication despite language barriers.

SPECIAL INTERESTS & ACTIVITIES

Community Service
- Chai Lifeline Volunteer, an organization that supports cancer patients and their families. Maintained ongoing relationships with seriously ill youngsters. Participated in "Big Brother" program for two years.

Team Sports
- Captain of college basketball team, 2 years.

International Travel
- Extensive travel to over 10 European countries, as well as trips to the Middle East. Enjoy experiencing and learning about other cultures, history, and customs.

Foreign Languages
- Write and speak Hebrew.
- Conversational Yiddish — an international dialect of German.

Reading
- Avid reader. Especially enjoy financial publications.

Young Adult. Intern. Reverse Chronological. Recent MPA graduate seeks Program Officer/Researcher position with nonprofit or public policy organization. Requirements: Bachelor's degree (preferably Master's),[1] strong research, writing, and legislative skills,[2] experience working on policy and advocacy campaigns,[3] solid Microsoft Office skills,[4] and strong attention to detail and ability to multi-task.[5]

ROCHELLE HENDERSON

Brooklyn, NY
Cell: 888-444-9090
E-mail: r_henderson@ny-u.edu

EXPERIENCE

[dates]   **UNITED NATIONS DEVELOPMENT PROGRAMME**   New York, N.Y.
Programme Assistant Intern, Equator Initiative   [dates]
Mid-term Evaluation Intern, United Nations Capital Development Fund   [dates]
- Researched and wrote [2] reports and position papers on capacity building in local communities.
- Authored and edited [2] articles for *Between the Lines* newsletter.
- Evaluated and analyzed documents to extract recommendations for improving design and cost effectiveness of microfinance donor training workshops.

[dates]   **NEW YORK UNIVERSITY SCHOOL OF MEDICINE**   New York, N.Y.
Research Associate, [2] Center for Immigrant Health
- Conducted highly detailed [5] research in English and Spanish on quality of medical services for immigrant populations for advocacy campaign,[3]
- Designed and implemented quality assurance mechanisms to improve accuracy of study's data.[5]
- Supervised and trained staff of 9 research interns.

[dates]   **PEACE CORPS**   Tarija, Bolivia
Gender and Development Representative   [dates]
Natural Resources Management Extensionist   [dates]
- Directed all logistical components, drafted budget, and raised funds for 4-day national gender and development conference for 35 high school students and 5 community representatives.
- Selected to use participatory modules to train 28 volunteers for gender mainstream projects.
- Managed locally focused natural resources projects for over 80 indigenous women.
- Planned, prioritized, and managed multiple tasks and assignments in fast-paced environment.[5]

[dates]   **WORLD WILDLIFE FUND**   Washington, D.C.
Government Relations Intern [2]
- Wrote and edited documents on environmental legislation and international development concerns to educate staff on policy issues. Represented lobbyist at World Bank and Capitol Hill meetings.

[dates]   **THE WHITE HOUSE**   Washington, D.C.
President's Council on Sustainable Development Intern [2]
- Prepared overviews of environmentally sustainable strategies presented to international delegations.
- Edited *Towards a Sustainable America* report presented to President William Clinton.

EDUCATION   **Master of Public Administration,[1]** New York University, New York, N.Y., [date]
Specialization: International Public and Nonprofit Management and Policy
Bachelor of Arts,[1] Environmental Science and Policy, Hood College, Frederick, Md., [date]
Concentration: Environmental Policy; Minors: Sociology and International Economics

COMPUTERS   Microsoft Office [4] (Word, Excel, Outlook, PowerPoint, Access, Visio) and SPSS
LANGUAGES   Fluent in Spanish. Intermediate proficiency in Portuguese and Quechua.

Young Professional. Graphic Artist/Visual Information Specialist. Reverse chronological. Graphic Artist seeks corporate communications graphics position. Requirements: Bachelor's degree,[1] 3 years' experience in graphics design and photography,[2] experience in production management and utilizing video, 35MM and audio equipment,[3] knowledge of advertising and marketing communications,[4] excellent communications skills,[5] and willing to travel 50% of the time.[6]

SCOTT E. PASQUALE

Cell: 111.444.4444

340 Decatur Lane
Baton Rouge, LA 70801

E-mail: spasquale@gmail.com

GRAPHIC ARTIST/VISUAL INFORMATION SPECIALIST

Skilled graphic artist, photographer, and video producer with three years' professional experience.[2] Creative and resourceful in coordinating and producing training videos, photography for print and Web and graphic design. Proficient in production management, as well as use of video, graphics software, 35 MM, digital and audio equipment and systems [3] to produce advertising and marketing materials, Web content, and training programs.[4] Strong communications skills;[5] able to travel.[6]

Professional Experience	**Computer and Information Specialist** *Training Professionals, Inc.; Baton Rouge, La.* • Maintain Web site utilizing HTML, scanning and forms management • Develop graphics, photographic images, and content for print and electronic media • Maintain customer service, evaluate customer feedback, and determine appropriate action • Produce videos and edit into training films • Photograph training sessions for Web site production	[dates]
	Commercial Photography Intern and Independent Contractor *Online Real Estate Listing Service; New Orleans, La.* *Judith Salmona, Freelance Photographer; Kenner, La.* • Accomplish portrait, real estate, and documentary photographic assignments • Produce professional quality custom color prints and graphic images • Scan negatives and slides; manipulate and correct images • Maintain and service printing and graphics equipment • Organize and catalog negatives and proof sheets	[dates]
	Technical Supervisor: *Performance Anxiety* **Installation** *Smith College; Northampton, Mass.* • Produced interactive video exhibition combining real-time computer image processing with variety of short videos • Used Image software and Infusion Systems' I-Cube X hardware	[dates]
Education	**B.A.,**[1] Visual and Performing Arts, Louisiana State University, Baton Rouge, La. *Relevant Coursework:* Introduction to Computers, Programming in C, HTML, Dreamweaver, Illustrator, Quark, Macromedia Flash, B&W Photography, Color Photography, Advanced Photography, Electronic Image Processing, Final Cut Pro, Alternative Processes, Visual Concepts, Ideas in the Arts, Introduction to Recording Techniques, History of Photography, Contemporary Art in Process, History of Film, American Life in Films	[date]
Skills	*Computer:* Macintosh and PC – Word, Excel, PowerPoint, Photoshop, Illustrator, Acrobat, QuarkXpress, Flash, digital imaging, scanning, Corel Draw, non-linear video production and editing, C Programming, HTML Web page development, database management *Photography:* digital video production, 35mm photography, B&W and color processing, printing and toning, studio portraiture, and dry mounting	

Young Professional. Sales and Marketing Manager. Hybrid. Seeks Marketing Coordinator position in larger company in advertising field. Requirements: 3-5 years of marketing experience – printing industry experience a plus,[1] degree in business, marketing, advertising or related discipline,[2] highly motivated,[3] detail and goal-oriented,[4] and high proficiency with MS Word, Excel, PowerPoint – Quark and Photoshop a plus.[5]

YOEL MORECK

Las Vegas, NV
Cell: 555-333-3939
Email: yoel_morick@gmail.com
Twitter: @YMoreck

MARKETING COORDINATOR with 5 years of marketing experience.[1]

- Sales, marketing, and advertising in printing/publishing,[1] real estate, and landscaping.

- Highly motivated,[3] with demonstrated ability to develop and maintain new sales territories and accounts, create new revenue streams, and increase profits.

- Strong ability to develop customer rapport and build loyal relationships.

- Excellent attention to detail and ability to meet and surpass sales goals.[4]

SALES & MARKETING EXPERIENCE

Sales and Marketing Manager/Field Supervisor
Local Lawn Services, Las Vegas, Nev.   [dates]

Recruited to spearhead sales and marketing efforts for this growing landscaping company.

Marketing: Develop marketing and advertising programs and materials, including direct mail and internet. Conduct market and customer research and develop new revenue streams to build business. Advise on market penetration and business development strategies.

Sales: Manage customer relationships from initial contact through consultation/estimate and service delivery. Develop sales leads, estimate projects, and write service contracts. Determine customer needs and recommend best options. Resolve customer problems and follow up to ensure customer satisfaction and loyalty.

Management: Analyze business operations and processes and identify improvements. Review profit and loss statements; recommend ways to reduce costs and maximize profits. Develop and implement policies. Direct laborers onsite; track time and attendance.

Key Accomplishments:

- Achieved year-on-year growth, increasing revenue by 31% in first year to $550,000; and an additional 18% the following year, for total revenue of $650,000. Established 70+ new accounts.

- Authored 14-page Employee Handbook; developed formal standards and policies for labor staff.

- Created new business line, hardscaping. Also created Web site for retail mulch sales.

Account Executive
Star Publishing, Las Vegas, Nev.   [dates]

Sold advertising to local and national clients for primarily business-to-business publications, including area chamber of commerce directories. Total circulation was approximately 100,000.

Maintained established accounts and developed new leads and clients. Consulted directly with clients' executive staffs to secure ad sales. Kept track of and met multiple, concurrent publication deadlines. Worked with creative design staff to develop advertising concepts and content. Managed full sales-cycle, ensuring client satisfaction.

YOEL MORECK   Page 2   Cell: 555-333-3939

Key Accomplishments:

- Consistently met/exceeded sales goals; sold $100,000 of advertising in 6 months.
- Established territory for newly won contract — Susquehanna Chamber of Commerce Quality of Life Guide, a full-color directory. Landed 35 new accounts, worth $35,000.

President

Your Lawn and Garden, LLC, Henderson, Nev.   [dates]

Founder/operator of landscaping business. Oversaw all aspects of company start-up and operation, including sales and marketing, business development, accounting, and management.

Researched market and identified specific demographics of targeted client base. Developed marketing strategy; created and distributed advertising materials. Managed customer relationships; met with potential clients, negotiated contract, and closed sale. Directed staff of 1-3, coordinating projects and ensuring completion.

Sales Manager

Sailor's Restaurant and Seaside Guide, San Francisco, Calif.   [dates]

Sold advertising for 2 regional editions of full-color, glossy boating magazine, circulation of 110,000.

Created sales territory for new regional edition of this yearly publication, distributed at local marinas. Generated leads through direct contact and cold calls. Clients included hotels, restaurants, yacht brokers, and retail shops. Negotiated contracts, established payment schedules, and designed ads. Managed billing and publication distribution. Once established, maintained and expanded client base.

OTHER WORK EXPERIENCE

Flight Attendant

Delta Airlines, Las Vegas, Nev.   [dates]

Provided customer service, resolved passenger and employee problems, and responded to emergency situations. As Chief Purser, supervised crews of 2-10; provided liaison with captain. Received numerous commendations and customer appreciation letters.

Editor: [dates]

Created and published 20-page bimonthly staff newsletter. Selected and compiled content and artwork; edited, formatted, designed, proofread, and laid out publication.

EDUCATION

B.S.,[2] **Marketing,** in progress, University of Nevada, Las Vegas, Nev.; 96 credits. Expected graduation: [date]

A.A.,[2] **Business,** City College of San Francisco, San Francisco, Calif.,   [date]

COMPUTER SKILLS: [5] MS Word, Excel, Outlook, Publisher, PowerPoint; Photoshop; ACT! database

Young Professional. Associate Editor. Reverse chronological. Journalist seeks features/projects designer position. Requirements: 3 years of weekly newsroom design experience,[1] solid news judgment,[2] communication skills,[3] attention to detail,[4] and knowledge of InDesign.[5]

JANCIE ULREY
Boston, MA • Mobile: 617-777-6767 • Email: jan_ulrey@gmail.com

JOURNALIST/LAYOUT & DESIGN SPECIALIST

OBJECTIVE: Features/Projects Designer

PROFILE: Nearly six years' experience in weekly newspaper settings, serving as writer, editor and page designer.[1] Passionate about newsgathering and creating eye-catching, reader-friendly content. Solid news judgment and design skills,[2] coupled with imagination and creativity, able to produce aesthetically pleasing pages. Organized, detail-oriented [4] and deadline-driven. Strong time management and communications skills;[3] excel in team and individual work settings. Proficient in AP Style. **Computer Skills:** Word, Outlook, Excel, PowerPoint, Access; Quark Express; InDesign;[5] Photoshop; HTML

~ **A.A.S.,** Communications, Bunker Hill Community College, Boston, Mass., [date] ~

RELEVANT EXPERIENCE

Associate Editor   [dates]
Bay Windows   Boston, Mass.

Design, layout and write for weekly newspaper, averaging 64-136 pages, with circulation of 16,000.

- Design/Layout: Plan and execute advertising and editorial page design, including front and back pages, news and features sections, headlines, column titles, and cutlines. Review weekly ad sales and determine page count and color slots. Formulate layout design and presentation using InDesign, including style and size of type, photographs, and graphics. Take layout direction from editor and work with advertising and design staff to correct problems. Use Photoshop to make color corrections on photos and crop and rotate images; track photo archives.

- Writing/Editing: Research, develop and write news and feature stories. Contribute to editorial planning, develop story ideas and arrange and conduct interviews. Review copy and correct errors in content, grammar and punctuation, following appropriate formatting and AP style guidelines. Write/rewrite cutlines and headlines. Correct final copy and prepare files for Web upload.

Key Accomplishments:
- Successfully completed layout/production on largest paper (136 pages) in publication's history for 30th anniversary issue.
- Supported new editor, staff writer and editorial assistant during major staff transition.
- Wrote over 40 feature and news stories while handling design/production responsibilities.

Staff Writer   [dates]
The Sunday Voice   Cambridge, Mass.

Key player on four-person staff of this small weekly community newspaper.

- Writing/Content Selection: Contributed to and/or managed news coverage, determining emphasis, length, and format. Wrote hard/soft news, including school news and obituaries. Gathered information through research, interviews, experience, and attendance of events.

- Production/Administration: Planned and executed layout of school news section and obituaries, as well as determined page count and scanned photos. Edited and proofread editorial content. Assumed managing editor's duties as needed, leading news meetings, assigning stories, and gathering news content. Also, screened phone calls and purchased supplies.

Mid-Career Trades. HVAC expert. Functional. Experienced heating/cooling specialist seeks HVAC Manager, Technical Training & Service position. Requirements: Min. 15 years of experience in theory and practice of HVAC – installation, service, repairs, heat pumps, air conditioners, gas/oil furnaces, boilers, and standard controls,[1] strong communication and leadership skills,[2] must be performance-driven, motivated,[3] and computer savvy. [4]

GREG BOREK
903 Longmeadow Lane • Raleigh, NC 27602
Cell: 999-333-2323 • Email: greg_borek@comcast.net

HVAC/Refrigeration Systems Expert

OBJECTIVE: HVAC Manager, Technical Training and Service

AREAS OF EXPERTISE

- **HVAC/R Expert**, with over 20 years' experience. Highly skilled in every phase of heating and air conditioning, chillers, heat pumps, furnaces, and boilers for residential, commercial, plumbing and refrigeration lines: **design, installation, troubleshooting, service, and repair.**[1] Experienced with Metasys and Johnson 350 controller. Proficient in Control systems design and installation–Analog and DDC.

- Experienced **project manager and team leader,**[2] with jobs averaging $500,000, up to 500 tons. Adept at estimating job schedules, choosing quality, cost-effective materials and designing and installing control systems, as well as supervising apprentices, journeymen and subcontractors on the job.

- Mentor, coach, and train junior staff. Develop and implement work standards and provide guidance on technical processes, safety, and operations.

- Performance-driven and motivated;[3] consistently complete job ahead of schedule and under budget. Regularly receive written and verbal recognition and bonuses.

- Strong customer service, interpersonal and communications skills.[2]

- Skilled at any and all **electrical** or **electronic diagnosis** and **repair**.

- Knowledgeable A/C systems **programmer**; PC proficient and familiar with HVACPRO software.[4]

CERTIFICATIONS

North Carolina Licensed Journeyman, #6666; EPA Certified, Universal & Automotive, #999999999

SAMPLE PROJECTS

Designed and installed controls systems for:
  WNCN 17 NBC • Fool Lion food stores
  Borders book stores • Wake Forest University

Installed & set up Metasys system for:
  Durham Regional Hospital • CVS drugstores
  State government building, Raleigh

WORK HISTORY

Johnson Controls, _Controls Technician_	[dates]
Aire Right Mechanical, _Commercial A/C_	[dates]
Servicemark Mechanical Services, _Residential A/C and Refrigeration; Appliance Repair_	[dates]

EDUCATION/SPECIALIZED TRAINING

Metasys ASC engineering, Johnson Controls, [date]
DDC control, M & M Controls, [date]
Trane Microcontrol Voyager, Trane, [date]
Pneumatic Controls I & II, [date]
Honeywell: Fireye, M & M Controls, [date]

Carrier Parker System, Carrier, [date]
Wake Tech. Comm. College, 36 credits [dates]
Diploma, Roosevelt High, Raleigh, SC [date]

Mid-Career Professional. Project Manager. Reverse chronological. PM seeks Managerial HRIS (Human Resource Information Systems) position. Requirements: Bachelor's degree in computer science, management information systems, or equivalent, MS/MBA a plus,[1] five+ years increasing responsibility in HR Technology and/or HR discipline leading medium to large scale projects,[2] three+ years experience in project management,[3] knowledge of current HRIS technology,[4] good analytical, interpersonal, leadership and managerial skills,[5] and strong oral and written communication skills.[6]

JANICE E. DEMER

Anaheim, CA   Day/night: 999-555-5555   E-mail: Janiceedemer@aol.com

MANAGER
HUMAN RESOURCE INFORMATION SYSTEMS

- Project Management
- Implementation Consultant
- Quality Customer Service
- Corporate Start-ups
- Procedural Development
- Corporate & Government Contracts

- Skilled Negotiator
- Strategic Planner
- Sales Process/Full Life Cycle
- Market/Competitor Research
- Product Solutions
- Payroll

Over 5 years' solid career history in HRIS operations including start-ups, reviewing and determining software solutions for payroll and HR issues, training, and large scale project management.[2] Keen eye for analyzing problems and determining viable solutions. Demonstrated experience in effectively managing implementation cycles. Expertly control high-level client problem resolution. Develop and establish 'customer service first' environments, attaining significant levels of customer retention. Proven ability to build and lead teams, establish rapport and manage personnel.[5] Excellent written, presentation, and negotiation skills.[6]

TECHNICAL PROFICIENCY [4]

Web Based Recruiting Tools	HRIS	LANs/WANs	Visio	Word
Internet & Research	Web-based HR/PR	Pivotal	Networks	Excel
Database Management	Tools	MS Project	Access	Outlook
Client Server Technology	SQL Reporting			PowerPoint

PROFESSIONAL EXPERIENCE

Treemont Employer Services, Irvine, Calif.   [dates]
Treemont is a payroll and HR solutions outsourcing company.

Project Manager [3]   [dates]
- Implement and manage responsibilities of multiple, integrated projects. Ensure consistent success of service initiatives across customer segments and business units.
- Collaborate with senior and functional managers to plan business and technology initiatives and budgets. Use formal and informal networks to accomplish objectives.
- Manage cost, schedules and performance of large, highly complex projects. Fully accountable for complex/diverse projects with high degree of business risk.

Janice Demer, Page 2

Key Projects:
- Managed multi-product Web-based implementation worth $250K. Successfully moved a 4,000 employee global client from Windows-based PR/HR software to a Web-based HR/Payroll package. Supervised project team of 17, completing project on time and under budget.
- Carefully managed sensitive outstanding balance issue with hostile client. Directed team of five to troubleshoot complex issues, retain the account, and collect balance in full, equaling $400K.

System Consultant   [dates]
- Generated leads and secured new HRIS clients. Created and delivered proposals and demonstrations to key management personnel (user, technical user, buyer and decision-makers), meeting customer specific requirements. Maintained $8.2 million quota annually. Proposed product solutions and applications working with IT directors for system requirements and functionality. Wrote RFPs.
- Effectively tailored responses and proposals using strategic models to best position firm in marketplace. Managed large and complex client accounts, averaging 500 to 5,000 personnel.
- Reviewed current technology trends. As product expert, educated field staff on cutting edge advances in payroll & HR, recruiting, employee self-service and benefit outsourcing.

Account Executive   [dates]
- Selected at regional level for special project team studying customer retention to proactively manage and develop profitable, long-term customers.
- Met with clients to ensure complete customer satisfaction. Reviewed and recommended solutions to HRIS problems and suggested specific software. Managed conflict resolution.
- Developed account strategies to establish trends and identify opportunities to capitalize on retaining and growing customer base. Coordinated customer training. Negotiated long-term agreements.

Consultant/Implementations   [dates]
- Analyzed customers' payroll needs and provided recommendations for streamlining payroll processes. Negotiated contracts up to $5M.
- Trained customers on Source 500 software. Provided quality on-going customer support, ensuring successful implementation of payroll, human resources, and tax filing accounts.

Mountain High Health Services, Villa Park, Calif.
                                                                                                               [dates]
Mountain High held a government contract for the military insurance program—housing multiple large databases with hundreds of thousands of files and records.

Operations Supervisor
- Developed and implemented start-up plans/operations/audits to employ and operate call center with 700 employees. Implemented new database software and controlled large databases.
- Hired and trained 60 direct-report employees, set-up department, and staffed call center with 500 additional personnel. Determined all staffing requirements, providing timely hiring and training.

EDUCATION

    M.A.,[1] Information Access and Management, University of California, Irvine, GPA: 4.0   [date]
    B.A., Human Resources Management, California State University Fullerton, GPA: 3.85   [date]

Project Management Institute, Irvine, Calif., Member

Careers in Contemporary Business

You'll be hitting the job market soon—if you haven't already. Regardless of what industry you want to work in—financial services, marketing, travel, construction, hospitality, manufacturing, wireless communications—you need an education. Attending college and taking a business course like this one gives you an edge because business skills and knowledge are needed in many different fields. But education comes in many forms. In addition to taking classes, you should try to gain related real-life experience. A summer job, an internship, or even a volunteer opportunity can give you excellent experience that you can build on once you graduate. Cooperative education programs and work-study programs can also give you hands-on experience while you pursue your education. While many students across the country will be doing the same thing, you can set yourself apart through your work ethic and initiative.

You will be responsible for earning a living once you leave school—if you aren't already doing so. Your level of education will probably influence your earnings. Table E.1 shows some hard facts about earnings as reported by the U.S. Census Bureau. Not only is there a wide discrepancy between earnings for high-school graduates and college graduates, but there is still a gap between earnings for men and women.[1]

Keep in mind that while a degree may help you get in the door for certain job interviews and may put you on a path for advancement, it doesn't guarantee success; you have to achieve that yourself.

Companies plan their hiring strategies carefully in order to attract and keep the most productive, creative employees and avoid the cost of rehiring. So, soon-to-be graduates still need to be on their toes. But creativity has never been in short supply among business students, and by the time you finish this class—and college—you will be well equipped to take on the challenge. You'll be

Yuri Arcurs/iStockphoto

Table E.1 — Average Annual Earnings of Workers by Educational Level

GENDER & AGE	HIGH SCHOOL	COLLEGE
Men: 18 to 24 years	$25,153	$37,429
Men: 25 to 34 years	35,995	66,731
Men: 35 to 44 years	47,149	92,776
Women: 18 to 24 years	21,389	33,693
Women: 25 to 34 years	30,092	49,996
Women: 35 to 44 years	23,120	62,358

Source: "Average Earnings of Year-Round, Full-Time Workers by Educational Attainment," *Current Population Reports,* U.S. Census Bureau, http://www.census.gov, accessed May 31, 2011.

able to think of your hunt for employment as a course in itself, at the end of which you will have a job. And you will be on your way toward a rewarding business career.

During this course, you are exposed to all the functional areas of business. You learn how firms are organized and operated. You find out who does what in a company. Gradually, you identify industries and disciplines—such as sales, finance, or product design—that interest you. And you learn about many organizations, large and small—who founded them, what products they offer, how they serve their customers, and what types of decisions they make. In short, you gain knowledge about business that you can apply to your career search and life.

Choosing a career is an important life decision. It sets you on a path that will influence where you live, how much money you earn, what type of people you meet, and what you do every day. And whether your goal is to operate an organic farm or to rise high in the ranks of a major corporation, you'll need to understand the principles of business. Even if you think you're headed down a different path, business skills may prove to be important. In addition, many fields are beginning to recognize the importance of a broader base of knowledge than specialized technical skills, and business knowledge is part of that base.

For example, engineers used to rely almost solely on a foundation of technical skill and expertise. But experts in the industry now report a trend toward a more well-rounded education. While engineers still need a strong technical foundation, they need additional skills as well. "There's no question that the employee who can do five things is harder to get rid of than the one who can only do one or two," says an engineer who held onto his job during the economic downturn. "The more diverse your toolset, the more stable your job will be."[2] That's why this appendix discusses the best way to approach career decisions and to prepare for an *entry-level job*—your first permanent employment after leaving school. We then look at a range of business careers and discuss employment opportunities in a variety of fields.

It's important to remember that you'll be looking for a job regardless of the state of the overall economy, whether it's sluggish or booming. You'll read about job cuts and unemployment rates, hiring freezes and wage increases. But if you stay flexible and are ready to work—just about any time and anywhere—you'll succeed.[3]

Internships—A Great Way to Acquire Real-World Experience

Many business students complete one or more *internships* prior to completing their academic careers. Some arrange internships during the summer, while others work at them during a semester away from college. An internship gives you hands-on experience in a real business environment, whether it's in banking, the hotel industry, or retailing. Not only does an internship teach you how a business runs, but it can also help you decide whether you want to pursue a career in a particular industry. You might spend a summer interning in the admissions department of a hospital and then graduate with your job search focused on hospital administration. Or you might decide you'd much rather work for a magazine publisher or a construction company.

When you apply for an internship, don't expect to be paid much, if at all. The true value of an internship lies in its hands-on experience. An internship bridges the theory–practice educational gap. It will help carry you from your academic experience to your professional future. Also keep in mind that, as an intern, you will not be running a department. People may not ask for your input or ideas. You may work in the warehouse or copy center. You might be answering phones or entering data. But it is important to make the most of your internship. Because many companies make permanent job offers—or offers to enter paid training programs—to the best interns, you'll want to stand out.

Internships can serve as critical networking and job-hunting tools. In many instances, they lead to future employment opportunities, allowing students to demonstrate technical proficiency while providing cost-effective employee training for the company. Even if you don't end up being hired by the company for which you interned, the experience is extremely valuable to your job hunt. One study estimates that almost one-third of all entry-level hires had internships prior to being hired. PricewaterhouseCoopers hired 91 percent of its entry-level employees from its pool of interns during one recent year.[4]

With this information in mind, start thinking the way a professional does now. Here are some tips for a successful internship experience. These guidelines are also helpful for your first job.

- **Dress like a professional.** Dress appropriately for your future career. During an interview visit, look around to see what employees are wearing. If you have any questions, ask your supervisor.

- **Act like a professional.** Arrive on time to work. Be punctual for any meetings or assignments. Ask questions and listen to the answers carefully. Complete your work thoroughly and on time. Maintain good etiquette on the phone, in meetings, and in all interactions with other people.

- **Stand out.** Work hard and show initiative, but behave appropriately. Don't try to use authority that you do not have. Show that you are willing to learn.

- **Be evaluated.** Even if your internship does not include a formal evaluation, ask your employer how you are doing to learn about your strengths and weaknesses.

- **Keep in touch.** Once you complete your internship, stay in touch periodically with the firm so that people know what you are currently doing.

An excellent source of information about the nation's outstanding internships can be found at your local bookstore—*The Best 109 Internships*, 9th edition, published by The Princeton Review. The same organization also publishes *The Internship Bible*, which is also helpful.

In addition to an internship, you can build your résumé with work and life experience through volunteer opportunities, extracurricular activities, and summer or off-campus study programs. *Cooperative education* also provides valuable experience. Cooperative education programs are similar to internships, but the jobs themselves usually pay more. These programs may take place during the summer or during the school year—typically, students might take classes one semester and hold jobs the next semester. Most cooperative programs are specific to a major field of study, such as retailing or information technology. At your cooperative job, you'll be treated like a real full-time employee, meaning you'll work long hours and probably have more responsibility that you would as an intern. And depending on how these programs are scheduled, you might add a semester or two to your college education. But in the long run, you will gain knowledge and work experience that will serve you well as you build your career.[5]

Self-Assessment For Career Development

You are going to spend a lot of time during your life working, so why not find a job—or at least an industry—that interests you? To choose the line of work that suits you best, you must first understand yourself. Self-assessment involves looking in the mirror and seeing the real you—with all your strengths and weaknesses. It means answering some tough questions. But being honest with yourself pays off because it will help you find a career that is challenging, rewarding, and meaningful to you. As you get to know yourself better, you may discover that helping other people really makes you happy. You may realize that to feel secure, you need to earn enough to put away substantial savings. Or you might learn that you are drawn to risks and the unknown, characteristics that might point you toward owning your own business someday. Each of these discoveries provides you with valuable information in choosing a career.

Many resources are available to help you in selecting a career. They include school libraries, career guidance and placement offices, counseling centers, and online job-search services. They include alumni from your college, as well as friends, family, and neighbors. Don't forget the contacts you make during an internship—they can help you in many ways. Ask questions of anyone you know—a local retailer, banker, or restaurant owner. Most people will be happy to speak with you or arrange a time to do so.

If you are interested in a particular industry or company, you might be able to arrange an informational interview—an appointment with someone who can provide you with more knowledge about an industry or career path. This type of interview is different from one that follows your application for a specific job, although it may ultimately lead to that. The informational interview can help you decide whether you want to pursue a particular avenue of employment. It also gives you some added experience in the interview process—without the pressure. To arrange an interview, tap anyone you know—friends of your parents, local businesspeople, or coordinators of not-for-profit organizations. Colleges often have databases of graduates who are working in various fields who are willing to talk with students on an informational basis, so be sure to start your search right at your own school.

To help you get started asking and answering the questions that will help you begin looking in the right direction, you can visit a number of Web sites that offer online career assessment tests. Career Explorer, at http://www.careerexplorer.net is one such site; LiveCareer at http://www.livecareer.com is another. These sites and others, such as Monster's Career Fit Indicator at http://www.monster.com, help you identify your interests, strengths, and weaknesses—including some that may surprise you.[6] In addition, follow the self-assessment process outlined in the next section to learn more about yourself.

The Self-Assessment Process

For a thorough assessment of your goals and interests, follow these steps:

1. **Outline your career interests.** What field or work activities interest you? What rewards do you want to gain from work?

2. **Outline your career goals.** What do you want to achieve through your career? What type of job can you see yourself doing? Where do you see yourself in a year? In five years? Do you have an ultimate dream job? How long are you willing to work to reach it? Write your goals down so that you can refer to them later.

3. **Make plans to reach your goal.** Do you need more education? Does the career require an apprenticeship or a certain number of years on the job? Outline the requirements you'll need to meet in order to reach your goal.

4. **List your skills and specific talents.** Write down your strengths—job skills you already have, as well as skills you have developed in life. For instance, you might know how to use financial software, and you might be good at negotiating with people. In addition, your school's career development office probably has standardized tests that can help determine your aptitude for specific careers. However, take these only as a guideline. If you really want to pursue a certain career, go for it.

5. **List your weaknesses.** This can be tough—it can also be fun. If you are shy about meeting new people, put shyness on your list. If you are quick to argue, admit it. If you aren't the best business-letter writer or think you're terrible at math, confess to yourself. This list gives you an opportunity to see where you need improvement—and take steps to turn weaknesses into strengths.

6. **Briefly sketch out your educational background.** Write down the schools, colleges, and special training programs you have attended, along with any courses you plan to complete before starting full-time employment. Make a candid assessment of how your background matches up with the current job market. Then make plans to complete any further education you may need.

7. **List the jobs you have held.** Include jobs that paid, internships, and volunteer opportunities. They all gave you valuable experience. As you make your list, think about what you liked and disliked about each. Maybe you liked working with the general public as a supermarket cashier. Perhaps you enjoyed caring for animals at a local shelter.

8. **Consider your hobbies and personal interests.** Many people have turned hobbies and personal pursuits into rewarding careers. Mick Jagger, lead singer of the Rolling Stones, has a master's degree from the London School of Economics. Without it, he probably wouldn't have been able to manage his rock group's vast business dealings. Jake Burton Carpenter earned a bachelor's degree in economics, but he loved winter sports. So he started a snowboard manufacturing company—and revolutionized the way people get from the top of a snowy mountain to the bottom. Cooking and catering star Paula Deen needed to support her young family. She loved the cooking from her own region—the South—so she opened a small business in which she and her boys delivered freshly made bag lunches to local businesses. Today she is a celebrity with her own television show, cookbooks, Web site, retail products, and more.[7] Turning a hobby into a career doesn't happen overnight, though, nor is it easy. It requires the same amount of research and hard work as any other business. But for many people, it is a labor of love—and ultimately succeeds because they refuse to give up.

Job Search Guidelines

Once you have narrowed your choice of career possibilities to two or three that seem right for you, get your job search under way. The characteristics that made these career choices attractive to you are also likely to catch the attention of other job seekers, so you must expect competition. Locate available positions that interest you; then be resourceful! Your success depends on gathering as much information as possible.

Register at Your Career Center

Register at your school's career center. Establish an applicant file, including letters of recommendation and supporting personal information. Most placement offices send out periodic lists of new job vacancies by e-mail, so be sure to get your name and e-mail address on the list. Visit the office regularly, and become a familiar face. Find out how the office arranges interviews with company representatives who visit campus. If your school has a career event, be sure to attend.

Preparing Your Job Credentials

Most placement or credential files include the following information:

1. letters of reference from people who know you well—instructors and employers
2. transcripts of course work to date
3. personal data form to report factual information
4. statement of career goals.

The career center will provide you with special forms to help you to develop your file. Often, these forms can be completed online. Prepare the forms carefully, since employers are always interested in your written communication skills. Keep a copy of the final file for later use in preparing similar information for other employment sources. Check back with the career center to make sure your file is in order, and update it whenever necessary to reflect additional academic accomplishments and added work experiences.

Letters of reference are very important, because they give prospective employers both personal and professional insights about you. They can influence a hiring decision. So, make a careful list of people who might be willing to write letters of reference. Your references should not be family members or close friends. Instead, choose a coach, an instructor, a former employer, or someone else whose knowledge could contribute to your job application. A soccer coach could vouch for your hard work and determination. A music teacher might be able to detail how well you accept instruction. A former employer might describe your punctuality and ability to get along with others. If possible, include someone from your school's business faculty on your list of references, or at least one of your current instructors.

Always ask people personally for letters of reference. Be prepared to give them brief outlines of your academic preparation, along with information about your job interests and career goals. This information will help them prepare their letters quickly and efficiently. It also shows that you are serious about the task and respect their time. Remember, however, that these people are very busy. Allow them at least a couple of weeks to prepare their reference letters; then follow up politely on missing ones. Always call or write to thank them for writing the letters.

Finding Employment through the Internet

The Internet plays an important role in connecting employers and job seekers. Companies of all sizes post their job opportunities on the Web, both on their own sites and on job sites such as Monster.com, Yahoo! HotJobs.com, and CareerBuilder.com. Specialized or niche sites such as Accounting.com and TechCareers.com are also gaining popularity. Some sites are free to applicants, while others charge a subscription fee. Figure E.1 provides a sampling of general and more-focused career sites.

Career Web sites typically offer job postings, tips on creating an effective résumé, a place to post your résumé, and advice on interviews and careers. If this sounds easy, keep in mind that these sites may receive hundreds of thousands of hits each day from job hunters, which means you have plenty of competition. This doesn't mean you shouldn't use one of these sites as part of your job search; just don't make it your sole source. Savvy job seekers often find that their time is better spent zeroing in on niche boards offering more focused listings. Naturally, if a particular company interests you, go to the firm's Web site, where available positions will be posted. If you are interested in applying for a job at the accounting firm Ernst & Young, go to http://www.ey.com. If you are looking for a job with Whole Foods Market, visit http://www.wholefoods.com. And if you fancy yourself working for an outdoor retailer, go to Recreational Equipment Inc. (REI) at http://www.rei.com.

Newspapers, the source for traditional classified want ads, also post their ads on the Web. Job seekers can even visit sites that merge ads from many different newspapers into one searchable database, such as CareerBuilder (http://www.careerbuilder.com). Some sites go a step farther and create separate sections for each career area. For example, entire sections may be devoted to accounting, marketing, and other business professions. Searches can then be narrowed according to geographic location, entry level, company name, job title, job description, and other categories.

As mentioned earlier, you can connect with potential employers by posting your résumé on job sites. Employers search the résumé database for prospects with the right qualifications. One commonly used approach is for an employer to list one or more *keywords* to select

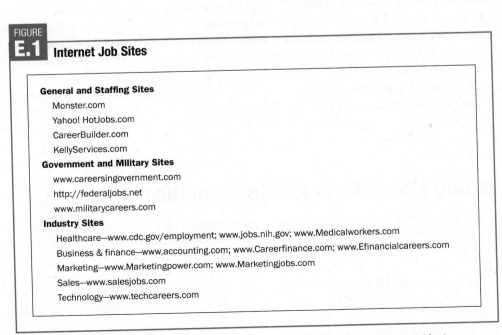

FIGURE E.1 Internet Job Sites

General and Staffing Sites
Monster.com
Yahoo! HotJobs.com
CareerBuilder.com
KellyServices.com

Government and Military Sites
www.careersingovernment.com
http://federaljobs.net
www.militarycareers.com

Industry Sites
Healthcare—www.cdc.gov/employment; www.jobs.nih.gov; www.Medicalworkers.com
Business & finance—www.accounting.com; www.Careerfinance.com; www.Efinancialcareers.com
Marketing—www.Marketingpower.com; www.Marketingjobs.com
Sales—www.salesjobs.com
Technology—www.techcareers.com

Source: "Index of Useful Internet Resources," *Career Planning & Placement Center*, University of Southern California, http://careers.usc.edu, accessed May 10, 2010.

candidates for personal interviews—for example, "retail sales experience," "network architecture," or "spa management"—and then browse the résumés that contain all the required keywords. Employers also scan résumés into their human resource database, and then when a manager requests, say, ten candidates, the database is searched by keywords that have been specified as part of the request. Job seekers are responding to this computer screening of applicants by making sure that relevant keywords appear on their résumés.

The *Contemporary Business* Web site hosts a comprehensive job and career assistance section. The site is updated frequently to include the best job and career sites for identifying and landing the career you want, as well as current strategies for getting the best results from your Web-based career-search activities.

Finding Employment through Other Sources

The importance of registering at your college's career planning or placement office was noted earlier. If you have completed formal academic coursework at more than one institution, you may be able to set up a placement file at each. In addition, you may want to contact private and public employment services available in your location or in the area where you would like to live.

Private Employment Agencies These firms often specialize in certain types of jobs—such as marketing, finance, sales, or engineering—offering services for both employers and job candidates that are not available elsewhere. Many private agencies interview, test, and screen job applicants so that potential employers do not have to do so. Job candidates benefit from the service by being accepted by the agency and because the agency makes the first contact with the potential employer.

A private employment agency usually charges the prospective employer a fee for finding a suitable employee. Other firms charge job seekers a fee for helping find them a job. Be sure that you understand the terms of any agreement you sign with a private employment agency.

State Employment Offices Don't forget to check the employment office of your state government. Remember that in many states, these public agencies process unemployment compensation applications along with other related work. Because of the mix of duties, some people view state employment agencies as providing services for semiskilled or unskilled workers. However, these agencies *do* list jobs in many professional categories and are often intimately involved with identifying job finalists for major new facilities moving to your state. In addition, many of the jobs listed at state employment offices may be with state or federal agencies and may include professionals such as accountants, attorneys, healthcare professionals, and scientists.

Learning More About Job Opportunities

Carefully study the various employment opportunities you have identified. Obviously, you will like some more than others, but you can examine a variety of factors when assessing each job possibility:

- actual job responsibilities
- industry characteristics
- nature of the company
- geographic location

- salary and opportunities for advancement
- contribution of the job to your long-range career objectives.

Too many job applicants consider only the most striking features of a job, perhaps its location or the salary offer. However, a comprehensive review of job openings should provide a balanced perspective of the overall employment opportunity, including both long-run and short-run factors.

Building a Résumé

Regardless of how you locate job openings, you must learn how to prepare and submit a *résumé*, a written summary of your personal, educational, and professional achievements. The résumé is a personal document covering your educational background, work experience, career preferences and goals, and major interests that may be relevant. It also includes such basic contact information as your home and e-mail addresses, as well as your telephone number. It should *not* include information on your age, marital status, race, or ethnic background.

Your résumé is usually your formal introduction to an employer, so it should present you in the best light, accentuating your strengths and potential to contribute to a firm as an employee. However, it should *never* contain embellishments or inaccuracies. You don't want to begin your career with unethical behavior, and an employer is bound to discover any discrepancies in fact—either immediately or during the months following your employment. Either event typically results in short-circuiting your career path.

Organizing Your Résumé

The primary purpose of a résumé is to highlight your qualifications for a job, usually on a single page. An attractive layout facilitates the employer's review of your qualifications. You can prepare your résumé in several ways. You may use narrative sentences to explain job duties and career goals, or you may present information in outline form. A résumé included as part of your credentials file at the career center on campus should be quite short. Remember to design it around your specific career objectives.

Figures E.2, E.3, and E.4 illustrate different ways to organize your résumé—by *reverse chronology*, or time; by *function*; and by *results*. Regardless of which format you select, you will want to include the following: a clearly stated objective, your work or professional experience, your education, your personal interests such as sports or music, and your volunteer work. While all three formats are acceptable, one study showed that 78 percent of employers preferred the reverse chronological format—with the most recent experience listed first—because it was easiest to follow.

Tips for Creating a Strong Résumé

Your résumé should help you stand out from the crowd, just as your college admissions application did. A company may receive hundreds or even thousands of résumés, so you want yours to be on the top of the stack. Here are some do's and don'ts:

Do:

- State your immediate objective clearly. If you are applying for a specific job, say so. State why you want the job and why you want to work at this particular company.

- Use terms related to your field, so that a human resource manager can locate them quickly. If you are submitting your résumé online, use words that will create an

FELICIA SMITH-WHITEHEAD
4265 Popular Lane
Cleveland, Ohio 44120
216-555-3296
FeliciaSW@gmail.com

OBJECTIVE
Challenging office management position in a results-oriented company where my organizational and people skills can be applied; leading to an operations management position.

WORK EXPERIENCE
ADM Distribution Enterprises, Cleveland, Ohio   2011–Present
Office Manager of leading regional soft-drink bottler. Coordinate all bookkeeping, correspondence, scheduling of 12-truck fleet to serve 300 customers, promotional mailings, and personnel records, including payroll. Install computerized systems.

Merriweather, Hicks & Bradshaw Attorneys, Columbus, Ohio   2009–2011
Office Supervisor and Executive Assistant for Douglas H. Bradshaw, Managing Partner. Supervised four clerical workers and two paraprofessionals, automated legal research and correspondence functions, and assisted in coordinating outside services and relations with other firms and agencies. Promoted three times from Secretary to Office Supervisor.

Conner & Sons Custom Coverings, Cleveland, Ohio   2005–2009
Secretary in father's upholstery and awning company. Performed all office functions over the years, running the office when the owner was on vacation.

EDUCATION
McBundy Community College, Associate's Degree in Business   2009
Mill Valley High School, Honors   2005

COMPUTER SKILLS
Familiar with Microsoft Office and Adobe Acrobat

LANGUAGE SKILLS
Fluent in Spanish (speaking and writing)
Adequate speaking and writing skills in Portuguese

PERSONAL
Member of various community associations; avid reader; enjoy sports such as camping and cycling; enjoy volunteering in community projects.

automatic "match" with a job description or field. If you are applying for an entry-level job in marketing, the phrase "communication skills" is likely to generate a match. You can identify such words and phrases by reading job descriptions online.

- Provide facts about previous jobs, internships, cooperative education programs, or volunteer work, including results or specific achievements. Include any projects or tasks you undertook through your own initiative.

- Emphasize your education if you are a recent graduate. Place it closer to the top of your résumé instead of the bottom.

- Highlight your strengths and skills, such as research, writing, or organizing.

- Write clearly and concisely.

Enrique Garcia
Five Oceanside Drive, Apt. 6B
Los Angeles, CA 90026
215-555-7092
EGARCIA@hotmail.com

Objective
Joining a growth-oriented company that values highly productive employees. Seeking an opportunity that leads to senior merchandising position.

Professional Experience
Administration
Management responsibilities in a major retailing buying office, coordinated vendor-relation efforts. Supervised assistant buyers.

Category Management
Experience in buying home improvement and sport and recreation categories.

Planning
Chaired a team charged with reviewing the company's annual vendor evaluation program.

Problem Solving
Successfully developed a program to improve margins in the tennis, golf, and fishing lines.

Work Experience
Senior Buyer for Southern California Department Stores   2010–Present

Merchandiser for Pacific Discount Stores, a division of Southern   2008–2010
California Department Stores

Education
Bachelor's Degree
California State University–San Bernardino   2006–2008

Associate's Degree
Los Angeles City College   2004–2006

- Proofread your résumé carefully for grammar, usage, and typographical errors. Refer to a dictionary or style manual.

- Keep your résumé to a single page.

Don't:

- Offer any misleading or inaccurate information.

- Make vague statements, such as "I work well with others," or "I want a position in business."

- State your objective as, "to run this company" or to "advance as quickly as possible."

- Include a salary request.

- Make demands about vacation time, work hours, or excessive benefits.

- Highlight your weaknesses.

- Submit a résumé with typos or grammatical errors.

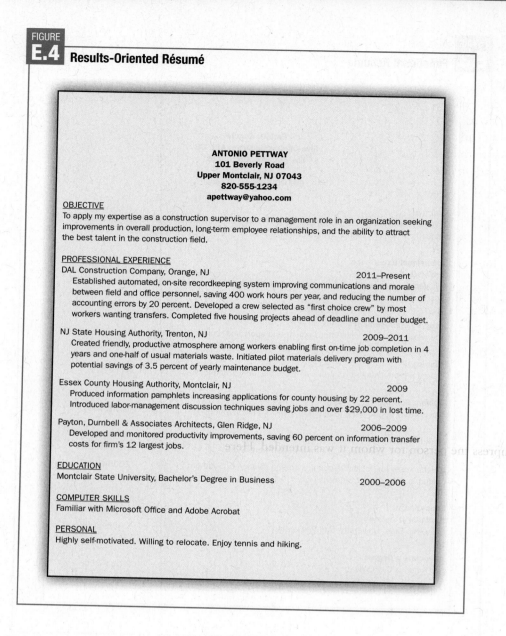

ANTONIO PETTWAY
101 Beverly Road
Upper Montclair, NJ 07043
820-555-1234
apettway@yahoo.com

OBJECTIVE
To apply my expertise as a construction supervisor to a management role in an organization seeking improvements in overall production, long-term employee relationships, and the ability to attract the best talent in the construction field.

PROFESSIONAL EXPERIENCE
DAL Construction Company, Orange, NJ   2011–Present
  Established automated, on-site recordkeeping system improving communications and morale between field and office personnel, saving 400 work hours per year, and reducing the number of accounting errors by 20 percent. Developed a crew selected as "first choice crew" by most workers wanting transfers. Completed five housing projects ahead of deadline and under budget.

NJ State Housing Authority, Trenton, NJ   2009–2011
  Created friendly, productive atmosphere among workers enabling first on-time job completion in 4 years and one-half of usual materials waste. Initiated pilot materials delivery program with potential savings of 3.5 percent of yearly maintenance budget.

Essex County Housing Authority, Montclair, NJ   2009
  Produced information pamphlets increasing applications for county housing by 22 percent. Introduced labor-management discussion techniques saving jobs and over $29,000 in lost time.

Payton, Durnbell & Associates Architects, Glen Ridge, NJ   2006–2009
  Developed and monitored productivity improvements, saving 60 percent on information transfer costs for firm's 12 largest jobs.

EDUCATION
Montclair State University, Bachelor's Degree in Business   2000–2006

COMPUTER SKILLS
Familiar with Microsoft Office and Adobe Acrobat

PERSONAL
Highly self-motivated. Willing to relocate. Enjoy tennis and hiking.

- Use slang or other inappropriate phrases or comments.
- Include pictures or graphics, or use fancy type fonts.[8]

Take your time with your résumé; it is one of the most important documents you'll create during your career. If you need help, go to your school's career center. If you are dealing with an employment agency, a counselor there should be able to help as well.

Keep in mind that you will probably have to modify your résumé at times to tailor it to a particular company or job. Again, take the time to do this; it may mean the difference between standing out and being lost in a sea of other applicants.

Preparing Your Cover Letter

In most cases, your résumé will be accompanied by a *cover letter*. This letter should introduce you, explain why you are submitting a résumé (cite the specific job opening if possible), and let the recipient know where you can be reached for an interview. An effective cover letter will make the recipient want to take the next step and read your résumé. Here are a few tips for preparing an outstanding letter:

- Write the letter to a specific person, if possible. A letter addressed to "to whom it may concern" may never reach the right person. Call the company or check its Web site for the name of the person to whom you should send your letter. It might be someone in human resources or a person in the department where you'd actually be working. Be sure to obtain the person's title if possible (such as general manager or director), and spell the person's name correctly.

- Introduce yourself and explain the purpose of your letter—to apply for a job.

- Describe briefly an example of your best work or most ambitious project.

- Keep it short—a page is acceptable, half a page even better.

- Request an interview.

- Thank the person for his or her time and consideration.

- Make sure all your contact information is in the letter—name, address, home phone number, cell phone number, and e-mail address.

- Proofread your letter carefully.[9]

Submitting Your Online Résumé

You may write a sparkling cover letter and stellar résumé, but if your online submission is blocked or tossed aside by an automated processing system, it won't have a chance to impress the person for whom it was intended. Here are a few tips for making certain your letter and résumé reach their mark.

- Review the formatting of your résumé to make sure it will appear the same to the recipient as it does to you. Delete any unusual symbols or fonts.

- Use keywords that create a match and allow your résumé through the company's filter. This aplies to the subject line of your email as well, which should be specific and contain keywords such as "application for sales trainee job."

- Include your cover letter in the e-mail.

- Send your résumé in the body of the e-mail—not as an attachment. This is more convenient for the recipient, and it also avoids the disaster of having your attachment automatically deleted by an antivirus system.

- Do not send graphics, because they may be blocked or deleted as well.

- If you are answering an ad, read the instructions for application and follow them exactly.[10]

The Job Interview

Congratulations! You've prepared an effective résumé, and you've been contacted for an interview. An interview is more than a casual conversation. During an interview, at least one manager will learn about you, and you'll learn more about the company and the job. Although you may feel nervous about the interview, you can control some of its outcome by doing your homework: planning and preparing for this important encounter with your potential employer. Before you meet with an interviewer, learn everything you can about the firm. The simplest way to do this is to visit the company's Web site. You can also check with your school's career center. If you know anyone who works for the company, you may ask the person about the firm. Try to learn the answers to the following questions about the organization:

- What does the firm do—manufacture clothing, market snack foods, produce films, sell cars? If you are applying for a job at a large corporation, zero in on the division for which you would be working.

- What is the company's mission? Many firms include a statement about their purpose in the business world—to supply affordable energy to communities, to serve fresh food, to make communication easier. Understanding why the company exists will help you grasp where it is headed and why.

- Where, when, and by whom was the company founded? Learn a little about the history of the firm.

- What is its position in the marketplace? Is it a leader or is it trying to gain a competitive advantage? Who are its main competitors?

- Where is the firm based? Does it have facilities located around the country and the world, or is it purely local?

- How is the company organized? Are there multiple divisions and products?

- Learning about the firm indicates to the interviewer that you have initiative and motivation, as well as an interest in the firm's culture and history. You have taken the time and effort to find out more about the organization, and your enthusiasm shows.

Tips for Successful Interviewing

An interview is your personal introduction to the company. You want to make a good impression, but you also want to find out whether you and the firm are a good fit. Although the interviewer will be asking most of the questions, you will want to ask some, as well. People who conduct interviews say that the most important qualities candidates can exhibit are self-confidence, preparedness, and an ability to communicate clearly.

When you are contacted for an interview, find out the name(s) of the person or people who will be interviewing you. It's also appropriate to ask whether the initial interview will be with a human resource manager or with the person to whom you would be reporting on the job, or both. Many people who conduct initial job interviews work in their firms' human resource divisions. These interviewers act as gatekeepers and can make recommendations to managers and supervisors about which individuals to interview further or hire. Managers who head the units in which an applicant will be employed may get involved later in the hiring process. Some hiring decisions come from human resource personnel together with the immediate supervisor of the prospective employee. In other cases, immediate supervisors make the decision alone. At your interview, keep in mind the following tips.

Do:

- **Dress appropriately.** Dress as if it is your first day of work at the firm. Conceal any tattoos or body piercings and wear simple jewelry.

- **Arrive a few minutes early.** This gives you time to relax and take in the surroundings. It also shows that you are punctual and care about other people's time.

- **Introduce yourself with a smile and a handshake.** Be friendly, but not overly familiar.

- **Be yourself—at your best.** Don't suddenly adopt a new personality. But try to be confident, polite, respectful, and interested in the people who are spending time with you. Be sure to thank each person who interviews you.

- **Listen.** Pay attention to what the interviewer is saying. If something is unclear to you, ask for clarification. Turn off your cell phone. Your full attention should be on the conversation you are having in the interview.

- **Use appropriate language.** As in your résumé and cover letter, be sure to use correct English. You don't need to be stiff or formal, but avoid slang or phrases that you know are inappropriate for the situation.

- **Be positive in your outlook.** Be enthusiastic about the firm and the job, but don't go overboard.

Don't:

- **Talk too much.** Avoid telling the interviewer a lot about your personal life, or why you left a particular job. Answer questions honestly and thoroughly, but don't dip into irrelevant details.

- **Be arrogant or aggressive.** Self-confidence is a good trait, but don't miss the mark by behaving in an arrogant or condescending manner. Certainly don't become aggressive, demanding that the interviewer offer you the job or even another interview.

- **Act indifferent or bored.** This may not be the job you ultimately want, but treat the interview and the interviewer with respect and attention. If you make a good impression, the firm is likely to keep your name on file—and that dream job may appear after all.

- **Don't get ahead of yourself.** This is not the time to discuss salary, vacation, or benefits.[11]

Answering and Asking Questions

In a typical format, the interviewer gives you ample opportunity to talk about yourself and your goals. You want to present your thoughts clearly and concisely, in an organized fashion, without rambling on to unrelated topics. The interviewer may wait until you are finished or prompt you to talk about certain subjects by asking questions. Be as specific as possible when answering questions. The questions that interviewers ask often include the following:

- "Why do you want this job?"

- "Why do you want to work in this field?"

- "What are your short-term goals? Long-term objectives?"

- "Where do you see yourself in five years? In ten years?"

- "What are your strengths? What are your weaknesses?"

- "What motivates you?"

- "Describe a situation in which you made a tough decision or solved a problem."

- "What did you like best about your last job? What did you like least?"

- "Why did you leave your last job?"

- "Why should my firm hire you?"

- "Are you considering other jobs or companies?"

Some of these questions may seem tougher than others, but you can reduce your anxiety by preparing for them. First, figure out which questions you fear the most. Then think about possible answers that are both truthful and positive. Rehearse your delivery in front of a mirror or with a friend.[12]

At some point, the interviewer will probably ask you whether you have any questions of your own. It's a good idea to come prepared with some questions, but others may arise during the interview. Try to keep your list concise, say three or four of your most important questions. The questions you ask reflect just as much about you as the answers you give to the interviewer's questions. Here is a sample of appropriate questions for the initial interview:

- "Could you clarify a certain aspect of the job responsibilities for me?"
- "Do people who start in entry-level jobs at this company tend to develop their careers here?"
- "In what ways could I perform above and beyond the job requirements?"

At some point during your conversation, the interviewer may give you an idea of the salary range for the job. If not, he or she will do so during a subsequent interview. You may ask about the range, but do not ask exactly how much you will be paid if you get the job. Keep in mind that usually there is little or no negotiation of an entry-level salary. However, you may ask if there is a probationary period with a review at the end of the period. Here are a few other questions *not* to ask:

- "When will I be promoted?"
- "How much time off do I get?"
- "When will I get my first raise?"
- "How many people are applying for this job?"
- "What are my chances of getting this job?"

At the end of the interview, be sure to thank the interviewer with a smile and a handshake, even if you both know the job is not for you. Again, another opportunity may come along in the future and you want to leave the door open. When you get home, write a note or e-mail the interviewer, thanking him or her for time spent with you. Thank-you notes really do make a lasting impression on a person, and it gives you another chance to reinforce your interest.

A successful first interview often leads to a second. The purpose of this interview is to better determine your specific qualifications and fit with the company. You may be introduced to more people—potential coworkers, people in other divisions, or sales staff. You may have another meeting with human resource staff members in which you'll learn more about salary, employee benefits, the firm's code of ethics, and the like. Depending on the type of job, you might be asked to take some skills tests. If you are entering a training program for a bank, you might be required to take some math-oriented tests. If you are going to work for a publisher, you might be asked to take an editing test or do some proofreading. If you are applying for a job as a sales representative, you may be given a test that assesses your personality traits. Don't be intimidated by these tests—you are not expected to know everything or be perfect—just do your best.

Making the Employment Decision

After receiving your résumé, conducting one or two interviews, and administering a skills test, a potential employer knows a lot about you. You should also know a lot about the company. If the experience has been positive on both sides, you may be offered a job. If you have interviewed at several companies and are offered more than one job, congratulations! You may receive a phone call, followed by a letter outlining the offer in writing. Whether you receive one offer or several, thank the person making the offer. If you choose to accept immediately, feel free to do so. If you have doubts about the job or need to decide between two, it is appropriate to ask for 24 hours to respond. If you must decline an offer, do so promptly and politely. After all, you may end up working for that firm sometime in the future. If you get a few rejections before you receive an offer, don't give up. Every application and interview adds to your experience.

As you think about an offer, consider the aspects that are most important. You'll want to choose a job that comes closest to your career interests and objectives. But don't rule out the element of surprise—you might wind up with a job you like in an industry you'd never considered before. Don't worry too much about the salary. The point of an entry-level job is to set you on a forward path. And keep in mind that your first job won't be your last. Once you have accepted an offer, you'll be given a start date as well as the name of the person to whom you should report on arrival. Congratulations, you are now a member of the workforce!

Congratulations! You've accepted an offer for your first job. You are now a member of the workforce.

Dean Mitchell/iStockphoto

Nontraditional Students

Take a quick glance around your class. You'll likely see classmates of all ages. Some will fall into the traditional college age group of 18 to 22, but many don't. Perhaps you are a veteran returning from military duty overseas. Maybe you have been engaged in a full-time career but want to broaden your education. Students who fall outside the 18- to 22-year-old age group are often referred to as *nontraditional students*, but these students have become the norm on many campuses. Homemakers returning to school to freshen up their résumés before returning to the workforce and workers who have been laid off due to an economic downturn are other examples of nontraditional students. As diverse as this group is, they share one thing in common: they are older than traditional students. This means that they face different challenges—but also enjoy some advantages over their younger classmates.

One major challenge faced by nontraditional students is scheduling. Often they are juggling the responsibilities of work, school, and family. They may have to study at odd times—during meals, while commuting, or after putting the kids to bed. If they are switching careers, they may be learning an entirely new set of skills, as well. But nontraditional students have an important advantage: experience. Even experience in an unrelated field is a plus. Older students know how organizations operate. Often, they have developed useful skills in human relations, management, budgeting, and communications. Even a former stay-home parent has skills in all of these areas. Through observing other people's successes and failures—as well as living through their own—they have developed an inventory of what to do and what not to do. So, in some ways, these students have a head start on their younger counterparts. But they also face the reality that they have fewer years in which to develop a career.

The Job Market: Where Do You Fit In?

The industry you choose, and the career you follow within it, are part of a bigger picture. They reflect the needs of society, changing populations, developing technology, and the overall economy. For instance, the U.S. population is expected to increase at a slower rate of growth for the foreseeable future than during the previous two decades. The U.S. workforce will continue to become more diverse, with Hispanics accounting for the largest share of jobs among minorities, while Asians represent the fastest-growing group of employees. The size of the Hispanic workforce is expected to increase from 14 percent to 17 percent. White, non-Hispanic workers will make up a declining share of the workforce, falling from approximately 69 percent to about 65 percent.[13]

The number of women in the workforce is growing at a faster rate than that of men. The male labor force is expected to grow by 7.5 percent by the year 2018, compared with almost 9 percent for women. So the men's share of the labor force will likely continue to decrease, while the women's share will increase.[14]

All of these facts combine to shape a picture of the needs of U.S. society and the workforce available to serve it. As the Baby Boom generation ages, the age group between 55 and 64 will increase by about one third. Thus, the United States will need more healthcare services, as well as other services for an aging population, such as assisted living facilities and leisure and hospitality. The group between the ages 35 and 44 will decrease by almost 6 percent, while the youth population between 16 and 24 will decline by about 1 percent. But today's younger workers are receiving more education and training to fill the need for professional and business service workers. These projections affect both the workforce and the types of goods and services needed to satisfy consumers. So jobs in education and healthcare services will increase by more than 5 million and in professional and business services by a little more than 4 million.[15]

Careers in service-providing industries continue a long-term rise. Service jobs in healthcare and social assistance will increase by about 26 percent by the year 2018, while manufacturing jobs will continue to shrink. But industries that produce certain types of goods, such as those related to the needs of an aging population and those related to green technologies or products, will probably increase.[16]

The good news is that even in a weaker job market, employers are looking to hire recent college graduates. In fact, some continue to offer signing bonuses and other incentives in order to secure the best workers. Why? Continuing to hire entry-level employees makes good business sense. The National Associate of Colleges and Employers (NACE) reports that college hiring is actually on the rise.[17] Some of the hot jobs can be found in accounting, sales, management training, engineering, and business services. So celebrate your graduation, and keep your résumé current and your outlook positive: a job is out there for you.

A Long-Range View of Your Career

Choosing a career is an important life decision. A career is a professional journey—regardless of whether you want to run a small restaurant or a branch bank, whether you are fascinated by language or math, whether you prefer to work with animals or people. In the end, you hope to contribute something good to society while enjoying what you do—and make a reasonable living at it.

Throughout your career, it is important to stay flexible and continue learning. Challenging new skills will be required of managers and other businesspeople during these first decades of the 21st century. Remain open to unexpected changes and opportunities that can help you learn and develop new skills. Keep in mind that your first job will not be your last. But tackle that first job with the same enthusiasm you'd have if someone asked you to run the company itself, because everything you learn on that job will be valuable at some point during your career—and someday you may actually run the company.

Finally, if you haven't already started your career search, begin now. Do this by talking with various resources, lining up an internship, looking for a part-time job on or off campus, or volunteering for an organization. Register with the campus career center long before you graduate. Then, when you reach your final semester, you'll be well on your way to beginning the career you want.

We are confident that this textbook presents a panorama of career options for you. Whatever you decide, be sure it is right for you—not your friends, your instructors, or your parents. As the old saying goes, "You pass this way just once." Enjoy the journey!

More Career Information on the *Contemporary Business* Web Site

More career information is available to students using *Contemporary Business* at the book's Web site.

The "Management Careers" section on the Web site enables you to learn more about business careers and to locate currently posted job opportunities. The site provides a vast number of career resources such as links to job sites, career guidance sites, and the like. Also, many links include extensive career information and guidance, such as interviewing techniques and tips for résumé writing.

■ Projects and Teamwork Applications

1. Visit one of the job Web sites such as CareerBuilder or Monster and research an industry in which you think you might be interested. Prepare a report on what you learned about the field. Was the site helpful? What types of jobs were available in the field? Based on your report, do you plan to pursue this industry or select another field?

2. Prepare your résumé following the procedures outlined earlier in this section. Exchange your résumé with a classmate so you can critique each other's resume. Then revise and proofread your résumé.

3. Go online to the Web site for a specific company for which you might be interested in working. Click on the "Careers" or "Job Opportunities" section of the site, and read carefully the job descriptions for any entry-level positions and the procedure for applying for them. Also review any general information about career development at the firm. Write a cover letter as if you were actually applying for one of the jobs.

4. With a classmate, practice interviewing for the job you selected in the previous question. Prepare questions for each other and take turns interviewing and being interviewed. What parts of the interview did you handle well? What could you improve?

5. Think about where you would like to be in your career in five years and write about your plans. Share your plans with the class, then seal them in an envelope. Keep the envelope and open it in five years to see how close you came to your predictions.

| Glossary |

360-degree performance review employee performance review that gathers feedback from co-workers, supervisors, managers, and sometimes customers.

401(k) plan retirement savings plan to which employees can make pretax contributions; employers often make additional contributions to the plan.

accounting process of measuring, interpreting, and communicating financial information to support internal and external business decision making.

accounting cycle set of activities involved in converting information and individual transactions into financial statements.

accounting equation relationship that states that assets must always equal the sum of liabilities and owners' equity.

accrual accounting accounting method that records revenues and expenses when they occur, not necessarily when cash actually changes hands.

acquisition agreement in which one firm purchases another.

activity ratios measures of how efficiently a firm utilizes its assets.

actuarial table probability of the number of events that are expected to occur within a given year.

advertising paid nonpersonal communication usually targeted at large numbers of potential buyers.

affective conflict disagreement that focuses on individuals or personal issues.

affinity program marketing effort sponsored by an organization that solicits involvement by individuals who share common interests and activities.

affirmative action programs programs designed by employers to increase job opportunities for women, minorities, disabled people, and other protected groups

agency legal relationship whereby one party, called a *principal,* appoints another party, called an *agent,* to enter into contracts with third parties on the principal's behalf.

alien corporation firm incorporated in one nation and operating in another nation.

angel investors wealthy individuals who invest directly in a new venture in exchange for an equity stake.

appellate courts courts that hear appeals of decisions made at the general trial court level; both the federal and state systems have appellate courts.

application service provider (ASP) outside supplier that provides both the computers and the application support for managing an information system.

arbitration bringing in an impartial third party called an arbitrator to render a binding decision in a dispute.

assembly line manufacturing technique that carries the product on a conveyor system past several workstations where workers perform specialized tasks.

asset anything of value owned by a firm.

asset intensity amount of assets needed to generate a given level of sales.

autocratic leadership management approach whereby leaders make decisions on their own without consulting employees.

balance of payments overall money flows into and out of a country.

balance of trade difference between a nation's exports and imports.

balance sheet statement of a firm's financial position—what it owns and claims against its assets—at a particular point in time.

balanced budget situation in which total revenues raised by taxes and fees equal total proposed government spending for the year.

bankruptcy legal nonpayment of financial obligations.

banner ad ad placed by an organization on another organization's Web site; interested parties click on the ad for more information.

benchmarking process of determining how well other companies perform business functions or tasks.

blog online journal written by a blogger.

board of directors governing body of a corporation.

bot short for *robot*—a program that allows online shoppers to compare prices for a specific product at several e-tailers.

botnet a network of PCs that have been infected with one or more data-stealing viruses.

boycott effort to prevent people from purchasing a firm's goods or services.

brand name, term, sign, symbol, design, or some combination that identifies the products of one firm and differentiates them from competitors' offerings.

brand equity added value that a respected and successful name gives to a product.

brand name part of a brand consisting of words or letters that form a name that identifies and distinguishes an offering from those of competitors.

brand name part of the brand consisting of words or letters included in a name used to identify and distinguish the firm's offerings from those of competitors.

branding process of creating an identity in consumers' minds for a good, service, or company; a major marketing tool in contemporary business.

breach of contract violation of a valid contract.

breakeven analysis pricing-related technique used to determine the minimum sales volume a product must generate at a certain price level to cover all costs.

budget organization's plan for how it will raise and spend money during a given period of time.

budget deficit situation in which the government spends more than the amount of money it raises through taxes.

budget surplus excess funding that occurs when government spends less than the amount of funds raised through taxes and fees.

business all profit-seeking activities and enterprises that provide goods and services necessary to an economic system.

business (B2B) product good or service purchased to be used, either directly or indirectly, in the production of other goods for resale.

business ethics standards of conduct and moral values regarding right and wrong actions in the work environment.

business incubator local programs designed to provide low-cost shared business facilities to small start-up ventures.

business intelligence activities and technologies for gathering, storing, and analyzing data to make better competitive decisions.

business interruption insurance type of insurance that protects firms from financial losses resulting from the suspension of business operations.

business law aspects of law that most directly influence and regulate the management of business activity.

business plan written document that provides an orderly statement of a company's goals, methods, and standards.

business-to-business (B2B) e-business electronic business transactions between organizations using the Internet.

business-to-consumer (B2C) e-business selling directly to consumers over the Internet.

call provision right of the issuer to buy a bond back from the investor before maturity at a specified price.

capital production inputs consisting of technology, tools, information, and physical facilities.

capital investment analysis process of comparing the costs and benefits of a long-term asset investment.

capital structure mix of a firm's debt and equity capital.

capitalism economic system that rewards firms for their ability to perceive and serve the needs and demands of consumers; also called the private enterprise system.

cash budget budget that shows cash inflows and outflows during a period of time.

cash flow sources of cash minus uses of cash during a specified period of time.

cash value policy type of life insurance that combines insurance protection with a savings feature.

category advisor vendor that is designated by the business customer as the major supplier to assume responsibility for dealing with all the other vendors for a project and presenting the entire package to the business buyer.

category manager person who oversees an entire group of products and assumes profit responsibility for the product group.

cause advertising form of institutional advertising that promotes a specific viewpoint on a public issue as a way to influence public opinion and the legislative process.

cause marketing marketing that promotes a cause or social issue, such as preventing child abuse, anti-littering efforts, and stop-smoking campaigns.

Central America–Dominican Republic Free Trade Agreement (CAFTA-DR) agreement among the United States, Costa Rica, the Dominican Republic, El Salvador, Guatemala, Honduras, and Nicaragua to reduce tariffs and trade restrictions.

centralization decision making based at the top of the management hierarchy.

certified management accountant (CMA) management accountant who meets specified educational and experience requirements and has passed an examination covering management accounting topics.

certified public accountant (CPA) public accountant who meets specified educational and experiential requirements and has passed a comprehensive examination on accounting theory and practice.

chain of command set of relationships that indicates who directs which activities and who reports to whom.

channel conflict conflict between two or more members of a supply chain, such as a manufacturer, wholesaler, or retailer.

chief information officer (CIO) executive responsible for managing a firm's information system and related computer technologies.

Class-Action Fairness Act of 2005 law that moves most large, multistate class-action lawsuits to federal courts, ensures judicial oversight of plaintiffs' compensation, bases lawyers' compensation on awards actually distributed or actual time spent, and ensures plaintiffs' interests are protected equally with their lawyers'.

classic entrepreneur person who identifies a business opportunity and allocates available resources to tap that market.

click-through rate number of visitors who click on a Web banner ad.

cloud computing powerful servers store applications software and databases for users to access the software and databases via the Web using anything from a PC to a smart phone.

cobranding cooperative arrangement in which two or more businesses team up to closely link their names on a single product.

code of conduct formal statement that defines how an organization expects its employees to resolve ethical issues.

cognitive ability tests tests that measure job candidates' abilities in perceptual speed, verbal comprehension, numerical aptitude, general reasoning, and spatial aptitude.

cognitive conflict disagreement that focuses on problem- and issue-related differences of opinion.

collective bargaining process of negotiation between management and union representatives.

comarketing cooperative arrangement in which two businesses jointly market each other's products.

committee organization organizational structure that places authority and responsibility jointly in the hands of a group of individuals rather than a single manager.

common law body of law arising out of judicial decisions, some of which can be traced back to early England.

common stock (Chap. 5, p. 173) shares that give owners voting rights but only residual claims to the firm's assets and income distributions.

communication meaningful exchange of information through messages.

communism economic system in which all property would be shared equally by the people of a community under the direction of a strong central government.

compensation amount employees are paid in money and benefits.

competition battle among businesses for consumer acceptance.

competitive differentiation unique combination of organizational abilities, products, and approaches that sets a company apart from competitors in the minds of customers.

competitive pricing strategy that tries to reduce the emphasis on price competition by matching other firms' prices and concentrating their own

marketing efforts on the product, distribution, and promotional elements of the marketing mix.

compressed workweek scheduling option that allows employees to work the regular number of hours per week in fewer than the typical five days.

computer-aided design (CAD) process that allows engineers to design components as well as entire products on computer screens faster and with fewer mistakes than they could achieve working with traditional drafting systems.

computer-aided manufacturing (CAM) computer tools to analyze CAD output and enable a manufacturer to analyze the steps that a machine must take to produce a needed product or part.

computer-based information systems information systems that rely on computer and related technologies to store information electronically in an organized, accessible manner.

computer-integrated manufacturing (CIM) production system in which computers help workers design products, control machines, handle materials, and control the production function in an integrated fashion.

conceptual skills ability to see the organization as a unified whole and to understand how each part interacts with others.

conflict when one person or group's needs do not match those of another, and attempts may be made to block the opposing side's intentions or goals.

conflict of interest situation in which an employee must choose between a business's welfare and personal gain.

conglomerate merger merger that combines unrelated firms, usually with the goal of diversification, spurring sales growth, or spending a cash surplus in order to avoid a takeover attempt.

consumer (B2C) product good or service that is purchased by end users.

consumer behavior actions of ultimate consumers directly involved in obtaining, consuming, and disposing of products and the decision processes that precede and follow these actions.

consumer orientation business philosophy that focuses first on determining unmet consumer wants and needs and then designing products to satisfy those needs.

Consumer Price Index (CPI) measurement of the monthly average change in prices of goods and services.

consumerism public demand that a business consider the wants and needs of its customers in making decisions.

contingency planning plans that allow a firm to resume operations as quickly and as smoothly as possible after a crisis while openly communicating with the public about what happened.

contract legally enforceable agreement between two or more parties regarding a specified act or thing.

controlling function of evaluating an organization's performance against its objectives.

convenience product item the consumer seeks to purchase frequently, immediately, and with little effort.

conversion rate percentage of visitors to a Web site who actually make a purchase.

convertible securities bonds or preferred stock issues that are convertible into a set number of shares of the issuing company's common stock.

cooperative organization whose owners join forces to collectively operate all or part of the functions in their business.

cooperative advertising allowances provided by marketers in which they share the cost of local advertising of their firm's product or product line with channel partners.

copyright protection of written material such as textbooks, designs, cartoon illustrations, photos, and computer software.

core inflation rate inflation rate of an economy after energy and food prices are removed.

corporate charter legal document that formally establishes a corporation.

corporate culture organization's system of principles, beliefs, and values.

corporate philanthropy effort of an organization to make a contribution to the communities in which it earns profits.

corporate Web site Web site designed to increase a firm's visibility, promote its offerings, and provide information to interested parties.

corporation legal organization with assets and liabilities separate from those of its owner(s).

cost-based pricing formulas that calculate total costs per unit and then add markups to cover overhead costs and generate profits.

countertrade barter agreement whereby trade between two or more nations involves payment made in the form of local products instead of currency.

creative selling persuasive type of promotional presentation.

creativity capacity to develop novel solutions to perceived organizational problems.

credit receiving money, goods, or services on the basis of an agreement between the lender and the borrower that the loan is for a specified period of time with a specified rate of interest.

critical path sequence of operations that requires the longest time for completion.

critical thinking ability to analyze and assess information to pinpoint problems or opportunities.

cross-functional team a team made up of members from different functions, such as production, marketing, and finance.

cyclical unemployment people who are out of work because of a cyclical contraction in the economy.

damages financial payments to compensate for a loss and related suffering.

data raw facts and figures that may or may not be relevant to a business decision.

data mining computer searches of customer data to detect patterns and relationships.

data warehouse customer database that allows managers to combine data from several different organizational functions.

database centralized integrated collection of data resources.

debenture unsecured corporate bond.

debt capital funds obtained from borrowing.

debt financing borrowed funds that entrepreneurs must repay.

decentralization decision makeup based at lower levels of the organization.

decision making process of recognizing a problem or opportunity, evaluating alternative solutions, selecting and implementing an alternative, and assessing the results.

decision support system (DSS) gives direct support to businesspeople during the decision-making process.

deflation opposite of inflation, occurs when prices continue to fall.

delegation managerial process of assigning work to employees.

demand willingness and ability of buyers to purchase goods and services.

demand curve graph of the amount of a product that buyers will purchase at different prices.

democratic leadership management approach whereby leaders delegate assignments, ask employees for suggestions, and encourage their participation.

demographic segmentation dividing markets on the basis of various demographic or socioeconomic characteristics such as gender, age, income, occupation, household size, stage in family life cycle, education, or ethnic group.

demographics statistical characteristics of the segment of the market that might purchase a product.

departmentalization process of dividing work activities into units within the organization.

deregulation regulatory trend toward elimination of legal restraints on competition in industries previously served by a single firm in an attempt to improve customer service and lower prices through increased competition.

devaluation reduction in a currency's value relative to other currencies or to a fixed standard.

direct distribution channel marketing channel that moves goods directly from producer to ultimate user.

directing guiding and motivating employees to accomplish organizational objectives.

disability income insurance type of insurance that pays benefits to those who cannot work due to some sort of disability.

discrimination biased treatment of a job candidate or employee.

dispatching phase of production control in which the manager instructs each department on what work to do and the time allowed for its completion.

display ad glossy-looking online ad often targeted at a specific user.

distribution channel path through which products—and legal ownership of them—flow from producer to consumers or business users.

distribution channels path that products – and legal ownership of them – follow from producer to consumers to business user.

diversity blending individuals of different genders, ethnic backgrounds, cultures, religions, ages, and physical and mental abilities to enhance a firm's chances of success.

divestiture sale of assets by a firm.

domestic corporation firm that operates in the state where it is incorporated.

double-entry bookkeeping process by which accounting transactions are entered; each individual transaction always has an offsetting transaction.

downsizing process of reducing the number of employees within a firm by eliminating jobs.

dumping selling products abroad at prices below production costs or below typical prices in the home market to capture market share from domestic competitors.

economics social science that analyzes the choices people and governments make in allocating scarce resources.

electronic bulletin board Internet chat room that allows users to post and read messages on a specific topic.

electronic business (e-business) conducting business via the Internet.

electronic data interchange (EDI) computer-to-computer exchanges of invoices, purchase orders, price quotations, and other information between buyers and sellers.

electronic exchange online marketplace that caters to an industry's specific needs.

electronic shopping cart file that holds items that the online shopper has chosen to buy.

electronic storefront company Web site that sells products to customers.

electronic wallet secure computer data file set up by an online shopper at an e-business site that contains credit card and personal identification information.

embargo total ban on importing specific products or a total halt to trading with a particular country.

employee benefits additional compensation such as vacation, retirement plans, profit-sharing, health insurance, gym membership, child and elder care, and tuition reimbursement, paid entirely or in part by the company.

employee ownership business ownership in which workers buy shares of stock in the company that employs them.

employee stock-ownership plan (ESOP) plan that benefits employees by giving them ownership stakes in the companies for which they work.

empowerment (Chap. 7, p. 235) giving employees shared authority, responsibility, and decision making with their managers.

employee separation broad term covering the loss of an employee for any reason, voluntary or involuntary.

encryption process of encoding data for security purposes, using software that encodes and scrambles messages.

end-use segmentation marketing strategy that focuses on the precise way a B2B purchaser will use a product.

enterprise zones specific geographic areas designated for economic revitalization.

entrepreneur person who seeks a profitable opportunity and takes the necessary risks to set up and operate a business.

entrepreneurship willingness to take risks to create and operate a business.

environmental impact study analyzes how a proposed plant would affect the quality of life in the surrounding area.

e-procurement use of the Internet by business and government agencies to solicit bids and purchase goods and services from suppliers.

Equal Employment Opportunity Commission (EEOC) this commission created to increase job opportunities for women and minorities and to help end discrimination based on race, color, religion, disability, gender, or national origin in any personnel action.

equilibrium price prevailing market price at which you can buy an item.

equity capital funds obtained from owners.

equity financing funds invested in new ventures in exchange for part ownership.

equity theory an individual's perception of fair and equitable treatment.

European Union (EU) 27-nation European economic alliance.

event marketing marketing or sponsoring short-term events such as athletic competitions and cultural and charitable performances.

everyday low pricing (EDLP) is a strategy devoted to maintaining continuous low prices rather than relying on short-term price cuts such as cents-off coupons, rebates, and special sales.

exchange control restriction on importation of certain products or against certain companies to reduce trade and expenditures of foreign currency.

exchange process activity in which two or more parties give something of value to each other to satisfy perceived needs.

exchange rate value of one nation's currency relative to the currencies of other countries.

exclusive distribution distribution strategy involving limited market coverage by a single retailer or wholesaler in a specific geographical territory.

executive summary one- to two-page snapshot of what the overall business plan explains in detail.

executive support system (ESS) lets senior executives access the firm's primary databases, often by touching the computer screen, pointing and clicking a mouse, or using voice recognition.

expansionary monetary policy increases the money supply in an effort to cut the cost of borrowing, which encourages business decision makers to make new investments, in turn stimulating employment and economic growth.

expectancy theory the process people use to evaluate the likelihood that their efforts will yield the results they want, along with the degree to which they want those results.

expert system computer program that imitates human thinking through complicated sets of "if-then" rules.

exports domestically produced goods and services sold in other countries.

external communication meaningful exchange of information through messages transmitted between an organization and its major audiences.

extranet secure network used for e-business and accessible through an organization's Web site; available to external customers, suppliers, and other authorized users.

factoring selling receivables to another party, called a factor, for cash.

factors of production four basic inputs for effective operation: natural resources, capital, human resources, and entrepreneurship.

fair trade a market-based approach to pay higher prices to producers on exports from developing countries to developed countries in order for the developing countries to obtain better trading conditions and promote sustainability.

family brand brand name used to identify several different, but related, products.

family leave the Family and Medical Leave Act of 1993 states that businesses with 50 or more employees must provide unpaid leave up to 12 weeks annually for any employee who wants time off for the birth or adoption of a child, to become a foster parent, or to care for a seriously ill relative, spouse, or self if he or she has a serious health condition or injury.

Federal Deposit Insurance Corporation (FDIC) federal agency that insures deposits at commercial and savings banks.

Federal Open Markets Committee Fed body that has primary responsibility for money policy.

Federal Reserve System (Fed) central bank of the United States.

fee-for-service plan traditional form of health insurance in which the insured chooses his or her healthcare provider, pays for treatment, and is reimbursed by the insurance company; also called an indemnity plan.

finance planning, obtaining, and managing the company's funds to accomplish its objectives as effectively and efficiently as possible.

finance charge the difference between the amount borrowed and the amount repaid on a loan.

Financial Accounting Standards Board (FASB) organization that interprets and modifies GAAP in the United States.

financial institutions intermediary between savers and borrowers, collecting funds from savers and then lending the funds to individuals, businesses, and governments.

financial managers executive who develops and implements the firm's financial plan and determines the most appropriate sources and uses of funds.

financial markets market in which securities are bought and sold.

financial plan document that specifies the funds needed by a firm for a period of time, the timing of inflows and outflows, and the most appropriate sources and uses of funds.

financial system process by which money flows from savers to users.

financing section section of a business plan that demonstrates the cost of the product, operating expenses, expected sales revenue and profit, and the amount of the business owner's own funds that will be invested to get the business up and running.

firewall limit data transfers to certain locations and log system use so that managers can identify attempts to log on with invalid passwords and other threats to a system's security.

fiscal policy government spending and taxation decisions designed to control inflation, reduce unemployment, improve the general welfare of citizens, and encourage economic growth.

flexible benefit plan benefit system that offers employees a range of options from which they may choose the types of benefits they receive.

flexible manufacturing system (FMS) production facility that workers can quickly modify to manufacture different products.

flexible work plan employment that allows personnel to adjust their working hours and places of work to accommodate their personal needs.

flextime scheduling system that allows employees to set their own work hours within constraints specified by the firm.

follow-up phase of production control in which employees and their supervisors spot problems in the production process and determine needed adjustments.

foreign corporation firm that operates in states where it is not incorporated.

Foreign Corrupt Practices Act federal law that prohibits U.S. citizens and companies from bribing foreign officials to win or continue business.

foreign licensing agreement international agreement in which one firm allows another to produce or sell its product, or use its trademark, patent, or manufacturing processes, in a specific geographical area in return for royalties or other compensation.

formal communication channel messages that flow within the chain of command defined by an organization.

franchise contractual agreement in which a franchisee gains the right to produce and/or sell the franchisor's products under that company's brand name if they agree to certain operating requirements.

franchisee individual or business firm purchasing a franchise.

franchising contractual business arrangement between a manufacturer or other supplier, and a dealer such as a restaurant operator or retailer.

franchisor firm whose products are sold to customers by the franchisee.

free-rein leadership management style of leaders who believe in minimal supervision and leave most decisions to their subordinates.

frequency marketing marketing initiative that rewards frequent purchases with cash, rebates, merchandise, or other premiums.

frictional unemployment applies to members of the workforce who are temporarily not working but are looking for jobs.

General Agreement on Tariffs and Trade (GATT) international trade accord that substantially reduced worldwide tariffs and other trade barriers.

generally accepted accounting principles (GAAP) principles that encompass the conventions, rules, and procedures for determining acceptable accounting practices at a particular time.

geographical segmentation dividing an overall market into homogeneous groups on the basis of their locations.

global business strategy offering a standardized, worldwide product and selling it in essentially the same manner throughout a firm's domestic and foreign markets.

goal target, objective, or result that someone tries to accomplish.

goal-setting theory says that people will be motivated to the extent to which they accept specific, challenging goals and receive feedback that indicates their progress toward goal achievement.

government bonds bonds issued by the U.S. Department of the Treasury.

grapevine internal information channel that transmits information from unofficial sources.

green marketing a marketing strategy that promotes environmentally safe products and production methods.

grid computing consists of a network of smaller computers running special software.

grievance formal complaint filed by an employee or a union that management is violating some provision of a union contract.

gross domestic product (GDP) sum of all goods and services produced within a country's boundaries during a specific time period, such as a year.

guerrilla marketing innovative, low-cost marketing effort designed to get consumers' attention in unusual ways.

hardware all tangible elements of a computer system.

health insurance category of insurance that pays for losses due to illness or injury.

high-context culture society in which communication depends not only on the message itself but also on nonverbal cues, past and present experiences, and personal relationships between the parties.

home-based businesses firm operated from the residence of the business owner.

horizontal merger merger that joins firms in the same industry for the purpose of diversification, increasing customer bases, cutting costs, or expanding product lines.

human resource management function of attracting, developing, and retaining employees who can perform the activities necessary to accomplish organizational objectives.

human resources production inputs consisting of anyone who works, including both the physical labor and the intellectual inputs contributed by workers.

human skills interpersonal skills that enable a manager to work effectively with and through people; the ability to communicate with, motivate, and lead employees to accomplish assigned activities.

hygiene factors factors that if present are essential to job satisfaction, although they cannot motivate an employee.

hyperinflation economic situation characterized by soaring prices.

imports foreign goods and services purchased by domestic customers.

income statement financial record of a company's revenues, expenses, and profits over a period of time.

individual brand different brand names given to each product within a line.

inflation rising prices caused by a combination of excess consumer demand and increases in the costs of raw materials, component parts, human resources, and other factors of production.

infomercial form of broadcast direct marketing; 30-minute programs that resemble regular TV programs, but are devoted to selling goods or services.

informal communication channel messages outside formally authorized channels within an organization's hierarchy.

information knowledge gained from processing data.

information system organized method for collecting, storing, and communicating past, present, and projected information on internal operations and external intelligence.

infrastructure basic systems of communication, transportation, and energy facilities in a country.

initial public offering (IPO) sale of stock to the public for the first time.

insider trading use of material nonpublic information about a company to make investment profits.

institutional advertising involves messages that promote of concepts, ideas, philosophies, or goodwill for industries, companies, organizations, or government entities.

insurable interest demonstration that a direct financial loss will result if some event occurs.

insurable risk requirement that a pure risk must meet for an insurer to agree to provide coverage.

insurance contract by which the insurer for a fee agrees to reimburse the insured a sum of money if a loss occurs.

integrated marketing communications (IMC) coordination of all promotional activities—media advertising, direct mail, personal selling, sales promotion, and public relations—to produce a unified customer-focused message.

integrity adhering to deeply felt ethical principles in business situations.

intensive distribution distribution strategy that involves placing a firm's products in nearly every available outlet.

International Accounting Standards Board (IASB) established in 1973 to promote worldwide consistency in financial reporting practices.

International Financial Reporting Standards (IFRS) standards and interpretations adopted by the IASB.

international law regulations that govern international commerce.

International Monetary Fund (IMF) organization created to promote trade, eliminate barriers, and make short-term loans to member nations that are unable to meet their budgets.

International Organization for Standardization (ISO) organization whose mission is to develop and promote International Standards for business, government and society to facilitate global trade and cooperation.

intranet computer network that is similar to the Internet but limits access to authorized users.

intrapreneurship process of promoting innovation within the structure of an existing organization.

introduction section of a business plan that describes the company, the management team, and the product in detail.

inventory control function requiring production and operations managers to balance the need to keep stock on hand to meet demand against the costs of carrying inventory.

investment-grade bond bond with a rating of BBB or above.

job enlargement job design that expands an employee's responsibilities by increasing the number and variety of tasks assigned to the worker.

job enrichment change in job duties to increase employees' authority in planning their work, deciding how it should be done, and learning new skills.

job rotation systematically moving employees from one job to another.

job sharing program management decision that allows two or more employees to divide the tasks of one job.

joint venture partnership between companies formed for a specific undertaking.

judiciary court system, or branch of government that is responsible for settling disputes by applying laws.

just-in-time (JIT) system broad management philosophy that reaches beyond the narrow activity of inventory control to influence the entire system of production and operations management.

labor union group of workers who have banded together to achieve common goals in the areas of wages, hours, and working conditions.

law standards set by government and society in the form of either legislation or custom.

law of large numbers concept that seemingly random events will follow predictable patterns if enough events are observed.

leadership ability to direct or inspire people to attain certain goals.

leverage increasing the rate of return on funds invested by borrowing funds.

leverage ratios measures of the extent to which a company relies on borrowed funds.

leveraged buyouts (LBOs) transaction in which public shareholders are bought out and the firm reverts to private status.

LEED (Leadership in Energy and Environmental Design) voluntary certification program administered by the U.S. Green Building Council, aimed at promoting the most sustainable construction processes available.

liability claims against assets by creditors.

liability insurance a type of insurance that protects people against financial losses to others for acts for which the insured was responsible.

life insurance a type of insurance that protects people against the financial losses that occur with premature death.

lifestyle entrepreneur person who starts a business to reduce work hours and create a more relaxed lifestyle.

lifetime value of a customer revenues and intangible benefits (referrals and customer feedback) from a customer over the life of the relationship, minus the amount the company must spend to acquire and serve that customer.

limit order order that puts a ceiling or floor on a security purchase or sale.

limited-liability company (LLC) corporation that secures the corporate advantage of limited liability while avoiding the double taxation characteristic of corporations.

line manager executive involved with the functions of production, financing, or marketing.

line organization organizational structure that establishes a direct flow of authority from the chief executive to subordinates.

line-and-staff organization structure that combines the direct flow of authority of a line organization with staff departments that support the line departments.

liquidity ratios measures of a firm's ability to meet its short-term obligations.

listening receiving a message and interpreting its intended meaning by grasping the facts and feelings it conveys.

local area networks (LANs) computer networks that connect machines within limited areas, such as a building or several nearby buildings.

lockout management decision to put pressure on union members by closing the firm.

logistics process of coordinating flow of goods, services, and information among members of the supply chain.

low-context culture society in which communication tends to rely on explicit written and verbal messages.

macroeconomics study of a nation's overall economic issues, such as how an economy maintains and allocates resources and how a government's policies affect the standards of living of its citizens.

make, buy, or lease decision choosing whether to manufacture a needed product or component in house, purchase it from an outside supplier, or lease it.

malware any malicious software program designed to infect computer systems.

managed care plan healthcare plan in which most, if not all, of the insured's healthcare bills are paid by the insurance company; in exchange, the insured has much less say over his or her treatment.

management process of achieving organizational objectives through people and other resources.

management accountant accountant who works for a firm and provides accounting services to that firm.

management by objectives systematic approach that allows managers to focus on attainable goals and to achieve the best results based on the organization's resources.

management development program training designed to improve the skills and broaden the knowledge of current and potential executives.

management information system (MIS) information system designed to produce reports for managers and other professionals.

management support systems information systems that are designed to provide support for effective decision making.

manufacturer's (national) brand brand offered and promoted by a manufacturer or producer.

market order order that instructs the investor's broker to obtain the best possible price.

market penetration percentage of the market that has purchased your product.

market segmentation process of dividing a total market into several relatively homogeneous groups.

marketable securities low-risk securities with short maturities.

marketing the activity, set of institutions, and processes for creating, communicating, delivering, and exchanging offerings that have value for customers, clients, partners, and society at large.

marketing concept companywide consumer orientation to promote long-run success.

marketing mix blending the four elements of marketing strategy—product, distribution, promotion, and pricing—to satisfy chosen customer segments.

marketing research collecting and evaluating information to support marketing decision making.

marketing strategy section of a business plan that presents information describing the market's need for a product and how the business will satisfy it.

marketing Web site Web site whose main purpose is to increase purchases by visitors.

Maslow's hierarchy of needs theory of motivation proposed by Abraham Maslow. According to the theory, people have five levels of needs that they seek to satisfy: physiological, safety, social, esteem, and self-actualization.

mass production system for manufacturing products in large quantities through effective combinations of employees with specialized skills, mechanization, and standardization.

materials requirement planning (MRP) computer-based production planning system that lets a firm ensure that it has all the parts and materials it needs to produce its output at the right time and place and in the right amounts.

matrix structure project management structure that links employees from different parts of the organization to work together on specific projects.

mediation dispute resolution process that uses a third party, called a mediator, to make recommendations for settling labor–management differences.

Medicare public health insurance program for those 65 or older.

merger agreement in which two or more firms combine to form one company.

microeconomics study of small economic units, such as individual consumers, families, and businesses.

microloans small-business loans often used to buy equipment or operate a business.

middle management second tier in the management pyramid that focuses on specific operations within the organizations.

mission statement written explanation of an organization's business intentions and aims.

missionary selling indirect form of selling in which the representative promotes goodwill for a company or provides technical or operational assistance to the customer.

mixed market economy economic system that draws from both types of economies, to different degrees.

monetary policy government actions to increase or decrease the money supply and change banking requirements and interest rates to influence bankers' willingness to make loans.

money market instruments short-term debt securities issued by financial institutions, companies, and governments.

monopolistic competition market structure in which large numbers of buyers and sellers exchange heterogeneous products so each participant has some control over price.

monopoly market situation in which a single seller dominates trade in a good or service for which buyers can find no close substitutes.

morale mental attitude of employees toward their employer and jobs.

motivator factors factors that can produce high levels of motivation when they are present.

multidomestic business strategy developing and marketing products to serve different needs and tastes of separate national markets.

multinational corporation (MNC) firm with significant operations and marketing activities outside its home country.

municipal bonds bonds issued by state and local governments.

mutual fund financial intermediary that pools funds from investors by selling shares of itself and uses the funds to purchase securities.

national debt money owed by government to individuals, businesses, and government agencies who purchase Treasury bills, Treasury notes, and Treasury bonds sold to cover expenditures.

natural resources all production inputs that are useful in their natural states, including agricultural land, building sites, forests, and mineral deposits.

nearshoring outsourcing production or services to locations near a firm's home base.

negotiable instrument commercial paper that is transferable among individuals and businesses.

net worth the difference between an individual or household's assets and liabilities.

newsgroup noncommercial online forum.

nonpersonal selling consists of advertising, sales promotion, direct marketing, and public relations.

nonprogrammed decision complex and unique problem or opportunity with important consequences for the organization.

nonverbal communication transmission of messages through actions and behaviors.

North American Free Trade Agreement (NAFTA) agreement among the United States, Canada, and Mexico to break down tariffs and trade restrictions.

not-for-profit corporation organization whose goals do not include pursuing a profit.

not-for-profit organizations organization that has primary objectives such as public service rather than returning a profit to its owners.

objectives guideposts by which managers define the organization's desired performance in such areas as new-product development, sales, customer service, growth, environmental and social responsibility, and employee satisfaction.

odd pricing pricing method using uneven amounts, which appear less than they really are to consumers.

offshoring relocation of business processes to lower-cost locations overseas.

oligopoly market structure in which relatively few sellers compete and high start-up costs form barriers to keep out new competitors.

on-demand computing firms essentially rent the software time from application providers and pay only for their usage of the software.

on-the-job training training method that teaches an employee to complete new tasks by performing them under the guidance of an experienced employee.

open book management practice of sharing financial information with employees and teaching them how to understand and use financial statements.

open market operations technique in which the Fed buys or sells government bonds to affect the supply of money and credit.

operational planning detailed standards that guide implementation of tactical plans.

operational support systems information systems designed to produce a variety of information on an organization's activities for both internal and external users.

order processing form of selling, mostly at the wholesale and retail levels, that involves identifying customer needs, pointing them out to customers, and completing orders.

organization structured group of people working together to achieve common goals.

organization chart visual representation of a firm's structure that illustrates job positions and functions.

organization marketing marketing strategy that influences consumers to accept the goals of, receive the services of, or contribute in some way to an organization.

organizing process of blending human and material resources through a formal structure of tasks and authority; arranging work, dividing tasks among employees, and coordinating them to ensure implementation of plans and accomplishment of objectives.

outsourcing using outside vendors to produce goods or fulfill services and functions that were previously handled in-house or in-country.

owners' equity funds contributed by owners plus profits not distributed to owners in the form of cash dividends.

ownership utility orderly transfer of goods and services from the seller to the buyer; also called possession utility.

pacing program company-initiated and financed program to develop new products.

paid time off (PTO) bank of time that employees can use for holidays, vacation, and sick days.

partnership association of two or more persons who operate a business as co-owners by voluntary legal agreement.

patent guarantee to an inventor exclusive rights to an invention for 17 years.

penetration pricing strategy that sets a low price as a major marketing tactic.

performance appraisal evaluation of and feedback on an employee's job performance.

perpetual inventory system that continuously monitors the amount and location of a company's stocks.

person marketing use of efforts designed to attract the attention, interest, and preference of a target market toward a person.

personal financial management study of the economic factors and personal decisions that affect a person's financial well-being.

personal selling the most basic form of promotion: a direct person-to-person promotional presentation to a potential buyer.

PERT (Program Evaluation and Review Technique) chart that seeks to minimize delays by coordinating all aspects of the production process.

phishing high-tech scam that uses authentic looking e-mail or pop-up ads to get unsuspecting victims to reveal personal information.

physical distribution actual movement of products from producer to consumers or business users.

picketing workers marching at a plant entrance to protest some management practice.

place marketing attempt to attract people to a particular area, such as a city, state, or nation.

place utility availability of a product in a location convenient for customers.

planned economy government controls determine business ownership, profits, and resource allocation to accomplish government goals rather than those set by individual firms.

planning process of anticipating future events and conditions and determining courses of action for achieving organizational objectives.

podcast audio or video blog.

point-of-purchase (POP) advertising displays or demonstrations that promote products when and where consumers buy them, such as in retail stores.

pollution environmental damage caused by a company's products or operating processes.

pop-up ad Internet ad that pops-up in a new window; interested parties can click on the ad for more information.

positioning concept in which marketers attempt to establish their products in the minds of customers by communicating to buyers meaningful distinctions about the attributes, price, quality, or use of a good or service.

potential sales revenue amount of revenue the business would collect if its market penetration were 100 percent.

preferred stock shares that give owners limited voting rights, and the right to receive dividends or assets before owners of common stock.

premium amount paid by the insured to the insurer to exchange for insurance coverage.

pre-roll video ad a short advertising video clip that begins automatically whenever a user visits a particular Web site.

prestige pricing establishes a relatively high price to develop and maintain an image of quality and exclusiveness.

price exchange value of a good or service.

primary market financial market in which firms and governments issue securities and sell them initially to the general public.

private enterprise system economic system that rewards firms for their ability to identify and serve the needs and demands of customers.

private equity funds investment companies that raise funds from individuals and institutional investors and use the funds to take large stakes in a wide range of public and private companies.

private exchange secure Web site at which a company and its suppliers share all types of data related to e-business, from product design through order delivery.

private placements sale of securities to a small number of investors.

private property most basic freedom under the private enterprise system; the right to own, use, buy, sell, and bequeath land, buildings, machinery, equipment, patents, individual possessions, and various intangible kinds of property.

private (store) brand product that is not linked to the manufacturer, but instead carries the label of a retailer or wholesaler.

privatization conversion of government-owned and operated companies into privately held businesses.

problem-solving team temporary combination of workers who gather to solve a specific problem and then disband.

process control systems operational support system to monitor and control physical processes.

product bundle of physical, service, and symbolic attributes designed to satisfy buyers' wants.

product advertising consists of messages designed to sell a particular good or service.

product liability the responsibility of manufacturers for injuries and damages caused by their products.

product life cycle four basic stages—introduction, growth, maturity, and decline—through which a successful product progresses.

product line group of related products marked by physical similarities or intended for the same market.

product mix the assortment of product lines and individual goods and services that a firm offers to consumers and business users.

product placement form of promotion in which marketers pay fees to have their products showcased in various media, ranging from newspapers and magazines to television and movies.

production use of resources, such as people and machinery, to convert materials into finished goods and services.

production and operations management oversee the production process by managing people and machinery in converting materials and resources into finished goods and services.

production control creates a well-defined set of procedures for coordinating people, materials, and machinery to provide maximum production efficiency.

production planning phase of production control that determines the amount of resources (including raw materials and other components) a firm needs in order to produce a certain output.

productivity relationship between the number of units produced and the number of human and other production inputs necessary to produce them.

product-related segmentation dividing consumer markets into groups based on benefits sought by buyers, usage rates and loyalty levels.

profitability objectives common objectives included in the strategic plans of most firms.

profitability ratios measures of a company's overall financial performance by evaluating its ability to generate revenues in excess of expenses.

profits rewards for businesspeople who take the risks involved to offer goods and services to customers.

programmed decision simple, common, and frequently occurring problem for which a solution has already been determined.

promotion function of informing, persuading, and influencing a purchase decision.

promotional mix combination of personal and nonpersonal selling components designed to meet the needs of their firm's target customers and effectively and efficiently communicate its message to them.

property and liability insurance general category of insurance that protects against losses due to a number of perils.

psychographic segmentation dividing consumer markets into groups with similar attitudes, values, and lifestyles.

public accountant accountant who provides accounting services to other organizations.

public insurance agency public agency that provides certain types of insurance coverage.

public ownership organization owned and operated by a unit or agency of government.

public relations organization's communications and relationships with its various public audiences.

publicity nonpersonal stimulation of demand for a good, service, place, idea, event, person, or organization by unpaid placement of information in print or broadcast media.

pulling strategy promote a product by generating consumer demand for it, primarily through advertising and sales promotion appeals.

pure competition market structure, in which large numbers of buyers and sellers exchange homogeneous products and no single participant has a significant influence on price.

pure risk type of risk where there is only the possibility of loss.

pushing strategy personal selling to market an item to wholesalers and retailers in a company's distribution channels.

quality control measuring output against established quality standards.

quality good or service that is free of deficiencies.

quota limit set on the amounts of particular products that can be imported.

ratio analysis commonly used tool for measuring the financial strength of a firm.

recession cyclical economic contraction that lasts for six months or longer.

recycling reprocessing of used materials for reuse.

regulated monopolies local, state or federal government grants exclusive rights in a certain market to a single firm.

relationship era the business era in which firms seek ways to actively nurture customer loyalty by carefully managing every interaction.

relationship management collection of activities that build and maintain ongoing, mutually beneficial ties with customers and other parties.

relationship marketing developing and maintaining long-term, cost-effective exchange relationships with partners.

restrictive monetary policy reducing the money supply to curb rising prices, overexpansion, and concerns about overly rapid economic growth.

retailer distribution channel members that sell goods and services to individuals for their own use rather than for resale.

risk uncertainty about loss or injury.

risk-return trade-off process of maximizing the wealth of the firm's shareholders by striking the optimal balance between risk and return.

robot reprogrammable machine capable of performing numerous tasks that require manipulation of materials and tools.

routing phase of production control that determines the sequence of work throughout the facility and specifies who will perform each aspect of production at what location.

rule of indemnity requirement that the insured cannot collect more than the amount of the loss and cannot collect for the same loss more than once.

S corporation corporations that do not pay corporate taxes on profits; instead, profits are distributed to shareholders, who pay individual income taxes.

salary pay calculated on a periodic basis, such as weekly or monthly.

sales law law governing the sale of goods or services for money or on credit.

sales promotion consists of forms of promotion such as coupons, product samples, and rebates that support advertising and personal selling.

Sarbanes-Oxley Act federal legislation designed to deter and punish corporate and accounting fraud and corruption and to protect the interests of workers and shareholders through enhanced financial disclosures, criminal penalties on CEOs and CFOs who defraud investors, safeguards for whistle-blowers, and establishment of a new regulatory body for public accounting firms.

scheduling development of timetables that specify how long each operation in the production process takes and when workers should perform it.

search marketing paying search engines, such as Google, a fee to make sure that the company's listing appears toward the top of the search results.

seasonal unemployment joblessness of workers in a seasonal industry.

secondary market collection of financial markets in which previously issued securities are traded among investors.

Secure Sockets Layer (SSL) technology that secures a Web site by encrypting information and providing authentication.

securities financial instruments that represent obligations on the part of the issuers to provide the purchasers with expected stated returns in the funds invested or loaned.

seed capital initial funding needed to launch a new venture.

selective distribution distribution strategy in which a manufacturer selects only a limited number of retailers to distribute its product lines.

self-managed team work team that has the authority to decide how its members complete their daily tasks.

sell-off transaction in which assets are sold by one firm to another.

serial entrepreneur person who starts one business, runs it, and then starts and runs additional businesses in succession.

server the heart of a midrange computer network

set-aside program component of a government contract specifying that certain government contracts (or portions of those contracts) are restricted to small businesses and/or to women- or minority-owned companies.

sexism discrimination against members of either sex, but primarily affecting women.

sexual harassment unwelcome and inappropriate actions of a sexual nature in the workplace.

shopping product item typically purchased only after the buyer has compared competing products in competing stores.

skimming pricing strategy that sets an intentionally high price relative to the prices of competing products.

skunkworks project initiated by a company employee who conceives the idea, convinces top management of its potential, and then recruits human and other resources from within the firm to turn it into a commercial project.

small business independent business with fewer than 500 employees, not dominant in its market.

Small Business Administration (SBA) principal government agency concerned with helping small U.S. firms.

Small Business Investment Company (SBIC) business licensed by the Small Business Administration to provide loans to small businesses.

social audits formal procedure that identifies and evaluates all company activities that relate to social issues such as conservation, employment practices, environmental protection, and philanthropy.

social entrepreneur person who recognizes societal problems and uses business principles to develop innovative solutions.

social responsibility business's consideration of society's well-being and consumer satisfaction, in addition to profits.

socialism economic system characterized by government ownership and operation of major industries such as communications.

software all the programs, routines, and computer languages that control a computer and tell it how to operate.

sole proprietorship business ownership in which there is no legal distinction between the sole proprietor's status as an individual and his or her status as a business owner.

sovereign wealth funds government-owned investment companies

spam popular name for junk e-mail.

span of management number of subordinates a manager can supervise effectively.

specialty advertising promotional items that prominently display a firm's name, logo, or business slogan.

specialty product item that a purchaser is willing to make a special effort to obtain.

speculative (junk) bond a bond with a rating below BB.

speculative risk type of risk where the possibility of gain and loss both exist.

spin-off transaction in which divested assets form a new company.

sponsorship involves providing funds for a sporting or cultural event in exchange for a direct association with the event.

spyware software that secretly gathers user information through the user's Internet connections without his or her knowledge, usually for advertising purposes.

staff manager executive who provides information, advice, or technical assistance to aid line managers; does not have the authority to give orders outside his or her own department or to compel line managers to take action.

stakeholders customers, investors, employees, and public affected by or with an interest in a company.

standard of living necessities, comforts, and luxuries one seeks to obtain or to maintain.

statement of cash flows statement showing the sources and uses of cash during a period of time.

statement of owners' equity record of the change in owners' equity from the end of one fiscal period to the end of the next.

statutory law written law, including state and federal constitutions, legislative enactments, treaties of the federal government, and ordinances of local governments.

stock market (exchanges) market in which shares of stock are bought and sold by investors.

stock options rights to buy a specified amount of company stock at a given price within a given time period.

stockholders owners of a corporation due to their purchase of stock in the corporation.

strategic alliance partnership formed to create a competitive advantage for the businesses involved; in international business, a business strategy in which a company finds a partner in the country where it wants to do business.

strategic planning process of determining the primary objectives of an organization and then acting and allocating resources to achieve those objectives.

strike temporary work stoppage by employees until a dispute is settled or a contract signed.

structural unemployment people who remain unemployed for long periods of time, often with little hope of finding new jobs like their old ones.

subcontracting international agreement that involves hiring local companies to produce, distribute, or sell goods or services in a specific country or geographical region.

subprime mortgage loan made to a borrower with a poor credit rating.

supervisory management first-line management; includes positions such as supervisor, line manager, and group leader; responsible for assigning nonmanagerial employees to specific jobs and evaluating their performance every day.

supply willingness and ability of sellers to provide goods and services.

supply chain complete sequence of suppliers that contribute to creating a good or service and delivering it to business users and final consumers.

supply curve graph that shows the relationship between different prices and the quantities that sellers will offer for sale, regardless of demand.

sustainable the capacity to endure in ecology.

SWOT analysis SWOT is an acronym for *strengths, weaknesses, opportunities,* and *threats.* By systematically evaluating all four of these factors, a firm can then develop the best strategies for gaining a competitive advantage.

synergy notion that a combined firm is worth more than the two firms are individually.

tactical planning implementing the activities specified by strategic plans.

target market group of people toward whom an organization markets its goods, services, or ideas with a strategy designed to satisfy their specific needs and preferences.

tariff tax imposed on imported goods.

tax assessment by a governmental unit.

team group of people with certain skills who are committed to a common purpose, approach, and set of performance goals.

team cohesiveness extent to which team members feel attracted to the team and motivated to remain part of it.

team diversity variances or differences in ability, experience, personality, or any other factor on a team.

team level average level of ability, experience, personality, or any other factor on a team.

team norm standard of conduct shared by team members that guides their behavior.

technical skills manager's ability to understand and use techniques, knowledge, and tools and equipment of a specific discipline or department.

technology business application of knowledge based on scientific discoveries, inventions, and innovations.

telecommuter home-based employee.

telemarketing personal selling conducted entirely by telephone, which provides a firm's marketers with a high return on their expenditures, an immediate response, and an opportunity for personalized two-way conversation.

tender offer offer made by a firm to the target firm's shareholders specifying a price and the form of payment.

term policy pure type of life insurance policy providing only a death benefit.

test marketing introduction of a new product supported by a complete marketing campaign to a selected city or TV coverage area.

Theory X assumption that employees dislike work and will try to avoid it.

Theory Y assumption that employees enjoy work and seek social, esteem, and self-actualization fulfillment.

Theory Z assumption that employee involvement is key to productivity and quality of work life.

time utility availability of a good or service when customers want to purchase it.

top management managers at the highest level of the management pyramid who devote most of their time to developing long-range plans for their organizations.

tort civil wrong inflicted on another person or the person's property.

trade credit credit extended by suppliers in which the buyer agrees to pay for goods and services received now at a later date.

trade promotion sales promotion geared to marketing intermediaries rather than to final consumers.

trademark brand a legal protection that has been given.

transaction management building and promoting products in the hope that enough customers will buy them to cover costs and earn profits.

transaction processing systems operational support system to record and process data from business transactions.

trends consumer and business tendencies or patterns that firms can exploit to gain market share in an industry.

trial courts federal and state courts of general jurisdiction.

Trojan horse program that claims to do one thing but in reality does something else, usually something malicious.

underwriting process used by an insurance company to determine who, or what, to insure and how much to charge.

unemployment rate percentage of the total workforce actively seeking work but are currently unemployed.

Uniform Commercial Code The basis of U.S. business law; referred to as UCC.

utility power of a good or service to satisfy a want or need.

vendor-managed inventory process in which the producer and the retailer agree that the producer (or the wholesaler) will determine how much of a product a buyer needs and automatically ship new supplies when needed.

venture capital money invested in a business by another business firm or group of individuals in exchange for an ownership share.

venture capitalists business firms or groups of individuals that invest in new and growing firms in exchange for an ownership share.

vertical merger merger that combines firms operating at different levels in the production and marketing process.

virtual private networks (VPNs) secure connections between two points on the Internet.

virtual team group of geographically or organizationally dispersed coworkers who use a combination of telecommunications and information technologies to accomplish an organizational task.

viruses programs that secretly attach themselves to other programs (called *hosts*) and change them or destroy data.

vishing variation on phishing that involves a voice system in which the intended victim receives a voice message directing him or her to reveal personal financial information.

VoIP alternative to traditional telecommunication services provided by companies such as Verizon and Qwest.

volume objectives bases pricing decisions on market share, the percentage of a market controlled by a certain company or product.

wage pay based on an hourly rate or the amount of work accomplished.

Web-to-store use of the Web to aid shoppers at brick-and-mortar retailers.

wheel of retailing theory of retailing in which new retailers gain a competitive foothold by offering low prices and limited services and then add services and raise prices, creating opportunities for new low-price competitors.

whistle-blowing employee's disclosure to company officials, government authorities, or the media of illegal, immoral, or unethical practices committed by an organization.

wholesaler distribution channel member that sells primarily to retailers, other wholesalers, or business users.

wide area networks (WANs) tie larger geographical regions together by using telephone lines and microwave and satellite transmission.

WiFi wireless network that connects various devices and allows them to communicate with one another through radio waves.

wiki Web page that can be edited by users.

work team relatively permanent group of employees with complementary skills who perform the day-to-day work of organizations.

World Bank organization established by industrialized nations to lend money to less developed countries.

World Trade Organization (WTO) 153-member international institution that monitors GATT agreements and mediates international trade disputes.

worm small piece of software that exploits a security hole in a network to replicate itself.

Notes

Chapter 1

1. "Google Android Surpasses Apple's iPhone in Total U.S. Subscribers," *Compelling Mind*, January 9, 2011, http://www.compellingmind.com; "Google Projects for Android: Google APIs," Google, http://code.google.com, accessed January 9, 2011; Raquel P. Gomez, "Add Charm to Android's List of Assets," *Philippine Daily Inquirer*, January 9, 2011, http://www.inquirer.net; Julio Ojeda-Zapata, "Tech Test Drive: Google Gambles That Should Pay Off," *TwinCities.com*, January 7, 2011, http://www.twincities.com; Olivia Oran, "10 Top Android Apps for 2011," *TheStreet for Newsweek*, December 30, 2010, http://www.newsweek.com; Jason Del Rey, "App Time," *Inc*, December 2010–January 2011, p. 116; Daniel Lyons, "Android Invasion," *Newsweek*, October 3, 2010, http://www.newsweek.com.

2. "Quick Facts About Nonprofits," National Center for Charitable Statistics, http://nccs.urban.org/statistics, accessed January 11, 2011.

3. "Quick Facts About Nonprofits," National Center for Charitable Statistics, http://nccs.urban.org/statistics, accessed January 11, 2011.

4. Organization Web site, http://www.stjude.org, accessed February 9, 2010.

5. "American Red Cross Contributes an Initial $10 Million to Assist Japan's Earthquake and Tsunami Survivors," *American Red Cross*, March 15, 2011, http://www.redcross.org.

6. LiveStrong, http://www.livestrong.org, accessed January 11, 2011.

7. "Kindle App Gets Side-loading, Background Downloading," *Yahoo! News*, January 10, 2011, http://news.yahoo.com.

8. "UPS Partners With Red Cross," *Atlanta Business Chronicle*, January 11, 2011, http://www.bizjournals.com; Hugh Collins, "UPS Launches Marketing Campaign to Promote Logistics Business," *Daily Finance*, September 13, 2010, http://www.dailyfinance.com.

9. "100 Best Companies to Work For: #1 SAS," *CNNMoney.com*, http://money.cnn.com, accessed February 4, 2010.

10. Max Chafkin, in "Entrepreneurs We Love," *Inc.*, December 2010/January 2011, p. 96.

11. Ian King and Adam Satarino, "Microsoft to Unveil Apple iPad Competition," *The Olympian*, December 28, 2010, http://www.theolympian.com.

12. Jeffry Bartash, "FCC to Force Cable Operators to Share Sports Channels," January 20, 2010, http://www.marketwatch.com.

13. http://www.sba.gov/advo/stats/sbfaq.pdf

14. Company Web site, http://www.competitivelawn.com, accessed January 11, 2011; Eric Hansen, "That's Opportunity Knocking," *Portfolio.com*, http://www.portfolio.com, accessed January 11, 2011.

15. Dan Macsai, "eBay Dials M for Makeover," *Fast Company*, December 2010/January 2011, pp. 42–44.

16. Company Web site, "History," http://www.graniterock.com, accessed February 9, 2010.

17. "Best Global Brands—2010 Rankings," *Interbrand*, http://www.interbrand.com, accessed January 11, 2011.

18. Mack Collier, "Examples of Great Company Blogs," http://www.searchengineguide.com, accessed February 4, 2010.

19. Company Web site, http://www.overstock.com, accessed January 11, 2011; "Overstock.com Ranked Top Ten of Best Places to Work in Corporate America," December 15, 2010, http://investors.overstock.com.

20. "R.C. Bigelow Company," Connecticut Clean Energy Fund, press release, http://www.ctcleanenergy.com, accessed February 4, 2010.

21. Christine Lagoria, in "Entrepreneurs We Love," *Inc.*, December 2010/January 2011, p. 104.

22. Company Web site, http://www.solarcity.com, accessed January 11, 2011.

23. Helen Coster, "Ranking the World's Most Sustainable Companies," *Forbes*, January 27, 2010, http://www.forbes.com.

24. "Census: More Diversity, Slower Growth in U.S.A. 2050," U.S. Census Bureau Press Release, in *IMDiversity.com*, http:www.imdiversity.com, accessed January 11, 2011.

25. "The 2010 DiversityInc. Top 50 List," *DiversityInc*, March 19, 2010, http://www.diversityinc.com.

26. "Exclusive Data on Discrimination at Work," *DiversityInc*, April 15, 2010, http://www.diversityinc.com.

27. Matthew J. Mowry, "Celebrating Business Excellence," *Business NH Magazine*, May 2011, p. 54.

28. Mitch Weiss and Samantha Bomkamp, "Sully Retires: Chelsey Sullenberger, 'Miracle on the Hudson' Pilot, Retiring," *Huffington Post*, March 3, 2010, http://www.huffingtonpost.com.

29. "World's Most Admired Companies 2010," *Fortune*, http://inoney.cnn.com, accessed January 14, 2011.

Chapter 2

1. Company Web site, http://pharmajet.com, accessed January 17, 2011; "PharmaJet to Appear on 21st Century Healthcare," *Emailwire.com*, December 23, 2010, http://www.pharmajet.com; Ariel Schwartz, "The Future of Prison Technology: Not As Scary As It Seems?" *Fast Company.com*, November 23, 2010, http://www.fastcompany.com; Jeff Bailey, "Unstuck," *Inc.*, October 2010, pp. 91–97.

2. Betsy Feldman, "When the Storm Hits," *Fortune*, August 16, 2010, p. 12.

3. "Recall of Tylenol, Benadryl, Sudafed, Sinutab Issued Over Sanitary Problems," *AboutLawsuits.com*, January 17, 2011, http://www.aboutlaws.com; Company Web site, http://www.jnj.com, accessed January 17, 2011.

4. Company Web site, "Sustainability," http://www.walmartstores.com, accessed January 17, 2011.

5. "Questions and Findings from the 2009 ERC National Business Ethics Survey," *i-Sight*, September 30, 2010, http://i-sight.com.

6. Daniel Franklin, "Just Good Business," *The Economist*, http://www.economist.com, accessed January 17, 2011.

7. "Questions and Findings from the 2009 ERC National Business Ethics Survey," *i-Sight*, September 30, 2010, http://i-sight.com.

8. "2010 Data Breach Stats," *Identify Theft Resource Center*, December 29, 2010, http://itrc.org.

9. Jim Dwyer, "H & M Says It Will Stop Destroying Unworn Clothing," *The New York Times*, January 6, 2010; Jim Dwyer, "A Clothing Clearance Where More Than Just the Prices Have Been Slashed," *The New York Times*, January 5, 2010, http://www.nytimes.com.

10. Damon van der Linde, "Blood Diamond Trade Resuming in Zimbabwe?" *International Business Times*, January 12, 2011, http://www.ibtimes.com; "UAE Joins Ban on Zimbabwe's Blood Diamonds," *Arabian Business.com*, December 23, 2010, http://www.arabianbusiness.com.

11. "Resigned: City Worker Who Lied On Resume Steps Down from Plush Post," 19 Action News, http://www.woio.com, January 20, 2010.

12. "Internet Abuse at Work," *Memory Spy*, December 15, 2010, http://memoryspy.com.

13. U.S. Department of Commerce, Office of the Inspector General, "American Recovery and Reinvestment Act of 2009 Whistleblower Protection," http://www.nist.gov/recovery/upload/whistleblower_factsheet.pdf, accessed February 4, 2010.

14. "Virgin America Is Investigated by FAA & OSHA for 'Cooking Maintenance Log Books,'" *PR Log*, January 11, 2011, http://www.prlog.org.

15. Company Web site, http://www.lockheedmartin.com/index.html, accessed February 4, 2010.

16. Company Web site, http://www.syrusglobal.com/sg/, accessed February 4, 2010.

17. Umaimah Mendhro and Abhinav Sinha, "Three Keys to Staying Ethical in the Age of Madoff," *Forbes.com*, February 6, 2009, http://www.forbes.com.

18. "Mercadien Donates Hundreds of Toys for Children in Need," Company Web site, http://www.mercadien.com, accessed January 18, 2011.

19. Marisa Novello, "Couple's Business Venture Comes Full Circle," *Exeter Newsletter*, January 18, 2011, p. A8.

20. Company Web site, http://www.subway.com/, accessed February 4, 2010; Jared Foundation, http://www.jaredfoundation.org, accessed February 4, 2010; "The Jared Foundation," North American Association of SUBWAY Franchises, http://www.naasf.org, accessed February 10, 2010; "SUBWAY's Jared Fogle Retires Famous Fat Pants," February 12, 2009, Bison Franchise, http://www.bison.com.

21. Tyler Kepner, "McGwire Admits That He Used Steroids," *The New York Times*, January 11, 2010, http://www.nytimes.com.

22. Damian Joseph, "Score Two for Sustainability," *Fast Company*, November 2010, p. 54.

23. Company Web site, http://www.chevrolet.com/volt, accessed January 18, 2011.

24. Dana Capiello and Matthew Daly, "Spill Report Rekindles Democratic Push for Reform," *Associated Press*, January 11, 2011, http://news.yahoo.com: "Gulf Oil Spill Findings: Prison Time Unlikely," *CBS News*, January 6, 2011, http://www.cbsnews.com.

25. Institute of Scrap Recycling Industries, http://www.isri.org, accessed January 18, 2011.

26. Mickey Meece, "Giving Those Old Gadgets a Proper Green Burial," *The New York Times*, January 5, 2011, http://www.nytimes.com.

27. Martin LaMonica, "Bill Gates Investing in Vinod Khosla Green-Tech Fund," *CNET News*, January 25, 2010, http://news.cnet.com.

28. Company Web site, http://www.mars.com/global/index.aspx, accessed February 12, 2010.

29. U.S. Bureau of Labor Statistics, "Table 4. Quartiles and Selected Deciles of Usual Weekly Earnings of Full-Time Wage and Salary Workers by Selected Characteristics, Fourth Quarter 2009 Averages, Not Seasonally Adjusted," http://www.bls.gov, accessed February 12, 2010.

30. "Cheerios Spoonfuls of Stories," http://www.spoonfulsofstoriescontest.com/rules/, accessed January 18, 2011.

31. "Making the Best Better," *Benton County Daily Record*, June 4, 2010, p. 1.

32. "Brand Partnerships," General Mills Web site, http://www.generalmills.com, accessed February 14, 2010.

33. "UPS Pilots Volunteer to Help Haiti Relief Effort," *Forbes.com*, January 14, 2010, http://www.forbes.com.

34. "Salmonella Concerns Prompt Voluntary Recalls of Some Natural Balance Dry Dog Food, Pro-Pet Dog Vitamins," *Los Angeles Times*, June 27, 2010, http://latimes.com/news/blogs.

35. "Dannon to Pay $45M to Settle Yogurt Lawsuit," *ABC News*, February 26, 2010, http://abcnews.go.com.

36. "FDA Warns Consumers about Counterfeit Alli," http://www.fda.gov, accessed February 13, 2010.

37. "eBay Rules and Policies," eBay, http://pages.ebay.com/help/policies/overview.html, accessed February 14, 2010.

38. "Teen Workers," U.S. Department of Labor, http://www.osha.gov/SLTC/teenworkers.html, accessed February 14, 2010; Youth Rules!, http://youthrules.dol.gov, accessed February 14, 2010.

39. "2010 Working Mother 100 Best Companies," *Working Mother*, http://www.workingmother.com, accessed January 18, 2011.

40. Robert Smithson, "Is Unlimited Vacation Time a Recipe for Business Success?" *Kelowna Capital News,* February 16, 2010, http://www.bclocalnews.com.

41. EEOC Web site, http://www.eeoc.gov, accessed January 18, 2011.

42. Steven Greenhouse, "Democrats Working to Overturn Justices on Age Bias," *The New York Times*, October 6, 2009, http://www.nytimes.com; Warren Richey, "Supreme Court Sets High Bar For Age-Bias Suits," *Christian Science Monitor*, June 18, 2009, http://www.csmonitor.com.

43. "Conference Board Job Satisfaction Survey Finds Older Workers as Dissatisfied as Others," *Aging Workforce News*, January 10, 2010, http://www.agingworkforcenews.com.

44. U.S. Department of Labor, *Occupational Outlook Handbook 2010–11,* http://www.bls.gov, accessed February 17, 2010.

45. U.S. Equal Employment Opportunity Commission, "Sexual Harassment," http://archive.eeoc.gov/types/sexual_harassment.html, accessed February 17, 2010.

46. Russell Cawyer, "Bill to Add Lilly Ledbetter Act Provisions to Texas Labor Code Enrolled," *Texas Employment Law Update*, January 6, 2011, http://www.texasemploymentlawupdate.com; S. 181: Lilly Ledbetter Fair Pay Act of 2009, http://www.govtrack.us/congress/bill.xpd?bill=s111-181&tab=summary, accessed February 14, 2010; Sheryl Gay Stolberg, "Obama Signs Equal-Pay Legislation," *The New York Times*, January 29, 2009.

47. Laura Fitzpatrick, "Why Do Women Still Earn Less Than Men?" *Time*, April 20, 2010, http://www.time.com.

Chapter 3

1. Jenna Fryer, "Fox Sports Chairman Calls for Shorter NASCAR Races," *ThatsRacin'.com*, January 25, 2011, http://www.thatsracin.com; "Sunoco Offering Free Fuel, 2011 Explorer in Contest," *Sponsor Release*, January 6, 2011, http://www.nascar.com; "TMS Announces Plans for Pit Stop Park," *Track Release*, January 6, 2011, http://www.nascar.com: "Tracks, Networks Team Up to Sell Naming Rights," *Sporting News Wire Service*, January 4, 2011, http://www.nascar.com; David Caraviello, "Top 5: Issues Facing NASCAR," NASCAR Web site, January 1, 2011, http://www.nascar.com; Jim Peltz, "NASCAR Is Looking to Snap Out of Its Attendance and Ratings Slumps," *Los Angeles Times*, July 22, 2010, http://articles.latimes.com; Nate Ryan, "Lower Prices, Promotions Don't Stop NASCAR Attendance Drop," *USA Today*, May 7, 2010, http://www.usatoday.com.

2. "Worldwide Top 10 Video Games," *VGChartz.com*, January 15, 2011, http://www.vgchartz.com.

3. Curt Hopkins, "Hulu To Begin Charging for Programming," *ReadWriteWeb*, April 22, 2010, http://www.readwriteweb.com.

4. Jad Mouawad, "Demand for Oil Set to Rise Anew," *The New York Times*, February 15, 2010, http://www.nytimes.com.

5. "Top 100 Retailers," *Stores*, July 2010, http://www.stores.org.

6. Pascal Fletcher, "Freeze Mauls Florida Citrus, Significant Damage Seen," *Reuters*, January 11, 2010, http://www.reuters.com.

7. "Vietnam's Shrimp Industry Booming," *Associated Press*, January 4, 2011, http://www.oregonlive.com; Stephan Dinan, "Obama Noshes on Gulf Seafood to Stimulate Industry," *The Washington Times*, August 11, 2010, http://www.washingtontimes.com.

8. Bettina Wassener, "Fed's Move Prompts Drop in Asian Stocks, Oil and Gold, but Dollar Rises," *The New York Times*, February 20, 2010, http://www.nytimes.com; Lewa Pardomuan, "Gold Slips 1 Percent after Fed Raises Discount Rate," *Reuters*, February 19, 2010, http://www.reuters.com.

9. William Spain, "Fast-Food Outlook: Intense Competition, Margin Pressures," *MarketWatch*, January 14, 2010, http://www.marketwatch.com.

10. "Google vs. Microsoft," *Business Exchange*, January 26, 2011, http://bx.businessweek.com; Austin Carr, "Can Bing Catch Google? Microsoft Spends Millions on ESPN, Jay-Z Partnerships," *Fast Company.com*, January 25, 2011, http://www.fastcompany.com.

11. "FCC Order on Exclusive Marketing and Bulk Billing Agreements," National Apartment Association, March 3, 2010, http://www.naahq.org.

12. Air Canada Web site, http://www.aircanada.com, accessed January 26, 2011.

13. *World Factbook*, Central Intelligence Agency, http://www.cia.gov, accessed January 26, 2011.

14. Steve Pendlebury, "Number of Millionaires in U.S. Rebounds," *AOL News*, March 10, 2010, http://www.aolnews.com.

15. *Occupational Outlook Handbook 2010–1011 Edition*, Bureau of Labor Statistics, http://www.bls.gov, accessed January 26, 2011.

16. World Bank Web site, http://web.worldbank.org, accessed February 4, 2010; "Disaster Experts Share Lessons for Haiti," http://web.worldbank.org; Jack Ewing, "Emerging Economies Gain a Voice at Davos," *The New York Times*, January 26, 2010, http://www.nytimes.com.

17. "U.S. And World Population Clocks," U.S. Census Bureau, http://www.census.gov. accessed January 26, 2011.

18. Jonathan Carr, "CPSC Opens Office in China," Weil, Gotshal & Manges LLP, January 13, 2011, http://product-liability.weil.com.

19. Guy Montague-Jones, "Asian Consumers Thirst After Healthy Soft Drinks," *Beverage Daily.com*, December 15, 2010, http://www.beveragedaily.com.

Chapter 4

1. "Ford Figo Review," *CarDekho.com*, http://www.cardekho.com, accessed January 30, 2011; "Ford Figo, Yamaha Honored By ET ZigWheels," *One India*, January 25, 2011, http://living.oneindia.com; "Ford Figo, Yamaha SZ-X Bag Top Honours at ET ZigWheels Awards," *The Economic Times*, January 24, 2011, http://economictimes.indiatimes.com; "A Double Victory for Ford Figo at the CNBC TV18-Overdrive Awards," Ford India Web site, January 5, 2011, http://www.india.ford.com; Nick Kurczewski, "Ford Figo Brings 'Cool' to India," *The New York Times*, March 10, 2010, http://wheels.blogs.nytimes.com.

2. CIA *World FactBook*, "United States," www.cia.gov, accessed February 24, 2011.

3. U.S. Census Bureau, "International Data Base," www.census.gov, accessed February 24, 2011; "You Think! But Do You Know?" World Bank, http://youthink.worldbank.org, accessed February 24, 2011.

4. CIA, *World FactBook*, www.cia.gov, accessed February 24, 2011.

5. Company Web site, http://walmartstores.com, "International," accessed January 31, 2011; "Walmart Stores—Global 500," *Fortune*, http://money.cnn.com, accessed January 31, 2011.

6. "Top Ten Countries with Which the U.S. Trades, for the Month of December 2009," http://www.census.gov, accessed January 31, 2011.

7. *The 2010 Statistical Abstract: State Rankings*, U.S. Census Bureau, http://www.census.gov, accessed January 31, 2011; Daniel Workman, "Top U.S. states for Exported Goods," *Suite101*, June 6, 2010, http://www.suite101.com.

8. Company Web site, Sahar Saffron, http://safarsaffron.com, accessed February 24, 2011; http://www.spiceadvice.com, accessed February 24, 2011.

9. "New IBM Global R&D Lab to Open in Australia," *IBM Press Room*, October 14, 2010, http://www.ibm.com.

10. U.S. Census Bureau, "Exhibit 1. U. International Trade in Goods and Services, January 2007 to December 2009," www.census.gov, accessed February 24, 2011.

11. James T. Reddy, "Disney to Build Shanghai Theme Park," *The Wall Street Journal*, November 7, 2010, http://online.wsj.com

12. Bank for International Settlements, http://www.bis.org., accessed February 24, 2011.

13. "Kraft Foods to Expand China Presence," *The Economic Times*, September 13, 2010, http://www.economictimes.indiatimes.com.

14. Tanya Mohn, "Going Global, Stateside," *The New York Times*, www.nytimes.com, February 24, 2011.

15. "India Needs 400 Airports to Cater to People's Needs," *LiveMint*, www.livemint.com, posted March 3, 2010; Samar Halarnkar, "Delhi Airport's T3: Bags Packed, Ready to Go," *LiveMint*, www.livemint.com, posted February 28, 2010.

16. Matt Hamblen, "Vodafone Says it Had to Cut Mobile Service in Egypt," *Computerworld*, January 31,2011, http://www.computerworld.com.

17. "Recent FCPA and Anti-Corruption News Highlights the Ever-Growing Importance of Effective FCPA Compliance Programs," *Proskauer LLC*, April 22,2010, http://www.proskauer.com.

18. David Segal, "Its Italy Too Italian?" *The New York Times*, July 31, 2010, http://www.nytimes.com.

19. Jessica Anne D. Hermosa, "Electronics Boost Seen with Removal of EU Tariffs," *GMA News.TV*, January 17, 2011, http://www.gmanews.tv.

20. "Administering Sugar Imports," The U.S. Department of Agriculture Foreign Agricultural Service, http://www.fas.usda.gov, accessed February 24, 2011.

21. April Joyner, "Passions: Greg Lueck," *Inc.*, December 2010–January 2011, pp. 36–37.

22. World Trade Organization, "Lamy Calls for March Stocktaking to 'Inject Political Energy and Momentum' in the Negotiations," www.wto.org, February 22 and 23, 2010.

23. "G7 to Forgive Haiti Foreign Debt," *ABC News*, www.abc.net.au, February 7, 2010; press release, "World Bank Statement on Haiti Debt," The World Bank, www.worldbank.org, January 21, 2010.

24. CIA *World Factbook*, "United States," https://www.cia.gov, accessed February 24, 2011.

25. CIA *World Factbook*, "Canada," https://www.cia.gov, accessed February 24, 2011.

26. CIA *World Factbook*, "Mexico," https://www.cia.gov, accessed February 24, 2011.

27. "The Member Countries of the European Union," *Europa*, http://europa .eu, accessed February 4, 2011.

28. Ryan Underwood, "Should You Consider an International Franchise?" *Inc.*, February 1, 2011, http://www.inc.com; Ryan Underwood, "How to Support Global Online Sales," *Inc.*, December 1, 2011, http://www.inc.com.

29. Company Web site, Fuel Systems Solutions, www.fuelsystemssolutions .com, accessed February 24, 2011.

30. Company Web site, http://www.dominosbiz.com, accessed February 4, 2011.

31. Company Web site, Morinaga Co., www.morinagamilk.co.jp, accessed February 24, 2011.

32. Kate O'Sullivan, "Best Buys in Offshore Manufacturing," CFO.com, www.cfo.com, February 18, 2010.

33. "Polaris Acquires Engine Developer Swissauto," *Motorcycle-USA*, www.motorcycle-usa.com, February 3, 2010.

34. Company Web site, "Alcoa Best in Class in Covalence Ethical Reputation Ranking," February 2, 2011, http://www.alcoa.com.

End of Part 1: Launching Your Global Business and Economics Career

1. U.S. Department of Labor, "Tomorrow's Jobs," Occupational Outlook Handbook, 2010–2011 edition, U.S. Bureau of Labor Statistics, http://www.bls.gov.

2. U.S. Department of Labor, "Economists," Occupational Outlook Handbook, 2010–2011 edition, U.S. Bureau of Labor Statistics, http://www.bls.gov.

3. Adapted from Michael R. Czinkota, Ilkka A. Ronkainen, and Michael H. Moffett, "Criteria for Selecting Managers for Overseas Assignments," in International Business, 7th ed. (Mason, OH: SouthWestern, 2005), Table 19.2, p. 634.

4. "In the Money," *The Economist*, www.economist.com, accessed February 28, 2011.

5. Sattar Bawany, "Transition Coaching Helps Ensure Success for Global Assignments," Today's Manager, January 2008, accessed at Entrepreneur .com, March 17, 2010.

Chapter 5

1. Dewey Weber Surf Boards Web site, http://www.deweyweber.com, accessed March 31, 2011; Hansen Surfboards. http://www.hansensurf .com, accessed January 2, 2011; Lost Enterprises, http://www .lostenterprises.com, accessed January 2, 2011; Patrick Rizzo, "U.S. Surfboard Makers Thrive in Choppy Waters," *MSBNC.com*, August 5, 2011, http://www.msnbc.com.

2. "Advocacy Small Business Statistics and Research," U.S. Small Business Administration, http://web.sba.gov/faqs, accessed April 2, 2010.

3. Ibid.

4. Ibid.

5. "An Innovative Green Startup: Zimride Wins OG25 Competition," *Opportunity Green*, September 24, 2010, http://www.opportunitygreen.com.

6. "CEO of ModCloth, Eric Koger, Wins Entrepreneur of the Year," *Press Release*, June 22, 2010, ModCloth Web site, http://www.modcloth.com.

7. U.S. Department of Agriculture, *Agricultural Fact Book*, pp. 12–23, http://www.usda.gov/factbook, accessed April 2, 2010.

8. Cider Hill Farm Web site, http://www.ciderhill.com, accessed January 2, 2011.

9. "Advocacy Small Business Statistics and Research."

10. EBeanstalk Web site, http://www.ebeanstalk.com, accessed January 3, 2011; "Toy Testers to the Rescue," *ABC News*, http://abcnews.com. accessed April 2, 2010.

11. Shobhana Chandra and Alex Kowalski, "U.S. Economy: Sales, Small-Business Optimism Climb," *Bloomberg Business Week*, December 14, 2010, http://www.businessweek.com; "Advocacy Small Business Statistics and Research."

12. "The Small Business Advocate—December 2010," *U.S. Small Business Administration*, http://www.sba.gov/advocacy.

13. "Advocacy Small Business Statistics and Research."

14. "Small Business Jobs Act of 2010," *U.S. Small Business Administration*, http://www.sba.gov, accessed January 4, 2011.

15. Facebook Web site, http://www.facebook.com, accessed January 3, 2011.

16. Jennifer Wang, "Who's Your Daddy?" *Entrepreneur*, December 2010, p. 67.

17. Jennifer Wang, "MicroGreen," *Entrepreneur*, December 2010, p. 67.

18. "Advocacy Small Business Statistics and Research."

19. Ibid.

20. Krispy Kreme Web site, http://www.krispykreme.com, accessed January 3, 2011.

21. Patricia Schaefer, "The Seven Pitfalls of Business Failure and How to Avoid Them," *BusinessKnowHow.com,* http://www.businessknowhow.com/Startup/business-failure.htm, accessed April 2, 2010.

22. Ibid.

23. "Advocacy Small Business Statistics and Research."

24. Fantastic Fortunes Web site, htip://www.fantasticfortunecookies.com, accessed January 3, 2011; David Liscio, "NH Gourmet Cookie Company Brings Products to North Shore," *The Daily Item of Lynn*, October 19, 2010, http://www.thedailyitemoflynn.com.

25. "Advocacy Small Business Statistics and Research."

26. U.S. Department of Labor, "As an Employer, Are you Engaged in Commerce or in an Industry or Activity Affecting Commerce?" e-laws, Family and Medical Leave Act Advisor, http://www.dol.gov, accessed April 2, 2010.

27. "Business Tax Credits," IRS, http://www.irs.gov/business/small, accessed January 3, 2011.

28. TOMs Shoes Web site, http://www.tomsshoes.com/Our-Movement, accessed January 3, 2011.

29. "Top 10 Tips for Writing Your Business Plan," *AllBusiness*, http://www.allbusiness.com/, accessed April 2, 2010.

30. "Performance Stats for the SBA," *Inc.,* http://www.inc.com, accessed April 2, 2010.

31. "Programs and Services to Help You Start, Grow and Succeed," Small Business Administration, http://www.sba.gov/financialassistance, accessed April 2, 2010.

32. Ibid.

33. "Q&A For Small Business Owners," Small Business Administration, http://www.sba.gov, accessed April 2, 2010.

34. "Small Business Jobs Act of 2010," U.S. Small Business Administration, http://www.sba.gov, accessed January 4, 2011.

35. "Fact Sheet About U.S. Small Business Administration Disaster Loans," Small Business Administration, http://www.sba.gov, accessed April 2, 2010.

36. "Support Your Business with a Team of Experts," Small Business Administration, http://www.sba.gov/localresources/index.html, accessed April 2, 2010.

37. "Mission," Thurston County Economic Development Council, http://www.thurstonedc.com, accessed April 2, 2010.

38. Thurston County EDC Web site, http://www.thurstonedc.com, accessed January 4, 2011.

39. National Business Incubator Association, http://www.nbia.org, accessed January 2, 2011.

40. National Venture Capital Association, http://www.nvca.org, accessed January 2, 2011.

41. "Key Facts About Women-Owned Businesses," Center for Women's Business Research, http://www.womensbusinessresearchcenter.org/research/keyfacts, accessed January 2, 2011.

42. The Marketing Zen Group, http://www.marketingzen.com, accessed January 2, 2011.

43. "Mentor-Protégé Program," Small Business Administration, http://www.sba.gov, accessed April 2, 2010.

44. International Franchise Association, http://www.franchise.org, accessed January 2, 2011.

45. Baskin-Robbins Web site, http://www.baskinrobbins.com, accessed January 2, 2011.

46. Subway Web site, http://www.subway.com, accessed April 2, 2010.

47. Edward N. Levitt, "What's So Great About Franchising?" *Franchise Trade*, http://www.franchisetrade.com, accessed April 2, 2010.

48. Ibid.

49. "Why People Are Drawn to Franchising," http://www.articles.directory.com, accessed April 2, 2010.

50. Levitt, "What's So Great About Franchising?"

51. "How Much Does a Franchise Cost?" *AllBusiness.com,* http://www.allbusiness.com, accessed April 2, 2010.

52. Levitt, "What's So Great About Franchising?"

53. "Top Franchises By Investment Level," *Franchise Business Review*, 2010 Franchise Satisfaction Awards, http://fbr50.com, accessed January 2, 2011.

54. Chris Morran, "Judge Dismisses Burger King Franchisee Suit Over Pricing Limits," *The Consumerist*, November 24, 2010, http://consumerist.com.

55. Sylvia Cochran, "Current Class Action Suits," *Yahoo! Contributor Network*, April 12, 2010, http://www.associatedcontent.com.

56. Internal Revenue Service, "IRS Launches Study of S Corporation Reporting Compliance," http://www.irs.gov, accessed April 2, 2010.

57. "The World of Employee Ownership," National Center for Employee Ownership, http://www.nceo.org, accessed January 3, 2011.

58. Michael J. Conway, JD, and Stephen J. Baumgartner, MSc, "The Family-Owned Business," *Graziado Business Report,* Pepperdine University, http://gbr.pepperdine.edu, accessed April 2, 2010.

59. Squamscott Beverages Web site, http://www.nhsoda.com, accessed January 3, 2011; Lara Bricker, "Soda Sparkles on West Coast," *Seacoast Sunday,* http://www.seascoastonline.com, accessed January 3, 2011.

60. "About City Year," http://www.cityyear.org, accessed January 3, 2011.

61. "Company Directory by Business Classification," Hoover's, http://www.hoovers.com, accessed April 2, 2010.

62. "Amtrak," Federal Railroad Administration, http://www.fra.dot.gov, accessed April 2, 2010.

63. "Cabot's Cooperative Heritage," Cabot Creamery, http://www.cabotcheese.coop, accessed April 2, 2010.

64. Ibid.

65. Cecilia Kang, "Comcast–NBC Universal Merger Gains Support in FCC," *The Washington Post,* December 31, 2010, http://www.washingtonpost.com.

66. "Pfizer Buying Synbiotics to Expand Animal Business," *Reuters,* December 29, 2010, http://www.reuters.com.

67. Robin Wauters, "Nokia, Pearson Set up Digital Education Joint Venture in China," *TechCrunch,* February 1, 2010, http://techcrunch.com.

68. "About City Year" and "City Year Tumblr," http://www.cityyear.org, accessed January 3, 2011.

Chapter 6

1. Tesla Web site, http://www.teslamotors.com, accessed February 7, 2011; "Tesla Celebrates Opening of Milan Store on Feb. 11," *EVWind,* February 7, 2011, http://www.evwind.es; Lewis Page, "Elon Musk Looking to Get Into Black Spy Sat Market," *The Register,* February 1, 2011, http://www.theregister.co.uk; Marjorie Censer, "SpaceX Leases New Office in Chantilly," *Capital Business,* January 31, 2011, http://www.washingtonpost.com; Paul Lilly, "Tesla CEO Predicts Auto Industry Will be Fully Electric by 2030," *MaximumPC,* January 25, 2011, http://www.maximumpc.com; W. J. Hennigan, "SpaceX Aims for Next Milestone: Carrying Astronauts," *Los Angeles Times,* January 24, 2011, http://www.latimes.com; Andy Pasztor, "Launch Signals New Space Race," *The Wall Street Journal,* December 9, 2010, http://online.wsj.com; Chester Dawson and Yoshio Takahashi, "Tesla Plans Japan Push," *The Wall Street Journal,* November 15, 2010, http://online.wsj.com; Max Chafkin, "The Explorer," *Inc.,* October 2010, pp. 81–88.

2. Walmart Web site, http://investors.walmartstores.com, accessed March 4, 2011.

3. Bloody Mary Web site, http://www.dearbloodymary.com, accessed February 9, 2011.

4. David Port, "Earn Your Bones with a Doggie Daycare," *Entrepreneur's StartUps,* March 2010, http://www.entrepreneur.com.

5. Video, from *Forbes.com Video Network,* on Stella & Dot Web site, http://home.stella&dot.com, accessed February 9, 2011.

6. Cooperative Web site, http://www.lijjat.com, accessed February 9, 2011.

7. "Kauffman Index of Entrepreneurial Activity, http://www.kauffman.org, accessed March 4, 2011.

8. Janet Steele Holloway, "Disabled Vet Designs the Perfect Tech Job," *Women Entrepreneur,* February 4, 2010, http://www.womenentrepreneur.com.

9. David Port, "Fitness Franchise Flexes Its Muscle," *Entrepreneur's StartUps,* March 2010, http://www.entrepreneur.com.

10. Liz Welch, "John Vechey: PopCap, Making Big Bucks out of Little Games," *Inc.,* October 2010, pp. 101–102.

11. Office of Advocacy, U.S. Small Business Administration, "The Facts About Small Businesses," http://www.sba.gov, accessed March 4, 2011.

12. Hannah Seligson, "Nine Young Chinese Entrepreneurs to Watch," *Forbes.com,* February 28, 2010, http://www.forbes.com.

13. Mike Kessler, "The Outdoorsman," in "Dream Companies," *Inc.,* October 2010, pp. 71–72.

14. "Kauffman Index of Entrepreneurial Activity."

15. Bhati Bead Web site, http://www.bhatibeads.com, accessed March 4, 2011.

16. Niels Bosma, Kent Jones, Erkko Autio and Jonathan Levie, "Global Entrepreneurial Monitor: Executive Report," http://www.gemconsortium.org, accessed March 4, 2011.

17. "About Global Entrepreneurship Week," http://www.unleashingideas.org, accessed February 10, 2011.

18. "Entrepreneurship and Innovation Group," Northeastern University, http://www.cba.neu.edu, accessed March 4, 2011.

19. "Leadership and Career Connections," Students in Free Enterprise, http://www.sife.org, accessed March 4, 2011.

20. Mark Henricks, "Honor Roll," *Entrepreneur,* http://www.entrepreneur.com, accessed March 4, 2011.

21. Max Chafkin, "Ge Wang: For Turning the App into an Art Form," in "Entrepreneurs We Love," *Inc.,* December 2010/January 2011, p. 114.

22. Jason Daley "Tearing Down the Walls," *Entrepreneur,* December 2010, pp. 57–62.

23. "Kauffman Index of Entrepreneurial Activity."

24. "Cool College Startups 2010," *Inc.com,* http://www.inc.com, accessed March 10, 2010.

25. Ibid.

26. Leigh Buchanan, "For Staying True," in "Entrepreneurs We Love," *Inc.,* December 2010/January 2011, pp. 102–103.

27. "Accidental Inventions" *Popular Science.com,* http://www.popsci.com/technology, accessed February 11, 2011.

28. "A Day in the Life of an Entrepreneur," *Princeton Review,* http://www.princetonreview.com, accessed March 4, 2011.

29. "Oprah Winfrey—About.com Readers' Most Admired Entrepreneur," http://www.entrepreneurs.about.com, accessed March 4, 2011.

30. "Apple's Steve Jobs Most Admired Entrepreneur Among Teens," *ABC News Radio,* October 7, 2010, http://abcnewsradioonline.com.

31. Issie Lapowsky, "Because When His City Needs Him, He Is Right There," in "Entrepreneurs We Love," *Inc.,* December 2010/January 2011, p. 114.

32. Company Web site, http://www.bobbibrowncosmetics.com, accessed March 15, 2010; Bobbi Brown and Athena Schindelheim, "How I Did It," *Inc.,* http://www.inc.com, accessed March 4, 2011.

33. Lubbers Farm Web site, http://www.lubbersfarm.com, accessed February 11, 2011.

34. Donna Fenn, "The Kid Behind a $170 Million Website," *Inc.com*, http://www.inc.com, accessed March 4, 2011.

35. Funeraltech Web site, http://twitter.com/funeraltech, accessed February 11, 2011; "Cool College Startups 2010."

36. Mitnick Security Consulting Web site, http://www.mitnicksecurity.com, accessed February 12, 2011; Elinor Mills, "For Kevin Mitnick, Staying Legal Is Job No. 1," *CNET News,* August 10, 2010, http://news.cnet.com.

37. BraunAbility Web site, http://www.braunability.com, accessed February 12, 2011.

38. Retro Fitness Web sites, http://www.retrofitness.net, and http://www.retrofranchising.com, accessed February 12, 2011; and Jason Daley, "What, No Leotard?" *Entrepreneur,* March 2010, http://www.entrepreneur.com.

39. Tracy Stapp, "Young and Growing," *Entrepreneur,* March 2010, http://www.entrepreneur.com.

40. Robert Tuchman, "The Passion's Only as Good As the Plan," *Entrepreneur,* March 5, 2010, http://www.entrepreneur.com.

41. Able Planet Web site, http://www.ableplanet.com, accessed February 12, 2011.

42. Able Planet Web site, http://www.ableplanet.com, accessed February 12, 2011.

43. Helen Coster, "Offshore Odysseys Is No Typical Timeshare," *Forbes,* January 18, 2010, http://www.forbes.com.

44. Darren Dahl, "How to Read a Term Sheet," *Inc.*, March 1, 2010, http://www.inc.com.

45. Immigration Act of 1990 (IMMACT 90), http://www.labor.state.ny.us, accessed March 4, 2011.

46. Michael Goldman, Inc., http://www.michaelgoldman.com, accessed February 12, 2011.

47. Marc Gunther, "3M's Innovation Revival," *CNN Money,* September 24, 2010, http://money.cnn.com.

48. Marc Gunther, "3M's Innovation Revival," *CNN Money,* September 24, 2010, http://money.cnn.com.

End of Part 2: Launching Your Entrepreneurial Career

1. Michael Ames, cited in "Is Entrepreneurship for You?" Small Business Administration, http://www.sba.gov, accessed February 18, 2011.

2. U.S. Department of Labor, "Overview of the 2008–18 Projections" *Occupational Outlook Handbook,* 2010–2011 edition, Bureau of Labor Statistics, http://www.bls.gov, accessed February 18, 2011.

3. Alex Salkever, "The Furniture Company Wanted to Sell Him Its Buildings—and Close Down. Should He Buy the Company, Too?" *Inc.,* November 2007, pp. 60–65.

4. U.S. Department of Labor, "Management, Scientific, and Technical Consulting Services," *Career Guide to Industries, 2010–2011 Edition,* Bureau of Labor Statistics, http://www.bls.gov, accessed February 18, 2011.

5. U.S. Small Business Administration, "Protecting Your Ideas," http://www.sba.gov, accessed February 18, 2011.

Chapter 7

1. "Xerox at a Glance," Company Web site, http://www.xerox.com, accessed February 15, 2011; "Ursula Burns Profile," *Wall Street Journal Online,* http://topics.wsj.com, accessed February 15, 2011; "Remove Water, Add Profit: Xerox Announces New Production Inkjet System," Company Web site, February 14, 2011, http://news.xerox.com; "Restructure Dents Xerox Earnings," *The Age,* January 27, 2011, http://www.theage.au; Roger Cheng, "Tech Executives: Schools, Immigration Key to Innovation," *Digits,* January 7, 2011, http://blogs.wsj.com; Geoff Golvin, "Ursula Burns Launches Xerox Into the Future,: *CNN Money.com* April 22, 2010, http://money.cnn.com.

2. "The Stop and Shop Supermarket Company," *Hoovers.com,* http://www.hoovers.com, accessed February 24, 2011.

3. David Lidsky, "Who's Next: Laura Ipsen," *Fast Company,* December 2010/ January 2011, pp. 39–40.

4. "*BusinessWeek* Names Customer Service Champs," *Customers 1ˢᵗ Blogspot,* February 23, 2010, http://www.customers1stblogspot.com.

5. Cold Stone Creamery Web site, http://www.coldstonecreamery.com, accsed February 15, 2011.

6. "Zappos.com Power by Service," http://about.zappos.com, accessed February 15, 2011.

7. Helen Coster, "The State of the CEO in 2010," *Forbes.com,* January 21, 2010, http://www.forbes.com.

8. Kurt Badenhausen, "Names You Need to Know in 2011: Todd Combs," *Forbes,* November 12, 2010, http://blogs.forbes.com.

9. Christopher Steiner, "Go Green and Stay in the Black," *Forbes.com,* March 8, 2010, http://www.forbes.com.

10. Sarah E. Needleman, "Business Owners Try to Motivate Employees," *The Wall Street Journal,* January 14, 2010, http://online.wsj.com.

11. "The Most Innovating and Promising College Startups," *Grasshopper Group,* August 5, 2010, http://grasshoppergroup.com.

12. "The Most Innovating and Promising College Startups," *Grasshopper Group,* August 5, 2010, http://grasshoppergroup.com.

13. Coster, "The State of the CEO in 2010."

14. "Mattel Named One of the World's Most Ethical Companies Again in 2010," *Forbes.com,* March 22, 2010, http://www.forbes.com.

15. "Interview with Mark Zuckerberg," *Baturaja Online,* January 10, 2011, http://status.baturajaonline.com; Jason Kincaid, "Mark Zuckerberg on Facebook's Strategy for China (And His Wardrobe)," *TechCruch,* October 16, 2010, http://techcrunch.com.

16. Staples Announces Finalists of Global Search for the Next Green Office Product," *Boston.com,* March 24, 2010, http://finance.boston.com.

17. Ibid.

18. Savious Kwinika, "South Africa Stricke," *The Christian Science Monitor,* August 18, 2010, http://www.csmonitor.com; David Daly, "Wave of Airline Strikes Sweeps Europe," *The New York Times,* March 22, 2010, http://www.nytimes.com.

19. Company Web site, http://www.starbucks.com, accessed February 24, 2011; "Starbucks News! 2010," *Coffee Club Network,* January 22, 2010, http://www.cofeeclubnetwork.com.

20. "Starbucks news! 2010," *Coffee Club Network.*

21. Piperlime We site, http://www.piperlime.com, accessed February 16, 2011.

22. Andria Chang, "Piperlime Brand Adding Zest to Gap," *MarketWatch,* February 16, 2011, http://www.marketwatch.com.

23. "The Most Innovating and Promising College Startups," *Grasshopper Group,* August 5, 2010, http://grasshoppergroup.com.

24. "How Companies Manage the Front Line Today," *McKinsey & Company,* pp 1–2.

25. Jena McGregor, Alli McConnon, and David Kiley, "Customer Service in a Shrinking Economy," *BusinessWeek,* March 9, 2010, http://www.businessweek.com.

26. Company Web site, http://www.apple.com, accessed February 24, 2011.

27. "CR's 100 Best Corporate Citizens 2010," *CR Magazine,* http://www.thecro.org, accessed February 16, 2011.

28. "Denise Morrison to Replace Douglas Conant at Campbell Soup," *FoodProcessing.com,* September 30, 2010, http://www.foodprocessing.com.

29. Scott D. Anthony, "Google's Management Style Grows Up," *BusinessWeek,* March 9, 2010, http://www.businessweek.com.

30. Dean Foust, "US Airways: After the Miracle on the Hudson," *BusinessWeek,* March 9, 2010, http://www.businessweek.com.

31. "Corporate Information," Google Web site, http://www.google.com/corporate/culture.html, accessed February 24, 2011.

32. "Culture," Walt Disney Company Web site, http://corporate.disney.go.com/careers/culture.html, accessed February 24, 2011.

33. Ben Fritz, "Company Town," *Los Angeles Times,* March 30, 2010, http://latimesblogs.latimes.com.

34. Petswelcome.com Web site, http://www.petswelcom.com, accessed February 16, 2011.

35. Procter & Gamble Web site, http://www.pg.com, accessed February 16, 2011.

36. Brandon Gutman, "Zappos' Marketing Chief: 'Customer Service Is the New Marketing!' " *Fast Company,* March 15, 2010, www.fastcompany.com.

37. Mike Gordon, Chris Musso, Eric Rebentisch, and Nisheeth Gupta, "The Path to Successful New Products," *McKinsey Quarterly,* January 7, 2010, http://www.forbes.com.

38. Jason Del Rey, "How I Did It: Omniture's Josh James," *Inc.com,* March 1, 2010, http://www.inc.com.

Chapter 8

1. Bonna Johnson, "Gaylord to Raise Level at Opryland Hotel," *The Tennessean,* February 8, 2011, http://www.knoxnews.com; Joe Edwards, "Opryland Hotel Reopens After Flood Damage," *Associated Press,* November 16, 2010, http://www.msnbc.com; "Opryland Hotel Reopens After Flood," *NewsChannel5.com,* November 14, 2010, http://www.newschannel5.com; "Gaylord to Lay Off 1,700 Employees," *WKRN-TV Nashville,* June 2, 2010, http://www.wrkn.com; "Opryland Damage Estimates at Least $50M," *WKRN-TV Nashville,* May 7, 2010, http://www.wkrn.com.

2. Heather R. Huhman, "5 Job Skills in Demand 2011," *Careerealism,* February 13, 2011, http://www.careerealism.com.

3. Mark Kolakowski, "Find a Job Online," *About.com,* http://financecareers.about.com, accessed February 22, 2011.

4. Jobs in Pods, http://www.jobsinpods.com, accessed March 4, 2011.

5. "Uniform Employee Selection Guidelines Interpretation and Clarification," *Uniform Guidelines.com,* http://www.uniformguidelines.com, accessed March 4, 2011.

6. Peter M. LaSorsa, "UPS Settles EEOC Lawsuit for $46,000," *Illinois Sexual Harassment Attorney Blog,* February 20, 2010, http://www.illinoissexualharassmentblog.com.

7. Hank Hayes, "Tennessee House Subcommittee Advances English-Only Bill," *Times News.net.* March 3, 2010, http://www.timesnews.net.

8. "The True Cost of (Mis) Hiring," *Automation,* http://www.automation.com, accessed February 22, 2011.

9. "Nugget Market" in "100 Best Companies to Work For," *CNN Money.com,* January 2011, http://money.cnn.com.

10. "McDonald's Puts Apprenticeships on the Menu," updated February 7, 2011, McDonald's Web site, http://www.aboutmcdonalds.com.

11. "Welcome to EYU," http://www.ey.com, accessed March 4, 2011.

12. Denise H. Horton, "High-Tech Training for Georgia's Companies," Technical College System of Georgia, http://www.dtae.org, accessed February 22, 2011.

13. Glimmerglass Web site, http://www.glimmerglassgroup.com, accessed March 4, 2011.

14. Julia Werdigier, "Rothschilds Bring in an Outsider to Run the Show," *The New York Times,* March 29, 2010, http://www.nytimes.com.

15. Samuel A. Culbert, "Yes, Everyone Really Does Hate Performance Reviews," *The Wall Street Journal,* April 19, 2010, http://finance.yahoo.com.

16. "Turn Your Performance Review System into One That Works," *Quality Digest Magazine,* http://www.qualitydigest.com, accessed March 4, 2011.

17. Halogen Software Web site, http://www.halogensoftware.com, accessed February 23, 2011.

18. "25 Top-Paying Companies," *CNN Money.com,* January 26, 2011, http://money.cnn.com.

19. "S.181 Lilly Ledbetter Fair Pay Act of 2009," *Open Congress,* http://www.opencongress.org, accessed March 4, 2011.

20. "Employer Costs for Employee Compensation," Bureau of Labor Statistics, March 10, 2010, http://www.bls.gov.

21. "Paid Family Leave," Employment Development Department, http://www.edd.ca.gov, accessed March 4, 2011.

22. Lance Whitney, "SAS, Google Top Fortune's Best-Employer List," *CNET News,* January 25, 2010, http://news.cnet.com.

23. Raytheon Solipsys Web site, http://www.solipsys.com, accessed February 23, 2011.

24. "Advantages and Disadvantages of Paid Time Off," *The Thriving Small Business,* March 19, 2010, http://www.thethrivingsmallbusiness.com.

25. Steven Greenhouse, "Flex Time Flourishes in Accounting Industry," *The New York Times,* January 7, 2011, http://nytimes.com.

26. "Things You Should Know About BidShift," San Angelo Community Medical Center, http://www.sacmc.com, accessed March 4, 2011.

27. "Truth and Myths of Work/Life Balance," *Workforce Management,* http://www.workforce.com, accessed February 24, 2011.

28. "Economists Push for Federal Job-Sharing Program," *Washington Independent,* February 24, 2010, http://washingtonindependent.com.

29. "Study: Remote-Work Programs Benefit Employers Too," *Microsoft News Center,* March 11, 2010, http://www.microsoft.com.

30. "Telework Week: February 14th–18th 2011," *Telecommute & Telework News,* November 19, 2010, http://www.telecommutenews.com.

31. Lisa Orrell, "5 Tips to Retain Gen Y Talent," *Women Entrepreneur,* April 12, 2010, http://www.womenentrepreneur.com.

32. Marshall Goldsmith, "How to Keep Good Employees in a Bad Economy," February 26, 2010, http://blogs.hbr.org.

33. Dustin Ensinger, "Why Layoffs Are Not Beneficial to Companies," *Economy in Crisis,* February 8, 2010, http://www.economyincrisis.org.

34. Ibid.

35. "MySpace Prepares Downsizing, Layoffs Ahead of Possible Sale," *Fox Business,* January 4, 2011, http://www.foxbusiness.com; "One is Five European Companies Expected to Downsize in 2011 and 2012," *Burson-Marsteller,* October 15, 2010, http://burson-marsteller.eu.

36. Tim Worstall, "Can Oz Compete in the Outsourcing Market?" *Channel Register,* February 14, 20111, http://www.sourcingmag.com; "Virgin Brand Damaged by IT Outsourcing Failure," *The Outsource Blog,* September 28, 2010, http://www.theoutsourceblog.com.

37. "Maslow's Hierarchy of Needs," *Accel-Team.com,* http://www.accel-team.com, accessed March 4, 2011.

38. Maggie Ginsberg-Schutz, "Best Places to Work 2010," *Madison Magazine,* http://www.madisonmagazine.com, accessed February 24, 2011.

39. Kenneth A. Dodge, "Make CEOs Help the Little Guy," *Post-Gazette,* February 7, 2010, http://www.post-gazette.com.

40. "Our Company," The Pampered Chef, http://www.pamperedchef.com, accessed March 4, 2011.

41. "Rotational Training Programs," http://www.emc.com, accessed March 4, 2011.

42. "Union Members Summary," Bureau of Labor Statistics, January 22, 2010, http://www.bls.gov.

43. "Major Work Stoppages (or Dearth Thereof) in 2010," *U.S. Bureau of Labor Statistics,* February 9, 2011, http://mrzine.monthlyreview.org.

44. A.G. Sulzberger, "For Wisconsin Lawmakers, a Hero's Homecoming," *The New York Times,* March 12, 2011, http://nytimes.com.

45. Ibid.

46. James Sherk, "Majority of Union Members Now Work for the Government," *The Heritage Foundation,* January 22, 2010, no. 2773.

Chapter 9

1. "Teamwork for Humanity," Mayo Clinic Web site, http://www.mayoclinic.org, accessed February 28, 2011; "Transform 2011," *Center for Innovation,* http://centerforinnovation.mayo.edu, accessed February 28, 2011; Jeff Hansel, "At Mayo, MSNBC Host Highlights Clinic's Teamwork," *PostBulletin.com,* January 27, 2011, http://www.postbulletin.com; Lauren Venoy, "Having a Heart: My Mayo Moment," *Sharing Mayo Clinic,* September 7, 2010, http://sharing.mayoclinic.org; Uri Neren, "Why Innovation Thrives at the Mayo Clinic," *Harvard Business Review,* August 16, 2010, http://blogs.hbr.org; "Mayo Clinic Center for Innovation to Sponsor a Collaborative Symposium on Innovations in Health Care Experience and Delivery," Mayo Clinic Web site, http://www.mayoclinic.org.

2. Anderson & Associates Web site, http://www.andassoc.com, accessed March 1, 2011; Su Clauson-Wicker, "Warm Hearth CEO Ferne Moschella: Seeing the Trees & the Forest," *Ampersand,* January/February 2011, Vol. 24, Issue I, http://www.andassoc.com.

3. Lebanon Valley Brethren Home, http://www.lvbh.org, accessed March 1, 2011; Becka Livesay, "The Culture Change Way: Empowering Direct Care Workers to Improve Care," *Direct Care Alliance,* March 2010, http://blog.directcarealliance.org.

4. "A Statistical Profile of Employee Ownership," The National Center for Employee Ownership, updated March 2010, http://www.nceo.org.

5. "Employee Stock Options and Ownership (ESOP)," http://www.referenceforbusiness.com, accessed March 8, 2011.

6. "A Statistical Profile of Employee Ownership," The National Center for Employee Ownership, updated March 2010, http://www.nceo.org.

7. "Employee Ownership as a Retirement Plan," The National Center for Employee Ownership, http://www.nceo.org, accessed March 8, 2011.

8. "Employee Stock Options Fact Sheet," The National Center for Employee Ownership, http://www.nceo.org, accessed March 8, 2011.

9. Ibid.

10. Toyota Web site, http://www.toyota.com/safety/smart-team, accessed March 1, 2011.

11. "Our Core Values," Whole Foods Market Web site, http://www.wholefoodsmarket.com, accessed March 1, 2011.

12. Lisa Arthur, "We Twitter, So Now Let's Chatter," *Forbes.com,* October 5, 2010, http://blogs.forbes.com.

13. BBC Web site, http://www.bbc.co.uk, accessed May 10, 2010; Lynda Gratton, Andreas Voigt, and Tamara Erickson, "Bridging Faultlines in Diverse Teams," *MIT Sloan Management Review,* Summer 2007, pp. 22–29.

14. Sedona Spirit Yoga & Hiking, http://www.yogalife.net, accessed March 2, 2011.

15. CEO Chef Web site, http://ceochef.com, accessed March 2, 2011.

16. "Alliance with Rock Valley Designed to Better Prepare Public School Graduates for College," District 205 Web Site, http://webs.rps.com, accessed March 8, 2011.

17. Michiel Kruyt, Judy Malan, and Rachel Tuffield, "Three Steps to Building a better Top Team," *Forbes.com,* February 22, 2011; Nick Grabbe, "Experts: Don't Fear Workplace Conflict," *Gazettenet.com,* March 10, 2010, http://www.gazettenet.com.

18. Mike Ramsey, "U.S. Ends Toyota Probe," *The Wall Street Journal,* February 25, 2011, http://online.wsj.com.

19. Mike Ramsey, "U.S. Ends Toyota Probe," *The Wall Street Journal,* February 25, 2011, http://online.wsj.com.

20. David Woods, "i-level Redesigns Its Employee Reward Communication Strategy," *HR Magazine,* March 8, 2010, http://www.humanresourcesmagazine.co.uk.

21. Norma Chew, "Are You a Good Listener?" *Associated Content,* http://www.associatedcontent.com, accessed March 8, 2011.

22. "Why Outsource Email?" DakotaPro.biz Web site, http://www.dakotapro.biz, accessed March 8, 2011.

23. "Expand Trust in Your Organization," *Peter Stark.com,* http://www.peterstark.com, accessed March 8, 2011.

24. Susan Adams, "Ten Questions You'd Better Ask Your Boss," *Forbes.com,* January 4, 2011, http://www.forbes.com.

25. John Boe, "How to Read Your Prospect Like a Book!" John Boe International, http://johnboe.com, accessed March 8, 2011.

26. Toni Bowers, "Company Settles Facebook/NLRB Case of Employee Firing," *Tech Republic,* February 8, 2011, http://techrepublic.com; Steven Greenhouse, "Company Accused of Firing Over Facebook Post," *The New York Times,* November 8, 2010, http://www.nytimes.com.

27. American Medical Response Web site, http://www.amr.net, accessed March 2, 2011; Toni Bowers, "Company Settles Facebook/NLRB Case of Employee Firing," *Tech Republic,* February 8, 2011, http://www.techrepublic.com.

28. "Keep Current with Latest AMR News," AMR Web site, http://www.amr.net, accessed March 2, 2011; Mike Ramsey, "U.S. Ends Toyota Probe," *The Wall Street Journal,* February 25, 2011, http://online.wsj.com; Toni Bowers, "Company Settles Facebook/NLRB Case of Employee Firing," *Tech Republic,* February 8, 2011, http://www.techrepublic.com.

Chapter 10

1. "Boeing 737 Production Rate increases to 35 Per Month," Boeing Web site, http://boeing.mediaroom.com, accessed March 9, 2011; Dean Radford, "Boeing's 737 Production Increase to Mean About 1,200 New Jobs in Renton," *Renton Reporter,* March 2, 2011, http://www.pnwlocalnews.com; Bernard Choi, "Delivering 737s on Demand," *Boeing Features,* September 20, 2010, http://www.boeing.com; John Ostrower, "Boeing to Re-evaluate 777 and 737 Production Rates," *Air Transport Intelligence News,* September 3, 2010, http://www.flightglobal.com.

2. "William Levitt," *Entrepreneur,* http://www.entrepreneur.com, accessed April 26, 2010.

3. "Marysville Auto Plant," Honda of America Mfg., Inc., http://www.ohio.honda.com, accessed March 9, 2011.

4. Company Web site, http://www.shibuidesignsltd.com, accessed March 9, 2011.

5. Company Web site, http://www.chobani.com, accessed March 9, 2011.

6. "LEED," U.S. Green Building Council Web site, http://www.usgbc.org, accessed May 27, 2010.

7. "Saks Will Use Kiva Robots," *The Boston Globe,* January 26, 2010, http://www.boston.com.

8. Brady Weber, "Machine Vision Protects Pharmaceutical Packaging," *Control Engineering,* February 1, 2010, http://www.controleng.com.

9. Clara Maria Cabrera, "CAD/CAM Dental Technology," *Associated Content,* http://www.associatedcontent.com, accessed April 26, 2010.

10. "World Pharma Manufacturing Summit 2011," summit Web site, http://www.wpms.org.cn.en, accessed March 9, 2011.

11. Company Web site, http://www.manroland.com, accessed March 9, 2011.

12. Anupam Govil, "Shifting of the Global Sourcing Axis," *Near Shore Americas,* April 6, 2010, http;//www.nearshoreamericas.com.

13. "World Premiere of the New Passat for the USA," Company Web site, January 10, 2011, http://www.volkswagengroupamerica.com.

14. "Holland Car's Assembly Line to Evolve," *Fortune,* April 18, 2010, http://www.addisfortune.com.

15. "Advantages and Disadvantages of Outsourcing," *The Thriving Small Business,* February 8, 2010, http://www.thethrivingsmallbusiness.com.

16. "Profile of American Apparel," *Market Research News,* December 20, 2010, http://www.salisonline.org.

17. "Supplier Mangement," Ariba Web site, http://www.ariba.com, accessed April 26, 2010.

18. Shruti Date Singh, "Deere Shortage Prompts Kansas Farmer to Buy Dragotec," *Bloomberg Businessweek,* April 26, 2010, http://www.businessweek.com.

19. "Roundy's Implements Inventory Management System," *Supermarket News,* January 6, 2010, http://www.supermarketnews.com.

20. "Velvac Chooses Datalliance's Vendor Managed Inventory Program," *Truckinginfo.com,* February 1, 2010, http://www.truckinginfo.com.

21. "Seattle Children's Hospital Saves $2.5 Million in First Year with Streamlined Inventory Distribution," http://www.hfma.org, accessed April 26, 2010.

22. "Turtle Wax," Solarsoft Web site, http://www.solarsoft.com, accessed March 9, 2011.

23. Judy Miller, "Still Made in America: The Super Bowl Footballs from Ada, Ohio," *Encyclopedia Britannica Blog,* February 1, 2010, http://www.britannica.com.

24. JETCAM Web site, http://www.jetcam.com, accessed April 26, 2010.

25. Company Web site, http://www.sleepmaster.co.uk, accessed March 9, 2011; "Success Stories: Sleepmaster, Ltd.," *Usersolutions.com,* http://www.usersolutions.com, accessed March 9, 2011.

26. Linda Doell, "Toxic Waste Nuclear Sludge Candy Recalled Over Lead Levels," *Wallet Pop,* January 14, 2011, http://www.walletpop.com.

27. Jamie Liddell, "Top Ten Tips for Better Benchmarking," *SSON Network,* http://www.ssonetwork.com, accessed April 26, 2010.

28. Vic Nanda, "Preempting Problems," *Six Sigma Forum Magazine,* February 2010, pp. 9–18.

29. "Maintaining the Benefits and Continual Improvement," International Organization for Standardization, http://www.iso.org, accessed April 26, 2010.

Part 3 Launching Your Management Career

1. U.S. Department of Labor, "Tomorrow's Jobs," *Occupational Outlook Handbook, 2010–2011 edition,* Bureau of Labor Statistics, accessed March 18, 2011, http://www.bls.gov.

2. U.S. Department of Labor, "Administrative Services Managers," *Occupational Outlook Handbook, 2010–2011 edition,* Bureau of Labor Statistics, accessed March 18, 2011, http://www.bls.gov.

3. U.S. Department of Labor, "Construction Managers," *Occupational Outlook Handbook, 2010–2011 edition,* Bureau of Labor Statistics, accessed March 18, 2011, http://www.bls.gov.

4. U.S. Department of Labor, "Food Service Managers," *Occupational Outlook Handbook, 2010–2011 edition,* Bureau of Labor Statistics, accessed March 18, 2011, http://www.bls.gov.

5. U.S. Department of Labor, "Human Resources, Training, and Labor Relations Managers and Specialists," *Occupational Outlook Handbook, 2010–2011 edition,* Bureau of Labor Statistics, accessed March 18, 2011, http://www.bls.gov.

6. U.S. Department of Labor, "Lodging Managers," *Occupational Outlook Handbook, 2010–2011 edition,* Bureau of Labor Statistics, accessed March 18, 2011, http://www.bls.gov.

7. U.S. Department of Labor, "Medical and Health Services Managers," *Occupational Outlook Handbook, 2010–2011 edition,* Bureau of Labor Statistics, accessed March 18, 2011, http://www.bls.gov.

8. U.S. Department of Labor, "Purchasing Managers, Buyers, and Purchasing Agents," *Occupational Outlook Handbook, 2010–2011 edition,* Bureau of Labor Statistics, accessed March 18, 2011, http://www.bls.gov.

9. U.S. Department of Labor, "Industrial Production Managers," *Occupational Outlook Handbook, 2010–2011 edition,* Bureau of Labor Statistics, accessed March 18, 2011, http://www.bls.gov.

Chapter 11

1. Patricio Robles, "Netflix's Biggest Competition? Facebook," *Econsultancy,* March 10, 2011, http://econsultancy.com; "Netflix Changing the Way You Add DVDs to Queue," *iMarkinteractive,* January 19, 2011, http://www.imarkinteractive.com; Jamie Odell, "Removing 'Add to DVD Queue' from Streaming Devices," *Netflix,* January 17, 2011, http://blog.netflix.com; Jesse Noyes, "2011: The Year of Living Netflix," *b2c Marketing Insider,* December 31, 2010, http://www.marketing-insider.com; "Android Getting Netflix in 2011," Mobile Marketing Watch, November 16, 2010, http://www.mobilemarketingwatch.com; Ryan Nakashima and Michael Liedtke, "Netflix Streaming Selection Expands to Include Paramount, Lionsgate, MGM Movies," *Huffington Post,* August 10, 2010, http://www.huffingtonpost.com.

2. American Marketing Association, "Definition of Marketing," accessed March 25, 2011.

3. Company Web site, http://www.target.com, accessed March 25, 2011; Brad Gilligan, "Target Starts Mobile Coupon Program," *All Tech Considered,* March 11, 2010, http://www.npr.org; Business Wire, "Target Launches First-Ever Scannable Mobile Coupon Program," *MarketWatch,* March 10, 2010, http://www.marketwatch.com; Marguerite Reardon, "Attention Shoppers: Target Offers Mobile Coupons," *CNET News,* March 10, 2010, http://news.cnet.com.

4. "Kindle Puts Readers and Friends on Same Page," *Physorg,* February 7, 2011, http://www.physorg.com; "Barnes & Noble Nook Color" *Geek News Central,* January 29, 2011, http://www.geeknewscentral.com; Rachel Metz, "Amazon Releasing Kindle Software for Android," *Physorg,* May 18, 2010, http://www.physorg.com.

5. "Scope of the Nonprofit Sector," *Independent Sector,* http://independentsector.org, accessed March 15, 2011.

6. "Volunteering in the United States, 2010," *Bureau of Labor Statistics,* January 26, 2011, http://www.bls.gov.

7. "Volunteer Programs—Hometown Huddle," *Join the Team,* https://www.jointheateam.com, accessed March 16, 2011; "Hometown Huddle," *United Way,* http://liveunited.org.

8. Company Web site, http://www.avoncompany.com, accessed March 25, 2011; "Avon Foundation for Woman Grants $500,000 to the U.S. Department of State Secretary's Fund for Global Women's Leadership," Press Release, March 11, 2010, http://multivu.prnewswire.com.

9. "Celebrity Ads Among Most Memorable of 2011 Oscar Commercials," *Nielsen Ratings,* March 3, 2011, http://blog.nielsen.com.

10. Olympics 2012 Web site, http://www.london2012.com, accessed March 20, 2011.

11. "Tour de Cure 2010," American Diabetes Association, http://tour.diabetes.org, accessed March 25, 2011.

12. "2011 United Way Alternative Spring Break," http://liveunited.org, accessed March 20, 2011.

13. Donna Fenn, "Ten College Startups That Want to Change the World," *BNET,* March 2, 2011, http://www.bnet.com.

14. Patrick J. Sauer, "Give and Go," *Fast Company,* November 2010, pp. 64–67.

15. Take Care Clinic Web site, http://www.takecarehealth.com, accessed March 25, 2011; BusinessWire, "Take Care Clinics at Select Walgreens Offer Families Convenient and Affordable Option for Camp and Sports Physicals," Press Release, MarketWatch, March 10, 2010, http://www.marketwatch.com; Pamela Lewis Dolan, "Retail Clinics: Struggling to Find Their Place," *American Medical News,* March 1, 2010, http://www.ama-assn.org/amednews.

16. Marco Lui, "Subway Plans to Open 500 Stores across China in Next Five Years," *BusinessWeek,* March 11, 2010, http://www.businessweek.com; Farah Master, "Subway Eyes Matching McDonalds in China in 10 Years," *Reuters,* March 8, 2010, http://www.reuters.com.

17. Blank Label Web site, http://www.blanklabel.com, accessed March 20, 2011; Spreadshirt Web site, http://www.spreadshirt.com, accessed March 20, 2011.

18. Chris Foreman, "iPhone Still Second-Place US Smartphone While Android Grows," *Ars Technica,* March 11, 2010, http://arstechnica.com; Philip Elmer-DeWitt, "ComScore: Android Gains on the iPhone," *Fortune Brainstorm Tech,* March 10, 2010, http://brainstormtech.blogs.fortune.cnn.com.

19. Christopher T. Heun, "Procter & Gamble Readies Online Market-Research Push," *InformationWeek,* http://www.informationweek.com, accessed March 25, 2011; Mark Clothier, "P&G's McDonald Pins Growth on Closer Shave than Mumbai Barber," *BusinessWeek,* March 11, 2010, http://www.businessweek.com.

20. Stephanie Rosenbloom, "In Bid to Sway Sales, Cameras Track Shoppers," *The New York Times,* March 20, 2010, http://www.nytimes.com.

21. Clothier, "P&G's McDonald Pins Growth on Closer Shave."

22. Pottery Barn Kids Web site, http://www.potterybarnkids.com, accessed March 20, 2011; Timothy Lorang, "The State of Social Media for Your Small Business," Image Media Partners, March 7, 2011, http://www.imagemediapartners.com.

23. IdeaStorm Web site, http://www.ideastorm.com, accessed March 20, 2011.

24. Declan McCullagh, "Why No One Cares about Privacy Anymore," *CNET News,* March 12, 2010, http://news.cnet.com; Leah Betancourt, "How Companies Are Using Your Social Media Data," *Mashable,* March 2, 2010, http://mashable.com; Jim Cooper, "Yahoo's Carol Bartz Touts Data," *Mediaweek,* March 1, 2010, http://www.mediaweek.com.

25. Company Web site, http://turiyamedia.com, accessed March 25, 2011; "Turiya Media Targets Game Publishers with Behavioral Data Mining," *GamesBeat,* March 10, 2010, http://games.venturebeat.com.

26. Alex Priest, "Pew Study Shows Social Media use Nearly Double Among Older Users," *Technorati,* August 27, 2010, http://www.technorati.com; Pew Internet Organization Web site, August 27, 2010, http://pewinternet.org.

27. Damon Darlin, "Always Pushing Beyond the Envelope," *The New York Times,* August 7, 2010, http://www.nytimes.com.

28. Nelson Ireson, "2012 Ford Police Interceptor: Taurus Does Law and Order," *Motor Authority,* March 12, 2010, http://www.motorauthority.com; Brent Snavely, "Ford to Unveil Police Interceptor," *Frreep.com,* March 12, 2010, http://www.freep.com; "Ford Unveils Next-Generation, V-6-Only Taurus Police Car," *USA Today,* March 12, 2010, http://content.usatoday.com.

29. Kristina Knight, "Study: Online Hubs Change Women's Offline Shopping Habits," *Biz Report,* May 19, 2010, http://www.bizreport.com.

30. Aileen Lee, "Why Women Rule the Internet," *TechCrunch,* March 20, 2011, http://techcrunch.com.

31. Aileen Lee, "Why Women Rule the Internet," *TechCrunch,* March 20, 2011, http://techcrunch.com.

32. U.S. Census Bureau, "Resident Population Projections by Sex and Age: 2010 to 2050," *Statistical Abstract of the United States,* http://www.census.gov, accessed March 25, 2010.

33. Paul Briand, "Baby Boomers Shunning Usual Retirement Haunts," *Examiner.com,* March 26, 2010, http://www.examiner.com.

34. "Nielsen: Shopping Habits by Generation," *Convenience Store News,* March 29, 2010, http://www.csnews.com.

35. "Mun2 Premiers Second Season of 'The mun2 Look,'" *Its Reality TV,* March 3, 2011, http://www.itsrealitytv.com.

36. Emily Maltby, "Immigrant Entrepreneurs Top List," *The Wall Street Journal Blogs,* March 7, 2011, http://blogs.wsj.com.

37. Company Web site, http://www.gmblogs.com, accessed March 25, 2011.

38. "Where Does the Money Go?" *Visual Economics,* http://www.visualeconomics.com, accessed March 21, 2011; Ruth Mantell, "Despite Tough Times, Parents Spend Big on Kids," *MarketWatch,* May 4, 2010, http://www.marketwatch.com.

39. IKEA Web site, "People & the Environment," http://www.ikea.com and http://www.mypaper.se, accessed March 21, 2011.

40. "Sodexho Marriott Services," *Claritas,* www.claritas.com, accessed March 25, 2011.

41. Jennifer Booton, "McCafe, Oatmeal Help Boost McDonald's February Sales," *Fox Business,* March 8, 2011, http://www.foxbusiness.com.

42. Resources for Entrepreneurs staff, "Consumer Habits Could Be Permanently Changed by Recession," *Resources for Entrepreneurs,* March 25, 2010, http://www.gaebler.com.

43. Company Web site, http://www.timberland.com, accessed March 21, 2011.

44. Company Web site, http://www.atlantis.com, accessed March 21, 2011.

45. Company Web site, http://www.apple.com/ipod/nike, accessed March 25, 2011.

46. Company Web site, http://www.netcall.com, accessed March 25, 2011.

Chapter 12

1. Company Web site, http://www.bagbalm.com, accessed March 22, 2011; "Offering Soothing Skin Solutions" and "Where Can I Find Bag Balm?" J J Smith Co. Web site, http://jjsmithco.net, accessed March 22, 2011; "Bag Balm Uses," *Mahalo,* http://www.mahalo.com, accessed March 22, 2011; Norm Siegel, "Protect Your Dog's Feet From Salt," *Examiner.com,* http://www.examiner.com, accessed March 22, 2011; "Bag Balm Becomes Popular Problem Salver," *Associated Press,* February 1, 2010, http://www.cbsnews.com.

2. Stan Schroeder, "Gartner: Most Kids Will Use PCs with Touchscreens by 2015," *Mashable,* April 7, 2010, http://mashable.com.

3. Associated Press, "Pepsi to Distribute New Line of Tampico Drinks," *msn.com,* April 9, 2010, http://news.moneycentral.msn.com.

4. "The Most Innovating and Promising College Startups," *Grasshopper Group,* August 5, 2010, http://grasshoppergroup.com.

5. Joachim Ebert, Shiv Shivaraman, and Paul Carrannanto, "Driving Growth through Ultra-Low-Cost Product Development," *Industry Week,* February 17, 2010, http://www.industryweek.com.

6. Kathy Erickson, "Nook or Kindle? New Developments in 2011 Creating a Stir," *Ezine Articles,* January 28, 2011, http://ezinearticles.com; "Barnes & Noble NOOKcolor Wins Last Gadget Standing 2011," *citybizlist,* January 10, 2011, http://nework.citybizlist.com.

7. Alfred Poor, "HDTV Almanac—LED Backlight Prices Falling," *HDTV Magazine,* February 22, 2010, http://www.hdtvmagazine.com.

8. Company Web site, http://www.bagbalm.com, accessed March 22, 2011.

9. Matthew Moskovciak, "Blu-ray Quick Guide," *CNET Reviews,* February 25, 2010, http://reviews.cnet.com.

10. Company Web site, http://www.chase.com, accessed March 25, 2011.

11. Michael Leddy, "Advice Students: Twenty Uses for a Post-It Note," *Lifehack,* September 27, 2010, http://www.lifehack.org.

12. Company Web site, http://www.febreze.com, accessed March 25, 2011; *PR Newswire,* "P&G Leads 2010 Edison Best New Product Award Finalists with Five Nods," Press Release, February 11, 2010, http://www.prnewswire.com.

13. "New Helmet Blocks Rifle Shots," *Military.com,* February 4, 2011, http://www.military.com.

14. Company Web site, http://www.ea.com, accessed March 25, 2011; Ben Gilbert, "Report: EA Planning Premium, Pre-Launch DLC for Retail Games at $10–$15," *Joystiq,* March 22, 2010 http://www.joystiq.com.

15. "Top 10 Worst Beauty Products Ever," *Beauty High,* March 2, 2011, http://www.beautyhigh.com; "Worst Products of CES 2011," *Huffington Post,* January 19, 2011, http://www.huffingtonpost.com.

16. Company Web site, http://www.ikea.com, accessed March 28, 2011; CBS4, "Centennial IKEA Construction Begins May 4," April 20, 2010, http://cbs4denver.com.

17. J. Jennings Moss, "The Brand Stand," *Portfolio.com*, April 12, 2010, http://www.portfolio.com; "Survey: FedEx in Top 10 for Brand Awareness," *Memphis Business Journal*, April 12, 2010, http://memphis.bizjournals.com.

18. Company Web site, http://www.quiznos.com, accessed March 25, 2011; Quiznos, "Quiznos Rolls Out Green Packaging," Press Release, February 23, 2010, http://www.chainleader.com.

19. "FDA Issues Open Letter on Nutrition Labeling," *Packaging Digest*, March 4, 2010, http://www.packagingdigest.com; Robin Shreeves, "FDA Could Pull Foods over Labeling," *MNN Mother Nature Network*, March 4, 2010, http://www.mnn.com; U.S. Food and Drug Administration, "FDA Calls on Food Companies to Correct Labeling Violations; FDA Commissioner Issues an Open Letter to the Industry," March 3, 2010, http://www.fda.gov.

20. "What Are Unlocked Cell Phones?" *wiseGEEK*, March 24, 2011, http://www.wisegeek.com; Phil Goldstein, "Google's Nexus One Promises New Distribution Channel for Smartphones," *FierceWireless*, January 5, 2010, http://www.fiercewireless.com; Tom Krazit, "Google's Mobile Hopes Go Beyond Nexus One," *CNET News*, January 5, 2010, http://new.cnet.com.

21. Company Web site, "FedEx International," http://www.fedex.com, accessed March 28, 2011.

22. U.S. Census Bureau, *"County Business Patterns,"* http://www.census.gov, accessed May 24, 2010; Bureau of Labor Statistics, "Occupational Outlook Handbook, 2010–11 Edition," http://www.bls.gov, accessed March 25, 2011.

23. Company Web site, http://www.acehardware.com, accessed March 28, 2011.

24. U.S. Census Bureau, "Quarterly Retail E-Commerce Sales, 4th Quarter 2009," February 16, 2010, http://www.census.gov.

25. Company Web site, http://saksfifthavenue.com, accessed April 30, 2010; Kelly O'Reilly, "Saks' Special Delivery to 10022-SHOE," *NBC New York*, March 15, 2010, http://www.nbcnewyork.com; Jennifer Paull, "Saks Fifth Avenue Introduces Special Delivery: The Hottest Designer Shoes for Spring," *StyleList*, March 14, 2010, http://www.stylelist.com.

26. Company Web site, http://www.seventhgeneration.com, accessed March 28, 2011; Romy Ribitzky, "Talking about an Ad Generation," *Portfolio.com*, February 11, 2010, http://www.portfolio.com; Romy Ribitzky, "7 Facts about Seventh Generation," *Portfolio.com*, February 11, 2010, http://www.portfolio.com; Elaine Wong, "How Seventh Generation Is Going Mainstream," *Brandweek*, January 26, 2010, http://www.brandweek.com.

27. Company Web site, http://www.polaroid.com, accessed March 25, 2011; "Starlight to Expand Digital Entertainment Product Category under the Polaroid Brand," press release, March 24, 2010, http://www.foxbusiness.com.

28. Company Web site, http://www.traderjoes.com, accessed March 28, 2011.

29. Petco Web site, http://www.petco.com; and PetSmart Web site, http://www.petsmart.com, both accessed March 29, 2011.

30. Company Web site, http://www.victoriagardensie.com, accessed April 30, 2010; Kristi Reedy, "Victoria Gardens Adds Sponsors to Offer Shoppers a True Lifestyle Center," press release, March 23, 2010, http://www.free-press-release.com.

31. My Starbucks Idea Web site, http://mystarbucksidea.force.com, accessed March 29, 2011, "Starbucks Gets Its Business Brewing Again with Social Media," *Advertising Age*, February 22, 2010, http://adage.com.

32. James Kanter, "Luxury Goods May Pick and Choose Venues for Sales," *The New York Times*, April 20, 2010, http://www.nytimes.com.

33. Company Web site, "About Us," http://www.easy.com, accessed April 30, 2010.

34. Samuel Axon, "How Small Businesses Are Using Social Media for Real Results," *Mashable*, March 22, 2010, http://mashable.com.

35. Best Buy Web site, http://www.bestbuy.com, accessed March 29, 2011.

36. "Top 10 Outlet Stores in America," *Marie Claire*, http://www.marieclaire.com, accessed March 29, 2011.

37. "Nano-Based RFID Tags Could Replace Bar Codes," *Science Daily*, March 19, 2010, http://www.sciencedaily.com; "Verayo Launches Next Generation of Unclonable RFID Chips," *BusinessWire*, March 2, 2010, http://www.businesswire.com.

38. "Trucking Statistics," *Truck Info*, http://www.truckinfo.net, accessed April 30, 2010.

39. Association of American Railroads, "Class I Railroad Statistics," April 12, 2010, http://www.aar.org; Vince Bond Jr., "Freight Trains Pull Their Weight in Energy Savings," *Great Lakes Echo*, January 12, 2010, http://greatlakesecho.org.

Chapter 13

1. San Francisco Giants Web site, http://www.sanfrancisco.giants.mib.com, accessed March 30, 2011; Jerry Beach, "Texas Rangers vs. San Francisco Giants World Series Creates Ticket Frenzy in Both Markets," *Ticket News*, October 25, 2010, http://www.ticketnews.com; Jerry Beach, "Dynamic Pricing Pays Offs for San Francisco Giants Tickets," *Ticket News*, October 4, 2010, http://www.ticketnews.com.

2. Aaron Perlut, "CMOs Must Ask Whether Campaigns Triangulate," *Forbes.com*, March 30, 2011, http://www.blogs.forbes.com.

3. Rebecca Ruiz, "Ten Misleading Drug Ads," *Forbes.com*, February 2, 2010, http://www.forbes.com.

4. Sarah Nassauer, "A New Sales Model: Employees," *The Wall Street Journal*, March 17, 2011. p. D3.

5. "San Diego McDonald's to Promo Frappes with Taxi Tops," *QSR Web*, April 6, 2010, http://www.qsrweb.com; Mike Hughlett, "McDonald's Frappes Spreading in Chicago Area," *Chicago Breaking Business*, February 2, 2010, http://www.chicagobreakingbusiness.com.

6. Nat Ives, "American Idol Returns to Dominance in Product Placement," *Advertising Age*, March 16, 2011, http://www.adage.com.

7. Ibid.

8. Mark Wyatt, "Guerilla [sic] Marketing Meets Social Media," *Articlesbase*, February 8, 2010, http://www.articlesbase.com.

9. David Griner, "To Hell and Back: EA's Guerrilla Marketing Campaign for 'Dante's Inferno,' " *AdFreak.com*, Spring 2010, http://adweek.blogs.com.

10. Jim Tierney, "Live from NEMOA: Why Your Brand Should Be Like Elvis," *Multichannel Merchant*, March 11, 2010, http://www.multichannelmerchant.com.

11. Bradley Johnson, "Top 100 Global Advertisers See World of Opportunity," *Advertising Age*, December 6, 2010, http://adage.com.

12. Ibid.

13. Company Web site, http://www.avonfoundation.org, accessed April 1, 2011.

14. "Foundation Fact Sheet," Bill and Melinda Gates Foundation, http://www.gatesfoundation.org, accessed Aplrl 8, 2011.

15. Google Web site, http://www.google.com/tv, accessed April 1, 2011.

16. Ibid.

17. Web TV Evolution: Insights and Statistics," *Online Marketing Trends*, February 1, 2011, http://www.onlinemarketing-trends.com; Erick Schonfeld, "Estimate: 800,000 U.S. Households Abandoned Their TVs for the Web," *TechCrunch*, April 13, 2010, http://techcrunch.com; John Latchem, "More U.S. Homes Have Game Consoles than Cable Boxes," *Home Media Magazine*, March 3, 2010, http://www.homemediamagazine.com.

18. "2011 Super Bowl Commercial Costs," http://www.superbowl-commercials.org, accessed April 1, 2011; "Most Expensive Television Commercial of All Time," *Hole in the Hull*, January 31, 2011, http://www.holeinthehull.com.

19. "Internet Radio—Traditional Radio's Future?" *Radio News*, April 7, 2010, http://www.radiostreamingnews.com.

20. "Google Audio Ads—The Future of Radio Advertising?" *Broadcast Advertising*, February 14, 2010, http://broadcastadvertising.doodig.com.

21. Larry Riggs, "Credit Card Mailings Expected to Rebound," *Chief Marketer*, February 8, 2011, http://chiefmarketer.com.

22. "Facts and Figures," *Outdoor Advertising Association of America*, http://www.oaaa.org, accessed April 1, 2011.

23. Clear Channel Outdoor Advertising, "Reach the Mobile Consumer," http://www.clearchanneloutdoor.com, accessed April 8, 2011; Schaller Consulting, *The New York City Taxicab Factbook*, 2006, http://www.schallerconsult.com; Dave Bradley, "Taxi Top Digital Advertising—What Next?" *EzineArticles.com*, March 2, 2010, http://ezinearticles.com; North Park University, "North Park Launches 2010 Outdoor Advertising Campaign," January 15, 2010, http://www.northpark.edu.

24. Natalie Zmuda, "Coca-Cola Gets Hands-on with Its Own Digital Billboards," *Advertising Age*, February 18, 2010, http://adage.com; "CBS Outdoor Brings 3D Outdoor Advertising to New York's Grand Central Station," press release, February 10, 2010, http://www.marketwatch.com.

25. Mike Sachoff, "Local Online Ad Revenue to Top $42 Billion," *Web Pro News*, March 21, 2011, http://www.webpronews.com.

26. Ford Motor Company Web site, http://www.fiestamovement2.com, accessed April 8, 2011; Jay Yarow, "YouTube Turning a Profit? Eric Schmidt 'Assumes' It Is," *Business Insider*, January 22, 2010, http://www.businessinsider.com; Grant McCracken, "How Ford Got Social Marketing Right," *Harvard Business Review*, January 7, 2010, http://blogs.hbr.org.

27. Jimm Fox, "Web Video Practices? Salesforce.com Chooses YouTube," *One Market Media*, February 6, 2011, http://onemarketmedia.com; Jimm Fox, "Top Viral Videos of 2010," *One Market Media*, December 29, 2010, http://onemarketmedia.com.

28. BzzAgent Web site, http://aboutbzzagent.com, accessed April 8, 2011; Andrew M. Kaikati, "Let's Make a Deal," *The Wall Street Journal*, January 25, 2010, http://online.wsj.com.

29. "Top NASCAR Team Helps Marketing for Lowes, Pepsi, DuPont and GoDaddy," *Quarterly Retail Review*, March 27, 2011, http://www.quarterlyretailreview.com.

30. "Effective Infomercials," Infomercial DRTV, http://www.infomercialdrtv.com, accessed April 8, 2011.

31. Edward C. Baig, "Target Puts Mobile Coupons on Customers' Cellphones," *USA Today*, March 11, 2010, http://www.usatoday.com; Phil Wahba, "Coupon Use Up 27 Pct Last Year—Inmar," *Shop Talk*, January 25, 2010, http://blogs.reuters.com.

32. Maisie Ramsay, "Verizon Drops Mail-In Rebate on Palm Pre, Pixi Plus," *Wireless Week*, March 5, 2010, http://www.wirelessweek.com; Rick Broida, "Take the Hassles Out of Mail-in Rebates," *The Washington Post*, February 9, 2010, http://www.washingtonpost.com.

33. Dan Fletcher, "How Facebook Is Redefining Privacy," *Time*, May 20, 2010, http://www.time.com; "Point of Purchase Marketing Turns to Digital Options," *POP Displays*, April 3, 2010, http://popdisplays.theproductjudge.com; Kunur Patel, "Forget Foursquare: Why Location Marketing Is New Point-of-Purchase," *Advertising Age*, March 22, 2010, http://adage.com.

34. U.S. Department of Labor, Economic News Release, Table 5. Employment by Major Occupational Group, 2008 and Projected 2018, December 11, 2009, http://data.bls.gov, accessed April 1, 2011.

35. Gary Strauss, "For the Wealthy, a Return to Luxury Spending," *USA Today*, February 21, 2011, http://www.usatoday.com.

36. Matthew Hathaway, "Recession-Weary Consumers Find Haggling Can Cut Costs," *Chicago Tribune*, March 14, 2010, http://articles.chicagotribune.com; Michael S. Rosenwald, "In Tough Economic Times, Shoppers Take Haggling to New Heights," *The Washington Post*, January 31, 2010, http://www.washingtonpost.com.

37. Lee Howard, "Pfizer Ups Its Commitment to E-Marketing," *The Day*, January 21, 2010, http://www.allbusiness.com.

38. Federal Trade Commission, "Q&A for Telemarketers and Sellers About the Do Not Call Provisions of the FTC's Telemarketing Sales Rule," *FTC Business Alert*, http://www.ftc.gov, accessed April 8, 2011.

39. Barbara Weaver Smith, "Ten Tactics to Drive B2B Sales with Social Media," *Blog World*, March 30, 2011, http://www.blogworld.com.

40. Nat Robinson, "SlideRocket Presentation Tip—4 Ways For Using MultiMedia Strategically," *SlideRocket*, April 1, 2010, http://www.sliderocket.com.

41. Marisa Novello, "Outpouring of Support for Local Merchant," *Exeter NewsLetter*, March 11, 2011, p. A3.

42. Susan G. Komen Race for the Cure Web site, http://ww5.komen.org, accessed April 8, 2011.

43. Elaine Wong, "Dove Super Bowl Spot Scores Initial Points with Men," *Brandweek*, February 9, 2010, http://www.brandweek.com; Jack Neff and Rupal Parekh, "Dove Takes Its New Men's Line to the Super Bowl," *Advertising Age*, January 5, 2010, http://adage.com. Reproduced with kind permission of Unilever PLC and group companies.

44. Elliot Zwiebach, "Family Dollar Plans Consumables Promotions," *Supermarket News*, March 30, 2011, http://supermarketnews.com.

45. Sean Poulter, "The High Price of Fashion: Sales of Luxury It Bags Soar by 60%," *Mail Online*, March 12, 2010, http://www.dailymail.co.uk.

46. Richard Esposito, "'Wise Guys' Accused of Scalping $29 Million in Springsteen, Yankees, Miley Cyrus Tickets," *ABC News*, March 1, 2010, http://abcnews.go.com.

47. Alex Mindlin, "Vowel Sounds Influence Consumers' Price Perceptions," *The New York Times*, January 18, 2010, http://www.cnbc.com.

Part 4: Launching Your Marketing Career

1. U.S. Department of Labor, "Market and Survey Researchers," *Occupational Outlook Handbook, 2010–2011*, Bureau of Labor Statistics, accessed April 18, 2011, http://www.bls.gov.

2. U.S. Department of Labor, "Advertising Sales Agents," *Occupational Outlook Handbook, 2010–2011*, Bureau of Labor Statistics, accessed April 18, 2011, http://www.bls.gov.

3. U.S. Department of Labor, "Advertising and Public Relations Services," *Occupational Outlook Handbook, 2010–2011*, accessed April 18, 2011, http://www.bls.gov.

4. Ibid.

Chapter 14

1. Shopkick Web site, http://www.shopkick.com, accessed April 6, 2011; Carol Wersich, "New Mobile Shopping Application Available Through Smartphones," *Courier Press*, April 5, 2011, http://www.courierpress.com; Dan Frommer, "Shopkick Passes 1 Million Users," *Business Insider*, March 9, 2011, http://www.businessinsider.com; Stephanie Clifford, "Aisle By Aisle, an App That Pushes Bargains," *The New York Times*, August 17, 2010, http://www.nytimes.com; Jefferson Graham, "Shopkick App Can Lead You to Discounts and Sales," *USA Today*, August 11, 2010, http://www.usatoday.com.

2. Fred Cummins, "The Changing Focus of the CIO in 2010," hp Community Home, February 3, 2010, http://www.communities.hp.com; Galen Gruman, "2010 CIO Priorities Shift to Lightweight Services, Virtualization," *InfoWorld*, January 19, 2010, http://www.infoworld.com; SearchCIO.com staff, "IT Salary Survey: How CIO, IT Salaries Vary by Industry," *SearchCIO.com*, January 7, 2010, http://searchcio.techtarget.com.

3. "Truecount, Trimble Partner for Retail RFID," *Apparel*, March 28, 2011, http://apparel.edgl.com/home.

4. IEEE Computer Society, "History of Computing Timeline," http://www.computer.org; Computer History Museum Web site, http://www.computerhistory.org, accessed May 24, 2010; Roy Schestowitz, "Computer History Development Timeline: Microsoft Perspective," *Techrights*, February 4, 2010, http://techrights.org.

5. "Best 5 Laptops," *CNET Reviews*, April 4, 2011, http://reviews.cnet.com; "Best Netbooks," *CNET Reviews*, April 4, 2011, http://reviews.cnet.com; Tim Gideon, "The Best Tablet at CES 2011," *PC Magazine*, January 7, 2011, http://www.pcmag.com.

6. Jakob Nielsen, "10 Best Intranets of 2011," *useit.com*, January 4, 2011, http://www.useit.com.

7. Company Web site, http://www.virtual.com, accessed April 7, 2011.

8. Zach Epstein, "Google May Finally Be Adding VoIP to Google Voice," *BGR*, March 8, 2011, http://www.bgr.com; Elliott Drucker, "Tech Insights—The Future of Voice," *Wireless Week*, March 7, 2010, http://www.wirelessweek.com; "Future of VOIP in 2010, a New Beginning?" Cheapest VOIP Calls.net, January 2010, http://cheapestvoipcalls.net.

9. Diane Bartz, "Apple Users Lose Some Immunity to Cybercrime," *Reuters*, April 20, 2010, http://ca.news.yahoo.com; IDG News Service, "E-Crime Reporting Format Draws Closer to a Standard," *Reuters*, March 23, 2010, http://www.reuters.com; Sue Marquette Poremba, "Report: Dangers of Cyber Crime on the Rise," *IT Business Edge*, January 27, 2010, http://www.itbusinessedge.com.

10. "Data Theft Crisis Spreads to Best Buy, Walgreens," *CBS News*, April 3, 2011, http://www.cbsnews.com.

11. Juan Carlos Perez, "Report: Mysterious Facebook Web Search Box Could Be Malware," *Network World*, March 25, 2011, http://www.networkworld.com; Elinor Mills, "Malware Delivered by Yahoo, Fox, Google Ads," *CNET News*, March 22, 2010, http://news.cnet.com.

12. Tony Bradley, "McAfee Debacle Shows Why Malware Defense Must Evolve," *TechWorld*, April 28, 2010, http://www.techworld.com.

13. Associated Press, "Mastermind of World's Worst Computer Virus Still at Large," *Fox News*, March 4, 2010, http://www.foxnews.com.

14. "New Security Threat Against 'Smart Phone' Users, Researchers Show," *Science Daily*, February 22, 2010, http://www.sciencedaily.com.

15. Tim Greene, "IBM: Mobile Phone and Cloud Security Issues Can Bite Unwary IT Departments," *Network World.com*, March 31, 2011, http://www.networkworld.com.

16. "Data Loss Statistics," Boston Computing Network, http://www.bostoncomputing.net, accessed May 24, 2010.

17. Antony Savvas, "Radley Bags Safer Data With New Backup System," *CSO Security and Risk*, March 26, 2011, http://www.csoonline.com; "FalconStor: Disaster Recovery Solutions Need to Make Applications Available, Not Just Replicate Data," *Zycko News*, March 23, 2011, http://www.zycko.com.

18. "Bureau of Labor Statistics, "Work-at-Home Patterns by Occupation," *Issues in Labor Statistics*, http://www.bls.gov, accessed April 8, 2011.

19. Infosys Web site, http://www.infosys.com, accessed April 8, 2011; "Infosys Technologies to Manage Microsoft's Internal IT Service," press release, April 13, 2010, http://www.infosys.com.

Part 5: Launching Your Information Technology and Accounting Career

1. U.S. Department of Labor, "Tomorrow's Jobs," *Occupational Outlook Handbook, 2010–2011*, Bureau of Labor Statistics, accessed April 11, 2011, http://www.bls.gov.

2. U.S. Department of Labor, "Accountants and Auditors," *Occupational Outlook Handbook, 2010–2011*, Bureau of Labor Statistics, accessed April 11, 2011, http://www.bls.gov.

3. U.S. Department of Labor, "Computer Software Engineers," *Occupational Outlook Handbook, 2010–2011*, Bureau of Labor Statistics, accessed April 11, 2011, http://www.bls.gov.

4. U.S. Department of Labor, "Computer and Information Systems Managers," *Occupational Outlook Handbook, 2010–2011*, Bureau of Labor Statistics, accessed June 28, 2010, http://www.bls.gov.

Chapter 15

1. Company Web site, http://www.deloitte.com, accessed April 12, 2011; Marc E. Babej, "Deloitte: Consumers Are Feeling the Gas and Food Price Crunch—Is Your Company Ready?" *Forbes.com*, April 12, 2011, http://blogs.forbes.com; Anne D'Innocenzio, "Stores Expected to Report

Disappointing January," *ABC News,* February 2, 2011, http://abcnews .go.com; "The 2011 Outlook," *Consulting Magazine,* January 28, 2011, http://www.consultingmage.com.

2. Bureau of Labor Statistics, *Occupational Outlook Handbook, 2010–2011* Edition, http://data.bls.gov.

3. "Spring Accounting Grads Fare Better in Hiring than Their Peers," *Accounting Web,* April 23, 2010, http://www.accountingweb.com.

4. "Tax-Aide," AARP, http://www.aarp.org, accessed April 13, 2011.

5. "The 2010 *Accounting Today* Top 100 Firms," March 15, 2010, http://www .webcpa.com.

6. "A New Way to Attract Accounting Talent? E&Y Might Be Onto Something Big," *Accounting WEB,* February 22, 2011, http://www.accountingweb.com.

7. FASB Web site, http://www.fasb.org, accessed June 1, 2010.

8. Johnson & Johnson financial statements, *MSN Investor,* http://moneycentral.msn.com, accessed June 1, 2010.

9. "Mobile Computing Takes Accountants to a New Level of Productivity," *Accounting WEB,* March 14, 2011, http://www.accountingweb.com.

10. John Adams, "Success Story," *US Banker,* January 2010, http://www .americanbanker.com.

11. "Bullish Peso Bets Jump 35% to $5 Billion As Exports Climb: Mexico Credit," *Bloomberg.com,* April 14, 2011, http://www.bloomberg.com.

12. "Despite Uncertainty, Initial Response to SEC's IFRS Announcement Finds Executives Won't Delay Their Own IFRS Planning," *PR Newswire,* March 9, 2010, http://www.prnewswire.com.

13. Ernst & Young, "SEC Reaffirms Its Commitment to IFRS," *Hot Topic,* February 24, 2010, http://www.ey.com; Ra'id Marie, "IFRS vs. GAAP— What Does This Have to Do with the Financial Crisis?" Meirc Training and Consulting, January 17, 2010, http://www.meirc.com.

Chapter 16

1. Sam's Club Web site, http://www.samsclub.com, accessed April 19, 2011; Anita Campbell, "Sam's Club Dives Into Small Business Lending," *Small Business Trends,* October 21, 2010, http://smallbiztrends.com; "It Sam's Club the Answer to the Small Business Credit Crunch?" *Small Business Labs,* July 14, 2010, http://www.smallbizlabs.com; Mae Anderson, "Sam's Club Will Offer Small Business Loans," *Huffington Post,* July 6, 2010, http://www.huffingtonpost.com.

2. Rowena Mason, "A Bloody Nose for Sir William Castell at BP's AGM," *The Telegraph,* April 15, 2011, http://www.telegraph.co.uk; Anya Kamanetz, "Not So Slick," *Fast Company,* October 2010, pp. 56–58. Andrew Ross Sorkin, ed., "S&P Cuts BP Ratings, Citing Liabilities and Politics," *The New York Times,* June 17, 2010, http://dealbook.blogs.nytimes.com; "BP Suspends Dividend after Deepwater Horizon Spill," *MarketWatch,* June 16, 2010, http://www.marketwatch.com; Peter Nicholas, "BP Will Create Fund to Pay Claims," *Los Angeles Times,* June 16, 2010, http://articles .latimes.com; AP/1010WINS, "Scientists: BP Oil Spill Leaking Up to 2.52M Gallons a Day," *1010WINS.com,* June 15, 2010, http://www .1010wins.com; Ben Baden, "The Case for (and against) BP Cutting Its Dividend," *U.S. News & World Report,* June 14, 2010, http://www.usnews .com; Jeff Plungis and Christopher Condon, "U.S. Lawmakers Say BP

Should Suspend Dividends, Ads (Update 2)," *Bloomberg Businessweek,* June 9, 2010, http://www.businessweek.com; "Gulf of Mexico Oil Spill Worst in U.S. History," *MarketWatch,* May 27, 2010, http://www.marketwatch.com.

3. "European Financial Stability Bonds Issued," *New Europe,* February 6, 2011, http://www.neurope.eu; Catarina Saraiva, William Selway, and Brendan A. McGrail, "California Markets Second-Biggest Taxable Bond Sale of 2010," *Bloomberg.com,* March 25, 2010, http://www.bloomberg.com.

4. "The 17 Most Important IPOs to Watch for in 2011," *24/7 Wall Street,* January 12, 2011, http://247wallst.com.

5. "NYSE Euronext Announces First Quarter 2010 Financial Results," news release, May 4, 2010, http://www.nyse.com; "New York Stock Exchange," *Money-Zine,* http://www.money-zine.com, accessed June 21, 2010.

6. Rule 300. Trading Licenses, NYSE Euronext, 2010, http://www.nyse.com; Trading Licenses, NYSE Price List 2010, http://www.nyse.com, accessed June 21, 2010.

7. Federal Deposit Insurance Corporation, "Statistics on Depository Institutions Report," http://www2.fdic.gov, accessed April 19, 2011.

8. "Debit Cards—Holders, Number, Transactions, and Volume, 2000 and 2008, and Projections, 2011", U.S. Census Bureau, http://www.census.gov, accessed April 27, 2011.

9. "In the Know," *ABA Center for Banking Information,* American Bankers Association, http://www.aba.com, accessed April 19, 2011.

10. Federal Deposit Insurance Corporation, "Table S112. Assets, FDIC-Insured Savings Institutions, United States and Other Areas," http://www2.fdic .gov, accessed June 21, 2010.

11. Federal Deposit Insurance Corporation, "Table S114. Federal Deposit Insurance Corporation, Loans and Leases, FDIC-Insured Savings Institutions, United States and Other Areas," http://www2.fdic.gov, accessed June 21, 2010.

12. "America's Largest Credit Unions," *Credit Union Access,* http://creditunionaccess.com, accessed June 21, 2010; Donna Fuscaldo, "Can You Join a Credit Union?" *Bankrate.com,* April 21, 2010, http://www.bankratecom.

13. "Life Insurance: The Life/Health Insurance Industry," Insurance Information Institute, http://www.iii.org, accessed April 19, 2011.

14. "Retirement Funds," Insurance Information Institute, http://www.iii.org, accessed April 19, 2011; Mary Williams Walsh, "Public Pension Funds Are Adding Risk to Raise Returns," *The New York Times,* March 8, 2010, http://www.nytimes.com.

15. *2010 Investment Company Factbook,* Table 9, Number of Shareholder Accounts of the U.S. Mutual Fund Industry, and Table 1 Total Net Assets, Number of Funds, Number of Share Classes, and Number of Shareholder Accounts of the U.S. Mutual Fund Industry, http://www.icifactbook.org, accessed June 21, 2010; "Frequently Asked Questions about 401(k) Plans," Investment Company Institute, http://www.ici.org, accessed June 21, 2010; Investment Company Institute, "Trends in Mutual Fund Investing, March 2010," April 19, 2010, http://www.ici.org.

16. Investment Company Institute, "Trends in Mutual Fund Investing, March 2010."

17. Elizabeth MacDonald, "Banks, Companies That Tapped Fed Reserve Rescue Programs," *Fox Business,* March 31, 2011, http:/www .foxbusiness.com; Federal Reserve press release, January 12, 2010,

http://www.federalreserve.gov, accessed June 21, 2010; Board of Governors of the Federal Reserve System, "Term Auction Facility Questions and Answers," http://www.federalreserve.gov, accessed June 21, 2010.

18. "Top Banks in the World," *Bankers Almanac,* February 16, 2011, http://www.bankersalmanac.com.

Chapter 17

1. Michael V. Copeland, "What HP Really Bought from Palm: A Mobile Future, Untethered from Microsoft," *CNN Money,* February 9, 2011, http://tech.fortune.cnn.com; Sue Marek, "HP's $1.2B Purchase of Palm May Be a Win for the Enterprise," *Fierce Wireless,* April 29, 2010, http://www.fiercewireless.com; Dan Frommer, "Why HP Is Buying Palm and Why It Will Fail," *Business Insider,* April 28, 2010, http://www.businessinsider.com; Allen Tsai, "HP Buys Palm for $1.2 Billion," *Mobiledia,* April 28, 2010, http://www.mobiledia.com; "HP To Acquire Palm for $1.2 Billion," *HP Web site,* April 28, 2010, http://www.hp.com.

2. "For S&P CFOs, Pay Is Down, Bonuses Are Up," *Equilar,* June 24, 2010. http://www.equilar.com.

3. Ibid.

4. "Airbus A380 Customers," Airbus Web site, March 2011, http://www.airbus.com.

5. Genco Marketplace Web site, https://www.gencomarketplace.com, accessed April 26, 2011.

6. Horatiu Boerlu, "BMW Super Bowl Ad Shot Around Spartanburg," *BMW Blog,* February 6, 2011, http://www.bmwblog.com.

7. BMW Factory Web site, http://www.bmwusfactory.com, accessed April 27, 2011.

8. Federal Reserve Bank of St. Louis, Series: AEXUSUK, U.S./U.K. Foreign Exchange Rate, May 11, 2010, http://research.stlouisfed.org.

9. Federal Reserve Board, "Commercial Paper," Federal Reserve Release, May 13, 2010, http://federalreserve.gov.

10. Maxwell Murphy, "Update: Barnes & Noble Drops on Suspended Dividends, No Guidance," *Dow Jones Newswires,* February 22, 2011, http://online.wsj.com.

11. Federal Reserve Board, Commercial Paper Outstanding, Federal Reserve Release, May 12, 2010, http://federalreserve.gov.

12. Dena Aubin, "CORRECTED—US Companies Sell Debt at Fastest Pace since March," *Reuters,* June 23, 2010, http://www.reuters.com; Michael Aneiro, "Credit Markets Pub on the Brakes," *The Wall Street Journal,* May 29, 2010, http://www.online.wsj.com.

13. Board of Governors of the Federal Reserve System, "Federal Reserve Statistical Release, Z.1, Flow of Funds Accounts of the United States," March 12, 2009, http://www.federalreserve.gov.

14. "DFJ Portfolio," DFJ Web site, http://www.dfj.com, accessed April 27, 2011.

15. "Moody's May Downgrade DynCorp's 'Ba3' Rating," *MarketWatch,* April 12, 2010, http://www.marketwatch.com.

16. "Saudi Alwaleed Backs Citigroup Reverse Stock Split," *Reuters,* April 9, 2011, http://en.news.maktoob.com.

17. Andrew Ross Sorkin, ed., "Hedge Fund Strategies, at Smaller Prices," *The New York Times.com,* January 11, 2010, http://dealbook.blogs.nytimes.com.

18. Margie Lindsay, "Global Hedge Fund AUM Hits $1.8 Trillion," *Hedge Funds Review,* March 8, 2010, http://www.hedgefundsreview.com.

19. "2011 Mergers & Acquisitions Outlook and 2010 Summary," *The Investment Blog,* January 17, 2011, http://investmentblog.wordpress.com; Ashlee Vance, "With McAfee Deal, Intel Looks for Edge," *The New York Times,* August 19, 2010, http://www.nytimes.com.

20. Emre Peker, "Cerberus Taps Banks for LBO as Leveraged Loan Rally Spurs M&As," *Bloomberg Businessweek,* May 14, 2010, http://www.businessweek.com; David Russell, "LBOs Loom as Credit Market Recovers," Nasdaq, March 19, 2010, http://www.nasdaq.com.

Part 6: Launching Your Finance Career

1. U.S. Department of Labor, "Tomorrow's Jobs," *Occupational Outlook Handbook, 2010–2011,* Bureau of Labor Statistics, accessed May 19, 2011, http://www.bls.gov.

2. National Association of Colleges and Employers, "Starting Salary Offers to College Class of 2010 Decline," accessed at http://www.career.vt.edu, accessed July 8, 2010.

3. U.S. Department of Labor, "Financial Managers," *Occupational Outlook Handbook, 2010–2011,* Bureau of Labor Statistics, accessed May 19, 2011, http://www.bls.gov.

Appendix A

1. "The Top Ten Legal Outsourcing Companies in India," *Chillibreeze,* http://www.chillibreeze.com, accessed May 9, 2011; "LPO Regulatory Trends in 2011," *Fronterion,* January 27, 2011, http://fronterion.com; Mian Ridge, "The Outsource Trend: It's Not Just Call Centers in India Anymore," *Christian Science Monitor,* January 19, 2011, http://www.csmonitor.com; Heather Timmons, "Outsourcing to India Draws Western Lawyers," *The New York Times,* August 4, 2010, http://www.nytimes.com.

2. "Frivolous Lawsuits," *NFIB,* http://www.nfib.com, accessed May 7, 2010.

3. "All States Have Silly Laws," http://foodstamp.aphsa.org/olwkshps/AllSatesHaveSillyLaws.pdf, accessed May 7, 2010.

4. "United States Court of Appeals for the Fourth Circuit," http://www.ca4.uscourts.gov, accessed May 7, 2010.

5. "The Justices' Caseload," The Supreme Court of the United States, http://www.supremecourt.gov, accessed May 7, 2010.

6. "Lieff Cabraser Announces Class Action Lawsuit Against China Electric Motor, Inc.," *Press Release,* April 14, 2011, http://www.lieffcabraser.com; "New Report Shows Rise in China Class Action Investor Lawsuits," *Reverse Merger Report,* January 20, 2011, http://reversemerger.dealflow.com.

7. "Brief Summary of the Dodd-Frank Wall Street Reform and Consumer Protection Act," U.S. Government Web site, http://www.banking.senate.gov, and http://www.treasury.gov, accessed May 10, 2011, Beverly Blair Harzog, "New Credit Card Rules' Double Standard," *CNN Money.com,* February 22, 2010, http://money.cnn.com.

8. Andrew Ramonas, "Senate Passes Short-Term Patriot Act Reauthorization," *Main Justice,* February 25, 2010, http://www.mainjustice.com.

9. Rob Pegoraro, "Court Cuts FCC's Net-Neutrality Power; Now What?" *The Washington Post,* April 7, 2010, http://voices.washingtonpost.com.

10. U.S. Treasury Web site, http://www.treasury.gov, accessed May 10, 2011.

11. "Food and Drug Administration Amendments Act (FDAAA) of 2007," U.S. Food and Drug Administration, http://www.fda.gov, accessed May 7, 2010.

12. Ameet Sachdev, "EEOC Sues Law Firm for Age Discrimination," *AARP Bulletin Today*, February 2, 2010, http://bulletin.aarp.org.

13. Miguel Helft, "Judge Sides With Google in Viacom Video Suit," *The New York Times*, June 23, 2010, http://www.nytimes.com; "Google's YouTube Secrets Exposed in Viacom Case," *Huffington Post*, April 15, 2010, http://www.huffingtonpost.com.

14. Kelly Kunsch, "Commercial Law and the Uniform Code," *Seattle University School of Law*, http://www.law.seattle.edu, accessed May 7, 2010.

15. Charles V. Bagli, "Court Upholds Columbia Campus Expansion Plan," *The New York Times*, June 24, 2010, http://www.nytimes.com.

16. "Utah Eminent Domain Law: Governor Signs Bill Authorizing Eminent to Domain To Take Federal Land," *Huffington Post*, March 29, 2010, http://www.huffingtonpost.com.

17. Mark Sweney, "Google Wins Louis Vuitton Trademark Case," *The Guardian*, March 23, 2010, http://www.guardian.co.uk.

18. "Senate Judiciary Committee Unveils Details of Patent Reform Agreement," *Law Updates.com*, March 9, 2010, http://www.lawupdates.com.

19. Dominic Rushe, "US Judge Writes Unhappy Ending for Google's Online Library Plans," *The Guardian*, March 23, 2011, http://www.guardian.co.uk.

20. "New Wisconsin Law in Toxic Tort Litigation," *Martindale.com*, April 21, 2011, http://www.martindale.com.

21. Duff Wilson, "Sharp Increase in March in Personal Bankruptcies," *The New York Times*, April 1, 2010, http://www.nytimes.com.

Appendix B

1. Aaron Smith, "Joplin Tornado Damage Could Total $3 Billion," *CNN Money*, May 24, 2011, http://money.cnn.com; Noam Cohen, "Tornado Hits Missouri City, Killing Many," *The New York Times*, May 22, 2011, http://www.nytimes.com; David Ranii, "Home Insurance Unlikely to Jump After Tornadoes," *The Cary News*, May 11, 2011, http://www.carynews.com; Phillip Rawls, "Alabama Tornado Damage Could Approach Record $2 Billion," *Huffpost Green*, May 11, 2011, http://www.huffingtonpost.com; "Alabama Sees Tornado Insured Losses Exceeding $2B," *Business Insurance*, May 4, 2011, http://www.businessinsurance.com; Trang Do, "DeKalb Co. Tornado Victim Without Insurance Coverage," *Live5news.com*, May 5, 2011, http://www.live5news.com; Aaron Dimick, "Home Insurance May Not Cover Certain Tornado Damage," *WEAU News*, April 29, 2011, http://www.weau.com; Ben Garbarek, "Insurance Concerns Loom After Tornadoes," *NBC12.com*, April 19, 2011, http://www.nbc12.com.

2. *ACLI Lilfe Insurance Fact Book 2009*, http://www.acli.com, accessed May 11, 2011.

3. Robert P. Hartwig, "2010—Year End Results," Insurance Information Institute, http://www.iii.org, accessed May 11, 2011.

4. "Home Buyers Insurance Checklist," Insurance Information Institute, http://www.iii.org, accessed May 9, 2010.

5. "Insurance Requirements," Walmart Web site, http://walmartstores.com, accessed May 11, 2011.

6. "Healthcare Reform Legislation Update 2010," *JLBH Health*, March 22, 2010, http://www.jlbghealth.com.

Appendix C

1. "Credit Card Debt Statistics," *Money-zine.com*, http://www.money-zine.com, accessed May 16, 2011; Jessica Silver-Greenberg and Mary Pilon, "Cards Return to School," *Wall Street Journal*, May 7, 2011, http://online.wsj.com; Courtney Robishaw, "Student Debt Tops $1 Trillion," *Daily Campus*, May 5, 2011, http: ///www.dailycampus.com; Tamar Lewin, "Burden of College Loans on Graduates Grows," *The New York Times*, April 11, 2011, http://www.nytimes.com; Michelle Singletary, "Despite New Card Law, Credit Card Companies Still Targeting Young Adults," *Washington Post*, January 12, 2011, http: //www.washingtonpost.com: Mary Pilon, "Students Still Targets of Credit-Card Offers," *Wall Street Journal*, January 8, 2011, http://online.wsj.com: "Student Debt Crisis threatens US Economy," *IBTimes*, December 28, 2010, http://www.ibtimes.com.

2. "Income, Poverty, and Health Insurance Coverage in the United States," U.S. Census Bureau, http://www.census.gov, accessed May 16, 2011.

3. "How Many Workers Are Postponing Retirement? Why?" *Employee Benefit Research Institute*, March 2011, http://www.ebri.org.

4. "Personal Bankruptcy Filings Reach Five-Year High," *Clear Bankruptcy*, July 16, 2010, http://www.clearbankruptcy.com.

5. "Consumer Credit," *Federal Reserve Statistical Release*, May 7, 2010, http://federalreserve.gov.

6. Keith Cronin, "Avoiding Credit Card Debt in College," *Campus Life*, May 8, 2010, http://campuslife.suite101.com.

Appendix D

1. Next Restaurant Web site, http://www.nextrestaurant.com, accessed May 13, 2011; Carey Polis and Colin Sterling, "Grant Achatz's Next Restaurant Tickets Selling for up to $3,000," *Huffpost Food*, April 8, 2011, http: //www.huffingtonpost.com: Julia Moskin, "The Perfect Menu. Now Change It," *The New York Times*, February 15, 2011, http://www.nytimes.com; Joel Stein, "Sneak Preview: A Taste of Grant Achatz's Next Menu," *Time*, December 9, 2010, http://www.time.com; Pete Wells, "In Chicago, the Chef Grant Achatz Is Selling Tickets to His New Restaurant," *The New York Times*, May 5, 2010, http://www.nytimes.com; "US Next Hot Restaurant Will Require Prepaid Tickets," *AOL News*, May 5, 2010, http://www.aolnews.com; Chuck Sudo, "Achatz's Next Two Projects: Time Travel, Cocktails," *Chicagoist*, May 4, 2010, http://chicagoist.com; Paul Frumkin.

Appendix E

1. "Average Earnings of Year-Round, Full-Time Workers by Educational Attainment," *Current Population Reports*, U.S. Census Bureau, http://www.census.gov, accessed May 31, 2011.

2. Henry Devries, "How to Get a Job in Embedded Engineering," *San Diego News Network*, April 27, 2010, http://www.sdnn.com.

3. "College Grad Job Search Strategies," *JobDoc*, March 15, 2010, http://www.boston.com.

4. Lindsey Gerdes, "Best Places to Intern," *Bloomberg Businessweek*, December 10, 2009, http://www.businessweek.com.

5. "The Cooperative Education Model, National Commission for Cooperative Education, http://www.co-op.edu, accessed May 10, 2010.

6. "More Free Assessment Tests," *Career Explorer,* http://www .careerexplorer.net, accessed May 31, 2011; "Assessment Exercises," *Monster Careers,* http://www.monstercareeres.com, accessed May 31, 2011.

7. "Paula's Story," *Paula Deen.com,* http://www.pauladeen.com, accessed May 31, 2011.

8. Kim Isaacs, "Five Resume Tips for College Students," *Monster.com,* accessed May 31, 2011; "Top 10 Professional Resume Writing Tips for 2010," *An Elite Resume,* http://aneliteresume.com, accessed May 31, 2011; "Five Tips for Better Resume Writing," *Resume Writing for Dummies,* http:// www.dummies.com, accessed May 31, 2011.

9. Kat Neville, "What Makes a Great Cover Letter, According to Companies?" *Smashing Magazine,* March 25, 2010, http://www .smashingmagazine.com.

10. "Tips for Submitting Your Online Resume," *An Elite Resume,* http://aneliteresume.com, accessed May 31, 2011.

11. Carole Martin, "Ten Tips to Boost Your Interview Skills," *Monster.com,* http://career-advice.monster.com, accessed May 31, 2011.

12. Jerome Young, "How to Answer the Hard Interview Questions," *Forbes .com,* April 9, 2010, http://www.forbes.com.

13. "Overview of the 2008–2018 Projections," U.S. Bureau of Labor Statistics, http://data.bls.gov, accessed May 31, 2011.

14. Ibid.

15. Ibid.

16. Ibid.

17. Anthony Balderama, "What Kind of Job Market Can the Class of 2010 Expect?" *The Work Buzz,* April 15, 2010, http://www.theworkbuzz.com.

Name Index

R

Subject Index